LIFE-SPAN DEVELOPMENT

FIFTH EDITION

LIFE-SPAN DEVELOPMENT

JOHN W. SANTROCK

UNIVERSITY OF TEXAS AT DALLAS

WCB Brown &
Benchmark
PUBLISHERS

Madison, Wisconsin • Dubuque, Iowa

Book Team

Executive Editor *Michael Lange*
Developmental Editors *Sheralee Connors/Ted Underhill*
Production Editor *Peggy Selle*
Designers *K. Wayne Harms/Gail Ryan*
Art Editor *Rachel Imsland*
Photo Editor *Carol A. Judge*
Permissions Coordinator *Karen L. Storlie*
Visuals/Design Developmental Consultant *Marilyn A. Phelps*
Visuals/Design Freelance Specialist *Mary L. Christianson*
Marketing Manager *Steven Yetter*
Advertising Coordinator *Michael Matera*

WCB Brown & Benchmark

A Division of Wm. C. Brown Communications, Inc.

Executive Vice President/General Manager *Thomas E. Doran*
Vice President/Editor in Chief *Edgar J. Laube*
Vice President/Marketing and Sales Systems *Eric Ziegler*
Director of Production *Vickie Putman Caughron*
Director of Custom and Electronic Publishing *Chris Rogers*

WCB Wm. C. Brown Communications, Inc.

President and Chief Executive Officer *G. Franklin Lewis*
Corporate Senior Vice President and Chief Financial Officer *Robert Chesterman*
Corporate Senior Vice President and President of Manufacturing *Roger Meyer*

The credits section for this book begins on page C-1 and is considered
an extension of the copyright page.

Cover image of Monet, Poppyfield, 1873, detail. Paris, Musee d'Orsay. (Art Resource)

Copyedited by Wendy E. Nelson

A special thank-you to Borders Book Store in Madison, Wisconsin for the photos of
the self-help books in this text.

A Times Mirror Company

Library of Congress Catalog Card Number: 93–73056

ISBN 0–697–14503–4 (cloth)
    0–697–14504–2 (paper)

Printed in the United States of America by Wm. C. Brown Communications, Inc.,
2460 Kerper Boulevard, Dubuque, IA 52001

10 9 8 7 6 5 4 3 2 1

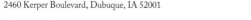

To my parents, Ruth and John Santrock

BRIEF CONTENTS

Contents

SECTION ONE

The Life-Span Developmental Perspective

All the world is a stage,
And all the men and women merely players;
They have their exits and their entrances,
And one man in his time plays many parts.

—William Shakespeare

CHAPTER 1

Introduction 5

The first cry of a newborn in Chicago or Zamboango, in Amsterdam or Rangoon, has the same pitch and key, each saying, "I am! I have come through! I am a member of the human family.". . . babies arriving, suckling, growing into youths restless and questioning. Then as grown-ups they seek and hope. They mate, toil, fish, quarrel, sing, fight, pray.

—Carl Sandburg

CHAPTER 2

The Science of Life-Span Development 31

There is nothing quite so practical as a good theory.

—Kurt Lewin

SECTION TWO

Beginnings

*What endless questions vex the
thought, of whence and whither,
when and how.*

—Sir Richard Burton

CHAPTER 3

Biological Beginnings   73

*The frightening part about heredity and environment is
that we parents provide both.*

—Notebook of a Printer

CHAPTER 4

Prenatal Development and Birth   95

*What web is this
Of will be, is, and was?*

—Jorge Luis Borges

SECTION SIX

Adolescence

In no order of things is adolescence the simple time of life.

—Jean Erskine Stewart

CHAPTER 11

Socioemotional Development in Middle and Late Childhood   309

Children know nothing about childhood and have little to say about it. They are too busy becoming something they have not quite grasped yet, something which keeps changing. . . . Nor will they realize what is happening to them until they are too far beyond it to remember how it felt.

—Alistair Reed

CHAPTER 12

Physical and Cognitive Development in Adolescence   347

In youth, we clothe ourselves with rainbows, and go brave as the zodiac.

—Ralph Waldo Emerson

CHAPTER 13

Socioemotional Development in Adolescence   377

"Who are you?" said the caterpillar. Alice replied rather shyly, "I—I hardly know, sir, just at present—at least I know who I was when I got up this morning, but I must have changed several times since then."

—Lewis Carroll

CHAPTER 14

Physical and Cognitive Development in Early Adulthood   405

We are born twice over; the first time for existence, the second for life; once as human beings and later as men or as women.

—Jean-Jacques Rousseau

SECTION EIGHT

Middle Adulthood

Generations will depend on the ability of every procreating individual to face his children.

—Erik Erikson

CHAPTER 16

Physical and Cognitive Development in Middle Adulthood 463

The first forty years of life furnish the text, while the remaining thirty supply the commentary.

—Schopenhauer

CHAPTER 17

Socioemotional Development in Middle Adulthood 483

The generations of living things pass in a short time, and like runners hand on the torch of life.

—Lucretius

SECTION TEN

Death and Dying

Years following years steal something every day:
At last they steal us from ourselves away.

—Alexander Pope

CHAPTER 21

Death and Dying   575

Man is the only animal that finds his own existence a
problem he has to solve and from which he cannot escape.
In the same sense man is the only animal who knows he
must die.

—Erich Fromm

EPILOGUE

The Journey of Life   594

CONCEPT TABLES

SOCIOCULTURAL WORLDS OF DEVELOPMENT

PERSPECTIVES ON PARENTING AND EDUCATION

LIFE-SPAN PRACTICAL KNOWLEDGE

LIFE-SPAN HEALTH
AND WELL-BEING

PREFACE

This is the fifth edition of *Life-Span Development*. When I began writing the first edition of the book I was 37 years old. Across the five editions, I have aged from the latter part of early adulthood into middle age, my children have moved through adolescence and into early adulthood, one of them got married, both of them graduated from college and established careers (Tracy sells cellular phones, and Jennifer is a professional tennis player), and I became a grandfather. I gained a few gray hairs and finally, after several false starts, learned how to use a computer for word processing. I also gave up tennis but still exercise regularly, and I have been painting expressionist art since 1989.

The journey through the human life span, if anything, grows in fascination for me. This is an exciting time to study and write about life-span development. Scholars around the world are making new discoveries and developing new insights about every period of the human life cycle at a much faster pace than in previous decades. The field of life-span development is mature enough that the knowledge that is being gained can be applied to peoples' lives to improve their adaptation, health, and well-being.

As in the past three revisions, I have carefully added to, subtracted from, integrated, and simplified the material for this fifth edition of the book. I retained the core ideas on life-span development from the fourth edition. However, I made some significant changes that involved extensively updating the research knowledge base that is the foundation of what we know about the human life span. And I significantly expanded the discussions of applying what we know about life-span development to the everyday lives of people in different periods of development.

SCIENCE AND RESEARCH

Above all else the fifth edition of *Life-Span Development* is an extremely up-to-date presentation of the research in the three primary domains of human development: biological processes, cognitive processes, and socioemotional processes. Research on biological, cognitive, and socioemotional processes continues to represent the core of this book. This core includes classic and leading-edge research. Approximately 30 percent of the references in this edition are new. More than 375 references come from 1993, 1994, and in-press sources.

APPLICATIONS

I hope that when students complete this book, they not only have a much better understanding of the scientific basis of life-span development, but also increase their wisdom about their own personal journeys through the human life span. To this end, the fifth edition of *Life-Span Development* includes more discussion of health, well-being, and practical applications than the fourth edition did. Three new features appear at least once in every chapter: (1) Life-Span Health and Well-Being, (2) Perspectives on Parenting and Education, and (3) Life-Span Practical Knowledge.

WRITING AND PEDAGOGY

I continue to strive to make this book more student-friendly. I have explored alternative ways of presenting ideas and continue to ask college students of all ages to give me feedback on which strategies are the most effective. Covering the entire life span in one book and in one course is a challenging task. To incorporate the basic core knowledge of the field of life-span development, present the latest advancements on the scientific front, and describe practical applications in each period of development requires careful consideration of what to include in a book of this nature (as well as what to exclude), and how to include it.

This challenging task requires clear writing and an effective pedagogical system. In constructing the fourth and fifth editions, I rewrote virtually every paragraph and section—adding, subtracting, integrating, and simplifying. *Life-Span Development* also has a carefully designed pedagogical system that will benefit student learning. The key features of the learning system are presented in the visual section of the preface, "To the Student."

MOTIVATION

Students learn best when they are highly motivated and interested in what they are reading and experiencing. It is important to be motivated right from the start, so each chapter of the book begins with a high-interest piece, Images of Life-Span Development, that should motivate students to read the chapter.

For example, a new introductory piece for chapter 1 motivates students to think about why Alice Walker became Alice Walker and why Jeffrey Dahmer became Jeffrey Dahmer. The increased applications, in the fifth edition, to the real lives of people at different periods of development should also motivate students, because they will increasingly be able to perceive how the material relates to their own journeys through the human life span. I have also tried to communicate the discoveries in life-span development with energy and enthusiasm and to provide lively examples of each concept I introduce. I also personally chose virtually every photograph in this book, because I believe the combination of the right photograph with the right words improves student motivation and learning. I also extensively participated in the design of the book and created a number of visual figures that combine photographs with figure information or summaries of concepts, because I also believe these enhance student learning and motivation. We also know that learning is facilitated when the learner is in a good mood—to that end, cartoons are also used at appropriate places in the text.

In summary, I have tried to convey the complex and exciting story of how we develop, and how we become who we are, in a manner that is both informative *and* enjoyable. If students are bored with this book, don't learn effectively from it, or don't feel they have more wisdom about their own journeys through the human life span upon finishing it, then I will not have reached the goals I set for this fifth edition.

OTHER HIGHLIGHTS AND CHANGES IN THE FIFTH EDITION

Other highlights and changes in the fifth edition of *Life-Span Development* include increased and updated coverage of culture, ethnicity, and gender; health and well-being; families and parenting; and many other content areas for each period of development. The discussion of methods was moved to chapter 2, and the presentation of theories in that chapter was streamlined. This allowed me to expand the discussion of contemporary and life-span developmental issues in chapter 1. It also provides a cohesive, integrated presentation of the main themes of a science of life-span development—theories and methods—in a single chapter. An epilogue, "The Journey of Life," appears in the book for the first time. It combines words and photographs to stimulate students to reflect on what they have learned about the human life span. The discussion of adult development and aging continues to be given considerable attention in an effort to present a balanced treatment of all periods of life-span development; a much stronger emphasis on successful aging characterizes the fifth edition of *Life-Span Development*. The former summary outline at the end of each chapter has been replaced with a section called "Conclusions," which briefly highlights the main topics covered in the chapter and reminds students to reread the concept tables for an overall summary of the chapter. This change eliminates the redundancy of information that appeared in both the second or third concept table and the summary in the fourth edition of the book.

SUPPLEMENTARY MATERIALS

Brown & Benchmark Publishers has gathered a group of talented individuals with many years of experience in teaching life-span development to create supplementary materials that will assist instructors and students who use this text. The supplements are designed to make it as easy as possible to customize the entire package for the unique needs of professors and their students.

Instructor's Course Planner The key to this teaching package was created by Allen H. Keniston and Blaine F. Peden of the University of Wisconsin–Eau Claire. Allen and Blaine are both award winning teachers and active members of The Council of Teachers of Undergraduate Psychology. This flexible planner provides a variety of useful tools to enhance your teaching efforts, reduce your workload, and increase your enjoyment. For each chapter of the text, the planner provides an outline, overview, learning objectives, and key terms. These items are also contained in the Student Study Guide. The planner also contains lecture suggestions, classroom activities, discussion questions, integrative essay questions, a film list, and a transparency guide. It contains an abundance of handouts and exercises for stimulating classroom discussion and encouraging critical thinking.

The **Test Item File** was constructed by Bradley Caskey of the University of Wisconsin–River Falls. Brad is also an award winning teacher and has worked extensively with the Educational Testing Service (ETS) as a writer of test items for the Advanced Placement Test for Psychology. This comprehensive test bank includes over 2,000 new multiple-choice test questions that are keyed to the text and learning objectives. Each item is designated as factual, conceptual, or applied as defined by the first three levels of Benjamin Bloom's *Taxonomy of Educational Objectives* (1956).

The questions in the Test Item File are available on **MicroTest III**, a powerful but easy-to-use test-generating program by Chariot Software Group. MicroTest is available for DOS, Windows, and Macintosh. With MicroTest, you can easily select questions from the Test Item File and print a test and an answer key. You can customize questions, headings, and instructions, you can add or import questions of your own, and you can print your test in a choice of fonts if your printer supports them. You can obtain a copy of MicroTest III by contacting your local Brown & Benchmark sales representative or by phoning Educational Resources at 800–338–5371.

The **Student Study Guide** was also created by Allen H. Keniston and Blaine F. Peden of the University of Wisconsin–Eau Claire. For each chapter of the text, the student is provided with an outline, an overview, learning objectives, key terms, a guided review, study questions (with answers provided for self-testing), and an integration and application question. The study guide begins with the section "Developing Good Study Habits" to help students study more effectively and efficiently.

The **Brown & Benchmark Human Development Transparency/Slide Set** 2e is brand new and consists of 100 newly developed acetate transparencies or slides. These full-color transparencies, selected by author John Santrock and Lynne Blesz Vestal, include graphics from the text and various outside sources and were expressly designed to provide comprehensive coverage of all major topic areas generally covered in life-span development. A comprehensive annotated guide provides a brief description for each transparency and helpful suggestions for use in the classroom.

A large selection of **Videotapes,** including *Seasons of Life,* and *Childhood,* is also available to instructors, based upon the number of textbooks ordered from Brown & Benchmark Publishers by your bookstore.

The AIDS Booklet, 3e by Frank D. Cox of Santa Barbara City College, is a brief but comprehensive introduction to the Acquired Immune Deficiency Syndrome which is caused by HIV (Human Immunodeficiency Virus) and related viruses.

The Critical Thinker, written by Richard Mayer and Fiona Goodchild of the University of California, Santa Barbara, uses excerpts from introductory psychology text-books to show students how to think critically about psychology. Either this or the AIDS booklet are available at no charge to first-year adopters of our textbook or can be purchased separately.

Our **Custom Publishing Service** also allows you to have your own notes, handouts, or other classroom materials printed and bound very inexpensively for your course use, either as part of your custom designed textbook or separately. Contact your Brown & Benchmark representative for details.

A **Customized Transparency Program** is available to adopters for *Life-Span Development,* fifth edition, based on the number of textbooks ordered. Consult your Brown & Benchmark representative for ordering policies.

The **Human Development Interactive Videodisc Set** produced by Roger Ray of Rollins College, brings life-span development to life with instant access to over 30 brief video segments from the highly acclaimed *Seasons of Life* series. The 2-disc set can be used alone for selecting and sequencing excerpts, or in tandem with a Macintosh computer to add interactive commentary capability, as well as extra video and search options. Consult your Brown & Benchmark sales representative for details.

The Brain Modules on Videodisk, created by WNET New York, Antenne 2 TV/France, the Annenberg/CPB Foundation, and Professor Frank J. Vattano of Colorado State University, is based upon the Peabody award-winning series "The Brain." Thirty segments averaging 6 minutes each, vividly illustrate an array of psychology topics. Consult your Brown & Benchmark sales representative for details.

ACKNOWLEDGMENTS

This book was produced by many minds and hands. Brown & Benchmark Publishers has provided excellent support for the book. Michael Lange, Acquisitions Editor, is a wonderful editor, whose friendship and guidance I cherish. Sheralee Connors and Ted Underhill, Developmental Editors, showed a special enthusiasm for this book and should feel a sense of pride in having competently guided it through the revision process! The production team deserves special thanks for their excellent work: Peggy Selle, production editor; K. Wayne Harms and Gail Ryan, designers; Karen Storlie, permissions editor; Carol Judge, photo editor; and Rachel Imsland, art editor. Thanks also go to Allen Keniston and Blaine Peden, who prepared an excellent Student Study Guide and a very useful Instructor's Course Planner, and to Bradley Caskey, who prepared the Test Item File.

The fifth edition of this book benefited enormously from a carefully selected board of reviewers who provided in-depth reviews of chapters dealing with their areas of expertise and/or a page-by-page analysis of the entire manuscript. For their generous help and countless good ideas, I would like to thank:

Susan E. Allen, *Baylor University*

Frank R. Asbury, *Valdosta State College*

Daniel R. Bellack, *Trident Technical College*

Kathleen Crowley-Long, *College of Saint Rose*

Margaret Sutton Edmonds, *University of Massachussetts–Boston*

Martha M. Ellis, *Collin County Community College*

Tom Frangicetto, *Northampton Community College*

J. Steven Fulks, *Utah State University*

Cathy Furlong, *Tulsa Junior College*

Mary Ann Goodwyn, *Northeast Louisiana University*

Sharon C. Hott, *Allegany Community College*

Joseph C. LaVoie, *University of Nebraska at Omaha*

Kelli Meland, *Sullivan County Community College*

Heather E. Metcalfe, *University of Windsor*

James Turcott, *Kalamazoo Valley Community College*

Nancy C. White, *Coastal Carolina Community College*

I also remain indebted to the following individuals who reviewed previous editions and whose helpful guidance has been carried forward into the current edition of this text:

Joanne M. Alegre, *Yavajai College*

Helen E. Benedict, *Baylor University*

James A. Blackburn, *University of Wisconsin–Madison*

Belinda Blevin-Knabe, *University of Arkansas–Little Rock*

Donald Bowers, *Community College of Philadelphia*

Joan B. Cannon, *University of Lowell*

Shirley Feldman, *Stanford University*

Linda E. Flickinger, *St. Clair Community College*

Duwayne Furman, *Western Illinois University*

David Goldstein, *Temple University*

Peter C. Gram, *Pensacola Junior College*

Michael Green, *University of North Carolina*

Stephen Hoyer, *Pittsburgh State University*

Kathleen Day Hulbert, *University of Lowell*

Seth Kalichman, *Loyola University*

Karen Kirkendall, *Sangamon State University*

Jean Hill Macht, *Montgomery County Community College*

Salvador Macias, *University of South Carolina–Sumter*
Teri M. Miller-Schwartz, *Milwaukee Area Technical College*
Martin D. Murphy, *University of Akron*
Malinda Muzi, *Community College of Philadelphia*
Gordon K. Nelson, *Pennsylvania State University*
Stuart Offenbach, *Purdue University*
Sandra Osborne, *Montana State University*
Richard Pierce, *Pennsylvania State University–Altoona*
Susan Nakayama Siaw, *California State Polytechnic University*
Vicki Simmons, *University of Victoria*
Jon Snodgrass, *California State University–LA*
Donald Stanley, *North Dallas County College*
Lori L. Temple, *University of Nevada, Las Vegas*
B. D. Whetstone, *Birmingham Southern College*
Sarah White, *Reynolds Community College*
Lyn W. Wickelgren, *Metropolitan State College*
Ann M. Williams, *Luzerne County Community College*

The quality of this text is greatly due to the ideas and insights of many other colleagues. I would like to thank the following individuals for sharing their thoughts and beneficial suggestions for improving *Life-Span Development:*

Berkeley Adams, *Jamestown Community College*
Jack Busky, *Harrisburg Area Community College*
Jeri Carter, *Glendale Community College*
Vincent Castranovo, *Community College of Philadelphia*
Ginny Chappeleau, *Muskingum Area Technical College*
M. A. Christenberry, *Augusta College*
Cynthia Crown, *Xavier University*
Diane Davis, *Bowie State University*
Doreen DeSantio, *West Chester University*
Jill De Villiers, *Smith College*
Richard Ewy, *Penn State University*
Roberta Ferrara, *University of Kentucky*
John Gat, *Humboldt State University*
Marvin Gelman, *Montgomery County College*
Rebecca J. Glare, *Weber State College*

Judy Goodell, *National University*
Robert Heavilin, *Greater Hartford Community College*
Sharon Holt, *Allegany Community College*
Erwin Janek, *Henderson State University*
James Jasper-Jacobsen, *Indiana University–Purdue*
Ursula Joyce, *St. Thomas Aquinas College*
Barbara Kane, *Indiana State University*
James L. Keeney, *Middle Georgia College*
Elinor Kinarthy, *Rio Hondo College*
A. Klingner, *Northwest Community College*
Jane Krump, *North Dakota State College of Science*
Joe LaVoie, *University of Nebraska*
Karen Macrae, *University of South Carolina*
Robert C. McGinnis, *Ancilla College*
Clara McKinney, *Barstow College*
Michael Newton, *Sam Houston State University*
Beatrice Norrie, *Mount Royal College*
Jean O'Neil, *Boston College*
David Pipes, *Caldwell Community College*
Bob Rainey, *Florida Community College*
H. Ratner, *Wayne State University*
Russell Riley, *Lord Fairfax Community College*
Clarence Romeno, *Riverside Community College*
Paul Roodin, *SUNY–Oswego*
Ron Russac, *University of North Florida*
Cynthia Scheibe, *Ithaca College*
Robert Schell, *SUNY–Oswego*
Owen Sharkey, *University of Prince Edward Island*
Donald Stanley, *North Harris Community College*
Barbara Thomas, *National University*
James Turcott, *Kalamazoo Valley Community College*
Stephen Truhon, *Winston-Salem State University*
Myron D. Williams, *Great Lakes Bible College*

A final note of thanks goes to my wife, Mary Jo, for her continued support of my work and for the companionship she has provided.

To the Student

How the Learning System Works

This book contains a number of learning devices, each of which presents the field of life-span development in a meaningful way. The learning devices in *Life-Span Development* will help you learn the material more effectively.

Chapter Outlines

Each chapter begins with an outline, showing the organization of topics by heading levels. The outline functions as an overview to the arrangement and structure of the chapter.

Images of Life-Span Development

Opening each chapter is an imaginative, high-interest piece, focusing on a topic related to the chapter's content.

Preview

This brief introductory section describes the chapter's main themes.

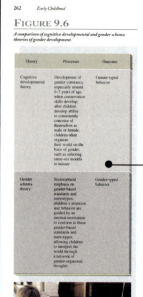

Critical Thinking Questions

Three or more critical thinking questions are embedded in the text of every chapter. These questions will challenge you to think more deeply about the content of the chapter.

Visual Figures and Tables

These include both a description of important content information and photographs that illustrate the content. Some are summaries of important ideas contained in the text.

Life-Span Practical Knowledge

This boxed insert provides a review of a recommended or controversial book that appears one or more times in each chapter.

Photographs and Legends

Special attention was given to the selection of photographs for *Life-Span Development*. Several experts on life-span development sent photographs to be included in the text. Legends were carefully written to clarify and elaborate concepts.

Key Term Definitions

Key terms appear in boldface type. Their definitions immediately follow in italic type. This provides you with a clear understanding of important concepts.

Perspectives on Parenting and Education

This feature explores parenting and education across the human life span and stimulates discussion through a variety of topics that relate to the chapters. One of these boxed inserts appears in every chapter.

Sociocultural Worlds of Development

Life-Span Development gives special attention to the cultural, ethnic, and gender worlds of individuals. Each chapter has one or more boxed inserts that highlight the sociocultural dimensions of life-span development.

Socioemotional Development in Early Childhood 241

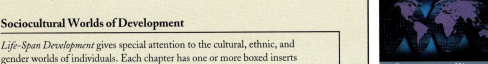

SOCIOCULTURAL WORLDS OF DEVELOPMENT 9.1

Black and Hispanic Family Orientations

In the 1985 Children's Defense Fund study "Black and White Children in America: Key Facts" (Edelman, 1987), Black children were three times as likely as White children to

- be poor
- live with a parent who was separated from a spouse
- die of child abuse

five times as likely to

- be dependent on welfare

and twelve times as likely to

- live with a parent who never married

Nonetheless, it is important to keep in mind that millions of Black American families are not on welfare, have children who stay in school and out of trouble, and find ways to cope with and overcome problems they experience during difficult times. In 1967, Martin Luther King, Jr., reflected on the Black American family and gave the following caution: "As public awareness of the predicament of the Black family increases, there will be danger and opportunity. The opportunity will be to deal fully rather than haphazardly with the problem as a whole, as a social catastrophe brought on by many years of oppression. The danger is that the problems will be attributed to innate Black weaknesses and used to justify further neglect and to rationalize continued oppression." In today's world, Dr. King's words still ring true. (McLoyd, in press; Ogbu, 1989; Spencer & Dornbusch, 1990).

The Black cultural tradition of an extended family household—in which one or several grandparents, uncles, aunts, siblings, or cousins, either live together or provide support—has helped many Black parents cope with adverse social conditions such as economic impoverishment (McAdoo, 1988). The Black extended family can be traced to the African heritage of many Black Americans, where in many cultures a newly married couple does not move away from relatives. Instead, the extended family assists its members with basic family functions. Researchers have found that the extended Black family helps to reduce the stress of poverty and single parenting through emotional support, sharing of income and economic responsibility, and surrogate parenting (McAdoo, 1988). The presence of grandmothers in the households of many Black adolescents and their infants has been an important support system for both the teenage mother and the infant (Stevens, 1984). Active and involved extended family support systems also help a parent or parents from other ethnic minority groups cope with poverty and its related stress.

A basic value in Mexico is represented by the saying "As long as our family stays together, we are strong." Mexican children are brought up to stay close to their family, often playing with siblings rather than with schoolmates or neighborhood children, as American children usually do. Unlike the father in many American families, the Mexican father is the undisputed authority on all family matters and is usually obeyed without question. The mother is revered as the primary source of affection and care. This emphasis on family attachment leads the Mexican to say, "I will achieve mainly because of my family, and for my family, rather than myself." By contrast, the self-reliant American would say, "I will achieve mainly because of my ability and initiative and for myself rather than for my family." Unlike most Americans, families in Mexico tend to stretch out in a network of relatives that often runs to scores of individuals.

Both cultures—Mexican and American—have undergone considerable change in recent decades. Whether Mexican children will gradually take on the characteristics of American children, or whether American children will shift closer to Mexican children, is difficult to predict. The cultures of both countries will probably move to a new order more in keeping with future demands, retaining some common features of the old while establishing new priorities and values (Holtzmann, 1982).

Although Black children are more likely than White children to be poor and live with a parent who has been separated from a spouse, it is important to keep in mind that millions of Black American families are not on welfare, have considerable family support, and find ways to effectively cope with stress. The extended family, especially grandmothers, plays an especially important role in Black American children's development.

Concept Tables

Two or three times in each chapter we review what has been discussed so far in that chapter by displaying the information in concept tables. This learning device helps you get a handle on material several times a chapter.

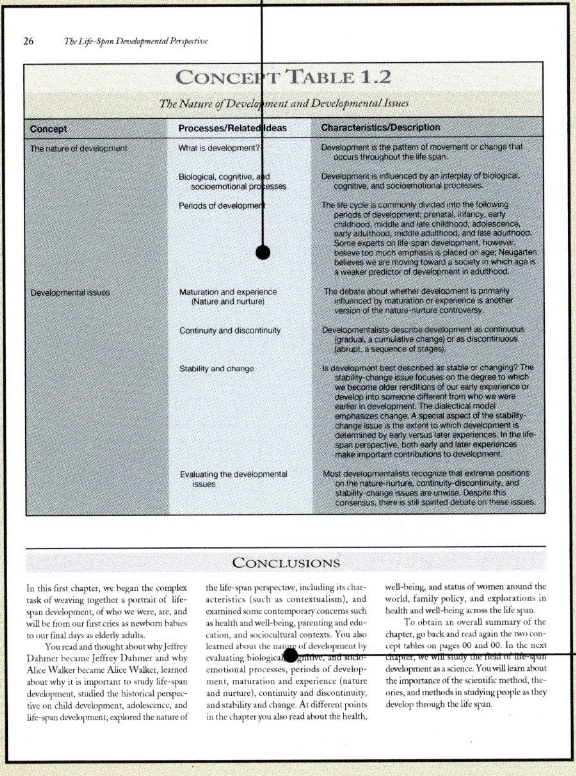

26 *The Life-Span Developmental Perspective*

CONCEPT TABLE 1.2

The Nature of Development and Developmental Issues

Concept	Processes/Related Ideas	Characteristics/Description
The nature of development	What is development?	Development is the pattern of movement or change that occurs throughout the life span.
	Biological, cognitive, and socioemotional processes	Development is influenced by an interplay of biological, cognitive, and socioemotional processes.
	Periods of development	The life cycle is commonly divided into the following periods of development: prenatal, infancy, early childhood, middle and late childhood, adolescence, early adulthood, middle adulthood, and late adulthood. Some experts on life-span development, however, believe too much emphasis is placed on age; Neugarten believes we are moving toward a society in which age is a weaker predictor of development in adulthood.
Developmental issues	Maturation and experience (Nature and nurture)	The debate about whether development is primarily influenced by maturation or experience is another version of the nature-nurture controversy.
	Continuity and discontinuity	Developmentalists describe development as continuous (gradual, a cumulative change) or as discontinuous (abrupt, a sequence of stages).
	Stability and change	Is development best described as stable or changing? The stability-change issue focuses on the degree to which we become older renditions of our early experience or develop into someone different from who we were earlier in development. The dialectical model emphasizes change. A special aspect of the stability-change issue is the extent to which development is determined by early versus later experiences. In the life-span perspective, both early and later experiences make important contributions to development.
	Evaluating the developmental issues	Most developmentalists recognize that extreme positions on the nature-nurture, continuity-discontinuity, and stability-change issues are unwise. Despite this consensus, there is still spirited debate on these issues.

CONCLUSIONS

In this first chapter, we began the complex task of weaving together a portrait of life-span development, of who we were, are, and will be from our first cries as newborn babies to our final days as elderly adults.

You read and thought about why Jeffrey Dahmer became Jeffrey Dahmer and why Alice Walker became Alice Walker, learned about why it is important to study life-span development, studied the historical perspective on child development, adolescence, and life-span development, explored the nature of the life-span perspective, including its characteristics (such as contextualism), and examined some contemporary concerns such as health and well-being, parenting and education, and sociocultural contexts. You also learned about the nature of development by evaluating biological, cognitive, and socioemotional processes, periods of development, maturation and experience (nature and nurture), continuity and discontinuity, and stability and change. At different points in the chapter you also read about the health, well-being, and status of women around the world, family policy, and explorations in health and well-being across the life span.

To obtain an overall summary of the chapter, go back and read again the two concept tables on pages 00 and 00. In the next chapter, we will study the field of life-span development as a science. You will learn about the importance of the scientific method, theories, and methods in studying people as they develop through the life span.

Conclusions Section

At the end of each chapter, a section called "Conclusions" helps you to review the main ideas of the entire chapter.

Life-Span Health and Well-Being

At the end of each chapter, this feature explores health and well-being across the life span.

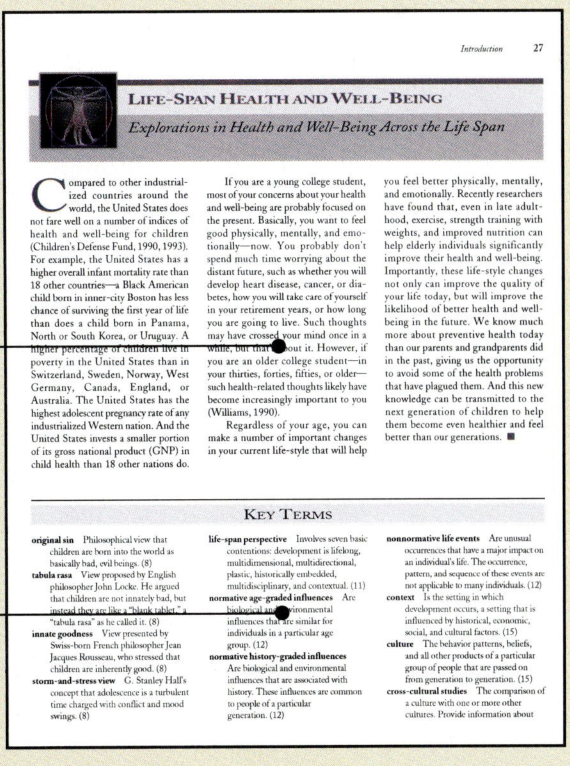

Introduction 27

LIFE-SPAN HEALTH AND WELL-BEING

Explorations in Health and Well-Being Across the Life Span

Compared to other industrialized countries around the world, the United States does not fare well on a number of indices of health and well-being for children (Children's Defense Fund, 1990, 1993). For example, the United States has a higher overall infant mortality rate than 18 other countries—a Black American child born in inner-city Boston has less chance of surviving the first year of life than does a child born in Panama, North or South Korea, or Uruguay. A higher percentage of children live in poverty in the United States than in Switzerland, Sweden, Norway, West Germany, Canada, England, or Australia. The United States has the highest adolescent pregnancy rate of any industrialized Western nation. And the United States invests a smaller portion of its gross national product (GNP) in child health than 18 other nations do.

If you are a young college student, most of your concerns about your health and well-being are probably focused on the present. Basically, you want to feel good physically, mentally, and emotionally—now. You probably don't spend much time worrying about the distant future, such as whether you will develop heart disease, cancer, or diabetes, how you will take care of yourself in your retirement years, or how long you are going to live. Such thoughts may have crossed your mind once in a while, but that's about it. However, if you are an older college student—in your thirties, forties, fifties, or older—such health-related thoughts likely have become increasingly important to you (Williams, 1990).

Regardless of your age, you can make a number of important changes in your current life-style that will help you feel better physically, mentally, and emotionally. Recently researchers have found that, even in late adulthood, exercise, strength training with weights, and improved nutrition can help elderly individuals significantly improve their health and well-being. Importantly, these life-style changes not only can improve the quality of your life today, but will improve the likelihood of better health and well-being in the future. We know much more about preventive health today than our parents and grandparents did in the past, giving us the opportunity to avoid some of the health problems that have plagued them. And this new knowledge can be transmitted to the next generation of children to help them become even healthier and feel better than our generations. ■

KEY TERMS

original sin Philosophical view that children are born into the world as basically bad, evil beings. (8)
tabula rasa View proposed by English philosopher John Locke. He argued that children are not innately bad, but instead they are like a "blank tablet," a "tabula rasa" as he called it. (8)
innate goodness View presented by Swiss-born French philosopher Jean Jacques Rousseau, who stressed that children are inherently good. (8)
storm-and-stress view G. Stanley Hall's concept that adolescence is a turbulent time charged with conflict and mood swings. (8)
life-span perspective Involves seven basic contentions: development is lifelong, multidimensional, multidirectional, plastic, historically embedded, multidisciplinary, and contextual. (11)
normative age-graded influences Are biological and environmental influences that are similar for individuals in a particular age group. (12)
normative history-graded influences Are biological and environmental influences that are associated with history. These influences are common to people of a particular generation. (12)
nonnormative life events Are unusual occurrences that have a major impact on an individual's life. The occurrence, pattern, and sequence of these events are not applicable to many individuals. (12)
context Is the setting in which development occurs, a setting that is influenced by historical, economic, social, and cultural factors. (15)
culture The behavior patterns, beliefs, and all other products of a particular group of people that are passed on from generation to generation. (15)
cross-cultural studies The comparison of a culture with one or more other cultures. Provide information about

Key Terms

Key Terms are listed with definitions and page references. They also are defined again in a page-referenced glossary at the end of the book.

LIFE-SPAN DEVELOPMENT

The Life-Span Developmental Perspective

All the world's a stage, And all the men and women merely players; They have their exits and their entrances, And one man in his time plays many parts . . .

—William Shakespeare

This book is about human development—its universal features, its individual variations, its nature. Every life is distinct, a new biography in the world. Examining the shape of human development allows us to understand it better. *Life-Span Development* is about the rhythm and meaning of people's lives, about turning mystery into understanding, and about weaving a portrait of who each of us was, is, and will be. In Section One, you will read two chapters: Introduction (chapter 1) and "The Science of Life-Span Development" (chapter 2).

Monet, Train in the
Countryside, detail.

1

Introduction

We reach backward to our parents and forward to our children, and through their children to a future we will never see, but about which we need to care.

—Carl Jung

> *The first cry of a newborn in Chicago or Zamboango, in Amsterdam or Rangoon, has the same pitch and key, each saying, "I am! I have come through! I belong! I am a member of the human family." . . . babies arriving, suckling, growing into youths restless and questioning. Then as grown-ups they seek and hope. They mate, toil, fish, quarrel, sing, fight, pray.*
>
> —Carl Sandburg, *The Family of Man*, 1955

IMAGES OF LIFE-SPAN DEVELOPMENT

How Did Jeffrey Dahmer Become Jeffrey Dahmer and Alice Walker Become Alice Walker?

On page 45 of Jeffrey Dahmer's Ohio high school yearbook is a photograph of 45 honor society students lined up shoulder to shoulder. Except for one of them, their hair is well combed, their smiles confident. But one senior three rows from the top has no smile, no eyes, no face at all—his image was reduced to a silhouette by an annoyed student editor before the yearbook went to the printer. The silhouette belonged to Jeffrey Dahmer, whose grades ranged from A's to D's. He fell far short of honor society qualifications, but he sneaked into the photo session as if he belonged. The photo session took place just 2 months before the day in the spring of 1978 when, by his account, he killed his first victim with a barbell.

That was 13 years before Dahmer confessed to one of the most horrific strings of slayings in modern times. In all the years he cried out for attention, the photo session was one of the few times he got caught. By then he had learned to hide his contradictory emotions behind a mask of normalcy. It was a mask no one pulled down until one night in 1991 when a man in handcuffs dashed out of Dahmer's bizarrely cluttered apartment in a tough Milwaukee neighborhood, called the police, and stammered that

Dahmer had tried to kill him. At least 17 other victims did not get away (Barron & Tabor, 1991).

Jeffrey Dahmer had a troubled childhood. His parents constantly bickered before they divorced, his mother had emotional problems and doted on his younger brother, he felt that his father neglected him, and he had been sexually abused by another boy when he was 8 years old. But the vast majority of individuals who suffer through such childhood pains never go on to commit the grisly crimes that Dahmer committed (Goleman, 1991).

A decade before Dahmer's first murder, Alice Walker, who would later win a Pulitzer Prize for her book *The Color Purple*, spent her days battling racism in Mississippi. She had recently won her first writing fellowship, but rather than use the money to follow her dream of moving to Senegal, Africa, she put herself into the heart and heat of the civil rights movement. Walker grew up knowing the brutal effects of poverty and racism. Born in 1944, she was the eighth child of Georgia sharecroppers who earned $300 a year. When Walker was 8, her brother accidentally shot her in the left eye with a BB gun. By the time her parents got her to the hospital a week

Alice Walker won the Pulitzer Prize for her book The Color Purple. *Like the characters in her book (especially the women), Walker overcame pain and anger to triumph and celebrate the human spirit.*

later (they had no car), she was blind in that eye and it had developed a disfiguring layer of scar tissue. Despite the counts against her, Walker went on to become an essayist, a poet, an award-winning novelist, a short-story writer, and a social activist who, like her characters (especially the women), has overcome pain and anger.

THE LIFE-SPAN PERSPECTIVE

Why study life-span development? What is the history of interest in life-span development? What are the characteristics of life-span development? What are some contemporary concerns?

Why Study Life-Span Development?

Why study life-span development? Perhaps you are or will be a parent or teacher. Responsibility for children is or will be a part of your everyday life. The more you learn about them, the better you can deal with them. Perhaps you hope to gain some insight into your own history—as an infant, a child, an adolescent, or a young adult. Perhaps you want to know more about what your life will be like as you grow through the adult years—as a middle-aged adult, as an adult in old age, for example. Or perhaps you just stumbled onto this course, thinking that it sounded intriguing and that the topic of the human life cycle would raise some provocative and intriguing issues about our lives as we grow and develop. Whatever your reasons, you will discover that the study of life-span development *is* provocative, *is* intriguing, and *is* filled with information about who we are, how we have come to be this way, and where our future will take us.

This book tells the story of human development from conception to death—from the point in time when life begins until the point in time when it ends, at least life as we know it. You will see yourself as an infant, as a child, and as an adolescent, and be stimulated to think about how those years influenced the kind of individual you are today. And you will see yourself as a young adult, as a middle-aged adult, and as an adult in old age, and be stimulated to think about how your experiences today will influence your development through the remainder of your adult years.

The Historical Perspective

Interest in children has a long and rich history. Interest in adolescents is more recent, and interest in adults has begun to develop seriously only in the latter half of the twentieth century (Havighurst, 1973).

FIGURE 1.1

These artistic impressions show how children were viewed as miniature adults earlier in history. Artists' renditions of children as miniature adults may have been too stereotypical.

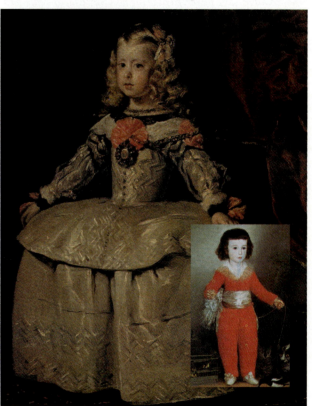

Child Development

Childhood has become such a distinct period that it is hard to imagine it was not always thought of in that way. However, in medieval times, laws generally did not distinguish between childhood offenses and adult offenses. After analyzing samples of art, along with available publications, historian Philippe Aries (1962) concluded that European societies did not accord any special status to children prior to 1600. In the paintings he studied, children were often dressed in small versions of adult clothing (see figure 1.1).

Were children actually treated as miniature adults with no special status in medieval Europe? Aries's interpretation has been criticized. Aries primarily sampled aristocratic, idealized subjects, which led to the overdrawn conclusion that children were treated as miniature adults and not accorded any special status (Borstelmann, 1983). In medieval times, children did often work, and their emotional bond with parents may not have been as strong as it is for many children today. However, in medieval times, childhood was probably recognized as a distinct phase of life more than Aries believed. Also, we know that in ancient Egypt, Greece, and Rome, rich conceptions of children's development were held.

Throughout history, philosophers have speculated at length about the nature of children and how they should be reared. Three such philosophical views are based on the notions of original sin, tabula rasa, and innate goodness. In the perspective of **original sin,** *especially advocated during the Middle Ages, children were perceived as being basically bad, as being born into the world as evil beings.* The goal of child rearing was salvation, which was believed to remove sin from the child's life. Toward the end of the seventeenth century, the **tabula rasa** *view was proposed by English philosopher John Locke. He argued that children are not innately bad, but instead they are like a "blank tablet," a "tabula rasa" as he called it.* Locke believed that childhood experiences are important in determining adult characteristics. He advised parents to spend time with their children and help them become contributing members of society. In the eighteenth century, the **innate goodness** *view was presented by Swiss-born French philosopher Jean Jacques Rousseau, who stressed that children are inherently good.* Rousseau said that because children are basically good, they should be permitted to grow naturally with little parental monitoring or constraint.

During the past century and a half, interest in the nature of children and ways to improve their well-being have continued to be important concerns of our society. We now conceive of childhood as a highly eventful and unique period of life that lays an important foundation for the adult years and is highly differentiated from them. In most approaches to childhood, distinct periods are identified in which special skills are mastered and new life tasks are confronted. Childhood is no longer seen as an inconvenient "waiting" period during which adults must suffer the incompetencies of the young. We now value childhood as a special time of growth and change, and we invest great resources in caring for and educating our children. We protect them from the excesses of adult work through strict child labor laws; we treat their crimes against society under a special system of juvenile justice; and we have government provisions for helping them when ordinary family support systems fail or when families seriously interfere with the child's well-being (Cohen & Naimark, 1991).

Adolescence

Twentieth-century poet-essayist Roger Allen once remarked, "In case you are worried about what's going to become of the younger generation, it's going to grow up and start worrying about the younger generation." Virtually every society has worried about its younger generation, but it was not until the beginning of the twentieth century that the scientific study of adolescence appeared. In 1904, American psychologist G. Stanley Hall wrote the first scientific book on the nature of adolescence. The **storm-and-stress view** *is G. Stanley Hall's concept that adolescence is a turbulent time charged with conflict and mood swings.* Thoughts, feelings, and actions oscillate between conceit and humility, good and temptation, and happiness and sadness. The adolescent may be nasty to a peer one moment and kind the next moment, or may want to be alone, but seconds later seek companionship.

In youth, we clothe ourselves with rainbows, and go as brave as the zodiac.

—Ralph Waldo Emerson,
The Conduct of Life, 1860

As we move toward the close of the twentieth century, experts on adolescence are trying to dispel the myth that adolescents are abnormal and deviant (Feldman & Elliott, 1990). Too often all adolescents are stereotyped and described in sweeping generalizations based on a small group of highly visible adolescents. An investigation by Daniel Offer and his colleagues (1988) documented that the vast majority of adolescents are competent human beings who are not experiencing deep emotional turmoil. The self-images of adolescents were sampled from around the world—from the United States, Australia, Bangladesh, Hungary, Israel, Japan, Taiwan, Turkey, and West Germany. A positive self-image characterized three of every four adolescents studied. The adolescents were moving toward adulthood with a healthy integration of their identity, being happy most of the time, enjoying life, valuing work and school, having positive feelings about their family and friends, expressing confidence in their sexual selves, and believing they have the ability to cope with life's stresses—not exactly a storm-and-stress portrayal of adolescence.

Critical Thinking

In what ways are today's adolescents the same as or different from the adolescents of 10 years ago? 20 years ago?

Although adolescence has a biological base, sociohistorical conditions contributed to the emergence of the concept of adolescence. American society may have "inflicted" the status of adolescence on its youth through child-saving legislation (Elder, Caspi, & Burton, 1988; Fasick, 1994; Lapsley, Enright, & Serlin, 1985). By developing laws for youth only, the adult power structure placed young people in a submissive position that restricted their options, encouraged dependency, and made their move into the world of adult work more manageable. From 1890 to 1920, virtually every state developed laws that excluded youth from work and required them to attend school. In this time frame, a 600 percent increase in the number of high

FIGURE 1.2

Two contrasting perspectives on developmental change. *In the traditional perspective, dramatic change occurs in infancy and early childhood, while little or no change takes place in adult development. In the life-span perspective, developmental change takes place throughout the human life cycle.*

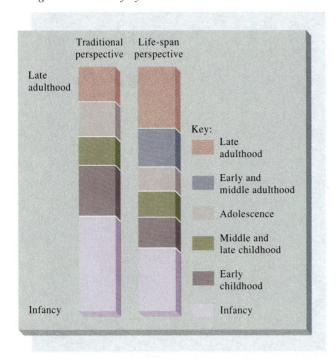

FIGURE 1.3

The aging of America. (a) *Millions of Americans over age 65 from 1900 to the present and projected to the year 2040.* (b) *Millions of Americans over age 85 in 1980 and projected in the year 2040.*

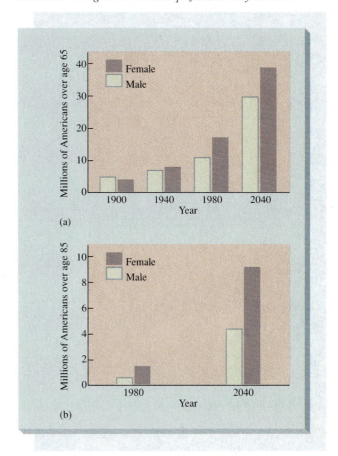

TABLE 1.1

Human Life Expectancy at Birth From Prehistoric to Contemporary Times

Time Period	Average Life Expectancy (in years)
Prehistoric Times	18
Ancient Greece	20
Middle Ages, England	33
1620, Massachusetts Bay Colony	35
19th Century, England	41
1900, USA	47
1915, USA	54
1954, USA	70
1992, USA	75

Source: Data from Monroe Lerner, "When, Why, and Where People Die" in E. S. Shneidman (ed.), *Death: Current Perspectives*, 2d ed., pp. 89–91, 1980.

school graduates occurred! (Tyack, 1976). And by 1950, the developmental period we refer to as "adolescence" had come of age. Not only did it possess physical and social identity, but it possessed legal identity as well. By this time, every state had developed special laws for youth between the ages of 16 and 21.

Life-Span Development

The *traditional approach* to development emphasizes extreme change from birth to adolescence, little or no change in adulthood, and decline in old age. By contrast, the *life-span approach* emphasizes that developmental change occurs during adulthood as well as during childhood (Baltes, Featherman, & Lerner, 1990; Pollock & Greenspan, 1994). Figure 1.2 reveals how the traditional view of development contrasts with the life-span perspective. In the traditional view, notice the powerful role allotted to infancy and early childhood and the absence of change in early and middle adulthood.

The adult part of the life cycle that first aroused the interest of life-span researchers was toward the end of the cycle: aging (Riegel, 1977). Improvements in sanitation, nutrition, and medical knowledge led to dramatic increases in life expectancy. In table 1.1, the average life expectancy of individuals from prehistoric to contemporary times is shown. Until the twentieth century, most individuals did not live to be 50 years of age. In 1900, only 1 American in 25 was over 65; today, 9 in 25 live to be this old. By the middle of the next century, 1 American in 4 will be 65 years of age or older. Figure 1.3a shows

FIGURE 1.4

Maximum recorded life spans for different species.

Species (common name)	Maximum life span (years)
Human	120
Galápagos turtle	100+
Indian elephant	70
Chinese alligator	52
Golden eagle	46
Gorilla	39
Common toad	36
Domestic cat	27
Domestic dog	20
Vampire bat	13
House mouse	3

Source: After Kirkwood (1985), p. 34. Comparative and evolutionary aspects of longevity. In C. E. Finch & E. L. Schneider (Eds.), *Handbook of the Biology of Aging.* (2nd ed.). New York: Van Nostrand Reinhold.

the number (in millions) of Americans over 65 in 1900, 1940, and 1980, and the projected number for the year 2040. Not only will we experience a substantial increase in the number of people over 65, but the same trend will occur for individuals over the age of 85 (see figure 1.3b).

Although we are living longer, on the average, than we did in the past, the maximum life span of humans has not changed since the beginning of recorded history. The upper boundary of the life span is approximately 120 years, and, as indicated in figure 1.4, our only competition from other species for the maximum recorded life span is the Galápagos turtle.

For too long we believed that development was something that happened only to children. To be sure, growth and development are dramatic in the first two decades of life, but a great deal of change goes on in the next five or six decades of life, too. In the words of American developmental psychologists Robert Sears and Shirley Feldman (1973):

> But the next five or six decades are every bit as important, not only to those adults who are passing through them but to their children, who must live with and understand parents and grandparents. The changes in body, personality, and abilities through these later decades is great. There are severe developmental tasks imposed by marriage and parenthood, by the waxing and waning of physical prowess and of some intellectual capacities, by the children's flight from the nest, by the achievement of an occupational plateau, and by the facing of retirement and the prospect of final extinction. Parents have always been fascinated by their children's development, but it is high time adults began to look objectively at themselves, to examine the systematic changes in their own physical, mental, and emotional qualities, as they pass through the life cycle, and to get acquainted with the limitations and assets they share with so many others of their age. (pp. v–vi)

Our society's increasing interest in older adults is reflected by a law enacted by Congress in 1986, which states that employers can no longer require workers to retire when they

Paul Baltes (center) is shown here with his research colleagues at the Max Planck Institute of Human Development in Berlin, Germany. Baltes has developed a number of important ideas about the life-span perspective and conducted many research studies documenting the nature of developmental changes in adulthood. His most recent research interests have focused on the developmental aspects of wisdom in adulthood.

reach age 70—with exceptions for certain occupations, such as police officers and pilots (Riley, 1989). This act does not end discrimination, but it does increase the freedom of choice of many older adults and sends a strong message that the work contributions of older adults are valued. This act may signify a reversal of the century-long decline in labor force participation of workers over the age of 65.

As the elderly population continues to grow into the twenty-first century, life-span developmentalists are concerned that an increasing number of older adults will be without either a spouse or children, who have traditionally been main sources of support for older adults (Zarit & Reid, 1994). In recent decades, American adults were less likely to be married, more likely to be childless, and more likely to be living alone than earlier in the twentieth century. As these individuals become older, their need for social relationships, networks, and supports appears to be increasing at the same time as the supply is dwindling. (More about the role of social supports for older adults appears in chapter 20.)

Characteristics of the Life-Span Perspective

In this book we take a life-span perspective on understanding development. What does it mean to adopt a life-span perspective? According to life-span development expert Paul Baltes (1987), the **life-span perspective** *involves seven basic contentions: Development is lifelong, multidimensional, multidirectional, plastic, historically embedded, multidisciplinary, and contextual.*

> *When we truly comprehend and enter the rhythm of life, we shall be able to bring together the daring of youth with the discipline of age in a way that does justice to both.*
>
> —J. S. Bixler,
> *Two Blessings of Joseph*

Development is *lifelong*. No age period dominates development. Researchers increasingly study the experiences and psychological orientations of adults at different points in their development. Development includes both gains and losses, which interact in dynamic ways throughout the life cycle (Baltes, 1989; Lerner, 1990).

Development is *multidimensional*. Development consists of biological, cognitive, and social dimensions. Even within a dimension such as intelligence, there are many components, such as abstract intelligence, nonverbal intelligence, social intelligence, and so on.

Development is *multidirectional*. Some dimensions or components of a dimension may increase in growth, while others decrease. For example, older adults may become wiser by being able to call on experience as a guide to intellectual decision making, but perform more poorly on tasks that require speed in processing information.

Development is *plastic*. Depending on the individual's life conditions, development may take many paths. A key developmental research agenda is the search for plasticity and its constraints. For example, researchers have demonstrated that the reasoning abilities of older adults can be improved through training (Smith & Baltes, 1991; Willis & Schaie, 1994).

Development is *embedded in history*, being influenced by historical conditions. The experiences of 40-year-olds who lived through the Great Depression were very different from the experiences of 40-year-olds who lived in the optimistic aftermath of World War II. The career orientation of many 30-year-old females in the 1990s is very different from what the career orientation of most 30-year-old females was in the 1950s.

Development is *studied by a number of disciplines*. Psychologists, sociologists, anthropologists, neuroscientists, and medical researchers all study human development and share a concern for unlocking the mysteries of development throughout the life span.

Development is *contextual*. The individual continually responds to and acts on contexts, which include a person's biological makeup, physical environment, and social, historical, and cultural contexts. In the contextual view, individuals are thought of as changing beings in a changing world. A summary of the characteristics of the life-span perspective is presented in figure 1.5.

The life-span perspective has benefitted the health and well-being of individuals, families, and communities. Many different careers now include positions that involve an application of knowledge about life-span development. For example, a knowledge of life-span development is relevant to genetic counselors and family planning specialists, health specialists and nurses, directors of day-care centers and preschool teachers, crisis intervention counselors, juvenile probation officers, social workers and therapists, and gerontologists (those who study or work with older adults).

Contextualism: Age–Graded, History–Graded, and Nonnormative Influences

One characteristic of the life-span perspective—contextualism—merits further attention. In the contextual view, development can be understood as the outcome of the interaction among three systems: (1) normative age-graded influences, (2) normative history-graded influences, and (3) nonnormative life events (Baltes, 1987).

Normative age-graded influences *are biological and environmental influences that are similar for individuals in a particular age group.* These influences include biological processes such as puberty and menopause, and they include sociocultural, environmental processes such as entry into formal education (usually at about age 6 in most cultures) and retirement (usually occurring in the fifties and sixties).

Normative history-graded influences *are biological and environmental influences that are associated with history. These influences are common to people of a particular generation.* Normative history-graded influences include economic changes (the Great Depression of the 1930s), war (World War II in the 1940s), the changing roles of women, the computer revolution, and political upheaval and change (such as the decrease in hardline communism in the late 1980s and early 1990s).

Nonnormative life events *are unusual occurrences that have a major impact on an individual's life. The occurrence, pattern, and sequence of these events are not applicable to many individuals.* These events do not follow a general and predictable course. Such events may include the death of a parent when a child is young, pregnancy in early adolescence, a disaster (such as a fire that destroys a home), or an accident (such as a serious car wreck). Nonnormative life events can also include positive occurrences such as winning a lottery or being offered a unique career opportunity with special privileges. An important aspect of understanding the role of nonnormative life events is how individuals adapt to them.

FIGURE 1.5

Characteristics of the life-span perspective.

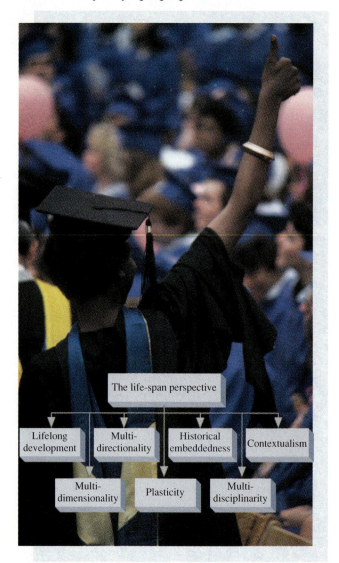

Some Contemporary Concerns

Consider some of the topics you read about in newspapers and magazines every day: genetic research, child abuse, homosexuality, mental retardation, parenting, intelligence, career changes, divorce, addiction and recovery, the increasing ethnic minority population, gender issues, mid-life crises, stress and health, retirement, and aging. What the experts are discovering in each of these areas has direct and significant consequences for understanding children and adults and our decisions as a society about how they should be treated.

An important theme of this textbook is to provide detailed, contemporary coverage of the roles that health and well-being, parenting and education, and sociocultural contexts play in life-span development.

LIFE-SPAN PRACTICAL KNOWLEDGE 1.1

Familyhood

(1992) by Dr. Lee Salk. New York: Simon & Schuster.

Familyhood is about the importance of the family in children's lives and about nurturing the family values that matter. Lee Salk was a well-known clinical psychologist who championed better lives for children for many years. He died in 1992.

Salk says that while the structure of families has changed enormously in recent years because of high divorce rates, increasing numbers of stepfamilies, and huge numbers of working-mother families, the values the family cherishes most have not changed. Relying on information from a comprehensive family values survey, Salk describes how parents today still have the following needs, wants, and values:

- They want family members to provide emotional support for one another.
- They want children to show respect for their parents.
- They believe parents should also show respect for their children.
- They think that parents should show mutual respect for each other.
- They believe that family members should take responsibility for their own actions.
- They think that family members should try to understand and listen to each other.

Salk draws on his extensive background in counseling parents to provide advice on how to make the family a place where people care about each other and transmit important family values.

Health and Well-Being

We have become a nation obsessed with health and well-being. Whether we are healthy, exercise regularly, and adopt good nutritional patterns, or are in poor health, are couch potatoes, and fill our veins with cholesterol, it is impossible to avoid reading about, hearing about, and observing the interest in health and well-being in our society. The AIDS epidemic, starving children in Somalia, the poor quality of health care that many American families receive compared to their counterparts in other industrialized nations, the ever-present stress in many people's lives, the succumbing of many people to lives of alcohol and drug abuse, the rapidly expanding elderly population and how its health care will be provided, and how we can effectively cope with major life events such as the death of a loved one, divorce, and the loss of a job, as well as the countless daily hassles that infuse our lives—these are among the innumerable issues and dilemmas we face as we make the long journey through the human life span (Shonkoss, in press).

Asian physicians around 2600 B.C. and Greek physicians around 500 B.C. recognized that good habits are essential for good health. They did not blame the gods for illness and think that magic would cure it. They realized that people have some control over their health and well-being. A physician's role was that of a guide, assisting patients in restoring a natural and emotional balance.

As we approach the twenty-first century, once again we recognize the power of life-styles and psychological states in promoting health and well-being. We are returning to the ancient view that the ultimate responsibility for individuals' health and well-being throughout the human life span rests with the individuals themselves.

Our coverage of health and well-being in this book will be integrated into our discussion of life-span development in every chapter. Their importance is also highlighted in each chapter by (1) a "Life-Span Health and Well-Being" section, a chapter-ending piece that focuses on some aspect of the chapter's contents related to health and well-being, and (2) "Life-Span Practical Knowledge" inserts that briefly review outstanding or controversial books that will expand your understanding of how to improve your health and well-being in your everyday life.

Parenting and Education

We hear a great deal from both experts and popular writers about pressures on contemporary families. The number of families in which both parents work is increasing; at the same time, the number of one-parent families has risen over the past two decades as a result of a climbing divorce rate. With more children being raised by single parents or by parents who are both working—parents who have much less time to spend with their children—the quality of child care is of concern to many. Are working parents better at using the smaller amount of time they have with their children? How troubled should we be about the increasing number of latchkey children—those at home alone after school, waiting for parents to return from work? We can begin to answer these questions by seeing what developmental experts have discovered about such issues: for instance, how working parents use their time with their children, and the nature of their parenting approaches and behaviors; how various day-care arrangements influence children's social and intellectual growth in relation to home-care arrangements; and how children are affected by being unsupervised for hours every day after school (Lamb, 1994; Lerner & Abrams, 1994; McCartney & others, 1993).

Families, of course, do not consist just of parents with young children. The family life cycle also includes middle-aged parents and the aging couple. We now have special concerns about the strains placed on middle-aged parents, many of whom have to care for not only their own children and adolescents, but also their own aging parents, who are living to a much older age than did past generations. It has also become apparent that widows and divorced women may be in particular danger of having to live in poverty.

During the past decade, the American educational system has come under attack (Holtzmann, 1992). A national commission appointed by the Office of Education concluded that children are poorly prepared for the increasingly complex future they will be asked to face in our society. The problems are legion: The skills of those entering the teaching profession are declining; adolescents are graduating from high school with primary-grade-level reading and math skills; there is a shortage of qualified math and science teachers; students are spending less time in academic classroom work; school curricula are unchallenging and don't require much thinking; and there is a high dropout rate over the 4 years of high school. Solutions to these problems are not easy to come by. However, in searching for solutions, policy makers often turn to developmentalists, because, to design an engaging curriculum, a planner must know what engages and motivates children (Gardner, 1993). To improve our national effort in teaching thinking skills, planners must understand what thinking is and how it changes across the school years (Kuhn, 1991). To understand the roots of social difficulties encountered by so many of today's youth— difficulties that lead them to drop out of school in droves— planners need to understand the nature of the transition from childhood to adolescence and the ways in which schools address this change (Entwisle & Alexander, 1992; Kuhn, 1993; Seidman & others, in press).

Discussions of parenting and education are woven into every chapter of *Life-Span Development*. Also, each chapter has one boxed insert, related to the chapter's contents, called "Perspectives on Parenting and Education."

Sociocultural Contexts

The tapestry of American culture has changed dramatically in recent years. Nowhere is the change more noticeable than in the increasing ethnic diversity of America's citizens (see figure 1.6). Ethnic minority groups—Black American, Hispanic American (American Indian), and Asian—made up 20 percent of all individuals under the age of 17 in 1989. By the year 2000, one-third of all schoolchildren will fall into this category. This changing demographic tapestry promises not only the richness that diversity produces, but also difficult challenges in extending the American dream to individuals of all ethnic groups. Historically, most ethnic minorities have found themselves at the bottom of the economic and social order. They have been

FIGURE 1.6

Ethnic minority population increases in the United States. The *percentage of Black American, Hispanic American, and Asian American individuals increased far more from 1980 to 1988 than did the percentage of whites. Shown here are two Korean-born children on the day they became United States citizens. Asian American children are the fastest-growing group of ethnic minority children.*

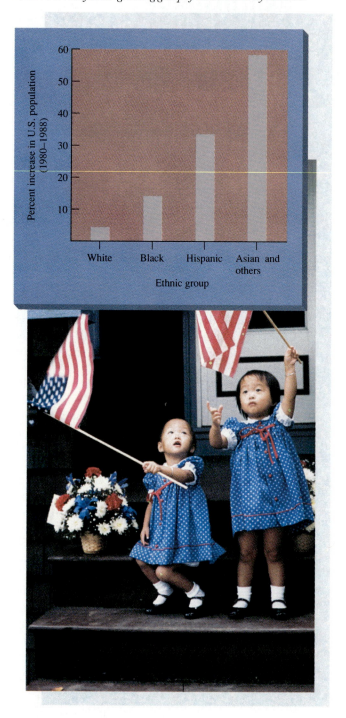

disproportionately represented among the poor and the inadequately educated. Half of all Black American children and one-third of all Hispanic American children live in poverty. School dropout rates for minority youth reach the alarming rate of 60 percent in some urban areas. These population trends and our nation's inability to prepare many ethnic minority individuals for full participation in American life have produced an imperative for the social institutions that serve ethnic minorities (Allen & Santrock, 1993; Bennett, 1994; Jones, 1994; Kreutzer & Fritz, in press; Lee & Hall, 1994, Marin, 1994; Sue, 1993; Triandis, 1994). Schools, social services, health and mental health agencies, juvenile probation services, and other programs need to become more sensitive to ethnic issues and to provide improved services to ethnic minority and low-income individuals.

An important point to keep in mind is that not only is there ethnic diversity within a culture such as the United States; there is also diversity within each ethnic group (McAdoo, 1993). Not all Black Americans live in low-income circumstances. Not all Hispanic Americans are Catholic. Not all Asian Americans are geniuses. Not all Native Americans are high school dropouts. It is easy to fall into the trap of stereotyping an ethnic group and thinking that all of its members are alike. A more accurate ethnic group portrait is one of heterogeneity.

Sociocultural contexts of development include four important concepts: context, culture, ethnicity, and gender. These concepts are central to our discussion of life-span development, so we need to clearly define them. **Context** *is the setting in which development occurs, a setting that is influenced by historical, economic, social, and cultural factors.* To sense how important context is in studying development, consider a researcher who wants to discover whether today's college students are more racially tolerant than they were a decade ago (Allen & Santrock, 1993). Without reference to the historical, economic, social, and cultural aspects of race relations, the students' racial tolerance cannot be fully understood. Every individual's development occurs in a cultural backdrop of contexts. These contexts or settings include homes, schools, peer groups, churches, cities, neighborhoods, communities, university laboratories, the United States, China, Mexico, Japan, Egypt, Somalia, and many others—each with meaningful historical, economic, social, and cultural legacies.

Three sociocultural contexts that many developmentalists believe merit special attention are culture, ethnicity, and gender. **Culture** *is the behavior patterns, beliefs, and all other products of a particular group of people that are passed on from generation to generation.* The products result from the interaction between groups of people and their environment over many years. A cultural group can be as large as the United States or as small as an African hunter-gatherer group. Whatever its size, the group's culture influences the behavior of its members (Brislin, 1993; Cole, 1993; Lonner & Malpass, 1994). For example, the United States is an achievement-oriented culture with a strong work ethic, but recent comparisons of American and Japanese children revealed that the Japanese are better at math, spend more time working on math in school, and do more math homework than Americans (Stevenson, Chen, &

Lee, 1993). **Cross-cultural studies**—*the comparison of a culture with one or more other cultures*—*provide information about the degree to which human development is similar, or universal, across cultures, or to what degree it is culture-specific.*

> *Our most basic link is that we all inhabit the same planet. We all breathe the same air. We all cherish our children's future.*
>
> —John F. Kennedy

Ethnicity (the word *ethnic* comes from the Greek word for "nation") *is based on cultural heritage, nationality characteristics, race, religion, and language.* Ethnicity is central to the development of an **ethnic identity,** *which is a sense of membership based on the shared language, religion, customs, values, history, and race of an ethnic group.* Each of you is a member of one or more ethnic groups. Your ethnic identity reflects your deliberate decision to identify with an ancestor or ancestral group. If you are of Native American and African ancestry, you might choose to align yourself with the traditions of Native Americans, although an outsider might believe that your identity is African American. The dramatic increase in ethnic minority group population in the United States is shown in figure 1.6.

> *We need every human gift and cannot afford to neglect any gift because of artificial barriers of sex or race or class or national origin.*
>
> —Margaret Mead, *Male and Female* (1949)

A third very important aspect of sociocultural contexts that is receiving increased attention is gender (Beale, 1994; Caplan & Caplan, 1994; Denmark & Paludi, 1993; Gilligan, 1992; Golombok & Firush, 1994). **Gender** *is the sociocultural dimension of being female or male. Sex refers to the biological dimension of being female or male.* Few aspects of our development as human beings are more central to our identity and our social relationships than our gender or sex. Society's gender attitudes are changing. But how much? Is there a limit to how much society should determine what is appropriate behavior for females and males? These are among the provocative questions about gender we will explore in *Life-Span Development.*

Critical Thinking

Health and well-being, family issues, educational reform, and sociocultural issues involving culture, ethnicity, and gender are concerns in development. What other contemporary concerns related to human development can you generate?

We will integrate the discussion of sociocultural contexts into the discussion of each chapter of the book. Each chapter also has one boxed insert—called "Sociocultural Worlds of Development"—that is related to the chapter's contents. To read the first boxed insert, turn to Sociocultural Worlds of Development 1.1, where we evaluate the health, well-being, and status of women around the world.

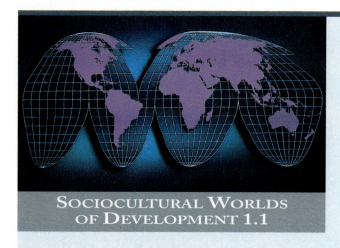

**SOCIOCULTURAL WORLDS
OF DEVELOPMENT 1.1**

*Women's Struggle for Equality:
An International Journey*

What are the political, economic, educational, and psychosocial conditions of women around the world? Frances Culbertson (1991), president of the Clinical Psychology of Women section of the American Psychological Association, recently summarized these conditions.

Women and Politics

In politics, too often women are treated like burdens rather than assets. Especially in developing countries, women marry early and have many children quickly, in many cases before their undernourished bodies have an opportunity to mature. In such developing countries, women need greater access to education, work, health care, and especially family planning. Some experts on women's issues believe that these needs would have a better chance of being met if women were more strongly represented at the decision-making and managerial levels of governments and international organizations. For example, in 1990, less than 10 percent of the members of national legislatures were women, and for every 100 ministerial-level positions around the world only 5 were filled by women (Sadik, 1991).

Women and Employment

Women's work around the world is more limiting and narrower than that of men (Monagle, 1990). Bank tellers and secretaries are most often women. Domestic workers in North America and in Central and South America are most often women. Around the world, jobs defined as women's work too often carry low pay, low status, and little security. Two authors described many of these circumstances as "job ghettos" (Seager & Olson, 1986). In 1990 the only countries in the world that had maternity leave and guaranteed jobs on the basis of national law were Brazil, Chile, Mexico, Finland, Switzerland, Germany, Italy, Egypt, Syria, Russia, Japan, and Thailand. Among the major countries without these provisions were the United States, England, and France.

Women and Education

The countries with the fewest women being educated are in Africa, where in some areas women are receiving no education

at all. Canada, the United States, and Russia have the highest percentage of educated women (Seager & Olson, 1986). In developing countries, 67 percent of the women and 50 percent of the men over the age of 25 have never been to school. In 1985, 80 million more boys than girls were in primary and secondary educational settings around the world.

Women and Psychosocial Issues

Women around the world, in every country, experience violence, often by someone close to them. In Canada 10 percent of the women report that they have been beaten in their homes by the man they live with, and in the United States almost 2 million women are beaten in their homes each year (Seager & Olson, 1986). In a recent survey, "The New Woman Ethics Report," wife abuse was listed as number one among 15 of the most pressing concerns facing society today (Johnson, 1990). Although most countries around the world now have battered women's shelters, there are some countries where beating women continues to be accepted and expected.

In a recent investigation of depression in high-income countries, the women were twice as likely as the men to be diagnosed as being in depression (Nolen-Hoeksema, 1990). In the United States, from adolescence through adulthood, females are more likely to be depressed than males (McGrath & others, 1993). There are many sociocultural inequities and experiences that have contributed to the greater incidence of depression in females than males.

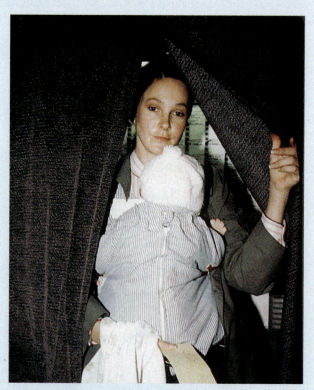

Around the world women too often are treated as burdens rather than assets in the political process. Few women have leadership positions in government. Some experts on women's issues believe that if women are to gain more access to work, education, health care, and family planning, they need to be more strongly represented at the decision making and managerial levels of government and business.

Marian Wright Edelman, president of the Children's Defense Fund (shown here interacting with a young child), has been a tireless advocate of children's rights and has been instrumental in calling attention to the needs of children.

Social Policy

Social policy *is a national government's course of action designed to influence the welfare of its citizens.* A current trend is to conduct developmental research that produces knowledge that will lead to wise and effective decision making about social policy (McLoyd, 1993; Takanish & DeLeon, 1994). When more than 20 percent of all children and more than half of all ethnic minority children are being raised in poverty, when 40 to 50 percent of all children can expect to spend at least 5 years in a single-parent home, when children and young adolescents are giving birth, when the use and abuse of drugs is widespread, when the specter of AIDS is present, and when the provision of health care for the elderly is inadequate, our nation needs revised social policy.

The shape and scope of social policy is strongly tied to our political system (Garwood & others, 1989). Our country's policy agenda and whether the welfare of the nation's citizens will be improved are influenced by the values held by individual lawmakers, the nation's economic strengths and weaknesses, and partisan politics.

If our American way of life fails the child, it fails us all.
—Pearl Buck, *The Child Who Never Grew*

Marian Wright Edelman, president of the Children's Defense Fund, has been a tireless advocate of children's rights. Especially troublesome to Edelman (1992, 1994) are the indicators of social neglect that place the United States at or near the lowest rank for industrialized nations in the treatment of children. Edelman says that parenting and nurturing the next generation of children is our society's most important function and that we need to take it more seriously than we have in the past. She points out that we hear a lot from politicians these days about "family values," but that when we examine our nation's policies for families, they don't reflect the politicians' words. Family policy is an

Maggie Kuhn, founder of the Gray Panthers, has actively sought to improve society's image of the elderly, obtain better living conditions for the elderly, and gain political clout. Her Gray Panthers group—with more than 80,000 members—pressures Congress on everything from health insurance to housing costs for the elderly.

important dimension of social policy, and you can read more about it in Perspectives on Parenting and Education 1.1.

Our aging society and older persons' status in this society raise policy issues about the well-being of older adults. There is a special concern about escalating health-care costs and the access of elderly to adequate health care.

Who should get the bulk of government dollars for improved well-being? Children? Their parents? The elderly? **Generational inequity,** *which is a social policy concern, is the condition in which an aging society is being unfair to its younger members because older adults pile up advantages by receiving inequitably large allocations of resources, such as Social Security and Medicare.* Generational inequity raises questions about whether the young should have to pay for the old and whether an "advantaged" older population is using up resources that should go to disadvantaged children (Hirshorn, 1991; Sapp, 1991). The argument is that older adults are advantaged because they have publicly provided pensions, health care, food stamps, housing subsidies, tax breaks, and other benefits that younger groups do not have.

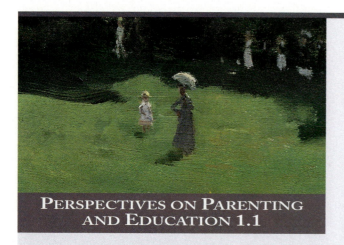

PERSPECTIVES ON PARENTING AND EDUCATION 1.1

Family Policy

The last decade has been one of extremes with respect to family policy in the United States, ranging from efforts to dismantle welfare programs to modest efforts at reform (Berardo, 1990). Controversy has focused on the ability of government intervention to reduce poverty and promote family well-being. The Family Support Act was passed in 1988, linking family welfare payments to job training or work obligations and strengthening child support enforcement strategies, so that families would ultimately become economically independent.

Much of the controversy surrounding family policy involves a lack of agreement on objectives. A major barrier to sound family policy is its emotional nature, often visible in the actions and statements of highly vocal pressure groups. Policy makers often become enmeshed in hotly debated ideological and moral issues, such as family planning and abortion, or child care and parental leave legislation. At this point, there is no clear indication that sharp differences over the role of families and government will be resolved in favor of rational solutions in the near future (Berardo, 1990).

According to social commentator Richard Louv (1990), a successful family policy will primarily be shaped not by committees and lobbyists in Washington, D.C., but by parents themselves, when they come to understand their need for each other and the interconnectedness of families, schools, and communities.

Family policies can be divided into those that help parents in their "breadwinning" roles and those that concentrate on their nurturing and caregiving roles (Kamerman & Kahn, 1978). Breadwinning family policy supports the family as a viable economic unit, either by maintaining a certain minimal family income or by providing for the care of children while parents work. Nurturing and caregiving family policy focuses on the internal life of the family by promoting positive family functioning and the development and well-being of individual family members.

Consider the plight of the homeless. As many as 100,000 American children spend the night in emergency shelters, in abandoned buildings, or on the street. Homeless children have

more health problems than other children in poverty who live in homes, and homeless children have high rates of hunger and malnutrition. They also often display developmental delays in motor and language skills (Bassuk, 1991; Rafferty & Shinn, 1991).

Some people maintain that homeless families only need housing. Others argue that homeless families need a broader economic package of affordable housing, decent jobs, child care, and health care (Shinn & Gillespie, 1994). And yet others stress that homeless families need more than economic assistance, that the factors that precipitated their plight and the harmful effects of being homeless call for additional support—a "caregiving package" that includes services such as home management training, parental support groups, and parent education (Bassuk, Carman, Weinreb, 1990; Jacobs, Little, & Almeida, 1993; Little, in press). In the last decade, public support for caregiving and nurturing policies has increased, but less so than support for economic assistance.

The family policies of the United States are overwhelmingly treatment-oriented. Only those families and individuals who already have problems are eligible; few preventive programs are available on any widespread basis. For example, families on the verge of having their children placed in foster care are eligible, and often required, to receive counseling; families in which problems are brewing but are not yet full blown usually cannot qualify for public services (Jacobs & Davies, 1991). Most experts on family policy believe more attention should be given to preventing family problems (Snow & Bradford, 1994).

What are some of the family policy issues involved in helping the homeless?

CONCEPT TABLE 1.1

The Life–Span Perspective

Concept	Processes/Related Ideas	Characteristics/Description
Why study life-span development?	Reasons	Responsibility for children is or will be a part of our everyday lives. The more we learn about children, the more we can better deal with them and assist them in becoming competent human beings. Life-span development gives us insights about our development as adults as well.
An historical perspective on life-span development	Its nature	Interest in children has a long and rich history. In the Renaissance, philosophical views were prominent, including the notions of original sin, tabula rasa, and innate goodness. The scientific study of adolescence was promoted by G. Stanley Hall in the early 1900s. His storm-and-stress view contrasts with the belief that sociohistorical conditions produced the concept of adolescence. The traditional approach emphasizes extensive change in childhood but stability in adulthood; the life-span perspective emphasizes that change is possible throughout the life span.
Characteristics of the life-span perspective	Their nature	The life-span perspective involves seven basic contentions: Development is lifelong, multidimensional, multidirectional, plastic, historically embedded, contextual, and multidisciplinary.
	Contextualism	In the contextualist view, development can be understood as the outcome of the interaction of normative age-graded influences, normative history-graded influences, and nonnormative life events.
Some contemporary concerns	Their nature	Today, the development and well-being of children and adults capture the interest of the public, scientists, and policy makers. Among the important contemporary concerns are family issues, parenting, education, sociocultural contexts, and social policy. Three important sociocultural contexts are culture, ethnicity, and gender.

While the trend of greater services for the elderly has been occurring, the percentage of children in poverty has been rising.

Life-span developmentalist Bernice Neugarten (1988) says the problem should be viewed not as one of generational inequity, but rather as a major shortcoming of our broader economic and social policies. She believes we should develop a spirit of support for improving the range of options of all people in our society.

At this point we have discussed a number of ideas about why we should study life-span development, a historical perspective on life-span development, the life-span perspective, and contemporary concerns. A summary of these ideas is presented in concept table 1.1.

THE NATURE OF DEVELOPMENT

Each of us develops partly like all other individuals, partly like some other individuals, and partly like no other individuals. Most of the time, our attention is directed to an individual's uniqueness. But psychologists who study life-span development are drawn to our shared as well as our unique characteristics. As humans, we all have traveled some common paths. Each of us—Leonardo Da Vinci, Joan of Arc, George Washington, Martin Luther King, Jr., yourself—walked at about 1 year, talked at about 2 years, engaged in fantasy play as a young child, and became more independent as a youth. Each of us, if we live long enough, will experience hearing problems and the deaths of family members and friends.

> *Each of you, individually, walkest with the tread of a fox,*
> *but collectively ye are geese.*
>
> —Solon, Ancient Greece

Just what do psychologists mean when they speak of an individual's "development"? **Development** *is the pattern of movement or change that begins at conception and continues through the life cycle.* Most development involves growth, although it also includes decay (as in death and dying). The pattern of movement is complex because it is the product of several processes—biological, cognitive, and social.

Biological, Cognitive, and Socioemotional Processes

Biological processes *involve changes in the individual's physical nature.* Genes inherited from parents, the development of the brain, height and weight gains, changes in motor skills, the hormonal changes of puberty, and cardiovascular decline all reflect the role of biological processes in development.

Cognitive processes *involve changes in the individual's thought, intelligence, and language.* Watching a colorful mobile swinging above the crib, putting together a two-word sentence, memorizing a poem, imagining what it would be like to be a movie star, and solving a crossword puzzle all reflect the role of cognitive processes in development.

Socioemotional processes *involve changes in the individual's relationships with other people, changes in emotions, and changes in personality.* An infant's smile in response to her mother's touch, a young boy's aggressive attack on a playmate, a girl's development of assertiveness, an adolescent's joy at the senior prom, and the affection of an elderly couple all reflect the role of the social processes in development.

> *The chess-board is the world. The pieces are the phenomena of the universe. The rules of the game are what we call laws of nature.*
>
> —Thomas Henry Huxley, 1868
>
> *I think, therefore I am.*
> —Rene Descartes
>
> *Man is by nature a social animal.*
> —Aristotle

Remember as you read about biological, cognitive, and socioemotional processes that they are intricately interwoven. You will read about how socioemotional processes shape cognitive processes, how cognitive processes promote or restrict socioemotional processes, and how biological processes influence cognitive processes, for example. Although it is helpful to study the different processes involved in children's development in separate sections of the book, keep in mind that you are studying the development of an integrated individual with a mind and body that are interdependent (see figure 1.7).

FIGURE 1.7

Biological, cognitive, and socioemotional processes in life-span development. Changes in development are the result of biological, cognitive, and socioemotional processes. These processes are interwoven in the development of the individual through the human life cycle.

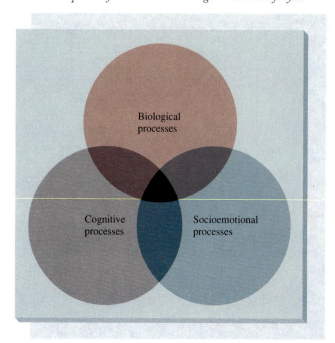

Periods of Development

For the purposes of organization and understanding, we commonly describe development in terms of periods. The most widely used classification of developmental periods involves the following sequence: prenatal period, infancy, early childhood, middle and late childhood, adolescence, early adulthood, middle adulthood, and late adulthood. Approximate age ranges are listed below for the periods to provide a general idea of when a period begins and ends.

The **prenatal period** *is the time from conception to birth.* It is a time of tremendous growth—from a single cell to an organism complete with brain and behavioral capabilities, produced in approximately a 9-month period.

Infancy *is the developmental period extending from birth to 18 or 24 months.* Infancy is a time of extreme dependence upon adults. Many psychological activities are just beginning—language, symbolic thought, sensorimotor coordination, and social learning, for example.

Early childhood *is the developmental period extending from the end of infancy to about 5 or 6 years; this period is sometimes called the "preschool years."* During this time, young children learn to become more self-sufficient and to care for themselves, develop school readiness skills (following instructions, identifying letters), and spend many hours in play with peers. First grade typically marks the end of early childhood.

Middle and late childhood *is the developmental period extending from about 6 to 11 years of age, approximately corresponding to the elementary school years; this period is sometimes called the "elementary school years."* The fundamental skills of reading, writing, and arithmetic are mastered. The child is formally exposed to the larger world and its culture. Achievement becomes a more central theme of the child's world, and self-control increases.

Adolescence *is the developmental period of transition from childhood to early adulthood, entered at approximately 10 to 12 years of age and ending at 18 to 22 years of age.* Adolescence begins with rapid physical changes—dramatic gains in height and weight, changes in body contour, and the development of sexual characteristics such as enlargement of the breasts, development of pubic and facial hair, and deepening of the voice. At this point in development, the pursuit of independence and an identity are prominent; thought is more logical, abstract, and idealistic; and more and more time is spent outside of the family.

Early adulthood *is the developmental period beginning in the late teens or early twenties and lasting through the thirties.* It is a time of establishing personal and economic independence, a time of career development, and, for many, a time of selecting a mate, learning to live with someone in an intimate way, starting a family, and rearing children.

Middle adulthood *is the developmental period beginning at approximately 35 to 45 years of age and extending to the sixties.* It is a time of expanding personal and social involvement and responsibility; of assisting the next generation in becoming competent, mature individuals; and of reaching and maintaining satisfaction in one's career.

Late adulthood *is the developmental period beginning in the sixties or seventies and lasting until death.* It is a time of adjustment to decreasing strength and health, life review, retirement, and adjustment to new social roles.

> *One's children's children's children. Look back to us as we look to you; we are related by our imaginations. If we are able to touch, it is because we have imagined each other's existence, our dreams running back and forth along a cable from age to age.*
>
> —Roger Rosenblatt, 1986

Life-span developmentalists are increasingly making a distinction between two age groups in late adulthood: the *young old,* or *old age* (65 to 74 years of age), and the *old old,* or *late old age* (75 years and older) (Baltes, Smith, & Staudinger, in press; Charness & Bosman, 1992). Still others distinguish the *oldest old* (85 years and older) from younger older adults (Johnson, 1994; Pearlin, 1994). Beginning in the sixties and extending to more than 100 years of age, late adulthood has the longest span of any period of development. Combining this lengthy span with the dramatic increase in the number of adults living to older ages, we will see increased attention given to differentiation of the late adulthood period.

Bernice Neugarten was one of the pioneers in conceptualizing the nature of adulthood and aging. She believes that social and contextual factors play important roles in adult development. And she says that age is rapidly becoming a weaker predictor of adult behavior and life events.

The periods of the human life cycle are shown in figure 1.8 along with the processes of development—biological, cognitive, and socioemotional. The interplay of these processes produces the periods of the human life cycle.

In our description of the periods of the life cycle, we placed approximate age bands on the periods. However, one expert on life-span development, Bernice Neugarten (1980, 1988; Neugarten & Neugarten, 1989), believes we are rapidly becoming an age-irrelevant society. She says we are already familiar with the 28-year-old mayor, the 35-year-old grandmother, the 65-year-old father of a preschooler, the 55-year-old widow who starts a business, and the 70-year-old student. Neugarten says that she has had difficulty clustering adults into age brackets that are characterized by particular issues. She stresses that choices and dilemmas do not spring forth at 10-year intervals, and decisions are not made and then left behind as if they were merely beads on a chain. Neugarten argues that most adulthood themes appear and reappear throughout life's human cycle. The issues of intimacy and freedom can haunt couples throughout their relationship. Feeling the pressure of time, reformulating goals, and coping with success and failure are not the exclusive property of adults of a particular age.

FIGURE 1.8

Processes and periods of life-span development. *The unfolding of the life cycle's periods of development is influenced by the interplay of biological, cognitive, and socioemotional processes.*

Periods of development

Processes of development

Biological processes

Cognitive processes   Socioemotional processes

Late adulthood

Middle adulthood

Early adulthood

Adolescence

Middle and late childhood

Early childhood

Infancy

Prenatal period

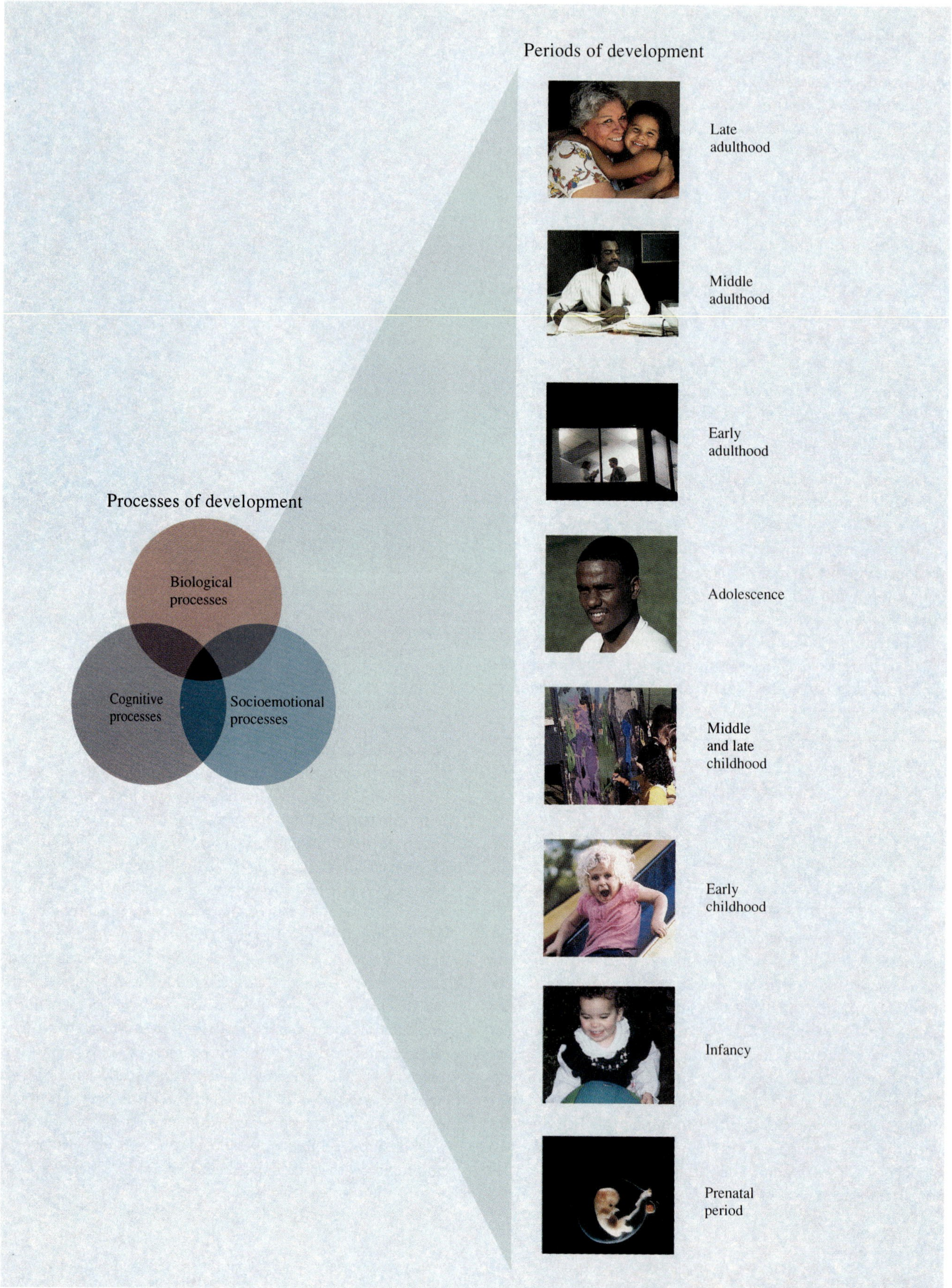

When individuals report how happy they are and how satisfied they are with their lives, no particular age group reports that they are happier or more satisfied than any other age group (Stock & others, 1983). In one report of life-satisfaction in eight Western European countries, there was no difference in the percentage who reported an overall satisfaction with life at different ages: 78 percent of 15- to 24-year-olds, 78 percent of 35- to 44-year-olds, and 78 percent of those 65 years and older (Ingelhart & Rabier, 1986). Similarly, slightly less than 20 percent of each of the age groups reported that they were "very happy."

Why might older people report just as much happiness and life satisfaction as younger people? Every period of the life cycle has its stresses, its pluses and minuses, its hills and valleys. While adolescents must cope with developing an identity, feelings of insecurity, mood swings, and peer pressure, the majority of adolescents develop positive perceptions of themselves, feelings of competence about their skills, positive relationships with friends and family, and an optimistic view of their future. And while older adults face a life of reduced income, less energy, decreasing physical skills, and concerns about death, they are also less pressured to achieve and succeed, have more time for leisurely pursuits, and have accumulated many years of experience that help them adapt to their lives with a wisdom they may not have had in their younger years. Since growing older is a certain outcome of living, we can derive considerable pleasure from knowing that we are likely to be just as happy as older adults as when we were younger (Myers, 1992).

Maturation and Experience (Nature and Nurture)

Not only can we think of development as produced by the interplay of biological, cognitive, and social processes, but also by the interplay of maturation and experience. **Maturation** *is the orderly sequence of changes dictated by the genetic blueprint we each have.* Just as a sunflower grows in an orderly way—unless flattened by an unfriendly environment—so does the human grow in an orderly way, according to the maturational view. The range of environments can be vast, but the maturational approach argues that the genetic blueprint produces communalities in our growth and development. We walk before we talk, speak one word before two words, grow rapidly in infancy and less so in early childhood, experience a rush of sexual hormones in puberty after a lull in childhood, reach the peak of our physical strength in late adolescence and early adulthood and then decline, and so on. The maturationists acknowledge that extreme environments—those that are psychologically barren or hostile—can depress development, but they believe basic growth tendencies are genetically wired into the human.

By contrast, other psychologists emphasize the importance of experiences in life-span development. Experiences run the gamut from the individual's biological environment—nutrition, medical care, drugs, and physical accidents—to the social environment—family, peers, schools, community, media, and culture.

The debate about whether development is primarily influenced by maturation or by experience has been a part of psychology since its beginning. This debate is often referred to

FIGURE 1.9

Continuity and discontinuity in development. *Is our development like that of a seedling gradually growing into a giant oak? Or is it more like that of a caterpillar suddenly becoming a butterfly?*

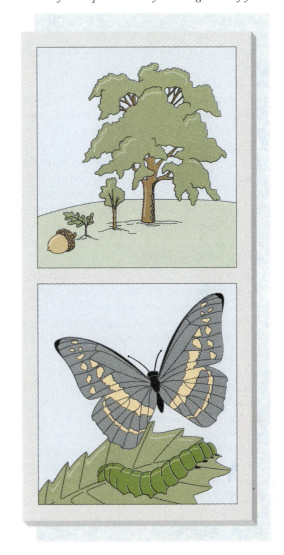

as the **nature-nurture controversy.** *Nature refers to an organism's biological inheritance, "nurture" to environmental experiences. The "nature" proponents claim biological inheritance is the most important influence on development, and the "nurture" proponents claim that environmental experiences are the most important.*

Continuity and Discontinuity

Think about your development for a moment. Did you gradually become the person you are, like the slow, cumulative growth of a seedling into a giant oak? Or did you experience sudden, distinct changes in your growth, like the way a caterpillar changes into a butterfly (see figure 1.9)? For the most part, developmentalists who emphasize experience have described development as a gradual, continuous process; those who emphasize maturation have described development as a series of distinct stages.

Some developmentalists emphasize **continuity of development,** *the view that development involves gradual, cumulative change from conception to death.* A child's first word, while seemingly an abrupt, discontinuous event, is actually the result of weeks and months of growth and practice. Puberty, while also seemingly an abrupt, discontinuous occurrence, is actually a gradual process occurring over several years.

Other developmentalists emphasize **discontinuity of development,** *the view that development involves distinct stages in the life span.* Each of us is described as passing through a sequence of stages in which change is qualitatively rather than quantitatively different. As the oak moves from seedling to giant oak, it becomes *more* oak—its development is continuous. As the caterpillar changes to a butterfly, it is not just more caterpillar, it is a *different kind* of organism—its development is discontinuous. For example, at some point a child moves from not being able to think abstractly about the world to being able to. This is a qualitative, discontinuous change in development, not a quantitative, continuous change.

Stability and Change

Another important developmental topic is the **stability-change issue,** *which addresses whether development is best described by stability or by change. The stability-change issue involves the degree to which we become older renditions of our early experience or whether we develop into someone different from who we were at an earlier point in development.* Will the shy child who hides behind the sofa when visitors arrive be a wallflower at college dances, or will the child become a sociable, talkative individual? Will the fun-loving, carefree adolescent have difficulty holding down a 9-to-5 job as an adult or become a straitlaced, serious conformist?

One of the reasons adult development was so late in being studied was the predominant belief for many years that nothing much changes in adulthood. The major changes were believed to take place in childhood, especially during the first 5 years of life. Today, most developmentalists believe that some change is possible throughout the human life cycle, although they disagree, sometimes vehemently, about just how much change can take place, and how much stability there is. The important issue of stability and change in development will reappear on many occasions in our journey through the human life cycle.

The issue of stability and change raises the question, Which is the more dominant and desired characteristic of human development: stability or change? Some life-span developmentalists, such as Klaus Riegel (1975), have argued that change, not stability, is the key to understanding development. Riegel's view is called the **dialectical model,** *which states that each individual is continually changing because of various forces that push and pull development forward. In the dialectical model, each person is viewed as acting on and reacting to social and historical conditions.* Consider the push and pull between independence and dependence. In the first year of life, the infant is dependent on parents for support and sustenance. In the second year of life, as development proceeds, the infant becomes more independent, seeking to engage in more autonomous adventures. But as toddlers encounter fears and stressors, their independent efforts become moderated as they sense their need to maintain some dependence on their parents. Thus the push and pull between independence and dependence continues throughout life, waxing and waning, as we, others, and sociohistorical conditions develop and change. As individuals enter adolescence, they push for independence from their parents, who struggle to pull them toward dependence. All adolescents push for independence, but sociohistorical conditions influence the intensity of the push. The rebelliousness of adolescents of the late 1960s and the 1970s can be partly understood as a reaction to their parents' conservative values, which were likely an outgrowth of the difficult times of the depression and World War II. In subsequent years, the so-called generation gap between parents and adolescents decreased as both parents and adolescents, as well as sociohistorical conditions, changed. In the dialectical model, such change also characterizes the push and pull that we experience in the development of masculinity-femininity, competitiveness-cooperation, introversion-extraversion, and so on.

An important dimension of the stability-change issue is the extent to which early experiences (especially in infancy) or later experiences are the key determinants of a person's development. That is, if infants experience negative, stressful circumstances in their lives, can those experiences be overcome by later, more positive experiences? Or are the early experiences so critical, possibly because they are the infant's first, prototypical experiences, that they cannot be overridden by an enriched environment later in development?

The early-later experience issue has a long history and continues to be hotly debated among developmentalists. Some believe that unless infants experience warm, nurturant caregiving in the first year or so of life, their development will never be optimal (Bowlby, 1989; Sroufe, in press). Plato was sure that infants who were rocked frequently became better athletes. Nineteenth-century New England ministers told parents in Sunday sermons that the way they handled their infants would determine their children's future character. The emphasis on the importance of early experience rests on the belief that each life is an unbroken trail on which a psychological quality can be traced back to its origin (Kagan, 1984, 1992).

The early-experience doctrine contrasts with the later-experience view that, rather than there being statuelike permanence after change in infancy, development continues to be like the ebb and flow of a river. The later-experience advocates argue that children are malleable throughout development and that later sensitive caregiving is just as important as earlier sensitive caregiving. A number of life-span developmentalists, who focus on the entire lifespan rather than only on child development, stress that too little attention has been given to later experiences in development (Baltes, 1987). They argue that early experiences are important contributors to development, but no more important than later experiences. Jerome Kagan (1992) points out that even children who show the qualities of an inhibited temperament, which is linked to heredity, have the capacity to change their behavior. In his research, almost one-third of a group of children who had an inhibited temperament at 2 years of age were not unusually shy or fearful when they were 4 years of age (Kagan & Snidman, 1991).

People in Western cultures, especially those steeped in the Freudian belief that the key experiences in development are children's relationships with their parents in the first 5 years of life, have tended to support the idea that early experiences are more important than later experiences (Chan, 1963; Lamb & Sternberg, 1992). By contrast, the majority of people in the world do not share this belief. For example, people in many Asian countries believe that experiences occurring after about 6 to 7 years of age are more important aspects of development than earlier experiences. This stance stems from the long-standing belief in Eastern cultures that children's reasoning skills begin to develop in important ways in the middle childhood years.

Evaluating the Developmental Issues

As we further consider these three salient developmental issues—nature and nurture, continuity and discontinuity, and stability and change—it is important to point out that most life-span developmentalists recognize that extreme positions on these issues are unwise. Development is not all nature or all nurture, not all continuity or all discontinuity, and not all stability or all change. Both nature and nurture, continuity and discontinuity, stability and change characterize our development through the human life cycle. For example, in considering the nature-nurture issue, the key to development is the *interaction* of nature and nurture rather than either factor alone (Baumrind, 1993; Plomin, 1993; Scarr, 1993); an individual's cognitive development, for instance, is the result of heredity-environment interaction, not heredity or environment alone. (Much more about the role of heredity-environment interaction appears in chapter 3.)

Although most developmentalists do not take extreme positions on these three important issues, there is, nonetheless, spirited debate about how strongly development is influenced by each of these factors. Are girls less likely to do well in math because of their "feminine" nature, or because of society's masculine bias? How extensively can the elderly be trained to reason more effectively? How much, if at all, does our memory decline in old age? Can techniques be used to prevent or reduce the decline? For children who experienced a world of poverty, neglect by parents, and poor schooling in childhood, can enriched experiences in adolescence remove the "deficits" they encountered earlier in their development? The answers given by developmentalists to such questions depend on their stances regarding the issues of nature and nurture, continuity and discontinuity, and stability and change. The answers to these questions also influence public policy decisions about children, adolescents, and adults, and influence how we each live our lives as we go through the human life cycle.

At this point we have discussed a number of ideas about the nature of development and issues in development. A summary of these ideas is presented in concept table 1.2.

CONCEPT TABLE 1.2

The Nature of Development and Developmental Issues

Concept	Processes/Related Ideas	Characteristics/Description
The nature of development	What is development?	Development is the pattern of movement or change that occurs throughout the life span.
	Biological, cognitive, and socioemotional processes	Development is influenced by an interplay of biological, cognitive, and socioemotional processes.
	Periods of development	The life cycle is commonly divided into the following periods of development: prenatal, infancy, early childhood, middle and late childhood, adolescence, early adulthood, middle adulthood, and late adulthood. Some experts on life-span development, however, believe too much emphasis is placed on age; Neugarten believes we are moving toward a society in which age is a weaker predictor of development in adulthood.
Developmental issues	Maturation and experience (Nature and nurture)	The debate about whether development is primarily influenced by maturation or experience is another version of the nature-nurture controversy.
	Continuity and discontinuity	Developmentalists describe development as continuous (gradual, a cumulative change) or as discontinuous (abrupt, a sequence of stages).
	Stability and change	Is development best described as stable or changing? The stability-change issue focuses on the degree to which we become older renditions of our early experience or develop into someone different from who we were earlier in development. The dialectical model emphasizes change. A special aspect of the stability-change issue is the extent to which development is determined by early versus later experiences. In the life-span perspective, both early and later experiences make important contributions to development.
	Evaluating the developmental issues	Most developmentalists recognize that extreme positions on the nature-nurture, continuity-discontinuity, and stability-change issues are unwise. Despite this consensus, there is still spirited debate on these issues.

CONCLUSIONS

In this first chapter, we began the complex task of weaving together a portrait of life-span development, of who we were, are, and will be from our first cries as newborn babies to our final days as elderly adults.

You read and thought about why Jeffrey Dahmer became Jeffrey Dahmer and why Alice Walker became Alice Walker, learned about why it is important to study life-span development, studied the historical perspective on child development, adolescence, and life-span development, explored the nature of the life-span perspective, including its characteristics (such as contextualism), and examined some contemporary concerns such as health and well-being, parenting and education, and sociocultural contexts. You also learned about the nature of development by evaluating biological, cognitive, and socioemotional processes, periods of development, maturation and experience (nature and nurture), continuity and discontinuity, and stability and change. At different points in the chapter you also read about the health, well-being, and status of women around the world, family policy, and explorations in health and well-being across the life span.

To obtain an overall summary of the chapter, go back and read again the two concept tables on pages 19 and 26. In the next chapter, we will study the field of life-span development as a science. You will learn about the importance of the scientific method, theories, and methods in studying people as they develop through the life span.

LIFE-SPAN HEALTH AND WELL-BEING

Explorations in Health and Well-Being Across the Life Span

Compared to other industrialized countries around the world, the United States does not fare well on a number of indices of health and well-being for children (Children's Defense Fund, 1990, 1993). For example, the United States has a higher overall infant mortality rate than 18 other countries—a Black American child born in inner-city Boston has less chance of surviving the first year of life than does a child born in Panama, North or South Korea, or Uruguay. A higher percentage of children live in poverty in the United States than in Switzerland, Sweden, Norway, West Germany, Canada, England, or Australia. The United States has the highest adolescent pregnancy rate of any industrialized Western nation. And the United States invests a smaller portion of its gross national product (GNP) in child health than 18 other nations do.

If you are a young college student, most of your concerns about your health and well-being are probably focused on the present. Basically, you want to feel good physically, mentally, and emotionally—now. You probably don't spend much time worrying about the distant future, such as whether you will develop heart disease, cancer, or diabetes, how you will take care of yourself in your retirement years, or how long you are going to live. Such thoughts may have crossed your mind once in a while, but that's about it. However, if you are an older college student—in your thirties, forties, fifties, or older—such health-related thoughts likely have become increasingly important to you (Williams, 1990).

Regardless of your age, you can make a number of important changes in your current life-style that will help you feel better physically, mentally, and emotionally. Recently researchers have found that, even in late adulthood, exercise, strength training with weights, and improved nutrition can help elderly individuals significantly improve their health and well-being. Importantly, these life-style changes not only can improve the quality of your life today, but will improve the likelihood of better health and well-being in the future. We know much more about preventive health today than our parents and grandparents did in the past, giving us the opportunity to avoid some of the health problems that have plagued them. And this new knowledge can be transmitted to the next generation of children to help them become even healthier and feel better than our generations. ■

KEY TERMS

original sin   Philosophical view that children are born into the world as basically bad, evil beings. (8)

tabula rasa   View proposed by English philosopher John Locke. He argued that children are not innately bad, but instead they are like a "blank tablet," a "tabula rasa" as he called it. (8)

innate goodness   View presented by Swiss-born French philosopher Jean Jacques Rousseau, who stressed that children are inherently good. (8)

storm-and-stress view   G. Stanley Hall's concept that adolescence is a turbulent time charged with conflict and mood swings. (8)

life-span perspective   Involves seven basic contentions: development is lifelong, multidimensional, multidirectional, plastic, historically embedded, multidisciplinary, and contextual. (11)

normative age-graded influences   Are biological and environmental influences that are similar for individuals in a particular age group. (12)

normative history-graded influences   Are biological and environmental influences that are associated with history. These influences are common to people of a particular generation. (12)

nonnormative life events   Are unusual occurrences that have a major impact on an individual's life. The occurrence, pattern, and sequence of these events are not applicable to many individuals. (12)

context   Is the setting in which development occurs, a setting that is influenced by historical, economic, social, and cultural factors. (15)

culture   The behavior patterns, beliefs, and all other products of a particular group of people that are passed on from generation to generation. (15)

cross-cultural studies   The comparison of a culture with one or more other cultures. Provide information about the degree to which human development is similar, or universal, across cultures, or to what degree it is culture-specific. (15)

ethnicity   Is based on cultural heritage, nationality characteristics, race, religion, and language. (15)

ethnic identity   A sense of membership based on the shared language, religion, customs, values, history, and race of an ethnic group. (15)

gender   The sociocultural dimension of being female or male. (15)

social policy   A national government's course of action designed to influence the welfare of its citizens. (17)

generational inequity   A social policy concern which is the condition in which an aging society is being unfair to its younger members because older adults pile up advantages by receiving inequitably large allocations of resources, such as Social Security and Medicare. (17)

development   The pattern of movement or change that begins at conception and continues through the life cycle. (20)

biological processes   Involve changes in the individual's physical nature. (20)

cognitive processes   Involve changes in the individual's thought, intelligence, and language. (20)

socioemotional processes   Involve changes in the individual's relationships with other people, changes in emotions, and changes in personality. (20)

prenatal period   The time from conception to birth. (20)

infancy   The developmental period extending from birth to 18 or 24 months. (20)

early childhood   The developmental period extending from the end of infancy to about 5 or 6 years; this period is sometimes called the "preschool years." (20)

middle and late childhood   The developmental period extending from about 6 to 11 years of age, approximately corresponding to the elementary school years; this period is sometimes called the "elementary school years." (21)

adolescence   The developmental period of transition from childhood to early adulthood, entered at approximately 10 to 12 years of age and ending at 18 or 22 years of age. (21)

early adulthood   The developmental period beginning in the late teens or early twenties and lasting through the thirties. (21)

middle adulthood   The developmental period beginning at approximately 35 to 45 years of age and extending to the sixties. (21)

late adulthood   The developmental period beginning in the sixties or seventies and lasting until death. (21)

maturation   The orderly sequence of changes dictated by each person's genetic blueprint. (23)

continuity of development   This view states that development involves gradual, cumulative change from conception to death. (24)

discontinuity of development   This view states that development involves distinct stages in the life span. (24)

stability-change issue   Addresses whether development is best described by stability or by change. The stability-change issue involves the degree to which we become older renditions of our early experience or whether we develop into someone different from who we were at an earlier point in development. (24)

dialectical model   States that each individual is continually changing because of various forces that push and pull development forward. In the dialectical model, each person is viewed as acting on and reacting to social and historical conditions. (24)

Romare Bearden, The
Piano Lesson, detail

The Science of Life-Span Development

*Truth is arrived at by the painstaking
process of eliminating the untrue.*

—Arthur Conan Doyle,
Sherlock Holmes

There is nothing quite so practical as a good theory.

Kurt Lewin, psychologist, 1890–1947

IMAGES OF LIFE-SPAN DEVELOPMENT

Erikson and Piaget as Children

Imagine that you have developed a major theory of development. What would influence someone like you to construct this theory? A person interested in developing such a theory usually goes through a long university training program that culminates in a doctoral degree. As part of the training, the future theorist is exposed to many ideas about a particular area of development, such as biological, cognitive, or socioemotional development. Another factor that could explain why someone develops a particular theory is that person's life experiences. Two important developmental theorists, whose views we will describe later in the chapter, are Erik Erikson and Jean Piaget. Let's examine a portion of their lives as they were growing up to discover how their experiences might have contributed to the theories they developed.

Erik Homberger Erikson was born in 1902 near Frankfort, Germany, to Danish parents. Before Erik was born, his parents separated and his mother left Denmark to live in Germany. At age 3, Erik became ill, and his mother took him to see a pediatrician named Homberger. Young Erik's mother fell in love with the pediatrician, married him, and named Erik after his new stepfather.

Erik attended primary school from age 6 to 10 and then the gymnasium (high school) from 11 to 18. He studied art and a number of languages rather than science courses such as biology and chemistry. Erik did not like the atmosphere of formal schooling, and this was reflected in his grades. Rather than go to

college at age 18, the adolescent Erikson wandered around Europe, keeping a diary about his experiences. After a year of travel through Europe, he returned to Germany and enrolled in art school, became dissatisfied, and enrolled in another. Later he traveled to Florence, Italy. Psychiatrist Robert Coles described Erikson at this time:

> To the Italians he was . . . the young, tall, thin Nordic expatriate with long, blond hair. He wore a corduroy suit and was seen by his family and friends as not odd or "sick" but as a wandering artist who was trying to come to grips with himself, a not unnatural or unusual struggle. (Coles, 1970, p. 15)

The second major theorist whose life we will examine is Jean Piaget. Piaget (1896–1980) was born in Neuchâtel, Switzerland. Jean's father was an intellectual who taught young Jean to think systematically. Jean's mother was also very bright. His father had an air of detachment from his mother, whom Piaget described as prone to frequent outbursts of neurotic behavior.

In his autobiography, Piaget detailed why he chose to study cognitive development rather than social or abnormal development:

> I started to forego playing for serious work very early.
> Indeed, I have always detested

any departure from reality, an attitude which I relate to . . . my mother's poor health. It was this disturbing factor which at the beginning of my studies in psychology made me keenly interested in psychoanalytic and pathological psychology. Though this interest helped me to achieve independence and widen my cultural background, I have never since felt any desire to involve myself deeper in that particular direction, always much preferring the study of normalcy and of the workings of the intellect to that of the tricks of the unconscious. (Piaget, 1952a, p. 238)

These excerpts from Erikson's and Piaget's lives illustrate how personal experiences might influence the direction in which a particular theorist goes. Erikson's own wanderings and search for self contributed to his theory of identity development, and perhaps Piaget's intellectual experiences with his parents and schooling contributed to his emphasis on cognitive development.

Critical Thinking

What personal experiences in your own life might influence the kind of developmental theory you would construct?

PREVIEW

Some individuals have difficulty thinking of life-span development as being a science in the same way physics, chemistry, and biology are sciences. Can a discipline that studies how babies develop, parents nurture children, adolescents' thoughts change, adults form intimate relationships, and aging adults engage in self-control, be equated with disciplines that investigate the molecular structure of a compound and how gravity works? Science is not defined by *what* it investigates but by *how* it investigates. Whether you are studying photosynthesis, butterflies, Saturn's moons, or human development, it is the way you study that makes the approach scientific or not.

In this chapter, we will study three key ingredients of life-span development as a science—the scientific method, theories, and methods. You also will learn about how to be a wise consumer of information about life-span development.

THEORY AND THE SCIENTIFIC METHOD

According to nineteenth-century French mathematician Henri Poincaré, "Science is built of facts the way a house is built of bricks, but an accumulation of facts is no more science than a pile of bricks a house." Science *does* depend upon the raw material of facts or data, but as Poincaré indicated, science is more than just facts. As you will soon learn, psychology's theories are more than just facts; they are the mortar that tie the facts together.

A **theory** *is a coherent set of ideas that helps to explain data and to make predictions.* A theory has **hypotheses,** *assumptions that can be tested to determine their accuracy.* For example, a theory about depression among the elderly would explain our observations of depressed elderly individuals and predict why elderly people get depressed. We might predict that elderly individuals get depressed because they fail to focus on their strengths but instead dwell excessively on their shortcomings. This prediction would help to direct our observations by telling us to look for overexaggerations of weaknesses and underestimations of strengths and skills.

The **scientific method** *is an approach that can be used to discover accurate information about behavior and development, which includes the following steps: identify and analyze the problem, collect data, draw conclusions, and revise theories.*

Critical Thinking

Theories help us to make predictions about how we develop and how we behave. Do you believe that we can predict an individual's behavior and development? Explain your answer.

For example, you decide that you want to help elderly individuals overcome their depression. You *identified a problem,* which does not seem to be a difficult task. But as part of this first step, you need to go beyond a general description of the problem by isolating, analyzing, narrowing, and focusing on what you hope to investigate. What specific strategies do you want to use to reduce depression among the elderly? What aspect of depression do you want to study—its biological characteristics, cognitive characteristics, or behavioral characteristics? One group of psychologists believe the cognitive and behavioral aspects of depression can be improved through a course on coping with depression (Lewinsohn & others, 1991; Zeiss and Lewinsohn, 1986). One of the course's components involves teaching elderly individuals to control their negative thoughts. In this first step of the scientific method, the researchers identified and analyzed a problem.

The next step in the scientific method involves *collecting information (data).* Psychologists observe behavior and draw inferences about thoughts and emotions. For example, in the investigation of depression among the elderly, you might observe how effectively individuals who complete the course of coping with depression monitor their moods and engage in an active life-style.

Once psychologists collect data, they use statistical (mathematical) procedures to understand the meaning of quantitative data. Psychologists then draw conclusions. In the investigation of the elderly's depression, statistics help the researchers determine whether their observations are due to chance. After psychologists analyze data, they compare their findings with what others have discovered about the same issue or problem.

The final step in the scientific method is *revising theory.* Psychologists have developed a number of theories about why people become depressed and how they can cope with depression. Data such as those collected in our hypothetical study force us to study existing theories of depression to determine if they are accurate. Over the years, some theories of life-span development have been discarded and others revised.

THEORIES OF DEVELOPMENT

We will briefly explore five major theoretical perspectives on development: psychoanalytic, cognitive, behavioral/social learning, ethological, and ecological. You will read more about these theories at different points in later chapters in the book.

The diversity of theories makes understanding life-span development a challenging undertaking. Just when you think one theory has the correct explanation of life-span development, another theory crops up and makes you rethink your earlier conclusion. To keep from getting frustrated, remember that life-span development is a complex, multifaceted topic and no single theory has been able to account for all aspects of it. Each theory has contributed an important piece to the life-span development puzzle. While the theories sometimes disagree about certain aspects of life-span development, much of their information is complementary rather than contradictory. Together they let us see the total landscape of life-span development in all its richness.

Psychoanalytic Theories

For psychoanalytic theorists, development is primarily unconscious—that is, beyond awareness—and is heavily colored by emotion. Psychoanalytic theorists believe that behavior is merely a surface characteristic and that to truly understand development we have to analyze the symbolic meanings of behavior and the deep inner workings of the mind. Psychoanalytic theorists also stress that early experiences with parents extensively shape our development. These characteristics are highlighted in the main psychoanalytic theory, that of Sigmund Freud.

Freud's Theory

Freud (1856–1939) developed his ideas about psychoanalytic theory from work with mental patients. He was a medical doctor who specialized in neurology. He spent most of his years in Vienna, though he moved to London near the end of his career because of the Nazis' anti-Semitism.

> *The passions are at once temptors and chastisers. As temptors, they come with garlands of flowers on brows of youth; as chastisers, they appear with wreaths of snakes on the forehead of deformity. They are angels of light in their delusion; they are fiends of torment in their inflictions.*
>
> —Henry Giles

Sigmund Freud

Freud (1917) believed that personality has three structures: the id, the ego, and the superego. The **id** is *the Freudian structure of personality that consists of instincts, which are an individual's reservoir of psychic energy.* In Freud's view, the id is totally unconscious; it has no contact with reality. As children experience the demands and constraints of reality, a new structure of personality emerges—the **ego,** *the Freudian structure of personality that deals with the demands of reality.* The ego is called the "executive branch" of personality, because it makes rational decisions. The id and the ego have no morality. They do not take into account whether something is right or wrong. The **superego** *is the Freudian structure of personality that is the moral branch of personality and does take into account whether something is right or wrong.* Think of the superego as what we often refer to as our "conscience." You probably are beginning to sense that both the id and the superego make life rough for the ego. Your ego might say, "I will have sex only occasionally and be sure to take the proper precautions, because I don't want the intrusion of a child in the development of my career." However, your id is saying, "I want to be satisfied; sex is pleasurable." Your superego is at work too: "I feel guilty about having sex."

Remember that Freud considered personality to be like an iceberg; most of personality exists below our level of awareness, just as the massive part of an iceberg is beneath the surface of the water. Figure 2.1 illustrates this analogy.

FIGURE 2.1

Conscious and unconscious processes: The iceberg analogy. This rather odd-looking diagram illustrates Freud's belief that most of the important personality processes occur below the level of conscious awareness. In examining people's conscious thoughts and their behaviors, we can see some reflections of the ego and the superego. Whereas the ego and superego are partly conscious and partly unconscious, the primitive id is the unconscious, totally submerged part of the iceberg.

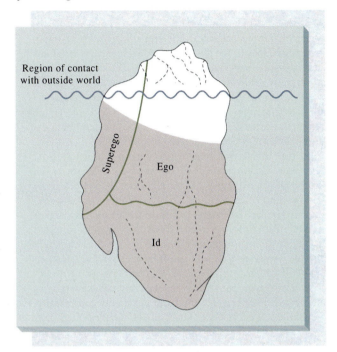

How does the ego resolve the conflict between its demands for reality, the wishes of the id, and constraints of the superego? Through **defense mechanisms,** *the psychoanalytic term for unconscious methods, the ego distorts reality, thereby protecting it from anxiety.* In Freud's view, the conflicting demands of the personality structures produce anxiety. For example, when the ego blocks the pleasurable pursuits of the id, inner anxiety is felt. This diffuse, distressed state develops when the ego senses that the id is going to cause harm to the individual. The anxiety alerts the ego to resolve the conflict by means of defense mechanisms.

> *They cannot scare me with their empty spaces*
> *Between stars—on stars where no human race is.*
> *I have it in me so much nearer home*
> *To scare myself with my own desert places.*
> —Robert Frost

Repression *is the most powerful and pervasive defense mechanism, according to Freud; it works to push unacceptable id impulses out of awareness and back into the unconscious mind.* Repression is the foundation from which all other defense mechanisms work; the goal of every defense mechanism is to *repress,* or push threatening impulses out of awareness. Freud said that our early childhood experiences, many of which he believed were

sexually laden, are too threatening and stressful for us to deal with consciously. We reduce the anxiety of this conflict through the defense mechanism of repression.

As Freud listened to, probed, and analyzed his patients, he became convinced that their problems were the result of experiences early in life. Freud believed that we go through five stages of psychosexual development and that at each stage of development we experience pleasure in one part of the body more than in others. **Erogenous zones,** *according to Freud, are the parts of the body that have especially strong pleasure-giving qualities at each stage of development.*

Freud thought that the adult personality is determined by the way conflicts between the early sources of pleasure—the mouth, the anus, and then the genitals—and the demands of reality are resolved. When these conflicts are not resolved, the individual may become fixated at a particular stage of development. For example, a parent may wean a child too early, be too strict in toilet training, punish the child for masturbation, or smother the child with warmth. We will return to the idea of fixation and how it may show up in an adult's personality, but first we need to learn more about the early stages of personality development.

The **oral stage** *is the first Freudian stage of development, occurring during the first 18 months of life, in which the infant's pleasure centers around the mouth.* Chewing, sucking, and biting are the chief sources of pleasure. These actions reduce tension in the infant.

The **anal stage** *is the second Freudian stage of development, occurring between 1½ and 3 years of age, in which the child's greatest pleasure involves the anus or the eliminative functions associated with it.* In Freud's view, the exercise of anal muscles reduces tension.

The **phallic stage** *is the third Freudian stage of development, which occurs between the ages of 3 and 6; its name comes from the Latin word* phallus, *which means "penis."* During the phallic stage, pleasure focuses on the genitals as the child discovers that self-manipulation is enjoyable.

"So, Mr. Fenton . . . Let's begin with your mother."

THE FAR SIDE cartoon by Gary Larson is reprinted by permission of Chronicle Features, San Francisco, CA.

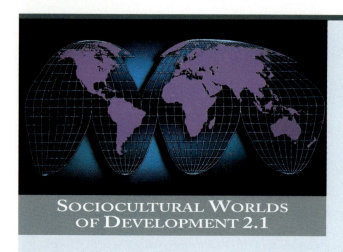

SOCIOCULTURAL WORLDS OF DEVELOPMENT 2.1

Culture- and Gender-Based Criticisms of Freud's Theory

The Oedipus complex was one of Freud's most influential concepts pertaining to the importance of early psychosexual relationships for later personality development. Freud's theory was developed during the Victorian era of the late nineteenth century, when the male was dominant and the female was passive, and when sexual interests, especially the female's, were repressed. According to Freud, the sequence of events in the phallic stage for the girl begins when she realizes that she has no penis. According to Freud, she recognizes that the penis is superior to her own anatomy, and thus develops *penis envy*. Since her desire for having a penis can never be satisfied directly, Freud said, the young girl develops a wish to become impregnated by her father. Holding her mother responsible for her lack of a penis, she renounces her love for her mother and becomes intensely attached to her father, thus forming her own version of the Oedipus complex, sometimes referred to as the "Electra complex." Thus the sequence of events becomes

reversed: for the boy, the Oedipal complex produces castration anxiety; whereas for the girl, penis envy—the parallel to castration anxiety—occurs first and leads to the formation of the Oedipus complex (Hyde, 1985).

Many psychologists believe Freud overemphasized behavior's biological determinants and did not give adequate attention to sociocultural influences and learning. In particular, his view on the differences between males and females, including their personality development, has a strong biological flavor, relying mainly on anatomical differences. That is, Freud argues that because they have a penis, boys are likely to develop a dominant, powerful personality, and that girls, because they do not have a penis, are likely to develop a submissive, weak personality. In basing his view of male/female differences in personality development on anatomical differences, Freud ignored the enormous impact of culture and experience in determining the personalities of the male and the female.

More than half a century ago, English anthropologist Bronislaw Malinowski (1927) observed the behavior of the Trobriand islanders of the Western Pacific. He found that the Oedipus complex is not universal but depends on cultural variations in families. The family pattern of the Trobriand islanders is different than found in many cultures. In the Trobriand islands, the biological father is not the head of the household; this role is reserved for the mother's brother, who acts as a disciplinarian. Thus, the Trobriand islanders tease apart the roles played by the same person in Freud's Vienna and in many other cultures. In Freud's view, this different family constellation should make no difference: The Oedipus complex should still emerge, in which the father is the young boy's hated rival for the mother's love. However, Malinowski found no indication of conflict between fathers and sons in the Trobriand islanders, though he did observe some negative feelings directed by the boy toward the maternal uncle. Thus, the young boy feared the man who was the authoritarian figure in his life, which in the Trobriand island culture was the maternal uncle, not the

In Freud's view, the phallic stage has a special importance in personality development because it is during this period that the Oedipus complex appears. This name comes from Greek mythology, in which Oedipus, the son of the King of Thebes, unwittingly kills his father and marries his mother. The **Oedipus complex** *is the Freudian concept in which the young child develops an intense desire to replace the parent of the same sex and enjoy the affections of the opposite-sexed parent.* Freud's concept of the Oedipus complex has been criticized by some psychoanalysts and writers. To learn more about culture- and gender-based criticisms of Freud's theory, turn to Sociocultural Worlds of Development 2.1.

How is the Oedipus complex resolved? At about 5 to 6 years of age, children recognize that their same-sex parent might punish them for their incestuous wishes. To reduce this conflict, the child identifies with the same-sex parent, striving to be like him or her. If the conflict is not resolved, though, the individual may become fixated at the phallic stage.

The **latency stage** *is the fourth Freudian stage of development, which occurs between approximately 6 years of age and puberty; the child represses all interest in sexuality and develops social and intellectual skills.* This activity channels much of the child's energy into emotionally safe areas and helps the child forget the highly stressful conflicts of the phallic stage.

The **genital stage** *is the fifth and final Freudian stage of development, occurring from puberty on. The genital stage is a time of sexual reawakening; the source of sexual pleasure now becomes someone outside of the family.* Freud believed that unresolved conflicts with parents reemerge during adolescence. When resolved, the individual is capable of developing a mature love relationship and functioning independently as an adult.

Freud's theory has undergone significant revisions by a number of psychoanalytic theorists. Many contemporary psychoanalytic theorists place less emphasis on sexual instincts and more emphasis on cultural experiences as determinants of an individual's development. Unconscious thought remains a central

Karen Horney developed the first feminist-based criticism of Freud's theory. Horney's model emphasizes women's positive qualities and self-evaluation.

Nancy Chodorow has developed an important contemporary feminist revision of psychoanalytic theory that emphasizes the meaningfulness of emotions for women.

father. In sum, Malinowski's study documented that it was not the sexual relations within the family that created conflict and fear for a child, a damaging finding for Freud's Oedipus-complex theory.

The first feminist-based criticism of Freud's theory was proposed by psychoanalytic theorist Karen Horney (1967). She developed a model of women with positive feminine qualities and self-evaluation. Her critique of Freud's theory included

reference to a male-dominant society and culture. Rectification of the male bias in psychoanalytic theory continues today. For example, Nancy Chodorow (1978, 1989) emphasizes that many more women then men define themselves in terms of their relationships and connections to others. Her feminist revision of psychoanalytic theory also emphasizes the meaningfulness of emotions for women, as well as the belief that many men use the defense mechanism of denial in self-other connections.

theme, but most contemporary psychoanalysts believe that conscious thought makes up more of the iceberg than Freud envisioned. Next, we explore the ideas of an important revisionist of Freud's ideas—Erik Erikson.

Erikson's Theory

Erik Erikson (1902–1994) recognized Freud's contributions but believed that Freud misjudged some important dimensions of human development. For one, Erikson (1950, 1968) says we develop in *psychosocial stages,* in contrast to Freud's psychosexual stages. For another, Erikson emphasizes developmental change throughout the human life cycle, whereas Freud argued that our basic personality is shaped in the first 5 years of life. In Erikson's theory, eight stages of development unfold as we go through the life cycle. Each stage consists of a unique developmental task that confronts individuals with a crisis that must be faced. For Erikson, this crisis is not a catastrophe but a turning point of increased vulnerability

and enhanced potential. The more individuals resolve the crises successfully, the healthier their development will be.

Trust versus mistrust *is Erikson's first psychosocial stage, which is experienced in the first year of life. A sense of trust requires a feeling of physical comfort and a minimal amount of fear and apprehension about the future.* Trust in infancy sets the stage for a lifelong expectation that the world will be a good and pleasant place to live.

Autonomy versus shame and doubt *is Erikson's second stage of development, occurring in late infancy and toddlerhood (1–3 years).* After gaining trust in their caregivers, infants begin to discover that their behavior is their own. They start to assert their sense of independence or autonomy. They realize their *will.* If infants are restrained too much or punished too harshly, they are likely to develop a sense of shame and doubt.

Initiative versus guilt *is Erikson's third stage of development, occurring during the preschool years.* As preschool children encounter a widening social world, they are challenged more

LIFE-SPAN PRACTICAL KNOWLEDGE 2.1

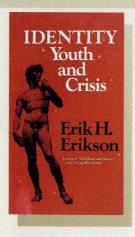

Identity: Youth and Crisis
(1968) by Erik H. Erikson.
New York: W. W. Norton.

Erik Erikson is one of the leading theorists in the field of life-span development. In *Identity: Youth and Crisis,* he outlines his eight stages of life-span development and provides numerous examples from his clinical practice to illustrate the stages. Special attention is given to the fifth stage in Erikson's theory, identity versus identity confusion. Especially worthwhile are Erikson's commentaries about identity development in different cultures.

Two other Erikson books that are excellent reading on life-span development are *Young Man Luther* and *Gandhi's Truth.* If you are interested in learning more about your development of your identity, you will find any of these three books to provide many insights about your pursuit of who you are, what you are all about, and where you are going in life.

Erik Erikson with his wife, Joan, who is an artist. Erikson generated one of the most important developmental theories of the twentieth century.

than when they were infants. Active, purposeful behavior is needed to cope with these challenges. Children are asked to assume responsibility for their bodies, their behavior, their toys, and their pets. Developing a sense of responsibility increases initiative. Uncomfortable guilt feelings may arise, though, if the

child is irresponsible and is made to feel too anxious. Erikson has a positive outlook on this stage. He believes that most guilt is quickly compensated for by a sense of accomplishment.

Industry versus inferiority *is Erikson's fourth developmental stage, occurring approximately in the elementary school years.* Children's initiative brings them in contact with a wealth of new experiences. As they move into middle and late childhood, they direct their energy toward mastering knowledge and intellectual skills. At no other time is the child more enthusiastic about learning than at the end of early childhood's period of expansive imagination. The danger in the elementary school years is the development of a sense of inferiority—of feeling incompetent and unproductive. Erikson believes that teachers have a special responsibility for children's development of industry. Teachers should "mildly but firmly coerce children into the adventure of finding out that one can learn to accomplish things which one would never have thought of by oneself" (Erikson, 1968, p. 127).

Identity versus identity confusion *is Erikson's fifth developmental stage, which individuals experience during the adolescent years. At this time individuals are faced with finding out who they are, what they are all about, and where they are going in life.* Adolescents are confronted with many new roles and adult statuses—vocational and romantic, for example. Parents need to allow adolescents to explore many different roles and different paths within a particular role. If the adolescent explores such roles in a healthy manner and arrives at a positive path to follow in life, then a positive identity will be achieved. If an identity is pushed on the adolescent by parents, if the adolescent does not adequately explore many roles, and if a positive future path is not defined, then identity confusion reigns.

Know thyself, for once we know ourselves, we may learn how to care for ourselves, otherwise we never shall.

—Socrates

Intimacy versus isolation *is Erikson's sixth developmental stage, which individuals experience during the early adulthood years. At this time, individuals face the developmental task of forming intimate relationships with others.* Erikson describes intimacy as finding oneself yet losing oneself in another. If the young adult forms healthy friendships and an intimate close relationship with another individual, intimacy will be achieved; if not, isolation will result.

Generativity versus stagnation *is Erikson's seventh developmental stage, which individuals experience during middle adulthood.* A chief concern is to assist the younger generation in developing and leading useful lives—this is what Erikson means by *generativity.* The feeling of having done nothing to help the next generation is *stagnation.*

> *You come to a place in your life when what you've been is going to form what you will be. If you've wasted what you have in you, it's too late to do much about it. If you've invested yourself in life, you're pretty certain to get a return. If you are inwardly a serious person, in the middle years it will pay off.*
>
> —Lillian Hellman

Integrity versus despair *is Erikson's eighth and final developmental stage, which individuals experience during late adulthood.* In the later years of life, we look back and evaluate what we have done with our lives. Through many different routes, the older person may have developed a positive outlook in most or all of the previous stages of development. If so, the retrospective glances will reveal a picture of a life well spent, and the person will feel a sense of satisfaction—integrity will be achieved. If the older adult resolved many of the earlier stages negatively, the retrospective glances likely will yield doubt or gloom—the despair Erikson talks about.

Erikson does not believe the proper solution to a stage crisis is always completely positive in nature. Some exposure or commitment to the negative end of the person's bipolar conflict is sometimes inevitable—you cannot trust all people under all circumstances and survive, for example. Nonetheless, in the healthy solution to a stage crisis, the positive resolution dominates. A summary of Erikson's stages is presented in figure 2.2.

Cognitive Theories

Whereas psychoanalytic theories stress the importance of children's unconscious thoughts, cognitive theories emphasize their conscious thoughts. Two important cognitive theories are Piaget's cognitive development theory and information-processing theory.

Piaget's Theory

The famous Swiss psychologist Jean Piaget (1896–1980) stressed that children actively construct their own cognitive worlds; information is not just poured into their minds from the environment. Piaget believes that children adapt their thinking to include new ideas, because additional information furthers understanding.

Piaget's theory will be covered in greater detail later in this book when we discuss cognitive development in infancy, early childhood, middle and late childhood, and adolescence. Here we briefly present the main ideas of his theory. In Piaget's view, two processes underlie the individual's construction of the world: organization and adaptation. To make sense of our world, we organize our experiences. For example, we separate important ideas from less important ideas. We connect one idea to another. But we not only organize our observations and experiences, we also *adapt* our thinking to include new ideas. Piaget (1954) believed that we adapt in two ways: assimilation and accommodation.

Assimilation *occurs when individuals incorporate new information into their existing knowledge.* **Accommodation** *occurs when individuals adjust to new information.* Consider a circumstance in which a 7-year-old girl is given a hammer and nails to hang a picture on the wall. She has never used a hammer, but from observation and vicarious experience she realizes that a hammer is an object to be held, that it is swung by the handle to hit the nail, and that it is usually swung a number of times. Recognizing each of these things, she fits her behavior into information she already has (assimilation). However, the hammer is heavy, so she holds it near the top. She swings too hard and the nail bends, so she adjusts the pressure of her strikes. These adjustments reveal her ability to alter her conception of the world slightly (accommodation).

Piaget thought that assimilation and accommodation operate even in the very young infant's life. Newborns reflexively suck everything that touches their lips (assimilation), but after several months of experience, they construct their understanding of the world differently. Some objects, such as fingers and the mother's breast, can be sucked, and others, such as fuzzy blankets, should not be sucked (accommodation).

Critical Thinking

What experiences in your own life provide examples of Piaget's concepts of assimilation and accommodation?

Piaget also believed that we go through four stages in understanding the world. Each of the stages is age-related and consists of distinct ways of thinking. Remember, it is the *different* way of understanding the world that makes one stage more advanced than another; knowing *more* information does not make the child's thinking more advanced, in the Piagetian view. This is what Piaget meant when he said the child's cognition is *qualitatively* different in one stage compared to another. What are Piaget's four stages of cognitive development like?

The **sensorimotor stage,** *which lasts from birth to about 2 years of age, is the first Piagetian stage. In this stage, infants construct an understanding of the world by coordinating sensory experiences (such as seeing and hearing) with physical motoric actions—hence the term* sensorimotor. At the beginning of this stage, newborns have little more than reflexive patterns with which to work. At the end of the stage, 2-year-olds have complex sensorimotor patterns and are beginning to operate with primitive symbols.

FIGURE 2.2

Erikson's eight stages of development.

Erikson's stages	Developmental period	Characteristics
Trust versus mistrust	Infancy (first year)	A sense of trust requires a feeling of physical comfort and a minimal amount of fear about the future. Infants' basic needs are met by responsive, sensitive caregivers.
Autonomy versus shame and doubt	Infancy (second year)	After gaining trust in caregivers, infants start to discover that they have a will of their own. They assert their sense of autonomy, or independence. They realize their will. If infants are restrained too much or punished too harshly, they are likely to develop a sense of shame and doubt.
Initiative versus guilt	Early childhood (preschool years, ages 3–5)	As preschool children encounter a widening social world, they are challenged more and need to develop more purposeful behavior to cope with these challenges. Children are now asked to assume more responsibility. Uncomfortable guilt feelings may arise, though, if the children are irresponsible and are made to feel too anxious.
Industry versus inferiority	Middle and late childhood (elementary school years, 6 years– puberty)	At no other time are children more enthusiastic than at the end of early childhood's period of expansive imagination. As children move into the elementary school years, they direct their energy toward mastering knowledge and intellectual skills. The danger at this stage involves feeling incompetent and unproductive.

Erikson's stages	Developmental period	Characteristics
Identity versus identity confusion	Adolescence (10 to 20 years)	Individuals are faced with finding out who they are, what they are all about, and where they are going in life. An important dimension is the exploration of alternative solutions to roles. Career exploration is important.
Intimacy versus isolation	Early adulthood (20s, 30s)	Individuals face the developmental task of forming intimate relationships with others. Erikson described intimacy as finding oneself yet losing oneself in another person.
Generativity versus stagnation	Middle adulthood (40s, 50s)	A chief concern is to assist the younger generation in developing and leading useful lives.
Integrity versus despair	Late adulthood (60s –)	Individuals look back and evaluate what they have done with their lives. The retrospective glances can either be positive (integrity) or negative (despair).

TABLE 2.1

Piaget's Stages of Cognitive Development

Stage	Description	Age Range
Sensorimotor	An infant progresses from reflexive, instinctual action at birth to the beginning of symbolic thought. The infant constructs an understanding of the world by coordinating sensory experiences with physical actions.	Birth to 2 years
Preoperational	The child begins to represent the world with words and images; these words and images reflect increased symbolic thinking and go beyond the connection of sensory information and physical action.	2 to 7 years
Concrete operational	The child can now reason logically about concrete events and classify objects into different sets.	7 to 11 years
Formal operational	The adolescent reasons in more abstract and logical ways. Thought is more idealistic.	11 to 15 years

Jean Piaget, the famous Swiss developmental psychologist, changed the way we think about the development of children's minds. For Piaget, a child's mental development is a continuous creation of increasingly complex forms.

The **preoperational stage,** *which lasts from approximately 2 to 7 years of age, is the second Piagetian stage. In this stage, children begin to represent the world with words, images, and drawings.* Symbolic thought goes beyond simple connections of sensory information and physical action. However, although preschool children can symbolically represent the world, according to Piaget, they still lack the ability to perform what

Piaget calls "operations"—internalized mental actions that allow children to do mentally what they previously did physically.

The **concrete operational stage,** *which lasts from approximately 7 to 11 years of age, is the third Piagetian stage. In this stage, children can perform operations, and logical reasoning replaces intuitive thought as long as reasoning can be applied to specific or concrete examples.* For instance, concrete operational thinkers cannot imagine the steps necessary to complete an algebraic equation, which is too abstract for thinking at this stage of development.

The **formal operational stage,** *which appears between the ages of 11 and 15, is the fourth and final Piagetian stage. In this stage, individuals move beyond the world of actual, concrete experiences and think in abstract and more logical terms.* As part of thinking more abstractly, adolescents develop images of ideal circumstances. They may think about what an ideal parent is like and compare their parents with this ideal standard. They begin to entertain possibilities for the future and are fascinated with what they can be. In solving problems, formal operational thinkers are more systematic, developing hypotheses about why something is happening the way it is, then testing these hypotheses in a deductive fashion. Piaget's stages are summarized in table 2.1.

The Information-Processing Approach

The **information-processing approach** *is concerned with how individuals process information about their world—how information enters our minds, how it is stored and transformed, and how it is retrieved to perform such complex activities as problem solving and reasoning.* A simple model of cognition is shown in figure 2.3. Cognition begins when information from the world is detected through sensory and perceptual processes. Then information is stored, transformed, and retrieved through the processes of memory. Notice in our model that information can flow back and forth between memory and perceptual processes. For example, we are good at remembering the faces we see, yet our memory of an individual's face may be different from how

FIGURE 2.3

A model of cognition.

the individual actually looks. Keep in mind that our information-processing model is a simple one, designed to illustrate the main cognitive processes and their interrelations. We could have drawn other arrows—between memory and language, between thinking and perception, and between language and perception, for example. Also, it is important to know that the boxes in the figure do not represent sharp, distinct stages in processing information. There is continuity and flow between the cognitive processes as well as overlap.

> *Man is a reed, the weakest in nature; but he is a thinking reed.*
>
> —Pascal, 1670

Behavioral and Social Learning Theories

Behaviorists believe we should examine only what can be directly observed and measured. At approximately the same time as Freud was interpreting his patients' unconscious minds through early childhood experiences, behaviorists such as Ivan Pavlov and John B. Watson were conducting detailed observations of behavior in controlled laboratory circumstances. Out of the behavioral tradition grew the belief that development is observable behavior, learned through experience with the environment. The two versions of the behavioral approach that are prominent today are the view of B. F. Skinner and social learning theory.

Skinner's Behaviorism

Behaviorism *emphasizes the scientific study of observable behavioral responses and their environmental determinants.* In Skinner's behaviorism, the mind, conscious or unconscious, is not needed to explain behavior and development. For Skinner, development is behavior. For example, observations of Sam reveal that his behavior is shy, achievement-oriented, and caring. Why is Sam's behavior this way? For Skinner, rewards and punishments in Sam's environment have shaped him into a shy, achievement-oriented, and caring person. Because of interactions with family members, friends, teachers, and others, Sam has *learned* to behave in this fashion.

Critical Thinking

Think about your life during the last month. How did rewards and punishments influence the way you behaved during this time frame?

Since behaviorists believe that development is learned and often changes according to environmental experiences, it follows that rearranging experiences can change development. For behaviorists, shy behavior can be transformed into outgoing behavior; aggressive behavior can be shaped into docile behavior; lethargic, boring behavior can be turned into enthusiastic, interesting behavior.

Social Learning Theory

Some psychologists believe that the behaviorists basically are right when they say development is learned and is influenced strongly by environmental experiences. However, they believe that Skinner went too far in declaring that cognition is unimportant in understanding development. **Social learning theory** *is the view of psychologists who emphasize behavior, environment, and cognition as the key factors in development.*

The social learning theorists say we are not like mindless robots, responding mechanically to others in our environment. Neither are we like weathervanes, behaving like a communist in the presence of a communist or like a John Bircher in the presence of a John Bircher. Rather, we think, reason, imagine, plan, expect, interpret, believe, value, and compare. When others try to control us, our values and beliefs allow us to resist their control.

American psychologists Albert Bandura (1977, 1986, 1989, 1991, 1994) and Walter Mischel (1973, 1984) are the main architects of the contemporary version of social learning theory, which was labeled *cognitive social learning theory* by Mischel (1973). Bandura believes we learn by observing what others do. Through observational learning (also called "modeling" or "imitation"), we cognitively represent the behavior of others and then possibly adopt this behavior ourselves. For example, a young boy may observe his father's aggressive outbursts and hostile interchanges with people; when observed with his peers, the young boy's style of interaction is highly aggressive, showing the same characteristics as his father's behavior. Or a young female executive adopts the

Albert Bandura has been one of the leading architects of the contemporary version of social learning theory—cognitive social learning theory.

dominant and sarcastic style of her boss. When observed interacting with one of her subordinates, the young woman says, "I need this work immediately if not sooner; you are so far behind you think you are ahead!" Social learning theorists believe we acquire a wide range of such behaviors, thoughts, and feelings through observing others' behavior; these observations form an important part of our development. To read about the importance of observational learning in parent-child relationships, turn to Perspectives on Parenting and Education 2.1.

Social learning theorists also differ from Skinner's behavioral view by emphasizing that we can regulate and control our own behavior. For example, another young female executive who observed her boss behave in a dominant and sarcastic manner toward employees found the behavior distasteful and went out of her way to encourage and support her subordinates. Imagine that someone tries to persuade you to join a particular social club on campus and makes you an enticing offer. You reflect about the offer, consider your interests and beliefs, and make the decision not to join. Your *cognition* (your thoughts) leads you to control your behavior and resist environmental influence in this instance.

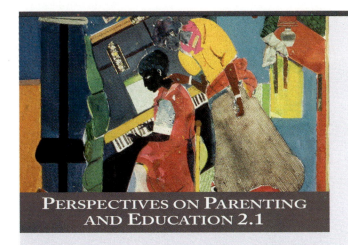

PERSPECTIVES ON PARENTING AND EDUCATION 2.1

Observing and Imitating Parents

Think for a moment about the thousands of hours most children spend observing their parents' behavior. Often on a daily basis, children watch and listen to their parents comment about their work and careers, observe whether they drink too much or not at all, experience their model of marital relationships and whether their mother and father argue a lot or very little, see and hear if they solve problems calmly or with great discharge of anger, view whether they are generous toward others or are more selfish, and see how male and female adults act.

Why are children motivated to imitate their parents' behaviors? Children can gain and maintain their parents' affection and avoid punishment by behaving like their parents. Children also acquire a sense of mastery over their environment by imitating the behavior of warm, competent, and powerful parents.

One issue in observational learning is whether parents can get by with telling their children, "Do what I say, not what I do," and not harm their children's development. Such parents often hope that by rewarding their children's positive behavior and/or punishing their negative behaviors, they still can engage in their own maladaptive, selfish, and inappropriate ways without jeopardizing their children's development. Imitation often occurs without parents knowingly trying to influence their children, but when parents verbalize standards and try to get children to abide by them, they are usually consciously shaping their children's behavior.

Child developmentalists believe a "do as I say, but not as I do" approach by parents is not a wise parenting strategy. Children who see their parents attend church regularly and hear them talk about how moral they are, but then observe them cheat on their income tax, never give money to charity,

turn down requests to help others in need, and treat others with little respect, will often imitate their parents' *actions* rather than their *words*. In the case of children's imitation of parents, then, a familiar saying often holds true: Actions speak louder than words.

How much children learn by observing parents also is influenced by what children see are the consequences of that behavior for the parent. If parental models are rewarded for their behavior, children are more likely to imitate their behavior than if the parents receive no reward or are punished for their behavior. The consequences to the model can be either external (someone else says or does something positive to the parents after the parent engages in a particular action) or internal (the parent engages in self-reinforcement by showing pleasure after performing a behavior). For example, a father may give to a charity and subsequently smile and say how good it made him feel. The father's children observe these consequences and then may imitate the father's kind, generous behavior as long as it makes the children feel good. Parents may find it ineffective to exhort their children to share their toys because children will not feel good letting others share what they want themselves. However, if children see their parents derive pleasure from sharing, the self-sacrificing behavior probably will bring more joy to the children. Thus, imitation is an important part of the process in getting children to behave in kind ways toward others (Jensen & Kingston, 1986).

Observational learning is a primary way children learn from their parents.

FIGURE 2.4

Bandura's model of the reciprocal influence of behavior, personal and cognitive factors, and environment. *P(C) stands for personal and cognitive factors, B for behavior, and E for environment. The arrows reflect how relations between these factors are reciprocal rather than unidirectional. Examples of personal factors include intelligence, skills, and self-control.*

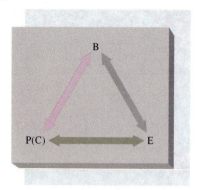

Albert Bandura, *SOCIAL FOUNDATIONS OF THOUGHT AND ACTION: A Social Cognitive Theory,* © 1986, p. 24. Reprinted by permission of Prentice-Hall, Inc., Englewood Cliffs, NJ.

Bandura's (1986, 1989, 1991) most recent model of learning and development involves behavior, the person, and the environment. As shown in figure 2.4, behavior, cognitive and other personal factors, and environmental influences operate interactively. Behavior can influence cognition and vice versa, the person's cognitive activities can influence the environment, environmental influences can change the person's thought processes, and so on.

Let's consider how Bandura's model might work in the case of a college student's achievement behavior. As the student diligently studies and gets good grades, her behavior produces positive thoughts about her abilities. As part of her effort to make good grades, she plans and develops a number of strategies to make her studying more efficient. In these ways, her behavior has influenced her thought and her thought has influenced her behavior. At the beginning of the semester, her college made a special effort to involve students in a study skills program. She decided to join. Her success, along with that of other students who attended the program, has led the college to expand the program next semester. In these ways, environment influenced behavior, and behavior changed the environment. And the college administrators' expectations that the study skills program would work made it possible in the first place. The program's success has spurred expectations that this type of program could work in other colleges. In these ways, cognition changed the environment, and the environment changed cognition. Expectations are an important variable in Bandura's model.

Like the behavioral approach of Skinner, the social learning approach emphasizes the importance of empirical research in studying children's development. This research focuses on the processes that explain children's development—the social and cognitive factors that influence what children are like.

Ethological Theories

Sensitivity to different kinds of experience varies over the life cycle. The presence or absence of certain experiences at

FIGURE 2.5

Konrad Lorenz, a pioneering student of animal behavior, is followed through the water by three imprinted greylag geese. *Lorenz described imprinting as rapid, innate learning within a critical period that involves attachment to the first moving object seen. For goslings, the critical period is the first 36 hours after birth.*

particular times in the life span influences individuals well beyond the time they first occur. Ethologists believe that most psychologists underestimate the importance of these special time frames in early development and the powerful roles that evolution and biological foundations play in development (Charlesworth, 1992; Hinde, 1992).

> *The tide of evolution carries everything before it, thoughts no less than bodies, and persons no less than nations.*
>
> —George Santayana,
> *Little Essays,* 1920

Ethology emerged as an important view because of the work of European zoologists, especially Konrad Lorenz (1903–1989). **Ethology** *stresses that behavior is strongly influenced by biology, is tied to evolution, and is characterized by critical or sensitive periods.*

Working mostly with greylag geese, Lorenz (1965) studied a behavior pattern that was considered to be programmed within the birds' genes. A newly hatched gosling seemed to be born with the instinct to follow its mother. Observations showed that the gosling was capable of such behavior as soon as it hatched. Lorenz proved that it was incorrect to assume that such behavior was programmed in the animal. In a remarkable set of experiments, Lorenz separated the eggs laid by one goose into two groups. One group he returned to the goose to be hatched by her; the other group was hatched in an incubator. The goslings in the first group performed as predicted; they followed their mother as soon as they hatched. However, those in the second group, which saw Lorenz when they first hatched, followed him everywhere, as though he were their mother. Lorenz marked the goslings and then placed both groups under a box. Mother goose and "mother" Lorenz stood aside as the box lifted. Each group of goslings went directly to its "mother" (see figure 2.5). Lorenz called this process **imprinting,** *the ethological concept of rapid, innate learning within a limited critical period of time that involves attachment to the first moving object seen.*

Urie Bronfenbrenner (above with his grandson) has developed ecological theory, a perspective that is receiving increased attention. His theory emphasizes the importance of both micro and macro dimensions of the environment in which the child lives.

The ethological view of Lorenz and the European zoologists forced American developmental psychologists to recognize the importance of the biological basis of behavior. However, the research and theorizing of ethology still seemed to lack some ingredients that would elevate it to the ranks of the other theories discussed so far in this chapter. In particular, there was little or nothing in the classical ethological view about the nature of social relationships across the human life cycle, something that any major theory of development must explain. Also, its concept of **critical period,** *a fixed time period very early in development during which certain behaviors optimally emerge,* seemed to be overdrawn. Classical ethological theory was weak in stimulating studies with humans. Recent expansion of the ethological view has improved its status as a viable developmental perspective.

Like behaviorists, ethologists are careful observers of behavior. Unlike behaviorists, ethologists believe that laboratories are not good settings for observing behavior; rather, they meticulously observe behavior in its natural surroundings, in homes, playgrounds, neighborhoods, schools, hospitals, and so on.

Ecological Theory

Ethological theory places a strong emphasis on the biological foundations of development. In contrast to ethological theory, Urie Bronfenbrenner (1917–   ) has proposed a strong environmental view of development that is receiving increased attention. **Ecological theory** *is Bronfenbrenner's sociocultural view of development, which consists of five environmental systems ranging from the fine-grained inputs of direct interactions with social agents to the broad-based inputs of culture. The five systems in Bronfenbrenner's ecological theory are the microsystem, mesosystem, exosystem, macrosystem, and chronosystem.* Bronfenbrenner's (1979, 1986, 1989, 1993) ecological model is shown in figure 2.6. The **microsystem** *in Bronfenbrenner's ecological theory is the setting in which the individual lives. These contexts include the person's*

FIGURE 2.6

Bronfenbrenner's ecological theory of development, which consists of five environmental systems: microsystem, mesosystem, exosystem, macrosystem, and chronosystem.

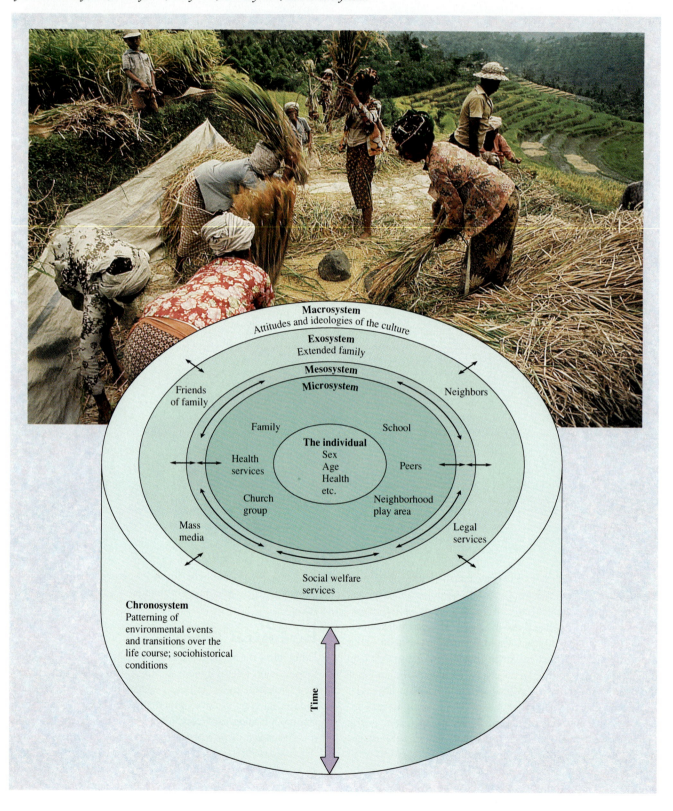

family, peers, school, and neighborhood. It is in the microsystem that the most direct interactions with social agents take place—with parents, peers, and teachers, for example. The individual is not viewed as a passive recipient of experiences in these settings, but as someone who helps to construct the settings. Bronfenbrenner points out that most research on sociocultural influences has focused on microsystems.

The **mesosystem** *in Bronfenbrenner's ecological theory involves relations between microsystems or connections between contexts. Examples are the relation of family experiences to school experiences, school experiences to church experiences, and family experiences to peer experiences.* For example, children whose parents have rejected them may have difficulty developing positive relations with teachers. Developmentalists increasingly believe it is important to observe behavior in multiple settings—such as family, peer, and school contexts—to obtain a more complete picture of the individual's development.

The **exosystem** *in Bronfenbrenner's ecological theory is involved when experiences in another social setting—in which the individual does not have an active role—influence what the individual experiences in an immediate context.* For example, work experiences may affect a woman's relationship with her husband and their child. The mother may receive a promotion that requires more travel, which might increase marital conflict and change patterns of parent-child interaction. Another example of an exosystem is the city government, which is responsible for the quality of parks, recreation centers, and library facilities for children and adolescents. And yet another example is the federal government through its role in the quality of medical care and support systems for the elderly.

The **macrosystem** *in Bronfenbrenner's ecological theory involves the culture in which individuals live.* Remember from chapter 1 that *culture* refers to the behavior patterns, beliefs, and all other products of a group of people that are passed on from generation to generation. Remember also that *cross-cultural studies*—the comparison of one culture with one or more other cultures—provide information about the generality of development.

The **chronosystem** *in Bronfenbrenner's ecological theory involves the patterning of environmental events and transitions over the life course and sociohistorical circumstances.* For example, in studying the effects of divorce on children, researchers have found that the negative effects often peak in the first year after the divorce and that the effects are more negative for sons than for daughters (Hetherington, 1989; Hetherington, Cox, & Cox, 1982). By 2 years after the divorce, family interaction is less chaotic and more stable. With regard to sociocultural circumstances, women today are much more likely to be encouraged to pursue a career than they were 20 or 30 years ago. In ways such as these, the chronosystem has a powerful impact on our development.

An Eclectic Theoretical Orientation

An **eclectic theoretical orientation** *does not follow any one theoretical approach, but rather selects and uses whatever is considered the best in all theories.* No single theory described in this chapter is indomitable or capable of explaining entirely the rich complexity of development. Each of the theories has made important contributions to our understanding of development, but none provides a complete description and explanation. Psychoanalytic theory best explains the unconscious mind. Erikson's theory best describes the changes that occur in adult development. Piaget's theory is the most complete description of cognitive development. The behavioral and social learning and ecological theories have been the most adept at examining the environmental determinants of development. The ethological theories have made us aware of biology's role and the importance of sensitive periods in development. It is important to recognize that, although theories are helpful guides, relying on a single theory to explain development is probably a mistake.

An attempt was made in this chapter to present five theoretical perspectives objectively. The same eclectic orientation will be maintained throughout the book. In this way, you can view the study of development as it actually exists—with different theorists making different assumptions, stressing different empirical problems, and using different strategies to discover information.

These theoretical perspectives, along with research issues that were discussed in chapter 1 and methods that will be described shortly, provide a sense of development's scientific nature. Table 2.2 compares the main theoretical perspectives in terms of how they view important developmental issues and the methods they prefer to use when they study development.

In thinking about theories of life-span development, be sure to keep in mind the life-span perspective discussed in chapter 1. Recall that the life-span perspective developed only recently, and that many of the theories presented in this chapter were already in place when the life-span perspective was formulated. As a perspective, the life-span view coordinates a number of theoretical principles about the nature of development. Although these principles of the life-span perspective are not new, the strength of the beliefs and the coordination of principles represent a novel, unique approach to development (Baltes, 1987).

Remember that from a life-span perspective, development is seen as lifelong, multidirectional, multidimensional, plastic, historically embedded, contextual, and multidisciplinary. By considering the ideas of various developmental theorists discussed in this chapter along with the characteristics of the life-span perspective, we can get a sense of the theoretical concepts that are important in understanding life-span development. You may want to review the characteristics of the life-span perspective at this time (see chapter 1) as you think about taking an eclectic approach to life-span development.

At this point we have discussed a number of ideas about the scientific method and theories of development. A summary of these ideas is presented in concept table 2.1. Next, we explore the methods developmentalists use, beginning with the measures they use.

TABLE 2.2

A Comparison of Theories and the Issues and Methods in Development

Theory	Issues and Methods			
	Continuity/ Discontinuity, Stability/Change	Biological and Environmental Factors	Importance of Cognition	Research Methods
Psychoanalytic	Discontinuity between stages—continuity between early experiences and later development; early family experiences very important; later changes in development emphasized in Erikson's theory	Freud's biological determination interacting with early family experiences; Erikson's more balanced biology-culture interaction perspective	Emphasized, but in the form of unconscious thought	Clinical interviews, unstructured personality tests, psychohistorical analyses of lives
Cognitive	Discontinuity between stages—continuity between early experiences and later development in Piaget's theory; has not been important to information-processing psychologists	Piaget's emphasis on interaction and adaptation; environment provides the setting for cognitive structures to develop; information-processing view has not addressed this issue extensively, but mainly emphasizes biology-environment interaction	The primary determinant of behavior	Interviews and observations
Behavioral and social learning	Continuity (no stages); experience at all points of development important	Environment viewed as the cause of behavior in both views	Strongly deemphasized in the behavioral approach but an important mediator in social learning	Observation, especially laboratory observation
Ethological	Discontinuity but no stages; critical or sensitive periods emphasized; early experience very important	Strong biological view	Not emphasized	Observation in natural settings
Ecological	Little attention to continuity/discontinuity; change emphasized more than stability	Strong environmental view	Not emphasized	Varied methods; especially stresses importance of collecting data in different social contexts

MEASURES

Systematic observations can be conducted in a variety of ways. For example, we can watch behavior in the laboratory or in a more natural setting such as a home or a street corner. We can question people using interviews and surveys, develop and administer standardized tests, conduct case studies, or carry out physiological research or research with animals. To help you understand how psychologists use these methods, we will apply each method to the study of aggression.

Observations

Sherlock Holmes chided Watson, "You see but you do not observe." We look at things all the time, but casually watching a mother and her infant is not scientific observation. Unless you are a trained observer and practice your skills regularly, you may not know what to look for, and you may not remember what you saw, and you may not communicate your observations effectively.

For observations to be effective, we have to know what we are looking for, who we are observing, when and where we will observe, how the observations will be made, and in what form

CONCEPT TABLE 2.1

Theory and the Scientific Method, and Theories of Development

Concept	Processes/Related Ideas	Characteristics/Description
Theory and the scientific method	Theory	Theories are general beliefs that help us to explain what we observe and make predictions. A good theory has hypotheses, which are assumptions to be tested.
	The scientific method	The scientific method is a series of procedures (identifying and analyzing a problem, collecting data, drawing conclusions, and revising theory) to obtain accurate information.
Theories of child development	Psychoanalytic theories	Two important psychoanalytic theories are Freud's and Erikson's. Freud said personality is made up of three structures—id, ego, and superego—and that most of children's thoughts are unconscious. The conflicting demands of personality structures produce anxiety. Defense mechanisms, especially repression, protect the ego and reduce anxiety. Freud was convinced that problems develop because of early childhood experiences. He said individuals go through five psychosexual stages—oral, anal, phallic, latency, and genital. During the phallic stage, the Oedipus complex is a major source of conflict. Culture- and gender-based criticisms of psychoanalytic theory have been made. Erikson developed a theory that emphasizes eight psychosocial stages of development: trust vs. mistrust, autonomy vs. shame and doubt, initiative vs. guilt, industry vs. inferiority, identity vs. identity confusion, intimacy vs. isolation, generativity vs. stagnation, and integrity vs. despair.
	Cognitive theories	Two important cognitive theories are Piaget's cognitive developmental theory and information-processing theory. Piaget said that we are motivated to understand our world and that we use the processes of organization and adaptation (assimilation, accommodation) to do so. According to Piaget, children go through four stages of cognitive development: sensorimotor, preoperational, concrete operational, and formal operational. Information-processing theory is concerned with how individuals process information about their world, including how information gets into the mind, how it is stored and transformed, and how it is retrieved to allow us to think and solve problems.
	Behavioral and social learning theories	Behaviorism emphasizes that cognition is not important in understanding behavior. Development is observed behavior, which is determined by rewards and punishments in the environment, according to B. F. Skinner, a famous behaviorist. Social learning theory, developed by Albert Bandura and others, states that the environment is an important determinant of behavior, but so are cognitive processes. People have the ability to control their own behavior, in the social learning view.
	Ethological theories	Konrad Lorenz was one of the important developers of ethological theory. Ethology emphasizes the biological and evolutionary basis of development. Imprinting and critical periods are key concepts.
	Ecological theory	In Bronfenbrenner's ecological theory, five environmental systems are important: microsystem, mesosystem, exosystem, macrosystem, and chronosystem.
	Eclectic theoretical orientation	No single theory can explain the rich, awesome complexity of life-span development. Each of the theories has made a different contribution, and it probably is a wise strategy to adopt an eclectic theoretical perspective as we attempt to understand life-span development. As a perspective, the life-span view coordinates a number of theoretical principles about the nature of development. By considering the ideas of the life-span perspective along with the developmental theories discussed in this chapter, we can get a sense of the theoretical concepts that are important in understanding life-span development.

they will be recorded. That is, our observations have to be made in some *systematic* way. Consider aggression. Do we want to study verbal or physical aggression, or both? Do we want to study children or adults, or both? Do we want to evaluate them in a university laboratory, at work, at play, or at all of these locations? A common way to record our observations is to write them down, using shorthand or symbols; however, tape recorders, video cameras, special coding sheets, and one-way mirrors are used increasingly to make observations more efficient and more objective (Roberts, 1993).

When we observe, frequently it is necessary to *control* certain factors that determine behavior but are not the focus of our inquiry. For this reason, much psychological research is conducted in a **laboratory,** *a controlled setting from which many of the complex factors of the "real world" are removed.* For example, Albert Bandura (1965) brought children into a laboratory and had them observe an adult repeatedly hit a plastic, inflated Bobo doll about 3 feet tall. Bandura wondered to what extent the children would copy the adult's behavior. After the children saw the adult attack the Bobo doll, they also hit the inflated toy aggressively. By conducting his experiment in a laboratory with adults the children did not know as models, Bandura had complete control over when the child witnessed aggression, how much aggression the child saw, and what form the aggression took. Bandura could not have had as much control in his experiment if other factors—such as parents, siblings, friends, television, and a familiar room—had been present.

Laboratory research, however, does have some drawbacks. First, it is almost impossible to conduct without the participants' knowing they are being studied. Second, the laboratory setting may be *unnatural* and therefore cause unnatural behavior from the participants. Subjects usually show less aggressive behavior in a laboratory than in a more familiar natural setting, such as a park or at home. They also show less aggression when they are unaware they are being observed than when they are aware that an observer is studying them. Third, some aspects of life-span development are difficult if not impossible to examine in a laboratory. Certain types of stress are difficult (and unethical) to study in the laboratory, such as recreating the circumstances that stimulate marital conflict.

Although laboratory research is a valuable tool for developmentalists, naturalistic observation provides insight we sometimes cannot achieve in the laboratory. In **naturalistic observation,** *the scientist observes behavior in real-world settings and makes no effort to manipulate or control the situation.* Developmentalists conduct naturalistic observations at day-care centers, hospitals, schools, parks, homes, malls, dances, and so on. In contrast to Bandura's observations of aggression in a laboratory, developmentalists observe the aggression of children in nursery schools, of adolescents on street corners, and of marital partners at home (Bronfenbrenner, 1989; Patterson, Capaldi, & Bank, 1991).

Interviews and Questionnaires

Sometimes the best and quickest way to get information from people is to ask them for it. Psychologists use interviews and questionnaires to find out about an individual's experiences and attitudes. Most interviews occur face-to-face, although they can take place over the telephone.

Interviews range from being highly unstructured to being highly structured. Examples of unstructured interview questions are these: How aggressive do you see yourself as being? and How aggressive is your child? Examples of structured interview questions are these: In the last week, how often did you yell at your spouse? and How often in the last year was your child involved in fights at school? Structure is imposed by the questions themselves, or the interviewer can categorize answers by asking the respondent to choose from several options. For example, in the question about your level of aggressiveness, you might be asked to choose from "highly aggressive," "moderately aggressive," "moderately unaggressive," and "highly unaggressive." In the question about how often you yelled at your spouse in the last week, you might be asked to choose "0," "1–2," "3–5," "6–10," or "more than 10 times."

An experienced interviewer knows how to put respondents at ease and encourage them to open up. A competent interviewer is sensitive to the way the person responds to questions and often probes for more information. A person may respond with fuzzy statements to questions about the nature of marital conflict, for example, "Well, I don't know whether we have a lot of conflict or not." The skilled interviewer pushes for more specific, concrete answers, possibly asking, "If you had it to do over, would you get married?" or "Tell me the worst things you and your husband said to each other in the last week." Using these interviewing strategies forces researchers to be involved with, rather than detached from, their subjects, which yields a better understanding of development.

Psychologists also use questionnaires or surveys to gather information. A **questionnaire** *is similar to a highly structured interview except that respondents read the questions and mark their answers on paper rather than respond verbally to the interviewer.* One major advantage of surveys and questionnaires is that they can easily be given to a large number of people. Good surveys have concrete, specific, and unambiguous questions and allow assessment of the authenticity of the replies.

Case Studies

A **case study** *is an in-depth look at one individual; it is used mainly by clinical psychologists when the unique aspects of an individual's life cannot be duplicated, for either practical or ethical reasons.* A case study provides information about an individual's fears, hopes, fantasies, traumatic experiences, upbringing, family relationships, health, or anything that helps the psychologist understand the person's mind and behavior.

Traumatic experiences have produced some truly fascinating case studies in psychology. Consider the following. A 26-year-old male schoolteacher met a woman with whom he fell intensely in love. But several months after their love affair began, he became depressed, drank heavily, and talked about suicide. The suicidal ideas progressed to images of murder and suicide. His actions became bizarre. On one occasion he punctured the tires of her car. On another he stood on the roadside where she frequently passed in her car, extending his hand in his pocket so she would think he was holding a gun. His relationship with the woman vacillated between love and hate. Only 8 months after meeting her, the teacher shot her while he was a passenger in the car she was driving. Soon after the act, he ran to a telephone booth to call his priest. The girlfriend died (Revitch & Schlesinger, 1978).

This case reveals how depressive moods and bizarre thinking can precede violent acts, such as murder. Other vivid case studies appear throughout this text, among them a modern-day wild child named Genie, who lived in near isolation during her childhood.

Case histories provide dramatic, in-depth portrayals of people's lives, but we need to exercise caution when generalizing about this information. The subject of a case study is unique, with a genetic makeup and experiences no one else shares. In addition, case studies involve judgments of unknown reliability, in that no check is usually made to see if other psychologists agree with the observations.

Standardized Tests

Standardized tests *require people to answer a series of written or oral questions. They have two distinct features. First, psychologists usually total an individual's score to yield a single score, or a set of scores, that reflects something about the individual. Second, psychologists compare the individual's score to the scores of a large group of similar people to determine how the individual responded relative to others.* Scores are often described in percentiles. For example, if you scored in the 92nd percentile on the SAT, this measure tells you how much higher or lower you scored than the large group of individuals who previously took the test. Among the most widely used standardized tests in psychology are the Stanford-Binet intelligence test and the Minnesota Multiphasic Personality Inventory (MMPI).

To continue our look at how psychologists use different methods to evaluate aggression, consider the MMPI, which includes a scale to assess an individual's delinquency and antisocial tendencies. The items on this scale ask you to respond about whether you are rebellious, impulsive, and have trouble with authority figures. The 26-year-old teacher who murdered his girlfriend would have scored high on a number of the MMPI scales, including one designed to measure how strange and bizarre our thoughts and ideas are.

Cross-Cultural Research and Research With Ethnic Minority Groups

Researchers who are unfamiliar with the cultural and ethnic groups they are studying must take extra precautions to shed any biases they bring with them from their own culture. For example, they must make sure they construct measures that are meaningful for each of the cultural or ethnic minority groups being studied (Berry, 1980; Berry & others, in press).

In conducting research on cultural and ethnic minority issues, investigators distinguish between the emic approach and the etic approach. In the **emic approach**, *the goal is to describe behavior in one culture or ethnic group in terms that are meaningful and important to the people in that culture or ethnic group, without regard to other cultures or ethnic groups.* In the **etic approach**, *the goal is to describe behavior so that generalizations can be made across cultures.* That is, the emic approach is culture-specific; the etic approach is culture-universal. If researchers construct a questionnaire in an emic fashion, their concern is only that the questions are meaningful to the particular culture or ethnic group being studied. If, however, the researchers construct a questionnaire in an etic fashion, they want to include questions that reflect concepts familiar to all cultures involved (Atkinson, Morten, & Sue, 1993; Berry, 1969, 1990).

How might the emic and etic approaches be reflected in the study of family processes? In the emic approach, the researchers might choose to focus only on middle-class White families, without regard for whether the information obtained in the study can be generalized or is appropriate for ethnic minority groups. In a subsequent study, the researchers may decide to adopt an etic approach by studying not only middle-class White families, but also lower-income White families, Black American families, Hispanic American families, and Asian American families. In studying ethnic minority families, the researchers would likely discover that the extended family is more frequently a support system in ethnic minority families than in White American families. If so, the emic approach would reveal a different pattern of family interaction than would the etic approach, documenting that research with middle-class White families cannot always be generalized to all ethnic groups.

Let's go back to the study of aggression. Cross-cultural psychologists have found that aggression is universal, appearing in every culture. In this sense, it is an etic behavior; however, the expression of aggression may be culture-specific, so aggression is also an emic behavior. For example, the !Kung of southern Africa actively dissuade one another from behaving aggressively, whereas the Yanomamo Indians of South America promote aggression. Yanomamo youths are told that adult status cannot be achieved unless they are capable of killing, fighting, and pummeling others.

Cross-cultural psychologist Joseph Trimble (1989) is especially concerned about researchers' tendencies to use ethnic gloss when they select and describe ethnic groups. By **ethnic gloss,** Trimble means *using an ethnic label, such as Black, Hispanic, Asian, or Native American, in a superficial way that makes an ethnic group seem more homogeneous than it actually is.* For example, the following is an unsuitable description of a research sample, according to Trimble: "The subjects included 28 Blacks, 22 Hispanics, and 24 Whites." An acceptable description of each of the groups requires much more detail about the participants' country of origin, socioeconomic status, language, and ethnic self-identification, such as this: "The 22 subjects were Mexican Americans from low-income neighborhoods in the southwestern area of Los Angeles. Twelve spoke Spanish in the home, while 10 spoke English; 11 were born in the United States, 11 were born in Mexico; 16 described themselves as Mexican, 3 as Chicano, 2 as American, and 1 as Latino." Trimble believes that ethnic gloss can cause researchers to obtain samples of ethnic groups and cultures that are not representative of their ethnic and cultural diversity, leading to overgeneralizations and stereotypes.

In a recent symposium on racism in developmental research (Bloom, 1992; Lee, 1992; Padilla & Lindholm, 1992), the participants concluded that we need to include more ethnic minority individuals in our developmental research. Historically, ethnic minority individuals have essentially been discounted from research and viewed simply as variations from the norm or average. The development of nonmainstream individuals has been viewed as "confounds" or "noise" in data, and consequently researchers have deliberately excluded them from the samples they have selected. Because ethnic minority individuals have been excluded from research for so long, there likely is more variation in people's real lives than our research data have indicated in the past.

Physiological Research and Research With Animals

Two additional methods that psychologists use to gather data are physiological research and research with animals. Research on the biological basis of behavior and technological advances continue to produce remarkable insights about mind and behavior. For example, researchers have found that electrical stimulation of certain areas of the brain turns docile, mild-mannered people into hostile, vicious attackers, and higher concentrations of some hormones have been associated with anger in adolescents (Susman & Dorn, 1991).

Since much physiological research cannot be carried out with humans, psychologists sometimes use animals. Animal studies permit researchers to control their subjects' genetic background, diet, experiences during infancy, and many other factors. In studying humans, psychologists treat these factors as random variation, or "noise," that may interfere with accurate results. In addition, animal researchers can investigate the effects of treatments (brain implants, for example) that would be unethical with humans. Moreover, it is possible to track the entire life cycle of some animals over a relatively short period of time. Laboratory mice, for instance, have a life span of approximately 1 year.

Multimeasure, Multisource, Multicontext Approach

The various methods have their strengths and weaknesses. Direct observations are extremely valuable tools for obtaining information about development, but there are some things we cannot observe in people—their moral thoughts, their inner feelings, their arguments with parents, how they acquire information about sex, and so on. In such instances, other measures, such as interviews, questionnaires, and case studies, may be valuable. Because virtually every method has limitations, many investigators use multiple measures in assessing development. For example, a researcher might ask individuals about their aggressive behavior, check with their friends, observe them carefully at home and in their neighborhood, and in the case of children, interview their friends, observe the children at school during recess, and ask teachers to rate the children's aggression. Researchers hope that the convergence of multimeasure, multisource, and multicontext information provides a more comprehensive and valid assessment of development.

STRATEGIES FOR SETTING UP RESEARCH STUDIES

How can we determine if responding nurturantly to an infant's cries increases attachment to the caregiver? How can we determine if listening to rock music lowers an adolescent's grades? How can we determine if an active life-style in old age increases longevity? When designing research to answer such questions, a developmentalist must decide whether to use a correlational strategy or an experimental strategy.

Correlational Strategy

In the **correlational strategy,** *the goal is to describe the strength of the relation between two or more events or characteristics. This is a useful strategy because the more strongly events are correlated (related, or associated), the more effectively we can predict one from the other.* For example, consider one of our major national health problems, high blood pressure. If we find that high blood pressure is strongly associated with an inability to manage stress, then we can use the inability to manage stress to predict high blood pressure.

Often the next step is to conclude from such evidence that one event causes the other. Following this line of reasoning, we would erroneously conclude that the inability to manage stress causes high blood pressure. Why is this reasoning faulty? Why doesn't a strong correlation between two events mean that one event causes the other? A strong correlation could mean that the inability to manage stress causes high blood pressure; on the other hand, it could mean that high blood pressure causes an inability to manage stress. A third possibility also exists: Although strongly correlated, the inability to manage stress and high blood pressure might not

FIGURE 2.7

Possible explanations of correlational data. *An observed correlation between two events cannot be used to conclude that one event causes a second event. Other possibilities are that the second event causes the first event or that a third, unknown event causes the correlation between the first two events.*

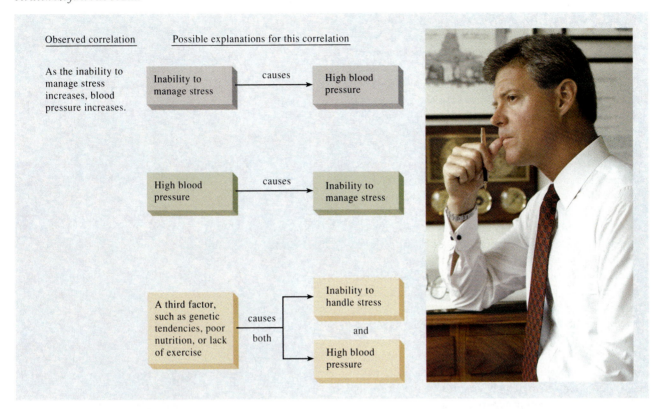

cause each other at all. It's possible that a third factor, such as a genetic tendency, poor nutrition, or a lack of exercise, underlies their association (see figure 2.7).

To ensure that your understanding of correlation is clear, let's look at another example. Suppose that people who make a lot of money have higher self-esteem than those who make less money. We could mistakenly interpret this to mean that making a lot of money causes us to have high self-esteem. What are the two other interpretations we need to consider? It could be that developing high self-esteem causes us to make a lot of money, or that a third factor, such as education, social upbringing, or genetic tendencies, causes the correlation between making a lot of money and high self-esteem. Throughout this text, you will read about numerous studies that were based on a correlational strategy. Keep in mind how easy it is to assume causality when two events or characteristics are merely correlated.

Experimental Strategy

While the correlational strategy only allows us to say that two events are related, the **experimental strategy** *allows us to precisely determine behavior's causes. The psychologist accomplishes this task by performing an experiment, a carefully regulated setting in which one or more of the factors believed to influence the behavior being studied is manipulated and all others are held constant.* If the

behavior under study changes when a factor is manipulated, we say that the manipulated factor causes the behavior to change. Experiments are used to establish cause and effect between events, something correlational studies cannot do. *Cause* is the event being manipulated, and *effect* is the behavior that changes because of the manipulation. Remember that in testing correlation, nothing is manipulated; in an experiment, the researcher actively changes an event to see the effect on behavior.

The following example illustrates the nature of an experiment. The problem to be studied is whether aerobic exercise during pregnancy affects the development of the infant. We need to have one group of pregnant women engage in aerobic exercise and the other not engage in aerobic exercise. We randomly assign our subjects to these two groups. **Random assignment** *occurs when researchers assign subjects by chance to experimental and control conditions, thus reducing the likelihood that the results of the experiment will be due to some preexisting differences in the two groups.* For example, random assignment greatly reduces the probability of the two groups differing on such factors as age, social class, prior aerobic exercise, intelligence, health problems, alertness, and so on.

The **independent variable** *is the manipulated, influential, experimental factor in the experiment. The label* independent *is used because this variable can be changed independently of other factors.*

In the aerobic exercise experiment, the amount of aerobic exercise was the independent variable. The experimenter manipulated the amount of the aerobic exercise by having the pregnant women engage in aerobic exercise four times a week under the direction of a trained instructor.

The **dependent variable** *is the factor that is measured in an experiment; it may change because of the manipulation of the independent variable. The label* dependent *is used because this variable depends on what happens to the subjects in the experiment.* In the aerobic exercise experiment, the dependent variable was represented by two measures—breathing and sleeping patterns of the infants. The subjects' responses on these measures depended on the influence of the independent variable (whether or not pregnant women engaged in aerobic exercise). An illustration of the nature of the experimental strategy, applied to the aerobic exercise study, is presented in figure 2.8. In our experiment, we tested the two sets of offspring during the first week of life. We found that the experimental group infants had more regular breathing and sleeping patterns than their control group counterparts. We conclude that aerobic exercise by pregnant women promotes more regular breathing and sleeping patterns in newborn infants.

Remember that the correlational study of the relation between stress and blood pressure gave us little indication of whether stress influences blood pressure, or vice versa. A third factor may have caused the correlation. A research study that determined if stress management reduces high blood pressure will help you to understand further the experimental strategy (Irvine & others, 1986). Thirty-two males and females with high blood pressure were randomly assigned to either a group who were trained in relaxation and stress management (experimental group) or a group who received no training (control group). The independent variable consisted of ten weekly 1-hour sessions that included educational information about the nature of stress and how to manage it, as well as extensive training in learning to relax and control stress in everyday life. The blood pressure of both groups was assessed before the training program and 3 months after it was completed. Nurses who were unaware of which group the subjects had been in measured blood pressure at the 3-month follow-up. The results indicated that the relaxation and stress management program (the independent variable) was effective in reducing high blood pressure.

It might seem as if we should always choose an experimental strategy over a correlational strategy, because the experimental strategy gives us a better sense of the influence of one variable on another. Are there instances when a correlational strategy might be preferred? Three such instances are (1) when the focus of the investigation is so new that we have little knowledge of which variables to manipulate (as when AIDS first appeared), (2) when it is physically impossible to manipulate the variables (such as factors involved in suicide), and (3) when it is unethical to manipulate the variables (for example, in determining the association between illness and exposure to dangerous chemicals).

FIGURE 2.8

Principles of experimental strategy: the effects of aerobic exercise by pregnant women on their newborns' breathing and sleeping patterns.

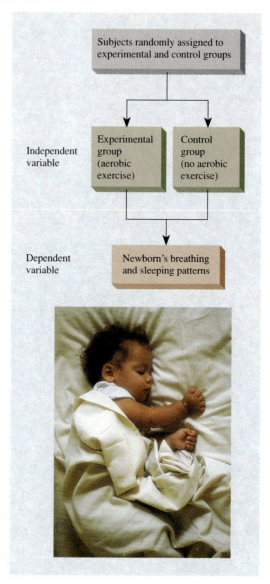

TIME SPAN OF INQUIRY

A special concern of developmentalists is the time span of a research investigation. Studies that focus on the relation of age to some other variable are common in life-span development. We have several options: We can study different individuals of different ages and compare them; we can study the same individuals as they age over time; or we can use some combination of these two approaches.

Cross-Sectional Approach

The **cross-sectional approach** *is a research strategy in which individuals of different ages are compared at one time.* A typical

FIGURE 2.9

A comparison of cross-sectional and longitudinal approaches.

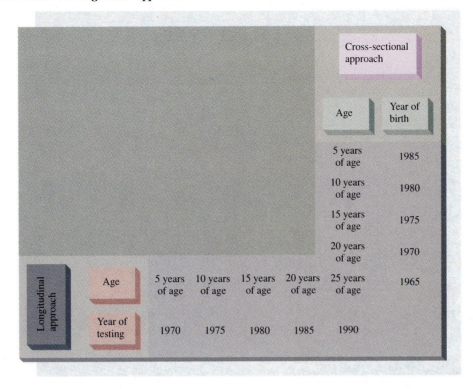

cross-sectional study might include a group of 5-year-olds, 8-year-olds, and 11-year-olds; another might include a group of 15-year-olds, 25-year-olds, and 45-year-olds. The different groups can be compared with respect to a variety of dependent variables: IQ, memory, peer relations, attachment to parents, hormonal changes, and so on. All of this can be accomplished in a short time. In some studies data are collected in a single day. Even in large-scale cross-sectional studies with hundreds of subjects, data collection does not usually take longer than several months to complete.

The main advantage of the cross-sectional study is that the researcher does not have to wait for the individuals to grow up or become older. Despite its time efficiency, the cross-sectional approach has its drawbacks. It gives no information about how individuals change or about the stability of their characteristics. The increases and decreases of development—the hills and valleys of growth and development—can become obscured in the cross-sectional approach. For example, in a cross-sectional approach to perceptions of life satisfaction, average increases and decreases might be revealed. But the study would not show how the life satisfaction of individual adults waxed and waned over the years. It also would not tell us whether adults who had positive or negative perceptions of life satisfaction as young adults maintained their relative degree of life satisfaction as middle-aged or older adults. Although cross-sectional studies cannot answer such questions, longitudinal studies can.

Longitudinal Approach

The **longitudinal approach** *is a research strategy in which the same individuals are studied over a period of time, usually several years or more.* For example, if a study of life satisfaction were conducted longitudinally, the same adults might be assessed periodically over a 70-year time span—at the ages of 20, 35, 45, 65, and 90, for example. The cross-sectional and longitudinal research designs are compared in figure 2.9.

Although longitudinal studies provide a wealth of information about such important issues as stability and change in development and the importance of early experience for later development, they are not without their problems. They are expensive and time-consuming. The longer the study lasts, the more subjects drop out—they move, get sick, lose interest, and so forth. Subjects can bias the outcome of a study, because those who remain may be dissimilar to those who drop out. Those individuals who remain in a longitudinal study over a number of years may be more compulsive and conformity-oriented, for example, Or they might have more stable lives.

Sequential Approach

Sometimes developmentalists also combine the cross-sectional and longitudinal approaches to learn about life-span development (Schaie, 1973, 1989, 1991, 1994). The **sequential approach** *is the combined cross-sectional, longitudinal design. In most instances, this approach starts with a cross-sectional study* *that includes individuals of different ages. A number of months or years after the initial assessment, the same individuals are tested again—this is the longitudinal aspect of the design. At this later time, a new group of subjects is assessed at each age level.* The new groups at each level are added at the later time to control for changes that might have taken place in the original group of subjects—some may have dropped out of the study, or retesting might have improved their performance, for example. The sequential approach is complex, expensive, and time-consuming, but it does provide information that is impossible to obtain from cross-sectional or longitudinal approaches alone. The sequential approach has been especially helpful in examining cohort effects in life-span development, which we discuss next.

Critical Thinking

You are faced with the task of designing an investigation of intergenerational relations. What problem do you want to study? What measure(s) would you use? What strategy would you follow— experimental or correlational? What would be the time span of your inquiry?

Cohort Effects

Cohort effects *are due to a subject's time of birth or generation but not to actual age.* For example, cohorts can differ in years of education, child-rearing practices, health, attitudes toward sex, religious values, and economic status (see figure 2.10). Cohort effects are important because they can powerfully affect the dependent measures in a study ostensibly concerned with age. Researchers have shown that cohort effects are especially important to investigate in the assessment of adult intelligence (Schaie, 1993; Schaie, Willis, & O'Hanlon, in press; Willis, 1990; Willis & Schaie, 1986). Individuals born at different points in time—such as 1920, 1940, and 1960—have had varying opportunities for education, while individuals born in earlier years have had less access.

The mark of the historic is the nonchalance with which it picks up an individual and deposits him in a trend, like a house playfully moved in a tornado.

—Mary McCarthy,
On the Contrary, 1961

Now that we have considered the main ways that developmentalists conduct research, it is also important to consider whether research on life-span development is value free, how life-span development research can become less sexist, and what ethical issues must be considered in developmental research.

REDUCING SEXIST RESEARCH

Traditional science is presented as being value free and thus a more valid way of studying mental processes and behavior. However, there is a growing consensus that the sciences in general, and psychology in particular, are not value free (Matlin,

1993; Paludi, 1992). A special concern is that the vast majority of psychological research has been male oriented and male dominated. Some researchers believe male-dominated sciences such as psychology need to be challenged to examine the world in a new way, one that incorporates girls' and women's perspectives and respects their ethnicity, sexual orientation, age, and socioeconomic status (Denmark & others, 1988; McHugh, Koeske, & Frieze, 1986; Quina, 1986). For example, Florence Denmark and her colleagues (1988) provided the following three recommendations as guidelines for nonsexist research:

1. Research methods:
   - Problem: The selection of research participants is based on stereotypic assumptions and does not allow for generalizations to other groups.
   - Example: On the basis of stereotypes about who should be responsible for contraception, only females are studied.
   - Correction: Both sexes should be studied before conclusions are drawn about the factors that determine contraceptive use.
2. Data analysis:
   - Problem: Gender differences are inaccurately magnified.
   - Example: While only 24 percent of the females were found to . . . fully 28 percent of the males were. . . .
   - Correction: The results should include extensive descriptions of the data so that inappropriate presentation of differences are not exaggerated.
3. Conclusions:
   - Problem: The title or abstract (a summary) of an article makes no reference to the limitations of the study participants and implies a broader scope of the study than is warranted.
   - Example: A study purporting to be about "perceptions of the disabled" uses only blind, White subjects. . . .
   - Correction: Use more precise titles and clearly describe the sample and its selection criteria in the abstract or summary.

Florence Denmark (shown here talking with a group of students) has developed a number of guidelines for nonsexist research. Denmark and others believe that psychology needs to be challenged to examine the world in a new way, one that incorporates girls' and women's perspectives.

FIGURE 2.10

Cohort effects. *Cohort effects are due to a person's time of birth or generation but not actually to age. Think for a moment about growing up in* (a) *the Roaring Twenties,* (b) *the Great Depression,* (c) *the 1940s and World War II,* (d) *the 1950s,* (e) *the late 1960s, and* (f) *the 1990s. How might an individual's development be different depending on which of these time frames dominated that person's life?*

ETHICS IN RESEARCH ON LIFE-SPAN DEVELOPMENT

When Anne and Pete, two 19-year-old college students, agreed to participate in an investigation of dating couples, they did not consider that the questionnaire they filled out would get them to think about issues that might lead to conflict in their relationship and possibly end it. One year after this investigation, nine of ten participants said that they had discussed their answers with their dating partner (Rubin & Mitchell, 1976). In most instances, the discussions helped to strengthen the relationships, but in some instances the participants used the questionnaire as a springboard to discuss problems or concerns previously hidden. One participant said, "The study definitely played a role in ending my relationship with Larry." In this circumstance, the couple had different views about how long they expected to be together. She anticipated that the relationship would end much sooner than Larry thought. Discussion of their answers to the questions brought the long-term prospects of the relationship out in the open, and eventually Larry found someone who was more interested in marrying him.

At first glance, you would not think that a questionnaire on dating relationships would have any substantial impact on the participants' behavior. But psychologists increasingly recognize that considerable caution must be taken to ensure the well-being of subjects in a study of life-span development. Today colleges and universities have review boards that evaluate the ethical nature of research conducted at their institutions. Proposed research plans must pass the scrutiny of an ethics research committee before the research can be initiated. In addition, the American Psychological Association (APA) has developed guidelines for its members' ethics.

The code of ethics adopted by APA instructs researchers to protect their subjects from mental and physical harm. The best interests of the subjects need to be kept foremost in the researcher's mind. All subjects must give their informed consent to participate in the research study, which requires that subjects know what their participation will involve and any risks that might develop. For example, research subjects who date one another should be told beforehand that a questionnaire might stimulate thought about issues they might not anticipate. The subjects should also be informed that in some instances a discussion of the issues raised can improve their dating relationships, while in other cases, it can worsen the relationship and even terminate it. After informed consent is given, the subject reserves the right to withdraw from the study at any time while it is being conducted.

Special ethical concerns govern the conduct of research with children. First, if children are to be studied, informed consent from parents or legal guardians must be obtained. Parents have the right to a complete and accurate description of what will be done with their children and may refuse to let them participate. Second, children have rights, too. The psychologist is obliged to explain precisely what the child will experience. The child may refuse to participate, even after parental permission has been given. If so, the researcher must not test the child. Also, if a child becomes upset during the research study, it is the

psychologist's obligation to calm the child. If the psychologist fails to do so, the activity must be discontinued. Third, the psychologist must always weigh the potential for harming children against the prospects of contributing some clear benefits to them. If there is the chance of harm—as when drugs are used, social deception takes place, or the child is treated aversively (that is, punished or reprimanded)—the psychologist must convince a group of peers that the benefits of the experience clearly outweigh any chance of harm. Fourth, since children are in a vulnerable position and lack power and control when facing an adult, the psychologist should always strive to make the professional encounter a positive and supportive experience.

BEING A WISE CONSUMER OF INFORMATION ABOUT LIFE-SPAN DEVELOPMENT

We live in an information society in which there is a vast amount of information about life-span development available for public consumption. The information varies greatly in quality. How can you become a wise consumer of information about life-span development?

Be Cautious About What Is Reported in the Media

Research and clinical findings about life-span development are increasingly talked about in the media. Television, radio, newspapers, and magazines frequently report on research and clinical findings about life-span development that are likely to interest the general public. Many professional, mental health, and psychological organizations regularly supply the media with information about life-span development. In many cases, this information has been published in professional journals or has been presented at national meetings. And most major colleges and universities have a media relations department that contacts the press about current research by their faculty.

Not all information about life-span development that is presented for public consumption comes from professionals with excellent credentials and reputations at colleges, universities, and applied settings. Journalists, television reporters, and other media personnel are not scientifically and clinically trained. It is not an easy task for them to sort through the widely varying material they come across and make sound decisions about which information about life-span development should be presented to the public.

Unfortunately, the media often focus on sensational and dramatic findings about life-span development. They want you to read what they have written or stay tuned and not flip to another channel. They can capture your attention and keep it by presenting dramatic, sensational, and surprising information. As a consequence, media presentations of information about life-span development tend to go beyond what actual research articles and clinical findings actually say. Consider such magazine article titles as "How To Turn Your 2-Year-Old Into a Genius," "Ten Steps To Help You Stop Aging," or "How You

Can Live To Be 130." We have no evidence to support such claims, but their sensational nature attracts our attention.

Even when excellent research and clinical findings are presented to the public, it is difficult for media personnel to adequately inform people about what has been found and the implications for their lives. For example, throughout this text you will be introduced to an entirely new vocabulary. Each time we present a new concept, we precisely define it and also give examples of it. We have an entire book to carry out our task of carefully introducing, defining, and elaborating on key concepts and issues, research, and clinical findings about life-span development. However, the media do not have the luxury of time and space to go into considerable detail and specify the limitations and qualifications of research and clinical findings. They often have only a few minutes or a few lines to summarize as best they can the complex findings of a study about life-span development.

These are some of the ways you can think critically about the psychological information you see, hear, or read: Understand the distinction between nomothetic research and idiographic needs. Be aware of the tendency to overgeneralize from a small sample or a unique clinical sample. Know that a single study is often not the final and definitive word about an issue or topic. Be sure you understand why causal conclusions cannot be drawn from a correlational study. And always consider the source of the information about life-span development and evaluate its credibility.

Know How To Distinguish Between Nomothetic Research and Idiographic Needs

Nomothetic research *is conducted at the level of the group.* Most research on life-span development is nomothetic research. Individual variations in how infants, children, and adults respond are often not a main focus of the research. For example, a study of 50 divorced women and 50 married women might find that divorced women, as a group, cope less well with stress than married women. That is a nomothetic finding that applies to divorced women as a group. In this particular study, it is likely that some of the divorced women were coping better with stress than some of the married women—not as many, but some. Indeed, it is entirely possible that the two or three women who were coping the very best with stress were divorced women; and yet the findings will still be reported as showing that divorced women (as a group) cope less well with stress than married women (as a group).

As a consumer of information about life-span development, you want to know what the information means for you *individually,* not necessarily for a group of people. **Idiographic needs** *refer to what is important for the individual, not the group.* The failure of the media to adequately distinguish between nomothetic research and idiographic needs is not entirely their fault. Researchers have not adequately done this either. The research they conduct too often fails to examine the overlap between groups and tends to present only the differences that are found. And when those differences are reported, frequently they are reported as if there is no overlap between the groups being compared (in our example, divorced women and married women), when in reality there is substantial overlap. If you read a study in a research journal or a media report of a study that states that divorced women cope less well with stress than married women, remember that it does not mean that all divorced women cope less well than all married women. It simply means that as a group married women cope better.

Recognize How Easy It Is to Overgeneralize From a Small or Clinical Sample

There often isn't space or time in media presentations of information about life-span development to go into details about the nature of the sample. Sometimes you will get basic information about the sample's size—whether it is based on 10 subjects, 50 subjects, or 200 subjects, for example. In many cases, small or very small samples require that care be exercised in generalizing to a larger population of individuals. For instance, if a study of divorced children is based on only 10 or 20 children, what is found in the study may not generalize to all divorced children, because the sample investigated may have some unique characteristics. The sample might come from families who have substantial economic resources, are White American, live in a suburb of a small southern town, and are all undergoing psychotherapy. In this study, then, we clearly would be making unwarranted generalizations if we thought the findings also characterize divorced children from families who have moderate to low incomes, are from other ethnic backgrounds, live in different locations, and are not undergoing psychotherapy.

Be Aware That a Single Study Is Usually Not the Defining Word About Any Aspect of Life-Span Development

The media may identify an interesting piece of research about life-span development and claim that it is something phenomenal with far-reaching implications. Such studies and findings do occur, but it is rare for a single study to provide earth-shattering and conclusive answers, especially answers that apply to all people. In fact, in most domains of life-span development where there have been a large number of investigations, it is not unusual to find conflicting results about a particular topic or issue. Answers to these questions usually emerge after many scientists have conducted similar investigations that produce a consensus of results. Thus, a report of one study should not be taken as the absolute, final truth about some aspect of life-span development.

Remember That Causal Conclusions Cannot Be Made From Correlational Studies

Drawing causal conclusions from correlational studies is one of the most common mistakes made by the media. In studies in which an experiment has not been conducted (remember that

CONCEPT TABLE 2.2

Methods and How To Be a Wise Consumer of Information About Life-Span Development

Concept	Processes/Related Ideas	Characteristics/Description
Measures	Observation	Observation is a key ingredient in research that includes laboratory and naturalistic observation.
	Interviews and questionnaires	These are used to assess perceptions and attitudes.
	Case studies	Case studies provide an in-depth look at an individual. Caution in generalizing is warranted.
	Standardized tests	Standardized tests are designed to assess an individual's characteristics relative to those of a large group of similar individuals.
	Cross-cultural research and research with ethnic minority groups	This research focuses on the culture-universal (etic approach) and culture-specific (emic approach) nature of mind and behavior. A special concern in research with ethnic minority groups is ethnic gloss. In the past, ethnic minority individuals have often been excluded from research because researchers wanted to reduce variation in their data. We need to include more ethnic minority individuals in research.
	Physiological research and research with animals	Physiological research provides information about the biological basis of behavior. Since much physiological research cannot be carried out with humans, psychologists sometimes use animals. Animal studies permit researchers to control genetic background, diet, experiences in infancy, and countless other factors. One issue is the extent to which research with animals can be generalized to humans.
	Multiple measures, sources, and contexts	Researchers are increasingly adopting a multimeasure, multisource, multicontext approach.
Strategies for setting up research studies	Correlational strategy	This strategy describes how strongly two or more events or characteristics are related. It does not allow causal statements.
	Experimental strategy	This strategy involves manipulation of influential factors—independent variables—and measurement of their effect on the dependent variables. Subjects are randomly assigned to experimental and control groups in many studies. The experimental strategy can reveal the causes of behavior and tell us how one event influenced another.

in an experiment, subjects are randomly assigned to treatments or experiences), two variables or factors may be related to each other. However, causal interpretations cannot be made when two or more factors are simply correlated or related to each other. In the case of divorce, a headline might read, "Divorce Causes Children To Have Problems in School." We read the article and find out the headline was derived from the results of a research study. Because obviously, for ethical or practical purposes, we do not randomly assign children to families that will become divorced or stay intact, this headline is based on

a correlational study, and the causal statement is inaccurate. At least some of the children's problems in school probably occurred prior to the divorce of their parents. Other factors, such as poor parenting practices, low socioeconomic status, a difficult temperament, and low intelligence, may also contribute to children's problems in school and not be a direct consequence of divorce itself. What we can say, based on such studies, if the data warrant it, is that divorce is related to or associated with problems in school. What we cannot legitimately say, based on such studies, is that divorce causes problems in school.

Concept	Processes/Related Ideas	Characteristics/Description
Time span of inquiry	Cross-sectional approach	Individuals of different ages are compared all at one time.
	Longitudinal approach	The same individuals are studied over a period of time, usually several years or more.
	Sequential approach	A combined cross-sectional, longitudinal approach that highlights the importance of cohort effects in life-span development.
	Cohort effects	Cohort effects are due to a subject's time of birth or generation, but not to actual age. The study of cohort effects emphasizes the importance of considering the historical dimensions of development.
Reducing sexist research	Its nature	A special concern is that the vast majority of research in psychology has been male oriented and male dominated. Some researchers believe that developmentalists need to be challenged to examine development in a new way, one that incorporates girls' and women's perspectives. Recommendations have been made for conducting nonsexist research.
Ethics in research on life-span development	Their nature	Researchers must ensure the well-being of subjects in life-span development research. The risk of mental and physical harm must be reduced, and informed consent should be obtained. Special ethical considerations are involved when children are research subjects.
Being a wise consumer of information about life-span development	Its nature	In many instances the quality of information you read about life-span development, especially in the media, varies greatly. Being a wise consumer involves understanding the distinction between nomothetic research and idiographic needs, being aware of the tendency to overgeneralize from a small sample or a unique sample, knowing that a single study is often not the defining word about an issue or problem, understanding why causal conclusions cannot be drawn from a correlational study, and always considering the source of the information and evaluating its credibility.

Always Consider the Source of the Information and Evaluate Its Credibility

Studies are not automatically accepted by the research community. Researchers usually have to submit their findings to a research journal where it is reviewed by their colleagues, who make a decision about whether to publish the paper or not. Although the quality of research in journals is not uniform, in most cases the research has undergone far greater scrutiny and more careful consideration of the quality of the work than is the case for research or any other information that has not gone through the journal process. And within the media, we can distinguish between what is presented in respected newspapers, such as the *New York Times* and the *Washington Post,* as well as credible magazines, such as *Time* and *Newsweek,* and much less respected and less credible tabloids, such as the *National Inquirer* and the *Star.*

At this point, we have studied a number of ideas about measures, strategies for setting up research studies, time span of inquiry, reducing sexist research, ethics in research, and being a wise consumer of information about life-span development. A summary of these ideas is presented in concept table 2.2.

LIFE-SPAN HEALTH AND WELL-BEING

Cultural Expectations and Support for Health and Well-Being

In chapters 1 and 2, we have emphasized the importance of sociocultural factors in life-span development. Some cultures place a high premium on the health and well-being of their members, while others pay less attention to health and well-being. And within our culture, our circle of friends and family, and the community in which we live, either reinforce a healthy lifestyle or present us with barriers to optimal well-being.

In the contexts in which you live, does the atmosphere promote health and well-being or present barriers to them?

To determine the cultural contexts of your health and well-being, for each of the following statements place a check in each box for which the statement is true. After these lists of statements you will find an explanation of how to interpret your responses (Allen & Allen, 1986).

Cultural Contexts That Enhance Health and Well-Being

		Household, Close Friends, Family	Community
1.	The people around me exercise regularly and at a level that is healthy for them	☐	☐
2.	People look at exercise as a source of pleasure instead of a grind	☐	☐
3.	People balance their food intake with their physical exercise as they grow older	☐	☐
4.	People pay a good deal of attention to the nutritional value of the foods they eat	☐	☐
5.	People rarely have coffee and a roll instead of a nutritional breakfast in the morning	☐	☐
6.	The people around me rarely have a drink when they really don't want one; they rarely drink just because others do	☐	☐
7.	People rarely drive when they are drowsy or under the influence of alcohol or medication	☐	☐
8.	People wear seat belts even when they feel it is inconvenient to do so	☐	☐
9.	People perceive stress to be something they can do something about	☐	☐
10.	People ask for help if their work begins to overload them	☐	☐
11.	People understand the harmful effects that continued stress can have on their lives	☐	☐
12.	People handle conflicts with others in constructive ways	☐	☐

	Household, Close Friends, Family	Community
13. People achieve an adequate balance between rest and play in their lives	☐	☐
14. People enjoy their lives as much as they are capable of doing	☐	☐
15. People rarely have coffee, cola drinks, and other caffeine-based beverages	☐	☐
16. People rarely keep their feelings bottled up inside; they feel comfortable in openly expressing them	☐	☐

Cultural Contexts That Are Barriers to Health and Well-Being

	Household, Close Friends, Family	Community
1. People use their cars and public transportation to go short distances	☐	☐
2. People look at being just a little overweight as being natural, especially for older people	☐	☐
3. People see desserts—such as cake, pie, pudding, and ice cream—as an expected part of lunch or dinner	☐	☐
4. People associate overindulging in food with relaxation, pleasure, and social relationships	☐	☐
5. People smoke cigarettes, pipes, or cigars	☐	☐
6. People feel that somehow the illness and death statistics about smoking do not apply to them	☐	☐
7. The host or hostess of a party repeatedly checks to make sure that everyone's glass is full and drinks are continually being replenished	☐	☐
8. People mention with pride their own ability, or a friend's ability, to consume large amounts of alcohol	☐	☐
9. Waiters and waitresses and others in restaurants expect that people will be having a drink before dinner	☐	☐
10. People ignore safety hazards or violations instead of correcting them	☐	☐
11. People perceive that safety rules and regulations are something that others should follow but they don't	☐	☐
12. People overextend themselves physically in ways that endanger and harm their bodies	☐	☐
13. People disregard physicians' advice and endanger their health	☐	☐
14. People continue to drive when physical disability hinders their ability to drive safely	☐	☐

	Household, Close Friends, Family	Community
15. People think it is OK to drive over the posted speed limit as long as they don't get caught	☐	☐
16. People take on more responsibility than they can handle	☐	☐
17. People bury their creative urges and talents	☐	☐
18. People work so hard that they tend to lose contact with other important dimensions of their lives, such as their spouse, children, friends, hobbies, and other interests	☐	☐
19. People don't seek help with emotional problems until they become very severe	☐	☐

To determine whether the cultural contexts in which you live support or are barriers to your health and well-being, simply total the number of checks you made in the boxes under enhancing health and well-being and the number of checks under barriers. If you made more checks under enhancement, then you live in cultural contexts that support your health and well-being; but if you made more checks under barriers, you live in an environment that is impeding your ability to attain health and well-being. ■

CONCLUSIONS

A discipline that studies how babies develop, parents nurture children, adults form intimate relationships, and aging adults engage in self-control can be a science just as much as disciplines that investigate how gravity works or what the molecular structure of a compound is. Science is determined not by what it investigates but rather by how it investigates.

We began the study of life-span development as a science by examining the nature of theory and the scientific method. Then we evaluated five main theories of development—psychoanalytic (Freud and Erikson), cognitive (Piaget and the information-processing approach), behavioral/social learning (Skinner and Bandura), ethological (Lorenz), and ecological (Bronfenbrenner)—as well as an eclectic theoretical orientation. We studied a variety of measures that can be used to collect information about life-span development, such as observation, interviews and questionnaires, case studies, standardized tests, cross-cultural research and research with ethnic minority individuals, physiological research and research with animals, and a multimeasure, multisource, multicontext approach. We also examined strategies for setting up research studies, time spans of inquiry, reducing sexist research, ethics in research, and how to be a wise consumer of information about life-span development. At different points in the chapter we also read about Erikson and Piaget as children, culture- and gender-based criticisms of Freud's theory, observing and imitating parents, and cultural expectations and support for health and well-being.

Don't forget that you can obtain an overall summary of the chapter by again reading the two concept tables on pages 51 and 62. This concludes Section One of the book. In Section Two, we will explore the beginning of life-span development, starting with chapter 3, "Biological Beginnings."

KEY TERMS

theory A coherent set of ideas that helps to explain data and to make prediction. (33)

hypotheses Assumptions that can be tested to determine their accuracy. (33)

scientific method An approach, that can be used to discover accurate information about behavior and development, it includes the following steps: identify and analyze the problem, collect data, draw conclusions, and revise theories. (33)

id The Freudian structure of personality that consists of instincts, which are an individual's reservoir of psychic energy. (34)

ego The Freudian structure of personality that deals with the demands of reality. (34)

superego The Freudian structure of personality that is the moral branch of personality. (34)

defense mechanisms The psychoanalytic term for unconscious methods, the ego uses to distort reality, thereby protecting it from anxiety. (35)

repression The most powerful and pervasive defense mechanism, (according to Freud) it works to push unacceptable id impulses out of awareness and back into the unconscious mind. (35)

erogenous zones The parts of the body that have especially strong pleasure-giving qualities at each stage of development. (35)

oral stage The first Freudian stage of development, occurring during the first 18 months of life, in which the infant's pleasure centers around the mouth. (35)

anal stage The second Freudian stage of development, occurring between 1½ and 3 years of age, in which the child's greatest pleasure involves the anus or the eliminative functions associated with it. (35)

phallic stage The third Freudian stage of development, which occurs between the ages of 3 and 6; its name comes from the Latin word phallus, which means "penis." (35)

Oedipus complex The Freudian concept in which the young child develops an intense desire to replace the parent of the same sex and enjoy the affections of the opposite-sexed parent. (36)

latency stage The fourth Freudian stage of development, which occurs between approximately 6 years of age and puberty; the child represses all interest in sexuality and develops social and intellectual skills. (36)

genital stage The fifth and final Freudian stage of development, occurring from puberty on. The genital stage is a time of sexual reawakening; the source of sexual pleasure now becomes someone outside of the family. (36)

trust versus mistrust Erikson's first psychosocial stage, which is experienced in the first year of life. A sense of trust requires a feeling of physical comfort and a minimal amount of fear and apprehension about the future. (37)

autonomy versus shame and doubt Erikson's second stage of development, occurring in late infancy and toddlerhood (1–3 years). (37)

initiative versus guilt Erikson's third stage of development, occurring during the preschool years. (37)

industry versus inferiority Erikson's fourth developmental stage, occurring approximately in the elementary school years. (38)

identity versus identity confusion Erikson's fifth developmental stage, which individuals experience during the adolescent years. At this time individuals are faced with finding out who they are, what they are all about, and where they are going in life. (38)

intimacy versus isolation Erikson's sixth developmental stage, which individuals experience during the early adulthood years. At this time, individuals face the developmental task of forming intimate relationships with others. (39)

generativity versus stagnation Erikson's seventh developmental stage, which individuals experience during middle adulthood. (39)

integrity versus despair Erikson's eighth and final developmental stage, which individuals experience during late adulthood. (39)

assimilation Occurs when individuals incorporate new information into their existing knowledge. (39)

accommodation Occurs when individuals adjust to new information. (39)

sensorimotor stage (Lasts from birth to about 2 years of age) the first Piagetian stage; infants construct an understanding of the world by coordinating sensory experiences (such as seeing and hearing) with physical, motoric actions—hence the term sensorimotor. (39)

preoperational stage (Lasts from approximately 2 to 7 years of age) the second Piagetian stage; children begin to represent the world with words, images, and drawings. (42)

concrete operational stage (Lasts from approximately 7 to 11 years of age) the third Piagetian stage; children can perform operations, and logical reasoning replaces intuitive thought as long as reasoning can be applied to specific or concrete examples. (42)

formal operational stage (Appears between the ages of 11 and 15) the fourth and final Piagetian stage; individuals move beyond the world of actual, concrete experiences and think in abstract and more logical terms. (42)

information-processing approach Concerned with how individuals process information about their world—how information enters our minds, how it is stored and transformed, and how it is retrieved to perform such complex activities as problem solving and reasoning. (42)

behaviorism Emphasizes the scientific study of observable behavioral responses and their environmental determinants. (44)

social learning theory The view of psychologists who emphasize behavior, environment, and cognition as the key factors in development. (44)

ethology Stresses that behavior is strongly influenced by biology, is tied to evolution, and is characterized by critical or sensitive periods. (46)

imprinting The ethological concept of rapid, innate learning within a limited critical period of time that involves attachment to the first moving object seen. (46)

critical period A fixed time period very early in development during which certain behaviors optimally emerge. (47)

ecological theory Bronfenbrenner's sociocultural view of development consists of five environmental systems ranging from the fine-grained inputs of direct interactions with social agents to the broad-based inputs of culture. (47)

microsystem The setting in which the individual lives; includes the person's family, peers, school, and neighborhood. It is in the microsystem that the most direct interactions with social agents take place—with parents, peers, and teachers, for example. (47)

mesosystem Relations between microsystems or connections between contexts, such as the relation of family experiences to school experiences, school experiences to church experiences, or family experiences to peer experiences. (49)

exosystem When experiences in another social setting—in which the individual does not have an active role—influence what the individual experiences in an immediate context. (49)

macrosystem The culture in which individuals live. (49)

chronosystem The patterning of environmental events and transitions over the life course and sociohistorical circumstances. (49)

eclectic theoretical orientation Does not follow any one theoretical approach, but rather selects and uses whatever is considered the best in all theories. (49)

laboratory A controlled setting from which many of the complex factors of the "real world" are removed. (52)

naturalistic observation A method in which the scientist observes behavior in real world settings and makes no effort to manipulate or control the situation. (52)

questionnaire Similar to a highly structured interview except that respondents read the questions and mark their answers on paper rather than respond verbally to the interviewer. (52)

case study An in-depth look at one individual; it is used mainly by clinical psychologists when the unique aspects of an individual's life cannot be duplicated, for either practical or ethical reasons. (52)

standardized tests   Require people to answer a series of written or oral questions. They have two distinct features: first, psychologists usually total an individual's score to yield a single score, or a set of scores, that reflects something about the individual; second, psychologists compare the individual's score to the scores of a large group of similar people to determine how the individual responded relative to others. (53)

emic approach   The goal is to describe behavior in one culture or ethnic group in terms that are meaningful and important to the people in that culture or ethnic group, without regard to other cultures or ethnic groups. (53)

etic approach   The goal is to describe behavior so that generalizations can be made across cultures. (53)

ethnic gloss   Using an ethnic label, such as Black, Hispanic, Asian, or Native American, in a superficial way that makes an ethnic group seem more homogeneous than it actually is. (54)

correlational strategy   The goal is to describe the strength of the relation between two or more events or characteristics. This is a useful strategy because the more strongly events are correlated (related, or associated), the more effectively we can predict one from the other. (54)

experimental strategy   Allows investigators to precisely determine behavior's causes. The psychologist accomplishes this task by performing an experiment, a carefully regulated setting in which one or more of the factors believed to influence the behavior being studied is manipulated and all others are held constant. (55)

random assignment   When researchers assign subjects by chance to experimental and control conditions, thus reducing the likelihood that the results of the experiment will be due to some preexisting differences in the two groups. (55)

independent variable   The manipulated, influential, experimental factor in the experiment. (55)

dependent variable   The factor that is measured in an experiment; it may change because of the manipulation of the independent variable. (56)

cross-sectional approach   A research strategy in which individuals of different ages are compared at one time. (56)

longitudinal approach   A research strategy in which the same individuals are studied over a period of time, usually several years or more. (57)

sequential approach   Combined cross-sectional, longitudinal design. (57)

cohort effects   Effects that are due to a subject's time of birth or generation but not to actual age. (58)

nomothetic research   Research conducted at the level of the group. (61)

idiographic needs   Needs that refer to what is important for the individual, not the group. (61)

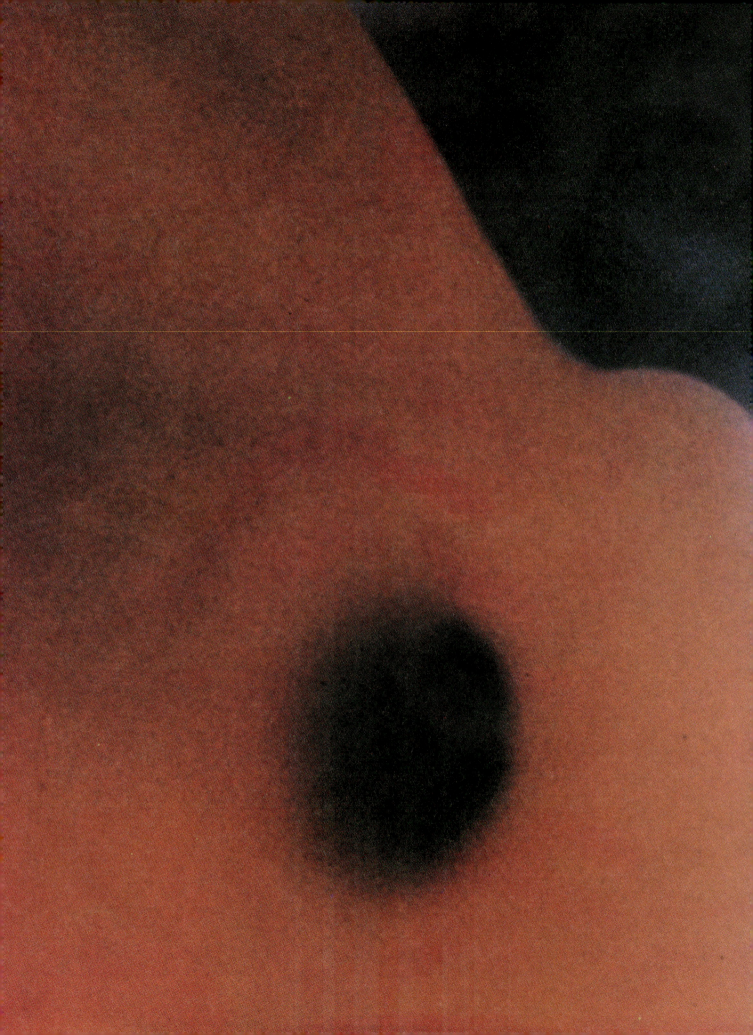

Beginnings

What endless questions vex the thought, of whence and whither, when and how.

—Sir Richard Burton,
Kasidah

The rhythm and meaning of life involve beginnings. Questions are raised about how, from so simple a beginning, endless forms develop and grow and mature. What was this organism, what will this organism be? Section Two contains two chapters: "Biological Beginnings" (chapter 3) and "Prenatal Development and Birth" (chapter 4).

Picasso, Child with Dove,
detail.

Biological Beginnings

*There are one hundred and ninety-three
species of monkeys and apes. One-
hundred and ninety-two of them are
covered with hair. The exception is the
naked ape self-named, homo-sapiens.*

—Desmond Morris,
The Naked Ape, 1967

> *The frightening part about heredity and environment is that we parents provide both.*
>
> —Notebook of a Printer

IMAGES OF LIFE-SPAN DEVELOPMENT

The Jim and Jim Twins

Jim Springer and Jim Lewis are identical twins. They were separated at 4 weeks of age and did not see each other again until they were 39 years old. Both worked as part-time deputy sheriffs, vacationed in Florida, drove Chevrolets, had dogs named Toy, and married and divorced women named Betty. One twin named his son James Allan, and the other named his son James Alan. Both liked math but not spelling, enjoyed carpentry and mechanical drawing, chewed their fingernails down to the nubs, had almost identical drinking and smoking habits, had hemorrhoids, put on 10 pounds at about the same point in development, first suffered headaches at the age of 18, and had similar sleep patterns.

Jim and Jim had some differences. One wore his hair over his forehead, the other slicked it back and had sideburns. One expressed himself best orally, the other was more proficient in writing. But for the most part, their profiles were remarkably similar.

Another pair of identical twins who were separated as infants, Daphne and Barbara, were called the "giggle sisters" because they were always making each other laugh. A thorough search of their adoptive families' histories revealed no gigglers. Both sisters handled stress by ignoring it, avoided conflict and controversy whenever possible, and showed no interest in politics.

Two other female identical twin sisters were separated at 6 weeks and reunited in their fifties. Both had nightmares, which they described in hauntingly similar ways: Both dreamed of doorknobs and fishhooks in their mouths as they smothered to death! The

The Jim twins: how coincidental? Springer, left, and Lewis were unaware of each other for 40 years.

nightmares began during early adolescence and had stopped in the last 10 to 12 years. Both women were bed wetters until about 12 or 13 years of age, and they reported educational and marital histories that were remarkably similar.

These sets of twins are part of the Minnesota Study of Twins Reared Apart, directed by Thomas Bouchard and his colleagues. They bring identical twins (identical genetically, because they come from the same egg) and fraternal twins (dissimilar genetically, because they come from two eggs) from all over the world to Minneapolis to investigate their lives. The twins are given a number of personality tests, and detailed medical histories are obtained, including information about diet, smoking, exercise habits, chest X rays, heart stress tests, and EEGs (brain-wave tests). The twins are interviewed and asked more than 15,000 questions about their family and childhood environment, personal interests, vocational orientation, values, and aesthetic judgments. They also are given ability and intelligence tests (Bouchard & others, 1981; Bouchard & others, 1990).

Critics of the Minnesota identical twins study point out that some of the separated twins were together several months prior to their adoption, that some of the twins had been reunited prior to their testing (in some cases, a number of years earlier), that adoption agencies often place twins in similar homes, and that even strangers who spend several hours together and start comparing their lives are likely to come up with some coincidental similarities (Adler, 1991). Still, even in the face of such criticism, the Minnesota study of identical twins indicates how scientists have recently shown an increased interest in the genetic basis of human development, and that we need further research on genetic and environmental factors.

PREVIEW

The examples of Jim and Jim, the giggle sisters, and the identical twins who had the same nightmares stimulate us to think about our genetic heritage and the biological foundations of our existence. Organisms are not like billiard balls, moved by simple, external forces to predictable positions on life's pool table. Environmental experiences and biological foundations work together to make us who we are. Our coverage of life's biological beginnings focuses on evolution, genetics, heredity's influence on development, and the interaction of heredity and environment.

THE EVOLUTIONARY PERSPECTIVE

In evolutionary time, humans are relative newcomers to Earth, yet we have established ourselves as the most successful and dominant species. If we think of past evolutionary time as being a calendar year, humans arrived here in late December (Sagan, 1977). As our earliest ancestors left the forest to feed on the savannas, and finally to form hunting societies on the open plains, their minds and behaviors changed. How did this evolution come about?

Natural Selection

Natural selection *is the evolutionary process that favors individuals of a species that are best adapted to survive and reproduce.* To understand natural selection, let's return to the middle of the nineteenth century, when Charles Darwin was traveling around the world observing many different species of animals in their natural surroundings. Darwin (1859), who published his observations and thoughts in *On the Origin of Species,* observed that most organisms reproduce at rates that would cause enormous increases in the population of most species, yet populations remain nearly constant. He reasoned that an intense, constant struggle for food, water, and resources must occur among the many young born each generation, because many of the young do not survive. Those that do survive pass their genes on to the next generation. Darwin believed that those who do survive to reproduce are probably superior in a number of ways to those who do not. In other words, the survivors are better adapted to their world than the nonsurvivors. Over the course of many generations, organisms with the characteristics needed for survival would comprise a larger percentage of the population. Over many, many generations, this could produce a gradual modification of the whole population. If environmental conditions change, however, other characteristics might develop, moving the process in a different direction.

Over a million species have been classified—from bacteria to blue whales, with many varieties of beetles in between.

The work of natural selection produced the disappearing acts of moths and the quills of porcupines. And the effects of evolution produced the technological advances, intelligence, and longer parental care of human beings.

What seest thou else in the dark backward and abysm of time.

—William Shakespeare,
The Tempest

I am a brother to dragons, and a companion to owls.
—Job 30:29

Generally, evolution proceeds at a very slow pace. The lines that led to the emergence of human beings and the great apes diverged about 14 million years ago! Modern humans, *Homo sapiens,* came into existence only about 50,000 years ago. And the beginning of civilization as we know it began about 10,000 years ago. No sweeping evolutionary changes in humans have occurred since then—for example, our brain is not ten times as big, we do not have a third eye in the back of our head, and we haven't learned to fly.

Although no dramatic evolutionary changes have occurred since *Homo sapiens* first appeared on the fossil record 50,000 years ago, there have been sweeping cultural changes. Biological evolution shaped human beings into a culture-making species. More information about the human species as a culture-making species appears in Sociocultural Worlds of Development 3.1.

Sociobiology

Sociobiology *is a contemporary evolutionary view that emphasizes the power of genes in determining behavior and explains complex social interactions that natural selection cannot. It states that all behavior is motivated by the desire to contribute one's genetic heritage to the greatest number of descendants.* That is, sociobiologists believe that an organism is motivated by a desire to dominate the gene pool (Wilson, 1975).

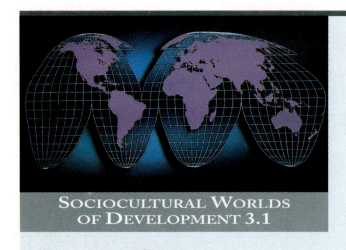

SOCIOCULTURAL WORLDS OF DEVELOPMENT 3.1

The Human Species Is a Culture-Making Species

Unlike all other animal species, which evolve in blind response to random changes in their environment, humans have considerable control over their own evolution. We change today primarily through *cultural evolution*. For example, we've made some astonishing accomplishments in the past 10,000 years or so, ever since we developed language. Biological (Darwinian) evolution continues in our species, but its rate, compared with cultural evolution, is so slow that its impact seems almost negligible. There is no evidence, for example, that brain size or structure has changed since *Homo sapiens* first appeared on the fossil record about 50,000 years ago.

As humans evolved, we acquired knowledge and passed it on from generation to generation. This knowledge, which originally instructed us in how to hunt, make tools, and communicate, became our culture. The accumulation of knowledge has gathered speed—from a slow swell to a meteoric rise. Hunter-gatherer tribes, characteristic of early human society, changed over thousands of years into small agricultural communities. With people rooted in one place, cities grew and flourished. Life within those cities remained relatively unchanged for generations. Then industrialization put a dizzying speed on cultural change. Now technological advances in communication and transportation—computers, FAX machines, the SST—transform everyday life at a staggering pace.

Whatever one generation learns, it can pass to the next through writing, word of mouth, ritual, tradition, and a host of other methods humans have developed to assure their culture's continuity (Gould, 1981). By creating cultures, humans have built, shaped, and carved out their own environments. The human species is no longer primarily at nature's mercy. Rather, humans are capable of changing their environment to fit their needs (McCandless & Trotter, 1977).

More than 99 percent of all humans now live in a different kind of environment from that in which the species evolved. By creating cultures, humans have, in effect, built, shaped, and carved out their own environments.

Even complex social behaviors, such as altruism, aggression, and socialization, have been explained as expressions of the urge to propagate our own genes. Take altruism, for example. Parents are likely to risk their own lives to save their children from a blazing fire. Although the parents may die, their children's genes survive, increasing the probability that their genes will dominate the gene pool. Similarly, males have been said to be more aggressive than females because the males' former role as hunters required them to be aggressive if they were to be successful.

Since evolution's imperative, according to sociobiologists, is to spread our genes, men and women have evolved different strategies for doing so. Sperm is abundant; men produce billions in a lifetime. However, women have a limited number of eggs, only about 400 in a lifetime. Men have the potential, then, to produce many more offspring than do women. To ensure that they spread their genes, it is to a male's advantage to impregnate as many females as possible. Given that women have few eggs and gestation takes a long time, it is to a woman's advantage to choose a mate who will protect her. This, say some sociobiologists, explains why women tend to be monogamous and men do not.

Sociobiologists point to animal models to support their theories. For example, the males of most species initiate sexual behavior more frequently than females. In some species, such as seals, cattle, and elephants, the male maintains a large harem of females to inseminate and protect. Some human societies incorporate this reproductive strategy into their culture (Hinde, 1984). Sociobiologists also contend that the universality of certain behaviors, such as incest taboos and religious laws, are proof that such behaviors are genetic.

Sociobiology is controversial. Critics argue that sociobiology does not adequately consider human adaptability and experience and that it reduces human beings to mere automatons caught in the thrall of their genes. They point out that sociobiologists explain things only after the fact, with no evidence of the predictive ability that would characterize a good theory. Male aggression is said to be a sociobiological imperative, but only after sociobiologists have seen that males do indeed behave more

FIGURE 3.1

Facts about chromosomes, DNA, and genes. (a) *The body contains billions of cells that are organized into tissue and organs.* (b) *Each cell contains a central structure, the nucleus, which controls reproduction.* (c) *Chromosomes reside in the nucleus of each cell. The male's sperm and the female's egg are specialized reproductive cells that contain chromosomes.* (d) *At conception the offspring receives matching chromosomes from the mother's egg and the father's sperm.* (e) *The chromosomes contain DNA, a chemical substance. Genes are short segments of the DNA molecule. They are the units of hereditary information that act as a blueprint for cells to reproduce themselves and manufacture the proteins that sustain life. The rungs in the DNA ladder are an important location of genes.*

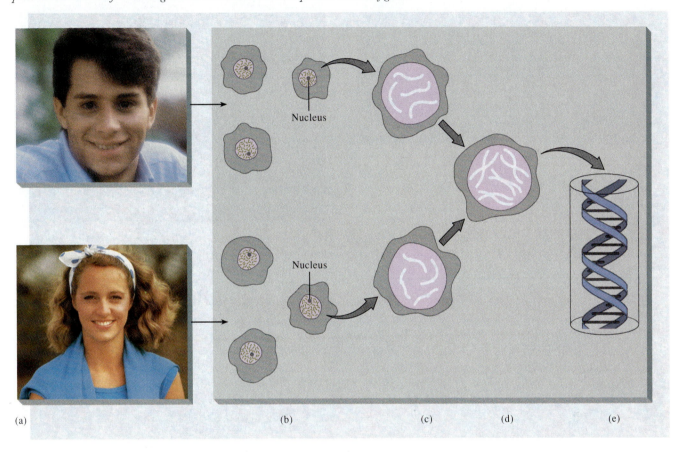

(a)　　　　　　(b)　　　　(c)　　　　(d)　　　　(e)

aggressively than females. Much of the evidence to support sociobiology is based on animal research. Critics assert that findings from animal research cannot always be generalized to humans. Further, some critics see sociobiology as little more than a justification to discriminate against women and minorities under a scientific umbrella, using genetic determinism as an excuse for ignoring the social injustice and discrimination that contribute to inequality (Paludi, 1992).

HEREDITY

Every species must have a mechanism for transmitting characteristics from one generation to the next. This mechanism is explained by the principle of genetics. Each of us carries a genetic code that we inherited from our parents. This code is located within every cell in our bodies. Our genetic codes are alike in one important way—they all contain the human genetic code. Because of the human genetic code, a fertilized human egg cannot grow into an egret, eagle, or elephant.

What Are Genes?

Each of us began life as a single cell weighing about one twenty-millionth of an ounce! This tiny piece of matter housed our entire genetic code—information about who we would become. These instructions orchestrated growth from that single cell to a person made of trillions of cells, each containing a perfect replica of the original genetic code.

The nucleus of each human cell contains 46 **chromosomes,** *which are threadlike structures that come in 23 pairs, one member of each pair coming from each parent. Chromosomes contain the remarkable genetic substance deoxyribonucleic acid, or DNA.* **DNA** *is a complex molecule that contains genetic information.* DNA's "double helix" shape looks like a spiral staircase. **Genes,** *the units of hereditary information, are short segments of the DNA "staircase." Genes act as a blueprint for cells to reproduce themselves and manufacture the proteins that maintain life.* Chromosomes, DNA, and genes can be mysterious. To help you turn mystery into understanding, refer to figure 3.1.

FIGURE 3.2

Union of sperm and egg.

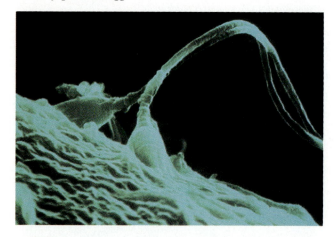

The turtle lives 'twixt plated decks
Which practically conceal its sex.
I think it clever of the turtle
In such a fix to be so fertile.

—Ogden Nash,
Many Long Years Ago, 1945

Gametes *are human reproduction cells, which are created in the testes of males and the ovaries of females.* **Meiosis** *is the process of cell division in which each pair of chromosomes in the cell separates, with one member of each pair going into each gamete, or daughter cell.* Thus, each human gamete has 23 unpaired chromosomes. **Reproduction** *takes place when a female gamete (ovum) is fertilized by a male gamete (sperm)* (see figure 3.2). A **zygote** *is a single cell formed through fertilization.* In the zygote, two sets of unpaired chromosomes combine to form one set of paired chromosomes—one member of each pair coming from the mother and the other member from the father. In this manner, each parent contributes 50 percent of the offspring's heredity.

Reproduction

The ovum is about 90,000 times as large as a sperm. Thousands of sperm must combine to break down the ovum's membrane barrier to allow even a single sperm to penetrate the membrane barrier. Ordinarily, females have two X chromosomes and males have one X and one Y chromosome. Because the Y chromosome is smaller and lighter than the X chromosome, Y-bearing sperm can be separated from X-bearing sperm in a centrifuge. This raises the possibility that the offspring's sex can be controlled. Not only are the Y-bearing sperm lighter, but they are more likely than the X-bearing sperm to coat the ovum. This results in the conception of 120 to 150 males for every 100 females. But males are more likely to die (spontaneously abort) at every stage of prenatal development, so only about 106 are born for every 100 females.

Reproduction's fascinating moments have been made even more intriguing in recent years. **In vitro fertilization** *is conception outside the body.* Consider the following situation. The year is 1978. One of the most dazzling occurrences of the 1970s is

FIGURE 3.3

In vitro fertilization. In vitro fertilization is conception outside of the womb. Here sperm meets egg in a laboratory dish.

about to unfold. Mrs. Brown is infertile, but her physician informs her of a new procedure that could enable her to have a baby. The procedure involves removing the mother's ovum surgically, fertilizing it in a laboratory medium with live sperm cells obtained from the father or another male donor (see figure 3.3), storing the fertilized egg in a laboratory solution that substitutes for the uterine environment, and finally implanting the egg in the mother's uterus. For Mrs. Brown, the procedure was successful, and 9 months later her daughter Louise was born.

Since the first in vitro fertilization in the 1970s, variations of the procedure have brought hope to childless couples. A woman's egg can be fertilized with the husband's sperm, or the husband and wife may contribute their sperm and egg and let the resulting embryo be carried by a third party, who essentially is donating her womb. Researchers have not found any developmental deficiencies in children born through in vitro fertilization.

Approximately 10 to 15 percent of couples in the United States are estimated to experience infertility, which is defined as the inability to conceive a child after 12 months of regular intercourse without contraception. The cause of infertility may rest with the woman or the man. The woman may not be ovulating, she may be producing abnormal ova, her fallopian tubes may be blocked, or she may have a disease that prevents implantation of the ova. The man may produce too few sperm, the sperm may lack motility (the ability to move adequately), or he may have a blocked passageway. In one recent investigation, long-term use of cocaine by men was related to low sperm count, low motility, and a high number of abnormally formed sperm (Bracken & others, 1990). Cocaine-related infertility appears to be reversible if users stop taking the drug for at least 1 year. In some cases of infertility, surgery may correct the problem; in others, hormone-based drugs may improve the probability of having a child. However, in some instances fertility drugs have caused superovulation, producing as many as three or more babies at a time. A summary of some of infertility's causes and solutions is presented in table 3.1.

LIFE-SPAN PRACTICAL KNOWLEDGE 3.1

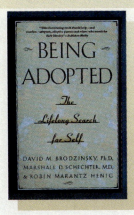

Being Adopted

(1992) by David Brodzinsky, Marshall Schecter, and Robin Henig.
New York: Doubleday.

This book provides an excellent overview of how adoption influences people's lives throughout the human life span, including a discussion of how adoption ties in with Erikson's stages of the human life cycle. Adoptees, adoptive parents, professionals, and other interested individuals will find the book to be a rich source of information about the special hurdles that adoptees and adopters must manage.

TABLE 3.1

Fertility Problems and Solutions

Females	
Problem	Solution
Damaged fallopian tubes	Surgery, in vitro fertilization
Abnormal ovulation	Hormone therapy, antibiotics, in vitro fertilization
Pelvic inflammatory disease (PID)	Antibiotics, surgery, change in birth control methods
Endometriosis*	Antibiotics, hormone therapy, surgery, artificial insemination
Damaged ovaries	Surgery, antibiotics, hormone therapy
Hostile cervical mucus	Antibiotics, artificial insemination, hormone therapy
Fibroid tumor	Surgery, antibiotics
Males	
Problem	Solution
Low sperm count	Antibiotics, hormone therapy, artificial insemination, lowered testicular temperature
Dilated veins around testicle	Surgery, lowered testicular temperature, antibiotics
Damaged sperm ducts	Surgery, antibiotics
Hormone deficiency	Hormone therapy
Sperm antibodies	Antibiotics, in vitro fertilization

*Endometriosis occurs when the uterine lining grows outside of the uterus and causes bleeding, blocking, or scarring that can interfere with conception or pregnancy.

Source: Data from A. Toth, *The Fertility Solution,* 1991.

While surgery and fertility drugs can solve the infertility problem in some cases, another choice is to adopt a child. At the time of the adoption, most adoptive parents receive little information about the child's family history, and, in turn, the child's biological parents are given little information about the adoptive parents. This policy has been followed by most adoption agencies as being in the child's best interests, but it is currently being challenged by a number of activist groups who argue that to seal records at the time of adoption violates the basic rights of persons to know about themselves (Nickman, 1992). Researchers have found that adopted children often are more at risk for psychological and school-related problems than nonadopted children (Brodzinky & others, 1984), although some adopted children adapt well to their circumstances (Marquis & Detweiler, 1985). Some adopted children show difficulties during adolescence, when, as part of their search for identity, they feel a void and incompleteness because they do not know their biological family's history.

A question that virtually every adoptive parent wants answered is, "Should I tell my adopted child that he or she is adopted? If so, when?" Most psychologists believe that adopted children should be told that they are adopted, because they will eventually find out anyway. Many children begin to ask where they came from when they are approximately 4 to 6 years of age. This is a natural time to begin to respond in simple ways to children about their adopted status. Clinical psychologists report that one problem that sometimes surfaces is the desire of adoptive parents to make life too perfect for the adoptive child and to present a perfect image of themselves to the child. The result too often is that adopted children feel that they cannot release any angry feelings and openly discuss problems in this climate of perfection (Warshak, 1993).

Abnormalities in Genes and Chromosomes

What are some abnormalities in genes and chromosomes? What tests can be used to determine the presence of these abnormalities?

Abnormalities

Geneticists and developmentalists have identified a range of problems caused by major gene or chromosome defects (Holmes, 1992; Miller, 1992). **Phenylketonuria (PKU)** *is a genetic disorder in which the individual cannot properly metabolize protein. Phenylketonuria is now easily detected, but if left untreated, mental retardation and hyperactivity result.* When detected, the disorder is treated by diet to keep a poisonous substance from entering the nervous system. Phenylketonuria involves a recessive gene and occurs about once in every 10,000 to 20,000 live births. Phenylketonuria accounts for about 1 percent of institutionalized mentally retarded individuals and it occurs primarily in whites.

Down syndrome, *the most common genetically transmitted form of mental retardation, is caused by the presence of an extra (47th) chromosome.* An individual with Down syndrome has a round face, a flattened skull, an extra fold of skin over the eyelids, a protruding tongue, short limbs, and retardation of motor and mental abilities. It is not known why the extra chromosome is present, but the health of the male sperm or female ovum may be involved (Vining, 1992). Women between the ages of 18 and 38 are less likely to give birth to a Down syndrome child than are younger or older women. Down syndrome appears approximately once in every 700 live births. Black children are rarely born with Down syndrome.

Sickle-cell anemia, *which occurs most often in Blacks, is a genetic disorder affecting the red blood cells.* A red blood cell is usually shaped like a disk, but in sickle-cell anemia, a change in a recessive gene modifies its shape to a hook-shaped "sickle." These cells die quickly, causing anemia and early death of the individual because of their failure to carry oxygen to the body's cells. About 1 in 400 Black babies is affected. One in 10 Black Americans is a carrier, as is 1 in 20 Latin Americans (Whaley & Wong, 1988).

Other disorders are associated with sex-chromosome abnormalities. Remember that normal males have an X chromosome and a Y chromosome, and normal females have two X chromosomes. **Klinefelter syndrome** *is a genetic disorder in which males have an extra X chromosome, making them XXY instead of XY.* Males with this disorder have undeveloped testes, and they usually have enlarged breasts and become tall. Klinefelter syndrome occurs approximately once in every 3,000 live male births.

Turner syndrome *is a genetic disorder in which females are missing an X chromosome, making them XO instead of XX.* These females are short in stature and have a webbed neck. They may be mentally retarded and sexually underdeveloped. Turner syndrome occurs approximately once in every 3,000 live female births.

The **XYY syndrome** *is a genetic disorder in which the male has an extra Y chromosome. Early interest in this syndrome involved the belief that the Y chromosome found in males contributed to male*

FIGURE 3.4

Amniocentesis being performed on a pregnant woman.

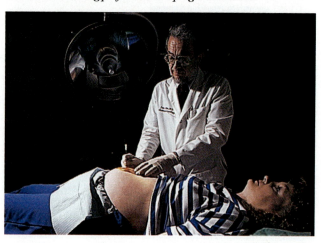

aggression and violence. It was then reasoned that if a male had an extra Y chromosome, he would likely be extremely aggressive and possibly develop a violent personality. However, researchers subsequently found that XYY males were no more likely to commit crimes than XY males (Witkin & others, 1976).

We have discussed six genetic disorders—phenylketonuria, Down syndrome, sickle-cell anemia, Klinefelter syndrome, Turner syndrome, and the XYY syndrome. A summary of these genetic disorders, as well as some other common ones, appears in table 3.2.

Each year in the United States, approximately 100,000 to 150,000 infants are born with a genetic disorder or malformation. These infants comprise about 3 to 5 percent of the 3 million births and account for at least 20 percent of infant deaths. Prospective parents increasingly are turning to genetic counseling for assistance, wanting to know their risk of having a child born with a genetic defect or malformation (Bernhardt & Pyeritz, 1992; Carey, 1992; Hirschhorn, 1992; Langlois, 1992).

Critical Thinking

Imagine that you want to start a family. Probe your family background. What questions would you want to ask a genetic counselor?

Tests to Determine Abnormalities

Scientists have developed a number of tests to determine whether the fetus is developing normally, among them amniocentesis, ultrasound sonography, the chorionic villus test, and the maternal blood test, each of which we now discuss in turn.

Amniocentesis *is a prenatal medical procedure in which a sample of amniotic fluid is withdrawn by syringe and tested to discover if the fetus is suffering from any chromosomal or metabolic disorders. Amniocentesis is performed between the 12th and 16th weeks of pregnancy.* The later amniocentesis is performed, the better the diagnostic potential. The earlier it is performed, the more useful it is in deciding whether a pregnancy should be terminated (see figure 3.4).

TABLE 3.2

Genetic Disorders and Conditions

Name	Description	Treatment	Incidence	Prenatal Detection	Carrier Detection
Anencephaly	Neural tube disorder that causes brain and skull malformations; most children die at birth.	Surgery	1 in 1,000	Ultrasound, amniocentesis	None
Cystic fibrosis	Glandular dysfunction that interferes with mucus production; breathing and digestion are hampered, resulting in a shortened life span.	Physical and oxygen therapy, synthetic enzymes, and antibiotics	1 in 2,000	Amniocentesis	Family history, DNA analysis
Down syndrome	Extra or altered 21st chromosome causes mild to severe retardation and physical abnormalities.	Surgery, early intervention, infant stimulation, and special learning programs	1 in 800 women; 1 in 350 women over 35	AFP, CVT, amniocentesis	Family history chromosomal analysis
Hemophilia	Lack of the clotting factor causes excessive internal and external bleeding.	Blood transfusions and/or injections of the clotting factor	1 in 10,000 males	CVT, amniocentesis	Family history, DNA analysis
Klinefelter syndrome	An extra X chromosome causes physical abnormalities.	Hormone therapy	1 in 800 males	CVT, amniocentesis	None
Phenylketonuria (PKU)	Metabolic disorder that, left untreated, causes mental retardation.	Special diet	1 in 14,000	CVT, amniocentesis	Family history, blood test
Pyloric stenosis	Excess muscle in upper intestine causes severe vomiting and death if not treated.	Surgery	1 in 200 males; 1 in 1,000 females	None	None
Sickle-cell anemia	Blood disorder that limits the body's oxygen supply. It can cause joint swelling, sickle-cell crises, heart and kidney failure.	Penicillin, medication for pain, antibiotics, and blood transfusions	1 in 500 Black children (lower among other groups)	CVT, amniocentesis	Blood test
Spina bifida	Neural tube disorder that causes brain and spine abnormalities.	Corrective surgery at birth, orthopedic devices, and physical/medical therapy	2 in 1,000	AFP, ultrasound, amniocentesis	None
Tay-Sachs disease	Deceleration of mental and physical development caused by an accumulation of lipids in the nervous system; few children live to age 5.	Medication and special diet	1 in 30 American Jews is a carrier	CVT, amniocentesis	Blood test
Thalassemia	Group of inherited blood disorders that causes anemic symptoms ranging from fatigue and weakness to liver failure.	Blood transfusions and antibiotics	1 in 400 children of Mediterranean descent	CVT, amniocentesis	Blood test
Turner syndrome	A missing or altered X chromosome may cause mental retardation and/or physical abnormalities.	Hormone therapy	1 in 3,000 females	None	Blood test

Ultrasound sonography *is a prenatal medical procedure in which high-frequency sound waves are directed into the pregnant woman's abdomen.* The echo from the sounds is transformed into a visual representation of the fetus's inner structures. This technique has been able to detect such disorders as microencephaly, a form of mental retardation involving an abnormally small brain. Ultrasound sonography is often used in conjunction with amniocentesis to determine the precise location of the fetus in the mother's abdomen (see figure 3.5).

As scientists have searched for more accurate, safe assessments of high-risk prenatal conditions, they have developed a new test. The **chorionic villus test (CVT)** *is a prenatal medical procedure in which a small sample of the placenta is removed at some point between the 8th and the 11th week of pregnancy.* Diagnosis takes approximately 10 days. The chorionic villus test allows a decision about abortion to be made near the end of the first trimester of pregnancy, a point when abortion is safer and less traumatic than after amniocentesis in the second trimester.

LIFE-SPAN PRACTICAL KNOWLEDGE 3.2

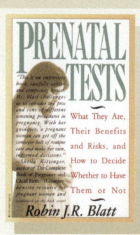

Prenatal Tests
(1988) by Robin J. R. Blatt.
New York: Vintage Books.

Prenatal Tests is a comprehensive guide to available prenatal tests, their benefits and risks, and how to decide whether to have them or not. The author challenges women to consider the pros and cons of different screening procedures in pregnancy. With her guidance, a pregnant woman can avoid the conveyor belt of routine care and make her own, informed decisions. The book also provides valuable information for the partners of pregnant women, addressing the emotional and ethical aspects of decision making that couples face when considering prenatal testing.

FIGURE 3.5

A 6-month-old infant poses with the ultrasound sonography record taken 4 months into the baby's prenatal development.

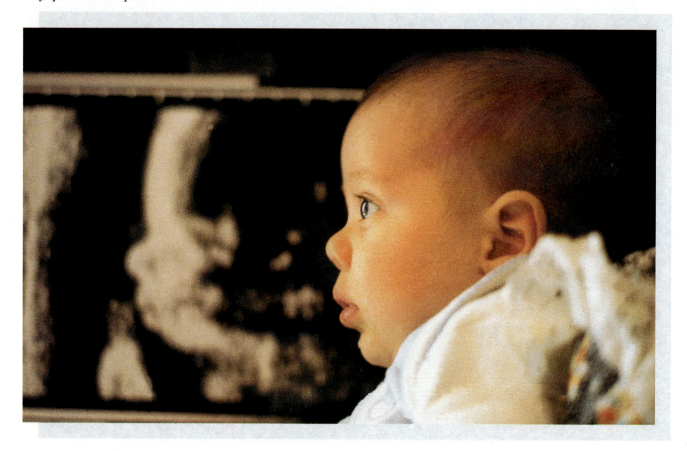

CONCEPT TABLE 3.1

The Evolutionary Perspective and Genetics

Concept	Processes/Related Ideas	Characteristics/Description
The evolutionary perspective	Natural selection	Natural selection is the process that favors the individuals of a species that are best adapted to survive and produce. This concept was originally proposed by Charles Darwin. Although no dramatic evolutionary changes have occurred in humans since *Homo sapiens* first appeared in the fossil record 50,000 years ago, there have been sweeping cultural changes. Biological evolution shaped human beings into a culture-making species.
	Sociobiology	Sociobiology argues that all behavior is motivated by a desire to dominate the gene pool. Critics say that sociobiology ignores the environmental determinants of behavior and is biased against females.
Genes, chromosomes, and reproduction	Genes and chromosomes	The nucleus of each human cell contains 46 chromosomes, which are composed of DNA. Genes are short segments of DNA and act as a blueprint for cells to reproduce and manufacture proteins that maintain life.
	Reproduction	Genes are transmitted from parents to offspring by gametes, or sex cells. Gametes are formed by the splitting of cells, a process called "meiosis." Reproduction takes place when a female gamete (ovum) is fertilized by a male gamete (sperm) to create a single-celled ovum. In vitro fertilization has helped to solve some infertility problems. Approximately 10 to 15 percent of couples in the United States experience infertility problems, some of which can be corrected through surgery or fertility drugs. Another choice for infertile couples is adoption.
Abnormalities in genes and chromosomes	The range of problems	A range of problems are caused by major gene or chromosome defects, among them the PKU, Down syndrome, sickle-cell anemia, Klinefelter syndrome, Turner syndrome, and the XYY syndrome.
	Genetic counseling and tests	Genetic counseling has increased in popularity as couples desire information about their risk of having a defective child. Amniocentesis, ultrasound sonography, the chorionic villus test, and the maternal blood test are used to determine the presence of defects after pregnancy has begun.

These techniques provide valuable information about the presence of birth defects, but they also raise issues pertaining to whether an abortion should be obtained if birth defects are present.

The **maternal blood test** *(alpha-fetoprotein test—AFP) is a prenatal diagnostic technique that is used to assess blood alphaprotein level, which is associated with neural tube defects.* This test is administered to women 14 to 20 weeks into pregnancy only when they are at risk for bearing a child with defects in the formation of the brain and spinal cord.

So far in this chapter, we have discussed the evolutionary perspective, genes, chromosomes, reproduction, and abnormalities in genes and chromosomes. For a summary of these ideas, see concept table 3.1.

GENETIC PRINCIPLES AND METHODS

What are some basic genetic principles that affect children's development? What methods do behavior geneticists use to study heredity's influence? How does heredity influence such aspects of children's development as their intelligence? And how do heredity and environment interact to produce children's development?

Some Genetic Principles

Genetic determination is a complex affair, and much is unknown about the way genes work. But a number of genetic principles have been discovered, among them the principles of dominant-recessive genes, sex-linked genes, polygenically inherited characteristics, reaction range, and canalization.

According to the **dominant-recessive genes principle,** *if one gene of the pair is dominant and one is recessive (goes back or recedes), the dominant gene exerts its effect, overriding the potential influence of the other, recessive gene. A recessive gene exerts its influence only if the two genes of a pair are both recessive.* If you inherit a recessive gene for a trait from each of your parents, you will show the trait. If you inherit a recessive gene from only one parent, you may never know you carry the gene. Brown eyes, farsightedness, and dimples rule over blue eyes, nearsightedness, and freckles in the world of dominant-recessive genes. Can two brown-eyed parents have a blue-eyed child? Yes, they can, if each parent has a dominant gene for brown eyes and a recessive gene for blue eyes: Since dominant genes override recessive genes, the parents have brown eyes. But both are carriers of blueness and can pass on their recessive genes for blue eyes. With no dominant gene to override them, the recessive genes will make the child's eyes blue. Figure 3.6 illustrates the dominant-recessive genes principle.

For thousands of years, people wondered what determined whether we become male or female. Aristotle believed that the father's arousal during intercourse determined the offspring's sex. The more excited the father was, the more likely it would be a son, he reasoned. Of course, he was wrong, but it was not until the 1920s that researchers confirmed the existence of human sex chromosomes, 2 of the 46 chromosomes human beings normally carry. As we saw earlier, ordinarily females have two X chromosomes and males have an X and a Y. (Figure 3.7 shows the chromosomal makeup of a male and a female.)

Genetic transmission is usually more complex than the simple examples we have examined thus far. **Polygenic inheritance** *is a genetic principle describing the interaction of many genes to produce a particular characteristic.* Few psychological characteristics are the result of single pairs. Most are determined by the interaction of many different genes. There are as many as 50,000 or more genes, so you can imagine that possible combinations of these are staggering in number. Traits produced by this mixing of genes are said to be polygenically determined.

FIGURE 3.6

How brown-eyed parents can have a blue-eyed child. Although both parents have brown eyes, each parent can have a recessive gene for blue eyes. In this example both parents have brown eyes, but each parent carries the recessive gene for blue eyes. Therefore, the odds of their child having blue eyes is one in four—the probability the child will receive a recessive gene (b) from each parent.

B = gene for brown eyes
b = gene for blue eyes

That which comes of a cat will catch mice.
—English Proverb

No one possesses all the characteristics that our genetic structure makes possible. **Genotype** *is the person's genetic heritage, the actual genetic material.* However, not all of this genetic material is apparent in our observed and measurable characteristics. **Phenotype** *is the way an individual's genotype is expressed in observed and measurable characteristics.* Phenotypes include physical traits, such as height, weight, eye color, and skin pigmentation, and psychological characteristics, such as intelligence, creativity, personality, and social tendencies.

For each genotype, a range of phenotypes can be expressed. Imagine that we could identify all the genes that would make a person introverted or extraverted. Would measured introversion-extraversion be predictable from knowledge of the specific genes? The answer is no, because even if our genetic model were adequate, introversion-extraversion is a characteristic shaped by experience throughout life. For example, parents may push an introverted child into social situations and encourage the child to become more gregarious.

To understand how introverted a person is, think about a series of genetic codes that predispose the child to develop in a particular way, and imagine environments that are responsive

FIGURE 3.7

The genetic difference between males and females. *Set* (a) *shows the chromosome structure of a male, and set* (b) *shows the chromosome structure of a female. The last pair of 23 pairs of chromosomes is in the bottom right box of each set. Notice that the Y chromosome of the male is smaller than that of the female. To obtain this kind of chromosomal picture, a cell is removed from a person's body, usually from the inside of the mouth. The chromosomes are magnified extensively and then photographed.*

(a)

(b)

or unresponsive to this development. For example, the genotype of some persons may predispose them to be introverted in an environment that promotes a turning inward of personality, yet in an environment that encourages social interaction and out-goingness, these individuals may become more extraverted. However, it would be unlikely for the individual with this introverted genotype to become a strong extravert. The term **reaction range** *is used to describe the range of phenotypes for each genotype, suggesting the importance of an environment's restrictiveness or enrichment* (see figure 3.8).

Sandra Scarr (1984) explains reaction range this way: Each of us has a range of potential. For example, an individual with "medium-tall" genes for height (genes for medium-tall height)

who grows up in a poor environment may be shorter than average. But in an excellent nutritional environment, the individual may grow up taller than average. However, no matter how well fed the person is, someone with "short" genes will never be taller than average. Scarr believes that characteristics such as intelligence and introversion work the same way. That is, there is a range within which the environment can modify intelligence, but intelligence is not completely malleable. Reaction range gives us an estimate of how modifiable intelligence is.

Genotypes, in addition to producing many phenotypes, may show the opposite track for some characteristics—those that are somewhat immune to extensive changes in the environment.

FIGURE 3.8

Although each genotype responds favorably to improved environments, some are more responsive to environmental deprivation and enrichment than are others.

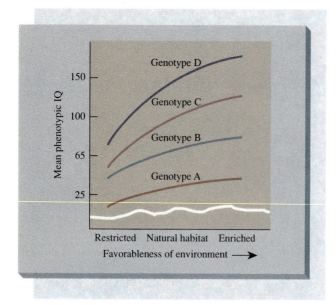

Identical twins develop from a single fertilized egg that splits into two genetically identical organisms. Twin studies compare identical twins with fraternal twins. Fraternal twins develop from separate eggs, making them genetically less similar than identical twins.

These characteristics seem to stay on a particular developmental course regardless of the environmental assaults on them (Waddington, 1957). **Canalization** *is the term chosen to describe the narrow path or developmental course that certain characteristics take. Apparently, preservative forces help to protect or buffer a person from environmental extremes.* For example, American developmental psychologist Jerome Kagan (1984) points to his research on Guatemalan infants who had experienced extreme malnutrition as infants yet showed normal social and cognitive development later in childhood. And some abused children do not grow up to be abusers themselves.

However, it is important to recognize that although the genetic influence of canalization exerts its power by keeping organisms on a particular developmental path, genes alone do not directly determine human behavior (Cairns, 1991; Gottlieb, 1991; Lerner, 1991). Developmentalist Gilbert Gottlieb (1991) points out that genes are an integral part of the organism, but that their activity (genetic expression) can be affected by the organism's environment. For example, hormones that circulate in the blood make their way into the cell, where they influence the cell's activity. The flow of hormones themselves can be affected by environmental events such as light, day length, nutrition, and behavior.

Methods Used by Behavior Geneticists

Behavior genetics *is concerned with the degree and nature of behavior's hereditary basis.* Behavior geneticists assume that behaviors are jointly determined by the interaction of heredity and environment (Goldsmith, 1994). To study heredity's influence on behavior, behavior geneticists often use either twin studies or adoption studies.

In a **twin study,** *the behavior of identical twins is compared with the behavior of fraternal twins.* **Identical twins** *(called "monozygotic" twins) develop from a single fertilized egg that splits into two genetically identical replicas, each of which becomes a person.* **Fraternal twins** *(called "dizygotic" twins) develop from separate eggs, making them genetically less similar than identical twins.* Although fraternal twins share the same womb, they are no more alike genetically than are nontwin brothers and sisters, and they may be of different sexes. By comparing groups of identical and fraternal twins, behavior geneticists capitalize on the basic knowledge that identical twins are more similar genetically than are fraternal twins. In one twin study, 7,000 pairs of Finnish identical and fraternal twins were compared on the personality traits of extraversion (outgoingness) and neuroticism (psychological instability) (Rose & others, 1988). On both of these personality traits, identical twins were much more similar than fraternal twins, suggesting the role of heredity in both traits. However, several issues crop up as a result of twin studies. Adults may stress the similarities of identical twins more than those of fraternal twins, and identical twins may perceive themselves as a "set" and play together more than fraternal twins. If so, observed similarities in identical twins could be environmentally influenced.

In an **adoption study,** *investigators seek to discover whether the behavior and psychological characteristics of adopted children are more like their adoptive parents, who provided a home environment, or their biological parents, who contributed their heredity.* In one investigation, the educational levels attained by biological parents were better predictors of adopted children's IQ scores than were the IQs of the children's adopted parents (Scarr &

THE WIZARD OF ID

By permission of Johnny Hart and Creators Syndicate, Inc.

Weinberg, 1983). Because of the genetic relation between the adopted children and their biological parents, the implication is that heredity influences children's IQ scores.

Heredity's Influence on Development

What aspects of development are influenced by genetic factors? They all are. However, behavior geneticists are interested in more precise estimates of a characteristic's variation that can be accounted for by genetic factors. Intelligence and temperament are among the most widely investigated aspects of heredity's influence on development.

Arthur Jensen (1969) sparked a lively, and at times hostile, debate when he presented his thesis that intelligence is primarily inherited. Jensen believes that environment and culture play only a minimal role in intelligence. He examined several studies of intelligence, some of which involved comparisons of identical and fraternal twins. Remember that identical twins have identical genetic endowments, so their IQs should be similar. Fraternal twins and ordinary siblings are less similar genetically, so their IQs should be less similar. Jensen found support for his argument in these studies. Studies with identical twins produced an average correlation of .82; studies with ordinary siblings produced an average correlation of .50. Note the difference of .32. To show that genetic factors are more important than environmental factors, Jensen compared identical twins reared together with those reared apart; the correlation for those reared together was .89 and for those reared apart it was .78 (a difference of .11). Jensen argued that if environmental influences were more important than genetic influences, then siblings reared apart, who experienced different environments, should have IQs much farther apart.

Many scholars have criticized Jensen's work. One criticism concerns the definition of intelligence itself. Jensen believes that IQ as measured by standardized intelligence tests is a good indicator of intelligence. Critics argue that IQ tests tap only a narrow range of intelligence. Everyday problem solving, work, and social adaptability, say the critics, are important aspects of intelligence not measured by the traditional intelligence tests used in Jensen's sources. A second criticism is that most investigations of heredity and environment do not include environments that differ radically. Thus, it is not surprising that many genetic studies show environment to be a fairly weak influence on intelligence.

Developmentalists have a special interest in intervening in the lives of children who live in impoverished circumstances. To read about the effects of early intervention on intelligence in impoverished contexts, turn to Perspectives on Parenting and Education 3.1.

HEREDITY-ENVIRONMENT INTERACTION AND DEVELOPMENT

A common misconception is that behavior geneticists only analyze the effects of heredity on development. They do believe heredity plays an important role in development, but they also carve up the environment's contribution to heredity-environment interaction.

Passive Genotype-Environment, Evocative Genotype-Environment, and Active Genotype-Environment Interactions

Parents not only provide the genes for the child's biological blueprint for development; they also play important roles in determining the types of environments their children will encounter. Behavior geneticist Sandra Scarr (1992; Scarr & McCartney, 1983; Scarr & Ricciuti, in press) believes that the environments parents select for their children depend to some degree on the parents' own genotypes. Behavior geneticists believe heredity and environment interact in this manner in three ways: passively, evocatively, and actively. **Passive genotype-environment interactions** *occur when parents who are genetically related to the child provide a rearing environment for the child.* For example, parents may have a genetic predisposition to be intelligent and read skillfully. Because they read well and enjoy reading, they provide their children with books to read, with the likely outcome that their children will become skilled readers who enjoy reading.

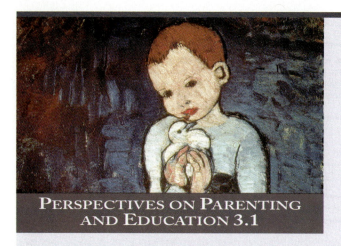

PERSPECTIVES ON PARENTING AND EDUCATION 3.1

The Effects of Early Intervention on Intelligence

Researchers are increasingly interested in manipulating the environment early in children's lives when they are perceived to be at risk for impoverished intelligence. In a program conducted in North Carolina by Craig Ramey and his associates (1988), pregnant women with IQs averaging 80 were recruited for a study. After their babies were born, half of the infants were cared for during the day at an educational day-care center and half were reared at home by their mothers. Both groups of children were given medical care and dietary supplements, and their families were given social services if they requested them.

At the age of 3, the children who attended the educational day-care center had significantly higher IQs than the home-reared children. This difference was likely due to the decline in the IQs of the home-reared children during the period from 12 to 18 months of age. By the time the children were 5 years old, 39 percent of the home-reared children had IQs below 85 but only 11 percent of the educational day-care children had IQs this low.

Some parents, such as those in Ramey's study, have difficulty providing an adequate environment for the intellectual needs of their infants. Once these difficulties are a repetitive part of the family system, then change efforts probably will be more difficult and costly. Early intervention in the family system is directed at changing parental adaptive and responsive functioning so that permanent negative effects are minimized (Heinicke, Beckwith, & Thompson, 1988).

A second example of a successful early intervention program was conducted in Houston, Texas, with low-income Mexican-American families (Johnson & McGowan, 1984). The Mexican-American children were 1 year old at the beginning of the intervention, which lasted for 2 years. A family educator visited each home twice a week during the first year of the program to encourage parents to teach their infants and to be sensitive to their developmental needs. On weekends, the whole family participated in groups to discuss ways to improve family communication. In the program's second year, toddlers went to an educational day-care center four mornings each week while their mothers participated in group discussion sessions focused on family issues and parenting.

In this study, the families who experienced the intervention were compared with a control group of families from similar backgrounds who did not receive parent education, educational day care, or any other services. The intervention program was successful. Mothers in the intervention program created a more stimulating home environment for their children, gave them more affection, and encouraged them to talk more than the control group mothers did. And, at both 2 and 3 years of age, the intervention children had higher IQs than the control group children.

In another investigation, the Infant Health and Development Program, early intervention with low-birthweight children revealed that both home visitation and an educational child curriculum improved the children's IQ, decreased behavior problems, and improved the home environment (Infant Health and Development Program Staff, 1990; Liaw & others, 1994). The intervention was more effective with mothers with low educational attainment than with those with high educational attainment, more effective for Black than White children, and more effective for most at-risk children (Brooks-Gunn & others, 1992; Brooks-Gunn & others, in press).

Intervention programs have the most positive effects on children's well-being when they (a) begin as early as possible, (b) provide services to parents as well as to the child, (c) have a low child-teacher ratio, (d) have high parental involvement, and (e) have frequent contacts (Bronfenbrenner, 1974; Bryant & Ramey, 1987; Lazar & Darlington, 1982; McKey & others, 1985; Schorr, 1988). In one review of family intervention studies, intervention was more effective when there were eleven or more contacts between the intervenor and the family (Heinicke, Beckwith, & Thompson, 1988). While eleven sessions is a somewhat arbitrary number, it does indicate that a certain duration of contact is necessary for intervention success.

Craig Ramey's research has documented that high-quality early educational day care can significantly raise the intelligence of young children from impoverished environments.

Evocative genotype-environment interactions *occur because a child's genotype elicits certain types of physical and social environments.* For example, active, smiling babies receive more social stimulation than passive, quiet babies. Cooperative, attentive children evoke more pleasant and instructional responses from the adults around them than uncooperative, distractible children.

Active (niche-picking) genotype-environment interactions *occur when children seek out environments they find compatible and stimulating. "Niche-picking" means finding a niche or setting that is especially suited to the child's abilities.* Children select from their surrounding environment some aspects that they respond to, learn about, or ignore. Their active selections of certain aspects of their environment are related to their particular genotypes. Some children, because of their genotype, have the sensorimotor skills to perform well at sports. Others, because of their genotype, may have more ability in music. Children who are athletically inclined are more likely to actively seek out sports environments in which they can perform well, while children who are musically inclined are more likely to spend time in musical environments in which they can successfully perform their skills.

Scarr (1992; Scarr & McCartney, 1983) believes that the relative importance of the three kinds of genotype-environment interaction changes as children develop from infancy through adolescence. In infancy, much of the environment that children experience is provided by adults. When those adults are genetically related to the child, the environment they provide is related to their own characteristics and genotypes. Although infants are active in structuring their experiences by actively attending to what is available to them, they cannot seek out and build their own environmental niches as much as older children can. Therefore, passive genotype-environment interactions are more common in the lives of infants and young children than they are for older children, who can extend their experiences beyond the family's influences and create their environments to a greater degree.

Shared and Nonshared Environmental Influences

Behavior geneticists also believe that another way the environment's role in heredity-environment interaction can be carved up is to consider the experiences that children have in families that are common with other children living in the same home and those that are not common or shared. Behavior geneticist Robert Plomin (1991; Plomin & Daniels, 1987) believes that common rearing and shared environment account for little of the variation in children's personality or interests. In other words, even though two children live under the same roof with the same parents, their personalities are often very different.

Shared environmental influences *are children's common experiences, such as their parents' personalities and intellectual orientation, the family's social class, and the neighborhood in which they live.* By contrast, **nonshared environmental influences** *are a child's own unique experiences, both within the family and outside the family, that are not shared with another sibling.* Parents often do interact differently with each sibling, and

Sandra Scarr has developed a number of important theoretical ideas and conducted a number of research investigations on the roles of heredity and environment in children's development. She believes that the environments parents select for their children depend to some degree on the parents' own genotype. Scarr's critics believe she greatly underestimates the role of environment in development.

siblings interact differently with parents. Siblings often have different peer groups, different friends, and different teachers at school.

Not all developmentalists accept the shared/nonshared environmental view. Parenting experts Eleanor Maccoby (1992) and Diana Baumrind (in press) argue that there are a number of important aspects of family contexts that are shared by all family members. After all, children observe how parents are treating their siblings, and they learn from what they observe as well as what they experience directly. And atmospheres and moods tend to be spread to whoever is in the room.

The Contemporary Heredity-Environment Controversy

As we have just seen, Sandra Scarr (1991, 1992, 1993) believes that heredity plays a powerful role in children's development. Her theory of genotype → environment effects essentially states that genotypes drive experiences. Scarr also stresses that unless a child's family is specifically abusive or fails to provide what she calls "average expectable" conditions in which the species has evolved, parental differences in child rearing styles, social class, and income have small effects on differences in children's intelligence, personality, and interests. Scarr also has presented the provocative view that biology makes nonrisk infants invulnerable to lasting, negative effects of day care. In sum, Scarr stresses that except in extreme instances of abused and at-risk children, environmental experiences play a minimal, if any, role in determining differences in children's cognitive and socioemotional development.

Not surprisingly, Scarr's beliefs have generated considerable controversy in the field of child development. Among Scarr's critics, Diana Baumrind (1993), Eleanor Maccoby (1992), and Jacquelyne Jackson (1993) point to a number of loopholes in her arguments. They conclude that Scarr has not adequately defined what an "average expectable" environment is, that good parenting optimizes both normal and vulnerable children's development, and that her interpretations of behavior genetics studies go far beyond what is possible, given their inherit limitations.

Scarr (1993) responds to such criticisms by arguing that understanding children's development requires describing it under the umbrella of evolutionary theory and that many developmentalists do not adequately give attention to the important role that biology plays in children's development. She, as well as other biologically-oriented theorists (Goldsmith, in press; Wachs, in press), feel their critics often misinterpret what they say. Scarr says that social reformers oppose her ideas because they believe they cause pessimism for social change. She responds that she is simply motivated to discover the facts about the roles of genes and environment in determining human development. Scarr says that all children should have an opportunity to become species-normal, culturally appropriate, and uniquely themselves—their own versions of Georgia O'Keefe and Martin Luther King. She continues that many children in today's world lack those opportunities and that their needs should be addressed. However, she concludes that humanitarian concerns should not drive developmental theory and that developmental theory has to have a strong biological orientation to be accurate.

In conclusion, virtually all developmentalists today are interactionists in that they believe heredity and environment interact to determine children's development. However, in their effort to more precisely determine heredity's and environment's role, Scarr argues that heredity plays a powerful role in heredity-environmental interaction, while Baumrind, Maccoby, and Jackson believe the environment is a much stronger influence on children's development than Scarr acknowledges.

Conclusions About Heredity-Environment Interaction

In sum, both genes and environment are necessary for a person to even exist. Heredity and environment operate together—or cooperate—to produce a person's intelligence, temperament, height, weight, ability to pitch a baseball, reading talents, and so on (Loehlin, 1992; Plomin & others, 1994; Rowe, in press; Scarr, 1992). Without genes, there is no person; without environment, there is no person (Scarr & Weinberg, 1980). If an attractive, popular, intelligent girl is elected president of her senior class in high school, should we conclude that her success is due to heredity or due to environment? Of course, the answer is both. Because the environment's influence depends on genetically endowed characteristics, we say the two factors *interact*.

Critical Thinking

Beyond the fact that heredity and environment always interact to produce development, first argue for heredity's dominance in this interaction, and, second, argue for environment's dominance.

A summary of the main ideas in our discussion of genetic principles and methods, heredity's influence on development, and how heredity and environment interact to produce development is presented in concept table 3.2. In the next chapter, we will continue to discuss biological beginnings, turning to the nature of prenatal development and birth.

CONCLUSIONS

Biological beginnings raise questions of how we as a species came to be, how parents' genes are shuffled to produce a particular child, and how much experience can go against the grain of heredity.

In this chapter, we read about the Jim and Jim twins and studied the evolutionary perspective, in which we discussed natural selection and sociobiology; the nature of heredity; what genes are; how reproduction takes place; some abnormalities in genes and chromosomes; genetic principles; methods used by behavior geneticists; heredity's influence on development; and what heredity-environment interaction is like. Behavior geneticists believe that it is important to consider passive genotype-environment, evocative genotype-environment, and active genotype-environment interactions, as well as shared and nonshared environmental experiences. At different points in the chapter we also studied the human species as a culture-making species, the effects of early intervention on intelligence, and genetic counseling.

Remember that you can obtain an overall summary of the chapter by again reading the two concept tables on pages 83 and 91. In the next chapter, we continue our exploration of biological beginnings in the form of the dramatic unfolding of prenatal development and birth.

CONCEPT TABLE 3.2

Genetic Principles and Methods, Heredity, and Heredity–Environment Interaction

Concept	Processes/Related Ideas	Characteristics/Description
Genetic principles and methods	Genetic principles	Genetic transmission is complex, but some principles have been worked out, among them principles of dominant-recessive genes, sex-linked genes, polygenic inheritance, genotype-phenotype distinction, reaction range, and canalization.
	Methods used by behavior geneticists	Behavior genetics is the field concerned with the degree and nature of behavior's hereditary basis. Among the most important methods used by behavior geneticists are twin studies and adoption studies.
Heredity's influence on development	Its scope	All aspects of development are influenced by heredity.
	Intelligence	Jensen's argument that intelligence is primarily due to heredity sparked a lively, and at times bitter, debate. Intelligence is influenced by heredity, but not as strongly as Jensen envisioned.
Heredity-environment interaction and development	Passive genotype-environment, evocative genotype-environment, and active genotype-environment interactions	Scarr believes that the environments parents select for their own children depend to some degree on the parents' genotypes. Behavior geneticists believe heredity and environment interact in this manner in three ways: passively, evocatively, and actively. Passive genotype-environment interactions occur when parents who are genetically related to the child provide a rearing environment for the child. Evocative genotype-environment interactions occur because a child's genotype elicits certain types of physical and social environments. Active (niche-picking) genotype-environment interactions occur when children seek out environments they find compatible and stimulating. Scarr believes that the relative importance of these three forms of genotype-environment interaction changes as children develop.
	Shared and nonshared environments	Shared environmental experiences are children's common experiences, such as their parents' personalities and intellectual orientation, the family's social class, and the neighborhood in which they live. Nonshared environmental experiences are the child's own unique experiences, both within the family and outside the family, that are not shared by another sibling. Plomin argues that it is nonshared environmental experiences that primarily make up the environment's contribution to why one sibling's personality is different from another's.
	The contemporary heredity/environment controversy	Scarr's genotype → environment theory has generated considerable controversy. She argues that except in extreme abuse and at risk conditions, the environment plays a minimal role in determining differences in children's cognitive and socioemotional development. A number of criticisms of her view have been offered.
	Conclusions about heredity-environment interaction	Heredity and environment interact to produce human development. Without genes, there is no person; without environment, there is no person.

LIFE-SPAN HEALTH AND WELL-BEING

Genetic Counseling

Bob and Mary Sims have been married for several years. They would like to start a family, but they are frightened. The newspapers and popular magazines are full of stories about infants who are born prematurely and don't survive, infants with debilitating physical defects, and babies found to have congenital mental retardation. The Simses feel that to have such a child would create a social, economic, and psychological strain on them and on society.

Accordingly, the Simses turn to a genetic counselor for help. Genetic counselors are usually physicians or biologists who are well versed in the field of medical genetics. They are familiar with the kinds of problems that can be inherited, the odds for encountering them, and helpful measures for offsetting some of their effects. The Simses tell their counselor that there has been a history of

mental retardation in Bob's family. Bob's younger sister was born with Down syndrome, a form of mental retardation. Mary's older brother has hemophilia, a condition in which bleeding is difficult to stop. They wonder what the chances are that a child of theirs might also be retarded or have hemophilia and what measures they can take to reduce their chances of having a mentally or physically defective child.

The counselor probes more deeply, because she understands that these facts in isolation do not give her a complete picture of the possibilities. She learns that no other relatives in Bob's family are retarded and that Bob's mother was in her late forties when his younger sister was born. She concludes that the retardation was due to the age of Bob's mother and not to some general tendency for members of his family to inherit retardation. It

is well known that women over 40 have a much higher probability of giving birth to retarded children than younger women. Apparently, in women over 40, the ova (egg cells) are not as healthy as in women under 40.

In Mary's case the counselor determines that there is a small but clear possibility that Mary may be a carrier of hemophilia and may transmit that condition to a son. Otherwise, the counselor can find no evidence from the family history to indicate genetic problems.

The decision is then up to the Simses. In this case, the genetic problem will probably not occur, so the choice is fairly easy. But what should parents do if they face the strong probability of having a child with a major birth defect? Ultimately, the decision depends on the couple's ethical and religious beliefs. ■

KEY TERMS

natural selection   The evolutionary process that favors individuals of a species that are best adapted to survive and reproduce. (75)

sociobiology   Emphasizes the power of genes in determining behavior and explains complex social interactions that natural selection cannot. It states that all behavior is motivated by the desire to contribute one's genetic heritage to the greatest number of descendants. (75)

chromosomes   Threadlike structures that come in 23 pairs, one member of each pair coming from each parent. Chromosomes contain the remarkable genetic substance deoxyribonucleic acid or DNA. (77)

DNA   A complex molecule that contains genetic information. (77)

genes   The units of hereditary information are short segments of the

DNA "staircase." Genes act as a blueprint for cells to reproduce themselves and manufacture the proteins that maintain life. (77)

gametes   Human reproduction cells created in the testes of males and the ovaries of females. (78)

meiosis   The process of cell division in which each pair of chromosomes in the cell separates, with one member of each pair going into each gamete, or daughter cell. (78)

reproduction   When a female gamete (ovum) is fertilized by a male gamete (sperm), the reproduction process begins. (78)

zygote   A single cell formed through fertilization. (78)

in vitro fertilization   Conception outside the body. (78)

phenylketonuria   A genetic disorder in which the individual cannot properly metabolize protein. Phenylketonuria is

now easily detected, but if left untreated, mental retardation and hyperactivity result. (80)

Down syndrome   The most common genetically transmitted form of mental retardation is caused by the presence of an extra (47th) chromosome. (80)

sickle-cell anemia   Occurs most often in Blacks that is a genetic disorder affecting the red blood cells. (80)

Klinefelter syndrome   A genetic disorder in which males have an extra X chromosome, making them XXY instead of XY. (80)

Turner syndrome   A genetic disorder in which females are missing an X chromosome, making them XO instead of XX. (80)

XYY syndrome   A genetic disorder in which the male has an extra Y chromosome. (80)

amniocentesis A prenatal medical procedure in which a sample of amniotic fluid is withdrawn by syringe and tested to discover if the fetus is suffering from any chromosomal or metabolic disorders. (80)

ultrasound sonography A prenatal medical procedure in which high-frequency sound waves are directed into the pregnant woman's abdomen. (81)

chorionic villus test A prenatal medical procedure in which a small sample of the placenta is removed at some point between the 8th and 11th week of pregnancy. (81)

maternal blood test (Alpha-fetoprotein test—AFP) a prenatal diagnostic technique that is used to assess blood alphaprotein level, which is associated with neural tube defects. (83)

dominant-recessive genes principle If one gene of the pair is dominant and one is recessive (goes back or recedes), the dominant gene exerts its effect, overriding the potential influence of the other, recessive gene. A recessive gene exerts its influence only if the two genes of a pair are both recessive. (84)

polygenic inheritance A genetic principle describing the interaction of many genes to produce a particular characteristic. (84)

genotype The person's genetic heritage, the actual genetic material. (84)

phenotype The way an individual's genotype is expressed in observed and measurable characteristics. (84)

reaction range Used to describe the range of phenotypes for each genotype, suggesting the importance of an environment's restrictiveness or enrichment. (85)

canalization Describes the narrow path or developmental course that certain characteristics take. Apparently, preservative forces help to protect or buffer a person from environmental extremes. (86)

behavior genetics The branch of genetics that is concerned with the degree and nature of behavior's hereditary basis. (86)

twin study When the behavior of identical twins is compared with the behavior of fraternal twins. (86)

identical twins (Called "monozygotic" twins) develop from a single fertilized egg that splits into two genetically identical replicas, each of which becomes a person. (86)

fraternal twins (Called "dizygotic" twins) develop from separate eggs, making them genetically less similar than identical twins. (86)

adoption study Investigators seek to discover whether the behavior and psychological characteristics of adopted children are more like their adoptive parents, who provided a home environment, or their biological parents, who contributed their heredity. (86)

passive genotype-environment interactions When parents who are genetically related to the child provide a rearing environment for the child. (87)

evocative genotype-environment interactions When a child's genotype elicits certain types of physical and social environments. (89)

active (niche-picking) genotype environment interactions When children seek out environments they find compatible and stimulating. "Niche-picking" means finding a niche or setting that is especially suited to the child's abilities. (89)

shared environmental influences Children's common experiences, such as their parents' personalities and intellectual orientation, the family's social class, and the neighborhood in which they live. (89)

nonshared environmental influences The child's own unique experiences, both within the family and outside the family, that are not shared with another sibling. (89)

Morisot, The Cradle, detail.

C H A P T E R

4

Prenatal Development and Birth

*The history of man for nine months
preceding his birth would, probably, be
far more interesting, and contain events
of greater moment than all three score
and ten years that follow it.*

—Samuel Taylor Coleridge

*What web is this
Of will be, is, and was?*

—Jorge Luis Borges

IMAGES OF LIFE-SPAN DEVELOPMENT

Jim and Sara, an Expectant Couple

Although Jim and Sara did not plan to have a baby, they did not take precautions to prevent it, and it was not long before Sara was pregnant (Colt, 1991). Jim and Sara read the popular pregnancy book *What to Expect When You're Expecting* (Eisenberg, Murkoff, & Hathaway, 1989). They found a nurse-midwife they liked and invented a pet name—Bibinello—for the fetus. They signed up for birth preparation classes, and each Friday night for 8 weeks they faithfully practiced simulated contractions. They drew up a birth plan that included their decisions about such matters as the type of care provider they wanted to use, the birth setting they wanted, and various aspects of labor and birth. They moved into a larger apartment so the baby could have its own room and spent weekends browsing through garage sales and second-hand stores to find good prices on baby furniture—a crib, a high chair, a stroller, a changing table, a crib mobile, a swing, a car seat.

Jim and Sara also spent a lot of time talking about Sara's pregnancy, what kind of parents they wanted to be, and what their child might be like. They also discussed what changes in their life the baby would make. One of their concerns was that Sara's maternity leave would only last 6 weeks. If she wanted to stay home longer, she would have to quit her job, something she and Jim were not sure they could afford. These are among the many questions that expectant couples face.

PREVIEW

This chapter includes further information about expectant parents and chronicles the truly remarkable developments from conception through birth. Imagine . . . at one time you were an organism floating around in a sea of fluid in your mother's womb. Let's now explore what your development was like from the time you were conceived through the time you were born.

PRENATAL DEVELOPMENT

Imagine how you came to be. Out of hundreds of eggs and millions of sperm, one egg and one sperm united to produce you. Had the union of sperm and egg come a day or even an hour earlier or later, you might have been very different—maybe even of the opposite sex. Remember from chapter 3 that conception occurs when a single sperm cell from the male unites with an ovum (egg) in the female's fallopian tube in a process called "fertilization." Remember also that the fertilized egg is called a "zygote." By the time the zygote ends its 3- to 4-day journey through the fallopian tube and reaches the uterus, it has divided into approximately 12 to 16 cells.

The Course of Prenatal Development

Prenatal development is commonly divided into three main periods: germinal, embryonic, and fetal.

The Germinal Period

The **germinal period** *is the period of prenatal development that takes place in the first 2 weeks after conception. It includes the creation of the zygote, continued cell division, and the attachment of the zygote to the uterine wall.* By approximately 1 week after conception, the zygote is composed of 100 to 150 cells. The differentiation of cells has already commenced as inner and outer layers of the organism are formed. The **blastocyst** *is the inner*

FIGURE 4.1

Significant developments in the germinal period.

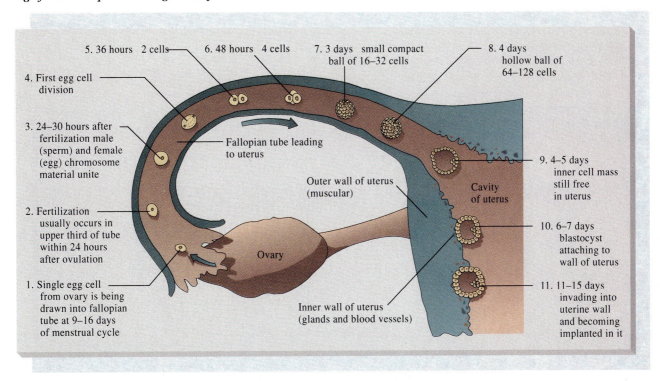

5. 36 hours 2 cells

6. 48 hours 4 cells

7. 3 days small compact ball of 16–32 cells

8. 4 days hollow ball of 64–128 cells

4. First egg cell division

3. 24–30 hours after fertilization male (sperm) and female (egg) chromosome material unite

Fallopian tube leading to uterus

Outer wall of uterus (muscular)

Cavity of uterus

9. 4–5 days inner cell mass still free in uterus

2. Fertilization usually occurs in upper third of tube within 24 hours after ovulation

Ovary

10. 6–7 days blastocyst attaching to wall of uterus

1. Single egg cell from ovary is being drawn into fallopian tube at 9–16 days of menstrual cycle

Inner wall of uterus (glands and blood vessels)

11. 11–15 days invading into uterine wall and becoming implanted in it

layer of cells that develops during the germinal period. These cells later develop into the embryo. The **trophoblast** *is the outer layer of cells that develops during the germinal period. It later provides nutrition and support for the embryo.* **Implantation,** *the attachment of the zygote to the uterine wall, takes place about 10 days after conception.* Figure 4.1 illustrates some of the most significant developments during the germinal period.

The Embryonic Period

The **embryonic period** *is the period of prenatal development that occurs from 2 to 8 weeks after conception. During the embryonic period, the rate of cell differentiation intensifies, support systems for the cells form, and organs appear.* As the zygote attaches to the uterine wall, its cells form two layers. The mass of cells is now called an "embryo." The embryo's **endoderm** *is the inner layer of cells, which will develop into the digestive and respiratory systems.* The outer layer of cells is divided into two parts. The **ectoderm** *is the outermost layer, which will become the nervous system, sensory receptors (ear, nose, and eyes, for example), and skin parts (hair and nails, for example).* The **mesoderm** *is the middle layer, which will become the circulatory system, bones, muscle, excretory system, and reproductive system.* Every body part eventually develops from these three layers. The endoderm primarily produces internal body parts, the mesoderm primarily produces parts that surround the internal areas, and the ectoderm primarily produces surface parts.

*If I could have watched you grow
As a magical mother might,
If I could have seen through my
magical transparent belly,
There would have been such
ripening within . . .*

—Anne Sexton, *Little Girl,
My String Bean, My Lovely Woman*

As the embryo's three layers form, life-support systems for the embryo mature and develop rapidly. These life-support systems include the placenta, the umbilical cord, and the amnion. The **placenta** *is a life-support system that consists of a disk-shaped group of tissues in which small blood vessels from the mother and the offspring intertwine but do not join.* The **umbilical cord** *is a life-support system, containing two arteries and one vein, that connects the baby to the placenta.* Very small molecules—oxygen, water, salt, food from the mother's blood, and carbon dioxide and digestive wastes from the embryo's blood—pass from mother to infant and from infant to mother. Large molecules cannot pass through the placental wall; these include red blood cells and harmful substances such as most bacteria, maternal wastes, and hormones. The mechanisms that govern the transfer of substances across the placental barrier are complex and are still not entirely understood (Rosenblith, 1992). Figure 4.2 provides an

FIGURE 4.2

The placenta and the umbilical cord. Maternal blood flows through the uterine arteries to the spaces housing the placenta and returns through the uterine veins to maternal circulation. Fetal blood flows through the umbilical arteries into the capillaries of the placenta and returns through the umbilical veins to the fetal circulation. The exchange of materials takes place across the layer separating the maternal and fetal blood supplies, so the bloods never come into contact. Note: *The area bound by the square is enlarged in the right half of the illustration. Arrows indicate the direction of blood flow.*

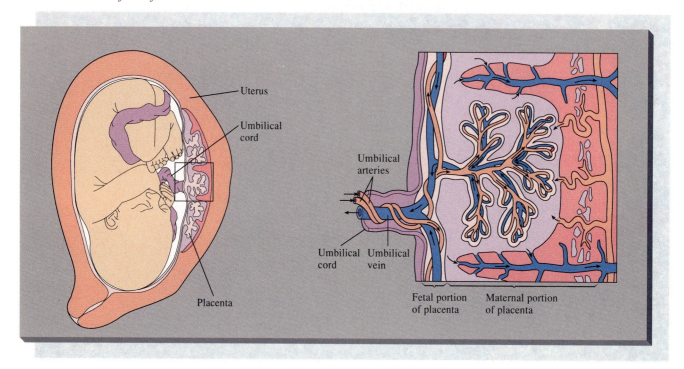

illustration of the placenta, the umbilical cord, and the nature of blood flow in the expectant mother and developing child in the uterus. The **amnion,** *a bag or envelope that contains a clear fluid in which the developing embryo floats, is another important life-support system.* Like the placenta and umbilical cord, the amnion develops from the fertilized egg, not from the mother's own body. At approximately 16 weeks, the kidneys of the fetus begin to produce urine. This fetal urine remains the main source of the amniotic fluid until the third trimester, when some of the fluid is excreted from the lungs of the growing fetus. Although the volume of the amniotic fluid increases tenfold from the 12th to the 40th week of pregnancy, it is also removed in various ways. Some is swallowed by the fetus, and some is absorbed through the umbilical cord and the membranes covering the placenta. The amniotic fluid is important in providing an environment that is temperature and humidity controlled, as well as shockproof.

> *The history of man for nine months preceding his birth would, probably, be far more interesting, and contain events of greater moment than all three score and ten years that follow it.*
>
> —Samuel Taylor Coleridge

Before most women even know they are pregnant, some important embryonic developments take place. In the 3rd week, the neural tube that eventually becomes the spinal cord forms. At about 21 days, eyes begin to appear, and at 24 days the cells for the heart begin to differentiate. During the 4th week, the first appearance of the urogenital system is apparent, and arm and leg buds emerge. Four chambers of the heart take shape, and blood vessels surface. From the 5th to the 8th week, arms and legs differentiate further; at this time, the face starts to form but still is not very recognizable. The intestinal tract develops and the facial structures fuse. At 8 weeks, the developing organism weighs about one-thirtieth of an ounce and is just over 1 inch long. **Organogenesis** *is the process of organ formation that takes place during the first 2 months of prenatal development.* When organs are being formed, they are especially vulnerable to environmental changes. Later in the chapter, we will describe the environmental hazards that are harmful during organogenesis.

The Fetal Period

The **fetal period** *is the prenatal period of development that begins 2 months after conception and lasts for 7 months, on the average.* Growth and development continue their dramatic course during this time. Three months after conception, the fetus is about 3 inches long and weighs about 1 ounce. It has become active,

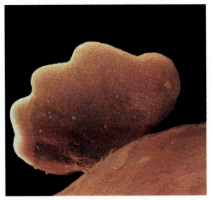

The hand of an embryo at 6 weeks.

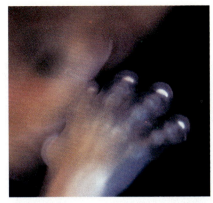

Fingers and thumb with pads seen at 8 weeks.

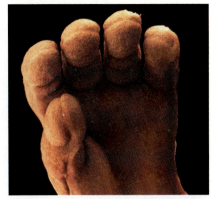

The finger pads have regressed by 13 weeks.

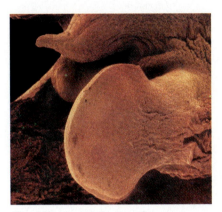

Toe ridges emerge after 7 weeks.

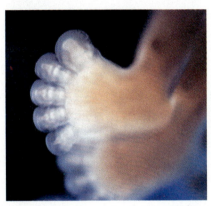

Toe pads and the emerging heel are visible by 9 weeks.

The toe pads have regressed by 13 weeks.

The fingers and toes form rapidly during the first trimester. After 13 weeks of pregnancy, the hands and feet already look remarkably similar to those of a mature human although they are still smaller than an adult's fingernail.

moving its arms and legs, opening and closing its mouth, and moving its head. The face, forehead, eyelids, nose, and chin are distinguishable, as are the upper arms, lower arms, hands, and lower limbs, and the genitals can be identified as male or female. By the end of the 4th month, the fetus has grown to 5½ inches in length and weighs about 4 ounces. At this time, a growth spurt occurs in the body's lower parts. Prenatal reflexes are stronger; arm and leg movements can be felt for the first time by the mother.

> *So the riders of the darkness pass on their circuits: the luminous island of the self trembles and waits, waits for us all, my friends, where the sea's big brush recolors the dying lives, and the unborn smiles.*
>
> —Lawrence Durrell

By the end of the 5th month, the fetus is about 10 to 12 inches long and weighs ½ to 1 pound. Structures of the skin have formed—toenails and fingernails, for example. The fetus is more active, showing a preference for a particular position in the womb. By the end of the 6th month, the fetus is about 14 inches long and already has gained another half pound to a pound. The eyes and eyelids are completely formed, and a fine layer of hair covers the head. A grasping reflex is present, and irregular breathing occurs. By the end of the 7th month, the fetus is 14 to 17 inches long and has gained another pound, now weighing 2½ to 3 pounds. During the 8th and 9th months, the fetus grows longer and gains substantial weight—about another 4 pounds. At birth, the average American baby weighs 7 to 7½ pounds and is about 20 inches long. In the last 2 months, fatty tissues develop and the functioning of various organ systems—heart and kidneys, for example—steps up.

We have described a number of developments in the germinal, embryonic, and fetal periods. An overview of some of the main developments we have discussed and some more specific changes in prenatal development are presented in figure 4.3.

Miscarriage and Abortion

A miscarriage, or spontaneous abortion, happens when pregnancy ends before the developing organism is mature enough to survive outside the womb. The embryo separates from the uterine wall and is expelled by the uterus. About 15 to 20 percent of all pregnancies end in a spontaneous abortion, most in the first 2 to 3 months. Many spontaneous abortions occur without the mother's knowledge, and many involve an embryo or fetus that was not developing normally.

FIGURE 4.3

The three trimesters of prenatal development.

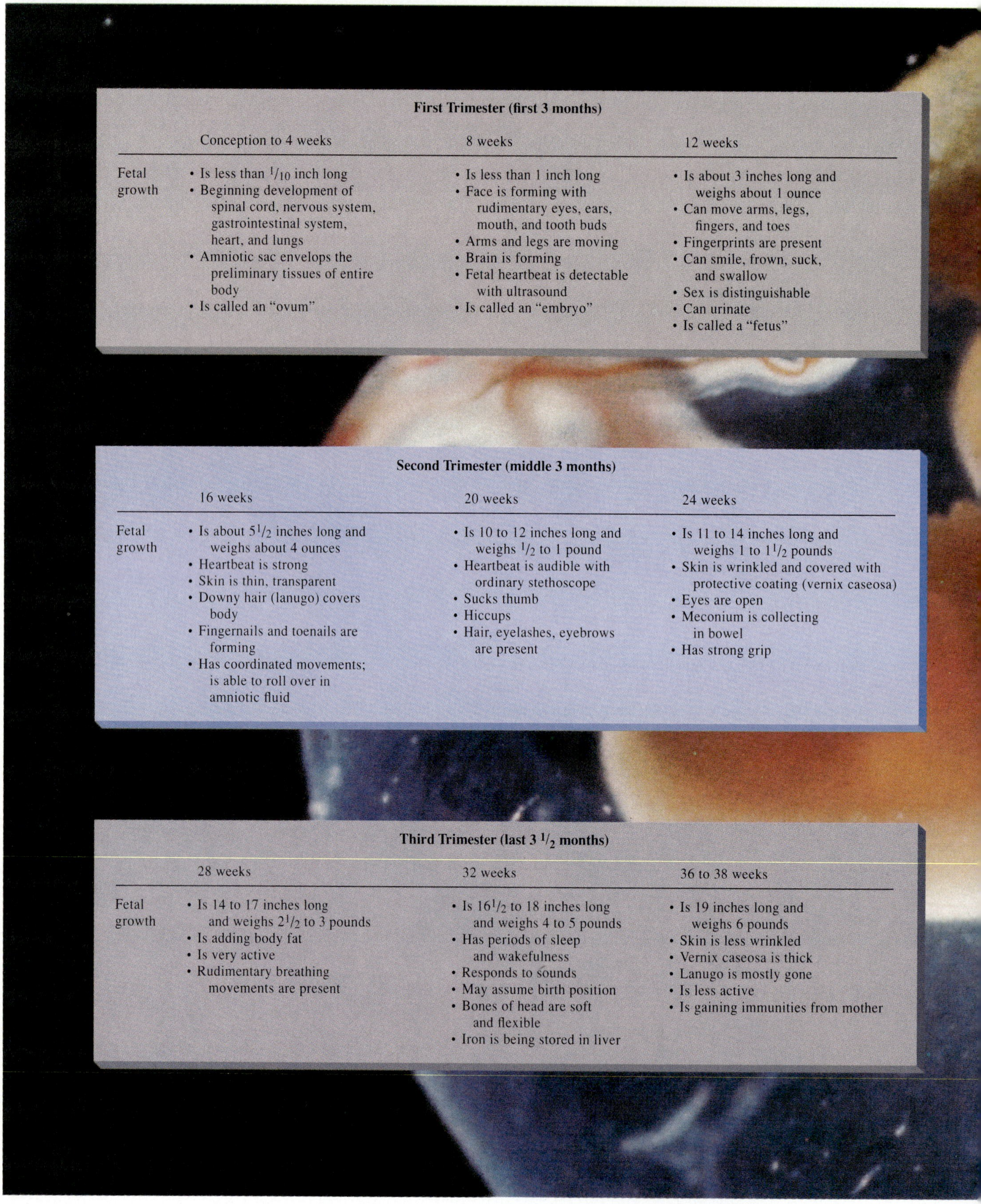

First Trimester (first 3 months)

	Conception to 4 weeks	8 weeks	12 weeks
Fetal growth	• Is less than $1/10$ inch long • Beginning development of spinal cord, nervous system, gastrointestinal system, heart, and lungs • Amniotic sac envelops the preliminary tissues of entire body • Is called an "ovum"	• Is less than 1 inch long • Face is forming with rudimentary eyes, ears, mouth, and tooth buds • Arms and legs are moving • Brain is forming • Fetal heartbeat is detectable with ultrasound • Is called an "embryo"	• Is about 3 inches long and weighs about 1 ounce • Can move arms, legs, fingers, and toes • Fingerprints are present • Can smile, frown, suck, and swallow • Sex is distinguishable • Can urinate • Is called a "fetus"

Second Trimester (middle 3 months)

	16 weeks	20 weeks	24 weeks
Fetal growth	• Is about $5^1/2$ inches long and weighs about 4 ounces • Heartbeat is strong • Skin is thin, transparent • Downy hair (lanugo) covers body • Fingernails and toenails are forming • Has coordinated movements; is able to roll over in amniotic fluid	• Is 10 to 12 inches long and weighs $1/2$ to 1 pound • Heartbeat is audible with ordinary stethoscope • Sucks thumb • Hiccups • Hair, eyelashes, eyebrows are present	• Is 11 to 14 inches long and weighs 1 to $1^1/2$ pounds • Skin is wrinkled and covered with protective coating (vernix caseosa) • Eyes are open • Meconium is collecting in bowel • Has strong grip

Third Trimester (last 3 $1/2$ months)

	28 weeks	32 weeks	36 to 38 weeks
Fetal growth	• Is 14 to 17 inches long and weighs $2^1/2$ to 3 pounds • Is adding body fat • Is very active • Rudimentary breathing movements are present	• Is $16^1/2$ to 18 inches long and weighs 4 to 5 pounds • Has periods of sleep and wakefulness • Responds to sounds • May assume birth position • Bones of head are soft and flexible • Iron is being stored in liver	• Is 19 inches long and weighs 6 pounds • Skin is less wrinkled • Vernix caseosa is thick • Lanugo is mostly gone • Is less active • Is gaining immunities from mother

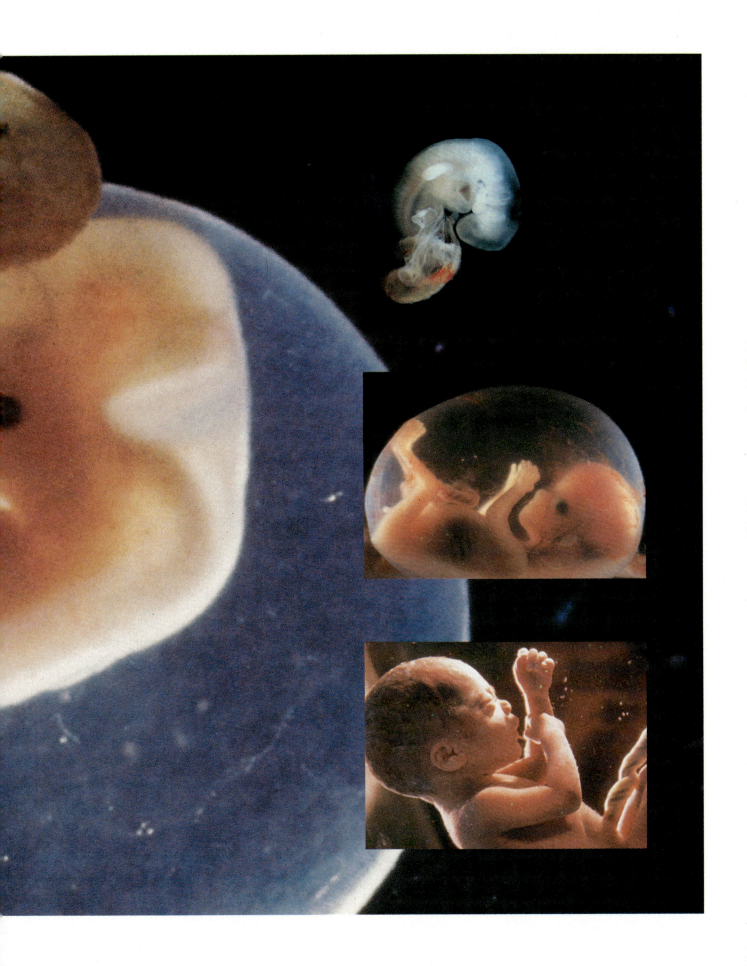

LIFE-SPAN PRACTICAL KNOWLEDGE 4.1

What To Expect When You're Expecting

(1989, 2nd ed.) by Arlene Eisenberg, Heidi Murkoff, and Sandee Hathaway. New York: Workman.

What To Expect When You're Expecting is a month-by-month, step-by-step guide to pregnancy and childbirth. The authors are a mother-and-daughters team, and the book was the result of the fact that the second author (Heidi Eisenberg Murkoff) had an unnecessarily worry-filled pregnancy. The book tries to put expectant parents' normal fears into perspective by giving them comprehensive information and helping them to enjoy this transition in their lives.

This is an excellent book for expectant parents. It is reassuring, thorough, and filled with charts and lists that make understanding pregnancy an easier task. One of the book's enthusiasts said that having access to this book is like having an experienced mother nearby whom you can always call with questions like, "Hey, did you get leg cramps in the fifth month of pregnancy?"

Early in history, it was believed that a woman could be frightened into a miscarriage by loud thunder or a jolt in a carriage. Today, we recognize that this is highly unlikely; the developing organism is well protected. Abnormalities of the reproductive tract and viral or bacterial infections are more likely to cause spontaneous abortions. In some cases, severe traumas may be at fault.

Critical Thinking

What are the arguments for and against abortion? Where do you stand on this sensitive ethical issue? Why?

Deliberate termination of pregnancy is a complex issue, medically, psychologically, socially, and legally (Schaff, 1992). Carrying a baby to term may affect a woman's health, the woman's pregnancy may have resulted from rape or incest, the woman may not be married, or perhaps she is poor and wants to continue her education. Abortion is legal in the United States; in 1973, the Supreme Court ruled that any woman can obtain an abortion during the first 6 months of pregnancy, a decision that continues to generate ethical objections from antiabortion forces. The Supreme Court also has ruled that abortion in the first trimester is solely the decision of the mother and her doctor. Court cases also have added the point that the baby's father and the parents of minor girls do not have any say during this time frame. In the second trimester, states can legislate the time and method of abortion for protection of the mother's health. In the third trimester, the fetus's right to live is a critical concern.

What are the psychological effects of having an abortion? In 1989, a research review panel appointed by the American Psychological Association examined more than 100 investigations of the psychological effects of abortion. The panel's conclusions follow. Unwanted pregnancies are stressful for most women. However, it is common for women to report feelings of relief as well as feelings of guilt after an abortion. These feelings are usually mild and tend to diminish rapidly over time without adversely affecting the woman's ability to function. Abortion is more stressful for women who have a history of serious emotional problems and who are not given support by family or friends. According to the American Psychological Association report, only a small percentage of women fall into these high-risk categories. If an abortion is performed, it should involve not only competent medical care but care for the woman's psychological needs as well.

Teratology and Hazards to Prenatal Development

Some expectant mothers carefully tiptoe about in the belief that everything they do and feel has a direct effect on their unborn child. Others behave casually, assuming that their experiences will have little effect. The truth lies somewhere between these two extremes. Although living in a protected, comfortable environment, the fetus is not totally immune to the larger world surrounding the mother. The environment can affect the child in many well-documented ways. Thousands of babies born deformed or mentally retarded every year are the result of events that occurred in the mother's life, as early as 1 or 2 months before conception.

Teratology

A **teratogen,** (the word comes from the Greek word *tera* meaning "monster") *is any agent that causes a birth defect. The field of study that investigates the causes of birth defects is called "teratology."* A specific teratogen (such as a drug) usually does not cause a specific birth defect (such as malformation of the legs). So

FIGURE 4.4

Teratogens and the timing of their effects on prenatal development. *The danger of structural defects caused by teratogens is greatest early in embryonic development. This is the period of organogenesis, and it lasts for several months. Damage caused by teratogens during this period is represented by the dark-colored bars. Later assaults by teratogens typically occur during the fetal period and, instead of causing structural damage, are more likely to stunt growth or cause problems of organ function.*

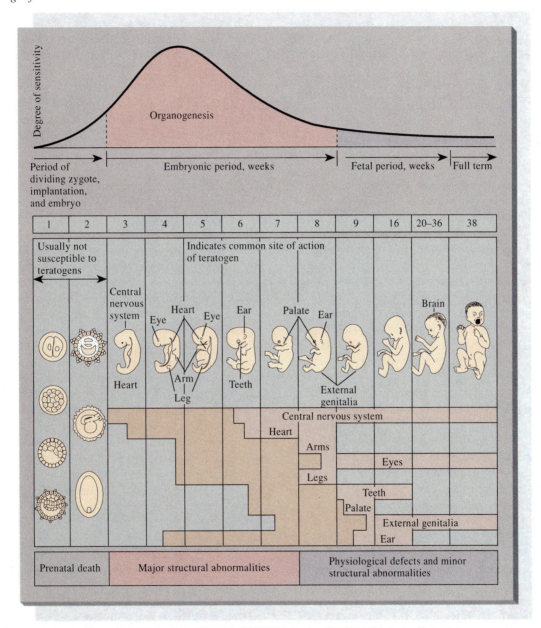

From Keith L. Moore, *The Developing Human: Clinically Oriented,* 4th ed. Copyright © 1988 W. B. Saunders, Philadelphia, PA. Reprinted by permission.

many teratogens exist that practically every fetus is exposed to at least some teratogens. For this reason, it is difficult to determine which teratogen causes which birth defect. In addition, it may take a long time for the effects of a teratogen to show up; only about half of all potential effects appear at birth.

Despite the many unknowns about teratogens, scientists have discovered the identity of some of these hazards to prenatal development and the particular point of fetal development at which they do their greatest damage (Little, 1992). As figure 4.4 shows, sensitivity to teratogens begins about 3 weeks after conception. The probability of a structural defect is greatest early in the embryonic period, because this is when organs are being formed. After organogenesis is complete, teratogens are less likely to cause anatomical defects. Exposure later, during the fetal period, is more likely to stunt growth or to create problems in the way organs function. The precision of organogenesis is evident; teratologists point out that the brain is most vulnerable at 15 to 25 days after conception, the eye at 24 to 40 days, the heart at 20 to 40 days, and the legs at 24 to 36 days.

In the following sections, we will explore how certain environmental agents influence prenatal development: maternal diseases and conditions, the mother's age, nutrition, emotional states and stress, drugs, and environmental hazards.

Maternal Diseases and Conditions

Maternal diseases or infections can produce defects by crossing the placental barrier, or they can cause damage during the birth process itself. Rubella (German measles) is a maternal disease that can damage prenatal development. A rubella outbreak in 1964–1965 resulted in 30,000 prenatal and neonatal (newborn) deaths, and more than 20,000 infants were born with malformations, including mental retardation, blindness, deafness, and heart problems. The greatest damage occurs when mothers contract rubella in the 3rd and 4th weeks of pregnancy, although infection during the 2nd month is also damaging. Elaborate preventive efforts now ensure that rubella will never again have the disastrous effects it had in the mid-1960s. A vaccine that prevents German measles is routinely administered to children, and women who plan to have children should have a blood test before they become pregnant to determine if they are immune to the disease.

Syphilis (a sexually transmitted disease) is more damaging later in prenatal development—4 months or more after conception. Rather than affecting organogenesis, as rubella does, syphilis damages organs after they have formed. Damage includes eye lesions, which can cause blindness, and skin lesions. When syphilis is present at birth, other problems involving the central nervous system and gastrointestinal tract can develop. Most states require that pregnant women be given a blood test to detect the presence of syphilis.

Another infection that has received widespread attention recently is genital herpes. Newborns contract this virus when they are delivered through the birth canal of a mother with genital herpes. About one-third of babies delivered through an infected birth canal die; another one-fourth become brain damaged. If a pregnant woman detects an active case of genital herpes close to her delivery date, a cesarean section can be performed (in which the infant is delivered through the mother's abdomen) to keep the virus from infecting the newborn (Byer & Shainberg, 1991).

The importance of women's health to the health of their offspring is nowhere better exemplified than when the mother has acquired immune deficiency syndrome (AIDS). As the number of women with AIDS grows, more children are born exposed to and infected with AIDS (*The Health of America's Children*, 1992; Whalen & Henker, 1994; Wolters & others, 1994).

AIDS was the eighth leading cause of death among children from 1 to 4 years of age in 1989. Through the end of 1991, AIDS had been diagnosed in 3,123 children younger than 13. The number of pediatric AIDS cases does not include as many as 10,000 children infected with HIV who have not yet suffered the full effects of AIDS. Black and Latino children make up 83 percent of all pediatric AIDS cases. The majority of mothers who transmit HIV to their offspring were infected through intravenous drug use or heterosexual contact with injecting drug users.

There are three ways a mother with AIDS can infect her offspring: (1) during gestation, across the placenta; (2) during delivery, through contact with maternal blood or fluids; and (3) postpartum, through breast-feeding. Approximately one-third of infants born to infected mothers will ultimately become infected with the HIV virus themselves (Caldwell & Rogers, 1991). Babies born to AIDS-infected mothers can be (1) infected and symptomatic (showing AIDS symptoms), (2) infected but asymptomatic (not showing AIDS symptoms), or (3) not infected at all. An infant who is infected and asymptomatic may still develop HIV symptoms up until 15 months of age.

The Mother's Age

When the mother's age is considered in terms of possible harmful effects on the fetus and infant, two time periods are of special interest: adolescence and the thirties and beyond. Approximately one of every five births is to an adolescent; in some urban areas, the figure reaches as high as one in every two births. Infants born to adolescents are often premature. The mortality rate of infants born to adolescent mothers is double that of infants born to mothers in their twenties. Although such figures probably reflect the mother's immature reproductive system, they also may involve poor nutrition, lack of prenatal care, and low socioeconomic status. Prenatal care decreases the probability that a child born to an adolescent girl will have physical problems. However, adolescents are the least likely of women in all age groups to obtain prenatal assistance from clinics, pediatricians, and health services.

Increasingly, women are seeking to establish their careers before beginning a family, delaying childbearing until their thirties. Down syndrome, a form of mental retardation, is related to the mother's age. A baby with Down syndrome rarely is born to a mother under the age of 30, but the risk increases after the mother reaches 30. By age 40, the probability is slightly over 1 in 100 and, by age 50, it is almost 1 in 10. The risk also is higher before age 18.

Women also have more difficulty becoming pregnant after the age of 30 (Toth, 1991). In one investigation, the clients of a French fertility clinic all had husbands who were sterile (Schwartz & Mayaux, 1982). To increase their chances of having a child, they were artificially inseminated once a month for 1 year. Each woman had 12 chances to become pregnant. Seventy-five percent of the women in their twenties became pregnant, 62 percent of the women 31 to 35 years old became pregnant, and only 54 percent of the women over 35 years old became pregnant.

We still have much to learn about the role of the mother's age in pregnancy and childbirth. As women remain active, exercise regularly, and are careful about their nutrition, their reproductive systems may remain healthier at older ages than was thought possible in the past. Indeed, as we will see next, the mother's nutrition influences prenatal development.

Nutrition

A developing fetus depends completely on its mother for nutrition, which comes from the mother's blood. Nutritional status is not determined by any specific aspect of diet; among the important factors are the total number of calories and the appropriate levels of protein, vitamins, and minerals. The mother's nutrition even influences her ability to reproduce. In extreme instances of malnutrition, women stop menstruating, thus precluding conception, and children born to malnourished mothers are more likely to be malformed (Rosso, 1992).

One investigation of Iowa mothers documents the important role of nutrition in prenatal development and birth (Jeans, Smith, & Stearns, 1955). The diets of 400 pregnant women were studied, and the status of their newborns was assessed. The mothers with the poorest diets were more likely to have offspring who weighed the least, had the least vitality, were born prematurely, or died. In another investigation, diet supplements given to malnourished mothers during pregnancy improved the performance of their offspring during the first 3 years of life (Werner, 1979).

Emotional States and Stress

Tales abound about the way a mother's emotional state affects the fetus. For centuries, it was thought that frightening experiences—a severe thunderstorm or a family member's death—would leave birthmarks on the child or affect the child in more serious ways. Today, we believe that the mother's stress can be transmitted to the fetus, but we have gone beyond thinking that these happenings are somehow magically produced (Parker & Barrett, 1992). We now know that when a pregnant woman experiences intense fears, anxieties, and other emotions, physiological changes occur—among them, increased respiration and glandular secretions. For example, producing adrenaline in response to fear restricts blood flow to the uterine area and may deprive the fetus of adequate oxygen.

Nothing vivifies, and nothing kills, like the emotions.

—Joseph Roux,
Meditations of a Parish Priest, 1886

The mother's emotional state during pregnancy can influence the birth process, too. An emotionally distraught mother might have irregular contractions and a more difficult labor, which can cause irregularities in the baby's oxygen supply or tend to produce irregularities after birth. Babies born after extended labor also may adjust more slowly to their world and be more irritable. One investigation revealed a connection between the mother's anxiety during pregnancy and the newborn's condition (Ottinger & Simmons, 1964). In this study, mothers answered a questionnaire about their anxiety every 3 months during pregnancy. When the babies were born, the babies' weights, activity levels, and crying were assessed. The babies of the more anxious mothers cried more before feedings and were more active than the babies born to the less anxious mothers.

Drugs

How do drugs affect prenatal development? Some pregnant women take drugs, smoke tobacco, and drink alcohol without thinking about the possible effects on the fetus. Occasionally a rash of deformed babies are born, bringing to light the damage drugs can do to a developing fetus. This happened in 1961, when many pregnant women took a popular tranquilizer, thalidomide, to alleviate their morning sickness. In adults, the effects of thalidomide are mild; in embryos, however, they are devastating. Not all infants were affected in the same way. If the mother took thalidomide on day 26 (probably before she knew she was pregnant), an arm might not grow. If she took the drug 2 days later, the arm might not grow past the elbow. The thalidomide tragedy shocked the medical community and parents into the stark realization that the mother does not have to be a chronic drug user for the fetus to be harmed. Taking the wrong drug at the wrong time is enough to physically handicap the offspring for life.

Heavy drinking by pregnant women can also be devastating to offspring (Coles, Platzman, & Smith, 1991; Jensen & Nanson, 1993). **Fetal alcohol syndrome (FAS)** *is a cluster of abnormalities that appear in the offspring of mothers who drink alcohol heavily during pregnancy.* The abnormalities include facial deformities and defective limbs, face, and heart. Most of these children are below average in intelligence, and some are mentally retarded. Although no serious malformations such as those produced by FAS are found in infants born to mothers who are moderate drinkers, in one investigation infants whose mothers drank moderately during pregnancy (for example, one to two drinks a day) were less attentive and alert, with the effects still present at 4 years of age (Streissguth & others, 1984).

Expectant mothers are becoming more aware that alcohol and pregnancy do not mix. In a recent study of 1,712 pregnant women in 21 states, the prevalence of alcohol consumption by pregnant women declined from 32 percent in 1985 to 20 percent in 1988 (Serdula & others, 1991). The declines in drinking were greatest among the oldest and most educated pregnant women—19 percent of pregnant college graduates drank in 1988, a decline from the 41 percent rate in 1985. However, no decline in drinking was found among the least educated and youngest pregnant women. The proportion of drinkers

FIGURE 4.5

The effects of smoking by expectant mothers on fetal weight. *Throughout prenatal development, the fetuses of expectant mothers who smoke weigh less than the fetuses of expectant mothers who do not smoke.*

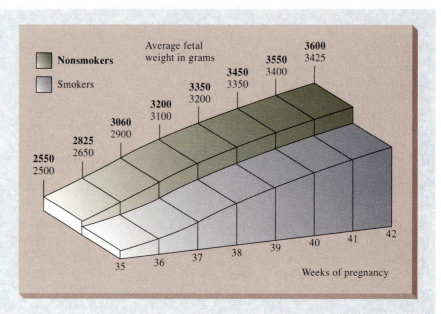

among pregnant women with only a high school education stayed at 23 percent from 1985 to 1988.

Cigarette smoking by pregnant women can also adversely influence prenatal development, birth, and postnatal development (Bloch, 1992; Chasnoff, 1991; Fried & O'Connell, 1991; Johnson & others, 1993; Streissguth & others, 1991). Fetal and neonatal deaths are higher among smoking mothers; also prevalent are a higher incidence of preterm births and lower birthweights (see figure 4.5). In one investigation, prenatal exposure to cigarette smoking was related to poorer language and cognitive development at 4 years of age (Fried & Watkinson, 1990). In another study, mothers who smoked during pregnancy had infants who were awake more on a consistent basis—an expected finding, since the active ingredient in cigarettes is the stimulant nicotine (Landesman-Dwyer & Sackett, 1983). Respiratory problems and sudden infant death syndrome (also known as crib death) are also more common among the offspring of mothers who smoked during pregnancy (Schoendorf & Kiely, 1992). Intervention programs designed to get pregnant women to stop smoking are successful in reducing some of smoking's negative effects on offspring, especially in raising their birthweights (Sexton & Hebel, 1984; Vorhees & Mollnow, 1987).

Critical Thinking

How can we reduce the number of offspring born to drug dependent mothers? If you had 100 million dollars to spend to help remedy this problem, what would you do?

Marijuana use by pregnant women also has detrimental effects on a developing child (Day, 1991). Marijuana use by pregnant mothers is associated with increased tremors and startles among newborns (Fried, Watkinson, & Dillon, 1987) and poorer verbal and memory development at 4 years of age (Fried & Watkinson, 1990).

It is well documented that infants whose mothers are addicted to heroin show several behavioral difficulties (Hans, 1989; Hutchings & Fifer, 1986). The young infants of these mothers are addicted and show withdrawal symptoms characteristic of opiate abstinence, such as tremors, irritability, abnormal crying, disturbed sleep, and impaired motor control. Behavioral problems are still often present at the first birthday, and attention deficits may appear later in the child's development.

With the increased use of cocaine in the United States, there is growing concern about its effects on the embryos, fetuses, and infants of pregnant cocaine users (Davis & Mercier, 1992). Cocaine use during pregnancy has recently attracted considerable attention because of concerns about possible harm to the developing embryo and fetus (Ahl, 1993; Chasnoff & others, 1992; Hawley, 1993; Scafidi & Wheenclen, 1993; Wootton & Miller, 1994). The most consistent finding is that infants born to cocaine abusers have reduced birthweight and length (Chasnoff & others, 1989). There are increased frequencies of congenital abnormalities in the offspring of cocaine users during pregnancy, but other factors in the drug addict's life-style, such as malnutrition and other substance abuse, may be responsible for the congenital abnormalities (Eyler, Behnke, &

TABLE 4.1

Drug Use During Pregnancy

Drug	Effects on Fetus and Offspring	Safe Use of the Drug
Alcohol	Small amounts increase risk of spontaneous abortion. Moderate amounts (1–2 drinks a day) are associated with poor attention in infancy. Heavy drinking can lead to fetal alcohol syndrome. Some experts believe that even low to moderate amounts, especially in the first 3 months of pregnancy, increase the risk of FAS.	Avoid use.
Nicotine	Heavy smoking is associated with low-birthweight babies, which means the babies may have more health problems than other infants. Smoking may be especially harmful in the second half of pregnancy.	Avoid use.
Tranquilizers	Taken during the first 3 months of pregnancy, they may cause cleft palate or other congenital malformations.	Avoid use if you might become pregnant and during early pregnancy. Use only under a doctor's supervision.
Barbiturates	Mothers who take large doses may have babies who are addicted. Babies may have tremors, restlessness, and irritability.	Use only under a doctor's supervision.
Amphetamines	They may cause birth defects.	Use only under a doctor's supervision.
Cocaine	Cocaine may cause drug dependency and withdrawal symptoms at birth, as well as physical and mental problems, especially if the mother uses cocaine in the first 3 months of pregnancy. There is a higher risk of hypertension, heart problems, developmental retardation, and learning difficulties.	Avoid use.
Marijuana	It may cause a variety of birth defects and is associated with low birth-weight and height.	Avoid use.

Source: Modified from the National Institute on Drug Abuse.

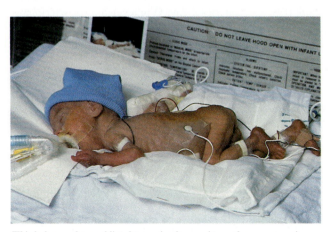

This baby was born addicted to cocaine because its mother was a cocaine addict. Researchers have found that the offspring of women who use cocaine during pregnancy often have hypertension and heart damage. Many of these infants face a childhood full of medical problems.

Stewart, 1990; Little & others, 1989; Stewart, 1990). For example, cocaine users are more likely to smoke cigarettes and marijuana, drink alcohol, and take amphetamines than are cocaine nonusers (Little & others, 1989). Teasing apart these potential influences from the effects of cocaine use itself has not yet been adequately accomplished. Obtaining valid information about the frequency and type of drug use by mothers is also complicated, since many mothers fear prosecution or loss of custody because of their drug use.

A list of the effects of cocaine and of various other drugs, on offspring, and some guidelines for safe use of these drugs, are presented in table 4.1.

Environmental Hazards

Radiation, chemicals, and other hazards in our modern industrial world can endanger the fetus. For instance, radiation can cause a gene mutation, an abrupt but permanent change in genetic material. Chromosomal abnormalities are higher among the offspring of fathers exposed to high levels of radiation in their occupations (Schrag & Dixon, 1985). Radiation from X rays also can affect the developing embryo and fetus, with the most dangerous time being the first several weeks after conception, when women do not yet know they are pregnant.

LIFE-SPAN PRACTICAL KNOWLEDGE 4.2

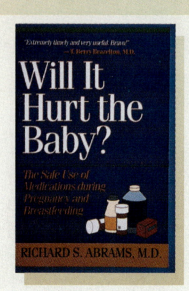

Will It Hurt the Baby?

(1990) by Richard Abrams. Reading, MA: Addison-Wesley.

Will It Hurt the Baby? examines the safe use of medication during pregnancy and breast-feeding. The author is a professor of medicine and pediatrics at the University of Colorado School of Medicine. Abrams describes the trend toward eliminating medication during pregnancy, but believes that in some cases a drug's benefits outweigh its risks. He discusses 15 common medical problems women face during pregnancy, their symptoms, and special concerns about them. He also describes nine environmental and occupational hazards during pregnancy, such as food additives, pesticides, and physical exertion. In a final section of almost 300 pages, hundreds of drugs, from acetaminophen (Tylenol) to zidovudine (AZT), are evaluated.

This is a good reference guide for expectant mothers and breast-feeding mothers. Respected pediatrician T. Berry Brazelton (1990) commented that the book is timely and useful.

It is important for women and their physicians to weigh the risk of an X ray when an actual or potential pregnancy is involved.

Environmental pollutants and toxic wastes are also sources of danger to unborn children. Researchers have found that various hazardous wastes and pesticides cause defects in animals exposed to high doses. Among the dangerous pollutants and wastes are carbon monoxide, mercury, and lead. Some children are exposed to lead because they live in houses where lead-based paint flakes off the walls, or near busy highways, where there are heavy automobile emissions from leaded gasoline. Researchers believe that early exposure to lead affects children's mental development. For example, in one investigation, 2-year-old infants who prenatally had high levels of lead in their umbilical cord blood performed poorly on a test of mental development (Bellinger & others, 1987).

Researchers also have found that the manufacturing chemicals known as PCBs are harmful to prenatal development. In one investigation, the extent to which pregnant women ate PCB-polluted fish from Lake Michigan was examined, and subsequently their newborns were observed (Jacobson & others, 1984). Women who had eaten more PCB-polluted fish were more likely to have smaller, preterm infants who were more likely to react slowly to stimuli. And in one recent study, prenatal exposure to PCBs was associated with problems in visual discrimination and short-term memory in 4-year-old children (Jacobson & others, 1992).

A current environmental concern involves women who spend long hours in front of video display terminals. The fear is that low levels of electromagnetic radiation from the video display terminal adversely affect their offspring. In one investigation, 2,430 telephone operators were studied (Schnorr & others, 1991). Half of the women worked at video display terminals, half did not. During the 4 years of the study, 730 women became pregnant, some more than once, for a total of 876 pregnancies. Over the 4 years, there was no significant difference in miscarriage rates between the two groups. The researchers concluded that working at a video display terminal does not increase miscarriage risk. Critics point out that there was no check for early fetal loss and that all of the women were younger than 34 years of age, so whether the findings hold for early fetal loss and older women will have to await further research. In this study, miscarriages were higher among women who had more than 8 alcoholic drinks per month or smoked more than 20 cigarettes a day. While video display terminals may not be related to miscarriage, they are associated with an increase in a variety of problems involving eye strain and the musculoskeletal system.

Another environmental concern is **toxoplasmosis,** *a mild infection that causes coldlike symptoms or no apparent illness in adults. However, toxoplasmosis can be a teratogen for the unborn baby, causing possible eye defects, brain defects, and premature birth.* Cats are common carriers of toxoplasmosis, especially outdoor cats who eat raw meat, such as rats and mice. The toxoplasmosis organism passes from the cat in its feces and lives up to 1 year. The expectant mother may pick up these organisms by handling cats or cat litter boxes, or by working in soil where cats have buried their feces. Eating raw or undercooked meat is another way of acquiring the disease. To avoid getting toxoplasmosis, expectant mothers need to wash their hands after handling cats, litter boxes, and raw meat. In addition, pregnant women should make sure that all meats are thoroughly cooked before eating them.

Critical Thinking

Where do you stand on the issue of the fertile woman's right to work at jobs that may have detrimental effects on her health and the health of the fetus? Defend your argument.

CONCEPT TABLE 4.1

The Course of Prenatal Development, Miscarriage and Abortion,
and Teratology and Hazards to Prenatal Development

Concept	Processes/Related Ideas	Characteristics/Description
The course of prenatal development	Germinal period	This period begins at conception and lasts about 10 to 14 days. The fertilized egg is called a "zygote." The period ends when the zygote attaches to the uterine wall.
	Embryonic period	The embryonic period lasts from about 2 weeks to 8 weeks after conception. The embryo differentiates into three layers, life-support systems develop, and organ systems form (organogenesis).
	Fetal period	The fetal period lasts from about 2 months after conception until 9 months or when the infant is born. Growth and development continue their dramatic course, and organ systems mature to the point where life can be sustained outside the womb.
Miscarriage and abortion	Their nature and ethical issues	A miscarriage, or spontaneous abortion, happens when pregnancy ends before the developing organism is mature enough to survive outside the womb. Estimates indicate that about 15 to 20 percent of all pregnancies end this way, many without the mother's knowledge. Induced abortion is a complex issue—medically, psychologically, and socially. An unwanted pregnancy is stressful for the woman, regardless of how it is resolved.
Teratology and hazards to prenatal development	Teratology	Teratology is the field that investigates the causes of congenital (birth) defects. Any agent that causes birth defects is called a "teratogen."
	Maternal diseases and conditions	Maternal diseases and infections can cause damage by crossing the placental barrier, or they can be destructive during the birth process. Among the maternal diseases and conditions believed to be involved in possible birth defects are rubella, syphilis, genital herpes, AIDS, the mother's age, nutrition, and emotional state and stress.
	Drugs	Thalidomide was a tranquilizer given to pregnant mothers to alleviate their morning sickness. In the early 1960s, thousands of babies were malformed as a consequence of their mothers' having taken this drug. Alcohol, tobacco, heroin, and cocaine are other drugs that can adversely affect prenatal and infant development.
	Environmental hazards	Among the environmental hazards that can endanger the fetus are radiation in occupations and X rays, environmental pollutants, toxic wastes, toxoplasmosis, and prolonged exposure to heat in saunas and hot tubs.

Yet another recent environmental concern for expectant mothers is prolonged exposure to heat in saunas or hot tubs that may raise the mother's body temperature, creating a fever that endangers the fetus. The high temperature of a fever may interfere with cell division and may cause birth defects or even fetal death if the fever occurs repeatedly for prolonged periods of time. Prenatal experts recommend that if the expectant mother wants to take a sauna or bathe in a hot tub, she should take her oral temperature while she is exposed to the heat. When her body temperature rises a degree or more, she should get out and cool down. Ten minutes is a reasonable length of time for expectant mothers to spend in a sauna or a hot tub, since body temperature does not usually rise in this length of time. If the expectant mother feels uncomfortably hot in a sauna or a hot tub, she should get out even if she has only been there for a short time.

At this point we have discussed a number of ideas about the course of prenatal development, miscarriage and abortion, and teratology and hazards to prenatal development. A summary of these ideas is presented in concept table 4.1.

BIRTH

After the long journey of prenatal development, birth takes place. Among the important topics related to birth that we will explore in this section are stages of birth, delivery complications, and the use of drugs during childbirth; preterm infants; and measures of neonatal health and responsiveness.

Stages of Birth

The birth process occurs in three stages. For a woman having her first child, the first stage lasts an average of 12 to 24 hours; it is the longest of the three stages. In the first stage, uterine contractions are 15 to 20 minutes apart at the beginning and last up to a minute. These contractions cause the woman's cervix to stretch and open. As the first stage progresses, the contractions come closer together, appearing every 2 to 5 minutes. Their intensity increases, too. By the end of the first birth stage, contractions dilate the cervix to an opening of about 4 inches so that the baby can move from the uterus to the birth canal.

Children sweeten labors . . .
—Frances Bacon, *Essays,* 1625

The second birth stage begins when the baby's head starts to move through the cervix and the birth canal. It terminates when the baby completely emerges from the mother's body. This stage lasts approximately 1½ hours. With each contraction, the mother bears down hard to push the baby out of her body. By the time the baby's head is out of the mother's body, the contractions come almost every minute and last for about a minute.

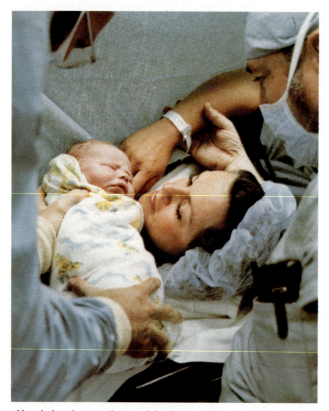

After the long journey of prenatal development, birth takes place, at which time the baby is on a threshold, between two worlds.

Afterbirth *is the third stage, at which time the placenta, umbilical cord, and other membranes are detached and expelled.* This final stage is the shortest of the three birth stages, lasting only minutes.

Delivery Complications

Complications can accompany the baby's delivery. **Precipitate delivery** *is a form of delivery that takes place too rapidly. A precipitate delivery is one in which the baby takes less than 10 minutes to be squeezed through the birth canal.* This deviation in delivery can disturb the infant's normal flow of blood, and the pressure on the infant's head can cause hemorrhaging. On the other hand, **anoxia,** *the insufficient supply of oxygen to the infant,* can develop if the delivery takes too long. Anoxia can cause brain damage.

The **breech position** *is the baby's position in the uterus that causes the buttocks to be the first part to emerge from the vagina.* Normally, the crown of the baby's head comes through the vagina first, but in 1 of every 25 babies, the head does not come through first. Breech babies' heads are still in the uterus when the rest of their bodies are out, which can cause respiratory problems. Some breech babies cannot be passed through the cervix and must be delivered by cesarean section.

A **cesarean section** *is the surgical removal of the baby from the uterus.* A cesarean section is usually performed if the baby is in a breech position, if it is lying crosswise in the uterus, if the baby's head is too large to pass through the mother's pelvis, if the baby develops complications, or if the mother is bleeding vaginally. The benefits and risks of cesarean section delivery are debated. Cesarean section deliveries are safer than breech deliveries, but a higher infection rate, a longer hospital stay, greater expense, and the stress that accompanies any surgery characterize cesarean section deliveries. Some critics believe that in the United States too many babies are delivered by cesarean section. More cesarean sections are performed in the United States than in any other industrialized nation. From 1979 to 1987, the cesarean section rate increased almost 50 percent in the United States alone, to an annual rate of 24 percent (Marieskind, 1989). However, a growing use of vaginal birth after a previous cesarean, greater public awareness, and peer pressure in the medical community are beginning to slow the rate of increase (Enkin, 1989; Marieskind, 1989).

The Use of Drugs During Childbirth

Drugs can be used to relieve pain and anxiety and to speed delivery during the birth process. Drugs are most frequently used during delivery to relieve the expectant mother's pain or anxiety. A wide variety of tranquilizers, sedatives, and analgesics are used for this purpose (Nelson, 1992). Researchers are interested in the effects of these drugs because they can cross the placental barrier, and because their use is so widespread. One survey of hospitals found that only 5 percent of deliveries involve no anesthesia (Brackbill, 1979).

Oxytocin, *a hormone that stimulates and regulates the rhythmicity of uterine contractions, has been widely used as a drug to speed delivery. Controversy surrounds the use of this drug.* Some physicians argue that it can save the mother's life or keep the infant from being damaged. They also stress that using the drug allows the mother to be well rested and prepared for the birth process. Critics argue that babies born to mothers who have taken oxytocin are more likely to have jaundice; that induced labor requires more painkilling drugs; and that greater medical care is required after the birth, resulting in the separation of the infant and mother.

Critical Thinking

After reading the information on the use of drugs during childbirth, what considerations would be foremost in your mind if your offspring was about to be born? What questions about the use of drugs during delivery would you want to ask the individuals responsible for delivering the baby?

The following conclusions can be reached, based on research about the influence of drugs during delivery (Rosenblith, 1992):

1. Few research studies have been done, and many that have been completed have had methodological problems. However, not all drugs have similar effects. Some—tranquilizers, sedatives, and analgesics, for example—do not seem to have long-term effects. Other drugs—oxytocin, for example—are suspected of having long-term effects.
2. The degree to which a drug influences the infant is usually small. Birthweight and social class, for instance, are more powerful predictors of infant difficulties than are drugs.
3. A specific drug may affect some infants but not others. In some cases, the drug may have a beneficial effect, whereas in others it may be harmful.
4. The overall amount of medication may be an important factor in understanding drug effects on delivery.

Next, we discuss a number of the increasing variety of childbirth strategies. In the last several decades, a growing number of expectant mothers have chosen to have a prepared, or natural, childbirth. One aspect of prepared childbirth is an attempt to minimize the use of medication.

Childbirth Strategies

In the past two decades, the nature of childbirth has changed considerably. Where heavy medication was once the norm, now natural, or prepared, childbirth has become increasingly popular. Today, husbands much more frequently participate in childbirth. Alternative birthing centers and birthing rooms have become standard in many maternity units, and the acceptance of midwives has increased. Before we examine some of these contemporary trends in childbirth strategies, let's explore the nature of standard childbirth.

Standard Childbirth

In the standard childbirth procedure that has been practiced for many years—and the way you probably were delivered—

the expectant mother is taken to a hospital, where a doctor is responsible for the baby's delivery. To prepare the pregnant woman for labor, her pubic hair is shaved and she is given an enema. She then is placed in a labor room, which is often filled with other pregnant women, some of whom are screaming. When she is ready to deliver, she is taken to the delivery room, which looks like an operating room. She is laid on the table and the physician, along with an anesthetist and a nurse, delivers the baby.

What could be wrong with this procedure? Critics list three things: (1) Important individuals related to the mother are excluded from the birth process. (2) The mother is separated from her infant in the first minutes and hours after birth. (3) Giving birth is treated like a disease, and a woman is thought of as a sick patient (Rosenblith, 1992). As we will see next, some alternatives differ radically from this standard procedure.

The Leboyer Method

The **Leboyer method,** *developed by French obstetrician Frederick Leboyer, intends to make the birth process less stressful for infants. Leboyer's procedure is referred to as "birth without violence."* He describes standard childbirth as "torture" (Leboyer, 1975). He vehemently objects to holding newborns upside down and slapping or spanking them, putting silver nitrite into their eyes, separating them immediately from their mothers, and scaring them with bright lights and harsh noises in the delivery room. Leboyer also criticizes the traditional habit of cutting the umbilical cord as soon as the infant is born, a situation that forces the infant to immediately take in oxygen from the air to breathe. Leboyer believes that the umbilical cord should be left intact for several minutes to allow the newborn a chance to adjust to a world of breathing air. In the Leboyer method, the baby is placed on the mother's stomach immediately after birth so the mother can caress the infant. Then the infant is placed in a bath of warm water to relax. Although most hospitals do not use the soft lights and warm baths that Leboyer suggests, they sometimes do place the newborn on the mother's stomach immediately after birth, believing that it will stimulate mother-infant bonding.

> *We must respect this instant of birth, this fragile moment. The baby is between two worlds, on a threshold, hesitating . . .*
>
> —Frederick Leboyer,
> *Birth Without Violence*

Prepared, or Natural, Childbirth

Prepared, or natural, childbirth, *includes being informed about what will happen during the procedure, knowing about comfort measures for childbirth, anticipating that little or no medication will be used, and expecting to participate in decision making if complications arise* (Bean, 1990). Medical treatment is used when there is a reason, but it should always be done with care and concern for the expectant mother and the offspring. Prepared childbirth assumes the presence and support of a partner or friend, and in some cases a labor-support person identified through local childbirth education groups. At least two persons, including the laboring woman, are needed to work with each contraction.

Prepared childbirth includes a number of variations. Consider the following three instances of prepared childbirth. The first woman in labor lies awake under light medication with an intravenous needle in her arm into which a nearby pump introduces a labor stimulant. She is attached to electronic monitoring devices and confined to the bed. A second woman is wearing her own clothes, sitting in a rocking chair in a birthing room, relaxing, attending to her breathing, and sipping a glass of cider with none of the above medications or equipment being used. At her infant's birth there will be no gowns or masks, and she will give birth in the birthing room instead of being moved to the delivery room. An older child who has learned about childbirth may even be in the room, preparing to welcome the new sibling. The third woman and her husband are "prepared" parents, who may or may not have attended cesarean preparation classes, but agree that cesarean birth is required. Both parents are in the delivery room and she is awake. Despite obvious involvement of the couple in the decision to have the cesarean birth, no one has yet described a cesarean birth as "natural."

A basic philosophy of prepared childbirth is that information and teaching methods should support parent confidence, provide the knowledge required to carry out normal childbirth, and explain how the medical system functions in childbirth. Professional disciplines involved in childbirth now go beyond obstetrics (with its main emphasis on pathology rather than normal birth) and also include nursing, public health, education, physical therapy, psychology, sociology, and physiology. Each of these areas has contributed to teaching programs and provided increased knowledge about childbirth. But never to be overlooked is the input to health professionals from parents themselves.

The **Lamaze method** *has become a widely used childbirth strategy; it is a form of prepared or natural childbirth developed by Fernand Lamaze, a pioneering French obstetrician.* It has become widely accepted by the medical profession and involves helping the expectant mother to cope actively with the pain of childbirth and to avoid or reduce medication. Lamaze training for parents is available on a widespread basis in the United States and usually consists of six weekly classes. In these classes, the pregnant woman learns about the birth process and is trained in breathing and relaxation exercises. As the Lamaze method has grown in popularity, it has become more common for the father to participate in the exercises and to assist in the birth process.

Lamaze exercises and breathing have much in common with the other methods of prepared childbirth, with the exception that breathing techniques are more central to the method; Lamaze breathing is very active. Whatever the method of prepared childbirth that expectant couples choose, each will provide information about birth, ways of relaxing and releasing muscle tension, breathing patterns to relieve anxiety and bring adequate oxygen to the contracting uterine muscle, ways to avoid hyperventilation (overbreathing), and basic physical conditioning exercises.

New for the Nineties

Among the current changes in childbirth are shifts in emphases, new choices, and an understanding of obstetrical terminology. And an increasing number of instructors report that they are now using a more eclectic approach to childbirth, drawing information from several different methods (Bean, 1990). Let's examine some of these trends in more detail:

- Breathing methods continue to be important but are more flexible in accord with the individual needs of the expectant mother. In general, breathing is becoming less active and less vigorous, with more attention given to other methods of providing comfort. However, some prepared childbirth instructors believe that the importance of breathing should not be downplayed too much.

- New ways of teaching relaxation are offered, including guided mental imagery, massage, and meditation.

- The use of warm water for comfort is recognized, and many hospitals have showers in their labor and delivery areas. Some hospitals have introduced Jacuzzies.

- A more homelike institutional environment is believed to be important.

- Stress from intense lighting and an intrusive environment can inhibit uterine contraction, possibly slowing labor and even making the introduction of medication necessary. Hospitals are moving in the direction of having most nonsurgical births, including anesthetized births, in homelike birthing rooms that are quiet, peaceful, and less intensely lit.

- Walking during labor and the use of varied body positions during labor and birth are encouraged. For many women, the squatting position is the most comfortable and effective position.

- The "nothing by mouth" policy during labor is being seriously questioned and reexamined. Light food was initially introduced in home birth and freestanding birthing centers. It is now beginning to be offered in some hospitals.

- The use of midwife-assisted birth is becoming more widespread, allowing longer and more informative prenatal visits, labor support, and less use of medication.

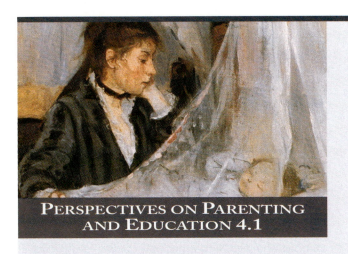

PERSPECTIVES ON PARENTING AND EDUCATION 4.1

Becoming Knowledgeable About Pregnancy, Prenatal Development, and Childbirth Strategies

Two important aspects of parenting and education for expectant parents are, first, becoming knowledgeable about pregnancy and prenatal development, and, second, learning about different childbirth strategies and considering childbirth classes.

Early prenatal classes may include both couples in early pregnancy and couples in prepregnancy (Olds, London, & Ladewig, 1988). The classes often focus on such topics as:

- Changes in the development of the embryo and the fetus
- Self-care during pregnancy
- Fetal development concerns and environmental dangers for the fetus
- Sexuality during pregnancy
- Birth settings and types of care providers
- Nutrition, rest, and exercise
- Common discomforts of pregnancy, and relief measures
- Psychological changes in both the expectant mother and her partner
- Information needed to get the pregnancy off to a good start

Early classes also may include information about factors that place the expectant mother at risk for preterm labor and recognition of the possible signs and symptoms of preterm labor. Prenatal education classes may include information on the advantages and disadvantages of breast- and bottle-feeding (we will discuss this issue in chapter 5). Researchers have found that the majority of expectant mothers (50 to 80 percent) have made this infant feeding decision prior to the 6th month of pregnancy. Therefore, information about the issues involved in breast- versus bottle-feeding in an early prenatal education class is helpful (Aberman & Kirchoff, 1985).

So far, the prenatal education classes we have described focus on expectant couples in the first trimester of pregnancy. The later classes—those when the expectant mother is in the second or third trimester of pregnancy—often focus on preparation for the birth, infant care and feeding, postpartum self-care, and birth choices. Much more about these topics appears in the next chapter.

What happens in childbirth classes? The format is often a six-part, 2-hour session with 1 hour of discussion and 1 hour of practicing techniques and exercises. Instructors, working with each couple in turn, teach fathers or other partners (often called "coaches") how to assist the woman in labor. One or more couples from previous classes may return for a visit, with their babies, to describe their childbirth experiences. This provides a valuable and interesting opportunity for expectant parents. Birth slides and films help make childbirth more real and less frightening. The Birth Atlas, a series of detailed, life-sized photographs of pregnancy, labor, and delivery from Maternity Center in New York City, is another educational tool widely used in childbirth classes throughout the United States. The purpose of the Birth Atlas is to show in precise detail how birth takes place and to help demystify birth.

The International Childbirth Education Association guide for childbirth educators endorses the concept of a health-care *circle* rather than a health-care *team*. The key person in the center of the health-care circle is the person seeking care, in this case the expectant mother. She selects the people around her for advice, information, care, and support. The circle may include family, friends, other expectant couples, obstetrician, midwife, nurse, or others. Communication, shared decision making, and her right to make informed choices are central to effective childbirth education.

- Parent-infant bonding, which we will discuss later in the chapter, is widely available and encouraged. Even if the baby is premature or ill, parents go to the intensive care nursery to see, touch, and talk to their newborn.
- Siblings and grandparents are welcome to touch and hold the baby in the hospital.
- Hospital stays have been shortened to 3 days or less, mainly because of recent government reimbursement regulations. Approximately 5 days are allowed for cesarean births.

- Increased amounts of time are spent discussing the pros and cons of various obstetrical and birthing options.

> *The strongest principle of human growth lies in human choice.*
>
> —Alexander Chase, *Perspectives*, 1966

In the 1990s, more prospective parents are becoming knowledgeable about pregnancy, prenatal development, and childbirth strategies. To read about how parents can gain this knowledge, see Perspectives on Parenting and Education 4.1.

The Father's Participation

In the past several decades, fathers increasingly have participated in childbirth. Fathers-to-be are now more likely to go to at least one meeting with the obstetrician or caregiver during the pregnancy, attend childbirth preparation classes, learn about labor and birth, and be more involved in the care of the young infant (Coleman & Coleman, 1991). The change is consistent with our culture's movement toward less rigid concepts of "masculine" and "feminine."

For many expectant couples today, the father is trained to be the expectant mother's coach during labor, helping her to learn relaxation methods and special breathing techniques for labor and birth. Most health professionals now believe that, just as with pregnancy, childbirth should be an intimate, shared moment between a couple who are creating a new life together. Nonetheless, some men do not want to participate in prepared childbirth, and some women also still prefer that their male partner not have a very active role. In such cases, other people can provide support for childbirth—mother, sister, friend, midwife, or physician, for example.

A father who is motivated to participate in childbirth has an important role at the mother's side. In the long stretches when there is no staff attendant present, the father can provide companionship, support, and encouragement. In difficult moments of examination or medication, he can be comforting. Initially, he may feel embarrassed to use the breathing techniques he learned in preparation classes, but he usually begins to feel more at home when he realizes he is performing a necessary function for the mother during each contraction.

Some individuals question whether the father is the best coach during labor. He may be nervous and feel uncomfortable in the hospital; and, never having gone through labor himself, he might not understand the expectant mother's needs as well as another woman might. There is no universal answer to this issue. Some laboring women want to depend on another woman, someone who has been through labor herself; others want their male partner to intimately share the childbirth experience. Many cultures exclude men from births, just as the American culture did until the last several decades. In some cultures, the woman's mother, or occasionally a daughter, serves as her assistant.

Critical Thinking

How actively should the husband be involved in childbirth? Why?

Siblings

If parents have a child and are expecting another, it is important for them to prepare the older child for the birth of a sibling (Simkin, Whalley, & Keppler, 1984). Sibling preparation includes providing the child with information about pregnancy, birth, and life with a newborn that is realistic and appropriate for the child's age.

Parents can prepare their older child for the approaching birth at any time during pregnancy. The expectant mother might announce the pregnancy early to explain her tiredness and vomiting. If the child is young and unable to understand waiting, parents may want to delay announcing the pregnancy until later, when the expectant mother's pregnancy becomes obvious and she begins to look "fat" to the child.

Parents may want to consider having the child present at the birth. Many family-centered hospitals, birth centers, and homebirths make this option available. Some parents wish to minimize or avoid separation from the older child, so they choose to give birth where sibling involvement is possible. These parents feel that if there is no separation, the child will not develop separation anxiety and will not see the new baby as someone who took the mother away. Sibling involvement in the childbirth may enhance the attachment between the older child and the new baby.

To help the child cope with the arrival of the new baby, parents can do the following:

- Before and after the birth, read books to the child about living with a new baby
- Plan to spend time alone with the older child and do what he or she wants to do
- Use the time when the baby is asleep and the parent is rested to give special attention to the older child
- Give a gift to the older child in the hospital or at home
- "Tell" the baby about his or her special older brother or sister when the older sibling is listening

Preterm Infants and Age–Weight Considerations

How can we distinguish between a preterm infant and a low-birthweight infant? What are the developmental outcomes for low-birthweight infants? Do preterm infants have a different profile from that of full-term infants? What conclusions can we reach about preterm infants?

Preterm and Low–Birthweight Infants

An infant is full-term when it has grown in the womb for the full 38 to 42 weeks between conception and delivery. A **preterm infant** *(also called a "premature" infant) is one who is born prior to 38 weeks after conception.* **Low-birthweight infants** *are infants born after a regular gestation period (the length of time between conception and birth) of 38 to 42 weeks, but who weigh less than 5½ pounds.* Both preterm and low-birthweight infants are considered high-risk infants (Crisafi & Driscoll, 1991; Smith, Ulvind, & Lindemann, 1994).

A "kilogram kid," weighing less than 2.3 pounds at birth. In the neonatal intensive care unit, banks of flashing lights, blinking numbers, and beeping alarms stand guard over kilogram kids, who are extreme preterm infants. They often lie on a water bed that gently undulates; the water bed is in an incubator that is controlled for temperature and humidity by the baby's own body. Such vital signs as brain waves, heartbeat, blood gases, and respiratory rate are constantly monitored. All of this care can be very expensive. Though the cost can usually be kept within five figures, 5 or 6 months of neonatal intensive care can result in expenses of as much as $300,000 or more.

In one study, an intervention program was implemented to improve the developmental outcomes of low-birthweight infants (Achenbach & others, 1990). The program was designed to enhance the mother's adjustment to the care of a low-birthweight infant by (a) enabling the mother to appreciate her baby's specific behavioral and temperamental characteristics; (b) sensitizing her to the baby's cues, especially those that signal stimulus overload, distress, and readiness for interaction; and (c) teaching her to respond appropriately to those cues, to facilitate mutually satisfying interactions. The intervention involved seven hospital sessions and four home sessions in which

a nurse helped mothers adapt to their low-birthweight babies. At age 7, the low-birthweight babies whose mothers had participated in the intervention program scored higher than a control group of low-birthweight babies on information-processing measures. The researchers commented that the intervention prevented cognitive lags among low-birthweight children and that long-term follow-ups are needed to overcome major biological and environmental risks.

A short gestation period does not necessarily harm an infant. It is distinguished from retarded prenatal growth, in which the fetus has been damaged (Kopp, 1983, 1987). The neurological development of a short-gestation infant continues after birth on approximately the same timetable as if the infant still were in the womb. For example, consider an infant born after a gestation period of 30 weeks. At 38 weeks, approximately 2 months after birth, this infant shows the same level of brain development as a 38-week fetus who is yet to be born.

Some infants are born very early and have a precariously low birthweight (Friedman & Caron, 1991; Thompson & Oehler, 1991). "Kilogram kids" weigh less than 2.3 pounds (which is 1 kilogram, or 1,000 grams) and are very premature. The task of saving such a baby is not easy. At the Stanford University Medical Center in Palo Alto, California, 98 percent of the preterm babies survive; however, 32 percent of those between 750 and 1,000 grams do not, and 76 percent of those below 750 grams do not. Approximately 250,000 preterm babies are born in the United States each year, and more than 15,000 of these weigh less than 1,000 grams.

Preterm infants have a different profile from that of full-term infants. For instance, Tiffany Field (1979) found that 4-month-old preterm infants vocalize less, fuss more, and avoid eye contact more than their full-term counterparts. Other researchers have found differences in the information-processing skills of preterm and full-term infants. In one investigation, Susan Rose and her colleagues (1988) found that 7-month-old high-risk preterm infants are less visually attentive to novelty and show deficits in visual recognition memory when compared with full-term infants.

Stimulation of Preterm Infants

Just three decades ago, preterm infants were perceived to be too fragile to cope well with environmental stimulation, and the recommendation was to handle such infants as little as possible. The climate of opinion changed when the adverse effects of maternal deprivation (mothers' neglect of their infants) became known and such deprivation was interpreted to include a lack of stimulation. A number of research studies followed that indicated a "more is better" approach in the stimulation of preterm infants. Today, however, experts on infant development argue that preterm infant care is far too complex to be described only in terms of amount of stimulation (Field, 1990; Lester & Tronick, 1990; Thoman, 1992).

Recently, experts on the stimulation of preterm infants held a roundtable discussion and offered the following recommendations (Lester & Tronick, 1990):

1. Preterm infants' responses to stimulation vary with their conceptual age, illness, and individual makeup. The immature brain of the preterm infant may be more vulnerable to excessive, inappropriate, or mistimed stimulation. The very immature infant should probably be protected from stimulation that could destabilize its homeostatic condition.

2. As the healthy preterm infant becomes less fragile and approaches term, the issue of what is appropriate stimulation should be considered. Infants' behavioral cues can be used to determine appropriate interventions. An infant's signs of stress or avoidance behaviors indicate that stimulation should be terminated. Positive behaviors indicate that stimulation is appropriate.

3. Intervention with the preterm infant should be organized in the form of an individualized developmental plan. This plan should be constructed as a psychosocial intervention to include the parents and other immediate family members and to acknowledge the socioeconomic, cultural, and home environmental factors that will determine the social context in which the infant will be reared. The developmental plan should also include assessing the infant's behavior, working with the parents to help them understand the infant's medical and behavioral status, and helping the parents deal with their own feelings.

Some Conclusions About Preterm Infants

What conclusions can we draw from the results of research about preterm infants? Three such conclusions seem appropriate (Kopp, 1983, 1992; Kopp & Kaler, 1989):

1. As intensive care technology has improved, there have been fewer serious consequences of preterm births. For instance, from 1961 to 1965, the manner of feeding preterm infants changed, and intravenous fluid therapy came into use. From 1966 to 1968, better control of hypoxemia (oxygen deficiency) was gained. In 1971, artificial ventilation was introduced. In the mid-1970s, neonatal support systems became less intrusive and damaging to infants.

2. Infants born with a problem that is identifiable at birth are likely to have a poorer developmental future than infants born without a recognizable problem. For instance, extremely sick or extremely tiny babies are less likely to survive than healthy or normal-weight babies.

3. Social class differences are associated with preterm infants' development. The higher the socio-economic status, the more favorable is the developmental outcome for a newborn. Social class differences also are tied to many other differences. For example, the quality of the environment, tobacco and alcohol consumption, IQ, and knowledge of competent parenting strategies are associated with social class; less positive characteristics are associated with lower-class families.

Despite the advances made in prenatal care and technology in the United States, the availability of high-quality medical and educational services still needs much improvement (Brooks-Gunn, McCarton, & Tonascia, 1992). In some countries, especially in Scandinavia and Western Europe, more consistent, higher-quality prenatal care is provided than in the United States. To read further about the nature of prenatal care in different countries, turn to Sociocultural Worlds of Development 4.1.

Measures of Neonatal Health and Responsiveness

The **Apgar scale** *is a method widely used to assess the health of newborns at 1 and 5 minutes after birth. The Apgar scale evaluates infants' heart rate, respiratory effort, muscle tone, body color, and reflex irritability.* An obstetrician or nurse does the evaluation and gives the newborn a score, or reading, of 0, 1, or 2 on each of these five health signs (see figure 4.6). A total score of 7 to 10 indicates that the newborn's condition is good, a score of 5 indicates there may be developmental difficulties, and a score of 3 or below signals an emergency and indicates that the baby's survival may be in doubt.

Whereas the Apgar scale is used immediately after birth to identify high-risk infants who need resuscitation, the **Brazelton Neonatal Behavioral Assessment Scale** *is given several days after birth to assess the newborn's neurological development, reflexes, and reactions to people* (Brazelton, 1973; Brazelton, Nugent, & Lester, 1987). The Brazelton scale is usually given on the third day of life and then repeated several days later.

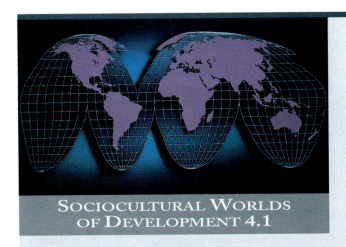

Prenatal Care in the United States and Around the World

As advanced a nation as the United States has become economically and technologically, it still has more low-birthweight infants than a number of other countries (Grant, 1994). As indicated in table 4.A, only 4 percent of the infants born in Sweden, Finland, the Netherlands, and Norway are low-birthweight, and only 5 percent of those born in New Zealand, Australia, France, and Japan are low-birthweight. In the United States, 7 percent of all infants are low-birthweight. Also, as indicated in table 4.A, in some developing countries, such as Bangladesh, where poverty is rampant and the health and nutrition of mothers is poor, the percentage of low-birthweight infants reaches as high as 50 percent of all infants.

In the United States, there also are discrepancies between the prenatal development and birth of Black infants and White infants. Black infants are twice as likely to: be born prematurely, have low birthweight, and have mothers who received late or no prenatal care; are three times as likely to have their mothers die in childbirth; and are five times as likely to be born to unmarried teenage mothers (Edelman, 1992).

In many of the countries with a lower percentage of low-birthweight infants than the United States, either free or very low-cost prenatal and postnatal care is available to mothers. This care includes paid maternity leave from work that ranges from 9 to 40 weeks (Miller, 1987). In Norway and the Netherlands, prenatal care is coordinated with a general practitioner, an obstetrician, and a midwife.

Pregnant women in the United States do not receive the uniform prenatal care that women in many Scandinavian and Western European countries receive. The United States does not have a national policy of health care that assures high-quality assistance for pregnant women. The cost of giving birth is approximately $4,000 in the United States (more than $5,000 for a cesarean birth), and more than 25 percent of all American women of prime childbearing age do not have insurance that will pay for hospital costs. More than one-fifth of all White mothers and one-third of all Black mothers do not receive prenatal care in the first trimester of their pregnancy. Five percent of White mothers and 10 percent of Black mothers receive no prenatal care at all (Wegman, 1986). Many infant-development researchers believe that the United States needs more comprehensive medical and educational services to improve the quality of prenatal care and reduce the percentage of low-birthweight infants.

TABLE 4.A
Percentage of Low-Birthweight Infants

Country	Low-Birthweight Infants (Percentage)
Bangladesh	50
India	30
Guatemala	18
Iran	14
Mexico	12
USSR	9
United States, Great Britain, Israel, Egypt	7
Canada, China	6
New Zealand, Australia, France, Japan	5
Sweden, Finland, the Netherlands, Norway	4

Source: Data from J. Grant, *State of the World's Children*, 1986.

FIGURE 4.6

The Apgar scale.

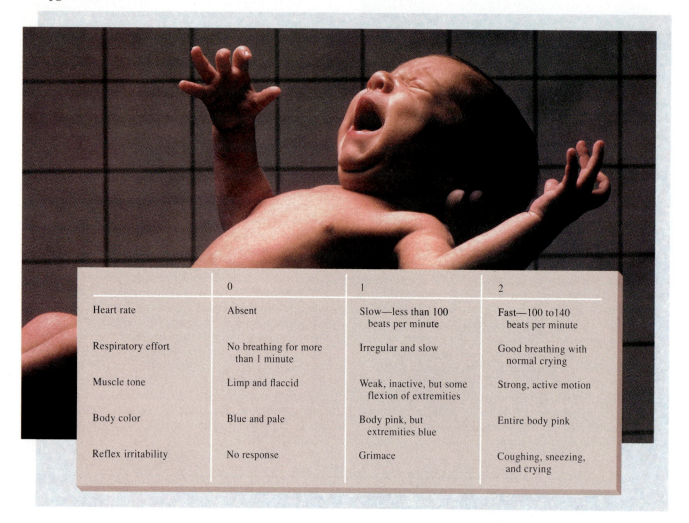

	0	1	2
Heart rate	Absent	Slow—less than 100 beats per minute	Fast—100 to 140 beats per minute
Respiratory effort	No breathing for more than 1 minute	Irregular and slow	Good breathing with normal crying
Muscle tone	Limp and flaccid	Weak, inactive, but some flexion of extremities	Strong, active motion
Body color	Blue and pale	Body pink, but extremities blue	Entire body pink
Reflex irritability	No response	Grimace	Coughing, sneezing, and crying

Twenty reflexes are assessed, along with reactions to circumstances such as the infant's reaction to a rattle. The examiner rates the newborn, or neonate, on each of 27 categories (see table 4.2). As an indication of how detailed the ratings are, consider item 15: "cuddliness." Nine categories are involved in assessing this item, with infant behavior scored on a continuum that ranges from the infant's being very resistant to being held to the infant's being extremely cuddly and clinging. The Brazelton scale not only is used as a sensitive index of neurological competence in the week after birth, but it also is used widely as a measure in many research studies on infant development. In recent versions of scoring the Brazelton scale, Brazelton and his colleagues (1987) categorize the 27 items into four categories—physiological, motoric, state, and interaction. They also classify the baby in global terms, such as "worrisome," "normal," or "superior," based on these categories.

A very low Brazelton score can indicate brain damage. However, if an infant merely seems sluggish in responding to social circumstances, parents are encouraged to give the infant attention and become more sensitive to the infant's needs (Brazelton, 1990). Parents are shown how the newborn can respond to people and how to stimulate such responses.

Researchers have found that the social interaction skills of both high-risk infants and healthy, responsive infants can be improved through such communication with parents (Widmayer & Field, 1980; Worobey & Belsky, 1982).

THE POSTPARTAL PERIOD

Many health professionals believe that the best postpartal care is family centered, using the family's resources to support an early and smooth adjustment to the newborn by all family members. What is the postpartal period? What physical changes does it involve? What emotional and psychological changes are encountered?

The Nature of the Postpartal Period

The **postpartal period** *(also called "postpartum period") is the period after childbirth or delivery. It is a time when the woman adjusts, both physically and psychologically, to the process of childbearing. It lasts for about 6 weeks or until the body has completed its adjustment and has returned to a near prepregnant state* (Olds, London, & Ladewig, 1988). Some health professionals refer

TABLE 4.2

The 27 Categories on the Brazelton Neonatal Behavioral Assessment Scale (NBAS)

1. Response decrement to repeated visual stimuli
2. Response decrement to rattle
3. Response decrement to bell

4. Response decrement to pinprick
5. Orienting response to inanimate visual stimuli
6. Orienting response to inanimate auditory stimuli

7. Orienting response to inanimate visual and auditory stimuli
8. Orienting response to animate visual stimuli—examiner's face
9. Orienting response to animate auditory stimuli—examiner's voice

10. Orienting response to animate visual and auditory stimuli
11. Quality and duration of alert periods
12. General muscle tone—in resting and in response to being handled, passive, and active

13. Motor activity
14. Traction responses as the infant is pulled to sit
15. Cuddliness—responses to being cuddled by examiner

16. Defensive movements—reactions to a cloth over the infant's face
17. Consolability with intervention by examiner
18. Peak of excitement and capacity to control self

19. Rapidity of buildup to crying state
20. Irritability during the examination
21. General assessment of kind and degree of activity

22. Tremulousness
23. Amount of startling
24. Lability of skin color—measuring autonomic lability

25. Lability of states during entire examination
26. Self-quieting activity—attempts to console self and control state
27. Hand-to-mouth activity

Adapted from *Cultural Perspectives on Child Development* edited by Wagner and Stevenson. Copyright © 1982 by W. H. Freeman and Company. Reprinted by permission.

to the postpartal period as the "fourth trimester." While the time span of the postpartal period does not necessarily cover 3 months, the terminology *fourth trimester* demonstrates the idea of continuity and the importance of the first several months after birth for the mother.

The postpartal period is influenced by what preceded it. During pregnancy the woman's body gradually adjusted to physical changes, but now it is forced to respond quickly. The method of delivery and circumstances surrounding the delivery affect the speed with which the woman's body readjusts during the postpartal period.

The postpartal period involves a great deal of adjustment and adaptation (Coleman & Coleman, 1991). The baby has to be cared for; the mother has to recover from childbirth; the mother has to learn how to take care of the baby; the mother needs to learn to feel good about herself as a mother; the father needs to learn how to take care of his recovering wife; the father needs to learn how to take care of the baby; and the father needs to learn how to feel good about himself as a father.

Physical Adjustments

The woman's body makes numerous physical adjustments in the first days and weeks after childbirth (Simkin, Whalley, &

Keppler, 1984). She may have a great deal of energy or feel exhausted and let down. Most new mothers feel tired and need rest. Although these changes are normal, the fatigue can undermine the new mother's sense of well-being and confidence in her ability to cope with a new baby and a new family life.

Involution *is the process by which the uterus returns to its prepregnant size 5 or 6 weeks after birth*. Immediately following birth, the uterus weighs 2 to 3 pounds. By the end of 5 or 6 weeks, the uterus weighs 2 to 3½ ounces and it has returned to its prepregnancy size. Nursing the baby helps to contract the uterus at a rapid rate.

After delivery, a woman's body undergoes sudden and dramatic changes in hormone production. When the placenta is delivered, estrogen and progesterone levels drop steeply and remain low until the ovaries start producing hormones again. The woman will probably begin menstruating again in 4 to 8 weeks if she is not breast-feeding. If she is breast-feeding, she may not menstruate for several months, though ovulation can occur during this time. The first several menstrual periods following delivery may be heavier than usual, but periods soon return to normal.

Some women and men want to resume sexual intercourse as soon as possible after the birth. Others feel constrained or afraid. A sore perineum (the area between the anus and vagina in the female), a demanding baby, lack of help, and extreme fatigue affect a woman's ability to relax and to enjoy making love. Physicians often recommend that women refrain from having sexual intercourse for approximately 6 weeks following the birth of the baby. However, it is probably safe to have sexual intercourse when the stitches heal, vaginal discharge stops, and the woman feels like it.

If the woman regularly engaged in conditioning exercises during pregnancy, exercise will help her to recover her former body contour and strength during the postpartal period. With a caregiver's approval, the woman can begin some exercises as soon as 1 hour after delivery. In addition to recommending exercise in the postpartal period for women, health professionals also increasingly recommend that women practice the relaxation techniques they used during pregnancy and childbirth. Five minutes of slow breathing on a stressful day in the postpartal period can relax and refresh the new mother as well as the new baby.

Emotional and Psychological Adjustments

Emotional fluctuations are common on the part of the mother in the postpartal period. These emotional fluctuations may be due to any of a number of factors: hormonal changes, fatigue, inexperience or lack of confidence with newborn babies, or the extensive time and demands involved in caring for a newborn. For some women, the emotional fluctuations decrease within several weeks after the delivery and are a minor aspect of their motherhood. For others, they are more long-lasting and may produce feelings of anxiety, depression, and difficulty in coping with stress. Mothers who have such feelings, even when they are getting adequate rest, may benefit from professional help in dealing with their problems. Following are some of the signs that may indicate a need for professional counseling about postpartal adaptation (Simkin, Whalley, & Keppler, 1984):

- Excessive worrying
- Depression
- Extreme changes in appetite
- Crying spells
- Inability to sleep

Another adjustment for the mother and for the father is the time and thought that go into being a competent parent of a young infant. It is important for both the mother and the father to become aware of the young infant's developmental needs—physical, psychological, and emotional. Both the mother and the father need to develop a comfortable relationship with the young infant.

Of special interest in parent-infant relationships is **bonding**, *the occurrence of close contact, especially physical, between parents and newborn in the period shortly after birth.* Some physicians believe that this period shortly after birth is critical in development; during this time, the parents and infant need to form an important emotional attachment that provides a foundation for optimal development in years to come. Special interest in bonding came about when some pediatricians argued that the circumstances surrounding delivery often separate mothers and

their infants, preventing or making difficult the development of a bond. The pediatricians further argued that giving the mother drugs to make her delivery less painful may contribute to the lack of bonding. The drugs may make the mother drowsy, thus interfering with her ability to respond to and stimulate the newborn. Advocates of bonding also assert that preterm infants are isolated from their mothers to an even greater degree than full-term infants, thereby increasing their difficulty in bonding.

Is there evidence that such close contact between mothers and newborns is absolutely critical for optimal development later in life? Although some research supports the bonding hypothesis (Klaus & Kennell, 1976), a growing body of research challenges the significance of the first few days of life as a critical period (Bakeman & Brown, 1980; Rode & others, 1981). Indeed, the extreme form of the bonding hypothesis—that the newborn must have close contact with the mother in the first few days of life to develop optimally—simply is not true.

Nonetheless, the weakness of the maternal-infant bonding research should not be used as an excuse to keep motivated mothers from interacting with their infants in the postpartum period, because such contact brings pleasure to many mothers. In some mother-infant pairs—such as those including preterm infants, adolescent mothers, or mothers from disadvantaged circumstances—the practice of bonding may set in motion a climate for improved interaction after the mother and infant leave the hospital (Maccoby & Martin, 1983).

The new baby also changes a mother's and father's relationship with each other. Among the questions that have to be dealt with are these: How will we share the housework and baby care? How can we find enough time for each other, when the baby takes up so much of our time? How can we arrange to get out of the house so we can enjoy some of the things we did before the baby came? At some point, new parents have to figure out which of their commitments are the most important, and which have to get less time or be dropped. Support from relatives, friends, and baby-sitters can help new parents find time to renew some of these activities they enjoyed earlier.

A special concern of many new mothers is whether they should stay home with the baby or go back to work. Some mothers want to return to work as soon as possible after the infant is born, others want to stay home with the infant for several months, then return to work, others want to stay home for a year before they return to work, and yet others, of course, did not work prior to baby's arrival and do not plan to do so in the future.

Critical Thinking

If you are a female, what would be the key factors for you in deciding whether to work or to stay home with the baby? If you are a male, what would you want your wife to do—work or stay home with the baby? What key factors underlie your preference?

Many women, because of a variety of pressures—societal, career, financial—do not have the option of staying at home after their babies are born (Eisenberg, Murkoff, & Hathaway, 1989). However, for women who have to make the choice, the process of decision making is often difficult and agonizing. By

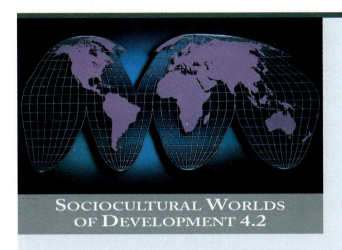

SOCIOCULTURAL WORLDS OF DEVELOPMENT 4.2

To Work or Not to Work

If a mother of a newborn is pondering the question of whether to work or not to work, asking herself the following questions may help her sort out which choice to make (Eisenberg, Murkoff, & Hathaway, 1989):

What are my priorities? The new mother can carefully consider what is most important in her life and rank order these on paper. Priorities might include her baby, her family, her career, financial security, and luxuries of life (such as vacations and entertainment). Her list may be different from that of a woman next door or a woman at the next desk. After charting her priorities, she can consider whether returning to employment or staying at home will best meet the most important of them.

Which full-time role suits my personality best? The woman might ask herself whether she is at her best at home with the baby or whether staying at home would make her feel impatient and tense. Will she be able to leave worries about her baby at home when she goes to her work? Will she worry about not being employed when she stays home with the baby? Or will an inability to compartmentalize her life keep her from doing her best at either job?

Would I feel comfortable having someone else take care of my baby? Does she feel no one else can do the job of caring for the baby as well as she can herself? Or does she feel secure that she can find (or has found) a person (or small-group situation) that can substitute well for her during the hours she is away from home?

How much energy do I have? Considerable physical and emotional stamina are needed to rise with a baby, get ready for work, put in a full day on the job, then return to the demands of the baby, home, and husband. What often suffers most when energy is lacking in the two-paycheck family with infants is the husband-wife relationship.

How do I feel about missing my baby's milestones? Will the mother mind hearing about some of the baby's milestones secondhand—the first time the baby laughs, sits alone, crawls, or walks? Will the mother feel hurt if the baby runs to the sitter instead of her when the baby is frightened or hurt? Does the mother feel that she can be synchronized with the baby's needs by just spending evenings and weekends together?

How stressful is the combination of my employment and the baby? If the mother's employment involves little stress and her baby is an easy baby to care for, then the employment may not present much of a problem. But if the mother's job is very stressful and her baby is difficult to care for (has physical problems, cries a lot, and so on), then she may have difficulty coping with both the job and the baby.

If I return to work, will I get adequate support from my husband or from some other source? Even superwomen can't, and should not be expected to, do everything alone. Will her husband be willing to do his share of babysitting, shopping, cooking, cleaning, and laundry? Is the couple able to afford outside help?

What is our financial situation? If she decides not to work, will it threaten the family's economic survival or just mean cutting down on some extras the couple has been enjoying? Are there ways of cutting back so that the mother's lack of income won't hurt so much? If the mother does go back to work, how much of a dent in her income will job-related costs such as clothes, travel, and child care make?

How flexible is my job? Will the mother be able to take time off if her baby or her sitter becomes sick? Will she be able to come in late or leave early if there is an emergency at home? Does her job require long hours, weekends, or travel? Is the mother willing to spend extended time away from the baby?

If I don't return to my job, how will it influence my career? Putting a career on hold can sometimes set the woman back when she eventually does return to employment. If the mother suspects this may happen, is she willing to make this sacrifice? Are there ways to keep in touch professionally during her at-home months (or years) without making a full-time commitment?

Whatever choice the woman makes, it is likely to require some sacrifices and misgivings. Such sacrifices and misgivings are normal; since we do not live in a perfect world, we have to learn to live and cope with some of them. However, if they begin to multiply and the mother finds her dissatisfaction outweighing her satisfaction, she may want to reassess the choice she made. A choice that seemed right in theory may not work out in practice.

turning to Sociocultural Worlds of Development 4.2, you can read about some of the questions women can ask themselves when they face the issue of whether they should stay home with the baby or return to work.

At this point we have discussed a number of ideas about preterm infants and age-weight considerations, measures of neonatal health and responsiveness, and the postpartal period. A summary of these ideas is presented in concept table 4.2.

CONCEPT TABLE 4.2

Birth and the Postpartal Period

Concept	Processes/Related Ideas	Characteristics/Description
Birth	Stages of birth	Three stages of birth have been defined. The first lasts about 12 to 24 hours for a woman having her first child. The cervix dilates to about 4 inches. The second stage begins when the baby's head moves through the cervix and ends with the baby's complete emergence. The third stage is afterbirth.
	Delivery complications	A baby can move through the birth canal too rapidly or too slowly. A delivery that is too fast is called "precipitate"; when delivery is too slow, anoxia my result. A cesarean section is the surgical removal of the baby from the uterus.
	The use of drugs during childbirth	A wide variety of tranquilizers, sedatives, and analgesics are used to relieve the expectant mother's pain and anxiety, and oxytocin is used to speed delivery. Birthweight and social class are more powerful predictors of problems than are drugs. A drug can have mixed effects, and the overall amount of medication needs to be considered.
	Childbirth strategies	In standard childbirth, the expectant mother is taken to the hospital, where a doctor is responsible for the baby's delivery. The birth takes place in a delivery room, which looks like an operating room, and medication is used in the procedure. Criticisms of the standard childbirth procedure have been made.
		The Leboyer method and prepared, or natural, childbirth are alternatives to standard childbirth. A widely practiced form of natural childbirth is the Lamaze method. Among the current changes in childbirth are shifts in emphases, new choices, and an increased understanding of obstetrical terminology. In the past several decades, fathers have increasingly participated in childbirth. Another special concern is the sibling's role in childbirth.
	Preterm infants and age-weight considerations	Preterm infants are those born after an abnormally short time period in the womb. Infants who are born after a regular gestation period of 38 to 42 weeks but who weigh less than 5½ pounds are called "low-birthweight" infants.

Concept	Processes/Related Ideas	Characteristics/Description
		As intensive care technology has improved, preterm babies have benefited considerably. Infants born with an identifiable problem have a poorer developmental future than those born without a recognizable problem. Social class differences are associated with the preterm infant's development.
	Measures of neonatal health and responsiveness	For many years the Apgar scale has been used to assess the newborn's health. A more recently developed test—the Brazelton Neonatal Behavioral Assessment Scale—is used for long-term neurological assessment. It assesses not only the newborn's neurological integrity but also social responsiveness.
The postpartal period	Its nature	The postpartal period (also called "postpartum period") is the period after childbirth or delivery. It is a time when the woman adjusts, both physically and psychologically, to the process of childbearing. It lasts for about 6 weeks or until the body has completed its adjustment.
	Physical adjustments	These include fatigue, involution (the process by which the uterus returns to its prepregnant size 5 or 6 weeks after birth), hormone changes that include a dramatic drop in estrogen and progesterone, consideration of when to resume sexual intercourse, and participation in exercises to recover former body contour and strength.
	Emotional and psychological adjustments	Emotional fluctuations on the part of the mother are common in the postpartal period. They may be due to hormonal changes, fatigue, inexperience or lack of confidence with newborn babies, or the extensive time and other demands involved in caring for a newborn. For some, the emotional fluctuations are minimal and disappear in several weeks; for others, they are more long-lasting. Another adjustment for both the mother and the father is the time and thought that go into being a competent parent of a young infant. Of special interest in parent-infant relationships is bonding, which has not been found to be critical in the development of a competent infant or child, but which may stimulate positive interaction between some mother-infant pairs. The new baby also changes the mother's and father's relationship with each other. A special concern of many new mothers is whether they should go back to work, or whether they should stay home with the infant.

LIFE-SPAN HEALTH AND WELL-BEING

The Power of Touch and Massage in Development

There has been a surge of interest recently in the roles of touch and massage in improving the growth, health, and well-being of infants and children. This interest has especially been stimulated by a number of research investigations by Tiffany Field, director of the Touch Research Institute at the University of Miami School of Medicine. In one investigation, 40 preterm infants who had just been released from an intensive care unit and placed in a transitional nursery were studied (Field, Scafidi, & Schanberg, 1987). Twenty of the preterm babies were given special stimulation with massage and exercise for three 15-minute periods at the beginning of 3 consecutive hours every morning for 10 weekdays. For example, each infant was placed on its stomach and gently stroked. The massage began with the head and neck and moved downward to the feet. It also moved from the shoulders down to the hands. The infant was then rolled over. Each arm and leg was flexed and extended; then both legs were flexed and extended. Next, the massage was repeated.

The massaged and exercised preterm babies gained 47 percent more weight than their preterm counterparts who were not massaged and exercised, even though both groups had the same number of feedings per day and averaged the same intake of formula. The increased activity of the massaged, exercised infants would seem to work against weight gain. However, similar findings have been discovered with animals. The increased activity may increase gastrointestinal and metabolic efficiency. The massaged infants were more active and alert, and they performed better on developmental tests. Also, their hospital stays were about 6 days shorter than those of the nonmassaged, nonexercised group, which saved about $3,000 per preterm infant. Field has recently replicated these findings with preterm infants in another study.

In a more recent study, Field (1992b) gave the same kind of massage (firm stroking with the palms of the hands) to preterm infants who were exposed to cocaine in utero. The infants also showed significant weight gain and improved scores on developmental tests. Currently, Field is using massage therapy with HIV-exposed preterm infants with the hope that their immune system functioning will be improved. Others she has targeted include infants of depressed mothers, infants with colic, infants and children with sleep problems, as well as children who have diabetes, asthma, and juvenile arthritis.

Field (1992b) also reports that touch has been helpful with children and adolescents who have touch aversions, such as children who have been sexually abused, autistic children, and adolescents with eating disorders. Field also is studying the amount of touch a child normally receives during school activities. She hopes that positive forms of touch will return to school systems where touching has been outlawed because of potential sex abuse lawsuits. ■

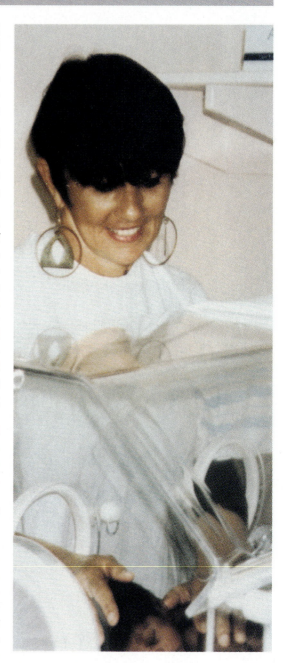

Shown here is Dr. Tiffany Field massaging a newborn infant. Dr. Field's research has clearly demonstrated the power of massage in improving the developmental outcome of at-risk infants. Under her direction The Touch Research Institute in Miami, Florida, was recently developed to investigate the role of touch in a number of domains of health and well-being.

CONCLUSIONS

When a species reproduces itself, life comes from life. Much of this chapter was about becoming. Pregnancy is a state of becoming. An unborn baby is becoming a person capable of life outside the mother's body. And a woman and a man are becoming parents.

In this chapter, you read about the course of prenatal development and its three main periods—germinal, embryonic, and fetal—as well as about miscarriage and abortion, teratology, and hazards to prenatal development, such as the mother's use of drugs. You also read about birth, including childbirth strategies, preterm infants, and age-weight considerations. And you studied the postpartal period and its physical and psychological adjustments. At different points in the chapter you also read about becoming knowledgeable and educated about pregnancy and childbirth strategies, prenatal care in the United States and around the world, issues involved in deciding whether and when to go back to work after having a baby, and the power of touch and massage in development.

Don't forget that you can obtain an overall summary of the chapter by again reading the two concept tables on pages 109 and 122. In the next chapter, we will continue to examine early aspects of the child's development, focusing on physical development in infancy.

KEY TERMS

germinal period   The period of prenatal development that takes place in the first two weeks after conception. It includes the creation of the zygote, continued cell division, and the attachment of the zygote to the uterine wall. (96)

blastocyst   The inner layer of cells that develops during the germinal period. These cells later develop into the embryo. (96)

trophoblast   The outer layer of cells that develops during the germinal period. It later provides nutrition and support for the embryo. (97)

implantation   The attachment of the zygote to the uterine wall, which takes place about ten days after conception. (97)

embryonic period   The period of prenatal development that occurs from two to eight weeks after conception. During the embryonic period, the rate of cell differentiation intensifies, support systems for the cells form, and organs appear. (97)

endoderm   The inner layer of cells, which will develop into the digestive and respiratory systems. (97)

ectoderm   The outermost layer, which will become the nervous system, sensory receptors (ear, nose, and eyes, for example), and skin parts (hair and nails, for example). (97)

mesoderm   The middle layer, which will become the circulatory system, bones, muscle, excretory system, and reproductive system. (97)

placenta   A life-support system that consists of a disk-shaped group of tissues in which small blood vessels from the mother and the offspring intertwine but do not join. (97)

umbilical cord   A life-support system, containing two arteries and one vein, that connects the baby to the placenta. (97)

amnion   A bag or envelope that contains a clear fluid in which the developing embryo floats and is another important life-support system. (98)

organogenesis   The process of organ formation that takes place during the first two months of prenatal development. (98)

fetal period   The prenatal period of development that begins two months after conception and lasts for seven months, on the average. (98)

teratogen   (The word comes from the Greek word *tera* meaning "monster.") Any agent that causes a birth defect. The field of study that investigates the causes of birth defects is called "teratology." (102)

fetal alcohol syndrome (FAS)   A cluster of abnormalities that appear in the offspring of mothers who drink alcohol heavily during pregnancy. (105)

toxoplasmosis   A mild infection that causes coldlike symptoms or no apparent illness in adults. However, toxoplasmosis can be a teratogen for the unborn baby, causing possible eye defects, brain defects, and premature birth. (108)

afterbirth   The third stage of birth, at which time the placenta, umbilical cord, and other membranes are detached and expelled. (110)

precipitate delivery   A form of delivery that takes place too rapidly. A precipitate delivery is one in which the baby takes less than ten minutes to be squeezed through the birth canal. (110)

anoxia   The insufficient supply of oxygen to the infant. (110)

breech position   The baby's position in the uterus that causes the buttocks to be the first part to emerge from the vagina. (110)

cesarean section   The surgical removal of the baby from the uterus. (110)

oxytocin   A hormone that stimulates and regulates the rhythmicity of uterine contractions, has been widely used as a drug to speed delivery. Controversy surrounds the use of this drug. (110)

Leboyer method   A childbirth strategy developed by Frederick Leboyer that intends to make the birth process less stressful for infants. Leboyer's procedure is referred to as "birth without violence." (111)

prepared, or natural, childbirth   Includes being informed about what will happen during the procedure, knowing about comfort measures for childbirth, anticipating that little or no medication will be used, and if complications arise, expecting to participate in a decision. (111)

Lamaze method   A widely used childbirth strategy developed by Fernand Lamaze, a pioneering French obstetrician, that is a form of natural childbirth. (112)

preterm infant   An infant who is born prior to 38 weeks (also called a "premature" infant). (114)

low-birthweight infants   Infants born after a regular gestation period (the length of time between conception and birth) of 38 to 42 weeks, but who weigh less than 5½ pounds. (114)

Apgar scale   A method widely used to assess the health of newborns at one and five minutes after birth. The Apgar scale evaluates infants' heart rate, respiratory effort, muscle tone, body color, and reflex irritability. (116)

Brazelton Neonatal Behavioral Assessment Scale   Given several days after birth to assess the newborn's neurological development, reflexes, and reactions to people. (116)

postpartal period   The period after childbirth or delivery that is also called the "postpartum period." It is a time when the woman adjusts, both physically and psychologically, to the process of childbearing. It lasts for about six weeks or until the body has completed its adjustment and has returned to a near prepregnant state. (118)

involution   The process by which the uterus returns to its prepregnant size five to six weeks after birth. (119)

bonding   The occurrence of close contact, especially physical, between parents and newborn in the period shortly after birth. (120)

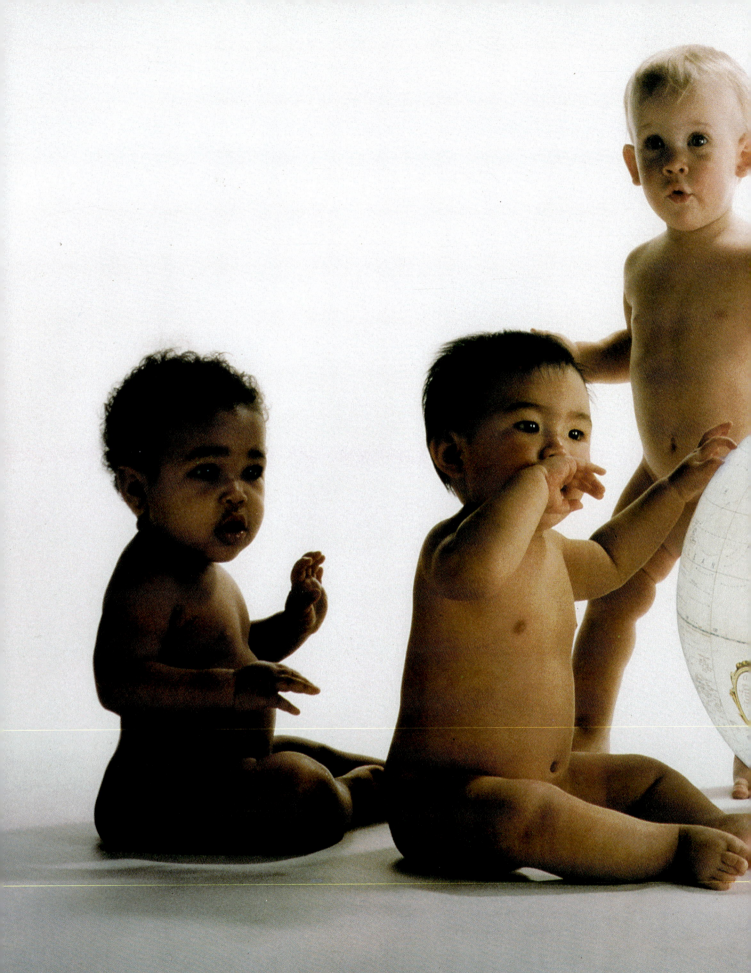

Infancy

Babies are such a nice way to start people.
—Don Herold

As newborns, we were not empty-headed organisms. We had some basic reflexes, among them crying, kicking, and coughing. We slept a lot, and occasionally we smiled, although the meaning of our first smiles was not entirely clear. We ate and we grew. We crawled and then we walked, a journey of a thousand miles beginning with a single step. Sometimes we conformed, sometimes others conformed to us. Our development was a continuous creation of more complex forms. Our helpless kind demanded the meeting eyes of love. We juggled the necessity of curbing our will with becoming what we could will freely. Section Three contains three chapters: "Physical Development in Infancy" (chapter 5), "Cognitive Development in Infancy" (chapter 6), and "Socioemotional Development in Infancy" (chapter 7).

Bill Rane, Mayan
Madonna, detail.

Physical Development in Infancy

Chapter Outline

LIFE-SPAN HEALTH AND WELL-BEING

Chapter Boxes

*Systematic reasoning is something we
could not, as a species of individuals, do
without. But neither, if we are to
remain sane, can we do without direct
perception . . . of the inner and outer
world into which we have been born.*

—Aldous Huxley

> *A baby is the most complicated object made by unskilled labor.*
>
> —Anonymous

IMAGES OF LIFE-SPAN DEVELOPMENT

Studying Newborns

The creature has poor motor coordination and can move itself only with great difficulty. Its general behavior appears to be disorganized, and, although it cries when uncomfortable, it uses few other vocalizations. In fact, it sleeps most of the time, about 16 to 17 hours a day. You are curious about this creature and want to know more about what it can do. You think to yourself, "I wonder if it can see. How could I find out?"

You obviously have a communication problem with the creature. You must devise a way that will allow the creature to "tell" you that it can see. While examining the creature one day, you make an interesting discovery. When you move a large object toward it, it moves its head backward, as if to avoid a collision with the object. The creature's head movement suggests that it has at least some vision.

In case you haven't already guessed, the creature you have been reading about is the human infant, and the role you played is that of a developmentalist interested in devising techniques to learn about the infant's visual perception. After years of work, scientists have developed research tools and methods sophisticated enough to examine the subtle abilities of infants and to interpret their complex actions. Videotape equipment allows researchers to investigate elusive behaviors, and high-speed computers make it possible to perform complex data analysis in minutes instead of months and years. Other sophisticated equipment is used to closely monitor respiration, heart rate, body movement, visual fixation, and sucking behavior, which provide clues to what is going on inside the infant.

PREVIEW

Among the first things developmentalists were able to demonstrate was that infants have highly developed perceptual motor systems. Until recently, though, even some nurses in maternity hospitals believed that newborns are blind at birth, and they told this to mothers. Most parents were also told that their newborns could not taste, smell, or feel pain. As you will discover later in this chapter, we now know that newborns can see (albeit fuzzily), taste, smell, and feel pain. Before we turn to the fascinating world of the infant's perception, we will discuss a number of ideas about infants' and toddlers' physical development.

PHYSICAL GROWTH AND DEVELOPMENT IN INFANCY

Infants' physical development in the first 2 years of life is extensive. At birth, neonates have a gigantic head (relative to the rest of the body) that flops around in an uncontrollable fashion; they also possess reflexes that are dominated by evolutionary movements. In the span of 12 months, infants become capable of sitting anywhere, standing, stooping, climbing, and usually walking. During the second year, growth decelerates, but rapid increases in such activities as running and climbing take place.

Let's now examine in greater detail the sequence of physical development in infancy by studying the infant's reflexes, cephalocaudal and proximodistal sequences, height and weight, gross and fine motor skills, the brain, infant states, nutrition, toilet training, and health.

Critical Thinking

Other than moving a large object toward a newborn's head to see if the newborn responds to it, can you think of other techniques that could be used to determine whether a newborn can see or not?

LIFE-SPAN PRACTICAL KNOWLEDGE 5.1

WHAT TO EXPECT THE FIRST YEAR

The comprehensive month-by-month guide that clearly explains everything parents need to know about the first year with a new baby.

Featuring a practical, illustrated Baby Care Primer, a First Aid Guide, and Best-Odds recipes.

With special sections on the older sibling, selecting the right physician, seasonal concerns and traveling with baby, managing childhood illnesses, and nurturing the adopted baby, the low-birthweight infant, and the baby with specific problems.

By Arlene Eisenberg, Heidi E. Murkoff, and Sandee E. Hathaway, B.S.N. Authors of *What to Expect When You're Expecting*.

With a Foreword by Henry Harris, M.D., F.A.A.P., Albert Einstein Medical Center, New York City.

What To Expect the First Year
(1989) by Arlene Eisenberg, Heidi Murkoff, and Sandee Hathaway. New York: Workman.

What To Expect the First Year provides a broad, developmental-milestone approach to infant development in the first year of life. This is an encyclopedic volume of facts and practical tips on how babies develop, how to become a better parent, and how to deal with problems when they arise. Developmental milestones are given for each month of the first year, along with potential health and behavioral problems. Many questions on parents' minds are asked and intelligently answered by the authors.

Reflexes

What is the nature of the infant's reflexes? The newborn is not an empty-headed organism. Among other things, it has some basic reflexes that are genetically carried survival mechanisms. For example, the newborn has no fear of water; it will naturally hold its breath and contract its throat to keep water out.

Reflexes govern the newborn's movements, which are automatic and beyond the newborn's control. They are built-in reactions to certain stimuli and provide young infants with adaptive responses to their environment before they have had the opportunity to learn. The **sucking reflex** *occurs when newborns automatically suck an object placed in their mouth. The sucking reflex enables newborns to get nourishment before they have associated a nipple with food.* The sucking reflex is an example of a reflex that is present at birth but later disappears. The **rooting reflex** *occurs when the infant's cheek is stroked or the side of the mouth is touched. In response, the infant turns its head toward the side that was touched, in an apparent effort to find something to suck.* The sucking and rooting reflexes disappear when the infant is about 3 to 4 months old. They are replaced by the infant's voluntary eating. The sucking and rooting reflexes have survival value for newborn mammals, who must find the mother's breast to obtain nourishment.

The **Moro reflex** *is a neonatal startle response that occurs in response to a sudden, intense noise or movement. When startled, the newborn arches its back, throws its head back, and flings out its arms and legs. Then the newborn rapidly closes its arms and legs to the center of its body.* The Moro reflex is a vestige from our primate ancestry and it too has survival value. This reflex, which is normal in all newborns, also tends to disappear at 3 to 4 months of age. Steady pressure on any part of the infant's body calms the infant after it has been startled. Holding the infant's arm flexed at the shoulder will quiet the infant.

The experiences of the first three years of life are almost entirely lost to us, and when we attempt to enter into a small child's world, we come as foreigners who have forgotten the landscape and no longer speak the native tongue.

—Selma Fraiberg

Some reflexes present in the newborn—coughing, blinking, and yawning, for example—persist throughout life. They are as important for the adult as they are for the infant. Other reflexes, though, disappear several months following birth as the infant's brain functions mature and voluntary control over many behaviors develops. The movements of some reflexes eventually become incorporated into more complex, voluntary actions. One important example is the **grasping reflex,** *which occurs when something touches the infant's palms. The infant responds by grasping tightly.* By the end of the third month, the grasping reflex diminishes and the infant shows a more voluntary grasp, which is often produced by visual stimuli. For example, when an infant sees a mobile whirling above its crib, it may reach out and try to grasp it. As its motor development becomes smoother, the infant will grasp objects, carefully manipulate them, and explore their qualities.

An overview of the main reflexes we have discussed, along with others, is given in figure 5.1.

Sucking is an especially important reflex: It is the infant's route to nourishment. The sucking capabilities of newborns vary considerably. Some newborns are efficient at forceful sucking and obtaining milk, others are not so adept and get tired before they are full. Most newborns take several weeks to establish a sucking style that is coordinated with the way the mother is holding the infant, the way milk is coming out of the bottle or breast, and the infant's sucking speed and temperament.

An investigation by pediatrician T. Berry Brazelton (1956) involved observations of infants for more than a year to determine the incidence of their sucking when they were nursing and how their sucking changed as they grew older. More than 85 percent of the infants engaged in considerable sucking behavior unrelated to feeding. They sucked their fingers, their fists, and pacifiers. By the age of 1 year, most had stopped the sucking behavior.

Parents should not worry when infants suck their thumbs, fist, or even a pacifier. Many parents, though, do begin to worry when thumb sucking persists into the preschool and elementary school years. As many as 40 percent of children continue to suck their thumbs after they have started school (Kessen, Haith, & Salapatek, 1970). Most developmentalists do not attach a great deal of significance to this behavior and are not aware of

FIGURE 5.1

Infant reflexes.

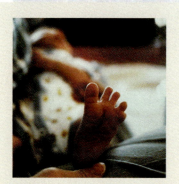

Babinski reflex

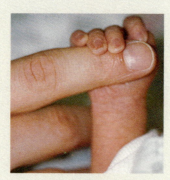

Grasping reflex

Moro reflex

Reflex	Stimulation	Infant's Response	Developmental Pattern
Blinking	Flash of light, puff of air	Closes both eyes	Permanent
Babinski	Sole of foot stroked	Fans out toes, twists foot in	Disappears 9 months to 1 year
Grasping	Palms touched	Grasps tightly	Weakens after 3 months, disappears after 1 year
Moro (startle)	Sudden stimulation, such as hearing loud noise or being dropped	Startles, arches back, throws head back, flings out arms and legs and then rapidly closes them to center of body	Disappears 3 to 4 months
Rooting	Cheek stroked or side of mouth touched	Turns head, opens mouth, begins sucking	Disappears 3 to 4 months
Stepping	Infant held above surface and feet lowered to touch surface	Moves feet as if to walk	Disappears 3 to 4 months
Sucking	Object touching mouth	Sucks automatically	Disappears 3 to 4 months
Swimming	Infant put face down in water	Makes coordinated swimming movements	Disappears 6 to 7 months
Tonic neck	Infant placed on back	Forms fists with both hands and usually turns head to the right (sometimes called the "fencer's pose" because the infant looks like it is assuming a fencer's position)	Disappears 2 months

parenting strategies that might contribute to it. Individual differences in children's biological makeup may be involved to some degree in the continuation of sucking behavior.

Nonnutritive sucking, *sucking behavior unrelated to the infant's feeding,* is used as a measure in a large number of research studies with young infants, because young infants quit sucking when they attend to something, such as a picture or a vocalization. Nonnutritive sucking, then, is one of the ingenious ways developmentalists study the young infant's attention and learning.

Cephalocaudal and Proximodistal Sequences

The **cephalocaudal pattern** *is the sequence in which the greatest growth always occurs at the top—the head—with physical growth in size, weight, and feature differentiation gradually working its way down from top to bottom (to neck, shoulders, middle trunk, and so on).* This same pattern occurs in the head area; the top parts of the head—the eyes and brain—grow faster than the lower parts—such as the jaw. An extraordinary proportion of the total body is occupied by the head during prenatal development and early infancy.

The **proximodistal pattern** *is the sequence in which growth starts at the center of the body and moves toward the extremities.* An example of this is the early maturation of muscular control of the trunk and arms as compared with that of the hands and fingers.

Height and Weight

The average North American newborn is 20 inches long and weighs 7½ pounds. Ninety-five percent of full-term newborns are 18 to 22 inches long and weigh between 5½ and 10 pounds. In the first several days of life, most newborns lose 5 to 7 percent of their body weight before they learn to adjust to neonatal feeding. Once infants adjust to sucking, swallowing, and digesting, they grow rapidly, gaining an average of 5 to 6 ounces per week during the first month. By 4 months, they have doubled their birthweight, and they have nearly tripled it by their first birthday. Infants grow about 1 inch per month during the first year, reaching approximately 1½ times their birth length by their first birthday.

Infants' rate of growth is considerably slower in the second year of life. By 2 years of age, infants weigh approximately 26 to 32 pounds, having gained a quarter to half a pound per month during the second year; now they have reached about one-fifth of their adult weight. At 2 years of age, the average infant is 32 to 35 inches in height, which is nearly one-half of their adult height. A summary of changes in height and weight during the first 18 months of life is shown in figure 5.2.

Gross and Fine Motor Skills

Gross motor skills *involve large muscle activities such as moving one's arms and walking.* **Fine motor skills** *involve more finely tuned movements, such as finger dexterity.* Let's examine the changes in gross and fine motor skills in the first 2 years of life.

Gross Motor Skills

At birth, the infant has no appreciable coordination of the chest or arms, but in the first month the infant can lift its head from a prone position. At about 3 months, the infant can hold its chest up and use its arms for support after being in a prone position. At 3 to 4 months, infants can roll over, and at 4 to 5 months they can support some weight with their legs. At about 6 months, infants can sit without support, and by 7 to 8 months they can crawl and stand without support. At approximately 8 months, infants can pull themselves up to a standing position, at 10 to 11 months they can walk using furniture for support (this is called "cruising"), and at 12 to 13 months the average infant can walk without assistance. A summary of the developmental accomplishments in gross motor skills during the first year is shown in figure 5.3. The actual month at which the milestones occur varies by as much as 2 to 4 months, especially among older infants. What remains fairly uniform, however, is the sequence of accomplishments. An important implication of these infant motor accomplishments is the increasing degree of independence they bring. Older infants can explore their environment more

extensively and initiate social interaction with caregivers and peers more readily than when they were younger.

> *A baby is an angel whose wings decrease as his legs increase.*
>
> —French Proverb

In the second year of life, toddlers become more motorically skilled and mobile. They are no longer content with being in a playpen and want to move all over the place. Child development experts believe that motor activity during the second year is vital to the child's competent development and that few restrictions, except for safety purposes, should be placed on their motoric adventures (Fraiberg, 1959).

By 13 to 18 months, toddlers can pull a toy attached to a string, use their hands and legs to climb up a number of steps, and ride four-wheel wagons (White, 1988). By 18 to 24 months, toddlers can walk fast or run stiffly for a short distance, balance on their feet in a squat position while playing with objects on the floor, walk backward without losing their balance, stand and kick a ball without falling, stand and throw a ball, and jump in place (Schirmer, 1974).

Fine Motor Skills

Infants have hardly any control over fine motor skills at birth, although they have many components of what later become finely coordinated arm, hand, and finger movements (Rosenblith, 1992). The development of such behaviors as reaching and grasping becomes increasingly more refined during the first 2 years of life. Initially, infants show only crude shoulder and elbow movements, but later show wrist movements, hand rotation, and coordination of the thumb and forefinger. The maturation of hand-eye coordination over the first 2 years of life is reflected in the improvement of fine motor skills.

The Brain

As an infant walks, talks, runs, shakes a rattle, smiles, and frowns, changes in its brain are occurring. Consider that the infant began life as a single cell and 9 months later was born with a brain and nervous system that contained approximately 100 billion nerve cells. Indeed, at birth, the infant probably had all of the nerve cells (neurons) it is going to have in its entire life. However, at birth and in early infancy, the connectedness of these neurons is impoverished. As the infant ages from birth to 2 years, the interconnection of neurons increases dramatically as the dendrites (the receiving parts) of the neurons branch out (see figure 5.4).

At birth, the newborn's brain is about 25 percent of its adult weight, and by the second birthday it is about 75 percent of its adult weight.

Infant States

To chart and understand the infant's development, developmentalists have constructed classifications of infants' states (Berg & Berg, 1987; Brown, 1964; Colombo, Moss, & Horowitz, 1989). *States* is an abbreviated term for states of consciousness,

FIGURE 5.2

Developmental changes in height and weight from birth to 18 months. *The numbers on the colored lines in the charts refer to the percentiles for infants' height and weight at different months of age compared with other infants of the same age. The 50th percentile indicates that half of the infants of a particular age are taller and half are shorter. The 10th percentile tells us that 10 percent of the infants of that age are shorter and 90 percent are taller.*

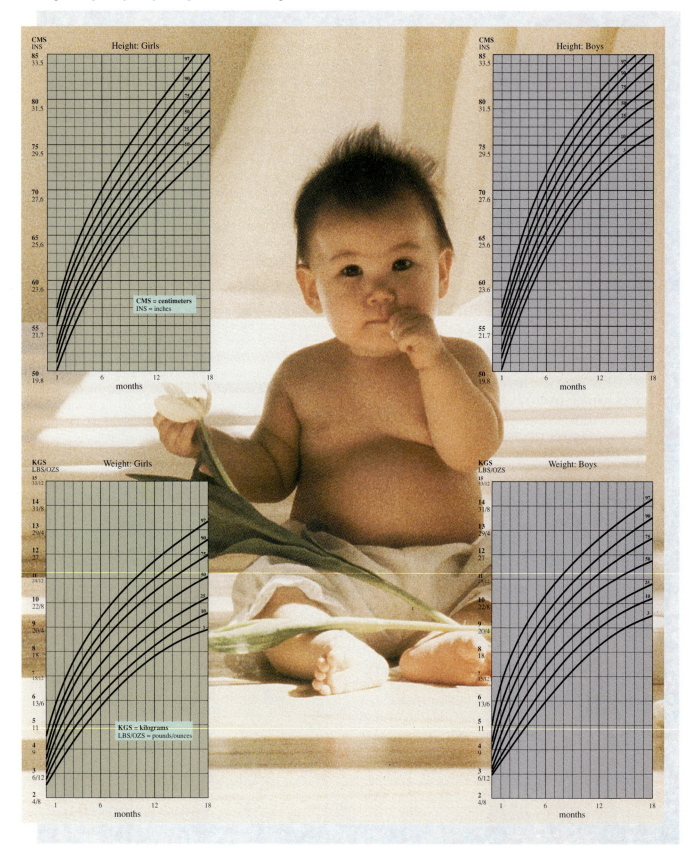

FIGURE 5.3

Developmental accomplishments in gross motor skills during the first 15 months.

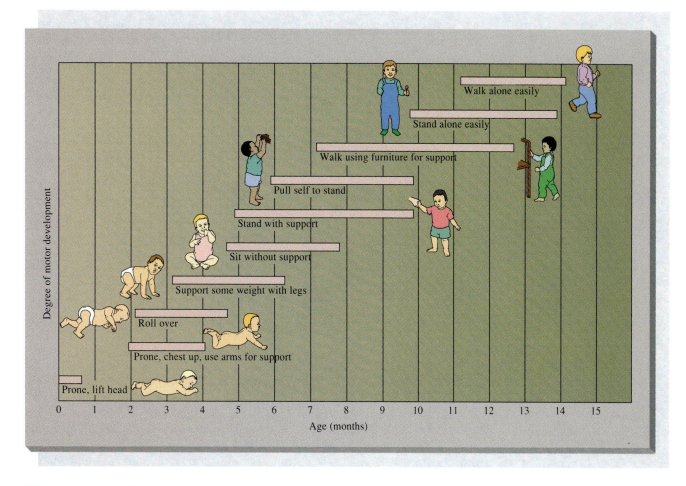

FIGURE 5.4

The development of dendritic spreading. *Note the increase in connectedness between neurons over the course of the first 2 years of life.*

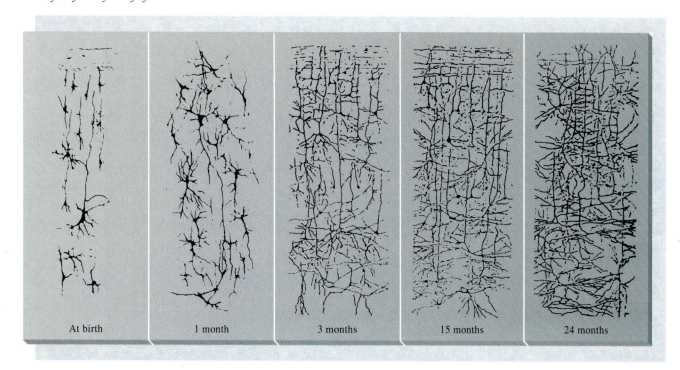

| At birth | 1 month | 3 months | 15 months | 24 months |

LIFE-SPAN PRACTICAL KNOWLEDGE 5.2

Solve Your Child's Sleep Problems

(1985) by Richard Ferber. New York: Simon & Schuster.

Solve Your Child's Sleep Problems helps parents to recognize when their infant or child has a sleep problem and tells them what to do about the problem. Author Richard Ferber is director of the Center for Pediatric Sleep Disorders at Children's Hospital in Boston. Among the topics covered are basic information about normal and abnormal sleep patterns in infants and children, the sleepless child, sleep rhythm disorders, interruptions during sleep, and other problems such as snoring and head-banging. An appendix provides suggestions for further reading, such as children's books on bedtime, sleep, and dreams, as well as information about organizations that might help parents who have infants or children with sleep disorders.

This is an excellent self-help book. It is clearly written, and the author's prescriptions are humane and wise.

---

or the level of awareness that characterizes the individual. The following is one possible classification scheme, describing seven infant states (Brown, 1964):

1. *Deep sleep.* The infant lies motionless with eyes closed, has regular breathing, makes no vocalization, and does not respond to outside stimulation.
2. *Regular sleep.* The infant moves very little, breathing might be raspy or involve wheezing, and respirations may be normal or move from normal to irregular.
3. *Disturbed sleep.* There is a variable amount of movement, the infant's eyelids are closed but might flutter, breathing is irregular, and there may be some squawks, sobs, and sighs.
4. *Drowsy.* The infant's eyes are open or partly open and appear glassy, there is little movement (although startles and free movement may occur), vocalizations are more regular than in disturbed sleep, and some transitional sounds may be made.
5. *Alert activity.* This is the state most often viewed by parents as being awake. The infant's eyes are open and bright. The infant makes a variety of free movements, it may fret, and its skin may redden. There may be irregular breathing when the infant feels tension.
6. *Alert and focused.* This kind of attention is often seen in older children but is unusual in the neonate. The child's eyes are open and bright. Some motor activity may occur, but it is integrated around a specific activity. This state may occur when focusing on a sound or visual stimulus.
7. *Inflexibly focused.* In this state, the infant is awake but does not react to external stimuli; two examples are sucking and wild crying. During wild crying, the infant may thrash about, but the eyes are closed as screams pour out.

Using classification schemes such as the one just described, researchers have identified many different aspects of infant development. One such aspect is the sleeping-waking cycle. When we were infants, sleep consumed more of our time than it does now. Newborns sleep for 16 to 17 hours a day, although some sleep more, and others less. The range is from a low of about 10 hours to a high of about 21 hours (Parmalee, Wenner, & Schulz, 1964). The longest period of sleep is not always between 11 P.M. and 7 A.M. Although total sleep remains somewhat consistent for young infants, their sleep during the day does not always follow a rhythmic pattern. An infant might change from sleeping several long bouts of 7 or 8 hours to sleeping three or four shorter sessions only several hours in duration. By about 1 month of age, most infants have begun to sleep longer at night, and by about 4 months of age they usually have moved closer to adultlike sleep patterns, spending their longest span of sleep at night and their longest span of waking during the day (Coons & Guilleminault, 1984).

> *Sleep that knits up the ravelled sleave of care . . .*
> *Balm of hurt minds, nature's second course.*
> *Chief nourisher in life's feast.*
>
> —William Shakespeare

A special concern about infant sleep is **sudden infant death syndrome (SIDS),** *a condition that occurs when an infant stops breathing, usually during the night, and suddenly dies without apparent cause.* Approximately 13 percent of infant deaths are due to SIDS; for infants between 10 days after birth and 1 year of age, SIDS results in more deaths than any other factor. While we do not know exactly what causes SIDS, infants who die from the condition reveal biological vulnerabilities early in their development, including a greater incidence of prematurity, low birthweight, low Apgar scores, and respiratory problems (Barness & Gilbert-Barness, 1992; Buck & others, 1989; Woolsey, 1992).

Nutrition

Four-month-old Robert lives in Bloomington, Indiana, with his middle-class parents. He is well nourished and healthy. By contrast, 4-month-old Nikita lives in Ethiopia. Nikita and his parents live in impoverished conditions. Nikita is so poorly nourished that he has become emaciated and lies near death. The lives of Robert and Nikita reveal the vast diversity in nutritional status among today's children. Our coverage of infant nutrition begins with information about nutritional needs and eating behavior, then turns to the issue of breast- versus bottle-feeding, and concludes with an overview of malnutrition.

Nutritional Needs and Eating Behavior

The importance of adequate energy and nutrient intake consumed in a loving and supportive environment during the infant years cannot be overstated (Pipes, 1988). From birth to 1 year of age, human infants triple their weight and increase their length by 50 percent. Individual differences of infants in nutrient reserves, body composition, growth rates, and activity patterns make defining actual nutrient needs difficult. However, because parents need guidelines, nutritionists recommend that infants consume approximately 50 calories per day for each pound they weigh—more than twice an adult's requirement per pound.

Breast- Versus Bottle-Feeding

Human milk, or an alternative formula, is the baby's source of nutrients and energy for the first 4 to 6 months. For years, developmentalists and nutritionists have debated whether breast-feeding an infant has substantial benefits over bottle-feeding. The growing consensus is that breast-feeding is better for the baby's health (Eiger, 1992; Worthington-Roberts, 1988). Breast-feeding provides milk that is clean and digestible and helps immunize the newborn from disease. Breast-fed babies gain weight more rapidly than do bottle-fed babies. However, only about one-half of mothers nurse newborns, and even fewer continue to nurse their infants after several months. Most mothers who work outside the home find it impossible to breast-feed their young infants for many months. Even though breast-feeding provides more ideal nutrition, some researchers argue that there is no long-term evidence of physiological or psychological harm to American infants when they are bottle-fed (Caldwell, 1964; Ferguson, Harwood, & Shannon, 1987; Forsyth, Leventhal, & McCarthy, 1985). Despite these researchers' claims that no long-term negative consequences of bottle-feeding have been documented in American children, the American Academy of Pediatrics, the majority of physicians and nurses, and two leading publications for parents—the *Infant Care Manual* and *Parents* magazine—endorse breast-feeding as having physiological and psychological benefits (Young, 1990).

There is a consensus among experts that breast-feeding is the preferred practice, especially in developing countries where inadequate nutrition and poverty are common. In 1991, the Institute of Medicine, part of the National Academy of Sciences, issued a report that women should be encouraged to breast-feed their infants exclusively for the first 4 to 6 months of life. According to the report, the benefits of breast-feeding

Human milk, or an alternative formula, is a baby's source of nutrients for the first 4 to 6 months. The growing consensus is that breast-feeding is better for the baby's health, although controversy still swirls about the issue of breast- versus bottle-feeding.

are protection against some gastrointestinal infections and food allergies for infants, and possible reduction of osteoporosis and breast cancer for mothers. Nonetheless, while the majority of experts recommend breast-feeding, the issue of breast- versus bottle-feeding continues to be hotly debated. Many parents, especially working mothers, are now following a sequence of breast-feeding in the first several months and bottle-feeding thereafter. This strategy allows the mother's natural milk to provide nutritional benefits to the infant early in development and permits mothers to return to work after several months. Working mothers are also increasingly using "pumping," in which they use a pump to extract breast milk that can be stored for later feeding of the infant when the mother is not present.

Critical Thinking

If and when you become a parent, what considerations would you have about the nutrition your infant gets? How important do you believe breast-feeding is for the infant's development? Explain.

Malnutrition in Infancy

Marasmus *is a wasting away of body tissues in the infant's first year, caused by severe deficiency of protein and calories.* The infant becomes grossly underweight, and its muscles atrophy.

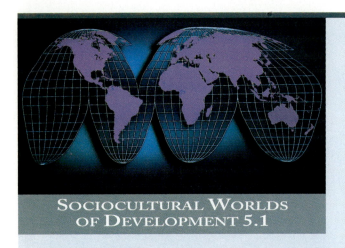

Children Living Hungry in America

Harlingen, Texas, is a heavily Chicano city of approximately 40,000 near the Rio Grande. At Su Clinica ("Your Clinic"), which serves many Chicano residents, poverty and unemployment are evident in the waiting list of 800 families needing low-cost care. Many of the Chicanos working in Texas agriculture receive no health care benefits, and few make even the minimum wage. Farm workers usually get less than $1.50 an hour for working long days in the pesticide-infected fields. The infant mortality rate for the region is listed as good by the U.S. government, but this description is wrong. Many of the deaths are not counted. A baby dies and is buried. People outside the family seldom know. Many infants and young children experi-

ence growth problems because they do not get enough to eat. This is not unique to Harlingen, Texas; many other locations in the United States have their share of impoverished families who have difficulty making ends meet and putting food on the table. Hunger and poverty are seen in the children of poor Mississippi tenant farmers, in the children of laid-off coal miners in West Virginia, in neglected children in the ghettos of New York and Chicago, and in the increasing number of homeless families across the nation. In many instances, these children are the victims of silent undernutrition, less dramatic than in Africa or Bangladesh, but no less real (Brown & Pizer, 1987).

Many locations in the United States, including the ghettos of many large American cities, have impoverished families that have difficulty making ends meet and putting food on the table.

The main cause of marasmus is early weaning from breast milk to inadequate nutrients such as unsuitable and unsanitary cow's milk formula. Something that looks like milk, but is not, usually a form of tapioca or rice, also may be used. In many of the world's developing countries, mothers used to breast-feed their infants for at least 2 years. To become more modern, they stopped breast-feeding much earlier and replaced it with bottle-feeding. Comparisons of breast-fed and bottle-fed infants in such countries as Afghanistan, Haiti, Ghana, and Chile document that the rate of infant death is much greater among bottle-fed than among breast-fed infants, with bottle-fed infants sometimes dying at a rate five times higher than breast-fed infants (Grant, 1994). So far our discussion of malnutrition has focused on developing countries, but hunger is also a problem in some areas of the United States. To read about children living hungry in America, turn to Sociocultural Worlds of Development 5.1.

Toilet Training

Being toilet trained is a physical and motor skill that is expected to be attained in the North American culture by 3 years of age (Charlesworth, 1987). By the age of 3, 84 percent of children

are dry throughout the day and 66 percent are dry throughout the night. The ability to control elimination depends both on muscular maturation and on motivation. Children must be able to control their muscles to eliminate at the appropriate time, and they must also want to eliminate in the toilet or potty rather than in their pants.

Currently, there is a trend toward beginning toilet training later than in the past. Many of today's parents begin the toilet training of their toddlers at about 20 months to 2 years. Developmentalists now realize that cognitive maturity needs to be added to muscular maturation and motivation for appropriate toilet training to take place. Toddlers need to be able to understand instructions and the need for accomplishing the task. Developmentalists also recommend that toilet training be accomplished in a warm, relaxed, supportive manner.

At this point we have discussed a number of ideas about infants' reflexes, cephalocaudal and proximodistal sequences, height and weight, gross and fine motor skills, the brain, infant states, nutrition, and health. A summary of these ideas is presented in concept table 5.1. Next, we turn our attention to the fascinating sensory and perceptual worlds of infants.

CONCEPT TABLE 5.1

Physical Growth and Development in Infancy

Concept	Processes/Related Ideas	Characteristics/Description
Reflexes	Their nature	The newborn is no longer viewed as a passive, empty-headed organism. Newborns are limited physically, though, and reflexes—automatic movements—govern the newborn's behavior.
	Sucking	For infants, sucking is an important means of obtaining nutrition, as well as a pleasurable, soothing activity. Nonnutritive sucking is of interest to researchers because it provides a means of evaluating attention.
Cephalocaudal and proximodistal patterns	Their nature	The cephalocaudal pattern is growth from the top down; the proximodistal pattern is growth from the center out.
Height and weight	Their nature	The average North American newborn is 20 inches long and weighs 7½ pounds. Infants grow about 1 inch per month during the first year and nearly triple their weight by their first birthday. Infants' rate of growth is slower in the second year.
Gross and fine motor skills	Gross motor skills	Gross motor skills involve large muscle activities such as moving one's arms and walking. A number of gross motor milestones occur in infancy, among them walking at an average age of 12 to 13 months.
	Fine motor skills	Fine motor skills involve more finely tuned movements than gross motor skills, and include such skills as finger dexterity. A number of fine motor milestones occur in infancy, among them the development of reaching and grasping skills.
States	Classification	Researchers have put together different classification systems; one involves seven infant state categories, including deep sleep, drowsy, alert and focused, and inflexibly focused.
	The sleeping-waking cycle	Newborns usually sleep 16 to 17 hours a day. By 4 months, they approach adultlike sleeping patterns. REM sleep, during which children and adults are most likely to dream, occurs much more in early infancy than in childhood and adulthood. The high percentage of REM sleep—about half of neonatal sleep—may be a self-stimulatory device, or it may promote brain development. Sudden infant death syndrome (SIDS) is a condition that occurs when an infant stops breathing and suddenly dies without apparent cause.
Nutrition	Nutritional needs and eating behavior	Infants need to consume approximately 50 calories per day for each pound they weigh.
	Breast- versus bottle-feeding	The growing consensus is that breast-feeding is superior to bottle-feeding, but the increase in working mothers has meant fewer breast-fed babies. A current trend is for working mothers to breast-feed infants in the first several months to build up the infant's immune system, then bottle-feed after they have returned to work.
	Malnutrition	Severe infant malnutrition is still prevalent in many parts of the world. Severe protein-calorie deficiency can cause marasmus, a wasting away of body tissues. It is mainly caused by early weaning from breast milk.
Toilet training	Its nature	Being toilet trained is a physical and motor skill that is expected to be attained by 3 years of age in the North American culture. Currently, there is a trend toward beginning toilet training later than in the past; many of today's parents begin toilet training their toddlers at about 20 months to 2 years.

SENSORY AND PERCEPTUAL DEVELOPMENT

At the beginning of this chapter, you read about how newborns come into the world equipped with sensory capacities. What are sensation and perception? Can a newborn see, and, if so, what can it perceive? What about the other senses—hearing, smell, taste, touch, and pain? What are they like in the newborn, and how do they develop in infancy? What kind of visual, auditory, and tactile stimulation is appropriate for infants? These are among the intriguing questions we will now explore.

What Are Sensation and Perception?

How does a newborn know that her mother's skin is soft rather than rough? How does a 5-year-old know what color his hair is? How does an 8-year-old know that summer is warmer than winter? How does a 10-year-old know that a firecracker is louder than a cat's meow? Infants and children "know" these things because of their senses. All information comes to the infant through the senses. Without vision, hearing, touch, taste, smell, and other senses, the infant's brain would be isolated from the world; the infant would live in dark silence, a tasteless, colorless, feelingless void.

Sensation *occurs when information contacts sensory receptors— the eyes, ears, tongue, nostrils, and skin.* The sensation of hearing occurs when waves of pulsating air are collected by the outer ear and transmitted through the bones of the inner ear to the auditory nerve. The sensation of vision occurs as rays of light contact the two eyes and become focused on the retina. **Perception** *is the interpretation of what is sensed.* The information about physical events that contacts the ears may be interpreted as musical sounds, for example. The physical energy transmitted to the retina may be interpreted as a particular color, pattern, or shape.

Visual Perception

How do we see? Anyone who has ever taken pictures while on vacation appreciates the miracle of perception. The camera is no match for it. Consider a favorite scenic spot that you visited and photographed sometime in the past. Compare your memory of this spot to your snapshot. Although your memory may be faulty, there is little doubt that the richness of your perceptual experience is not captured in the picture. The sense of depth that you felt at this spot probably is not conveyed by the snapshot. Neither is the subtlety of the colors you perceived nor the intricacies of textures and shapes. Human vision is complex, and its development is complex too.

The Newborn's Vision

Psychologist William James (1890/1950) called the newborn's perceptual world a "blooming, buzzing confusion." Was James right? A century later we can safely say that he was wrong. Infants' perception of visual information is *much* more advanced than previously thought (Bahrick, 1992; Bower, 1989; 1993).

Our tour of visual perception begins with the pioneering work of Robert Fantz (1963). Fantz placed infants in a "looking chamber" that had two visual displays on the ceiling above the infant's head. An experimenter viewed the infant's eyes by looking through a peephole. If the infant was fixating on one of the displays, the experimenter could see the display's reflection in the infant's eyes. This allowed the experimenter to determine how long the infant looked at each display. In figure 5.5, you can see Fantz's looking chamber and the results of his experiment. The infants preferred to look at patterns rather than at color or brightness. For example, they preferred to look at a face, a piece of printed matter, or a bull's-eye longer than at red, yellow, or white discs. In another experiment, Fantz found that younger infants—only 2 days old—looked longer at patterned stimuli, such as faces and concentric circles, than at red, white, or yellow discs. Based on these results, pattern perception likely has an innate basis, or at least is acquired after only minimal environmental experience. The newborn's visual world is not the blooming, buzzing confusion William James imagined.

Just how well can infants see? The newborn's vision is estimated to be 20/200 to 20/600 on the well-known Snellen chart that you are tested with when you have your eyes examined (Haith, 1991). This is about 10 to 30 times lower than normal adult vision (20/20). By 6 months of age, however, vision is 20/100 or better (Banks & Salapatek, 1983).

Infants' Perception of Faces

The human face is perhaps the most important visual pattern for the newborn to perceive. The infant masters a sequence of steps in progressing toward full perceptual appreciation of the face (Gibson, 1969). At about 3½ weeks, the infant is fascinated with the eyes, perhaps because the infant notices simple perceptual features such as dots, angles, and circles. At 1 to 2 months of age, the infant notices and perceives contour. At 2 months and older, the infant begins to differentiate facial features; the eyes are distinguished from other parts of the face, the mouth is noticed, and movements of the mouth draw attention to it. By 5 months of age, the infant has detected other features of the face—its plasticity, its solid, three-dimensional surface, the oval shape of the head, and the orientation of the eyes and the mouth. Beyond 6 months of age, the infant distinguishes familiar faces from unfamiliar faces—mother from stranger, masks from real faces, and so on.

An important question that most parents would like to have answered for them is, "How much stimulation should I give the baby?" Another question they might ask is, "How much and what kind of visual stimulation should I give the baby?" To read about these topics, turn to Perspectives on Parenting and Education 5.1.

Depth Perception

How early can infants perceive depth? To investigate this question, infant perception researchers Eleanor Gibson and Richard Walk (1960) conducted a classic experiment. They constructed a miniature cliff with a drop-off covered by glass. The motivation for this experiment arose when Gibson was eating a picnic lunch on the edge of the Grand Canyon. She wondered

FIGURE 5.5

Fantz's experiment on infants' visual perception. (a) *Infants 2 to 3 months old preferred to look at some stimuli more than others. In Fantz's experiment, infants preferred to look at patterns rather than at color or brightness. For example, they looked longer at a face, a piece of printed matter, or a bulls-eye than at red, yellow, or white discs.* (b) *Fantz used a "looking chamber" to study infants' perception of stimuli.*

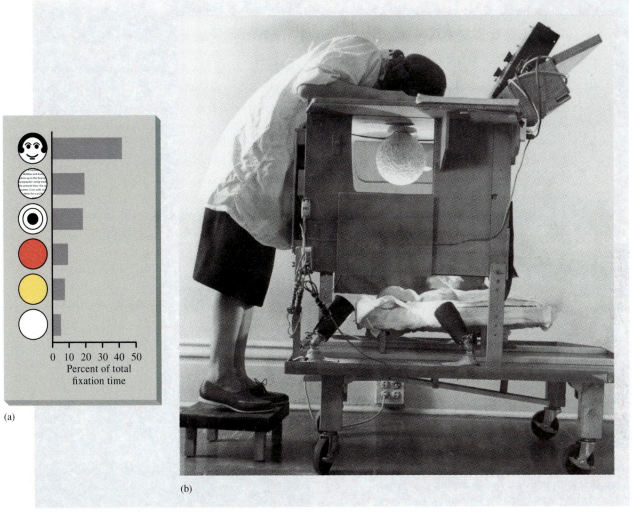

(a)

(b)

(a) Modified from "The Origin of Form Perception" by R. L. Fantz. Copyright © 1961 by Scientific American, Inc. All rights reserved.

whether an infant looking over the canyon's rim would perceive the dangerous drop-off and back up. In their laboratory, Gibson and Walk placed infants on the edge of a visual cliff and had their mothers coax them to crawl onto the glass (see figure 5.6). Most infants would not crawl out on the glass, choosing instead to remain on the shallow side, indicating that they could perceive depth. However, because the 6- to 14-month-old infants had extensive visual experience, this research did not answer the question of whether depth perception is innate.

Exactly how early in life does depth perception develop? Since younger infants do not crawl, this question is difficult to answer. Research with 2- to 4-month-old infants shows differences in heart rate when these infants are placed directly on the deep side of the visual cliff instead of on the shallow side (Campos, Langer, & Krowitz, 1970). However, an alternative interpretation is that young infants respond to differences in some visual characteristics of the deep and shallow cliffs, with no actual knowledge of depth.

The Young Infant's Built-In Knowledge of How the Perceptual World Works

Infant perception researcher Elizabeth Spelke (1988, 1991) has revealed that babies as young as 4-months of age have a rudimentary knowledge of the way the perceptual world works, or should work. She places babies before a puppet stage, where she shows them a series of unexpected actions—for example, a ball seems to roll through a solid barrier, another seems to leap between two platforms, and a third appears to hang in midair. Spelke measures the babies' looking time and records longer intervals for unexpected than expected actions. Spelke concludes that babies must have some basic knowledge about the way physical objects work in the perceptual world. Spelke says that

PERSPECTIVES ON PARENTING AND EDUCATION 5.1

The Right Stimulation and Suggested Activities for Visual Stimulation of Infants

Some parents don't interact with their infants often enough and don't provide them with adequate experiences to stimulate their senses. Other well-meaning parents may actually overstimulate their babies.

Infants do need a certain amount of stimulation to develop their perceptual skills. Infants should not be unattended for long stretches of time in barren environments. Many babies born into impoverished families, as well as babies in "warehouse" day-care centers with many babies per caregiver and an absence of appropriate stimuli and toys, are at risk for receiving inadequate sensory stimulation.

Caregivers should play with infants, give them toys, and periodically provide them with undivided attention during the course of the day. Some infant experts, however, worry that some parents, often those who want to have a "superbaby," may give their infant too much stimulation, which can cause the infant to become confused, irritated, or withdrawn (Bower, 1977; White & Held, 1966). Such parents likely place too much pressure on the infant's developing sensory systems and cause more damage than good.

In thinking about what the "right" amount and type of stimulation is, it is important to recognize that what is right may differ from one baby to another. Some infants have a low threshold for sensory stimulation—that is, they can't handle a heavy load of stimulation, and they become overwhelmed and cry and fuss when they are frequently exposed to it. Other infants have a high threshold for sensory stimulation—they like a lot of sensory stimulation and can benefit from it (Korner, 1971; Zuckerman, 1979).

In sum, it is important for parents to be sensitive to their infant's stimulation needs and monitor when the infant "senses" too little or too much stimulation. The following are some suggested activities for visual, auditory, and tactile stimulation of infants at different developmental levels (Whaley & Wong, 1988):

- Birth to 1 month:
  Look at the infant within close range.
  Hang a bright, shiny object within 8 to 10 inches of the infant's face and in midline.

- 2–3 months:
  Provide bright objects.
  Make the room bright with pictures or mirrors on the wall.
  Take the infant to different rooms while you do chores.
  Place the infant in an infant seat for a vertical view of the environment.

- 4–6 months:
  Position the infant to see in a mirror.
  Give brightly colored toys to the infant to grasp (toys that are small enough to grasp).

- 6–9 months:
  Give the infant large toys with bright colors, movable parts, and noisemakers.
  Place the infant in front of a mirror; the infant will enjoy patting the mirror, making sounds at the image.
  The infant enjoys peekaboo, especially hiding its face in a towel.
  Make funny faces to encourage imitation.
  Give the infant paper to tear and crumble.
  Give the infant a ball of yarn or string to pull apart.

- 9–12 months:
  Show the infant large pictures in books.
  Take the infant to places where there are animals, many people, different objects (for example, a shopping center).
  Play ball by rolling a ball to the infant, demonstrating how to "throw" it back.
  Demonstrate building a two-block tower.

At 4 to 6 months, infants can be positioned to see in a mirror and they can be given brightly colored toys that are small enough for them to grasp.

FIGURE 5.6

Examining infants' depth perception on the visual cliff. *The apparatus consists of a board laid across a sheet of heavy glass, with a patterned material directly beneath the glass on one side and several feet below it on the other. Placed on the center board, the child crawls to its mother across the "shallow" side. Called from the "deep" side, the child pats the glass but, despite this tactual evidence that the cliff is a solid surface, the child refuses to cross over to the mother.*

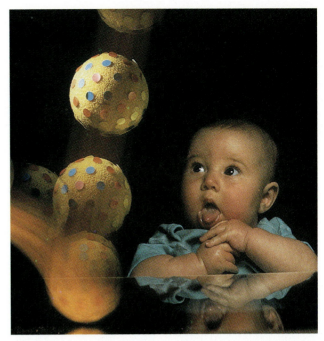

Above, a 4-month-old in Elizabeth's Spelke's infant perception laboratory is tested to determine if it knows that an object in motion will not stop in midair. Spelke believes the young infant's knowledge about how the perceptual world works is innate.

at such young ages when infants can't yet talk about objects, move around objects, manipulate objects, or even see objects with high resolution, they seem to be able to recognize where a moving object is when it has left their visual field and make inferences about where it should be when it comes into their sight again.

Spelke and an increasing number of other infant perception researchers, believe that young infants have a biologically programmed core knowledge about the way the perceptual world works.

Hearing

What is the nature of hearing in newborns? Can the fetus hear? What types of auditory stimulation should be used with infants at different points in the first year? We examine each of these questions.

Immediately after birth, infants can hear, although their sensory thresholds are somewhat higher than those of adults (Trehub & others, 1991). That is, a stimulus must be louder to be heard by a newborn than it must be to be heard by an adult. Also, in one recent study, as infants aged from 8 to 28 weeks, they became more proficient at localizing sounds (Morrongiello, Fenwick, & Chance, 1990). Not only can newborns hear, but the possibility has been raised that the fetus can hear as it nestles within its mother's womb. Let's examine this possibility further.

The fetus can hear sounds in the last few months of pregnancy: the mother's voice, music, and so on. Given that the fetus can hear sounds, two psychologists wanted to find out if listening to Dr. Seuss's classic story *The Cat in the Hat*, while still in the mother's womb, would produce a preference for hearing the story after birth (DeCasper & Spence, 1986). Sixteen pregnant women read *The Cat in the Hat* to their fetuses twice a day over the last 6 weeks of their pregnancies. When the babies were born, they were given a choice of listening to either *The Cat in the Hat* or a story with a different rhyme and pace, *The King, the Mice, and the Cheese.* They made their choices by varying their sucking rate. Sucking at one rate (slowly, for example) resulted in their hearing a recording of one of the stories, and sucking at another rate resulted in hearing a recording of the other story. The newborns preferred listening to *The Cat in the Hat,* which they had heard frequently as a fetus (see figure 5.7).

Two important conclusions can be drawn from this investigation. First, it reveals how ingenious scientists have become at assessing the development not only of infants but of fetuses as well, in this case discovering a way to "interview" newborn babies who cannot yet talk. Second, it reveals the remarkable ability of an infant's brain to learn even before birth.

FIGURE 5.7

(a) *Pregnant mothers read* The Cat in the Hat *to their fetuses during the last few months of pregnancy.* (b) *When the babies were born, they preferred listening to a recording of their mothers reading* The Cat in the Hat, *as evidenced by their sucking on a nipple that produced this recording.*

(a)

(b)

Touch and Pain

Do newborns respond to touch? What activities can adults engage in that involve tactile (touch) stimulation at various points in the infant's development? Can newborns feel pain?

Touch in the Newborn

Newborns do respond to touch. A touch to the cheek produces a turning of the head, whereas a touch to the lips produces sucking movements. An important ability that develops in infancy is to connect information about vision with information about touch. One-year-olds clearly can do this, and it appears that 6-month-olds can too (Acredolo & Hake, 1982). Whether still-younger infants can coordinate vision and touch is yet to be determined.

Pain

If and when you have a son and need to consider whether he should be circumcised, the issue of an infant's pain perception probably will become important to you. Circumcision is usually performed on young boys about the third day after birth. Will your young son experience pain if he is circumcised when he is 3 days old? Increased crying and fussing occur during the circumcision procedure, suggesting that 3-day-old infants experience pain (Gunnar, Malone, & Fisch, 1987; Porter, Porges, & Marshall, 1988).

In the investigation by Megan Gunnar and her colleagues (1987), the healthy newborn's ability to cope with stress was evaluated. The newborn infant males cried intensely during the circumcision, indicating that it was stressful. The researchers pointed out that it is rather remarkable that the newborn infant does not suffer serious consequences from the surgery. Rather, the circumcised infant displays amazing resiliency and ability to cope. Within several minutes after the surgery, the infant can nurse and interact in a normal manner with his mother. And, if allowed to, the newly circumcised newborn drifts into a deep sleep that seems to serve as a coping mechanism. In this experiment, the time spent in deep sleep was greater in the 60 to 240 minutes after the circumcision than before it.

For many years, doctors have performed operations on newborns without anesthesia. This accepted medical practice was followed because of the dangers of anesthesia and the supposition that newborns do not feel pain. Recently, as researchers have convincingly demonstrated that newborns can feel pain, the long-standing practice of operating on newborns without anesthesia is being challenged.

FIGURE 5.8

Newborns' preference for the smell of their mother's breast pad. In the experiment by MacFarlane (1975), 6-day-old infants preferred to smell their mother's breast pad over a clean one that had never been used, but 2-day-old infants did not show this preference, indicating that this odor preference requires several days of experience to develop.

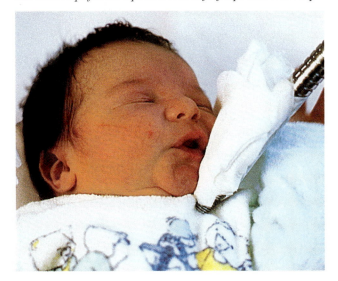

Smell

Newborn infants can differentiate odors. For example, by the expressions on their faces, they seem to indicate that they like the way vanilla and strawberry smell but do not like the way rotten eggs and fish smell (Steiner, 1979). In one investigation, young infants who were breast-fed showed a clear preference for smelling their mother's breast pad when they were 6 days old (MacFarlane, 1975). However, when they were 2 days old, they did not show this preference (compared to a clean breast pad), indicating that they require several days of experience to recognize this odor (see figure 5.8).

Taste

Sensitivity to taste may be present before birth. When saccharin was added to the amniotic fluid of a near-term fetus, increased swallowing was observed (Windle, 1940). Sensitivity to sweetness is clearly present in the newborn. When sucks on a nipple are rewarded with a sweetened solution, the amount of sucking increases (Lipsitt & others, 1976). In another investigation, newborns showed a smilelike expression after being given a sweetened solution but pursed their lips after being given a sour solution (Steiner, 1979). And in one study, 1- to 3-day-old infants cried much less when they were given sucrose through a pacifier (Smith, Fillion, & Blass, 1990).

Intermodal Perception

Are young infants so competent that they can relate and integrate information through several senses? **Intermodal perception** *is the ability to relate and integrate information about two or more sensory modalities, such as vision and hearing.* An increasing number of developmentalists believe that young infants experience related visual and auditory worlds (Bahrick, 1988; Gibson & Spelke, 1983; Rose & Ruff, 1987). Keep in mind, though, that intermodal perception in young infants remains a controversial concept. For example, in one investigation of 6-month-old infants, the auditory sense dominated the visual sense, restricting intermodal perception (Lewkowicz, 1988).

The claim that the young infant can relate information from several senses has been addressed by two important theoretical perspectives. The **direct-perception view** *states that infants are born with intermodal perception abilities that enable them to display intermodal perception early in infancy.* In this view, infants only have to attend to the appropriate sensory information; they do not have to build up an internal representation of the information through months of sensorimotor experiences. In contrast, the **constructivist view** *advocated by Piaget states that the main perceptual abilities—visual, auditory, and tactile, for example—are completely uncoordinated at birth and that young infants do not have intermodal perception.* According to Piaget, only through months of sensorimotor interaction with the world is intermodal perception possible. For Piaget, infant perception involves a representation of the world that builds up as the infant constructs an image of experiences.

Critical Thinking

Increasingly, developmentalists have been surprised by the early competencies of newborns and young infants. Are we going too far in believing that newborns and young infants are competent in dealing with their world, or are they really as sophisticated as the new wave of research seems to suggest?

Although the intermodal perception and direct-perception/constructivist arguments have not completely been settled, we now know that young infants know a lot more than we used to think they did (Bertenthal, 1993; Bower, 1989, 1993; Mandler, 1990, in press, a, b). They see and hear more than we used to think was possible.

At this point, we have discussed a number of ideas about perceptual development in infancy. A summary of these ideas is presented in concept table 5.2.

CONCEPT TABLE 5.2

Sensory and Perceptual Development in Infancy

Concept	Processes/Related Ideas	Characteristics/Description
What are sensation and perception?	Sensation	When information contacts sensory receptors—eyes, ears, tongue, nostrils, and skin—sensation occurs.
	Perception	Perception is the interpretation of what is sensed.
Visual perception	The newborn's visual world	William James said it is a blooming, buzzing confusion; he was wrong. The newborn's perception is more advanced than we previously thought.
	Visual preferences	Fantz's research—showing that infants prefer striped to solid patches—demonstrated that newborns can see.
	Quality of vision	The newborn's vision is about 20/600 on the Snellen chart; by 6 months, vision has improved to at least 20/100.
	The human face	The face is an important visual pattern for the newborn. The infant gradually masters a sequence of steps in perceiving the human face.
	Depth perception	A classic study by Gibson and Walk (1960) demonstrated, through the use of a visual cliff, that 6-month-old infants can perceive depth.
	Built-in perceptual knowledge	An increasing number of researchers, such as Spelke, believe the young infant has a built-in knowledge about how the perceptual world works.
Hearing	Hearing in the fetus and newborn	The fetus can hear several weeks before birth; immediately after birth, newborns can hear, although their sensory threshold is higher than that of adults.
Touch and pain	Touch in the newborn	Newborns do respond to touch.
	Pain	Newborns can feel pain. Research on circumcision shows that 3-day-old males experience pain and can adapt to stress.
Smell and taste	Their nature	Both of these senses are present in the newborn.
Intermodal perception	Its nature	There is considerable interest today in the infant's ability to relate information across perceptual modalities; the coordination and integration of perceptual information across two or more modalities—such as the visual and auditory senses—is called "intermodal perception." Research indicates that infants as young as 4 months of age have intermodal perception. The direct-perception and constructivist views are two important views of perception that make predictions about intermodal perception.

LIFE-SPAN HEALTH AND WELL-BEING

Babies Don't Need Exercise Classes

Six-month-old Andrew doesn't walk yet, but his mother wants him to develop his physical skills optimally. Three times a week, she takes him to a recreation center, where he participates with other infants in swimming and gymnastics classes. With the increased interest of today's adults in aerobic exercise and fitness, some parents have tried to give their infants a head start on becoming physically fit and physically talented. However, the American Academy of Pediatricians recently issued a statement that recommends against structured exercise classes for babies. Pediatricians are seeing more bone fractures and dislocations and more muscle strains in babies now than in the past. They point out that when an adult is stretching and moving an infant's limbs, it is easy to go beyond the infant's physical limits without knowing it.

The physical fitness classes for infants range from passive fare—with adults putting infants through the paces—to programs called "aerobic" because they demand crawling, tumbling, and ball skills. However, exercise for infants is not aerobic. They cannot adequately stretch their bodies to achieve aerobic benefits.

Swimming classes before early childhood also have a downside. No one would disagree with the desire of parents that their infants learn to swim so they will not drown. However, some infants who take swimming lessons develop "infant water intoxification" by swallowing too much water (White, 1990). Water intoxification occurs when an individual swallows enough water to lower the sodium (salt) content of the blood, which makes the brain swell and can lead to a stupor, coma, or seizure. Because of the potential danger of infant water intoxification, the YMCA and the Council for National Co-operation in Aquatics state that children under age 3 should not be involved in organized swimming instruction classes. Also, children cannot cognitively learn to swim until they are 3 or 4 years of age. It is not uncommon for 4-year-olds who have had swim classes since

Mothers and their babies in a swimming class. Pediatricians and child psychologists recommend that exercise classes, even swimming classes, for infants are unnecessary—and possibly produce more negative than positive outcomes.

infancy to become suddenly terrified of the water because, for the first time, they understand that they could drown.

For optimal physical development, babies simply need touch, face-to-face contact, and brightly colored toys they can manipulate. If infants are not couch potatoes who are babysat extensively by a television set, their normal play will provide them with all the fitness training they need.

What types of exercise activities and toys are developmentally appropriate for infants in the first year of life? Among the recommended activities are these (Whaley & Wong, 1988):

- Birth to 1 month: Rock the infant, place it in a cradle.
  Use a carriage for walks.
- 2–3 months: Use a cradle gym.
  Take the infant for rides in a car.
  Exercise the infant's body by gently moving the infant's extremities.
- 4–6 months: Use a stroller.
  Bounce the infant on your lap while holding the infant in standing position.
  Help the infant roll over.

Support the infant in a sitting position, let the infant lean forward to gain balance.

In the first 6 months, suggested toys designed to give the infant developmentally appropriate exercise are crib exercisers, crib gyms, rocking cribs or cradles, and weighted or suction toys.

- 6–9 months: Place the infant on the floor to crawl, roll over, and sit.
  Hold the infant upright to bear its weight and bounce.
  Pick up—say "up."
  Put down—say "down."
  Place toys out of reach; encourage the infant to get them.
  Play pat-a-cake.
- 9–12 months: Give large push-pull toys to encourage walking.
  Place furniture in a circle to encourage cruising.

In the second half of the first year, suggested toys designed to give the infant developmentally appropriate exercise are exercise crib toys, activity boxes for the crib, push-pull toys, and swings. ∎

CONCLUSIONS

It once was believed that the newborn infant was virtually an empty-headed organism that experienced the world as a blooming, buzzing confusion. Today, child developmentalists believe that the young infant has far more advanced capabilities.

In this chapter, you initially learned how newborns can be studied, and then read about physical growth and development in infancy. Among the topics you studied were the nature of the infant's reflexes, cephalocaudal and proximodistal sequences, height and weight gains, gross and fine motor skills, the development of the brain, infant states, nutrition, including the controversial issue of breast- versus bottle-feeding, and toilet training. Then you learned about the nature of sensation and perception, how the infant's visual perception changes, as well as what the infant's hearing, touch, pain, smell, and taste are like. You read about the infant's intermodal perception abilities and studied how researchers can find out about the way newborns perceive their world, and you gave some thought to children living hungry in America, the right stimulation and suggested activities for visual stimulation of infants, and why babies don't need exercise classes.

Remember that you can obtain an overall summary of the chapter by again reading the two concept tables on pages 141 and 148. Of course, the infant's development involves more than physical, motor, and perceptual development. In the next chapter, we will study how infants develop cognitively.

KEY TERMS

sucking reflex   A reflex that occurs when newborns automatically suck an object placed in their mouth. The sucking reflex enables newborns to get nourishment before they have associated a nipple with food. (133)

rooting reflex   A reflex that occurs when the infant's cheek is stroked or the side of the mouth is touched. In response, the infant turns its head toward the side that was touched, in an apparent effort to find something to suck. (133)

Moro reflex   A neonatal startle response that occurs in response to sudden, intense noise or movement. When startled, the newborn arches its back, throws its head back, and flings out its arms and legs. Then the newborn rapidly closes its arms and legs to the center of its body. (133)

grasping reflex   A reflex that occurs when something touches the infants' palms. The infant responds by grasping tightly. (133)

nonnutritive sucking   Sucking behavior unrelated to the infants' feeding. (134)

cephalocaudal pattern   The sequence in which the greatest growth always occurs at the top—the head—with physical growth in size, weight, and feature differentiation gradually working its way down from top to bottom (to neck, shoulders, middle trunk, and so on). (134)

proximodistal pattern   The sequence in which growth starts at the center of the body and moves toward the extremities. (135)

gross motor skills   Skills that involve large muscle activities such as moving one's arms and walking. (135)

fine motor skills   Skills that involve more finely tuned movements, such as finger dexterity. (135)

sudden infant death syndrome (SIDS)   A condition that occurs when an infant stops breathing, usually during the night, and suddenly dies without apparent cause. (138)

marasmus   A wasting away of body tissues in the infant's first year, caused by severe deficiency of protein and calories. (139)

sensation   Sensation occurs when information contacts sensory receptors—the eyes, ears, tongue, nostrils, and skin. (142)

perception   The interpretation of what is sensed. (142)

intermodal perception   The ability to relate and integrate information about two or more sensory modalities, such as vision and hearing. (147)

direct-perception view   A view that states that infants are born with intermodal perception abilities that enable them to display intermodal perception early in infancy. (147)

constructivist view   A view advocated by Piaget that states that the main perceptual abilities—visual, auditory, and tactile, for example—are completely uncoordinated at birth and that young infants do not have intermodal perception. (147)

Thomas Eakins, Baby at Play, detail.

Cognitive Development in Infancy

*I wish I could travel by the road that
crosses the baby's mind, and out beyond
all bounds; where messengers run
errands for no cause between the
kingdoms of kings of no history; where
Reason makes kites of her laws and flies
them, and Truth sets Fact free from its
fetters.*

—Rabindranoth Tagore, 1913

There was a child who went forth every day
And the first object he looked upon, that object he became.
And that object became part of him for the day, or a
certain part of the day, or for many years,
or stretching cycles of years.

—Walt Whitman

IMAGES OF LIFE-SPAN DEVELOPMENT

The Doman "Better Baby Institute" and What Is Wrong With It

Matthew is 1 year old. He has already seen over 1,000 flash cards with pictures of shells, flowers, insects, flags, countries, and words on them. His mother, Billie, has made almost 10,000 of the 11-inch-square cards for Matthew and his 4-year-old brother, Mark. Billie has religiously followed the regimen recommended by Glenn Doman, the director of the Philadelphia Institute for the Achievement of Human Potential and the author of *How to Teach Your Baby to Read.* Using his methods, learned in a course called "How to Multiply Your Baby's Intelligence," Billie is teaching Matthew Japanese and even a little math. Mark is learning geography, natural science, engineering, and fine arts, as well.

Parents using the card approach print one word on each card using a bright red felt-tipped pen. The parent repeatedly shows the card to the infant while saying the word aloud. The first word is usually *mommy,* then comes *daddy,* the baby's name, parts of the body, and all the things the infant can touch. Infants are lavishly praised when they recognize the word. The idea is to imprint the large red words in the infant's memory, so that in time the baby accumulates an impressive vocabulary and begins to read. The parent continues to feed the infant with all manner of information in small, assimilable bits, just as Billie Rash has done with her two boys.

With this method, children should be reading by 2 years of age, and by 4 or 5 should have begun mastering some

These infants and toddlers are being taught in the manner recommended by Glenn Doman, which emphasizes the acceleration of learning to read by intensely exposing children to flash cards with many different words on them. Most developmental psychologists believe there is something fundamentally wrong with Doman's approach. They believe that, rather than pouring information into children's minds in the way Doman advises, children should be permitted to explore their environment spontaneously and to construct their knowledge independently.

math and be able to play the violin, not to mention the vast knowledge of the world they should be able to display because of a monumental vocabulary. Maybe the SAT or ACT test you labored through on your way to college might have been conquered at the age of 6 if your parents had only been enrolled in the "How to Multiply Your Baby's Intelligence" course and made 10,000 flash cards for you.

Is this the best way for an infant to learn? A number of developmentalists believe Doman's "better baby institute" is a money-making scheme and is not based on sound scientific evidence. They believe

that we should not be trying to accelerate the infant's learning so dramatically. Rather than pour information into infants' minds, we should permit infants more time to spontaneously explore the environment and construct their knowledge. Jean Piaget called "What should we do to foster cognitive development?" the American question, because it was asked of him so often when he lectured to American audiences. Developmentalists worry that children exposed to Doman's methods will burn out on learning. What is more important is providing a rich and emotionally supportive atmosphere for learning.

PREVIEW

The excitement and enthusiasm about infant cognition have been fueled by an interest in what an infant knows at birth and soon after, by continued fascination about innate and learned factors in the infant's cognitive development, and by controversies about whether infants construct their knowledge (as Piaget believed) or whether they know their world more directly. In this chapter we will study Piaget's theory of infant development, a new perspective on cognitive development in infancy, information processing in infancy, individual differences in intelligence, and language development.

PIAGET'S THEORY OF INFANT DEVELOPMENT

The poet Noah Perry once asked, "Who knows the thoughts of a child?" Piaget knew as much as anyone. Through careful, inquisitive interviews and observations of his own three children—Laurent, Lucienne, and Jacqueline—Piaget changed the way we think about children's conception of the world. Remember that we studied a general outline of Piaget's theory in chapter 2. It may be helpful for you to review the basic features of his theory at this time.

Piaget believed that the child passes through a series of stages of thought from infancy to adolescence. Passage through the stages results from biological pressures to *adapt* to the environment (through assimilation and accommodation) and to organize structures of thinking. The stages of thought are *qualitatively* different from one another; the way children reason at one stage is very different from the way they reason at another stage. This contrasts with the quantitative assessments of intelligence made through the use of standardized intelligence tests, where the focus is on what the child knows, or how many questions the child can answer correctly (Ginsburg & Opper, 1988). According to Piaget, the mind's development is divided into four such qualitatively different stages: sensorimotor, preoperational, concrete operational, and formal operational. Here our concern is with the stage that characterizes infant thought—the sensorimotor stage.

> *We are born capable of learning.*
> —Jean-Jacques Rousseau

The Stage of Sensorimotor Development

Piaget's sensorimotor stage lasts from birth to about 2 years of age, corresponding to the period of infancy. During this time, mental development is characterized by considerable progression in the infant's ability to organize and coordinate sensations with physical movements and actions—hence, the name *sensorimotor* (Piaget, 1952).

At the beginning of the sensorimotor stage, the infant has little more than reflexive patterns with which to work. By the end of the stage, the 2-year-old has complex sensorimotor patterns and is beginning to operate with a primitive system of symbols. Unlike other stages, the sensorimotor stage is subdivided into six substages, each of which involves qualititative changes in sensorimotor organization. The term **scheme** *(or schema) refers to the basic unit (or units) for an organized pattern of sensorimotor functioning.*

Piaget was a masterful observer of his three children. The following observation of his son, Laurent, provides an excellent example of the infant's emerging coordination of visual and motor schemes, and eloquently portrays how infants learn about their hands.

At 2 months, Laurent by chance discovers his right index finger and looks at it briefly. Several days later, he briefly inspects his open right hand, which he perceived by chance. About a week later, he follows its spontaneous movement for a moment, then he holds his two fists in the air and looks at the left one. Then he slowly brings it toward his face and rubs his nose with it, then his eye. A moment later the left hand again approaches his face. He looks at it and touches his nose. He does that again and laughs five or six times while moving the left hand to his face. He seems to laugh before the hand moves, but looking has no influence on its movement. Then he rubs his nose. At a given moment, he turns his head to the left, but looking has no effect on the direction of the hand's movement. The next day, the same reaction occurs. And then, another day later, he looks at his right hand, then at his clasped hands. Finally, on the day after that, Piaget says, Laurent's looking acts on the orientation of his hands, which tend to remain in the visual field (Piaget, 1936).

Within a given substage, there may be different schemes—sucking, rooting, and blinking in substage 1, for example. In substage 1, the schemes are basically reflexive in nature. From substage to substage, the schemes change in organization. This change is at the heart of Piaget's description of the stages. The six substages of sensorimotor development are (1) simple reflexes; (2) first habits and primary circular reactions; (3) secondary circular reactions; (4) coordination of secondary circular reactions; (5) tertiary circular reactions, novelty, and curiosity; and (6) internalization of schemes.

Simple reflexes *is Piaget's first sensorimotor substage, which corresponds to the first month after birth. In this substage, the basic means of coordinating sensation and action is through reflexive behaviors, such as rooting and sucking, which the infant has at birth.* In substage 1, the infant exercises these reflexes. More importantly, the infant develops an ability to produce behaviors that resemble reflexes in the absence of obvious reflexive stimuli. The newborn may suck when a bottle or nipple is only nearby, for example. When the baby was just born, the bottle or nipple would have produced the sucking pattern only when placed directly in its mouth or touched to the lips. Reflexlike actions in the absence of a triggering stimulus are evidence that the infant is initiating action and is actively structuring experiences in the first month of life.

First habits and primary circular reactions *is Piaget's second sensorimotor substage, which develops between 1 and 4 months of age. In this substage, the infant learns to coordinate sensation and types of schemes or structures—that is, habits and primary circular reactions.* A *habit* is a scheme based upon a simple reflex, such as sucking, that has become completely divorced from its eliciting stimulus. For example, an infant in substage 1 might suck when orally stimulated by a bottle or when visually shown the bottle, but an infant in substage 2 might exercise the sucking scheme even when no bottle is present.

A **primary circular reaction** *is a scheme based upon the infant's attempt to reproduce an interesting or pleasurable event that initially occurred by chance.* In a popular Piagetian example, a child accidentally sucks his fingers when they are placed near his mouth; later, he searches for his fingers to suck them again, but the fingers do not cooperate in the search because the infant cannot coordinate visual and manual actions. Habits and circular reactions are stereotyped, in that the infant repeats them the same way each time. The infant's own body remains the center of attention; there is no outward pull by environmental events.

Secondary circular reactions *is Piaget's third sensorimotor substage, which develops between 4 and 8 months of age. In this substage, the infant becomes more object-oriented or focused on the world, moving beyond preoccupation with the self in sensorimotor interactions.* The chance shaking of a rattle, for example, may fascinate the infant, and the infant will repeat this action for the sake of experiencing fascination. The infant imitates some simple actions of others, such as the baby talk or burbling of adults, and some physical gestures. However, these imitations are limited to actions the infant is already able to produce. Although directed toward objects in the world, the infant's schemes lack an intentional, goal-directed quality.

Coordination of secondary circular reactions *is Piaget's fourth sensorimotor substage, which develops between 8 and 12 months of age. In this substage, several significant changes take place involving the coordination of schemes and intentionality.* Infants readily combine and recombine previously learned schemes in a *coordinated way.* They may look at an object and grasp it simultaneously, or visually inspect a toy, such as a rattle, and finger it simultaneously in obvious tactile exploration. Actions are even more outwardly directed than before. Related to this coordination is the second achievement—the presence of *intentionality*, the separation of means and goals in accomplishing simple feats. For example, infants might manipulate a stick (the means) to bring a desired toy within reach (the goal). They may knock over one block to reach and play with another one.

Tertiary circular reactions, novelty, and curiosity *is Piaget's fifth sensorimotor substage, which develops between 12 and 18 months of age. In this substage, infants become intrigued by the variety of properties that objects possess and by the multiplicity of things they can make happen to objects.* A block can be made to fall, spin, hit another object, slide across the ground, and so on. Tertiary circular reactions are schemes in which the infant purposely explores new possibilities with objects, continually changing what is done to them and exploring the results. Piaget says that this stage marks the developmental starting point for human curiosity and interest in novelty. Previous circular reactions have been devoted exclusively to reproducing former events, with the exception of imitation of novel acts, which occurs as early as substage 4. The tertiary circular act is the first to be concerned with novelty.

Internalization of schemes *is Piaget's sixth and final sensorimotor substage, which develops between 18 and 24 months of age. In this substage the infant's mental functioning shifts from a purely sensorimotor plane to a symbolic plane, and the infant develops the ability to use primitive symbols.* For Piaget, a *symbol* is an internalized sensory image or word that represents an event. Primitive symbols permit the infant to think about concrete events without directly acting them out or perceiving them. Moreover, symbols allow the infant to manipulate and transform the represented events in simple ways. In a favorite Piagetian example, Piaget's young daughter saw a matchbox being opened and closed; sometime later, she mimicked the event by opening and closing her mouth. This was an obvious expression of her image of the event. In another example, a child opened a door slowly to avoid disturbing a piece of paper lying on the floor on the other side. Clearly, the child had an image of the unseen paper and what would happen to it if the door opened quickly. However, developmentalists have debated whether 2-year-olds really have such representations of action sequences at their command (Corrigan, 1981).

Read further about Piaget's six substages of infant cognitive development in figure 6.1, where you will find suggestions for a day-care curriculum based on those substages.

Object Permanence

Object permanence *is the Piagetian term for one of an infant's most important accomplishments: understanding that objects and events continue to exist even when they cannot directly be seen, heard, or touched.* Imagine what thought would be like if you could not distinguish between yourself and your world. Your thought would be chaotic, disorganized, and unpredictable. This is what the mental life of a newborn is like, according to Piaget. There is no self-world differentiation and no sense of object permanence (Piaget, 1952). By the end of the sensorimotor period, however, both are present.

The principal way that object permanence is studied is by watching an infant's reaction when an interesting object or event disappears (see figure 6.2). If infants show no reaction, it is assumed they believe the object no longer exists. By contrast, if infants are surprised at the disappearance and search for the object, it is assumed they believe it continues to exist.

At this point we have discussed a number of characteristics of Piaget's stage of sensorimotor thought. To help you remember the main characteristics of sensorimotor thought, turn to figure 6.3.

Although Piaget's stage sequence is the best summary of what might happen as the infant fathoms the permanence of things in the world, some contradictory findings have emerged. Piaget's stages broadly describe the interesting changes reasonably well, but the infant's life is not so neatly packaged into distinct stages as Piaget believed. Some of Piaget's explanations for the causes of change are debated.

A New Perspective on Cognitive Development in Infancy

In the past decade, a new understanding of infants' cognitive development has been emerging. For many years, Piaget's ideas were so widely known and respected that, to many psychologists, one aspect of development seemed certain: Human infants go through a long, protracted period during which they cannot think (Mandler, 1990, 1992, in press, a, b). They can learn to recognize things and smile at them, to crawl, and to manipulate objects, but they do not yet have concepts and ideas. Piaget believed that only near the end of the sensorimotor stage of development, at about $1\frac{1}{2}$ to 2 years of age, do infants learn how to represent the world in a symbolic, conceptual manner.

Piaget constructed his view of infancy mainly by observing the development of his own three children. Very few laboratory techniques were available at the time. Recently, however, sophisticated experimental techniques have been devised to study infants, and there is now a large number of research studies on infant cognitive development. Much of the new research suggests that Piaget's theory of sensorimotor development will have to be modified substantially.

Piaget's theory of sensorimotor development has been attacked from two sources. First, extensive research in the area of infant perceptual development suggests that a stable and differentiated perceptual world is established much earlier in infancy than Piaget envisioned. Second, researchers recently have found that memory and other forms of symbolic activity occur by at least the second half of the first year.

Perceptual Development

In chapter 5, we described research on infants' perceptual development, indicating that a number of theorists, such as Eleanor Gibson (1989), Elizabeth Spelke (1988, 1991), and Tom Bower (1989, 1993), believe that infants' perceptual abilities are highly developed very early in development. For example, Spelke has demonstrated that infants as young as

4 months of age have intermodal perception—the ability to coordinate information from two or more sensory modalities, such as vision and hearing. Other research by Spelke (1988) and by Renée Baillargeon (1987, 1991) documents that infants as young as 4 months expect objects to be substantial—in the sense that the objects cannot move through other objects; neither can other objects move through them—and permanent, in the sense that the objects are assumed to continue to exist when hidden. In sum, the perceptual development researchers believe that infants see objects as bounded, unitary, solid, and separate from their background, possibly at birth or shortly thereafter, but definitely by 3 to 4 months of age. Young infants still have much to learn about objects, but the world appears both stable and orderly to them and, thus, capable of being conceptualized.

Conceptual Development

It is more difficult to study what infants are thinking about than what they see. Still, researchers have devised ways to assess whether or not infants are thinking. One strategy is to look for symbolic activity, such as using a gesture to refer to something. Piaget (1952) used this strategy to document infants' motor recognition. For example, he observed his 6-month-old daughter make a gesture when she saw a familiar toy in a new location. She was used to kicking at the toy in her crib. When she saw it across the room, she made a brief kicking motion. However, Piaget did not consider this to be true symbolic activity because it was a motor movement, not a purely mental act. Nonetheless, Piaget suggested that his daughter was referring to, or classifying, the toy through her actions (Mandler, 1990). In a similar way, infants whose parents use sign language have been observed to start using conventional signs at about 6 to 7 months of age (Bonvillian, Orlansky, & Novack, 1983).

In summary, the recent research on infants' perceptual and conceptual development suggests that infants have more sophisticated perceptual abilities and can begin to think earlier than Piaget envisioned. These researchers believe that infants either are born with or acquire these abilities early in their development (Mandler, 1990, 1992). Information-processing psychologists have made important contributions to the new perspective on infant cognition.

The Information-Processing Perspective and Infant Development

Unlike Piaget, information-processing psychologists do not describe infancy as a stage or a series of substages. Rather, they emphasize the importance of such cognitive processes as attention, memory, and thinking in the way the infant processes information about the world (Rose, 1992).

Piaget believed that the infant's ability to construct sensorimotor schemas, establish a coherent world of objects and events suitable to form the content of ideas, imitate, and form images that can stand for things is completed in the second half of the second year. However, many information-processing

FIGURE 6.1

Piagetian sensorimotor substages and caregiver strategies. *As more infants spend much of their day in day-care centers, it is important for the caregivers to interact in effective ways with the infants and for the day-care center to develop a curriculum that is appropriate for infant cognitive development. Following is a developmentally appropriate curriculum for infant cognitive development that was proposed by educator and developmentalist LaVisa Wilson (1990).*

Piagetian Substage	Materials	Examples of Caregiver Strategies	
Substage 1: Simple reflexes (birth–1 month)	Visually attractive crib and walls next to crib, objects near crib; occasional music, singing, talking, chimes	Provide nonrestrictive clothes, uncluttered crib, to allow freedom of movement; provide environment that commands attention during the infant's periods of alertness.	
Substage 2: First habits and primary circular reactions (1–4 months)	Face and voice, musical toys, musical mobile, rattle; objects infant can grasp and are safe to go in the infant's mouth; objects the infant can grasp and lift	Provide change in infant's environment; carry infant around, hold infant, place infant in crib; observe, discuss, record changes in the infant; turn on musical toys and place where the infant can see them; place objects in the infant's hands or within the infant's reach; provide clothes that allow freedom of movement; provide time and space for repetition of behaviors.	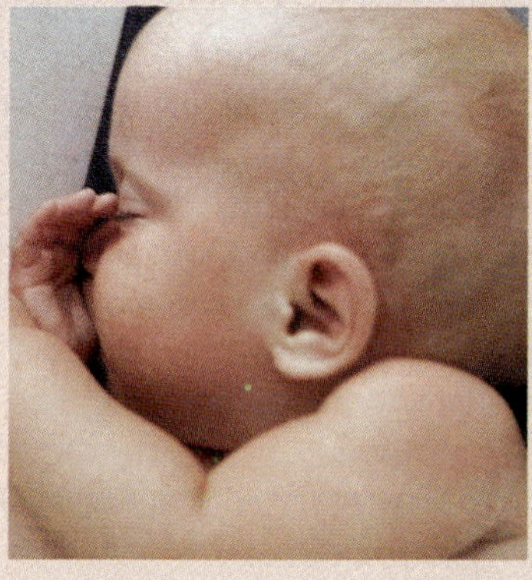
Substage 3: Secondary circular reactions (4–8 months)	Objects that attract attention (of contrasting colors, that change in sounds, have a variety of textures or designs); toys; balls	Watch movements the infant repeats, as when a waving arm hits the crib gym and then this action is repeated; provide materials that facilitate such repetitions (new items on the crib gym, for example); place blocks, dolls, ball, and other toys near the infant so they can be reached; initiate action, wait for the infant to imitate it, then repeat the action (smile, open mouth, for example).	

Piagetian Substage	Materials	Examples of Caregiver Strategies
Substage 4: Coordination of secondary circular reactions (8–12 months)	Toys, visually attractive objects	Place objects near the infant; play hide-the-doll-under-the-blanket; place the block behind you; verbalize your own actions, such as "I put the ball behind me"; introduce new copy games; allow time and space for the infant to play.
Substage 5: Tertiary circular reactions, novelty, and curiosity (12–18 months)	Blanket, paper, toys, dolls, spoon, interesting objects; water toys, water basin; narrow-neck milk carton and different sizes and shapes of objects	Play game of hide-the-object with infant—hide the object while the infant watches, let infant watch you move the object to a different place under the blanket, and ask "Where is it?" "Can you find it?"; observe and allow infant to find the object, praise infant for good watching and thinking; allow infant to play with water and toys to discover different actions of water and of the objects in the water; provide time and materials that stimulate infant to think and try out new ideas; ask questions but do not tell answers or show infant; encourage infant to pretend—to drink from a pretend bottle like baby Gwen, to march like Pearl, to pick up toys; allow infant to repeat own play and develop own preferences.
Substage 6: Internalization of schemes (18–24 months)	Objects that attract attention (of contrasting colors, that change in sounds, have a variety of textures or designs); toys; balls	Allow toddler time to figure out solutions; allow toddler time to think and search for objects; observe toddler's representations and identify the ideas that seem important to the toddler; allow the toddler to act out conflict in play with toys and materials; observe toddler's play and identify consistent themes; provide clothes and materials that help the toddler pretend to be someone else.

FIGURE 6.2

Object permanence. *Piaget thought that object permanence was one of infancy's landmark cognitive accomplishments. For this 5-month-old boy, "out-of-sight" is literally out of mind. The infant looks at the toy monkey (left), but when his view of the toy is blocked (right), he does not search for it. Eventually, he will search for the hidden toy monkey, reflecting the presence of object permanence.*

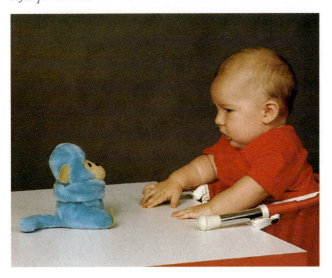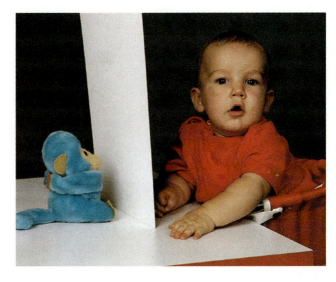

FIGURE 6.3

Piaget's description of the main characteristics of sensorimotor thought.

Ability to organize and coordinate sensations with physical movements

Is nonsymbolic through most of its duration

Consists of six substages of cognitive development

Object permanence develops

psychologists believe the young infant is more competent than Piaget believed, with attentional, symbolic, imitative, and conceptual capabilities present earlier in infant development than Piaget envisioned (Haith, 1992; Mandler, 1990; Meltzoff, 1992).

Habituation and Dishabituation

If a stimulus—a sight or sound—is presented to infants several times in a row, they usually pay less attention to it each time, suggesting they are bored with it. This is the process of **habituation**—*repeated presentation of the same stimulus that causes reduced attention to the stimulus.* **Dishabituation** *is an infant's renewed interest in a stimulus.* Among the measures infant researchers use to study whether habituation is occurring are sucking behavior (sucking behavior stops when the young infant attends to a novel object), heart and respiration rates, and the length of time the infant looks at an object. Newborn infants can habituate to repetitive stimulation in virtually every stimulus modality—vision, hearing, touch, and so on (Rovee-Collier, 1987). However, habituation becomes more acute over the first 3 months of life. The extensive assessment of habituation in recent years has resulted in its use as a measure of an infant's maturity and well-being. Infants who have brain damage or have suffered birth traumas such as lack of oxygen do not habituate well and may later have developmental and learning problems.

> *Man is the only animal that can be bored.*
> —Erich Fromm, *The Sane Society*, 1955

A knowledge of habituation and dishabituation can benefit parent-infant interaction. Infants respond to changes in stimulation. If stimulation is repeated often, the infant's response will decrease to the point that the infant no longer responds to the parent. In parent-infant interaction, it is important for parents to do novel things and to repeat them often until the infant stops responding. The wise parent senses when the infant shows an interest and that many repetitions of the stimulus may be necessary for the infant to process the information. The parent stops or changes behaviors when the infant redirects her attention (Rosenblith, 1992).

Memory

Memory *is a central feature of cognitive development, pertaining to all situations in which an individual retains information over time.* Sometimes information is retained for only a few seconds, and at other times it is retained for a lifetime. Memory is involved when we look up a telephone number and dial it, when we remember a telephone number and dial it, when we remember the name of our best friend from elementary school, when an infant remembers who her mother is, and when an older adult remembers to keep a doctor's appointment.

> *Life is all memory, except for the one present moment that goes by you so quick you hardly catch it going.*
>
> —Tennessee Williams,
> *The Milk Train Doesn't Stop Here Anymore,* 1963

Popular child-rearing expert Penelope Leach (1983) tells parents that 6-to-8-month old babies cannot hold in their mind a picture of their mother or father. And historically psychologists have believed that infants cannot store memories until they have the language skills required to form them and retrieve them. Recently, though, child development researchers have revealed that infants as young as three months of age show memory skills (Grunwald & others, 1993).

In one study, infants were placed in large black boxes where they laid and looked up at TV screens, viewing a sequence of colorful objects that appear (Canfield & Haith, 1991). Using an infrared camera linked to a computer, the babies' eye movements were monitored. After only five tries the babies can anticipate where the next object will appear. With just a little more practice, they predicted a four-step sequence and most can still remember it up to two weeks later!

Carolyn Rovee-Collier (1987) has also found that infants can remember surprisingly intricate material. In a characteristic experiment, she places a baby in a crib underneath an elaborate mobile, ties one of the baby's ankles to it with a satin ribbon, then observes as the baby kicks and makes it move. Weeks later, when the baby's feet are left untied and the mobile is returned to the crib, the baby will try to kick it again, apparently remembering when it kicked earlier (see figure 6.4). However, if the mobile's makeup is changed even slightly, the baby doesn't kick at it. Then as soon as the familiar and expected are brought back into the context, the baby remembers and begins kicking. According to Rovee-Collier, even by 2½ months the baby's memory is incredibly detailed.

Nancy Myers and her colleagues (1987) have found that an infant's experience at 6 months of age can be remembered two years later. They placed sixteen 6-month old babies in a dark room with objects that made different sounds. Using infrared cameras they observed how and when the infants reached for

FIGURE 6.4

The technique used in Rovee-Collier's investigation of infant memory. *The mobile is connected to the infant's ankle by the ribbon and moves in direct proportion to the frequency and vigor of the infant's kicks. This infant is in a reinforcement period. During this period the infant can see the mobile, but because the ribbon is attached to a different stand, she cannot make the mobile move. Baseline activity is assessed during a nonreinforcement period prior to training, and all retention tests are also conducted during periods of nonreinforcement. As can be seen, this infant has already learned and is attempting to make the mobile move by kicking her leg with the ribbon attachments.*

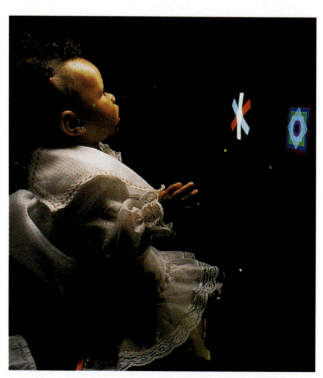

Researchers use a variety of ingenious techniques to study the infant's cognitive development. In researcher Mark Johnson's laboratory, at Carnegie Mellon University, babies have shown an ability to organize their world and to anticipate future events by learning and remembering sequences of colorful images on TV monitors.

objects. Two years later, the same children were brought back into the laboratory, along with a control group of 16 other 2½-year-old children (Perris & others, 1990). The experimental group revealed the same behavior they had shown at 6 months, reaching for the objects and displaying no fear, but fewer control group children reached for the objects and many of them cried. The experiment demonstrates that young children can remember experiences up to two years earlier when put in the same context.

In summary, the capacity for memory appears much earlier in infancy than we used to believe, and is also more precise than earlier conclusions suggested.

Imitation

Can infants imitate someone else's emotional expressions? If an adult smiles, will the baby follow with a smile? If an adult protrudes her lower lip, wrinkles her forehead, and frowns, will the baby show a saddened look? If an adult opens his mouth, widens his eyes, and raises his eyebrows, will the baby follow suit? Could infants only a few days old do these things?

> *We are, in truth, more than half what we are by imitation.*
> —Lord Chesterfield, *Letters to His Son,* 1750

Infant development researcher Andrew Meltzoff (1990; Meltzoff & Kuhl, 1989; Meltzoff & Moore, 1992) has conducted numerous studies of the imitative abilities of infants. He believes infants' imitative abilities are biologically based, because infants can imitate a facial expression within the first few days after birth, before they have had the opportunity to observe social agents in their environment engage in tongue protrusion and other behaviors. He also emphasizes that the infant's imitative abilities are not like what ethologists conceptualize as a hardwired, reflexive, innate releasing mechanism, but rather involve flexibility, adaptability, and intermodal perception. In Meltzoff's observations of infants in the first 72 hours of life, the infants gradually displayed a full imitative response of an adult's facial expression, such as tongue protrusion or a wide-opening of the mouth (see figure 6.5). Initially, the young infant may only get its tongue to the edge of its lips, but after a number of attempts and observations of the adult behavior, the infant displays a more full-blown response.

Meltzoff has also studied **deferred imitation,** *which is imitation that occurs after a time delay of hours or days.* In one investigation, Meltzoff (1988) demonstrated that 9-month-old infants could imitate actions they had seen performed 24 hours earlier. Each action consisted of an unusual gesture—for example, pushing a recessed button in a box (which produced a beeping sound). Piaget believed that deferred imitation does not occur until about 18 months of age; Meltzoff's research suggests that it occurs much earlier in infant development.

In sum, rather than assuming that infants' conceptual functioning—involving such important cognitive processes as memory and deferred imitation—can occur only as an outcome of a

FIGURE 6.5

Infant imitation. Infant development researcher Andrew Meltzoff displays tongue protrusion in an attempt to get the infant to imitate his behavior. Researchers have demonstrated that young infants can imitate adult behaviors far earlier than traditionally believed.

lengthy sensorimotor stage, information-processing psychologists believe that infants either are born with these capabilities or acquire them much earlier in infancy than Piaget believed. As we will see next, a third perspective on infant cognition also differs from Piaget's approach.

INDIVIDUAL DIFFERENCES IN INTELLIGENCE

So far we have stressed general statements about how the cognitive development of infants progresses, emphasizing what is typical of the largest number of infants or the average infant. But the results obtained for most infants do not apply to all infants. Individual differences in infant cognitive development have been studied primarily through the use of developmental scales or infant intelligence tests (Columbo & Fagen, 1991; Green, 1991; Horowitz, 1991).

It is advantageous to know whether an infant is advancing at a slow, a normal, or an advanced pace of development. In chapter 4, we discussed the Brazelton Neonatal Behavioral Assessment Scale, which is widely used to evaluate newborns. Developmentalists also want to know how development proceeds during the course of infancy. If an infant advances at an especially slow rate, then some form of enrichment may be necessary. If an infant develops at an advanced pace, parents may be advised to provide toys that stimulate cognitive growth in slightly older infants.

The infant testing movement grew out of the tradition of IQ testing with older children. However, the measures that assess infants are necessarily less verbal than IQ tests that assess the intelligence of older children. The infant developmental

LIFE-SPAN PRACTICAL KNOWLEDGE 6.1

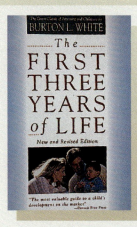

The First Three Years of Life
(1990, rev. ed.) by Burton White. New York: Prentice-Hall.

The First Three Years of Life presents a broad-based approach to how parents can optimally rear their infants and young children. Author Burton White is director of the Center for Parent Education in Newton, Massachusetts, and was formerly the director of the Harvard Preschool Project that focused on young children's learning. White strongly believes that most parents in America fail to provide an adequate intellectual and social foundation for their child's development, especially between the ages of 8 months and 3 years of age. White provides in-depth portrayals of motor, sensory, emotional, sociability, and language milestones at different points in the first 3 years of life. He gives specific recommendations for how parents should interact with their children, as well as criticisms of inappropriate strategies.

White's book is controversial. Some educational, parenting, and child clinical experts praise the book. Others, such as Susan Keyes of Harvard University and Sibylee Escalona of Albert Einstein College of Medicine, fault White for his rigid emphasis on critical periods and time frames for certain learning to occur, for failing to capture at least some variability in recommended parenting practices, and for recommending that mothers should spend most of their waking hours in the infant's and child's life, stimulating and monitoring the infant's and child's learning and development. White has been especially hard hit with the last criticism—he does not believe that mothers should work outside of the home during the infant's first 3 years of life, which critics say places an unnecessary burden of guilt on the high percentage of working mothers with infants and toddlers. However, he has excellent recommendations for how to handle spoiling, which toys to buy and which to not buy at different developmental levels, how to handle sibling rivalry, and how to discipline children.

---

scales contain far more items related to perceptual motor development. They also include measures of social interaction.

The most important early contributor to the developmental testing of infants was Arnold Gesell (1934). He developed a measure that was used as a clinical tool to help sort out potentially normal babies from abnormal ones. This was especially useful to adoption agencies who had large numbers of babies awaiting placement. Gesell's examination was used widely for many years and is still frequently used by pediatricians in their assessment of normal and abnormal infants. The version of the Gesell test now used has four categories of behavior: motor, language, adaptive, and personal-social. The **developmental quotient (DQ)** *is an overall developmental score that combines subscores in motor, language, adaptive, and personal-social domains in the Gesell assessment of infants.* However, overall scores on tests like the Gesell do not correlate highly with IQ scores obtained later in childhood. This is not surprising, because the items on the developmental scales are considerably less verbal in nature than the items on intelligence tests given to older children.

The **Bayley Scales of Infant Development,** *developed by Nancy Bayley (1969), are widely used in the assessment of infant development. The current version has three components: a mental scale, a motor scale, and an infant behavior profile.* Unlike Gesell, whose scales were clinically motivated, Bayley wanted to develop scales that could document infant behavior and predict later development. The early version of the Bayley scales covered only the first year of development; in the 1950s, the scales were extended to assess older infants. In 1993, the Bayley-II was published with updated norms for diagnostic assessment at a younger age.

Because our discussion centers on the infant's cognitive development, our primary interest is on Bayley's mental scale, which includes assessment of the following:

- Auditory and visual attention to stimuli
- Manipulation, such as combining objects or shaking a rattle
- Examiner interaction, such as babbling and imitation
- Relation with toys, such as banging spoons together
- Memory involved in object permanence, as when the infant finds a hidden toy
- Goal-directed behavior that involves persistence, such as putting pegs in a board
- Ability to follow directions and knowledge of objects' names, such as understanding the concept of "one"

How well should a 6-month-old perform on the Bayley mental scale? The 6-month-old infant should be able to vocalize pleasure and displeasure, persistently search for objects that are just out of immediate reach, and approach a mirror that is placed in front of the infant by the examiner. How well should a 12-month-old perform? By 12 months of age, the infant should be able to inhibit behavior when commanded to do so, imitate words the examiner says (such as *Mama*), and respond to simple requests (such as "Take a drink").

Infant tests of intelligence have been valuable in assessing the effects of malnutrition, drugs, maternal deprivation, and environmental stimulation on the development of infants. They have met with mixed results in predicting later intelligence. Global developmental quotient or IQ scores for infants have not been good predictors of childhood intelligence. However, specific aspects of infant intelligence are related to specific aspects of childhood intelligence. For example, in one investigation, infant language abilities as assessed by the Bayley test predicted language, reading, and spelling ability at 6 to 8 years of age (Siegel, 1989). Infant perceptual motor skills predicted visuospatial, arithmetic, and fine motor skills at 6 to 8 years of age. These results indicate that an item analysis of infant scales like Bayley's can provide information about the development of specific intellectual functions.

Critical Thinking

Is an older infant's intelligence just quantitatively different from a younger infant's intelligence, or is it qualitatively different? How would Piaget have answered this question?

The explosion of interest in infant development has produced many new measures, especially tasks that evaluate the way infants process information (Rose, 1989). Evidence is accumulating that measures of habituation and dishabituation predict intelligence in childhood (Bornstein, 1989; McCall & Carriger, 1993; Sigman & others, 1989; Slater & others, 1989). Less cumulative attention in the habituation situation and greater amounts of attention in the dishabituation situation reflect more efficient information processing. Both types of attention—decrement and recovery—when measured in the first 6 months of infancy, are related to higher IQ scores on standardized intelligence tests given at various times between infancy and adolescence. In sum, more-precise assessments of the infant's cognition with information-processing tasks involving attention have led to the conclusion that continuity between infant and childhood intelligence is greater than was previously believed (Bornstein & Krasnegor, 1989).

It is important, however, not to go too far and think that the connections between early infant cognitive development and later childhood cognitive development are so strong that no discontinuity takes place. Rather than asking whether cognitive development is continuous *or* discontinuous, perhaps we should be examining the ways cognitive development is both continuous *and* discontinuous (Cardon & others, 1992; Pomerleau, 1989; Sternberg & Okagaki, 1989). Some important changes in cognitive development take place after infancy, changes that underscore the discontinuity of cognitive development. We will describe these changes in cognitive development in subsequent chapters that focus on later periods of development.

So far we have discussed a number of ideas about cognitive development in infancy. A summary of these ideas is presented in concept table 6.1. Next we will study another key dimension of the infant's development—language.

LANGUAGE DEVELOPMENT

In 1799, a nude boy was observed running through the woods in France. The boy was captured when he was approximately 11 years old. It was believed he had lived in the wild for at least 6 years. He was called the "Wild Boy of Aveyron" (Lane, 1976). When the boy was found, he made no effort to communicate. Even after a number of years he never learned to communicate effectively. The Wild Boy of Aveyron raises an important issue in language, namely, what are the biological, environmental, and cultural contributions to language? Later in the chapter we will describe a modern-day wild child named Genie, who will shed some light on this issue. Indeed, the contributions of biology, environment, and culture figure prominently into our discussion of language.

What Is Language?

Every human culture has language. Human languages number in the thousands, differing so much on the surface that many of us despair at learning more than even one. Yet all human languages have some common characteristics. **Language** *is a system of symbols used to communicate with others. In humans, language is characterized by infinite generativity and rule systems.* **Infinite generativity** *is an individual's ability to generate an infinite number of meaningful sentences using a finite set of words and rules, which makes language a highly creative enterprise.* Language's rule systems include phonology, morphology, syntax, semantics, and pragmatics, each of which we now discuss in turn.

Language is made up of basic sounds or *phonemes*. In the English language there are approximately 36 phonemes. **Phonology** *is the study of a language's sound system.* Phonological rules ensure that certain sound sequences occur (for example, *sp, ba,* or *ar*) and others do not (for example, *zx* or *qp*). A good example of a phoneme in the English language is /k/, the sound represented by the letter *k* in the word *ski* and the letter *c* in the word *cat*. While the /k/ sound is slightly different in these two words, the variation is not distinguished, and the /k/ sound is described as a single phoneme. In some languages, such as Arabic, this kind of variation represents separate phonemes.

Morphology *refers to the rules for combining morphemes; a morpheme is the smallest string of sounds that gives meaning to what we say and hear.* Every word in the English language is made up of one or more morphemes. Some words consist of a single morpheme (for example, *help*), while others are made up of more than one morpheme (for example, *helper* has two morphemes, *help* + *er*, with the morpheme *er* meaning "one who"; in this case "one who helps"). However, as shown in the previous example, not all morphemes are words (for example, *pre-, tion,* and *-ing*). Just as the rules that govern phonemes ensure that certain sound sequences occur, the rules that govern morphemes ensure that certain strings of sounds occur in particular sequences. For example, we would not reorder *helper* to *erhelp*.

Syntax *involves the way words are combined to form acceptable phrases and sentences.* Because you and I share the same syntactic understanding of sentence structure, if I say to you "Bob

CONCEPT TABLE 6.1

Infant Cognitive Development

Concept	Processes/Related Ideas	Characteristics/Description
Piaget's theory of infant development	Sensorimotor stage	This stage lasts from birth to about 2 years of age and involves progression in the infant's ability to organize and coordinate sensations with physical movements. The sensorimotor stage has six substages: simple reflexes; first habits and primary circular reactions; secondary circular reactions; coordination of secondary circular reactions; tertiary circular reactions, novelty, and curiosity; and internalization of schemes.
	Object permanence	Object permanence refers to the development of the ability to understand that objects and events continue to exist even though the infant no longer is in contact with them. Piaget believed that this ability develops over the course of the six substages.
A new perspective on cognitive development in infancy	Its nature	In the past decade, a new understanding of infants' cognitive development has been emerging. Piaget's theory has been attacked from two sources. First, extensive research in perceptual development suggests that a stable and differentiated perceptual word is established much earlier than Piaget envisioned. Second, researchers recently have found that memory and other forms of symbolic activity occur by at least the second half of the first year.
Information processing	The information processing perspective and infant development	Unlike Piaget, information-processing psychologists do not describe infancy as a stage or series of substages of sensorimotor development. Rather, they emphasize the importance of cognitive processes such as attention, memory, and thinking. The information-processing psychologists believe that the young infant is more competent than Piaget envisioned, that attentional, symbolic, imitative, and conceptual abilities occur much earlier in development than Piaget thought.
	Habituation and dishabituation	Habituation is the repeated presentation of the same stimulus, causing reduced attention to the stimulus. If a different stimulus is presented and the infant pays attention to it, dishabituation is occurring. Newborn infants can habituate, but habituation becomes more acute over the first 3 months of infancy.
	Memory	Memory is the retention of information over time. Memory develops much earlier in infancy than once was believed and is more specific than earlier conclusions suggested.
	Imitation	Infants can imitate the facial expressions of others in the first few days of life. Meltzoff demonstrated that deferred imitation occurs at about 9 months of age, much earlier than Piaget believed.
Individual differences in intelligence	History	Developmental scales for infants grew out of the tradition of IQ testing with older children. These scales are less verbal than IQ tests. Gesell was an early developer of an infant test. His scale is still widely used by pediatricians; it provides a developmental quotient (DQ).
	Bayley scales	The developmental scales most widely used today, developed by Nancy Bayley, consist of a motor scale, a mental scale, and an infant behavior profile.
	Conclusions about infant tests and continuity in mental development	Global infant intelligence measures are not good predictors of childhood intelligence. However, specific aspects of infant intelligence, such as information-processing tasks involving attention, have been better predictors of childhood intelligence, especially in a specific area. There is both continuity and discontinuity between infant cognitive development and cognitive development later in childhood.

"If you don't mind my asking, how much does a sentence diagrammer pull down a year?"
Reprinted with the permission of Bob Thaves.

slugged Tom" and "Bob was slugged by Tom," you know who did the slugging and who was slugged in each case. You also understand that "You didn't stay, did you?" is grammatically correct and that "You didn't stay, didn't you?" is unacceptable and ambiguous.

A concept closely related to syntax is **grammar,** *the formal description of syntactical rules.* In elementary school and high school, most of us learned rules about sentence structure. Linguists devise rules of grammar that are similar to those you learned in school but are much more complex and powerful. Many contemporary linguists distinguish between the "surface" and "deep" structure of a sentence. **Surface structure** *is the actual order of words in a sentence;* **deep structure** *is the syntactic relation of the words in a sentence.* By applying syntactic rules in different ways, one sentence (the surface structure) can have two very different deep structures. For example, consider this sentence: "Mr. Smith found drunk on lawn." Was Mr. Smith drunk, or did he find a drunk on the lawn? Either interpretation fits the sentence, depending on the deep structure applied.

> *The adjective is the banana peel of the parts of speech.*
> —Clifton Fadiman, *Reader's Digest,* 1956

Semantics *refers to the meaning of words and sentences.* Every word has a set of semantic features. *Girl* and *woman,* for example, share the same semantic features as the words *female* and *human* but differ in regard to age. Words have semantic restrictions on how they can be used in sentences. The sentence *The bicycle talked the boy into buying a candy bar* is syntactically correct but is semantically incorrect. The sentence violates our semantic knowledge—bicycles do not talk.

> *A person gets from a symbol the meaning he puts into it, and what is one man's comfort and inspiration is another's jest and scorn.*
> —Justice Robert Jackson

A final set of language rules involves **pragmatics**—*the ability to engage in appropriate conversation.* Certain pragmatic rules ensure that a particular sentence will be uttered in one context and not in another. For example, you know that it is appropriate to say "Your new haircut certainly looks good" to someone who just had his or her hair styled, but that it is inappropriate to say "That new hairstyle makes you look awful." Through pragmatics we learn to convey intended meaning with words, phrases, and sentences. Pragmatics helps us to communicate more smoothly with others (Anderson, 1989).

> *Words not only affect us temporarily; they change us, they socialize us and they unsocialize us.*
> —David Riesman

Do we learn this ability to generate rule systems for language and then use them to create an almost infinite number of words, or is it the product of biology and evolution?

Biological Influences

How strongly is language influenced by biological evolution? Do animals have language? Is there a critical period for language? We consider each of these questions in turn.

Biological Evolution

A number of experts stress the biological foundations of language (Chomsky, 1957; Howe, 1993; Maratsos, 1983; Miller, 1981). They believe it is undeniable that biological evolution shaped humans into linguistic creatures. In terms of biological evolution, the brain, nervous system, and vocal system changed over hundreds of thousands of years. Prior to *Homo sapiens,* the physical equipment to produce language was not present. *Homo sapiens* went beyond the groans and shrieks of their predecessors with the development of abstract speech. Estimates vary as to how long ago humans acquired language—from about 20,000 to 70,000 years ago. In evolutionary time, then, language is a very recent acquisition.

Biological Prewiring

Linguist Noam Chomsky (1957) believes humans are biologically prewired to learn language at a certain time and in a certain way. He said that children are born into the world with a **language acquisition device (LAD),** *a biological prewiring that enables the child to detect certain language categories, such as phonology, syntax, and semantics.* LAD is an innate grammatical ability that underlies all human languages.

Do Animals Have Language?

Many animal species have complex and ingenious ways to signal danger and to communicate about basic needs, such as food and sex. For example, in one species of firefly, the females have learned to imitate the flashing signal of another species to lure the aliens into their territory. Then they eat the aliens. However, is this language in the human sense? What about higher animals, such as apes? Is ape language similar to human language? Can we teach human language to apes?

Some researchers believe that apes can learn language. One celebrity in this field is the chimp Washoe, who was adopted when she was about 10 months old (Gardner & Gardner, 1971). Since apes do not have the vocal apparatus to speak, the researchers tried to teach Washoe American Sign Language, which is one of the sign languages of the deaf. Washoe used sign language during everyday activities, such as meals, play, and car rides. In 2 years, Washoe learned 38 signs, and by the age of 5 she had a vocabulary of 160 signs. Washoe learned how to put signs together in novel ways, such as "you drink" and "you me tickle." A number of other efforts to teach language to chimps have had similar results (Premack, 1986).

The debate about chimpanzees' ability to use language focuses on two key issues. Can apes understand the meaning of symbols—that is, can they comprehend that one thing stands for another—and can apes learn syntax—that is, can they learn the mechanics and rules that give human language its creative productivity? The first of these issues may have been settled recently by Sue Savage-Rumbaugh and her colleagues (1993). They claim that pygmy chimpanzees have a communication system that can combine a set of visual geometric symbols and responses to spoken English words (see figure 6.6). They state that these animals often come up with novel combinations of words and that their language knowledge is broader than that of common chimpanzees.

The debate over whether or not animals can use language to express thoughts is far from resolved. Researchers agree that animals can communicate with each other and that some can be trained to manipulate languagelike symbols. However, although such accomplishments may be remarkable, they fall far short of human language, with its infinite number of novel phrases to convey the richness and subtleties of meaning that are the foundation of human relationships.

Is There a Critical Period for Learning Language?

Former secretary of state Henry Kissinger's heavy German accent illustrates the theory that there is a critical period for learning language. According to this theory, people who emigrate after the age of 12 will probably speak the new country's language with a foreign accent the rest of their lives, but if people emigrate as young children, the accent goes away as the new language is learned (Asher & Garcia, 1969). Acquiring an accent is less related to how long you have lived somewhere than to the age at which you moved there. For example, if you move to a certain part of New York City before you turn 12, you'll probably "tawk" like a native. Apparently, puberty marks the close of a critical period for acquiring the phonological rules of various languages and dialects.

The stunted language development of a modern "wild child" also supports the idea of there being a critical period for language acquisition. In 1970 a California social worker made a routine visit to the home of a partially blind woman who had applied for public assistance. The social worker discovered that the woman and her husband had kept their 13-year-old daughter Genie locked away from the world. Kept in almost total isolation during childhood, Genie could not

FIGURE 6.6

Sue Savage-Rumbaugh with a chimp in front of a board with languagelike visual geometric symbols. Rumbaugh and her colleagues claim that these pygmy chimpanzees have a communication system in which they generate novel combinations of words.

speak or stand erect. During the day, she was left to sit naked on a child's potty seat, restrained by a harness her father had made—she could move only her hands and feet. At night she was placed in a kind of straitjacket and caged in a crib with wire mesh sides and a cover. Whenever Genie made a noise, her father beat her. He never communicated with her in words but growled and barked at her instead.

Genie spent a number of years in extensive rehabilitation programs, such as speech therapy and physical therapy (Curtiss, 1977). She eventually learned to walk with a jerky motion and to use the toilet. Genie also learned to recognize many words and to speak in rudimentary sentences. At first she spoke in one-word utterances. Later she was able to string together two-word combinations, such as "big teeth," "little marble," and "two hand." Consistent with the language development of most children, three-word combinations followed—for example, "small two cup." Unlike normal children, however, Genie did not learn how to ask questions and she doesn't understand grammar.

Genie was not able to distinguish between pronouns or passive and active verbs. Four years after she began stringing words together, her speech still sounded like a garbled telegram. As an adult she speaks in short, mangled sentences, such as "father hit leg," "big wood," and "Genie hurt."

Children who are abandoned, abused, and not exposed to language for years, such as Genie, rarely learn to speak normally. Such tragic evidence supports the critical-period hypothesis in language development.

Behavioral and Environmental Influences

Behaviorists view language as just another behavior, like sitting, walking, or running. They argue that language represents chains of responses (Skinner, 1957) or imitation (Bandura, 1977). But many of the sentences we produce are novel; we have not heard them or spoken them before. For example, a child hears the sentence "The plate fell on the floor" and then says, "My mirror fell on the blanket," after dropping the mirror on the blanket. The behavioral mechanisms of reinforcement and imitation cannot completely explain this.

While spending long hours observing parents and their young children, child language researcher Roger Brown (1973) searched for evidence that parents reinforce their children for speaking in grammatical ways. He found that parents sometimes smiled and praised their children for sentences they liked, but that they also reinforced sentences that were ungrammatical. Brown concluded that no evidence exists to document that reinforcement is responsible for language's rule systems.

Another criticism of the behavioral view is that it fails to explain the extensive orderliness of language. The behavioral view predicts that vast individual differences should appear in children's speech development because of each child's unique learning history. But as we have seen, a compelling fact about language is its structure and ever-present rule systems. All infants coo before they babble. All toddlers produce one-word utterances before two-word utterances, and all state sentences in the active form before they state them in the passive form.

However, we do not learn language in a social vacuum. Most children are bathed in language from a very early age. We need this early exposure to language to acquire competent language skills (Adamson, 1992; Schegloff, 1989). The Wild Boy of Aveyron did not learn to communicate effectively after being reared in social isolation for years. Genie's language was rudimentary even after a number of years of extensive training.

Today, most language acquisition researchers believe that children from a wide variety of cultural contexts acquire their native language without explicit teaching, in some cases without apparent encouragement (Rice, 1993). Thus, the necessary aspects of learning a language seem to be quite minimal. However, the facilitative effects usually require more support and involvement on the part of caregivers and teachers. A special concern involves children who grow up in poverty-infested

areas and are not exposed to guided participation in language. In Sociocultural Worlds of Development 6.1, you can read about how the rich language tradition of Black Americans is being shut down in such poverty conditions.

One intriguing role of the environment in the young child's acquisition of language is called **motherese,** *the way mothers and other adults often talk to babies in a higher-than-normal frequency, greater-than-normal pitch, and simple words and sentences.* It is hard to talk in motherese when not in the presence of a baby. But as soon as you start talking to a baby, you immediately shift into motherese. Much of this is automatic and something most parents are not aware they are doing. Motherese has the important functions of capturing the infant's attention and maintaining communication (Snow, 1989). When parents are asked why they use baby talk, they point out that it is designed to teach their baby to talk. Older peers also talk baby talk to infants, but observations of siblings indicate that the affectional features are dropped when sibling rivalry is sensed (Dunn & Kendrick, 1982).

Are there strategies other than motherese that adults use to enhance the child's acquisition of language? Four candidates are recasting, echoing, expanding, and labeling. **Recasting** *is phrasing the same or a similar meaning of a sentence in a different way, perhaps turning it into a question.* For example, if the child says, "The dog was barking," the adult can respond by asking, "When was the dog barking?" The effects of recasting fit with suggestions that "following in order to lead" helps a child to learn language. That is, letting a child initially indicate an interest and then proceeding to elaborate that interest—commenting, demonstrating, and explaining—enhance communication and help language acquisition. In contrast, an overly active, directive approach to communicating with the child may be harmful (Rice, 1989).

Echoing *is repeating what the child says to you, especially if it is an incomplete phrase or sentence.* **Expanding** *is restating what the child has said in a linguistically sophisticated form.* **Labeling** *is identifying the names of objects.* Young children are forever being asked to identify the names of objects. Roger Brown (1986) identified this as "the great word game" and claimed that much of the early vocabulary acquired by children is motivated by this adult pressure to identify the words associated with objects.

The use of labeling can often be pursued by parents when they identify, as best they can, what the baby is attending to at the moment. To read further about parents' identification of objects with words and the use of live, concrete talk to infants, turn to Perspectives on Parenting and Education 6.1.

How Language Develops

In describing language, we have touched on language development many times. You just read about the motherese that parents use with their infants. Earlier we discussed the Wild Boy of Aveyron, Genie, and Washoe. Now let's

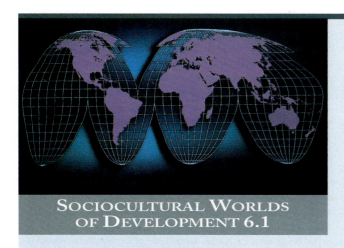

SOCIOCULTURAL WORLDS OF DEVELOPMENT 6.1

Language Traditions in Black Americans and Urban Poverty

Shirley Heath (1989) examined the language traditions of Black Americans from low-income backgrounds. She traced some aspects of Black English to the time of slavery. Heath also examined how those speech patterns have carried over into Black English today. She found that agricultural areas in the southern United States have an especially rich oral tradition.

Specifically she found that in this rich oral tradition adults do not simplify or edit their talk for children, in essence challenging the children to be highly active listeners. Also, adults ask only "real questions" of children—that is, questions for which the adult does not already know the answer. Adults also engage in a type of teasing with children, encouraging them to use their wits in communication. For example, a grandmother might pretend that she wants to take a child's hat and then starts a lively exchange in which the child must understand many subtleties or argument, mood, and humor—does Grandma really want my hat? Is she mad at me? Is she making a joke? Can I persuade her to give it back to me? Finally, there is an appreciation of wit and flexibility in how language is used, as well as an acknowledgement of individual differences—one person might be respected for recounting stories, another for negotiating and peace-making skills.

Heath argues that the language tradition she describes is richly varied, cognitively demanding, and well suited to many real-life situations. She says that the oral and literary traditions among poor Blacks in the cities are well suited for many job situations. Years ago many inner-city jobs required only that a person follow directions in order to perform repetitive tasks. Today many positions require continuous interactions involving considerable flexibility in language, such as the ability to persuade co-workers or to express dissatisfaction, in a subtle way, for example.

Despite its utility in many job situations, the rich language tradition possessed by low-income Black Americans does not meet with the educational priorities of our nation's schools. Too often schools stress rote memorization, minimizing group interaction and discouraging individual variations in communicative style. Also, the language tradition of Black culture is rapidly dying in the face of current life among poor Blacks, where the structure of low-income, frequently single-parent families often provides little verbal stimulation for children. In sum, the rich language tradition of many Black Americans is too often being squashed in the classroom and neglected at home, despite its utility in many real-world circumstances.

One mother agreed to let researcher Shirley Heath (in press) tape-record her interactions with her children over a 2-year period and to write notes about her activities with them. Within 500 hours of tape and more than 1,000 lines of notes, the mother initiated talk with her three preschool children on only 18 occasions (other than giving them a brief directive or asking a quick question). Few of the mother's conversations involved either planning or executing actions with or for her children.

Heath (1989) points out that the lack of family and community supports is widespread in urban housing projects, especially among Black Americans. The deteriorating, impoverished conditions of these inner-city areas severely impede the ability of young children to develop the cognitive and social skills they need to function competently.

Children who grow up in low-income, poverty-ridden neighborhoods of large cities often experience a lack of family and community support, which can seriously undermine the development of their cognitive and social skills.

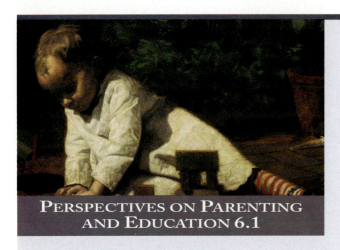

PERSPECTIVES ON PARENTING AND EDUCATION 6.1

Live, Concrete Parent Talk to Infants

Most parents are interested in how to talk to babies, especially what to say to them at different points in infant development. Infancy expert Burton White (1990) described appropriate ways for caregivers to interact with infants to promote their language development. An overview of White's ideas follows.

Some parents do not talk to their baby in the first several months or even the entire first year, waiting until the baby speaks its first word before beginning to do much talking to the infant. However, it is unquestionably a good idea for parents to begin talking to their babies right from the start. The best language teaching occurs when the talking is begun earlier than the first intelligible speech from an infant.

To assure good early language learning, it is important to talk in particular ways to babies. This particular method involves identifying, as well as the parent is able, what the baby is attending to at the moment. For the first 2 years of life, infants mainly orient to the here and now. They are simply incapable of understanding references to nonpresent objects. Talking about a trip that will be taken in a week is much less likely to register with the infant than comments about the parent's own face or the baby's hand, if that is what the baby is looking at. Diaper changing, bath, and playtimes lend themselves nicely to identifying what the baby is attending to at the moment and then talking directly to the baby about the situation in simple, normal language. For example, the parent can talk about the sock she is putting on the infant, the toy she is holding before the baby, or some feature of the baby's fingers.

Another important consideration for parents interested in promoting their infant's language development involves looking and listening to language. A typical example in the second year of life is the toddler who sees and hears the mother and older sibling talking at a level that is within the toddler's capacity to understand. A distinction can be made between *live language*—spoken language the infant may overhear or spoken language directed toward the infant by another person—and *mechanical language*—spoken language delivered by a television set, a radio, or a record or tape player. White argues that the more live language directed at toddlers—especially about what they seem to be attending to at the moment—the better for their language development.

It is also important for parents to act like they understand the toddler's words even when they don't. Correcting the toddler or trying to make the toddler say a word again "properly" only bores the toddler (Leach, 1990). As we have seen, toddlers are primarily developing language rather than imitating it, so parents' corrections will not have much effect anyway. The toddler's own words will develop into something more correct in time, but not under the caregiver's direct commands. Toddlers' own words are the best they have to offer at that point in development. Remember also that it is pleasure, affection, and excitement that motivate early talk. Refusing to hand the infant her bottle until she says "milk" instead of "bah-boo" will make her frustrated and cross. You are more likely to get tears than words.

It is unquestionably a good idea for parents to begin talking to their babies right at the start. The best language teaching occurs when the talking is begun before the infant becomes capable of its first intelligible speech.

examine in greater detail the developmental changes in language that take place in infancy.

In the first few months of life, infants show a startle response to sharp noises. Then, at 3 to 6 months, infants begin to show an interest in sounds, play with saliva, and respond to voices. During the next 3 to 6 months, infants begin to babble, emitting such sounds as "goo-goo" and "ga-ga." The start of

babbling is determined mainly by biological maturation, not reinforcement, hearing, or caregiver-infant interaction. Even deaf babies babble for a time (Lenneberg, Rebelsky, & Nichols, 1965). The purpose of the baby's earliest communication is to attract attention from parents and others in the environment. Infants engage the attention of others by making or breaking eye contact, by vocalizing sounds, or by performing manual

Around the world, young children learn to speak in two-word utterances, in most cases at about 18 to 24 months of age.

actions such as pointing. All of these behaviors involve the aspect of language we have called "pragmatics."

At approximately 6 to 9 months, infants begin to understand their first words. **Receptive vocabulary** *refers to the words an individual understands.* While infants' receptive vocabulary begins to develop in the second half of the first year, its growth increases dramatically in the second year from an average of 12 words understood at the first birthday to an estimated 300 words or more understood at the second birthday. At approximately 9 to 12 months, infants first begin to understand instructions, such as "wave bye-bye."

Children pick up words as pigeons peas.
—John Ray, *English Proverbs*, 1670

So far we have not mentioned *spoken* vocabulary, which begins when the infant utters its first word, a milestone anticipated by every parent. This event usually occurs at about 10 to 15 months of age. Many parents view the onset of language development as coincident with this first word, but as we have seen, some significant language milestones have already occurred. The infant's spoken vocabulary rapidly increases once the first word is spoken, reaching an average of 200 to 275 words by the age of 2.

A child's first words include those that name important people (*dada*), familiar animals (*kitty*), vehicles (*car*), toys (*ball*), food (*milk*), body parts (*eye*), clothes (*hat*), household items (*clock*), or greeting terms (*bye*). These were the first words of babies 50 years ago, and they are the first words of babies today (Clark, 1983). At times it is hard to tell what these one-word utterances mean. One possibility is that they stand for an entire sentence in the infant's mind. Because of the infant's limited cognitive or linguistic skills, possibly only one word comes out instead of the whole sentence. The **holophrase hypothesis** *is the concept that a single word is used to imply a complete sentence; this is characteristic of an infant's first words.*

By the time children are 18 to 24 months of age, they usually utter two-word statements. During this two-word stage, they quickly grasp the importance of expressing concepts and

of the role that language plays in communicating with others. To convey meaning with two-word utterances, the child relies heavily on gesture, tone, and context. The wealth of meaning children can communicate with a two-word utterance includes (Slobin, 1972):

- Identification: See doggie.
- Location: Book there.
- Repetition: More milk.
- Nonexistence: Allgone thing.
- Negation: Not wolf.
- Possession: My candy.
- Attribution: Big car.
- Agent-action: Mama walk.
- Action-direct object: Hit you.
- Action-indirect object: Give papa.
- Action-instrument: Cut knife.
- Question: Where ball?

One of the most striking aspects of this list is that it is used by children all over the world. The examples are taken from utterances in English, German, Russian, Finnish, Turkish, and Samoan, but the entire list could be made up from examples from a 2-year-old's speech in any language.

Telegraphic speech *is the use of short and precise words to communicate; it is characteristic of young children's two-word utterances.* When we send telegrams, we try to be short and precise, excluding any unnecessary words. As indicated in the examples of telegraphic speech from children from around the world, articles, auxiliary verbs, and other connectives are usually omitted. Of course telegraphic speech is not limited to two-word utterances. "Mommy give ice cream" and "Mommy give Tommy ice cream" are also examples of telegraphic speech.

A summary of the developmental milestones in language we have discussed so far appears in figure 6.7. Notice that the last entry for language accomplishments in infancy is the length of spoken sentences, which we consider next.

One- and two-word utterances classify children's language development in terms of number of utterances. In expanding this concept, Roger Brown (1973) proposed the **mean length of utterance (MLU),** *an index of language development based on the number of words per sentence a child produces in a sample of about 50 to 100 sentences, is a good index of language maturity.* Brown identified five stages based on MLU:

Stage	MLU
1	1+ to 2.0
2	2.5
3	3.0
4	3.5
5	4.0

The first stage begins when the child generates sentences consisting of more than one word, such as the examples we gave of two-word utterances. The 1+ designation suggests that the

FIGURE 6.7

Brown's stages of language development.

Stage	Age range (months)	Mean length of utterance (average number of words per sentence)	Characteristics	Typical sentences
1	12–26	1.00–2.00	Vocabulary consists mainly of nouns and verbs with a few adjectives and adverbs; word order is preserved	Baby bath.
2	27–30	2.00–2.50	Correct use of plurals; use of past tense, use of *be*, definite and nondefinite articles, some prepositions	Cars go fast.
3	31–34	2.50–3.00	Use of yes-no questions, *wh*-questions (who, what, where); use of negatives and imperatives	Put the baby down.
4	35–40	3.00–3.75	Embedding one sentence within another	That's the truck mommy buyed me.
5	41–46	3.75–4.50	Coordination of simple sentences and propositional relations	Jenny and Cindy are sisters.

From J. U. Dumtschin, "Recognize Language Development and Delay in Early Childhood" in *Young Children,* March 1988: 16–24. Copyright © 1988 by the National Association for the Education of Young Children. Reprinted by permission.

average number of words in each utterance is greater than one but not yet two, because some of the child's utterances are still holophrases. This stage continues until the child averages two words per utterance. Subsequent stages are marked by increments of 0.5 in mean length of utterance.

Brown's stages are important for several reasons. First, children who vary in chronological age by as much as one-half to three-fourths of a year still have similar speech patterns. Second, children with similar mean lengths of utterance have similar rule systems that characterize their language. In some ways, then, MLU is a better indicator of language development than is chronological age. Figure 6.8 shows the individual variation in chronological age that characterizes children's MLU.

As we have just seen, language unfolds in a sequence. At every point in development, the child's linguistic interaction with parents and others obeys certain principles (Conti-Ramsden & Snow, 1991; Maratsos, 1991). Not only is the development strongly influenced by the child's biological wiring, but the language environment the child is bathed in from an early age is far more intricate than was imagined in the past (von Tetzchner & Siegel, 1989). The main ideas we have discussed about language development are summarized in concept table 6.2. In the next chapter, we will continue our discussion of infant development, turning to information about the infant's social worlds.

FIGURE 6.8

An examination of MLU in three children. *Shown here is the average length of utterances generated by three children ranging in age from 1½ to just over 4 years.*

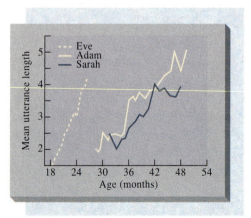

Critical Thinking

In our discussion of language, we have emphasized the role of biological and environmental factors. How might cognitive factors be involved in language development?

CONCEPT TABLE 6.2

Language Development

Concept	Processes/Related Ideas	Characteristics/Description
What is language?	Its nature	Language involves a system of symbols we use to communicate with each other. The system is characterized by infinite generativity and rule systems. The rule systems include phonology, morphology, syntax, semantics, and pragmatics.
Biological influences	Biological evolution	The fact that biological evolution shaped humans into linguistic creatures is undeniable.
	Biological prewiring	Chomsky argues that humans are biologically prewired to learn language and have a language acquisition device.
	Do animals have language?	Animals clearly can communicate, and pygmy chimpanzees and sea lions can be taught to use symbols. Whether animals have all of the properties of human language is debated.
	Is there a critical period for learning language?	The experiences of Genie and other children suggest that the early years of childhood are a critical time for learning language. If exposure to language does not occur before puberty, lifelong deficits in grammar occur.
Behavioral and environmental influences	The behavioral view	Language is just another behavior. Behaviorists believe language is learned primarily through reinforcement and imitation, although these probably play a facilitative rather than a necessary role.
	Environmental influences	Most children are bathed in language early in their development. Among the ways adults teach language to infants are motherese, recasting, echoing, expanding, and labeling. Parents should talk to infants extensively, especially about what the baby is attending to at the moment. Talk should be primarily live talk, not mechanical talk.
How language develops	Some developmental milestones	Among the milestones in infant language development are babbling (3 to 6 months), first words understood (6 to 9 months), the growth of receptive vocabulary (reaches 300 or more words at age 2), first instructions understood (9 months to 1 year), first word spoken (10 to 15 months), and the growth of spoken vocabulary (reaches 200 to 275 words at age 2).
	Holophrase, telegraphic speech, and mean length of utterance	The holophrase hypothesis states that a single word is often used to imply a complete sentence; it characterizes infants' first words. At 18 to 24 months of age, infants often speak in two-word utterances. Telegraphic speech is the use of short and precise words to communicate—this characterizes toddlers' two-word utterances. Brown developed the concept of mean length of utterance (MLU). Five stages of MLU have been identified, providing a valuable indicator of language maturity.

LIFE-SPAN HEALTH AND WELL-BEING

Malnutrition in Infancy and Children's Intelligence

In this chapter we explored the nature of infant cognitive development. Might there be some aspects of infants' health and well-being that undermine optimal cognitive growth and development? Nutritional intake, prenatal and postnatal factors, infections, accidents, and other assorted trauma can influence the infant's and child's intelligence. Recognizing that nutrition is important for the child's growth and development, the government provides money for school lunch programs. When we think about how nutrition affects development, we usually think of physical development, such as skeletal growth, body shape, and susceptibility to disease. What we often fail to recognize is that nutrition can also affect cognitive and social development. In recent years, developmentalists have shown a special concern about malnutrition in infancy and how it can restrict the child's cognitive development (Mortimer, 1992; Super, Herrera, & Mora, 1990).

In one investigation, two groups of extremely malnourished 1-year-old South African infants were studied (Bayley, 1970). The children in one group were given adequate nourishment during the next 6 years; no intervention took place in the lives of the other group of children. After the seventh year, the poorly nourished group of children performed much worse on tests of intelligence than did the adequately nourished group. Recently, other researchers have documented that nutritional supplements early in development can improve the cognitive de-

The recent crisis in Somalia brought to light how extensive malnutrition is in some developing countries. Both moderate and severe malnutrition can have detrimental effects, not only on children's physical growth and development, but also on their cognitive and social growth.

velopment of malnourished children (Engle, 1991; Gorman & Politt, 1991; Super, Herrera, & Mora, 1991).

Malnutrition in infancy can also be detrimental to children's social development. In one investigation, the diets of rural Guatemalan infants were associated with their social development at the time they entered elementary school (Barrett, Radke-Yarrow, & Klein, 1982). Children whose mothers had been given nutritional supplements during pregnancy and who themselves had been given

more nutritious, high-calorie foods in their first 2 years of life were more active, more involved, more helpful with their peers, less anxious, and happier than their counterparts who were not given nutritional supplements. The undernourished Guatemalan infants were only mildly undernourished in infancy, underscoring how important it is for parents to be attentive to the nutritional needs of their infants.

In the most recent research on early supplementary feeding and children's cognitive development, Ernesto Pollitt and his colleagues (1993) conducted a longitudinal investigation over two decades in rural Guatemala. They found that early nutritional supplements in the form of protein and increased calories can have positive long-term consequences for cognitive development. The researchers also found that the relation of nutrition to cognitive performance was moderated both by the time period during which the supplement was given and by the sociodemographic context. For example, children in the lowest socioeconomic groups benefitted more than did children in the higher socioeconomic groups. And, although there still was a positive nutritional influence when supplementation began after 2 years of age, the effect on cognitive development was less powerful.

In sum, good nutrition in infancy is important not only for the child's physical growth and development, but for cognitive and social development as well. ∎

CONCLUSIONS

Our knowledge of infant cognitive development has greatly expanded in the last two decades. We now know that infants have more sophisticated cognitive skills than we used to think.

We began this chapter with a look at the Doman "better baby institute" and sharply criticized its approach of pouring high-level knowledge into infants' minds. We studied Piaget's theory of infant development, focusing on the stage of sensorimotor development and object permanence. The new perspective on cognitive development in infancy reveals that infants have more-sophisticated perceptual

abilities, and can begin to think earlier, than Piaget envisioned. The new perspective involves taking an information-processing perspective on infant cognition and also includes the roles of habituation and dishabituation, memory, and imitation in development. We also studied individual differences in intelligence in infancy, with special emphasis on the developmental testing of infants. Our coverage of language development focused on what language is, biological evolution, biological prewiring, whether animals have language, whether there is a critical period for learning language, behavioral and environmental influences, and how language develops in infancy. At different points in the chapter you also read about language traditions in Black Americans and urban poverty, the importance of live, concrete parent talk to infants, and the influence of malnutrition in infancy on children's intelligence.

Don't forget that you can obtain an overall summary of the chapter by again reading the two concept tables on pages 165 and 173. In the next chapter, we turn our attention to the study of socioemotional development in infancy.

KEY TERMS

scheme (or schema)   Stage that refers to the basic unit (or units) for an organized pattern of sensorimotor functioning. (155)

simple reflexes   Piaget's first sensorimotor substage that corresponds to the first month after birth. In this substage, the basic means of coordinating sensation and action is through reflexive behaviors, such as rooting and sucking, which the infant has at birth. (156)

first habits and primary circular reactions   Piaget's second sensorimotor substage that develops between one and four months of age. In this substage, the infant learns to coordinate sensation and types of schemes or structures— that is, habits and primary circular reactions. (156)

primary circular reaction   A scheme based upon the infants attempt to reproduce an interesting or pleasurable event that initially occurred by chance. (156)

secondary circular reaction   Piaget's third sensorimotor substage that develops between four and eight months of age. In this substage, the infant becomes more object-orientated or focused on the world, moving beyond preoccupation with the self in sensorimotor interactions. (156)

coordination of secondary circular reactions   Piaget's fourth sensorimotor substage that develops between 8 and 12 months of age. In this substage, several significant changes take place involving the coordination of schemes and intentionality. (156)

tertiary circular reactions, novelty, and curiosity   Piaget's fifth sensorimotor substage that develops between 12 and 18 months of age. In this substage, infants become intrigued by the variety of properties that objects possess and by the multiplicity of things they can make happen to objects. (156)

internalization of schemes   Piaget's sixth and final sensorimotor substage that develops between 18 and 24 months of age. In this substage, the infant's mental functioning shifts from a purely sensorimotor plane to a symbolic plane, and the infant develops the ability to use primitive symbols. (156)

object permanence   The Piagetian term for one of an infant's most important accomplishments: understanding that objects and events continue to exist even when they cannot directly be seen, heard, or touched. (156)

habituation   Repeated presentation of the same stimulus that causes reduced attention to the stimulus. (160)

dishabituation   An infant's renewed interest in a stimulus. (160)

memory   A central feature of cognitive development, pertaining to all situations in which an individual retains information over time. (161)

deferred imitation   Imitation that occurs after a time delay of hours or days. (162)

developmental quotient (DQ)   An overall developmental score that combines subscores in motor, language, adaptive, and personal-social domains in the Gesell assessment of infants. (163)

Bayley Scales of Infant Development   Scales developed by Nancy Bayley that are widely used in the assessment of infant development. The current version has three components: a mental scale, a motor scale, and an infant behavior profile. (163)

language   A system of symbols used to communicate with others. In humans, language is characterized in infinite generativity and rule systems. (164)

infinite generativity   An individual's ability to generate an infinite number of meaningful sentences using a finite set of words and rules, which makes language a highly creative enterprise. (164)

phonology   The study of a language's sound system. (164)

morphology   The rules for combining morphemes; a morpheme is the smallest string of sounds that gives meaning to what we say and hear. (164)

syntax   The way words are combined to form acceptable phrases and sentences. (164)

grammar   The formal description of syntactical rules. (166)

surface structure   The actual order of words in a sentence. (166)

deep structure   The syntactic relation of words in a sentence. (166)

semantics   The meaning of words and sentences. (166)

pragmatics   The ability to engage in appropriate conversation. (166)

language acquisition device (LAD)   A biological prewiring that enables the child to detect certain language categories, such as phonology, syntax, and semantics. (166)

motherese   The way mothers and other adults often talk to babies in a higher-than-normal frequency, greater-than-normal pitch, and simple words and sentences. (168)

recasting   Phrasing the same or similar meaning of a sentence in a different way; perhaps turning it into a question. (168)

echoing   Repeating what the child says to you, especially if it is an incomplete phrase or sentence. (168)

expanding   Restating what the child has said in a linguistically sophisticated form. (168)

labeling   Identifying the names of objects. (168)

receptive vocabulary   The words an individual understands. (171)

holophrase hypothesis   The concept that a single word is used to imply a complete sentence; this is characteristic of an infant's first words. (171)

telegraphic speech   The use of short and precise words to communicate; it is characteristic of young children's two-word utterances. (171)

mean length of utterance (MLU)   An index of language development based on the number of words per sentence a child produces in a sample of about 50 to 100 sentences; is a good index of language maturity. (171)

Diego Rivera, Delfino Flores, detail.

Socioemotional Development in Infancy

*A child forsaken, waking suddenly,
Whose gaze affeard on all things round
doth rove,
And seeth only that it cannot see
The meeting eyes of love.*

—George Eliot

> *Out of the conflict between trust and mistrust, the infant develops hope,*
> *which is the earliest form of what gradually becomes faith in adults.*
>
> —Erik Erikson

IMAGES OF LIFE-SPAN DEVELOPMENT

The Newborn Opossum, Wildebeest, and Human

The newborns of some species function independently in the world; other species are not so independent. At birth, the opossum is still considered fetal and is capable of finding its way around only in its mother's pouch, where it attaches itself to her nipple and continues to develop.

This protective environment is similar to the uterus. By contrast, the newborn wildebeest must run with the herd moments after birth. Its behavior often is far more adult than the opossum's, although the wildebeest does not have to obtain

food through suckling. The maturation of the human infant lies somewhere between these two extremes; much learning and development must take place before the infant can sustain itself (Maccoby, 1980).

Variations in the dependency of newborns of different species. (a) The newborn opossum is fetal, capable of finding its way around only in its mother's pouch, where it attaches itself to one of her nipples and continues to develop. (b) By contrast, the wildebeest runs with the herd moments after birth. (c) The human newborn's maturation lies somewhere in between that of the opossum and that of the wildebeest.

PREVIEW

Because it cannot sustain itself, the human infant requires extensive care. What kind of care is needed, and how does the infant start down the road to social maturity? Much of the interest in infant care focuses on attachment and parent-infant interaction, although the roles of day care and temperament in infant development are also important considerations. Among the other topics we will address are emotional development, personality development, adapting caregiving to the developmental status of the infant and toddler, and problems and disorders. To begin, we explore some basic aspects of family processes.

FAMILY PROCESSES

Most of us began our lives in families and spent thousands of hours during our childhood interacting with our parents. Some of you are already parents; others of you may become parents. What is the nature of family processes?

Reciprocal Socialization

For many years, socialization between parents and children was viewed as a one-way process: Children were considered to be the products of their parents' socialization techniques. Today, however, we view parent-child interactions as reciprocal. **Reciprocal socialization** *is the view that socialization is bidirectional; children socialize parents just as parents socialize children.* For example, the interaction of mothers and their infants is symbolized as a dance or a dialogue in which successive actions of the partners are closely coordinated. This coordinated dance or dialogue can assume the form of mutual synchrony (each person's behavior depends on the partner's previous behavior). Or it can be reciprocal in a more precise sense; the actions of the partners can be matched, as when one partner imitates the other or when there is mutual smiling (Cohn & Tronick, 1988).

When reciprocal socialization has been investigated in infancy, mutual gaze or eye contact has been found to play an important role in early social interaction (Fogel, Toda, & Kawai, 1988). In one investigation, the mother and infant engaged in a variety of behaviors while they looked at each other; by contrast, when they looked away from each other, the rate of such behaviors dropped considerably (Stern & others, 1977). In sum, the behaviors of mothers and infants involve substantial interconnections, mutual regulation, and synchronization.

Scaffolding *describes an important caregiver's role in early parent-child interaction. Through their attention and choice of behaviors, caregivers provide a framework around which they and their infants interact. One function scaffolding serves is to introduce infants to social rules, especially turn taking* (Bruner, 1989). For example, in the game peekaboo, the mother initially covers her baby, then removes the covering, and finally registers "surprise" at the baby's reappearance. As infants become more skilled at peekaboo, the infants do the covering and uncovering. Other caregiver-infant games that involve scaffolding and its turn-taking sequences are pat-a-cake and so-big (Field, 1987). In one investigation, infants who had more extensive scaffolding experiences with their parents, especially in the form of turn taking, were more likely to take turns as they interacted with their peers (Vandell & Wilson, 1988).

The Family as a System

As a social system, the family can be thought of as a constellation of subsystems defined in terms of generation, gender, and role. Divisions of labor among family members define particular subunits, and attachments define others. Each family member is a participant in several subsystems—some dyadic (involving two people), some polyadic (involving more than two people). The father and child represent one dyadic subsystem, the mother and father another; the mother-father-child represent one polyadic subsystem, the mother and two siblings another (Belsky, Rovine, & Fish, 1989).

An organizational scheme that highlights the reciprocal influences of family members and family subsystems is shown in figure 7.1 (Belsky, 1981). As the arrows in the figure show, marital relations, parenting, and infant behavior can have both direct and indirect effects on each other. An example of a direct effect is the influence of the parents' behavior on the child; an example of an indirect effect is how the relationship between the spouses mediates the way a parent acts toward the child. For example, marital conflict might reduce the efficiency of parenting, in which case marital conflict would be an indirect effect on the child's behavior. In the family system, the infant's most important experiences involve the process of attachment.

ATTACHMENT

A small curly-haired girl named Danielle, age 11 months, begins to whimper. After a few seconds, she begins to wail. The psychologist observing Danielle is conducting a research study on the nature of attachment between infants and their mothers. Subsequently, the mother reenters the room, and Danielle's crying ceases. Quickly, Danielle crawls over to where her

FIGURE 7.1

Interaction between children and their parents: direct and indirect effects.

FIGURE 7.2

Harlow's classic "contact comfort" study. Regardless of whether they were fed by a wire mother or by a cloth mother, the infant monkeys overwhelmingly preferred to be in contact with the cloth mother, demonstrating the importance of contact comfort in attachment.

mother is seated and reaches out to be held. This scenario is one of the main ways that psychologists study the nature of attachment during infancy.

What Is Attachment?

In everyday language, *attachment* refers to a relationship between two individuals who feel strongly about each other and do a number of things to continue the relationship. Many pairs of people are attached: relatives, lovers, a teacher and a student. In the language of developmental psychology, though, attachment is often restricted to a relationship between particular social figures and a particular phenomenon that is thought to reflect unique characteristics of the relationship. In this case,

the developmental period is infancy, the social figures are the infant and one or more adult caregivers, and the phenomenon is a bond (Bowlby, 1969, 1989). To summarize, **attachment** *is a close emotional bond between the infant and the caregiver.*

There is no shortage of theories about infant attachment. Freud believed that infants become attached to the person or object that provides oral satisfaction; for most infants, this is the mother, since she is most likely to feed the infant.

However, is feeding as important as Freud thought? A classic study by Harry Harlow and Robert Zimmerman (1959) suggests that the answer is no. These researchers evaluated whether feeding or contact comfort was more important to infant attachment. Infant monkeys were removed from their mothers at birth and reared for 6 months by surrogate (substitute) "mothers." One of the mothers was made of wire, the other of cloth (see figure 7.2). Half of the infant monkeys were fed by the wire mother, half by the cloth mother. Periodically, the amount of time the infant monkeys spent with either the wire or the cloth monkey was computed. Regardless of whether they were fed by the wire or the cloth mother, the infant monkeys spent far more time with the cloth mother. This study clearly demonstrated that feeding is not the crucial element in the attachment process and that contact comfort is important.

Most toddlers develop a strong attachment to a favorite soft toy or a particular blanket. Toddlers may carry the toy or blanket with them everywhere they go, just as Linus does in the "Peanuts" cartoon strip, or they may run for the toy or blanket only in moments of crisis, such as after an argument or a fall. By the time they have outgrown the security object, all that may be left is a small fragment of the blanket, or an animal that is hardly recognizable, having had a couple of new faces and all its seams resewn half a dozen times. If parents try to replace the security object with something newer, the toddler will resist. There is nothing abnormal about a toddler carrying around a security blanket. Children know that the blanket or teddy bear is not their mother, and yet they react affectively to these objects and derive comfort from them as if they were their mother. Eventually, they abandon the security object as they grow up and become more sure of themselves.

Might familiarity breed attachment? The famous study by ethologist Konrad Lorenz (1965) suggests that the answer is yes. Remember from our description of this study in chapter 2 that newborn goslings became attached to "father" Lorenz rather than to their mother because he was the first moving object they saw. The time period during which familiarity is important for goslings is the first 36 hours after birth; for human beings, it is more on the order of the first year of life.

Erik Erikson (1968) believes that the first year of life is the key time frame for the development of attachment. Recall his proposal—also discussed in chapter 2—that the first year of life represents the stage of trust versus mistrust. A sense of trust requires a feeling of physical comfort and a minimal amount of fear and apprehension about the future. Trust in infancy sets the stage for a lifelong expectation that the world will be a good and pleasant place to be. Erikson believes that responsive, sensitive parenting contributes to an infant's sense of trust.

The ethological perspective of British psychiatrist John Bowlby (1969, 1989) also stresses the importance of attachment in the first year of life and the responsiveness of the caregiver. Bowlby believes that an infant and its mother instinctively form an attachment. He argues that the newborn is biologically equipped to elicit the mother's attachment behavior. The baby cries, clings, coos, and smiles. Later, the infant crawls, walks, and follows the mother. The infant's goal is to keep the mother nearby. Research on attachment supports Bowlby's view that, at about 6 to 7 months of age, the infant's attachment to the caregiver intensifies (Sroufe, 1985).

Individual Differences

Although attachment to a caregiver intensifies midway through the first year, isn't it likely that some babies have a more positive attachment experience than others? Mary Ainsworth (1979) thinks so and says that, in **secure attachment,** *infants use the caregiver, usually the mother, as a secure base from which to explore*

The attachment theorists argue that early experiences play an important role in a child's later social development. For example, Bowlby and Ainsworth argue that a secure attachment to the caregiver in infancy is related to the development of social competence during the childhood years.

the environment. Ainsworth believes that secure attachment in the first year of life provides an important foundation for psychological development later in life. The caregiver's sensitivity to the infant's signals increases secure attachment. The securely attached infant moves freely away from the mother but processes her location through periodic glances. The securely attached infant responds positively to being picked up by others and, when put back down, freely moves away to play. An insecurely attached infant, by contrast, avoids the mother or is ambivalent toward her, fears strangers, and is upset by minor, everyday separations.

Ainsworth believes that insecurely attached infants can be classified as either anxious-avoidant or anxious-resistant, making three main attachment categories: secure (type B), anxious-avoidant (type A), and anxious-resistant (type C). **Type B babies** *use the caregiver as a secure base from which to explore the environment.* **Type A babies** *exhibit insecurity by avoiding the mother (for example, ignoring her, avoiding her gaze, and failing to seek proximity).* **Type C babies** *exhibit insecurity by resisting the mother (for example, clinging to her but at the same time fighting against the closeness, perhaps by kicking and pushing away).*

I am what I hope and give.
—Erik Erikson

Why are some infants securely attached and others insecurely attached? Following Bowlby's lead, Ainsworth believes that attachment security depends on how sensitive and responsive a caregiver is to an infant's signals. For example, infants who are securely attached are more likely to have mothers who are more sensitive, accepting, and expressive of affection toward them than those who are insecurely attached (Pederson & others, 1989).

If early attachment to a caregiver is important, it should relate to a child's social behavior later in development. Research by Alan Sroufe (1985, 1990; Hiester, Carlson, & Sroufe, 1993) documents this connection. In one investigation, infants who were securely attached to their mothers early in infancy were less frustrated and happier at 2 years of age than their insecurely attached counterparts (Matas, Arend, & Sroufe, 1978). In another longitudinal investigation, securely attached infants were more socially competent and had better grades in the third grade (Egeland, 1989). Linkages between secure attachment and many other aspects of children's competence have been found (Gruys, 1993; Waters & others, 1994).

Attachment, Temperament, and the Wider Social World

Not all developmentalists believe that a secure attachment in infancy is the only path to competence in life. Indeed, some developmentalists believe that too much emphasis is placed on the importance of the attachment bond in infancy. Jerome Kagan (1987, 1989), for example, believes that infants are highly resilient and adaptive; he argues that they are evolutionarily equipped to stay on a positive developmental course even in the face of wide variations in parenting. Kagan and others stress that genetic and temperament characteristics play more important roles in a child's social competence than the attachment theorists, such as Bowlby, Ainsworth, and Sroufe, are willing to acknowledge (Calkins & Fox, 1992; Fish, 1989; Fox & others, 1989). For example, infants may have inherited a low tolerance for stress; this, rather than an insecure attachment bond, may be responsible for their inability to get along with peers.

Another criticism of attachment theory is that it ignores the diversity of socializing agents and contexts that exist in an infant's world (Thompson, 1991). In some cultures, infants show attachments to many people. Among the Hausa, both grandmothers and siblings provide a significant amount of care to infants (Super, 1980). Infants in agricultural societies tend to form attachments to older siblings who are assigned a major responsibility for younger siblings' care. The attachments formed by infants in group care in Israeli kibbutzim provide another challenge to the singular attachment thesis.

Researchers recognize the importance of competent, nurturant caregivers in an infant's development—at issue, though, is whether or not secure attachment, especially to a single caregiver, is critical.

FATHERS AS CAREGIVERS FOR INFANTS

Can fathers take care of infants as competently as mothers can? Observations of fathers and their infants suggest that fathers have the ability to act sensitively and responsively with their infants (Parke & Sawin, 1980; Parke & Stearns, 1993). Probably the strongest evidence of the plasticity of male caregiving abilities is derived from information about male primates who are notoriously low in their interest in offspring but are forced to live with infants whose female caregivers are absent. Under these circumstances, the adult male competently rears the infants.

Remember, however, that although fathers can be active, nurturant, involved caregivers with their infants, many do not choose to follow this pattern.

Do fathers behave differently toward infants than mothers do? Whereas maternal interactions usually center around child-care activities—feeding, changing diapers, bathing—paternal interactions are more likely to include play. Fathers engage in more rough-and-tumble play, bouncing infants, throwing them up in the air, tickling them, and so on (Lamb, 1986). Mothers do play with infants, but their play is less physical and arousing than that of fathers.

In stressful circumstances, do infants prefer their mother or father? In one investigation, twenty 12-month-olds were observed interacting with their parents (Lamb, 1977). With both parents present, the infants preferred neither their mother nor their father. The same was true when the infants were alone with the mother or the father. However, the entrance of a stranger, combined with boredom and fatigue, produced a shift in the infants' social behavior toward the mother. In stressful circumstances, then, infants show a stronger attachment to the mother.

Might the nature of parent-infant interaction be different in families that adopt nontraditional gender roles? This question was investigated by Michael Lamb and his colleagues (1982). They studied Swedish families in which the fathers were the primary caregivers of their firstborn, 8-month-old infants. The mothers were working full-time. In all observations, the mothers were more likely to discipline, hold, soothe, kiss, and talk to the infants than were the fathers. These mothers and fathers dealt with their infants differently, along the lines of American fathers and mothers following traditional gender roles. Having fathers assume the primary caregiving role did not substantially alter the way they interacted with their infants. This may be for biological reasons or because of deeply ingrained socialization patterns in cultures.

In Sweden, mothers or fathers are given paid maternity or paternity leave for up to 9 months. Sweden and many other European countries have well-developed child-care policies. To learn about these policies, turn to Sociocultural Worlds of Development 7.1. In Sweden, day care for infants under 1 year of age is usually not a major concern, because one parent is on paid leave for child care. As we will see, since the United States does not have a policy of paid leave for child care, day care in the United States has become a major national concern.

DAY CARE

Each weekday at 8 A.M., Ellen Smith takes her 1-year-old daughter Tanya to the day-care center at Brookhaven College in Dallas. Then Mrs. Smith goes to work and returns in the afternoon to take Tanya home. After 3 years, Mrs. Smith reports that her daughter is adventuresome and interacts confidently with peers and adults. Mrs. Smith believes that day care has been a wonderful way to raise Tanya.

In Los Angeles, however, day care has been a series of horror stories for Barbara Jones. After 2 years of unpleasant experiences with sitters, day-care centers, and day-care homes, Mrs. Jones has quit her job as a successful real estate agent to stay

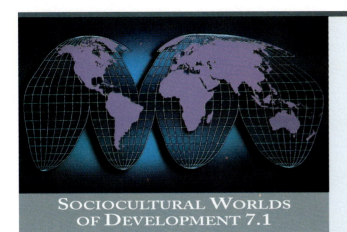

SOCIOCULTURAL WORLDS OF DEVELOPMENT 7.1

Child–Care Policy Around the World

Sheila Kamerman (1989) surveyed the nature of child-care policies around the world, giving special attention to European countries. Maternity and paternity policies for working parents include paid, job-protected leaves, which are sometimes supplemented by additional unpaid, job-protected leaves. Child-care policy packages also often include full health insurance. An effective child-care policy is designed to get an infant off to a competent start in life and to protect maternal health while maintaining income. More than a hundred countries around the world have such child-care policies, including all of Europe, Canada, Israel, and many developing countries (Kamerman & Kahn, 1988). Infants are assured of at least 2 to 3 months of maternal/paternal care, and in most European countries 5 to 6 months.

The maternity policy as now implemented in several countries involves a paid maternity leave that begins 2 to 6 weeks prior to expected childbirth and lasts from 8 to 20 or even 24 weeks after birth. This traditional maternal policy stems from an effort to protect the health of pregnant working women, new mothers, and their infants. Only since the 1960s has the maternity policy's link with employment become strong. A second child-care policy emphasizes the importance of parenting and recognizes the potential of fathers as well as mothers to care for their infants. In Sweden a parent insurance benefit provides protection to the new mother before birth and for 6 to 12 weeks after birth but then allows the father to participate in the postchildbirth leave. Approximately one-fourth of Swedish fathers take at least part of the postchildbirth leave, in addition to the 2 weeks of paid leave all fathers are entitled to at the time of childbirth. In a typical pattern in Sweden, the working mother might take off 3 months, after which she and her husband might share child care between them, each working half-time for 6 months. In addition, Swedish parents have the option of taking an unpaid but fully protected job leave until their child is 18 months old, and to work a 6-hour day (without a reduction in pay) from the end of the parental leave until their child is 8 years old.

In sum, almost all the industrialized countries other than the United States have recognized the importance of developing maternity/paternity policies that allow working parents some time off after childbirth to physically recover, to adapt to parenting, and to improve the well-being of the infant. These policies are designed to let parents take maternity/paternity leave without losing employment or income.

Provision of day care in most developing countries has improved, but this often has been in a form that denies access to the poorest children. In some locations in India, mobile day-care centers have provided intensive integrated child services to young children in slum settlements within large cities and rural villages.

home and take care of her 2½-year-old daughter Gretchen. "I didn't want to sacrifice my baby for my job," said Mrs. Jones, who was unable to find good substitute day-care homes. When she put Gretchen into a day-care center, she said that she felt her daughter was being treated like a piece of merchandise—dropped off and picked up.

Many parents worry whether day care will adversely affect their children. They fear that day care will reduce their infants' emotional attachment to them, retard the infants' cognitive development, fail to teach them how to control anger, and allow them to be unduly influenced by their peers. How extensive is day care? Are the worries of these parents justified?

In the 1990s, far more young children are in day care than at any other time in history; about 2 million children currently receive formal, licensed day care, and more than 5 million children attend kindergarten. Also, uncounted millions of children are cared for by unlicensed baby-sitters. Day care clearly has become a basic need of the American family (Caldwell, 1991; Phillips, 1989).

The type of day care that young children receive varies extensively. Many day-care centers house large groups of children and have elaborate facilities. Some are commercial operations, others are nonprofit centers run by churches, civic groups, and employers. Child care is frequently provided in private homes, at times by child-care professionals, at others by mothers who want to earn extra money.

The quality of care children experience in day care varies extensively (Phillips, in press). Some caregivers have no training, others have extensive training; some day-care centers have a low caregiver-child ratio, others have a high caregiver-child ratio. Some experts have recently argued that the quality of day care most children receive in the United States is poor. Infant researcher Jay Belsky (1989) not only believes that the quality of day care children experience is generally poor, but he also believes this translates into negative developmental outcomes for children. Belsky concludes that extensive day-care experience during the first 12 months of life—as typically experienced in the United States—is associated with insecure attachment as well as increased aggression, noncompliance, and possibly social withdrawal during the preschool and early elementary school years.

One study supports Belsky's beliefs (Vandell & Corasaniti, 1988). Extensive day care in the first year of life was associated with long-term negative outcomes. In contrast to children who began full-time day care later, children who began full-time day care (defined as more than 30 hours per week) as infants were rated by parents and teachers as being less compliant and as having poorer peer relations. In the first grade, they received lower grades and had poor work habits by comparison.

Belsky's conclusions about day care are controversial. Other respected researchers have arrived at a different conclusion; their review of the day-care research suggests no ill effects of day care (Andersson, 1992; Broberg, Hwang, & Chase, 1993; Caughy, DiPietro, & Strobino, in press; Clarke-Stewart, 1989; Field, in press; Scarr, 1984; Scarr, Lande, & McCartney, 1989).

What can we conclude? Does day care have adverse effects on children's development? Trying to combine the results into an overall conclusion about day-care effects is a problem because of the different types of day care children experience and the different measures used to assess outcome (Lamb, Sternberg, & Prodromidis, 1992; Park & Honing, 1991). Belsky's analysis does suggest that parents should be very careful about the quality of day care they select for their infants, especially those 1 year of age or less. Even Belsky agrees, though, that day care itself is not the culprit; rather it is the quality of day care that is problematic in this country. Belsky acknowledges that no evidence exists to show that children in high-quality day care are at risk in any way (Belsky, 1989; Doll, 1988).

What constitutes a high-quality day-care program for infants? The demonstration program developed by Jerome Kagan, Kearsley, and Zelazo (1978) at Harvard University is exemplary. The day-care center included a pediatrician, a nonteaching director, and an infant-teacher ratio of 3 to 1. Teachers' aides assisted at the center. The teachers and aides were trained to smile frequently, to talk with the infants, and to provide them with a safe environment that included many stimulating toys. No adverse effects of day care were observed in this project. More information about what to look for in a quality day-care center is presented in table 7.1. Using such criteria, Carolee Howes (1988) discovered that children who entered low-quality child care as infants were least likely to be socially competent in early childhood; such children were less compliant, less self-controlled, less task-oriented, more hostile, and have more problems in peer interaction.

Critical Thinking

If your own children were attending day care, which of the criteria listed in table 7.1 would you feel were most important? Are there criteria not listed that you believe should be considered?

Edward Zigler (1987) proposed a solution to the day-care needs of families. Zigler says that we should think of school not as an institution, but rather as a building, one that is owned by tax-paying parents who need day care for their children. Part of the school building would be for teaching and part would be for child care and supervision. This system could provide parents with competent developmental child-care services. Zigler believes it should be available to every child over the age of 3. He does not think children should start formal schooling at age 3; they would be in the schools only for day care. At the age of 5, children would start kindergarten, but only for half days. If the child has a parent at home, the child would spend the remainder of the day at home. If the parents are working, the child would spend the second half of the day in the day-care part of the school. For children aged 6 to 12, after-school and vacation care would be available to those who need it.

Zigler does not believe that teachers should provide day care; they are trained as educators and are too expensive. What we need, he says, is a child development associate, someone who is trained to work with children, someone we can afford to pay. This is a large vision, one that involves a structural change in society and a new face for our school system. As Zigler remembers, between the fall of 1964 and the summer of 1965, we managed to put 560,000 children into Head Start programs, an educational program for impoverished children. He believes we can do the same thing with day care (Trotter, 1987). Despite the efforts of Zigler and others, the child-care bills currently being introduced in Congress still do not adequately address the quality of child care and the low pay of child-care workers (DeAngelis, 1990).

We have all the knowledge necessary to provide absolutely first-rate child care in the United States. What is missing is the commitment and the will.

—Edward Zigler, 1987

In our discussion of attachment, we learned that some developmentalists believe temperament plays a more important role in infant development than many attachment enthusiasts take it to play. Next we look more closely at temperament's effects on children's development.

LIFE-SPAN PRACTICAL KNOWLEDGE 7.1

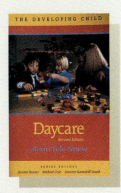

Daycare

(1993, rev. ed.) by Alison Clarke-Stewart. Cambridge, MA: Harvard University Press.

This book draws on extensive research to survey the social, political, and economic contexts of day care. The author discusses options and consequences to help parents make informed choices. She provides a broad overview of day care's role in contemporary society, and evaluates the emergence and current state of institutional day care in schools and businesses. The book includes a checklist parents can use to assess their own arrangements.

TABLE 7.1

Quality Day Care

What constitutes quality child care? The following recommendations were made by the National Association for the Education of Young Children (1986). They are based on a consensus arrived at by experts in early childhood education and child development. It is especially important that parents meet the adults who will care for their child. They are responsible for every aspect of the program's operation.

The adult caregivers.

- The adults should enjoy and understand how infants and young children grow.
- There should be enough adults to work with a group and to care for the individual needs of children. More specifically, there should be no more than four infants for each adult caregiver, no more than eight 2- to 3-year-old children for each caregiver, and no more than ten 4- to 5-year-old children for each adult caregiver.
- Caregivers should observe and record each child's progress and development.

The program activities and equipment.

- The environment should foster the growth and development of young children working and playing together.
- A good center provides appropriate and sufficient equipment and play materials and makes them readily available.
- Infants and children should be helped to increase their language skills and to expand their understanding of the world.

The relation of staff to families and the community.

- A good program should consider and support the needs of the entire family. Parents should be welcome to observe, discuss policies, make suggestions, and work in the activities of the center.
- The staff in a good center should be aware of and contribute to community resources. The staff should share information about community recreational and learning opportunities with families.

The facility and the program should be designed to meet the varied demands of infants and young children, their families, and the staff.

- The health of children, staff, and parents should be protected and promoted. The staff should be alert to the health of each child.
- The facility should be safe for children and adults.
- The environment should be spacious enough to accommodate a variety of activities and equipment. More specifically, there should be a minimum of 35 square feet of usable playroom floor space indoors per child and 75 square feet of play space outdoors per child.

T ABLE 7.2

Chess and Thomas's Dimensions and the Basic Clusters of Temperament

Temperament Dimension	Description	Temperament Cluster		
		Easy Child	Difficult Child	Slow-to-Warm-Up Child
Rhythmicity	Regularity of eating, sleeping, toileting	Regular	Irregular	
Activity level	Degree of energy movement		High	Low
Approach-withdrawal	Ease of approaching new people and situations	Positive	Negative	Negative
Adaptability	Ease of tolerating change in routine plans	Positive	Negative	Negative
Sensory threshold	Amount of stimulation required for responding			
Predominant quality of mood	Degree of positive or negative affect	Positive	Negative	
Intensity of mood expression	Degree of affect when pleased, displeased, happy, sad	Low to moderate	High	Low
Distractibility/attention span/persistence	Ease of being distracted			

Note: This table identifies those dimensions that were critical in spotting a basic cluster of temperament and the level of responsiveness for each critical feature. A blank space indicates that the dimension was not strongly related to a basic cluster of temperament.

TEMPERAMENT

Temperament *is an individual's behavioral style and characteristic way of responding.* Developmentalists are especially interested in the temperament of infants (Parker & Barrett, 1992). Some infants are extremely active, moving their arms, legs, and mouths incessantly. Others are tranquil. Some children explore their environment eagerly for great lengths of time. Others do not. Some infants respond warmly to people. Others fuss and fret. All of these behavioral styles represent a person's temperament (Carson & Bittner, 1993; Goldsmith & others, 1991; Gottfried & Lussier, 1993; Mehegany, 1992; Rothbart & Ahadi; 1993).

A widely debated issue in temperament research is just what the key dimensions of temperament are. Psychiatrists Alexander Chess and Stella Thomas (Chess & Thomas, 1977; Thomas & Chess, 1987, 1991) believe there are three basic types, or clusters, of temperament—easy, difficult, and slow to warm up.

1. An **easy child** *is generally in a positive mood, quickly establishes regular routines in infancy, and adapts easily to new experiences.*
2. A **difficult child** *tends to react negatively and cry frequently, engages in irregular daily routines, and is slow to accept new experiences.*
3. A **slow-to-warm-up child** *has a low activity level, is somewhat negative, shows low adaptability, and displays a low intensity of mood.*

Different dimensions make up these three basic clusters of temperament. The three basic clusters and their dimensions are shown in table 7.2. In their longitudinal investigation, Chess and Thomas found that 40 percent of the children they studied could be classified as easy, 10 percent as difficult, and 15 percent as slow to warm up. Researchers have found that these three basic clusters of temperament are moderately stable across the childhood years.

Critical Thinking

Consider your own temperament. Does it fit into one of the clusters described by Chess and Thomas? How stable has your temperament been in the course of your development? What factors contributed to this stability or lack of stability?

Other researchers suggest that temperament is composed of different basic components. Personality psychologist Arnold Buss and behavior geneticist Robert Plomin (1984, 1987) believe that infants' temperament falls into three basic categories: emotionality, sociability, and activity level. **Emotionality** *is the tendency to be distressed.* It reflects the arousal of a person's sympathetic nervous system. During infancy, distress develops into two separate emotional responses: fear and anger. Fearful infants try to escape something that is unpleasant; angry ones protest it. Buss and Plomin argue that children are labeled "easy" or "difficult" on the basis of their emotionality.

Sociability *is the tendency to prefer the company of others to being alone.* It matches a tendency to respond warmly to others. **Activity level** *involves tempo and vigor of movement.* Some children walk fast, are attracted to high-energy games, and jump or bounce around a lot; others are more placid.

Some experts on temperament believe there should be even further differentiation of certain domains of temperament (Eisenberg, 1992). For example, in the general domain of social withdrawal, researchers are beginning to distinguish between shyness (inhibited and awkward behavior with strangers or acquaintances, accompanied by feelings of tension and a desire to escape), introversion (a nonfearful preference for not affiliating with others), sociability (a preference for affiliating with others), and extraversion (the tendency to seek social interaction as a source of stimulation rather than out of true social interest in others).

A number of scholars, including Chess and Thomas, conceive of temperament as a stable characteristic of newborns that comes to be shaped and modified by the child's later experiences (Goldsmith, 1988; Thomas & Chess, 1987). This raises the question of heredity's role in temperament. Twin and adoption studies have been conducted to answer this question (Braungart & others, 1992; Emde & others, 1992; Plomin & others, 1993; Matheny, Dolan, & Wilson, 1976; Robinson & others, 1992). The researchers find a heritability index in the range of .50 to .60, suggesting a moderate influence of heredity on temperament. However, the strength of the association usually declines as infants become older (Goldsmith & Gottesman, 1981). This finding supports the belief that temperament becomes more malleable with experience. Alternatively, it may be that, as a child becomes older, behavior indicators of temperament are more difficult to spot.

The consistency of temperament depends, in part, on the "match" or "fit" between the child's nature and the parent's nature (Nitz & Lerner, 1991; Plomin & Thompson, 1987; Rothbart, 1988). Imagine a high-strung parent with a child who is difficult and sometimes slow to respond to the parent's affection. The parent may begin to feel angry or rejected. A father who does not need much face-to-face social interaction will find it easy to manage a similarly introverted baby, but he may not be able to provide an extraverted baby with sufficient stimulation. Parents influence infants, but infants also influence parents. Parents may withdraw from difficult children, or they may become critical and punish them; these responses may make the difficult child even more difficult. A more easygoing parent may have a calming effect on a difficult child or may continue to show affection even when the child withdraws or is hostile, eventually encouraging more competent behavior.

In sum, heredity does seem to influence temperament. However, the degree of influence depends on parents' responsiveness to their children and on other environmental childhood experiences.

At this point we have discussed a number of ideas about family processes, attachment, fathers as caregivers for infants, day care, and temperament. A summary of these ideas is presented in concept table 7.1. Next we turn our attention to the study of children's emotional development.

EMOTIONAL DEVELOPMENT

Children's worlds are filled with emotions and emotional experiences. What is the nature of children's emotions? How do emotions develop in infancy?

The Nature of Children's Emotions

What is an emotion? What are the functions of emotion in children? What is the role of emotion in parent-infant relationships?

Defining Emotion

Defining emotion is difficult because it is not easy to tell when a child or an adult is in an emotional state. Is a child in an emotional state when her heart beats fast, her palms sweat, and her stomach churns? Or is she in an emotional state when she smiles or grimaces? The body and face play important roles in understanding children's emotion, although psychologists debate how important each is in determining whether a child is in an emotional state (Harris, 1989). For our purposes, we will define **emotion** as *feeling or affect that involves a mixture of physiological arousal (a fast heartbeat, for example) and overt behavior (a smile or grimace, for example).*

> *Blossoms are scatter'd by the wind*
> *And the wind cares nothing, but*
> *The blossoms of the heart*
> *No wind can touch.*
>
> —Youshida Kenko,
> *The Harvest of Leisure,* 1330

When we think about children's emotions, a few dramatic feelings, such as rage, fear, and glorious joy, usually spring to mind. But emotions can be subtle as well—the feeling a mother has when she holds her baby, the mild irritation of boredom, and the uneasiness of being in a new situation.

Psychologists have classified emotions in many different ways, but one characteristic of almost all classifications is whether an emotion is positive or negative (Pennebaker, 1992). **Positive affectivity (PA)** *refers to the range of positive emotions, from high energy, enthusiasm, and excitement to calm, quiet, and withdrawn. Joy, happiness, and laughter involve positive affectivity.* **Negative affectivity (NA)** *refers to emotions that are negatively toned, such as anxiety, anger, guilt, and sadness.* PA and NA are independent dimensions, in that a child can be high along both dimensions at the same time (for example, in a high-energy state and enthusiastic yet angry).

Functions of Emotions in Children's Development

The three main functions of emotions are adaptation and survival, regulation, and communication (Bretherton & others, 1986).

With regard to adaptation and survival, various fears—such as fear of the dark and fear of sudden changes in the environment—are adaptive, because there are clear links

CONCEPT TABLE 7.1

Family Processes, Attachment, Fathers as Caregivers
for Infants, Day Care, and Temperament

Concept	Processes/Related Ideas	Characteristics/Description
Family processes	Reciprocal socialization	Children socialize their parents just as parents socialize their children. Scaffolding, synchronization, and mutual regulation are important dimensions of reciprocal socialization.
	The family as a system	The family is a system of individuals interacting with different subsystems, some dyadic, others polyadic. Belsky's model describes direct and indirect effects.
Attachment	What is attachment?	Attachment is a relationship between two people in which each person feels strongly about the other and does a number of things to ensure the relationship's continuation. In infancy, attachment refers to the bond between the caregiver and the infant. Feeding is not the critical element in attachment, although contact comfort, familiarity, and trust are important. Bowlby's ethological theory stresses that the caregiver and infant instinctively trigger attachment. Attachment to the caregiver intensifies at about 6 to 7 months.
	Individual differences	Ainsworth believes that individual differences in attachment can be classified into secure, avoidant, and resistant categories. Ainsworth believes that securely attached babies have sensitive and responsive caregivers. In some investigations, secure attachment is related to social competence later in childhood.
	Attachment, temperament, and the wider social world	Some developmentalists believe that too much emphasis is placed on the role of attachment; they believe that genetics and temperament, on the one hand, and the diversity of social agents and contexts, on the other, deserve more credit.
Fathers as caregivers for infants	Nature of father-infant interaction	Fathers have increased their interaction with their children, but they still lag far behind mothers, even when mothers are employed. Fathers can act sensitively to the infant's signals, but most of the time they do not. The mother's role in the infant's development is primarily caregiving. That of the father involves playful interaction. Infants generally prefer their mother under stressful circumstances. Even in nontraditional families, as when the father is the main caregiver, the behaviors of mothers and fathers follow traditional gender lines.
Day care	Its nature	Day care has become a basic need of the American family; more children are in day care today than at any other time in history.
	Quality of care and effects on development	The quality of day care is uneven. Belsky concluded that most day care is inadequate and that extensive day care in the first 12 months of an infant's life has negative developmental outcomes. Other experts disagree with Belsky. Day care remains a controversial topic. Quality day care can be achieved, and it seems to have few adverse effects on children.
Temperament	Its nature	Temperament is behavioral style; temperament has been studied extensively. Chess and Thomas described three temperamental clusters—easy, difficult, and slow to warm up. Temperament is influenced strongly by biological factors in early infancy but becomes more malleable with experience. An important consideration is the fit of the infant's temperament with the parents' temperament.

between the arousal of such feelings and possible dangers. With regard to regulation, emotions influence the information children select from the perceptual world and the behaviors they display. For example, children who are feeling happy are more likely to attend to what they are studying and learning than children who are feeling sad. And with regard to communication, children use emotions to inform others about their feelings and needs. Children who smile are likely telling others that they are feeling pleasant; children who cry are often communicating that something is unpleasant for them.

Affect in Parent–Child Relationships

Emotions are the first language that parents and infants communicate with before the infant acquires speech (Maccoby, 1992). Infants react to their parents' facial expressions and tones of voice. In return, parents "read" what the infant is trying to communicate, responding appropriately when their infants are either distressed or happy.

The initial aspects of infant attachment to parents are based on affectively toned interchanges, as when an infant cries and the caregiver sensitively responds to the infant (Berlin, 1993; Hommerding & Kriger, 1993). By the end of the first year, a mother's facial expression—either smiling or fearful—influences whether an infant will explore an unfamiliar environment. And when children hear their parents quarreling, they often react with distressed facial expressions and inhibited play (Cummings, 1987). Exceptionally well-functioning families often include humor in their interactions, sometimes making each other laugh and developing light, pleasant mood states to defuse conflicts. And when a positive mood has been induced in the child, the child is more likely to comply with a parent's directions (Lay, Waters, and Park, 1989).

Infant and adult affective communicative capacities make possible coordinated infant-adult interactions (Holt & Fogel, 1993; Tronick, 1989). The face-to-face interactions of even 3-month-old infants and their adults are bidirectional (mutually regulated). That is, infants modify their affective displays and behaviors on the basis of their appreciation of their parents' affective displays and behaviors. This coordination has led to characterizations of the mother-infant interaction as "reciprocal" or "synchronous." These terms are attempts to capture the quality of interaction when all is going well.

Emotional Development in Infancy

Infants express some emotions earlier than others. Let's examine the developmental timetable for the expression of emotions, and then explore in detail two important emotionally expressive behaviors—crying and smiling.

Developmental Timetable of Emotions

To determine whether infants are actually expressing a particular emotion, we need some system for measuring emotions. Carroll Izard (1982) developed such a system. The **Maximally Discriminative Facial Movement Coding System,** *called "MAX" for short, is Izard's system of coding infants' facial expressions related to emotion. Using MAX, coders watch slow-motion*

FIGURE 7.3

The developmental course of facial expressions of emotions.

Emotional expression	Approximate time of emergence
Interest, neonatal smile (a sort of half smile that appears spontaneously for no apparent reason),* startled response,* distress,* disgust	Present at birth
Social smile	4 to 6 weeks
Anger, surprise, sadness	3 to 4 months
Fear	5 to 7 months
Shame/shyness	6 to 8 months
Contempt, guilt	2 years

* These expressions are precursors of the social smile and the emotions of surprise and sadness, which appear later. No evidence exists to suggest that they are related to inner feelings when they are observed in the first few weeks of life.

and stop-action videotapes of infants' facial reactions to stimuli. Among the stimulus conditions are giving an infant an ice cube, putting tape on the backs of the infant's hands, handing the infant a favorite toy and then taking it away, separating the infant from the mother and then reuniting them, having a stranger approach the infant, restraining the infant's head, placing a ticking clock next to the infant's ear, popping a balloon in front of the infant's face, and giving the infant camphor to sniff and lemon rind and orange juice to taste. To give just one example of how an emotion is coded, anger is indicated when the infant's brows are sharply lowered and drawn together, eyes are narrowed or squinted, and mouth is open in an angular, square shape. Based on Izard's classification system, interest, distress, and disgust are present at birth, a social smile appears at about 4 to 6 weeks, anger, surprise, and sadness emerge at about 3 to 4 months, fear is displayed at about 5 to 7 months, shame and shyness are displayed at about 6 to 8 months, and contempt and guilt don't appear until 2 years of age. A summary of the approximate timetable for the emergence of facial expressions of emotions is shown in figure 7.3.

Crying

Crying is the most important mechanism newborns have for communicating with their world (Gustafson, Green, & Kalinowski, 1993; Rosenblith, 1992). This is true for the first cry, which tells the mother and doctor the baby's lungs have filled with air. Cries also may tell physicians or researchers something about the central nervous system.

Babies don't have just one type of cry. They have at least three (Wasz-Hockert & others, 1968; Wolff, 1969). The **basic cry** *is a rhythmic pattern that usually consists of a cry, followed by a briefer silence, then a shorter inspiratory whistle that is somewhat higher in pitch than the main cry, then another brief rest before the next cry.* Some infancy experts believe that hunger is one of the conditions that incites the basic cry. The

anger cry *is a variation of the basic cry. However, in the anger cry more excess air is forced through the vocal cords. The anger cry gets its name from mothers who infer exasperation or rage from it. The* **pain cry,** *which is stimulated by high-intensity stimuli, differs from other types of cries in that there is a sudden appearance of loud crying without preliminary moaning, and a long initial cry followed by an extended period of breath holding.*

Most parents, and adults in general, can determine whether an infant's cries signify anger or pain (Barr, Desilets, & Rortman, 1991; Zeskind, Klein, & Marshall, 1992). Parents also can distinguish the cries of their own baby better than those of a strange baby (Wiesenfeld, Malatesta, & DeLoache, 1981). There is little consistent evidence to support the idea that mothers or females, but not fathers or males, are innately programmed to respond nurturantly to an infant's crying (Rosenblith, 1992).

To soothe or not to soothe? Should a crying baby be given attention and soothed, or does this spoil the infant? Many years ago the famous behaviorist John Watson (1928) argued that parents spend too much time responding to infant crying. As a consequence, he said, parents are actually rewarding infant crying and increasing its incidence. More recently, by contrast, ethnologically oriented infant experts Mary Ainsworth (1979) and John Bowlby (1989) stress that you can't respond too much to infant crying in the first year of life. They believe that the caregiver's quick, comforting response to the infant's cries is an important ingredient in the development of secure attachment. In one of Ainsworth's studies, mothers who responded quickly to their infants when they cried at 3 months of age had infants who cried less later in the first year of life (Bell & Ainsworth, 1972). On the other hand, behaviorist Jacob Gewirtz (1977) found that a caregiver's quick, soothing response to crying increased subsequent crying.

Controversy, then, still swirls about the issue of whether parents should respond to an infant's cries. However, many developmentalists increasingly argue that an infant cannot be spoiled in the first year of life, which suggests that parents should quickly soothe a crying infant rather than be unresponsive: In this manner infants will likely develop a sense of trust and secure attachment to the caregiver in the first year of life.

Smiling

Smiling is another important communicative affective behavior of the infant. Two types of smiling can be distinguished in infants—one reflexive, the other social. A **reflexive smile** *does not occur in response to external stimuli. It appears during the first month after birth, usually during irregular patterns of sleep, not when the infant is in an alert state.* By contrast, a **social smile** *occurs in response to an external stimulus, which, early in development, typically is in response to a face.* Social smiling does not occur until 2 to 3 months of age (Emde, Gaensbauer, & Harmon, 1976), although some researchers believe that infants grin in response to voices as early as 3 weeks of age (Sroufe & Waters, 1976). The power of the infant's smiles was appropriately captured by British attachment theorist John Bowlby (1969): "Can we doubt that the more and better an infant smiles

the better he is loved and cared for? It is fortunate for their survival that babies are so designed by nature that they beguile and enslave mothers."

He who binds himself to joy
Does the winged life destroy;
But he who kisses the joy as it
Flies lives in eternity's sun rise.

—William Blake

PERSONALITY DEVELOPMENT

The individual characteristics of the infant that are often thought of as central to personality development are trust, the self, and independence.

Trust

According to Erik Erikson (1968), the first year of life is characterized by the trust-versus-mistrust stage of development. Following a life of regularity, warmth, and protection in the mother's womb, the infant faces a world that is less secure. Erikson believes that infants learn trust when they are cared for in a consistent, warm manner. If the infant is not well fed and kept warm on a consistent basis, a sense of mistrust is likely to develop.

Earlier we briefly described Erikson's ideas about the role of trust in attachment. His thoughts have much in common with Mary Ainsworth's concept of secure attachment. The infant who has a sense of trust is likely to be securely attached and to have confidence to explore new circumstances; the infant who has a sense of mistrust is likely to be insecurely attached and to not have such confidence and positive expectations.

Trust versus mistrust is not resolved once and for all in the first year of life; it arises again at each successive stage of development. There is both hope and danger in this. Children who enter school with a sense of mistrust may trust a particular teacher who has taken the time to make herself trustworthy. With this second chance children overcome their early mistrust. By contrast, children who leave infancy with a sense of trust can still have their sense of mistrust activated at a later stage, perhaps if their parents are separated or divorced under conflicting circumstances. An example is instructive (Elkind, 1970). A 4-year-old boy was being seen by a clinical psychologist at a court clinic because his adoptive parents, who had had him for 6 months, now wanted to give him back to the agency. They said he was cold and unloving, stole things, and could not be trusted. He was indeed a cold and apathetic boy, but with good reason. About a year after his illegitimate birth, he was taken away from his mother, who had a drinking problem, and was shuttled back and forth among several foster homes. At first he tried to relate to people in the foster homes, but the relationships never had an opportunity to develop, because he was moved so frequently. In the end, he gave up trying to reach out to others, because the inevitable separations hurt too much.

Reprinted with special permission of North America Syndicate.

Like the burned child who dreads the flame, this emotionally burned child shunned the pain of close relationships. He had trusted his mother, but now he trusted no one. Only years of devoted care and patience could now undo the damage to this child's sense of trust.

Critical Thinking

In addition to the description of the 4-year-old boy from an adopted family, can you think of other examples in which trust during infancy is an important aspect of development? Try to come up with at least two other specific cases.

The Developing Sense of Self and Independence

Individuals carry with them a sense of who they are and what makes them different from everyone else. They cling to this identity and begin to feel secure in the knowledge that this identity is becoming more stable. Real or imagined, this sense of self is a strong motivating force in life. When does the individual begin to sense a separate existence from others?

Children begin to develop a sense of self by learning to distinguish themselves from others. To determine whether infants can recognize themselves, psychologists have used mirrors. In the animal kingdom, only the great apes learn to recognize their reflection in the mirror, but human infants accomplish this feat by about 18 months of age. How does the mirror technique work? The mother puts a dot of rouge on her infant's nose. The observer watches to see how often the infant touches his nose. Next, the infant is placed in front of a mirror and observers detect whether nose touching increases (Lewis & Feinman, 1991; Lewis & others, 1989). In two independent investigations in the second half of the second year of life, infants recognized their own image and coordinated the image they saw with the actions of touching their own body (Amsterdam, 1968; Lewis & Brooks-Gunn, 1979).

Not only does the infant develop a sense of self in the second year of life, but independence becomes a more central theme in the infant's life as well. The theories of Margaret Mahler and Erik Erikson have important implications for both

Erikson believes that autonomy versus shame and doubt is the key developmental theme of the toddler years.

self-development and independence. Mahler (1979) believes that the child goes through a separation and then an individuation process. Separation involves the infant's movement away from the mother, and individuation involves the development of self.

> *We learn to curb our will and keep our overt actions within the bounds of humanity, long before we can subdue our sentiments and imaginations in the same mild tone.*
>
> —William Hazlitt, 1826

LIFE-SPAN PRACTICAL KNOWLEDGE 7.2

Touchpoints

(1992) by T. Berry Brazelton.
Reading, MA: Addison-Wesley.

Touchpoints is pediatrician T. Berry Brazelton's most recent book. Covering the period from pregnancy to first grade, Brazelton focuses on the concerns and questions that parents have about the child's feelings, behavior, and development. The book's title derives from Brazelton's belief that there are universal spurts of development, and trying times of adaptation that accompany them, throughout childhood. Section I chronicles development from pregnancy through 3 years; Section II describes a number of challenges to development, from allergies to toilet training; and Section III focuses on important figures in the child's development, such as fathers, mothers, grandparents, friends, caregivers, and the child's doctor.

Erikson (1968), like Mahler, believes that independence is an important issue in the second year of life. Erikson describes the second stage of development as the stage of autonomy versus shame and doubt. Autonomy builds on the infant's developing mental and motor abilities. At this point in development, not only can infants walk, but they can also climb, open and close, drop, push and pull, hold and let go. Infants feel pride in these new accomplishments and want to do everything themselves, whether it is flushing a toilet, pulling the wrapping off a package, or deciding what to eat. It is important for parents to recognize the motivation of toddlers to do what they are capable of doing at their own pace. Then they can learn to control their muscles and their impulses themselves. But when caregivers are impatient and do for toddlers what they are capable of doing themselves, shame and doubt develop. Every parent has rushed a child from time to time. It is only when parents consistently overprotect toddlers or criticize accidents (wetting, soiling, spilling, or breaking, for example) that children develop an excessive sense of shame and doubt about their ability to control themselves and their world.

I am what I can will freely.
—Erik Erikson, 1968

Erikson also believes that the stage of autonomy versus shame and doubt has important implications for the development of independence and identity during adolescence. The development of autonomy during the toddler years gives adolescents the courage to be independent individuals who can choose and guide their own future.

Too much autonomy, though, can be as harmful as too little. A 7-year-old boy who had a heart condition learned quickly how afraid his parents were of any signs of his having cardiac problems. It was not long before he ruled the household. The family could not go shopping or for a drive if the boy did not approve. On the rare occasions his parents defied him, he would get angry, and his purple face and gagging would frighten them into submission. This boy actually was scared of his power and eager to relinquish it. When the parents and the boy realized this, and recognized that a little shame and doubt were a healthy opponent of an inflated sense of autonomy, the family began to function much more smoothly (Elkind, 1970).

Consider also Robert, age 22 months, who has just come home from watching his 5-year-old brother, William, take a swimming lesson. Their mother has gone in the kitchen to get dinner ready when she hears a scream. She hurries into the living room and sees Robert's teeth sunk into William's leg. The next day, Robert is playing with a new game and he can't get it right. He hurls it across the room and just misses his mother. That night his mother tells him it is time for bed. Robert's response: "No." Sometimes the world of 2-year-olds becomes very frustrating. Much of their frustration stems from their inability to control the adult world. Things are too big to manage, to push around, or to make happen. Toddlers want to be in the driver's seat of every car and to push every cart by themselves. Two-year-olds want to play the dominant role in almost every situation. When things don't go their way, toddlers can become openly defiant, even though they were placid as babies earlier in life. Called the "terrible twos" by Arnold Gesell, this developmental time frame can try the patience of the most even-tempered parents. Nonetheless, calm, steady affection and firm patience can help to disperse most of toddlerhood's tensions. Fortunately, the defiance is only temporary in most children's development.

PROBLEMS AND DISORDERS

Problems and disorders in infancy can arise for a number of reasons. All development—normal and abnormal—is influenced by the interaction of heredity and environment. In a comprehensive study of children at risk, a variety of biological, social, and developmental characteristics were identified as predictors of problems and disturbances at age 18. They included moderate to severe perinatal (at or near birth) stress and birth defects, low socioeconomic status at 2 to 10 years of age, level of maternal education below 8 years, low family stability between 2 and 8 years, very low or very high infant responsiveness at 1 year, a Cattell score below 80 at age 2 (the Cattell is one of the early measures of infant intelligence), and the need for long-term mental health services or placement in a learning-disability class at age 10. When four or more of these factors were present, the stage was set for serious coping problems in the second decade of life (Werner & Smith, 1982). Among the problems in infancy that deserve special consideration are child abuse and autism.

Child Abuse

Unfortunately, parental hostility toward children in some families escalates to the point where one or both parents abuse the children. Child abuse is an increasing problem in the United States. Estimates of its incidence vary, but some authorities say that as many as 500,000 children are physically abused every year. Laws in many states now require doctors and teachers to report suspected cases of child abuse, yet many cases go unreported, especially those of battered infants.

Child abuse is such a disturbing circumstance that many people have difficulty understanding or sympathizing with parents who abuse or neglect their children (Crittenden, 1988a, 1988b; Martin, 1992). Our response is often outrage and anger directed at the parent. This outrage focuses our attention on parents as bad, sick, monstrous, sadistic individuals who cause their children to suffer. Experts on child abuse believe that this view is too simple and deflects attention away from the social context of the abuse and parents' coping skills. It is especially important to recognize that child abuse is a diverse condition, that it is usually mild to moderate in severity, and that it is only partially caused by individual personality characteristics of parents (Emery, 1989).

The Multifaceted Nature of Child Maltreatment

Whereas the public and many professionals use the term *child abuse* to refer to both abuse and neglect, developmentalists increasingly are using the term *child maltreatment.* This term reduces the emotional impact of the term *abuse* and acknowledges that maltreatment includes several different conditions. Among the different types of maltreatment are physical and sexual abuse; fostering delinquency; lack of supervision; medical, educational, and nutritional neglect; and drug or alcohol abuse. In one large survey, approximately 20 percent of the reported cases involved abuse alone, 46 percent neglect alone, 23 percent both abuse and neglect, and 11 percent sexual abuse (American Association for Protecting Children, 1986). Abused children are more likely to be angry or wary than neglected children, who tend to be passive (Lynch & Roberts, 1982).

Severity of Abuse

The concern about child abuse began with the identification of the "battered child syndrome" and has continued to be associated with severe, brutal injury for several reasons. First, the media tend to underscore the most bizarre and vicious incidents. Second, much of the funding for child abuse prevention, identification, and treatment depends on the public's perception of the horror of child abuse and the medical profession's lobby for funds to investigate and treat abused children and their parents. The emphasis is often on the worst cases. These

Dante Cicchetti has significantly advanced our knowledge of maltreated children. He and his colleagues at Mount Hope Family Center in Rochester, New York, have developed a model of intervention with maltreated children that is receiving increased attention.

horrific cases do exist, and are indeed terrible, but they make up only a small minority of abused children. Less than 1 percent of abused children die, and another 11 percent suffer life-threatening, disabling injuries (American Association for Protecting Children, 1986). By contrast, almost 90 percent suffer temporary physical injuries. These milder injuries, though, are likely to be experienced repeatedly in the context of daily hostile family exchanges. Similarly, neglected children, who suffer no physical injuries, often experience extensive, long-term psychological harm.

The Cultural Context of Maltreatment

The extensive violence that takes place in the American culture is reflected in the occurrence of violence in the family (Gelles & Conte, 1990). A regular diet of violence appears on television screens, and parents often resort to power assertion as a disciplinary-technique. In China, where physical punishment is rarely used to discipline children, the incidence of child abuse is reported to be very low. In the United States, many abusing parents report that they do not have sufficient resources or help from others. This may be a realistic evaluation of the situation experienced by many low-income families, who do not have adequate preventive and supportive services (Rodriguez-Haynes & Crittenden, 1988).

Community support systems are especially important in alleviating stressful family situations, thereby helping to prevent child abuse. An investigation of the support systems in 58 counties in New York State revealed a relation between the incidence of child abuse and the absence of support systems available to the family (Garbarino, 1976). Both family resources—relatives and friends, for example—and such formal community

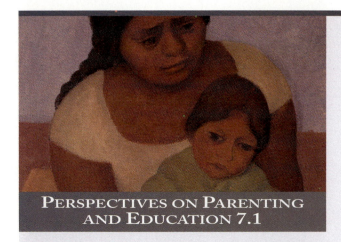

PERSPECTIVES ON PARENTING AND EDUCATION 7.1

Shattered Innocence—The Sexual Abuse of Children

Headlines about day-care-center scandals and feminist protests against sexist exploitation have increased public awareness of what we now know is a widespread problem: sexual abuse of children. A 1984 Gallup poll of 2,000 men and women in 210 Canadian communities found that 22 percent of the respondents were sexually abused as children. Clearly, children's sexual abuse is more widespread than was thought in the past. One reason the problem of children's sex-

ual abuse was a dark secret for so long is that people understandably kept this painful experience to themselves.

The sexual abuse of children occurs most often between the ages of 9 and 12, although the abuse of 2- and 3-year-olds is not unusual. The abuser is almost always a man, and typically he is known to the child, often being a relative. In many instances, the abuse is not limited to a single episode. No race, ethnic group, or economic class is immune.

While children do not react uniformly to sexual abuse, certain behaviors and feelings occur with some regularity. The immediate effects include sleeping and eating disorders, anger, withdrawal, and guilt. The children often appear to be afraid or anxious. Two additional signs occur so often that professionals rely on them as indicators of abuse when they are present together. The first is sexual preoccupation—excessive or public masturbation and an unusually strong interest in sexual organs, play, and nudity. The second sign consists of a host of physical complaints or problems, such as rashes, headaches, and vomiting, all without medical explanation. When it is discovered that these children have been sexually abused, a check of their medical records usually produces years of such mysterious ailments. While there are patterns in the immediate effects of sexual abuse of children, it is far more difficult to connect such abuse with later psychological problems. It is impossible to say that every child who has been abused will develop this or that problem, and we still have not developed a profile of the child abuse victim that everyone can agree upon.

support systems as crisis centers and child abuse counseling were associated with a reduction in child abuse.

Family Influences

To understand abuse in the family, the interactions of all family members need to be considered, regardless of who actually performs the violent acts against the child (Daro, 1988; Margolin, 1994). For example, even though the father may be the one who physically abuses the child, contributions by the mother, the child, and siblings also should be evaluated. Many parents who abuse their children come from families in which physical punishment was used. These parents view physical punishment as a legitimate way of control-

ling the child's behavior, and physical punishment may be a part of this sanctioning. Children themselves may unwittingly contribute to child abuse: An unattractive child may receive more physical punishment than an attractive child, and a child from an unwanted pregnancy may be especially vulnerable to abuse (Harter, Alexander, & Neimeyer, 1988). Husband-wife violence and financial problems may result in displaced aggression toward a defenseless child. Displaced aggression is commonly involved in child abuse.

In recent years a special concern has been the sexual abuse of children. To read about sexual abuse of children, see Perspectives on Parenting and Education 7.1.

Infantile Autism

As its name suggests, **infantile autism** *has its onset in infancy. It is a severe developmental disorder that includes deficiencies in social relationships, abnormalities in communication, and restricted, repetitive, and stereotyped patterns of behavior* (Dawson, 1989; Hertzig & Shapiro, in press; Rutter & Schopler, 1987; Tager-Flusberg, in press). Social deficiencies include a failure to use an eye-to-eye gaze to regulate social interaction, rarely seeking others for comfort or affection, rarely initiating play with others, and having no peer relations involving mutual sharing of interests and emotions. As babies, these children require very little from their parents. They do not demand much attention, and they do not reach out (literally or figuratively) for their parents. They rarely smile. When someone tries to hold them, they usually withdraw by arching their backs and pushing away. In their cribs or playpens, they appear oblivious to what is going on around them, often sitting and staring into space for long periods of time.

In addition to these social deficiencies, autistic children also show communication abnormalities that focus on the problems of using language for social communication: poor synchrony and lack of reciprocity in conversation, and stereotyped, repetitive use of language. As many as one of every two autistic children never learns to speak. **Echolalia** *is a speech disorder associated with autism in which children echo what they hear.* For example, if you ask, "How are you, Chuck?" Chuck responds, "How are you, Chuck?" Autistic children also confuse pronouns, inappropriately substituting *you* for *I,* for example.

Stereotyped patterns of behavior by autistic children include compulsive rituals, repetitive motor mannerisms, and distress over changes in small details of the environment. Rearrangement of a sequence of events or even furniture in the course of a day may cause autistic children to become extremely upset, suggesting that they are not flexible in adapting to new routines and changes in their daily lives.

What causes autism? Autism seems to involve some form of organic brain dysfunction and may also have a hereditary basis. There has been no satisfactory evidence developed to document that family socialization causes autism (Rutter & Schopler, 1987).

At this point we have studied a number of ideas about children's emotions, emotional development, personality development, and problems and disorders. A summary of these ideas is presented in concept table 7.2.

CONCLUSIONS

From birth, babies are wrapped in a socioemotional world with their caregivers. Babies and their caregivers communicate with each other through emotions, their senses, and their words. Through interaction with their caregivers, infants learn to adapt to their world.

We began this chapter by briefly examining how the human infant cannot sustain itself and therefore requires extensive care. Next we described some basic ideas about family processes. Much of the interest in the infant's social world has focused on attachment—we considered what attachment is, individual differences in attachment (secure and insecure), and the relation of attachment to temperament and the wider social world. We evaluated fathers as caregivers for infants and the role of day care in children's lives and how it affects their development. We learned that temperament is an important aspect of the infant's development, and explored the important worlds of infants' emotional and personality development. And we discussed two problems and disorders—child abuse and infantile autism. At different points in the chapter we also studied child-care policy around the world, child sexual abuse, and the personal characteristics of competent caregivers.

Remember that by again reading the two concept tables on pages 188 and 196 you can obtain an overall summary of the chapter. This chapter concludes our coverage of infant development. Next, we will turn our attention to Section Three, "Early Childhood," beginning with chapter 8, "Physical and Cognitive Development in Early Childhood."

CONCEPT TABLE 7.2

Emotional Development, Personality Development, and Problems and Disorders

Concept	Processes/Related Ideas	Characteristics/Description
The nature of children's emotion	What is emotion?	Emotion is feeling or affect that involves a mixture of physiological arousal and overt behavior. Emotions can be classified in terms of positive affectivity and negative affectivity.
	Functions of emotions in children's development	The three main functions are adaptation and survival, regulation, and communication.
	Affect in parent-child relationships	Emotions are the first language that parents and infants communicate with before the infant acquires speech. Infant and adult affective communicative capacities make possible coordinated infant-adult interaction.
Emotional development in infancy	Developmental timetable of emotions	Izard developed the Maximally Discriminative Facial Coding System (MAX) for coding infants' expression of emotions. Based on this coding system, interest, distress, and disgust are present at birth, a social smile appears at about 4 to 6 weeks, anger, surprise, and sadness emerge at about 3 to 4 months, fear is displayed at about 5 to 7 months, shame and shyness emerge at about 6 to 8 months, and contempt and guilt appear at about 2 years of age.
	Crying	Crying is the most important mechanism newborns have for communicating with their world. Babies have at least three types of cries—basic cry, anger cry, and pain cry. Most parents, and adults in general, can tell whether an infant's cries signify anger or pain. Controversy still swirls about whether babies should be soothed when they cry. An increasing number of developmentalists support Ainsworth's and Bowlby's idea that infant crying should be responded to immediately in the first year of life.
	Smiling	Smiling is an important communicative affective behavior of the infant. Two types of smiling can be distinguished in infants: reflexive and social.
Personality development	Trust	Erikson argues that the first year is characterized by the crisis of trust versus mistrust; his ideas about trust have much in common with Ainsworth's concept of secure attachment.
	Developing a sense of self and independence	At some point in the second half of the second year of life, the infant develops a sense of self. Independence becomes a central theme in the second year of life. Mahler argues that the infant separates herself from the mother and then develops individuation. Erikson stresses that the second year of life is characterized by the stage of autonomy versus shame and doubt.
Problems and disorders	Child abuse	An understanding of child abuse requires information about cultural, familial, and community influences. Sexual abuse of children is now recognized as a more widespread problem than was believed in the past.
	Infantile autism	Infantile autism is a severe disorder that first appears in infancy. It involves an inability to relate to people, speech problems, and upsets over changes in routine or environment. Autism seems to involve some form of organic brain and genetic dysfunction.

LIFE-SPAN HEALTH AND WELL-BEING

The Personal Characteristics of Competent Caregivers

Much of the health and well-being of infants is in the hands of caregivers. Whether the caregivers are parents or day-care personnel, these adults play significant roles in infants' lives. What are the personal characteristics of competent caregivers? That question was recently addressed by child-care expert LaVisa Wilson (1990). She believes the following personal characteristics define competent caregivers:

- *Competent caregivers are physically healthy.* Good health is necessary to provide the high level of energy required for competent caregiving. In day care, good health is required to resist the variety of illnesses to which caregivers are exposed.

- *Competent caregivers are mentally healthy.* In daily interactions with infants, caregivers need to provide physical closeness and nurturance for an extended period of time, to give emotionally more than they often receive, and to be patient longer than they would like. Emotionally stable caregivers who have learned how to cope with a variety of emotional demands in their daily experiences are often able to encourage mental health in others.

- *Competent caregivers have a positive self-image.* Feelings of self-confidence and positive self-worth show that caregivers believe in themselves. Caregivers who have positive self-images are people who infants and toddlers want to approach rather than avoid.

- *Competent caregivers are flexible.* Competent caregivers do not get upset if they have to change the daily schedule, daily plans, or responsibilities.

- *Competent caregivers are patient.* Infants and toddlers are very demanding and require considerable attention and monitoring, which can stretch the caregiver's patience. However, competent caregivers show patience as they respond to the infants' and toddlers' needs.

- *Competent caregivers are positive models for infants.* Caregivers' behaviors are observed and imitated by infants and toddlers. Competent caregivers monitor their own behavior, knowing it is a model for infants and toddlers.

- *Competent caregivers are open to learning.* Competent caregivers seek to develop additional skills and are open to new insights, understanding, and skills.

- *Competent caregivers enjoy caregiving.* Competent caregivers gain considerable enjoyment and satisfaction in providing effective, high-quality care for infants and toddlers. Competent caregivers reflect these positive feelings as they interact with infants and toddlers. ■

KEY TERMS

reciprocal socialization   The view that socialization is bidirectional; children socialize parents just as parents socialize children. (179)

scaffolding   An important caregiver's role in early parent-child interaction. Through their attention and choice of behaviors, caregivers provide a framework around which they and their infants interact. One function scaffolding serves is to introduce infants to social rules, especially turntaking. (179)

attachment   A close emotional bond between the infant and the caregiver. (180)

secure attachment   Infants use the caregiver, usually the mother, as a secure base from which to explore the environment. Ainsworth believes that secure attachment in the first year of life provides an important foundation for psychological development later in life. (181)

type B babies   Babies who use the mother as a secure base from which to explore the environment. (181)

type A babies   Babies who exhibit insecurity by avoiding the mother (for example, ignoring her, avoiding her gaze, and failing to seek proximity). (181)

type C babies   Babies who exhibit insecurity by resisting the mother (for example, clinging to her but at the same time fighting against the closeness, perhaps by kicking and pushing away). (181)

temperament   An individual's behavioral style and characteristic way of responding. (186)

easy child   A child who is generally in a positive mood, quickly establishes regular routines in infancy, and adapts easily to new experiences. (186)

difficult child   A child who tends to react negatively and cry frequently, engages in irregular daily routines, and is slow to accept new experiences. (186)

slow-to-warm-up child   A child who has a low activity level, is somewhat negative, shows low adaptability, and displays a low intensity of mood. (186)

emotionality   The tendency to be distressed. (186)

sociability   The tendency to prefer the company of others to being alone. (187)

activity level   The tempo and vigor of movement. (187)

emotion   Feeling or affect that involves a mixture of physiological arousal (a rapid heartbeat, for example) and overt behavior (a smile or grimace, for example). (187)

positive affectivity (PA)   The range of positive emotions, from high energy, enthusiasm, and excitement, to calm, quiet, and withdrawn. Joy, happiness, and laughter involve positive affectivity. (187)

negative affectivity (NA)   Emotions that are negatively toned, such as anxiety, anger, guilt, and sadness. (187)

Maximally Discriminative Facial Movement Coding System ("MAX" for short)   Izard's system of coding facial expressions related to emotion. Using MAX, coders watch slow-motion and stop-action videotapes of infants' facial reactions to stimuli. (189)

basic cry   A rhythmic pattern that usually consists of a cry, followed by a briefer silence, then a shorter inspiratory whistle that is somewhat higher in pitch than the main cry, then another brief rest before the next cry. (189)

anger cry   A variation of the basic cry. However, in the anger cry more excess air is forced through the vocal cords. The anger cry gets its name from mothers who infer exasperation or rage from it. (190)

pain cry   Stimulated by high intensity stimuli and differs from other types of cries in that there is a sudden appearance of loud crying without preliminary moaning, and a long initial cry followed by an extended period of breath holding. (190)

reflexive smile   A smile that does not occur in response to external stimuli. It appears during the first month after birth, usually during irregular patterns of sleep, not when an infant is in an alert state. (190)

social smile   A smile that occurs in response to an external stimulus, which, early in development, typically is in response to a face. (190)

infantile autism   A severe developmental disorder that includes deficiencies in social relationships, abnormalities in communication, and restricted, repetitive, and stereotyped patterns of behavior; onset is in infancy. (195)

echolalia   A speech disorder associated with autism in which children echo what they hear. (195)

Early Childhood

You are troubled at seeing him spend his early years doing nothing. What! Is it nothing to be happy? Is it nothing to skip, to play, to run about all day long? Never in his life will he be so busy as now.

—Jean-Jacques Rousseau

In early childhood, our greatest untold poem was being only 4 years old. We skipped and ran and played all day long, never in our lives so busy, busy being something we had not quite grasped yet. Who knew our thoughts, which we worked up into small mythologies all our own? Our thoughts and images and drawings took wings. The blossoms of our heart, no wind could touch. Our small world widened as we discovered new refuges and new people. When we said "I," we meant something totally unique, not to be confused with any other. Section Four consists of two chapters: "Physical and Cognitive Development in Early Childhood" (chapter 8) and "Socioemotional Development in Early Childhood" (chapter 9).

Diego Rivera, Delfino
Flores, detail.

C H A P T E R

8

Physical and Cognitive Development in Early Childhood

*The greatest poem ever known
Is one all poets have outgrown;
The poetry, innate, untold,
Of being only four years old.*

—Christopher Morley

All the sun long I was running . . .

—Dylan Thomas

IMAGES OF LIFE-SPAN DEVELOPMENT

Tony's Physical Development

At 2 years of age, Tony is no saint. Tony's growing demand for autonomy keeps his mother busy hour after hour. Only a year earlier, he had learned to walk. Now he is running away from her into neighbors' yards and down the aisles of grocery stores. Trying out his new skills, he is constantly testing his parents and finding out the limits of his behavior.

By about his third birthday, Tony's behavior takes a slightly different turn. His temper tantrums have not entirely disappeared—the "terrible twos" can last into the fourth year—but much of his negative behavior has gone away. Every week produces a palate of new words and new tricks of climbing, skipping, and jumping. Tony is beginning to be able to make his body do what he wants it to do. As he moves through the preschool years, he learns how to draw and how to play different ball games. He is boastful, too, about his newly developed competencies. Tony says, "I'm bigger now, aren't I?"

"I'm not a little baby anymore am I?" Tony is right. He is not a baby anymore. His babyhood is gone.

By 4 years of age, Tony has become even more adventuresome, exploring his world with fascination and abandon. By age 5, Tony is a self-assured child. He has good coordination and he delights at alarming his parents with his hair-raising stunts on any object suitable for climbing.

PREVIEW

Children make considerable strides in physical and cognitive development in early childhood. After briefly charting some of the developmental milestones in body growth and motor development, we will explore the importance of good nutrition and health in early childhood. Then we will study many different facets of young children's cognitive worlds, including Piaget's stage of preoperational thought, how young children process information, their language development, and early childhood education.

PHYSICAL DEVELOPMENT IN EARLY CHILDHOOD

Remember from chapter 5 that an infant's growth in the first year is extremely rapid and follows cephalocaudal and proximodistal patterns. Around their first birthday, most infants begin to walk. During an infant's second year, the growth rate begins to slow down, but both gross and fine motor skills progress rapidly. The infant develops a sense of mastery through increased proficiency in walking and running. Improvement in fine motor skills—such as being able to turn the pages of a book one at a time—also contributes to the infant's sense of mastery in the second year. The growth rate continues to slow down in early childhood; otherwise, we would be a species of giants.

Passing hence from infancy, I came to boyhood, or rather it came to me, displacing infancy, nor did that depart—and yet it was no more.

—Confessions of St. Augustine

Height and Weight

The average child grows 2½ inches in height and gains between 5 to 7 pounds a year during early childhood. As the preschool child grows older, the percentage of increase in height and weight decreases with each additional year. Figure 8.1 shows the average height and weight of children as they age from 2 to 6 years. Girls are only slightly smaller and lighter than boys during these

FIGURE 8.1

Average height and weight of girls and boys from 2 to 6 years of age.

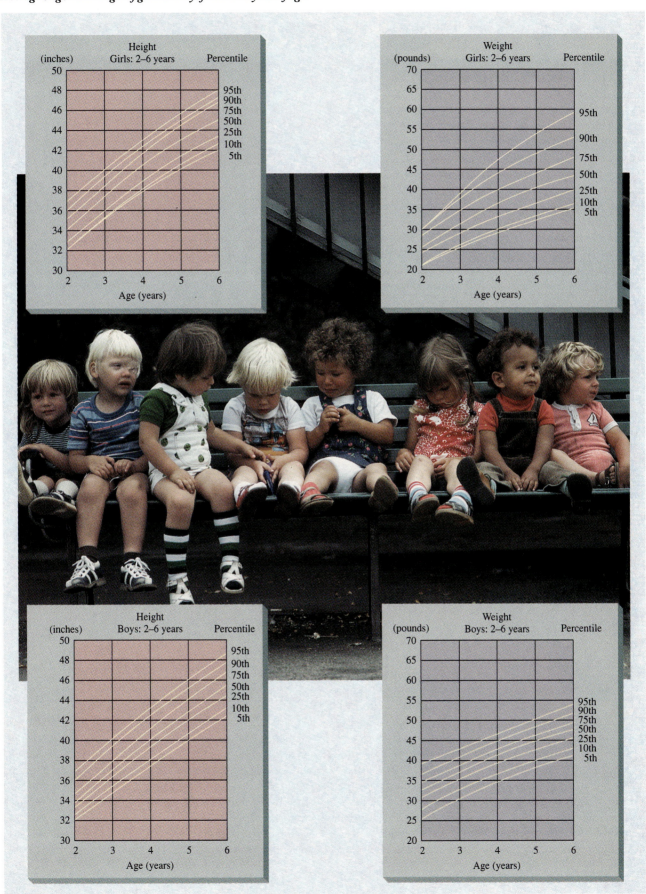

years, a difference that continues until puberty. During the preschool years, both boys and girls slim down as the trunk of their bodies lengthens. Although their heads are still somewhat large for their bodies, by the end of the preschool years, most children have lost their top-heavy look. Body fat also shows a slow, steady decline during the preschool years, so that the chubby baby often looks much leaner by the end of early childhood. Girls have more fatty tissue than boys, and boys have more muscle tissue.

Growth patterns vary individually. Think back to your preschool years. This was probably the first time you noticed that some children were taller than you, some shorter; that some were fatter, some thinner; that some were stronger, some weaker. Much of the variation is due to heredity, but environmental experiences are involved to some extent. A review of the heights and weights of children around the world concluded that the two most important contributors to height differences are ethnic origin and nutrition (Meredith, 1978). Urban, middle-class, and firstborn children were taller than rural, lower-class, and later-born children. Children whose mothers smoked during pregnancy were half an inch shorter than children whose mothers did not smoke during pregnancy. In the United States, Black children are taller than white children.

Why are some children unusually short? The culprits are congenital factors (genetic or prenatal problems), a physical problem that develops in childhood, or an emotional difficulty. In many cases, children with congenital growth problems can be treated with hormones. Usually this treatment is directed at the pituitary, the body's master gland, located at the base of the brain. This gland secretes growth-related hormones. With regard to physical problems that develop during childhood, malnutrition and chronic infections can stunt growth, although if the problems are properly treated, normal growth usually is attained. **Deprivation dwarfism** *is a type of growth retardation caused by emotional deprivation; children are deprived of affection, which causes stress and alters the release of hormones by the pituitary gland.* Some children who are not dwarfs may also show the effects of an impoverished emotional environment, although most parents of these children say they are small and weak because they have a poor body structure or constitution.

The Brain

One of the most important physical developments during early childhood is the continuing development of the brain and nervous system. While the brain continues to grow in early childhood, it does not grow as rapidly as in infancy. By the time children have reached 3 years of age, the brain is three-quarters of its adult size. By age 5, the brain has reached about nine-tenths of its adult size.

The brain and the head grow more rapidly than any other parts of the body. The top parts of the head, the eyes, and the brain grow faster than the lower portions, such as the jaw. Figure 8.2 reveals how the growth curve for the head and brain advances more rapidly than the growth curve for height and weight. At 5 years of age, when the brain has attained approximately 90 percent of its adult weight, the

FIGURE 8.2

Growth curves for the head and brain and for height and weight.
The more-rapid growth of the brain and head can be easily seen.
Height and weight advance more gradually over the first two decades
of life (Damon, 1977).

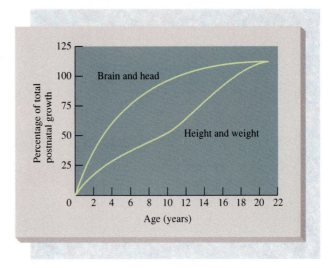

5-year-old's total body weight is only about one-third of what it will be when the child reaches adulthood.

Some of the brain's increase in size is due to the increase in the number and size of nerve endings within and between areas of the brain. These nerve endings continue to grow at least until adolescence. Some of the brain's increase in size also is due to the increase in **myelination,** *a process in which nerve cells are covered and insulated with a layer of fat cells. This process has the effect of increasing the speed of information traveling through the nervous system.* Some developmentalists believe myelination is important in the maturation of a number of children's abilities. For example, myelination in the areas of the brain related to hand-eye coordination is not complete until about 4 years of age. Myelination in the areas of the brain related to focusing attention is not complete until the end of middle and late childhood (Tanner, 1978).

> *Swiftly the brain becomes an enchanted loom, where millions of flashing shuttles weave a dissolving pattern—always a meaningful pattern—though never an abiding one.*
>
> Sir Charles Sherrington, 1906

The increasing maturation of the brain, combined with opportunities to experience a widening world, contribute enormously to children's emerging cognitive abilities. Consider a child who is learning to read and is asked by the teacher to read aloud to the class. Input from the child's eyes is transmitted to the child's brain, then passed through many brain systems, which translate (process) the patterns of black and white into codes for letters, words, and associations. The output occurs in the form of messages to the child's lips and tongue. The child's own gift of speech is possible because brain systems are organized in ways that permit language processing.

Motor Development

Running as fast as you can, falling down, getting right back up and running just as fast as you can . . . building towers with blocks . . . scribbling, scribbling, and more scribbling . . . cutting paper with scissors. During your preschool years you probably developed the ability to perform all of these activities.

Gross Motor Skills

The preschool child no longer has to make an effort simply to stay upright and to move around. As children move their legs with more confidence and carry themselves more purposefully, the process of moving around in the environment becomes more automatic (Poest & others, 1990).

At 3 years of age, children are still enjoying simple movement such as hopping, jumping, and running back and forth, just for the sheer delight of performing these activities. They take considerable pride in showing how they can run across a room and jump all of 6 inches. The run-and-jump will win no Olympic gold medals, but for the 3-year-old the activity is a source of considerable pride and accomplishment.

By 4 years of age, children are still enjoying the same kind of activities, but they have become more adventurous. They scramble over low jungle gyms as they display their athletic prowess. Although they have been able to climb stairs with one foot on each step for some time now, they are just beginning to be able to come down the same way. They still often revert to marking time on each step.

By 5 years of age, children are even more adventuresome than when they were 4. As our description of Tony at the beginning of the chapter indicated, it is not unusual for self-assured 5-year-olds to perform hair-raising stunts on practically any climbing object. Five-year-olds run hard and enjoy races with each other and their parents.

You probably have arrived at one important conclusion about preschool children: They are very, very active. Indeed, researchers have found that 3-year-old children have the highest activity level of any age in the entire human life span. They fidget when they watch television. They fidget when they sit at the dinner table. Even when they sleep, they move around quite a bit. Because of their activity level and the development of large muscles, especially in the arms and legs, preschool children need daily exercise.

Fine Motor Skills

At 3 years of age, children are still emerging from the infant ability to place and handle things. Although they have had the ability to pick up the tiniest objects between their thumb and forefinger for some time now, they are still somewhat clumsy at it. Three-year-olds can build surprisingly high block towers, each block being placed with intense concentration but often not in a completely straight line. When 3-year-olds play with a form board or a simple jigsaw puzzle, they are rather rough in placing the pieces. Even when they recognize the hole a piece

fits into, they are not very precise in positioning the piece. They often try to force the piece in the hole or pat it vigorously.

At 4 years of age, children's fine motor coordination has improved substantially and become much more precise. Sometimes 4-year-old children have trouble building high towers with blocks because in their desire to place each of the blocks perfectly they may upset those already stacked. By age 5, children's fine motor coordination has improved further. Hand, arm, and body all move together under better command of the eye. Mere towers no longer interest the 5-year-old, who now wants to build a house or a church complete with steeple, though adults may still need to be told what each finished project is meant to be.

Handedness

For centuries left-handers have suffered unfair discrimination in a world designed for the right-hander. Even the devil himself was portrayed as a left-hander. For many years, teachers forced all children to write with their right hand even if they had a left-hand tendency. Fortunately, today most teachers let children write with the hand they favor.

Some children are still discouraged from using their left hand, even though many left-handed individuals have become very successful. Their ranks include Leonardo da Vinci, Benjamin Franklin, and Pablo Picasso. Each of these famous men was known for his imagination of spatial layouts, which may be stronger in left-handed individuals. Left-handed athletes also are often successful; since there are fewer left-handed athletes, the opposition is not as accustomed to the style and approach of "lefties." Their serve in tennis spins in the opposite direction, their curve ball in baseball swerves the opposite way, and their left foot in soccer is not the one children are used to defending against. Left-handed individuals also do well intellectually. In an analysis of the Scholastic Aptitude Test (SAT) scores of more than 100,000 students, 20 percent of the top scoring group was left-handed, which is twice the rate of left-handedness found in the general population (Bower, 1985). Quite clearly, many left-handed people are competent in a wide variety of human activities ranging from athletic skills to intellectual accomplishments.

When does hand preference develop? Adults usually notice a child's hand preference during early childhood, but researchers have found handedness tendencies in the infant years. Even newborns have some preference for one side of their body over the other. In one research investigation, 65 percent of infants turned their head to the right when they were lying on their stomachs in the crib. Fifteen percent preferred to face toward the left. These preferences for the right or left were related to later handedness (Michel, 1981). By about 7 months of age, infants prefer grabbing with one hand or the other, and this is also related to later handedness (Ramsay, 1980). By 2 years of age, about 10 percent of children favor their left hand (Hardyck & Petrinovich, 1977). Many preschool children, though, use both hands, with a clear hand preference not completely distinguished until later in development. Some children use one hand for writing and drawing, and the other hand for throwing a ball.

My oldest daughter, Tracy, confuses the issue even further. She writes left-handed and plays tennis left-handed, but she plays golf right-handed. During her early childhood, her handedness was still somewhat in doubt. My youngest daughter, Jennifer, was left-handed from early in infancy. Their left-handed orientation has not handicapped them in their athletic and academic pursuits, although Tracy once asked me if I would buy her a pair of left-handed scissors.

Nutrition

Four-year-old Bobby is on a steady diet of double cheeseburgers, french fries, and chocolate milkshakes. Between meals he gobbles up candy bars and marshmallows. He hates green vegetables. Only a preschooler, Bobby has already developed poor nutrition habits. What are a preschool child's energy needs? What is a preschooler's eating behavior like?

> *Spinach: Divide into little piles. Rearrange again into new piles. After five or six maneuvers, sit back and say you are full.*
>
> —Delia Ephron

Energy Needs

Feeding and eating habits are important aspects of development during early childhood. What children eat affects their skeletal growth, body shape, and susceptibility to disease. Recognizing that nutrition is important for the child's growth and development, the federal government provides money for school lunch programs. An average preschool child requires 1,700 calories per day. Energy requirements for individual children are determined by the **basal metabolism rate (BMR)**, *which is the minimum amount of energy a person uses in a resting state.* Energy needs of individual children of the same age, sex, and size vary. Reasons for these differences remain unexplained. Differences in physical activity, basal metabolism, and the efficiency with which children use energy are among the candidates for explanation (Pipes, 1988).

Eating Behavior

A special concern in our culture is the amount of fat we consume. Although some health-conscious mothers provide too little fat in their children's diets, other parents raise their children on diets that are too high in fat. Our busy life-styles, in which we often eat on the run and pick up fast-food meals, probably contribute to the increased fat levels in children's diets. Although most fast-food meals are high in protein, especially meat and dairy products, the average American child does not need to be concerned about getting enough protein. What must be of concern is the vast number of young children who are being weaned on fast foods that are high in fat. Eating habits become ingrained very early in life, and unfortunately it is during the preschool years that many people get their first taste of fast foods.

Being overweight can be a serious problem in early childhood. Consider Ramon, a kindergartner who always begged to stay inside to help during recess. His teacher noticed that Ramon never joined the running games the small superheroes played as they propelled themselves around the playground. Ramon is an overweight 4-year-old boy. Except for extreme cases of obesity, overweight preschool children are usually not encouraged to lose a great deal of weight, but to slow their rate of weight gain so that they will grow into a more normal weight for their height by thinning out as they grow taller. Prevention of obesity in children includes helping children and parents see food as a way to satisfy their hunger and nutritional needs, not as a proof of love or as a reward for good behavior. Snack foods should be low in fat, simple sugars, and salt, and high in fiber. Routine physical activity should be a daily occurrence. The child's life should be centered around activities, not meals (Javernik, 1988).

The State of Illness and Health in the World's Children

A special concern is the state of children's illness and health in developing countries around the world. One death of every three in the world is the death of a child under the age of 5 (Grant, 1993). Every week, more than a quarter of a million children die in developing countries in a quiet carnage of infection and undernutrition. The leading cause of childhood death in the world is dehydration and malnutrition as a result of diarrhea. Approximately 70 percent of the more than 40 million children killed by diarrhea in 1989 could have been saved if parents had available a low-cost breakthrough known as **oral rehydration therapy (ORT),** *a treatment involving a range of techniques designed to prevent dehydration during episodes of diarrhea by giving the child fluids by mouth.*

Most child malnutrition and deaths could now be prevented by parental actions that are almost universally affordable and based on knowledge that is already available. Making sure that parents know they can improve their children's health by adequate birth spacing, care during pregnancy, breast-feeding, immunization, special feeding before and after illness, and regular checkups of the children's weight can overcome many causes of malnutrition and poor growth.

> *A simple child,*
> *That lightly draws its breath,*
> *What should it know of death?*
> —William Wordsworth

Among the nations with the highest mortality rate under age 5 are Asian nations, such as Afghanistan, and African nations, such as Ethiopia (Grant, 1993). In Afghanistan, in 1986, for every 1,000 children born alive, 325 died before the age of 5; in Ethiopia, the figure was 255 per 1,000. Among the countries with the lowest mortality rate under age 5 are Scandinavian countries, such as Sweden and Finland, where only 7 of every

Although oral rehydration therapy is being used in Bangladesh, 10 percent of all children born in Bangladesh die before reaching the age of 5 from dehydration and malnutrition brought about by diarrhea.

1,000 children born died before the age of 5 in 1986. The United States mortality rate under age 5 is better than that of most countries, but, of 131 countries for which figures were available in 1986, 20 countries had better rates than the United States. In 1986, for every 1,000 children born alive in the United States, 13 died before the age of 5.

Fortunately, in the United States the dangers of many diseases such as measles, rubella (German measles), mumps, whooping cough, diphtheria, and polio are no longer present. The vast majority of children in the United States have been immunized against such major childhood diseases. It is important, though, for parents to recognize that these diseases, while no longer afflicting our nation's children, do require a sequence of vaccinations. Without the vaccinations, children can still get the diseases.

Critical Thinking

What responsibility do the wealthier nations of the world have for fostering and financially supporting health and nutrition services for children in developing countries? Explain.

The disorders most likely to be fatal during the preschool years are birth defects, cancer, and heart disease. Death rates from these problems have been reduced in recent years because of improved treatments and health care (Garrison & McQuiston, 1989).

At this point we have discussed a number of ideas about physical development in early childhood. A summary of these ideas is presented in concept table 8.1. Now we turn our attention to cognitive development in early childhood.

COGNITIVE DEVELOPMENT IN EARLY CHILDHOOD

The cognitive world of the preschool child is creative, free, and fanciful. In their art, suns sometimes show up as green, and skies as yellow. Cars float on clouds, pelicans kiss seals, and people look like tadpoles. Preschool children's imagination works overtime, and their mental grasp of the world improves. Our coverage of cognitive development in early childhood focuses on Piaget's stage of preoperational thought, information processing, language development, Vygotsky's theory of development, and early childhood education.

Piaget's Stage of Preoperational Thought

Remember from chapter 6 that, during Piaget's sensorimotor stage of development, the infant progresses in the ability to organize and coordinate sensations and perceptions with physical movements and actions. What kinds of changes take place in the preoperational stage?

Since this stage of thought is called "preoperational," it would seem that not much of importance occurs until fullfledged operational thought appears. Not so! The preoperational stage stretches from approximately 2 to 7 years of age.

CONCEPT TABLE 8.1

Physical Development in Early Childhood

Concept	Processes/Related Ideas	Characteristics/Description
Physical development	Height and weight	The average child grows 2½ inches in height and gains between 5 to 7 pounds a year during early childhood. Growth patterns vary individually, though. Some children are unusually short because of congenital problems, a physical problem that develops in childhood, or emotional problems.
	The brain	The brain is a key aspect of growth. By age 5, the brain has reached nine-tenths of its adult size. Some of its increase in size is due to increases in the number and size of nerve endings, some to myelination. Increasing brain maturation contributes to improved cognitive abilities.
Motor development	Gross motor skills	Gross motor skills increase dramatically during early childhood. Children become increasingly adventuresome as their gross motor skills improve. Young children's lives are extremely active, more active than at any other point in the life cycle.
	Fine motor skills	These also improve substantially during early childhood.
	Handedness	At one point, all children were taught to be right-handed. In today's world, the strategy is to allow children to use the hand they favor. Left-handed children are as competent in motor skills and intellect as right-handed children. Both genetic and environmental explanations of handedness have been given.
Nutrition	Energy needs	Energy needs increase as children go through the childhood years. Energy requirements vary according to basal metabolism, rate of growth, and level of activity.
	Eating behavior	There are a number of daily routines in eating behavior that 3-, 4-, and 5-year-old children follow. Many parents are raising children on diets that are too high in fat and sugar. Children's diets should include well-balanced proportions of fats, carbohydrates, protein, vitamins, and minerals. Eating too many sweets is often a contributing factor to eating problems in early childhood.
The state of illness and health in the world's children	Extent of children's deaths and their prevention	One of every three deaths in the world is that of a child under 5. Every week, more than a quarter of a million children die in developing countries. The most frequent cause of children's death is diarrhea. Oral rehydration therapy can be used to prevent death from diarrhea. Most child malnutrition and death could be prevented by parental actions that are affordable and based on knowledge available today.
	Death and illness in the United States compared to other countries	The United States has a relatively low mortality rate for children, compared to other countries, although the Scandinavian countries have the lowest rates. The disorders most likely to be fatal for American children in the preschool years are birth defects, cancer, and heart disease.

It is a time when stable concepts are formed, mental reasoning emerges, egocentrism begins strongly and then weakens, and magical beliefs are constructed. Preoperational thought is anything but a convenient waiting period for concrete operational thought, although the label *preoperational* emphasizes that the child at this stage does not yet think in an operational way.

What are operations? **Operations** *are internalized sets of actions that allow the child to do mentally what was done physically before.* Operations are highly organized and conform to certain rules and principles of logic. The operations appear in one form in concrete operational thought and in another form in formal operational thought. Thought in the preoperational stage is flawed

"Mrs. Hammond! I'd know you anywhere from little Billy's portrait of you."
Drawing by Frascino; © 1988 The New Yorker Magazine, Inc.

FIGURE 8.3

(a) *A 3½-year-old's symbolic drawing. Halfway into this drawing, the 3½-year-old artist said it was "a pelican kissing a seal." (b) This 11-year-old's drawing is neater and more realistic but also less inventive.*

and not well organized. Preoperational thought is the beginning of the ability to reconstruct at the level of thought what has been established in behavior. Preoperational thought also involves a transition from primitive to more sophisticated use of symbols. Preoperational thought can be divided into two substages: the symbolic function substage and the intuitive thought substage.

Symbolic Function Substage

The **symbolic function substage** *is the first substage of preoperational thought, occurring roughly between the ages of 2 and 4. In this substage, the young child gains the ability to mentally represent an object that is not present.* The ability to engage in such symbolic thought is called "symbolic function," and it vastly expands the child's mental world. Young children use scribbled designs to represent people, houses, cars, clouds, and so on.

> *The youth of art is,*
> *like the youth of anything else*
> *its most interesting period.*
> —Samuel Butler

Possibly because young children are not very concerned about reality, their drawings are fanciful and inventive. Suns are blue, skies are yellow, and cars float on clouds in their symbolic, imaginative world. One 3½-year-old looked at a scribble he had just drawn and described it as a pelican kissing a seal (see figure 8.3a). The symbolism is simple but strong, like abstractions found in some modern art. As Picasso commented, "I used to draw like Raphael but it has taken me a lifetime to draw like young children." In the elementary school years, a child's drawings become more realistic, neat, and precise (see figure 8.3b). Suns are yellow, skies are blue, and cars travel on roads (Winner, 1986).

FIGURE 8.4

The three mountains task. View 1 shows the child's perspective from where he or she is sitting. View 2 is an example of the photograph the child would be shown mixed in with others from different perspectives. To correctly identify this view, the child has to take the perspective of a person sitting at spot (b). Invariably, a preschool child who thinks in a preoperational way cannot perform this task. When asked what a view of the mountains looks like from position (b), the child selects a photograph taken from location (a), the child's view at the time.

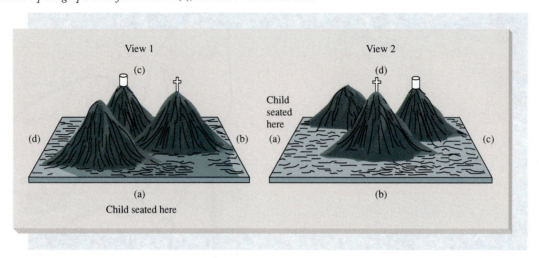

Egocentrism *is a salient feature of preoperational thought. It is the inability to distinguish between one's own perspective and someone else's perspective.* The following telephone conversation between 4-year-old Mary, who is at home, and her father, who is at work, typifies Mary's egocentric thought:

Father: Mary, is Mommy there?

Mary: (Silently nods.)

Father: Mary, may I speak to Mommy?

Mary: (Nods again silently.)

Mary's response is egocentric in that she fails to consider her father's perspective before replying. A nonegocentric thinker would have responded verbally.

Piaget and Barbel Inhelder (1969) initially studied young children's egocentrism by devising the three mountains task (see figure 8.4). The child walks around the model of the mountains and becomes familiar with what the mountains look like from different perspectives. The child can see that different objects are on the mountains as well. The child is then seated on one side of the table on which the mountains are placed. The experimenter takes a doll and moves it to different locations around the table, at each location asking the child to select one photo from a series of photos that most accurately reflects the view the doll is seeing. Children in the preoperational stage often pick the photo that shows the view they have rather than the view the doll has. Perspective taking does not seem to develop uniformly in the preschool child, who frequently shows perspective-taking skills on some tasks but not others (Shantz, 1983).

False would be a picture which insisted on the brutal egocentrism of the child, and ignored the physical beauty which softens it.

—A. A. Milne

Animism, *another facet of preoperational thought, is the belief that inanimate objects have "lifelike" qualities and are capable of action.* The young child might show animism by saying, "That tree pushed the leaf off, and it fell down," or "The sidewalk made me mad; it made me fall down." The young child who uses animism fails to distinguish the appropriate occasions for using human and nonhuman perspectives. Some developmentalists, though, believe that animism represents incomplete knowledge and understanding, not a general conception of the world (Dolgin & Behrend, 1984).

Intuitive Thought Substage

Tommy is 4 years old. Although he is starting to develop his own ideas about the world in which he lives, his ideas are still simple and he is not very good at thinking things out. He has difficulty understanding events he knows are taking place but cannot see. His fantasized thoughts bear little resemblance to reality. He cannot yet answer the question, What if? in any reliable way. For example, he has only a vague idea of what would happen if a car hit him. He also has difficulty negotiating traffic, because he cannot do the mental calculations necessary to estimate whether an approaching car will hit him when he crosses the road (Goodman, 1979).

FIGURE 8.5

Sorting objects. (a) *A random array of objects.* (b) *An ordered array of objects.*

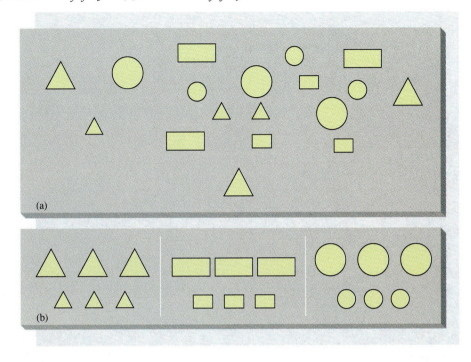

The **intuitive thought substage** *is the second substage of pre-operational thought, occurring between approximately 4 and 7 years of age. In this substage, children begin to use primitive reasoning and want to know the answers to all sorts of questions. Piaget called this time period "intuitive" because young children seem so sure about their knowledge and understanding, yet are so unaware of how they know what they know.* That is, they say they know something but know it without the use of rational thinking.

An example of young children's reasoning ability is the difficulty they have putting things into correct categories. Faced with a random collection of objects that can be grouped together on the basis of two or more properties, preoperational children are seldom capable of using these properties consistently to sort the objects into appropriate groupings. Look at the collection of objects in figure 8.5a. You would respond to the direction "Put the things together that you believe belong together" by sorting the characteristics of size and shape together. Your sorting might look something like that shown in figure 8.5b. In the social realm, the 4-year-old girl might be given the task of dividing her peers into groups according to whether they are friends and whether they are boys or girls. She would be unlikely to arrive at the following classification: friendly boys, friendly girls, unfriendly boys, unfriendly girls. Another example of classification shortcomings involves the preoperational child's understanding of religious concepts (Elkind, 1976). When asked, "Can you be a Protestant and an American at the same time?" 6- and 7-year-olds usually say no; 9-year-olds are likely to say yes, understanding that objects can be cross-classified simultaneously.

Many of these examples show a characteristic of preoperational thought called **centration**—*the focusing, or centering, of attention on one characteristic to the exclusion of all others.* Centration is most clearly evidenced in young children's lack of **conservation**—*a belief in the permanence of certain attributes of objects or situations in spite of superficial changes.* To adults, it is obvious that a certain amount of liquid stays the same regardless of a container's shape. But this is not obvious at all to young children; instead, they are struck by the height of the liquid in the container. In Piaget's most famous conservation task, a child is presented with two identical beakers, each filled to the same level with liquid (see figure 8.6). When asked if these beakers have the same amount of liquid, the child usually says yes. Then the liquid from one beaker is poured into a third beaker, which is taller and thinner than the first two. The child is then asked if the amount of liquid in the tall, thin beaker is equal to that which remains in one of the original beakers. Children who are less than 7 or 8 years old usually say no and justify their answers in terms of the differing height or width of the beakers. Older children usually answer yes and justify their answers appropriately ("If you poured the milk back, the amount would still be the same").

In Piaget's theory, failing the conservation-of-liquid task is a sign that children are at the preoperational stage of cognitive development, whereas passing this test is a sign that they are at the concrete operational stage. In Piaget's view, preoperational children fail to show not only conservation of liquid but also conservation of number, matter, length, volume, and area (see figure 8.7).

Some developmentalists do not believe Piaget was entirely correct in his estimate of when children's conservation skills emerge. For example, Rochel Gelman (1969; Gelman & Baillargeon, 1983) has shown that, when an experimenter instructs a child to attend to relevant aspects of the conservation

FIGURE 8.6

Piaget's conservation task. *The beaker test is a well-known Piagetian test to determine whether a child can think operationally—that is, can mentally reverse actions and show conservation of the substance. (a) Two identical beakers are presented to the child. Then, the experimenter pours the liquid from B into C, which is taller and thinner than A or B. (b) The child is asked if these beakers (A and C) have the same amount of liquid. The preoperational child says no. When asked to point to the beaker that has more liquid, the preoperational child points to the tall, thin beaker.*

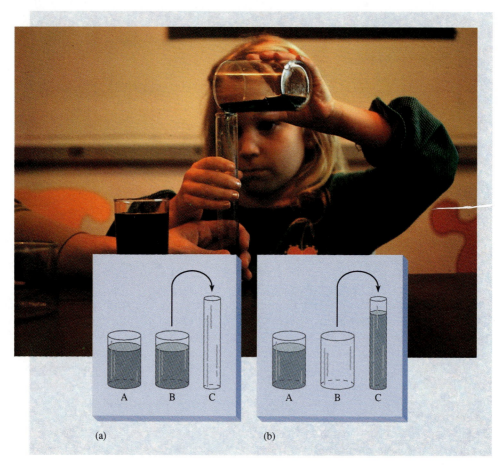

(a)   (b)

task, the child is more likely to conserve. Gelman has also demonstrated that attentional training on one type of task, such as number, improves the preschool child's performance on another type of task, such as mass. Thus, Gelman believes that conservation appears earlier than Piaget thought and that the process of attention is especially important in explaining conservation.

Critical Thinking

Is preoperational thought something that develops through maturation, or is it something that can be taught? Explain your answer.

Yet another characteristic of preoperational children is that they ask a barrage of questions. Children's earliest questions appear around the age of 3, and by the age of 5 they have just about exhausted the adults around them with "why" questions.

"I still don't have all the answers, but I'm beginning to ask the right questions."

Drawing by Lorenz; © 1989 The New Yorker Magazine, Inc.

FIGURE 8.7

Some dimensions of conservation: number, matter, length, volume, and area.

Type of conservation	Initial presentation	Manipulation	Preoperational child's answer
Number	Two identical rows of objects are shown to the child, who agrees they have the same number.	One row is lengthened and the child is asked whether one row now has more objects.	Yes, the longer row.
Matter	Two identical balls of clay are shown to the child. The child agrees that they are equal.	The experimenter changes the shape of one of the balls and asks the child whether they still contain equal amounts of clay.	No, the longer one has more.
Length	Two sticks are aligned in front of the child. The child agrees that they are the same length.	The experimenter moves one stick to the right, then asks the child if they are equal in length.	No, the one on the top is longer.
Volume	Two balls are placed in two identical glasses with an equal amount of water. The child sees the balls displace equal amounts of water.	The experimenter changes the shape of one of the balls and asks the child if it still will displace the same amount of water.	No, the longer one on the right displaces more.
Area	Two identical sheets of cardboard have wooden blocks placed on them in identical positions. The child agrees that the same amount of space is left on each piece of cardboard.	The experimenter scatters the blocks on one piece of cardboard and then asks the child if one of the cardboard pieces has more space covered.	Yes, the one on the right has more space covered up.

Their questions yield clues about their mental development and reflect intellectual curiosity. These questions signal the emergence of children's interest in reasoning and figuring out why things are the way they are. Here are some samples of the questions children ask during the questioning period of 4 to 6 years of age (Elkind, 1976):

"What makes you grow up?"
"What makes you stop growing?"
"Why does a lady have to be married to have a baby?"
"Who was the mother when everybody was a baby?"
"Why do leaves fall?"
"Why does the sun shine?"

At this point we have discussed a number of characteristics of preoperational thought. To help you remember these characteristics, turn to figure 8.8.

Earlier we mentioned that Gelman's research demonstrated that children may fail a Piagetian task because of their failure to attend to relevant dimensions of the task—length, shape, density, and so on. Gelman and other developmentalists also believe that many of the tasks used to assess cognitive development

FIGURE 8.8

Preoperational thought's characteristics.

More symbolic than sensorimotor thought

Inability to engage in operations; can't mentally reverse actions: lacks conservation skills

Egocentric (inability to distinguish between own perspective and someone else's)

Intuitive rather than logical

may not be sensitive to the child's cognitive abilities. Thus, rather than revealing limitations in a child's cognitive development, the tasks may merely be revealing their own limitations for assessing children's cognitive development. Gelman's research reflects the thinking of information-processing psychologists, who place considerable importance on the tasks and procedures involved in assessing children's cognition.

Information Processing

Not only can we study the stages of cognitive development that young children go through, as Piaget did, but we can also study the different cognitive processes of young children's mental worlds. Two limitations on preschool children's thoughts are in attention and memory, important domains involved in the way young children process information. Advances in these two domains are made during early childhood. What are the limitations and advances in attention and memory during the preschool years?

Attention

In chapter 6 we discussed attention in the context of habituation, which is something like being bored, in that the infant becomes disinterested in a stimulus and no longer attends to it. Habituation can be described as a decrement in attention, while dishabituation is the recovery of attention. The importance of these aspects of attention in infancy for the preschool years was underscored by research showing that both decrement and recovery of attention, when measured in the first 6 months of infancy, were associated with higher intelligence in the preschool years (Bornstein & Sigman, 1986).

Although the infant's attention has important implications for cognitive development in the preschool years, the child's ability to pay attention changes significantly during the preschool years. The toddler wanders around, shifting attention from one activity to another, generally seeming to spend little time focused on any one object or event. By comparison, the preschool child might be observed watching television for a half hour. In one investigation, young children's attention to television in the natural setting of the home was videotaped (Anderson & others, 1985). Ninety-nine families comprising 460 individuals were observed for 4,672 hours. Visual attention to television dramatically increased during the preschool years.

One deficit in attention during the preschool years concerns those dimensions that stand out or are *salient* compared to those that are relevant to solving a problem or performing well on a task. For example, a problem might have a flashy, attractive clown that presents the directions for solving a problem. Preschool children are influenced strongly by the features of the task that stand out, such as the flashy, attractive clown. After the age of 6 or 7, children attend more efficiently to the dimensions of the task that are relevant, such as the directions for solving a problem. Developmentalists believe this change reflects a shift to cognitive control of attention so that children act less impulsively and reflect more (Paris & Lindauer, 1982).

Memory

Memory is a central process in children's cognitive development; it involves the retention of information over time. Conscious memory comes into play as early as 7 months of age, although children and adults have little or no memory of events

FIGURE 8.9

Purple bangas who sneeze at people and merds who laugh but don't like mushrooms.

experienced before the age of 3. Among the interesting questions about memory in the preschool years are those involving short-term memory.

> *I come into the fields and spacious palaces of my memory, where are treasures of countless images of things in every manner.*
>
> —St. Augustine

In **short-term memory,** *individuals retain information for up to 15 to 30 seconds, assuming there is no rehearsal.* Using rehearsal, we can keep information in short-term memory for a much longer period. One method of assessing short-term memory is the memory-span task. If you have taken an IQ test, you were probably exposed to one of these tasks. You simply hear a short list of stimuli—usually digits—presented at a rapid pace (one per second, for example). Then you are asked to repeat the digits. Research with the memory-span task suggests that short-term memory increases during early childhood. For example, in one investigation, memory span increased from about 2 digits in 2- to 3-year-old children to about 5 digits in 7-year-old children; yet between 7 and 13 years of age, memory span increased only by 1½ digits (Dempster, 1981). Keep in mind, though, the individual differences in memory span, which is why IQ and various aptitude tests are used.

Why are there differences in memory span because of age? Rehearsal of information is important; older children rehearse the digits more than younger children. Speed and efficiency of processing information are important, too, especially the speed with which memory items can be identified. For example, in one investigation, children were tested on their speed at repeating words presented orally (Case, Kurland, & Goldberg,

1982). Speed of repetition was a powerful predictor of memory span. Indeed, when the speed of repetition was controlled, the 6-year-olds' memory spans were equal to those of young adults!

Critical Thinking

How extensively do you think children's memory span can be improved through the use of strategies? Are there limits on how much improvement can be made? Explain your answer.

The speed-of-processing explanation highlights an important point in the information-processing perspective. That is, the speed with which a child processes information is an important aspect of the child's cognitive abilities.

Task Analysis

Another major emphasis in the information-processing perspective is identifying the components of the task the child is performing (Klahr, 1989). Information-processing psychologists are intrigued by the possibility that if tasks are made interesting and simple, children may display greater cognitive maturity than Piaget realized. This strategy was followed to determine if preschool children could reason about a *syllogism*—a type of reasoning problem consisting of two premises, or statements assumed to be true, plus a conclusion (Hawkins & others, 1984). To simplify problems, words such as *some* and *all* were made implicit rather than explicit. The problems focused on fantasy creatures alien to practical knowledge. Imagine how wide a child's eyes become when told stories about purple bangas who sneeze at people and merds who laugh don't like mushrooms (see figure 8.9). The following are two syllogisms that were read to children:

Every banga is purple.
Purple animals always sneeze at people.
Do bangas sneeze at people?

Merds laugh when they're happy.
Animals that laugh don't like mushrooms.
Do merds like mushrooms?

By simplifying the problem and making its dimensions more understandable to young children, the researchers demonstrated that preschool children can reason about syllogisms.

The Child's Theory of Mind

Children are very curious about the nature of the human mind and developmentalists have shown a flurry of recent interest in children's thoughts about how the human mind exists (Barsch & Wellman, 1993; Delcielo & others, 1993; DeLoache, 1993; Gopik & Wellman, 1993; Olson, 1993; Zelazo & Frye, 1993).

The following account of children's developing knowledge of the mind was proposed by John Flavell, Patricia Miller, and Scott Miller (1993). It includes children's awareness that the mind exists, has connections to the physical world, is separate from the physical world, can represent objects and events accurately or inaccurately, and actively mediates the interpretation of reality and the emotion experienced.

A first developmental acquisition is knowing that such a thing as a mind exists. By the age of 2 or 3, chidren refer to needs, emotions, and mental states—"I need my Mommy," "Tom feels bad," and "I forgot my doll." They also use intentional action or desire words, such as "wants to." Cognitive terms such as know, remember, and think usually appear after perceptual and emotional terms, but often are used by the age of 3. Later children make finer distinctions between such mental phenomena as guessing versus knowing, believing versus fantasizing, and intending versus not on purpose.

At about 2–3 years of age, children develop the knowledge that people can be "cognitively connected" to objects and events in the external world in such ways as seeing them, hearing them, liking them, wanting them, fearing them, and so on. By their awareness of the connections among stimuli, mental states, and behavior, young children possess a rudimentary mental theory of human action (Wellman, 1988). On the input side, two-year-olds sometimes hide objects so that another person cannot see them, which involves manipulating stimuli to produce a certain perceptual state in another person. On the output side (mind to behavior), older 2-year-old children can predict action and emotional expression based on desires, as when comprehending that a child wants a cookie, tries to get one, and is happy if successful. However, 2-year-olds cannot predict actions based on beliefs (Wellman & Woolley, 1990). For instance, if Ann wants to find her toy but can't find it in one location, children predict she would be sad and look for it in another location. However, they don't know that Ann's beliefs about possible locations influence where she will look.

In addition to inferring connections from stimuli to mental states, or from mental states to behavior or emotion, 3-year-olds also can often infer mental states from behavior. When children use spontaneous language, they sometimes explain action by referring to mental causes. For example, a 3-year-old explains that he has paint on his hands because he thought his hands were paper, which gives new meaning to the term "finger painting!" (Wellman, 1988). In sum, children acquire knowledge about links between stimuli, mental states, and behavior fairly early in their development.

Young children also develop an understanding that the mind is separate from the physical world. They know that the mind is different from rocks, roller skates, and even the head (Wellman & Estes, 1986). For example, a 3-year-old who is told that one boy has a cookie and that another boy is thinking about cookie knows which cookie can be seen by others, touched, eaten, shared, and saved for later. Three-year-olds also know that they can fantasize about things that don't exist, such as Martians, ghosts, or dragons (Wellman & Estes, 1986).

Children develop an understanding that the mind can represent objects and events accurately or inaccurately. Understanding of false beliefs usually appears in 4- or 5-year-old children, but not 3-year-olds. Consider the following story acted out for children with dolls. A boy places some chocolate in a blue cupboard and then goes out to play. While he is outside, his mother moves the chocolate to a green cupboard. When the boy returns and wants the chocolate, the subject is asked where the boy will look for it. Three-year-olds usually say "the green cupboard," where the chocolate actually is, even though the boy had no way of knowing the chocolate was moved (Wimmer & Permer, 1983). Thus, 3-year-olds do not understand that a person acts on the basis of what he or she believes to be true rather than what they themselves know to be true in reality. By contrast, 4- and 5-year-old children usually understand false beliefs.

Finally, children also develop an understanding that the mind actively mediates the interpretation of reality and the emotion experienced. The shift from viewing the mind as passive to viewing it as active appears in children's knowledge that prior experiences influence current mental states, which in turn affect emotions and social inferences. In the elementary school years, children change from viewing emotions as caused by external events without any mediation by internal states, to viewing emotional reactions to an external event as influenced by a prior emotional state, experience, or expectations (Gnepp, 1989). For example, 6-year-old children do not understand that a child would be sad or scared when his friends suggest they ride bikes if that child previously was almost hit by a car when she could not stop her bike because her legs were too short.

In summary, young children are very curious about the human mind. By the age of 3, they turn some of their thoughts inward and understand that they and others have internal mental states (Flavell, Miller, & Miller, 1993). Beginning at about 3 years of age, children also show an understanding that the internal desires and beliefs of a person can be connected to that person's actions (Wellman, 1990; Wellman & Gelman, 1992). Young children also know that they cannot physically touch thoughts, believe that a person has to see an object to know it, and grasp that their mental image of an object represents something that exists in the world (Wellman, 1990).

Language Development

Young children's understanding sometimes gets way ahead of their speech. One 3-year-old, laughing with delight as an abrupt summer breeze stirred his hair and tickled his skin, commented, "It did winding me!" Adults would be understandably perplexed if a young child ventured, "Anything is not to break, only plates and glasses," when she meant, "Nothing is breaking except plates and glasses." Many of the oddities of young children's language sound like mistakes to adult listeners. But from the children's point of view, they are not mistakes; they represent the way young children perceive and understand their world at that point in their development.

Elaboration of Brown's Stages

In chapter 6, we briefly described Roger Brown's five stages of language development. Remember that Brown (1973, 1986) believes that mean length of utterance (MLU) is a good index of a child's language maturity. He identified five stages of a child's language development based on MLU. Other aspects of the stages include an age range, characteristics, and typical sentences.

In stage 1, occurring from 12 to 26 months of age, the MLU is 1.00 to 2.00. Vocabulary consists mainly of nouns and verbs, with several adjectives and adverbs. Word order is preserved. Typical sentences are "Mommy bye-bye" and "Big doggie."

In stage 2, occurring from 27 to 30 months, MLU is 2.00 to 2.50. Plurals are correctly formed, past tense is used, *be* is used, definite (*the*) and indefinite (*a, an*) articles are used, and so are some prepositions. Typical sentences are "Dolly in bed," "Them pretty," and "Milk's all gone."

In stage 3, occurring from 31 to 34 months of age, MLU is 2.50 and 3.00. Yes-no questions appear, *wh-* questions (*who, what, where*) proliferate, negatives (*no, not, non*) are used, and so are imperatives (commands or requests). Typical sentences are "Daddy come home?" and "Susie no want milk."

In stage 4, occurring from 35 to 40 months, MLU is 3.00 to 3.75. One sentence is sometimes embedded in another. Typical sentences include, "I think it's red," and "Know what I saw."

In stage 5, occurring from 41 to 46 months, MLU is 3.75 to 4.50. Simple sentences and propositional relations are coordinated. Typical sentences are "I went to Bob's and had ice cream" and "I like bunnies 'cause they're cute."

> But whatever the process, the result is wonderful, gradually from naming an object we advance step-by-step until we have traversed the vast difference between our first stammered syllable and the sweep of thought in a line of Shakespeare.
>
> —Helen Keller

Roger Brown, shown talking with a young girl, has been a pioneer in providing rich insights about children's language development. Among his contributions is the concept of MLU, or mean length of utterance, which has been documented as a good index of a child's language maturity.

Rule Systems

Remember from our discussion of language development in chapter 6 that language consists of rule systems such as those involving morphology, syntax, semantics, and pragmatics. What kinds of changes take place in these rule systems during early childhood?

As children move beyond two-word utterances, there is clear evidence that they know morphology rules. Children begin using the plurals and possessive forms of nouns (such as *dogs* and *dog's*), putting appropriate endings on verbs (such as *-s* when the subject is third-person singular, *-ed* for the past tense, and *-ing* for the present progressive tense), using prepositions (such as *in* and *on*), articles (such as *a* and *the*), and various forms of the verb *to be* (such as "I was going to the store"). Some of the best evidence for changes in children's use of morphological rules occur in their overgeneralizations of the rules. Have you ever heard a preschool child say "foots" instead of "feet," or "goed" instead of "went?" If you do not remember having heard such oddities, talk to some parents who have young children, or to the young children themselves. You will hear some interesting errors in the use of morphological rule endings.

In a classical experiment, Jean Berko (1958) presented preschool children and first-grade children with cards such as one with a "wug" on it — a "wug" is a small yellow animal that looks like a baby chicken. They were told, "This is a wug." Then, they were informed, "Now there is another one. There are two of them. There are two ____." In supplying the missing word, children had to say it correctly. "Wugs" is the correct response. Although the children's words were not perfect, they were much better than chance. Moreover, the children demonstrated their knowledge of morphological rules not only with the plural forms of nouns ("There are two wugs"), but with possessive forms of nouns and the third-person singular and past-tense forms of verbs. What makes the study by Berko impressive is that most of the words were fictional, created for the experiment. Thus, the children could not base their responses on remembering past instances of hearing the words. Instead they were forced to rely on *rules*.

Similar evidence that children learn and actively apply rules can be found at the level of syntax (Howe, 1992). After advancing beyond two-word utterances, children speak word sequences that show a growing mastery of complex rules for how words should be ordered. Consider the case of *wh-* questions: "Where is Daddy going?" and "What is that boy doing?" for example. To ask these questions properly, the child has to know two important differences between *wh-* questions and simple affirmative statements (such as "Daddy is going to work" and "That boy is waiting on the school bus"). First, a *wh-* word must be added at the beginning of the sentence. Second, the auxiliary verb must be "inverted"—that is, exchanged with the subject of the sentence. Young children learn quite early where to put the *wh-* word, but they take much longer to learn the auxiliary-inversion rule. Thus, it is common to hear preschool children asking such questions as "Where daddy is going?" and "What that boy is doing?"

As children move into the elementary school years, they become skilled at using syntactical rules to construct lengthy and complex sentences (Singer, 1991). Sentences such as "The man who fixed the house went home" and "I don't want you to use my bike" are impressive demonstrations of how the child can use syntax to combine ideas into a single sentence. How young children achieve the mastery of such complex rules and yet struggle with relatively simple arithmetic rules is a mystery we must still solve.

Regarding semantics, as children move beyond the 2-word stage, their knowledge of meanings also rapidly advances (Rice, 1991). The speaking vocabulary of a 6-year-old child ranges from 8,000 to 14,000 words (Carey, 1977). Assuming that word learning began when the child was 12 months old, this translates into a rate of 5 to 8 new word meanings a day between the ages of 1 and 6. After 5 years of word learning, the 6-year-old child does not slow down. According to some estimates, the average child of this age is moving along at the awe-inspiring rate of 22 words a day (Miller, 1981)! How would you fare if you were given the task of learning 22 new words every day? It is truly miraculous how quickly children learn language (Winner & Gardner, 1988).

Although there are many differences between a 2-year-old's language and a 6-year-old's language, none are more important than those pertaining to pragmatics—rules of conversation (Becker, 1991; Forrester, 1992; Garton, 1992; Shugar & Kmita, 1991). A 6-year-old is simply a much better conversationalist than a 2-year-old. What are some of the improvements in pragmatics that are made in the preschool years? At about 3 years of age, children improve in their ability to talk about things that are not physically present; that is, they improve their command of the characteristic of language known as "displacement." One way displacement is revealed is in games of pretend. Although a 2-year-old might know the word *table*, he is unlikely to use this word to refer to an imaginary table that he pretends is standing in front of him. But a child over 3 probably has this ability, even if he does not always use it. There are large individual differences in preschoolers' talk about imaginary people and things.

Vygotsky's Theory of Development

Children's cognitive and language development do not develop in a social vacuum. Lev Vygotsky (1896–1934), a Russian psychologist, recognized this important point about the child's mind more than half a century ago. Vygotsky's theory is receiving increased attention as we move toward the close of the twentieth century (Belmont, 1989; Butterworth, 1993; Glick, 1991; Light & Butterworth, 1993; Rogoff, 1993; Rogoff & Morelli, 1989; Wertsch & Tulviste, 1992). Before we turn to Vygotsky's ideas on language and thought, and culture and society, let's examine his important concept of the zone of proximal development.

Zone of Proximal Development

The **zone of proximal development (ZPD)** *is Vygotsky's term for tasks too difficult for children to master alone, but that can be mastered with the guidance and assistance of adults or more skilled children.* Thus, the lower limit of the ZPD is the level of problem solving reached by a child working independently. The upper limit is the level of additional responsibility the child can accept with the assistance of an able instructor (see figure 8.10). Vygotsky's emphasis on ZPD underscored his belief in the importance of social influences on cognitive development and the role of instruction in children's development (Steward, 1994).

The ZPD is conceptualized as a measure of learning potential. IQ is also a measure of learning potential. However, IQ emphasizes that intelligence is a property of the child, while ZPD emphasizes that learning is interpersonal, a dynamic social event that depends on a minimum of two minds, one better informed or more drilled than the other. It is inappropriate to say that the child *has* a ZPD; rather, a child *shares* a ZPD with an instructor.

The practical teaching involved in ZPD begins toward the zone's upper limit, where the child is able to reach the goal only through close collaboration with the instructor. With adequate continuing instruction and practice, the child organizes and masters the behavioral sequences necessary to perform the target skill. As the instruction continues, the performance transfers from the instructor to the child as the teacher gradually reduces the explanations, hints, and demonstrations until the child is able to adequately perform alone. Once the goal is achieved, it may become the foundation for the development of a new ZPD.

Learning by toddlers provides an example of how the ZPD works. The toddler has to be motivated and must be involved

FIGURE 8.10

Vygotsky's zone of proximal development has a lower limit and an upper limit. *Tasks in the ZPD are too difficult for the child to perform alone. They require assistance from an adult or a skilled child. As children experience the verbal instruction or demonstration, they organize the information in their existing mental structures so they can eventually perform the skill or task alone.*

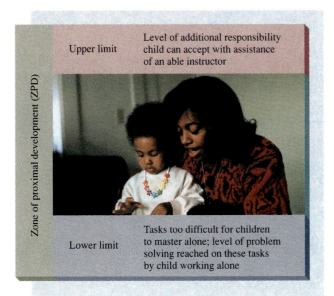

Upper limit — Level of additional responsibility child can accept with assistance of an able instructor

Zone of proximal development (ZPD)

Lower limit — Tasks too difficult for children to master alone; level of problem solving reached on these tasks by child working alone

Vygotsky said that language and thought initially develop independently of each other but eventually merge.

Two principles govern the merging of thought and language. First, all mental functions have external or social origins. Children must use language and communicate with others before they focus inward to their own mental processes. Second, children must communicate externally and use language for a long period of time before the transition from external to internal speech takes place. This transition period occurs between 3 and 7 years of age and involves talking to oneself. After a while, the self-talk becomes second nature to children and they can act without verbalizing. When this occurs, children have internalized their egocentric speech in the form of inner speech, which becomes the thoughts of the child. Vygotsky believed that children who engage in a large amount of private speech are more socially competent than those who do not use it extensively. He argued that private speech represents an early transition in becoming more socially communicative.

Vygotsky's theory challenges Piaget's ideas on language and thought. Vygotsky argued that language, even in its earliest forms, is socially based, whereas Piaget emphasized young children's egocentric and nonsocially oriented speech. Young children talk to themselves to govern their behavior and to guide themselves (Duncan, 1991). By contrast, Piaget stressed that young children's egocentric speech reflects social and cognitive immaturity.

Culture and Society

Many developmentalists who work in the field of culture and development find themselves comfortable with Vygotsky's theory, which focuses on the sociocultural context of development (Rogoff & Morelli, 1989). Vygotsky's theory offers a portrayal of human development as being inseparable from social and

in activities that involve the skill at a reasonably high level of difficulty—that is, toward the zone's upper end. The teacher must have the know-how to exercise the target skill at any level required by the activity, and must be able to locate and stay in the zone. The teacher and the child have to adapt to each other's requirements. The reciprocal relationship between the toddler and the teacher adjusts dynamically as the division of labor is negotiated and aimed at increasing the weaker partner's share of the goal attainment.

In one research investigation of toddler-mother dyads, the pair was put to work on a number of problems with arrays of various numbers (few versus many objects) and varying complexity (simple counting versus number reproduction) (Saxe, Guberman, & Gearhart, 1987). The mothers were told to treat this as an opportunity to encourage learning and understanding in their children. Based on videotaped interactions of the mothers and their toddlers, the mothers adjusted their task goals to meet their children's abilities. Importantly, the mothers also adjusted the quality of their assistance during the problem-solution period in direct response to the children's successes and failures. Vygotsky's concept of the zone of proximal development is also being effectively applied to teaching children math and how to read (Cox, 1993; Lightfoot, 1993).

Language and Thought

In Vygotsky's view, the child's mental or cognitive structures are made of relations between mental functions. The relation between language and thought is believed to be especially important in this regard (Langer, 1969; Vygotsky, 1962).

Lev Vygotsky (1896–1934), shown here with his daughter, believed that children's cognitive development is advanced through social interaction with skilled individuals embedded in a sociocultural backdrop.

cultural activities. Vygotsky emphasized how the development of mental processes such as memory, attention, and reasoning involve learning to use the inventions of society, such as language, mathematical systems, and memory devices. He also emphasized how children are aided in development by the guidance of individuals who are already skilled in these tools. Vygotsky's emphasis on the role of culture and society in cognitive development contrasts with Piaget's description of the child as a solitary little scientist.

Vygotsky stressed both the institutional and the interpersonal levels of social contexts. At the institutional level, cultural history provides organizations and tools useful to cognitive activity through institutions such as schools, inventions such as computers, and literacy. Institutional interaction gives the child broad behavioral and societal norms to guide their lives. The interpersonal level has a more direct influence on the child's mental functioning. According to Vygotsky (1962), skills in mental functioning develop through immediate social interaction. Information about cognitive tools, skills, and interpersonal relations are transmitted through direct interaction with people. Through the organization of these social interactional experiences embedded in a cultural backdrop, children's mental development matures.

Early Childhood Education

With increased understanding of how young children develop and learn has come greater emphasis on the education of young children. We explore the following questions about early childhood education: What is child-centered kindergarten? What are developmentally appropriate and inappropriate practices in programs for young children? Does it really matter if children attend preschool before kindergarten? What are the effects of early childhood education? What is the nature of education for disadvantaged young children?

Child–Centered Kindergarten

Kindergarten programs vary a great deal. Some approaches place more emphasis on young children's social development, others on their cognitive development. Some experts on early childhood education believe that the curriculum of too many of today's kindergarten and preschool programs place too much emphasis on achievement and success, putting pressure on young children too early in their development (Bredekamp & Shepard, 1989; Burts & others, in press; Charlesworth, 1989; Elkind, 1987, 1988; Moyer, Egertson, & Isenberg, 1987). Placing such heavy emphasis on success is not what kindergartens were originally intended to do. In the 1840s, Friedrich Froebel's concern for quality education for young children led to the founding of the kindergarten, literally "a garden for children." The founder of the kindergarten understood that, like growing plants, children require careful nurturing. *Unfortunately, too many of today's kindergartens have forgotten the importance of careful nurturing for our nation's young children.*

> *Learning is an ornament in prosperity, a refuge in adversity.*
>
> —Aristotle

In the **child-centered kindergarten,** *education involves the whole child and includes concern for the child's physical, cognitive, and social development. Instruction is organized around the child's needs, interests, and learning styles. The process of learning, rather than what is learned, is emphasized.* Each child follows a unique developmental pattern, and young children learn best through firsthand experiences with people and materials. Play is extremely important in the child's total development. *Experimenting, exploring, discovering, trying out, restructuring, speaking, and listening* are all words that describe excellent kindergarten programs. Such programs are closely attuned to the developmental status of 4- and 5-year-old children. They are based on a state of being, not on a state of becoming (Ballenger, 1983).

Developmentally Appropriate and Inappropriate Practices in the Education of Young Children

It is time for number games in a kindergarten class at the Greenbrook School in South Brunswick, New Jersey. With little prodding from the teacher, twenty-three 5- and 6-year-old children pick up geometric puzzles, playing cards, and counting equipment from the shelves lining the room. At one round table, some young children fit together brightly colored shapes. One girl forms a hexagon out of triangles. Other children gather around her to count up how many parts were needed to make the whole. After about half an hour the children prepare for story time. They put away their counting equipment and sit in a circle around one young girl. She holds up a giant book about a character named Mrs. Wishywashy, who insists on giving the farm animals a bath. The children recite the whimsical lines, clearly enjoying one of their favorite stories. The hallway outside the kindergarten is lined with drawings depicting the children's own interpretations of the book. After the first reading, volunteers act out various parts of the book. There is not one bored face in the room (Kantrowitz & Wingert, 1989).

This is not reading, writing, and arithmetic the way most individuals remember it. A growing number of educators and psychologists believe that preschool and young elementary school children learn best through active, hands-on teaching methods like games and dramatic play. They know that children develop at varying rates and that schools need to allow for these individual differences. They also believe that schools should focus on improving children's social development as well as their cognitive development. Educators refer to this type of schooling as **developmentally appropriate practice,** *which is based upon knowledge of the typical development of children within an age span (age appropriateness) as well as the uniqueness of the child (individual appropriateness). Developmentally appropriate practice contrasts with*

LIFE-SPAN PRACTICAL KNOWLEDGE 8.1

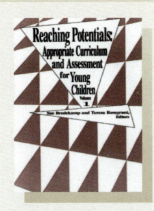

Reaching Potentials: Appropriate Curriculum and Assessment for Young Children, vol. 1 (1992) edited by Sue Bredekamp and Teresa Rosegrant. Washington, DC: National Association for the Education of Young Children.

This excellent book addresses how to help young children reach their full potential—not only their academical and vocational potential, but, just as importantly, their full potential as healthy, sensitive, caring, and contributing members of society. The authors argue that curriculum, assessment, and teaching practices help to determine whether these potentials are reached. The book closely follows the guidelines for appropriate curriculum content and assessment developed by the National Association for the Education of Young Children (NAEYC), a highly respected organization of early childhood educators. Bredekamp is the editor of NAEYC's position statements on accreditation, developmentally appropriate education, and standardized testing.

---

developmentally inappropriate practice, which ignores the concrete, hands-on approach to learning. Direct teaching largely through abstract, paper-and-pencil activities presented to large groups of young children is believed to be developmentally inappropriate.

One of the most comprehensive documents addressing the issue of developmentally appropriate practice in early childhood programs is the position statement by the NAEYC (National Association for the Education of Young Children, 1986; Bredekamp, 1987). This document represents the expertise of many of the foremost experts in the field of early childhood education. By turning to figure 8.11, you can examine some of the NAEYC recommendations for developmentally appropriate practice. In one recent study, children who attended developmentally appropriate kindergartens displayed more appropriate classroom behavior, had better conduct records, and better work-study habits in the first grade than children who attended developmentally inappropriate kindergartens (Hart & others, 1993).

A special worry of early childhood educators is that the back-to-basics movement that has recently characterized educational reform is filtering down to kindergarten. Another worry is that many parents want their children to go to school earlier than kindergarten for the purpose of getting a "head start" in achievement.

Does It Really Matter if Children Attend Preschool before Kindergarten?

According to child developmentalist David Elkind (1987, 1988), parents who are exceptionally competent and dedicated and who have both the time and the energy can provide the basic ingredients of early childhood education in their home. If parents have the competence and resources to provide young children with a variety of learning experiences and exposure to other children and adults (possibly through neighborhood play groups), along with opportunities for extensive play, then home schooling may sufficiently educate young children. However, if parents do not have the commitment, the time, the energy, and the resources to provide young children with an environment that approximates a good early childhood program, then it *does* matter whether a child attends preschool. In this case, the issue is not whether preschool is important, but whether home schooling can closely duplicate what a competent preschool program can offer.

We should always keep in mind the unfortunate idea of early childhood education as an early start to ensure the participants will finish early or on top in an educational race (NAEYC, 1990; Willer & Bredekamp, 1990). Elkind (1988) points out that perhaps the choice of the phrase *head start* for the education of disadvantaged children was a mistake. "Head Start program" does not imply a race. Not surprisingly, when middle-class parents heard that low-income children were getting a "head start," they wanted a head start for their own young children. In some instances, starting children in formal academic training too early can produce more harm than good. In Denmark, where reading instruction follows a language experience approach and formal instruction is delayed until the age of 7, illiteracy is virtually nonexistent. By contrast, in France, where state-mandated formal instruction in reading begins at age 5, 30 percent of the children have reading problems. Education should not be stressful for young children. Early childhood education should not be solely an academic prep school.

Preschool is rapidly becoming a norm in early childhood education. Twenty-three states already have legislation pending to provide schooling for 4-year-old children, and there are already many private preschool programs. The increase in public preschools underscores the growing belief that early childhood education should be a legitimate component of public education. There are dangers, though. According to child developmentalist David Elkind (1988), early childhood education is often not well understood at higher levels of education. The danger is that public preschool education for 4-year-old children will become little more than a downward extension of traditional elementary education. This is already occurring in preschool programs in which testing, workbooks, and group drill are imposed on 4- and 5-year-old children.

FIGURE 8.11

Developmentally appropriate and inappropriate practice in early childhood education: NAEYC recommendations.

Component	Appropriate practice	Inappropriate practice
Curriculum goals 	Experiences are provided in all developmental areas—physical, cognitive, social, and emotional.	Experiences are narrowly focused on cognitive development without recognition that all areas of the child's development are interrelated.
	Individual differences are expected, accepted, and used to design appropriate activities.	Children are only evaluated against group norms, and all are expected to perform the same tasks and achieve the same narrowly defined skills.
	Interactions and activities are designed to develop children's self-esteem and positive feelings toward learning.	Children's worth is measured by how well they conform to rigid expectations and perform on standardized tests.
Teaching strategies 	Teachers prepare the environment for children to learn through active exploration and interaction with adults, other children, and materials.	Teachers use highly structured, teacher-directed lessons almost exclusively.
	Children select many of their own activities from among a variety the teacher prepares.	The teacher directs all activity, deciding what children will do and when.
	Children are expected to be mentally and physically active.	Children are expected to sit down, be quiet, and listen, or do paper-and-pencil tasks for long periods of time. A major portion of time is spent passively sitting, watching, and listening.
Guidance of socioemotional development 	Teachers enhance children's self-control by using positive guidance techniques such as modeling and encouraging expected behavior, redirecting children to a more acceptable activity, and setting clear limits.	Teachers spend considerable time enforcing rules, punishing unacceptable behavior, demeaning children who misbehave, making children sit and be quiet, or refereeing disagreements.
	Children are provided many opportunities to develop social skills such as cooperating, helping, negotiating, and talking with the person involved to solve interpersonal problems.	Children work individually at desks and tables most of the time and listen to the teacher's directions to the total group.

Critical Thinking

Most of you went to preschool or kindergarten. Can you remember what it was like? In what ways could the kindergarten you attended have been improved? How can we make our nation's preschool education programs better?

Elkind believes that early childhood education should become a part of public education, but on its own terms. Early childhood should have its own curriculum, its own methods of evaluation and classroom management, and its own teacher-training programs. Although there may be some overlap with the curriculum, evaluation, classroom management, and teacher training at the upper levels of schooling, they certainly should not be identical.

Researchers are already beginning to document some of the stress that increased academic pressure can bring to young children (Burts, Charlesworth, & Fleege, 1991; Burts & others, in press; Charlesworth & others, in press). In one investigation, Diane Burts and her colleagues (1989) compared the frequencies of stress-related behaviors observed in young children in classrooms with developmentally appropriate and developmentally inappropriate instructional practices. They found that children in the developmentally inappropriate classrooms

Component	Appropriate practice	Inappropriate practice
Language development, literacy, and cognitive development	Children are provided many opportunities to see how reading and writing are useful before they are instructed in letter names, sounds, and word identification. Basic skills develop when they are meaningful to children. An abundance of these activities is provided to develop language and literacy: listening to and reading stories and poems, taking field trips, dictating stories, participating in dramatic play; talking informally with other children and adults; and experimenting with writing.	Reading and writing instruction stresses isolated skill development, such as recognizing single letters, reading the alphabet, singing the alphabet song, coloring within predefined lines, or being instructed in correct formation of letters on a printed line.
	Children develop an understanding of concepts about themselves, others, and the world around them through observation, interacting with people and real objects, and seeking solutions to concrete problems. Learning about math, science, social studies, health, and other content areas is integrated through meaningful activities.	Instruction stresses isolated skill development through memorization. Children's cognitive development is seen as fragmented in content areas such as math or science, and times are set aside for each of these.
Physical development	Children have daily opportunities to use large muscles, including running, jumping, and balancing. Outdoor activity is planned daily so children can freely express themselves.	Opportunity for large muscle activity is limited. Outdoor time is limited because it is viewed as interfering with instructional time, rather than as an integral part of the children's learning environment.
	Children have daily opportunities to develop small muscle skills through play activities, such as puzzles, painting, cutting, and similar activities.	Small motor activity is limited to writing with pencils, coloring predrawn forms, or engaging in similar structured lessons.
Aesthetic development and motivation	Children have daily opportunities for aesthetic expression and appreciation through art and music. A variety of art media is available.	Art and music are given limited attention. Art consists of coloring predrawn forms or following adult-prescribed directions.
	Children's natural curiosity and desire to make sense of their world are used to motivate them to become involved in learning.	Children are required to participate in all activities to obtain the teacher's approval, to obtain extrinsic rewards like stickers or privileges, or to avoid punishment.

exhibited more stress-related behaviors than children in the developmentally appropriate classrooms. In another investigation, children in a high academically oriented early childhood education program were compared with children in a low academically oriented early childhood education program (Hirsch-Pasek & others, 1989). No benefits appeared for children in the high academically oriented early childhood education program, but some possible harmful effects were noted. Higher test anxiety, less creativity, and a less positive attitude toward school characterized the children who attended the high academic program more than the low academic program.

One of the concerns of Americans is that our school-children fare poorly when their achievement test scores in math and science are compared with the test scores of schoolchildren from many other industrialized nations, especially such Asian nations as Japan and China (McKnight & others, 1987). Many Americans attribute the differences in achievement scores to a rigid Asian system that sets young children in a lockstep march from cradle to college. In fact, the early years of Japanese schooling are anything but a boot camp. To read further about the nature of early childhood education in Japan, turn to Sociocultural Worlds of Development 8.1.

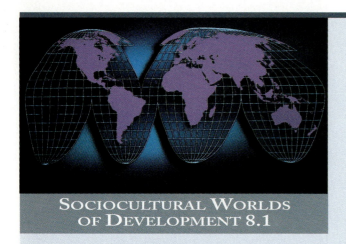

SOCIOCULTURAL WORLDS OF DEVELOPMENT 8.1

Early Childhood Education in Japan

In a time of low academic achievement by children in the United States, many Americans are turning to Japan, a country of high academic achievement and economic success, for possible answers. However, the answers provided by Japanese preschools are not the ones Americans expected to find. In most Japanese preschools, surprisingly little emphasis is put on academic instruction. In one investigation, 300 Japanese and 210 American preschool teachers, child development specialists, and parents were asked about various aspects of early childhood education (Tobin, Wu, & Davidson, 1989). Only 2 percent of the Japanese respondents listed "to give children a good start academically" as one of their top three reasons for a society to have preschools. In contrast, over half the American respondents chose this as one of their top three choices. To prepare children for successful careers in first grade and beyond, Japanese schools do not teach reading, writing, and mathematics, but rather skills such as persistence, concentration, and the ability to function as a member of a group. The vast majority of young Japanese children are taught to read at home by their parents.

In the recent comparison of Japanese and American preschool education, 91 percent of Japanese respondents chose providing children with a group experience as one of their top three reasons for a society to have preschools (Tobin, Wu, & Davidson, 1989). Sixty-two percent of the more individually oriented Americans listed group experience as one of their top three choices. An emphasis on the importance of the group seen in Japanese early childhood education continues into elementary school education.

Lessons in living and working together grow naturally out of the Japanese culture. In many Japanese kindergartens, children wear the same uniforms, including caps, which are of different colors to indicate the classrooms to which they belong. They have identical sets of equipment, kept in identical drawers and shelves. This is not intended to turn the young children into robots, as some Americans have observed, but to impress on them that other people, just like themselves, have needs and desires that are equally important (Hendry, 1986).

Like in America, there is diversity in Japanese early childhood education. Some Japanese kindergartens have specific aims, such as early musical training or the practice of Montessori methods (Hendry, 1986). In large cities, some kindergartens are attached to universities that have elementary and secondary schools. Some Japanese parents believe that if their young children attend a university-based program, it will increase the children's chances of eventually being admitted to top-rated schools and universities. Several more-progressive programs have introduced free play as an antidote for the heavy intellectualizing in some Japanese kindergartens.

In Japan, learning how to cooperate and participating in group experiences are viewed as extremely important reasons for the existence of early childhood education.

The Effects of Early Childhood Education

Because kindergarten and preschool programs are so diverse, it is difficult to draw overall conclusions about their effects on children's development. Nonetheless, in one review of early childhood education's influence (Clarke-Stewart and Fein, 1983), it was concluded that children who attend preschool or kindergarten

- interact more with peers, both positively and negatively
- are less cooperative with and responsive to adults than home-reared children

- are more socially competent and mature in that they are more confident, extraverted, assertive, self-sufficient, independent, verbally expressive, knowledgeable about the social world, comfortable in social and stressful circumstances, and better adjusted when they go to school (exhibiting more task persistence, leadership, and goal direction, for example)
- are less socially competent in that they are less polite, less compliant to teacher demands, louder, and more aggressive and bossy, especially if the school or family supports such behavior

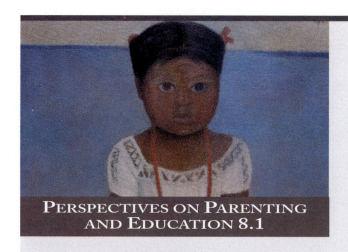

PERSPECTIVES ON PARENTING AND EDUCATION 8.1

The Role of Parenting in Young Children's Learning and Education

Mothers and fathers play important roles in the development of young children's positive attitudes toward learning and education. In one investigation, mothers and their preschool children were evaluated and then the children's academic competence was assessed when they were in sixth grade (Hess & others, 1984). Maternal behavior in the preschool years was related to the children's academic competence in sixth grade. The best predictors of academic competence in sixth grade were the following maternal behaviors shown during the preschool years:

effective communication with the child, a warm relationship with the child, positive expectations for achievement, use of rule-based rather than authority-based discipline, and not believing that success in school was based on luck.

The father's involvement with the child can also help to build positive attitudes toward school and learning. Competent fathers of preschool children set aside regular time to be with the child, listen to the child and respond to questions, become involved in the child's play, and show an interest in the child's preschool and kindergarten activities. Fathers can help with the young child's schooling in the following ways (Swick & Manning, 1983):

- Supporting their children's efforts in school and their children's unique characteristics
- Helping children with their problems when the children seek advice
- Communicating regularly with teachers
- Participating in school functions

The relationship between the school and the parents of young children is an important aspect of preschool and kindergarten education. Schools and parents can cooperate to provide young children with the best possible preschool and kindergarten experience, and a positive orientation toward learning. In one investigation, the most important factor in contributing to the success of the preschool program was the positive involvement of the parents in their young children's learning and education (Lally, Mangione, & Honig, 1987).

In sum, early childhood education generally has a positive effect on children's development, since the behaviors just mentioned—while at times negative—seem to be in the direction of developmental maturity, in that they increase as the child ages through the preschool years.

It is important to keep in mind that young children's development occurs in a number of different settings, not just schools, and that relationships in one of those settings—the family—are also important influences. To read about the role of parenting in young children's learning and education, turn to Perspectives on Parenting and Education 8.1.

Education for Disadvantaged Children

For many years, children from low-income families did not receive any education before they entered the first grade. In the 1960s, an effort was made to try to break the cycle of poverty and poor education for young children in the United States through compensatory education. **Project Head Start** *is a compensatory education program designed to provide children from low-income families the opportunity to acquire the skills and experiences important for success in school.* Project Head Start began in the summer of 1965, funded by the Economic Opportunity Act, and it continues to serve disadvantaged children today.

Initially, Project Head Start consisted of many different types of preschool programs in different parts of the country. Little effort was made to find out whether some programs

The preschool children shown here are attending a Head Start program, a national effort to provide children from low-income families the opportunity to experience an enriched environment.

worked better than others, but it became apparent that some programs did work better than others. **Project Follow Through** *was implemented in 1967 as an adjunct to Project Head Start. In Project Follow Through, different types of educational programs were devised to determine which programs were the most effective. In the Follow Through programs, the enriched programs were carried through the first few years of elementary school.*

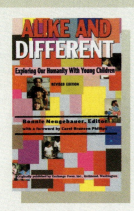
Were some Follow Through programs more effective than others? Many of the different variations were able to produce the desired effects in children. For example, children in academically oriented, direct-instruction approaches did better on achievement tests and were more persistent on tasks than were children in the other approaches. Children in affective education approaches were absent from school less often and showed more independence than children in other approaches. Thus, Project Follow Through was important in demonstrating that variation in early childhood education does have significant effects in a wide range of social and cognitive areas (Stallings, 1975).

The effects of early childhood compensatory education continue to be studied, and recent evaluations support the positive influence on both the cognitive and the social worlds of disadvantaged young children (Haskins, 1989; Kagan, 1988; Lee, Brooks-Gunn, & Schnur, 1988). Of special interest are the long-term effects such intervention might produce. Model preschool programs lead to lower rates of placement in special education, dropping out of school, grade retention, delinquency, and use of welfare programs. Such programs might also lead to higher rates of high school graduation and employment. For every dollar invested in high-quality, model preschool programs, taxpayers receive about $1.50 in return by the time the participants reach the age of 20 (Haskins, 1989). The benefits include savings on public school education (such as special-education services), tax payments on additional earnings, reduced welfare payments, and savings in juvenile justice system costs. Predicted benefits over a lifetime are much greater to the taxpayer, a return of $5.73 on every dollar invested.

One long-term investigation of early childhood education was conducted by Irving Lazar, Richard Darlington, and their colleagues (1982). They pooled their resources into what they called a "consortium for longitudinal studies," developed to share information about the long-term effects of preschool programs so that better designs and methods could be created. When the data from the eleven different early education studies were analyzed together, the children ranged in age from 9 to 19 years. The early education models varied substantially, but all were carefully planned and executed by experts in early childhood education. Outcome measures included indicators of school competence (such as special education and grade retention), abilities (as measured by standardized intelligence and achievement tests), attitudes and values, and impact on the family. The results indicated substantial benefits of competent preschool education with low-income children on all four dimensions investigated. In sum, ample evidence indicates that well-designed and well-implemented early childhood education programs with low-income children are successful (Darlington, 1991; Haskins, 1989; Kagan, 1988).

Although educational intervention in impoverished young children's lives is important, not all Head Start programs are created equal (Piotrowski & others, 1994). Edward Zigler and his colleagues (Zigler & Muenchow, 1992; Zigler & Styfco, 1994) concluded that 40 percent of the 1,400 Head Start programs are of questionable quality. More attention needs to be given to developing consistently high-quality Head Start programs. One high-quality early childhood education program (although not a Head Start program) is the Perry Preschool program in Ypsilanti, Michigan, that was designed by David Weikart (1982, 1993). The Perry Preschool program is a two-year preschool program that includes weekly home visits from program personnel. In a recent analysis of the long-term effects of the program, as young adults the Perry Preschool children had higher high school graduation rates, more are in the workforce, fewer need welfare, crime rates are lower among them, and there are fewer teen pregnancies than a control group from the same background who did not get the enriched early childhood education experience (Weikart, 1993).

At this point we have discussed a number of ideas about young children's cognitive development. A summary of these ideas is presented in concept table 8.2.

LIFE-SPAN HEALTH AND WELL-BEING

Early Interventions That Work

Children's health expert Lisbeth Schorr (1989) discussed society's stake in improving services to young children, especially poor children, and considered the attributes of early interventions that work. Investment in improved services to young children is increasingly recognized as essential to the welfare of every American (Children's Defense Fund, 1992). Connections have been made between early interventions and later outcomes such as the incidence of welfare dependence, crime, adolescent pregnancy, and dropping out of school (Schorr, 1989).

According to Schorr (1989), a number of early-intervention programs do work. How and why do they work? Schorr says there are four reasons.

1. *Successful programs are comprehensive and intensive.* They provide access to a wide array of services. Low-income families usually don't have the energy or the skills to wend their way through the maze of eligibility determinations and other hoops they must jump through to obtain support. Flexible access to a wide range of programs is more important for them than for middle-class families.
2. *In successful programs, staff have the time, training, and skills that are needed to build relationships of trust and respect with children and families.* The leaders and workers in successful programs know that *how* services are provided is just as important as *what* is provided. Such programs emphasize the importance of listening to parents, exchanging information rather

than lecturing, and helping parents gain greater control over their own lives and act more effectively on behalf of their children.

3. *Successful programs deal with the child as part of the family, and the family as part of the neighborhood and community.* For instance, the nurse in a high-quality program not only responds to a child's recurrent diarrhea, but goes beyond that problem and asks whether the child's health is threatened by circumstances for which the family needs support and services it is not getting. The successful school also enlists parents as collaborators in giving children reasons to learn.

Whether they focus on children or on parents, successful programs usually follow a *two-generational approach.* They might offer support to parents who need help with their lives as adults before they can effectively use services that are directed at children. They take into account the world inhabited by those they serve—rural health clinics deliver clean water, home visitors help young mothers plan their return to school or employment while teaching them about effective child rearing, and the Head Start teacher knows when a family is threatened by eviction.

4. *Successful programs cross long-standing professional and bureaucratic boundaries.* They are prepared to provide a wide range of services in nontraditional settings, including homes, and at

nontraditional hours. Nurses may offer family support, social workers might collaborate with teachers and physicians, and psychologists might listen to a mother's anxieties about her children in the course of taking her to the market. No one says, "This may be what you need, but helping you get it is not part of my job or in my jurisdiction."

Brief sketches of two programs illustrate how these characteristics can be implemented. The first is a Head Start program in Baltimore, Maryland, that serves children who have a history of lead poisoning. The children's breakfast and lunch are planned around their special nutritional needs, and their activities stress the structure, stimulation, and verbal exchange that are absent from many of their lives. Next door, the mothers meet with staff who assist them in developing better parenting skills and new approaches to nutrition. The pediatric department that sponsors the program works with local health and housing agencies to get the lead paint out of the homes (Schorr, 1988).

The second successful early intervention, Homebuilders, was started by a small Catholic family-service agency in Tacoma, Washington, and now is spreading to other parts of the country. Homebuilders work to keep families together that are threatened with the removal of a child because of abuse or neglect. The staff works with families, mainly in the family's own home, during crises, for a period of as much as 2 months. Its master's-level professionals have caseloads of no more than two or three families at a time. ■

CONCEPT TABLE 8.2

Cognitive Development in Early Childhood

Concept	Processes/Related Ideas	Characteristics/Description
Piaget's stage of preoperational thought	Its nature	This is the beginning of the ability to reconstruct at the level of thought what has been established in behavior, and a transition from primitive to more sophisticated use of symbols. The child does not yet think in an operational way.
	Symbolic function substage	This substage occurs roughly between 2 and 4 years of age and is characterized by symbolic thought, egocentrism, and animism.
	Intuitive thought substage	This substage stretches from approximately 4 to 7 years of age. It is called "intuitive" because the children seem so sure about their knowledge, yet they are so unaware of how they know what they know. The preoperational child lacks conservation and asks a barrage of questions.
Information processing	Attention	The child's attention dramatically improves during early childhood. One deficit in attention in early childhood is that the child attends to the salient rather than the relevant features of a task.
	Memory	Significant improvement in short-term memory occurs during early childhood. For example, memory span increases substantially in early childhood. Increased use of rehearsal and increased speed of processing are related to young children's memory improvement.
	Task analysis	Information-processing advocates believe a task's components should be analyzed. By making tasks more interesting and simple, researchers have shown that some aspects of children's cognitive development occur earlier than had been thought possible.
	The child's theory of mind	Young children are curious about the nature of the human mind. Children develop an awareness that the mind exists, has connections to the physical world, is separate from the physical world, can represent objects accurately or inaccurately, and actively mediates the interpretation of reality and the emotion experienced.
Language development	Elaboration of Brown's stages	Roger Brown's five stages represent a helpful model for describing young children's language development. They involve mean length of utterance, age ranges, characteristics of language, and sentence variations.
	Rule systems	Rule systems involve changes in phonology, morphology, syntax, semantics, and pragmatics during the early childhood years.
Vygotsky's theory of development	Zone of proximal development	ZPD is Vygotsky's term for tasks too difficult for children to master alone, but that can be mastered with the guidance and assistance of adults or more skilled children.

Concept	Processes/Related Ideas	Characteristics/Description
	Language and thought	These develop independently and then merge. The merging occurs between 3 and 7 years of age and involves private speech (talking to oneself).
	Culture and society	Vygotsky's theory stresses how the child's mind develops in the contexts of the sociocultural world. Cognitive skills develop through social interactions embedded in a cultural backdrop.
Early childhood education	Child-centered kindergarten	Child-centered kindergarten involves the education of the whole child, with emphasis on individual variation, the process of learning, and the importance of play in development.
	Developmentally appropriate and inappropriate practices in the education of young children	Developmentally appropriate practice is based on knowledge of the typical development of children within an age span (age appropriateness), as well as the uniqueness of the child (individual appropriateness). Developmentally inappropriate practice ignores the concrete, hands-on approach to learning. Direct teaching largely through abstract, paper-and-pencil activities presented to large groups of young children is believed to be developmentally inappropriate. The National Association for the Education of Young Children has been a strong proponent of developmentally appropriate practice and has developed extensive recommendations for its implementation.
	The importance of children attending preschool before kindergarten	Parents can educate their young children just as effectively as schools can. However, many parents do not have the commitment, time, energy, and resources needed to provide young children with an environment that approaches a competent early childhood education program. Too often, parents see education as a race, and preschool as a chance to get ahead in the race. However, education is not a race, and it should not be stressful for young children. Public preschools are appearing in many states. A concern is that they should not become merely simple versions of elementary school. Early childhood education has some issues that overlap with those of upper levels of schooling, but in many ways the agenda of early childhood education is different.
	The influence of early childhood education on children's development	This is difficult to evaluate. The effects overall seem to be positive, but outcome measures reveal areas in which social competence is more positive, others in which it is less positive.
	Education for disadvantaged young children	Compensatory education has tried to break through the poverty cycle with programs like Head Start and Follow Through. Long-term studies reveal that model preschool programs have positive effects on development.

CONCLUSIONS

Although young children's physical growth is slower than in infancy, their lives are very, very active—the most active of any period in the human life span. As their thinking develops, young children construct all sorts of ideas about what is happening in their world.

In this chapter, we began by studying physical development in early childhood, charting young children's growth in height and weight, the brain, and motor development (gross motor skills, fine motor skills), as well as evaluating the nature of handedness. We also learned about young children's nutrition, including energy needs, eating behavior, and the state of illness and health in the world's children. Then we turned our attention to a number of facets of young children's cognitive development, including Piaget's stage of preoperational thought and its two substages (symbolic function, intuitive thought), information processing (attention, memory, task analysis, and the young child's theory of mind), language development, and Vygotsky's theory and the increased attention it is receiving. We also examined a number of aspects of early childhood education, including child-centered education, the increasing interest in developmentally appropriate and inappropriate practice, whether it really matters if children attend preschool before kindergarten, the effects of early childhood education, and education for disadvantaged children. At different points in the chapter, you also read about early childhood education in Japan, and the role of parenting in young children's learning and education.

Don't forget that you can obtain a summary of the entire chapter by again reading the two concept tables on pages 210 and 230. In the next chapter we will study young children's socioemotional development.

KEY TERMS

deprivation dwarfism   A type of growth retardation caused by emotional deprivation; children are deprived of affection, which causes stress and alters the release of hormones by the pituitary gland. (206)

myelination   A process in which nerve cells are covered and insulated with a layer of fat cells. This process has the effect of increasing the speed of information traveling through the nervous system. (206)

basal metabolism rate (BMR)   The minimum amount of energy a person uses in a resting state. (208)

oral rehydration therapy (ORT)   A treatment involving a range of techniques designed to prevent dehydration during episodes of diarrhea by giving the child fluids by mouth. (208)

operations   Internalized sets of actions that allow the child to do mentally what was done physically before. (210)

symbolic function substage   The first substage of preoperational thought, occurring roughly between the ages of 2 and 4. In this substage, the young child gains the ability to mentally represent an object that is not present. (211)

egocentrism   A salient feature of preoperational thought. It is the inability to distinguish between one's own perspective and someone else's perspective. (212)

animism   Another facet of preoperational thought is the belief that inanimate objects have "lifelike" qualities and are capable of action. (212)

intuitive thought substage   The second substage of preoperational thought occurring between approximately 4 and 7 years of age. In this substage, children begin to use primitive reasoning and want to know the answers to all sorts of questions. Piaget called this time period *intuitive* because young children seem so sure about their knowledge and understanding, yet are so unaware of how they know what they know. (213)

centration   The focusing or centering of attention on one characteristic to the exclusion of all others. (213)

conservation   A belief in the permanence of certain attributes of objects or situations in spite of superficial changes. (213)

short-term memory   Individuals retain information for up to 15 to 30 seconds, assuming there is no rehearsal. (217)

zone of proximal development (ZPD)   Vygotsky's term for tasks too difficult for children to master alone, but that can be mastered with the guidance and assistance of adults or more skilled children. (220)

child-centered kindergarten   Education that involves the whole child and that includes concern for the child's physical, cognitive, and social development. Instruction is organized around the child's needs, interests, and learning styles. The process of learning, rather than what is learned, is emphasized. (222)

developmentally appropriate practice   Schooling based on the knowledge of the typical development of children within an age span (age appropriateness) as well as the uniqueness of the child (individual appropriateness). Developmentally appropriate practice contrasts with developmentally inappropriate practice, which ignores the concrete, hands-on approach to learning. Direct teaching largely through abstract, paper-and-pencil activities presented to large groups of young children is believed to be developmentally inappropriate. (222)

Project Head Start   A compensatory education program designed to provide children from low-income homes the opportunity to acquire skills and experiences important for success in school. (227)

Project Follow Through   Implemented in 1967 as an adjunct to Project Head Start. In Project Follow Through, different types of educational programs were devised to determine which programs were most effective. In the Follow Through programs, the enriched programs were carried through the first few years of elementary school. (227)

John Santrock,
The Family.

Socioemotional Development in Early Childhood

It is a happy talent to know how to play.

—Emerson, *Journals,* 1834

In the sun that is young once only
Time let me play.

—Dylan Thomas

IMAGES OF LIFE-SPAN DEVELOPMENT

The Diversity of Families and Parenting

Children grow up in a diversity of families. Some children live in families that have never experienced divorce, some live virtually their entire childhood in single-parent families, and yet others live in stepfamilies. Some children live in poverty, others in economically advantaged families. Some children's mothers work full-time and place them in day care, while some mothers stay home with their children. Some children grow up in an Anglo-American culture, others in ethnic minority cultures. Some children have siblings, others don't. Some children's parents treat them harshly and abuse them, other children have parents who nurture and support them.

In thinking about the diversity of families and parenting, consider the following two circumstances and predict how they might influence the child's development:

A young mother is holding an infant in her arms and trying to keep track of two boys walking behind her (Dash, 1986). The younger boy, who is about 3, clutches an umbrella but seems to be having trouble with it. He drags its curved handle along the ground, and that irritates his mother. She tells him to carry the umbrella right or she will knock the (expletive) out of him. "Carry it right, I said," she says, and then she slaps him in the face, knocking him off balance. She rarely nurtures her son and has beaten him so hard that at times he has bruises that don't go away for days. The mother lives in the poverty of an inner city and she is unemployed. She is unaware of how her own life stress affects her parenting behavior.

Now consider another child, who is growing up in a very different family environment:

A 28-year-old mother is walking along the street with her 4-year-old daughter. They are having a conversation about her daughter's preschool. As the conversation continues, they smile back and forth several times as the daughter describes some activities she did. As they reach home, the mother tells her daughter that she loves her and gives her a big hug. The mother lives in an economically advantaged suburb, and the preschool her daughter attends has high ratings. The mother reports that she sincerely enjoys being with her daughter and loves to plan enjoyable things for her to do.

PREVIEW

The young boy's mother was experiencing the strains of poverty, which was impairing her ability to effectively rear him. In the second example, the mother and daughter had a warm, enjoyable relationship. In this chapter we will study different types of parenting styles and how they influence children's development. We also will explore other dimensions of families in young children's lives, along with peer relations, play, television, the self, gender, and moral development.

CHEEVERWOOD   **by Michael Fry**

© *1994 Michael Fry.*

FAMILIES

In chapter 7, we learned that attachment is an important aspect of family relationships during infancy. Remember that some experts believe attachment to a caregiver during the first several years of life is the key ingredient in the child's social development, increasing the probability the child will be socially competent and well adjusted in the preschool years and beyond. We also learned that other experts believe secure attachment has been overemphasized and that the child's temperament, other social agents and contexts, and the complexity of the child's social world are also important in determining the child's social competence and well-being. Some developmentalists also emphasize that the infant years have been overdramatized as determinants of lifespan development, arguing that social experiences in the early childhood years and later deserve more attention than they have sometimes been given.

In this chapter, we will discuss early childhood experiences beyond the attachment process as we explore the different types of parenting styles to which children are exposed, sibling relationships, and how more children are now experiencing socialization in a greater variety of family structures than at any other point in history. Keep in mind, as we discuss these aspects of families, the importance of viewing the family as a system of interacting individuals who reciprocally socialize and mutually regulate each other.

Parenting Styles

Parents want their children to grow into socially mature individuals, and they may feel frustrated in trying to discover the best way to accomplish this. Developmentalists have long searched for the ingredients of parenting that promote competent social development in children. For example, in the 1930s, John Watson argued that parents were too affectionate with their children. In the 1950s, a distinction was made between physical and psychological discipline, with psychological discipline, especially reasoning, emphasized as the best way to rear a child. In the 1970s and beyond, the dimensions of competent parenting have become more precise.

Especially widespread is the view of Diana Baumrind (1971), who believes parents should be neither punitive nor aloof, but should instead develop rules for their children and be affectionate with them. She emphasizes three types of parenting that are associated with different aspects of the child's social behavior: authoritarian, authoritative, and laissez-faire (permissive). More recently, developmentalists have argued that permissive parenting comes in two different forms: permissive-indulgent and permissive-indifferent. What are these forms of parenting like?

Authoritarian parenting *is a restrictive, punitive style that exhorts the child to follow the parent's directions and to respect work and effort. The authoritarian parent places firm limits and controls on the child with little verbal exchange allowed. Authoritarian parenting is associated with children's social incompetence.* For example, an authoritarian parent might say, "You do it my way or else. There will be no discussion!" Children of authoritarian parents are often anxious about social comparison, fail to initiate activity, and have poor communication skills. And in one recent study, early harsh discipline was associated with child aggression (Weiss & others, 1992).

> *There's no vocabulary for love within a family, love that's lived in but not looked at, love within the light of which all else is seen, the love within which all other love finds speech. This love is silent.*
>
> —T. S. Eliot, *The Elder Statesman*

Authoritative parenting *encourages children to be independent but still places limits and controls on their actions. Extensive verbal give-and-take is allowed, and parents are warm and nurturant toward the child. Authoritative parenting is associated with children's social competence.* An authoritative parent might put his arm around the child in a comforting way and say, "You know you should not have done that; let's talk about how you can handle the situation better next time." Children whose parents are authoritative are socially competent, self-reliant, and socially responsible.

LIFE-SPAN PRACTICAL KNOWLEDGE 9.1

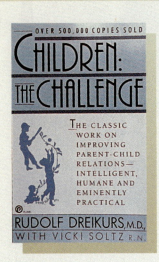

Children: The Challenge

(1964) by Rudolph Dreikurs.
New York: Hawthorn Books.

Children: The Challenge tells parents how to discipline their children more effectively. Author Rudolph Dreikurs was a Viennese psychiatrist who collaborated with famous psychoanalyst Alfred Adler in conducting child guidance clinics. Dreikurs, who came to the United States in 1937 and soon became a highly respected authority on child rearing, teaches parents how to understand their children and meet their needs. He stresses that the main reason for children's misbehavior is discouragement. Discouraged children often demand undue attention, he says,

and parents usually respond to this negative attention-seeking behavior by trying to impose their will on the children, who in turn keep misbehaving; thus, parents who get caught up in this cycle are actually rewarding their children for misbehavior. Dreikurs counsels parents on how to become calm and pleasant when disciplining the child, and he recommends family discussion for solving family problems. This book is easy to read, the examples are clear and plentiful, and the author discusses a wide range of situations calling for discipline. Although it was written three decades ago, the book is still one of the books on parental discipline most widely recommended by mental health professionals.

Permissive parenting comes in two forms: permissive-indifferent and permissive-indulgent (Maccoby & Martin, 1983). **Permissive-indifferent parenting** *is a style in which the parent is very uninvolved in the child's life; it is associated with children's social incompetence, especially a lack of self-control.* This parent cannot answer the question, "It is 10 P.M. Do you know where your child is?" Children have a strong need for their parents to care about them; children whose parents are permissive-indifferent develop the sense that other aspects of the parents' lives are more important than they are. Children whose parents are permissive-indifferent are socially incompetent—they show poor self-control and do not handle independence well.

Permissive-indulgent parenting *is a style of parenting in which parents are highly involved with their children but place few demands or controls on them. Permissive-indulgent parenting is associated with children's social incompetence, especially a lack of self-control.* Such parents let their children do what they want, and the result is that the children never learn to control their own behavior and always expect to get their way. Some parents deliberately rear their children in this way because they believe the combination of warm involvement with few restraints will produce a creative, confident child. One boy I knew whose parents deliberately reared him in a permissive-indulgent manner moved his parents out of their bedroom suite and took it over for himself. He is now 18 years old and has not learned to control his behavior; when he can't get something he wants, he still throws temper tantrums. As you might expect, he is not very popular with his peers. Children whose parents are permissive-indulgent rarely learn respect for others and have difficulty controlling their behavior.

> *Parenting is a very important profession, but no test of fitness for it is ever imposed in the interest of children.*
>
> —George Bernard Shaw,
> *Everybody's Political About What,* 1944

The four classifications of parenting just discussed involve combinations of acceptance and responsiveness, on the one hand, and demand and control, on the other. How these dimensions combine to produce authoritarian, authoritative, permissive-indifferent, and permissive-indulgent parenting is shown in figure 9.1.

Adapting Parenting to Developmental Changes in the Child

Parents also need to adapt their behavior to the child, based on the child's developmental maturity. Parents should not treat the 5-year-old same as the 2-year-old. The 5-year-old and the 2-year-old have different needs and abilities. In the first year, parent-child interaction moves from a heavy focus on routine caretaking—feeding, changing diapers, bathing, and soothing—to later include more noncaretaking activities like play and visual-vocal exchanges. During the child's second and third years, parents often handle disciplinary matters by physical manipulation: They carry the child away from a mischievous activity to the place they want the child to go; they put fragile and dangerous objects out of reach; they sometimes spank. But as the child grows older, parents turn increasingly

FIGURE 9.1

Classification of parenting styles. *The four types of parenting styles (authoritative, authoritarian, permissive-indulgent, and permissive-indifferent) involve the dimensions of acceptance and responsiveness, on the one hand, and demand and control, on the other.*

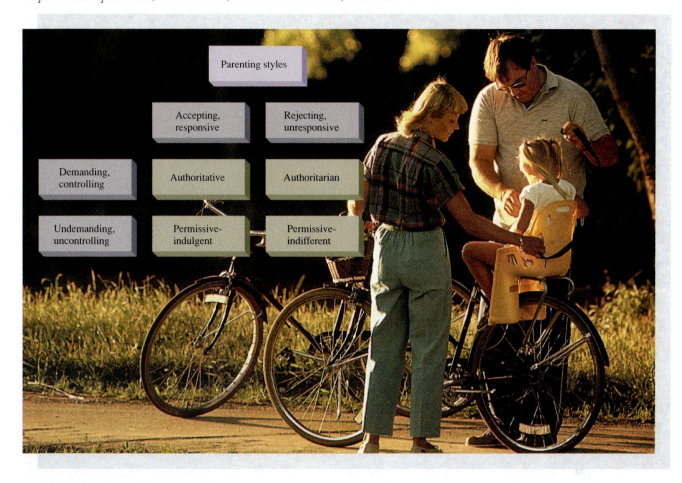

to reasoning, moral exhortation, and giving or withholding special privileges. As children move toward the elementary school years, parents show them less physical affection.

Cultural, Ethnic, and Social Class Variations in Families

Cultures vary on a number of issues involving families, such as what the father's role in the family should be, the extent to which support systems are available to families, and how children should be disciplined. Although there are cross-cultural variations in parenting (Whiting & Edwards, 1988), in one study of parenting behavior in 186 cultures around the world, the most common pattern was a warm and controlling style, one that was neither permissive nor restrictive (Rohner & Rohner, 1981). The investigators commented that the majority of cultures have discovered, over many centuries, a "truth" that only recently emerged in the Western world—namely, that

children's and adolescents' healthy social development is most effectively promoted by love and at least some moderate parental control.

Ethnic minority families differ from White American families in their size, structure, and composition, their reliance on kinship networks, and their levels of income and education (Chase-Lansdale, Brooks-Gunn, & Zamsky, in press; MacPhee, Fritz, & Miller–Heyl, 1993; Voight & Hans, 1993). Large and extended families are more common among ethnic minority groups than among White Americans (Wilson, 1989). For example, more than 30 percent of Hispanic American families consist of five or more individuals (Keefe & Padilla, 1987). Black American and Hispanic American adolescents interact more with grandparents, aunts, uncles, cousins, and more-distant relatives than do White American adolescents.

Single-parent families are more common among Black Americans and Hispanic Americans than among White Americans. In comparison with two-parent households, single

LIFE-SPAN PRACTICAL KNOWLEDGE 9.2

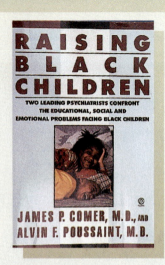

Raising Black Children

(1992) by James P. Comer and Alvin E. Poussaint. New York: Plume.

Raising Black Children is written by two of the most highly respected experts on Black children—James Comer and Alvin Poussaint, professors of psychiatry at Yale and Harvard, respectively. Comer and Poussaint argue that Black parents face additional difficulties in raising emotionally healthy Black children because of race and income problems. Comer and Poussaint's guide contains almost 1,000 child-rearing questions they have repeatedly heard from Black parents across the income spectrum. The authors give advice to parents on many issues, including how to improve the Black child's self-esteem and identity, how to confront racism, how to teach their children to handle anger, conflict, and frustration, and how to deal with the mainstream culture and retain a Black identity. This is an excellent book for Black parents that includes wise suggestions that are not in most child-rearing books (almost all others are written for White parents and do not deal with special problems faced by ethnic minority parents or parents from low-income backgrounds).

The Hispanic family reunion of the Limon family in Austin, Texas. Hispanic American children often grow up in families with a network of relatives that runs into scores of individuals. Large and extended families are more common among Hispanic Americans than among Anglo-Americans.

parents often have more limited resources of time, money, and energy. This shortage of resources may prompt them to encourage early autonomy among their children (Spencer & Dornbusch, 1990). Also, ethnic minority parents are less well educated and engage in less joint decision making than White American parents. And ethnic minority children are more likely to come from low-income families than are White American children (Committee for Economic Development, 1987; McLoyd, in press). Although impoverished families often raise competent youth, poor parents may have a diminished capacity for supportive and involved parenting (McLoyd, in press).

Some aspects of home life can help to protect ethnic minority children from social patterns of injustice (Spencer & Dornbusch, 1990). The community and family can filter out destructive racist messages, parents can provide alternate frames of reference than those presented by the majority, and parents can also provide competent role models and encouragement (Bowman & Howard, 1985; Jones, 1990). And the extended family system in many ethnic minority families provides an important buffer to stress (Munsch, Wampler, & Dawson, 1992). To read further about the extended family system in Black American and Hispanic American families, turn to Sociocultural Worlds of Development 9.1.

In America and most Western cultures, social class differences in child-rearing have been found. Working class and low-income parents often place a high value on external characteristics such as obedience and neatness, whereas middle-class families often place a high value on internal characteristics, such as self-control and delay of gratification. There are social class differences not only in child-rearing values but also in parenting behaviors. Middle-class parents are more likely to explain something, use verbal praise, use reasoning to accompany their

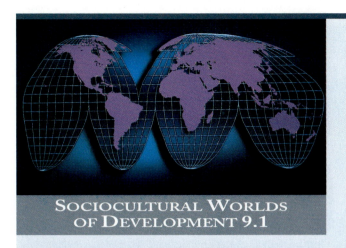

SOCIOCULTURAL WORLDS OF DEVELOPMENT 9.1

Black and Hispanic Family Orientations

In the 1985 Children's Defense Fund study "Black and White Children in America: Key Facts" (Edelman, 1987), Black children were three times as likely as White children to

- be poor
- live with a parent who was separated from a spouse
- die of child abuse

five times as likely to

- be dependent on welfare

and twelve times as likely to

- live with a parent who never married

Nonetheless, it is important to keep in mind that millions of Black American families are not on welfare, have children who stay in school and out of trouble, and find ways to cope with and overcome problems they experience during difficult times. In 1967, Martin Luther King, Jr., reflected on the Black American family and gave the following caution: "As public awareness of the predicament of the Black family increases, there will be danger and opportunity. The opportunity will be to deal fully rather than haphazardly with the problem as a whole, as a social catastrophe brought on by many years of oppression. The danger is that the problems will be attributed to innate Black weaknesses and used to justify further neglect and to rationalize continued oppression." In today's world, Dr. King's words still ring true. (McLoyd, in press; Ogbu, 1989; Spencer & Dornbusch, 1990).

The Black cultural tradition of an extended family household—in which one or several grandparents, uncles, aunts, siblings, or cousins, either live together or provide support—has helped many Black parents cope with adverse social conditions such as economic impoverishment (McAdoo, 1988). The Black extended family can be traced to the African heritage of many Black Americans, where in many cultures a newly married couple does not move away from relatives. Instead, the extended family assists its members with basic family functions. Researchers have found that the extended Black family helps to reduce the stress of poverty and single parenting through emotional support, sharing of income and economic responsibility, and surrogate parenting (McAdoo, 1988). The presence of grandmothers in the households of many Black adolescents and their infants has been an important support system for both the teenage mother and the infant (Stevens, 1984). Active and involved extended family support systems also help a parent or parents from other ethnic minority groups cope with poverty and its related stress.

A basic value in Mexico is represented by the saying "As long as our family stays together, we are strong." Mexican children are brought up to stay close to their family, often playing with siblings rather than with schoolmates or neighborhood children, as American children usually do. Unlike the father in many American families, the Mexican father is the undisputed authority on all family matters and is usually obeyed without question. The mother is revered as the primary source of affection and care. This emphasis on family attachment leads the Mexican to say, "I will achieve mainly because of my family, and for my family, rather than myself." By contrast, the self-reliant American would say, "I will achieve mainly because of my ability and initiative and for myself rather than for my family." Unlike most Americans, families in Mexico tend to stretch out in a network of relatives that often runs to scores of individuals.

Both cultures—Mexican and American—have undergone considerable change in recent decades. Whether Mexican children will gradually take on the characteristics of American children, or whether American children will shift closer to Mexican children, is difficult to predict. The cultures of both countries will probably move to a new order more in keeping with future demands, retaining some common features of the old while establishing new priorities and values (Holtzmann, 1982).

Although Black children are more likely than White children to be poor and live with a parent who has been separated from a spouse, it is important to keep in mind that millions of Black American families are not on welfare, have considerable family support, and find ways to effectively cope with stress. The extended family, especially grandmothers, plays an especially important role in Black American children's development.

discipline, and ask their children questions. By contrast, parents in low-income and working-class households are more likely to discipline their children with physical punishment and criticize their children more (Heath, 1983; Kohn, 1977).

Sibling Relationships and Birth Order

Sandra describes to her mother what happened in a conflict with her sister:

> We had just come home from the ball game. I sat down on the sofa next to the light so I could read. Sally [the sister] said, "Get up. I was sitting there first. I just got up for a second to get a drink." I told her I was not going to get up and that I didn't see her name on the chair. I got mad and started pushing her. Her drink spilled all over her. Then she got really mad; she shoved me against the wall, hitting and clawing at me. I managed to grab a handful of hair.

At this point, Sally comes into the room and begins to tell her side of the story. Sandra interrupts, "Mother, you always take her side." Sound familiar? Any of you who have grown up with siblings probably have a rich memory of aggressive, hostile interchanges; but sibling relationships have many pleasant, caring moments as well. Children's sibling relationships include helping, sharing, teaching, fighting, and playing. Children can act as emotional supports, rivals, and communication partners (Cicirelli, 1994; Eisenberg, Wolfe & Mick, 1993). More than 80 percent of American children have one or more siblings (brothers or sisters). Because there are so many possible sibling combinations, it is difficult to generalize about sibling influences. Among the factors to be considered are the number of siblings, age of siblings, birth order, age spacing, sex of siblings, and whether sibling relationships are different from parent-child relationships.

Critical Thinking

Sibling rivalry is common in families. What aspects of family life are likely to increase sibling rivalry? What techniques could be used to reduce sibling conflict?

Is sibling interaction different from parent-child interaction? There is some evidence that it is. Observations indicate that children interact more positively and in more varied ways with their parents than with their siblings (Baskett & Johnson, 1982). Children also follow their parents' dictates more than those of their siblings, and they behave more negatively and punitively with their siblings than with their parents.

In some instances, siblings may be stronger socializing influences on the child than parents are (Cicirelli, 1977). Someone close in age to the child—such as a sibling—may be able to understand the child's problems and be able to communicate more effectively than parents can. In dealing with peers, coping with difficult teachers, and discussing taboo subjects such as sex, siblings may be more influential in the socialization process than parents.

> *Big sisters are the crab grass in the lawn of life.*
> —Charles Schulz, *Peanuts*

Birth order is a special interest of sibling researchers. When differences in birth order are found, they usually are explained by variations in interactions with parents and siblings associated with the unique experiences of being in a particular position in the family. This is especially true in the case of the firstborn child (Murphy, 1993; Teti & others, 1993). The oldest child is the only one who does not have to share parental love and affection with other siblings—until another sibling comes along. An infant requires more attention than an older child; this means that the firstborn sibling now gets less attention than before the newborn arrived. Does this result in conflict between parents and the firstborn? In one research study, mothers became more negative, coercive, and restraining and played less with the firstborn following the birth of a second child (Dunn & Kendrick, 1982). Even though a new infant requires more attention from parents than does an older child, an especially intense relationship is often maintained between parents and firstborns throughout the life cycle. Parents have higher expectations for firstborn children than for later-born children; they put more pressure on them for achievement and responsibility, and interfere more with their activities (Rothbart, 1971).

Birth order is also associated with variations in sibling relationships. The oldest sibling is expected to exercise self-control and show responsibility in interacting with younger siblings. When the oldest sibling is jealous or hostile, parents often protect the younger sibling. The oldest sibling is more dominant, competent, and powerful than the younger siblings; the oldest sibling is also expected to assist and teach younger siblings. Indeed, researchers have shown that older siblings are both more antagonistic—hitting, kicking, and biting—and more nurturant toward their younger siblings than vice versa (Abramovitch & others, 1986). There is also something unique about same-sex sibling relationships. Aggression and dominance occur more in same-sex relationships than in opposite-sex sibling relationships (Minnett, Vandell, & Santrock, 1983).

Given the differences in family dynamics involved in birth order, it is not surprising that firstborns and later-borns have different characteristics. Firstborn children are more adult oriented, helpful, conforming, anxious, and self-controlled than their siblings. Parents give more attention to first-borns and this is related to first-borns' nurturant behavior (Stanhope & Corter, 1993). Parental demands and high standards established for firstborns result in these children excelling in academic and professional endeavors. Firstborns are overrepresented in *Who's Who* and Rhodes scholars, for example. However, some of the same pressures placed on firstborns for high achievement may be the reason they also have more guilt, anxiety, difficulty in coping with stressful situations, and higher admission to child guidance clinics.

What is the only child like? The popular conception is that the only child is a "spoiled brat" with such undesirable characteristics as dependency, lack of self-control, and self-centered behavior. But researchers present a more positive portrayal of the only child, who often is achievement oriented and displays

The one-child family is becoming much more common in China because of the strong motivation to limit population growth in the People's Republic of China. The policy is still new, and its effects on children have not been fully examined.

FIGURE 9.2

Percentage of children under 18 living with one parent in 1980 and 1991. Shown here is the breakdown for Black, White, and Hispanic families. Note the substantially higher percentage of Black single-parent families.

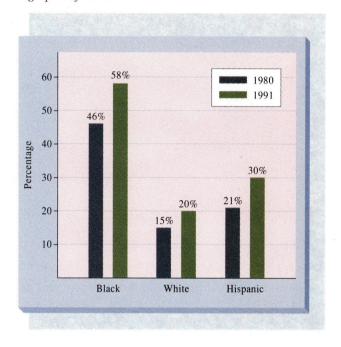

a desirable personality, especially in comparison to later-borns and children from large families (Falbo & Polit, 1986; Falbo & Poston, 1993; Thomas, Coffman, & Kipp, 1993).

So far our consideration of birth-order effects suggests that birth order might be a strong predictor of behavior. However, an increasing number of family researchers believe that birth order has been overdramatized and overemphasized. The critics argue that, when all of the factors that influence behavior are considered, birth order itself shows limited ability to predict behavior. Consider just sibling relationships alone. They vary not only in birth order, but also in number of siblings, age of siblings, age spacing of siblings, and sex of siblings.

Consider also the temperament of siblings. Researchers have found that siblings' temperamental traits ("easy" and "difficult," for example), as well as differential treatment of siblings by parents, influence how siblings get along (Stocker & Dunn, 1991). Siblings with "easy" temperaments who are treated in relatively equal ways by parents tend to get along with each other the best, whereas siblings with "difficult" temperaments, or whose parents have given one of them preferential treatment, get along the worst.

Beyond temperament and differential treatment of siblings by parents, think about some of the other important factors in children's lives that influence their behavior beyond birth order. They include heredity, models of competency or incompetency that parents present to children on a daily basis, peer influences, school influences, socioeconomic factors, sociohistorical factors, cultural variations, and so on. When someone says firstborns are always like this, but last-borns are always like that, you now know that they are making overly simplistic

statements that do not adequately take into account the complexity of influences on a child's behavior. Keep in mind, though, that, although birth order itself may not be a good predictor of adolescent behavior, sibling relationships and interaction are important dimensions of family processes.

The Changing Family in a Changing Society

Children are growing up in a greater variety of family structures than ever before in history. Many mothers spend the greatest part of their day away from their children, even their infants. More than one of every two mothers with a child under the age of 5 is in the labor force; more than two of every three with a child from 6 to 17 years of age is. And the increasing number of children growing up in single-parent families is staggering. As shown in figure 9.2, a substantial increase in the number of children under the age of 18 who live in a single-parent family occurred between 1980 and 1991. Also note that a much higher percentage of Black families than White families or Hispanic families are single-parent families. If current trends continue, by the year 2000 one in every four children will also have lived a portion of their lives in a stepparent family. And, as we saw in chapter 7, fathers perform more child-rearing duties than in the past.

Working Mothers

Because household operations have become more efficient and family size has decreased in America, it is not certain that children with mothers working outside the home actually receive

LIFE-SPAN PRACTICAL KNOWLEDGE 9.3

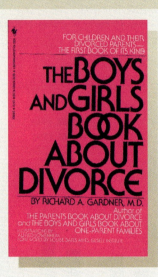

The Boys and Girls Book About Divorce

(1983) by Richard Gardner.
Northvale, NJ: Jason Aronson.

The Boys and Girls Book About Divorce is written for children to help them cope with their parents' separation and divorce. Author Richard Gardner is a child psychiatrist who is on the faculty of Columbia University College of Physicians and Surgeons. Most of what Gardner tells children comes from his therapy experiences with children from divorced homes. He talks directly to children about their feelings after the divorce, who is and is not to blame for the divorce, parents' love for their children, how to handle their angry feelings, and their fear of being left alone and abandoned. Then he tells children how to get along better with their divorced mother and father, as well as many other challenging and emotional circumstances the children are likely to face.

The Boys and Girls Book About Divorce is an excellent book and is most appropriate for children 10 to 12 years or older. A good book for younger children whose parents divorce is *Dinosaurs Divorce* (1986) by Laurene Brown and Marc Brown.

---

less attention than children in the past whose mothers were not employed. Outside employment—at least for mothers with school-age children—may simply be filling time previously taken up by added household burdens and more children. It also cannot be assumed that if the mother did not go to work, the child would benefit from the time freed up by streamlined household operations and smaller families. Mothering does not always have a positive effect on the child. The educated, nonworking mother may overinvest her energies in her children, fostering an excess of worry and discouraging the child's independence. In such situations, the mother may give more parenting than the child can profitably handle.

As Lois Hoffman (1989) comments, maternal employment is a part of modern life. It is not an aberrant aspect of it, but a response to other social changes, one that meets needs that cannot be met by the previous family ideal of a full-time mother and homemaker. Not only does it meet the parent's needs, but in many ways it may be a pattern better suited to socializing children for the adult roles they will occupy. This is especially true for daughters, but it is also true for sons. The broader range of emotions and skills that each parent presents is more consistent with this adult role. Just as his father shares the breadwinning role and the child-rearing role with his mother, so the son, too, will be more likely to share these roles. The rigid gender-role stereotyping perpetuated by the divisions of labor in the traditional family is not appropriate for the demands that will be made on children of either sex as adults. The needs of the growing child require the mother to loosen her hold on the child, and this task may be easier for the working woman whose job is an additional source of identity and self-esteem. Overall, researchers have found no detrimental effects of maternal employment on children's development (Gottfried, 1993; Richards & Duckett, 1994). Working and non-working mothers have similar attitudes toward parenting (O'Brien, 1993).

A common experience of working mothers (and working fathers) is feeling guilty about being away from their children. The guilt may be triggered by parents missing their child, worrying that their child is missing them, being concerned about the implications of working (such as whether the child is receiving good child-care), and worrying about the long-term effects of working (such as whether they are jeopardizing the child's future). To reduce guilt, the guilt needs to be acknowledged. Pediatrician T. Berry Brazelton (1983) believes that parents respond to guilt either by admitting it and working through it or by denying it and rationalizing it away. The latter tendency is not recommended. Working parents' guilt can also be reduced if they begin paying closer attention to how their children are doing.

Effects of Divorce on Children

Two main models have been proposed to explain how divorce affects children's development: the father-absence model and the multiple-factor model. The **family structure model** *states that any differences in children from different family structures are due to the family structure variations, such as the father's being absent in one set of the families.* However, family structure (such as father-present versus father-absent) is only one of many factors that influence children's development and adjustment in single-parent families. Even when researchers compare the development of children in more precise family structures (such as divorced versus widowed), there are many factors other than family structure that need to be examined to explain the child's development. As we see next, a second model of the effects of divorce on children's development goes beyond the overly simplistic family structure model.

The **multiple-factor model of divorce** *takes into account the complexity of the divorce context and examines a number of influences on the child's development, including not only family structure, but also the strengths and weaknesses of the child prior to the divorce, the*

LIFE-SPAN PRACTICAL KNOWLEDGE 9.4

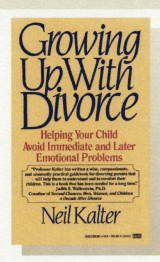

Growing Up With Divorce

(1990) by Neil Kalter. New York: Free Press.

Growing Up With Divorce is written for divorced parents and provides them with information to help their children avoid emotional problems. Neil Kalter is a child clinical psychologist who is director of the Center for the Child and Family at the University of Michigan. Kalter offers practical strategies for parents to help their children cope with the anxiety, anger, and confusion that can appear immediately after the separation or divorce, or that may develop after a number of years. Separate problems and concerns of children of different ages and sexes at each stage of divorce are portrayed. In a recent national survey of self-help books, this was the highest rated book in the divorce category for parents. Divorce expert Robert Weiss praised the book and said that parents in any divorced circumstance can benefit from it. Well-known authority on divorce Judith Wallerstein advises divorced parents that Kalter's book is a treasure of valuable advice for comforting their children.

nature of the events surrounding the divorce itself, the type of custody involved, visitation patterns, socioeconomic status, and postdivorce family functioning. Researchers are finding that the availability and use of support systems (relatives, friends, housekeepers), an ongoing positive relationship between the custodial parent and the ex-spouse, authoritative parenting, financial resources, and the child's competencies at the time of the divorce are important factors in how successfully the adolescent adapts to the divorce of her or his parents (Barber & others, 1992; Block, Block, & Gjerde, 1986; Ceballo & Olson, 1993; Gunnoe, 1994; Hetherington, 1993, 1994, in press; Hetherington & Clingempeel, 1992; Miller, Kliewer, & Burkeman, 1993; Santrock & Warshak, 1986; Wallerstein, 1989). Thus, just as the family structure factor of birth order by itself is not a good predictor of children's development, neither is the family structure factor of father absence. In both circumstances—birth order and father absence—there are many other factors that always have to be taken into consideration when explaining the child's development is at issue. Let's further examine what some of those complex factors are in the case of children whose parents divorce.

Age and Developmental Changes

The age of the child at the time of the divorce needs to be considered. Young children's responses to divorce are mediated by their limited cognitive and social competencies, their dependency on their parents, and possibly inferior day care (Hetherington, Hagan, & Anderson, 1989). The cognitive immaturity that creates considerable anxiety for children who are young at the time of their parents' divorce may benefit the children over time. Ten years after the divorce of their parents, adolescents had few memories of their own earlier fears and suffering or their parents' conflict (Wallerstein, Corbin, & Lewis, 1988). Nonetheless, approximately one-third of these children continued to express anger about not being able to grow up in an intact, never-divorced family. Those who were adolescents at the time of their parents' divorce were more likely to remember the conflict and stress surrounding the divorce some 10 years later, in their early adult years. They, too, expressed disappointment at not being able to grow up in an intact family and wondered if their life would not have been better if they had been able to do so. And in one study, adolescents who experienced the divorce of their parents during adolescence were more likely to have drug problems than adolescents whose parents were divorced when the adolescents were children or than adolescents living in continuously married families (Needle, Su, & Doherty, 1990).

Evaluations of children and adolescents 6 years after the divorce of their parents by developmental psychologist E. Mavis Hetherington and her colleagues (1989) found that living with a mother who did not remarry had long-term negative effects on boys, with deleterious outcomes appearing consistently from kindergarten to adolescence. No negative effects on preadolescent girls were found. However, at the onset of adolescence, early-maturing girls from divorced families engaged in frequent conflict with their mothers, behaved in noncompliant ways, had lower self-esteem, and experienced more problems in heterosexual relationships.

Conflict

Many separations and divorces are highly emotional affairs that immerse the child in conflict. Conflict is a critical aspect of family functioning that often outweighs the influence of family structure on the child's development. For example, children in divorced families low in conflict function better than children in intact, never-divorced families high in conflict (Black & Pedro-Carroll, 1993; Rutter, 1983; Wallerstein, 1989). Although the escape from conflict that divorce provides may be a positive benefit for children, in the year immediately following the divorce, the conflict does not decline but increases. At this time, children—especially boys—in divorced families show more adjustment problems than children in intact families with both parents present. During the first year after the divorce, the quality of parenting the child experiences is often poor; parents seem to be preoccupied with their own needs and adjustment—experiencing anger, depression, confusion, and emotional instability—which inhibits their ability to respond sensitively to the child's needs. During the second year after the divorce, parents are more effective in their child-rearing duties, especially with daughters (Hetherington, in press; Hetherington, Anderson, & Hagan, 1991; Hetherington, Cox, & Cox, 1982; Hetherington, Hagan, & Anderson, 1989).

Sex of the Child and the Nature of Custody

The sex of the child and the sex of the custodial parent are important considerations in evaluating the effects of divorce on children. One research study directly compared 6- to 11-year-old children living in father-custody and mother-custody families (Santrock & Warshak, 1979, 1986). On a number of measures, including videotaped observations of parent-child interaction, children living with the same-sex parent were more socially competent—happier, more independent, with higher self-esteem, and more mature—than children living with the opposite-sex parent. Some researchers have recently found support for the same-sex parent-child custodial arrangement (Camara & Resnick, 1988; Furstenberg, 1988), while others have found that, regardless of their sex, adolescents are better adjusted in mother-custody or joint-custody families than in father-custody families (Buchanan, Maccoby, & Dornbusch, 1992).

Critical Thinking

Imagine you are a judge in a custodial dispute. What are some of the key factors you would consider in awarding custody?

Conclusions About Children in Divorced Families

In sum, large numbers of children are growing up in divorced families. Most children initially experience considerable stress when their parents divorce, and they are at risk for developing problem behaviors. However, divorce can also remove children from conflicted marriages. Many children emerge from divorce as competent individuals. In recent years, developmentalists have moved away from the view that single-parent families are atypical or pathological, focusing more on the diversity of children's responses to divorce and the factors that facilitate or disrupt children's development and adjustment (Hetherington, Hagan, & Anderson, 1989). To read about parenting recommendations for communicating more effectively with children about divorce, turn to Perspectives on Parenting and Education 9.1.

Depressed Parents

Although depression has traditionally been perceived as a problem of the individual, today we believe that this view is limited. Researchers have found an interdependence between depressed

persons and their social contexts—this is especially true in the case of parents' depression and children's adjustment (Campbell & others, 1993; Downey & Coyne, 1990; Goodman & others, 1993; Kaslow, Deering, & Racusin, 1994; Sameroff & others, 1993). Depression is a highly prevalent disorder—so prevalent it has been called the common cold of mental disorders. It occurs often in the lives of women of child-bearing age—about 8%, a figure that rises to 12% for women who have recently given birth (O'Hara, 1986). As a result, large numbers of children are exposed to depressed parents.

Research on the children of depressed parents clearly documents that depression in parents is associated with problems of adjustment and disorders, especially depression, in their children (Downey & Coyne, 1990; Radke-Yarrow & others, 1992). Depressed mothers show lower rates of behavior and show constricted affect, adopt less-effortful control strategies with their children, and sometimes act hostile and negative toward them as well. In considering the effects of parental depression on children it is important to evaluate the social context of the family (Hammen, 1993). For example, marital discord and stress may precede, precipitate, or co-occur with maternal depression. In such instances, it may be marital turmoil that is the key factor that contributes to children's adjustment problems, not parental depression per se (Gelfand, Teti, & Fox, 1992).

Thus far, we have discussed a number of ideas about family relationships in early childhood. A summary of these ideas is presented in concept table 9.1. We now turn to the intriguing world of children's peer relations and play.

PEER RELATIONS

As children grow older, peer relations consume increasing amounts of their time. What is the function of a child's peer group? Although children spend increasingly more time with peers as they become older, are there ways in which family and peer relations are coordinated?

Peer Group Functions

Peers *are children of about the same age or maturity level.* Same-age peer interaction fills a unique role in our culture (Hartup, 1976). Age grading would occur even if schools were not age graded and children were left alone to determine the composition of their own societies. One of the most important functions of the peer group is to provide a source of information and comparison about the world outside the family. Children receive feedback about their abilities from their peer group. Children evaluate what they do in terms of whether it is better than, as good as, or worse than what other children do. It is hard to do this at home because siblings are usually older or younger.

Are peers necessary for development? When peer monkeys who have been reared together are separated, they become depressed and less advanced socially (Suomi, Harlow, & Domek, 1970). The human development literature contains a classic example of the importance of peers in social development. Anna Freud (Freud & Dann, 1951) studied six children

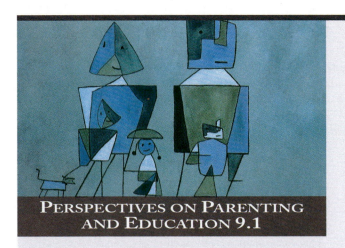

PERSPECTIVES ON PARENTING AND EDUCATION 9.1

Parenting Recommendations: Communicating With Children About Divorce

Ellen Galinsky and Judy David (1988) developed a number of guidelines for communicating with young children about divorce.

Explaining the Separation

As soon as the daily activities in the home make it obvious that one parent is leaving, tell the children. If possible, both parents should be present when the children are made aware of the separation to come. The reasons for the separation are very difficult for young children to understand. No matter what parents tell children, children can find reasons to argue against the separation. A child may say something like, "If you don't love each other anymore, you need to start trying harder." One set of parents told their 4-year-old, "We both love you. We will both always love you and take care of you, but we aren't going to live in the same house anymore. Daddy is moving to an apartment near the stores where we shop." It is extremely important for parents to tell the children who will take care of them and to describe the specific arrangements for seeing the other parent.

Explaining That the Separation Is Not the Child's Fault

Young children often believe their parents' separation or divorce is their own fault. Therefore, it is important to tell children that they are not the cause of the separation. Parents need to repeat this a number of times.

Explaining That It May Take Time to Feel Better

It is helpful to tell young children that it's normal to not feel good about what is happening, and that lots of other children feel this way when their parents become separated. It is also okay for divorced parents to share some of their emotions with children, by saying something like, "I'm having a hard time since the separation, just like you, but I know it's going to get better after a while." Such statements are best kept brief, and should not criticize the other parent.

Keeping the Door Open for Further Discussion

Tell your children to come to you anytime they want to talk about the separation. It is healthy for children to get their pent-up emotions out in the open for discussion with their parents, and to learn that the parents are willing to listen to their feelings and fears.

Providing As Much Continuity As Possible

The less children's worlds are disrupted by the separation, the easier their transition to a single-parent family will be. This means maintaining as much as possible the rules already in place. Children need parents who care enough to not only give them warmth and nurturance, but also set reasonable limits. If the custodial parent has to move to a new home, it is important to preserve as much of what is familiar to the child as possible. In one family, the child helped to arrange her new room exactly as it had been prior to the divorce. If children must leave friends behind, it is important for parents to help the children stay in touch by phone or by letter. Keeping the child busy and involved in the new setting can also keep their minds off of their stressful thoughts about the separation.

Providing Support for Your Children and Yourself

After a divorce or separation, parents are as important to children as before the divorce or separation. Divorced parents need to provide children with as much support as possible. Parents function best when other people are available to give them support as adults and as parents. Divorced parents can find people who provide practical help and with whom they can talk about their problems. Too often divorced parents criticize themselves and say they feel that they don't deserve help. One divorced parent commented, "I've made a mess of my life. I don't deserve anybody's help." However, seeking out others for support and feedback about problems can make the transition to a single-parent family more bearable.

CONCEPT TABLE 9.1

Families

Concept	Processes/Related Ideas	Characteristics/Description
Parenting styles	The four major categories	Authoritarian, authoritative, permissive-indifferent, and permissive-indulgent are four main categories of parenting. Authoritative parenting is associated with children's social competence more than the other styles.
Adapting parenting to developmental changes in the child	Its nature	Parents need to adapt their interaction strategies as the child grows older, using less physical manipulation and more reasoning in the process.
Cultural, social class, and ethnic variations in families	Cross-cultural and social class comparisons	Authoritative parenting is the most common child-rearing pattern around the world. Working-class and low-income parents place a higher value on external characteristics, middle-class parents place a higher value on internal characteristics, and these social classes vary in their child-rearing patterns.
	Ethnic variations	Ethnic minority families differ from White American families in their size, structure, and composition, their reliance on kinship networks, and their levels of income and education.
Sibling relationships and birth order	Sibling relationships	More than 80 percent of American children have one or more siblings. Siblings interact with each other in more negative, less positive, and less varied ways than parents and children interact. In some cases, siblings are stronger socializing influences than parents.
	Birth order	The relationship of the firstborn child and parents seems to be especially close and demanding, which may account for the greater achievement orientation and anxiety in firstborn children. Some critics argue that birth order is not a good predictor of behavior.
The changing family	Working mothers	A mother's working full-time outside the home can have both positive and negative effects on the child; there is no indication that long-term effects are negative overall.
	Divorce	Two main models of divorce effects have been proposed: the family structure model and the multiple-factor model. The family structure model that emphasizes only family structure effects is overly simplistic. The contemporary multiple-factor model takes into account the complexity of the divorce context, including conflict and postdivorce family functioning. Among the important factors in understanding the effects of divorce on children are age and developmental changes, conflict, sex of the child, and the nature of custody. In recent years, developmentalists have moved away from the model of single-parents as atypical or pathological, focusing more on the diversity of children's responses to divorce and the factors that facilitate or disrupt the adjustment of children in these family circumstances.
Depressed parents	Effects on children	Depression is especially prominent in women of child-bearing age. Depression in parents is associated with problems of adjustment and disorders, especially depression, in their children. In considering the role of depressed parents in children's problems, it is important to evaluate the social context of the family, especially marital discord.

FIGURE 9.3

Peer aggression: the influence of the relationship history of each peer.

from different families who banded together after their parents were killed in World War II. Intensive peer attachment was observed; the children formed a tightly knit group, dependent on one another and aloof with outsiders. Even though deprived of parental care, they neither became delinquent nor developed serious mental disorders.

Thus, good peer relations may be necessary for normal social development. Social isolation, or the inability to "plug in" to a social network, is linked with many problems and disorders

Peers are children who are of about the same age or maturity level. From the peer group, children receive feedback about their abilities and they learn about a world outside of their family.

ranging from delinquency and problem drinking to depression (Kupersmidt & Coie, 1990; Simons, Conger, & Wu, 1992). In one investigation, poor peer relations in childhood was associated with a tendency to drop out of school and delinquent behavior in adolescence (Roff, Sells, & Golden, 1972). In another investigation, harmonious peer relations in adolescence was related to positive mental health at midlife (Hightower, 1990).

The Distinct but Coordinated Worlds of Parent-Child and Peer Relations

What are some of the similarities and differences between peer and parent-child relationships? Children touch, smile, frown, and vocalize when they interact with parents and peers. However, rough-and-tumble play occurs mainly with other children, not with adults, and, in times of stress, children often move toward their parents rather than toward their peers.

A number of theorists and researchers argue that parent-child relationships serve as emotional bases for exploring and enjoying peer relations (Allen, Bell, & Boykin, 1994; Brown, 1994; Crockenberg & Lourie, 1993; Leonoff, 1993; Lollis, 1993; Mize & others, 1993). In one study, the relationship history of each peer helped to predict the nature of peer interaction (Olweus, 1980; see figure 9.3). Some boys were highly aggressive ("bullies") and other boys were the recipients of aggression ("whipping boys") throughout their preschool years. The bullies and the whipping boys had distinctive relationship histories. The bullies' parents frequently rejected

LIFE-SPAN PRACTICAL KNOWLEDGE 9.5

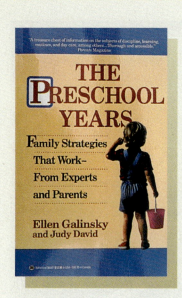

The Preschool Years

(1988) by Ellen Galinsky and Judy David. New York: Times Books.

The Preschool Years describes normal child development in the 3- to 5-year-old age period and provides recommendations to parents for how to cope with specific problems in this period of development. Author Ellen Galinsky is co-president of the Family and Work Institute in New York City, and she is a former president of the National Association for the Education of Young Children. Coauthor Judy David is Galinsky's research associate.

The *Preschool Years* presents a wealth of information about children's development in early childhood. The book is an excellent resource guide for children's growth and development during this time frame. The authors sort through what researchers have found out about young children's development and make practical suggestions for parents based on the research. They present a wide range of helpful strategies for solving children's everyday problems in the preschool years. All of the chapters are full of examples of young children's interchanges with people, including parents, teachers, and peers. The chapters focus on discipline, learning and growth, at-home and away-from-home routines, happy and sad times, family relationships, family work, work and family life, and schools and child care. This is an outstanding book for the parents of preschool children.

them, were authoritarian, and were permissive about their sons' aggression, and the bullies' families were characterized by discord. By contrast, the whipping boys' parents were anxious and overprotective, taking special care to have their sons avoid aggression. The well-adjusted boys in the study were much less likely to be involved in aggressive peer interchanges than were the bullies and whipping boys. Their parents did not sanction aggression, and the parents' responsive involvement with their sons promoted the development of self-assertion rather than aggression or wimpish behavior.

Parents also may model or coach their children in the ways of relating to peers. In one investigation, parents indicated they recommended specific strategies to their children regarding peer relations (Rubin & Sloman, 1984). For example, parents told their children how to mediate disputes or how to become less shy with others. They also encouraged them to be tolerant and to resist peer pressure. In another study, parents who frequently initiated peer contacts for their preschool children had children who were more accepted by their peers and who had higher levels of prosocial behavior (Ladd & Hart, 1992).

A key aspect of peer relations can be traced to basic life-style decisions by parents (Cooper & Ayers-Lopez, 1985). Parents' choices of neighborhoods, churches, schools, and their own friends influence the pool from which their children might select possible friends. For example, the chosen schools can lead to specific grouping policies, as well as particular academic and extracurricular activities. In turn, such factors affect which students their children meet, their purposes in interacting, and eventually who become friends. Classrooms in which teachers encourage more cooperative peer interchanges, for instance, have fewer isolates.

In sum, parent-child and peer worlds are coordinated but distinct. Earlier we indicated that rough-and-tumble play occurs mainly with other children and not in parent-child interaction, and that children often turn to parents, not peers, for support in times of stress. Peer relations also are more likely to consist of interaction on a much more equal basis than are parent-child relations. Because parents have greater knowledge and authority, children must often learn how to conform to rules and regulations laid down by parents. With peers, children learn to formulate and assert their own opinions, appreciate the perspective of peers, cooperatively negotiate solutions to disagreements, and evolve standards of conduct that are mutually acceptable.

PLAY

An extensive amount of peer interaction during childhood involves play. But although peer interaction can involve play, social play is but one type of play. Just what is play? **Play** *is a pleasurable activity that is engaged in for its own sake.* Our coverage of play includes its functions, Parten's classic study of play, and types of play.

Play's Functions

Play is essential to the young child's health. As today's children move into the twenty-first century and continue to experience pressure in their lives, play becomes even more crucial. Play increases affiliation with peers, releases tension, advances cognitive development, increases exploration, and provides a safe haven in which to engage in potentially dangerous behavior. Play increases the probability that children will converse and interact with each other. During this interaction, children practice the roles they will assume later in life.

For Freud and Erikson, play was an especially useful form of human adjustment, helping the child master anxieties and conflicts. Because tensions are relieved in play, the child can cope with life's problems. Play permits the child to work off excess physical energy and to release pent-up tensions. **Play therapy** *allows the child to work off frustrations and is a medium through which the therapist can analyze the child's conflicts and ways of coping with them. Children may feel less threatened and be more likely to express their true feelings in the context of play.*

Piaget (1962) saw play as a medium that advances children's cognitive development. At the same time, he said that children's cognitive development *constrains* the way they play. Play permits children to practice their competencies and acquired skills in a relaxed, pleasurable way. Piaget believed that cognitive structures need to be exercised, and play provides the perfect setting for this exercise. For example, children who have just learned to add or multiply begin to play with numbers in different ways as they perfect these operations, laughing as they do so.

Vygotsky (1962), whose developmental theory was discussed in chapter 8, also believed that play is an excellent setting for cognitive development. He was especially interested in the symbolic and make-believe aspects of play, as when a child substitutes a stick for a horse and rides the stick as if it were a horse (Smolucha, 1989). For young children, the imaginary situation is real. Parents should encourage such imaginary play, because it advances the child's cognitive development, especially creative thought (Arman-Nolley, 1989).

> *And that park grew up with me; that small world widened as I learned its secret boundaries, as I discovered new refuges in the woods and jungles: hidden homes and lairs for the multitudes of imagination, for cowboys and Indians. . . . I used to dawdle on half holidays along the bent and devon-facing seashore, hoping for gold watches or the skull of a sheep or a message in a bottle to be washed up by the tide.*
>
> —Dylan Thomas

Daniel Berlyne (1960) described play as being exciting and pleasurable in itself because it satisfies the exploratory drive each of us possesses. This drive involves curiosity and a desire for information about something new or unusual. Play is a means whereby children can safely explore and seek out new information—something they might not otherwise do. Play encourages this exploratory behavior by offering children the possibilities of novelty, complexity, uncertainty, surprise, and incongruity.

Parten's Classic Study of Play

Many years ago, Mildred Parten (1932) developed an elaborate classification of children's play. Based on observations of children in free play at nursery school, Parten arrived at these play categories:

1. **Unoccupied play** *occurs when the child is not engaging in play as it is commonly understood and may stand in one spot, look around the room, or perform random movements that do not seem to have a goal.* In most nursery schools, unoccupied play is less frequent than other forms of play.
2. **Solitary play** *occurs when the child plays alone and independently of others.* The child seems engrossed in the activity and does not care much about anything else that is happening. Two- and 3-year-olds engage more frequently in solitary play than older preschoolers do.
3. **Onlooker play** *occurs when the child watches other children play.* The child may talk with other children and ask questions but does not enter into their play behavior. The child's active interest in other children's play distinguishes onlooker play from unoccupied play.
4. **Parallel play** *occurs when the child plays separately from others, but with toys like those the others are using or in a manner that mimics their play.* The older children are, the less frequently they engage in this type of play, although even older preschool children engage in parallel play quite often.
5. **Associative play** *occurs when play involves social interaction with little or no organization.* In this type of play children seem to be more interested in each other than in the tasks they are performing. Borrowing or lending toys and following or leading one another in line are examples of associative play.
6. **Cooperative play** *involves social interaction in a group with a sense of group identity and organized activity.* Children's formal games, competition aimed at winning, and groups formed by the teacher for doing things together are examples of cooperative play. Cooperative play is the prototype for the games of middle childhood. Little cooperative play is seen in the preschool years.

Types of Play

Parten's categories represent one way of thinking about the different types of play. However, today researchers and practitioners who are involved with children's play believe other types of play are important in children's development. Whereas

Parten's categories emphasize the role of play in the child's social world, the contemporary perspective on play emphasizes both the cognitive and the social aspects of play. Among the most widely studied types of children's play today are sensorimotor/practice play, pretense/symbolic play, social play, constructive play, and games (Bergin, 1988). We consider each of these types of play in turn.

Sensorimotor/Practice Play

Sensorimotor play *is behavior engaged in by infants to derive pleasure from exercising their existing sensorimotor schemas.* The development of sensorimotor play follows Piaget's description of sensorimotor thought, which we discussed in chapter 8. Infants initially engage in exploratory and playful visual and motor transactions in the second quarter of the first year of life. By 9 months of age, infants begin to select novel objects for exploration and play, especially those that are responsive, such as toys that make noise or bounce. By 12 months of age, infants enjoy making things work and exploring cause and effect. At this point in development, children like toys that perform when they act on them.

In the second year, infants begin to understand the social meaning of objects, and their play reflects this awareness. And 2-year-olds may distinguish between exploratory play that is interesting but not humorous, and "playful" play, which has incongruous and humorous dimensions (McGhee, 1984). For example, a 2-year-old might "drink" from a shoe or call a dog a "cow." When 2-year-olds find these deliberate incongruities funny, they are beginning to show evidence of symbolic play and the ability to play with ideas.

Practice play *involves the repetition of behavior when new skills are being learned or when physical or mental mastery and coordination of skills are required for games or sports. Sensorimotor play, which often involves practice play, is primarily confined to infancy, while practice play can be engaged in throughout life.* During the preschool years, children often engage in play that involves practicing various skills. Estimates indicate that practice play constitutes about one-third of the preschool child's play activities, but less than one-sixth of the elementary school child's play activities (Rubin, Fein, & Vandenberg, 1983). Practice play contributes to the development of coordinated motor skills needed for later game playing. While practice play declines in the elementary school years, practice play activities such as running, jumping, sliding, twirling, and throwing balls or other objects are frequently observed on the playgrounds at elementary schools. These activities appear similar to the earlier practice play of the preschool years, but practice play in the elementary school years differs from earlier practice play because much of it is ends rather than means related. That is, elementary school children often engage in practice play for the purpose of improving motor skills needed to compete in games or sports.

Pretense/Symbolic Play

Pretense/symbolic play *occurs when the child transforms the physical environment into a symbol* (DeHart & Smith, 1991; Fein, 1986; Howes, Unger & Seidner, 1989; Rogers & Sawyers, 1988). Between 9 and 30 months of age, children increase their use of objects in symbolic play. They learn to transform objects—substituting them for other objects and acting toward them as if they were these other objects. For example, a preschool child treats a table as if it is a car and says, "I'm fixing the car," as he grabs a leg of the table.

Many experts on play consider the preschool years the "golden age" of symbolic/pretense play that is dramatic or sociodramatic in nature (Bergin, 1988; Singer & Singer, 1988). This type of make-believe play often appears at about 18 months of age and reaches a peak at 4 to 5 years of age, then gradually declines. In the early elementary school years, children's interests often shift to games.

Catherine Garvey (1977) has spent many years observing young children's play. She indicates that three elements are found in almost all of the pretend play she has observed: props, plot, and roles. Children use objects as *props* in their pretend play. Children can pretend to drink from a real cup or from a seashell. They can even create a make-believe cup from thin air, if nothing else is available. Most pretend play also has a story line, though the *plot* may be quite simple. Pretend play themes often reflect what children see going on in their lives, as when they play family, school, or doctor. Fantasy play can also take its theme from a story children have heard, or a show they have seen. In pretend play, children try out many different *roles*. Some roles, like mother or teacher, are derived from reality. Other roles, like cowgirls or Superman, come from fantasy.

Social Play

Social play *is play that involves social interaction with peers.* Parten's categories, which we described earlier, are oriented toward social play. Social play with peers increases dramatically during the preschool years. In addition to general social play with peers and group pretense or sociodramatic play, another form of social play is rough-and-tumble play. The movement patterns of rough-and-tumble play are often similar to those of hostile behavior (running, chasing, wrestling, jumping, falling, hitting), but in rough-and-tumble play these behaviors are accompanied by signals such as laughter, exaggerated movement, and open rather than closed hands that indicate that this is play (Bateson, 1956).

Constructive Play

Constructive play *combines sensorimotor/practice repetitive activity with symbolic representation of ideas. Constructive play occurs when children engage in self-regulated creation or construction of a product or a problem solution.* Constructive play increases in the preschool years as symbolic play increases and sensorimotor play decreases. In the preschool years, some practice play is replaced by constructive play. For example, instead of moving their fingers around and around in finger paint (practice play), children are more likely to draw the outline of a house or a person in the paint (constructive play). Some researchers have found that constructive play is the most common type of play during the preschool years (Hetherington, Cox, & Cox, 1979; Rubin, Maioni, & Hornung, 1976). Constructive play is also a frequent form of play in the elementary school years, both in and out of the classroom. Constructive play is one of the few playlike activities allowed in work-centered classrooms. For example, having children create a play about a social studies topic involves constructive play. Whether such activities are considered play by children usually depends on whether they get to choose whether to do it (it is play) or whether the teacher imposes it (it is not play), and also whether it is enjoyable (it is play) or not (it is not play) (King, 1982).

Constructive play can also be used in the elementary school years to foster academic skill learning, thinking skills, and problem solving. Many educators plan classroom activities that include humor, encourage playing with ideas, and promote creativity (Bergin, 1988). Educators also often support the performance of plays, the writing of imaginative stories, the expression of artistic abilities, and the playful exploration of computers and other technological equipment. However, distinctions between work and play frequently become blurred in the elementary school classroom.

Games

Games *are activities engaged in for pleasure that include rules and often competition with one or more individuals.* Preschool children may begin to participate in social game play that involves simple rules of reciprocity and turn taking, but games take on a much more salient role in the lives of elementary school children. In one investigation, the highest incidence of game playing occurred between 10 and 12 years of age (Eiferman, 1971). After age 12, games decline in popularity, often being replaced by practice play, conversations, and organized sports (Bergin, 1988).

In the elementary years, games feature the meaningfulness of a challenge (Eiferman, 1971). This challenge is present if two or more children have the skills required to play and understand the rules of the game. Among the types of games children engage in are steady or constant games, such as tag, which are played consistently; recurrent or cyclical games, such as marbles or hopscotch, which seem to follow cycles of popularity and decline; sporadic games, which are rarely played; and one-time games, such as hula hoop contests, which rise to popularity once and then disappear.

In sum, play is a multidimensional, complex concept. It ranges from an infant's simple exercise of a newfound sensorimotor talent to a preschool child's riding a tricycle to an older child's participation in organized games. A visual portrayal of the different types of play is shown in figure 9.4.

TELEVISION

Few developments in society in the second half of the twentieth century have had a greater impact on children than television has. Many children spend more time in front of the television set than they do with their parents. Although it is only one of the many mass media that affect children's behavior, television is the most influential. The persuasion capabilities of television are staggering; the 20,000 hours of television watched by the time the average American adolescent graduates from high school are greater than the number of hours spent in the classroom.

Television's Many Roles

Although television can have a negative influence on children's development by taking them away from homework, making them passive learners, teaching them stereotypes, providing them with violent models of aggression, and presenting them with unrealistic views of the world, television can have a positive influence on children's development by presenting motivating educational programs, increasing children's information about the world beyond their immediate environment, and providing models of prosocial behavior (Esty & Fisch, 1991).

> *Television is a medium of entertainment which permits millions of people to listen to the same joke at the same time, and yet remain lonesome.*
>
> —T. S. Eliot

Television has been called many things, not all of them good. Depending on one's point of view, it may be a "window on the world," the "one-eyed monster," or the "boob tube." Television has been attacked as one of the reasons why scores on national achievement tests in reading and mathematics are lower now than in the past. Television, it is claimed, attracts children away from books and schoolwork. In one study, children who read printed materials, such as books, watched television less than those who did not read (Huston, Seigle, & Bremer, 1983). Furthermore, critics argue that television trains children to become passive learners: rarely, if ever, does television require active responses from the observer.

"Mrs. Horton, could you stop by school today?"

© Martha Campbell.

FIGURE 9.4

Five important types of children's play are (a) *sensorimotor/practice play,* (b) *pretense/ symbolic play,* (c) *social play,* (d) *constructive play, and* (e) *games. What type of play is represented in the large background photograph?*

(a) (b) (c) (d) (e)

Television also is said to deceive; that is, it teaches children that problems are resolved easily and that everything always comes out right in the end. For example, TV detectives usually take only 30 to 60 minutes to sort through a complex array of clues to reveal the killer—and they *always* find the killer! Violence is a way of life on many shows, where it is all right for police to use violence and to break moral codes in their fight against evildoers. The lasting results of violence are rarely brought home to the viewer. A person who is injured suffers for only a few seconds; in real life, the person might need months or years to recover, or might not recover at all. Yet one out of every two first-grade children says that the adults on television are like adults in real life (Lyle & Hoffman, 1972).

A special concern is how ethnic minorities are portrayed on television (Greenberg & Brand, 1994). Ethnic minorities have historically been underrepresented and misrepresented on television. Ethnic minority characters—whether Black, Asian, Hispanic, or Native American—have traditionally been presented as less dignified and less positive than White characters (Condry, 1989). In one investigation, character portrayals of ethnic minorities were examined during heavy children's viewing hours (weekdays 4–6 P.M. and 7–11 P.M.) (Williams & Condry, 1989). The percentage of White characters far exceeded the actual percentage of Whites in the United States; the percentage of Black, Asian, and Hispanic characters fell short of the population statistics. Hispanic characters were especially underrepresented—only 0.6 percent of the characters were

Hispanic, while the Hispanic population in the United States is 6.4 percent of the total U.S. population. Minorities tended to hold lower-status jobs and were more likely than Whites to be cast as criminals or victims.

There are some positive aspects to television's influence on children. For one, television presents children with a world that is different than the one in which they live. It exposes children to a wider variety of viewpoints and information than they might get from only their parents, teachers, and peers. And some television programs have educational and developmental benefits. One of television's major programming attempts to educate children is "Sesame Street," which is designed to teach children both cognitive and social skills. The program began in 1969 and is still going strong.

"Sesame Street" demonstrates that education and entertainment can work well together. Through "Sesame Street," children experience a world of learning that is both exciting and entertaining. "Sesame Street" also follows the principle that teaching can be accomplished in both direct and indirect ways. Using the direct way, a teacher might tell children exactly what they are going to be taught and then teach them. However, in real life, social skills are often communicated in indirect ways. Rather than merely telling children, "You should cooperate with others," TV can show children so that children can figure out what it means to be cooperative and what the advantages are.

Amount of Television Watching by Children

Just how much television do young children watch? They watch a lot, and they seem to be watching more all the time. In the 1950s, 3-year-old children watched television for less than 1 hour a day; 5-year-olds watched just over 2 hours a day. But in the 1970s, preschool children watched television for an average of 4 hours a day; elementary school children watched for as long as 6 hours a day (Friedrich & Stein, 1973). In the 1980s, children averaged 11 to 28 hours of television per week (Huston, Watkins, & Kunkel, 1989), which is more than for any other activity except sleep. Of special concern is the extent to which children are exposed to violence and aggression on television. Up to 80 percent of the prime-time shows include violent acts, including beatings, shootings, and stabbings. The frequency of violence increases on the Saturday morning cartoon shows, which average more than 25 violent acts per hour.

Effects of Television on Children's Aggression and Prosocial Behavior

What are the effects of television violence on children's aggression? Does television merely stimulate a child to go out and buy a Star Wars ray gun, or can it trigger an attack on a playmate? When children grow up, can television violence increase the likelihood they will violently attack someone?

In one longitudinal investigation, the amount of violence viewed on television at age 8 was significantly related to the seriousness of criminal acts performed as an adult (Huesmann, 1986). In another investigation, long-term exposure to television violence was significantly related to the likelihood of aggression in 1,565 12- to 17-year-old boys (Belson, 1978). Boys who watched the most aggression on television were the most likely to commit a violent crime, swear, be aggressive in sports, threaten violence toward another boy, write slogans on walls, or break windows. These investigations are *correlational* in nature, so we cannot conclude from them that television violence causes children to be more aggressive, only that watching television violence is *associated* with aggressive behavior. In one experiment, children were randomly assigned to one of two groups: One watched television shows taken directly from violent Saturday morning cartoon offerings on 11 different days; the second group watched television cartoon shows with all of the violence removed (Steur, Applefield, & Smith, 1971). The children were then observed during play at their preschool. The preschool children who saw the TV cartoon shows with violence kicked, choked, and pushed their playmates more than the preschool children who watched nonviolent TV cartoon shows. Because children were randomly assigned to the two conditions (TV cartoons with violence versus nonviolent TV cartoons), we can conclude that exposure to TV violence *caused* the increased aggression in children in this investigation.

Although some critics have argued that the effects of television violence do not warrant the conclusion that TV violence causes aggression (Freedman, 1984), many experts argue that TV violence can induce aggressive or antisocial behavior in children (Comstock, 1991; Condry, 1989; Gunter, 1994; Liebert & Sprafkin, 1988; Roberts, 1993). Of course, television is not the *only* cause of aggression. There is no *one* single cause of any social behavior. Aggression, like all other social behaviors, has a number of determinants.

Children need to be taught critical viewing skills to counter the adverse effects of television violence. In one investigation, elementary school children were randomly assigned to either an experimental or a control group (Huesmann & others, 1983). In the experimental group, children assisted in making a film to help children who had been fooled or harmed by television. The children also composed essays that focused on how television is not like real life and why it is bad to imitate TV violence or watch too much television. In the control group, children received no training in critical viewing skills. The children who were trained in critical viewing skills developed more negative attitudes about TV violence and reduced their aggressive behavior.

Television can also teach children that it is better to behave in positive, prosocial ways than in negative, antisocial ways. Aimee Leifer (1973) demonstrated that television is associated with prosocial behavior in young children: she selected a number of episodes from the television show "Sesame Street" that reflected positive social interchanges. She was especially interested in situations that taught children how to use their social skills. For example, in one interchange, two men were fighting over the amount of space available to them; they gradually began to cooperate and to share the space. Children who watched these episodes copied these behaviors, and in later social situations they applied the prosocial lessons they had learned.

So far, we have discussed a number of ideas about peers, play, and television. A summary of these ideas is presented in concept table 9.2. Now we turn our attention to children's personality development in early childhood, beginning with the self.

CONCEPT TABLE 9.2

Peers, Play, and Television

Concept	Processes/Related Ideas	Characteristics/Description
Peers	The nature of peer relations	Peers are powerful social agents. The term *peers* refers to children who are of about the same age or maturity level. Peers provide a source of information and comparison about the world outside the family.
	The distinct but coordinated worlds of parent-child and peer relations	Peer relations are both like and unlike family relations. Children touch, smile, and vocalize when they interact with parents and peers. However, rough-and-tumble play occurs mainly with peers. In times of stress, children generally seek out their parents. Healthy family relations usually promote healthy peer relations.
Play	Play's functions	Affiliation with peers, tension release, advances in cognitive development, exploration, and provision of a safe haven in which to engage in potentially dangerous activities are among the benefits of play.
	Parten's classic study of play	Parten developed the categories of unoccupied, solitary, onlooker, parallel, associative, and cooperative play. Three-year-olds engage in more solitary play and parallel play than 5-year-olds, and 5-year-olds engage in cooperative and associative play more than other types of play.
	Types of play	The contemporary perspective emphasizes both the cognitive and social aspects of play. Among the most widely studied aspects of children's play today are sensorimotor/practice play, pretense/symbolic play, social play, constructive play, and games.
Television	Its effects on children	Although television can have a negative influence on children's development by taking them away from homework, making them passive learners, teaching them stereotypes, providing them with violent models of aggression, and presenting them with unrealistic views of the world, television can have a positive influence by presenting motivating educational programs, increasing children's information about the world beyond their immediate environment, and providing models of prosocial behavior. Children watch huge amounts of television, with preschool children watching an average of 4 hours a day. Up to 80 percent of the prime-time shows have violent episodes. Television violence is not the only cause of children's aggression, but most experts conclude that it can induce aggression and antisocial behavior in children. Prosocial behavior on television is associated with increased positive behavior by children.

THE SELF

We learned in chapter 7 that toward the end of the second year of life children develop a sense of self. During early childhood, some important developments in the self take place. Among these developments are facing the issue of initiative versus guilt and enhanced self-understanding.

Initiative Versus Guilt

According to Erikson (1968), the psychosocial stage that characterizes early childhood is *initiative versus guilt*. By now, children have become convinced that they are a person of their own;

during early childhood, they must discover what kind of person they will become. They intensely identify with their parents, who most of the time appear to them to be powerful and beautiful, although often unreasonable, disagreeable, and sometimes even dangerous. During early childhood, children use their perceptual, motor, cognitive, and language skills to make things happen. They have a surplus of energy that permits them to forget failures quickly and to approach new areas that seem desirable—even if they seem dangerous—with undiminished zest and some increased sense of direction. On their own *initiative*, then, children at this stage exuberantly move out into a wider social world.

The great governor of initiative is *conscience*. Children now not only feel afraid of being found out, but they also begin to hear the inner voice of self-observation, self-guidance, and self-punishment. Their initiative and enthusiasm may bring them not only rewards, but also punishments. Widespread disappointment at this stage leads to an unleashing of guilt that lowers the child's self-esteem.

Whether children leave this stage with a sense of initiative that outweighs their sense of guilt depends in large part on how parents respond to their self-initiated activities. Children who are given freedom and opportunity to initiate motor play such as running, bike riding, sledding, skating, tussling, and wrestling have their sense of initiative supported. Initiative is also supported when parents answer their children's questions and do not deride or inhibit fantasy or play activity. In contrast, if children are made to feel that their motor activity is bad, that their questions are a nuisance, and that their play is silly and stupid, then they often develop a sense of guilt over self-initiated activities that may persist through life's later stages (Elkind, 1970).

Self-Understanding

Self-understanding *is the child's cognitive representation of self, the substance and content of the child's self-conceptions.* For example, a 5-year-old girl understands that she is a girl, has blond hair, likes to ride her bicycle, has a friend, and is a swimmer. An 11-year-old boy understands that he is a student, a boy, a football player, a family member, a video-game lover, and a rock music fan. A child's self-understanding is based on the various roles and membership categories that define who children are (Harter, 1988). Though not the whole of personal identity, self-understanding provides its rational underpinnings (Damon & Hart, 1988, 1992).

The rudimentary beginning of self-understanding begins with self-recognition, which takes place by approximately 18 months of age. Since children can verbally communicate their ideas, research on self-understanding in childhood is not limited to visual self-recognition, as it was during infancy. Mainly by interviewing children, researchers have probed children's conceptions of many aspects of self-understanding, including mind and body, self in relation to others, and pride and shame in self. In early childhood, children usually conceive of the self in physical terms. Most young children think the self is part of their body, usually their head. Young children usually confuse self, mind, and body (Broughton, 1978). Because the self is a body part for them, they describe it along many material dimensions, such as size, shape, and color. Young children distinguish themselves from others through many different physical and material attributes. Says 4-year-old Sandra, "I'm different from Jennifer because I have brown hair and she has blond hair." Says 4-year-old Ralph, "I am different from Hank because I am taller, and I am different from my sister because I have a bicycle."

Researchers also believe that the *active dimension* is a central component of the self in early childhood (Keller, Ford, & Meacham, 1978). If we define the category *physical* broadly enough, we can include physical actions as well as body image and material possessions. For example, preschool children often describe themselves in terms of activities like play. In sum, in early childhood, children frequently think of themselves in terms of a physical self or an active self.

GENDER

Few aspects of children's social development are more central to their identity and to their social relationships than their sex or gender. What exactly do we mean by gender? What are the biological, cognitive, and social influences on gender?

What Is Gender?

While sex refers to the biological dimension of being male or female, **gender** *refers to the social dimension of being male or female.* Two aspects of gender bear special mention—gender identity and gender role. **Gender identity** *is the sense of being male or female, which most children acquire by the time they are 3 years old.* **Gender role** *is a set of expectations that prescribe how females and males should think, act, and feel.*

Biological Influences

It was not until the 1920s that researchers confirmed the existence of human sex chromosomes, the genetic material that determines our sex. In chapter 3, you learned that humans normally have 46 chromosomes arranged in pairs. The 23rd pair may have two X chromosomes to produce a female, or it may have an X and a Y chromosome to produce a male.

In the first few weeks of gestation, female and male embryos look alike. Male sex organs start to differ from female sex organs when XY chromosomes in the male embryo trigger the secretion of **androgen,** *the main class of male sex hormones.* Low levels of androgen in a female embryo allow the normal development of female sex organs.

Although rare, an imbalance in this system of hormone secretion can occur during fetal development. If there is insufficient androgen in a male embryo or an excess of androgen in a female embryo, the result is an individual with both male and female sex organs, a hermaphrodite. When genetically female (XX chromosomes) infants are born with masculine-looking genitals, surgery at birth can achieve a genital/genetic match. **Estrogen** *is the main class of female sex hormones.* At puberty, the production of estrogen begins to influence both physical development and behavior, but before then these females often behave in a "tomboyish" manner, acting more aggressively than most girls. They also dress and play in ways that are more characteristic of boys than girls (Ehrhardt, 1987; Money, 1987).

Is the behavior of these surgically corrected girls due to their prenatal hormones, or is it the result of their social experiences? Experiments with various animal species reveal that when male hormones are injected into female embryos, the females develop masculine physical traits and behave more aggressively (Hines, 1982). However, in humans, hormones exert less control over behavior. Perhaps because these girls look more masculine, they are treated more like boys and so adopt their boyish ways.

Although prenatal hormones may or may not influence gender behavior, psychoanalytic theorists, such as Sigmund Freud and Erik Erikson, have argued that an individual's genitals do play a pivotal role. Freud argued that human behavior and history are directly influenced by sexual drives and suggested that gender and sexual behavior are essentially unlearned and instinctual. Erikson went even further: He argued that, because of genital structure, males are more intrusive and aggressive, females more inclusive and passive. Erikson's critics contend that he has not given enough credit to experience, and they argue that women and men are more free to choose their behavior than Erikson allowed. In response, Erikson has clarified his view, pointing out that he never said that biology is the sole determinant of differences between the sexes. Biology, he said, interacts with both cultural and psychological factors to produce behavior.

No one argues about the presence of genetic, biochemical, and anatomical differences between the sexes. Even child developmentalists with a strong environmental orientation acknowledge that boys and girls are treated differently because of their physical differences and their different roles in reproduction. The importance of biological factors is not at issue. What is at issue is the directness or indirectness of their effects on social behavior (Huston, 1983). For example, if a high androgen level directly influences the central nervous system, which in turn increases activity level, then the biological effect on behavior is direct. By contrast, if a child's high level of androgen produces strong muscle development, which in turn causes others to expect the child to be a good athlete and, in turn, leads the child to participate in sports, then the biological effect on behavior is indirect.

Although virtually everyone thinks that children's behavior as males or females is due to an interaction of biological and environmental factors, an interactionist position means different things to different people (Bancroft & Reinisch, 1990; Hinde, 1992; Maccoby, 1987b; Money, 1987). For some, it suggests that certain environmental conditions are required before preprogrammed dispositions appear. For others, it suggests that a particular environment will have different effects depending on the child's predispositions. For still others, it means that children shape their environments, including their interpersonal environment, and vice versa. The processes of influence and counterinfluence unfold over time. Throughout development, males and females actively construct their own versions of acceptable masculine and feminine behavior patterns.

Social Influences

In our culture, adults discriminate between the sexes shortly after the infant's birth. The "pink and blue" treatment may be applied to boys and girls before they leave the hospital. Soon afterward, differences in hairstyles, clothes, and toys become obvious. Adults and peers reward these differences throughout development. And boys and girls learn gender roles through imitation or observational learning by watching what other people say and do. In recent years, the idea that parents are the critical socializing agents in gender-role development has come

under fire (Huston, 1983). Parents are only one of many sources through which the individual learns gender roles (Beal, 1994). Culture, schools, peers, the media, and other family members are others. Yet it is important to guard against swinging too far in this direction because—especially in the early years of development—parents are important influences on gender development.

Identification and Social Learning Theories

Two prominent theories address the way children acquire masculine and feminine attitudes and behaviors from their parents. **Identification theory** *stems from Freud's view that the preschool child develops a sexual attraction to the opposite-sex parent, then by approximately 5 or 6 years of age renounces this attraction because of anxious feelings, and subsequently identifies with the same-sex parent, unconsciously adopting the same-sex parent's characteristics.* However, today many child developmentalists do not believe gender development proceeds on the basis of identification, at least not in terms of Freud's emphasis on childhood sexual attraction. Children become gender-typed much earlier than 5 or 6 years of age, and they become masculine or feminine even when the same-sex parent is not present in the family.

> *Children need models rather than critics.*
> —Joseph Joubert

The **social learning theory of gender** *emphasizes that children's gender development occurs through observation and imitation of gender behavior, and through the rewards and punishments children experience for gender appropriate and inappropriate behavior.* Unlike identification theory, social learning theory argues that sexual attraction to parents is not involved in gender development. (A comparison of identification and social learning views is presented in figure 9.5.) Parents often use rewards and punishments to teach their daughters to be feminine ("Karen, you are being a good girl when you play gently with your doll") and masculine ("Keith, a boy as big as you is not supposed to cry"). Peers also extensively reward and punish gender behavior. And by observing adults and peers at home, at school, in the neighborhood, and on television, children are widely exposed to a myriad of models who display masculine and feminine behavior. Critics of the social learning view argue that gender development is not as passively acquired as it indicates. Later we will discuss the cognitive views on gender development, which stress that children actively construct their gender world.

Parental Influences

Parents, by action and by example, influence their children's gender development. Both mothers and fathers are psychologically important in children's gender development. Mothers are more consistently given responsibility for nurturance and physical care; fathers are more likely to engage in playful interaction and be given responsibility for ensuring that boys and girls conform to existing cultural norms. And whether or not they have more influence on them, fathers are more involved in socializing their

FIGURE 9.5

A comparison of identification and social learning views of gender development. Parents influence their children's gender development by action and by example.

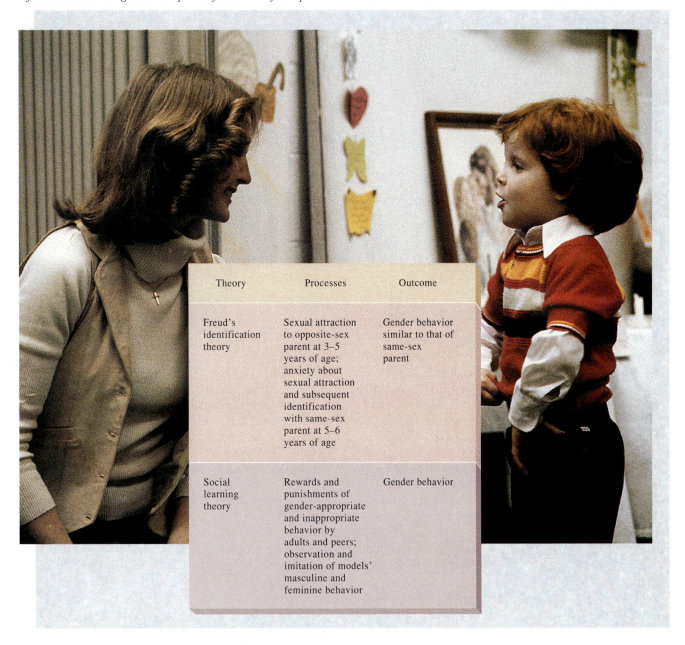

Theory	Processes	Outcome
Freud's identification theory	Sexual attraction to opposite-sex parent at 3–5 years of age; anxiety about sexual attraction and subsequent identification with same-sex parent at 5–6 years of age	Gender behavior similar to that of same-sex parent
Social learning theory	Rewards and punishments of gender-appropriate and inappropriate behavior by adults and peers; observation and imitation of models' masculine and feminine behavior	Gender behavior

sons than their daughters (Lamb, 1986). Fathers seem to play an especially important part in gender-role development—they are more likely than mothers to act differently toward sons and daughters and thus contribute more to distinctions between the genders (Huston, 1983).

Many parents encourage boys and girls to engage in different types of play and activities (Fagot, Leinbach, & O'Boyle, 1992). Girls are more likely to be given dolls to play with during childhood and, when old enough, are more likely to be assigned baby-sitting duties. Girls are encouraged to be more nurturant and emotional than boys, and their fathers are more likely to engage in aggressive play with their sons than with their daughters. As adolescents increase in age, parents permit boys more freedom than girls, allowing them to be away from home and stay out later without supervision. When parents place severe restrictions on their adolescent sons, it has been found to be especially disruptive to the sons' development (Baumrind, 1989).

Peer Influences

Parents provide the earliest discrimination of gender roles in development, but, before long, peers join the societal process of responding to and modeling masculine and feminine behavior. Children who play in sex-appropriate activities tend to be rewarded for doing so by their peers. Those who play in

As reflected in this tug-of-war battle between boys and girls, the playground in elementary school is like going to "gender school." Elementary school children show a clear preference for being with and liking same-sex peers. Eleanor Maccoby (at right) has studied children's gender development for many years. She believes peers play especially strong roles in socializing each other about gender roles.

cross-sexed activities tend to be criticized by their peers or left to play alone. Children show a clear preference for being with and liking same-sex peers (Buhrmester, 1993; Maccoby, 1989, 1993), and this tendency usually becomes stronger during the middle and late childhood years (Hayden-Thomson, Rubin, & Hymel, 1987). After extensive observations of elementary school playgrounds, two researchers characterized the play settings as "gender school," pointing out that boys teach one another the required masculine behavior and enforce it strictly (Luria & Herzog, 1985). Girls also pass on the female culture and mainly congregate with one another. Individual "tomboy" girls can join boys' activities without losing their status in the girls' groups, but the reverse is not true for boys, reflecting our society's greater sex-typing pressure for boys.

Peer demands for conformity to gender role become especially intense during adolescence. Although there is greater social mixing of males and females during early adolescence, in both formal groups and in dating, peer pressure is strong for the adolescent boy to be the very best male possible and for the adolescent girl to be the very best female possible.

School and Teacher Influences

In a recent Gallup poll, 80 percent of the respondents agreed that the federal government should promote educational programs intended to reduce such social problems as poverty and unequal educational opportunities for minorities and females (Gallup & Clark, 1987). Discriminatory treatment on the basis of gender can be found across all ability groups, but in many cases the stereotypically less-valued group (in this case, females)

is treated as though they are a lower-ability group. For example, girls with strong math abilities are frequently given fewer quality instructional interactions from teachers than their male counterparts (Eccles, MacIver, & Lange, 1986). And minority females are given fewer teacher interactions than other females, who are given fewer than Black males, who are given fewer than White males (Sadker, Sadker, & Klein, 1986).

In one study, researchers were trained in an observation system to collect data in more than a hundred fourth-, sixth-, and eighth-grade classrooms (Sadker & Sadker, 1986). At all three grade levels, male students were involved in more interactions than female students, and male students were given more attention from teachers. Male students were also given more remediation, more criticism, and more praise than female students.

Historically, education in the United States has been male defined rather than gender balanced. In many instances, traditional male activities, especially White male activities, have been the educational norm. Although females mature earlier, are ready for verbal and math training at a younger age, and have control of fine motor skills earlier than males, educational curricula have been constructed mainly to mirror the development of males. Decisions about the grade in which students should read *Huckleberry Finn*, do long division, or begin to write essays are based primarily on male developmental patterns. Some experts believe that this state of educational affairs means that some girls may become bored or give up, with most girls learning simply to hold back, be quiet, and smile (Shakeshaft, 1986).

Media Influences

As we have described, children encounter masculine and feminine roles in their everyday interactions with parents, peers, and teachers. The messages carried by the media about what is appropriate or inappropriate for males and for females are important influences on gender development as well.

A special concern is the way females are pictured on television. In the 1970s, it became apparent that television was portraying females as less competent than males. For example, about 70 percent of the prime-time characters were males, men were more likely to be shown in the work force, women were more likely to be shown as housewives and in romantic roles, men were more likely to appear in higher-status jobs and in a greater diversity of occupations, and men were presented as more aggressive and constructive (Sternglanz & Serbin, 1974).

In the 1980s, television networks became more sensitive to how males and females were portrayed on television shows. Consequently, many programs now focus on divorced families, cohabitation, and women in high-status roles. Even with the onset of this type of programming researchers continue to find that television portrays males as more competent than females (Durkin, 1985). In one investigation, young adolescent girls indicated that television occupations are more extensively stereotyped than real-life occupations (Wroblewski & Huston, 1987).

Gender-role stereotyping also appears in the print media. In magazine advertising, females are shown more often in advertisements for beauty products, cleaning products, and home appliances, while males are shown more often in advertisements for cars, liquor, and travel. As with television programs, females are being portrayed as more competent in advertisements than in the past, but advertisers have not yet given them equal status with males.

So far in our discussion of gender, we have seen that both biological and social factors play important roles in children's gender development. Recently, many child developmentalists have also recognized the important role that cognitive factors play.

Cognitive Influences

What is the cognitive developmental view of gender? What is the gender schema theory of gender development? What role does language play in gender development? We consider each of these questions in turn.

Cognitive Developmental Theory

In the **cognitive developmental theory of gender,** *children's gender typing occurs after they have developed a concept of gender. Once they consistently conceive of themselves as male or female, children often organize their world on the basis of gender.* Initially developed by psychologist Lawrence Kohlberg (1966), this theory argues that gender development proceeds in the following way: A child realizes, "I am a girl; I want to do girl things; therefore, the opportunity to do girl things is rewarding." Having acquired the ability to categorize, children then strive toward consistency in the use of categories and behavior. Kohlberg based his ideas on Piaget's cognitive developmental theory. As children's cognitive development matures, so does their understanding of gender. Although 2-year-olds can apply the labels *boy* and *girl* correctly to themselves and others, their concept of gender is simple and concrete. Preschool children rely on physical features, such as dress and hairstyle, to decide who falls into which category. Girls are people with long hair, they think, whereas boys are people who never wear dresses. Many preschool children believe that people can change their own gender at will by getting a haircut or a new outfit. They do not yet have the cognitive machinery to think of gender as adults do. According to Kohlberg, all the reinforcement in the world won't modify that fact. However, by the concrete operational stage (the third stage in Piaget's theory, entered at about 6 or 7 years of age), children understand gender constancy—that a male is still a male regardless of whether he wears pants or a skirt, or his hair is short or long (Tavris & Wade, 1984). When their concept of gender constancy is clearly established, children are then motivated to become a competent, or "proper" girl or boy. Consequently, she or he finds female or male activities rewarding and imitates the behavior of same-sex models.

> *Childhood decides.*
> —Jean-Paul Sartre

Gender Schema Theory

A **schema** *is a cognitive structure, a network of associations that organizes and guides an individual's perceptions.* A **gender schema** *organizes the world in terms of female and male.* **Gender schema theory** *states that an individual's attention and behavior are guided by an internal motivation to conform to gender-based sociocultural standards and stereotypes* (Bem, 1981; Levy, 1991; Levy & Carter, 1989; Liben & Signorella, 1987, 1993; Martin, 1989, 1993; Martin & Halverson, 1987; Martin & Rose, 1991; Rose & Martin, 1993). Gender schema theory suggests that "gender typing" occurs when individuals are ready to encode and organize information along the lines of what is considered appropriate or typical for males and females in a society. Whereas Kohlberg's cognitive developmental theory argues that a particular cognitive prerequisite—gender constancy—is necessary for gender typing, gender schema theory states that a general readiness to respond to and categorize information on the basis of culturally defined gender roles fuels children's gender-typing activities. A comparison of the cognitive developmental and gender schema theories is presented in figure 9.6.

While researchers have shown that the appearance of gender constancy in children is related to their level of cognitive development, especially the acquisition of conservation skills (which supports the cognitive developmental theory of gender) (Emmerich & others, 1977; Serbin & Sprafkin, 1986), they have also shown that young children who are pre-gender-constant have more gender-role knowledge than the cognitive developmental theory of gender predicts (which supports gender schema theory) (Carter & Levy, 1988; Carter & Taylor, in press).

FIGURE 9.6

A comparison of cognitive developmental and gender schema theories of gender development.

Theory	Processes	Outcome
Cognitive developmental theory	Development of gender constancy, especially around 6–7 years of age, when conservation skills develop; after children develop ability to consistently conceive of themselves as male or female, children often organize their world on the basis of gender, such as selecting same-sex models to imitate	Gender-typed behavior
Gender schema theory	Sociocultural emphasis on gender-based standards and stereotypes; children's attention and behavior are guided by an internal motivation to conform to these gender-based standards and stereotypes, allowing children to interpret the world through a network of gender-organized thoughts	Gender-typed behavior

Today, gender schema theorists acknowledge that gender constancy is one important aspect of gender role development, but stress that other cognitive factors—such as gender schema—are also very important (Levy & Carter, 1989).

Critical Thinking

How do cognitive theories of gender differ from the social learning and identification theories of gender discussed earlier?

Two main theories about the structure of gender schema have been proposed. Janet Spence (1984, 1985) believes that monolithic concepts such as gender schema or sex-role identification are not very useful. Rather, she argues, gender-related phenomena are multidimensional in nature, and the different factors involved are somewhat independent of each other. From this perspective, consistency in stereotyping across domains and people would not be expected. Spence also stresses that gender schemas may be monolithic in their origin (that is, when they first appear in young children's minds), but that they become more differentiated across the life span (Bigler, Liben, & Yekel, 1992). The second main theory about the structure of gender schemas was proposed by Sandra Bem (1979, 1981), who argued that considerable consistency characterizes stereotyping across domains and people. Which theory is correct? Data have been offered in support of both theories, and the issue of consistency and independence across the domains of gender has not yet been settled.

The Role of Language in Gender Development

Gender is present in the language children use and encounter. (Hurt & Leinbach, 1993; Quay, Minore, & Frazier, 1993). The language that children hear most of the time is sexist. That is, the English language contains sex bias, especially through the use of *he* and *man* to refer to everyone (O'Donnel, 1989). For example, in one investigation, mothers and their 1- and 3-year-old children looked at popular children's books, such as *The Three Bears,* together (DeLoache, Cassidy, & Carpenter, 1987). The three bears were almost always referred to as boys; 95 percent of all characters of indeterminate gender were referred to by mothers as males.

MORAL DEVELOPMENT

People are hardly neutral about moral development. Many parents worry that their children are growing up without traditional values. Teachers complain that their students are unethical. What is moral development? What is Piaget's view of how children's moral reasoning develops? What is the nature of children's moral behavior? How do children's feelings contribute to their moral development?

What Is Moral Development?

Moral development *concerns rules and conventions about what people should do in their interactions with other people.* In studying these rules, developmentalists examine three different domains. First, how do children *reason* or *think* about rules for ethical conduct? For example, consider cheating. The child can be presented with a story in which someone has a conflict about whether or not to cheat in a particular situation, such as taking a test in school. The child is asked to decide what is appropriate for the character to do and why. The focus is on the *reasoning* children use to justify their moral decisions.

Second, how do children actually *behave* in moral circumstances? In our example of cheating, the emphasis is on observing the child's cheating and the environmental circumstances that produced and maintained the cheating. Children might be shown some toys and then be asked to select the one they believe is the most attractive. The experimenter then tells the young child that that particular toy belongs to someone else and is not to be played with. Observations of different conditions under which the child deviates from the prohibition or resists temptation are then conducted.

Third, how does the child *feel* about moral matters? In the example of cheating, does the child feel enough guilt to resist temptation? If children do cheat, do feelings of guilt after the transgression keep them from cheating the next time they face temptation? In the remainder of this section, we will focus on these three facets of moral development: thought, action, and feeling. Then we will evaluate the positive side of children's moral development: altruism.

Piaget's View of How Children's Moral Reasoning Develops

Interest in how the child thinks about moral issues was stimulated by Piaget (1932), who extensively observed and interviewed children from the ages of 4 to 12. He watched them play marbles, seeking to learn how they used and thought about the game's rules. He also asked children questions about ethical rules—theft, lies, punishment, and justice, for example. Piaget concluded that children think in two distinctly different ways about morality, depending on their developmental maturity. **Heteronomous morality** *is the first stage of moral development in Piaget's theory, occurring from approximately 4 to 7 years of age. Justice and rules are conceived of as unchangeable properties of the world, removed from the control of people.* **Autonomous morality** *is the second stage of moral development in Piaget's theory, displayed by older children (about 10 years of age and older). The child becomes aware that rules and laws are created by people and that, in judging an action, one should consider the actor's intentions as well as the consequences.* Children 7 to 10 years of age are in a transition between the two stages, evidencing some features of both.

Let's consider Piaget's two stages of moral development further. The heteronomous thinker judges the rightness or goodness of behavior by considering the consequences of the behavior, not the intentions of the actor. For example, the heteronomous thinker says that breaking twelve cups accidentally is worse than breaking one cup intentionally while trying to steal a cookie. For the moral autonomist, the reverse is true. The actor's intentions assume paramount importance. The heteronomous thinker also believes that rules are unchangeable and are handed down by all-powerful authorities. When Piaget suggested that new rules be introduced into the game of marbles, the young children resisted. They insisted that the rules had always been the same and could not be altered. By contrast, older children—who were moral autonomists—accept change and recognize that rules are merely convenient, socially agreed-upon conventions, subject to change by consensus.

The heteronomous thinker also believes in **immanent justice,** *the concept that if a rule is broken, punishment will be meted out immediately.* The young child believes that the violation is connected in some automatic way to the punishment. Thus, young children often look around worriedly after committing a transgression, expecting inevitable punishment. Older children, the moral autonomists, recognize that punishment is socially mediated and occurs only if a relevant person witnesses the wrongdoing and that, even then, punishment is not inevitable.

Piaget argued that, as children develop, they become more sophisticated in thinking about social matters, especially about the possibilities and conditions of cooperation. Piaget believed that this social understanding comes about through the mutual give-and-take of peer relations. In the peer group, where all members have similar power and status, plans are negotiated and coordinated, and disagreements are reasoned about and eventually settled. Parent-child relations, in which parents have the power and the child does not, are less likely to advance moral reasoning, because rules are often handed down in an authoritarian way. Later, in chapter 11, we will discuss another highly influential cognitive view of moral development, that of Lawrence Kohlberg.

Moral Behavior

The study of moral behavior has been influenced by social learning theory. The processes of reinforcement, punishment, and imitation are used to explain children's moral behavior. When children are rewarded for behavior that is consistent with laws and social conventions, they are likely to repeat that behavior. When models who behave morally are provided, children are likely to adopt their actions. And when children are punished for immoral behavior, those behaviors are likely to be reduced or eliminated. However, because punishment may have adverse side effects, it needs to be used judiciously and cautiously.

Another important point needs to be made about the social learning view of moral development: Moral behavior is influenced extensively by the situation. What children do in one situation is often only weakly related to what they do in other situations. A child may cheat in math class, but not in English class; a child may steal a piece of candy when others are not present, and not steal it when they are present; and so on. More than half a century ago, morality's situational nature was observed in a comprehensive study of thousands of children in many different situations—at home, at school, and at church, for example. The totally honest child was virtually nonexistent; so was the child who cheated in all situations (Hartshorne & May, 1928–1930).

Social learning theorists also believe that the ability to resist temptation is closely tied to the development of self-control. Children must overcome their impulses toward something they want that is prohibited. To achieve this self-control, they must learn to be patient and to delay gratification. Today, social learning theorists believe that cognitive factors are important in the child's development of self-control. For example, in one investigation, children's cognitive transformations of desired objects helped children to become more patient (Mischel & Patterson, 1976). Preschool children were asked to do a boring task. Close by was an exciting mechanical clown who tried to persuade the children to come play with him. The children who had been trained to say to themselves "I'm not going to look at Mr. Clown when Mr. Clown says to look at him" controlled their behavior and continued working on the dull task much longer than those who did not instruct themselves.

Moral Feelings

In chapter 2, we discussed Sigmund Freud's psychoanalytic theory, which describes the *superego* as one of the three main structures of personality—the id and ego being the other two. In Freud's classical psychoanalytic theory, the child's superego—the moral branch of personality—develops as the child resolves the Oedipus conflict and identifies with the same-sex parent in the early childhood years. Among the reasons why children resolve the Oedipus conflict is the fear of losing their parents' love and of being punished for their unacceptable sexual wishes toward the opposite-sex parent. To reduce anxiety, avoid punishment, and maintain parental affection, children form a superego by identifying with the same-sex parent. Through their identification with the same-sex parent, children internalize the parents' standards of right and wrong that reflect societal prohibitions. And the child turns inward the hostility that was previously aimed externally at the same-sex parent. This inwardly directed hostility is now felt self-punitively as guilt, which is experienced unconsciously (beyond the child's awareness). In the psychoanalytic account of moral development, the self-punitiveness of

guilt is responsible for keeping the child from committing transgressions. That is, children conform to societal standards to avoid guilt.

What is moral is what you feel good after and what is immoral is what you feel bad after.

—Ernest Hemingway,
Death in the Afternoon, 1932

Positive feelings such as empathy contribute to the child's moral development. **Empathy** *is reacting to another's feelings with an emotional response that is similar to the other's feelings* (Damon, 1988; Damon & Hart, 1992). Although empathy is experienced as an emotional state, it often has a cognitive component. The cognitive component is the ability to discern another's inner psychological states, or what is called "perspective taking." Young infants have the capacity for some purely empathic responses, but for effective moral action children need to learn how to identify a wide range of emotional states in others, and they need to learn to anticipate what kinds of action will improve another person's emotional state.

We have seen that classical psychoanalytic theory emphasizes the power of unconscious guilt in moral development. However, other theorists, such as Martin Hoffman and William Damon, emphasize the role of empathy. Today, many child developmentalists believe that both positive feelings, such as empathy, sympathy, admiration, and self-esteem, as well as negative feelings, such as anger, outrage, shame, and guilt, contribute to the child's moral development. When strongly experienced, these emotions influence children to act in accord with standards of right and wrong. Emotions such as empathy, shame, guilt, and anxiety over other people's violation of standards are present early in development and undergo developmental change throughout childhood and beyond (Damon, 1988; Damon & Hart, 1992). These emotions provide a natural base for the child's acquisition of moral values, both orienting children toward moral events and motivating children to pay close attention to such events. But moral emotions do not operate in a vacuum to build the child's moral awareness, and they are not sufficient in themselves to generate moral responsiveness. They do not give the "substance" of moral regulation—the actual rules, values, and standards of behavior that children need to understand and act on. Moral emotions are inextricably interwoven with the cognitive and social aspects of children's development.

Thus far, we have discussed a number of ideas about the self, gender, and moral development in young children. These ideas are summarized in concept table 9.3.

LIFE-SPAN HEALTH AND WELL-BEING

Some Working–Parent Solutions When Work/Family Interference Occurs

Ellen Galinsky is the copresident of the new Families and Work Institute in New York City and has been president of the National Association for the Education of Young Children. Judy David is a researcher on the Work and Family Life Studies Project at the Bank Street College of Education in New York. Galinsky and David (1988) offered these working-parent solutions when work and family interfere with each other.

Making a List of the Problems

The first step in handling work/family interference is to understand it. Making a list of its stressful dimensions helps because they become less confusing. A parent who is a teacher might have the following list:

Teaching problems at work:

- Administration—lack of understanding
- Budget—not enough money
- Demands from parents
- Needs of children
- Lack of classroom help

Problems at home:

- Finding time for everything
- Finding time for myself
- Coping with stress

Understanding Expectations and Determining if They Are Realistic

When the list of problems is completed, the next step is to understand the role of expectations in each situation—what are the "shoulds" and are they realistic? Some of this parent's stress involves her anger that things are not as they *should* be. A school administrator *should* manage the budget and resources better so she can teach more effectively; her pupils *should* be prepared better for school; her husband and children *should* know to help her; her home *should* be clean all of the time; she *should* do it all! Once she becomes aware of these expectations, the parent can begin understanding them better and start examining ways to cope with them more effectively.

Solving One Problem at a Time

The third step for the working parent is to decide how to go about solving one problem at a time. Too often working parents try to tackle everything at once. Selecting one problem to work on increases the working parent's likelihood of success.

Escaping

At times, each of us needs to escape from the routines of everyday life. So do working parents. For one employed parent, it might mean reading mystery novels for half an hour a day, even if the dishes are waiting to be done. For another, it might mean watching television while exercising on a stationary bicycle. For still another, it might mean a regular dinner with college friends.

Exercising

Exercise is a great stress reducer. Working parents can get up earlier and jog before breakfast, or possibly jog or work out during the lunch hour. Some join team sports or participate in an aerobics class.

Finding Social Support

Social support is important in helping working parents cope with stress. Working parents may need a variety of people to form networks of support—friends at work to talk with about office politics, as well as friends for talking about family issues, for example. Parents also can provide important support for each other. Compliments and thanks for helping out can be very satisfying when they are given by one spouse to another. ■

CONCEPT TABLE 9.3

The Self, Gender, and Moral Development

Concept	Processes/Related Ideas	Characteristics/Description
The self	Initiative versus guilt	Erikson believes early childhood is a period when the self involves resolving the conflict between initiative versus guilt.
	Self-understanding	Self-understanding is the child's cognitive representation of self—the substance and content of the child's self-conceptions. Self-understanding provides the rational underpinnings for identity. While a rudimentary form of self-understanding occurs at about 18 months in the form of self-recognition, in early childhood the physical and active self becomes a part of self-understanding.
Gender	What is gender?	*Sex* refers to the biological dimension of being male or female; *gender* refers to the social dimension of being male or female. Gender identity is the sense of being male or female, which most children acquire by 3 years of age. Gender role is the set of expectations that prescribe how females or males should think, act, and feel.
	Biological influences	Freud's and Erikson's theories promote the idea that anatomy is destiny. Hormones influence gender development, although often not as pervasively as in animals. Hermaphrodites are individuals whose genitals become intermediate male and female because of a hormonal imbalance. Today's child developmentalists are all interactionists when biological and environmental influences on gender are considered. However, interaction means different things to different people.
	Social influences	Both identification theory and social learning theory, while providing different perspectives on gender development, emphasize the adoption of parents' gender characteristics. Parents, by action and by example, influence gender development. Peers are especially adept at rewarding gender-appropriate behavior. Historically, in the United States, education has been male defined rather than gender balanced. Currently, an effort is being made to make schools more gender balanced. Despite improvements, television still portrays males as being more competent than females.

CONCLUSIONS

In early childhood, children's socioemotional worlds expand to include more time spent with peers and in play. Their small worlds widen as they discover new refuges and new people, although parents continue to play important roles in their development.

We began this chapter by considering the diversity of families and parenting. Then we evaluated parenting styles, adapting parenting to developmental changes in the child, cultural, ethnic, and social class variations in families, and sibling relationships and birth order. We also studied the changing family in a changing society, investigating how working

mothers and divorce affect children's development, as well as depressed parents. In discussing peer relations, we examined peer group functions and the distinct but coordinated worlds of parent-child and peer relations. Our coverage of play focused on its functions, Parten's classic study, and types of play. We also read about how television influences children's development. The self, gender, and moral development are other important dimensions of young children's socioemotional development. At different points in the chapter you also read about Black and Hispanic parenting orientations,

parenting recommendations for communicating with children about divorce, and some working-parent solutions for when work and family interfere with each other.

Don't forget that you can obtain an overall summary of the main ideas in this chapter by again reading the three concept tables on pages 248, 256, and 266. In the next section of the book, Section Five, we turn our attention to middle and late childhood, beginning with chapter 10, "Physical and Cognitive Development in Middle and Late Childhood."

Concept	Processes/Related Ideas	Characteristics/Description
	Cognitive influences	Both cognitive developmental theory and gender schema theory emphasize the role of cognition in gender development. In cognitive developmental theory, children's gender-typing occurs only after they have a concept of gender. In gender schema theory, children's attention and behavior are guided by an internal motivation to conform to gender-based, sociocultural standards and stereotypes. Gender is present in the language children use and encounter. Much of the language children hear is sexist.
Moral development	What is it?	Moral development concerns rules and regulations about what people should do in their interactions with others. Developmentalists study how children think, behave, and feel about such rules and regulations.
	Piaget's view	Piaget distinguished between the heteronomous morality of younger children and the autonomous morality of older children.
	Moral behavior	Moral behavior is emphasized by social learning theorists. They believe there is considerable situational variability in moral behavior and that self-control is an important aspect of understanding children's moral behavior.
	Moral feelings	In psychoanalytic theory, the superego is the moral branch of personality. The superego develops as the child resolves the Oedipus conflict and identifies with the same-sex parent in early childhood. Through identification, children internalize a parent's standards of right and wrong. Children conform to societal standards to avoid guilt. Positive emotions, such as empathy, are important in understanding children's moral development. Empathy is reacting to another's feelings with an emotional response that is similar to the other's feelings. Empathy often has a cognitive component—perspective taking. Both positive feelings, such as empathy, sympathy, admiration, and self-esteem, and negative feelings such as anger, outrage, shame, and guilt contribute to children's moral development. When strongly experienced, these emotions influence children to act in accord with moral standards. Moral emotions do not operate in a vacuum; they are interwoven with the cognitive and social aspects of moral development.

KEY TERMS

authoritarian parenting A restrictive, punitive style that exhorts the child to follow the parent's directions and to respect work and effort. The authoritarian parent places firm limits and controls on the child with little verbal exchange allowed. Authoritarian parenting is associated with children's social incompetence. (237)

authoritative parenting Encourages children to be independent but still places limits and controls on their actions. Extensive verbal give-and-take is allowed, and parents are warm and nurturant toward the child. Authoritative parenting is associated with children's social competence. (237)

permissive-indifferent parenting A style of parenting in which the parent is very involved in the child's life; it is associated with children's social incompetence, especially a lack of self-control. (238)

permissive-indulgent parenting A style of parenting in which parents are highly involved with their children but place few demands or controls on them. Permissive-indulgent parenting is associated with children's social incompetence, especially lack of self-control. (238)

family structure model States that any differences in children from different family structures are due to the family structure variations, such as the father's being absent in one set of the families. (244)

multiple-factor model of divorce   Takes into account the complexity of the divorce context and examines a number of influences on the child's development, including not only family structure, but also the strengths and weaknesses of the child prior to the divorce, the nature of the events surrounding the divorce itself, the type of custody involved, visitation patterns, socioeconomic status, and postdivorce family functioning. (244)

peers   Children of about the same age or maturity level. (246)

play   A pleasurable activity that is engaged in for its own sake. (250)

play therapy   Allows the child to work off frustrations and is a medium through which the therapist can analyze the child's conflicts and ways of coping with them. Children may feel less threatened and be more likely to express their true feelings in the context of play. (251)

unoccupied play   Occurs when the child is not engaging in play as it is commonly understood and may stand in one spot, look around the room, or perform random movements that do not seem to have a goal. (251)

solitary play   Occurs when the child plays alone and independently of others. (251)

onlooker play   Occurs when the child watches other children play. (251)

parallel play   Occurs when the child plays separately from others, but with toys like those the others are using or in a manner that mimics their play. (251)

associative play   Occurs when play involves social interaction with little or no organization. (251)

cooperative play   Involves social interaction in a group with a sense of group identity and organized activity. (251)

sensorimotor play   Behavior engaged in by infants to derive pleasure from exercising their existing sensorimotor schemas. (252)

practice play   Involves the repetition of behavior when new skills are being learned or when physical or mental mastery and coordination of skills are required for games or sports. Sensorimotor play, which often involves practice play, is primarily confined to infancy, while practice play can be engaged in throughout life. (252)

pretense/symbolic play   Occurs when the child transforms the physical environment into a symbol. (252)

social play   Play that involves social interactions with peers. (252)

constructive play   Combines sensorimotor/practice repetitive activity with symbolic representation of ideas. Constructive play occurs when children engage in self-regulated creation or construction of a product or a problem solution. (252)

games   Activities engaged in for pleasure that include rules and often competition with one or more individuals. (253)

self-understanding   The child's cognitive representation of self, the substance and content of the child's self-conceptions. (257)

gender   The social dimension of being male or female. (257)

gender identity   The sense of being male or female, which most children acquire by the time they are 3 years old. (257)

gender role   A set of expectations that prescribe how females and males should think, act, and feel. (257)

androgen   The main class of male sex hormones. (257)

estrogen   The main class of female sex hormones. (257)

identification theory   Stems from Freud's view that the preschool child develops a sexual attraction to the opposite-sex parent, then by approximately 5 or 6 years of age renounces this attraction because of anxious feelings, and subsequently identifies with the same-sex parent, unconsciously adopting the same-sex parent's characteristics. (258)

social learning theory of gender   Emphasizes that children's gender development occurs through observation and imitation of gender behavior, and through the rewards and punishments children experience for gender appropriate and inappropriate behavior. (258)

cognitive developmental theory of gender   Children's gender typing occurs after they have developed a concept of gender. Once they consistently conceive of themselves as male or female, children often organize their world on the basis of gender. (261)

schema   A cognitive structure, a network of associations that organizes and guides an individual's perceptions. (261)

gender schema   Organizes the world in terms of female and male. (261)

gender schema theory   States that an individual's attention and behavior are guided by an internal motivation to conform to gender-based sociocultural standards and stereotypes. (261)

moral development   Concerns rules and conventions about what people should do in their interactions with other people. (263)

heteronomous morality   The first stage of moral development in Piaget's theory, occurring from approximately 4 to 7 years of age. Justice and rules are conceived of as unchangeable properties of the world, removed from the control of people. (263)

autonomous morality   The second stage of moral development in Piaget's theory, displayed by older children (about 10 years of age and older). The child becomes aware that rules and laws are created by people and that, in judging an action, one should consider the actor's intentions as well as the consequences. (263)

immanent justice   The concept that if a rule is broken, punishment will be meted out immediately. (263)

empathy   Reacting to another's feelings with an emotional response that is similar to the other's feelings. (264)

Middle and Late Childhood

Blessed be childhood, which brings something of heaven into the midst of our rough earthliness.

—Henri Frédéric Amiel, *Journal,* 1868

In middle and late childhood, children are on a different plane, belonging to a generation and feeling all their own. It is the wisdom of the human life cycle that at no time are children more ready to learn than during the period of expansive imagination at the end of early childhood. Children develop a sense of wanting to make things, and not just to make them, but to make them well and even perfectly. Their thirst is to know and to understand. They are remarkable for their intelligence and for their curiosity. Their parents continue to be important influences in their lives, but their growth also is shaped by successive choirs of friends. They don't think much about the future or about the past, but they enjoy the present moment. Section Five consists of two chapters, "Physical and Cognitive Development in Middle and Late Childhood" (chapter 10) and "Socioemotional Development in Middle and Late Childhood" (chapter 11).

Paul Klee, The Gifted Boy, detail.

Physical and Cognitive Development in Middle and Late Childhood

*Children are remarkable for their
intelligence and ardor, for their
curiosity, their intolerance of shams,
the clarity . . . of their vision.*

—Aldous Huxley

Every forward step we take we leave some phantom of ourselves behind.

—John Lancaster Spalding

IMAGES OF LIFE-SPAN DEVELOPMENT

Training Children for the Olympics in China

Standing on the balance beam at a sports school in Beijing, China, 6-year-old Zhang Liyin stretches her arms outward as she gets ready to perform a backflip. She wears the bright-red gymnastic suit of the elite—a suit given to only the best ten girls in her class of 6- to 8-year-olds. But her face wears a dreadful expression; she can't drum up enough confidence to do the flip. Maybe it is because she has had a rough week; a purple bruise decorates one leg, and a nasty gash disfigures the other. Her coach, a woman in her twenties, makes Zhang jump from the beam and escorts her to the high bar, where she is instructed to hang for 3 minutes. If Zhang falls, she must pick herself up and try again. But she does not fall, and she is escorted back to the beam, where her coach puts her through another tedious routine.

Zhang attends the sports school in the afternoon. The sports school is a privilege given to only 260,000 of China's 200 million students of elementary to college age. The Communist party has decided that sports is one avenue China can pursue to prove that China has arrived in the modern world. The sports schools designed to produce Olympic champions were the reason for China's success in the 1984, 1988, and 1992 Olympics. These schools are the only road to Olympic stardom in China. There are precious few neighborhood playgrounds. And for every 3.5 million people, there is only one gymnasium.

The training of future Olympians in the sports schools of China. Six-year-old Zhang Liyin (third from the left) hopes someday to become an Olympic gymnastics champion. Attending the sports school is considered an outstanding privilege; only 260,000 of China's 200 million children are given this opportunity.

Many of the students who attend the sports schools in the afternoon live and study at the schools as well. Only a few attend a normal school and then come to a sports school in the afternoon. Because of her young age, Zhang stays at home during the mornings and goes to the sports school from noon until 6 P.M. A part-timer like Zhang can stay enrolled until she no longer shows potential to move up to the next step. Any child who seems to lack potential is asked to leave.

Zhang was playing in a kindergarten class when a coach from a sports school spotted her. She was selected because of her broad shoulders, narrow hips, straight legs, symmetrical limbs, openminded attitude, vivaciousness, and outgoing personality. If Zhang continues to show progress, she could be asked to move to full-time next year. At age 7, she would then go to school there and live in a dorm 6 days a week. If she becomes extremely competent at gymnastics, Zhang could be moved to Shishahai, where the elite gymnasts train and compete (Reilly, 1988).

PREVIEW

By American standards, Zhang's life sounds rigid and punitive. Even though achievement in sports has a lofty status in American society, children are not trained with the intensity now being witnessed in China. Later in the chapter, we will discuss children's sports, physical fitness, and health. We begin the chapter by examining children's physical development in middle and late childhood, then turn our attention to a number of important aspects of children's cognitive development in this period of childhood.

PHYSICAL DEVELOPMENT IN MIDDLE AND LATE CHILDHOOD

How do children's bodies change in middle and late childhood? How much exercise do children get and how does it affect their development? What is the role of sports in children's development? What are children's stress and coping like? What kind of disabilities do handicapped children have, and how should they be educated?

Body Changes

The period of middle and late childhood involves slow, consistent growth. This is a period of calm before the rapid growth spurt of adolescence. Among the important aspects of body change in this developmental period are those involving the skeletal system, the muscular system, and motor skills.

The Skeletal and Muscular Systems

During the elementary school years, children grow an average of 2 to 3 inches a year until, at the age of 11, the average girl is 4 feet 10 inches tall and the average boy is 4 feet, 9½ inches tall. Children's legs become longer and their trunks slimmer. During the middle and late childhood years, children gain about 5 to 7 pounds a year. The weight increase is due mainly to increases in the size of the skeleton and muscular systems, as well as the size of some body organs. Muscle mass and strength gradually increase as "baby fat" decreases. The loose movements and knock-knee of early childhood give way to improved muscle tone. The increase in muscular strength is due to heredity and to exercise. Children double their strength capabilities during these years. Because of their greater number of muscle cells, boys are usually stronger than girls.

As children move through the elementary school years, they gain greater control over their bodies. Physical action is essential for them to refine their developing skills.

Motor Skills

During middle and late childhood, children's motor development becomes smoother and more coordinated than it was in early childhood. For example, only one child in a thousand can hit a tennis ball over the net at the age of 3, yet by the age of 10 or 11, most children can learn to play the sport. Running, climbing, skipping rope, swimming, bicycle riding, and skating are just a few of the many physical skills elementary school children can master. And when mastered, these physical skills are a source of great pleasure and accomplishment for children. In gross motor skills involving large muscle activity, boys usually outperform girls rather handily.

As children move through the elementary school years, they gain greater control over their bodies and can sit and attend for longer periods of time. However, elementary school children are far from physically mature, and they need to be active. They become more fatigued by long periods of sitting than by running, jumping, or bicycling. Physical action is essential for these children to refine their developing skills, such as batting a ball, skipping rope, or balancing on a beam. An important principle of practice for elementary school children, therefore, is that they should be engaged in *active,* rather than passive, activities (Katz & Chard, 1989).

> *The quality of life is determined by its activities.*
> —Aristotle, 4th Century B.C.

Increased myelinization—an insulation of the nerves that helps nerve impulses travel faster—of the central nervous system is reflected in the improvement of fine motor skills during middle and late childhood. Children's hands are used more adroitly as tools. Six-year-olds can hammer, paste, tie shoes, and fasten clothes. By 7 years of age, children's hands become steadier. At this age, children prefer a pencil to a crayon for printing, and reversal of letters is less common. Printing becomes smaller. From 8 to 10 years of age, the hands can be used independently with more ease and precision. Fine motor coordination develops to the point where children can write rather than print words. Letter size becomes smaller and more even. By 10 to 12 years of age, children begin to show manipulative skills similar to the abilities of adults. The complex, intricate, and rapid movements needed to produce fine-quality crafts or play a difficult piece on a musical instrument can be mastered. Girls usually outperform boys in fine motor skills.

Exercise

Many of our patterns of health and illness are long-standing. Our experiences as children contribute to our health practices as adults. Did your parents seek medical help at your first sniffle, or did they wait until your temperature reached 104 degrees? Did they feed you heavy doses of red meat and sugar or a more rounded diet with vegetables and fruit? Did they get you involved in sports or exercise programs, or did you lie around watching television all the time?

> *We are underexercised as a nation. We look instead of play. We ride instead of walk. Our existence deprives us of the minimum of physical activity essential for healthy living.*
> —John F. Kennedy, 1961

Are children getting enough exercise? The 1985 School Fitness Survey tested 18,857 children aged 6 to 17 on nine fitness tasks. Compared to a similar survey in 1975, virtually no improvement was made on the tasks. For example, 40 percent of the boys 6 to 12 years of age could do no more than one pull-up, and a full 25 percent could not do any! Fifty percent of the girls aged 6 to 17 and 30 percent of the boys aged 6 to 12 could not run a mile in less than 10 minutes. In the 50-yard dash, the adolescent girls in 1975 were faster than the adolescent girls in 1985.

Some experts suggest that television is at least partially to blame for the poor physical condition of our nation's children. In one investigation, children who watched little television were significantly more physically fit than their heavy-television-viewing counterparts (Tucker, 1987). The more children watch television, the more they are likely to be overweight. No one is quite sure whether this is because children spend their leisure time in front of the television set instead of chasing each other around the neighborhood or whether they tend to eat a lot of junk food they see advertised on television.

Some of the blame also falls on the nation's schools, many of which fail to provide physical education classes on a daily basis. In the 1985 School Fitness Survey, 37 percent of the children in the first through the fourth grades take gym classes only once or twice a week. The investigation also revealed that parents are poor role models when it comes to physical fitness. Less than 30 percent of the parents of children in grades 1 through 4 exercised 3 days a week. Roughly half said they never get any vigorous exercise. In another study, observations of children's behavior in physical education classes at four different elementary schools revealed how little vigorous exercise is done in these classes (Parcel & others, 1987). Children moved through space only 50 percent of the time they were in the class, and they moved continuously an average of only 2.2 minutes. In summary, not only do children's school weeks not include adequate physical education classes, but the majority of children do not exercise vigorously even when they are in such classes. Furthermore, most children's parents are poor role models for vigorous physical exercise.

Critical Thinking

Imagine that you are the physical education coordinator for the elementary schools in a large city. Describe the ideal program you would want to implement to improve children's physical fitness.

Sports

Sports have become an increasingly integral part of American culture. Thus, it is not surprising that more and more children become involved in sports every year. Both in public schools and in community agencies, children's sports programs that involve baseball, soccer, football, basketball, swimming, gymnastics, and other activities have grown to the extent that they have changed the shape of many children's lives.

Participation in sports can have both positive and negative consequences for children. Children's participation in sports can provide exercise, opportunities to learn how to compete, increased self-esteem, and a setting for developing peer relations and friendships. However, sports also can have negative outcomes for children: Too much pressure to achieve and win, physical injuries, a distraction from academic work, and unrealistic expectations for success as an athlete. Few people challenge the value of sports for children when conducted as part of a school physical education or intramural program, but some question the appropriateness of highly competitive, win-oriented sports teams in schools and community agencies.

Little League baseball, basketball, soccer, tennis, dance—as their motor development becomes smoother and more coordinated, children are able to master these activities more competently in middle and late childhood than they could in early childhood.

There is a special concern for children in "high pressure" sports settings involving championship play with accompanying media publicity. Some clinicians and child developmentalists believe such activities not only put undue stress on the participants, but also teach children the wrong values, namely, a "win-at-all costs" philosophy. The possibility of exploiting children through highly organized, win-oriented sports programs is an ever-present danger. Overly ambitious parents, coaches, and community boosters can unintentionally create a highly stressful atmosphere in children's sports. When parental, agency, or community prestige becomes the central focus of the child's participation in sports, the danger of exploitation is clearly present. Programs oriented toward such purposes often require long and arduous training sessions over many months and years, frequently leading to sports specialization at too early an age. In such circumstances, adults often transmit a distorted view of the role of the sport in the child's life, communicating to the child that the sport is the most important aspect of the child's existence.

Stress

Stress is a sign of the times. No one really knows whether today's children experience more stress than their predecessors did, but it does seem that their stressors have increased. Among the stress-related questions we examine are these: What is stress? How do cognitive factors influence stress? What roles do life events and daily hassles play in children's stress? And how do sociocultural factors influence the stress children experience?

What Is Stress?

Stress is not easy to define. Initially the term *stress* was loosely borrowed from physics. Humans, it was thought, are in some ways similar to physical objects such as metals that resist moderate outside forces but lose their resiliency at some point of greater pressure. But unlike metal, children can think and reason; they experience a myriad of social circumstances that make defining stress more complex in psychology than in physics (Hobfoll, 1989). Is stress the threats and challenges that the environment places on us (as when we say, "Sally's world is so stressful, it is overwhelming her")? Is stress our response to such threats and challenges (as when we say, "Bob is not coping well with the problems in his life; he is experiencing a lot of stress and his body is falling apart")? While there is continuing debate on whether stress is the threatening event or the response to those demands, we will define it broadly. **Stress** *is the response of individuals to the circumstances and events (called "stressors") that threaten them and tax their coping abilities.*

Cognitive Factors

Most of us think of stress as environmental events that place demands on an individual's life, events such as an approaching test, being in a car wreck, or losing a friend. While there are some common ways children and adults experience stress, not everyone perceives the same events as stressful. For example, one child may perceive an approaching test as threatening, another child may perceive it as challenging. To some degree, then, what is stressful for children depends on how they cognitively appraise and interpret events. This view has been presented most clearly by stress researcher Richard Lazarus (1966, 1990, 1993a, 1993b). **Cognitive appraisal** *is Lazarus's term that describes children's interpretations of events in their lives as harmful, threatening, or challenging, and their determination of whether they have the resources to effectively cope with the events.*

In Lazarus's view, events are appraised in two steps: primary appraisal and secondary appraisal. In **primary appraisal,** *children interpret whether an event involves harm or loss that has already occurred, a threat to some future danger, or a challenge to be overcome.* *Harm* is the child's appraisal of the damage the event has already inflicted. For example, if a child failed a test in school yesterday, the harm has already been done. *Threat* is the child's appraisal of potential future damage an event may bring. For example, failing the test may lower the teacher's opinion of the child and increase the probability the child will get a low grade at the end of the year. *Challenge* is the child's appraisal of the potential to overcome the adverse circumstances of an event and ultimately profit from the event. In the case of the child failing a test in school, the child may develop a commitment to never get into that situation again and become a better student.

After children cognitively appraise an event for its harm, threat, or challenge, Lazarus says they subsequently engage in secondary appraisal. In **secondary appraisal,** *children evaluate their resources and determine how effectively they can cope with the event.* This appraisal is called "secondary" because it comes after

LIFE-SPAN PRACTICAL KNOWLEDGE 10.1

To Listen to a Child

(1984) by T. Berry Brazelton.
Reading, MA: Addison-Wesley.

The focus in *To Listen to a Child* is primarily on problematic events that arise in the lives of children. Fears, feeding, sleeping problems, stomachaches, and asthma are among the normal problems of growing that Brazelton evaluates. He assures parents that it is only when parents let their own anxieties interfere that these problems (such as bed-wetting) become chronic and guilt-laden. Each chapter closes with practical guidelines for parents. A final chapter focuses on the hospitalized child, including how to prepare the child for a hospital stay and how to interact with the child at the hospital.

To Listen to a Child includes clearly explained examples and is warm, personal, and entertaining. It is a good resource book for parents to hold on to as their child ages through the childhood years and to consult when physical problems develop.

primary appraisal and depends on the degree to which the event has been appraised as harmful, threatening, or challenging. Coping involves a wide range of potential strategies, skills, and abilities for effectively managing stressful events. In the example of failing the exam, if the child learns that his or her parents will get a tutor to help him or her, then the child likely will be more confident in coping with the stress than if the parents provide no support.

Lazarus believes a child's experience of stress is a balance of primary and secondary appraisal. When harm and threat are high, and challenge and resources are low, stress is likely to be high; when harm and threat are low, and challenge and resources are high, stress is more likely to be moderate or low.

Life Events and Daily Hassles

Children can experience a spectrum of stresses, ranging from ordinary to severe. At the ordinary end are experiences that occur in most children's lives and for which there are reasonably well-defined coping patterns. For example, most parents are aware that siblings are jealous of each other and that when one sibling does well at something, the other sibling(s) will be jealous. They know how jealousy works and know ways to help children cope with it. More severe stress occurs when children become separated from their parents. Healthy coping patterns for this stressful experience are not as well spelled out. Some children are well cared for; others are ignored when there is a separation caused by divorce, death, illness, or foster placement. Even more severe are the experiences of children who have lived for years in situations of neglect or abuse. Victims of incest also experience severe stress, with few coping guidelines.

Recently, psychologists have emphasized that life's daily experiences as well as life's major events may be the culprits in stress. Enduring a tense family life and living in poverty do not show up on scales of major life events in children's development, yet the everyday pounding children take from these living conditions can add up to a highly stressful life and eventually psychological disturbance or illness (Compas, 1989; Creasy & others, 1993; Folkman & Lazarus, 1991).

Sociocultural Factors

Among the sociocultural factors involved in stress are acculturative stress and socioeconomic stress, each of which we consider in turn.

Acculturative Stress

Acculturation *is cultural change that results from continuous, first-hand contact between two distinctive cultural groups. Acculturative stress is the negative consequence of acculturation.* Members of ethnic minority groups have historically encountered hostility, prejudice, and lack of effective support during crises, which contributes to alienation, social isolation, and heightened stress (Huang & Gibbs, 1989). As upwardly mobile ethnic minority families have attempted to penetrate all-White neighborhoods, interracial tensions often mount. Similarly, racial tensions and hostility often emerge among the various ethnic minorities as they each struggle for limited housing and employment opportunities, seeking a fair share of a limited market. Clashes become inevitable as Hispanic family markets spring up in Black urban neighborhoods; as Vietnamese extended families displace Puerto Rican apartment dwellers; as the increasing enrollment of Asian students on college campuses is perceived as a threat to affirmative action policies by other non-White ethnic minority students. While race relations in the United States have historically been conceptualized as Black/White, this is no longer the only combination producing ethnic animosity.

As the number of Hispanics and Asians has increased dramatically, and as Native Americans have crossed the boundaries of their reservations, the visibility of these groups has brought them into contact not only with the mainstream White society, but with one another as well. Depending on the circumstances, this contact has sometimes been harmonious, sometimes antagonistic.

Although the dominant White society has tried on many occasions to enslave or dispossess entire populations, these ethnic minority groups have survived and flourished, showing remarkable resilience and adaptation in the face of severe stress and oppression (Phinney, Chavira, & Williamson, 1992; Rick & Foward, 1992; Root, 1992). Confronted with overt or covert attempts at segregation, they have developed their own communities and social structures, which include Black churches, Vietnamese mutual assistance associations, Chinese American family associations, Japanese-language schools, Indian "bands" and tribal associations, and Mexican American kin systems; at the same time they have learned to negotiate with the dominant White culture in America. They essentially have mastered two cultures and have developed impressive competencies and coping strategies for adapting to life in America. The resilience and adaptation shown by ethnic minority groups can teach us much about coping and survival in the face of overwhelming adversity (Jackson, 1992; Kavanaugh & Kennedy, 1992).

Socioeconomic Status

Poverty imposes considerable stress on children and their families (Aber, 1993; Belle, 1990; Huston, McLoyd & Coll, in press; McLoyd, 1993; Strawn, 1992). Chronic life conditions such as inadequate housing, dangerous neighborhoods, burdensome responsibilities, and economic uncertainties are potent stressors in the lives of the poor. The incidence of poverty is especially pronounced among ethnic minority children and their families (Richards & others, 1994). For example, Black women heading families face a risk of poverty that is more than 10 times that of White men heading families. Puerto Rican female family heads face a poverty rate that is almost 15 times that found among White male family heads (National Advisory Council on Economic Opportunity, 1980). Many individuals who become poor during their lives remain poor for 1 or 2 years. However, Blacks and female family heads are at risk for experiencing persistent poverty. The average poor Black child experiences poverty that will last almost 20 years (Wilson & Neckerman, 1986).

Poverty is related to threatening and uncontrollable events in children's lives (Belle, 1990; Russo, 1990). For example, poor females are more likely to experience crime and violence than are middle-class females. Poverty also undermines sources of social support that play a role in buffering the effects of stress. Sometimes just one person can make a difference in children's lives in low-income neighborhoods.

Protective Buffers

What are some of the factors that help children be resilient in the face of stressful circumstances and assaults on their health and well-being? In one large-scale investigation, Emmy Werner and Ruth Smith (1982) found that children greatly benefit from having a readily available support network of grandparents, neighbors, or relatives. In many instances, children who cope effectively with stress, threats, and assaults on their health and well-being have a cluster of protective factors, not just one or two. But if forced to pick one factor that above all others is the most important in helping children weather problems, Werner says, it is a basic, trusting relationship with an adult. In all of the protective clusters in Werner's study, there was not one that did not include that one good relationship, whether with a parent, a grand-

One of a child's most important protective buffers from stressors and problems is the long-term presence of a basic, trusting relationship with an adult.

parent, an older sibling, a teacher, or a mentor—someone consistent in the child's life who could say to the child, "You count. I love you and will care for you. I will always be there for you." Even children of abusive or schizophrenic parents sometimes prove to be resilient if they have had at least one good caring parent nurturing and protecting them—someone who serves as sort of a beacon in their lives.

Thomas Boyce (1991), pediatrics professor at the University of California, San Francisco, described an 8-year-old boy from an impoverished, rural Black family who had been abandoned by his mother. The boy also had "prune-belly syndrome," an abnormality of the abdominal musculature that left him with significant kidney and urinary problems, which required extensive surgery. But the boy had two nurturing, caring grandparents who had raised him from infancy. They consistently supported him and unfailingly accompanied him on his hospital visits. Despite his physical problems and the absence of his mother, the boy's school performance was superb.

Such protective factors in children's lives work best when they are long-lasting. There is no guarantee that the child will always be resilient, since families and children may experience a host of ups and downs as children develop. Children who cope well early in their development can have setbacks later because of family or school problems. In life, no child is unbreakable. Every child needs the care and support of at least one significant person throughout the childhood years for optimal development (Gelman, 1991).

TABLE 10.1

Estimates of the Percentage and Number of Handicapped Children in the United States

Handicap	Percentage of Population	Number of Children Ages 5 to 18
Visual impairment (includes blindness)	0.1	55,000
Hearing impairment (includes deafness)	0.5–0.7	275,000–385,000
Speech handicap	3.0–4.0	1,650,000–2,200,000
Orthopedic and health impairments	0.5	275,000
Emotional disturbance	2.0–3.0	1,100,000–1,650,000
Mental retardation (both educable and trainable)	2.0–3.0	1,100,000–1,650,000
Learning disabilities	2.0–3.0	1,100,000–1,650,000
Multiple handicaps	0.5–0.7	275,000–385,000
Total	10.6–15.0	5,830,000–8,250,000

Reprinted with the permission of Macmillan College Publishing Company from *The Exceptional Student in the Regular Classroom*, 3rd edition, by Bill R. Gearheart and Mel W. Weishahn. Copyright © 1984 by Macmillan College Publishing Company, Inc.

Handicapped Children

The elementary school years are a time when handicapped children become more sensitive about their differentness and how it is perceived by others. One 6-year-old girl came home from school and asked, "Am I disabled or handicapped?" Another articulate 6-year-old girl described in detail how her premature birth was the cause of her cerebral palsy: "I was a teensy-weensy baby. They put me in an incubator and I almost died." Later, when asked about being teased by her classmates because she could not walk, she replied, "I hate their guts, but if I said anything the teacher would get mad at me." A 7-year-old handicapped boy commented about how he had successfully completed a rocket-making course during the summer; he was the youngest and the most knowledgeable child in the class: "For the first time, some kids really liked me" (Howard, 1982). Life is not always fair, especially for handicapped children. As evidenced by the comments of the handicapped children just mentioned, adjusting to the world of peers and school is often painful and difficult. Our coverage of handicapped children focuses on the prevalence of handicaps and the education of handicapped children, learning disabilities, and attention-deficit hyperactivity disorder.

Prevalence of Handicaps and the Education of Handicapped Children

An estimated 10 to 15 percent of the United States population of children between the ages of 5 and 18 are handicapped in some way (see table 10.1). It is estimated that 0.1 percent are visually impaired and that 3 to 4 percent have speech handicaps. Estimates vary because of problems in classification and testing. Experts sometimes differ in how they define the various categories of handicapped children, and different tests may be used by different school systems or psychologists to assess whether a child is handicapped.

Public Law 94-142 *is the federal government's mandate to all states to provide a free, appropriate education for all children. This law, also called the "Education for All Handicapped Children Act," was passed by Congress in 1975. A key provision of the bill was the development of an individualized education program for each identified handicapped child.*

Public Law 94-142 mandates free, appropriate education for all children. A key provision of the bill was the development of an individualized education program for each identified handicapped child. Among the important issues involved in the education of handicapped children are mainstreaming and labeling.

Mainstreaming *occurs when handicapped children attend regular school classes with nonhandicapped children. In this way handicapped children enter the "mainstream" of education in the school and are not separated from nonhandicapped students.* However, even under PL 94-142, which emphasizes mainstreaming, certain types of handicapped children, such as those with hearing impairments, usually spend part of each day in separate classes taught by specially trained teachers. The results of mainstreaming have met with mixed results. In some schools, teachers assign children to environments that are not the best contexts for learning (Brady & others, 1988). Some people believe that mainstreaming means there will be a number of profoundly retarded, drugged children sitting in classrooms in dazed, unresponsive states. Others believe that including handicapped children in regular classrooms will detract from the quality of education given to nonhandicapped children. The picture is not as bleak as some of these criticisms suggest. Virtually all profoundly retarded children are institutionalized and will never be schooled in public classrooms. Only the mildly retarded are mainstreamed. Mainstreaming makes children and teachers more aware of the special needs of handicapped people.

In practice, mainstreaming has not been the simple solution its architects hoped for. Many handicapped children require extensive and expensive services to help them become effective learners in the regular classroom. As school systems have become increasingly strapped financially, many services for handicapped children have been cut back. Some teachers, already burdened with heavy course loads and time demands, have felt overwhelmed by the added requirement of developing special teaching arrangements for handicapped children. And the social interaction of handicapped and nonhandicapped children has not always gone smoothly in mainstreamed classrooms (Gallagher, Trohanis, & Clifford, 1989).

The hope that mainstreaming would be a positive solution for all handicapped children needs to be balanced with the reality of each individual handicapped child's life and that particular child's special needs. The specially tailored education program should meet with the acceptance of the child's parents, counselors, educational authorities, and, when feasible, the children themselves (Hallahan & others, 1988).

Is there a disadvantage to referring to these children as "handicapped" or "disabled"? Children who are labeled handicapped or disabled may feel permanently stigmatized and rejected, and they may be denied opportunities for full development. Children labeled as handicapped or disabled may be assigned to inferior educational programs or placed in institutions without the legal protection given to "normal" individuals. Paradoxically, however, if handicapped or disabled children are not labeled, they may not be able to take advantage of the special programs designed to help them (Hobbs, 1975; Home, 1988).

> ## Critical Thinking
>
> *Is mainstreaming the best way for handicapped children to be educated? What needs and concerns of handicapped and nonhandicapped children should be considered?*

There are no quick fixes for the education of handicapped children (Ysseldyke, Algozzine, & Thurlow, 1992). Progress has been made in recent years to provide supportive instruction for handicapped children, but increasing effort needs to be devoted to developing the skills of handicapped children (Hynd & Obrzut, 1986). Handicapped children have a strong will to survive, to grow, and to learn. They deserve our very best educational efforts (Wood, 1988).

Learning Disabilities

Paula doesn't like kindergarten and can't seem to remember the names of her teacher or classmates. Bobby's third-grade teacher complains that his spelling is awful and that he is always reversing letters. Ten-year-old Tim hates to read. He says it is too hard for him and the words just don't make any sense to him. Each of these children is learning disabled. Children with **learning disabilities** *(1) are of normal intelligence or above, (2) have difficulties in several academic areas but usually do not show deficits in others, and (3) are not suffering from some other conditions or disorders that could explain their learning problems.* (Reid, 1988). The breadth of definitions of learning disabilities has generated controversy about just what learning disabilities are (Chalfant, 1989; Gerber, 1992).

Within the global concept of learning disabilities fall problems in listening, thinking, memory, reading, writing, spelling, and math (Andrew & Conte, 1993; Jackson, Breitmeyer & Fletcher, 1993; Spear-Swerling & Sternberg, 1994). Attention deficits involving an inability to sit still, pay attention, and concentrate are also classified as learning disabilities. Estimates of the number of learning-disabled children in the United States are as broad as the definition, ranging from 1 percent to 30 percent (Lerner, 1988). The U.S. Department of Education puts the number of identified learning-disabled children between the ages of 3 and 21 at approximately 2 million.

Improving the lives of learning-disabled children will come from (1) recognizing the complex, multifaceted nature of learning disabilities (biological, cognitive, and social aspects of learning disabilities need to be considered) and (2) becoming more precise in our analysis of the learning environments in which learning-disabled children participate (Drew & Luftig, 1993; Vaughn, 1993; Lyytinen & others, 1994). The following discussion of one subtype of learning disability, attention-deficit hyperactivity disorder, exemplifies this complexity and preciseness.

Attention-Deficit Hyperactivity Disorder

Matthew failed the first grade. His handwriting was messy. He did not know the alphabet and never attended very well to the lessons the teacher taught. Matthew is almost always in motion. He can't sit still for more than a few minutes at a time. His mother describes him as very fidgety. Matthew has **attention-deficit hyperactivity disorder,** *or what is commonly called "hyperactivity." This disorder is characterized by a short attention span, distractibility, and high levels of physical activity* (Barkeley, 1989; Berman, 1992; O'Connor, Crowell, & Sprafkin, 1993). In short, these children do not pay attention and have difficulty concentrating on what they are doing. Estimates of the number of children with attention-deficit hyperactivity disorder vary from less than 1 percent to 5 percent. While young children or even infants may show characteristics of this disorder, the vast majority of hyperactive children are identified in the first three grades of elementary school, when teachers recognize that they have great difficulty paying attention, sitting still, and concentrating on their schoolwork.

What makes Jimmy so impulsive, Sandy so distractible, and Harvey so excitable? Possible causes include heredity, prenatal damage, diet, family dynamics, and the physical environment. As we saw in chapter 7, the influence of heredity on temperament is increasingly considered, with activity level being one aspect of temperament that differentiates one child from another very early in development. Approximately four times as many boys as girls are hyperactive. This sex difference may be due to differences in the brains of boys and girls determined by genes on the Y chromosome. The prenatal hazards we discussed in chapter 4 may also produce hyperactive behavior; excessive drinking by women during pregnancy is associated with poor attention and concentration by their offspring at 4 years of age, for example (Streissguth & others, 1984). With regard to diet, severe vitamin deficiencies can lead to attentional problems. Vitamin B deficiencies are of special concern. Caffeine and sugar may also contribute to attentional problems.

A wide range of psychotherapies and drug therapy have been used to improve the lives of hyperactive children. For unknown reasons, some drugs that stimulate the brains and behaviors of adults have a quieting effect on the brains and behaviors of children. The drugs most widely prescribed for hyperactive children are amphetamines, especially Ritalin. Amphetamines work effectively for some hyperactive children, but not all (Batshaw & Perret, 1986). As many as 20 percent of hyperactive children treated with Ritalin do not respond to it. Even when Ritalin works, it is also important to consider the social world of the hyperactive child. The teacher is especially important in this social world, helping to monitor the child's academic and social behavior to determine whether the drug works and whether the prescribed dosage is correct.

At this point we have discussed a number of ideas about physical development in middle and late childhood. A summary of these ideas is presented in concept table 10.1. Now we turn our attention to children's cognitive development.

COGNITIVE DEVELOPMENT IN MIDDLE AND LATE CHILDHOOD

Our coverage of children's cognitive development focuses on Piaget's theory and concrete operational thought, Piagetian contributions and criticisms, information processing, intelligence, and its variations, language, and achievement.

Piaget's Theory and Concrete Operational Thought

According to Piaget (1967), the preschool child's thought is preoperational. Preoperational thought involves the formation of stable concepts, the emergence of mental reasoning, the prominence of egocentrism, and the construction of magical belief systems. Thought during the preschool years is still flawed and not well organized. Piaget believed that concrete operational thought does not appear until about the age of 7, but as we learned in chapter 8, Piaget may have underestimated some of the cognitive skills of preschool children. For example, by carefully and cleverly designing experiments on understanding the

concept of number, Rochel Gelman (1972) demonstrated that some preschool children show conservation, a concrete operational skill. In chapter 8, we explored concrete operational thought by describing the preschool child's flaws in thinking about such concrete operational skills as conservation and classification; here we will cover the characteristics of concrete operational thought again, this time emphasizing the competencies of elementary school children. Applications of Piaget's ideas to children's education and an evaluation of Piaget's theory are also considered.

> *The thirst to know and understand . . . these are the goods in life's rich hand.*
>
> —Sir William Watson, 1905

Concrete Operational Thought

Remember that, according to Piaget, concrete operational thought is made up of operations—mental actions that allow the child to do mentally what was done physically before. Concrete operations are also mental actions that are reversible. In the well-known test of reversibility of thought involving conservation of matter, the child is presented with two identical balls of clay. The experimenter rolls one ball into a long, thin shape; the other remains in its original ball shape. The child is then asked if there is more clay in the ball or in the long, thin piece of clay. By the time children reach the age of 7 or 8, most answer that the amount of clay is the same. To answer this problem correctly, children have to imagine that the clay ball is rolled out into a long, thin strip and then returned to its original round shape. This type of imagination involves a reversible mental action. Thus, a concrete operation is a reversible mental action on real, concrete objects. Concrete operations allow the child to coordinate several characteristics rather than focus on a single property of an object. In the clay example, the preoperational child is likely to focus on height *or* width. The concrete operational child coordinates information about both dimensions.

Many of the concrete operations identified by Piaget focus on the ways children reason about the properties of objects. One important skill that characterizes the concrete operational child is the ability to classify or divide things into different sets or subsets and to consider their interrelationships. An example of the concrete operational child's classification skills involves a family tree of four generations (see figure 10.1) (Furth & Wachs, 1975). This family tree suggests that the grandfather (A) has three children (B, C, & D), each of whom has two children (E through J), and that one of these children (J) has three children (K, L, & M). A child who comprehends the classification system can move up and down a level (vertically), across a level (horizontally), and up and down and across (obliquely) within the system. The concrete operational child understands that person J can at the same time be father, brother, and grandson, for example. A summary of concrete operational thought's characteristics is shown in figure 10.2.

FIGURE 10.1

Classification: an important ability in concrete operational thought. *A family tree of four generations (I to IV): the preoperational child has trouble classifying the members of the four generations; the concrete operational child can classify the members vertically, horizontally, and obliquely (up and down and across).*

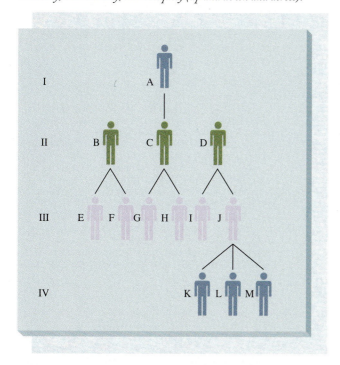

Piaget and Education

Piaget was not an educator and never pretended to be. But he did provide a sound conceptual framework from which to view educational problems. What are some of the principles in Piaget's theory of cognitive development that can be applied to children's education? David Elkind (1976) described three. First, the foremost issue in education is *communication*. In Piaget's theory, the child's mind is not a blank slate; on the contrary, the child has a host of ideas about the physical and natural world, but these ideas differ from those of adults. We must learn to comprehend what children are saying and to respond in the same mode of discourse that children use. Second, the child is always unlearning and relearning in addition to acquiring knowledge. Children come to school with their own ideas about space, time, causality, quantity, and number. Third, the child is by nature a knowing creature, motivated to acquire knowledge. The best way to nurture this motivation for knowledge is to allow the child to spontaneously interact with the environment; education needs to ensure that it does not dull the child's eagerness to know by providing an overly rigid curriculum that disrupts the child's own rhythm and pace of learning.

Piagetian Contributions and Criticisms

We have spent considerable time outlining Piaget's theory of cognitive development in this chapter and in chapters 2, 6, and 8. Let's briefly summarize some of Piaget's main contributions, and then enumerate criticisms of his theory.

FIGURE 10.2

Characteristics of concrete operational thought.

Can use operations, mentally reversing action; shows conservation skills

Logical reasoning replaces intuitive reasoning, but only in concrete circumstances

Not abstract (can't imagine steps in algebraic equation, for example)

Classification skills—can divide things into sets and subsets and reason about their interrelations

CONCEPT TABLE 10.1

Physical Development in Middle and Late Childhood

Concept	Processes/Related Ideas	Characteristics/Description
Body changes	The skeletal and muscular systems	During the elementary school years, children grow an average of 2 to 3 inches a year. Muscle mass and strength gradually increase. Legs lengthen and trunks slim down as "baby fat" decreases. Growth is slow and consistent.
	Motor skills	During the middle and late childhood years, children's motor development becomes smoother and more coordinated. Children gain greater control over their bodies and can sit and attend for longer frames of time. However, their lives should be activity oriented and very active. Increased myelinization of the central nervous system is reflected in improved fine motor skills. Improved fine motor development is reflected in children's handwriting skills over the course of middle and late childhood. Boys are usually better at gross motor skills, girls at fine motor skills.
Exercise and sports	Their nature	Every indication suggests that our nation's children are not getting enough exercise. Television viewing, parents being poor role models for exercise, and the lack of adequate physical education classes in schools may be the culprits. Children's participation in sports can have both positive and negative consequences.
Stress	What is stress?	Stress is the response of individuals to the circumstances and events, called "stressors," that threaten them and tax their coping abilities.
	Cognitive factors in stress	Lazarus believes that children's stress depends on how they cognitively appraise and interpret events. *Cognitive appraisal* is the term Lazarus uses to describe individuals' interpretation of events in their lives as harmful, threatening, or challenging (primary appraisal), and their determination of whether they have the resources to effectively cope with the event (secondary appraisal).
	Life events and daily hassles	Both life events—such as divorce, incest, death of a parent—and daily hassles—such as living in poverty—can cause stress.

Contributions

We owe Piaget the present field of cognitive development. We owe him a long list of masterful concepts of enduring power and fascination, such as the concepts of object permanence, conservation, assimilation, and accommodation. We also owe Piaget the currently accepted vision of children as active, constructive thinkers who, through their commerce with the environment, make themselves manufacturers of their own development (Flavell, 1992).

Piaget was a genius when it came to observing children; his astute observations showed us inventive ways to discover how children, and even infants, act on and adapt to their world. Piaget showed us some important things to look for in children's cognitive development, including the shift from preoperational to concrete operational thought. He also showed that we make experiences fit our cognitive framework yet simultaneously adapt our cognitive orientation to experience. Piaget also revealed how children's cognitive change is

Concept	Processes/Related Ideas	Characteristics/Description
	Sociocultural influences	*Acculturation* refers to cultural change that results from continuous, firsthand contact between two distinctive cultural groups. *Acculturative stress* refers to the negative consequences of acculturation. Members of ethnic minority groups have historically encountered hostility, prejudice, and lack of effective support during crises, which contribute to alienation, social isolation, and heightened stress. Poverty also imposes considerable stress on children and their families. Chronic life conditions such as inadequate housing, dangerous neighborhoods, burdensome responsibilities, and economic uncertainties are potent stresses in the lives of the poor. The incidence of poverty is especially pronounced among ethnic minority children and their families.
	Protective buffers	One of children's important protective buffers against stress is the long-term presence of a basic, trusting relationship with at least one adult. A readily available support network is also important.
Handicapped children	Prevalence of handicaps and the education of handicapped children	It is estimated that approximately 10 to 15 percent of children in the United States are handicapped in some way. Public Law 94-142 ordered free, appropriate education for every handicapped child. The law emphasizes an individually tailored education program for every child and provision of a least restrictive environment, which has led to extensive mainstreaming of handicapped children into the regular classroom. Mainstreaming has been a controversial topic. Another issue is the labeling of handicapped children and its benefits and drawbacks.
	Learning disabilities	Children with a learning disability have normal or above-normal intelligence, have difficulties in some areas but not others, and do not suffer from some other disorder that could explain their learning problems. Learning disabilities are complex and multifaceted and require precise analysis.
	Attention-deficit hyperactivity disorder	This is the technical term for what is commonly called "hyperactivity." This disorder is characterized by a short attention span, distractibility, and high levels of physical activity. Possible causes include heredity, prenatal damage, diet, family dynamics, and physical environment. Amphetamines have been used with some success in treatment, but they do not work with all hyperactive children.

likely to occur if their situations are structured to allow gradual movement to the next higher level (Beilin, 1992).

Criticisms

Piaget's theory has not gone unchallenged, however. Questions are raised about the following areas: estimates of the child's competence at different developmental levels; stages; training of children to reason at higher levels; and culture and education.

Estimates of Children's Competence

Some cognitive abilities emerge earlier than Piaget thought, and their subsequent development is more prolonged than he believed. As we saw earlier in the chapter, some aspects of object permanence emerge much earlier in infancy than Piaget believed. Even 2-year-olds are nonegocentric in some contexts—as when they realize that another person will not see an object they see if the person is blindfolded or is looking in a different direction

Piaget is shown sitting on a bench observing children. Piaget was a genius at observing children. By carefully observing and interviewing children, he constructed a comprehensive theory of children's cognitive development.

(Lempers, Flavell, & Flavell, 1977). Conservation of number has been demonstrated in children as young as 3 years of age, although Piaget thought it did not come about until 7 years of age. Young children are not as "pre" this and "pre" that (precausal, preoperational, and so on) as Piaget thought (Flavell, 1992). Some aspects of formal operational thinking that involve abstract reasoning do not consistently emerge in early adolescence as Piaget envisioned. And adults often reason in far more irrational ways than Piaget believed (Siegler, 1991). In sum, recent trends highlight the cognitive competencies of infants and young children and the cognitive shortcomings of adolescents and adults (Flavell, 1992).

Stages

Piaget conceived of stages as unitary structures of thought, so his theory assumes synchrony in development. That is, various aspects of a stage should emerge at about the same time. However, several concrete operational concepts do not appear in synchrony. For example, children do not learn to conserve at the same time as they learn to cross-classify.

Most contemporary developmentalists agree that children's cognitive development is not as grand-stage-like as Piaget thought. **Neo-Piagetians** *are developmentalists who have elaborated on Piaget's theory, believing children's cognitive development is more specific in many respects than he thought* (Case, 1987, 1992, 1993; Pascual-Leone, 1987). Neo-Piagetians don't believe that all of Piaget's ideas should be junked. However,

they argue that a more accurate vision of the child's cognitive development involves fewer references to grand stages and more emphasis on the roles of strategies, skills, how fast and automatically children can process information, the task-specific nature of children's cognition, and the importance of dividing cognitive problems into smaller, more precise steps.

Neo-Piagetians still believe that children's cognitive development contains some general properties (Flavell, 1992). They stress that there is a regular, maturation-based increase with age in some aspects of the child's information-processing capacity, such as how fast or efficiently the child processes information (Case, 1987, 1992; Demetriou & Efklides, in press; Fischer & Farrar, 1987; Halford, in press; Pascual-Leone, 1987; Sternberg, 1987a). As the child's information-processing capacity increases with increasing age, new and more complex forms of cognition in all content domains are possible, because the child can now hold in mind and think about more things at once. Canadian developmentalist Robbie Case (1985) argues, for example, that adolescents have increasingly more cognitive resources available than they did as children (because they can process information more automatically), they have more information-processing capacity, and they are more familiar with a range of content knowledge.

Training Children to Reason at a Higher Level

Children who are at one cognitive stage—such as preoperational thought—can be trained to reason at a higher cognitive stage—such as concrete operational thought. This poses a problem for Piaget, who argued that such training works only on a superficial level and is ineffective unless the child is at a transitional point from one stage to the next.

Culture and Education

Culture and education exert stronger influences on children's development than Piaget believed. The age at which individuals acquire conservation skills is associated to some extent with the degree to which their culture provides relevant practice. And in many developing countries, formal operational thought is rare. In chapter 8, we learned about the increased interest in how the child's cognitive development progresses through interaction with skilled adults and peers, and how children's embeddedness in a culture influences their cognitive growth. Such views, advocated by Vygotsky and his followers, stand in stark contrast to Piaget's view of the child as a solitary little scientist.

Information Processing

Among the highlights of changes in information processing during middle and late childhood are improvements in memory, schemata, and scripts. Remember also, from chapter 8, that the attention of most children improves dramatically during middle and late childhood, and that at this time children attend more to the task-relevant features of a problem than to the salient features.

An outstanding teacher and education in the logic of science and mathematics are important cultural experiences that promote the development of operational thought. Schooling and education likely play more important roles in the development of operational thought than Piaget envisioned.

> *Our life is what our thoughts make it.*
> —Marcus Aurelius,
> *Meditations*, 2nd Century B.C.

Memory

In chapter 8, we concluded that tasks involving short-term memory—the memory span task, for example—reveal a considerable increase in short-term memory during early childhood, but after the age of 7 do not show as much increase. Is the same pattern found for **long-term memory,** *a relatively permanent and unlimited type of memory?* Long-term memory increases with age during middle and late childhood. Two aspects of memory related to improvement in long-term memory are control processes and learner characteristics.

If we know anything at all about long-term memory, it is that long-term memory depends on the learning activities individuals engage in when learning and remembering information. **Control processes** *are cognitive processes that do not occur automatically but require work and effort. They are under the learner's conscious control and they can be used to improve memory. They are also appropriately called "strategies."* Three important control processes involved in children's memory are rehearsal, organization, and imagery.

Rehearsal is a control process that improves memory. It is the repetition of information after it has been presented. Rehearsal occurs, for instance, when children hear a phone number, then repeat the number several times to improve their memory of it. Researchers have found that children's spontaneous use of rehearsal increases between 5 and 10 years of age (Flavell, Beach, & Chinsky, 1966). The use of organization also improves memory. As with rehearsal, children in middle and late childhood are more likely to spontaneously

FIGURE 10.3

The keyword method. *To help children remember the state capitals, the keyword method was used. A special component of the keyword method is the use of mental imagery, which was stimulated by presenting the children with a vivid visual image, such as two apples being married. The strategy is to help the children associate* apple *with Annapolis and* marry *with Maryland.*

organize information to be remembered than are children in early childhood (Moely & others, 1969).

Another control process that develops as children move through middle and late childhood is imagery. A powerful imagery strategy is the *keyword method,* which has been used to practical advantage by teaching elementary school children how to quickly master new information such as foreign vocabulary words, the states and capitals of the United States, and the names of U.S. presidents. For example, in remembering that Annapolis is the capital of Maryland, children were taught the keywords for the states, such that when a state was given (Maryland), they could supply the keyword (*marry*) (Levin, 1980). Then children were given the reverse type of keyword practice with the capitals. That is, they had to respond with the capital (Annapolis) when given a keyword (*apple*). Finally, an illustration was provided (see figure 10.3). The keyword strategy's use of vivid mental imagery was effective in increasing children's memory of state capitals. Developmentalists today encourage the use of imagery in our nation's schools, believing that it helps to increase the child's memory (McDaniel & Pressley, 1987).

In addition to these control processes, characteristics of the child influence memory. Apart from the obvious variable of age, many characteristics of the child determine the effectiveness of memory. These characteristics include attitude, motivation, and health. However, the characteristic that has been examined the most thoroughly is the child's previously acquired knowledge. What the child knows has a tremendous effect on what the child remembers. In one investigation, 10-year-old children who were chess experts remembered chessboard positions much better than adults who did not play much chess (Chi, 1978). However, the children did not do as well as the adults when both groups were asked to remember a group of random numbers; the children's expertise in chess gave them superior memories, but only in chess.

Schema and Scripts

In chapter 9, we described gender schema theory and defined a *schema* as a cognitive structure, a network of associations that organizes and guides an individual's perceptions. Schema is an important cognitive concept in memory and information processing. Schemas come from prior encounters with the environment and influence the way children encode, make inferences about, and retrieve information. Children have schemas for stories, scenes, spatial layouts (a bathroom or a park, for example), and common events (such as going to a restaurant, playing with toys, or practicing soccer).

Children frequently hear and tell stories. And as they develop the ability to read, they are exposed to many kinds of stories in print. Simple stories have a structure to them, and after hearing enough stories, children develop a strong expectation about what kind of information will be contained in a story. This expectation is a *story schema.* For example, a story tells about what happens in a particular place and circumstance. This content is called the "setting." A story will also have at least one main character, the protagonist, who attempts to achieve some purposeful goal for some clear reason. The protagonist's actions are usually captured in one or more episodes of a story, which can be further broken down, depicting a fairly simple, one-episode story (see figure 10.4).

A decade of research has shown that children at a very young age are able to use structures like these to fill in missing information, remember better, and tell relatively coherent stories (Ackerman, 1988; Buss & others, 1983; Rahman & Bisanz, 1986; Stein & Glenn, 1979; Yussen & others, 1988). Changes occur throughout the childhood years, however, in children's abilities to identify salient events in stories, to unscramble mixed-up stories, and to keep multiple plot lines straight in their minds when facing more-complex stories involving several episodes and more than one major character.

A **script** *is a schema for an event* (Schank & Abelson, 1977). Children's first scripts appear very early in development, perhaps as early as the first year of life. Children clearly have scripts by the time they enter school (Firush & Cobb, 1989; Flannagan & Tate, 1989; Furman & Walden, 1989, 1990; Krackow, 1991). As they develop, their scripts become less crude and more sophisticated. For example, a 4-year-old's script for a restaurant might include information only about sitting down and eating food. By middle and late childhood, the child adds information to the restaurant script about the types of people who serve food, paying the cashier, and so on.

Metacognitive Knowledge

Metacognitive knowledge *is knowledge about cognition, the knowledge children have accumulated through experience, and stored in long-term memory, about the human mind and its workings.*

FIGURE 10.4

"Albert, the Fish," a representative story.

Setting	1	Once there was a big gray fish named Albert.
	2	He lived in a pond near the edge of a forest.
Initiating event	3	One day Albert was swimming around the pond.
	4	Then he spotted a big juicy worm on top of the water.
Internal response	5	Albert knew how delicious worms tasted.
	6	He wanted to eat that one for his dinner.
Attempt	7	So he swam very close to the worm.
	8	Then he bit into him.
Consequence	9	Suddenly, Albert was pulled through the water into a boat.
	10	He had been caught by a fisherman.
Reaction	11	Albert felt sad.
	12	He wished he had been more careful.

Cognitive developmentalist John Flavell has been a pioneer in providing insights into the ways in which children think.

According to one of the leading cognitive developmentalists, John Flavell (1985; Flavell, Miller, & Miller, 1993), metacognitive knowledge can be subdivided roughly into knowledge about *persons* (oneself as well as other human beings), *tasks,* and *strategies.*

Metacognitive knowledge about *persons* includes insights such as this: (Yussen & Levy, 1975): "People, including myself, have limits to the amount of information they can process. It is not possible to deal with all of the information that comes my way. If I worry too much about this, I will feel the stress of information overload." Metacognitive knowledge about *tasks* includes insights such as this: "Some conditions always make it harder or easier to solve a problem or complete a task. For example, the more time I have to solve a problem, the better I do. The fewer number of items I have to process (that is, attend to, remember, perceive), the easier it is for me to do." Metacognitive knowledge about *strategies* includes insights such as this: "Some cognitive steps will help me across a wide range of cognitive tasks (remembering, communicating, reading). However, some strategies will help me with some tasks more than others. For example, I can master a long list of names more effectively by using the imagery keyword method than by rehearsing the names by simple repetition."

Many developmentalists believe that metacognitive knowledge benefits school learning and that if students (especially younger ones) are deficient in metacognitive knowledge, this knowledge can possibly be taught to them (Flavell, 1985; Flavell, Miller, & Miller, 1993). Several researchers have developed school programs to impart metacognitive knowledge to children in the areas of reading comprehension, writing, and math. The research we discuss next, pertaining to the importance of cognitive monitoring in reading comprehension, is an excellent example of how metacognitive knowledge can be taught to children (Brown & Palincsar, 1984, 1989).

Cognitive Monitoring

Cognitive monitoring *is the process of taking stock of what you are currently doing, what you will do next, and how effectively the mental activity is unfolding.* When children engage in an activity like reading, writing, or solving a math problem, they are repeatedly called on to take stock of what they are doing and what they plan to do next (Baker & Brown, 1984; Brown, 1993; Brown & Palincsar, 1989). For example, when children begin to solve a math problem—especially one that might take a while to finish—they must figure out what kind of problem they are working on and what would be a good approach in solving it. Once they undertake a problem solution, it is helpful to check whether the solution seems to be working or whether some other approach would be better.

Instructional programs in reading comprehension (Brown & Palincsar, 1989; Brown & others, in press), writing (Scardamalia, Bereiter, & Steinbach, 1984), and mathematics (Schoenfeld, 1985) have been designed to foster the development of cognitive monitoring (Collins, Brown, & Newman, 1989; Glaser, 1989). Developmental psychologists Ann Brown and Annemarie Palincsar's program for reading comprehension is an excellent example of a cognitive monitoring instructional program. Students in the program acquire specific knowledge and also learn strategies for monitoring their understanding. **Reciprocal teaching** *is an instructional procedure used by Brown and Palincsar to develop cognitive monitoring; it requires that students take turns in leading a study group in the use of strategies for comprehending and remembering text content.* The instruction involves a small group of students, often working with an adult leader, actively discussing a short text, with the goal of *summarizing* it, asking *questions* to promote understanding, offering *clarifying* statements for difficult or confusing words and ideas, and *predicting* what will come next. The

procedure actively involves children, it teaches them some techniques to reflect on about their own understanding, and the group interaction is highly motivating and engaging. A flurry of recent research has documented the power of peer collaboration in learning (Grannott, 1993; Saxe & Guberman, 1993; Tudge & Winterhoff, 1993).

Critical Thinking

Much of the knowledge children are exposed to in the course of their education passes through their minds like grains of sand washed through a sieve. Children need to do more than just memorize or passively absorb new information. They must learn how to think critically. Currently, a number of psychologists and educators are studying children's critical thinking skills (Ennis, 1991; Jones, Idol, & Brandt, 1991; Perkins, Jay, & Tishman, 1993), although it is not a new idea. Educator John Dewey (1933) was working with a similar concept when he contrasted "reflective thinking" with "nonreflective thinking" in the use of formulas or rules to achieve goals. So was Gestalt psychologist Max Wertheimer (1945) when he distinguished between "productive thinking" and "blind induction." Although today's definitions vary, they all have in common the notion that **critical thinking** *involves grasping the deeper meaning of problems, keeping an open mind about different approaches and perspectives, and thinking reflectively rather than accepting statements and carrying out procedures without significant understanding and evaluation.* Another, often implicit assumption is that critical thinking is an important aspect of everyday reasoning (Galotti, 1989). Critical thinking can and should be used not just in the classroom, but outside it as well.

How can we cultivate the ability to think critically and clearly in children? According to a leading cognitive psychologist, Robert J. Sternberg (1987b), we need to teach children to use the right thinking processes, to develop problem-solving strategies, to improve their mental representation, to expand their knowledge base, and to become motivated to use their newly learned thinking skills.

To think critically—or to solve any problem or learn any new knowledge—children need to take an active role in learning. This means that children need to call on a variety of active thinking processes, such as these:

- Listening carefully
- Identifying or formulating questions
- Organizing their thoughts
- Noting similarities and differences
- Deducing (reasoning from the general to the specific)
- Distinguishing between logically valid and invalid inferences

Children also need to learn how to ask questions of clarification, such as "What is the main point?" "What do you mean by that?" and "Why?"

Good thinkers use more than just the right thinking processes. They also know how to combine them into workable strategies for solving problems. Rarely can a problem be solved by a single type of thought process used in isolation. Children need to learn how to combine thinking processes to master a new task. Critical thinking involves combining thought processes in a way that makes sense, not just by jumbling them together.

Children need to learn to see things from multiple points of view. Unless they can interpret information from more than one point of view, they may rely on an inadequate set of information. If children are not encouraged to seek alternative explanations and interpretations of problems and issues, their conclusions may be based solely on their own expectations, prejudices, stereotypes, and personal experiences, which may lead to erroneous conclusions.

It is important to keep in mind that thinking does not occur in the absence of knowledge. Children need *something* to think *about*. It is a mistake, however, to concentrate only on information, to the exclusion of thinking skills, because children simply would become individuals who have a lot of knowledge but are unable to evaluate and apply it. It is equally a mistake to concentrate only on thinking skills, because children would become individuals who know how to think but have nothing to think about. Also, researchers are increasingly finding that critical thinking programs are more effective when they are domain-specific rather than domain-general (Byrnes, 1993).

Critical Thinking

Imagine that you have been asked to develop an information-processing-based curriculum for first-grade students. What would the curriculum be like?

Finally, all of the thinking skills children could possibly master would be irrelevant if they were not actually put to use. Critical thinking is both a matter for academic study *and* a part of living. Children need to be motivated to put their critical thinking skills to practical use.

At this point we have discussed a number of ideas about Piaget's theory and concrete operational thought, Piagetian contributions and criticisms, and information processing in middle and late childhood. A summary of these ideas is presented in concept table 10.2. Now we turn our attention to the nature of children's intelligence.

Intelligence

Intelligence is an abstract concept that is difficult to define. While many psychologists and laypeople equate intelligence with verbal ability and problem-solving skills, others prefer to define it as the individual's ability to learn from and adapt to the experiences of everyday life. If we were to settle on a definition of intelligence based on these criteria, it would be that **intelligence** is *verbal ability, problem-solving skills, and the ability to learn from and adapt to the experiences of everyday life* (see figure 10.5).

As many men, as many minds; everyone his own way.

—Terence

The components of intelligence are very close to the information-processing and language skills we have discussed at various points in children's development. The difference between how we discussed information-processing skills and language and how we will discuss intelligence lies in the concepts of individual differences and assessment. Individual differences are simply the consistent, stable ways we differ from each other. The history of the study of intelligence has focused extensively on individual differences and their assessment. For example, an intelligence test will inform us whether a child can reason more logically than most other children who have taken the test. Our coverage of intelligence focuses on the components of intelligence, cultural bias, the use and misuse of intelligence tests, and the extremes of intelligence. As you think about intelligence, keep in mind our discussion of intelligence in chapter 3, in which we concluded that intelligence is influenced by the interaction of heredity and environment, rather than being a product of either factor alone.

One Face or Many?

Is it more appropriate to think of intelligence as an individual's general ability or as a number of specific abilities? As we explore different approaches to what intelligence is and how it should be measured, you will discover that intelligence is probably *both*.

In 1904, the French Ministry of Education asked psychologist Alfred Binet to devise a method that would determine which students did not profit from typical school instruction. School officials wanted to reduce overcrowding by placing into special schools those who did not benefit from regular classroom teaching. To meet this request, Binet and his student Theophile Simon developed an intelligence test. The test, referred to as the "1905 Scale," consisted of thirty items, ranging from the ability to touch one's nose or ear when asked to, to the ability to draw designs from memory and define abstract concepts.

Binet developed the concept of **mental age (MA)**—*an individual's level of mental development relative to others.* Binet reasoned that mentally retarded children would perform like normal children of a younger age. He developed norms for intelligence by testing fifty nonretarded children from 3 to 11 years of age. Children suspected of mental retardation were tested, and their performance was compared with children of the same chronological age in the normal sample. Average mental-age scores (MA) correspond to chronological age (CA), which is age since birth. A bright child has an MA above CA, a dull child has an MA below CA.

The term **intelligence quotient (IQ)** was devised by William Stern. *IQ is the child's mental age divided by chronological age multiplied by 100:*

$$IQ = \frac{MA}{CA} \times 100$$

If mental age is the same as chronological age, then the child's IQ is 100; if mental age is above chronological age, the IQ is more than 100; if mental age is below chronological age, the IQ is less than 100.

CONCEPT TABLE 10.2

Piaget's Theory and Concrete Operational Thought, Piagetian Contributions and Criticisms, and Information Processing

Concept	Processes/Related Ideas	Characteristics/Description
Piaget's theory and concrete operational thought	Concrete operational thought	Concrete operational thought is made up of operations, mental actions that allow the child to do mentally what was done before physically. Concrete operations are also mental actions that are reversible. The concrete operational child shows conservation and classification skills. The concrete operational child needs clearly available perceptual supports to reason; later in development, thought becomes more abstract.
	Piaget and education	Piaget's ideas have been applied extensively to children's education. Emphasis is on communication and the belief that the child has many ideas about the world, that the child is always learning and unlearning, and that the child is by nature a knowing creature.
Piagetian contributions and criticisms	Contributions	We owe Piaget the present field of cognitive development and a long list of meaningful concepts. Piaget also was a genius at observing children.
	Criticisms	Questions are raised about estimates of competence at different developmental levels; stages; training of children to reason at higher levels; and culture and education. Neo-Piagetians are developmentalists who have elaborated on Piaget's theory, believing children's cognitive development is more specific than he thought.
Information processing	Memory	Children's long-term memory improves during middle and late childhood. Control processes or strategies such as rehearsal, organization, and imagery are among the important influences that are responsible for improved long-term memory. Children's knowledge also influences their memory.
	Schema and scripts	A schema is a cognitive structure, a network of associations that organizes and guides an individual's perceptions. Schemas influence the way children process information. A script is a schema for an event.
	Metacognitive knowledge	This is acquired knowledge about cognitive matters, especially the way the human mind works. Many developmentalists believe metacognitive knowledge is beneficial in school learning.
	Cognitive monitoring	This is the process of taking stock of what one is currently doing, what will be done next, and how effectively the mental activity is unfolding. The source of much cognitive monitoring in children is other people. Instructional programs in reading comprehension, writing, and math have been designed to foster children's cognitive monitoring of these activities. Reciprocal teaching is an instructional procedure used to develop children's cognitive monitoring.
	Critical thinking	Critical thinking refers to grasping the deeper meaning of problems, keeping an open mind about different approaches and perspectives, and thinking reflectively rather than accepting statements and carrying out procedures without significant understanding and evaluation. To cultivate critical thinking in children, we need to teach them to use the right thinking processes, to develop problem-solving strategies, to improve their mental representation, to expand their knowledge base, and to become motivated to use their newly developed thinking skills.

FIGURE 10.5

Defining intelligence. Intelligence is an abstract concept that has been defined in various ways. The three most commonly agreed–upon aspects of intelligence are the following:
(a) *verbal ability, as reflected in the verbal skills of these students searching for library books;*
(b) *problem–solving skills, as reflected in the ability of this girl to solve the design problem presented her; and* (c) *ability to learn from and adapt to experiences of everyday life, as reflected in this handicapped child's adaptation to her inability to walk.*

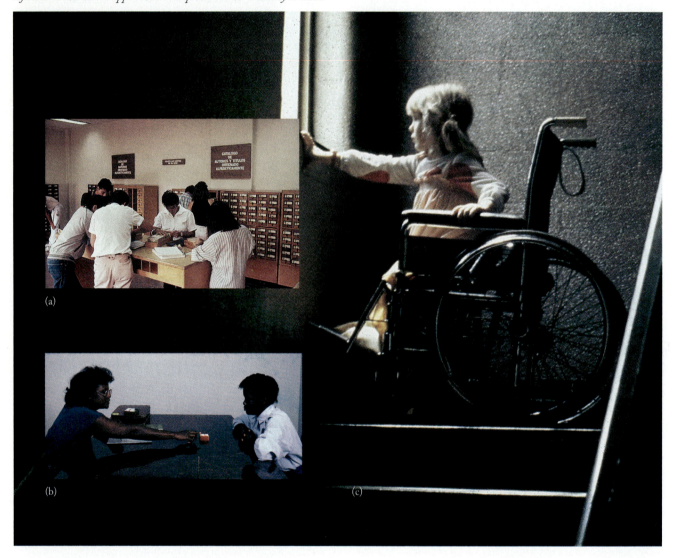

Over the years extensive effort has been expended to standardize the Binet test, which has been given to thousands of children and adults of different ages, selected at random from different parts of the United States. By administering the test to large numbers of individuals and recording the results, it has been found that intelligence measured by the Binet approximates a normal distribution (see figure 10.6). A **normal distribution** *is symmetrical with a majority of cases falling in the middle of the possible range of scores and few scores appearing toward the extreme of the range.*

The current Stanford-Binet (named after Stanford University, where revisions of the test were constructed) is given to persons from the age of 2 through adulthood. It includes a wide variety of items, some requiring verbal responses, others nonverbal responses. For example, items that characterize a 6-year-old's performance on the test include the verbal ability to define at least six words such as *orange* and *envelope,* and the nonverbal ability to trace a path through a maze. Items that reflect the average adult's intelligence include defining words such as *disproportionate* and *regard,* explaining a proverb, and comparing idleness and laziness.

The fourth edition of the Stanford-Binet was published in 1985 (Thorndike, Hagan, & Sattler, 1985). One important addition to this version is the analysis of responses in four content areas: verbal reasoning, quantitative reasoning, abstract/visual reasoning, and short-term memory (Keith & others, 1988). A general composite score is also obtained to reflect overall intelligence. The Stanford-Binet continues to be one of the most widely used individual tests of children's intelligence.

FIGURE 10.6

The normal curve and Stanford-Binet IQ scores. *The distribution of IQ scores approximates a normal curve. Most of the population falls in the middle range of scores. Notice that extremely high and extremely low scores are very rare. Slightly more than two-thirds of the scores fall between 84 and 116. Only about 1 in 50 individuals has an IQ of more than 132 and only about 1 in 50 individuals has an IQ of less than 68.*

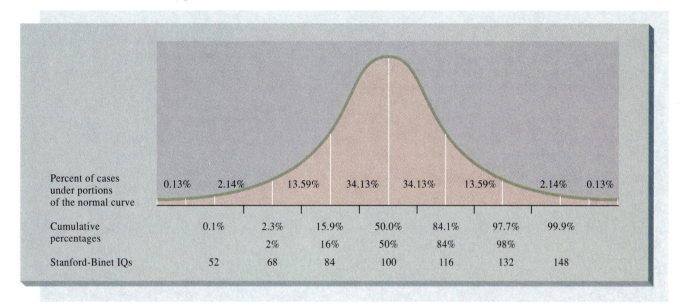

Percent of cases under portions of the normal curve	0.13%	2.14%	13.59%	34.13%	34.13%	13.59%	2.14%	0.13%
Cumulative percentages	0.1%	2.3%	15.9%	50.0%	84.1%	97.7%	99.9%	
		2%	16%	50%	84%	98%		
Stanford-Binet IQs	52	68	84	100	116	132	148	

Besides the Stanford-Binet, the other most widely used individual intelligence tests are the *Wechsler scales,* developed by David Wechsler. They include the Wechsler Adult Intelligence Scale—Revised (WAIS-R); the Wechsler Intelligence Scale for Children—Third Edition (WISC-III), for use with children between the ages of 6 and 16; and the Wechsler Preschool and Primary Scale of Intelligence—Revised (WPPSI-R), for use with children from the ages of 4 to 6½ (Wechsler, 1949, 1955, 1967, 1974, 1981, 1989, 1991).

The Wechsler scales not only provide an overall IQ, but the items are grouped according to twelve subscales, six verbal and six nonverbal. This allows the examiner to obtain separate verbal and nonverbal IQ scores and to see quickly in which areas of mental performance the child is below average, average, or above average. The inclusion of a number of nonverbal subscales makes the Wechsler test more representative of verbal *and* nonverbal intelligence; the Binet test includes some nonverbal items but not as many as the Wechsler scales. Several subscales on the Wechsler Intelligence Scale for Children—Third Edition are shown in figure 10.7 along with examples of the subscales.

"You're wise, but you lack tree smarts."
Drawing by D. Reilly; © 1988 The New Yorker Magazine, Inc.

Critical Thinking

How close are Piaget's view of intelligence and the intelligence test approach to intelligence? Explain your answer.

The contemporary theory of Robert J. Sternberg (1986, 1989) states that intelligence has three factors. **Triarchic theory** *is Sternberg's theory that intelligence consists of componential*

intelligence, experiential intelligence, and contextual intelligence. Consider Ann, who scores high on traditional intelligence tests like the Stanford-Binet and is a star analytical thinker; Todd, who does not have the best test scores but has an insightful and creative mind; and Art, a street-smart person who has learned to deal in practical ways with his world, although his scores on traditional IQ tests are low.

Sternberg calls Ann's analytical thinking and abstract reasoning *componential intelligence;* it is the closest to what we call "intelligence" in this chapter and what is commonly measured by intelligence tests. Sternberg calls Todd's insightful and creative

FIGURE 10.7

Sample subscales of the Wechsler Intelligence Scale for Children. *Remember that the Wechsler includes 11 subscales, 6 verbal and 5 nonverbal. Four of the subscales are shown here.*

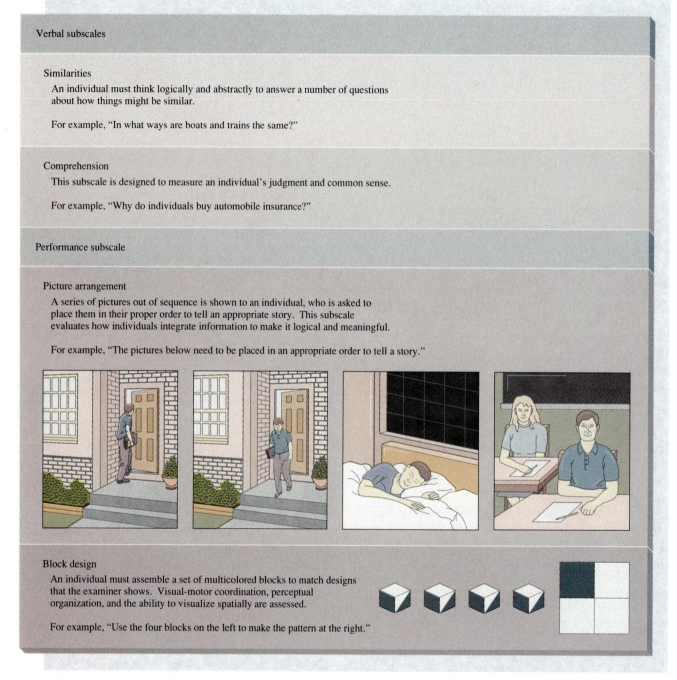

Verbal subscales

Similarities

An individual must think logically and abstractly to answer a number of questions about how things might be similar.

For example, "In what ways are boats and trains the same?"

Comprehension

This subscale is designed to measure an individual's judgment and common sense.

For example, "Why do individuals buy automobile insurance?"

Performance subscale

Picture arrangement

A series of pictures out of sequence is shown to an individual, who is asked to place them in their proper order to tell an appropriate story. This subscale evaluates how individuals integrate information to make it logical and meaningful.

For example, "The pictures below need to be placed in an appropriate order to tell a story."

Block design

An individual must assemble a set of multicolored blocks to match designs that the examiner shows. Visual-motor coordination, perceptual organization, and the ability to visualize spatially are assessed.

For example, "Use the four blocks on the left to make the pattern at the right."

thinking *experiential intelligence,* and he calls Art's street smarts and practical know-how *contextual intelligence.*

In Sternberg's view of componential intelligence, the basic unit in intelligence is a *component,* simply defined as a basic unit of information processing. Sternberg believes such components include the ability to acquire or store information; to retain or retrieve information; to transfer information; to plan, make decisions, and solve problems; and to translate our thoughts into performance. Notice the similarity

of these components to our description of information processing earlier in this chapter.

The second part of Sternberg's model focuses on experience. According to Sternberg, intellectual individuals have the ability to solve new problems quickly, but they also learn how to solve familiar problems in an automatic, rote way so their minds are free to handle other problems that require insight and creativity.

The third part of the model involves practical intelligence—such as how to get out of trouble, how to replace a fuse, and how to get along with people. Sternberg describes this practical or contextual intelligence as all of the important information about getting along in the real world that you are not taught in school. He believes contextual intelligence is sometimes more important than the "book knowledge" that is often taught in school.

Yet another developmental psychologist, Howard Gardner (1983, 1989), believes there are seven types of intelligence: verbal, mathematical, ability to spatially analyze the world, movement skills, insightful skills for analyzing ourselves, insightful skills for analyzing others, and musical skills. Gardner believes that each of the seven types of intelligence can be destroyed by brain damage, that each involves unique cognitive skills, and that each shows up in exaggerated fashion in both the gifted and idiot savants (individuals who are mentally retarded but who have unbelievable skill in a particular domain, such as drawing, music, or computing). I remember vividly an individual from my childhood who was mentally retarded but could instantaneously respond with the correct day of the week (say Tuesday or Saturday) when given any date in history (say June 4, 1926, or December 15, 1746).

Gardner is especially interested in musical intelligence, particularly when it is exhibited at an early age. He points out that musically inclined preschool children not only have the remarkable ability to learn musical patterns easily, but that they rarely forget them. He recounts a story about Stravinsky, who as an adult could still remember the musical patterns of the tuba, drums, and piccolos of the fife-and-drum band that marched outside his home when he was a young child.

To measure musical intelligence in young children, Gardner might ask a child to listen to a melody and then ask the child to recreate the tune on some bells he provides. He believes such evaluations can be used to develop a profile of a child's intelligence. He also believes that it is during this early time in life that parents can make an important difference in how a child's intelligence develops.

Critics of Gardner's approach point out that we have geniuses in many domains other than music. There are outstanding chess players, prize-fighters, writers, politicians, physicians, lawyers, preachers, and poets, for example; yet we do not refer to "chess intelligence," "prize-fighter intelligence," and so on.

Are Intelligence Tests Culturally Biased?

Many of the early intelligence tests were culturally biased, favoring urban children over rural children, middle-class children over lower-class children, and White children over minority children (Miller-Jones, 1989). The norms for the early tests were based almost entirely on White, middle-class children. And some of the items themselves were culturally biased. For example, one item on an early test asked what you should do if you find a 3-year-old child in the street; the correct answer was "Call the police." Children from impoverished inner-city families might not choose this answer if they have had bad experiences with the police; rural children might not choose it, because they may not have police nearby. Such items do not measure the knowledge necessary to adapt to one's environment or to be

TABLE 10.2

The Chitling Intelligence Test

1. A "gas head" is a person who has a
   a. fast-moving car
   b. stable of "lace"
   c. "process"
   d. habit of stealing cars
   e. long jail record for arson

2. "Bo Diddley" is a
   a. game for children
   b. down-home cheap wine
   c. down-home singer
   d. new dance
   e. Moejoe call

3. If a pimp is uptight with a woman who gets state aid, what does he mean when he talks about "Mother's day"?
   a. second Sunday in May
   b. third Sunday in June
   c. first of every month
   d. none of these
   e. first and fifteenth of every month

4. A "handkerchief head" is
   a. a cool cat
   b. a porter
   c. an Uncle Tom
   d. a hoddi
   e. a preacher

5. If a man is called a "blood," then he is a
   a. fighter
   b. Mexican-American
   c. Negro
   d. hungry hemophile
   e. red man, or Indian

6. Cheap chitlings (not the kind you purchase at a frozen-food counter) will taste rubbery unless they are cooked long enough. How soon can you quit cooking them to eat and enjoy them?
   a. 45 minutes
   b. 2 hours
   c. 24 hours
   d. 1 week (on a low flame)
   e. 1 hour

Answers: 1. c 2. c 3. e 4. c 5. c 6. c

Source: Adrian Dove, 1968.

"intelligent" in an inner-city minority neighborhood or in rural America (Scarr, 1984). The contemporary versions of intelligence tests attempt to reduce cultural bias (Angoff, 1989).

Even if the content of test items is appropriate, another problem may exist with intelligence tests. Since many questions are verbal in nature, minority groups may encounter problems in understanding the language of the questions (Gibbs & Huang, 1989). Minority groups often speak a language that is very different from standard English. Consequently, they may be at a disadvantage when they take intelligence tests oriented toward middle-class whites. Such cultural bias is dramatically underscored by tests like the one in table 10.2. The items in this test were developed to reduce the cultural disadvantage Black children might experience on traditional intelligence tests.

FIGURE 10.8

Iatmul and Caroline Islander intelligence. (a) *The intelligence of the Iatmul people of Papua, New Guinea, involves the ability to remember the names of many clans.* (b) *The Caroline Islands number 680 in the Pacific Ocean east of the Philippines. The intelligence of their inhabitants includes the ability to navigate by the stars.*

Culture-fair tests *are tests that are designed to reduce cultural bias.* Two types of culture-fair tests have been developed. The first includes items that are familiar to individuals from all socioeconomic and ethnic backgrounds, or items that are at least familiar to the people taking the test. A child might be asked how a bird and a dog are different, on the assumption that all children have been exposed to birds and dogs. The second type of culture-fair test has all the verbal items removed. Even though these tests are designed to be culture-fair, people with more education score higher on them than those with less education (Anastasi, 1988).

Culture-fair tests remind us that traditional intelligence tests are probably culturally biased, yet culture-fair tests do not provide a satisfactory alternative. Constructing a test that is truly culture-fair—one that rules out the role of experience emanating from socioeconomic and ethnic background—has been difficult and may be impossible. Consider, for example, that the intelligence of the Iatmul people of Papua, New Guinea, involves the ability to remember the names of some 10,000 to 20,000 clans; by contrast, the intelligence of islanders in the widely dispersed Caroline Islands involves the talent of navigating by the stars (see figure 10.8).

The Use and Misuse of Intelligence Tests

Psychological tests are tools. Like all tools, their effectiveness depends on the knowledge, skill, and integrity of the user. A hammer can be used to build a beautiful kitchen cabinet or it can be used as a weapon of assault. Like a hammer, intelligence tests can be used for positive purposes or they can be used abusively. It is important for both the test constructor and the test examiner to be familiar with the current state of scientific knowledge about intelligence and intelligence tests (Anastasi, 1988).

Even though they have limitations, intelligence tests are among psychology's most widely used tools. To be effective, though, intelligence tests must be viewed realistically. They should not be thought of as a fixed, unchanging indicator of a person's intelligence. They should also be used in conjunction with other information about a person and should not be relied upon as the sole indicator of intelligence. For example, an intelligence test should not be used as the sole indicator of whether a child should be placed in a special-education or gifted class. The child's developmental history, medical background, performance in school, social competencies, and family experiences should be taken into account, too.

The single number provided by many IQ tests can easily lead to stereotypes and expectations about a person. Many people do not know how to interpret the results of an intelligence test, and sweeping generalizations about a person are too often made on the basis of an IQ score. Imagine, for example, that you are a teacher sitting in the teacher's lounge the day after school has started in the fall. You mention a student—Johnny Jones—and a fellow teacher remarks that she had Johnny in class last year, and goes on to say that he was a real dunce, pointing out that his IQ is 78. You cannot help but remember this information, and it may lead you to think that Johnny Jones is not very bright so it is useless to spend much time teaching him. In this way, IQ scores are misused and stereotypes are formed (Rosenthal & Jacobsen, 1968).

We have a tendency in our culture to consider intelligence or a high IQ as the ultimate human value. It is important to keep in mind that our value as people includes other matters: consideration of others, positive close relationships, and competence in social situations, for example. The verbal and problem-solving skills measured on traditional intelligence tests are only one part of human competence.

Despite their limitations, when used judiciously by a competent examiner, intelligence tests provide valuable information about people. There are not many alternatives to intelligence tests. Subjective judgments about individuals simply reintroduce the biases the tests were designed to eliminate.

The Extremes of Intelligence

Intelligence tests have been used to discover indications of mental retardation or intellectual giftedness, the extremes of intelligence. At times intelligence tests have been misused for this purpose. Keeping in mind the theme that an intelligence test should not be used as the sole indicator of mental retardation or giftedness, we explore the nature of these intellectual extremes.

Mental Retardation

The most distinctive feature of mental retardation is inadequate intellectual functioning. Long before formal tests were developed to assess intelligence, the mentally retarded were identified by a lack of age-appropriate skills in learning and caring for themselves. Once intelligence tests were developed, numbers were assigned to indicate degree of mental retardation. It is not unusual to find two retarded individuals with the same low IQ, one of whom is married, employed, and involved in the community and the other requiring constant supervision in an institution. These differences in social competence led psychologists to include deficits in adaptive behavior in their definition of mental retardation. **Mental retardation** *is a condition of limited mental ability in which the individual has a low IQ, usually below 70 on a traditional intelligence test, and has difficulty adapting to everyday life.* About 5 million Americans fit this definition of mental retardation.

There are several classifications of mental retardation. About 89 percent of the mentally retarded fall into the mild category, with IQs of 55 to 70. About 6 percent are classified as moderately retarded, with IQs of 40 to 54; these people can attain a second-grade level of skills and may be able to support themselves as adults through some types of labor. About 3.5 percent of the mentally retarded are in the severe category, with IQs of 25 to 39; these individuals learn to talk and engage in very simple tasks but require extensive supervision. Less than 1 percent have IQs below 25; they fall into the profoundly mentally retarded classification and are in constant need of supervision.

Mental retardation can have an organic cause, or it can be social and cultural in origin. **Organic retardation** *is mental*

FIGURE 10.9

A Down syndrome child. What causes a child to develop Down syndrome? In what major classification of mental retardation does the condition fall?

retardation caused by a genetic disorder or by brain damage; organic refers to the tissues or organs of the body, so there is some physical damage in organic retardation. Down syndrome, one form of mental retardation, occurs when an extra chromosome is present in an individual's genetic makeup (see figure 10.9). It is not known why the extra chromosome is present, but it may involve the health or age of the female ovum or male sperm. Most people who suffer from organic retardation have IQs that range between 0 and 50.

Cultural-familial retardation *is a mental deficit in which no evidence of organic brain damage can be found; individuals' IQs range from 50 to 70.* Psychologists suspect that such mental deficits result from the normal variation that distributes people along the range of intelligence scores above 50, combined with growing up in a below-average intellectual environment (Hodapp, Burack, & Zigler, in press). As children, those who are familially retarded can be detected in schools, where they often fail, need tangible rewards (candy rather than praise), and are highly sensitive to

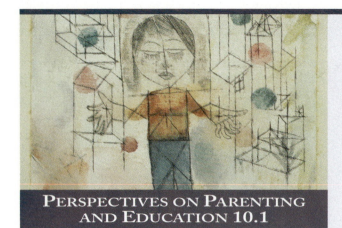

PERSPECTIVES ON PARENTING AND EDUCATION 10.1

Parenting and Gifted Children

While the parents of gifted children are blessed in many ways, they must deal with a number of issues related to their children's giftedness or talent (Keirouz, 1990). Parents often feel ambivalent about having their child labeled "gifted," proud that their child is talented but worried about how it will affect the child and whether the child will have a normal life. Parents of gifted children express concern over how to find the proper level of encouragement, fearing that they will overstimulate or understimulate the child. Parents want their gifted children to be able to reach their full potential. Some parents overindulge their

gifted child, which often increases the child's self-confidence but unfortunately carries with it the potential for having a spoiled and egocentric child. Heaping too much attention on a gifted child also has negative repercussions for nongifted siblings.

Researchers have found that nongifted siblings often do suffer from negative social comparison with the gifted sibling, have lower self-esteem than the gifted sibling, and show poorer emotional adjustment than the gifted sibling (Cornell & Grossberg, 1986). Friction between siblings is the greatest when the gifted child is the oldest (Bridges, 1973).

In addition to concerns about sibling issues, parents of gifted children also may worry about the education of their gifted child. Parents of gifted children may become critical of the school's efforts, or lack of efforts, to provide a positive, stimulating education for the gifted child. No matter how competent the efforts of the school or the teacher, some parents still criticize the education their gifted child is receiving.

Another important issue for parents to consider is that the gifted child's social and emotional growth may lag behind his or her intellectual growth and that the gifted child often does not have the same abilities in different domains of development. Parents should not expect the gifted child to be perfect. Even in the domain of their gifted talent, gifted children have "bad days" when they don't perform at their gifted level. Not recognizing these variations in gifted children can lead parents to have unrealistic expectations for their gifted children and harm their development.

---

what others—both peers and adults—want from them. However, as adults the familially retarded are usually invisible, perhaps because adult settings don't tax their cognitive skills as sorely. It may also be that the familially retarded increase their intelligence as they move toward adulthood (Sattler, 1988).

Giftedness

There have always been people whose abilities and accomplishments outshine others'—the whiz kid in class, the star athlete, the natural musician. People who are **gifted** *have above-average intelligence (an IQ of 120 or higher) and/or superior talent for something.* When it comes to programs for the gifted, most school systems select children who have intellectual superiority and academic aptitude. Children who are talented in the visual and performing arts (arts, drama, dance), athletics, or other special aptitudes tend to be overlooked.

Critical Thinking

What should be the criteria for placing a child in a gifted program?

Until recently giftedness and emotional distress were thought to go hand in hand. English novelist Virginia Woolf suffered from severe depression, for example, and eventually committed suicide. Sir Isaac Newton, Vincent van Gogh, Ann Sexton, Socrates, and Sylvia Plath all had emotional problems. However, these are the exception rather than the rule; in general, no relation between giftedness and mental disorders has

been found. A number of recent studies support the conclusion that gifted people tend to be more mature and have fewer emotional problems than others (Draper & others, 1993; Janos & Robinson, 1985).

Lewis Terman (1925) has followed the lives of approximately 1,500 children whose Stanford-Binet IQs averaged 150 into adulthood; the study will not be complete until the year 2010. Terman has found that this remarkable group is an accomplished lot: of the 800 males, 78 have obtained doctorates (they include two past presidents of the American Psychological Association), 48 have earned M.D.s, and 85 have been granted law degrees. Most of these figures are 10 to 30 times greater than those found among the 800 men of the same age chosen randomly as a comparison group. These findings challenge the commonly held belief that the intellectually gifted are emotionally disturbed or socially maladjusted. To learn more about gifted children, turn to Perspectives on Parenting and Education 10.1, where you can read about ways parents can effectively interact with their gifted children.

> *Never to be cast away are the gifts of the gods, magnificent.*
> —Homer, *The Iliad*, 9th Century B.C.

Creativity

Most of us would like to be both gifted and creative. Why was Thomas Edison able to invent so many things? Was he simply more intelligent than most people? Did he spend long hours toiling away in private? Surprisingly, when Edison was a young boy, his teacher told him he was too dumb to learn anything. Other famous people whose creative genius went unnoticed when they were young include Walt Disney, who was fired from a newspaper job because he did not have any good ideas; Enrico Caruso, whose music teacher told him that his voice was terrible; and Winston Churchill, who failed 1 year of secondary school.

Disney, Edison, Caruso, and Churchill were intelligent and creative men; however, experts on creativity believe that intelligence is not the same as creativity. One common distinction is between **convergent thinking,** *which produces one correct answer and is characteristic of the kind of thinking on standardized intelligence tests* and **divergent thinking,** *which produces many answers to the same question and is more characteristic of creativity* (Guilford, 1967). For example, the following is a typical problem on an intelligence test that requires convergent thinking: "How many quarters will you get in return for 60 dimes?" The following question, though, has many possible answers: "What image comes to mind when you hear the phrase 'sitting alone in a dark room'?" (Barron, 1989). Such responses as "the sound of a violin with no strings" and "patience" are considered creative answers. Conversely, common answers, such as "a person in a crowd" or "insomnia" are not very creative.

Creativity *is the ability to think about something in novel and unusual ways and to come up with unique solutions to problems.* When creative people, such as artists and scientists, are asked what enables them to solve problems in novel ways, they say that the ability to find affinities between seemingly unrelated elements plays a key role. They also say they have the time and independence in an enjoyable setting to entertain a wide range of possible solutions to a problem. How strongly is creativity related to intelligence? Although most creative people are quite intelligent, the reverse is not necessarily true. Many highly intelligent people (as measured by IQ tests) are not very creative.

Some experts remain skeptical that we will ever fully understand the creative process. Others believe that a psychology of creativity is in reach. Most experts agree, however, that the concept of creativity as spontaneously bubbling up from a magical well is a myth. Momentary flashes of insight, accompanied by images, make up only a small part of the creative process. At the heart of the creative process are ability and experience that shape an individual's intentional and sustained effort, often over the course of a lifetime (Baer, 1993).

> *The artist finds a greater pleasure in painting than in having completed the picture.*
>
> —Seneca

Language Development in Middle and Late Childhood

As children develop during middle and late childhood, changes in their vocabulary and grammar take place. Reading assumes a prominent role in their language world. An increasingly important consideration is bilingualism.

We will consider each of these aspects of children's language development in turn.

Vocabulary and Grammar

During middle and late childhood, a change occurs in the way children think about words. They become less tied to the actions and perceptual dimensions associated with words, and they become more analytical in their approach to words. For example, when asked to say the first thing that comes to mind when they hear a word, such as *dog,* preschool children often respond with a word related to the immediate context of a dog. A child might associate *dog* with a word that indicates its appearance (*black, big*) or to an action associated with it (*bark, sit*). Older children more frequently respond to *dog* by associating it with an appropriate category (*animal*) or to information that intelligently expands the context (*cat, veterinarian*) (Holzman, 1983). The increasing ability of elementary school children to analyze words helps them understand words that have no direct relation to their personal experiences. This allows children to add more abstract words to their vocabulary. For example, *precious stones* can be understood by understanding the common characteristics of *diamonds* and *emeralds.* Also, children's increasing analytic abilities allow them to distinguish between such similar words as *cousin* and *nephew* or *city, village,* and *suburb.*

Children make similar advances in grammar. The elementary school child's improvement in logical reasoning and analytical skills helps in the understanding of such constructions as the appropriate use of comparatives (*shorter, deeper*) and subjectives ("If you were president, . . ."). By the end of the elementary school years, children can usually apply many of the appropriate rules of grammar (de Villiers & de Villiers, 1978).

Reading

Reading becomes a special skill during the elementary school years. Not being a competent reader places children at a substantial disadvantage in relation to their peers.

In the history of learning-to-read techniques, three approaches have dominated: the ABC method, the whole-word method, and the phonics method. The **ABC method** *is a learning-to-read technique that emphasizes memorizing the names and letters of the alphabet.* The **whole-word method** *is a learning-to-read technique that emphasizes learning direct associations between whole words and their meanings.* The **phonics method** *is a learning-to-read technique that emphasizes the sounds that letters make when in words (such sounds can differ from the names of these letters, as when the sound of the letter C is not found in* cat). The ABC method is in ill repute today. Because of the imperfect relationship between the names of letters and their sounds in words, the technique is regarded as ineffective, if not harmful, in teaching children to read. Despite its poor reputation, the ABC method was the technique that taught many children in past generations to read successfully. Disputes in recent years have centered on the merits of the whole-word and phonics methods (Goswami & Bryant, 1990). Although some research has been done comparing these two techniques, the findings have not been conclusive (Carbo, 1987). However, there is evidence that drill practice with the sounds made by letters in

LIFE-SPAN PRACTICAL KNOWLEDGE 10.2

The New York Times Parents' Guide to the Best Books for Children

(1991) by Eden Lipson. New York: Random House.

This revised and updated edition includes book recommendations for children of all ages. More than 1,700 titles are evaluated. The six sections are organized according to reading level: wordless, picture, story, early reading, middle reading, and young adult. Each entry provides the essential information needed to become acquainted with the book's content and know where to find it in a local library or a bookstore. More than 55 indexes make it easy to match the right book to the right child. This is an extensive, thorough, competent guide to selecting children's books.

words (part of some phonics methods) improves reading ability (Williams, 1979). Many current techniques of reading instruction incorporate components of both wholeword and phonics (Karlin & Karlin, 1987).

Reading is more than the sum of whole-word and phonics methods. Information-processing skills are also involved in successful reading (Hall, 1989; Rieben & Perfetti, 1991). When children read, they process information and interpret it, so reading serves as a practical example to illustrate the information-processing approach we have talked about at various other times in this book. Remember that information processing is concerned with how children analyze the many different sources of information available to them in the environment and how they make sense of those experiences. When children read, for example, a rich and complex set of visual symbols is available to their senses. The symbols are associated with sounds, the sounds are combined to form words, and the words and large units that contain them (phrases, sentences, paragraphs) have conventional meanings. To read effectively, children must perceive and attend to words and sentences. They must also hold information in memory while processing new information. A number of information-processing skills, then, are involved in children's ability to read effectively.

Bilingualism

Octavio's Mexican parents moved to the United States 1 year before Octavio was born. They do not speak English fluently and have always spoken to Octavio in Spanish. At 6 years of age, Octavio has just entered the first grade at an elementary school in San Antonio, Texas, and he speaks no English. What is the best way to teach Octavio? How much easier would elementary school be for Octavio if his parents had been able to speak to him in Spanish *and* English when he was an infant?

Well over 6 million children in the United States come from homes in which English is not the primary language. Often, like Octavio, they live in a community in which non-English language is the main means of communication. These children face a more difficult task than most of us: They must master the native tongue of their family to communicate effectively at home, and they must also master English to make their

way in the larger society. The number of bilingual children is expanding at such a rapid rate in our country (some experts predict a tripling of their number early in the twenty-first century) that they constitute an important subgroup of language learners that society must deal with. Although the education of such children in the public schools has a long history, only recently has a national policy evolved to guarantee a high-quality language experience for them.

Bilingual education *refers to programs for students with limited proficiency in English that instruct students in their own language part of the time while they learn English.* The rationale for bilingual education was provided by the United States Commission on Civil Rights (1975): Lack of English proficiency is the main reason language minority students do poorly in school; bilingual education should keep students from falling far behind in a subject while they are learning English. Bilingual programs vary extensively in content and quality. At a minimum, they include instruction in English as a second language for students with limited English proficiency. Bilingual programs often include some instruction in Spanish as well. The largest number of bilingual programs in the United States are in Spanish, so our examples refer to Spanish, although the principles also apply to bilingual programs in other languages. Bilingual programs differ in the extent to which the Hispanic culture is taught to all students, and some bilingual programs teach Spanish to all students, regardless of whether their primary language is Spanish.

Most bilingual education programs are simply transitional programs developed to support students in Spanish until they can understand English well enough to function in the regular classroom, which is taught in English. A typical bilingual program begins teaching students with limited English proficiency in their primary language in kindergarten and then changes to English-only classes at the end of the first or second grade (Slavin, 1988).

Research evaluation of bilingualism has led to the conclusion that bilingualism does not interfere with performance in either language (Hakuta & Garcia, 1989). There is no evidence that the native language should be eliminated as early as possible because it might interfere with learning a second language.

What are the arguments for and against bilingual education?

Instead, higher degrees of bilingualism are associated with cognitive flexibility and improved concept formation (Diaz, 1983). These findings are based primarily on research in additive bilingual settings—that is, in settings where the second language is added as an enrichment to the native language and not at its expense. Causal relations between bilingualism and cognitive or language competence are difficult to establish, but, in general, positive outcomes are often noted in communities where bilingualism is not socially stigmatized.

Increasingly, researchers are recognizing the complexity of bilingualism's effects (Brislin, 1993; Fillmore, 1989). For example, as indicated earlier, the nature of bilingualism programs varies enormously—some are of excellent quality; others are of poor quality. Some teachers in bilingual education programs are completely bilingual; others are not. Some programs begin in kindergarten, others in elementary school. Some programs end in the first or second grade; others continue through the fifth or sixth grade. Some include instruction in Hispanic culture; others focus only on language instruction. Some researchers select outcome measures that include only proficiency in English; others focus on cognitive variables such as cognitive flexibility and concept formation; and still others include more social variables such as integration into the school, self-esteem, and attitude toward school. In sum, there is more to understanding the effects of bilingual education than simple language proficiency (Hakuta & Garcia, 1989).

One final point about bilingualism deserves attention. The United States is one of the few countries in the world in which most students graduate from high school knowing only their own language. For example, in Russia, schools have 10 grades, called forms, which correspond roughly to the 12 grades in American schools. Children begin school at age 7. In the third form, Russian students begin learning English. Because of the emphasis on teaching English in their schools, most Russian citizens today under the age of 35 speak at least some English (Cameron, 1988).

Critical Thinking

Assume that you have taken a position as a director of bilingual education in a large school system in a major U.S. city. What social policy on bilingual education would you urge the school board to adopt? Explain your answer.

Achievement

Yet another important dimension of cognitive development in middle and late childhood is children's achievement. We are a species motivated to do well at what we attempt, to gain mastery over the world in which we live, to explore with enthusiasm and curiosity unknown environments, and to achieve the heights of success. We live in an achievement-oriented world with standards that tell children success is important. The standards suggest that success requires a competitive spirit, a desire to win, a motivation to do well, and the wherewithal to cope with adversity and persist until an objective is reached. Some developmentalists, though, believe that we are becoming a nation of hurried, "wired" people who are raising our children to become the same way—uptight about success and failure and far too worried about what we accomplish in comparison to others (Elkind, 1981). It was in the 1950s that an interest in achievement began to flourish. The interest initially focused on the need for achievement.

The trouble with being in the rat race is that even when you win you are still a rat.

—Lily Tomlin

Need for Achievement

Think about yourself and your friends for a moment. Are you more achievement oriented than they are, or are you less so? If we asked you and your friends to tell stories about achievement-related themes, could we accurately determine which of you is the most achievement oriented?

Some individuals are highly motivated to succeed and expend a lot of effort striving to excel. Other individuals are not as motivated to succeed and don't work as hard to achieve. These two types of individuals vary in their **achievement motivation** (*or* **need for achievement**), *the desire to accomplish something, to reach a standard of excellence, and to expend effort to excel.* Borrowing from Henry Murray's (1938) theory and measurement of personality, psychologist David McClelland (1955) assessed achievement by showing individuals ambiguous pictures that were likely to stimulate achievement-related responses. The individuals were asked to tell a story about the picture, and their comments were scored according to how strongly they reflected achievement.

A host of studies have correlated achievement-related responses with different aspects of the individual's experiences and behavior. The findings are diverse, but they do suggest that

LIFE-SPAN PRACTICAL KNOWLEDGE 10.3

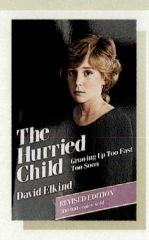

The Hurried Child

(1988, rev. ed.) by David Elkind. Reading, MA: Addison-Wesley.

The Hurried Child describes a pervasive and harmful circumstance that all too many American children face—that of growing up too fast and too soon. Author David Elkind is a highly respected expert on children's and adolescents' lives. Elkind says that today's American parents too often push their children to be "superkids" who are competent to deal with all of life's ups and downs. He

thinks parents invented the "superkid" to alleviate their own anxiety and guilt. But he doesn't just fault parents, also pointing the finger of blame at schools and media. According to Elkind, many parents' expectations for their children are unrealistic, not just about their children's academic journeys, but about their performance on athletic fields as well. Elkind recommends that parents respect children's own developmental timetables and needs, encourage children to play and fantasize, and make sure that their expectations and support are in reasonable balance.

achievement-oriented individuals have a stronger hope for success than a fear of failure, are moderate rather than high or low risk-takers, and persist for appropriate lengths of time in solving difficult problems (Atkinson & Raynor, 1974). Early research indicated that independence training by parents promoted children's achievement, but more-recent research reveals that parents, to increase achievement, need to set high standards for achievement, model achievement-oriented behavior, and reward their children for their achievements (Huston-Stein & Higgens-Trenk, 1978).

Intrinsic and Extrinsic Motivation

Our achievement motivation—whether in school, at work, or in sports—can be divided into two main types: **intrinsic motivation,** *the internal desire to be competent and to do something for its own sake;* and **extrinsic motivation,** *which is influenced by external rewards and punishments.* If you work hard in college because a personal standard of excellence is important to you, intrinsic motivation is involved. But if you work hard in college because you know it will bring you a higher-paying job when you graduate, extrinsic motivation is at work.

An important consideration when motivating a child to do something is whether or not to offer an incentive (Ames & Ames, 1989; Gottfried, Gottfried, & Bathurst, 1988; Rotter, 1989). If a child is not doing competent work, is bored, or has a negative attitude, it may be worthwhile to consider incentives to improve motivation. However, there are times when external rewards can get in the way of motivation. In one investigation, children with a strong interest in art spent more time in a drawing activity when they expected no reward than their counterparts who knew they would be rewarded (Lepper, Greene, & Nisbett, 1973).

Intrinsic motivation implies that internal motivation should be promoted and external factors deemphasized. In this way, children learn to attribute to themselves the cause of their success and failure, and especially how much effort they expend. But in reality, achievement is motivated by both internal

and external factors; children are never divorced from their external environment. Some of the most achievement-oriented children are those who have a high personal standard for achievement and are also highly competitive. In one investigation, low-achieving boys and girls who engaged in individual goal setting (intrinsic motivation) and were given comparative information about peers (extrinsic motivation) worked more math problems and got more of them correct than their counterparts who experienced either condition alone (Schunk, 1983). Other research suggests that social comparison by itself is not a wise strategy (Nicholls, 1984). The argument is that social comparison puts the child in an ego-involved, threatening, self-focused state rather than in a task-involved, effortful, strategy-focused state.

> *The reward of a thing well done is to have done it.*
> —Ralph Waldo Emerson, *Essays: Second Series,* 1844

Another important consideration is the role of the child's home environment in promoting internal motivation. In one investigation, Adele and Allen Gottfried (1989) found that greater variety of home experiences, parental encouragement of competence and curiosity, and home emphasis on academically related behaviors are related to children's internal motivation for achievement. And in a recent study, mothers who encouraged curiosity, persistence, and mastery had children with higher achievement than mothers who emphasized extrinsic consequences (Gottfried, Fleming, & Gottfried, in press).

An extremely important aspect of internal causes of achievement is *effort*. Unlike many causes of success, effort is under the child's control and is amenable to change (Jagacinski & Nicholls, 1990; Schunk, 1990). The importance of effort in achievement is recognized by most children. In one study, third through sixth-grade students felt that effort was the most effective strategy for good school performance (Skinner, Wellborn, & Connell, 1990).

Mastery Orientation Versus Helpless Orientation

Closely related to an emphasis on intrinsic motivation, attributions of internal causes of behavior, and the importance of effort in achievement is a mastery orientation (Le Gall, 1990). Developmental psychologists Valanne Henderson and Carol Dweck (1990) have found that children show two distinct responses to difficult or challenging circumstances: The **helpless orientation** *describes children who seem trapped by the experience of difficulty. They attribute their difficulty to a lack of ability.* They frequently say things like, "I'm not very good at this," even though they may have earlier demonstrated their ability through numerous successes. And once they view their behavior as failure, they often feel anxious about the situation and their performance worsens even further. The **mastery orientation** *describes children who are task oriented. Instead of focusing on their ability, they become concerned about their learning strategies.* Mastery-oriented children often instruct themselves to pay attention, to think carefully, and to remember strategies that have worked for them in previous situations. They frequently report feeling challenged and excited by difficult tasks rather than being threatened by them.

What psychological factors undergird the mastery and helpless achievement orientations? In one investigation, students were followed over the first few months of the seventh grade, their first year of junior high school (Henderson & Dweck, 1989). Students who believed that their intelligence is malleable and who had confidence in their abilities earned significantly higher grades than their counterparts who believed their intelligence is fixed and who did not have much confidence in their abilities. Students who believed that their intelligence is fixed also had higher levels of anxiety than students who believed it is changeable. Apparently, then, the way students think about their intelligence and their confidence in their abilities may affect their ability and desire to master academic material. Believing that learning new material increases one's intelligence may actually promote academic mastery.

In summary, we have seen that a number of psychological and motivational factors influence children's achievement. Especially important in the child's ability to adapt to new academic and social pressures are achievement motivation, internal attributions of effort, intrinsic motivation, and a mastery achievement orientation. Next, we examine the role of ethnicity in achievement.

Achievement in Ethnic Minority Children

Too often, the findings of research on minority groups are presented in terms of "deficits" by middle-class, white standards. Rather than characterizing individuals as *culturally different,* many conclusions unfortunately characterize the cultural distinctiveness of Blacks, Hispanics, and other minority groups as deficient in some way (Jones, 1990; Ramirez, 1990; Sue & Okazaki, 1990).

Much of the research on minority-group children is plagued by a failure to consider socioeconomic status (determined by some combination of education, occupation, and income). In many instances, when ethnicity *and* socioeconomic status (also called "social class") are investigated in the same study, social class is a far better predictor of achievement orientation than is ethnicity. Middle-class individuals fare better than their lower-class counterparts in a variety of achievement-oriented circumstances—expectations for success, achievement aspirations, and recognition of importance of effort, for example (McAdoo & McAdoo, 1985).

Educational psychologist Sandra Graham has conducted a number of investigations that reveal not only stronger social class than ethnic-group differences, but also the importance of studying minority-group motivation in the context of general motivational theory (Graham, 1986, 1987, 1990). Her inquiries focus on the causes Blacks give for their achievement orientation— why they succeed or fail, for example. She is struck by how consistently middle-class Black children do not fit our stereotypes of either deviant or special populations. They, like their middle-class white counterparts, have high expectations and understand that failure is often due to lack of effort rather than to luck.

It is always important to keep in mind the diversity that exists within an ethnic group (Slaughter-DeFoe & others, 1990). Consider Asian American children. Many Asian American children fit the "whiz kid, superachiever" image, but there are still many Asian American children who are struggling just to learn English. The "whiz kid" image fits many of the children of Asian immigrant families who arrived in the United States in the late 1960s and early 1970s. Many of these immigrants came from Hong Kong, South Korea, India, and the Philippines. The image also fits many of the more than 100,000 Indochinese (primarily Vietnamese) immigrants who arrived in the United States after the end of the Vietnam War in 1975. Both groups included mostly middle- and upper-income professional people who were reasonably well educated and who passed along a strong interest in education and a strong work ethic to their children. For thousands of other Asian Americans, including a high percentage of the 600,000 Indochinese refugees who fled Vietnam, Laos, and Cambodia in the late 1970s, the problems are legion. Many in this wave of refugees lived in poor surroundings in their homelands. They came to the United States with few skills and little education. They speak little English and have a difficult time finding decent jobs. They often share housing with relatives. Adjusting to school is difficult for their children; some drop out, and some are attracted to gangs and drugs. Better school systems use a variety of techniques to help these Asian Americans, including classes in English as a second language, as well as a range of social services.

American children are more achievement oriented than children in many countries. However, there has recently been concern about the achievement most American children display in comparison with children in other countries with strong educational orientations—Japan, China, and Russia, for example. To learn more about the achievement orientation of American children compared to Japanese and Chinese children, see Sociocultural Worlds of Development 10.1

At this point we have discussed a number of ideas about children's intelligence and its variations, creativity, language, and achievement. A summary of these ideas is presented in concept table 10.3.

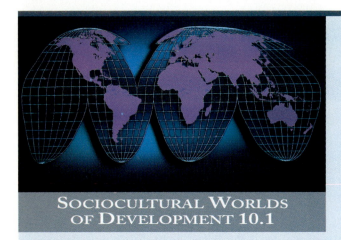

SOCIOCULTURAL WORLDS OF DEVELOPMENT 10.1

Achievement and Learning in Asian and American Children

In the last decade, the poor performance of American children in math and science has become well publicized. For example, in one recent cross-national comparison of the math and science achievement of 9- to 13-year-old students, the United States finished 13th (out of 15) in science and 15th (out of 16) in math achievement (Educational Testing Service, 1992). In this study, Korean and Taiwanese students placed first and second, respectively.

Harold Stevenson and his colleagues (Stevenson, Chen, & Lee, 1993; Stevenson & others, 1990) have conducted a series of cross-national studies of children's learning and achievement in various Asian countries and the United States over a period of about 15 years. Rather than just describe the deficiencies of the American children's achievement in comparison to children from other nations, Stevenson has sought to answer the all-important question, Why? He has found that contrary to popular stereotypes, Asian children's high level of achievement does not result from rote learning and repeated drilling in tension-filled schools. Rather, children are motivated to learn, and teaching is innovative and interesting in many Asian schools. Knowledge is not force-fed to children, but rather children are encouraged to construct their own ways of representing the knowledge. Long school days in Asia are punctuated by extended recess periods. Asian schools embrace many of the ideals Americans have for their own schools, but they are more successful in implementing them in interesting and productive ways that make learning more enjoyable for children.

These conclusions were reached by Stevenson and his colleagues following five different cross-national studies of children in the United States, China, Taiwan, and Japan. In these studies, Asian children consistently outperformed U.S. children in math. And the longer the children were in school, the wider the gap between the Asian and the American children's math scores became, with the lowest differential being in the first grade, the biggest in the eleventh grade.

To learn more about the reasons for these large cross-cultural differences in achievement, the researchers spent hundreds of hours observing in classrooms, interviewing teachers,

children, and mothers, and giving questionnaires to the fathers. They found that American parents' satisfaction with their children's achievement and education is high but that their standards are low in comparison with those of their Asian counterparts. And American parents emphasize that their children's math achievement is primarily determined by innate ability; Asian parents believe their children's math achievement is mainly the result of effort and training.

In 1990, President Bush and the nation's governors adopted a well-publicized goal: to change American education in ways that will help students to lead the world in math achievement by the year 2000. Stevenson (1992; Stevenson, Chen, & Lee, 1993) says that is unlikely to happen, because American standards and expectations for children's math achievement are too low by international standards.

Even though Asian students are doing so well in math achievement, might there be a dark underside of too much stress and tension in the students and their schools? Stevenson and his colleagues (1993) have not found that to be the case. They asked eleventh-grade students in Japan and the United States how often in the past month they had experienced feelings of stress, depression, aggression, and other problems, such as not being able to sleep well. They also asked the students how often they felt nervous when they took tests. On all of these characteristics, the Japanese students expressed less distress and reported fewer problems than did the American students. Such findings do not support the Western stereotype that Asian students are tense, wired individuals driven by relentless pressures for academic excellence.

Critics of cross-national studies say that such comparisons are flawed because countries vary greatly in the percentage of children who go to school, the curricula, and so forth. Even in face of such criticisms, there is a growing consensus, based on information collected by different research teams, that American children's achievement is very low, that American educators' and parents' expectations for children's math achievement are too low, and that American schools are long overdue for an extensive overhaul.

Asian grade schools intersperse studying with frequent periods of activities. This approach helps children maintain their attention and likely makes learning more enjoyable. Shown here are Japanese fourth-graders making wearable masks.

CONCEPT TABLE 10.3

Intelligence, Extremes of Intelligence, Creativity, Language Development, and Achievement

Concept	Processes/Related Ideas	Characteristics/Description
Intelligence	What is intelligence?	Intelligence is an abstract concept that is measured indirectly. Psychologists rely on intelligence tests to estimate intelligence. Verbal ability, problem-solving skills, and the ability to learn from and adapt to everyday life are involved in intelligence.
	One face or many?	The Binet and Wechsler scales are the most widely used individual tests of intelligence. Both evaluate intelligence as a general ability, while the Wechsler also evaluates a number of components of intelligence. Psychologists debate whether intelligence is a general ability or a number of specific abilities.
	Cultural bias	Early intelligence tests favored White, middle-class, urban individuals. Current tests try to reduce this bias. Culture-fair tests are alternatives to traditional tests, but most psychologists believe they cannot replace traditional tests.
	The use and misuse of intelligence tests	Despite limitations, when used by a judicious examiner, tests can be valuable tools for determining individual differences in intelligence. The tests should be used with other information about the individual. IQ scores can produce unfortunate stereotypes and expectations. Intelligence or a high IQ is not necessarily the ultimate human value.
The extremes of intelligence	Mental retardation	A mentally retarded child has a low IQ, usually below 70 on a traditional IQ test, and has difficulty adapting to everyday life. Classifications of mental retardation have been made. The two main types of retardation are organic and cultural-familial.
	Giftedness	A gifted child has above-average intelligence (an IQ of 120 or more) and/or superior talent for something.
Creativity	Its nature	Creativity is the ability to think about something in a novel or unusual way and to come up with unique solutions to problems.
Language development	Vocabulary and grammar	In middle and late childhood, children become more analytical and logical in their approach to words and grammar.
	Reading	In the history of learning to read, three techniques dominate: ABC, whole-word, and phonics. Current strategies often focus on a combination of the whole-word and phonics methods. However, reading is much more than the sum of these approaches. Understanding how reading works requires consideration of information processing.
	Bilingualism	This has become a major issue in our nation's schools, with debate raging over the best way to conduct bilingual education. No negative effects of bilingualism have been found, and bilingual education is often associated with positive outcomes, although causal relations are difficult to establish. Increasingly, researchers are recognizing the complexity of bilingual education.
Achievement	Its nature	Early interest, stimulated by McClelland's ideas, focused on the need for achievement. Contemporary ideas include the distinction between intrinsic and extrinsic motivation, a mastery orientation versus a helpless orientation, as well as a concern for achievement motivation in children from ethnic minority groups.

LIFE-SPAN HEALTH AND WELL-BEING

Madeline Cartwright: Making a Difference in North Philadelphia

Madeline Cartwright was formerly the principal of the James G. Blaine public school in a neighborhood enshrouded in poverty and rocked by violence. Cartwright became the principal of Blaine school in 1979. She grew up in Pittsburgh's poor Hill District, and she was determined to make a difference in North Philadelphia, one of America's most drug-ridden, devastated inner-city areas.

One of the first things Cartwright did when she became principal was to install a washer and dryer in the school's kitchen, where each morning she and her staff personally washed much of the children's clothing. A Philadelphia chemical company provided her with free soap powder. Cartwright said this is the only way many of the children in her school will know what it is like to have clean clothes. She is proud that the kids in her school "looked good and had clean clothes," and she knows it made them feel better about themselves.

The most important thing Cartwright did when she became the principal was to, as she said, "browbeat" parents into getting involved in the school. She told them that she came from the same circumstances they did and that, here at Blaine school, the children were going to get a better education and have a better life than most children who attended her elementary school when she was growing up. But she told the parents that this was only

Madeline Cartwright is an elementary school principal who has made a powerful difference in many impoverished children's lives. Especially important was Cartwright's persistence and persuasiveness in getting parents more involved in their children's education.

going to happen if they worked with her and became partners with the school in educating and socializing the children.

When she came to Blaine school, she told the parents, "This place is dirty! How can your kids go to school in a place like this!" One of the parents commented, "You must think you are in the suburbs." The parent expected the neighborhood and the school to be dirty. Cartwright told the parent, "The dirt in the suburbs is the same as the dirt in North Philadelphia—if you don't *move* it. And the same detergents work here."

Cartwright rounded up 18 parents and scrubbed the building until it was clean.

Blaine's school auditorium overflowed with parents when parent meetings were scheduled. Cartwright made children bring their parents to the meetings. She told the children, "Your parents need to know what we are doing in school." She gave the children a doughnut or a pretzel the next day if one of their parents came. She told the parents they could come to her if they had problems—that she could direct them to places and people who would help them solve their problems. Because of Cartwright's efforts, parents now feel comfortable at Blaine school.

Cartwright believes that a very important aspect of intervening in children's lives who come from low-income families is increasing the positive role models they see and with whom they can interact. She wants the state of Pennsylvania to set up "mentor houses," into which salvageable families can be moved. These vacant houses are located in better neighborhoods, and a family with positive values is appointed or paid to be a mentor or role model for the family. Says Cartwright, "I would like to be a mentor."

Some people would say that Cartwright's dreams are naive, but maybe not. One safe and clean school, one set of clean clothes, one clean toilet, one safe house—and then another safe school, and another, and another. Concludes Cartwright, "I'm telling you; there are things you can do!" (Louv, 1990). ■

CONCLUSIONS

In middle and late childhood, healthy and competent children lead active lives, seek to know and understand, and enjoy learning.

We began this chapter by exploring the physical development of children during middle and late childhood. This included the study of body changes, exercise, sports, stress, handicapped children, learning disabilities, and attention-deficit hyperactivity disorder. Then

we learned about Piaget's theory and concrete operational thought, Piagetian contributions and criticisms, information processing, the many faces of intelligence, including its extremes of mental retardation and giftedness, creativity, language development, and achievement. At different points in the chapter you read about how children are trained for the Olympics in China, achievement and learning

in Asian and American children, and Madeline Cartwright, who is making a difference in North Philadelphia.

Remember that you can obtain an overall summary of the entire chapter by again reading the three concept tables on pages 284, 291, and 305. In the next chapter we turn our attention to socioemotional development in middle and late childhood.

KEY TERMS

stress The response of individuals to the circumstances and events (called "stressors") that threaten them and tax their coping abilities. (277)

cognitive appraisal Lazarus's term that describes children's interpretations of events in their lives as harmful, threatening, or challenging and their determination of whether they have the resources to effectively cope with the events. (277)

primary appraisal Children interpret whether an event involves harm or loss that has already occurred, a threat to some future danger, or a challenge to be overcome. (277)

secondary appraisal Children evaluate their resources and determine how effectively they can cope with the event. (277)

acculturation Cultural change that results from continuous, firsthand contact between two distinctive cultural groups. Acculturative stress is the negative consequence of acculturation. (278)

Public Law 94–142 The federal government's mandate to all states to provide a free, appropriate education for all children. This law, also called the "Education for All Handicapped Children Act," was passed by Congress in 1975. A key provision of the bill was the development of an individualized education program for each identified handicapped child. (280)

mainstreaming Occurs when handicapped children attend regular school classes with nonhandicapped children. In this way handicapped children enter the "mainstream" of education in the school and are not separated from nonhandicapped students. (280)

learning disabilities (1) Are of normal intelligence or above, (2) have difficulties in several academic areas but usually do not show deficits in others, and (3) are not suffering from some other conditions or disorders that could explain their learning problems. (281)

attention-deficit hyperactivity disorder Commonly called "hyperactivity." This disorder is characterized by a short attention span, distractibility, and high levels of physical activity. (281)

neo-Piagetians Are developmentalists who have elaborated on Piaget's theory, believing children's cognitive development is more specific in many respects than he thought. (286)

long-term memory A relatively permanent and unlimited type of memory. (287)

control processes Are cognitive processes that do not occur automatically but require work and effort. They are under the learner's conscious control and they can be used to improve memory. They are also appropriately called "strategies." (287)

script A schema for an event. (288)

metacognitive knowledge Knowledge about cognition, the knowledge children have accumulated through experience, and stored in long-term memory about the human mind and its workings. (288)

cognitive monitoring The process of taking stock of what you are currently doing, what you will do next, and how effectively the mental activity is unfolding. (289)

reciprocal teaching An instructional procedure used by Brown and Palincsar to develop cognitive monitoring; it requires that students take turns in leading a study group in the use of strategies for comprehending and remembering text content. (289)

critical thinking Involves grasping the deeper meaning of problems, keeping an open mind about different approaches and perspectives, and thinking reflectively rather than accepting statements and carrying out procedures without significant understanding and evaluation. (289)

intelligence Verbal ability, problem-solving skills, and the ability to learn from and adapt to the experiences of everyday life. (290)

mental age (MA) An individual's level of mental development relative to others. (290)

intelligence quotient (IQ) Was devised by William Stern. IQ is the child's mental age divided by chronological age multiplied by 100. (290)

normal distribution Is symmetrical with a majority of cases falling in the middle of the possible range of scores and a few scores appearing toward the extremes of the range. (292)

triarchic theory Sternberg's theory that intelligence consists of componential intelligence, experiential intelligence, and contextual intelligence. (293)

culture-fair tests Tests that are designed to reduce cultural bias. (296)

mental retardation A condition of limited mental ability in which the individual has a low IQ, usually below 70 on a traditional intelligence test, and has difficulty adapting to everyday life. (297)

organic retardation Mental retardation caused by a genetic disorder or by brain damage; organic refers to the tissues or organs of the body, so there is some physical damage in organic retardation. (297)

cultural-familial retardation A mental deficit in which no evidence of organic brain damage can be found; individuals' IQs range from 50 to 70. Psychologists suspect that such mental deficits result from the normal variation that distributes people along the range of intelligence scores above 50, combined with growing up in a below-average intellectual environment. (297)

gifted Have above-average intelligence (an IQ of 120 or higher) and/or superior talent for something. (298)

convergent thinking Is characteristic of the kind of thinking on standardized intelligence tests, that produces one correct answer. (299)

divergent thinking Produces many answers to the same question and is more characteristic of creativity. (299)

creativity The ability to think about something in novel and unusual ways and to come up with unique solutions to problems. (299)

ABC method A learning-to-read technique that emphasizes memorizing the names and letters of the alphabet. (299)

whole-word method A learning-to-read technique that emphasizes learning direct associations between whole words and their meanings. (299)

phonics method A learning-to-read technique that emphasizes the sounds that letters make when in words (such sounds can differ from the names of these letters, as when the sound of the letter C is not found in cat). (299)

bilingual education Refers to programs for students with limited proficiency in English that instruct students in their own language part of the time while they learn English. (300)

achievement motivation (or **need for achievement**) The desire to accomplish something, to reach a standard of excellence, and to expend effort to excel. (301)

intrinsic motivation The internal desire to be competent and to do something for its own sake. (302)

extrinsic motivation Motivation influenced by external rewards and punishments. (302)

helpless orientation Describes children who seem trapped by the experience of difficulty. They attribute their difficulty to a lack of ability. (303)

mastery orientation Describes children who are task oriented. Instead of focusing on their ability, they become concerned about their learning strategies. (303)

Winslow Homer, Three Boys and a Kitten, detail.

Socioemotional Development in Middle and Late Childhood

*The little ones leaped, and shouted, and
Laugh'd and all the hills echoed.*

—William Blake

Children know nothing about childhood and have little to say about it. They are too busy becoming something they have not quite grasped yet, something which keeps changing. . . . Nor will they realize what is happening to them until they are too far beyond it to remember how it felt.

—Alistair Reed

IMAGES OF LIFE-SPAN DEVELOPMENT

Children's Perceptions of Morals on the Make-Believe Planet of Pax

Can children understand such concepts as discrimination, economic inequality, affirmative action, and comparable worth? Probably not if we use these terms, but might we be able to construct circumstances involving these concepts that they are able to understand? Phyllis Katz (1987) asked elementary school children to pretend that they had taken a long ride on a spaceship to a make-believe planet called "Pax." She asked for their opinions about various situations in which they found themselves. The situations involved conflict, socioeconomic inequality, and civil and political rights. For example, included in the conflict items was the question of what a teacher should do when two students were tied for a prize or when they have been fighting. The economic equality dilemmas included a proposed field trip that not all students could afford, a comparable worth situation in which janitors were paid more than teachers, and an employment situation that discriminated against those with dots on their noses instead of stripes. The rights items dealt with minority rights and freedom of the press.

The elementary school children did indeed recognize injustice and often came up with interesting solutions to problems. For example, all but two children believed that teachers should earn as much as janitors—the holdouts said teachers should make less because they stay in one room or because cleaning toilets is more disgusting and, therefore, deserves higher wages. Children were especially responsive to the economic inequality items. All but one thought that not giving a job to a qualified applicant who had different physical characteristics (a striped rather than a dotted nose) was unfair. The majority recommended an affirmative action solution—giving the job to the one from the discriminated minority. None of the children verbalized the concept of freedom of the press or seemed to understand that a newspaper has the right to criticize a mayor in print without being punished. What are our schools teaching children about democracy? Some of the courses of action suggested were intriguing. Several argued that the reporters should be jailed. One child said that, if she were the mayor being criticized, she would worry, make speeches, and say, "I didn't do anything wrong," not unlike what American presidents have done in recent years. Another said that the mayor should not put the newspaper people out of work, because that might make them print more bad things. "Make them write comics instead," he said. The children believed that poverty exists on Earth but mainly in Africa, big cities, or Vietnam. War was mentioned as the biggest problem on Earth, although children were not certain where it is presently occurring. Other problems mentioned were crime, hatred, school, smog, meanness, and Delta Airlines (the questions were asked in the summer of 1986, just after a Delta Airlines crash killed hundreds of passengers). Overall, the types of rules the children believed a society should abide by were quite sensible—almost all included the need for equitable sharing of resources and work and prohibitions against aggression.

PREVIEW

The socioemotional worlds of children become more complex and differentiated in middle and late childhood. Family relationships and peers continue their important roles in middle and late childhood. Schools and relationships with teachers become more structured aspects of the child's life. The child's self-understanding advances, and changes in gender and moral development characterize children's development during the elementary school years.

FAMILIES

As children move into the middle and late childhood years, parents spend considerably less time with them. In one investigation, parents spent less than half as much time with their children aged 5 to 12 in caregiving, instruction, reading, talking, and playing as when the children were younger (Hill & Stafford, 1980). This drop in parent-child interaction may be even more extensive in families with little parental education. Although parents spend less time with their children in middle and late childhood than in early childhood, parents continue to be extremely important socializing agents in their children's lives. What are some of the most important parent-child issues in middle and late childhood?

Parent-Child Issues

Parent-child interactions during early childhood focus on such matters as modesty, bedtime regularities, control of temper, fighting with siblings and peers, eating behavior and manners, autonomy in dressing, and attention seeking. While some of these issues—fighting and reaction to discipline, for example—are carried forward into the elementary school years, many new issues appear by the age of 7 (Maccoby, 1984). These include whether children should be made to perform chores, and, if so, whether they should be paid for them; how to help children learn to entertain themselves rather than relying on parents for everything; and how to monitor children's lives outside the family in school and peer settings.

School-related matters are especially important for families during middle and late childhood. School-related difficulties are the number one reason that children in this age group are referred for clinical help. Children must learn to relate to adults outside the family on a regular basis—adults who interact with the child much differently than parents. During middle and late childhood, interactions with adults outside the family involve more formal control and achievement orientation.

> *Of all the animals, the boy is the most unmanageable, inasmuch as he has the fountain of reason in him not yet regulated; He is the most insidious, sharp-witted, and insubordinate of animals. Wherefore he must be bound with many bridles.*
>
> —Plato, 350 B.C.

Discipline during middle and late childhood is often easier for parents than it was during early childhood; it may also be easier than during adolescence. In middle and late childhood, children's cognitive development has matured to the point where it is possible for parents to reason with them about resisting deviation and controlling their behavior. By adolescence, children's reasoning has become more sophisticated, and they may be less likely to accept parental discipline. Adolescents also push more strongly for independence, which contributes to parenting difficulties. Parents of elementary school children use less physical discipline than do parents of preschool children. By contrast, parents of elementary school children are more likely

to use deprivation of privileges, appeals directed at the child's self-esteem, comments designed to increase the child's sense of guilt, and statements indicating to the child that she is responsible for her actions.

During middle and late childhood, some control is transferred from parent to child, although the process is gradual and involves *coregulation* rather than control by either the child or the parent alone (Maccoby, 1984). The major shift to autonomy does not occur until about the age of 12 or later. During middle and late childhood, parents continue to exercise general supervision and exert control while children are allowed to engage in moment-to-moment self-regulation. This coregulation process is a transition period between the strong parental control of early childhood and the increased relinquishment of general supervision of adolescence.

During this coregulation, parents should

- monitor, guide, and support children at a distance;
- effectively use the times when they have direct contact with the child;
- strengthen in their children the ability to monitor their own behavior, to adopt appropriate standards of conduct, to avoid hazardous risks, and to sense when parental support and contact are appropriate.

In middle and late childhood, parents and children increasingly label each other and make attributions about each others' motives. Parents and children do not react to each other only on the basis of each others' past behavior; rather, their reactions to each other are based on how they interpret behavior and their expectations for behavior. Parents and children label each other broadly. Parents label their children as being smart or dumb, introverted or extraverted, mannerly or unruly, and lazy or hardworking. Children label their parents as being cold or warm, understanding or not understanding, and so on. Even though there are probably specific circumstances when children and parents do not conform to these labels, the labels represent a distillation of many hours, days, months, and years of learning what each other is like as a person.

Life changes in parents also influence the nature of parent-child interaction in middle and late childhood; parents become more experienced in child rearing. As child-rearing demands are reduced in middle and late childhood, mothers are more likely to consider returning to a career or beginning a new career. Marital relationships change, as less time is spent in child rearing and more time is spent in career development, especially for mothers.

Societal Changes in Families

As we discussed in chapter 9, increasing numbers of children are growing up in divorced and working-mother families. But there are several other major shifts in the composition of family life that especially affect children in middle and late childhood. Parents are divorcing in greater numbers than ever before, but many of them remarry. It takes time for parents to marry, have

LIFE-SPAN PRACTICAL KNOWLEDGE 11.1

Strengthening Your Stepfamily

(1986) by Elizabeth Einstein and Linda Albert. Circle Pines, MN: American Guidance Service.

This book covers many different types of stepfamilies. Stepfamily myths and unrealistic expectations that are common in stepfamilies are highlighted. The authors emphasize strategies for developing positive relationships between stepparents and stepchildren; they evaluate children's feelings and behaviors in stepfamilies, and they provide parental guidelines for helping children cope more effectively. The recommendations for dealing with stepfamily issues cover everything from daily routines to holiday celebrations.

children, get divorced, and then remarry. Consequently, there are far more elementary and secondary school children than infant or preschool children living in stepfamilies. In addition, an increasing number of elementary and secondary school children are latchkey children.

Stepfamilies

The number of remarriages involving children has steadily grown in recent years, although both the rate of increase in divorce and stepfamilies slowed in the 1980s. Stepfather families, in which a woman has custody of children from a previous marriage, make up 70 percent of stepfamilies. Stepmother families make up almost 20 percent of stepfamilies, and a small minority are blended, with both partners bringing children from a previous marriage. A substantial percentage of stepfamilies produce children of their own.

Like divorce, remarriage has also become commonplace in American society. The United States has the highest remarriage rate in the world, and Americans tend to remarry soon after divorce. Younger women remarry more quickly than older women, and childless women, divorced prior to the age of 25, have higher remarriage rates than women with children. The more money a divorced male has, the more likely he is to remarry, but for women the opposite is true. Remarriage satisfaction, similar to satisfaction in first marriages, appears to decrease over time (Guisinger & others, 1989). In fact, few differences have been found between the factors that predict marital satisfaction in first marriages and remarriage (Coleman & Ganong, 1990).

Just as couples who are first married, remarried individuals often have unrealistic expectations about their stepfamily. Thus, an important adjustment for remarried persons is to develop realistic expectations. Money and the complexities of family structure in the remarried family often contribute to marital conflict.

Many variations in remarriage have the potential for what is called **boundary ambiguity**—*the uncertainty in stepfamilies of who is in or out of the family and who is performing or responsible for certain tasks in the family system.* The uncertainty of boundaries likely increases stress for the family system and the probability of behavior problems in children.

Research on stepfamilies has lagged behind research on divorced families, but a number of investigators have turned their attention to this increasingly common family structure (Anderson, 1992; Hetherington, 1993; Hetherington & Clingempeel, 1992; Hetherington, Hagan, & Anderson, 1989; Lindner, 1992; Lyons & Barber, 1992; O'Connor, 1992; Santrock & Sitterle, 1987; Santrock, Sitterle, & Warshak, 1988). In one recent study, entrance of a stepfather when children were 9 years or older was associated with more problems than when the stepfather family was formed earlier (Hetherington, 1993). Following remarriage of their parents, children of all ages show a resurgence of behavior problems (Freeman, 1993). Younger children seem to eventually form an attachment to a stepparent and accept the stepparenting role. However, the developmental tasks facing adolescents make them especially vulnerable to the entrance of a stepparent. At the time when they are searching for an identity and exploring sexual and other close relationships outside the family, a nonbiological parent may increase the stress associated with these important tasks.

Following the remarriage of the custodial parent, an emotional upheaval usually occurs in girls, and problems in boys often intensify. Over time, preadolescent boys seem to improve more than girls in stepfather families. Sons who frequently are involved in conflicted or coercive relations with their custodial mothers probably have much to gain from living with a warm, supportive stepfather. In contrast, daughters who have a close relationship with their custodial mothers and considerable independence frequently find a stepfather both disruptive and constraining.

Critical Thinking

What might parents do to improve the adjustment of children in stepfamilies?

Children's relationships with their biological parents are more positive than with their stepparents, regardless of whether a stepmother or stepfather family is involved. However, stepfathers are often distant and disengaged from their stepchildren. As a rule, the more complex the stepfamily, the more difficult the child's adjustment. Families in which both parents bring children from a previous marriage have the highest level of behavioral problems.

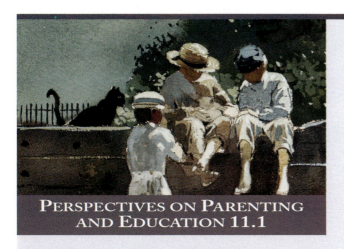

PERSPECTIVES ON PARENTING AND EDUCATION 11.1

Parenting and Children in Stepfamilies

What are some problems frequently encountered by stepfamilies? What are some ways to build a strong, positive stepfamily? William Gladden (1991) recently provided the following guidelines that address these questions.

Frequently Encountered Problems in Stepfamilies

- Adapting to multiple viewpoints, attitudes, and personalities.
- Arranging to comply with the visitation and other custodial rights granted by a court to the absent natural parent—holidays and vacations can pose special problems, for example.
- Conflicting ideas about how to discipline children and differing expectations about children.
- Continuing battles over child custody issues.
- Disagreements over expenses and how family finances are to be allocated.
- Feelings of anger, hurt, mistrust, or guilt regarding the ex-spouse that may be transferred to the new mate.
- Interference by in-laws, especially grandparents, who have an interest in the children.
- Reduced space, privacy, and personal time.
- Refusal of the children to follow the rules or wishes of the stepparent.

- Unwillingness of the children to accept the stepparent, with possible outright rejection of the stepparent.
- Rivalry between children for attention and affection, especially when stepsiblings are involved.
- Unresolved emotional problems of the children because of the disequilibrium they have experienced in their lives.
- Unresolved personal problems of parents, such as psychological or behavioral problems, that may accompany them into the newly created family.

Strategies for Building a Strong, Positive Stepfamily

- Communicate about and come to an agreement on rules of conduct.
- Try to develop and maintain a cooperative relationship with the absent natural parent who still has legal rights to the children.
- Develop good communications between family members and learn to communicate clearly.
- Provide the children with age-appropriate responsibilities.
- Make a commitment to talk about and resolve disagreements based on mutual respect and kindness.
- Don't avoid dealing with the personal problems that create stress in the stepfamily; find positive ways to cope with them.
- Openly express affection.
- Plan for at least one mealtime per day that includes all the stepfamily members.
- Plan for family group entertainment and recreation.
- Respect the individual privacy rights of each member of the stepfamily.
- Support each stepfamily member's interests, hobbies, and goals.
- If family conflicts seem irreconcilable, or if the behavior of a child poses serious problems, it is usually wise to seek professional help. Most communities also have stepfamily support groups whose members may share problems encountered by many stepfamilies. Such support groups can be especially beneficial for coping with stepfamily issues and problems.

In the recent investigation by E. Mavis Hetherington (1993, 1994, in press), both parenting techniques and the school environment were associated with whether children coped effectively both with living in divorced family and a stepfamily. From the first grade on, an authoritative environment (an organized predictable environment with clearly defined standards, and a responsive, nurturant environment) was linked with greater achievement and fewer problems in children than three other environments—authoritarian (coercive, power assertive, punitive, more criticism than praise, little responsiveness to individual children's needs, and low

nurturance), permissive (low structure, disorganized, and high warmth), and chaotic/neglecting (disorganized, ineffective, erratic though usually harsh control, unstructured, low expectations, and hostile relationships). In divorced families, when only one parent was authoritative, or when neither parent was authoritative, an authoritative school improved the child's adjustment. A chaotic/neglecting school environment had the most adverse effects on children, which were most marked when there was no authoritative parent in the home. To read further about stepfamily issues, turn to Perspectives on Parenting and Education 11.1.

Latchkey Children

We concluded in chapter 9 that the mother's working outside the home does not necessarily have negative outcomes for her children. However, a certain subset of children from working-mother families deserve further scrutiny: latchkey children. These children typically do not see their parents from the time they leave for school in the morning until about 6 or 7 P.M. They are called "latchkey" children because they are given the key to their home, take the key to school, and then use it to let themselves into the home while their parents are still at work. Latchkey children are largely unsupervised for 2 to 4 hours a day during each school week. During the summer months, they may be unsupervised for entire days, 5 days a week.

Thomas and Lynette Long (1983) interviewed more than 1,500 latchkey children. They concluded that a slight majority of these children had had negative latchkey experiences. Some latchkey children may grow up too fast, hurried by the responsibilities placed on them (Elkind, 1981). How do latchkey children handle the lack of limits and structure during the latchkey hours? Without limits and parental supervision, latchkey children find their way into trouble more easily, possibly stealing, vandalizing, or abusing a sibling. The Longs point out that 90 percent of the juvenile delinquents in Montgomery County, Maryland, are latchkey children. Joan Lipsitz (1983), in testifying before the Select Committee on Children, Youth, and Families, called the lack of adult supervision of children in the after-school hours one of today's major problems. Lipsitz calls it the "three-to-six o'clock problem" because it is during this time that the Center for Early Adolescence in North Carolina, of which Lipsitz is director, experiences a peak of referrals for clinical help. And in a 1987 national poll, teachers rated the latchkey children phenomenon the number one reason that children have problems in schools (Harris, 1987).

But while latchkey children may be vulnerable to problems, the experiences of latchkey children vary enormously, as do the experiences of all children with working mothers (Posner & Vandell, in press). Parents need to give special attention to the ways in which their latchkey children's lives can be effectively monitored. Variations in latchkey experiences suggest that parental monitoring and authoritative parenting help the child cope more effectively with latchkey experiences, especially in resisting peer pressure (Galambos & Maggs, 1989; Steinberg, 1986). The degree of developmental risk to latchkey children remains undetermined. One positive sign is that researchers are beginning to conduct more-precise analyses of children's latchkey experiences to determine which aspects of latchkey circumstances are the most detrimental (Rodman, Pratto, & Nelson, 1988; Steinberg, 1988).

PEER RELATIONS

During middle and late childhood, children spend an increasing amount of time in peer interaction. In one investigation, children interacted with peers 10 percent of their day at the age of 2, 20 percent at age 4, and more than 40 percent

between the ages of 7 and 11 (Barker & Wright, 1951). Episodes with peers totaled 299 per typical school day.

What do children do when they are with their peers? In one study, sixth graders were asked what they do when they are with their friends (Medrich & others, 1982). Team sports accounted for 45 percent of boys' activities but only 26 percent of girls'. General play, going places, and socializing were common listings for both sexes. Most peer interactions occur outside the home (although close to home), occur more often in private than in public places, and occur more between children of the same sex than between children of different sexes.

Peer Popularity, Rejection, and Neglect

Children often think, "What can I do to get all of the kids at school to like me?" or "What's wrong with me? Something must be wrong or I would be more popular." What makes a child popular with peers? Children who give out the most reinforcements are often popular. So is a child who listens carefully to other children and maintains open lines of communication. Being themselves, being happy, showing enthusiasm and concern for others, and being self-confident but not conceited are characteristics that serve children well in their quest for peer popularity (Hartup, 1983). In one study, popular children were more likely to communicate clearly with their peers, to elicit their peers' attention, and to maintain conversation with peers than were unpopular children (Kennedy, 1990).

Recently, developmentalists have distinguished between two types of children who are not popular with their peers: those who are neglected and those who are rejected (Albrecht & Silbereisen, 1992; Coie, 1993; Coie & Koeppl, 1990; Roedel & Bendixen, 1992). **Neglected children** *receive little attention from their peers but they are not necessarily disliked by their peers.* **Rejected children** *are disliked by their peers. They are more likely to be disruptive and aggressive than neglected children.* Rejected children often have more serious adjustment problems later in life than do neglected children (Kupersmidt & Patterson, 1993). For example, in one study, 112 fifth-grade boys were evaluated over a period of 7 years until the end of high school (Kupersmidt & Coie, 1990). The key factor in predicting whether rejected children would engage in delinquent behavior or drop out of school later during adolescence was aggression toward peers in elementary school.

Not all rejected children are aggressive (Bierman, Smoot, & Aumillel, 1993). Although aggression and its related characteristics of impulsiveness and disruptiveness underlie rejection about half the time, approximately 10 to 20 percent of rejected children are shy.

An important question to ask is how neglected children and rejected children can be trained to interact more effectively with their peers. The goal of training programs with neglected children is often to help them attract attention from their peers in positive ways and to hold their attention by asking questions, by listening in a warm and friendly way, and by saying things about themselves that relate to the peers' interests. They also are taught to enter groups more effectively (Duck, 1988).

The goal of training programs with rejected children is often to help them listen to peers and "hear what they say" instead of trying to dominate peer interactions. Rejected children are trained to join peers without trying to change what is taking place in the peer group. Children may need to be motivated to use these strategies by being persuaded that they work effectively and are satisfying. In some programs, children are shown videotapes of appropriate peer interaction; then they are asked to comment on them and to draw lessons from what they have seen. In other training programs, popular children are taught to be more accepting of neglected or rejected peers.

Social Cognition

Earlier we found that the mutual cognitions of children and parents become increasingly important in family relationships during middle and late childhood. Children's social cognitions about their peers also become increasingly important for understanding peer relationships in middle and late childhood. Of special interest are how children process information about peer relations and their social knowledge (Crick & Dodge, 1994; Dodge, 1993; Quiggle & others, 1992).

A boy accidentally trips and knocks a peer's soft drink out of his hand. The peer misinterprets the encounter as hostile, which leads him to retaliate aggressively against the boy. Through repeated encounters of this kind, other peers come to perceive the aggressive boy as habitually acting in inappropriate ways. Kenneth Dodge (1983) argues that children go though five steps in processing information about their social world: decoding social cues, interpreting, searching for a response, selecting an optimal response, and enacting. Dodge has found that aggressive boys are more likely to perceive another child's actions as hostile when the child's intention is ambiguous. And when aggressive boys search for cues to determine a peer's intention, they respond more rapidly, less efficiently, and less reflectively than nonaggressive children. These are among the social cognitive factors believed to be involved in the nature of children's conflicts (Shantz, 1988).

Social knowledge is also involved in children's ability to get along with peers. An important part of children's social life involves knowing what goals to pursue in poorly defined or ambiguous situations. Social relationship goals are also important, such as how to initiate and maintain a social bond. Children need to know what scripts to follow to get other children to be their friends. For example, as part of the script for getting friends, it helps to know that saying nice things, regardless of what the peer does or says, will make the peer like the child more.

From a social cognitive perspective, children who are maladjusted do not have adequate social cognitive skills to effectively interact with others (Kelly & de Armas, 1989; Weisberg, Caplan, & Sivo, 1989). One investigation explored the possibility that children who are maladjusted do not have the social cognitive skills necessary for positive social interaction (Asarnow & Callan, 1985). Boys with and without peer adjustment difficulties were identified, and their social cognitive skills were assessed. Boys without peer adjustment problems generated more alternative solutions to problems, proposed more assertive and mature solutions, gave less-intense aggressive solutions, showed more adaptive planning, and evaluated physically aggressive responses less positively than boys with peer adjustment problems.

The world of peers is one of varying acquaintances; children interact with some children they barely know and with friends for hours every day. It is to the latter type—friends—that we now turn.

Friends

"My best friend is nice. She is honest and I can trust her. I can tell her my innermost secrets and know that nobody else will find out about them. I have other friends, but she is my best friend. We consider each other's feelings and don't want to hurt each other. We help each other out when we have problems. We make up funny names for people and laugh ourselves silly. We make lists of which boys we think are the ugliest, which are the biggest jerks, and so on. Some of these things we share with other friends, some we don't." This is a description of a friendship by a 10-year-old girl. It reflects the belief that children are interested in specific peers—in Barbara and Tommy—not just any peers. They want to share concerns, interests, information, and secrets with them.

> *A man's growth is seen in the successive choirs of his friends.*
>
> —Ralph Waldo Emerson, 1841

Why are children's friendships important? They serve six functions: companionship, stimulation, physical support, ego support, social comparison, and intimacy/affection (Gottman & Parker, 1987). Concerning companionship, friendship provides children with a familiar partner and playmate, someone who is willing to spend time with them and join in collaborative activities. Concerning stimulation, friendship provides children with interesting information, excitement, and amusement. Concerning physical support, friendship provides time, resources, and assistance. Concerning ego support, friendship provides the expectation of support, encouragement, and feedback that helps children maintain an impression of themselves as competent, attractive, and worthwhile individuals. Concerning social comparison, friendship provides information about where the child stands vis-á-vis others and whether the child is doing OK. Concerning intimacy and affection, friendship provides children with a warm, close, trusting relationship with another individual in which self-disclosure takes place (see figure 11.1).

> *Hold a true friend with both hands.*
>
> —Nigerian proverb

Two of friendship's most common characteristics are intimacy and similarity. **Intimacy in friendships** *is defined as self-disclosure and the sharing of private thoughts.* Research reveals that intimate friendships may not appear until early adolescence (Berndt, 1982; Berndt & Perry, 1990; Buhrmester, 1989). Also,

FIGURE 11.1

Functions of children's friendships.

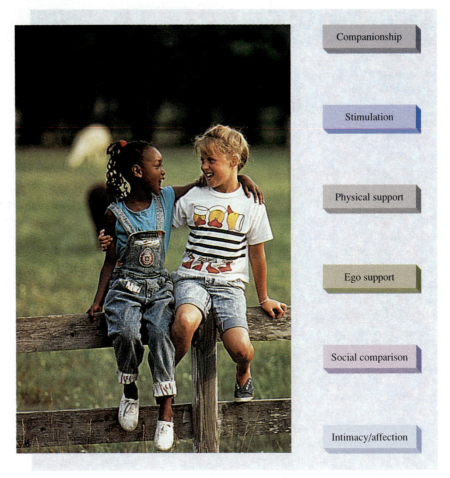

Companionship

Stimulation

Physical support

Ego support

Social comparison

Intimacy/affection

throughout childhood, friends are more similar than dissimilar in terms of age, sex, race, and many other factors. Friends often have similar attitudes toward school, similar educational aspirations, and closely aligned achievement orientations. Friends like the same music, the same kind of clothes, and the same kind of leisure activities.

Harry Stack Sullivan (1953) was the most influential theorist to discuss the importance of friendships. He argued that there is a dramatic increase in the psychological importance and intimacy of close friends during early adolescence. In contrast to other psychoanalytic theorists' narrow emphasis on the importance of parent-child relationships, Sullivan contended that friends also play important roles in shaping children's and adolescents' well-being and development. In terms of well-being, he argued that all people have a number of basic social needs, including the need for tenderness (secure attachment), playful companionship, social acceptance, intimacy, and sexual relations. Whether or not these needs are fulfilled largely determines our emotional well-being. For example, if the need for playful companionship goes unmet, then we become bored and depressed; if the need for social acceptance is not met, we suffer a lowered sense of self-worth. Developmentally, friends become increasingly depended upon to satisfy these needs during

adolescence, and thus the ups and downs of experiences with friends increasingly shape adolescents' state of well-being. In particular, Sullivan believed that the need for intimacy intensifies during early adolescence, motivating teenagers to seek out close friends. He felt that if adolescents failed to forge such close friendships, they would experience painful feelings of loneliness coupled with a reduced sense of self-worth.

SCHOOLS

It is justifiable to be concerned about the impact of schools on children: By the time students graduate from high school, they have spent 10,000 hours in the classroom. Children spend many years in schools as members of a small society in which there are tasks to be accomplished, people to be socialized and socialized by, and rules that define and limit behavior, feelings, and attitudes.

The world rests on the breath of the children in the schoolhouse.

—The Talmud

LIFE-SPAN PRACTICAL KNOWLEDGE 11.2

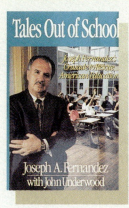

Tales Out of School
(1993) by J. Fernandez.
Boston: Little, Brown.

Author Fernandez was head of the Dade County School System in Florida and currently heads up the New York City school system. This book describes his crusade to improve America's schools and is a call to arms on behalf of America's children. Fernandez tells how we can restore order

and how we can achieve academic excellence in schools. Among the changes he recommends are more school-based management, in which principals, teachers, and parents collaborate in decision making about schools, and satellite schools, which are located in the workplace. This is a provocative book that provides a number of revolutionary ideas about revamping our nation's schools.

The Transition to Elementary School

For most children, entering the first grade signals a change from being a "homechild" to being a "schoolchild" in which new roles and obligations are experienced. Children take up a new role (being a student), interact and develop relationships with new significant others, adopt new reference groups, and develop new standards by which to judge themselves. School provides children with a rich source of new ideas to shape their sense of self (Stipek, 1992).

A special concern about children's early school experiences is emerging. Evidence is mounting that early schooling proceeds mainly on the basis of negative feedback. For example, children's self-esteem in the latter part of elementary school is lower than it is in the earlier part, and older children rate themselves as less smart, less good, and less hard-working than do younger ones (Blumenfeld & others, 1981). In one investigation, the first year of school was identified as a period of considerable importance in shaping achievement, especially for ethnic minority children (Alexander & Entwisle, 1988). Black and White children began school with similar achievement test scores, but by the end of the first year Black children's performance lagged noticeably behind that of White children, and the gap widened over the second year of schooling. The grades teachers gave to Black children in the first two grades of school also were lower than those they gave to White children.

Critical Thinking

Why does early elementary school involve so much negative feedback? What aspects of our culture and the nature of education are responsible?

In school as well as out of school, children's learning, like children's development, is *integrated* (NAEYC, 1988). One of the main pressures on elementary teachers has been the need to "cover the curriculum." Frequently, teachers have tried to do so by tightly scheduling discrete time segments for each subject.

This approach ignores the fact that children often do not need to distinguish learning by subject area. For example, they advance their knowledge of reading and writing when they work on social studies projects; they learn mathematical concepts through music and physical education (Katz & Chard, 1989; Van Deusen-Henkel & Argondizza, 1987). A curriculum can be facilitated by providing learning areas in which children plan and select their activities. For example, the classroom may include a fully equipped publishing center, complete with materials for writing, illustrating, typing, and binding student-made books; a science area with animals and plants for observation and books to study; and other similar areas (Van Deusen-Henkel & Argondizza, 1987). In this type of classroom, children learn reading as they discover information about science; they learn writing as they work together on interesting projects. Such classrooms also provide opportunities for spontaneous play, recognizing that elementary school children continue to learn in all areas through unstructured play, either alone or with other children.

Knowledge which is acquired under compulsion obtains no hold on the mind.

—Plato

Education experts Lillian Katz and Sylvia Chard (1989) described two elementary school classrooms. In one, children spent an entire morning making identical pictures of traffic lights. The teacher made no attempt to get the children to relate the pictures to anything else the class was doing. In the other class, children were investigating a school bus. They wrote to the district's school superintendent and asked if they could have a bus parked at their school for a few days. They studied the bus, discovered the functions of its parts, and discussed traffic rules. Then, in the classroom, they built their own bus out of cardboard. The children had fun, but they also practiced writing, problem solving, and even some arithmetic. When the class had their parents' night, the teacher was ready with reports on how each child was doing. However, all the parents wanted to see was the bus, because their children had been talking about it at home for weeks. Many contemporary education experts believe that this is the kind of education all children deserve. That is, they believe that children should be taught through concrete, hands-on experience.

Teachers

Teachers have a prominent influence in middle and late childhood. Teachers symbolize authority and establish the classroom's climate, conditions of interaction among students, and the nature of group functioning.

Almost everyone's life is affected in one way or another by teachers. You were influenced by teachers as you grew up; you may become a teacher yourself or work with teachers through counseling or psychological services; and you may one day have children whose education will be guided by many different teachers through the years. You can probably remember several of your teachers vividly: Perhaps one never smiled, another required you to memorize everything in sight, and yet another always appeared happy and vibrant and encouraged verbal interaction. Psychologists and educators have tried to create a profile of a good teacher's personality traits, but the complexity of personality, education, learning, and individual differences make the task difficult. Nonetheless, some teacher traits are associated with positive student outcomes more than others: enthusiasm, ability to plan, poise, adaptability, warmth, flexibility, and awareness of individual differences are a few (Gage, 1965). In one recent study, teacher support had a strong influence on students' achievement (Goodenow, 1993).

Erik Erikson (1968) believes that good teachers should be able to produce a sense of industry, rather than inferiority, in their students. Good teachers are trusted and respected by the community and know how to alternate work and play, study and games, says Erikson. They know how to recognize special efforts and to encourage special abilities. They also know how to create a setting in which children feel good about themselves and how to handle those children to whom school is not important. In Erikson's (1968) own words, children should be "mildly but firmly coerced into the adventure of finding out that one can learn to accomplish things which one would never have thought of by oneself" (p. 127).

Teacher characteristics and styles are important, but they need to be considered in concert with what children bring to the school situation (Linney & Seidman, 1989). Some children may benefit more from structure than others, and some teachers may be able to handle a flexible curriculum better than others. **Aptitude-treatment interaction (ATI)** *stresses the importance of children's aptitudes or characteristics and the treatments or experiences they are given in classrooms. Aptitude* refers to such characteristics as academic potential and personality characteristics on which students differ; *treatment* refers to educational techniques, such as structured versus flexible classrooms (Cronbach & Snow, 1977). Researchers have found that children's achievement level (aptitude) interacts with classroom structure (treatment) to produce the best learning (Peterson, 1977). For example, students who

are highly achievement oriented usually do well in a flexible classroom and enjoy it; low-achievement-oriented students usually fare worse and dislike the flexibility. The reverse often appears in structured classrooms.

Social Class and Ethnicity in Schools

Sometimes it seems as though the major function of schools has been to train children to contribute to a middle-class society. Politicians who vote on school funding have been from middle-class or elite backgrounds, school board members have often been from middle-class backgrounds, and principals and teachers also have had middle-class upbringing. Critics argue that schools have not done a good job of educating lower-class and ethnic minority children to overcome the barriers that block the enhancement of their positions (Falbo & Romo, 1994; Glasser, 1990; Holtzman, 1992; Huang & Gibbs, 1989).

My country is the world; My countrymen are mankind.
—William Lloyd Garrison, 1803

Teachers have lower expectations for children from low-income families than for children from middle-income families. A teacher who knows that a child comes from a lower-class background may spend less time trying to help the child solve a problem and may anticipate that the child will get into trouble. The teacher may believe that the parents in low-income families are not interested in helping the child, so she may make fewer efforts to communicate with them. There is evidence that teachers with lower-class origins may have different attitudes toward lower-class students than do teachers from middle-class origins (Gottlieb, 1966). Perhaps because they have experienced many inequities themselves, teachers with lower-class origins may be more empathetic to problems that lower-class children encounter. When asked to rate the most outstanding characteristics of their lower-class students, middle-class teachers checked lazy, rebellious, and fun-loving; lower-class teachers checked happy, cooperative, energetic, and ambitious. The teachers with lower-class backgrounds perceived the lower-class children's behaviors as adaptive; the middle-class teachers viewed the same behaviors as falling short of middle-class standards.

In his famous "I Have a Dream" speech, Martin Luther King said, "I have a dream that my four little children will one day live in a nation where they will not be judged by the color of their skin but by the content of their character." Children from lower-class backgrounds are not the only students who have had difficulties in school; so have children from different ethnic backgrounds (Fenzel & Magaletta, 1993; Tharp, 1989). In most American schools, Black Americans, Mexican Americans, Puerto Ricans, Native Americans, Japanese, and Asian Americans are minorities. Many teachers have been ignorant of the different cultural meanings non-Anglo children have learned in their communities (Huang & Gibbs, 1989). The social and academic development of children from minority groups depends on teacher expectations, the teacher's experience in working with children from different backgrounds, the curriculum,

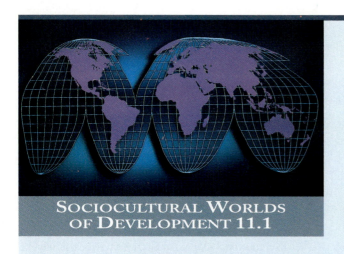

SOCIOCULTURAL WORLDS OF DEVELOPMENT 11.1

The Jigsaw Classroom

Aronson stressed that the reward structure of the elementary school classrooms needed to be changed from a setting of unequal competition to one of cooperation among equals, without making any curriculum changes. To accomplish this, he put together the *jigsaw classroom.* How might this work? Consider a class of thirty students, some White, some Black, some Hispanic. The lesson to be learned in the class focuses on the life of Joseph Pulitzer. The class might be broken up into five groups of six students each, with the groups being as equal as possible in terms of ethnic composition and academic achievement level. The lesson about Pulitzer's life could be divided into six parts, with one part given to each member of the six-person group. The parts might be paragraphs from Pulitzer's biography, such as how the Pulitzer family came to the United States, Pulitzer's childhood, his early work, and so on. The components are like parts of a jigsaw puzzle. They have to be put together to form the complete puzzle.

Each student in the group is given an allotted time to study her or his part. Then the group meets, and each member tries to teach a part to the group. After an hour or so, each member is tested on the entire life of Pulitzer, with each member receiving an individual rather than a group score. Each student, therefore, must learn the entire lesson; learning depends on the cooperation and effort of the other members. Aronson (1986) believes that this type of learning increases the students' interdependence through cooperatively working to reach the same goal.

The strategy of emphasizing cooperation rather than competition and the jigsaw classroom have been widely used in classrooms in the United States. A number of research studies reveal that this type of cooperative learning is associated with increased self-esteem, better academic performance, friendships among classmates, and improved interethnic perceptions (Aronson, 1986; Slavin, 1987, 1989).

While the cooperative classroom strategy has many merits, it may have a built-in difficulty that restricts its effectiveness. Academic achievement is as much an individual as a team "sport" (Brown, 1986). It is individuals, not groups, who enter college, take jobs, and follow careers. A parent with an advantaged child in the jigsaw classroom might react with increased ethnic hostility when the child brings home a lower grade than she had been used to getting before the jigsaw classroom was introduced. The child tells the father, "The teacher is getting us to teach each other. In my group, we have a kid named Carlos who can barely speak English." While the jigsaw classroom can be an important strategy for reducing interracial hostility, caution needs to be exercised in its use, because of the unequal status of the participants and the individual nature of achievement.

---

the presence of role models in the schools for minority students, the quality of relations between school personnel and parents from different ethnic, economic, and educational backgrounds, and the relations between the school and the community (Minuchin & Shapiro, 1983).

When the schools of Austin, Texas, were desegregated through extensive busing, the outcome was increased racial tension among Blacks, Mexican Americans, and Whites, producing violence in the schools. The superintendent consulted with Eliot Aronson, a prominent social psychologist, who was at the University of Texas at Austin at the time. Aronson thought it was more important to prevent racial hostility than to control it. This led him to observe a number of elementary school classrooms in Austin. What he saw was fierce competition between persons of unequal status. To learn how Aronson proposed to reduce the tension and fierce competition, turn to Sociocultural Worlds of Development 11.1.

American anthropologist John Ogbu (1974, 1986, 1989) proposed the controversial view that ethnic minority children are placed in a position of subordination and exploitation in the

American educational system. He believes that ethnic minority children, especially Black and Hispanic Americans, have inferior educational opportunities, are exposed to teachers and administrators who have low academic expectations for them, and encounter negative stereotypes about ethnic minority groups. Ogbu states that ethnic minority opposition to the middle-class White educational system stems from a lack of trust because of years of discrimination and oppression. Says Ogbu, it makes little sense for ethnic minority youth to do well academically if occupational opportunities are often closed to them.

> *Our most basic common link is that we all inhabit this planet. We all breathe the same air. We all cherish our children's future.*
>
> —John F. Kennedy, address.
> The American University, 1963

Completing high school, or even college, does not always bring the same job opportunities for many ethnic minority

Some critics argue that one of the main functions of schools has been to train children to contribute to a middle-class, White society. These critics argue that schools have not done a competent job of educating low-income, ethnic minority children.

James Comer (left) is shown with some of the inner-city Black American children who attend a school that became a better learning environment because of Comer's intervention. Comer is convinced that a strong, familylike atmosphere is a key to improving the quality of inner-city schools.

youth as for White youth (Entwisle, 1990). In terms of earnings and employment rates, Black American high school graduates do not do as well as their White counterparts. Many Hispanic American youth also give up in school, because, given the inadequate job opportunities awaiting them, they don't perceive any rewards for doing well in school.

According to American educational psychologist Margaret Beale Spencer and sociologist Sanford Dornbusch (1990), a form of institutional racism prevails in many American schools. That is, well-meaning teachers, acting out of misguided liberalism, often fail to challenge ethnic minority students. Knowing the handicaps these children face, some teachers accept a low level of performance from them, substituting warmth and affection for academic challenge and high standards of performance. Ethnic minority students, like their White counterparts, learn best when teachers combine warmth with challenging standards.

One person who is trying to do something about the poor quality of education for inner city children is Black American psychiatrist James Comer (1988, 1993). He has devised an intervention model that is based on a simple principle: Everyone with a stake in a school should have a say in how it's run. Comer's model calls for forming a school-governance team, made up of the principal, psychologists, and even cafeteria workers. The team develops a comprehensive plan for operating the school, including a calendar of academic and social events that encourage parents to come to school as often as possible. Comer is convinced that a strong family orientation is a key to educational success, so he tries to create a familylike environment in schools and also make parents feel comfortable in coming to their children's school. Among the reasons for Comer's concern about the lack of parental involvement in Black American and Hispanic American children's education is the high rate of single-parent families in these ethnic minority groups. A special concern is that 70 percent of the Black American and Hispanic American single-parent families headed by mothers are in poverty (McLoyd, in press). Poor school performance among many ethnic minority children is related to this pattern of single parenting and poverty (Dornbusch & others, 1985; Spencer & Dornbusch, 1990).

Thus far, we have discussed many ideas about families, peers, and schools in middle and late childhood. These ideas are summarized in concept table 11.1. We turn next to the continuing development of the self in middle and late childhood.

THE SELF

What is the nature of the child's self-understanding in the elementary school years? What is the role of perspective taking in self-understanding? What is the nature of children's self-esteem? What issue does Erikson believe children face in middle and late childhood?

The Development of Self-Understanding

In middle and late childhood, self-understanding increasingly shifts from defining oneself through external characteristics to defining oneself through internal characteristics. Elementary school children are also more likely to define themselves in terms of social characteristics and social comparisons.

In middle and late childhood, children not only recognize differences between inner and outer states, but are also more likely to include subjective inner states in their definition of self. For example, in one investigation, second-grade children were much more likely than younger children to name psychological characteristics (such as preferences or personality traits) in their self-definition and less likely to name physical characteristics (such as eye color or possessions) (Aboud & Skerry, 1983). For example, 8-year-old Todd includes in his self-description,

TABLE 11.1

Selman's Stages of Perspective Taking

Stage	Perspective-Taking Stage	Ages	Description
0	Egocentric viewpoint	3–6	Child has a sense of differentiation of self and other but fails to distinguish between the social perspective (thoughts, feelings) of other and self. Child can label other's overt feelings but does not see the cause-and-effect relation of reasons to social actions.
1	Social-informational perspective taking	6–8	Child is aware that other has a social perspective based on other's own reasoning, which may or may not be similar to child's. However, child tends to focus on one perspective rather than coordinating viewpoints.
2	Self-reflective perspective taking	8–10	Child is conscious that each individual is aware of the other's perspective and that this awareness influences self and other's view of each other. Putting self in other's place is a way of judging other's intentions, purposes, and actions. Child can form a coordinated chain of perspectives but cannot yet abstract from this process to the level of simultaneous mutuality.
3	Mutual perspective taking	10–12	Adolescent realizes that both self and other can view each other mutually and simultaneously as subjects. Adolescent can step outside the two-person dyad and view the interaction from a third-person perspective.
4	Social and conventional system perspective taking	12–15	Adolescent realizes mutual perspective taking does not always lead to complete understanding. Social conventions are seen as necessary because they are understood by all members of the group (the generalized other), regardless of their position, role, or experience.

From R. L. Selman, "The Development of Social-Cognitive Understanding: A Guide to Education and Clinical Practice" in *Moral Development and Behavior: Theory, Research and Social Issues,* Thomas Lickona (ed.). Copyright © 1986 Thomas Lickona. Reprinted by permission.

"I am smart and I am popular." Ten-year-old Tina says about herself, "I am pretty good about not worrying most of the time. I used to lose my temper but I'm better about that now. I also feel proud when I do well in school."

In addition to the increase of psychological characteristics in self-definition during the elementary school years, the *social aspects* of the self also increase at this point in development. In one investigation, elementary school children often included references to social groups in their self-descriptions (Livesly & Bromsley, 1973). For example, some children referred to themselves as Girl Scouts, as Catholics, or as someone who has two close friends.

Children's self-understanding in the elementary school years also includes increasing reference to *social comparison.* At this point in development, children are more likely to distinguish themselves from others in comparative rather than in absolute terms. That is, elementary-school-age children are no longer as likely to think about what *I* do or do not do, but are more likely to think about what I can do *in comparison with others.* This developmental shift provides an increased tendency of establishing one's differences from others as an individual. In a series of studies, Diane Ruble and her colleagues (1989) investigated children's

use of social comparison in their self-evaluations. Children were given a difficult task and then offered feedback on their own performance as well as information about the performances of other children their age. The children were then asked for self-evaluations. Children younger than 7 made virtually no reference to the information about other children's performances. However, children older than 7 often included socially comparative information in their self-descriptions.

The Role of Perspective Taking in Self-Understanding

Many child developmentalists believe that perspective taking plays an important role in self-understanding. **Perspective taking** *is the ability to assume another person's perspective and understand his or her thoughts and feelings.* Robert Selman (1980) has proposed a developmental theory of perspective taking that has been given considerable attention. He believes perspective taking involves a series of five stages, ranging from 3 years of age through adolescence (see table 11.1). These stages begin with the egocentric viewpoint in early childhood and end with in-depth perspective taking in adolescence.

CONCEPT TABLE 11.1

Families, Peers, and Schools

Concept	Processes/Related Ideas	Characteristics/Description
Families	Parent-child interaction and issues	Parents spend less time with children during middle and late childhood, including less time in caregiving, instruction, reading, talking, and playing. Nonetheless, parents still are powerful and important socializing agents during this period. New parent-child issues emerge, and discipline changes. Control is more coregulatory, children and parents label each other more, and parents mature just as children do.
	Societal changes in families	During middle and late childhood, two major changes in many children's lives are movement into a stepfamily and becoming a latchkey child. Just as divorce produces disequilibrium and stress for children, so does the entrance of a stepparent. Over time, preadolescent boys seem to improve more than girls in stepfather families. Adolescence appears to be an especially difficult time for adjustment to the entrance of a stepparent. An authoritative content in families and schools is associated with positive outcomes for children from divorced and stepfamily homes. Latchkey children may become vulnerable when they are not monitored by adults in the after-school hours.
Peers	Peer interaction	Children spend considerably more time with peers in middle and late childhood.
	Popularity, rejection, and neglect	Listening skills and effective communication, being yourself, being happy, showing enthusiasm and concern for others, and having self-confidence, but not being conceited, are predictors of peer popularity. The risk status of neglected children is unclear. Rejected children are at risk for the development of problems. A special interest focuses on improving the peer relations of neglected and rejected children.

To study children's perspective taking, Selman individually interviews the child, asking the child to comment on such dilemmas as the following:

Holly is an 8-year-old girl who likes to climb trees. She is the best tree climber in the neighborhood. One day while climbing down from a tall tree, she falls . . . but does not hurt herself. Her father sees her fall. He is upset and asks her to promise not to climb trees any more. Holly promises.

Later that day, Holly and her friends meet Shawn. Shawn's kitten is caught in a tree and can't get down. Something has to be done right away or the kitten may fall. Holly is the only one who climbs trees well enough to reach the kitten and get it down but she remembers her promise to her father (Selman, 1976, p. 302).

Subsequently, Selman asks the child a series of questions about the dilemma, such as:

- Does Holly know how Shawn feels about the kitten?
- How will Holly's father feel if he finds out she climbed the tree?
- What does Holly think her father will do if he finds out she climbed the tree?
- What would you do in this situation?

After analyzing children's responses to these dilemmas, Selman (1980) concluded that children's perspective taking follows the developmental sequence described in table 11.1.

Children's perspective taking not only can increase their self-understanding, but it can also improve their peer group status and the quality of their friendships. For example, in one

Concept	Processes/Related Ideas	Characteristics/Description
	Social cognition	Social information-processing skills and social knowledge are two important dimensions of social cognition in peer relations.
	Friends	Children's friendships serve six functions: companionship, stimulation, physical support, ego support, social comparison, and intimacy/affection. Intimacy and similarity are common characteristics of friendships. Harry Stack Sullivan was the most influential theorist to discuss the importance of friendships. He argued that there is a dramatic increase in the psychological importance and intimacy of close friends in early adolescence.
Schools	Transition to school	Children spend more than 10,000 hours in the classroom as members of a small society in which there are tasks to be accomplished, people to be socialized and socialized by, and rules that define and limit behavior. A special concern is that early schooling proceeds mainly on the basis of negative feedback to children. The curriculum in elementary schools should be integrated.
	Teachers	Teachers have prominent influences in middle and late childhood. Aptitude-treatment interaction is an important consideration.
	Social class and ethnicity	Schools have a stronger middle-class than lower-class orientation. Many lower-class children have problems in schools, as do children from ethnic minorities. Efforts are being made to reduce this bias, among them the jigsaw classroom. Ogbu proposed a controversial view that ethnic minority children are placed in a position of subordination and exploitation in the American educational system. Some experts believe a form of institutional racism exists in some schools because teachers fail to academically challenge ethnic minority students.

investigation, the most popular children in the third and eighth grades had competent perspective-taking skills (Kurdek & Krile, 1982). Children who are competent at perspective taking are better at understanding the needs of their companions, so they are likely to communicate more effectively with them (Hudson, Forman, & Brion-Meisels, 1982).

Self-Esteem and Self-Concept

What are self-esteem and self-concept? How are they measured? How do parent-child relationships contribute to self-esteem? How is group identity involved in children's self-esteem? And, how can children's self-esteem be enhanced?

What Are Self-Esteem and Self-Concept?

Self-esteem *is the global evaluative dimension of the self. Self-esteem is also referred to as self-worth or self-image.* For example, a child may perceive that she is not merely a person, but a *good* person. Of course, not all children have an overall positive image of themselves. **Self-concept** *refers to domain-specific evaluations of the self.* Children can make self-evaluations in many domains of their lives—academic, athletic, appearance, and so on. In sum, self-esteem refers to global self-evaluations, self-concept to more domain specific evaluations.

> *It is difficult to make people miserable when they feel worthy of themselves.*
>
> —Abraham Lincoln

Investigators have not always made clear distinctions between self-esteem and self-concept, sometimes using the terms interchangeably or not precisely defining them. As you read the remaining discussion of self-esteem and self-concept, the distinction between self-esteem as global self-evaluation and self-concept as domain-specific self-evaluation should help you to keep the terms straight.

Measuring Self-Esteem and Self-Concept

Measuring self-esteem and self-concept hasn't always been easy (Wylie, 1969; Yardley, 1987). Recently, different measures have been developed to assess children and adolescents.

Susan Harter has greatly advanced our knowledge of self-concept and self-esteem in children and adolescents. She has constructed excellent measures of perceived competence in different domains, provided insightful analyses of adolescents' self portrayals, and contributed to awareness of what causes low self-esteem.

Susan Harter's (1985) Self-Perception Profile for Children is a revision of her original instrument, The Perceived Competence Scale for Children (Harter, 1982). The **Self-Perception Profile for Children** *taps five specific domains of self-concept—scholastic competence, athletic competence, social acceptance, physical appearance, and behavioral conduct—plus general self-worth.* Harter's scale does an excellent job of separating children's self-evaluations in different skill domains, and when general self-worth is assessed, questions focus on the overall self evaluations rather than in specific skill domains.

The Self-Perception Profile for Children is designed to be used with third-grade through sixth-grade children. Harter also has developed a separate scale for adolescents, recognizing important developmental changes in self-perceptions. The Self-Perception Profile for Adolescents (Harter, 1989) taps eight domains—scholastic competence, athletic competence, social acceptance, physical appearance, behavioral conduct, close friendship, romantic appeal, and job competence—plus global self-worth. Thus, the adolescent version has three skill domains not present in the children's version—job competence, romantic appeal, and close friendship.

Parent–Child Relationships and Self–Esteem

In the most extensive investigation of parent-child relationships and self-esteem, a measure of self-esteem was given to elementary school boys, and the boys and their mothers were interviewed about their family relationships (Coopersmith, 1967). Based on these assessments, the following parenting attributes were associated with boys' high self-esteem:

- Expression of affection
- Concern about the child's problems
- Harmony in the home
- Participation in joint family activities
- Availability to give competent, organized help to the boys when they need it
- Setting clear and fair rules
- Abiding by these rules
- Allowing the children freedom within well-prescribed limits

Remember that these findings are correlational, so we cannot say that these parenting attributes *cause* children's high self-esteem. Such factors as parental acceptance and allowing children freedom within well-prescribed limits probably are important determinants of children's self-esteem, but we still must say *they are related to* rather than *they cause* children's self-esteem, based on the available research data.

Critical Thinking

Other than the parenting attributes described by Coopersmith, can you think of other ways children's self-esteem can be improved?

Group Identity and Self–Esteem

Children's group identity is also related to their self-esteem. **Social identity theory** *is social psychologist Henry Tajfel's (1978) theory that, when individuals are assigned to a group, they invariably think of that group as an in-group for them. This occurs because individuals want to have a positive self-image.* According to Tajfel, self-image consists of both a personal identity and many different social identities. Tajfel argues that individuals can improve their self-image by enhancing either their personal or their social identity. Tajfel believes that social identity is especially important. When children or adults compare the social identity of their group with the social identity of another group, they often maximize the distinctions between the two groups. For example, think of an adolescent's identity with the school's football or basketball team. When the school's teams win, students' self-images are enhanced, regardless of whether they play on the teams or not. Why? Because they have a social identity with the school and the school's teams.

As children and adults strive to promote their social identities, it is not long before proud, self-congratulatory remarks are interspersed with nasty comments about the opposing group(s). In a capsule, the theme becomes, "My group is good and I am good. Your group is bad and you are bad." So it goes with the sexes, ethnic groups, teams, social classes, religions, and countless other groups, all seeking to improve their respective self-images through social identity with the group and comparison of the group with other groups. These comparisons can easily lead to competition, conflict, and even a perception that discrimination against other groups is legitimate.

Tajfel showed that it does not take much to get children or adults to think in terms of "we" and "they," or in-group and out-group. He assigned children to two groups based on a trivial task. For example, one individual was assigned to one group because she overestimated the number of dots on a screen, and another individual was assigned to another group because he underestimated the number. Once assigned to the two groups, the members were asked to award amounts of money to pairs of other subjects. Those eligible to receive the money were anonymous except for their membership in one of the two groups Tajfel created. Invariably, the children acted favorably toward (awarded money to) members of their own group. It is no wonder, then, that if we favor our own group based on such trivial criteria, we will show intense in-group favoritism when differences are not as trivial.

Closely related to group identity and self-esteem is **ethnocentrism,** *the tendency to favor one's own group over other groups.* Ethnocentrism's positive side appears in the sense of in-group pride that fulfills our strong urge to attain and maintain a positive self-image. In-group pride has mushroomed as we approach the end of the twentieth century. Children observe and listen to their parents speak about Black pride, Hispanic pride, Native American pride, Irish pride, Italian pride, and so on. Unfortunately, sometimes prejudice develops. **Prejudice** *is an unjustified negative attitude toward an individual because of that person's membership in a group.* People can be prejudiced against groups of people made up of a particular ethnic group, sex, age, religion, or other detectable difference.

Many of the early attempts to assess the nature of self and self-concept in various ethnic groups compared Black and White individuals (Clark & Clark, 1939; Coopersmith, 1967; Deutsch, 1967). These reports indicated that Blacks, especially Black children, have a more negative self-concept than Whites. However, more-recent research suggests that Blacks, Mexican Americans, and Puerto Ricans have equally positive self-concepts and perhaps even higher self-esteem than Anglo-Americans (Allen & Majidi-Ahi, 1989; Powell & Fuller, 1972). A generation of ethnic awareness and pride appears to have advanced the self-esteem of ethnic minority group members.

Increasing Children's Self-Esteem

Four ways children's self-esteem can be improved are through (1) identifying the causes of low self-esteem and the domains of competence important to the self, (2) emotional support and social approval, (3) achievement, and (4) coping (see figure 11.2).

Identifying children's sources of self-esteem—that is, competence in domains important to the self—is critical to improving self-esteem. Self-esteem theorist and researcher Susan Harter (1990b) points out that the self-esteem enhancement programs of the 1960s, in which self-esteem itself was the target and individuals were encouraged to simply feel good about themselves, were ineffective. Rather, Harter believes that intervention must occur at the level of the *causes* of self-esteem if the individual's self-esteem is to improve significantly. Children have the highest self-esteem when they perform competently in domains important to the self. Therefore, children should be encouraged to identify and value areas of competence.

Emotional support and social approval in the form of confirmation from others also powerfully influence children's self-esteem (Harter, 1990b). Some children with low self-esteem come from conflicted families or conditions in which they experienced abuse or neglect—situations in which support is unavailable. In some cases, alternative sources of support can be implemented, either informally through the encouragement of a teacher, a coach, or other significant adult, or more formally, through programs such as Big Brothers and Big Sisters. While peer approval becomes increasingly important during adolescence, both adult and peer support are important influences on the adolescent's self-esteem.

Achievement also can improve children's self-esteem (Bednar, Wells, & Peterson, 1989). For example, the straightforward teaching of real skills to children often results in increased achievement and, thus, in enhanced self-esteem. Children develop higher self-esteem because they know the important tasks to achieve goals, and they have experienced performing them or similar behaviors. The emphasis on the importance of achievement in improving self-esteem has much in common with Bandura's cognitive social learning concept of *self-efficacy,* which refers to individuals' beliefs that they can master a situation and produce positive outcomes.

Self-esteem also is often increased when children face a problem and try to cope with it rather than avoid it (Bednar, Wells, & Peterson, 1989; Lazarus, 1991). If coping rather than avoidance prevails, children often face problems realistically, honestly, and nondefensively. This produces favorable self-evaluative thoughts, which lead to the self-generated approval that raises self-esteem. The converse is true of low self-esteem. Unfavorable self-evaluations trigger denial, deception, and

FIGURE 11.2

Four key aspects of improving self-esteem.

Identifying the
causes of low
self-esteem and
which domains of
competence are
important to
the self

Emotional
support and
social approval

Achievement

Coping

avoidance in an attempt to disavow that which has already been glimpsed as true. This process leads to self-generated disapproval as a form of feedback to the self about personal adequacy.

Industry Versus Inferiority

Erikson's fourth stage of the human life cycle, industry versus inferiority, appears during middle and late childhood. The term *industry* expresses a dominant theme of this period: Children become interested in how things are made and how they work. It is the Robinson Crusoe age, in that the enthusiasm and minute detail Crusoe uses to describe his activities appeal to the child's budding sense of industry. When children are encouraged in their efforts to make and build and work—whether building a model airplane, constructing a tree house, fixing a bicycle, solving an addition problem, or cooking—their sense of industry increases. However, parents who see their children's efforts at making things as "mischief" or "making a mess" encourage children's development of a sense of inferiority.

Children's social worlds beyond their families also contribute to a sense of industry. School becomes especially important in this regard. Consider children who are slightly below average in intelligence. They are too bright to be in special

classes but not bright enough to be in gifted classes. They fail frequently in their academic efforts, developing a sense of inferiority. By contrast, consider children whose sense of industry is derogated at home. A series of sensitive and committed teachers may revitalize their sense of industry (Elkind, 1970).

GENDER

In chapter 9, we discussed the biological, cognitive, and social influences on gender development. Gender is such a pervasive aspect of an individual's identity that we further consider its role in children's development here. Among the gender-related topics we examine are gender stereotypes, similarities, and differences; gender-role classification; and gender and ethnicity.

Gender-Role Stereotyping

Gender-role stereotypes *are broad categories that reflect our impressions and beliefs about females and males.* All stereotypes, whether they are based on gender, ethnicity, or other groupings, refer to an image of what the typical member of a particular social category is like. The world is extremely complex. Every day we are confronted with thousands of different stimuli. The use of stereotypes is one way we simplify this complexity. If we simply assign a label (such as *soft*) to someone, we then have much less to consider when we think about the individual. However, once labels are assigned, they are remarkably difficult to abandon, even in face of contradictory evidence.

> *What are little boys made of?*
> *Frogs and snails*
> *And puppy dogs' tails.*
>
> *What are little girls made of?*
> *Sugar and spice*
> *And all that's nice*
>
> —J. O. Halliwell,
> Nursery Rhymes of England, 1844

Many stereotypes are so general they are very ambiguous. Consider the stereotypes for masculine and feminine. Diverse behaviors can be called on to support each stereotype, such as scoring a touchdown or growing facial hair for "masculine" and playing with dolls or wearing lipstick for "feminine." The stereotype may be modified in the face of cultural change. At one point in history, muscular development may be thought of as masculine; at another point, it may be a more lithe, slender physique. The behaviors popularly agreed upon as reflecting a stereotype may also fluctuate according to socioeconomic circumstances. For example, lower socioeconomic groups might be more likely than higher socioeconomic groups to include "rough and tough" as part of a masculine stereotype.

Even though the behaviors that are supposed to fit the stereotype often do not, the label itself can have significant consequences for the individual. Labeling a male "feminine" and a female "masculine" can produce significant social reactions to the individuals in terms of status and acceptance in groups, for example (Mischel, 1970).

How widespread is feminine and masculine stereotyping? According to a far-ranging study of college students in thirty countries, stereotyping of females and males is pervasive (Williams & Best, 1982). Males were widely believed to be dominant, independent, aggressive, achievement oriented, and enduring, while females were widely believed to be nurturant, affiliative, less esteemed, and more helpful in times of distress.

In a more recent investigation, women and men who lived in more highly developed countries perceived themselves as more similar than women and men who lived in less-developed countries (Williams & Best, 1989). In the more highly developed countries, women were more likely to attend college and be gainfully employed. Thus, as sexual equality increases, male and female stereotypes, as well as actual behavioral differences, may diminish. In this investigation, women were more likely to perceive similarity between the sexes than men were (Williams & Best, 1989). And the sexes were perceived more similarly in Christian than in Muslim societies.

> *If you are going to generalize about women, you will find yourself up to here in exceptions.*
>
> —Dolores Hitchens, *In a House Unknown* (1973)

Gender-role stereotyping also changes developmentally. Stereotypical gender beliefs increase during the preschool years, peak in the early elementary school years, and then decrease in the middle and late elementary school years (Bigler, Liben, & Yekel, 1992). In one recent study, an age-related decrease in gender stereotyping was related to the acquisition of cognitive skills (Bigler & Liben, in press). Next we go beyond stereotyping and examine the similarities and differences between the sexes.

Gender Similarities and Differences

There is a growing consensus in gender research that differences between the sexes have often been exaggerated (Hyde, 1981; Hyde, 1994). Remember our discussion of reducing sexist research in psychology in chapter 2. It is not unusual to find statements such as the following: "While only 32 percent of the females were found to . . . fully 37 percent of the males were. . . ." This difference of 5 percent likely is a very small difference, and may or may not even be statistically significant or capable of being replicated in a separate study (Denmark & Paludi, in press). And when statements are made about female-male comparisons, such as "males outperform females in math," this does not mean all females versus all males. Rather, it usually means the average math achievement scores for males at certain ages are higher than the average math achievement scores for females. The math achievement scores of females and males overlap considerably, so that while an *average* difference may favor males, many females have higher math achievement than many males. Further, there is a tendency to think of differences between females and males as biologically based. Remember that when differences occur they may be socioculturally based.

Let's now examine some of the differences between the sexes, keeping in mind that (a) the differences are averages—not all females versus all males; (b) even when differences are reported, there is considerable overlap between the sexes; and (c) the differences may be due primarily to biological factors, sociocultural factors, or both. First, we examine physical and biological differences, and then we turn to cognitive and social differences.

From conception on, females are less likely than males to die, and females are less likely than males to develop physical or mental disorders. Estrogen strengthens the immune system, making females more resistant to infection, for example. Female hormones also signal the liver to produce more "good" cholesterol, which makes their blood vessels more elastic than males'. Testosterone triggers the production of low-density lipoprotein, which clogs blood vessels. Males have twice the risk of coronary disease as females. Higher levels of stress hormones cause faster clotting in males, but also higher blood pressure than in

FIGURE 11.3

Visuospatial ability of males and females. Notice that, although an average male's visuospatial ability is higher than an average female's, the overlap between the sexes is substantial. Not all males have better visuospatial ability than all females—the substantial overlap indicates that, although the average score of males is higher, many females outperform many males on such tasks.

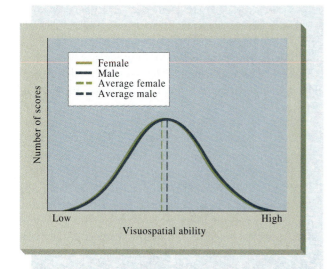

"So according to the stereotype, you can put two and two together, but I can read the handwriting on the wall."

abilities of females and males. Combined with the recent information about convergence in the verbal abilities of males and females (females used to have higher scores on the verbal section of the SAT, but now there are no differences, for example), we can conclude that cognitive differences between females and males do not exist in many areas, are disappearing in other areas, and are small when they do exist.

> *There is more difference within the sexes than between them.*
>
> —Ivy Compton-Burnett

Most males are more active and aggressive than most females (Maccoby, 1987a; Maccoby & Jacklin, 1974). The consistent difference in aggression often appears in children's development as early as 2 years of age. With regard to helping behavior, Alice Eagly and Maureen Crowley (1986) argue that the female gender role fosters helping that is nurturant and caring, whereas the male gender role promotes helping that is chivalrous. They found that males are more likely to help in situations in which there is a perceived danger and in which males feel most competent to help. For example, males are more likely than females to help when a person is standing by the roadside with a flat tire, a situation involving some danger and a circumstance in which many males feel a sense of competence—automobile problems. In contrast, if the situation involves volunteering time to help a disturbed child, most researchers have found more helping by females, because there is little danger present for the helper and because females feel more competent in nurturing (Hyde, 1990). As early as elementary school, girls show more caregiving behavior (Zahn-Waxler, 1990). However, in cultures where boys and girls both care for younger siblings, boys and girls are more similar in their nurturant behavior (Whiting, 1989). In one recent study, Judith Blakemore (1993) found that preschool girls spent more time with and nurtured babies more than preschool boys did.

Achievement

For some areas of achievement, gender differences are so large they can best be described as nonoverlapping. For example, no

females. Adult females have about twice the body fat of their male counterparts, most concentrated around breasts and hips. In males, fat is more likely to go to the abdomen. On the average, males grow to be 10 percent taller than females. Male hormones promote the growth of long bones; female hormones stop such growth at puberty. In sum, there are many physical differences between females and males. But are there as many cognitive differences?

According to a classic review of gender differences in 1974, Eleanor Maccoby and Carol Jacklin (1974) concluded that males have better math skills and better visuospatial ability (the kind of skills an architect would need to design a building's angles and dimensions), while females have better verbal abilities. More recently, Maccoby (1987a) revised her conclusion about several gender dimensions. She commented that the accumulation of research evidence now indicates that the verbal differences in males and females have virtually disappeared, but that the math and visuospatial differences are still present.

A number of researchers in the gender area point out that there are more cognitive similarities than differences between females and males. They also believe that the differences that do exist, such as the math and visuospatial differences, have been exaggerated. Males do outperform females in math, but only within a certain portion of the population—the gifted (Hyde, 1994). Further, males do not always outperform females on all visuospatial tasks—consistent differences occur only in the ability to rotate objects mentally (Linn & Peterson, 1986). And keep in mind our earlier comment about the considerable overlap that exists between females and males, even when differences are reported. Figure 11.3 shows the small average difference on visuospatial tasks that favors males, but also clearly reveals the substantial overlap in the visuospatial

Some of the brightest and most gifted girls do not have achievement and career aspirations that match their talents. Gender researchers hope that gender-role stereotypes that prevent girls from developing a more positive orientation toward math and science can be eliminated.

major league baseball players are female, and 96 percent of all registered nurses are female. In contrast, many measures of achievement-related behaviors do not reveal gender differences. For example, girls show just as much persistence at tasks. The question of whether males and females differ in their expectations for success at various achievement tasks is not yet settled (Eccles, 1987).

Because females are often stereotyped as less competent than males, incorporation of gender-role stereotypes into a child's self-concept could cause girls to have less confidence than boys in their general intellectual abilities. This could lead girls to have lower expectations for success at difficult academic and vocational activities. It could also lead girls to expect to have to work harder to achieve success at these activities than boys expect to have to work. Evidence supports these predictions (Eccles, Harold-Goldsmith, & Miller, 1989). Either of these beliefs could keep girls from selecting demanding educational or vocational options, especially if these options are not perceived as important or interesting.

A special concern is that some of the brightest and most gifted girls do not have achievement and career aspirations that match their talents. In one investigation, high-achieving girls had much lower expectations for success than high-achieving boys (Stipek & Hoffman, 1980). In the gifted research program at Johns Hopkins University, many mathematically precocious girls did select scientific and medical careers, although only 46 percent aspired to a full-time career, compared with 98 percent of the boys (Fox, Brody, & Tobin, 1979).

To help talented girls redirect their paths, some high schools are using programs developed by colleges and universities. Project CHOICE (Creating Her Options In Career Education) was designed by Case Western Reserve University to detect barriers in reaching one's potential. Gifted eleventh-grade females receive individualized counseling that includes interviews with female role models, referral to appropriate occupational groups, and information about career workshops.

A program at the University of Nebraska (Kerr, 1983) was successful in encouraging talented female high school students to pursue more prestigious careers. This was accomplished by individualized counseling and participation in a "Perfect Future Day," in which girls shared career fantasies and discussed barriers that might impede the fulfillment of their fantasies. Internal and external constraints were evaluated, gender-role stereotypes were discouraged, and high aspirations were applauded. Although these programs have shown short-term success in redirecting the career paths of high-ability females, in some instances the benefits fade over time—6 months or more, for example. It is important to be concerned about improving the awareness of career alternatives for all girls, however, and not just for those of high ability.

Emotion

Unless you've been isolated on a mountaintop away from people, television, magazines, and newspapers, you probably know the master stereotype about gender and emotion: She is emotional, he is not. This stereotype is a powerful and pervasive image in our culture (Shields, 1991a).

Is this stereotype confirmed when researchers study the nature of emotional experiences in females and males? Researchers have found that females and males are often more alike in the way they experience emotion than the master stereotype would lead us to believe. Females and males often use the same facial expressions, adopt the same language, and describe their emotional experiences similarly when they keep diaries about their life experiences. Thus, the master stereotype that females are emotional and males are not is simply that—a stereotype. Given the complexity and vast territory of emotion, we should not be surprised that this stereotype is not supported when actual emotional experiences are examined. Thus, for many emotional experiences, researchers do not find differences between females and males—both sexes are equally likely to feel love, jealousy, anxiety in new social situations, anger when they are insulted, grief when close relationships end, and embarrassment when they make mistakes in public (Tavris & Wade, 1984).

When we go beyond the master stereotype and consider some specific emotional experiences and the contexts in which emotions are displayed, gender does matter in understanding emotion (Shields, 1991a, 1991b). Consider anger. Males are more likely to show anger toward strangers, especially other males, when they feel they have been challenged, and males are more likely than females to turn their anger into aggressive action (Tavris, 1989). Female-male differences in emotion are more likely to occur in contexts that highlight social roles and relationships (Brown & others, 1993). For example, females are more likely than males to give accounts of emotion that include interpersonal relationships (Saarni, 1988). And females are more likely than males to express fear and sadness, especially when communicating with their friends and family.

Gender-Role Classification

How were gender roles classified in the past? What is androgyny? What is gender-role transcendence?

TABLE 11.2

The Bem Sex–Role Inventory: Are You Androgynous?

The following items are from the Bem Sex-Role Inventory. To find out whether you score as androgynous, first rate yourself on each item, on a scale from 1 (never or almost never true) to 7 (always or almost always true).

1. self-reliant	16. strong personality	31. makes decisions easily	46. aggressive
2. yielding	17. loyal	32. compassionate	47. gullible
3. helpful	18. unpredictable	33. sincere	48. inefficient
4. defends own beliefs	19. forceful	34. self-sufficient	49. acts as a leader
5. cheerful	20. feminine	35. eager to soothe hurt feelings	50. childlike
6. moody	21. reliable	36. conceited	51. adaptable
7. independent	22. analytical	37. dominant	52. individualistic
8. shy	23. sympathetic	38. soft-spoken	53. does not use harsh language
9. conscientious	24. jealous	39. likable	54. unsystematic
10. athletic	25. has leadership abilities	40. masculine	55. competitive
11. affectionate	26. sensitive to the needs of others	41. warm	56. loves children
12. theatrical	27. truthful	42. solemn	57. tactful
13. assertive	28. willing to take risks	43. willing to take a stand	58. ambitious
14. flatterable	29. understanding	44. tender	59. gentle
15. happy	30. secretive	45. friendly	60. conventional

SCORING

(a) Add up your ratings for items 1, 4, 7, 10, 13, 16, 19, 22, 25, 28, 31, 34, 37, 40, 43, 46, 49, 55, and 58. Divide the total by 20. That is your masculinity score.

(b) Add up your ratings for items 2, 5, 8, 11, 14, 17, 20, 23, 26, 29, 32, 35, 38, 41, 44, 47, 50, 53, 56, and 59. Divide the total by 20. That is your femininity score.

(c) If your masculinity score is above 4.9 (the approximate median for the masculinity scale) and your femininity score is above 4.9 (the approximate femininity median) then you would be classified as androgynous on Bem's scale.

From Janet S. Hyde, *Half the Human Experience: The Psychology of Women*, 3d ed. Copyright © 1985 D. C. Heath and Company, Lexington, MA. Reprinted by permission.

The Past

Not too long ago, it was accepted that boys should grow up to be masculine and that girls should grow up to be feminine, that boys are made of frogs and snails and puppy dogs' tails, and that girls are made of sugar and spice and all that's nice. Today, diversity characterizes gender roles and the feedback individuals receive from their culture. A girl's mother might promote femininity, the girl might be close friends with a tomboy, and the girl's teachers at school might encourage her assertiveness.

In the past, the well-adjusted male was expected to be independent, aggressive, and power oriented. The well-adjusted female was expected to be dependent, nurturant, and uninterested in power. Further, masculine characteristics were considered to be healthy and good by society; female characteristics were considered to be undesirable. A classic study in the early 1970s summarized the traits and behaviors that college students believed were characteristic of males and those they believed were characteristic of females (Broverman & others, 1972). The traits clustered into two groups that were labeled "instrumental" and "expressive." The instrumental traits paralleled the male's purposeful, competent entry into the outside world to gain goods for his family; the expressive traits paralleled the female's responsibility to be warm and emotional in the home. Such stereotypes are more harmful to females than to males because the characteristics assigned to males are more valued than those assigned to females. The beliefs and stereotypes have led to the negative treatment of females because of their sex, or what is called *sexism*. Females receive less attention in schools, are less visible in leading roles on television, are rarely depicted as competent, dominant characters in children's books, are paid

less than males even when they have more education, and are underrepresented in decision-making roles throughout our society, from corporate executive suites to Congress.

Androgyny

In the 1970s, as both males and females became dissatisfied with the burdens imposed by their strictly stereotyped roles, alternatives to "masculinity" and "femininity" were explored. Instead of thinking of masculinity and femininity as a continuum, with more of one meaning less of the other, it was proposed that individuals could show both expressive *and* instrumental traits. This thinking led to the development of the concept of **androgyny**, *the presence of desirable masculine and feminine characteristics in the same individual* (Bem, 1977; Spence & Helmreich, 1978). The androgynous individual might be a male who is assertive (masculine) and nurturant (feminine), or a female who is dominant (masculine) and sensitive to others' feelings (feminine).

Measures have been developed to assess androgyny. One of the most widely used gender measures, the Bem Sex-Role Inventory, was constructed by a leading early proponent of androgyny, Sandra Bem. To see what the items on Bem's measure are like, see table 11.2. Based on their responses to the items in the Bem sex-role inventory, individuals are classified as having one of four gender-role orientations: masculine, feminine, androgynous, or undifferentiated (see figure 11.4). The androgynous individual is simply a female or a male who has a high degree of both feminine (expressive) and masculine (instrumental) traits. No new characteristics are used to describe the androgynous individual. A feminine individual is high on

FIGURE 11.4

Gender-role classification.

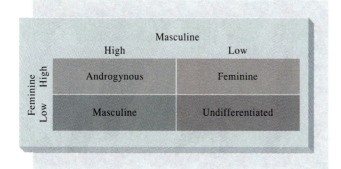

feminine (expressive) traits and low on masculine (instrumental) traits; a masculine individual shows the reverse of these traits. An undifferentiated person is not high on feminine or masculine traits.

Androgynous individuals are described as more flexible and more mentally healthy than either masculine or feminine individuals. Individuals who are undifferentiated are the least competent. To some degree, though, the context influences which gender role is most adaptive. In close relationships, a feminine or androgynous gender role may be more desirable because of the expressive nature of close relationships. However, a masculine or androgynous gender role may be more desirable in academic and work settings because of the instrumental nature of these settings. And the culture in which individuals live also plays an important role in determining what is adaptive. On the one hand, increasing numbers of children in the United States and other modernized countries such as Sweden are being raised to behave in androgynous ways. On the other hand, traditional gender roles continue to dominate the cultures of many countries around the world. To read about traditional gender-role practices in Egypt, as well as the nature of gender roles in China, turn to Sociocultural Worlds of Development 11.2.

Critical Thinking

How extensively are parents rearing their children to become androgynous? Are parents rearing their daughters to be more androgynous than they are their sons? Are middle-class parents more likely to rear their children to be androgynous than parents from low-income backgrounds? Explain.

Gender-Role Transcendence

Although the concept of androgyny was an improvement over exclusive notions of femininity and masculinity, it has turned out to be less of a panacea than many of its early proponents envisioned (Matlin, 1993; Paludi, 1992). Some theorists, such as Joseph Pleck (1981), believe that the idea of androgyny should be replaced with **gender-role transcendence,** *the belief that, when an individual's competence is at issue, it should not be conceptualized on the basis of masculinity,*

femininity, or androgyny, but rather on a person basis. Thus, rather than merging gender roles, or stereotyping people as masculine or feminine, Pleck believes we should begin to think about people as people. However, the concepts of androgyny and gender-role transcendence both draw attention away from women's unique needs and the power imbalance between women and men in most cultures (Hare-Muston & Maracek, 1988).

> *To be meek, patient, tactful, modest, honorable, brave, is not to be either manly or womanly; it is to be humane.*
>
> —Jane Harrison (1850–1928), English Writer

Ethnicity and Gender

Are gender-related attitudes and behavior similar across different ethnic groups? All ethnic minority females are females, and all ethnic minority males are males, so there are many similarities in the gender-related attitudes of females across different ethnic minority groups and of males across different ethnic minority groups. Nevertheless, the different ethnic and cultural experiences of Black American, Hispanic American, Asian American, and Native American females and males need to be considered in understanding their gender-related attitudes and behavior, because in some instances even small differences can be important. For example, the socialization of males and females in other cultures who subsequently migrate to America often reflects a stronger gap between the status of males and females than is experienced in America. Keeping in mind that there are many similarities between females in all ethnic minority groups and between males in all ethnic minority groups, we first examine information about females from specific ethnic minority groups and then discuss males from specific ethnic minority groups.

Ethnic Minority Females

Let's now consider the behavior and psychological orientations of females from specific ethnic minority groups, beginning with Black females, and then in turn, study Asian American females, Hispanic American females, and Native American females.

Researchers in psychology have only begun to focus on the behavior of Black females. For too long, Black females only served as a comparison group for White females on selected psychological dimensions, or they served as the subjects in studies in which the primary research interest related to poverty, unwed motherhood, and so on (Hall, Evans, & Selice, 1989). This narrow research approach could be viewed as attributing no personal characteristics to Black females beyond the labels given to them by society.

The nature and focus of psychological research on Black females has begun to change—to some extent paralleling societal changes (Hall, Evans, & Selice, 1989). In the last decade, more individualized, positive dimensions of Black females are being studied, such as self-esteem, achievement, motivation, and self-control. In the 1980s, psychological studies of Black females began to shift away from studies focused only on the

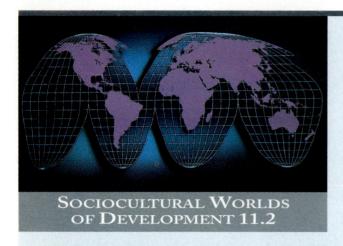

SOCIOCULTURAL WORLDS OF DEVELOPMENT 11.2

In Egypt near the Aswan Dam, women are returning from the Nile River, where they have filled their water jugs. How might gender-role socialization for girls in Egypt compare to that in the United States?

Gender Roles in Egypt and China

In recent decades, roles assumed by males and females in the United States have become increasingly similar—that is, androgynous. In many countries, though, gender roles have remained more gender-specific. For example, in Egypt, the division of labor between Egyptian males and females is dramatic: Egyptian males are socialized to work in the public sphere, females in the private world of home and child rearing. The Islamic religion dictates that the man's duty is to provide for his family, the woman's duty to care for her family and household (Dickersheid & others, 1988). Any deviations from this traditional gender-role orientation are severely disapproved of.

Egypt is not the only country in which males and females are socialized to behave, think, and feel in strongly gender-specific ways. Kenya and Nepal are two other cultures in which children are brought up under very strict gender-specific guidelines (Munroe, Himmin, & Munroe, 1984). In the People's Republic of China, the female's status has historically been lower than the male's. The teachings of the fifth century B.C. Chinese philosopher Confucius were used to reinforce the concept of the female as an inferior being. Beginning with the 1949 revolution in China, women began to achieve more economic freedom and more-equal status in marital relationships. However, even with the sanctions of a socialist government, the old patriarchal traditions of male supremacy in China have not been completely uprooted. Chinese women still make considerably less money than Chinese men in comparable positions, and in rural China a tradition of male supremacy still governs many women's lives.

Thus, in China, although females have made considerable strides, complete equality remains a distant objective. And in many cultures, such as Egypt and other countries where the Muslim religion predominates, gender-specific behavior is pronounced, and females are not given access to high-status positions.

In China, females and males are usually socialized to behave, feel, and think differently. The old patriarchal traditions of male supremacy have not been completely uprooted. Chinese women still make considerably less money than Chinese men, and, in rural China (such as here in the Lixian village of Sichuan), male supremacy still governs many women's lives.

problems of Black females and toward research on the positive aspects of Black females in a pluralistic society.

Black females, as well as other ethnic minority females, have experienced the double jeopardy of racism and sexism. The ingenuity and perseverance shown by ethnic minority females as they have survived and grown against the odds is remarkable. For example, 499 Black women earned doctoral degrees in 1986. This represents only 2 percent of the Ph.D.'s awarded (compared to the 6.4 percent of the general population represented by Black females). However, the positive side of these figures is that the Ph.D.'s earned by Black women in 1986 represented an almost 16 percent increase over the number earned in 1977. Despite such gains, our society needs to make a strong commitment to providing Black, and other ethnic minority, females with the opportunities they deserve (Young, 1993).

Asian females are often expected to carry on domestic duties, to marry, to become obedient helpers of their mothers-in-law, and to bear children, especially males (Nishio & Bilmes, 1993; Sue, 1989). In China, the mother's responsibility for the emotional nurturance and well-being of the family, and for raising children, derives from Confucian ethics (Huang & Ying, 1989). However, as China has become modernized, these roles have become less rigid. Similarly, in acculturated Chinese families in the United States, only derivatives of these rigidly defined roles remain. For example, Chinese American females are not entirely relegated to subservient roles.

Traditionally in Mexican families, women assume the expressive role of homemaker and caretaker of children. This continues to be the norm, although less so than in the past (Comas-Diaz, 1993; Domino, 1992; Ramirez, 1989). Historically, the Mexican female's role has been one of self-denial, and her needs were considered to be subordinate to those of other family members. Joint decision making and greater equality of males' and females' roles are becoming more characteristic of Mexican American families (Ramirez & Arce, 1981). Of special significance is the increased frequency of Mexican American women's employment outside the home, which in many instances has enhanced a wife's status in the family and in decision making (Baca Zinn, 1980; Espini, 1993; Knouse, 1992).

For Native Americans, the amount of social and governing control exhibited by women or men depends on the tribe (LaFromboise, 1993; LaFromboise & Low, 1989). For example, in the traditional matriarchal Navajo family, an older woman might live with her husband, her unmarried children, her married daughter, and the daughter's husband and children (Ryan, 1980). In patriarchal tribes, women function as the central "core" of the family, maintaining primary responsibility for the welfare of children. Grandmothers and aunts often provide child care. As with other ethnic minority females, Native American females who have moved to urban areas experience cultural conflict between traditional ethnic values and the values of the American society.

Ethnic Minority Males

Just as ethnic minority females have experienced considerable discrimination and have had to develop coping strategies in the face of adversity, so have ethnic minority males. As with ethnic minority females, our order of discussion will be Black males, Asian American males, Hispanic American males, and Native American males.

Some statistics provide a portrayal of the difficulties many Black males have faced (Purham & McDavis, 1993). Black American males of all ages are three times as likely as White males to live below the poverty line. Black males aged 20 to 44 are twice as likely to die as White males. Black male heads of household earn 70 percent of the income of their White male counterparts. Although they make up only 6.3 percent of the U.S. population, Black males comprise 42 percent of jail inmates and more than 50 percent of men executed for any reason in the last 50 years! Murder by gun is the leading cause of death among Black males aged 15 to 19, and the rates are escalating. From 1979 to 1989, the death rate by guns among this age group of Black males increased by 71 percent. In one recent study, the problem of inadequate male role models in Black American boys' development surfaced (Browne & others, 1993).

Such statistics do not tell the complete story (Evans & Whitfield, 1988). The sociocultural aspects of historical discrimination against an ethnic minority group must be taken into account to understand these statistics. Just as with Black females, researchers are beginning to focus on some of the more positive dimensions of Black males. For example, researchers are finding that Black makes are especially efficient at the use of body language in communication, decoding nonverbal cues, multilingual/multicultural expression, and improvised problem solving.

Asian cultural values are reflected in traditional patriarchal Chinese and Japanese families (Sue, 1989; Sue & Sue, 1993). The father's behavior in relation to other family members is generally dignified, authoritative, remote, and aloof. Sons are generally valued over daughters. Firstborn sons have an especially high status. As with Asian American females, the acculturation experienced by Asian American males has eroded some of the rigid gender roles that characterized Asian families in the past. Fathers still are often the figurative heads of families, especially when dealing with the public, but in private, they have relinquished some of their decision-making powers to their wives (Huang & Ying, 1989; Root, 1993).

In Mexican families, men traditionally assume the instrumental role of provider and protector of the family (Ramirez, 1989). The concept of machismo—being a macho man—continues to influence the role of the male and the patriarchal orientation of Mexican families, though less so than in the past. Traditionally, this orientation required men to be forceful and strong, and also to withhold affectionate emotions. Ideally, it involved a strong sense of personal honor, family, loyalty, and care for children, but it also has involved exaggerated masculinity and aggression (Trankina, 1983). The concepts of machismo and absolute patriarchy are currently diminishing in influence. Adolescent males are still given much more freedom than adolescent females in Mexican American families.

Some Native American tribes are also patriarchal, with the male being the head of the family and primary decision maker. In some tribes, though, child care is shared by men. For example, Mescalero Apache men take responsibility for children when not working away from the family (Ryan, 1980). Autonomy is highly valued among the male children in many Native American tribes, with the males operating semi-independently at an early age (LaFromboise & Low, 1989). As with Native American females, increased movement to urban areas has led to modifications in the values and traditions of some Native American males.

At this point we have discussed a number of ideas about gender. Another important topic in children's development that requires further discussion is moral development.

MORAL DEVELOPMENT

Remember from chapter 9 our description of Piaget's view of moral development. Piaget believed that younger children are characterized by heteronomous morality, but that by 10 years of age they have moved into a higher stage called "autonomous" morality. According to Piaget, older children consider the intentions of the individual, believe that rules are subject to change, and are aware that punishment does not always follow a wrongdoing. A second major cognitive perspective on moral development was proposed by Lawrence Kohlberg.

Kohlberg's Theory of Moral Development

Kohlberg stressed that moral development is based primarily on moral reasoning and unfolds in stages (Kohlberg, 1958, 1976, 1986). Kohlberg arrived at his view after some 20 years of using a unique interview with children. In the interview, children are presented with a series of stories in which characters face moral dilemmas. The following is the most popular Kohlberg dilemma:

> In Europe a woman was near death from a special kind of cancer. There was one drug that the doctors thought might save her. It was a form of radium that a druggist in the same town had recently discovered. The drug was expensive to make, but the druggist was charging ten times what the drug cost him to make. He paid $200 for the radium and charged $2,000 for a small dose of the drug. The sick woman's husband, Heinz, went to everyone he knew to borrow the money, but he could only get together $1,000 which is half of what it cost. He told the druggist that his wife was dying and asked him to sell it cheaper or let him pay later. But the

druggist said, "No, I discovered the drug, and I am going to make money from it." So Heinz got desperate and broke into the man's store to steal the drug for his wife. (Kohlberg, 1969, p. 379)

This story is one of eleven devised by Kohlberg to investigate the nature of moral thought. After reading the story, the interviewee answers a series of questions about the moral dilemma. Should Heinz have stolen the drug? Was stealing it right or wrong? Why? Is it a husband's duty to steal the drug for his wife if he can get it no other way? Would a good husband steal? Did the druggist have the right to charge that much when there was no law setting a limit on the price? Why or why not?

Based on the reasons interviewees gave in response to this and other moral dilemmas, Kohlberg believed three levels of moral development exist, each of which is characterized by two stages. A key concept in understanding moral development, especially Kohlberg's theory, is **internalization,** *the developmental change from behavior that is externally controlled to behavior that is internally controlled.*

Level One: Preconventional Reasoning

Preconventional reasoning *is the lowest level in Kohlberg's theory of moral development. At this level, the child shows no internalization of moral values—moral reasoning is controlled by external rewards and punishments.*

Stage 1. **Punishment and obedience orientation** *is the first stage in Kohlberg's theory of moral development. At this stage, moral thinking is based on punishment.* Children obey because adults tell them to obey.

Stage 2. **Individualism and purpose** *is the second stage in Kohlberg's theory of moral development. At this stage, moral thinking is based on rewards and self-interest.* Children obey when they want to obey and when it is in their best interest to obey. What is right is what feels good and what is rewarding.

Level Two: Conventional Reasoning

Conventional reasoning *is the second or intermediate level in Kohlberg's theory of moral development. At this level, the individual's internalization is intermediate. The person abides by certain standards (internal), but they are the standards of others (external), such as parents or the laws of society.*

Stage 3. **Interpersonal norms** *is the third stage in Kohlberg's theory of moral development. At this stage, the person values trust, caring, and loyalty to others as the basis of moral judgments.* Children often adopt their parents' moral standards at this stage, seeking to be thought of by their parents as a "good girl" or a "good boy."

Stage 4. **Social system morality** *is the fourth stage in Kohlberg's theory of moral development. At this stage, moral judgments are based on understanding the social order, law, justice, and duty.*

TABLE 11.3

Moral Reasoning at Kohlberg's Stages in Response to the "Heinz and the Druggist" Story

Stage Description	Examples of Moral Reasoning That Support Heinz's Theft of the Drug	Examples of Moral Reasoning That Indicate Heinz Should Not Steal the Drug
Preconventional morality		
Stage 1: Avoid punishment	Heinz should not let his wife die; if he does, he will be in big trouble.	Heinz might get caught and sent to jail.
Stage 2: Seek rewards	If Heinz gets caught, he could give the drug back and maybe they would not give him a long jail sentence.	The druggist is a businessman and needs to make money.
Conventional morality		
Stage 3: Gain approval/avoid disapproval especially with family	Heinz was only doing something that a good husband would do; it shows how much he loves his wife.	If his wife dies, he can't be blamed for it; it is the druggist's fault. He is the selfish one.
Stage 4: Conformity to society's rules	If you did nothing, you would be letting your wife die; it is your responsibility if she dies. You have to steal it with the idea of paying the druggist later.	It is always wrong to steal; Heinz will always feel guilty if he steals the drug.
Postconventional morality		
Stage 5: Principles accepted by the community	The law was not set up for these circumstances; taking the drug is not really right, but Heinz is justified in doing it.	You can't really blame someone for stealing, but extreme circumstances don't really justify taking the law in your own hands. You might lose respect for yourself if you let your emotions take over; you have to think about the long-term.
Stage 6: Individualized conscience	By stealing the drug, you would have lived up to society's rules, but you would have let down your conscience.	Heinz is faced with the decision of whether to consider other people who need the drug as badly as his wife. He needs to act by considering the value of all the lives involved.

Level Three: Postconventional Reasoning

Postconventional reasoning *is the highest level in Kohlberg's theory of moral development. At this level, morality is completely internalized and not based on others' standards.* The person recognizes alternative moral courses, explores the options, and then decides on a personal moral code.

Stage 5. **Community rights versus individual rights** *is the fifth stage in Kohlberg's theory of moral development. At this stage, the person understands that values and laws are relative and that standards may vary from one person to another.* The person recognizes that laws are important for society but knows that laws can be changed. The person believes that some values, such as liberty, are more important than the law.

Stage 6. **Universal ethical principles** *is the sixth and highest stage in Kohlberg's theory of moral development. At this stage, persons have developed a moral standard based on universal human rights.* When faced with a conflict between law and conscience, the person will follow conscience, even though the decision might involve personal risk.

Some specific responses to the dilemma of Heinz and the druggist are given in table 11.3, which should provide you with a better sense of reasoning at the six stages in Kohlberg's theory. Notice that whether Heinz steals the drug is not the important issue in Kohlberg's cognitive developmental theory. What is crucial is how the person reasons about the moral dilemma.

Kohlberg believed that these levels and stages occur in a sequence and are age related: Before age 9, most children reason about moral dilemmas in a preconventional way; by early adolescence, they reason in more conventional ways; and by early adulthood, a small number of people reason in postconventional ways. In a 20-year longitudinal investigation, the uses of stages 1 and 2 decreased (Colby & others, 1983). Stage 4, which did not appear at all in the moral reasoning of the 10-year-olds, was reflected in 62 percent of the moral thinking of the 36-year-olds. Stage 5 did not appear until the age of 20 to 22 and never characterized more than 10 percent of the individuals. Thus, the moral stages appeared somewhat later than Kohlberg initially envisioned, and the higher stages, especially stage 6, were extremely elusive. Recently, stage 6 was removed from the Kohlberg scoring manual, but it is still considered to be theoretically important in the Kohlberg scheme of moral development.

Kohlberg's Critics

Kohlberg's provocative theory of moral development has not gone unchallenged (Kurtines & Gewirtz, 1991; Puka, 1991). The criticisms involve the link between moral thought and moral behavior, the quality of the research, inadequate consideration of culture's role in moral development, and underestimation of the care perspective.

Moral Thought and Moral Behavior

Kohlberg's theory has been criticized for placing too much emphasis on moral thought and not enough emphasis on moral behavior. Moral reasons can sometimes be a shelter for immoral behavior. Bank embezzlers and presidents endorse the loftiest of moral virtues when commenting about moral dilemmas, but their own behavior may be immoral. No one wants a nation of cheaters and thieves who can reason at the postconventional level. The cheaters and thieves may know what is right, yet still do what is wrong.

Culture and Moral Development

Yet another criticism of Kohlberg's view is that it is culturally biased (Banks, 1993; Bronstein & Paludi, 1988; Miller, 1991; Miller & Bersoff, in press). A review of research on moral development in 27 countries concluded that moral reasoning is more culture-specific than Kohlberg envisioned and that Kohlberg's scoring system does not recognize higher-level moral reasoning in certain cultural groups (Snarey, 1987). Examples of higher-level moral reasoning that would not be scored as such by Kohlberg's system are values related to communal equity and collective happiness in Israel, the unity and sacredness of all life-forms in India, and the relation of the individual to the community in New Guinea. These examples of moral reasoning would not be scored at the highest level in Kohlberg's system because they do not emphasize the individual's rights and abstract principles of justice. One study assessed the moral development of 20 adolescent male Buddhist monks in Nepal (Huebner, Garrod, & Snarey, 1990). The issue of justice, a basic theme in Kohlberg's theory, was not of paramount importance in the monks' moral views, and their concerns about prevention of suffering and the role of compassion are not captured by Kohlberg's theory. In sum, moral reasoning is shaped more by the values and beliefs of a culture than Kohlberg acknowledged.

Critical Thinking

Can you think of some ways that children's moral development might vary across cultures, other than those variations described in this text?

Gender and the Care Perspective

Carol Gilligan (1982, 1990, 1991, 1992) believes that Kohlberg's theory of moral development does not adequately reflect relationships and concern for others. The **justice perspective** *is a moral perspective that focuses on the rights of the individual; individuals stand alone and independently make moral*

The main focus of adolescent Buddhist monks in Nepal is not on the issue of justice (as Kohlberg's theory argues it would be) but, rather, on the prevention of suffering and the importance of compassion.

decisions. Kohlberg's theory is a justice perspective. By contrast, the **care perspective** *is a moral perspective that views people in terms of their connectedness with others and emphasizes interpersonal communication, relationships with others, and concern for others. Gilligan's theory is a care perspective.* According to Gilligan, Kohlberg greatly underplayed the care perspective in moral development. She believes that this may have happened because he was a male, because most of his research was with males rather than females, and because he used male responses as a model for his theory.

In extensive interviews with girls from 6 to 18 years of age, Gilligan and her colleagues found that girls consistently interpret moral dilemmas in terms of human relationships and base these interpretations on listening and watching other people (Gilligan, 1990, 1992; Gilligan, Brown, & Rogers, 1990). According to Gilligan, girls have the ability to sensitively pick up different rhythms in relationships and often are able to follow the pathways of feelings. Gilligan believes that girls reach a critical juncture in their development when they reach adolescence. Usually around 11 to 12 years of age, girls become aware that their intense interest in intimacy is not prized by the male-dominated culture, even though society values women as caring and altruistic. The dilemma is that girls are presented with a choice that makes them look either selfish or selfless. Gilligan believes that, as adolescent girls experience this dilemma, they increasingly silence their "distinctive voice." Researchers have found support for Gilligan's claim that females' and males' moral reasoning often centers around different concerns and issues (Bussey & Maughan, 1982; Galotti,

Carol Gilligan (center) is shown with some of the students she has interviewed about the importance of relationships in a female's development. According to Gilligan, the sense of relationships and connectedness is at the heart of female development.

Kozberg, & Appleman, in press; Galotti, Kozberg, & Farmer, 1990; Hanson & Mullis, 1985; Lyons, 1983; Scheidel & Marcia, 1985). However, one of Gilligan's initial claims—that traditional Kohlbergian measures of moral development are biased against females—has been extensively disputed. For example, most research studies using the Kohlberg stories and scoring system do not find sex differences (Walker, 1984, 1991a, 1991b). Thus, the strongest support for Gilligan's claims comes from studies that focus on items and scoring systems pertaining to close relationships, pathways of feelings, sensitive listening, and the rhythm of interpersonal behavior (Galotti, Kozberg, & Farmer, 1990).

While females often articulate a care perspective and males a justice perspective, the gender difference is not absolute, and the two orientations are not mutually exclusive (Gilligan & Attanucci, 1988; Lyons, 1990; Rothbart, Hanley, & Albert, 1986). For example, in one study, 53 of 80 females and males showed either a care or a justice perspective, but 27 subjects used both orientations, with neither predominating (Gilligan & Attanucci, 1988).

Altruism

Altruism *is an unselfish interest in helping someone.* Human acts of altruism are plentiful—the hardworking laborer who places $5 in a Salvation Army kettle; rock concerts to feed the hungry, help farmers, and fund AIDS research; and the child who takes in a wounded cat and cares for it. How do psychologists account for such acts of altruism?

Reciprocity and exchange are involved in altruism. Reciprocity is found throughout the human world. Not only is it the highest moral principle in Christianity, but it is also present in every widely practiced religion in the world—Judaism, Hinduism, Buddhism, and Islam. Reciprocity encourages children to do unto others as they would have others do unto them. Human sentiments are wrapped up in this reciprocity. Trust is probably the most important principle over the long run in altruism. Guilt surfaces if the child does not reciprocate, and anger may result if someone else does not reciprocate. Not all altruism is motivated by reciprocity and exchange, but self-other interactions and relationships help us understand altruism's nature. The circumstances most likely to involve altruism are empathic emotion for an individual in need or a close relationship between benefactor and recipient (Batson, 1989).

William Damon (1988) described a developmental sequence of children's altruism, especially of sharing. Most sharing during the first 3 years of life is done for nonempathic reasons, such as for the fun of the social play ritual or out of mere imitation. Then, at about 4 years of age, a combination of empathic awareness and adult encouragement produces a sense of obligation on the part of the child to share with others. This obligation forces the child to share, even though the child may not perceive this as the best way to have fun. Most 4-year-olds are not selfless saints, however. Children believe they have an obligation to share but do not necessarily think they should be as generous to others as they are to themselves. Neither do their actions always support their beliefs, especially when the object of contention is a coveted one. What is important developmentally is that the child has developed an internal belief that sharing is an obligatory part of a social relationship and that this involves a question of right and wrong. However, a preschool child's sense of reciprocity constitutes not a moral duty but, rather, a pragmatic means of getting one's way. Despite their shortcomings, these ideas about justice formed in early childhood set the stage for giant strides that children make in the years that follow.

By the start of the elementary school years, children genuinely begin to express more objective ideas about fairness. These notions about fairness have been used throughout history to distribute goods and to resolve conflicts. They involve the principles of equality, merit, and benevolence. *Equality* means that everyone is treated the same. *Merit* means giving extra rewards for hard work, a talented performance, or other laudatory behavior. *Benevolence* means giving special consideration to individuals in a disadvantaged condition. Equality is the first of these principles used regularly by elementary school children. It is common to hear 6-year-old children use the word *fair* as synonymous with *equal* or *same*. By the mid to late elementary school years, children also believe that equity means special treatment for those who deserve it—the principles of merit and benevolence.

> *Every man takes care that his neighbor shall not cheat him. But a day comes when he begins to care that he does not cheat his neighbor. Then all goes well.*
>
> —Ralph Waldo Emerson

Missing from the factors that guide children's altruism is one that many adults might expect to be the most influential of all: the motivation to obey adult authority figures. Surprisingly, a number of studies have shown that adult authority has only a small influence on children's sharing. For example, when child developmentalist Nancy Eisenberg (1982) asked children to explain their own altruistic acts, they mainly gave empathic and pragmatic reasons for their spontaneous acts of sharing. Not one of the children referred to the demands of adult authority. Parental advice and prodding certainly foster standards of sharing, but the give-and-take of peer requests and arguments provides the most immediate stimulation of sharing. Parents may set examples that children carry into peer interaction and communication, but parents are not present during all of their children's peer exchanges. The day-to-day construction of fairness standards is done by children in collaboration and negotiation with each other. Over the course of many years and thousands of encounters, children's understanding of altruism deepens. With this conceptual elaboration, which involves such notions as equality, merit, benevolence, and compromise, come a greater consistency and generosity in children's sharing behavior (Damon, 1988; Damon & Hart, 1992).

> *Without civic morality communities perish; without personal morality their survival has no value.*
>
> —Bertrand Russell

At this point we have discussed a number of ideas about the self, gender, and moral development in children's lives. A summary of these ideas is presented in concept table 11.2.

CONCLUSIONS

Children's socioemotional development changes in many ways during the middle and late childhood years. These changes involve the self, gender, and moral development as the child interacts with others in the contexts of families, peers, and schools.

We began the chapter by exploring parent-child issues and societal changes in families; peer popularity, rejection, and neglect, social cognition, and friends; and the transition to school, teachers, and social class and ethnicity in schools. We then learned about the development of self-understanding, self-esteem, and self-concept; gender stereotyping, similarities, and differences, gender-role classification, and ethnicity and gender; and Kohlberg's theory of moral development, Kohlberg's critics, especially Carol Gilligan and other advocates of the care perspective, and altruism. At different points in the chapter we also studied children's perceptions of morals on the make-believe planet of Pax; parenting and children in stepfamilies; gender roles in Egypt and China; care, justice, and mixed care/justice considerations of girls; and a model school health program, Heart Smart.

Remember that you can obtain a summary of the entire chapter by again reading the two concept tables on pages 322 and 340. This concludes our discussion of middle and late childhood. In Section Six, we will follow children's development into adolescence, beginning with chapter 12, "Physical and Cognitive Development in Adolescence."

LIFE-SPAN HEALTH AND WELL-BEING

A Model School Health Program: Heart Smart

Exercise is an important component in the Bogalusa Heart Study, a large-scale investigation of children's health that involves an ongoing evaluation of 8,000 boys and girls in Bogalusa, Louisiana (Berensen, 1989; Downey & others, 1987). Observations show that the precursors of heart disease begin at a young age, with many children already possessing one or more clinical risk factors, such as hypertension or obesity. Based on the Bogalusa Heart Study, a cardiovascular health intervention model for children has been developed. The model is called "Heart Smart."

The school is the focus of the Heart Smart intervention. Since 95 percent of children and adolescents aged 5 to 18 are in school, schools are an efficient context in which to educate individuals about health. Special attention is given to teachers, who serve as role models. Teachers who value the role of health in life and who engage in health-enhancing behavior present children and adolescents with positive models for health. Teacher in-service education is conducted by an interdisciplinary team of specialists, including physicians, psychologists, nutritionists, physical educators, and exercise physiologists. The school's staff is introduced to heart health education, the nature of cardiovascular disease, and risk factors for heart disease. Coping behavior, exercise behavior, and eating behavior are discussed with the staff, and a Heart Smart curriculum is explained. For example, the Heart Smart curriculum for grade 5 includes the content areas of cardiovascular health (such as risk factors associated with heart disease), behavior skills (for example, self-assessment and monitoring), eating behavior (for example, the

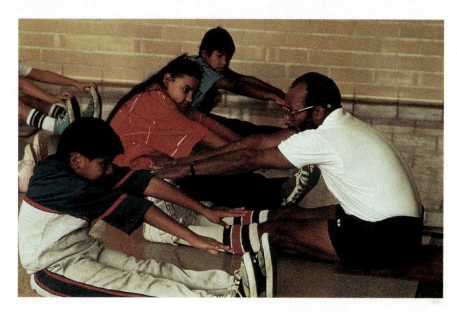

A gymnastics class for third and fourth grades at the Govalle School in Austin, Texas. One of the most important components of heart disease prevention programs is regular vigorous exercise.

effects of food on health), and exercise behavior (for example, the effects of exercise on the heart).

The physical education component of Heart Smart involves two to four class periods each week to incorporate a "Superkids-Superfit" exercise program. The physical education instructor teaches skills required by the school system plus aerobic activities aimed at cardiovascular conditioning, including jogging, race-walking, interval workouts, rope skipping, circuit training, aerobic dance, and games. Classes begin and end with 5 minutes of walking and stretching.

The school lunch program serves as an intervention site, where sodium, fat, and sugar levels are decreased. Children and adolescents are given reasons why they should eat healthy foods, such as a tuna sandwich, and why they should not eat unhealthy foods, such as a hot dog with chili. The school lunch program in-

cludes a salad bar, where children and adolescents can serve themselves. The amount and type of snack foods sold on the school premises are monitored.

High-risk children—those with elevated blood pressure, cholesterol, and weight—are identified as part of Heart Smart. A multidisciplinary team of physicians, nutritionists, nurses, and behavioral counselors work with the high-risk boys and girls and their parents through group-oriented activities and individual-based family counseling. High-risk boys and girls and their parents receive diet, exercise, and relaxation prescriptions in an intensive 12-session program, followed by long-term monthly evaluations.

Extensive assessment is a part of this ongoing program. Short-term and long-term changes in children's knowledge about cardiovascular disease and changes in their behavior are assessed. ■

CONCEPT TABLE 11.2

The Self, Gender, and Moral Development in Middle and Late Childhood

Concept	Processes/Related Ideas	Characteristics/Description
The self	Self-understanding	The internal self, the social self, and the socially comparative self become more prominent in self-understanding during middle and late childhood. Elementary-school-aged children increasingly describe themselves with internal, psychological characteristics. They are also more likely to define themselves in terms of social characteristics and social comparison.
	Perspective taking	This is the ability to assume another person's perspective and understand his or her thoughts and feelings. Selman proposed a developmental theory of perspective taking with five stages, ranging from 3 years of age through adolescence, beginning with the egocentric viewpoint in early childhood and ending with the in-depth perspective taking of adolescence.
	Self-esteem and self-concept	Self-esteem is the global evaluative dimension of the self. Self-esteem is also referred to as self-worth or self-image. Self-concept refers to domain-specific evaluations of the self. Researchers such as Susan Harter have constructed different measures for children and adolescents. Her measures assess self-evaluations in different skill domains as well as general self-worth. In Coopersmith's study, children's self-esteem was associated with such parenting attributes as parental acceptance and allowing children freedom within well-prescribed limits. It is important to remember that these associations are correlational in nature. Social identity theory is Tajfel's theory that, when individuals are assigned to a group, they invariably think of the group as an in-group for them. This occurs because they want to have a positive self-image. Tajfel believes self-image consists of a personal identity *and* many different social identities related to group membership and identity. Group identity often leads to competitiveness, and sometimes conflict, between groups. Closely related to group identity and self-esteem is ethnocentrism, the tendency to favor one's own group over other groups. The positive side of ethnocentrism is the sense of in-group pride, but sometimes a negative side—prejudice—develops. A special concern is the self-esteem of ethnic minority children. Four ways to increase children's self-esteem involve (1) identifying the causes of adolescents' low self-esteem and which domains of competence are important to the self, (2) emotional support and social approval, (3) achievement, and (4) coping.
Gender	Gender stereotypes	Gender-role stereotypes are broad categories that reflect our impressions and beliefs about males and females. These stereotypes are widespread around the world, especially emphasizing the male's power and the female's nurturance. However, in more highly developed countries, females and males are more likely to be perceived as more similar.
	Similarities and differences	Many gender researchers believe a number of differences between females and males have been exaggerated. In considering differences, it is important to recognize that the differences are averages; there is considerable overlap between the sexes; and the differences may be due primarily to biological factors, sociocultural factors, or both. There are a number of physical differences between the sexes, but cognitive differences are either small or nonexistent. At the level of the gifted, the average male does outperform the average female in math achievement. In terms of social behavior, males

Concept	Processes/Related Ideas	Characteristics/Description
		are more aggressive and active than females, but females are usually more adept at "reading" emotions, show more helping behavior, and have a wider social network than males. Overall, though, there are more similarities than differences between females and males. The social context plays an important role in gender differences and similarities.
	Achievement	Although the answer to the question of whether males and females differ in expectations for success is not yet settled, some of the brightest and most gifted girls do not have achievement and career aspirations that match their talents.
	Emotion	The master stereotype of gender and emotion is this: Females are emotional, males are not. This is a stereotype; emotion and gender are far more complex. When we go beyond the master stereotype and consider some of the specific dimensions of emotion and the contexts in which emotions are displayed, gender does matter in understanding emotion. Female-male differences in emotion are more likely to occur in contexts that highlight social roles and relationships.
How can gender roles be classified?	The past	In the past, a well-adjusted male was supposed to show instrumental traits, a well-adjusted female expressive traits. Masculine traits were more valued by society. Sexism was widespread.
	Androgyny	In the 1970s, alternatives to traditional masculinity and femininity were explored. It was proposed that individuals could show both expressive and instrumental traits. This thinking led to the development of the concept of androgyny, the presence of desirable masculine and feminine traits in one individual. Gender-role measures often categorize individuals as masculine, feminine, androgynous, or undifferentiated. Androgynous individuals are often flexible and mentally healthy, although the particular context and the individual's culture also determine the adaptiveness of a gender-role orientation.
	Gender-role transcendence	One alternative to the concept of androgyny is gender-role transcendence, but like the concept of androgyny, it draws attention away from the imbalance of power between males and females.
Ethnicity and gender	Similarities and differences	There are many similarities among the females in various ethnic minority groups and among the males in different ethnic minority groups, but even small differences can sometimes be important.
	Ethnic minority females	Researchers in psychology have only begun to focus on female behavior in specific ethnic groups in a positive way. Many ethnic minority females have experienced the double jeopardy of racism and sexism. In many instances, Asian American, Hispanic American, and Native American females have lived in patriarchal, male-dominated families, although gender roles have become less rigid in these ethnic groups in recent years.
	Ethnic minority males	Just as ethnic minority females have experienced considerable discrimination and have had to develop coping strategies in face of adversity, so have ethnic minority males. Just as they have with Black American females, researchers are beginning to focus more on the positive dimensions of Black American males. A patriarchal, male-dominant orientation has characterized many ethnic minority groups, such as

CONCEPT TABLE 11.2

Continued

Concept	Processes/Related Ideas	Characteristics/Description
		Asian American, Hispanic American, and Native American, although females are gaining greater decision-making power in these cultures, especially those who develop careers and work outside of the home.
Moral development	Kohlberg's theory	Kohlberg developed a provocative view of the development of moral reasoning. He argued that moral development consists of three levels—preconventional, conventional, and postconventional—and six stages (two at each level). Increased internalization characterizes movement to Levels 2 and 3. Kohlberg's longitudinal data show a relation of the stages to age, although the highest two stages, especially Stage 6, rarely appear.
	Kohlberg's critics	Criticisms include the claims that Kohlberg overemphasizes cognitive factors and underemphasizes behavior, underestimates culture's role, and inadequately considers the care perspective. Carol Gilligan advocates a stronger care perspective (which views people in terms of their connectedness to others and interpersonal communication). Gilligan also believes that early adolescence is a critical juncture in the development of a moral voice for females. Researchers have found support for Gilligan's claim that females' and males' moral reasoning often center around different concerns, although gender differences in Kohlberg's stages have not been found consistently. Studies that focus more extensively on the items pertaining to close relationships, and use scoring systems that emphasize connectedness, support Gilligan's claims.
	Altruism	Altruism is an unselfish interest in helping someone. Damon described a developmental sequence of altruism, especially sharing. Up to 3 years of age, sharing is done for nonempathic reasons; at about 4 years, the combination of empathic awareness and adult encouragement produces a sense of obligation to share; in the early elementary years, children begin to genuinely show more objective ideas about fairness, at which time the principle of equality is understood; in the middle to late elementary years, the principles of merit and benevolence are understood.

KEY TERMS

boundary ambiguity   The uncertainty in stepfamilies of who is in or out of the family and who is performing or responsible for certain tasks in the family system. (312)

neglected children   These children receive little attention from their peers but they are not necessarily disliked by their peers. (314)

rejected children   These children are more likely to be disruptive and aggressive than neglected children and are often disliked by their peers. (314)

intimacy in friendships   Self-disclosure and the sharing of private thoughts. (315)

aptitude-treatment interaction (ATI)   Stresses the importance of children's aptitudes or characteristics and the treatments or experiences they are given in classrooms. (318)

perspective taking   The ability to assume another person's perspective and understand his or her thoughts and feelings. (321)

self-esteem   The global evaluative dimension of the self. Self-esteem is also referred to as "self-worth" or "self-image." (323)

self-concept   Domain-specific evaluations of the self. (323)

Self-Perception Profile for Children   This self-concept measure has five specific domains—scholastic competence, athletic competence, social acceptance, physical appearance, and behavioral conduct—plus general self-worth. (324)

social identity theory   Social psychologist Henry Tajfel's (1978) theory that, when individuals are assigned to a group, they invariably think of that group as an in-group for them. This occurs because individuals want to have a positive image. (324)

ethnocentrism   The tendency to favor one's own group over other groups. (325)

prejudice   An unjustified negative attitude toward an individual because of that person's membership in a group. (325)

gender-role stereotypes   These are broad categories that reflect our impressions and beliefs about females and males. (326)

androgyny   The presence of desirable masculine and feminine characteristics in the same individual. (330)

gender-role transcendence   The belief that, when an individual's competence is at issue, it should not be conceptualized on the basis of masculinity, femininity, or androgyny, but rather on a person basis. (331)

internalization   The developmental change from behavior that is externally controlled to behavior that is internally controlled. (334)

preconventional reasoning   The lowest level in Kohlberg's theory of moral development. At this level, the child shows no internalization of moral values—moral reasoning is controlled by external rewards and punishments. (334)

punishment and obedience orientation   The first stage in Kohlberg's theory of moral development. At this stage, moral thinking is based on punishment. (334)

individualism and purpose   The second stage in Kohlberg's theory of moral development. At this stage, moral thinking is based on rewards and self-interest. (334)

conventional reasoning   The second or intermediate level in Kohlberg's theory of moral development. At this level, the individual's internalization is intermediate. The person abides by certain standards (internal), but they are the standards of others (external), such as parents or the laws of society. (334)

interpersonal norms   The third stage in Kohlberg's theory of moral development. At this stage, the person values trust, caring, and loyalty to others as the basis of moral judgments. (334)

social system morality   The fourth stage in Kohlberg's theory of moral development. At this stage, moral judgments are based on understanding the social order, law, justice, and duty. (334)

postconventional reasoning   The highest level in Kohlberg's theory of moral development. At this level, morality is completely internalized and not based on others' standards. (335)

community rights versus individual rights   The fifth stage in Kohlberg's theory of moral development. At this stage, the person understands that values and laws are relative and that standards may vary from one person to another. (335)

universal ethical principles   The sixth and highest stage in Kohlberg's theory of moral development. At this stage, persons have developed a moral standard based on universal human rights. (335)

justice perspective   A moral perspective that focuses on the rights of the individual; individuals stand alone and independently make moral decisions. Kohlberg's theory is a justice perspective. (336)

care perspective   A moral perspective that views people in terms of their connectedness with others and emphasizes interpersonal communication, relationships with others, and concern for others. Gilligan's theory is a care perspective. (336)

altruism   An unselfish interest in helping someone. (337)

In no order of things is adolescence the simple time of life.

—Jean Erskine Stewart

Adolescents feel like they will live forever. At times, they are sure that they know everything. They clothe themselves with rainbows and go brave as the zodiac, flashing from one end of the world to the other in both mind and body. In many ways, today's adolescents are privileged, wielding unprecedented economic power. At the same time, they move through a seemingly endless preparation for life. They try on one face after another, seeking to find a face of their own. In their most pimply and awkward moments, they become acquainted with sex. They play furiously at "adult games" but are confined to the society of their own peers. They want their parents to understand them. Their generation of young people is the fragile cable by which the best and the worst of their parents' generation is transmitted to the present. In the end, there are only two lasting bequests parents can leave youth, one being roots, the other wings. Section Six contains two chapters: "Physical and Cognitive Development in Adolescence" (chapter 12) and "Socioemotional Development in Adolescence" (chapter 13).

Carl Larsson, In the
Hawthorne Hedge, detail.

Physical and Cognitive Development in Adolescence

*What is formed for long duration arrives
slowly to its maturity.*

—Samuel Johnson, *The Rambler*, 1750

> *In youth, we clothe ourselves with rainbows, and go brave as the zodiac.*
>
> —Ralph Waldo Emerson, *The Conduct of Life*, 1860

IMAGES OF LIFE-SPAN DEVELOPMENT

Puberty's Mysteries and Curiosities

I am pretty confused. I wonder whether I am weird or normal. My body is starting to change, but I sure don't look like a lot of my friends. I still look like a kid for the most part. My best friend is only 13, but he looks like he is 16 or 17. I get nervous in the locker room during PE class because when I go to take a shower, I'm afraid somebody is going to make fun of me since I'm not as physically developed as some of the others.

Robert, age 12

I don't like my breasts. They are too small, and they look funny. I'm afraid guys won't like me if they don't get bigger.

Angie, age 13

I can't stand the way I look. I have zits all over my face. My hair is dull and stringy. It never stays in place. My nose is too big. My lips are too small. My legs are too short. I have four warts on my left hand, and people get grossed out by them. So do I. My body is a disaster!

Ann, age 14

I'm short and I can't stand it. My father is six feet tall, and here I am only five foot four. I'm 14 already. I look like a kid, and I get teased a lot, especially by other guys. I'm always the last one picked for sides in basketball because I'm so short. Girls don't seem to be interested in me either because most of them are taller than I am.

Jim, age 14

The comments of these four adolescents in the midst of pubertal change underscore the dramatic upheaval in our bodies following the calm, consistent growth of middle and late childhood. Young adolescents develop an acute concern about their bodies. When columnist Bob Greene (1988) dialed a party line called "Connections in Chicago" to discover what young adolescents were saying to each other, the first things the boys and girls asked for—after first names—were physical descriptions. The idealism of the callers was apparent. Most of the girls described themselves as having long blond hair, being 5 feet, 5 inches tall, and weighing about 110 pounds. Most of the boys said that they had brown hair, lifted weights, were 6 feet tall, and weighed 170 pounds.

PREVIEW

Puberty's changes are perplexing to adolescents as they go through them. Although the changes are perplexing and call for self-doubts, questions, fears, and anxieties, most of us survive the adolescent years quite well. In this chapter we will explore the nature of puberty and physical development in adolescence, as well as the cognitive changes that characterize adolescent development. Our coverage will include schools, problems and disorders, and the current status of adolescents and at-risk behavior. To begin, though, we consider the transition to adolescence.

TRANSITION TO ADOLESCENCE

As in the development of children, genetic, biological, environmental, and experiential factors interact in adolescent development, which is also characterized by continuity and discontinuity. The genes inherited from parents still influence thought and behavior during adolescence, but inheritance now interacts with the social conditions of the adolescent's world—with family, peers, friendships, dating, and school experiences. An adolescent has experienced thousands of hours of interaction with parents, peers, and teachers in the past 10 to 13 years of development. Still, new experiences and developmental tasks appear during adolescence. Relationships with parents take a different form, moments with peers become more intimate, and dating

From *Penguin Dreams and Stranger Things* by Berke Breathed. Copyright © 1985 by The Washington Post Writer Group. By permission of Little, Brown and Company.

occurs for the first time, as does sexual exploration and possibly intercourse. The adolescent's thoughts are more abstract and idealistic. Biological changes trigger a heightened interest in body image. Adolescence, then, has both continuity and discontinuity with childhood.

PHYSICAL DEVELOPMENT

In Norway, **menarche,** *first menstruation,* now occurs at just over 13 years of age, as opposed to 17 years of age in the 1840s. In the United States—where children mature up to a year earlier than children in European countries—the average age of menarche has declined from 14.2 years in 1900 to about 12.45 years today. The age of menarche has been declining at an average of about 4 months per decade for the past century (Petersen, 1989).

Fortunately, however, we are unlikely to see pubescent toddlers, since what has characterized the past century is special—most likely, a higher level of nutrition and health. The available information suggests that menarche began to occur earlier at about the time of the Industrial Revolution, a period associated with increased standards of living and advances in medical science.

Menarche is one event that characterizes puberty, but there are others. What are puberty's markers? What are the psychological accompaniments of puberty's changes?

Pubertal Change

Puberty *is a period of rapid skeletal and sexual maturation that occurs mainly in early adolescence.* However, puberty is not a single sudden event. It is part of a gradual process. We know when a young person is going through puberty, but pinpointing its beginning and its end is difficult. Except for menarche, which occurs rather late in puberty, no single marker heralds puberty. For boys, the first whisker or first wet dream are events that could mark its appearance, but both may go unnoticed.

Behind the first whisker in boys and widening of hips in girls is a flood of hormones, powerful chemical substances secreted by the endocrine glands and carried through the body by the bloodstream (Dyk, 1993). The concentrations of certain hormones increase dramatically during adolescence (Rabin & Chrousos, 1991; Susman & Dorn, 1991). **Testosterone** *is a hormone associated with the development of genitals, an increase in height, and a change in voice in boys.* **Estradiol** *is a hormone associated with breast, uterine, and skeletal development in girls.* In one investigation, testosterone levels increased eighteenfold in boys but only twofold in girls during puberty; estradiol increased eightfold in girls but only twofold in boys (Nottelmann & others, 1987).

> *Puberty: the time of life when the two sexes begin to first become acquainted.*
> —Samuel Johnson

These hormonal and body changes occur, on the average, about 2 years earlier in females (10½ years of age) than in males (12½ years of age) (see figure 12.1). Four of the most noticeable areas of body change in females are height spurt, menarche, breast growth, and growth of pubic hair; four of the most noticeable areas of body change in males are height spurt, penile growth, testes growth, and growth of pubic hair (Malina, 1991; Tanner, 1991). The normal range and average age for these characteristics are shown in figures 12.2 and 12.3. Among the most remarkable normal variations is that two boys (or two girls) may be the same chronological age, yet one may complete the pubertal sequence before the other has begun it. For most girls, the first menstrual period may occur as early as the age of 10 or as late as the age of 15½ and still be considered normal, for example (Brooks-Gunn, 1988, 1992; Hood, 1991; Paikoff, Buchanan, & Brooks-Gunn, 1991).

Psychological Accompaniments of Physical Changes

A host of psychological changes accompany an adolescent's physical development. Imagine yourself as you were beginning puberty. Not only did you probably think about yourself differently, but your parents and peers probably began acting differently toward you. Maybe you were proud of your changing

FIGURE 12.1

Pubertal growth spurt. *On the average, the growth spurt that characterizes pubertal change occurs 2 years earlier for girls (age 10½) than for boys (age 12½).*

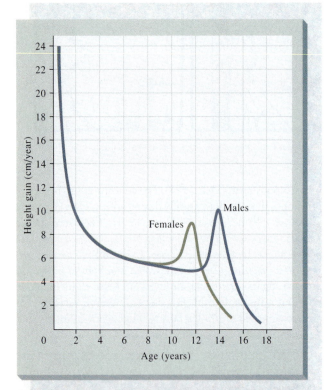

FIGURE 12.2

Normal range and average age of male sexual development.

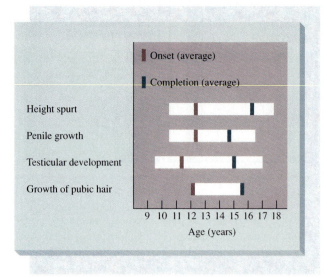

FIGURE 12.3

Normal range and average age of female sexual development.

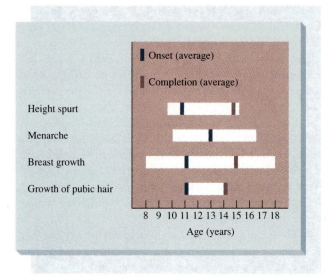

body, even though you were perplexed about what was happening. Perhaps your parents no longer perceived you as someone they could sit in bed and watch television with or as someone who should be kissed goodnight.

One thing is certain about the psychological aspects of physical change in adolescence: Adolescents are preoccupied with their bodies and develop individual images of what their bodies are like. Perhaps you looked in the mirror daily or even hourly to see if you could detect anything different about your changing body. Preoccupation with one's body image is strong throughout adolescence, but it is especially acute during puberty, a time when adolescents are more dissatisfied with their bodies than in late adolescence (Wright, 1989).

> *If we listen to boys and girls at the very moment they seem most pimply, awkward and disagreeable, we can partly penetrate a mystery most of us once felt heavily within us, and have now forgotten. This mystery is the very process of creation of man and woman.*
>
> —Colin Macinnes, *The World of Children*

Some of you entered puberty early, others late, and yet others on time. When adolescents mature earlier or later than their peers, might they perceive themselves differently? Some years ago, in the California Longitudinal Study, early-maturing boys perceived themselves more positively and had more successful peer relations than did their late-maturing counterparts (Jones, 1965). The findings for early-maturing girls were similar but not as strong as for boys. When the late-maturing boys were in their thirties, however, they had developed a stronger sense of identity than the early-maturing boys (Peskin, 1967). Possibly this occurred because the late-maturing boys had more time to explore life's options or because the early-maturing boys continued to focus on their advantageous physical status instead of on career development and achievement.

More-recent research confirms, though, that at least during adolescence it is advantageous to be an early-maturing rather than a late-maturing boy (Blyth, Bulcroft, & Simmons, 1981; Simmons & Blyth, 1987). The more-recent findings for girls suggest that early maturation is a mixed blessing: These girls experience more problems in school but also more independence and popularity with boys. The time that maturation is assessed also is a factor. In the sixth grade, early-maturing girls showed greater satisfaction with their figures than late-maturing girls, but, by the tenth grade, late-maturing girls were more satisfied. The reason for this is that, by late adolescence, early-maturing girls are shorter and stockier, whereas late-maturing girls are taller and thinner. Late-maturing girls in late adolescence have bodies that more closely approximate the current American ideal of feminine beauty—tall and thin.

In the last decade an increasing number of researchers have found that early maturation increases the vulnerability of girls to a number of problems (Brooks–Gunn & Paikoff, 1993; Stattin & Magnusson, 1990). Early maturing girls are more likely to smoke, drink, be depressed, and have an eating disorder; request earlier independence from their parents and have older friends; and their bodies likely elicit responses from males that lead to earlier dating and earlier sexual experiences (Gariulo & others, 1987; Magnusson, Stattin, & Allen, 1985).

In one study, early maturing girls had lower educational and occupational attainment in adulthood (Stattin & Magnusson, 1990). Apparently as a result of their social and cognitive immaturity, combined with early physical development, early maturing girls are easily lured into problem behaviors, not recognizing the possible long-term effects on their development (Petersen, 1993).

Some researchers now question whether the effects of puberty are as strong as once believed (Lerner, Petersen, & Brooks-Gunn, 1991; Montemayor, Adams, & Gulotta, 1990). Puberty affects some adolescents more strongly than others and some behaviors more strongly than others. Body image, dating interest, and sexual behavior are affected by pubertal change. The recent questioning of puberty's effects suggests that, if we look at overall development and adjustment in the human life cycle, pubertal variations (such as early and late maturation) are less dramatic than is commonly thought. In thinking about puberty's effects, keep in mind that an adolescent's world involves cognitive and social changes as well as physical changes. As with all periods of development, these processes work in concert to produce who we are in adolescence (Block, 1992; Eccles & Buchanan, 1992).

COGNITIVE DEVELOPMENTAL CHANGES

Adolescents' developing power of thought opens up new cognitive and social horizons. Their thought becomes more abstract, logical, and idealistic; more capable of examining one's own thoughts, others' thoughts, and what others are thinking about oneself; and more likely to interpret and monitor the social world. We will discuss, first, Piaget's view of adolescent thought, second, social cognition in adolescence, and third, decision making.

Formal Operational Thought

Piaget believed that formal operational thought comes into play between the ages of 11 and 15. Formal operational thought is more *abstract* than a child's thinking. Adolescents are no longer limited to actual concrete experience as the anchor of thought. Instead, they may conjure up make-believe situations, hypothetical possibilities, or purely abstract propositions and reason about them. The adolescent increasingly thinks about thought itself. One adolescent pondered, "I began thinking about why I was thinking what I was. Then I began thinking about why I was thinking about why I was thinking about what I was." If this sounds abstract, it is, and it characterizes the adolescent's increased interest in thought itself and the abstractness of thought.

> *The error of youth is to believe that intelligence is a substitute for experience, while the error of age is to believe that experience is a substitute for intelligence.*
>
> —Slyman Bryson

In addition to being abstract, adolescent thought is also idealistic. Adolescents begin to think about ideal characteristics for themselves and others and to compare themselves and others to these ideal standards. In contrast, children think more in terms of what is real and what is limited. During adolescence, thoughts often take fantasy flights into the future. It is not unusual for the adolescent to become impatient with these newfound ideal standards and to be perplexed over which of many ideal standards to adopt.

At the same time as adolescents think more abstractly and idealistically, they also think more logically (Kuhn, 1991). Adolescents begin to think more like a scientist, devising plans to solve problems and systematically testing solutions. This type of problem solving has an imposing name. **Hypothetical-deductive reasoning** *is Piaget's formal operational concept that*

FIGURE 12.4

Characteristics of formal operational thought. Adolescents begin to think in more abstract, idealistic, and logical ways than when they were children.

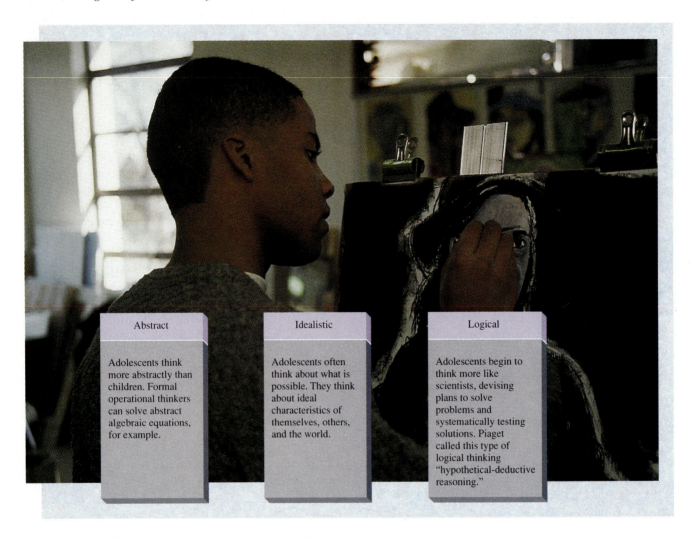

Abstract

Adolescents think more abstractly than children. Formal operational thinkers can solve abstract algebraic equations, for example.

Idealistic

Adolescents often think about what is possible. They think about ideal characteristics of themselves, others, and the world.

Logical

Adolescents begin to think more like scientists, devising plans to solve problems and systematically testing solutions. Piaget called this type of logical thinking "hypothetical-deductive reasoning."

adolescents have the cognitive ability to develop hypotheses, or best guesses, about ways to solve problems, such as an algebraic equation. They then systematically deduce, or conclude, which is the best path to follow in solving the problem. By contrast, children are more likely to solve problems in a trial-and-error fashion. Figure 12.4 summarizes the main features of formal operational thought.

Some of Piaget's ideas on formal operational thought are currently being challenged (Byrnes, 1988; Danner, 1989; Keating, in press; Lapsley, 1989; Overton & Byrnes, 1991; Overton & Montangero, 1991). There is much more individual variation in formal operational thought than Piaget envisioned. Only about one in three young adolescents is a formal operational thinker. Many American adults never become formal operational thinkers, and neither do many adults in other cultures. Consider the following conversation between a researcher and an illiterate Kpelle farmer in the West African country of Liberia (Scribner, 1977):

Researcher: All Kpelle men are rice farmers. Mr. Smith is not a rice farmer. Is he a Kpelle man?

Kpelle farmer: I don't know the man. I have not laid eyes on the man myself.

Members of the Kpelle culture who had gone through formal schooling answered the researcher in a logical way. As with our discussion of concrete operational thought in chapter 10, we find that cultural experiences influence whether individuals reach a Piagetian stage of thought. Education in the logic of science and mathematics is an important cultural experience that promotes the development of formal operational thinking.

Also, for adolescents who become formal operational thinkers, assimilation (incorporating new information into existing knowledge) dominates the initial development of formal operational thought and the world is perceived subjectively and idealistically. Later in adolescence, as intellectual balance is restored, these individuals accommodate (adjust to new information) to the cognitive upheaval that has occurred.

Social Cognition

Impressive changes in social cognition characterize adolescent development. Adolescents develop a special type of egocentrism, begin to think about personality not unlike the way personality theorists do, and monitor their social world in sophisticated ways.

Adolescent thought is egocentric. David Elkind (1976) believes that **adolescent egocentrism** *has two parts: an imaginary audience and a personal fable.* The **imaginary audience** *is the adolescent's belief that others are as preoccupied with her as she herself is.* Attention-getting behavior, so common in adolescence, reflects egocentrism and the desire to be on stage, noticed, and visible. Imagine the eighth-grade boy who thinks he is an actor and all the others are the audience as he stares at the small spot on his trousers. Imagine the seventh-grade girl who thinks that all eyes are riveted on her complexion because of the tiny blemish she has.

Jennifer talks with her best friend, Anne, about something she has just heard. "Anne, did you hear about Barbara. You know she fools around a lot. Well, the word is she is pregnant. Can you believe it? That would never happen to me." Later in the conversation, Anne tells Jennifer, "I really like Bob, but sometimes he is a jerk. He just can't understand me. He has no clue about what my personal feelings are." The **personal fable** *is the part of adolescent egocentrism that involves an adolescent's sense of uniqueness.* Adolescents' sense of personal uniqueness makes them feel that no one can understand how they really feel. For example, an adolescent girl thinks that in no way can her mother sense the hurt that she feels because her boyfriend broke up with her. As part of their effort to retain a sense of personal uniqueness, adolescents may craft a story about the self that is filled with fantasy, immersing themselves in a world that is far removed from reality. Personal fables frequently show up in adolescent diaries.

Developmentalists have increasingly studied adolescent egocentrism in recent years. The research interest focuses on what the components of egocentrism really are, the nature of self-other relationships, why egocentric thought emerges in adolescence, and the role of egocentrism in adolescent problems. For example, David Elkind (1985) believes that adolescent egocentrism is brought about by formal operational thought. Others, however, argue that adolescent egocentrism is not entirely a cognitive phenomenon. Rather, they think the imaginary audience is due to both the ability to think hypothetically (formal operational thought) and the ability to step outside oneself and anticipate the reactions of others in imaginative circumstances (perspective taking) (Lapsley, 1990, 1991; Lapsley & others, 1986; Lapsley & Murphy, 1985; Lapsley & Rice, 1988; O'Connor & Nikolic, 1990).

Some developmentalists believe that egocentrism may account for some of the seemingly reckless behavior of adolescents, including drug use, suicidal thoughts, and failure to use contraceptives during intercourse (Dolcini & others, 1989; Elkind, 1978). The reckless behavior may stem from

The colorful attire of this skateboarder reflects adolescent egocentrism. Attention-getting behavior reflects the desire to be on stage and noticed. The risk-taking behavior of skateboarding, as well as racing cars, taking drugs, and many other behaviors, reflects adolescents' sense of indestructibility. Joseph Conrad once commented, "I remember my youth and the feeling that never came back anymore—the feeling that I could last forever, outlast the sea, the earth, and all men."

the egocentric characteristics of uniqueness and invulnerability. In one investigation, eleventh- and twelfth-grade females who were high in adolescent egocentrism gave a lower estimate of the likelihood that they would get pregnant if they engaged in sex without contraception than did those who were low in adolescent egocentrism (Arnett, 1990).

Adolescents also begin to interpret personality not unlike the way personality theorists do (Barenboim, 1981, 1985). First, when adolescents are given information about another person, they consider previously acquired information and current information and do not rely solely on the concrete information at hand, as children do. Second, adolescents are more likely to detect the contextual or situational variability in their own and others' behavior rather than think that they and others always behave consistently. Third, rather than merely accepting surface traits as a valid description of another person or themselves, adolescents begin to look for deeper, more complex—even hidden—causes of personality.

As part of their increased awareness of others—including what others are doing and thinking—adolescents engage in social monitoring. For example, Bob, a 16-year-old, feels he does not know as much as he wants or needs to know about Sally, another 16-year-old. He also wants to know more about Sally's relationship with Brian, a 17-year-old. Bob decides that he wants to know more about the groups Sally belongs to—her student council friends, the clique she is in, and so on. Adolescents use a number of social monitoring methods on a daily basis. For example, an adolescent may check incoming information about an organization (school, club, or group of friends) to determine if it is consistent with the adolescent's impression of the group. Still another adolescent may question someone or paraphrase what that person has just said about her feelings to ensure that he has understood them correctly. Yet another adolescent may meet someone new and quickly think, "It's going to be hard to really get to know him" (Flavell, 1979).

Decision Making

Adolescence is a time of increased decision making (Beth-Marom & others, in press; Quaderel, Fischoff, & Davis, 1993). Adolescents make decisions about the future, which friends to choose, whether to go to college, which person to date, whether to have sex, whether to take drugs, whether to buy a car, and so on. How competent are adolescents at making decisions? Older adolescents are more competent than younger adolescents, who in turn are more competent than children (Keating, 1990). Young adolescents are more likely than children to generate options, to examine a situation from a variety of perspectives, to anticipate the consequences of decisions, and to consider the credibility of sources (Mann, Harmoni, & Power, in press). However, young adolescents are less competent at these decision-making skills than are older adolescents.

Transitions in decision making appear at approximately 11 to 12 years of age and at 15 to 16 years of age. For example, in one study, eighth-, tenth-, and twelfth-grade students were presented with dilemmas involving the choice of a medical procedure (Lewis, 1981). The oldest students were most likely to spontaneously mention a variety of risks, to recommend consultation with an outside specialist, and to anticipate future consequences. For example, when asked a question about whether to have cosmetic surgery, a twelfth-grader said that different aspects of the situation need to be examined along with its effects on the individual's future, especially relationships with other people. By contrast, an eighth-grader provided a more limited view, commenting on the surgery's effects on getting turned down for a date, the money involved, and being teased at school by peers.

However, the decision-making skills of older adolescents and adults are often far from perfect. And the ability to make decisions does not guarantee that such decisions will be made in everyday life, where breadth of experience often comes into play (Ganzel & Jacobs, 1992; Jacobs & Potenza, 1990; Keating, 1990; Keating, Menna, & Matthews, 1992). For example, driver-training courses improve the adolescent's cognitive and motor skills to levels equal to, or sometimes superior to, those

of adults. However, driver training has not been effective in reducing adolescents' high rate of traffic accidents (Potvin, Champagne, & Laberge-Nadeau, 1988). Thus, an important research agenda is to study the ways adolescents make decisions in practical situations.

Adolescents need more opportunities to practice and discuss realistic decision making. Many real-world decisions occur in an atmosphere of stress, involving such factors as time constraints and emotional involvement. One strategy to improve adolescent decision making about real-world choices involving such matters as sex, drugs, and daredevil driving is for schools to develop more opportunities for adolescents to engage in role playing and group problem-solving related to such circumstances (Mann, Harmoni, & Power, in press).

In some instances, adolescents' decision making may be blamed when in reality the problem involves society's orientation toward adolescents and its failure to provide adolescents with adequate choices (Keating, 1990). For example, a mathematically precocious ninth-grade girl may abandon mathematics, not because of poor decision-making skills, but because of a stronger motivation to maintain positive peer relations that would be threatened if she stayed on the math track. The decision of an adolescent in a low-income, inner-city area to engage in drug trafficking even at considerable risk may not be a consequence of the adolescent's failure to consider all of the relevant information, but may be the outcome of quite sophisticated thinking about risk-benefit ratios in oppressive circumstances offering limited or nonexistent options. As cognitive developmentalist Daniel Keating observes, if we dislike adolescents' choices, perhaps we need to provide them with better options from which to choose.

At this point we have discussed a number of ideas about adolescents' physical and cognitive development. A summary of these ideas is presented in concept table 12.1. Now we turn our attention to schools and their effects on adolescent development.

THE NATURE OF ADOLESCENTS' SCHOOLING

The impressive changes in adolescents' cognition lead us to examine the nature of schools for adolescents. In chapter 11, we discussed different ideas about the effects of schools on children's development. Here we focus more exclusively on the nature of secondary schools. Among the questions we try to answer are the following: What should be the function of secondary schools? What is the nature of the transition from elementary to middle or junior high school? Why do adolescents drop out of high school, and how can we reduce the number of dropouts?

In youth we learn, in age we understand.
—Marie Ebner von Eschenbach, *Aphorism*, 1904

CONCEPT TABLE 12.1

Physical and Cognitive Development in Adolescence

Concept	Processes/Related Ideas	Characteristics/Description
Transition to adolescence	Its nature	Both continuity and discontinuity characterize the transition from childhood to adolescence. Just as in the development of children, genetic, biological, environmental, and experiential factors interact in adolescent development.
Physical development	Pubertal change	Puberty is a period of rapid skeletal and sexual maturation that occurs mainly in early adolescence. Testosterone plays an important role in male pubertal development, estradiol in female pubertal development. The growth spurt for boys occurs about 2 years later than for girls, with 12½ being the average age of onset for boys, 10½ for girls. Individual maturation in pubertal change is extensive.
	Psychological accompaniments of pubertal changes	Adolescents show a heightened interest in their body image. Early maturation favors boys, at least during adolescence. As adults, though, late-maturing boys achieve more successful identities. Researchers are increasingly finding that early maturing girls are vulnerable to a number of problems.
	Are puberty's effects exaggerated?	Recently, some scholars have expressed doubt that puberty's effects on development are as strong as once believed. It is important to keep in mind that adolescent development is influenced by an interaction of biological, cognitive, and social factors, rather than being dominated by biology. While extremely early or late maturation may place an adolescent at risk, the overall effects of early and late maturation are not great. This is not to say that puberty and early or late maturation have no effect on development. They do, but puberty's changes always need to be considered in terms of the larger framework of interacting biological, cognitive, and social factors.
Cognitive development	Formal operational thought	Piaget believed that formal operational thought comes into play between 11 and 15 years of age. Formal operational thought is more abstract, idealistic, and logical than concrete operational thought. Piaget believed that adolescents become capable of using hypothetical deductive reasoning. Some of Piaget's ideas on formal operational thought are currently being challenged.
	Social cognition	Impressive changes in social cognition characterize adolescent development. Adolescents develop a special type of egocentrism that involves an imaginary audience and a personal fable about being unique. They begin to think about personality not unlike the way personality theorists do, and they monitor their social world in more sophisticated ways.
	Decision making	Adolescence is a time of increased decision making. Older adolescents are more competent at decision making than younger adolescents, who in turn are more competent than children. The ability to make decisions does not guarantee they will be made in practice, because in real life breadth of experience comes into play. Adolescents need more opportunities to practice and discuss realistic decision making. In some instances, adolescents' faulty decision making may be blamed when in reality the problem is society's orientation toward adolescents and failure to provide them with adequate choices.

The Controversy Surrounding Secondary Schools

During the twentieth century, schools have assumed a more prominent role in the lives of adolescents. From 1890 to 1920, virtually every state developed laws that excluded youth from work and required them to attend school. In this time frame, the number of high school graduates increased 600 percent (Tyack, 1976). By making secondary education compulsory, the adult power structure placed adolescents in a submissive position and made their move into the adult world of work more manageable. In the nineteenth century, high schools were mainly for the elite, with the main educational emphasis being on classical liberal arts courses. By the 1920s, educators perceived that the secondary school curriculum needed to be changed. Schools for the masses, it was thought, should not just involve intellectual training, but should also involve training for work and citizenship. The curriculum of secondary schools became more comprehensive and grew to include general education, college preparatory, and vocational education courses. As the twentieth century unfolded, secondary schools continued to expand their orientation, adding courses in music, art, health, physical education, and other topics. By the middle of the twentieth century, schools had moved further toward preparing students for comprehensive roles in life (Conant, 1959). Today, secondary schools have retained their comprehensive orientation, designed to train adolescents intellectually, but in many other ways as well, such as vocationally and socially.

Although there has been a consistent trend of increased school attendance for more than 150 years, the distress over alienated and rebellious youth led some social scientists to question whether secondary schools actually benefit adolescents. During the early 1970s, three independent panels agreed that high schools contribute to adolescent alienation and actually restrict the transition to adulthood (Brown, 1973; Coleman & others, 1974; Martin, 1976). These prestigious panels argued that adolescents should be given educational alternatives to the comprehensive high school, such as on-the-job community work, to increase their exposure to adult roles and to decrease their sense of isolation from adults. To some degree in response to these reports, a number of states lowered from 16 to 14 the age at which adolescents could leave school.

As we enter the last decade of the twentieth century, the back-to-basics movement has gained momentum, with proponents arguing that the main function of schools should be rigorous training of intellectual skills through subjects like English, math, and science (Kerns, 1988). Advocates of the back-to-basics movement point to the excessive fluff in secondary school curricula, with students being allowed to select from many alternatives that will not give them a basic education in intellectual subjects. Some critics also point to the extensive time students spend in extracurricular activities. They argue that schools should be in the business of imparting knowledge to adolescents and not be so concerned about their social and emotional lives. Related to the proverbial dilemma of schools' functions is whether schools should include a vocational curriculum in addition to training in basic subjects such as English, math, and science. Some critics of the fluff in secondary schools argue that the school day should be longer and that the school year should be extended into the summer months. Such arguments are made by critics who believe that the main function of schools should be the training of intellectual skills. Little concern for adolescents' social and emotional development appears in these arguments (Duke & Canady, 1991; Perkinson, 1991).

Should the main—and perhaps only—major goal of schooling for adolescents be the development of an intellectually mature individual? Or should schools also focus on the adolescent's maturity in social and emotional development? Should schools be comprehensive, providing a multifaceted curriculum that includes many electives and alternative subjects to basic core courses? These are provocative questions that continue to be heatedly debated in educational and community circles. To read further about secondary schools, turn to Sociocultural Worlds of Development 12.1, where we explore the nature of secondary schools in different countries.

The Transition to Middle or Junior High School

The emergence of junior high schools in the 1920s and 1930s was justified on the basis of physical, cognitive, and social changes that characterize early adolescence, as well as the need for more schools for the growing student population. Old high schools became junior high schools and new regional high schools were built. In most systems, the ninth grade remained a part of the high school in content, although physically separated from it in a 6-3-3 system. Gradually, the ninth grade has been restored to the high school as many school systems have developed middle schools that include the seventh and eighth grades, or sixth, seventh, and eighth grades. The creation of middle schools has been influenced by the earlier onset of puberty in recent decades.

One worry of educators and psychologists is that junior high and middle schools have simply become watered-down versions of high schools, mimicking their curricular and extracurricular schedules (Hill, 1980). The critics argue that unique curricular and extracurricular activities reflecting a wide range of individual differences in biological and psychological development in early adolescence should be incorporated into our junior high and middle schools. The critics also stress that many high schools foster passivity rather than autonomy, and that schools should create a variety of pathways for students to achieve an identity.

The transition to middle school or junior high school from elementary school interests developmentalists because, even though it is a normative experience for virtually all children, the transition can be stressful. Why? Because the transition takes place at a time when many changes—in the individual, in the family, and in school—are taking place simultaneously (Eccles & Midgely, 1990; Hawkins & Berndt, 1985; Hirsch, 1989; Simmons & Blyth, 1987). These changes include puberty and related concerns about body image; the emergence of at least

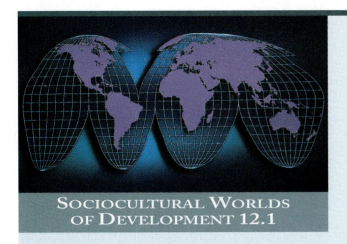

SOCIOCULTURAL WORLDS OF DEVELOPMENT 12.1

Cross-Cultural Comparisons of Secondary Schools

Secondary schools in different countries share a number of features, but differ on others (Cameron & others, 1983; George, 1987; Thomas, 1988). Let's explore the similarities and differences in secondary schools in six countries: Australia, Brazil, Germany, Japan, Russia, and the United States.

Most countries mandate that children begin school at 6 to 7 years of age and stay in school until they are 14 to 17 years of age. Brazil requires students to go to school only until they are 14 years of age, while Russia mandates that students stay in school until they are 17. Germany, Japan, Australia, and the United States require school attendance until 15 to 16 years of age.

Most secondary schools around the world are divided into two or more levels, such as middle school (or junior high school) and high school. However, Germany's schools are divided according to three educational ability tracks: (1) The main school provides a basic level of education, (2) the middle school gives students a more advanced education, and (3) the academic school prepares students for entrance to a university. German schools, like most European schools, offer a classical education, which includes courses in Latin and Greek.

Japanese secondary schools have an entrance exam, but secondary schools in the other five countries do not. Only Australia and Germany have comprehensive exit exams.

The United States is the only country in the world in which sports are an integral part of the public school system. Only a few private schools in other countries have their own sports teams, sports facilities, and highly organized sports events.

Curriculum is often similar in secondary schools in different countries, although there are some differences in content

and philosophy. For example, at least until recently, the secondary schools in Russia have emphasized the preparation of students for work, The "labor education program," which is part of the secondary school curriculum, includes vocational training and on-the-job experience. The idea is to instill in youth a love for manual work and a positive attitude about industrial and work organizations. Russian students who are especially gifted—academically, artistically, or athletically—attend special schools where they are encouraged to develop their talents and are trained to be the very best in their vocation. With the breakup of the Soviet Union, it will be interesting to follow what changes in education take place in Russia.

In Brazil, students are required to take Portuguese (the native language) and four foreign languages (Latin, French, English, and Spanish). Brazil requires these languages because of the country's international character and emphasis on trade and commerce. Seventh-grade students in Australia take courses in sheep husbandry and weaving, two areas of economic and cultural interest in the country. In Japan, students take a number of Western courses in addition to their basic Japanese courses; these courses include Western literature and languages (in addition to Japanese literature and language), Western physical education (in addition to Japanese martial arts classes), and Western sculpture and handicrafts (in addition to Japanese calligraphy). The Japanese school year is also much longer than that of other countries (225 days versus 180 days in the United States, for example).

The juku, or "cramming school," is available to Japanese children and adolescents in the summertime and after school. It provides coaching to help them improve their grades and their entrance exam scores for high schools and universities. The Japanese practice of requiring an entrance exam for high school is a rarity among the nations of the world.

some aspects of formal operational thought, including accompanying changes in social cognition; increased responsibility and independence in association with decreased dependency on parents; change from a small, contained classroom structure to a larger, more impersonal school structure; change from one teacher to many teachers and a small, homogeneous set of peers to a larger, more heterogeneous set of peers; and increased focus on achievement and performance, and their assessment. This

list includes a number of negative, stressful features, but there can be positive aspects to the transition. Students are more likely to feel grown up, have more subjects from which to select, have more opportunities to spend time with peers and to locate compatible friends, and enjoy increased independence from direct parental monitoring, and they may be more challenged intellectually by academic work.

When students make the transition from elementary school to middle or junior high school, they experience the **top-dog phenomenon,** *the circumstance of moving from the top position (in elementary school, being the oldest, biggest, and most powerful students in the school) to the lowest position (in middle or junior high school, being the youngest, smallest, and least powerful students in the school).* Researchers who have charted the transition from elementary to middle or junior high school find that the first year of middle or junior high school can be difficult for many students (Eccles & Midgely, 1990; Hawkins & Berndt, 1985; Simmons & Blyth, 1987). For example, in one investigation of the transition from sixth grade in an elementary school to the seventh grade in a junior high school, adolescents' perceptions of the quality of their school life plunged in the seventh grade (Hirsch & Rapkin, 1987). In the seventh grade, the students were less satisfied with school, were less committed to school, and liked their teachers less. The drop in school satisfaction occurred regardless of how academically successful the students were.

Effective Schools for Young Adolescents

What makes a successful middle school? Joan Lipsitz (1984) and her colleagues searched the nation for the best middle schools. Extensive contacts and observations were made. Based on the recommendations of education experts and observations in schools in different parts of the United States, four middle schools were chosen for their outstanding ability to educate young adolescents. What were these middle schools like? The most striking feature was their willingness and ability to adapt all school practices to the individual differences in physical, cognitive, and social development of their students. The schools took seriously the knowledge we have developed about young adolescents. This seriousness was reflected in the decisions about different aspects of school life. For example, one middle school fought to keep its schedule of minicourses on Friday so that every student could be with friends and pursue personal interests. Two other middle schools expended considerable energy on a complex school organization so that small groups of students worked with small groups of teachers who could vary the tone and pace of the school day, depending on the students' needs. Another middle school developed an advisory scheme so that each student had daily contact with an adult who was willing to listen, explain, comfort, and prod the adolescent. Such school policies reflect thoughtfulness and personal concern about individuals who have compelling developmental needs.

What does education often do? It makes a straight-cut ditch of a free, meandering brook.

—Henry David Thoreau

> ## Critical Thinking
>
> *Analyze your own middle school or junior high school. How did it measure up to Lipsitz's criteria for effective schools for young adolescents?*

Another aspect of the effective middle schools was that early in their existence—the first year in three of the schools and the second year in the fourth school—they emphasized the importance of creating an environment that was positive for adolescents' social and emotional development. This goal was established not only because such environments contribute to academic excellence, but also because social and emotional development are valued as intrinsically important in adolescents' schooling.

Recognizing that the vast majority of middle schools do not approach the excellent schools described by Joan Lipsitz (1984), in 1989 the Carnegie Corporation issued an extremely negative evaluation of our nation's middle schools. In the report, "Turning Points: Preparing American Youth for the 21st Century," the conclusion was put forth that most young adolescents attend massive, impersonal schools, learn from seemingly irrelevant curricula, trust few adults in school, and lack access to health care and counseling. The Carnegie report (1989) recommended the following:

- Develop smaller "communities" or "houses" to lessen the impersonal nature of large middle schools.

- Lower student-to-counselor ratios from several hundred-to-1 to 10-to-1.

- Involve parents and community leaders in schools.

- Develop curricula that produce students who are literate, understand the sciences, and have a sense of health, ethics, and citizenship.

- Have teachers team teach in more flexibly designed curriculum blocks that integrate several disciplines instead of presenting students with disconnected, rigidly separated 50-minute segments.

- Boost students' health and fitness with more in-school programs and help students who need public health care to get it.

Many of these same recommendations were echoed in a report from the National Governors' Association (*America in Transition,* 1989), which stated that the very structure of middle school education in America neglects the basic developmental needs of young adolescents. Many educators and psychologists strongly support these recommendations (Entwisle, 1990; MacIver & others, 1992). The Edna McConnell Clark

Foundation's Program for Disadvantaged Youth is an example of multiyear, multisite effort designed to implement many of the proposals for middle school improvement. The foundation has engaged the Center for Early Adolescence at the University of North Carolina to guide five urban school districts in their middle school reform (Scales, 1992). In sum, middle schools throughout the nation need a major redesign if they are to be effective in educating adolescents for becoming competent adults in the twenty-first century.

High School Dropouts

For many decades, dropping out of high school has been viewed as a serious educational and societal problem. By leaving high school before graduating, many dropouts take with them educational deficiencies that severely curtail their economic and social well-being throughout their adult lives (Rumberger, 1987). We will study the scope of the problem, the causes of dropping out, and ways to reduce dropout rates. While dropping out of high school often has negative consequences for youth, the picture is not entirely bleak (William T. Grant Foundation Commission on Work, Family, and Citizenship, 1988). Over the last 40 years, the proportion of adolescents who have not finished high school has decreased considerably. In 1940, more than 60 percent of all individuals 25 to 29 years of age had not completed high school. By 1986, this proportion had dropped to less than 14 percent. From 1973 to 1983, the annual dropout rate nationwide fell by almost 20 percent, from 6.3 to 5.2 percent.

Despite the decline in overall high school dropout rates, a major concern is the higher dropout rate of minority-group and low-income students, especially in large cities (Cohen, 1994). The student dropout rates of most minority groups have been declining, but they remain substantially above those of White adolescents. The proportion of Hispanic American youth who finish high school is not keeping pace with the gains by Black American and other minority groups. High school completion rates for Hispanic American youth dropped from 63 percent in 1985 to 56 percent in 1989; the completion rate was 52 percent in 1972. In contrast to the pattern among Hispanic American youth, the high school graduation rate for Black American youth increased from 67 percent in 1972 to 76 percent in 1989. The comparable rates for White youth remained the same—82 percent in both 1972 and 1989.

Dropout rates are also high for Native Americans (fewer than 10 percent graduate from high school) (LaFromboise & Low, 1989). In some inner-city areas the dropout rate for ethnic minority students is especially high, reaching more than 50 percent in Chicago, for example (Hahn, 1987).

Students drop out of schools for many reasons. In one investigation, almost 50 percent of the dropouts cited school-related reasons for leaving school, such as not liking school or being expelled or suspended (Rumberger, 1983). Twenty percent of the dropouts (but 40 percent of the Hispanic students) cited economic reasons for leaving school. One-third of the female students dropped out for personal reasons, such as pregnancy or marriage.

To help reduce the dropout rate, community institutions, especially schools, need to break down the barriers between work and school. Many youth step off the education ladder long before reaching the level needed for a professional career, often with nowhere to step next, and left to their own devices to search for work. These youth need more assistance than they are now receiving. Among the approaches worth considering are these (William T. Grant Foundation on Work, Family, and Citizenship, 1988):

- Monitored work experiences, such as through cooperative education, apprenticeships, internships, preemployment training, and youth-operated enterprises.
- Community and neighborhood services, including voluntary and youth-guided services.
- Redirected vocational education, the principal thrust of which should not be preparation for specific jobs but acquisition of basic skills needed for a wide range of jobs.
- Guarantees of continuing education, employment, or training, especially in conjunction with mentor programs.
- Career information and counseling to expose youth to job opportunities and career options as well as to successful role models.
- School volunteer programs, not only for tutoring but also for providing access to adult friends and mentors.

ADOLESCENT PROBLEMS AND DISORDERS

What are some of the major problems that adolescents may encounter? They include drug and alcohol abuse, delinquency, adolescent pregnancy, suicide, and eating disorders.

Drugs

The 1960s and 1970s were a time of marked increases in the use of illicit drugs. During the social and political unrest of those years, many youth turned to marijuana, stimulants, and hallucinogens. Increases in alcohol consumption by adolescents also were noted (Robinson & Greene, 1988). More precise data about drug use by adolescents have been collected in recent years. Each year since 1975, Lloyd Johnston, Patrick O'Malley, and Gerald Bachman (1993, 1994), working at the Institute of Social Research at the University of Michigan, have carefully monitored drug use by America's high school seniors in a wide range of public and private high schools. From time to time, they also sample the drug use of younger adolescents and adults as well.

In the most recent survey (1993), a downward trend of drug use by adolescents in the first several years of the 1990s was reversed. In 1993, adolescents showed a sharp rise in marijuana use, as well as an increase in the use of stimulants, LSD, and inhalents. An increase in cigarette smoking also occurred (Johnston, O'Malley, & Bachman, 1994). A special concern is the increased use of drugs by young adolescents. Also, it is important to note that adolescents in the United States have the highest rate of drug use among the world's industrialized nations. Let's further examine the use of alcohol and cocaine by adolescents.

Alcohol

Some mornings, 15-year-old Annie was too drunk to go to school. Other days, she'd stop for a couple of beers or a screwdriver on the way to school. She was tall, blonde, and good looking, and no one who sold her liquor, even at 8:00 in the morning, questioned her age. Where did she get her money? She got it from baby-sitting and from what her mother gave her to buy lunch. Annie used to be a cheerleader, but no longer; she was kicked off the squad for missing practice so often. Soon, she and several of her peers were drinking almost every morning. Sometimes, they skipped school and went to the woods to drink. Annie's whole life began to revolve around her drinking. This routine went on for 2 years. After a while, Annie's parents discovered her problem. Even though they punished her, it did not stop her drinking. Finally, this year, Annie started dating a boy she really liked and who would not put up with her drinking. She agreed to go to Alcoholics Anonymous and has just successfully completed treatment. She has abstained from drinking for 4 consecutive months now, and she hopes that her abstinence will continue.

Alcohol is the drug most widely used by adolescents in our society. For them, it has produced many enjoyable moments and many sad ones as well. Alcoholism is the third leading killer in the United States, with more than 13 million people classified as alcoholics, many of whom established their drinking habits during adolescence. Each year, approximately 25,000 people are killed and 1.5 million injured by drunk drivers. In 65 percent of the aggressive male acts against females, the offender is under the influence of alcohol (Goodman & others, 1986). In numerous instances of drunk driving and assaults on females, the offenders are adolescents.

How extensive is alcohol use by adolescents? Alcohol use by high school seniors has gradually declined. Monthly use declined from 72 percent in 1980 to 51 percent in 1993. The prevalence of drinking five or more drinks in a row in a 2-week interval fell from 41 percent in 1983 to 28 percent in 1993. Figure 12.5 shows the trends in the percentages of students at different grade levels who say they have been drunk in the last year and in the last 30 days. There remains a substantial gender difference in heavy adolescent drinking: 28 percent for females versus 46 percent for males in 1986, although this difference diminished gradually during the 1980s. However, data from college students show little drop in alcohol use and an increase in heavy drinking: 45 percent in 1986, up 2 percent from the previous year. Heavy drinking at parties among college males is common and is becoming more common (Johnston, O'Malley, & Bachman, 1994).

FIGURE 12.5

Trends in the percentage of 8th, 10th, and 12th graders who have been drunk in the last year and the last 30 days.

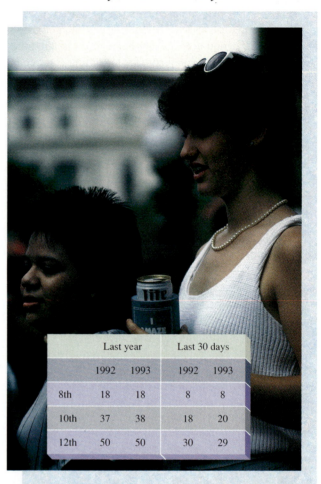

	Last year		Last 30 days	
	1992	1993	1992	1993
8th	18	18	8	8
10th	37	38	18	20
12th	50	50	30	29

Critical Thinking

Why do you think alcohol use has remained so high during adolescence?

Cocaine

Did you know that cocaine was once an ingredient in Coca-Cola? Of course, it has long since been removed from the soft drink. Cocaine comes from the coca plant, native to Bolivia and Peru. For many years, Bolivians and Peruvians chewed the plant to increase their stamina. Today, cocaine is usually snorted, smoked, or injected in the form of crystals or powder. The effect is a rush of euphoric feelings, which eventually wear off, followed by depressive feelings, lethargy, insomnia, and irritability.

Cocaine is a highly controversial drug. Users claim it is exciting, makes them feel good, and increases their confidence. It is clear, however, that cocaine has potent cardiovascular effects and is potentially addictive. The recent death of sports star Len Bias demonstrates how lethal cocaine can be. When the drug's effects are extreme, it can produce a heart attack, stroke, or brain

LIFE-SPAN PRACTICAL KNOWLEDGE 12.1

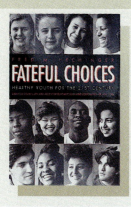

Fateful Choices
(1992) by Fred Hechinger.
New York: Hill & Wang.

The substance of this excellent book was provided by the Carnegie Council on Adolescent Development. One of the Carnegie Council's main themes comes through clearly here—linking health and education in the development of adolescents. The author provides valuable recommendations that can improve the health and well-being of all adolescents, especially those at risk for problems. Topics include adolescents at risk, adolescent pregnancy, drug abuse, nutrition and exercise, and youth organizations.

seizure. The increase in cocaine-related deaths is traced to very pure or tainted forms of the drug.

Cocaine use, which remained at peak levels throughout much of the 1980s, began an important decline in 1987 that continued through 1992 in high school and college students (Johnston, O'Malley, & Bachman, 1994). Among high school seniors, the proportion of cocaine users fell considerably from 1986 to 1993, from 6.2 percent to 1.3 percent. A large proportional drop in use was also observed among college students over the same time interval—from 7 percent to 1.0 percent. A growing proportion of high school seniors and college students are reaching the conclusion that cocaine use holds considerable, unpredictable risk.

The Roles of Development, Parents, and Peers in Adolescent Drug Abuse

Earlier, we discussed the statistics that place adolescents at risk for alcohol abuse. Researchers also have examined the factors that are related to drug use in adolescence, especially the roles of development, parents, peers, and schools.

Most adolescents become drug users at some point in their development, whether limited to alcohol, caffeine, and cigarettes, or extended to marijuana, cocaine, and hard drugs. A special concern involves adolescents using drugs as a way of coping with stress, which can interfere with the development of competent coping skills and responsible decision making. Researchers have found that drug use in childhood or early adolescence has more detrimental long-term effects on the development of responsible, competent behavior than when drug use occurs in late adolescence (Newcomb & Bentler, 1989). When they use drugs to cope with stress, young adolescents often enter adult roles of marriage and work prematurely, without adequate socioemotional growth, and experience greater failure in adult roles.

How early are adolescents beginning drug use? National samples of eighth- and ninth-grade students were included in the Institute for Social Research survey of drug use for the first time in 1991 (Johnston, O'Malley, & Bachman, 1992). Early on in the increase in drug use in the United States (late 1960s, early 1970s), drug use was much higher among college students than among high school students, who in turn had much higher rates of drug use than middle or junior high school students. However, today the rates for college and high school students are similar, and the rates for young adolescents are not as different from those for older adolescents as might be anticipated.

Parents, peers, and social support play important roles in preventing adolescent drug abuse (Cohen, Brook, & Kandel, 1991; Conger, Conger, & Simons, 1992; Dishion, 1992; Pentz, 1994; Tildesley & Duncan, 1994). A developmental model of adolescent drug abuse has been proposed by Judith Brook and her colleagues (Brook & Brook, in press; Brook & others, 1990). They believe that the initial step in adolescent drug abuse is laid down in the childhood years, when children fail to receive nurturance from their parents and grow up in conflict-ridden families. These children fail to internalize their parents' personality, attitudes, and behavior, and later carry this absence of parental ties into adolescence. Adolescent characteristics, such as lack of a conventional orientation and inability to control emotions, are then expressed in affiliations with peers who take drugs, which, in turn, leads to drug use. In recent studies, Brook and her colleagues have found support for their model (Brook & others, 1990).

Positive relationships with parents and others are important in reducing adolescents' drug use (Hughes, Power, & Francis, 1992; McMaster & Wintre, 1994). In one study, social support (which consisted of good relationships with parents, siblings, adults, and peers) during adolescence substantially reduced drug abuse (Newcomb & Bentler, 1988). In another study, adolescents were most likely to take drugs when both of their parents took drugs (such as tranquilizers, amphetamines, alcohol, or nicotine) and their peers took drugs (Kandel, 1974). To read about a successful school-based program designed to reduce adolescent substance abuse, turn to Perspectives on Parenting and Education 12.1.

Juvenile Delinquency

Arnie is 13 years old. His history includes a string of thefts and physical assaults. The first theft occurred when Arnie was 8; he stole a SONY walkman from an electronics store. The first physical assault took place a year later, when he shoved his 7-year-old brother up against the wall, bloodied his face, and then threatened to kill him with a butcher knife.

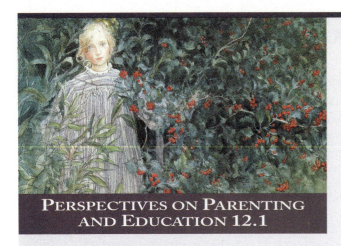

The Life Skills Training Program

Gilbert Botvin's Life Skills Training Program was selected as one of fourteen showcase programs by the American Psychological Association's Task Force on Promotion, Prevention, and Intervention Alternatives in Psychology (Price & others, 1988). Botvin's (1986) program was the only drug prevention/intervention program selected out of a field of 300 nominees.

According to Botvin, substance use is a socially learned, purposive, and functional behavior. His approach involves attempts to reduce pressure to smoke, to develop general personal competence, and to learn specific skills to resist peer pressure. The Life Skills Training curriculum consists of five main components:

1. Students are given information about the short-term and long-term consequences of substance abuse; biofeedback demonstrates the immediate effects of cigarette smoking.
2. Decision-making skills are taught to foster students' critical thinking. Counterarguments to advertising appeals are formulated.
3. Coping skills are taught so that students deal with stress more effectively.
4. Social skills training for resisting peer pressure is implemented. The training sessions include such topics as dealing with shyness, coping with dating, and assertiveness skills.
5. Self-improvement is emphasized by helping students to develop a positive self-image using learning principles.

The Life Skills Training Program consists of 20 sessions and is designed primarily for middle school and junior high school students. It is directed by a classroom teacher who uses a teacher's manual and receives one day of in-service training. Older peers (eleventh- and twelfth-graders) are also used as teachers after extensive training and on-site monitoring by the Life Skills Training staff.

Botvin has conducted a number of evaluations of the Life Skills Training Program and demonstrated that the program is effective in reducing cigarette smoking, alcohol use, and marijuana use. The greatest success has occurred when the sessions are led by older peers (Botvin, 1987).

Recently, the thefts and physical assaults have increased. In the last week, he stole a television set and struck his mother repeatedly and threatened to kill her. He also broke some neighborhood street lights and threatened some youths with a wrench and a hammer. Arnie's father left home when Arnie was 3 years old. Until the father left, his parents argued extensively and his father often beat up his mother. Arnie's mother indicates that when Arnie was younger, she was able to control his behavior; but in the last several years she has not been able to enforce any sanctions on his antisocial behavior. Because of Arnie's volatility and dangerous behavior, it was recommended that he be placed in a group home with other juvenile delinquents.

What Is Juvenile Delinquency?

The term **juvenile delinquency** *refers to a broad range of behaviors, from socially unacceptable behavior (such as acting out in school) to status offenses (such as running away) to criminal acts (such as burglary).* For legal purposes, a distinction is made between index offenses and status offenses. **Index offenses** *are criminal acts, whether they are committed by juveniles or adults. They include such acts as robbery, aggravated assault, rape, and homicide.* **Status offenses,** *such as running away, truancy, drinking under age, sexual promiscuity, and uncontrollability, are less serious acts. They are performed by youth under a specified age, which classifies*

them as juvenile offenses. States often differ in the age used to classify an individual as a juvenile or an adult. Approximately three-fourths of the states have established age 18 as a maximum for defining juveniles. Two states use age 19 as the cutoff, seven states use age 17, and four states use age 16. Thus, running away from home at age 17 may be an offense in some states but not in others.

What Are the Antecedents of Delinquency?

Predictors of delinquency include identity (negative identity), self-control (low degree), age (early initiation), sex (males), expectations for education (low expectations, little commitment), school grades (low achievement in early grades), peer influence (heavy influence, low resistance), socioeconomic status (low), parental role (lack of monitoring, low support, and ineffective discipline), and neighborhood quality (urban, high crime, high mobility). An overview of the antecedents of delinquency is presented in figure 12.6. Let's now look in greater detail at family processes and the role of socioeconomic status and neighborhood quality in delinquency.

Family Processes

There has been a long history of interest in defining the family factors that contribute to delinquency; the most recent focus has been on the nature of family support and family management

FIGURE 12.6

The antecedents of juvenile delinquency.

Antecedent	Association with delinquency	Description
Identity	Negative identity	Erikson believes delinquency occurs because the adolescent fails to resolve a role identity.
Self-control	Low degree	Some children and adolescents fail to acquire the essential controls that others have acquired during the process of growing up.
Age	Early initiation	Early appearance of antisocial behavior is associated with serious offenses later in adolescence. However, not every child who acts out becomes a delinquent.
Sex	Males	Boys engage in more antisocial behavior than girls do, although girls are more likely to run away. Boys engage in more violent acts.
Expectations for education and school grades	Low expectations and low grades	Adolescents who become delinquents often have low educational expectations and low grades. Their verbal abilities are often weak.
Parental influences	Monitoring (low), support (low), discipline (ineffective)	Delinquents often come from families in which parents rarely monitor their adolescents, provide them with little support, and ineffectively discipline them.
Peer influences	Heavy influence, low resistance	Having delinquent peers greatly increases the risk of becoming delinquent.
Socioeconomic status	Low	Serious offenses are committed more frequently by lower-class males.
Neighborhood quality	Urban, high crime, high mobility	Communities often breed crime. Living in a high-crime area, which also is characterized by poverty and dense living conditions, increases the probability that a child will become a delinquent. These communities often have grossly inadequate schools.

Adapted from *Adolescents at Risk: Prevalence and Prevention* by Joy G. Dryfoos. Copyright 1990 by Joy G. Dryfoos. Oxford University Press, Inc.

practices. Disruptions or omissions in the parents' applications of family support and management practices are consistently linked with antisocial behavior by children and adolescents (Novy & others, 1992). These family support and management practices include monitoring adolescents' whereabouts, using effective discipline for antisocial behavior, calling on effective problem-solving skills, and supporting the development of prosocial skills.

The parents of delinquents are less skilled in discouraging antisocial behavior than the parents of nondelinquents. Parental monitoring of adolescents is especially important in whether adolescents become delinquents. In one investigation, parental monitoring of adolescents' whereabouts was the most important family factor in predicting delinquency (Patterson & Stouthamer-Loeber, 1984). "It's 10 P.M., do you know where your children are?" seems to be an important question for parents to answer affirmatively. Family discord and inconsistent and inappropriate discipline also are associated with delinquency.

Social Class and Neighborhood Quality

Although juvenile delinquency is less exclusively a lower-class problem than it was in the past, some characteristics of the lower-class culture are likely to promote delinquency (Sampson & Laub, in press). The norms of many lower-class peer groups and gangs are antisocial, or counterproductive to the goals and norms of society at large. Getting into and staying out of trouble in some instances becomes a prominent feature of the lives of some adolescents from lower-class backgrounds. Status in the peer group may be gauged by how often the adolescent can engage in antisocial conduct yet manage to stay out of jail. Since lower-class adolescents have less opportunity to develop skills that are socially desirable, they may sense that they can gain attention and status by performing antisocial actions. Being "tough" and "masculine" are high-status traits for lower-class boys, and these traits often are gauged by adolescents' success in performing delinquent acts and getting away with them.

The nature of a community may contribute to delinquency (Chesney-Lind, 1989). In a community with a high crime rate, adolescents observe many models who engage in criminal activities and may be rewarded for their criminal accomplishments. Such communities often are characterized by poverty, unemployment, and feelings of alienation from the middle class. The quality of schools, funding for education, and organized neighborhood activities are other community factors that may be related to delinquency. Are there caring adults in the schools and neighborhood who can convince adolescents with delinquent tendencies that education is the best route to success? When family support becomes inadequate, then such community supports take on added importance in preventing delinquency.

A recent, special concern in low-income areas is escalating gang violence, which is being waged on a level more lethal than ever before. Knives and clubs have been replaced by grenades and automatic weapons, frequently purchased with money made from selling drugs. The lure of gang membership is powerful, especially for children and adolescents who are disconnected from family, school, work, and the community. Children as young as 9 to 10 years of age cling to the fringes of neighborhood gangs, eager to prove themselves worthy of membership by the age of 12. Once children are members of a gang, it is difficult to get them to leave. Recommendations for preventing gang violence include identifying disconnected children in elementary schools and initiating counseling with the children and their families.

Prevention and Intervention

Brief descriptions of the varied attempts to reduce delinquency would fill a large book. These attempts include forms of individual and group psychotherapy, family therapy, behavior modification, recreation, vocational training, alternative schools, survival camping and wilderness canoeing, incarceration and probation, "Big Brothers" and "Big Sisters," community organizations, and Bible reading (Gold & Petronio, 1980). However, surprisingly little is known about what actually does help to reduce delinquency, and in many instances, prevention and intervention have not been successful.

While few successful models of delinquency prevention and intervention have been identified, many experts on delinquency agree that the following points deserve closer examination as prevention and intervention possibilities (Dryfoos, 1990):

1. Programs should be broader than just focusing on delinquency. For example, it is virtually impossible to improve delinquency prevention without considering the quality of education available to high-risk youth. One successful program designed to curb delinquency is described in Sociocultural Worlds of Development 12.2.

2. Programs should have multiple components, because no one component has been found to be the "magic bullet" that decreases delinquency.

3. Programs should begin early in the child's development to prevent learning and conduct problems.

4. Schools play an important role. Schools with strong governance, fair discipline policies, student participation in decision making, and high investment in school outcomes by both students and staff have a better chance of curbing delinquency.

5. Efforts should often be directed at institutional rather than individual change. Especially important is upgrading the quality of education for disadvantaged children.

6. While point 5 is accurate, researchers have found that intensive individual attention and personalized planning also are important factors in working with children at high risk for becoming delinquent.

7. Program benefits often "wash out" after the program stops. Thus, maintenance programs and continued effort are usually necessary.

In her review of delinquency prevention, Joy Dryfoos (1990) also outlined what has *not* worked in preventing delinquency. Ineffective attempts include preventive casework, group counseling, pharmacological interventions (except for extremely violent behavior), work experience, vocational education, "scaring straight" efforts, and the juvenile justice system. Current school practices that are ineffective in reducing delinquency include suspension, detention, expulsion, security guards, and corporal punishment.

Adolescent Pregnancy

Angela is 15 years old and pregnant. She reflects, "I'm 3 months pregnant. This could ruin my whole life. I've made all of these plans for the future and now they are down the drain. I don't have anybody to talk to about my problem. I can't talk to my parents. There is no way they can understand." Pregnant adolescents were once practically invisible and unmentionable, but yesterday's secret has become today's national dilemma.

They are of different ethnic groups and from different places, but their circumstances have a distressing sameness. Each year more than 1 million American teenagers become pregnant, 4 out of 5 of them unmarried. Like Angela, many become pregnant in their early or middle adolescent years, 30,000 of them under the age of 15. In all, this means that 1 of every 10 adolescent females in the United States becomes pregnant each year, with 8 of the 10 pregnancies being unintended. As one 17-year-old Los Angeles mother of a 1-year-old boy said, "We are children having children." The only bright spot in the adolescent pregnancy statistics is that the adolescent pregnancy rate, after increasing during the 1970s, has leveled off and may even be beginning to decline.

The adolescent pregnancy rate in the United States is the highest of any in the Western world. It is more than twice the rate in England, France, or Canada; almost three times the rate

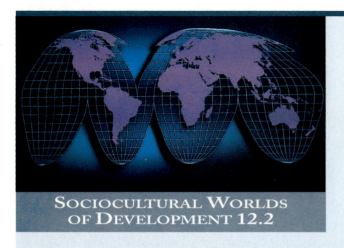

SOCIOCULTURAL WORLDS OF DEVELOPMENT 12.2

The Midnight Basketball League

The dark side of peer relations is nowhere more present than in the increasing number of youth gangs. Beginning in 1990, the Chicago Housing Authority began offering young gang members an alternative to crime—the Midnight Basketball League (MBL) (Simons, Finlay, & Yang, 1991). Most crimes were being committed between 10 P.M. and 2 A.M. by males in their late teens and early twenties. The MBL offers these males a positive diversion during the time they are most likely to get into trouble. There are eight teams in the housing projects and

160 players in all. The year-round program provides top-quality basketball shoes, uniforms, championship rings, all-star games, and award banquets.

Attitude is considered more important than ability, so most teams consist of one or two stars and eight or nine enthusiastic, mediocre to poor players. Different gang factions are represented on each team.

Basketball, however, is only one component of the MBL. To stay in the league, players must follow rules that prohibit fighting, unsportsmanlike behavior, profanity, drugs, alcohol, radios, and tape players. If they break the rules, they don't play basketball. Practices are mandatory, and so are workshops after each game. During the workshops, youth are encouraged to seek drug abuse counseling, vocational counseling and training, life skills advising, basic health care, adult education and GED services, and various social services. The program is funded by the Chicago Housing Authority and private donations.

In a recent year, not one of the MBL players had been in trouble, and 54 of the 160 participants registered for adult education classes once the season had ended. The program has been replicated in Hartford, CT, Louisville, KY, and Washington, DC. For more information about the MBL, contact Gil Walker, MBL Commissioner, Chicago Housing Authority, 534 East 37th Street, Chicago, IL 60653, 312–791–4768.

The Midnight Basketball League (MBL) was created in a high-crime neighborhood of Chicago to help combat the participation of youth in gangs. The comprehensive program includes not only a well-organized basketball league, but also a number of workshops to improve the high-risk youths' life skills and educational orientation. Gil Walker, MBL commissioner and organizer, is on the first row, far left.

in Sweden; and seven times the rate in the Netherlands (Alan Guttmacher Institute, 1990). Although American adolescents are no more sexually active than their counterparts in these other nations, they are many times more likely to become pregnant.

Adolescent pregnancy is a complex American problem, one that strikes many nerves. The subject of adolescent pregnancy touches on many explosive social issues: the battle over abortion rights, contraceptives and the delicate question of whether adolescents should have easy access to them, and the perennially touchy subject of sex education in the public schools (Hofferth, 1990; Stevens-Simon & McAnarney, 1992).

Dramatic changes involving sexual attitudes and social morals have swept through American culture in the last three decades. Adolescents actually gave birth at a higher rate in 1957 than they do today, but that was a time of early marriage, when almost 25 percent of 18- and 19-year-olds were married. The overwhelming majority of births to adolescent mothers in the 1950s occurred within a marriage and mainly involved females 17 years of age and older. Two or three decades ago, if an unwed adolescent girl became pregnant, in most instances her parents swiftly married her off in a shotgun wedding. If marriage was impractical, the girl would discreetly disappear, the child would be put up for adoption, and the predicament would never be discussed again. Abortion was not an option for most adolescent females until 1973, when the Supreme Court ruled it could not be outlawed.

In today's world of adolescent pregnancies, a different scenario unfolds. If the girl does not choose to have an abortion (45 percent of pregnant adolescent girls do), she usually keeps the baby and raises it without the traditional involvement of marriage. With the stigma of illegitimacy largely absent, girls are less likely to give up their babies for adoption. Fewer than 5 percent do, compared with about 35 percent in the early 1960s. However, although the stigma of illegitimacy has waned, the lives of most pregnant teenagers are anything but rosy.

The consequences of our nation's high adolescent pregnancy rate are of great concern (Dean, 1993; Jorgensen, 1993). Pregnancy in adolescence increases the health risks of both the child and the mother. Infants born to adolescent mothers are more likely to have low birthweights (a prominent cause of infant mortality), as well as neurological problems and childhood illnesses (Furstenberg, Brooks-Gunn, & Chase-Lansdale, 1989). Adolescent mothers often drop out of school, fail to gain employment, and become dependent on welfare. Although many adolescent mothers resume their education later in life, they generally do not catch up with women who postpone childbearing. In the National Longitudinal Survey of Work Experience of Youth, it was found that only half of the women 20 to 26 years old who first gave birth at age 17 had completed high school by their twenties. The percentage was even lower for those who gave birth at a younger age (Mott & Marsiglio, 1985). By contrast, among females who waited until age 20 to have a baby, more than 90 percent had obtained a high school education. Among the younger adolescent mothers, almost half had obtained a general equivalency diploma (GED), which does not often open up good employment opportunities.

These educational deficits have negative consequences for the young women themselves and for their children (Scott-Jones & White, 1990). Adolescent parents are more likely than those who delay childbearing to have low-paying, low-status jobs or to be umemployed. The mean family income of White females who give birth before age 17 is approximately half that of families in which the mother delays birth until her mid- or late twenties.

Serious, extensive efforts need to be developed to help pregnant adolescents and young mothers enhance their educational and occupational opportunities. Adolescent mothers also need extensive help in obtaining competent day care and in planning for the future (Barnet & others, 1992; Furstenberg, 1991). Experts recommend that, to reduce the high rate of teen pregnancy, adolescents need improved sex-education and family-planning information, greater access to contraception, and broad community involvement and support (Conger, 1988; Crockett & Chopak, 1993; Potthof, 1992; Treboux & Busch-Rossnagel, 1991). Another very important consideration, especially for young adolescents, is abstention, which is increasingly being included as a theme in sex-education classes.

Critical Thinking

You have been assigned to design a community program to reduce the rate of adolescent pregnancy in your community. What would the program be like?

In Holland and Sweden, as well as in other European countries, sex does not carry the mystery and conflict it does in American society. Holland does not have a mandated sex-education program, but adolescents can obtain contraceptive counseling at government-sponsored clinics for a small fee. The Dutch media also have played an important role in educating the public about sex through frequent broadcasts focused on birth control, abortion, and related matters. Most Dutch adolescents do not consider having sex without birth control.

Swedish adolescents are sexually active at an earlier age than American adolescents, and they are exposed to even more explicit sex on television. However, the Swedish National Board of Education has developed a curriculum that ensures that every child in the country, beginning at age 7, will experience a thorough grounding in reproductive biology and, by the ages of 10 or 12, will have been introduced to information about various forms of contraceptives. Teachers are expected to handle the subject of sex whenever it becomes relevant, regardless of the subject they are teaching. The idea is to dedramatize and demystify sex so that familiarity will make individuals less vulnerable to unwanted pregnancy and sexually transmitted diseases (Wallis, 1985). American society is not nearly so open about sex education.

Suicide

Suicide is a common problem in our society. Its rate has tripled in the past 30 years in the United States; each year, about 25,000 people take their own lives. Beginning at about the age of 15, the rate of suicide begins to rise rapidly. Suicide accounts for about 12 percent of the mortality in the adolescent and young adult age group (Brent, 1989). Males are about three times as likely to commit suicide as females; this may be because of their more active methods for attempting suicide—shooting, for example. By contrast, females are more likely to use passive

Our society has not handled adolescent sex very effectively. We tell adolescents that sex is fun, harmless, adult, and forbidden. Adolescents 13 years old going on 21 want to try out new things and take risks. They see themselves as unique and indestructible—pregnancy couldn't happen to them, they think. Add to this the adolescent's increasing need for love and commitment, and the result all too often is social dynamite.

TABLE 12.1

What to Do and What Not to Do When You Suspect Someone Is Likely to Commit Suicide

What to Do

1. Ask direct, straightforward questions in a calm manner: "Are you thinking about hurting yourself?"
2. Assess the seriousness of the suicidal intent by asking questions about feelings, important relationships, who else the person has talked with, and the amount of thought given to the means to be used. If a gun, pills, rope, or other means has been obtained and a precise plan developed, clearly the situation is dangerous. Stay with the person until help arrives.
3. Be a good listener and be very supportive without being falsely reassuring.
4. Try to persuade the person to obtain professional help and assist him or her in getting this help.

What Not to Do

1. Do not ignore the warning signs.
2. Do not refuse to talk about suicide if a person approaches you about it.
3. Do not react with horror, disapproval, or repulsion.
4. Do not give false reassurances by saying such things as "Everything is going to be OK." Also do not give out simple answers or platitudes, such as "You have everything to be thankful for."
5. Do not abandon the individual after the crisis has passed or after professional help has commenced.

From *Living with 10- to 15-Year-Olds: A Parent Education Curriculum* edited by Robin Pulver, second edition, 1992. Center for Early Adolescence, University of North Carolina at Chapel Hill, D-2 Carr Mill Town Center, Carrboro, NC. Reprinted by permission.

methods, such as sleeping pills, which are less likely to produce death. Although males commit suicide more frequently, females attempt it more frequently (Maltsberger, 1988).

Estimates indicate that, for every successful suicide in the general population, 6 to 10 attempts are made. For adolescents, the figure is as high as 50 attempts for every life taken. As many as two in every three college students has thought about suicide on at least one occasion; their methods range from overdosing on drugs to crashing into the White House in an airplane.

Why do adolescents attempt suicide? There is no simple answer to this important question (Cole, 1991). It is helpful to think of suicide in terms of proximal and distal factors. Proximal, or immediate, factors can trigger a suicide attempt. Highly stressful circumstances, such as the loss of a boyfriend or girlfriend, poor grades at school, or an unwanted pregnancy, can trigger a suicide attempt. Drugs also have been involved more often in recent suicide attempts than in attempts in the past (Rich, Young, & Fowler, 1986; Wagner, Cole, & Schwartzman, 1993).

Distal, or earlier, experiences often are involved in suicide attempts as well (Reinherz & others, 1994). A long-standing history of family instability and unhappiness may be present (Hodgmann, 1992; Tishler, 1992). Just as a lack of affection and emotional support, high control, and pressure for achievement by parents during childhood are related to adolescent depression, so are such combinations of family experiences likely to show up as distal factors in suicide attempts. Lack of supportive friendships also may be present (Rubenstein & others, 1989). In an investigation of suicide among gifted women, previous suicide attempts, anxiety, conspicuous instability in work and in relationships, depression, or alcoholism also were present in the women's lives (Tomlinson-Keasey, Warren, & Elliott, 1986). These factors are similar to those found to predict suicide among gifted men (Shneidman, 1971).

Just as genetic factors are associated with depression, so are they associated with suicide. The closer the genetic relationship a person has to someone who has committed suicide, the more likely that person is to commit suicide (Wender & others, 1986). Table 12.1 provides valuable information about what to do and what not to do when you suspect someone is contemplating suicide.

Eating Disorders

Fifteen-year-old Jane gradually eliminated foods from her diet to the point where she subsisted by eating *only* applesauce and eggnog. She spent hours observing her own body, wrapping her fingers around her waist to see if it was getting any thinner. She fantasized about becoming a beautiful fashion model who would wear designer bathing suits. Even when she reached 85 pounds, Jane still felt fat. She continued to lose weight, eventually emaciating herself. She was hospitalized and treated for **anorexia nervosa,** *an eating disorder that involves the relentless pursuit of thinness through starvation.* Eventually, anorexia nervosa can lead to death, as it did for popular singer Karen Carpenter.

Anorexia nervosa afflicts primarily females during adolescence and early adulthood (only about 5 percent of anorexics are male). Most individuals with this disorder are White and from well-educated, middle- and upper-income families. Although anorexics avoid eating, they have an intense interest in food; they cook for others, they talk about food, and they insist on watching others eat. Anorexics have a distorted body image, perceiving that they will look better even if they become skeletal. As self-starvation continues and the fat content of the body drops to a bare minimum, menstruation usually stops and behavior often becomes hyperactive (Polivy & Thomsen, 1987).

Numerous causes of anorexia nervosa have been proposed. They include societal, psychological, and physiological factors (Brooks-Gunn, 1993; Hepworth, 1994; Striegel-Moore & others, 1993). The societal factor most often held responsible is the current fashion of thinness. Psychological factors include a motivation for attention, a desire for individuality, a denial of sexuality, and a way of coping with overcontrolling parents. Anorexics sometimes have families that place high demands for achievement on them. Unable to meet their parents' high standards, anorexics feel unable to control their own lives. By limiting their food intake, anorexics gain a sense of self-control. Physiological causes focus on the hypothalamus, which becomes abnormal in a number of ways when an individual becomes anorexic. At this time, however, we are not exactly certain what causes anorexia nervosa.

Bulimia *is an eating disorder that involves a binge-and-purge sequence on a regular basis.* Bulimics binge on large amounts of food and then purge by self-induced vomiting or the use of a laxative. The binges sometimes alternate with fasting; at other times, they alternate with normal eating behavior. Like anorexia nervosa, bulimia is primarily a female disorder, and it has become prevalent among college women. Some estimates suggest that one in two college women binge and purge at least some of the time. However, recent estimates suggest that true bulimics—those who binge and purge on a regular basis—make up less than 2 percent of the college female population (Stunkard, 1987). Whereas anorexics can control their eating, bulimics cannot. Depression is a common characteristic of bulimics (Levy, Dixon, & Stern, 1989). Many of the same causes proposed for anorexia nervosa are offered for bulimia.

So far we have discussed a number of specific problems and disorders in adolescence. As we will soon see, many adolescents do not experience a single problem, but rather their problems are often interrelated.

Anorexia nervosa is an eating disorder that has appeared in an increasing number of adolescent females.

THE CURRENT STATUS OF ADOLESCENTS AND AT-RISK YOUTH

What is the current status of adolescents in the United States? Do adults have idealized images of adolescents, and does society communicate ambivalent messages to adolescents? Which youth are at risk? We consider each of these questions in turn.

LIFE-SPAN PRACTICAL KNOWLEDGE 12.2

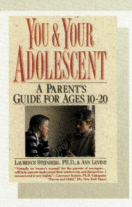

You and Your Adolescent
(1990) by Laurence Steinberg and Ann Levine. New York: Harper Perennial.

You and Your Adolescent provides a broad, developmental overview of adolescence with parental advice mixed in along the way. Author Laurence Steinberg is a professor of psychology at Temple University and a highly respected researcher in ado-

lescent development. The book is divided into the preteens (ages 10–13), the teens (14–17), and near adulthood (18–20). This is an excellent book for parents of adolescents. It educates parents about how adolescents develop (knowledge that, in the authors' view, will keep parents from making a lot of mistakes) and gives them valuable parenting strategies for coping with teenagers.

The Current Status of Adolescents

Today's adolescents face demands and expectations, as well as risks and temptations, that appear to be more numerous and complex than did adolescents only a generation ago (Feldman & Elliott, 1990; Hamburg, 1993; Hechinger, 1992). Nonetheless, contrary to the popular stereotype of adolescents as highly stressed and incompetent, the vast majority of adolescents successfully negotiate the path from childhood to adulthood (Offer & Church, 1991). By some criteria, today's adolescents are doing better than their counterparts from a decade or two earlier. Today, more adolescents complete high school, especially Black American adolescents. In the last few years, accidents and homicides have declined somewhat, as have drug use, juvenile delinquency, and adolescent pregnancy rates. The majority of adolescents today have positive self-conceptions and have positive relationships with others. Such contemporary findings do not reveal a portrayal of adolescence as a highly disturbed, overly stressful time period in the life cycle. Rather, the majority of adolescents find the transition from childhood to adulthood to be a time of physical, cognitive, and social development that provides considerable challenge, opportunities, and growth (Santrock, 1993; Takanishi, 1993).

Even though most adolescents experience the transition from childhood to adulthood more positively than is portrayed by many adults and the media, too many adolescents today are not provided with adequate opportunities and support to become competent adults (Lerner, Entwisle, & Hauser, 1994). In many ways, today's adolescents are presented with a less stable environment than adolescents of a decade or two ago were. High divorce rates, high adolescent pregnancy rates, and increased geographic mobility of families contribute to this lack of stability in adolescents' lives. Today's adolescents are exposed to a complex menu of life-style options through the media. And while the adolescent

drug use rate is beginning to show signs of decline, the rate of adolescent drug use in the United States is the highest of any country in the industrialized Western world. Many of today's adolescents face the temptations of drugs, as well as sexual activity, at increasingly young ages.

The above discussion underscores an important point about adolescents: They are not a homogeneous group of individuals. The majority of adolescents negotiate the lengthy path to adult maturity successfully, but too large a minority do not. Ethnic, cultural, gender, socioeconomic, age, and life-style differences influence the actual life trajectory of each adolescent.

Different portrayals of adolescence often emerge, depending on the particular group of adolescents being described. As we see next, some of the problems faced by today's adolescents involve adults' idealized images of what adolescence should be and society's ambivalent messages to adolescents.

Idealized Images of Adolescence and Society's Ambivalent Messages to Adolescents

Adolescent developmental researchers Shirley Feldman and Glenn Elliott (1990) recently described how our society seems to be uncertain about what adolescence should be or should not be. The following examples illustrate how adults' idealized images of adolescence and society's ambivalent messages to adolescents may contribute to adolescent problems:

- Many adults treasure the independence of youth, yet insist that adolescents do not have the maturity to make autonomous, competent decisions about their lives. Some of the ambiguity in messages about adult status and

LIFE-SPAN PRACTICAL KNOWLEDGE 12.3

All Grown Up and No Place To Go: Teenagers in Crisis

(1991) by David Elkind. Reading, MA: Addison-Wesley.

Elkind believes that raising teenagers in today's world is more difficult than ever. He argues that teenagers are expected to confront adult challenges too early in their development. By being pressured into adult roles too soon, today's youth are all grown up with no place to go, hence the title of the book. Elkind believes that the main reason teenagers are pressed into adult roles too early is that parents are more committed to their own self-fulfillment than to their adolescents'. These parents of the "me" generation are often too quick to accept their teenagers' outward sophistication as a sign of emotional maturity. Teens' emotional needs are also neglected by a school system that is up-to-date in computer gadgetry but bankrupt in responding to adolescents' emotional needs and individual differences, says Elkind. He also believes that the media exploit adolescents by appealing to their vulnerability to peer pressure.

maturity that society communicates to adolescents appears in the form of laws dictating that they cannot drive until they are 16, vote until they are 18, or drink until age 21, yet in some states, 14-year-olds now have the legal right to choose the parent with whom they want to live after a parental divorce and to override parental wishes about such medical matters as abortion and psychiatric care.

- Society's sexual messages to adolescents are especially ambiguous. Adolescents are somehow supposed to be sexually naive but become sexually knowledgeable. The message to many adolescents is this: You can experiment with sex and "sow your wild oats," but be sure to maintain high standards of maturity and safety. Adolescents must negotiate this formidable task in a society that cannot agree on how much and what kind of explicit sex education adolescents should be given. This same society sanctions alluring messages about the power and attractiveness of sexuality in the media.

- Laws prohibit adolescents from using alcohol, tobacco, or other drugs, and adults decry the high level of drug use by adolescents. Yet many of the very same adults who stereotype and criticize adolescents for their drug use are themselves drug abusers and heavy cigarette smokers.

- Society promotes education and the development of knowledge as essential to success as an adult. Yet adolescents frequently observe the rewards society doles out to individuals who develop their athletic skills and business acumen (White, 1993). As adolescents interact with adults who do not value the process of learning, adolescents may attach more importance to simply attaining a diploma than to the process of getting one.

At-Risk Youth

While adolescence is best viewed as a time of decision making and commitment rather than a time of crisis and pathology, a large subset of adolescents are at risk because their likelihood of becoming productive adults is limited. Four areas of special concern that make up a large portion of at-risk youth are delinquency, substance abuse, adolescent pregnancy, and school-related problems (Dryfoos, 1990, 1993). Earlier in the chapter, we considered each of these problems separately. However, there is a growing awareness that these high-risk behaviors often overlap, with many adolescents showing problems in more than one area (Scales, 1992). No actual data exist to quantify at-risk status of youth, but experts on adolescence estimate that *very high-risk youth*—those with multiple problem behaviors—make up about 5 to 10 percent of the adolescent population (Dryfoos, 1990, 1993). This group includes adolescents who have been arrested or have committed serious offenses, have dropped out of school or are behind their grade level, are users of "heavy" drugs, drink frequently, regularly use cigarettes and marijuana, and are sexually active but do not use contraception. Many but not all very high-risk youth "do it all."

High-risk youth include another 10 to 15 percent of the youth population. They participate in these same behaviors with a lower frequency and less deleterious consequences. They commit less-serious delinquent offenses; however, they are heavy users of alcohol, cigarettes, and marijuana; they engage in unprotected sexual intercourse; and they are behind in school. This group often engages in two or three problem behaviors. Overall, 2 to 3 million adolescents are at very high risk, while 3 to 4 million are at high risk (Dryfoos, 1990). Very-high-risk and high-risk adolescents are more often males than females, live in cities rather than suburban or rural areas, and often come from families that are poor and have low education levels.

In an analysis of successful programs focused on at-risk youth, conducted for the Carnegie Foundation, Joy Dryfoos (1990, 1993) found that two approaches had the widest application: providing individual attention to at-risk children and adolescents, and developing broad community-wide interventions. In successful programs, at-risk youth are attached to a responsible adult who pays attention to the adolescent's specific needs. For example, in substance abuse programs, a student assistance counselor might be available full-time for individual counseling. In delinquency prevention, a family worker might give "intensive" support to a predelinquent and the family so they will make the necessary changes to avoid repeated delinquent acts. In pregnancy prevention, a full-time social worker might be placed in the school system for individual counseling. In school remediation, a prevention specialist might work with at-risk adolescents and their families to improve school attendance.

The basic concept of community-wide programs is that, to improve the lives of at-risk youth, a number of programs and services need to be in place (Dryfoos, 1992). For example, a substance abuse program might involve a community-wide health promotion that uses local media and community education in conjunction with a substance abuse prevention curriculum in the schools. A delinquency program might consist of a neighborhood development program that includes local residents in neighborhood councils who work with schools, police, courts, gang leaders, and the media. A pregnancy prevention program might concentrate on community education through media and a speaker's bureau; training of parents, clergy, and other community leaders; and developing and implementing a comprehensive sex and family life education program in the schools. The problem of dropping out of school might be addressed by an all-out community effort involving schools and local businesses, local government agencies, and universities in planning, teacher training, and student training and job placement.

As the twenty-first century approaches, the well-being of adolescents should be one of America's foremost concerns. We all cherish the future of our youth, because they are the future of any society. Adolescents who do not reach their full potential, who are destined to make fewer contributions to society than it needs, and who do not take their place as productive adults diminish the power of that society's future (Horowitz & O'Brien, 1989).

At this point we have discussed a number of ideas about schools, problems and disturbances, and the current status of adolescents and at-risk youth. A summary of these ideas is presented in concept table 12.2.

CONCLUSIONS

After the slow growth of childhood, the rapid maturational changes of puberty arrive. And so do some impressive cognitive changes.

We began this chapter by considering puberty's mysteries and curiosities, then explored the transition to adolescence, pubertal change, and psychological accompaniments of pubertal change, with a special focus on early and late maturation. Our coverage of cognitive developmental changes involved formal operational thought, social cognition, especially adolescent egocentrism, and decision

making. Then we studied schools for adolescents, examining the controversy surrounding secondary schools, the transition to middle or junior high school, effective schools for young adolescents, and high school dropouts. We evaluated a number of problems and disorders in adolescents, including drug and alcohol abuse, delinquency, adolescent pregnancy, suicide, and eating disorders. We also considered the current status of adolescents and at-risk adolescents. At different points in the chapter we also examined secondary schools in different

countries, the life skills training program for reducing adolescent substance abuse, and guidelines for seeking therapy when an adolescent shows problem behavior.

Don't forget that you can obtain an overall summary of the chapter by again reading the two concept tables on pages 355 and 372. In the next chapter, we continue our discussion of adolescence, focusing on socioemotional development.

CONCEPT TABLE 12.2

*Schools, Problems and Disorders, and the Current Status
of Today's Adolescents and At–Risk Youth*

Concept	Processes/Related Ideas	Characteristics/Description
Schools	Function of schools	In the nineteenth century, secondary schools were for the elite. By the 1920s, they had changed, becoming more comprehensive and training adolescents for work and citizenship, as well as improving their intellect. The comprehensive high school remains today, but the function of secondary schools continues to be debated. Some maintain that the function should be intellectual development; others argue for more comprehensive functions.
	Transition to middle or junior high school	The emergence of junior high schools in the 1920s and 1930s was justified on the basis of physical, cognitive, and social changes in early adolescence and the need for more schools in response to a growing student population. Middle schools have become more popular in recent years, coinciding with puberty's earlier arrival. The transition to middle or junior high school coincides with many social, familial, and individual changes in the adolescent's life. The transition involves moving from the top-dog to the bottom-dog position. Successful schools for young adolescents take individual differences in development seriously, show a deep concern for what is known about early adolescence, and emphasize social and emotional development as much as intellectual development.
	High school dropouts	Dropping out has been a serious problem for decades. Many dropouts have educational deficiencies that curtail their economic and social well-being for much of their adult lives. Some progress has been made; dropout rates for most ethnic minority groups have declined in recent decades, although dropout rates for inner-city, low-income minorities are still precariously high. Students drop out of school for school-related, economic, and personal reasons. To reduce the dropout rate, community institutions, especially schools, need to break down the barriers between work and school.
Problems and disorders	Drugs and alcohol	The United States has the highest adolescent drug use rate of any industrialized nation. The 1960s and 1970s were a time of marked increase in adolescent drug use. Since the mid-1980s there has been a slight overall downturn in drug use among adolescents but in the early 1990s a slight upturn in use has been documented. Alcohol is the drug most widely used by adolescents; alcohol abuse by adolescents is a major problem. Heavy drinking is common. Cocaine is a highly controversial drug. Its use by high school seniors dropped off for the first time in 8 years in 1987, a trend that has continued. Development, parents, peers, and schools play important roles in adolescent drug use.

Concept	Processes/Related Ideas	Characteristics/Description
	Juvenile delinquency	Juvenile delinquency refers to a broad range of behaviors, from socially unacceptable behavior to status offenses to criminal acts. For legal purposes, a distinction is made between index offenses (criminal acts, whether committed by juveniles or by adults) and status offenses (performed by youth under a certain age). Predictors of delinquency include a negative identity, a low degree of self-control, early initiation of delinquency, being a male, low expectations for education and little commitment to education, heavy peer influence and low resistance to peer pressure, failure of parents to adequately monitor their adolescents, ineffective discipline by parents, and living in an urban, high-crime, mobile neighborhood. Successful programs do not focus on delinquency alone (rather, they include other components, such as education), have multiple components (but no one component is a "magic bullet"), begin early in the child's development, often involve schools, focus on institutions while also giving individualized attention to delinquents, and include maintenance.
	Suicide	The rate of suicide has increased. Beginning at about the age of 15, the rate of suicide increases dramatically. Both proximal and distal factors are involved in suicide's causes.
	Eating disorders	Anorexia nervosa and bulimia have increasingly become problems for adolescent females. Societal, psychological, and physiological causes of these disorders have been proposed.
The current status of adolescents and at-risk youth	The current status of adolescents	The majority of adolescents today successfully negotiate the path from childhood to adulthood. By some criteria, today's adolescents are also doing better than their counterparts from a decade or two earlier. However, too many of today's adolescents are not provided with adequate opportunities and support to become competent adults. In many ways, today's adolescents are presented with a less stable environment than a decade or two ago. It is important to view adolescents as a heterogeneous group because a different portrayal emerges depending on the particular set of adolescents being described.
	Idealized images of adolescence and society's ambivalent messages to adolescents	Our society seems to be uncertain about what adolescence should be or should not be. There are many areas, such as independence, sexuality, laws and values, and education, in which adults entertain idealized images of adolescents but communicate ambivalent messages to adolescents that may contribute to adolescents' problems.
	At-risk youth	There is a growing awareness that high-risk behaviors in adolescence often overlap with four areas of special concern: delinquency, substance abuse, adolescent pregnancy, and school-related problems. From 15 to 25 percent of adolescents are at risk because their likelihood of becoming productive adults is limited. Two approaches have the widest application to improving the lives of at-risk youth: providing individual attention to at-risk children and adolescents and developing broad community-wide interventions.

LIFE-SPAN HEALTH AND WELL-BEING

Some Guidelines for Seeking Therapy When an Adolescent Shows Problem Behaviors

Determining whether an adolescent needs professional help when she or he engages in problem behaviors is not an easy task. Adolescents, by nature, tend to have mercurial moods and engage in behaviors that are distasteful to adults and run counter to their values. In many cases, though, such behaviors are only part of the adolescent's search for identity, are normal, and do not require professional help. Too often when an adolescent first shows a problem behavior, such as drinking or stealing, parents panic and fear that their adolescent is going to turn into a drug addict or a hardened criminal. Such fears are usually not warranted—virtually every adolescent drinks alcohol at some point in their transition from childhood to adulthood, and, likewise, virtually every adolescent engages in at least one or more acts of juvenile delinquency. By overreacting to such initial occurrences of adolescent problem behaviors, parents can exacerbate their relationship with the adolescent and thereby contribute to increased parent-adolescent conflict.

What are the circumstances under which parents should seek professional help for their adolescent's problems? Laurence Steinberg and Ann Levine (1990) developed five guidelines for determining when to get professional help if an adolescent is showing problem behaviors:

- If the adolescent is showing severe problem behaviors, such as depression, anorexia nervosa, drug addiction, repeated delinquent acts, or serious school-related problems, parents should not try to treat these problems alone and probably should seek professional help for the adolescent.

Among the times when parents might think about seeking professional help for their adolescent are when the adolescent engages in frequent truancy, chronic running away, or repeated, hostile opposition to authorities. Family therapy (shown here), in which the adolescent as well as other family members, especially one or both parents, participate, is often recommended in such circumstances.

- If the adolescent has a problem, but the parents do not know what the problem is, they may want to seek professional help for the adolescent. An example is an adolescent who is socially withdrawn and doesn't have many friends, which could be due to extreme shyness, depression, stress at school, drug involvement, or any of a number of other reasons. If parents do not know what the adolescent's problem is, how can they help the adolescent? Professionals can often make specific diagnoses and provide recommendations for helping the adolescent.

- If parents have tried to solve the adolescent's problem but have not been successful and the problem continues to disrupt the adolescent's life, then parents may wish to seek professional help for the adolescent. Frequent truancy, chronic running

away, or repeated, hostile opposition to authority are examples of such problems.

- If parents realize they are part of the adolescent's problem, they may wish to seek professional help for the family. Constant, intense, bitter fighting that disrupts the everyday living of the family is a good example. Rarely is one individual the single cause of extensive family dissension. A therapist can objectively analyze the family's problems and help the family members to see why they are fighting so much and to find ways to reduce the fighting.

- When the family is under extensive stress (from the death of a family member or a divorce, for example) and the adolescent is not coping well (for example, becomes depressed or drinks a lot), professional help may be needed. ■

KEY TERMS

menarche A girl's first menstruation. (349)

puberty A period of rapid skeletal and sexual maturation that occurs mainly in early adolescence. (349)

testosterone Hormone is associated with the development of genitals, an increase in height, and a change of voice in boys. (349)

estradiol Hormone is associated with breast, uterine, and skeletal development in girls. (349)

hypothetical-deductive reasoning According to Piaget's formal operational concept, adolescents have the cognitive ability to develop hypotheses, or best guesses, about ways to solve problems, such as an algebraic equation. They then systematically deduce, or conclude, which is the best path for solving the problem. (352)

adolescent egocentrism David Elkind believes that adolescent egocentrism has two parts: an imaginary audience and a personal fable. (353)

imaginary audience According to Elkind, adolescents believe that others are as preoccupied with them as they are with themselves. (353)

personal fable According to Elkind, the adolescent's egocentrism involves a sense of uniqueness so that others cannot truly understand how she or he feels. (353)

top-dog phenomenon Includes the circumstance of moving from the top position (in elementary school, being the oldest, biggest, and most powerful students in the school) to the lowest position (in middle or junior high school, being the youngest, smallest, and least powerful students in the school). (358)

juvenile delinquency Refers to a broad range of behaviors, from socially unacceptable behavior (such as acting out in school) to status offenses (such as running away) to criminal offenses (such as burglary). (362)

index offenses Criminal acts, whether committed by juveniles or by adults. They include robbery, aggravated assault, rape, and homicide. (362)

status offenses Juvenile offenses such as running away, truancy, underage drinking, sexual promiscuity, and uncontrollability. They are less serious than index offenses. (362)

anorexia nervosa Eating disorder that involves the relentless pursuit of thinness through starvation. (368)

bulimia Eating disorder that involves a binge-and-purge sequence on a regular basis. (368)

Vincent van Gogh,
Camille Roulin,
Artes, detail.

13

Socioemotional Development
in Adolescence

*Youth is the time to go flashing from one
end of the world to the other, both in
mind and body.*

—Robert L. Stevenson

> *"Who are you?" said the caterpillar. Alice replied rather shyly, "I—I hardly know, sir, just at present—at least I know who I was when I got up this morning, but I must have changed several times since then."*
>
> —Lewis Carroll, *Alice in Wonderland*, 1865

IMAGES OF LIFE-SPAN DEVELOPMENT

A 15-Year-Old Girl's Self-Description

How do adolescents describe themselves? How would you have described yourself when you were 15 years old? What features would you have emphasized? The following is a self-portrait of one 15-year-old girl:

> What am I like as a person? Complicated! I'm sensitive, friendly, outgoing, popular, and tolerant, though I can also be shy, self-conscious, and even obnoxious. Obnoxious! I'd *like* to be friendly and tolerant all of the time. That's the kind of person I *want* to be, and I'm disappointed when I'm not. I'm responsible, even studious now and then, but on the other hand, I'm a goof-off, too, because if you're too studious, you won't be popular. I don't usually do that well at school. I'm a pretty cheerful person, especially with my friends, where I can even get rowdy. At home I'm more likely to be anxious around my parents. They expect me to get all A's. It's not fair! I worry about how I probably *should* get better grades. But I'd be mortified in the eyes of my friends. So I'm usually pretty stressed-out at home, or sarcastic, since my parents are always on my case. But I really don't understand how I can switch so fast. I mean, how can I be cheerful one minute, anxious the next, and then be sarcastic? Which one is the *real* me? Sometimes, I feel phony, especially around boys. Say I think some guy might be interested in asking me out. I try to act different, like Madonna. I'll be flirtatious and fun-loving. And then everybody, I mean *everybody* else is looking at me like they think I'm totally weird. Then I get self-conscious and embarrassed and become radically introverted, and I don't know who I really am! Am I just trying to impress them or what? But I don't really care what they think anyway. I don't *want* to care, that is. I just want to know what my close friends think. I can be my true self with my close friends. I can't be my real self with my parents. They don't understand me. What do *they* know about what it's like to be a teenager? They still treat me like I'm still a kid. At least at school people treat you more like you're an adult. That gets confusing, though. I mean, which am I, a kid or an adult? It's scary, too, because I don't have any idea what I want to be when I grow up. I mean, I have lots of *ideas.* My friend Sheryl and I talk about whether we'll be stewardesses, or teachers, or nurses, veterinarians, maybe mothers, or actresses. I know I *don't* want to be a waitress or a secretary. But how do you decide all of this? I really don't know. I mean, I think about it a lot, but I can't resolve it. There are days when I wish I could just become immune to myself. (Harter, 1990b, pp. 352–353).

PREVIEW

The 15-year-old girl's self-description that you just read exemplifies the increased interest in self-portrayal and search for an identity during adolescence. Later in the chapter we will explore the nature of identity development in adolescence, but before we get to the topic of identity we will examine these other aspects of adolescence: families, peers, and culture and rites of passage.

FAMILIES

In chapter 11 we discussed how, during middle and late childhood, parents spend less time with their children than in early childhood, discipline involves an increased use of reasoning and deprivation of privileges, there is a gradual transfer of control from parents to children but still within the boundary of coregulation, and parents and children increasingly respond to each other on the basis of labels. Some of the most important issues and questions that need to be raised about family relationships in adolescence are these: What is the nature of autonomy and attachment in adolescence? How extensive is parent-adolescent conflict, and how does it influence the adolescent's development? Does maturation of adolescents and parents influence how adolescents and parents interact?

Autonomy and Attachment

The adolescent's push for autonomy and responsibility puzzles and angers many parents. Parents see their teenager slipping from their grasp. They may have an urge to take stronger control as the adolescent seeks autonomy and responsibility. Heated emotional exchanges may ensue, with either side calling names, making threats, and doing whatever seems necessary to gain control. Parents may seem frustrated because they *expect* their teenager to heed their advice, to want to spend time with the family, and to grow up to do what is right (Collins & Luebker, 1993). Most parents anticipate that their teenager will have some difficulty adjusting to the changes that adolescence brings, but few parents can imagine and predict just how strong an adolescent's desires will be to spend time with peers or how much adolescents will want to show that it is they—not their parents—who are responsible for their successes and failures.

The ability to attain autonomy and gain control over one's behavior in adolescence is acquired through appropriate adult reactions to the adolescent's desire for control. At the onset of adolescence, the average individual does not have the knowledge to make appropriate or mature decisions in all areas of life. As the adolescent pushes for autonomy, the wise adult relinquishes control in those areas where the adolescent can make reasonable decisions but continues to guide the adolescent to make reasonable decisions in areas where the adolescent's knowledge is more limited. Gradually, adolescents acquire the ability to make mature decisions on their own.

But adolescents do not simply move away from parental influence into a decision-making process all their own. There is continued connectedness to parents as adolescents move toward and gain autonomy. In the last decade, developmentalists have begun to explore the role of secure attachment, and related concepts such as connectedness to parents, in adolescent development. They believe that attachment to parents in adolescence may facilitate the adolescent's social competence and well-being, as reflected in such characteristics as self-esteem, emotional adjustment, and physical health (Allen & others, 1994; Kobak & Cole, in press; Kobak & others, 1993; Onishi & Gjerde, 1994). For example, adolescents who have secure relationships with their parents have higher self-esteem and better emotional well-being (Armsden & Greenberg, 1987). In contrast, emotional detachment from parents is associated with greater feelings of parental rejection and a lower sense of one's own social and romantic attractiveness (Ryan & Lynch, 1989). Thus, attachment to parents during adolescence may serve the adaptive function of providing a secure base from which adolescents can explore and master new environments and a widening social world in a psychologically healthy manner. Secure attachment to parents may buffer adolescents from the anxiety and potential feelings of depression or emotional distress associated with the transition from childhood to adulthood. In one study, when young adolescents had a secure attachment to their parents, they perceived their family as cohesive and reported little social anxiety or feelings of depression (Papini, Roggman, & Anderson, 1990).

> *We cannot build the future for our youth, but we can build our youth for the future.*
>
> —Franklin D. Roosevelt, 1940

Secure attachment or connectedness to parents promotes competent peer relations and positive close relationships outside of the family. In one investigation in which attachment to parents and peers was assessed (Armsden & Greenberg, 1984), adolescents who were securely attached to parents were also securely attached to peers; those who were insecurely attached to parents were also more likely to be insecurely attached to peers. In another investigation, college students who were securely attached to their parents as young children were more likely to have securely attached relationships with friends, dates, and spouses than their insecurely attached counterparts (Hazen & Shaver, 1987). And in yet another investigation, older adolescents who had an ambivalent attachment history with their parents reported greater jealousy, conflict, and dependency along with less satisfaction in their relationship with their best friend than their securely attached counterparts (Fisher, 1990). There are times when adolescents reject closeness, connection, and attachment to their parents as they assert their ability to make decisions and to develop an identity. But for the most part, the worlds of parents and peers are coordinated and connected, not uncoordinated and disconnected (Haynie & McLellan, 1992).

Parent-Adolescent Conflict

While attachment and connectedness to parents remains strong during adolescence, the attachment and connectedness is not always smooth. Early adolescence is a time when conflict with parents escalates beyond childhood levels (Steinberg, 1993). This increase may be due to a number of factors: the biological changes of puberty, cognitive changes involving increased idealism and logical reasoning, social changes focused on independence and identity, maturational changes in parents, and violated expectations on the part of parents and adolescents. The adolescent compares her parents to an ideal standard and then criticizes the flaws. A 13-year-old girl tells her mother, "That is the tackiest-looking dress I have ever seen. Nobody would be caught dead wearing that." The adolescent demands logical explanations for comments and discipline. A 14-year-old boy tells his mother, "What do you mean I have to be home

FIGURE 13.1

Old and new models of parent-adolescent relationships.

Old model		New model		
Autonomy, detachment from parents; parent and peer worlds are isolated	Intense, stressful conflict throughout adolescence; parent-adolescent relationships are filled with storm and stress on virtually a daily basis	Attachment and autonomy; parents are important support systems and attachment figures; adolescent-parent and adolescent-peer worlds have some important connections	Moderate parent-adolescent conflict common and can serve a positive developmental function; conflict greater in early adolescence, especially during the apex of puberty	

at 10 P.M. because it's the way we do things around here? Why do we do things around here that way? It doesn't make sense to me."

Many parents see their adolescent changing from a compliant child to someone who is noncompliant, oppositional, and resistant to parental standards. When this happens, parents tend to clamp down and put more pressure on the adolescent to conform to parental standards (Collins, 1990). Parents often expect their adolescents to become mature adults overnight instead of understanding that the journey takes 10 to 15 years. Parents who recognize that this transition takes time handle their youth more competently and calmly than those who demand immediate conformity to adult standards. The opposite tactic—letting adolescents do as they please without supervision—is also unwise.

Conflict with parents does increase in early adolescence, but it does not reach the tumultuous proportions G. Stanley Hall envisioned at the beginning of the twentieth century (Kupersmidt & others, 1992). Rather, much of the conflict involves the everyday events of family life such as keeping a bedroom clean, dressing neatly, getting home by a certain time, not talking forever on the phone, and so on. The conflicts rarely involve major dilemmas like drugs and delinquency.

It is not unusual to hear parents of young adolescents ask, "Is it ever going to get better?" Things usually do get better as adolescents move from early to late adolescence. Conflict with parents often escalates during early adolescence, remains somewhat stable during the high school years, and then lessens as the adolescent reaches 17 to 20 years of age. Parent-adolescent relationships become more positive if adolescents go away to college than if they stay at home and go to college (Sullivan & Sullivan, 1980).

The everyday conflicts that characterize parent-adolescent relationships may actually serve a positive developmental function (Blos, 1989; Hill, 1983). These minor disputes and negotiations facilitate the adolescent's transition from being dependent on parents to becoming an autonomous individual. For example, in one investigation, adolescents who expressed disagreement with parents explored identity development more actively than adolescents who did not express disagreement with their parents (Cooper & others, 1982). One way for parents to cope with the adolescent's push for independence and identity is to recognize that adolescence is a 10- to 15-year transitional period in the journey to adulthood rather than an overnight accomplishment. Recognizing that conflict and negotiation can serve a positive developmental function can tone down parental hostility, too. Understanding parent-adolescent conflict, though, is not simple.

In sum, the old model of parent-adolescent relationships suggested that as adolescents mature they detach themselves from parents and move into a world of autonomy apart from parents. The old model also suggested that parent-adolescent conflict is intense and stressful throughout adolescence. The new model emphasizes that parents serve as important attachment figures and support systems as adolescents explore a wider, more complex social world. The new model also emphasizes that in the majority of families, parent-adolescent conflict is moderate rather than severe, and that the everyday negotiations and minor disputes are normal and can serve the positive developmental function of helping the adolescent make the transition from childhood dependency to adult independence (see figure 13.1).

When I was a boy of 14, my father was so ignorant I could hardly stand to have the man around. But when I got to be 21, I was astonished at how much he had learnt in 7 years.

—Mark Twain

It is not enough for parents to understand children. They must accord children the privilege of understanding them.

—Milton Sapirstein,
Paradoxes of Everyday Life, 1955

LIFE-SPAN PRACTICAL KNOWLEDGE 13.1

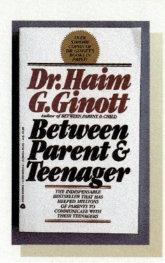

Between Parent & Teenager (1969) by Dr. Haim G. Ginott, New York: Avon.

Despite the fact that *Between Parent & Teenager* is well past its own adolescence (it was published in 1969), it continues to be one of the most widely read and recommended books for parents who want to communicate more effectively with their teenagers. Author Haim Ginott was a clinical psychologist at Columbia University who died in 1973. Ginott describes a number of commonsense solutions and strategies. For Ginott, parents' greatest challenge in the teenage years is to let go when they want to hold on—only by letting go can a peaceful and meaningful coexistence be reached between parents and teenagers. Throughout the book, Ginott connects with and educates parents through catchy phrases, such as *Don't collect thorns* (when parents see imperfections in themselves, they often expect perfection on the part of their teenagers) and *Don't step on corns* (adolescents have many imperfections about which they are very sensitive, ranging from zits to dimples; teenagers don't need parents to remind them of these imperfections). The book is very entertaining reading and is full of insightful interchanges between parents and teenagers. Ginott's strategies can make the world of parents and adolescents a kinder, gentler world.

Still, a high degree of conflict characterizes some parent-adolescent relationships. One estimate of the percentage of parents and adolescents who engage in prolonged, intense, repeated, unhealthy conflict is about one in five families (Montemayor, 1982). While this figure represents a minority of adolescents, it indicates that 4 to 5 million American families encounter serious, highly stressful parent-adolescent conflict. And this prolonged, intense conflict is associated with a number of adolescent problems—moving away from home, juvenile delinquency, school dropout, pregnancy and early marriage, joining religious cults, and drug abuse (Brook & others, 1990). To read about strategies for reducing parent-adolescent conflict, turn to Perspectives on Parenting and Education 13.1.

The Maturation of Adolescents and Parents

Physical, cognitive, and social changes in the adolescent's development influence the nature of parent-adolescent relationships. Parental changes also influence the nature of these relationships. Among the changes in the adolescent are puberty, expanded logical reasoning and increased idealistic and egocentric thought, violated expectations, changes in schooling, peers, friendship, and dating, and movement toward independence. Several investigations have shown that conflict between parents and adolescents is the most stressful during the apex of pubertal growth (Hill & others, 1985; Silverberg & Steinberg, 1990; Steinberg, 1981, 1988).

Parental changes include those involving marital dissatisfaction, economic burdens, career reevaluation and time perspective, and health and body concerns. Marital dissatisfaction is greater when the offspring is an adolescent rather than a child or an adult. A greater economic burden is placed on parents during the rearing of their adolescents. Parents may reevaluate their occupational achievement, deciding whether they have met their youthful aspirations for success. Parents may look to the future and think about how much time they have remaining to accomplish what they want. Adolescents, however, look to the future with unbounded optimism, sensing that they have an unlimited amount of time to accomplish what they desire. Health concerns and an interest in bodily integrity and sexual attractiveness become prominent themes of adolescents' parents. Even when their bodies and sexual attractiveness are not deteriorating, many parents of adolescents perceive that they are. By contrast, adolescents are beginning to reach the peak of their physical attractiveness, strength, and health. While both adolescents and their parents show a heightened preoccupation with their bodies, adolescents' outcomes are probably more positive.

Critical Thinking

As the parents of adolescents will be increasingly older in the future because of delays in marriage and childbearing, how do you think this will influence the nature of parent-adolescent relationships?

PEERS

In chapter 11, we discussed how children spend more time with their peers in middle and late childhood than in early childhood. We also found that friendships become more important in middle and late childhood, and that popularity with peers is a strong motivation for most children. Advances in cognitive development during middle and late childhood also allow children to

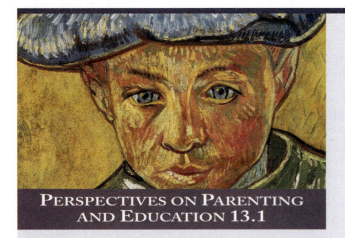

PERSPECTIVES ON PARENTING AND EDUCATION 13.1

Strategies for Reducing Parent–Adolescent Conflict

If parents and adolescents are immersed in conflict, are there ways parents can reduce the conflict? Laurence Steinberg has studied parent-adolescent conflict for a number of years. Steinberg (with Ann Levine, 1990) believes that the best way for parents to handle parent-adolescent conflict is through collaborative problem solving, the goal of which is discover a solution that satisfies both the parent and the adolescent. The approach works best at a time when neither the parent nor the adolescent will be distracted, when the discussion is restricted to a single issue, and when the adolescent's agreement to try to work out a solution is secured in advance. The collaborative problem solving approach consists of six basic steps:

1. *Establish ground rules for conflict resolution.* These rules are basically the rules of fighting fairly. Both the parent and the adolescent agree to treat each other with respect—no name-calling or putting each other down, for example—and to listen to each other's point of view. At the beginning of the discussion, the parent should provide a positive note by stating a desire to be fair.

2. *Try to reach a mutual understanding.* Step 2 involves taking turns being understood, which means that both the parent and the adolescent get the opportunity to say what the real problem is and how they feel about it. In this part of the discussion, it is important to focus on the issue, not on personalities.

3. *Try brainstorming.* Step 3 involves both the adolescent and the parent generating as many solutions to the problem as they can. At this point, no idea should be rejected because it is too crazy, too expensive, or too dumb. A time limit should be set—something like 5 or 10 minutes—for both parent and child to come up with as many ideas as possible for solving the conflict. Write down all of the possibilities.

4. *Try to come to an agreement about one or more solutions.* In step 4 of collaborative problem solving, both the parent and the adolescent select the options they like best. Every option should not be discussed because this can produce endless, sometimes fruitless, debate. In this step, the parent and the adolescent can see where their interests converge. Some give-and-take and some negotiation will probably be needed at this point. Neither the parent nor the adolescent should agree to something they find unacceptable.

5. *Write down the agreement.* While step 5 may sound formal, it should be followed because memories can become distorted. If either the parent or the adolescent breaks the agreement, the written statement can be consulted.

6. *Establish a time for a follow-up conversation to examine the progress that has been made.* Step 6 is just as important as the first five steps. Either the adolescent or the parent may not abide by the agreement, or the solution agreed upon may not be working out as well as was hoped and any new problem that arises will have to be addressed.

The six steps of collaborative problem solving can be applied to a number of parent-adolescent conflicts, including such issues as curfew, choice of friends, keeping a room clean, respect for adults, rules for dating, and so on. In some situations, parents and adolescents will not be able to reach an agreement. When the health and safety of the adolescent is at issue, it may be necessary for the parent to make a decision that is not agreed to by the adolescent. However, adolescents are often far more likely to go along with the direction of a parent's decisions if the adolescent is allowed to participate in the decision-making process and sees that the parent is taking the adolescent's needs and desires seriously.

Peer conformity becomes especially strong during the early adolescent years, as reflected in the uniform dress and behavior of these young adolescent "Madonnas."

Most adolescents conform to the mainstream standards of their peers. However, the rebellious or anticonformist adolescent reacts counter to the mainstream peer group's expectations, deliberately moving away from the actions or beliefs this group advocates.

take the perspective of their peers and friends more readily, and their social knowledge of how to make and keep friends increases.

Imagine you are back in junior or senior high school, especially during one of your good times. Peers, friends, cliques, dates, parties, and clubs probably come to mind. Adolescents spend huge chunks of time with peers, more than in middle and late childhood. Among the important issues and questions to be asked about peer relations in adolescence are these: What is the nature of peer pressure and conformity? How important are cliques in adolescence? How do children and adolescent groups differ? What is the nature of dating in adolescence?

Peer Pressure and Conformity

Consider the following statement made by an adolescent girl:

Peer pressure is extremely influential in my life. I have never had very many friends, and I spend quite a bit of time alone. The friends I have are older. . . . The closest friend I have had is a lot like me in that we are both sad and depressed a lot. I began to act even more depressed than before when I was with her. I would call her up and try to act even more depressed than I was because that is what I thought she liked. In that relationship, I felt pressure to be like her.

Conformity to peer pressure in adolescence can be positive or negative (Camarena, 1991; Foster-Clark & Blyth, 1991; Pearl, Bryan, & Herzog, 1990; Wall, 1993). Teenagers engage in all sorts of negative conformity behavior—use seedy language, steal, vandalize, and make fun of parents and teachers. However, a great deal of peer conformity is not negative and consists of the desire to be involved in the peer world, such as dressing like friends and wanting to spend huge chunks of time with members of a clique. Such circumstances may involve prosocial activities as well, as when clubs raise money for worthy causes.

During adolescence, especially early adolescence, we conformed more to peer standards than we did in childhood. Investigators have found that around the eighth and ninth grades, conformity to peers—especially to their antisocial standards—peaks (Berndt, 1979; Berndt & Perry, 1990; Leventhal, 1994). At this point adolescents are most likely to go along with a peer to steal hubcaps off a car, draw grafitti on a wall, or steal cosmetics from a store counter.

> *Each of you, individually, walkest with the tread of a fox, but collectively ye are geese.*
>
> —Solon, Ancient Greece

Cliques and Crowds

Most peer group relationships in adolescence can be categorized in one of three ways: the crowd, the clique, or individual friendships. The **crowd** *is the largest and least personal of adolescent groups.* Members of the crowd meet because of their mutual interest in activities, not because they are mutually attracted to each other. **Cliques** *are smaller, involve greater intimacy among members, and have more group cohesion than crowds.*

Allegiance to cliques, clubs, organizations, and teams exerts powerful control over the lives of many adolescents (McLellan, Haynie, & Strouse, 1993). Group identity often overrides personal identity. The leader of a group may place a member in a position of considerable moral conflict by asking, in effect, "What's more important, our code or your parents'?" or "Are you looking out for yourself, or the members of the group?" Such labels as *brother* and *sister* sometimes are adopted and used in the members' conversations with each other. These labels symbolize the bond between the members and suggest the high status of group membership.

One of the most widely cited studies of adolescent cliques and crowds is that of James Coleman (1961). Students from 10 high schools were asked to identify the leading crowds in their schools. They also were asked to identify the students who were the most outstanding in athletics, popularity, and various school activities. Regardless of the school sampled, the leading crowds were composed of athletes and popular girls. Much less power in the leading crowd was attributed to bright students.

Think about your high school years. What were the cliques, and which one were you in? Although the names of cliques change, we could go to almost any high school in the United States and find three to six well-defined cliques or

crowds. In one investigation, six peer group structures emerged: populars, unpopulars, jocks, brains, druggies, and average students (Brown & Mounts, 1989). The proportion of students in these cliques was much lower in multiethnic schools because of the additional existence of ethnically based crowds.

In one study, clique membership was associated with the adolescent's self-esteem (Brown & Lohr, 1987). Cliques included jocks (athletically oriented), populars (well-known students who lead social activities), normals (middle-of-the-road students who make up the masses), druggies or toughs (known for illicit drug use or other delinquent activities), and nobodies (low in social skills or intellectual abilities). The self-esteem of the jocks and the populars was highest, whereas that of the nobodies was lowest. One group of adolescents not in a clique had self-esteem equivalent to that of the jocks and the populars; this group was the independents, who indicated that clique membership was not important to them. Keep in mind that these data are correlational; self-esteem could increase an adolescent's probability of becoming a clique member, just as clique membership could increase the adolescent's self-esteem.

Adolescent Groups Versus Children Groups

Children groups differ from adolescent groups in several important ways. The members of children groups often are friends or neighborhood acquaintances, and their groups usually are not as formalized as many adolescent groups. During the adolescent years, groups tend to include a broader array of members. In other words, adolescents other than friends or neighborhood acquaintances often are members of adolescent groups. Try to recall the student council, honor society, or football team at your junior high school. If you were a member of any of these organizations, you probably remember that they were made up of many people you had not met before and that they were a more heterogeneous group than your childhood peer groups. For example, peer groups in adolescence are more likely to have a mixture of individuals from different ethnic groups than are peer groups in childhood.

As ethnic minority children move into adolescence and enter schools with more heterogeneous school populations, they become more aware of their ethnic minority status. Ethnic minority adolescents may have difficulty joining peer groups and clubs in predominantly White schools. Similarly, White adolescents may have peer relations difficulties in predominately ethnic minority schools. However, schools are only one setting in which peer relations take place; they also occur in the neighborhood and in the community.

Ethnic minority adolescents often have two sets of peer relationships, one at school, the other in the community. Community peers are more likely to be from their own ethnic group in their immediate neighborhood. Sometimes, they go to the same church and participate in activities together, such as Black History Week, Chinese New Year's, or Cinco de Mayo Festival. Because ethnic group adolescents usually have two sets of peers and friends, when researchers ask about their peers and friends, questions should focus on both relationships at school and relationships in the neighborhood and community. Ethnic minority group adolescents who are social isolates at school may be sociometric stars in their segregated neighborhood. Also, because adolescents are more mobile than children, inquiries should be made about the scope of their social networks (Gibbs & Huang, 1989; Mounts, 1992).

A well-known observational study by Dexter Dunphy (1963) supports the notion that opposite-sex participation in groups increases during adolescence. In late childhood, boys and girls participate in small, same-sex cliques. As they move into the early adolescent years, the same-sex cliques begin to interact with each other. Gradually, the leaders and high-status members form further cliques based on heterosexual relationships. Eventually, the newly created heterosexual cliques replace the same-sex cliques. The heterosexual cliques interact with each other in large crowd activities, too—at dances and athletic events, for example. In late adolescence, the crowd begins to dissolve as couples develop more serious relationships and make long-range plans that may include engagement and marriage (see figure 13.2).

Dating

Dating takes on added importance during adolescence (Connolly & Johnson, 1993; Dowdy & Howard, 1993). As Dick Cavett (1974) remembers, the thought of an upcoming dance or sock hop was absolute agony: "I knew I'd never get a date. There seemed to be only this limited set of girls I could and should be seen with, and they were all taken by the jocks." Adolescents spend considerable time either dating or thinking about dating, which has gone far beyond its original courtship function to become a form of recreation, a source of status and achievement, and a setting for learning about close relationships. One function of dating, though, continues to be mate selection.

He who would learn to fly one day must first learn to stand and walk and climb and dance: one cannot fly into flying.

—Friedrich Nietzsche, *Thus Spoke Zarathustra*, 1883

Most girls in the United States begin dating at the age of 14, whereas most boys begin sometime between the ages of 14 and 15 (Douvan & Adelson, 1966). The majority of adolescents have their first date between the ages of 12 and 16. Fewer than 10 percent have a first date before the age of 10, and by the age of 16, more than 90 percent have had at least one date. More than 50 percent of high school students average one or more dates per week (Dickinson, 1975). About 15 percent date less than once per month, and about three of every four students have gone steady at least once by the end of high school.

Female adolescents bring a stronger desire for intimacy and personality exploration to dating than do male adolescents (Duck, 1975). Adolescent dating is a context in which gender-related role expectations intensify. Males feel pressured to perform in "masculine" ways, and females feel pressured to perform in "feminine" ways. Especially in early adolescence, when pubertal changes are occurring, the adolescent male wants to show that he is the very best male possible, and the adolescent female wants to show that she is the very best female possible.

Dating scripts *are the cognitive models that adolescents and adults use to guide and evaluate dating interactions.* In one recent study, first dates were highly scripted along gender lines (Rose & Frieze, 1993). Males followed a proactive dating script, females a reactive one. The male's script involved initiating the date (asking for and planning it), controlling the public domain (driving and opening doors), and initiating sexual interaction (making physical contact, making out, and kissing). The female's script focused on the private domain (concern about appearance, enjoying the date), participating in the structure of the date provided by the male (being picked up, having doors opened), and responding to his sexual gestures. These gender differences give males more power in the initial stage of a relationship (McCormick & Jessor, 1983).

The sociocultural context exerts a powerful influence on adolescent dating patterns (Xiaohe & Whyte, 1990). Values and religious beliefs of people in various cultures often dictate the age at which dating begins, how much freedom in dating is allowed, whether dates must be chaperoned by adults or parents, and the roles of males and females in dating. For example, Hispanic American and Asian American cultures have more conservative standards regarding adolescent dating than does the Anglo-American culture. Dating may be a source of cultural conflict for many immigrants and their families who have come from cultures in which dating begins at a late age, little freedom in dating is allowed, dates are chaperoned, and adolescent girls' dating is especially restricted.

Critical Thinking

How do you think adolescents' observations of their parents' marital lives and their own relationships with their parents influence dating relationships in adolescence?

Thus far, we have discussed a number of ideas about families and peers during adolescence. A summary of these ideas is presented in concept table 13.1.

CULTURE AND ADOLESCENT DEVELOPMENT

Consider the flowering of a garden. Though differing in kind, color, form, and shape, yet, as flowers are refreshed by the waters of one spring, revived by the breath of one wind, invigorated by the rays of one sun, their diversity increases their charm and adds to their beauty. How unpleasing to the eye if all the flowers and the plants, the leaves and the blossoms, the fruits, and the trees of the garden were all of the same shape and color! Diversity of hues, form, and shape enriches and adorns the garden.

—Abud'l-Baha

FIGURE 13.2

Dunphy's progression of peer group relations in adolescence.

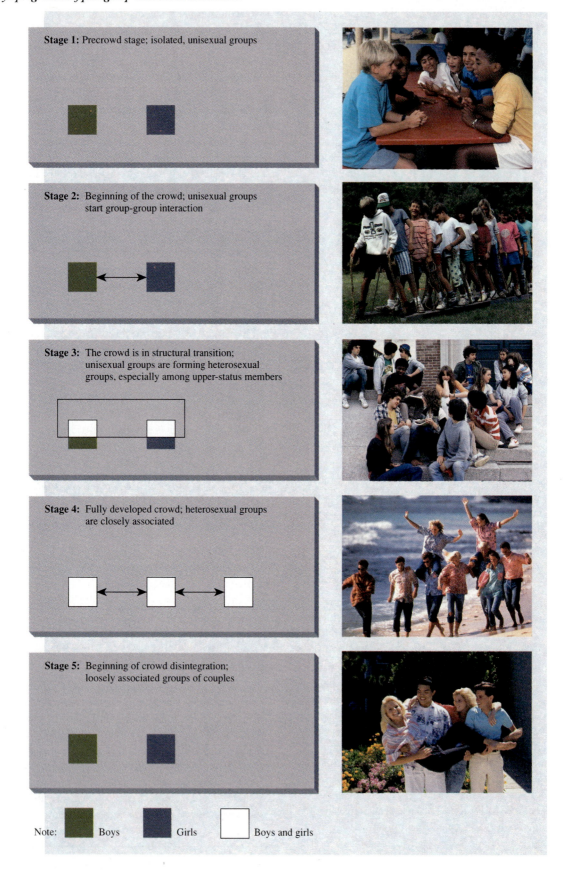

Stage 1: Precrowd stage; isolated, unisexual groups

Stage 2: Beginning of the crowd; unisexual groups start group-group interaction

Stage 3: The crowd is in structural transition; unisexual groups are forming heterosexual groups, especially among upper-status members

Stage 4: Fully developed crowd; heterosexual groups are closely associated

Stage 5: Beginning of crowd disintegration; loosely associated groups of couples

Note: Boys   Girls   Boys and girls

CONCEPT TABLE 13.1

Families and Peers

Concept	Processes/Related Ideas	Characteristics/Description
Families	Autonomy and attachment	Many parents have a difficult time handling the adolescent's push for autonomy, even though this push is one of the hallmarks of adolescent development. Adolescents do not simply move into a world isolated from parents; attachment to parents increases the probability that the adolescent will be socially competent and explore a widening social world in healthy ways.
	Parent-adolescent conflict	Conflict with parents often increases in early adolescence. Such conflict is usually moderate. The increase in conflict probably serves the positive developmental function of promoting autonomy and identity. A small subset of adolescents experience high parent-adolescent conflict that is related to various negative outcomes for adolescents.
	The maturation of the adolescent and parents	Physical, cognitive, and social changes in the adolescent's development influence parent-adolescent relationships. Parental changes—marital dissatisfaction, economic burdens, career reevaluation and time perspective, and health and body concerns—also influence parent-adolescent relationships.
Peers	Peer pressure and conformity	The pressure to conform to peers is strong during adolescence, especially during the eighth and ninth grades.
	Cliques and crowds	There are usually three to six well-defined cliques in every secondary school. Membership in certain cliques—especially jocks and populars—is associated with increased self-esteem. Independents also show high self-esteem.
	Children and adolescent groups	Children groups are less formal, less heterogeneous, and less heterosexual than adolescent groups. Dunphy found that the development of adolescent groups moves through five stages.
	Dating	Dating can be a form of mate selection, recreation, a source of status and achievement, and a setting for learning about close relationships. Most adolescents are involved in dating. Adolescent females appear to be more interested in intimacy and personality exploration than adolescent males are. Male dating scripts are proactive, females' reactive. Dating varies cross-culturally.

We live in an increasingly diverse world, one in which there is increasing contact between adolescents from different cultures and ethnic groups. How do adolescents vary cross-culturally? What rites of passage do adolescents experience? What is the nature of ethnic minority adolescents and their development?

Cross-Cultural Comparisons and Rites of Passage

Ideas about the nature of adolescents and orientation toward adolescents may vary from culture to culture and within the same culture over different time periods (Whiting, 1989). For example, some cultures (the Mangaian culture in the South Sea islands, for example) have more permissive attitudes toward adolescent sexuality than the American culture, and some cultures (the Ines Beag culture off the coast of Ireland, for example) have more conservative attitudes toward adolescent sexuality than the American culture. Over the course of the twentieth century, attitudes toward sexuality—especially for females—have become more permissive in the American culture.

Early in this century, overgeneralizations about the universal aspects of adolescents were made based on data and experience in a single culture—the middle-class culture of the United States (Havighurst, 1976). For example, it was believed that adolescents everywhere went through a period of "storm

These Congolese Kota boys painted their faces as part of a rite of passage to adulthood. What kinds of rites of passage do American adolescents have?

and stress" characterized by self-doubt and conflict. However, when Margaret Mead visited the island of Samoa, she found that the adolescents of the Samoan culture were not experiencing much stress.

As we discovered in chapter 1, **cross-cultural studies** *involve the comparison of a culture with one or more other cultures, which provides information about the degree to which development is similar, or universal, across cultures, or the degree to which it is culture-specific*. The study of adolescence has emerged in the context of Western industrialized society, with the practical needs and social norms of this culture dominating thinking about adolescents. Consequently, the development of adolescents in Western cultures has evolved as the norm for all adolescents of the human species, regardless of economic and cultural circumstances. This narrow viewpoint can produce

erroneous conclusions about the nature of adolescents. One variation in the experiences of adolescents in different cultures is whether the adolescents go through a rite of passage.

Some societies have elaborate ceremonies that signal the adolescent's move to maturity and achievement of adult status. A **rite of passage** *is a ceremony or a ritual that marks an individual's transition from one status to another. The most interest in rites of passage focuses on the transition to adult status*. In many primitive cultures, rites of passage are the avenue through which adolescents gain access to sacred adult practices, to knowledge, and to sexuality (MacDonald, 1991; Sommer, 1978). These rites often involve dramatic practices intended to facilitate the adolescent's separation from the immediate family, especially the mother. The transformation is usually characterized by some form of ritual death and rebirth, or by means of contact with the

LIFE-SPAN PRACTICAL KNOWLEDGE 13.2

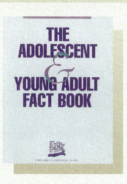

The Adolescent & Young Adult Fact Book

(1993) by Janet Simons, Belva Finlay, and Alice Yang. Washington, DC: Children's Defense Fund.

This book is filled with valuable charts showing the roles that poverty and ethnicity play in adolescent development. Many of the charts display information separately for Black American, Hispanic American, and Asian American adolescents. Special attention is given to prevention and intervention programs that work with adolescents from low-income and ethnic minority backgrounds. Topics discussed include families, health, substance abuse, crime, victimization, education, employment, sexual activity, and pregnancy.

spiritual world. Bonds are forged between the adolescent and the adult instructors through shared rituals, hazards, and secrets to allow the adolescent to enter the adult world. This kind of ritual provides a forceful and discontinuous entry into the adult world at a time when the adolescent is perceived to be ready for the change.

Africa has been the location of many rites of passage for adolescents, especially sub-Saharan Africa. Under the influence of Western culture, many of the rites are disappearing today, although some vestiges remain. In locations where formal education is not readily available, rites of passage are still prevalent.

Do we have such rites of passage for American adolescents? We certainly do not have universal formal ceremonies that mark the passage from adolescence to adulthood. Certain religious and social groups do have initiation ceremonies that indicate that an advance in maturity has been reached—the Jewish bar mitzvah, the Catholic confirmation, and social debuts, for example. School graduation ceremonies come the closest to being culture-wide rites of passage in the United States. The high school graduation ceremony has become nearly universal for middle-class adolescents and increasing numbers of adolescents from low-income backgrounds (Fasick, 1988). Nonetheless, high school graduation does not result in universal changes; many high school graduates continue to live with their parents, continue to be economically dependent on them, and continue to be undecided about career and life-style matters. Another rite of passage for increasing numbers of American adolescents is sexual intercourse (Allen & Santrock, 1993). By the end of adolescence, more than 70 percent of American adolescents have had sexual intercourse.

The absence of clear-cut rites of passage make the attainment of adult status ambiguous. Many individuals are unsure whether or not they have reached adult status. In Texas, the age for beginning employment is 15, but many younger adolescents and even children are employed, especially Mexican immigrants. The age for driving is 16, but when emergency need is demonstrated, a driver's license can be obtained at 15. Even at age 16, some parents may not allow their son or daughter to obtain a driver's license, believing they are too young for this responsibility. The age for voting is 18; the age for drinking has recently been raised to 21. Exactly when adolescents become adults in America has not been clearly delineated, as it has been in some primitive cultures where rites of passage are universal in the culture.

Now that we have discussed the importance of a global perspective in understanding adolescence and the nature of rites of passage, we turn our attention to the development of ethnic minority adolescents in the United States.

Ethnicity

First, we examine the nature of ethnicity and social class; second, we examine the nature of differences, and diversity; and, third, we study the aspects of value conflicts, assimilation, and pluralism.

Ethnicity and Social Class

Much of the research on ethnic minority adolescents has failed to tease apart the influences of ethnicity and social class. Ethnicity and social class can interact in ways that exaggerate the influence of ethnicity because ethnic minority individuals are overrepresented in the lower socioeconomic levels of American society (Spencer & Dornbusch, 1990). Consequently, researchers too often have given ethnic explanations of adolescent development that were largely due to socioeconomic status rather than ethnicity. For example, decades of research on group differences in self-esteem failed to consider the socioeconomic status of Black American and White American children and adolescents. When Black American adolescents from low-income backgrounds are compared with White American adolescents from middle-class backgrounds, the differences are often large but not informative because of the confounding of ethnicity and social class (Bell-Scott & Taylor, 1989; Spencer, 1987).

While some ethnic minority youth are from middle-class backgrounds, economic advantage does not entirely enable them to escape their ethnic minority status (Spencer & Dornbusch, 1990). Middle-class ethnic minority youth still encounter much of the prejudice, discrimination, and bias associated with being a member of an ethnic minority group. Often characterized as a "model minority" because of their strong achievement orientation and family cohesiveness, Japanese Americans still experience stress associated with ethnic minority status (Sue, 1990). Even though middle-class ethnic minority adolescents have more resources available to counter the destructive influences of prejudice and discrimination, they still cannot completely avoid the pervasive influence of negative stereotypes about ethnic minority groups.

> *In the end, antiblack, antifemale, and all forms of discrimination are equivalent to the same thing—antihumanism.*
>
> —Shirley Chisholm, *Unbought and Unbossed* (1970)

Not all ethnic minority families are poor. However, poverty contributes to the stressful life experiences of many ethnic minority adolescents. In a recent review, Vonnie McLoyd (in press) concluded that ethnic minority youth experience a disproportionate share of the adverse effects of poverty and unemployment in America today. Thus, many ethnic minority adolescents experience a double disadvantage: (a) prejudice, discrimination, and bias because of their ethnic minority status, and (b) the stressful effects of poverty.

Differences and Diversity

There are legitimate differences between various ethnic minority groups, and between ethnic minority groups and the majority White group (Allen & Santrock, 1993). Recognizing and respecting these differences is an important aspect of getting along with others in a diverse, multicultural world. Historical, economic, and social experiences produce differences in ethnic groups (Triandis, 1990, 1994). Individuals living in a particular ethnic or cultural group adapt to the values, attitudes, and stresses of that culture. Their behavior, while possibly different from yours, is, nonetheless, often functional for them. It is important for adolescents, as well as each of us, to take the perspective of individuals from ethnic and cultural groups that are different from ours and think, "If I were in their shoes, what kind of experiences might I have had?" "How would I feel if I were a member of their ethnic or cultural group?" "How would I think and behave if I had grown up in their world?" Such perspective taking often increases an adolescent's empathy and understanding of individuals from ethnic and cultural groups different from their own.

Unfortunately, the differences between ethnic minority groups and the White majority are emphasized by both society and science, with damaging results to ethnic minority individuals. Ethnicity has defined who will enjoy the privileges of citizenship and to what degree and in what ways (Jones, 1990, 1994). An individual's ethnic background has determined whether the individual will be alienated, oppressed, or disadvantaged, all too often humiliating and embarrassing ethnic minority individuals.

Another very important dimension to continually keep in mind when studying ethnic minority adolescents is their diversity, a point we made in chapter 1 but that deserves to be underscored again. Ethnic minority groups are not homogeneous; they have different social, historical, and economic backgrounds. For example, Mexican, Cuban, and Puerto Rican immigrants are all Hispanics, but they migrated for different reasons, came from varying socioeconomic backgrounds in their native countries, and experience different rates and types of employment in the United States (Ramirez, 1989). The federal government now recognizes the existence of 511 *different* Native American tribes, each having a unique ancestral background with differing values and characteristics. Asian Americans include the Chinese, Japanese, Filipinos, Koreans, and Southeast Asians, each group having a distinct ancestry and language. As an indication of the diversity of Asian Americans, they not only show high educational attainments but also include a high proportion of individuals with no education whatsoever (Sue & Okazaki, 1990). For example, 90 percent of Korean American males graduate from high school, but only 71 percent of Vietnamese American males do.

Sometimes well-meaning individuals fail to recognize the diversity within an ethnic group (Sue, 1990). Consider the circumstance of a sixth-grade teacher who goes to a human relations workshop and is exposed to the necessity of incorporating more ethnicity into her instructional planning. Since she has two Mexican American adolescents in her class, she asks them to be prepared to demonstrate to the class on the following Monday how they dance at home. The teacher expected both of them to perform Mexican folk dances, reflecting their ethnic heritage. The first boy got up in front of the class and began dancing in a typical American fashion. The teacher said, "No, I want you to dance like you and your family do at home, like you do when you have Mexican American celebrations." The boy informed the teacher that their family didn't dance that way. The second boy did demonstrate a Mexican folk dance to the class. The first boy was highly assimilated into the American culture and did not know how to dance Mexican folk dances. The second boy was less assimilated and came from a Mexican American family that had retained more of their Mexican heritage.

> *We all know we are unique individuals, but we tend to see others as representatives of groups.*
>
> —Deborah Tannen

This example illustrates the diversity and individual differences that exist within any ethnic minority group. Failure to recognize diversity and individual variations results in the stereotyping of an ethnic minority group.

Value Conflicts, Assimilation, and Pluralism

Stanley Sue (1990) believes that value conflicts are often involved when individuals respond to ethnic issues. These value conflicts have been a source of considerable controversy. According to Sue, without properly identifying the assumptions and effects of the conflicting values it is difficult to resolve ethnic minority issues. Let's examine one of these value conflicts,

Stanley Sue, shown lecturing to Asian Americans, has been an important advocate of increased research on ethnic minority issues in psychology. Sue has conducted extensive research on the role of ethnicity in abnormal behavior and psychotherapy. He also has provided considerable insight into ethnic minority issues.

assimilation versus pluralism, to see how it might influence an individual's response to an ethnic minority issue.

A faculty member commented that he was glad his psychology department was interested in teaching students about ethnic and cultural issues. He felt that by becoming aware of the cultures of different groups, students would improve their understanding of their own and other cultures. However, another faculty member disagreed. She felt that students' knowledge of ethnic minority issues and different cultures was a relevant concern, but she argued that the department's scarce resources should not be devoted to ethnic and cultural issues. She also believed that if too much attention is given to ethnic and cultural issues, it might actually increase the segregation of students, and even cause friction among ethnic and cultural groups. She commented that we all live in this society and therefore we must all learn the same skills to succeed. In Sue's (1990) perspective, a value conflict involving assimilation and pluralism underlies these opposing views about whether a psychology department should devote increased, or any, funds to teaching students about ethnicity and culture.

Assimilation *refers to the absorption of ethnic minority groups into the dominant group, which often means the loss of some or virtually all of the behavior and values of the ethnic minority group.* Individuals who adopt an assimilation stance usually advocate that ethnic minority groups should become more American. By contrast, **pluralism** *refers to the coexistence of distinct ethnic and cultural groups in the same society. Individuals who adopt a pluralism stance usually advocate that cultural differences be maintained and appreciated.*

For many years, an assimilation approach was thought to be the best course for American society, because it was believed that the mainstream was in many ways the superior culture. Even though many individuals today reject the notion that the mainstream culture is intrinsically superior to ethnic minority

cultures, the assimilation approach is currently resurfacing with a more complex face. Advocates of the assimilation approach now often use practical and functional arguments rather than intrinsic superiority arguments to buttress their point of view. For example, assimilation advocates stress that educational programs for immigrant children (Mexican, Chinese, and so on) should stress the learning of English as early as possible in education rather than provide a bilingual education. Their argument is that spending time on any language other than English may be a handicap, particularly because it is not functional in the classroom. By contrast, the advocates of pluralism argue that an English-only approach reasserts the mainstream-is-right-and-best belief. Thus, responses to the ethnic minority issue of bilingual education involve a clash of fundamental values. As Sue asks, how can one argue against the development of functional skills and, to some degree, the support of Americanization? Similarly, how can one doubt that pluralism, diversity, and respect for different cultures is a valid principle? Sue believes that the one-sidedness of the issue is the main problem. Advocates of assimilation often overlook the fact that a consensus may be lacking on what constitutes functional skills, or that a particular context may alter what skills are useful. For example, with the growth in the immigrant population, the ability to speak Spanish or Japanese may be an asset, as is the ability to interact and collaborate with diverse ethnic groups.

> *I am here and you will know that I am the best and will hear me. The color of my skin or the kink of my hair or the spread of my mouth has nothing to do with what you are listening to.*
>
> —Leontyne Price

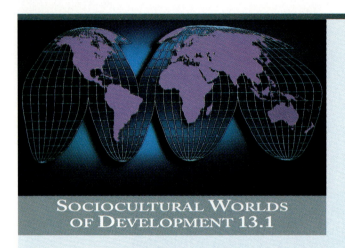

SOCIOCULTURAL WORLDS OF DEVELOPMENT 13.1

Education and the Development of Ethnic Minority Adolescents

Parents' attitudes and behavior can either improve or detract from adolescents' school performance (Spencer & Dornbusch, 1990). In one investigation that controlled for social class, authoritarian and permissive parenting were both associated with poor grades, while authoritative parenting was associated with better grades (Dornbusch & others, 1987). However, more than parenting styles are involved in understanding ethnic minority adolescents' school performance, because many Asian American adolescents' parents follow an authoritarian parenting style, yet

Asian American adolescents, especially Japanese and Chinese American, often excel in school. A special concern is the large number of Black and Hispanic adolescents who grow up in single-parent families. For example, half of Black American adolescents are likely to remain with a single parent through the end of adolescence, while only 15 percent of White American adolescents will (McLoyd, in press). Among ethnic minorities, about 70 percent of Black American and Hispanic American adolescents are raised by single mothers. Poor school performance among many ethnic minority youth is related to this pattern of single parenting and poverty (Dornbusch & others, 1985).

One program in Washington, DC, has helped many ethnic minority adolescents do better in school. In 1983, Dr. Henry Gaskins began an after-school tutorial program for ethnic minority students. For 4 hours every weeknight and all day Saturday, 80 students receive one-on-one assistance from Gaskins and his wife, two adult volunteers, and academically talented peers. Those who can afford it contribute 5 dollars to cover the cost of school supplies. In addition to tutoring in specific subjects, Gaskin's home-based academy helps students set personal goals and commit to a desire to succeed. Many of his students come from families in which the parents are high school dropouts and either can't or are not motivated to help their adolescent sons and daughters achieve in school. In addition, the academy prepares students to qualify for scholarships and college entrance exams. Gaskins recently received the President's Volunteer Action Award at the White House.

Dr. Henry Gaskins, here talking with three high school students, began an after-school tutorial program for ethnic minority students in 1983 in Washington, D.C. Volunteers like Dr. Gaskins can be especially helpful in developing a stronger sense of the importance of education in ethnic minority adolescents.

Parents play an important role in the education of ethnic minority adolescents, as demonstrated by this Hispanic American father at his daughter's high school graduation. Many Black and Hispanic American adolescents grow up in low-income, single-parent families and do not receive the support this Hispanic American girl has been given.

Sue believes that one way to resolve value conflicts about sociocultural issues is to conceptualize or redefine them in innovative ways. For example, in the assimilation/pluralism conflict, rather than assume that assimilation is necessary for the development of functional skills, one strategy is to focus on the fluctuating criteria defining those skills considered to be functional; another is to consider the possibility that developing functional skills does not prevent the existence of pluralism. For instance, the classroom instructor might use multicultural examples when teaching social studies, and still be able to discuss

both culturally universal (etic) and culturally specific (emic) approaches to American and other cultures.

Two important emphases in this text have been the importance of families and the importance of education in the development of children. In our discussions of ethnic minority children at different points in the book we have seen that, as with Anglo-American children, families and education play important roles in their lives. To read further about the nature of families, education, and ethnic minority adolescents, turn to Sociocultural Worlds of Development 13.1.

Now that we have considered a number of ideas about the role of culture in the adolescent's development, we turn our attention to one of the most important tasks of adolescence—the development of identity. We will consider the role of adolescence as a critical juncture in the identity development of ethnic minority adolescents as well.

IDENTITY

By far the most comprehensive and provocative story of identity development has been told by Erik Erikson. As you may remember from chapter 2, identity versus identity confusion is the fifth stage in Erikson's eight stages of the life cycle, occurring at about the same time as adolescence. It is a time of being interested in finding out who one is, what one is all about, and where one is headed in life.

> *The thoughts of youth are long, long thoughts.*
> —Henry Wadsworth Longfellow, 1858

During adolescence, worldviews become important to the individual, who enters what Erikson (1968) calls a "psychological moratorium," a gap between the security of childhood and the autonomy of adulthood. Adolescents experiment with numerous roles and identities they draw from the surrounding culture. Youth who successfully cope with these conflicting identities during adolescence emerge with a new sense of self that is both refreshing and acceptable. Adolescents who do not successfully resolve this identity crisis are confused, suffering what Erikson calls "identity confusion." This confusion takes one of two courses: The individuals withdraw, isolating themselves from peers and family; or they may lose their identity in the crowd.

Some Contemporary Thoughts About Identity

Contemporary views of identity development suggest several important considerations. First, identity development is a lengthy process; in many instances it is a more gradual, less cataclysmic transition than Erikson's term *crisis* implies. Second, identity development is extraordinarily complex (Marcia, 1980, 1987). Identity formation neither begins nor ends with adolescence. It begins with the appearance of attachment, the development of a sense of self, and the emergence of independence in infancy, and reaches its final phase with a life review and integration in old age. What is important about identity in adolescence, especially late adolescence, is that for the first time physical development, cognitive development, and social development advance to the point at which the individual can sort through and synthesize childhood identities and identifications to construct a viable pathway toward adult maturity. Resolution of the identity issue at adolescence does not mean identity will be stable through the remainder of one's life. A person who develops a healthy identity is flexible, adaptive, and open to changes in society, in relationships, and in careers. This openness

assures numerous reorganizations of identity features throughout the life of the person who has achieved identity.

> *In the beginning was alpha and the end is omega, but somewhere in between occurred delta, which is nothing less than the arrival of man himself into the daylight of . . . being himself and not being himself, of being at home and being a stranger.*
> —Walker Percy, *Message in the Bottle*

Identity formation does not happen neatly, and it usually does not happen cataclysmically. At the bare minimum, it involves commitment to a vocational direction, an ideological stance, and a sexual orientation. Synthesizing the identity components can be a long, drawn-out process with many negations and affirmations of various roles and faces. Identities are developed in bits and pieces. Decisions are not made once and for all, but have to be made again and again. And the decisions may seem trivial at the time: whom to date, whether or not to break up, whether or not to have intercourse, whether or not to take drugs, whether to go to college after high school or get a job, which major to choose, whether to study or whether to play, whether or not to be politically active, and so on. Over the years of adolescence, the decisions begin to form a core of what the individual is all about as a person—what is called "identity" (Archer, 1989; Papini, Micka, & Barnett, 1989).

The Four Statuses of Identity

Canadian psychologist James Marcia (1966, 1980, 1991) analyzed Erikson's theory of identity development and concluded that four identity statuses, or modes of resolution, appear in the theory: identity diffusion, identity foreclosure, identity moratorium, and identity achievement. The extent of an adolescent's commitment and crisis is used to classify the individual according to one of the four identity statuses. **Crisis** *is defined as a period of identity development during which the adolescent is*

"*Do you have any idea who I am?*"
Drawing by Koren; © 1988 The New Yorker Magazine, Inc.

FIGURE 13.3

Marcia's four statuses of identity.

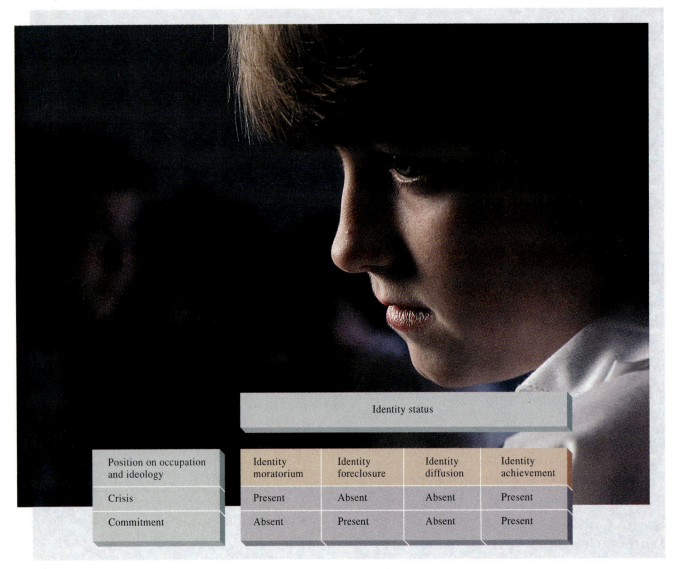

Identity status				
Position on occupation and ideology	Identity moratorium	Identity foreclosure	Identity diffusion	Identity achievement
Crisis	Present	Absent	Absent	Present
Commitment	Absent	Present	Absent	Present

choosing among meaningful alternatives. Most researchers now use the term *exploration* rather than *crisis,* although in the spirit of Marcia's original formulation, we will use the term *crisis.* **Commitment** *is defined as the part of identity development in which adolescents show a personal investment in what they are going to do.*

Identity diffusion *is the term Marcia uses to describe adolescents who have not yet experienced a crisis (that is, they have not yet explored meaningful alternatives) or made any commitments.* Not only are they undecided about occupational and ideological choices, they are also likely to show little interest in such matters. **Identity foreclosure** *is the term Marcia uses to describe adolescents who have made a commitment but have not experienced a crisis.* This occurs most often when parents hand down commitments to their adolescents, more often than not in an authoritarian manner. In these circumstances, adolescents have

not had adequate opportunities to explore different approaches, ideologies, and vocations on their own. **Identity moratorium** *is the term Marcia uses to describe adolescents who are in the midst of a crisis, but their commitments are either absent or only vaguely defined.* **Identity achievement** *is Marcia's term for adolescents who have undergone a crisis and have made a commitment.* Marcia's four statuses of identity are summarized in figure 13.3.

Developmental Changes

Young adolescents are primarily in Marcia's identity diffusion or moratorium statuses. At least three aspects of the young adolescent's development are important in identity formation (Marcia, 1987): Young adolescents must establish confidence in parental support, develop a sense of industry, and gain a self-reflective perspective on their future.

Some researchers believe the most important identity changes take place in youth rather than earlier in adolescence. For example, Alan Waterman (1985, 1989, 1992) has found that from the years preceding high school through the last few years of college, an increase in the number of individuals who are identity achieved occurs, along with a decrease in those who are identity diffused. College upperclassmen are more likely to be identity achieved than college freshmen or high school students. Many young adolescents are identity diffused. These developmental changes are especially true for vocational choice. For religious beliefs and political ideology, fewer college students have reached the identity achieved status, with a substantial number characterized by foreclosure and diffusion. Thus, the timing of identity may depend on the particular role involved, and many college students are still wrestling with ideological commitments (Arehart & Smith, 1990; Harter, 1990a, 1990b).

Many identity-status researchers believe that a common pattern of individuals who develop positive identities is to follow what are called "MAMA" cycles of *moratorium-achiever-moratorium-achiever* (Archer, 1989). These cycles may be recreated throughout life (Francis, Fraser, & Marcia, 1989). Personal, family, and societal changes are inevitable, and as they occur, the flexibility and skill required to explore new alternatives and develop new commitments are likely to facilitate an individual's coping skills.

> *As long as one keeps searching, the answers come.*
>
> —Joan Baez

Family Influences on Identity

Parents are important figures in the adolescent's development of identity. In studies that relate identity development to parenting styles, democratic parents, who encourage adolescents to participate in family decision making, foster identity achievement. Autocratic parents, who control the adolescent's behavior without giving the adolescent an opportunity to express opinions, encourage identity foreclosure. Permissive parents, who provide little guidance to adolescents and allow them to make their own decisions, promote identity diffusion (Bernard, 1981; Enright and others, 1980; Marcia, 1980).

In addition to studies on parenting styles, researchers have also examined the role of individuality and connectedness in the development of identity. Developmentalist Catherine Cooper and her colleagues (Carlson, Cooper, & Hsu, 1990; Cooper & Grotevant, 1989; Grotevant & Cooper, 1985) have demonstrated that the presence of a family atmosphere that promotes both individuality and connectedness are important in the adolescent's identity development. **Individuality** *consists of two dimensions: self-assertion, the ability to have and communicate a point of view; and separateness, the use of communication patterns to express how one is different from others.* **Connectedness** *also consists of two dimensions: mutuality, sensitivity to and respect for others' views; and permeability, openness to others' views.* In general, Cooper's research findings reveal

Margaret Beale Spencer, shown here talking with adolescents, believes that adolescence is often a critical juncture in the identity development of ethnic minority individuals. Most ethnic minority individuals consciously confront their ethnicity for the first time in adolescence.

that identity formation is enhanced by family relationships that are both individuated (encouraging adolescents to develop their own points of view) and connected (providing a secure base from which to explore the widening social worlds of adolescence).

Stuart Hauser and his colleagues (Hauser & Bowlds, 1990; Hauser & others, 1984) have also illuminated family processes that promote the adolescent's identity development. They have found that parents who use *enabling* behaviors (such as explaining, accepting, and giving empathy) facilitate the adolescent's identity development more than parents who use *constraining* behaviors (such as judging and devaluing). In sum, family interaction styles that give the adolescent the right to question and to be different, within a context of support and mutuality, foster healthy patterns of identity development (Harter, 1990b).

Cultural and Ethnic Aspects of Identity

Erikson is especially sensitive to the role of culture in identity development. He points out that, throughout the world, ethnic minority groups have struggled to maintain their cultural identities while blending into the dominant culture (Erikson, 1968). Erikson says that this struggle for an inclusive identity, or identity within the larger culture, has been the driving force in the founding of churches, empires, and revolutions throughout history.

For ethnic minority individuals, adolescence is often a special juncture in their development (Dreyer & others, 1994; Fraser, 1994; Phinney & others, 1994; Phinney & Cobb, 1993; Spencer & Dornbusch, 1990; Spencer & Markstrom-Adams, 1990). Although children are aware of some ethnic and cultural differences, most ethnic minority individuals consciously confront their ethnicity for the first time in adolescence. In contrast to children, adolescents have the ability to interpret ethnic and cultural information, to reflect on the past, and to speculate about the future (Harter, 1990a, 1990b). As they cognitively mature, ethnic minority adolescents become acutely aware of the evaluations of their ethnic group by the majority White culture (Comer, 1988; Ogbu, 1989). As one researcher commented, the young Black American child may learn that Black is beautiful, but conclude as an adolescent that White is powerful (Semaj, 1985).

Ethnic minority youths' awareness of negative appraisals, conflicting values, and restricted occupational opportunities can influence life choices and plans for the future (Spencer & Dornbusch, 1990). As one ethnic minority youth stated, "The future seems shut off, closed. Why dream? You can't reach your dreams. Why set goals? At least if you don't set any goals, you don't fail."

For many ethnic minority youth, a lack of successful ethnic minority role models with whom to identify is a special concern (Blash & Unger, 1992). The problem is especially acute for inner-city ethnic minority youth. Because of the lack of adult ethnic minority role models, some ethnic minority youth may conform to middle-class White values and identify with successful White role models. However, for many adolescents, their ethnicity and skin color limit their acceptance by the White culture. Thus, many ethnic minority adolescents have a difficult task: negotiating two value systems—that of their own ethnic group and that of the White society. Some adolescents reject the mainstream, foregoing the rewards controlled by White Americans; others adopt the values and standards of the majority White culture; and yet others take the difficult path of biculturality (Hiraga & others, 1993).

In one investigation, ethnic identity exploration was higher among ethnic minority than among White American college students (Phinney & Alipura, 1990). In this same investigation, ethnic minority college students who had thought about and resolved issues involving their ethnicity had higher self-esteem than their ethnic minority counterparts who had not. In another investigation, the ethnic identity development of Asian American, Black American, Hispanic American, and White American tenth-grade students in Los Angeles was studied (Phinney, 1989). Adolescents from each of the three ethnic minority groups faced a similar need to deal with their ethnic group identification in a predominantly White American culture. In some instances, the adolescents from the three ethnic minority groups perceived different issues to be important in their resolution of ethnic identity. For Asian American adolescents, pressures to achieve academically and concerns about quotas that make it difficult to get into good colleges were salient issues. Many Black American adolescent females discussed their realization that White American standards of beauty (especially hair and skin color) did not apply to them; Black American adolescent males were concerned with possible job discrimination and the need to distinguish themselves from a negative societal image of Black male adolescents. For Hispanic American adolescents, prejudice was a recurrent theme, as was the conflict of values between their Hispanic cultural heritage and the majority culture. To read further about identity development in ethnic minority youth, turn to Sociocultural Worlds of Development 13.2.

The contexts in which ethnic minority youth live influence their identity development. Many ethnic minority youth in the United States live in low income urban settings where support for developing a positive identity is absent. Many of these youth live in pockets of poverty, are exposed to drugs, gangs, and criminal activities, and interact with other youth and adults who have dropped out of school and/or are unemployed. In such settings, effective organizations and programs for youth can make important contributions to developing a positive identity.

Shirley Heath and Milbrey McLaughlin (1993) studied 60 different youth organizations that involved 24,000 adolescents over a period of five years. They found that these organizations were especially good at building a sense of ethnic pride in inner city ethnic youth. Heath and McLaughlin believe that many inner-city youth have too much time on their hands, too little to do, and too few places to go. Inner city youth want to participate in organizations that nurture them and respond positively to their needs and interests. Organizations that perceive youth as fearful, vulnerable, and lonely but also frame them as capable, worthy, and eager to have a healthy and productive life contribute in positive ways to the identity development of ethnic minority youth.

Gender and Identity Development

In Erikson's (1968) classic presentation of identity development, the division of labor between the sexes was reflected in his assertion that males' aspirations were mainly oriented toward career and ideological commitments, while females' were centered around marriage and childbearing. In the 1960s and 1970s researchers found support for Erikson's assertion about gender differences in identity. For example, vocational concerns were more central to the identity of males, and affiliative concerns were more important in the identity of females (LaVoie, 1976). However, in the last decade, as females have developed stronger vocational interests, sex differences are turning into sex similarities (Waterman, 1985).

Some investigators believe the order of stages proposed by Erikson are different for females and males. One view is that for males identity formation precedes the stage of intimacy, while for females intimacy precedes identity (Douvan & Adelson, 1966). These ideas are consistent with the belief that relationships and emotional bonds are more important concerns of females, while autonomy and achievement are more important concerns of males (Gilligan, 1990). In one study, the development of a clear sense of self by adolescent girls was related to their concerns about care and response in relationships (Rogers, 1987). In another investigation, a strong sense of self in college women was associated with their ability to solve problems of care in relationships while staying connected with both self and others (Skoe & Marcia, 1988). Indeed, conceptualization and measurement of identity development in females should include interpersonal content (Patterson, Sochting, & Marcia, 1992).

The task of identity exploration may be more complex for females than for males, in that females may try to establish

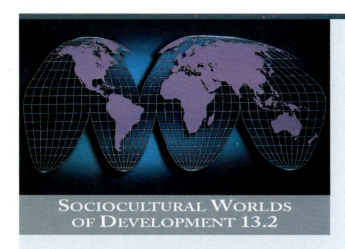

SOCIOCULTURAL WORLDS OF DEVELOPMENT 13.2

The Development of Identity in Native American Youth

Substandard living conditions, poverty, and chronic unemployment place many Native American youth at risk for school failure and poor health, which can contribute to problems in developing a positive identity (LaFromboise & Low, 1989; Spencer & Markstrom-Adams, 1990). A special concern is the negative image of Native Americans that has been perpetuated for centuries in the majority White American culture. To consider further the development of identity in Native American youth, we examine the experiences of a 12-year-old Hopi Indian boy.

The Hopi Indians are a quiet, thoughtful people who go to great lengths not to offend anyone. In a pueblo north of Albuquerque, a 12-year-old boy speaks: "I've been living in Albuquerque for a year. The Anglos I've met, they're different. I don't know why. In school, I drew a picture of my father's horse. One of the other kids wouldn't believe that it was ours. He said, 'You don't really own that horse.' I said, 'It's a horse my father rides, and I feed it every morning.' He said, 'How come?' I said, 'My uncle and my father are good riders, and I'm pretty good.' He said, 'I can ride a horse better than you, and I'd rather be a pilot.' I told him I never thought of being a pilot."

The 12-year-old Indian boy continues, "Anglo kids, they won't let you get away with anything. Tell them something, and fast as lightning and loud as thunder, they'll say, 'I'm better than you, so there!' My father says it's always been like that."

Native American adolescents are not really angry at or envious of White American adolescents. Maybe they are in awe of their future power; maybe they fear it. White American adolescents cannot keep from wondering if, in some way, they have missed out on something and may end up "losing" (Coles, 1986).

The following words of a Native American vividly capture some important ingredients of the 12-year-old boy's interest in a peaceful identity:

Rivers flow.
The sea sings.
Oceans roar.
Tides rise.
Who am I?

A small pebble
On a giant shore;
Who am I
To ask who I am?
Isn't it enough to be?

The Native American adolescent's quest for identity involves a cultural meshing of tribal customs and the technological educational demands of modern society.

identities in more domains than males. In today's world, the options for females have increased and thus may at times be confusing and conflicting, especially for females who hope to successfully integrate family and career roles (Archer, 1989, 1992; Archer & Waterman, 1994; Gilligan, 1990).

At this point we have studied a number of different ideas about culture and identity. A summary of these ideas is presented in concept table 13.2.

CONCEPT TABLE 13.2

Culture and Identity

Concept	Processes/Related Ideas	Characteristics/Description
Culture and rites of passage	Their nature	As in other periods of development, culture influences adolescents' development. Ceremonies mark an individual's transition from one status to another, especially into adulthood. In primitive cultures, rites of passage are often well defined. In contemporary America, rites of passage to adulthood are ill defined.
	Ethnicity	Much of the research on ethnic minority adolescents has not teased apart the influences of ethnicity and social class. Because of this failure, too often researchers have given ethnic explanations that were largely due to socioeconomic factors. While not all ethnic minority families are poor, poverty contributes to the stress of many ethnic minority adolescents. There are legitimate differences between many ethnic groups, and between ethnic groups and the White majority. Recognizing these differences is an important aspect of getting along with others in a diverse, multicultural world. Too often differences between ethnic groups and the White majority have been interpreted as deficits on the part of the ethnic minority group. Another important dimension of ethnic minority groups is their diversity. Ethnic minority groups are not homogeneous; they have different social, historical, and economic backgrounds. Failure to recognize diversity and individual variations results in the stereotyping of an ethnic minority group. Value conflicts are often involved when individuals respond to ethnic issues. One prominent value conflict involves assimilation versus pluralism.
Identity	Erikson's theory	This is the most comprehensive and provocative view of identity development. Identity versus identity confusion is the fifth stage in Erikson's life-cycle theory. During adolescence, worldviews become important and the adolescent enters a psychological moratorium, a gap between childhood security and adult autonomy.
	Some contemporary thoughts about identity	Identity development is extraordinarily complex. It is done in bits and pieces. For the first time in development, during adolescence, individuals are physically, cognitively, and socially mature enough to synthesize their lives and pursue a viable path toward adult maturity.

Concept	Processes/Related Ideas	Characteristics/Description
	The four statuses of identity	Marcia proposed that four statuses of identity exist, based on a combination of conflict and commitment: identity diffusion, identity foreclosure, identity moratorium, and identity achievement.
	Developmental changes	Some experts believe the main identity changes take place in late adolescence or youth rather than in early adolescence. College upperclassmen are more likely to have achieved identity than are freshmen or high school students, although many college students are still wrestling with ideological commitments. Individuals often follow "moratorium-achievement-moratorium-achievement" cycles.
	Family influences	Parents are important figures in adolescents' identity development. Democratic parenting facilitates identity development in adolescence; autocratic and permissive parenting do not. Cooper and her colleagues have shown that both individuation and connectedness in family relations make important contributions to adolescent identity development. Hauser has shown that enabling behaviors promote identity development more than constraining behaviors do.
	Cultural and ethnic influences	Erikson is especially sensitive to the role of culture in identity development, underscoring how throughout the world ethnic minority groups have struggled to maintain their cultural identities while blending into the majority culture. Adolescence is often a special juncture in the identity development of ethnic minority individuals, because for the first time they consciously confront their ethnic identity.
	Gender	While Erikson's classical theory argued for sex differences in identity development, more-recent studies have shown that as females have developed stronger vocational interests, sex differences in identity are turning into similarities. However, others argue that relationships and emotional bonds are more central to the identity development of females than males, and that female identity development today is more complex than male identity development.

LIFE-SPAN HEALTH AND WELL-BEING

Explorations in Education, Work, and Identity Development

Susan Harter (1990a, 1990b) addressed the importance of developing programs for youth that promote the *active* and *realistic* exploration of broad identity goals, such as educational and occupational choices. Such programs may take the form of on-the-job experiences, as in the Boston Compact Youth Incentive Program, which provides students with well-paying summer jobs if they maintain a good record of school attendance and performance. Another program strengthens the link between high school activities and the world of work and provides opportunities for exploring alternatives. This program emphasizes adolescents' choice of areas in which they are both interested and competent, letting them choose educational opportunities that further their development in these domains. This strategy is consistent with Harter's conclusion that the highest levels of self-esteem are found in individuals who are performing competently in domains that are important to them.

What are some other ways to improve identity development? One strategy is to encourage society to recognize the positive benefits of competence in many different domains, not just academic competence. Another strategy is to acknowledge that education is the primary means for achieving success, and to provide individuals with poor academic

Shown here is a scene from the movie Stand and Deliver, *in which Hispanic high school teacher Jaime Escalante (in the center with a cap) spent many evenings and weekends tutoring Hispanic students in math in addition to effectively teaching the students math in the classroom. Escalante's commitment and motivation were transferred to the students, many of whom obtained college scholarships and passed advanced placement tests in calculus.*

skills and low self-esteem better support and more individualized attention. The inspiration of Hispanic high school teacher Jaime Escalante, documented in the movie *Stand and Deliver*, reflects this latter strategy. Escalante was a California high school teacher who spent many evenings and weekends tutoring Hispanic students in math, in addition to effectively teaching the students math in the classroom. Escalante's commitment and motivation were transferred to

the Hispanic high school students, many of whom obtained college scholarships and passed advanced placement tests in calculus. Insisting that high school and college athletes maintain a respectable grade point average is a policy that endorses the importance of academic achievement and competence in other domains, as is the requirement that students maintain respectable grades to participate in jobs programs. ■

CONCLUSIONS

As adolescents wend their way from childhood to adulthood, they influence and are influenced by people in numerous social contexts, including family and peers, dating and school. And their quest for identity—to find out who they are, what they are all about, and where they are going—takes a more central place in their development.

The 15-year-old girl's self-description that began this chapter exemplified the increasing search for an identity during adolescence. We discussed adolescents and their families, including the nature of attachment and autonomy, parent-adolescent conflict, and the maturation of adolescents and parents. Our coverage of peers focused on peer pressure and conformity, cliques and crowds, adolescent groups compared to children groups, and dating. We also evaluated the role of culture, including cross-cultural comparisons, rites of passage, and ethnicity. And we devoted considerable time to investigating identity, including some contemporary thoughts about identity, the four statuses of identity, developmental changes, family influences, cultural and ethnic aspects, and gender. At different points in the chapter we also read about strategies for reducing parent-adolescent conflict, education and the development of ethnic minority adolescents, and explorations in education, work, and identity development.

Don't forget that you can obtain an overall summary of the chapter by again reading the two concept tables on pages 387 and 398. This concludes our coverage of adolescent development. In Section Seven, we continue our journey through the human life cycle, beginning with chapter 14, "Physical and Cognitive Development in Early Adulthood."

KEY TERMS

crowd The largest and least personal of adolescent groups. (384)

cliques Smaller groups that involve greater intimacy among members and have more cohesion than crowds. (384)

dating scripts The cognitive models that adolescents and adults use to guide and evaluate dating interactions. (385)

cross-cultural studies The comparison of a culture with one or more other cultures, which provides information about the degree to which development is similar (universal) across cultures or the degree to which it is culture-specific. (388)

rite of passage A ceremony or a ritual that marks an individual's transition from one status to another. Most rites of passage focus on the transition to adult status. (388)

assimilation The absorption of ethnic minority groups into the dominant group, which often involves the loss of some or virtually all of the behavior and values of the ethnic minority group. (391)

pluralism The coexistence of distinct ethnic and cultural groups in the same society. Individuals with a pluralist stance usually advocate that cultural differences should be maintained and appreciated. (391)

crisis James Marcia defines crisis as a period of identity development during which the adolescent is choosing among meaningful alternatives. (393)

commitment James Marcia defines commitment as the part of identity development in which adolescents show a personal investment in what they are going to do. (394)

identity diffusion James Marcia uses this term to describe adolescents who have not yet experienced a crisis (explored meaningful alternatives) or made any commitments. (394)

identity foreclosure Marcia uses this term to describe adolescents who have made a commitment but have not experienced a crisis. (394)

identity moratorium Marcia uses this term to describe adolescents who are in the midst of a crisis, but their commitments are either absent or vaguely defined. (394)

identity achievement Marcia's term for adolescents who have undergone a crisis and made a commitment. (394)

individuality According to Cooper and her colleagues, individuality consists of two dimensions: self-assertion (the ability to have and communicate a point of view) and separateness (the use of communication patterns to express how one is different from others). (395)

connectedness According to Cooper and her colleagues, connectedness consists of two dimensions: mutuality (sensitivity to and respect for others' views) and permeability (openness to others' views). (395)

Early Adulthood

How many roads must a man walk down before you call him a man?

—Bob Dylan

Early adulthood is a time for work and a time for love, sometimes leaving little time for anything else. For some of us, finding our place in adult society and committing to a more stable life take longer than we imagine. We still ask ourselves who we are and wonder if it isn't enough just to be. Our dreams continue and our thoughts are bold, but at some point we become more pragmatic. Sex and love are powerful passions in our lives—at times angels of light, at others fiends of torment. And we possibly will never know the love of our parents until we become parents ourselves. Section Seven contains two chapters: "Physical and Cognitive Development in Early Adulthood" (chapter 14) and "Socioemotional Development in Early Adulthood" (chapter 15).

Conservatory, Portrait
of Frida Kahlo, detail.

14

Physical and Cognitive Development in Early Adulthood

Chapter Outline

LIFE-SPAN HEALTH AND WELL-BEING

Chapter Boxes

Whatever you can do, or dream you can, begin it. Boldness has genius, power and magic in it.

—Johann Wolfgang von Goethe

We are born twice over; the first time for existence, the second for life;
once as human beings and later as men or as women.

—Jean-Jacques Rousseau

IMAGES OF LIFE-SPAN DEVELOPMENT

Tongue-in-Cheek Reasons Not To Take a Job

Robert is in his senior year of college and just had his 21st birthday last week. Looking to his future and pondering what life might be like over the next few years, he came up with the following tongue-in-cheek reasons not to take a job:

1. You have to work.
2. It's habit forming. Once you get a job, you'll want another, and then another. . . . It's better not to start at all. Why do you think they call it work?
3. Once you stop being a student, you can never go back. Remember those pathetic people who came

back to hang around your high school? You'll look even sillier showing up at mixers, pep rallies, and Sadie Hawkins dances after you have taken a position with some respectable accounting firm.

4. It's unbearably tedious. Not only that, but employees and their families are not eligible to win.
5. People will start calling you "mister" and "sir." Hippies will resent you and call you a "capitalist roader." People with better jobs will shake their heads and say, "What a waste of human talent."
6. Fully employed people can never have sex.

7. You will have to say nice things about the boss's new "flame-thrower red" polyester golf pants, laugh at the boss's jokes about people who mismanage their finances, and carry on endless conversations with your boss about "pennant rallies," "the primaries," and "resort areas." You will have to nod your head with conviction when he refers to his employees as a "team" that works together to "bring home the bacon."
8. If you take a job, you will be an adult. (*The Harvard Lampoon Big Book of College Life*)

PREVIEW

In this chapter, we explore what it is like to take a job, as part of our discussion of careers and work in early adulthood. You will also read about changes in cognitive development in early adulthood, the importance of sexuality in the early adulthood years, and physical changes in early adulthood. But first we will think about the transition from adolescence to adulthood.

THE TRANSITION FROM ADOLESCENCE TO ADULTHOOD

As Bob Dylan asked at the opening of Section VII, "How many roads must a man walk down before you call him a man?" When does an adolescent become an adult? In chapter 12, we saw that it is not easy to tell when a boy or girl enters adolescence. Many developmentalists, though, believe the task of determining adolescence's beginning is easier than determining its end and adulthood's beginning. Although no

consensus exists as to when adolescence is left behind and adulthood is entered, some criteria have been proposed.

Youth and the Criteria for Becoming an Adult

Faced with a complex world of work, with highly specialized tasks, many post-teenagers spend an extended period of time in technical institutes, colleges, and postgraduate centers to acquire specialized skills, educational experiences, and professional training. Their pay is poor and sporadic, and they may

LIFE-SPAN PRACTICAL KNOWLEDGE 14.1

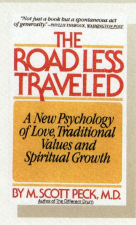

"Not just a book but a spontaneous act of generosity." –PHYLLIS THEROUX, WASHINGTON POST

THE ROAD LESS TRAVELED

A New Psychology of Love, Traditional Values and Spiritual Growth

BY M. SCOTT PECK, M.D.
Author of The Different Drum

The Road Less Traveled

(1978) by M. Scott Peck. New York: Simon & Schuster.

The Road Less Traveled presents a spiritually and emotionally based approach to self-fulfillment. Peck begins by stating that life is difficult and that we all suffer pain and disappointment. He believes we should face up to life's difficulties and not be lazy. Indeed, Peck equates laziness with the original sin, going on to say that people's tendency to avoid problems and emotional suffering is the root of mental disorders. Peck also believes that people are thirsting for integrity in their lives. They are not happy with a country that has "In God we trust" as one of its main emblems and at the same time still leads the world's arms race. They also can't tolerate being just Sunday-morning Christians, he says. To achieve integrity, Peck believes, people need to move spirituality into all phases of their lives.

Peck speaks of four important tools to use in life's journey: delaying gratification, accepting responsibility, dedication to the truth, and balancing. After a thorough analysis of each, Peck explores the will to use them, which he calls "love." Then he probes further and analyzes the relation of growth and religion, which leads him to examine the final step of "the road less traveled": grace. By grace, Peck means the whole range of human activities that support the human spirit. Grace operates at the interface between humans and God and at the frontier between unconscious and conscious thought, in Peck's view.

The Road Less Traveled has been an immensely popular book; it was on the *New York Times* best-sellers list for more than a year. Peck has developed a cultlike following, especially among young people. The book's enthusiasts say that Peck recognized some important voids in people's lives, especially the need for an integrated, spiritually based existence. Some critics say that Peck's ideas are not new and that his thoughts are occasionally fuzzy, especially when he arrives at the meeting point between God and humankind, and unconscious and conscious selves.

change residences frequently. Marriage and a family may be shunned. This period often lasts from 2 to 8 years, although it is not unusual for it to last a decade or longer.

Youth *is sociologist Kenneth Kenniston's term for the transitional period between adolescence and adulthood that is a time of extended economic and personal temporariness.* Kenniston (1970) argues that youth have not settled the questions whose answers once defined adulthood—questions about one's relation to the existing society, about vocation, and about social roles and lifestyles. Youth differs from adolescence because of youth's struggle between developing an autonomous self and becoming socially involved in contrast to adolescence's struggle for self-definition.

Critical Thinking

Other than economic independence and independent decision making, can you think of any other criteria for indicating the beginning of adult status?

Two criteria that have been proposed as signaling the end of youth and the beginning of early adulthood are economic independence and independent decision making. Probably the most widely recognized marker of entrance into adulthood is the occasion when the individual takes a more-or-less permanent full-time job. This usually occurs when the individual finishes school—high school for some, college for others, and graduate school for still others. For those who finish high school, move away from home, and assume a career, the transition to adulthood seems to have taken place. But one out of

every four individuals does not complete high school, and many individuals who finish college cannot find a job. Further, only a small percentage of graduates settle into jobs that remain permanent throughout their adult lives. Also, attaining economic independence from parents is usually a gradual, rather than an abrupt, process. It is not unusual to find college graduates getting a job and continuing to live, or returning to live, with their parents, especially in today's economic climate.

The ability to make decisions is another characteristic that often is not fully developed in youth. We refer broadly here to decision making about a career, about values, about family and relationships, and about life-style. As a youth, the individual may still be trying out many different roles, exploring alternative careers, thinking about a variety of life-styles, and considering the variety of relationships that are available. The individual who enters adulthood usually has made some of these decisions, especially in the areas of life-style and career.

While change characterizes the transition from adolescence to adulthood, keep in mind that considerable continuity still glues these periods together. Consider the data collected in a longitudinal study of more than 2,000 males from the time they were in the tenth grade until 5 years after high school (Bachman, O'Malley, & Johnston, 1978). Some of the males dropped out, others graduated from high school; some took jobs after graduating from high school, others went to college; some were employed, others were unemployed. The dominant picture of the males as they went through this 8-year period was stability rather than change. For example, the tenth-graders who had the highest self-esteem were virtually the same individuals who had the highest self-esteem 5 years after high school. A similar pat-terning was found for achievement orientation—those who were the most achievement oriented in the tenth grade remained the most achievement oriented 8 years later. Some environmental changes produced differences in this transition period. For example, marriage reduced drug use, unemployment increased it. Success in college and career increased achievement orientation; less education and poor occupational performance diminished achievement orientation.

> *The process of entering into adulthood is more lengthy and complex than has usually been imagined. It begins around 17 and continues until 33. . . . A young man needs about 15 years to emerge from adolescence, find his place in adult society and commit himself to a more stable life.*
>
> —Daniel J. Levinson, *Seasons of a Man's Life*, 1978

Transition From High School to College

Just as the transition from elementary school to middle or junior high school involves change and possible stress, so does the transition from high school to college. In many instances, there are parallel changes in the two transitions. Going from being a senior in high school to being a freshman in college replays the top-dog phenomenon of transferring from the oldest and most powerful group of students to the youngest and least powerful group of students that occurred earlier as adolescence began. For many of you, the transition from high school to college was not very long ago. You may vividly remember the feeling of your first days, weeks, and months on campus. You were called a "freshman." Dictionary definitions of *freshmen* describe such students as being in the first year of high school or college, and as novices and beginners. *Seniors* are designated as being in the final year of high school or college, and as above others in decision-making power. The transition from high school to college involves movement to a larger, more impersonal school structure; interaction with peers from more diverse geographical and sometimes more diverse ethnic backgrounds; and increased focus on achievement and its assessment (Belle & Paul, 1989; Upcraft & Gardner, 1989).

But, as with the transition from elementary to middle or junior high school, the transition from high school to college can involve positive features. Students are more likely to feel grown up, have more subjects from which to select, have more time to spend with peers, have more opportunities to explore different life-styles and values, enjoy greater independence from parental monitoring, and be challenged intellectually by academic work.

However, today's college freshmen appear to be experiencing more stress and depression than in the past, according to a survey of more than 300,000 freshmen at more than 500 colleges and universities (Astin, Green, & Korn, 1989). In 1987, 8.7 percent of freshmen reported feeling depressed often; in 1988, the figure rose to 10.5 percent. Fear of failing in a success-oriented world is frequently given as a reason for stress

The transition from high school to college often involves positive as well as negative features. In college, students are likely to feel grown up, be able to spend more time with peers, have more opportunities to explore different life-styles and values, and enjoy greater freedom from parental monitoring. However, college involves a larger, more impersonal school structure and an increased focus on achievement and its assessment.

and depression among college students. The pressure to succeed in college, get an outstanding job, and make lots of money is pervasive, according to many of the students.

Some college students report that they feel "burned out." **Burnout** *is a hopeless, helpless feeling brought on by relentless, work-related stress.* Burnout leaves its sufferers in a state of physical and emotional exhaustion that includes chronic fatigue and low energy. Burnout usually occurs not because of one or two traumatic events but because of a gradual accumulation of heavy, work-related stress (Garden, 1989; Pines & Aronson, 1988).

On a number of campuses, college burnout is the most common reason students leave school before earning their degrees, reaching a rate of 25 percent at some schools. Dropping out of college for a semester or two used to be considered a sign of weakness. Now sometimes called "stopping out" because the student fully intends to return, it may be encouraged for some students who feel overwhelmed with stress. Before recommending "stopping out" though, most counselors suggest first examining ways the overload could be reduced and possible coping strategies that would allow the student to remain in school. The simple strategy of taking a reduced or better-balanced class load sometimes works, for example. Most college counseling services have professionals who can effectively work with students to alleviate the sense of being overloaded and overwhelmed by life (Leafgren, 1989; Rayman & Garis, 1989).

PHYSICAL DEVELOPMENT

Physical status not only reaches its peak in early adulthood, it also begins to decline during this period. An interest in health has increased among young adults, with special concerns about diet, weight, exercise, and addiction.

The Peak and Slowdown in Physical Performance

For most of us, our peak physical performance is reached under the age of 30, often between the ages of 19 and 26. This peak of physical performance occurs not only for the average young adult, but for outstanding athletes as well. Even though athletes keep getting better—running faster, jumping higher, and lifting more weight—the age at which they reach their peak performance has remained virtually the same. Richard Schultz and Christine Curnow (1988) analyzed records from track and field, swimming, baseball, tennis, and golf to learn at which age athletes turned in their best performances. For example, in track and field they studied Olympic results from 1896 through 1980. Overall, the mean age of the winners from 1896 to 1936 was about the same as from 1948 to 1980. In the 1,500-meter race, the earlier winners averaged 25 years of age, the more-recent winners averaged 24.6 years of age. For marathoners, the average age of Olympic champions was 27. The average age for swimming champions was 20 years for males, 18 for females. This gender difference also held for track and field, although the difference was only 1 year. For professional baseball players, the mean age of peak performance was consistently 27 to 28 years, based on wins, strikeouts, and earned run averages for pitchers, and batting averages, home runs, and runs batted in for nonpitchers. For tennis and golf, world professional rankings were examined. In tennis, the champions' mean ages were 25.4 for males, 24.5 for females. In golf, stars' peak performances were 31 years for males, 30 years for females.

In sum, the strength and speed events peak relatively early, compared to those requiring more diverse motor and cognitive skills. In recent years, though, the "biological window" of peak performance has widened in some individual cases. Weight training, once unthinkable for female athletes, has become standard procedure for such athletic stars as Florence Griffith Joyner. Her ability to lift 320 pounds helped build the strength behind her explosive start and leg drive, which won her world records, at the age of 28, of 10.49 seconds in the 100 meters and 21.34 seconds in the 200 meters in the 1988 Olympics. Figure 14.1 summarizes the age of peak performances in professional baseball, the Olympics, tennis, and golf.

We not only reach our peak physical performance during early adulthood, but during this time we are also the healthiest. Few young adults have chronic health problems, and they have fewer colds and respiratory problems than when they were children. Most college students know what it takes to prevent illness and promote health. In one study, college students' ranking of health-protective activities—nutrition, sleep, exercise, watching one's weight, and so on—virtually matched that of licensed nurses (Turk, Rudy, & Salovey, 1984).

Although most college students know what it takes to prevent illness and promote health, they don't fare very well when it comes to applying this information to themselves. In one investigation, college students reported that they probably would never have a heart attack or drinking problem, but that other college students would (Weinstein, 1984). The college students

FIGURE 14.1

Age at peak performance by professional baseball players, Olympic champions, tennis players, and golfers.

Peak performances in baseball	
Pitchers	**Mean age**
Wins	27.3
Strikeouts	27.3
Earned run average	27.7
Nonpitchers	
Batting average	26.5
Home runs	27.3
Runs batted in	28.0

Peak performance age, by event	
Men	**Women**
18	Swimming
19	
20 Swimming	
21	
22	Running short distance
23 Running short distance	
24 Jumping	Running medium distance
Running medium distance	Tennis
Tennis	
25	
26	
27 Running long distance	Running long distance
28 Baseball	
29	
30	Golf
31 Golf	
32	

REPRINTED WITH PERMISSION FROM PSYCHOLOGY TODAY MAGAZINE. Copyright © 1988 (Sussex Publishers, Inc.).

also said no relation exists between their risk of heart attack and how much they exercise, smoke, or eat meat or high-cholesterol food such as eggs, even though they correctly recognized that factors such as family history influence risk. Many college students, it seems, have unrealistic, overly optimistic beliefs about their future health risks.

> *The tissue of life to be*
> *We weave with colors all our own*
> *And in the field of destiny*
> *We reap as we have sown.*
>
> John Greenleaf Whittier
> *Raphael*, 1842

As individuals move from adolescence to early adulthood, they often increase their use of drugs. For example, in one longitudinal investigation, as individuals moved from the tenth grade to 5 years after high school, they increased their cigarette smoking, drinking, marijuana smoking, and use of amphetamines, barbiturates, and hallucinogens (Bachman, O'Malley, & Johnston, 1978). Other data confirm that the period from late adolescence to the late twenties is a time of peak levels for many drugs (Johnston, O'Malley, & Bachman, 1987, 1993). Special concerns are the increase in party drinking by college students and the increased use of cocaine by young adults. Heavy party drinking by college males is common and becoming more common (Johnston, O'Malley, & Bachman, 1991). Fortunately, cocaine use by college students declined from 17.1 percent annual prevalence in 1986 to 3.0 percent in 1992. Still, the number of college students who use cocaine is precariously high, and is likely higher among noncollege youth.

In early adulthood, few individuals stop to think about how their personal life-styles will affect their health later in their adult lives. As young adults, many of us develop a pattern of not eating breakfast, not eating regular meals, and relying on snacks as our main food source during the day, eating excessively to the point where we exceed the normal weight for our age, smoking moderately or excessively, drinking moderately or excessively, failing to exercise, and getting by with only a few hours of sleep at night. These poor personal life-styles were associated with poor health in one investigation of 7,000 individuals from the ages of 20 to 70 (Belloc & Breslow, 1972). In the California Longitudinal Study—in which individuals were evaluated over a period of 40 years—physical health at age 30 predicted life satisfaction at age 70, more so for men than women (Mussen, Honzik, & Eichorn, 1982).

There are some hidden dangers in the peaks of performance and health in early adulthood. While young adults can draw on physical resources for a great deal of pleasure, often bouncing back easily from physical stress and abuse, this may lead them to push their bodies too far. The negative effects of abusing one's body may not show up in the first part of early adulthood, but they probably will surface later in early adulthood or in middle adulthood.

> *Life is not living, but living in health.*
> —Martial, *Epigrams*, A.D. 86

Not only do we reach our peak in physical performance during early adulthood, but it is during this age period that we also begin to decline in physical performance. Muscle tone and strength usually begin to show signs of decline around the age of 30. Sagging chins and protruding abdomens may also begin to appear for the first time. The lessening of physical abilities is a common complaint among the just-turned-thirties. Says one 30-year-old, "I played tennis last night. My knees are sore and my lower back aches. Last month, it was my elbow that hurt. Several years ago it wasn't that way. I could play all day and not be sore the next morning." Sensory systems show little change in early adulthood, but the lens of the eye loses some of its elasticity and becomes less able to change shape and focus on near objects. Hearing peaks in adolescence, remains constant in

the first part of early adulthood, and then begins to decline in the last part of early adulthood. And in the mid to late twenties, the body's fatty tissue increases.

> *After thirty, a body has a mind of its own.*
> —Bette Midler

The health profile of our nation's young adults can be improved by reducing the incidence of certain health-impairing life-styles, such as overeating, and by engaging in health-improving life-styles that include good nutrition and exercise.

Nutrition and Eating Behavior

A tall, slender female goes into the locker room of the fitness center, hurls her towel across the bench, looks squarely in the mirror and says, "You fat pig. You are nothing but a fat pig." The alarm goes off and 33-year-old Robert jumps out of bed, throws on his jogging shorts, and begins his daily predawn 3-mile-run. Returning to shower and dress, he too observes his body in the mirror, tugging at the flabby overhang and commenting, "Why did you eat that bowl of ice cream last night?"

We are a nation obsessed with food, spending an extraordinary amount of time thinking about, eating, and avoiding food. What causes us to be overweight? Which weight-loss program is the most effective?

What Causes People To Be Overweight?

The Chicago Bears' William "The Refrigerator" Perry ballooned to 350 pounds and Coach Mike Ditka suspended him, requiring him to enroll in a 28-day eating-disorders program. Like "The Refrigerator," many of us fight the "battle of the bulge." Although being overweight is a common problem for both men and women, more women view themselves as having a weight problem. After all, the female ideal is a thinner female than the average weight of the female population, so most women are heavier than the ideal (Fallon, 1990).

Understanding weight problems is complex, because body weight involves genetic inheritance, physiological mechanisms, cognitive factors, and environmental influences (Brownell, 1991). Until recently, the genetic component has been underestimated by scientists; recent research findings indicate that some individuals inherit a tendency to be overweight. Only 10 percent of children who do not have obese parents become obese themselves, whereas about 40 percent of children who have one obese parent become obese, and about 70 percent of children who have two obese parents become obese. The actual extent to which this is due to genes rather than to experiences with parents cannot be determined in human research, but animals can be bred to have a propensity for fatness (Blundell, 1984).

The amount of stored fat in your body is an important factor in your body weight's **set point,** *the weight maintained when no effort is made to gain or lose weight.* Fat is stored in adipose cells. When these cells are filled, you do not get hungry. When we gain weight, the number of fat cells increases, and we may not be able to get rid of them. A normal-weight individual has

FIGURE 14.2

Basal metabolic rate in females and males. *BMR varies with age and sex. Rates are usually higher for males and decline proportionately with age for both sexes.*

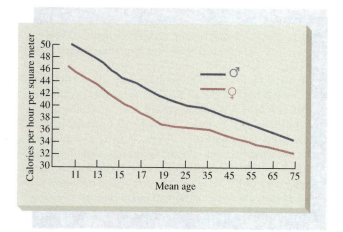

"Let's just go in and see what happens."

Drawing by Booth; © 1986 The New Yorker Magazine, Inc.

30 to 40 billion fat cells. An obese individual has 80 to 120 billion fat cells. Interestingly, adults who were not obese as children but who become overweight as adults have larger fat cells than their normal-weight counterparts, but they do not have more fat cells (VanItallie, 1984).

Health experts also point out that metabolic rate is important in understanding weight. **Basal metabolism rate (BMR)** *is the minimum amount of energy an individual uses in a resting state.* As shown in figure 14.2, BMR varies with age and sex. Rates decline precipitously during adolescence and then more gradually during adulthood, and they are slightly higher for males than females. Many individuals gradually increase their weight over a period of many years. Figure 14.2 suggests that to some degree the weight gain is due to a declining basal metabolism rate. The declining BMR underscores that to maintain weight in adulthood we have to reduce our food intake.

An Increasingly Heavy Population and Weight-Loss Programs

Our gustatory system and taste preferences developed at a time when reliable sources of food were scarce. Our earliest ancestors probably developed a preference for sweets, since ripe fruit, which is a concentrated source of sugar (and, thus, calories), was so accessible. Today we still have a "sweet tooth," but, instead of following our ancestors' healthy choice of vitamin- and mineral-rich fruits, many Americans snack on sweet foods filled with empty calories, like soft drinks and candy bars.

In the United States, approximately 50 percent of those who are middle-aged, and 25 percent of adolescents, are estimated to be overweight (Andres, 1989). Further, the proportion of American children who are overweight increased more than 50 percent from the 1960s to the 1980s (Dietz, 1986). Japanese youth are now turning to the fat-filled fast foods introduced by the United States, and they are the first generation of Japanese to have a significant increase in weight problems. In many industrialized countries, therefore, medical and mental health professionals have become increasingly concerned about getting children and teens to establish good eating habits early on. Eating patterns in childhood and adolescence are strongly associated with obesity in adulthood—80 percent of obese adolescents become obese adults, for example (Brone & Fisher, 1988).

Dieting

Ever since the ultra-slender fashion model Twiggy redefined the ideal feminine physique in the 1960s, losing weight has become a national obsession. At any one time, a third of American women and nearly a quarter of American men are trying to lose weight. The number of dollars spent on diet foods, books, and programs nearly doubled in the 1980s—to close to $30 billion (Brownell, 1990). Even ancient Roman women were known to starve themselves and engage in bulimic behaviors, but never before have women spent so much time, energy, and money on their weight. Since its inception in 1962, Weight Watchers alone has enrolled more than 15 million members, with more women than men joining this program. In spite of all these efforts, the percentage of overweight people has grown over the last 20 years. And, discouragingly, about 90 percent of dieters regain all or most of their lost weight within 1 to 5 years after the end of their diets.

Drugs and Weight Loss

Amphetamines are widely used by dieters because they diminish a person's appetite. Weight loss with amphetamines usually is short-lived, and these drugs often have adverse side effects, such as increased blood pressure and possible addiction. No drug currently is available that has been proven successful in long-term weight reduction (Logue, 1986). The ineffective drugs include over-the-counter drugs such as Dexatrim.

LIFE-SPAN PRACTICAL KNOWLEDGE 14.2

Over 1½ million copies sold
COVERT BAILEY
THE NEW
FIT OR FAT
The phenomenal best seller, completely revised, that guides you from fatness to fitness

The New Fit or Fat

(1991, rev. ed.) by Covert Bailey. Boston: Houghton Mifflin.

The New Fit or Fat describes ways to become healthy by developing better diet and exercise routines. Author Covert Bailey has an M.S. degree in nutritional biochemistry from MIT and heads the Bailey Fit-or-Fat Center in Oregon. Bailey argues that the basic problem for overweight people is not losing weight, which fat people do periodically, but gaining weight, which fat people do more easily than do those with a different body chemistry. He explores ways our bodies store fat and analyzes why crash diets don't work. He explains the relation between fat metabolism and weight, concluding that the ultimate cure for obesity is aerobic exercise coupled with a sensible low-fat diet.

This book was originally published in 1977 as *Fit or Fat;* the 1991 edition is greatly expanded, with new information on fitness life-styles and recent scientific advances. A new chapter also answers readers' most frequently asked questions about Bailey's views on diet and exercise. This book offers solid, no-nonsense advice on how to lose weight and become more physically fit.

Exercise and Weight Loss

Exercise is a much more attractive alternative than weight-loss drugs like amphetamines. Exercise not only burns up calories but also raises the metabolic rate; this beneficial effect persists for several hours after exercising. Exercise actually lowers your body's set point for weight, making it much easier to maintain a lower weight (Bennett & Gurin, 1982). Nonetheless, it is difficult to convince obese individuals to exercise. One reason is that added weight makes exercising itself more difficult to accomplish. Obese persons also often perceive that thin and normal-weight individuals ridicule and downplay their exercising efforts.

An additional problem is that moderate exercise does not reduce calorie consumption, and often individuals who exercise take in more calories than do their sedentary counterparts (Stern, 1984). Still, exercise combined with conscious self-control of eating habits can produce a viable weight loss (Ogden & Wardle, 1991; Polivy & Herman, 1991). When exercise is a component of weight-loss programs, individuals keep weight off longer than when they merely reduce the number of calories they consume.

Conclusions

Interest in the nature of obesity and its treatment shows no signs of abating. Perhaps we will discover ways to treat obesity more effectively, and possibly more-moderate weights—weights that are medically acceptable and achieved by appropriate nutrition and exercise—will become more fashionable as well. The important things to remember, for successful weight control, are these: (1) Don't diet, but change to habits that lead to slow, steady weight loss of less than a pound a week; (2) eat fewer calories and especially less fat; and (3) add regular exercise.

Everything we know about weight loss suggests that a combination of eating healthy foods and exercising works best.

Exercise

In 1961, President John F. Kennedy offered the following message: "We are underexercised as a nation. We look instead of play. We ride instead of walk. Our existence deprives us of the minimum of physical activity essential for healthy living." Without question, people are jogging, cycling, and aerobically exercising more today than in 1961, but far too many of us are still couch potatoes. **Aerobic exercise** *is sustained exercise— jogging, swimming, or cycling, for example—that stimulates heart and lung activity* (Cooper, 1970).

Research on the effects of exercise on health has focused mainly on preventing heart disease. Most health experts recommend that you should try to raise your heart rate to 60 percent of your maximum heart rate. Your maximum heart rate is calculated as 220 minus your age, times 0.6. So if you are 20, you should aim for an exercise heart rate of 120 ($220 - 20 = 200 \times 0.6 = 120$). People in some occupations get more vigorous exercise than those in others. For example, longshoremen have about half the risk of fatal heart attacks as co-workers such as crane drivers and clerks, whose jobs are less physically demanding. Further, one elaborate study of 17,000 male alumni of Harvard University found that those who played strenuous sports regularly had a lower risk of heart disease and were more likely to still be alive at follow-up assessments (Paffenbarger & others, 1986). Based on such findings, some health experts conclude that, regardless of other risk factors (smoking, high blood pressure, overweight, heredity), if you exercise enough to burn more than 2,000 calories a week, you can cut your risk of heart attack by an impressive two-thirds (Sherwood, Light, & Blumenthal, 1989). Burning up 2,000 calories a week through exercise requires a lot of effort, far more than most of us are willing to expend. Exercise you could do to burn 300 calories a day includes swimming or running for about 25 minutes, walking for 45 minutes at about 4 miles per hour, or aerobic dancing for 30 minutes.

The risk of heart attack can also be cut by as much as one-third over a 7-year period with such moderate exercise as rapid walking and gardening. The catch is that you have to spend an hour a day in these activities to get them to pay off. Going against the popular "no pain, no gain" popular philosophy, Robert Ornstein and David Sobel (1989) believe that exercise should be pleasurable, not painful. They point out that 20 percent of joggers running 10 miles a week suffer significant injuries, such as torn knee cartilage and pulled hamstring muscles. Ornstein and Sobel argue that most people can stay healthy by participating in exercise that burns up only 500 calories a week. They believe it is overkill to run 8-minute miles, 3 miles at a time, 5 days a week, for example. Not only are fast walking and gardening on their list of recommended exercises, so are 20 minutes of sex (110 calories), 20 minutes of playing with children (106 calories), and 45 minutes of dancing (324 calories).

Researchers have found that exercise benefits not only physical health, but mental health as well. In particular, exercise improves self-concept and reduces anxiety and depression (Doyne & others, 1987; Lobstein, Ismail, & Rasmussen, 1989; Ossip-Klein & others, 1989). In one study, 109 nonexercising volunteers were randomly assigned to one of four conditions: high-intensity aerobic training, moderate-intensity aerobic training, low-intensity nonaerobic training, and waiting list (Moses & others, 1989). In the high-intensity aerobic group, participants engaged in a continuous walk-jog program that elevated their heart rates to 70–75 percent of maximum. In the moderate-intensity aerobic group, participants engaged in walking or jogging that elevated their heart rates to 60 percent of maximum. In the low-intensity nonaerobic group, participants engaged in strength, mobility, and flexibility exercises in a slow, discontinuous manner for approximately 30 minutes. Those who were assigned to the exercise programs worked out

In one experiment, the self-concept of depressed women was improved by either weight lifting or running.

3 to 5 times a week. Those who were on the waiting list did not exercise. The programs lasted for 10 weeks. As expected, the group assigned to the high-intensity aerobic program showed the greatest aerobic fitness on a 12-minute walk-run. Fitness also improved for those assigned to moderate- and low-exercise programs. However, only the people assigned to the moderate-intensity aerobic training programs showed psychological benefits. These benefits appeared immediately in the form of reduced tension and anxiety and, after 3 months, improved ability to cope with stress. Perhaps the participants in the high-intensity program found the training too demanding, which is not so surprising, since these people were nonexercisers prior to the study. The superiority of the moderate aerobic training program

LIFE-SPAN PRACTICAL KNOWLEDGE 14.3

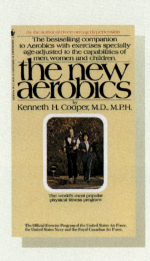

The New Aerobics

(1970) by Kenneth Cooper.
New York: Bantam.

The New Aerobics lays out Cooper's age-adjusted recommendations for aerobic exercise. The aerobic exercise program recommended by Cooper has been adopted by the United States Air Force, the United States Navy, and the Royal Canadian Air Force. The aerobics system is carefully planned to condition the heart, lungs, and body tissues of people who are in either fairly good health or poor health (the latter should always have a physical exam before embarking on any exercise program). The aerobic program uses common forms of exercise—walking, running, swimming, cycling, handball, squash, and basketball—to achieve desired results. Cooper developed a simple, easy-to-follow aerobics point system that is age-adjusted to the capabilities of women, men, and children.

More than any other person, Kenneth Cooper is responsible for getting many people off their couches and into a walking or jogging routine. His influence is international—in Brazil, when people go out for a jog, they call it "doing the Cooper." Two other books by Cooper that are very worthwhile are *The Aerobics Program for Well-Being* (1983) and *The New Aerobics for Women* (1988; coauthored with his wife, Mildred).

over the nonaerobic low-exercise program suggests that a minimum level of aerobic conditioning may be required to obtain important psychological benefits.

Research on the benefits of exercise suggests that both moderate and intense activities produce important physical and psychological gains (Brown, 1991; Plante & Rodin, 1990). Some people enjoy rigorous, intense exercise. Others enjoy more-moderate exercise routines. The enjoyment and pleasure we derive from exercise cooperate with its aerobic benefits to make exercise one of life's most important activities. And remember, regardless of your ultimate exercise program, health experts uniformly recommend that if you are unaccustomed to exercising, always start any exercise program slowly.

Addiction and Recovery

People can develop addictions to many different things, but addiction to drugs is the most prevalent and maladaptive addiction. For our purposes, **addiction** *is physical dependence on a drug.* **Withdrawal** *is the undesirable intense pain and craving experienced by an addict when the addictive drug is withheld.* **Psychological dependence** *is the need to take a drug to cope with problems and stress.* In both physical addiction and psychological dependence, the **psychoactive drug** (*any drug that acts on the nervous system to alter states of consciousness, modify perceptions, and change moods*) plays a powerful, usually disruptive role in the user's life.

Alcohol is the most widely abused psychoactive drug, although concern about cocaine abuse has heightened in recent years. More than 13 million people define themselves as alcoholics. Alcoholism is the third leading killer in the United States. Each year approximately 25,000 people are killed, and 1.5 million are injured, by drunk drivers. More than 50 percent of homicides involve the use of alcohol by either the offender or the victim, and 65 percent of aggressive sexual acts against women involve the use of alcohol by the offender. Alcohol costs the United States more than $40 billion each year in health costs, lost productivity, accidents, and crimes.

Alcohol acts on the body primarily as a depressant and slows down the brain's activities. This may seem surprising, since people who normally tend to be inhibited may begin to talk, dance, or socialize after a couple of drinks. People "loosen up" after one or two drinks because the areas in the brain involved in controlling inhibition and judgment *slow down*. As people drink more, their inhibitions become reduced even further and their judgments become increasingly impaired. Skills (such as driving) and intellectual functioning become impaired as more alcohol is consumed. Eventually the drinker becomes drowsy and falls asleep. With extreme intoxification, a person may lapse into a coma and die. Each of these effects varies with how the person's body metabolizes alcohol, body weight, the amount of alcohol consumed, and whether previous drinking has led to tolerance (Rivers, 1994).

Alcoholism tends to run in families. This fact has led researchers to search for the hereditary underpinnings of alcoholism (Prescott & others, 1994; Schuckit, 1994). Indeed, a common belief held by Americans is that alcoholism is a disease, which implies that it has hereditary/ biological causes. Experts on alcoholism differ on alcoholism's disease categorization. Some believe sociocultural experiences are just as important as genetic, biological factors in determining whether someone will become an alcoholic (Peele & Brodsky, 1991). In one recent investigation, the inheritance of alcoholic problems was assessed in a large number of twins (McGue, Pickens, & Svikis, 1992). There was no genetic tie with alcoholism for the female twins. The genetic-alcoholism link showed up in the male twins, but only if they became alcohol abusers before the age of 20. In all likelihood alcoholism is the result of a number of factors,

LIFE-SPAN PRACTICAL KNOWLEDGE 14.4

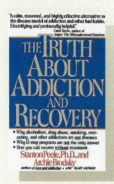

The Truth About Addiction and Recovery

(1991) by Stanton Peele and Archie Brodsky. New York: Simon & Schuster.

Drawing on recent research and detailed case studies, the authors conclude that addictions—whether to food, cigarettes, sex, alcohol, or drugs—are not diseases, and that they are not necessarily lifelong problems. Peele and Brodsky recommend a "life process" program for recovery that emphasizes coping with stress and achieving one's goals.

Separate chapters are included on alcoholism, various other drugs, smoking, gambling, and love and sex. You learn about skills that will help you take control of your life. You also learn to assess your values and what is really important to you, how to carry out plans of change, and where you have been and where you need to go. Distinguished psychotherapist Albert Ellis (1991) said this book should be required reading for people with addictions and for the people with whom they have close relationships.

including those that are biological, psychological, sociocultural, and possibly even spiritual in nature.

Recovery from an addiction is extremely difficult. Some type of therapy or ongoing self-help group is almost always needed for recovery. The most widespread and well-known self-help recovery group is Alcoholics Anonymous (AA) (Alcoholics Anonymous, 1976). AA groups are open and free to anyone—people with virtually any type of addiction or problem are welcome to attend. The average length of sobriety for AA members is 52 months; 29 percent stay sober for more than 5 years. Members range in age from teenagers to the elderly. Increasing numbers of young people have joined in recent years. About twice as many men as women belong. The principles of Alcoholics Anonymous have been revised and adapted by a number of other self-help groups, such as Narcotics Anonymous, Gamblers Anonymous, and Al-Anon.

The Alcoholics Anonymous program relies heavily on confession, group support, and spiritual commitment to God to help people cope with alcoholism. Individuals who attend AA are required to follow a 12-step program of confession, abstinence, and spiritual commitment. AA, however, is not without its critics. AA works for many, but not for all, alcoholics. Some agnostic or atheistic alcoholics have difficulty relating to AA's strong spiritual emphasis, although AA welcomes these individuals to join its groups. Three non-spiritually-oriented self-help groups that have sprung up in recent years as alternatives to AA are Rational Recovery (RR), Secular Organization for Sobriety (SOS), and Women for Sobriety (WFS). AA considers alcoholism a disease and urges members to accept their own helplessness against it; the newer groups emphasize the importance of taking personal responsibility for recovery (Ellis & Velton, 1992; Peele & Brodsky, 1991).

SEXUALITY

We do not need sex for everyday survival the way we need food and water, but we do need it for the survival of the species. Following are some of the inquiries about our sexual lives that we will examine: What is the nature of our sexual attitudes and behavior? What is the current status of our knowledge about AIDS? How sexually knowledgeable are Americans? What is the nature of the menstrual cycle and its hormonal fluctuations? How extensive is forcible sexual behavior, and what can be done about it?

Sexual Attitudes and Behavior

Gathering information about sexual attitudes and behavior has not always been a straightforward task. Consider how you would respond if someone asked you how often you have intercourse or how many different sexual partners you have had. When sexual surveys are conducted, the people most likely to respond are those with liberal sexual attitudes who engage in liberal sexual behaviors. Thus, what researchers know is limited by the reluctance of individuals to answer questions candidly about extremely personal matters and by an inability to get any answer, candid or otherwise, from individuals who believe that talking about sex with strangers should not be done (Allen & Santrock, 1993). With these cautions in mind, we will now examine a number of surveys of sexual attitudes and behavior at different points in the twentieth century, considering heterosexual and homosexual attitudes and behavior.

Heterosexual Attitudes and Behavior

Had you been a college student in 1940, you probably would have had a very different attitude toward many aspects of

LIFE-SPAN PRACTICAL KNOWLEDGE 14.5

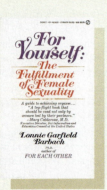

For Yourself

(1975) by Lonnie Barbach. New York: Doubleday.

For Yourself provides advice for women about how to achieve sexual fulfillment. Barbach addresses the worries that often distress nonorgasmic women and tells them how to achieve orgasm. She attacks the negative cultural attitudes that say women should not enjoy sex. A number of exercises that will enable women to achieve orgasm are presented—each exercise is accompanied by an explanation of why it can be effective as well as potential pitfalls to avoid. The book also includes many examples of the sexual lives of women Barbach has counseled in her sex therapy groups. A second book by Barbach, *For Each Other* (1982), is also a good choice; it devotes more time to achieving an orgasm with a sexual partner (especially the communication aspects of sexuality with a partner), women who rarely desire sex, and women who find sex painful.

Sexuality plays an important role in our lives. For most of us, sex has had its pleasurable and its unpleasurable moments. In thinking about the nature of sexuality, take a few moments and examine your own sexual history. What would you have changed? What would you like to be the same?

sexuality than you do today, especially if you are female. A review of college students' sexual practices and attitudes from 1900 to 1980 reveals two important trends (Darling, Kallon, & Van Duesen, 1984). First, the percentage of young people reporting intercourse has dramatically increased, and, second, the proportion of females reporting sexual intercourse has increased more rapidly than in the case of males, although males started off having intercourse more frequently. Prior to the 1970s, about twice as many college males as females reported they engaged in sexual intercourse, but since 1970 the number of males and females has become about equal. These changes suggest that major shifts in the standards governing sexual behavior have taken place—that is, movement away from a double standard in which it is more appropriate for males than females to have intercourse (Robinson & others, 1991).

Two surveys that included wider age ranges of adults verified these trends. Morton Hunt's survey of more than 2,000 adults in the 1970s revealed more permissiveness toward sexuality than Alfred Kinsey's inquiries in the 1940s (Hunt, 1974; Kinsey, Pomeroy, & Martin, 1948). Hunt's survey, however, may have overestimated sexual permissiveness, because it was based on a sample of *Playboy* magazine readers. Kinsey found that foreplay consisted of a kiss or two, but, by the 1970s, Hunt discovered that foreplay had lengthened, averaging 15 minutes. Hunt also found that individuals in the 1970s were using more varied sexual techniques in their lovemaking. Oral-genital sex, virtually taboo at the time of Kinsey's survey, was more accepted in the 1970s.

In one recent national survey of more than 2,000 adults in the United States, most of them practiced serial monogamy—a few exclusive relations, a faithful marriage, followed by divorce and additional relationships (Leigh, Temple, & Trocki, 1993). However, they usually do not protect one another with condoms, despite the risk of passing the AIDS virus from previous partners. And a minority (18%) had unprotected sex with multiple partners in a given year. In another recent national survey, the typical American male under 40 has had seven sex partners—but only one in the past 18 months (Alan Gouttmacher Institute, 1993).

Two more aspects of heterosexual attitudes and behavior are important to consider: the double standard mentioned earlier and the nature of extramarital sex. Although it has recently become more appropriate for females to engage in premarital sex, some vestiges of the double standard still exist (Erickson & Rapkin, 1991; Sprecher & McKinney, 1993; Wilkinson & Kitzinger, 1993). As one male adolescent remarked, "I feel a lot of pressure from my buddies to go for the score." Further evidence of physical and emotional exploitation of females was found in a survey of 432 14- to 18-year-old adolescents (Goodchilds & Zellman, 1984). Both male and female adolescents accepted the right of the male adolescent to be sexually aggressive but left matters up to the female to set the limits for the male's overtures. Yet another manifestation of the double standard is the mistaken belief that it is wrong for females to plan ahead to have sexual intercourse (by taking contraceptive precautions), but it is somewhat permissible for them to be swept away by the passion of the moment.

An individual's sexual preference—heterosexual, homosexual, or bisexual—is most likely determined by a mix of genetic, hormonal, cognitive, and environmental factors.

Critical Thinking

Why have we historically had a double standard in sexual relations?

The double standard is also at work in extramarital relations, although not as extensively as in earlier years. In Kinsey's research, about half of the husbands and one-fourth of the wives had engaged in sexual intercourse with someone other than their spouse during their marriage. In Hunt's survey in the 1970s, the figure was still about the same for men but had increased for women, especially for younger women—24 percent of wives under the age of 25 had experienced extramarital affairs, whereas only 8 percent had in the 1940s. The majority of men and women still disapprove of extramarital sex; in the Hunt survey, more than 80 percent said it is wrong.

Homosexual Attitudes and Behavior

Most individuals think that heterosexual and homosexual behavior are distinct patterns of behavior that can be easily defined. In fact, preference for a sexual partner of the same or opposite sex is not always a fixed decision, made once in life and adhered to forever. For example, it is not unusual for an individual, especially a male, to engage in homosexual experimentation in adolescence but not as an adult. Some individuals engage in heterosexual behavior during adolescence, then turn to homosexual behavior as adults. Homosexual behavior is common among prisoners and others with no alternative sexual partners. Sexual researchers report that lesbians are more likely to be involved in intimate, enduring relationships, have fewer sexual partners, and have fewer "one night stands" than are homosexual men (Bell & Weinberg, 1978).

Both the early (Kinsey) and the more recent (Hunt) surveys indicated that about 4 percent of the males and 3 percent of the females surveyed were exclusively homosexual. Although the incidence of homosexual behavior does not seem to have increased, attitudes toward homosexuality were becoming more permissive, at least until recently. In 1986 the Gallup Poll began to detect a shift in attitudes brought about by public awareness of acquired immune deficiency syndrome (AIDS).

For example, in 1985 slightly more than 40 percent of all Americans believed that "homosexual relations between consenting adults should be legal"; by 1986 the figure had dropped to just about 30 percent (Gallup Report, 1987). Individuals who have negative attitudes toward homosexuals also are likely to favor severe controls for AIDS, such as excluding AIDS carriers from the workplace and schools (Pryor & others, 1989).

Why are some individuals homosexual and others heterosexual? Speculation about this question has been extensive, but no firm answers are available (Rowlett, Patel, & Greydanus, 1992). Homosexual and heterosexual males and females have similar physiological responses during sexual arousal and are aroused by the same types of tactile stimulation. Investigators find no differences between homosexuals and heterosexuals for a wide range of attitudes, behaviors, and adjustments (Bell, Weinberg, & Mammersmith, 1981). Recognizing that homosexuality is not a form of mental illness, the American Psychiatric Association has discontinued its classification of homosexuality as a disorder, except in cases in which the individuals themselves consider the sexual orientation to be abnormal.

An individual's sexual orientation—heterosexual or homosexual—is most likely determined by a combination of genetic, hormonal, cognitive, and environmental factors

LIFE-SPAN PRACTICAL KNOWLEDGE 14.6

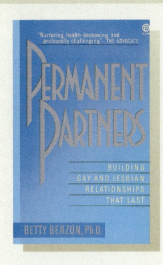

Permanent Partners

(1988) by Betty Berzon. New York: Dutton.

Permanent Partners presents the knowledge and understanding that will help gay and lesbian couples make their relationships work, satisfy, and last. Berzon examines the obstacles that same-sex couples face as they try to create a new life together. The author is a lesbian who has counseled same-sex couples for many years. Among the obstacles she explores are lack of visible long-term couples as role models; absence of support from society—from employers to landlords to insurers—

and too often from the gay or lesbian couple's families of origin; a "tradition of failure"; and the guidance gap, the lack of adequate advice for how to effectively build a life with another man or woman.

This is an excellent book on gay and lesbian relationships, both for gays and lesbians who are thinking about becoming coupled or are perplexed about their current relationships, and for anyone who wants to improve their understanding of gay and lesbian couples. Two other good books on gay and lesbian relationships are *The New Loving Someone Gay,* by Don Clark, and *Lesbian Couples,* by D. Merilee Clunis and G. Dorsey Green.

(McWhirter, Reinisch, & Sanders, 1989; Money, 1987; Savin-Williams & Rodriguez, 1993; Whitman, Diamond, & Martin, 1993). Most experts on homosexuality believe that no one factor alone causes homosexuality and that the relative weight of each factor may vary from one individual to the next. In effect, no one knows exactly what causes an individual to become a homosexual. Scientists have a clearer picture of what *does not* cause homosexuality. For example, children raised by gay or lesbian parents or couples are no more likely to be homosexual than are children raised by heterosexual parents. There also is no evidence that male homosexuality is caused by a dominant mother or a weak father, or that female homosexuality is caused by girls choosing male role models. One of the biological factors believed to be involved in homosexuality is prenatal hormone conditions (Ellis & Ames, 1987). In the second to fifth months after conception, the exposure of the fetus to hormone levels characteristic of females may cause the individual (male or female) to become attracted to males. If this "critical prenatal period hypothesis" turns out to be correct, it would explain why researchers and clinicians have found that a homosexual orientation is difficult to modify.

How can gays and lesbians adapt to a world in which they are a minority? According to psychologist Laura Brown (1989), gays and lesbians experience life as a minority in a dominant, majority culture. For lesbian women and gay men, developing a *bicultural identity* creates new ways of defining themselves. Brown believes that gays and lesbians adapt best when they don't define themselves in polarities, such as trying to live in an encapsulated gay or lesbian world completely divorced from the majority culture or completely accepting the dictates and bias of the majority culture. Balancing the demands of the two cultures—the minority gay/lesbian culture and the majority heterosexual culture—can often lead to more effective coping for homosexuals, says Brown.

A special concern in the lives of gays and lesbians is the bias and discrimination they face. In some instances, the bias has led to violence against homosexuals, violence not only toward them but toward their children as well. Becoming a more gentle, humane society requires that we reduce bias, discrimination, and prejudice not only against ethnic minority groups and women, but also against other minority groups, such as lesbians and gays (Gruskin, 1994). To become such a culture, each of us needs to be willing to ask how viewing certain human experiences through the lens of lesbian and gay realities might alter our understanding of those experiences (Brown, 1992).

AIDS

No single sexually transmitted disease (STD) has had a greater impact on sexual behavior, or created more public fear in the past decade, than AIDS. **AIDS** *is a sexually transmitted disease that is caused by a virus, human immunodeficiency virus (HIV), that destroys the body's immune system* (see figure 14.3). Following exposure to HIV, an individual is vulnerable to germs that a normal immune system could destroy. In 1981, when AIDS was first recognized in the United States, there were fewer than 60 reported cases. Beginning in 1990, according to Dr. Frank Press, president of the National Academy of Sciences, we started losing as many Americans each year to AIDS as the total number killed in the Vietnam War, almost 60,000 Americans. According to federal health officials, 1 to 1.5 million Americans are now asymptomatic carriers of AIDS—those who are infected with the virus and presumably capable of infecting others but who show no clinical symptoms of AIDS. The incidence of AIDS is especially high among ethnic minorities in the United States (Jemmott & Jones, 1993; Mays, 1991, 1993; Osmond & others, 1993). Although Blacks and Hispanics represented 12.3 percent and 8 percent of the United States population in 1988, 30 percent of the reported AIDS

FIGURE 14.3

The AIDS virus destroys the body's immune system. *This individual with AIDS is one of more than 60,000 Americans who die every year from AIDS.*

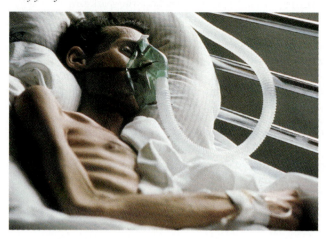

cases were Blacks and 14 percent were Hispanics. Much of the AIDS prevention literature, as well as the instructions included with condoms, require a high school reading proficiency. It is estimated that approximately 40 percent of adult Hispanics lack this proficiency.

In 1989 the first attempt to assess AIDS among college students was made. Tests of 16,861 students found 30 infected with the virus (American College Health Association, 1989). If the 12.5 million students attending college that year were infected in the same proportion, 25,000 students would have had the AIDS virus.

Experts say that AIDS can be transmitted only by sexual contact, the sharing of needles, or blood transfusions. Although 90 percent of all AIDS cases continue to occur among homosexual males and intravenous drug users, a disproportionate increase among females who are heterosexual partners of bisexual males or of intravenous drug users has been noted recently. This increase suggests that the risk of AIDS may be increasing among heterosexual individuals who have multiple sex partners (Boyer & Hein, 1991; Krijnen, van den Hoek, & Coutinho, 1994).

Remember that it is not who you are, but what you do, that puts you at risk for getting HIV. *Anyone* who is sexually active or uses intravenous drugs is at risk. No one is immune. Once an individual is infected, the prognosis is likely to be illness and death. The only *safe* behavior is abstinence from sex, which is not perceived as an option by most individuals. Beyond abstinence, there is only *safer* behavior, such as sex with a condom (Cox, 1994).

Just asking a date about his or her sexual behavior does not guarantee protection from AIDS and other sexually transmitted diseases. For example, in one investigation, 655 college students were asked to answer questions about lying and sexual behavior (Cochran & Mays, 1990). Of the 442 respondents who said they were sexually active, 34 percent of the males and 10 percent of the females said they had lied so their partner would have sex with them. Much higher percentages—47 percent of the men and 60 percent of the women—said they had been lied to by a potential sexual partner. When asked what aspects of their past they would be most likely to lie about, more than 40 percent of the men and women said they would understate the number of their sexual partners. Twenty percent of the men, but only 4 percent of the women, said they would lie about their results from an AIDS blood test. Let's now examine the course of AIDS.

In the first stage of the disease—*HIV+ and asymptomatic*—individuals do not show the characteristics of AIDS but can transmit the disease. It is estimated that 20 to 30 percent of those in Stage 1 will develop AIDS within 5 years. In Stage 2—*HIV+ and symptomatic*—an unknown number of those who had the silent infection develop symptoms, including swelling of the lymph glands, fatigue, weight loss, diarrhea, fever, and sweats. Many who are HIV+ and symptomatic continue to the final stage—*AIDS*. A person with AIDS has the symptoms of AIDS plus one or more diseases, such as pneumonia, which are fatal to AIDS patients because of their vulnerable immune systems. Although there is no known cure for AIDS, several drugs are being tested, including AZT, or zidovudine, approved by the FDA for treatment of the symptoms of AIDS in 1987.

Because it is possible, and even probable among high-risk groups, to have more than one STD at a time, efforts to prevent one disease can help reduce the prevalence of other diseases. Efforts to prevent AIDS can also help prevent adolescent pregnancy and other sex-related problems.

If you or someone you know would like more information about AIDS, you can call the National AIDS Hot Line at 1–800–342–7432, 8 A.M.–2 A.M. EST, 7 days a week. Given the increasing incidence of AIDS and other sexually transmitted diseases, it's crucial that both teenagers and adults understand these diseases and other aspects of sexuality. But how much do Americans really know about sex?

Sexual Knowledge

According to June Reinisch (1990), director of the Kinsey Institute for Sex, Gender, and Reproduction, the United States is a nation whose citizens know more about how their automobiles function than how their bodies function sexually. Reinisch directed a recent national assessment of basic sexual knowledge, given to 1,974 adults. Among the results of the assessment were the following:

- Sixty-five percent of the respondents did not know that most erection difficulties begin with physical problems.

- Seventy-five percent did not know that approximately 40 percent of all American men have had an extramarital affair (some experts believe that the rate of male infidelity is 60 percent or more).

- Fifty percent did not know that oil-based lubricants should not be used with condoms or diaphragms, since some can produce holes in less than 60 seconds.

LIFE-SPAN PRACTICAL KNOWLEDGE 14.7

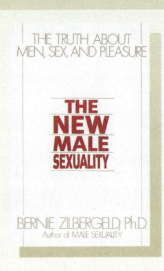

THE TRUTH ABOUT
MEN, SEX, AND PLEASURE

THE NEW MALE SEXUALITY

BERNIE ZILBERGELD, Ph.D.
Author of MALE SEXUALITY

The New Male Sexuality

(1992) by Bernie Zilbergeld.
New York: Bantam.

The New Male Sexuality is a very up-to-date, comprehensive book about male sexuality. An introductory section tackles male sexual myths and unrealistic expectations, and then turns to sexual reality and gives men a brief course in sexual knowledge. The next section explores better sex through topics such as how to be a good lover with your partner, how to be a better listener, touching, arousal, and how to keep the spark alive in long-standing relationships. A final section is devoted to resolving problems and includes discussion of ejaculatory control, erection difficulties, problems of sexual desire, and even advice for fathers on how to communicate more effectively about sex with their sons.

This is an excellent, easy-to-read, well-organized, authoritative guide to male sexuality. It is a giant step above the crass, how-to sex books that have populated the sex self-help sections of many bookstores in recent years.

And Americans adolescents also have woefully inadequate sexual knowledge. In one investigation, a majority of adolescents believed that pregnancy risk is greatest during menstruation (Zelnik & Kantner, 1977).

Of course, it's not that American adolescents and adults are sheltered from sexual messages. According to Reinisch, we are inundated with sexual messages, but not sexual facts. Sexual information is abundant, but much of it is misinformation (Haffner, 1993). In some cases, even sex-education teachers display sexual ignorance. One high school sex-education teacher referred to erogenous zones as "erroneous zones," possibly causing the students to wonder if their sexually sensitive zones were characterized by error!

Sexuality expert Seth Kalichman (1994) recently discussed some of the problems involved in exploring our sexual lives with others and in developing sexually responsive behavior in challenging situations. Kalichman believes that one of the most difficult aspects of developing our sexual identity is the lack of opportunity to define our values for ourselves. For example, when was the last time you had the opportunity to have an open conversation about such topics as sexual relationships, birth control, sexually transmitted diseases, premarital sexual relationships, extramarital sexual relationships, homosexuality, and bisexuality? How often do people with varying sexual backgrounds, orientations, and views come together and have nonconfrontational discussions?

Not only do we lack the opportunities to openly express our sexual views, we also rarely receive such shared information from others. Such exchanges hardly ever occur even in our most intimate relationships. This means that much of our sexuality is shaped within the confines of our own experience, often in informal ways through the family, peers, media, schools, and other social institutions.

One opportunity for individuals to openly explore their sexuality in the context of diverse others is in classes designed specifically for sex education. These classes often encourage discussion, use small groups for class projects, and bring in guest speakers from a variety of backgrounds.

The Menstrual Cycle and Hormones

From early adolescence until some point in middle adulthood, a woman's body undergoes marked changes in hormone levels that are associated with the menstrual cycle. The latter part of the menstrual cycle, from about day 22 on, is associated with a greater incidence of depression, anxiety, and irritability than is the middle of the menstrual cycle, when ovulation is occurring. Women show higher levels of self-esteem and confidence during ovulation in comparison to other phases of the menstrual cycle (Bardwick, 1971). The weight of the evidence shows that mood swings are definitely associated with the middle of the menstrual cycle and the later premenstrual phase. However, it is not entirely clear whether the mood changes are due to positive upswing of mood during the middle phase, a downward swing during the premenstrual phase, or a combination of both. Moreover, as many as 25 percent of all women report no mood shifts at all during these two phases (Hyde, 1985).

What causes the changes in mood that affect 75 percent of all women? Hormonal changes are clearly one factor. Female hormones reach their peak at about day 22 to day 24 of the menstrual cycle, just at the time when depression and irritability peak. By contrast, mood changes could affect hormone levels. If so, intense feelings of irritability and depression may feed back to the endocrine system and produce more estrogen.

So far we have discussed a number of important issues involving sexuality that include sexual attitudes and behavior,

AIDS, and the menstrual cycle. But it is important to also consider another topic involving sexuality—forcible sexual behavior.

Forcible Sexual Behavior

Most people choose to engage in sexual intercourse or other sexual activities, but, unfortunately, some people force others to engage in sex. **Rape** *is forcible sexual intercourse with a person who does not give consent.* Legal definitions of rape differ from state to state. For example, in some states, husbands are not prohibited from forcing their wives to have intercourse, although this law has been challenged in several states (Greenberg & others, 1989). Because of the difficulties involved in reporting rape, the actual incidence is not easily determined. It appears that rape occurs most often in large cities, where it has been reported that 8 of every 10,000 women 12 years and older are raped each year. Nearly 200,000 rapes are reported each year in the United States.

Why is rape so pervasive in the American culture? Feminist writers believe that males are socialized to be sexually aggressive, to regard women as inferior beings, and to view their own pleasure as the most important objective. Researchers have found the following characteristics common among rapists: aggression enhances the offender's sense of power or masculinity; rapists are angry at women generally; and they want to hurt their victims (Browne & Williams, 1993; Donat & D'Emilio, 1992; Gutek, 1993; Knight, Rosenberg, & Schneider, 1985).

An increasing concern is **date, or acquaintance, rape,** *which is coercive sexual activity directed at someone with whom the individual is at least casually acquainted.* Date rape is an increasing problem on college campuses (Lloyd, 1991). A survey of college women found that 24 percent had experienced unwanted attempts at intercourse, and 31 percent had been subjected to unwanted fondling of their genitals (Kavin & Parcell, 1977).

Rape is a traumatic experience for the victim and those close to her or him (Sorenson & White, 1992). The rape victim initially feels shock and numbness, and is often acutely disorganized. Some victims show their distress through words and tears; others show more internalized suffering. As victims strive to get their lives back to normal, they may experience depression, fear, and anxiety for months or years. Sexual dysfunctions, such as reduced sexual desire and the inability to reach orgasm, occur in 50 percent of all rape victims (Sprei & Courtoi, 1988). Many rape victims make changes in their life-style, moving to a new apartment or refusing to go out at night. A victim's recovery depends on both her coping abilities and her psychological adjustment prior to the assault. Social support from parents, spouse, and others close to her are important factors in recovery, as is the availability of professional counseling, which sometimes is obtained through a rape crisis center (Koss, 1990).

Most victims of rape are women. Male rape does occur, however. Men in prisons are especially vulnerable to rape, usually by heterosexuals who use rape as a means of establishing their domination and power. Though it might seem impossible for a man to be raped by a woman, a man's erection is not completely under his voluntary control, and some cases of male rape by women have been reported (Sarrel & Masters, 1982).

Although male victims account for fewer than 5 percent of all rapes, the trauma that males suffer is just as great as that experienced by females.

At this point we have discussed a number of ideas about the transition from adolescence to adulthood, physical development, and sexuality. A summary of these ideas is presented in concept table 14.1. Now we examine the possibility that cognitive changes take place in early adulthood.

COGNITIVE DEVELOPMENT

Do people continue to develop cognitively in adulthood, or are they as smart as they ever will be by the end of adolescence? Do people continue to develop their creative skills in adulthood, or are they as creative as they ever will be in childhood and adolescence?

Cognitive Stages

Piaget believed that an adolescent and an adult think in the same way. But some developmentalists believe it is not until adulthood that individuals consolidate their formal operational thinking. That is, they may begin to plan and hypothesize about problems as adolescents, but they become more systematic in approaching problems as adults. While some adults are more proficient than adolescents at developing hypotheses and deducing solutions to problems, many adults do not think in formal operational ways at all (Keating, 1980, 1990).

Other developmentalists believe that the absolute nature of adolescent logic and youth's buoyant optimism diminish in early adulthood. According to Gisela Labouvie-Vief (1982, 1986), a new integration of thought takes place in early adulthood. She thinks the adult years produce pragmatic constraints that require an adaptive strategy of less reliance on logical analysis in solving problems. Commitment, specialization, and channeling energy into finding one's niche in complex social and work systems replace the youth's fascination with idealized logic. If we assume that logical thought and buoyant optimism represent the criteria for cognitive maturity, we would have to admit that the cognitive activity of adults is too concrete and pragmatic. But from Labouvie-Vief's view, the adult's understanding of reality's constraints reflects cognitive maturity, not immaturity.

Critical Thinking

Other than an increase in pragmatic thinking, can you think of other ways that our cognitive development advances in early adulthood?

Our cognitive abilities are very strong during early adulthood, and they do show adaptation to the pragmatic aspects of our lives. Less clear is whether our logical skills actually decline. Competence as a young adult probably requires doses of both logical thinking skills and pragmatic adaptation to reality. For example, as architects design a building, they logically analyze and plan the structure but

CONCEPT TABLE 14.1

The Transition From Adolescence to Adulthood, Physical Development, and Sexuality

Concept	Processes/Related Ideas	Characteristics/Description
Transition from adolescence to adulthood	Youth	This transition was proposed by Kenniston; it is a period of economic and personal temporariness, and struggle between interest in autonomy and becoming socially involved. The period of youth averages 2 to 8 years but can be longer.
	Criteria for adulthood	Two criteria are economic independence and independent decision making. However, clear-cut criteria are yet to be established.
	Continuity and change	There is both change and continuity in the transition from adolescence to adulthood.
Physical development	The peak and slowdown in physical performance	Peak physical status is reached between ages 18 and 30, especially between 19 and 26. Health also peaks during these years. There is a hidden hazard in these peaks of physical performance and health; bad health habits may be formed. Toward the latter part of early adulthood, a detectable slowdown and decline in physical status is apparent.
	Nutrition and eating behavior	The causes for being overweight are complex and involve genetic factors, physiological mechanisms, cognitive factors, and environmental influences. We have become an increasingly heavy population, and weight-loss programs abound. Drugs have not effectively controlled weight over the long term. Exercise is one of the most effective ways to lose weight, especially when combined with less fat intake.
	Exercise	Both moderate and intense physical exercise produce important physical and psychological gains, such as lowered risk of heart disease and reduced anxiety. Experts increasingly recommend that your level of exercise should be pleasurable.
	Addiction and recovery	Addiction to drugs is a widespread problem in our society, with alcoholism being especially prevalent. Many people call alcoholism a disease, which implies that it has genetic, biological underpinnings, but alcoholism is likely caused by a number of factors, not just heredity alone. Recovery from an addiction is very difficult. Alcoholics Anonymous is a widespread self-help support group for alcoholics and people with other problems. Other, non-spiritually-oriented self-help support groups have recently sprung up.

understand the cost constraints, environmental concerns, and time it will take to get the job done effectively.

William Perry (1970) has also charted some important changes in the ways young adults think differently than adolescents. He believes adolescents often view the world in a basic dualistic fashion of polarities—right/wrong, we/they, or good/bad, for example. As youth mature and move into the adulthood years, they gradually become aware of the diversity of opinion and the multiple perspectives that others hold, which shakes their dualistic perceptions. Their *dualistic thinking* gives way to *multiple thinking,* as individuals come to understand that authorities may not have all of the answers. They begin to carve out their own territory of individualistic

thinking, often believing that others are entitled to their own opinions and that one's personal opinion is as good as anyone else's. As these personal opinions become challenged by others, multiple thinking yields to *relative subordinate thinking,* in which an analytical, evaluative approach to knowledge is consciously and actively pursued. Only in the shift to *full relativism* does the adult completely comprehend that truth is relative, that the meaning of an event is related to the context in which the event occurs and is confined to the framework that the knower uses to understand that event. In full relativism, the adult recognizes that relativism pervades all aspects of life, not just the academic world, and the adult also understands that knowledge is constructed, not given; it is contextual, not

Concept	Processes/Related Ideas	Characteristics/Description
Sexuality	Heterosexual attitudes and behavior	Heterosexual attitudes and behavior have become more liberal in the twentieth century, but some vestiges of the sexual double standard remain.
	Homosexual attitudes and behavior	Preference for a sexual partner of the same sex is not always a fixed decision. Rates of homosexual behavior have remained constant during the twentieth century. Until recently acceptance of homosexuality had been increasing, but the AIDS epidemic has reversed that trend. An individual's sexual orientation—whether heterosexual or homosexual—is likely to be determined by a mix of genetic, hormonal, cognitive, and environmental factors. A special concern is the bicultural adjustment of lesbians and gays, as well as bias and discrimination against homosexuals.
	AIDS	AIDS is caused by a virus, HIV (human immunodeficiency virus), that destroys the body's immune system. AIDS can be transmitted only through sexual contact, the sharing of needles, or blood transfusions. There is no known cure for AIDS.
	Sexual knowledge	According to a recent national survey, Americans are not very knowledgeable about sex. Many American adults and adolescents have misconceptions about sex.
	The menstrual cycle and hormones	The relation between the menstrual cycle and personality fluctuations in females have been studied, and there is a relation between mood swings and the middle and later premenstrual phases of the cycle.
	Forcible sexual behavior	Some individuals force others to engage in sexual activity. Rape is forcible sexual intercourse with a person who does not give consent. Legal definitions of rape vary from state to state. An increasing concern is date, or acquaintance, rape. Rape is a traumatic experience; a woman's recovery depends on her coping resources and how well adjusted she was prior to the assault. Male rape constitutes about 5 percent of all rape cases.

absolute. Perry's ideas have been widely used by educators and counselors in working with young adults in academic settings. Perry's ideas are oriented toward well-educated, bright individuals.

> *What can be known? The unknown. My true self runs toward a hill. More! O more! Visible.*
>
> —Theodore Roethke

Another perspective on adult cognitive change is offered by K. Warner Schaie (1977). He believes that Piaget's cognitive stages describe increasing efficiency in the *acquisition* of new information. It is doubtful that adults go beyond the powerful methods of scientific thinking characteristic of formal operational thought in their quest for knowledge. However, according to Schaie, adults do progress beyond adolescents in their *use* of intellect. For example, in early adulthood, we typically switch from acquiring knowledge to applying knowledge, using what we know to pursue careers and families. The **achieving stage** *is Schaie's early adulthood stage that involves the application of intelligence to situations that have profound consequences for achieving long-term goals, such as those involving careers and knowledge.* These solutions must be integrated into a life plan that extends far into the future.

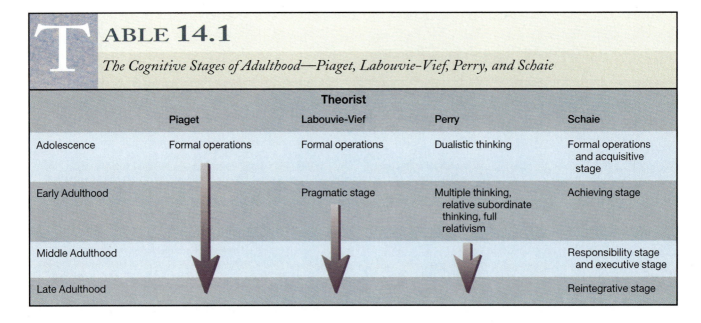

TABLE 14.1

The Cognitive Stages of Adulthood—Piaget, Labouvie-Vief, Perry, and Schaie

| | **Theorist** | | | |
	Piaget	Labouvie-Vief	Perry	Schaie
Adolescence	Formal operations	Formal operations	Dualistic thinking	Formal operations and acquisitive stage
Early Adulthood		Pragmatic stage	Multiple thinking, relative subordinate thinking, full relativism	Achieving stage
Middle Adulthood				Responsibility stage and executive stage
Late Adulthood				Reintegrative stage

Schaie believes that young adults who master the cognitive skills needed to monitor their own behavior, and have therefore acquired considerable independence, move on to the next stage that involves social responsibility. The **responsibility stage** *is Schaie's stage that occurs when a family is established and attention is given to the needs of a spouse and offspring.* Similar extensions of cognitive skills are needed as the individual's career develops and responsibility for others arises on the job and in the community. The responsibility stage often begins in early adulthood and extends into middle adulthood.

The **executive stage** *is Schaie's middle adulthood stage in which people are responsible for societal systems and organizations (government or business, for example). In the executive stage the individual develops an understanding of how societal organizations work and the complex relationships that are involved.* In middle age, individuals may become presidents of business firms, deans of academic institutions, officials of churches, or take other positions that require a knowledge of how an organization works and the complex relationships that are involved. Executives need to know who answers to whom, and for what purpose. They must monitor organizational activities over time (past, present, and future) and up and down the organizational hierarchy. Attainment of the executive stage, of course, depends on exposure to opportunities that permit the development and practice of relevant skills.

The **reintegrative stage,** *which occurs in late adulthood, is Schaie's final stage that involves older adults choosing to focus their energy on the tasks and activities that have meaning for them.* In late adulthood, the need to acquire knowledge declines further. The need to monitor decisions also declines, because the future appears short and inconsequential. Executive monitoring also declines because most individuals have retired from the position that required this type of intellectual application. What, then, is the nature of the older adult's cognitive stage? In Schaie's view, it is reintegrative, which closely corresponds to Erikson's final stage in the life cycle, integrity versus despair. Elderly people's

acquisition and application of knowledge is—to a greater extent than earlier in life—related to their interests, attitudes, and values. The elderly are less likely to waste time on tasks that have little or no meaning for them. They are less likely to expend effort to solve a problem unless that problem is one they face in their lives. For example, they tend to show little interest in abstract questions, such as "Which is better, communism or capitalism?" unless the questions relate to their motivation to make sense out of their lives as a whole, such as "What is the purpose of life?" or "What comes after death?" A summary of Schaie's adult cognitive stages, along with those proposed by Piaget, Labouvie-Vief, and Perry is presented in table 14.1.

Creativity

At the age of 30, Thomas Edison invented the phonograph, Hans Christian Anderson wrote his first volume of fairy tales, and Mozart composed *The Marriage of Figaro.* It hardly seems that these represent a decline in creativity during early adulthood. In several investigations, the quality of productivity of recognized adults was the highest during their thirties; approximately 80 percent of the most important creative contributions were completed by the age of 50 (Dennis, 1966; Lehman, 1960). In another approach, the total productivity, not just the superior works, of creative individuals in the arts, sciences, and humanities who had lived long lives was investigated (Dennis, 1966). The point in adult development at which creative production peaked varied from one discipline to another. In the humanities, the seventies was just as creative a decade as the forties. Artists and scientists, though, began to show a decline in creative productivity in their fifties. In all instances, the twenties was the least productive decade in terms of creativity. There are exceptions, of course. In the sciences, Benjamin Duggar discovered the antibiotic aureomycin when he was 72. The first major paper of Nobel laureates in science was published at the average age of 25. All laureates who were past 70, however, continued to publish scholarly papers in scientific journals. These data support the belief that individuals who are bright and productive during their early adult years maintain their creativity in their later years. It is inappropriate to conclude that there is a linear decrease in creativity during the adult years (Simonton, 1989).

CAREERS AND WORK

At age 21, Thomas Smith graduated from college and accepted a job as a science teacher at a high school in Boston. At age 26, Sally Caruthers graduated from medical school and took a job as an intern at a hospital in Los Angeles. At age 20, Barbara Breck finished her training at a vocational school and went to work as a computer programmer for an engineering firm in Chicago. Earning a living, choosing an occupation, establishing a career, and developing in a career—these are important themes of early adulthood.

Theories of Career Development

Three dominant theories describe the manner in which individuals make choices about careers—Ginzberg's developmental theory, Super's self-concept theory, and Holland's personality type theory.

Ginzberg's Developmental Theory

The **developmental theory of career choice** *is Eli Ginzberg's view that individuals go through three career choice stages—fantasy, tentative, and realistic* (Ginzberg & others, 1951). When asked what they want to be when they grow up, young children may answer "a doctor," "a superhero," "a teacher," "a movie star," "a sports star," or any number of other occupations. In childhood, the future seems to hold almost unlimited opportunities. Ginzberg argues that until about the age of 11, children are in the *fantasy stage* of career choice. From the ages of 11 to 17, adolescents are in the *tentative stage* of career development, a transition from the fantasy stage of childhood to the realistic decision making of young adulthood. He believes that adolescents progress from evaluating their interests (11 to 12 years of age) to evaluating their capacities (13 to 14 years of age) to evaluating their values (15 to 16 years of age). Thinking shifts from less subjective to more realistic career choices at around 17 to 18 years of age. The period from 17 to 18 years of age through the early twenties is called the *realistic stage* of career choice by Ginzberg. At this time, the individual extensively explores available careers, then focuses on a particular career, and finally selects a specific job within the career (such as family practitioner or orthopedic surgeon within the career of doctor).

Critics have attacked Ginzberg's theory on a number of grounds. For one, the initial data were collected from middle-class youth, who probably had more career options open to them. And, as with other developmental theories (such as Piaget's), the time frames are too rigid. Moreover, Ginzberg's theory does not take into account individual differences—some persons make mature decisions about careers (and stick with them) at much earlier ages than specified by Ginzberg. Not all

children engage in career fantasies either. In a revision of his theory, Ginzberg (1972) conceded that lower-class individuals do not have as many options available to them as middle-class individuals do. Ginzberg's general point—that at some time during late adolescence or early adulthood more realistic career choices are made—is probably correct.

Super's Self-Concept Theory

The **career self-concept theory** *is Donald Super's view that the individual's self-concept plays a central role in career choice. Super believes a number of developmental changes in vocational self-concept take place during the adolescent and young adulthood years* (Super, 1967, 1976). First, at about 14 to 18 years of age, adolescents develop ideas about work that mesh with their already existing global self-concept—this phase is called *crystallization.* Between 18 and 22 years of age, they narrow their career choices and initiate behavior that enables them to enter some type of career—this phase is called *specification.* Between 21 and 24 years of age, young adults complete their education or training and enter the world of work—this phase is called *implementation.* The decision on a specific, appropriate career is made between 25 and 35 years of age—this phase is called *stabilization.* Finally, after the age of 35, individuals seek to advance their careers and reach higher-status positions—this phase is called *consolidation.* The age ranges should be thought of as approximate rather than rigid. Super believes that career exploration in adolescence is a key ingredient of the adolescent's career self-concept. He constructed the Career Development Inventory to assist counselors in promoting adolescents' career exploration.

Holland's Personality Type Theory

Personality type theory *is vocational theorist John Holland's (1973, 1987) view that it is important to develop a match or fit between an individual's personality type and the selection of a particular career.* Holland believes that when individuals find careers that fit their personalities, they are more likely to enjoy the work and stay in their jobs longer than their counterparts who work at jobs not suited for their personalities. Holland proposes six basic career-related personality types: realistic, investigative, artistic, social, enterprising, and conventional (see figure 14.4).

Realistic. Individuals who have this type of vocational interest like the outdoors and working in manual activities. They are often less social, have difficulty in demanding situations, and prefer to work alone or with other realistic persons. Holland describes the realistic type as physically robust, practical, and often non- or anti-intellectual. A listing of the jobs associated with the realistic type shows a match with mostly blue-collar positions, such as labor, farming, truck driving, and construction, along with a few technical jobs such as engineer and pilot (Gottfredson & Holland, 1989; Lowman, 1991). The realistic type has the lowest prestige level of the six occupational interest types.

Investigative. The investigative type is interested in ideas more than in people, is rather indifferent to social relationships, is troubled by highly emotional situations, and may be perceived by others as being somewhat aloof and yet highly intelligent.

FIGURE 14.4

Holland's model of personality types and career choices.

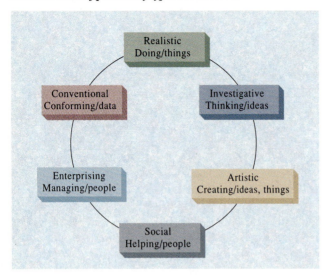

The educational level and the prestige level of the investigative type are the highest of the six types (Gottfredson, 1980). Most of the scientific, intellectually oriented professions fall into this category.

Artistic. The artistic type has a creative orientation. These individuals enjoy working with ideas and materials to express themselves in new ways. Artistic types often have a distaste for conformity, valuing freedom and ambiguity, and sometimes have difficulty in interpersonal relations. They tend to have high educational levels and experience moderate to high prestige. Relatively few artistic occupations exist, compared to the relatively large number of individuals who fall into the artistic type. As a result, some artistic types choose careers in their second or third most typical career type and express their artistic tendencies in hobbies and leisure.

Social. Oriented toward working through and with other people, social types tend to have a helping orientation. They enjoy nurturing and developing others, perhaps working to assist others in need, especially the less advantaged. Showing a much stronger interest in people than in intellectual pursuits, and often having excellent interpersonal skills, they are likely to be best equipped to enter "people" professions such as teaching, social work, counseling, and the like. The social type also has a high prestige rating.

Enterprising. Another type that is more oriented toward people than toward either things or ideas is the enterprising type. These individuals seek to dominate others, especially when they want to reach goals. Therefore, enterprising types are good at coordinating the work of others to accomplish a task. Their skills include being able to persuade other people to do something

and to adopt their own attitudes and choices. Ranking fourth of the sixth types in education and prestige, they match up best with such careers as sales, management, and politics.

Conventional. This type usually functions best in well-structured circumstances and jobs and is skilled at working with details. Conventional individuals like to work with numbers and perform clerical tasks, as opposed to working with ideas or people. They usually do not aspire to high-level positions in an organization. They are best suited for structured jobs such as bank tellers, secretaries, and file clerks. Of the six types, they show up in fifth place in education and prestige.

Evaluation of Holland's Theory. If all individuals (and careers) fell conveniently into Holland's personality types, career counselors would have an easy job. However, individuals are typically more varied and complex than Holland's theory suggests. Even Holland (1987) states that individuals rarely are pure types, and most persons are a combination of two or three types. Still, the basic idea of matching the abilities and attitudes of individuals to particular careers is an important contribution to the career development field. Holland's personality types are incorporated into the Strong-Campbell Interest Inventory, a widely used measure in career guidance.

Exploration, Planning, and Decision Making

At some point toward the end of adolescence or the beginning of early adulthood, most individuals enter some type of occupation. Exploration of a number of career options is widely recommended by career counselors. Individuals often approach career exploration and decision making with ambiguity, uncertainty, and stress (Lock, 1988). In one investigation of individuals after they left high school, over half the position changes (such as student to student, student to job, job to job) made between leaving school and the age of 25 involved floundering and unplanned changes. The young adults were neither systematic nor intentional in their career exploration and planning (Super, Kowalski, & Gotkin, 1967).

Predicting career choices and guiding individuals toward rewarding occupations is a complex undertaking (Vondracek, 1991). In the first several years of college, most students cannot accurately chart their career path through the adult years. Many students change majors while in college, discover that their employment after college is not directly related to their college major, and change careers during the course of adulthood (Rothstein, 1980). To some career counselors, the unpredictability of career pursuit by college students means that many students should not follow a path of narrow vocational training but rather should take a course of broad liberal education. Other career counselors believe that to increase the probability of getting a good job, an intense, focused course of study in a particular discipline is a wise strategy. To read about how to develop a personal, individualized career plan, turn to Perspectives on Parenting and Education 14.1.

LIFE-SPAN PRACTICAL KNOWLEDGE 14.8

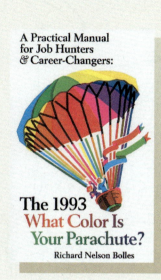

A Practical Manual for Job Hunters & Career-Changers:

The 1993 What Color Is Your Parachute?

Richard Nelson Bolles

What Color Is Your Parachute?

(1993) by Richard Bolles. Berkeley, CA: Ten Speed Press.

What Color Is Your Parachute? is an extremely popular book on job hunting. Author Richard Bolles is an Episcopal priest who changed from pastoral counseling to career counseling. *What Color Is Your Parachute?* was first published in 1970. Since 1975, an annual edition has appeared. This book has become the career seeker's bible. Bolles tries to answer your concerns about the job-hunting process and refers you to many sources that provide valuable information. Unlike many self-help books on job hunting, *What Color Is Your Parachute?* does not necessarily assume that you are a recent college graduate seeking your first job. Bolles also spends considerable time discussing job hunting for people seeking to change careers. He describes a number of myths about job hunting and successfully combats them. He also provides invaluable advice about where jobs are, what to do to get yourself hired, and how to cut through all of the red tape and confusing hierarchies of the business world to meet with the key people who are most likely to make the decision about whether to hire you or not.

What Color Is Your Parachute? was one of the 25 best self-help books in the recent national survey of clinical and counseling psychologists (Santrock, Minnett, & Campbell, 1994). Bolles writes in a warm, engaging, personal tone. His chatty comments are often witty and entertaining, and the book is attractively packaged with cartoons, drawings, and many self-administered exercises.

The Life Contour of Work in Adulthood

The occupational cycle has four main stages: selection and entry, adjustment, maintenance, and retirement (see figure 14.5). These stages are readily identifiable in careers that move in an orderly progression; they become more obscure in disorderly work patterns or work changes that require some form of readjustment. In chapter 16, we will discuss the stage of maintenance and career change in middle adulthood, and in chapter 19, we will address the stage of retirement and the work world of older adults. Here we focus on the two initial stages that take place primarily in early adulthood—selection and entry, and adjustment.

Entering an occupation signals the beginning of new roles and responsibilities for the individual. The career role is different from the role the individual might have had as a temporary or part-time worker during adolescence. Career role expectations for competence are high, and the demands are real for the young adult. When individuals enter a job for the first time, they may be confronted by unanticipated problems and conditions. Transitions are required as the individual tries to adjust to the new role. Meeting the expectations of a career and adjusting to a new role are crucial for the individual at this time in adult development (Heise, 1991; Smither, 1988).

Adjustment is the key label in the second stage of life's work contour. This is the period Daniel Levinson (1978) calls "Age 30 Transition" in men. According to Levinson, once an individual enters an occupation, he must develop a distinct occupational identity and establish himself in the occupational world. Along the way, he may fail, drop out, or begin a new path. He may stay narrowly on a single track or try several new directions before settling firmly on one. This adjustment phase

FIGURE 14.5

The life contour of work in adulthood. The occupational cycle has four main stages: selection and entry, adjustment, maintenance, and retirement.

The life contour of work in adulthood

Selection and entry | Adjustment | Maintenance | Retirement

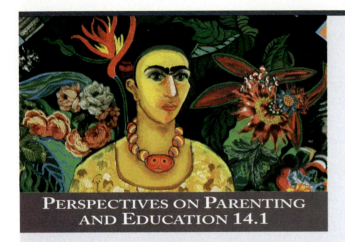

PERSPECTIVES ON PARENTING AND EDUCATION 14.1

Developing a Personal, Individualized Career Plan

Developing a good career plan is often perceived as a one-time event, a step toward making a single, major job commitment. However, each of us will likely experience changes during our lifetimes that will require modifications in our careers, adjustments in our career goals, and often a change of careers. In fact, the average worker now makes five or six job transitions (Hyatt, 1990).

The first job choice is like the first step on a long journey. It is useful to develop the expectation that change cannot be avoided and to have the assumption that change can usually be turned to your advantage. If you look at all the companies that merge, downsize, or even disappear, you can more easily accept the inevitability of change. Furthermore, change is inescapable because, as you have already read, individuals change developmentally as they age through the adult years. Such changes can have profound influences on career development.

In the widely popular book on job hunting and careers *What Color Is Your Parachute?* Richard Bolles (1994) emphasizes

"I don't have a parachute of any color."
© 1988 by Sidney Harris—Harvard Business Review.

that individuals need to use change to become wiser. It is our experiences that bring about change, so it is useful to understand the two aspects of experiences. The first aspect is the actual

---

lasts several years. A professional may spend several years in academic study while an executive may spend his early years in lower- or middle-management jobs. Hourly workers usually need several years to explore the work world, become familiar with the industry and the labor union, and move beyond the apprentice status to a permanent occupational role.

The level of attainment reached by individuals in their early thirties varies (Landy, 1989). A professional may just be getting started or may have already become well established and widely known. One executive may be on the bottom rung of the corporate ladder; another may be already near the top. An hourly worker may be an unskilled laborer without job security or a highly skilled craftsperson earning more than some executives or professionals.

We have seen how the early years of adulthood mark the development and integration of cognitive capacities that enable individuals to attain purposeful, organized mastery of their personal lives and work. We have also seen the importance of

work's role in our lives as young adults. Next, we consider one of the major changes in the work role.

Women and Work

Mary is a 26-year-old policewoman. Nancy is a 30-year-old electrical engineer. Barbara is a 32-year-old bricklayer. The occupations of these women underscore the dramatic changes of women's changing work roles.

Changing Women's Roles

The situation for women has changed dramatically. Modern contraceptive methods have made it possible for women to limit the number of children they have, and oftentimes to plan births to minimally disrupt their careers. With modern medical care, women have fewer complications during pregnancy and birth. Child rearing has changed, too. Domestic burdens are relatively light in modern society, and various types of child-care facilities have become available.

event, and the second aspect is the person's interpretation of and response to the event. One error in interpretation is to view one's past mistakes as harmful to one's career development. Rather, Bolles believes, the most important aspect of career development and adjustment is realizing that you will make mistakes but that positive change comes about by learning from these mistakes.

In addition to learning from our mistakes, it is important to consider other important components of a successful career plan, such as goals, hopes, and wishes, marketable skills, and personal fit (Waterman, 1991). Goals, wants, and wishes are our hopes for the future and the interests we want to pursue. In other words, they are what we would like to do, have, and be. Some people have no problems articulating goals, but most people don't find it that easy. If it is difficult for you, it might be best to begin with general goals, such as wanting to be happy (which is on everyone's list), and then work toward more specific goals (such as "I want to retire the December after I'm 60 years old," "I want to make enough money by the time I'm 30 to buy a Porsche," "I want to get my MBA degree by the age of 25 and work for a large oil company," or "I want to learn foreign languages and travel, the first time by being useful in the Peace Corps").

In thinking about goals, it is helpful to think about multiple categories, such as health/fitness, mental/intellectual, social interaction/special relationships, work/careers, etc. For some individuals, where a person lives is a category that is as important as, or even more important than, the type of career itself. Ardent surfers drive taxis just to be in Honolulu. Aspiring actors wait tables just to live in Hollywood. Some people refuse to live in a large city, others find heaven in Manhattan. For these individuals, the three most important aspects of a career are identical to those that real estate agents list as being what is most important to the monetary value of a house: location, location, location!

One person, already a systems analyst, didn't have location on his list of goals, wants, and wishes, but he did have the following: (1) losing 15 pounds and getting into good shape, (2) taking some management courses, (3) spending less time with people he cared little about and more with those he loved, and (4) becoming a manager in a computer-oriented department or company.

Like on any long journey, you need markers along the way to tell you that you are on track. These are your goals, the specific things that you will do and accomplish as you move through your career development. Every dream and vision you might develop about your future career development can be broken down into specific goals and time frames. Keeping your career dreams in focus, write down some of the specific work, job, and career goals you have for the next 20, 10, and 5 years. Be as concrete and specific as possible. In making up goals, start from the farthest point—20 years from now—and work backward. If you go the other direction, you run the risk of adopting goals that are not precisely and clearly related to your dreams (Jaffe & Scott, 1991).

To successfully compete in the job market, we must have not only goals, but also marketable skills. We need to ask ourselves what someone else will hire us to do in the current and future workplace. We need to consider current trends of employment and technology, thinking especially hard about the personal talents, abilities, and qualities for which employers are willing to pay good money. Again, it is helpful to make a list. Include the abilities, talents, aptitudes, skills, personality characteristics, and attitudes of yours that an employer is likely to find attractive. One way to accumulate items for a marketable-skills list is to brainstorm about all of your previous job experiences. And be sure to talk with others about your abilities, talents, and other qualities—they will probably have observed strengths you have that you haven't noticed about yourself.

The effect of these various changes has been to create a society that makes task demands on men and women that are vastly different from those of the past. Men no longer gain appreciable advantages from superior physical strength, women are no longer confined solely to bearing and rearing children and performing domestic tasks. Women who are economically independent do not have an economic need to marry, so they feel less pressure to marry. They may marry for other reasons, but marriage is not their only option. And those who choose not to be mothers, though married, may relate to men in markedly different ways than do women who do choose to be mothers.

Women in the Work Force

The changing role of women is evident in the increasing rate of women's employment (DeCorte, 1993; London & Greller, 1991; Morrison, 1993). In 1960, only one-third of women with children were employed; but in 1988, 55 percent of married women with infants and 61 percent of women with preschool children worked outside the home. Women's occupation are

also changing. Four in ten college women today intend to pursue careers in law, business, medicine, or engineering, while in 1970 only two in ten said they intended to pursue these male-dominated careers (Astin, Green, & Korn, 1987). In one recent investigation, gender-role orientation was related to females' stress in male-dominated occupations (Long, 1989). High-masculine (self-assertive) women reported less anxiety and strain in their jobs than did low-masculine women.

> *The test for whether or not you can hold a job should not be the arrangement of your chromosomes.*
>
> —Bella Abzug, *Bella!,* 1972

Today, women fill nearly one-third of management positions, an improvement from the 19 percent level in 1972, but most are in jobs with little authority and low pay (Paludi, 1992). Only 2 percent of senior executives are women, and only 1.7 percent of corporate officers of Fortune 500 companies are

The character played by Diane Keaton (above), in the movie Baby Boom, *lost her job when she couldn't find a way to juggle her career and family roles and still give her child adequate care and attention. A 1991 survey of 200 U.S. corporations found that their executives perceived flexible scheduling as the number one management issue. Some individuals are turning down higher-paying jobs to take jobs with more flexibility. In the remaining years of the 1990s, this is likely to be an increasing trend. The increased trend toward flexibility is reflected in* The Corporate Reference Guide to Work-Family Programs *that was released in 1991—of the 188 Fortune 1000 companies surveyed, 77 percent reported that they have instituted flexible scheduling, and 48 percent offer job sharing.*

women. A special concern about the career development of females, as well as ethnic minority individuals, is the experience of a "glass ceiling" in management. The glass ceiling concept was popularized in the 1980s to describe a subtle barrier that is virtually transparent, yet is so strong it prevents females from moving up in the management hierarchy. This discrimination still often portrays the "good manager" as "masculine" rather than "androgynous," or simply competent, in many organizations (Morrison & Von Glinow, 1990).

Dual-Career Marriage

As growing numbers of females pursue careers, they are faced with questions involving career and family (Anderson & Leslie, 1991; Gustafson & Magnusson, 1991; Spade & Reese, 1991; Steil & Weltman, 1991). Should they delay marriage and childbearing and establish their career first? Or should they combine their career, marriage, and childbearing in their twenties? Some females continue to embrace the domestic patterns of an earlier historical period. They have married, borne children, and committed themselves to full-time mothering. These "traditional" females have worked outside the home only intermittently, if at all, and have subordinated the work role to the family role. Many other females, though, have veered from this time-honored path. They have postponed motherhood, or in some cases chosen not to have children. They have developed committed, permanent ties to the workplace that resemble the

pattern once reserved only for men. When they have had children, they have strived to combine a career and motherhood. While there have always been "career" females, their numbers are growing at an unprecedented rate. More about work and family developmental paths is presented in Sociocultural Worlds of Development 14.1.

> *One can live magnificently in this world, if one knows how to work and how to love.*
>
> —Count Leo Tolstoy, 1856

Dual-career marriages can have advantages and disadvantages for individuals (Thompson & Walker, 1989; Zedeck & Mosier, 1990). Of course, one of the main advantages is financial. One of every three wives earns 30 to 50 percent of the family's total income, which helps to explain why most first-time home buyers are dual-career couples. In addition to their financial benefits, dual-career marriages can contribute to a more equal relationship between husband and wife and enhanced feelings of self-esteem for women. Among the possible disadvantages or stresses of dual-career marriages are added time and energy demands, conflict between work and family roles, competitive rivalry between husband and wife, and, if the family includes children, concerns about whether the children's needs are being adequately met.

Critical Thinking

As women's work roles have changed, what adaptations has this forced men to make?

Many men, especially those with low earnings, have a difficult time accepting their wives' employment. For example, in one investigation, married men who opposed their wives' employment were more depressed when their own earnings were low rather than high (Ulbrich, 1988). These men apparently experience a double insult to themselves as providers. Many husbands whose wives work report that they would like to have a wife who is a full-time homemaker. For example, in one study, although husbands appreciated their wives' earnings, they felt they had lost the services of a full-time homemaker—someone who is there when they get home, who cooks all their meals, and who irons all their clothes (Ratcliff & Bogdan, 1988). Some husbands, of course, encourage their wives' employment, or support their decision to pursue a career. In one investigation of high-achieving women, many of their husbands took pride in their wives' accomplishments and did not feel competitive with them (Epstein, 1987).

> *If . . . society will not admit of woman's free development, then society must be remolded.*
>
> —Elizabeth Murdoch

At this point we have discussed a number of ideas about cognitive development and careers and work in early adulthood. A summary of these ideas is presented in concept table 14.2.

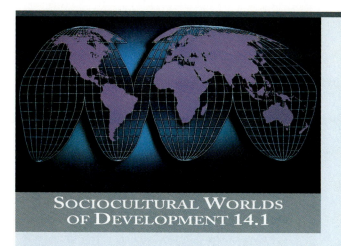

The Life and Career Paths of Joanne and Joan

The life paths of Joanne and Joan were very different (Gerson, 1986). Joanne grew up in a typical American family. While her father earned only a modest wage as a repairman, her mother stayed home to rear four children because both parents believed that full-time mothering for the children was more important than additional income. However, they hoped that Joanne would educate herself for a better life. But Joanne was more interested in dating than in schoolwork or in her part-time job at a fast-food restaurant. When she became pregnant at 17, she was happy to marry her boyfriend and assume the role of a full-time mother. Two children, several brief and disenchanting sales jobs and 10 years later, Joanne still finds satisfaction in full-time mothering. At times she feels financial pressure to give up homemaking for paid work and resents being snubbed when she says her family is her career. But every time she searches the want ads, she vividly remembers how much she disliked her temporary jobs. Since her husband earns enough money to make ends meet, the urge to go to work quickly passes. Instead, Joanne is seriously thinking about having another child.

Joanne's life history reflects the traditional model of female development. An adult woman chooses a domestic life for which she was prepared emotionally and practically since childhood. Approximately 20 percent of women from a variety of social class and family backgrounds are believed to follow this life course (Gerson, 1986). These women are insulated from events that might steer them away from their expected paths. They are neither pushed out of the home by economic necessity or marital instability nor pulled into the workplace by enticing opportunities. Instead, they remain committed to the domestic role that they assume is the woman's proper and natural place in society.

In contrast, consider Joan's path. Like Joanne, Joan believed as a child that when she grew up she would marry, have children, and live happily ever after as a housewife. She harbored a vague wish to go to college, but her father thought women should not go to college, and as a low-paid laborer he could not afford to send her to college, anyway. Joan worked after high school as a filing clerk and married Frank, a salesman, 2 years later. Within 6 months of the ceremony, she was pregnant and planning to stay home with her young child. But things changed soon after her daughter was born. Unlike Joanne, she became bored and unhappy as a full-time mother. Taking care of the baby was not the ultimate fulfillment for Joan. Motherhood was a mixture of feelings for her—alternately rewarding and frustrating, joyful and depressive. Despite her reluctance to admit these feelings to anyone but herself, a growing sense of emptiness and the need for additional income spurred Joan to look for paid work. She took a job as a bank teller, perceiving it to be a temporary way to boost family income. But the right time to quit never came. Frank's income consistently fell short of their needs, and as his work frustrations mounted, their marriage began to falter. When Frank pressured Joan to have another child, she began to think more seriously about whether she wanted to remain married to Frank. Just when the marriage seemed unbearable, Joan's boss gave her a chance to advance. She accepted the advance and decided to divorce Frank. Today, more than a decade later, Joan is dedicated to her career, aspires to upper-level management, and does not plan to remarry or expand her family beyond one child.

Joan's life represents an increasingly common pattern among women—one of rising work aspirations and ambivalence toward motherhood. Like their traditional counterparts, these women grew up wanting and preparing for a domestic role, only to find that events stimulated them to move in a different direction. About one-third of women today seem to follow this life pattern (Gerson, 1986). These women are more likely to experience unstable relationships with men, unanticipated opportunities for job advancement, economic squeezes at home, and disappointments with mothering and full-time homemaking. As a consequence, heightened work ambitions replace their earlier home-centered orientation. Although Joanne and Joan experienced similar childhood backgrounds and aspirations, their lives diverged increasingly as they were confronted with the opportunities and restrictions of early adulthood.

There are a number of other life trajectories that the career and family paths of women in early adulthood can take. More about the increasing dilemma of career and family roles appears in chapter 15 as we discuss the nature of marriage, family, and adult life-styles.

CONCEPT TABLE 14.2

Cognitive Development and Careers and Work

Concept	Processes/Related Ideas	Characteristics/Description
Cognitive development	Cognitive stages	It is not until adulthood that many individuals consolidate their formal operational thinking, and many other adults do not think in formal operational ways at all. Labouvie-Vief argues that young adults enter a pragmatic stage of thought. Perry theorized that as individuals move into adulthood, their thinking becomes more relativistic. Schaie proposed a sequence of cognitive stages: acquisitive, achieving, responsibility, executive, and reintegrative.
	Creativity	The highest productivity of superior works seems to be in the thirties, although when total productivity is considered, it depends on the discipline.
Careers and work	Theories of career development	Three major theories have been proposed—Ginzberg's developmental theory of career choice, Super's career self-concept theory, and Holland's personality-type theory.
	Exploration, planning, and decision making	Everything we know about career development suggests that young people should explore a variety of career options. Planning and decision making about careers is often disorganized and vaguely pursued. Predicting career choices and guiding individuals toward rewarding occupations is a complex undertaking.
	The life contour of work in adulthood	The contour follows this course: selection and entry, adjustment, maintenance, and retirement.
	Women and work	Women's roles have changed dramatically in recent years. There has been a tremendous influx of women into the labor force. Women have increased their presence in occupations previously dominated by men, although women, as well as ethnic minorities, still experience a "glass ceiling" in management. As greater numbers of women pursue careers, they face issues involving career and family. Dual-career marriages can involve advantages as well as stresses.

CONCLUSIONS

We don't stop developing at the end of adolescence. Our adult years are full of growth, change, new challenges, and development.

We began this chapter by exploring the transition from adolescence to adulthood and considered Kenniston's ideas about youth being a transitional period between adolescence and early adulthood. We also studied the transition from high school to college. Our coverage of physical development in early adulthood focused on the peak and slowdown in physical performance during these years, nutrition and eating behavior, exercise, and addiction. We also spent considerable time

evaluating sexuality, studying such topics as heterosexual and homosexual attitudes and behavior, the epidemic of AIDS, sexual knowledge, the menstrual cycle and hormones, and forcible sexual behavior. Then we examined the nature of cognitive changes in early adulthood, considering whether we enter any new cognitive stages in adulthood and when our creativity is most likely to peak. Our exploration of careers and work involved theories of career development, the importance of exploration, planning, and decision making, the life contour of work in adulthood, and women and work. At different

points in the chapter you also read about some tongue-in-cheek reasons not to take a job, thought about how to develop a personal, individualized career plan, studied the very different life and career plans of two women, Joanne and Joan, and examined the nature of women's health issues.

Don't forget that you can obtain a summary of the entire chapter by again reading the two concept tables on pages 422 and 432. In the next chapter we continue our coverage of adulthood development by studying socioemotional development in early adulthood.

LIFE-SPAN HEALTH AND WELL-BEING

Women's Health Issues

Women and men experience health and the health-care system differently (Paludi, 1992). Special concerns about women's health today focus on unintended and unwanted childbirth, abuse and violence, AIDS, the role of poverty in women's health, eating disorders, drug abuse, breast diseases, reproductive health, and the discrimination of the medical establishment against women.

The women's health movement in the United States rejected an assumption that was all too often made by the male medical profession: that women lose control of their bodies out of ignorance. Consciousness-raising groups and self-help groups were formed throughout the country to instruct women about their bodies, reproductive rights, nutrition, and health care. Information was also given on how to conduct breast and pelvic examinations. The Boston Women's Health Book Collective, which was formed in 1969, has, as one of its goals, to teach women about their physical and mental health. It published *The New Our Bodies, Ourselves* (1984) and *Ourselves Growing Older* (1987), which are excellent resources for information about women's health.

Although females are increasingly becoming physicians, medicine continues to be a male-dominated profession. All too often in this male-dominated world, women's physical complaints are devalued, interpreted as "emotional" rather than physical in origin, and dismissed as trivial. In one investigation, physicians described their men and women patients differently: The men were characterized as very direct, very logical, good decision makers, and rarely emotional, whereas the women were characterized as very excitable in minor crises, more easily influenced, less adventurous, less independent, very illogical, and even very sneaky (Broverman & others, 1970).

The issue of sex and gender bias has also recently been raised in selecting participants in medical research studies (Rabinowitz & Sechzur, 1994). Most medical research has been conducted with men, and frequently the results are generalized to women without apparent justification. For example, in a large-scale study involving 22,000 physicians that demonstrated the beneficial effect of an aspirin every other day on coronary heart disease, not a single woman was included in the study. Women's health advocates continue to press for greater inclusion of women in medical studies to reduce the bias that has characterized research on health, and they hope that the medical establishment will give increased attention to women's health concerns and treat women in less prejudiced and biased ways (Strickland, 1988). ■

KEY TERMS

youth   Kenneth Kenniston's term for the transitional period between adolescence and adulthood, which is a time of extended economic and personal temporariness. (407)

burnout   A feeling of hopelessness and helplessness brought on by relentless, work-related stress. (408)

set point   The weight one maintains when one makes no effort to gain or lose weight. (410)

basal metabolism rate (BMR)   The minimum amount of energy an individual uses in a resting state. (411)

aerobic exercise   Sustained exercise, such as jogging, swimming, or cycling, that stimulates heart and lung activity. (412)

addiction   Physical dependence on a drug. (414)

withdrawal   The undesirable, intense pain and craving experienced by an addict when the addictive drug is withheld. (414)

psychological dependence   The need to take a drug to cope with problems and stress. (414)

psychoactive drug   Any drug that acts on the nervous system to alter states of consciousness, modify perceptions, and change moods. (414)

AIDS (acquired immune deficiency syndrome)   A sexually transmitted disease that is caused by a virus, human immunodeficiency virus (HIV), that destroys the body's immune system. It is also transmitted by sharing needles and other contact with an infected person's blood. (418)

rape   Forcible sexual intercourse with a person who does not give consent. (421)

date or acquaintance rape   Coercive sexual activity directed at someone with whom the individual is at least casually acquainted. (421)

achieving stage   Schaie's early adulthood stage that involves the application of intelligence to situations that have profound consequences for achieving long-term goals, such as those involving careers and knowledge. (423)

responsibility stage   Schaie's adult stage when a family is established and attention is given to the needs of a spouse and offspring. (424)

executive stage   Schaie's middle adult stage in which people are responsible for societal systems and organizations. The individual develops an understanding of how societal organizations work and the complex relationships that are involved. (424)

reintegrative stage   Schaie's late adulthood, or final, stage, in which older adults choose to focus their energy on the tasks and activities that have meaning for them. (424)

developmental theory of career choice   In Eli Ginzberg's view, individuals go through three career choice stages: fantasy, tentative, and realistic. (425)

career self-concept theory   In Donald Super's view, an individual's self-concept plays a central role in career choice. Super believes that a number of developmental changes in vocational self-concept take place during the adolescent and young adulthood years. (425)

personality type theory   In John Holland's view, it is important to match an individual's personality with a particular career. (425)

Klimit, The Kiss, detail.

Socioemotional Development in Early Adulthood

Chapter Outline

LIFE-SPAN HEALTH AND WELL-BEING

Chapter Boxes

> Love is a canvas furnished by nature
> and embroidered by imagination.
>
> —Voltaire

> *Man is a knot, a web, a mesh into which relationships are tied.*
>
> —Saint-Exupéry

IMAGES OF LIFE-SPAN DEVELOPMENT

Edith, Phil, and Sherry, Searching for Love

Phil is a lovesick man. On two consecutive days he put expensive ads in New York City newspapers, urging, begging, pleading a woman named Edith to forgive him and continue their relationship. The first ad read as follows:

Edith
I was torn two ways.
Too full of child
to relinquish the lesser.
Older now,
a balance struck,
that child forever behind me.
Please forgive me,
reconsider.
Help make a new us;
better now than before.
                              Phil

This ad was placed in the *New York Post* at a cost of $3,600. Another full-page ad appeared in the *New York Times* at a cost of $3,408. Phil's ads stirred up quite a bit of interest. Forty-two Ediths responded; Phil said he thought the whole process would be more private. As Phil would attest, relationships are very important to us. Some of us will go to almost any length and spend large sums of money to restore lost relationships (Worschel & Cooper, 1979).

Sherry is not searching for a particular man. She is at the point where she is, well, looking for Mr. Anybody. Sherry is actually more particular than she says, although she is frustrated by what she calls the "great man shortage" in this country. According to the 1980 United States Census, for every 100 men over 15 years of age who have never been married or are widowed or divorced, there are 123 women; for Blacks the ratio is 100 men for every 133 women.

William Novak (1983), author of *The Great Man Shortage*, believes it is the quality of the gap that bothers most women. He says the quality problem stems from the fact that in the last two decades the combination of the feminist movement and women's tendency to seek therapy when their personal relationships do not work out has made women outgrow men emotionally. He points out that many women are saying to men, "You don't have to earn all the money anymore, and I don't want to have to do all the emotional work." Novak observes that the whole issue depresses many women because society has conditioned them to assume that their lack of a marriage partner is their fault. One 37-year-old woman told Novak, "I'm no longer waiting for a man on a white horse. Now I'd settle for the horse."

· PREVIEW ·

Our close relationships bring us warm and cherished moments. They can also bring us moments we would rather forget, moments that are highly stressful. Among the questions we ask and examine in this chapter are these: What attracts us to others, and what are love's faces? What is the nature of marriage and the family in early adulthood? What are the life-styles of single adults and divorced adults like? How do we juggle our motivation for both intimacy and independence? What is the nature of women's development, men's development, and gender issues? How much continuity and discontinuity is there between the adult and childhood years?

ATTRACTION, LOVE, AND CLOSE RELATIONSHIPS

What attracts us to others and motivates us to spend more time with them? And another question needs to be asked, one that has intrigued philosophers, poets, and songwriters for centuries: What is love? Is it lustful and passionate? Or should we be more cautious in our pursuit of love, as a Czech proverb advises, "Do not choose your wife at a dance, but in the fields among the harvesters."

Of equal importance is why relationships dissolve. Many of us know all too well that an individual we thought was a marvelous human being who we wanted to spend the rest of our life with may not turn out to be so marvelous after all. But often it is said that it is better to have loved and lost than never to have loved at all. Loneliness is a dark cloud over many individuals' lives, something few human beings want to feel. These are the themes of our exploration of close relationships: how they get started in the first place, the faces of love, and loneliness.

What Attracts Us to Others in the First Place?

Does just being around someone increase the likelihood of a relationship developing? Do birds of a feather flock together; that is, are we likely to associate with those who are similar to us? How important is the attractiveness of the other person?

Physical proximity does not guarantee that we will develop a positive relationship with an individual. Familiarity can breed contempt, but familiarity is a condition that is necessary for a close relationship to develop. For the most part, friends and lovers have been around each other for a long time; they may have grown up together, gone to high school or college together, worked together, or gone to the same social events. Once we have been exposed to someone for a period of time, what is it that makes the relationship breed friendship and even love?

Birds of a feather do indeed flock together. One of the most powerful lessons generated by the study of close relationships is that we like to associate with people who are similar to us. Our friends, as well as our lovers, are much more like us than unlike us. We have similar attitudes, behavior, and characteristics, as well as clothes, intelligence, personality, other friends, values, life-style, physical attractiveness, and so on. In some limited cases and on some isolated characteristics, opposites may attract. An introvert may wish to be with an extravert, or someone with little money may wish to associate with someone who has a lot of money, for example. But overall we are attracted to individuals with similar rather than opposite characteristics (Berndt & Perry, 1990). In one study, for example, the old adage "misery loves company" was supported as depressed college students preferred to meet unhappy others while nondepressed college students preferred to meet happy others (Wenzlaff & Prohaska, 1989).

THE FAR SIDE By GARY LARSON

And then, from across the room, their eyes met.

THE FAR SIDE cartoon by Gary Larson is reprinted by permission of Chronicle Features, San Francisco, CA.

> *Ask a toad what is beauty . . . he will answer that it is a female with two great round eyes coming out of her little head, a large flat mouth, a yellow belly and a brown back.*
> —Voltaire, *Philosophical Dictionary*, 1764

Consensual validation *provides an explanation of why individuals are attracted to people who are similar to them. Our own attitudes and behavior are supported when someone else's attitudes and behavior are similar to ours; their attitudes and behavior validate ours.* Also, because dissimilar others are unlike us and therefore more unknown, we may be able to gain more control over similar others, whose attitudes and behavior we can predict. And similarity implies that we will enjoy interacting with the other person in mutually satisfying activities, many of which require a partner with similarly disposed behavior and attitudes.

The Faces of Love

Love refers to a vast and complex territory of human behavior. How can we classify and study such a vast and complex phenomenon as love? A common classification is to describe four forms of love: altruism, friendship, romantic or passionate love, and affectionate or companionate love (Berscheid, 1988). We discussed altruism in chapter 11. Let's now examine friendship, romance or passionate love, and affectionate or companionate love.

FIGURE 15.1

Sample items from Rubin's loving and liking scales.

Love scale

1. I feel that I can confide in _____ about virtually everything.
2. If I could never be with _____ , I would feel miserable.
3. One of my primary concerns is _____ 's welfare.

Liking scale

1. I would highly recommend _____ for a responsible job.
2. Most people would react favorably to _____ after a brief acquaintance.
3. _____ is the sort of person whom I myself would like to be.

Critical Thinking

Think about your life and the lives of other people you know. What are the common faces of love that appear in each of your lives?

Friendship

For many of us, finding a true friend is not an easy task. In the words of American historian Henry Adams, "One friend in life is much, two are many, and three hardly possible." **Friendship** *is a form of close relationship that involves enjoyment (we like to spend time with our friends), acceptance (we accept our friends without trying to change them), trust (we assume our friends will act in our best interest), respect (we think our friends make good judgments), mutual assistance (we help and support our friends and they us), confiding (we share experiences and confidential matters with a friend), understanding (we feel that a friend knows us well and understands what we like), and spontaneity (we feel free to be ourselves around a friend)* (Davis, 1985). In an inquiry of more than 40,000 individuals, many of these characteristics were given when people were asked what a best friend should be like (Parlee, 1979).

How is friendship different from love? The difference can be seen by looking at the scales of liking and loving developed by social psychologist Zick Rubin (1970) (see figure 15.1). Rubin says that liking involves our sense that someone else is similar to us; it includes a positive evaluation of the individual. Loving, he believes, involves being close to someone; it includes dependency, a more selfless orientation toward the individual, and qualities of absorption and exclusiveness.

But friends and lovers are similar in some ways. Keith Davis (1985) revealed that friends and romantic partners share the characteristics of acceptance, trust, respect, confiding, understanding, spontaneity, mutual assistance, and happiness. However, he found that relationships with our spouses or lovers are more likely to also involve fascination and exclusiveness. Relationships with friends were perceived as more stable, especially more than those among unmarried lovers.

Romantic or Passionate Love

Romantic love *is also called "passionate love" or "Eros"; it has strong sexual and infatuation components, and it often predominates in the early part of a love relationship.* The fires of passion burn hot in romantic love. It is the type of love Juliet had in mind when she cried "O Romeo, Romeo, wherefore art thou Romeo?" It is the type of love portrayed in new songs that hit the charts virtually every week. It sells millions of books for writers like Danielle Steele. Well-known love researcher Ellen Berscheid (1988) says that it is romantic love we mean when we say that we are "in love" with someone. It is romantic love she believes we need to understand if we are to learn what love is all about.

> *I flee who chases me, and chase who flees me.*
> —Ovid, *The Loves*, A.D. 8

Romantic love is the main reason we get married. In 1967, a research study showed that men maintained that they would not get married if they were not "in love," women either were undecided or said that they would get married even if they did not love their prospective husband (Kephart, 1967). In the 1980s, women and men agreed that they would not get married unless they were "in love." And more than half of today's men and women say that not being "in love" is sufficient reason to dissolve a marriage (Simpson, Campbell, & Berscheid, 1986).

Romantic love is especially important among college students. In one investigation, unattached college males and females were asked to identify their closest relationship (Berscheid, Snyder, & Omoto, 1989). More than half named a romantic partner rather than a parent, sibling, or friend. It is about a romantic partner that an individual says, "I am *in love*," not just "I *love*."

The importance of romantic love appeared in a biography of actress Ingrid Bergman (Leamer, 1986). She once told a man she cared about him deeply, valued his friendship and affection, but simply was not in love with him. Upon hearing this, the man committed suicide. Romantic love has an awesome power—its fires are based on more than liking.

Romantic love includes a complex intermingling of different emotions—fear, anger, sexual desire, joy, and jealousy, for example. Note that not all of these emotions are positive. In one investigation, romantic lovers were more likely to be the cause of depression than friends (Berscheid & Fei, 1977).

Berscheid (1988; Berscheid, Snyder, & Omoto, 1989) believes sexual desire is vastly neglected in the study of romantic love. When pinned down to say what romantic love truly is, she

LIFE-SPAN PRACTICAL KNOWLEDGE 15.1

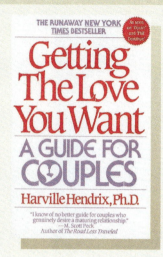

THE RUNAWAY NEW YORK TIMES BESTSELLER

As seen on *Oprah* and *Phil Donahue*

Getting The Love You Want

A GUIDE FOR COUPLES

Harville Hendrix, Ph.D.

"I know of no better guide for couples who genuinely desire a maturing relationship."
—M. Scott Peck
Author of *The Road Less Traveled*

Getting The Love You Want

(1988) by Harville Hendrix.
New York: Henry Holt.

Getting The Love You Want is a guide for couples to help them improve their relationships. The book is based on Hendrix's couple-workshop techniques that are designed to help couples construct conscious marriages, relationships based on awareness of unresolved childhood needs and conflicts that cause an individual to select a particular spouse. The author instructs readers how to conduct a 10-week course in marital therapy in the privacy of their homes. In stepwise fashion you learn how to communicate more clearly and sensitively, how to eliminate self-defeating behaviors, and how to focus your attention on meeting your partner's needs. Hendrix's goal is to transform the downward spiral of the struggle for power into a mutually beneficial relationship of emotional growth.

This is a good book for couples, especially those engulfed in conflicted relationships. Hendrix does an excellent job of helping you become aware of long-standing family-of-origin influences on your current relationships. His 10-week in-home workshop includes a variety of ingenious exercises.

---

concluded, "It's about 90 percent sexual desire." Berscheid said that this is still an inadequate answer but "to discuss romantic love without also prominently mentioning the role sexual arousal and desire plays in it is very much like printing a recipe for tiger soup that leaves out the main ingredient."

Affectionate or Companionate Love

Love is more than just passion. **Affectionate love,** *also called "companionate love," is the type of love that occurs when individuals desire to have the other person near and have a deep, caring affection for the person.*

There is a growing belief that the early stages of love have more romantic ingredients, but as love lasts, passion tends to give way to affection (Duck, 1993). Phillip Shaver (1986, 1993) described this developmental course. The initial phase of romantic love is fueled by a mixture of sexual attraction and gratification, a reduced sense of loneliness, uncertainty about the security of developing another attachment, and excitement from exploring the novelty of another human being. With time, sexual attraction wanes, attachment anxieties either lessen or produce conflict and withdrawal, novelty is replaced with familiarity, and lovers either find themselves securely attached in a deeply caring relationship or distressed—feeling bored, disappointed, lonely, or hostile, for example. In the latter case, one or both partners may eventually seek another close relationship.

Critical Thinking

When love ends, we seek to understand the reasons why the relationship did not work. What are some of the explanations we give as to why a relationship did not work? Are some of these explanations likely to be biased?

When two lovers go beyond their preoccupation with novelty, unpredictability, and the urgency of sexual attraction, they are more likely to detect deficiencies in each other's caring (Vannoy-Hiller & Philliber, 1989). This may be the point in a relationship when women, who often are better caregivers than men, sense that the relationship has problems. Wives are almost twice as likely as husbands to initiate a divorce (National Center for Health Statistics, 1989).

Friends, dates, lovers, and marital partners bring to their relationships a long history of relationships (Duck & Pond, 1989; Hartup, 1989). Each partner has internalized a relationship with parents, one that may have been (or continues to be) warm and affectionate or cold and aloof. One partner may have extensive experience in romantic relationships, the other little or none. These experiences are carried forward and influence our relationships with others. For example, adults who were securely attached to their parents as young children are more likely to have securely attached emotional relationships than are adults who were insecurely attached (Hazan & Shaver, 1987).

So far we have described two forms of love: romantic or passionate and affectionate or companionate. Robert J. Sternberg (1988, 1993) believes affectionate love actually consists of two types of love: intimacy and commitment. The **triangular theory of love** *is Sternberg's theory that love has three main forms: passion, intimacy, and commitment.* Passion, as we described earlier, is the physical and sexual attraction to a lover. Intimacy is the emotional feelings of warmth, closeness, and sharing in a relationship. Commitment is our cognitive appraisal of the relationship and our intent to maintain the relationship even in the face of problems. If only passion is present (with intimacy and commitment low or absent), *infatuation* is present. This might occur in an affair or a fling in which there

FIGURE 15.2

Sternberg's triangle of love.

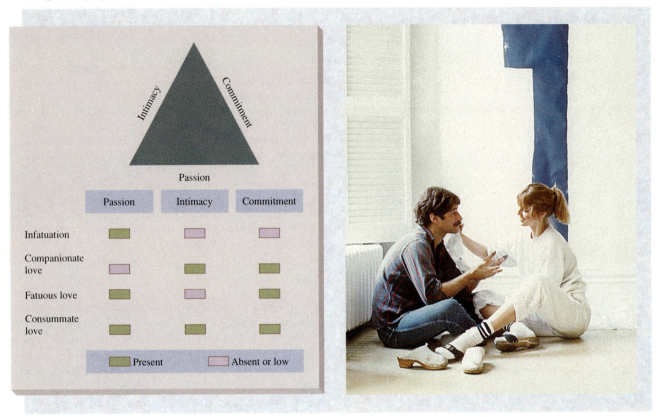

is little intimacy and even less commitment. If the relationship has intimacy and commitment, but passion is low or absent, *companionate* or *affectionate love* is present, a pattern often found in happy couples who have been married for many years. If passion and commitment are present but intimacy is not, Sternberg calls the relationship *fatuous love,* as when one person worships another from a distance. Only when all three of love's parts—passion, intimacy, and commitment—are present is the strongest, fullest type of love experienced, what Sternberg labels *consummate love* (see figure 15.2).

Loneliness

Some of us are lonely individuals. We may feel that no one knows us very well. We may feel isolated and sense that we do not have anyone we can turn to in times of need or stress. Our society's contemporary emphasis on self-fulfillment and achievement, the importance we attach to commitment in relationships, and the decline in stable close relationships are among the reasons feelings of loneliness are common today (de Jong-Gierveld, 1987).

Loneliness is associated with an individual's gender, attachment history, self-esteem, and social skills. A lack of time spent with females, on the part of both males and females, is associated with loneliness. Individuals who are lonely often have a history of poor relationships with their partners. Early experiences of rejection and loss (as when a parent dies) can cause a lasting effect of feeling alone. Lonely individuals often have low

self-esteem and tend to blame themselves more than they deserve for their inadequacies (Frankel & Prentice-Dunn, 1990). And lonely individuals are deficient in social skills (Riggio, Throckmorton, & DePaola, 1990; Jones, Hobbs, & Hockenbury, 1982). For example, they show inappropriate self-disclosure, self-attention at the expense of attention to a partner, or an inability to develop comfortable intimacy.

The social transition to college is a time when loneliness may develop as individuals leave behind the familiar world of their hometown and family. Many college freshmen feel anxious about meeting new people and developing a new social life. As one student commented:

> My first year here at the university has been pretty lonely. I wasn't lonely at all in high school. I lived in a fairly small town—I knew everyone and everyone knew me. I was a member of several clubs and played on the basketball team. It's not that way at the university. It is a big place and I've felt like a stranger on so many occasions. I'm starting to get used to my life here, and the last few months I've been making myself meet people and get to know them, but it hasn't been easy.

As reflected in the comments of this freshman, individuals usually can't bring their popularity and social standing from high school into the college environment. There may even be a dozen high school basketball stars, National Merit scholars, and former student council presidents in a single dormitory wing. Especially if students attend college away from home, they face the task of forming completely new social relationships.

In one investigation conducted 2 weeks after the school year began, 75 percent of 354 college freshmen said they felt lonely at least part of the time since arriving on campus (Cutrona, 1982). More than 40 percent said their loneliness was moderate to severe in intensity. Students who were the most optimistic and had the highest self-esteem were more likely to overcome their loneliness by the end of their freshmen year. Loneliness is not reserved only for college freshmen, though. It is not uncommon to find a number of upperclassmen who are also lonely.

How do you determine if you are lonely? Questions on scales of loneliness ask you to respond to questions such as these:

"I don't feel in tune with the people around me."
"I can't find companionship when I want it."

If you consistently respond that you never or rarely feel in tune with people around you and rarely or never can find companionship when you want it, you are likely to fall into the category of individuals described as moderately or intensely lonely.

How can individuals who are lonely reduce their loneliness? Two recommendations are to (1) change your actual social relations or (2) change your social needs and desires (Peplau & Perlman, 1982). Probably the most direct and satisfying way to become less lonely is to improve your social relations (Rokach, 1990). This can be accomplished by forming new relationships, by using your existing social network more competently, or by creating "surrogate" relationships with pets, television personalities, and the like. A second way to reduce loneliness is to reduce your desire for social contact. Over the short run, this might be accomplished by selecting activities you can enjoy alone rather than selecting activities that require someone's company. Over the long run, though, effort should be made to form new relationships. A third coping strategy some individuals unfortunately adopt is to distract themselves from their painful feelings by drinking to "drown their sorrows" or by becoming a workaholic. Some of the negative health consequences of loneliness may be the product of such maladaptive coping strategies (McWhirter, 1990). If you perceive yourself as being a lonely individual, you might consider contacting the counseling center at your college for advice on ways to reduce your loneliness and improve your social relations skills.

MARRIAGE AND THE FAMILY

Should I get married? If I wait any longer, will it be too late? Will I get left out? Should I stay single or is it too lonely a life? If I get married, do I want to have children? How will it affect my marriage? These are questions that many young adults pose to themselves as they consider their life-style options. But before we explore these life-style options, let's examine the nature of the family life cycle.

The Family Life Cycle

As we go through life, we are at different points in the family life cycle. The stages of the family cycle include leaving home and becoming a single adult, the joining of families through marriage (the new couple), becoming parents and a family with children, the family with adolescents, the family at mid-life, and the family in later life. A summary of these stages in the family life cycle is shown in figure 15.3, along with key aspects of emotional processes involved in the transition from one stage to the next, and changes in family status required for developmental change to take place (Carter & McGoldrick, 1989).

Leaving Home and Becoming a Single Adult

Leaving home and becoming a single adult *is the first stage in the family life cycle and involves launching.* **Launching** *is the process in which youths move into adulthood and exit their family of origin.* Adequate completion of launching requires that the young adult separate from the family of origin without cutting off ties completely or fleeing in a reactive way to find some form of substitute emotional refuge (Alymer, 1989). The launching period is a time for the youth and young adult to formulate personal life goals, to develop an identity, and to become more independent before joining with another person to form a new family. This is a time for young people to sort out emotionally what they will take along from the family of origin, what they will leave behind, and what they will create themselves into.

Complete cutoffs from parents rarely resolve emotional problems (Bowen, 1978; Carter & McGoldrick, 1989). The shift to adult-to-adult status between parents and children requires a mutually respectful and personal form of relating, in which young adults can appreciate parents as they are, needing neither to make them into what they are not nor to blame them for what they could not be. Neither do young adults need to comply with parental expectations and wishes at their own expense.

The Joining of Families Through Marriage: The New Couple

The **new couple** *is the second stage in the family life cycle, in which two individuals from separate families of origin unite to form a new family system.* This stage involves not only the development of a new marital system, but also a realignment with extended families and friends to include the spouse. Women's changing roles, the increasingly frequent marriage of partners from divergent cultural backgrounds, and the increasing physical distances between family members are placing a much stronger burden on couples to define their relationships for themselves than was true in the past (McGoldrick, 1989). Marriage is usually described as the union of two individuals, but in reality it is the union of two entire family systems and the development of a new, third system. Some experts on marriage and the family believe that marriage represents such a different phenomenon for women and men that we need to speak of "her" marriage and "his" marriage (Bernard, 1972). In the American society, women have anticipated marriage with greater enthusiasm and

FIGURE 15.3

The stages of the family life cycle.

Family life cycle stage	Emotional process of transition: Key principles	Changes in family status required to proceed developmentally
 1. Leaving home; Single young adults	Accepting emotional and financial responsibility for self	a. Differentiation of self in relation to family of origin b. Development of intimate peer relationships c. Establishment of self in relation to work and financial independence
 2. The joining of families through marriage: the new couple	Commitment to new system	a. Formation of marital system b. Realignment of relationships with extended families and friends to include spouse
 3. Becoming parents and families with children	Accepting new members into the system	a. Adjusting marital system to make space for child(ren) b. Joining in childrearing, financial, and household tasks c. Realignment of relationships with extended family to include parenting and grandparenting roles
 4. Families with adolescents	Increasing flexibility of family boundaries to include children's independence and grandparents' frailties	a. Shifting of parent-child relationships to permit adolescent to move in and out of system b. Refocus on midlife marital and career issues c. Beginning shift toward joint caring for older generation
 5. Mid-life families	Accepting a multitude of exits from and entries into the family system	a. Renegotiation of marital system as a dyad b. Development of adult to adult relationships between grown children and their parents c. Realignment of relationships to include in-laws and grandchildren d. Dealing with disabilities and death of parents (grandparents)
 6. Families in later life	Accepting the shifting of generational roles	a. Maintaining own and/or couple functioning and interests in face of physiological decline; exploration of new familial and social role options b. Support for a more central role of middle generation c. Making room in the system for the wisdom and experience of the elderly, supporting the older generation without overfunctioning for them d. Dealing with the loss of spouse, siblings, and other peers and preparation for own death. Life review and integration

more positive expectations than men have, although statistically it has not been a very healthy system for them.

Becoming Parents and Families With Children

Becoming parents and a family with children *is the third stage in the family life cycle. Entering this stage requires that adults now move up a generation and become caregivers to the younger generation.* Moving through this lengthy stage successfully requires a commitment of time as a parent, understanding the roles of parents, and adapting to developmental changes in children (Santrock, 1993). Problems that emerge when a couple first assumes the parental role are struggles with each other about taking responsibility, as well as refusal or inability to function as competent parents to children. We extensively discussed this stage of the family life cycle in chapters 7, 9, and 11.

> *We never know the love of our parents until we have become parents.*
>
> —Henry Ward Beecher, 1887

The Family With Adolescents

The **family with adolescents** *represents the fourth stage of the family life cycle. Adolescence is a period of development in which individuals push for autonomy and seek to develop their own identity.* The development of mature autonomy and identity is a lengthy process, transpiring over at least 10 to 15 years. Compliant children become noncompliant adolescents. Parents tend to adopt one of two strategies to handle noncompliance—they either clamp down and put more pressure on the adolescent to conform to parental values, or they become more permissive and let the adolescent have extensive freedom. Neither is a wise overall strategy; a more flexible, adaptive approach is best. We discussed the family with adolescents in chapter 13.

Mid-Life Families

The **family at mid-life** *is the fifth stage in the family cycle. It is a time of launching children, playing an important role in linking generations, and adapting to mid-life changes in development.* Until about a generation ago, most families were involved in raising their children for much of their adult lives until old age. Because of the lower birth rate and longer life of most adults, parents now launch their children about 20 years before retirement, which frees many mid-life parents to pursue other activities. We will discuss mid-life families in greater detail in chapter 17.

The Family in Later Life

The **family in later life** *is the sixth and final stage in the family life cycle. Retirement alters a couple's life-style, requiring adaptation.* Grandparenting also characterizes many families in this stage. We will discuss the family in later life in chapter 20.

Trends in Marriage

Until about 1930, the goal of a stable marriage was widely accepted as a legitimate endpoint of adult development. In the last 60 years, however, we have seen the emergence of personal fulfillment both inside and outside a marriage that competes with marriage's stability as an adult developmental goal. The changing norm of male-female equality in marriage has produced marital relationships that are more fragile and intense than they were earlier in the twentieth century (Cristianson & Pasch, 1993; Fincham, 1993; Margolin & Burman, 1993). More adults are remaining single longer in the 1990s, and the average duration of a marriage in the United States is currently just over 9 years. The divorce rate, which increased astronomically in the 1970s, has finally begun to slow down, although it still remains alarmingly high. Even with adults remaining single for longer and divorce being a frequent occurrence, Americans still show a strong predilection for marriage—the proportion of women who never marry has remained at about 7 percent throughout the twentieth century, for example.

> *When two people are under the influence of the most violent, most insane, most delusive, and most transient of passions, they are required to swear that they will remain in that excited, abnormal, and exhausting condition continuously until death do them part.*
>
> —George Bernard Shaw

The sociocultural context is a powerful influence on the nature of marriage. The age at which individuals marry, expectations about what the marriage will be like, and the developmental course of the marriage may vary not only across historical time within a given culture, but also across cultures. For example, a new marriage law took effect in China in 1981. The law sets a minimum age for marriage—22 years for males, 20 years for females. Late marriage and late childbirth are critical efforts in China's attempt to control population growth. More information about the nature of marriage in different cultures appears in Sociocultural Worlds of Development 15.1.

Marital Expectations and Myths

Among the explanations of our nation's high divorce rate and high degree of dissatisfaction in many marriages is that we have such strong expectations of marriage. We expect our spouse to simultaneously be a lover, a friend, a confidant, a counselor, a career person, and a parent, for example. In one research investigation, unhappily married couples expressed unrealistic expectations about marriage (Epstein & Eidelson, 1981). Underlying unrealistic expectations about marriage are numerous myths about marriage. A myth is a widely held belief unsupported by facts.

To study college students' beliefs in the myths of marriage, Jeffry Larson (1988) constructed a marriage quiz to measure

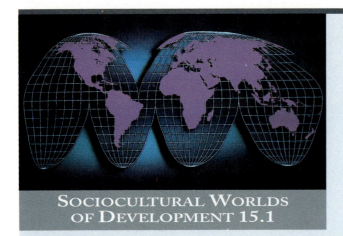

SOCIOCULTURAL WORLDS OF DEVELOPMENT 15.1

Marriage Around the World

The traits that people look for in a marriage partner vary around the world. In one large-scale study of 9,474 adults from 37 cultures on six continents and five islands, people varied the most on how much they valued chastity—desiring a marital partner with no previous experience in sexual intercourse (Buss & others, 1990). Chastity was the most important factor in marital selection in China, India, Indonesia, Iran, Taiwan, and the Palestinian Arab culture. Adults from Ireland and Japan placed moderate importance on chastity. In contrast, adults in Sweden, Finland, Norway, the Netherlands, and Germany generally said that chastity was not important in selecting a marital partner.

In this study, domesticity was also valued in some cultures and not in others. Adults from the Zulu culture in South Africa, Estonia, and Colombia placed a high value on housekeeping skills in their marital preference. By contrast, adults in the United States, Canada, and all Western European countries except Spain said that housekeeping was not an important trait in their partner.

Religion plays an important role in marital preferences in many cultures. For example, Islam stresses the honor of the male and the purity of the female. It also emphasizes the woman's role in childbearing, child rearing, educating children, and instilling the Islamic faith in their children.

International comparisons of marriage also reveal that individuals in Scandinavian countries marry late, whereas their counterparts in Eastern Europe marry early (Bianchi & Spani, 1986). In Denmark in the 1980s, for example, almost 80 percent of the women and 90 percent of the men aged 20 to 24 had never been married. In Hungary less than 40 percent of the women and 70 percent of the men the same age had never been married. In Scandinavian countries, cohabitation is popular among young adults; however, most Scandinavians eventually marry—in the 1980s, only 5 percent of the women and 11 percent of the men in their early forties had never been married. Some countries, such as Hungary, encourage early marriage and childbearing to offset current and future population losses. Like Scandinavian countries, Japan has a high proportion of unmarried young people, but, rather than cohabitating as the Scandinavians do, unmarried Japanese young adults live at home longer with their parents before marrying.

(a)   (b)   (c)

(a) *In Scandinavian countries, cohabitation is popular; only a small percentage of 20- to 24-year-olds are married.* (b) *Many Soviet-influenced countries encourage early marriage and childbearing to offset current and future population issues.* (c) *The Islam religion stresses the honor of the male and the purity of the female.*

college students' information about marriage and compared their responses with what is known about marriage in the research literature. The college students responded incorrectly to almost half of the items. Female students missed fewer items than male students, and students with a less romantic perception of marriage missed fewer items than more romantically inclined students. See figure 15.4 to take the marriage quiz.

Gender, Intimacy, and Family Work in Marriage

The experiences and implications of marriage may differ for the wife and for the husband (Thompson & Walker, 1989). This is especially true in the expression of intimacy and in family work. In one investigation, only one-third of married Black

LIFE-SPAN PRACTICAL KNOWLEDGE 15.2

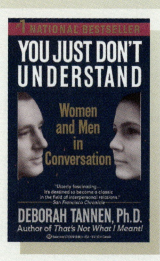

You Just Don't Understand

(1990) by Deborah Tannen.
New York: Ballantine.

This book is about how women and men communicate—or, all too often, miscommunicate—with each other. Author Deborah Tannen is an internationally recognized expert on communication in interpersonal relationships. Tannen says there are two important gender cultures in communication: rapport talk (female culture) and report talk (male culture). Rapport talk is the language of conversation and a way of establishing connections and negotiating relationships, which women feel more comfortable doing. Report talk is public speaking and talk that conveys information, which men feel more comfortable doing.

Tannen feels that both men and women need to make adjustments to improve their communication with each other. Women can push themselves to speak at the slightest pause; men can make women feel more comfortable speaking in groups and giving talks. This is an excellent book and helps women and men to understand each other's communication styles. It provides a guide for recognizing habits that get us in trouble.

FIGURE 15.4

The marriage quiz.

Take out a sheet of paper and number from 1 to 15. Answer each of the following items true or false. After completing the quiz, turn to the end of the chapter for the correct answers.

Marriage Quiz Items

1. A husband's marital satisfaction is usually lower if his wife is employed full time than if she is a full-time homemaker.
2. Today most young, single, never-married people will eventually get married.
3. In most marriages, having a child improves marital satisfaction for both spouses.
4. The best single predictor of overall marital satisfaction is the quality of a couple's sex life.
5. The divorce rate in America increased from 1960 to 1980.
6. A greater percentage of wives are in the work force today than in 1970.
7. Marital satisfaction for a wife is usually lower if she is employed full time than if she is a full-time homemaker.
8. If my spouse loves me, he/she should instinctively know what I want and need to be happy.
9. In a marriage in which the wife is employed full time, the husband usually assumes an equal share of the housekeeping.
10. For most couples, marital satisfaction gradually increases from the first years of marriage through the childbearing years, the teen years, the empty nest period, and retirement.
11. No matter how I behave, my spouse should love me simply because he/she *is* my spouse.
12. One of the most frequent marital problems is poor communication.
13. Husbands usually make more life-style adjustments in marriage than wives.
14. Couples who cohabitated before marriage usually report greater marital satisfaction than couples who did not.
15. I can change my spouse by pointing out his/her inadequacies, errors, etc.

women said they would go to their husbands first for support if they had a serious problem, such as being depressed or anxious (Brown & Gary, 1985). And only one-third of these women named their husbands as one of the three people closest to them. More men than women view their spouses as best friends (Rubin, 1984).

Wives consistently disclose more to their partners than husbands do (Peplau & Gordon, 1985). And women tend to express more tenderness, fear, and sadness than their partners. For many men, controlled anger is a common emotional orientation (Cancian & Gordon, 1988). A common complaint expressed by women in a marriage is that their husbands do not care about their emotional lives and do not express their own feelings and thoughts (Rubin, 1984). Women often point out that they have to literally pull things out of their husbands and push them to open up. Men frequently respond either that they are open or that they do not understand what their wives want from them. It is not unusual for men to protest that no matter how much they talk it is not enough for their wives. Women also say they want more warmth as well as openness from their husbands. For example, women are more likely than men to give their partners a spontaneous kiss or hug when something positive happens (Blumstein & Schwartz, 1983). Overall, women are more expressive and affectionate than men in marriage, and this difference bothers many women.

Not only are there gender differences in intimacy in marriages, but there are also strong gender differences in family work (Crosby & Jasker, 1993; Hood, 1993; Suitor, 1991; Thompson & Walker, 1989). Wives typically do much more family work than husbands (Warner, 1986). Most women and men agree that women should be responsible for family work and that men should "help out" (Szinovacz, 1984). Most wives report they are satisfied with the small amount of family work their husbands do (Peplau & Gordon, 1985). Most wives do

LIFE-SPAN PRACTICAL KNOWLEDGE 15.3

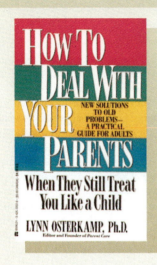

How To Deal With Your Parents

(1991) by Lynn Osterkamp.
New York: Berkley Books.

This book was written for adult children who want to understand and improve their relationships with their parents. Author Lynn Osterkamp is a nationally recognized expert on family conflict and communication. She helps young adults answer such important questions as these:

Why are so many grown-up people still worrying about what their parents think?
Why can't you talk to your parents the way you talk to other people?

Why do you keep having the same arguments?
How can you stop feeling guilty?
How can you cope with family gatherings, holidays?
How can you stay out of their relationship and keep them out of yours?
What role would you like your parents to play in your life today?
How can you make lasting changes?

The book is filled with personal accounts and gives young adults, as well as middle-aged adults, specific strategies for improving communication and resolving conflict with their parents.

"You have no idea how nice it is to have someone to talk to."
Copyright © 1964 Don Orehek

two to three times more family work than their husbands (Kamo, 1988). In one study, only 10 percent of husbands did as much family work as their wives (Berk, 1985). These "exceptional" men usually were in circumstances with many, usually young, children and a wife who worked full-time.

The nature of women's involvement in family work is often different from that of men's. Besides doing more, what women do and how they experience family work are different from men's experiences. The family work most women do is unrelenting, repetitive, and routine, often involving cleaning, cooking, child care, shopping, laundry, and straightening up. The family work most men do is infrequent, irregular, and nonroutine, often involving household repairs, taking out the garbage, mowing the lawn, yard work, and gardening. Women often report having to do several tasks at once, which may explain why they find domestic work less relaxing and more stressful than men do (Shaw, 1988).

Because family work is intertwined with love and embedded in family relations, it has complex and contradictory meanings (Marshall & Barnett, 1993). Most women experience family

tasks as mindless but essential work done for the people they love. Most women usually enjoy tending to the needs of their loved ones and keeping the family going, even if they do not find the activities enjoyable and fulfilling. Women experience both positive and negative family work conditions. They are unsupervised and rarely criticized, they plan and control their own work, and they have only their own standards to meet. However, women's family work is often worrisome, tiresome, menial, repetitive, isolating, unfinished, inescapable, and unappreciated. Thus, it is not surprising that many women have mixed feelings about family work.

The Parental Role

For many adults, the parental role is well planned and coordinated with other roles in life and is developed with the individual's economic situation in mind. For others, the discovery that they are about to become parents is a startling surprise. In either event, the prospective parents may have mixed emotions and romantic illusions about having a child. Parenting consists of a number of interpersonal skills and emotional demands, yet there is little in the way of formal education for this task. Most parents learn parenting practices from their own parents—some they accept, some they discard. Husbands and wives may bring different viewpoints of parenting practices to the marriage. Unfortunately, when methods of parents are passed on from one generation to the next, both desirable and undesirable practices are perpetuated.

The needs and expectations of parents have stimulated many myths about parenting (Okun & Rappaport, 1980):

- The birth of a child will save a failing marriage
- As a possession or extension of the parent, the child will think, feel, and behave like the parents did in their childhood

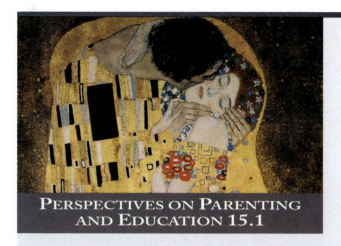

PERSPECTIVES ON PARENTING AND EDUCATION 15.1

Exploring the Mother's and the Father's Roles

What do you think of when you hear the word *motherhood?* If you are like most people, you associate motherhood with a number of positive images, such as warmth, selflessness, dutifulness, and tolerance (Matlin, 1993). And while most women expect that motherhood will be happy and fulfilling, the reality is that motherhood has been accorded relatively low prestige in our society (Hoffnung, 1984). When stacked up against money, power, and achievement, motherhood unfortunately doesn't fare too well, and mothers rarely receive the appreciation they warrant. When children don't succeed or they develop problems, our society has had a tendency to attribute the lack of success or the development of problems to a single source—mothers. One of psychology's most important lessons is that behavior is multiply determined. So it is with children's development—when development goes awry, mothers are not the single cause of the problems, even though our society stereotypes them in this way.

The role of the mother brings with it benefits as well as limitations. Although motherhood is not enough to fill most women's entire lives, for most mothers it is one of the most meaningful experiences in their lives (Hoffnung, 1984).

The father's role has undergone major changes (Biller, 1993; Bronstein, 1988; Lamb, 1986). During the colonial period in America, fathers were primarily responsible for moral teaching. Fathers provided guidance and values, especially through religion. With the Industrial Revolution, the father's role changed; he gained the responsibility as the breadwinner, a role that continued through the Great Depression. By the end of World War II, another role for fathers emerged, that of gender-role model. Although being breadwinner and moral guardian continued to be important father roles, attention shifted to the father's role as a male, especially for sons. Then, in the 1970s, the current interest in the father as an active, nurturant, caregiving parent emerged. Rather than being responsible only for the discipline and control of older children and for providing the family's economic base, the father now is being evaluated in terms of his active, nurturant involvement with his children (McBride, 1991).

Children's social development can significantly benefit from interaction with a caring, accessible, and dependable father who fosters a sense of trust and confidence (Ishii-Kuntz, 1994; Smith & Morgan, 1994). The father's positive family involvement assumes special importance in developing children's social competence, because he is often the only male the child encounters on a regular day-to-day basis.

Father-mother cooperation and mutual respect helps the child develop positive attitudes toward both males and females (Biller, 1993). It is much easier for working parents to cope with changing family circumstances and day-care issues when the father and mother equitably share child-rearing responsibilities. Mothers feel less stress and have more positive attitudes toward their husbands when they are supportive partners.

- Children will take care of parents in old age
- Parents can expect respect and get obedience from their children
- Having a child means that the parents will always have someone who loves them and is their best friend
- Having a child gives the parents a "second chance" to achieve what they should have achieved
- If parents learn the right techniques, they can mold their children into what they want
- It's the parents fault when children fail
- Mothers are naturally better parents than fathers
- Parenting is an instinct and requires no training

> *For years we have given scientific attention to the care and rearing of plants and animals, but we have allowed babies to be raised chiefly by tradition.*
>
> —Edith Belle Lowry, *False Modesty* (1912)

In earlier times, women considered being a mother a full-time occupation. Currently, there is a tendency to have fewer children, and, as birth control has become common practice, many individuals choose when they will have children and how many children they will raise. The number of one-child families is increasing, for example. Giving birth to fewer children and reduced demands of child care free a significant portion of a woman's life span for other endeavors. Three accompanying changes are that (1) as a result of the increase in working women, there is less maternal investment in the child's development; (2) men are apt to invest a greater amount of time in fathering; and (3) parental care in the home is often supplemented by institutional care (day care, for example). To read further about maternal and paternal roles, see Perspectives on Parenting and Education 15.1.

As more women show an increased interest in developing a career, they are not only marrying later, but also having children later. What are some of the advantages of having children early or late? Some of the advantages of having children early are these: The parents are likely to have more physical energy (for example, they can cope better with such matters as getting

CONCEPT TABLE 15.1

Attraction, Love, and Close Relationships, and Marriage and the Family

Concept	Processes/Related Ideas	Characteristics/Description
Attraction, love, and close relationships	What attracts us to others in the first place?	Familiarity precedes a close relationship. We like to associate with individuals who are similar to us.
	The faces of love	Berscheid believes love has four forms: altruism, friendship, romantic or passionate love, and affectionate or companionate love. Friends and lovers have similar and dissimilar characteristics. Romantic love is involved when we say we are "in love"; it includes passion, sexuality, and a mixture of emotions, some of which may be negative. Affectionate love is more important as relationships age. In Sternberg's triangular theory of love, love has three forms: passion, intimacy, and commitment. The high or low presence of these ingredients can produce infatuation, companionate love, fatuous love, or consummate love.
	Loneliness	An individual's gender, attachment history, self-esteem, and social skills are associated with loneliness. The transition to college is a time when loneliness often surfaces.
Marriage and the family	The family life cycle	There are six stages in the family life cycle: leaving home and becoming a single adult; the joining of families through marriage—the new couple; becoming parents and a family with children; the family with adolescents; the midlife family; and the family in later life.
	Trends in marriage	Even though adults are remaining single longer and the divorce rate is high, we still show a strong predilection for marriage. The age at which individuals marry, expectations about what the marriage will be like, and the developmental course of marriage may vary not only across historical time within a culture, but also across cultures.
	Marital expectations and myths	Unrealistic expectations and myths about marriage contribute to marital dissatisfaction and divorce.
	Gender, intimacy, and family work in marriage	Overall, women are more expressive and affectionate in marriage, and this difference bothers many women. Women do much more family work than men, and they experience family work differently than men do.
	The parental role	For some, the parental role is well planned and coordinated. For others, there is surprise and sometimes chaos. There are many myths about parenting, among them the myth that the birth of a child will save a failing marriage. Families are becoming smaller, and many women are delaying childbirth until they have become well established in a career. There are some advantages to having children earlier in adulthood, and some advantages to having them later.

up in the middle of the night with infants and waiting up until adolescents come home at night); the mother is likely to have fewer medical problems with pregnancy and childbirth; and the parents may be less likely to build up expectations for their children, as do many couples who have waited many years to have children. By contrast, there are also advantages to having children late: The parents will have had more time to consider their goals in life, such as what they want from their family and career roles; the parents will be more mature and will be able to benefit

from their life experiences to engage in more competent parenting; and the parents will be better established in their careers and have more income for child-rearing expenses (Olds, 1986).

At this point, we have discussed a number of ideas about attraction and close relationships, and about marriage and the family in early childhood. A summary of these ideas is presented in concept table 15.1. Next, we consider the diversity of lifestyles in adulthood.

THE DIVERSITY OF ADULT LIFE-STYLES

Today's adult life-styles are diverse. We have single-career families; dual-career families; single-parent families, including mother custody, father custody, and joint custody; the remarried or stepfamily; the kin family (made up of bilateral or intergenerationally linked members); and even the experimental family (individuals in multiadult households—communes—or cohabitating adults). And, of course, there are many single adults.

Single Adults

There is no rehearsal. One day you don't live alone, the next day you do. College ends. Your wife walks out. Your husband dies. Suddenly, you live in this increasingly modern condition, living alone. Maybe you like it, maybe you don't. Maybe you thrive on the solitude, maybe you ache as if in exile. Either way, chances are you are only half-prepared, if at all, to be sole proprietor of your bed, your toaster, and your time. Most of us were raised in the din and clutter of family life, jockeying for a place in the bathroom in the morning, fighting over the last piece of cake, and obliged to compromise on the simplest of choices—the volume of the stereo, the channel on the TV, for example. Few of us grew up thinking that home would be a way station in our life course (Schmich, 1987).

The number of individuals who live alone began to grow in the 1950s, but it was in the 1970s that the pace skyrocketed. In the decade of the seventies, the number of men living by themselves increased 97 percent, the number of women, 55 percent. In the eighties, the growth slowed considerably, but it continues and is expected to do so at least through the end of the century. In 1985, 20.6 million individuals lived alone in the United States, accounting for 11 percent of adults and 24 percent of all households. In some respects, the number of individuals living alone is a symptom of other changes: low birthrates, high divorce rates, long lives, and late marriages. But the group that grew the fastest in the 1970s was young adults living alone, the majority of them being young men. In that decade, the number of never-married people under 30 living by themselves more than tripled. For them, marriage was no longer the only way out of the house or the only route to sexual fulfillment.

A history of myths and stereotypes are associated with being single, ranging from "the swinging single" to "the desperately lonely, suicidal single." Most singles, of course, are somewhere between these extremes. Single adults are often challenged by others to get married so they will no longer be considered selfish, irresponsible, impotent, frigid, and immature. Clearly, though, being a single adult has some advantages—time to make decisions about one's life course, time to develop personal resources to meet goals, freedom to make autonomous decisions and pursue one's own schedule and interests, opportunity to explore new places and try out new things, and availability of privacy.

Common problems of single adults focus on intimate relationships with other adults, confronting loneliness, and finding a niche in a society that is marriage oriented. Many single adults cite personal freedom as one of the major advantages of being a single adult. One woman who never married commented, "I enjoy knowing that I can satisfy my own whims without someone else's interferences. If I want to wash my hair at two o'clock in the morning, no one complains. I can eat when I'm hungry and watch my favorite television shows without contradictions from anyone. I enjoy these freedoms. I would feel very confined if I had to adjust to another person's schedule."

Some adults never marry. Initially, they are perceived as living glamorous, exciting lives. But once we reach the age of 30, there is increasing pressure on us to settle down and get married. If a woman wants to bear children, she may feel a sense of urgency when she reaches 30. This is when many single adults make a conscious decision to marry or to remain single. As one 30-year-old male recently commented, "It's real. You are supposed to get married by 30—that is a standard. It is part of getting on with your life that you are supposed to do. You have career and who-am-I concerns in your 20s. In your 30s, you have to get on with it, keep on track, make headway, financially and familywise." But, to another 30-year-old, getting married is less important than buying a house and some property. A training manager for a computer company, Jane says, "I'm competent in making relationships and being committed, so I don't feel a big rush to get married. When it happens, it happens."

Divorced Adults

Divorce has become epidemic in our culture. Until recently, it was increasing annually by 10 percent, although its rate of increase is now slowing. While divorce has increased for all socioeconomic groups, those in disadvantaged groups have a higher incidence of divorce. Youthful marriage, low educational level, and low income are associated with increases in divorce. So too is premarital pregnancy. One investigation revealed that half of the women who were pregnant before marriage failed to live with the husband for more than 5 years (Sauber & Corrigan, 1970).

For those who do divorce, separation and divorce are complex and emotionally charged (Bursik, 1991). In one investigation, 6 of the 48 divorced couples continued to have sexual intercourse during the first 2 years after separation (Hetherington, Cox, & Cox, 1978). Prior social scripts and patterns of interaction are difficult to break. Although divorce is a marker event in the relationship between spouses, it often does not signal the end of the relationship. Attachment to each other endures regardless of whether the former couple respects, likes, or is satisfied with the present relationship. Former spouses often alternate between feelings of seductiveness and hostility. They may also have thoughts of reconciliation. And while at times they may express love toward their former mate, the majority of feelings are negative and involve anger and hate.

The stress of separation and divorce place both men and women at risk for psychological and physical difficulties (Chase-Lansdale & Hetherington, in press; Coombs, 1991; Guttman, 1993). Separated and divorced men and women have higher

Separation and divorce are highly charged emotional affairs. No one gets married to get divorced. Attachment in some form often continues after the separation and divorce. Prior social scripts and interactions are difficult patterns to break. Former spouses may vacillate between hostility and seduction.

rates of psychiatric disturbance, admission to psychiatric hospitals, clinical depression, alcoholism, and psychosomatic problems, such as sleep disturbances, than do married adults. There is increasing evidence that stressful events of many types—including marital separation—reduce the immune system's capabilities, rendering separated and divorced individuals vulnerable to disease and infection. In one investigation, the most recently separated women (1 year or less) were more likely to show impaired immunological functioning than women whose separations had occurred several years earlier (1 to 6 years) (Kiecolt-Glaser & Glaser, 1988). Also in this investigation, unhappily married individuals had immune systems that were not functioning as effectively as those of happily married individuals.

Special problems surface for the divorced woman who is a displaced homemaker. She assumed that her work would probably always be in the home. Although her expertise in managing the home may be considerable, future employers do not recognize this experience as work experience. Donna is typical of a divorced displaced homemaker. She married young, and at age 18 had her first child. Her work experience consisted of a part-time job as a waitress in high school. Now 32 with three children—aged 14, 12, and 6—her husband recently divorced her and married someone else. The child-support payments are barely enough for rent, clothing, and other necessities. Without any marketable skills, Donna is working as a salesclerk in a local department store. She cannot afford a housekeeper and worries about the children being unsupervised while she works. Creating a positive single identity is essential for divorced adults such as Donna, so they can come to grips with their loneliness,

lack of autonomy, and financial hardship (Ahrons & Rodgers, 1987; McLanahan & Booth, 1989). Men, however, do not go through a divorce unscathed. They usually have fewer rights to their children, experience a decline in income (though not nearly as great as that of their ex-wives), and receive less emotional support. Divorce can also have a negative impact on a man's career.

Intimacy, Independence, and Gender

As we go through our early adult years, most of us are motivated not only by intimacy but also by independence. What is the nature of intimacy's development? How do we juggle the motivation for intimacy and the motivation for independence? What is the nature of women's development and men's development?

Intimacy

On several occasions in this chapter we have described the importance of intimacy in close relationships—the self-disclosure of intimacy in friendships and the importance of intimacy in affectionate love. Now let's examine the importance of intimacy in development in greater detail.

We are what we love.
—Erik Erikson, 1968

Identity and Intimacy

As we go through our adult lives, most of us are motivated to successfully juggle the development of identity and intimacy. Recall from our discussion in chapter 13 that Erik Erikson (1968) believes that identity versus identity confusion—pursuing who we are, what we are all about, and where we are going in life—is the most important issue to be negotiated in adolescence. Erikson thinks that intimacy should come after individuals are well on their way to establishing stable and successful identities. Intimacy is another life crisis in Erikson's scheme—if intimacy is not developed in early adulthood, the individual may be left with what Erikson calls "isolation." Intimacy versus isolation is Erikson's sixth developmental stage, which individuals experience in early adulthood. At this time, individuals face the task of forming intimate relationships with others. Erikson describes intimacy as finding oneself yet losing oneself in another person. If young adults form healthy friendships and an intimate relationship with another individual, intimacy will be achieved; if not, isolation will result.

Intimacy is a difficult art.
—Virginia Woolf

An inability to develop meaningful relationships with others can be harmful to an individual's personality. It may lead individuals to repudiate, ignore, or attack those who frustrate them. Such circumstances account for the shallow, almost pathetic attempts of youth to merge themselves with a leader. Many youths want to be apprentices or disciples of leaders and adults who will shelter them from the harm of the "out-group" world. If this fails, and Erikson believes that it must, sooner or later the individuals recoil into a self-search to discover where they went wrong. This introspection sometimes leads to painful depression and isolation and may contribute to a mistrust of others and restrict the willingness to act on one's own initiative.

Styles of Intimate Interaction

Young adults show different styles of intimate interaction. Psychologist Jacob Orlofsky (1976) developed a classification of five styles of intimate relationships: intimate, preintimate, stereotyped, pseudointimate, and isolated. In the **intimate style,** *the individual forms and maintains one or more deep and long-lasting love relationships.* In the **preintimate style,** *the individual shows mixed emotions about commitment, an ambivalence that is reflected in the strategy of offering love without obligations or long-lasting bonds.* In the **stereotyped style,** *the individual has superficial relationships that tend to be dominated by friendship ties with same-sex rather than opposite-sex individuals.* In the **pseudointimate style,** *the individual maintains a long-lasting sexual attachment with little or no depth or closeness.* In the **isolated style,** *the individual withdraws from social encounters and has little or no attachment to same- or opposite-sex individuals.* Occasionally the isolate shows signs of developing close interpersonal relationships, but usually the interactions are stressful. In one investigation, intimate and preintimate individuals were more sensitive to their partners' needs and were more open in their friendships than were individuals in the three other intimacy statuses (Orlofsky, Marcia, & Lesser, 1973).

Levels of Relationship Maturity

A desirable goal is to develop a mature identity and have positive close relationships with others. Kathleen White and her colleagues (Paul & White, 1990; White & others, 1986; White & others, 1987) developed a model of relationship maturity that includes this goal at its highest level. Individuals are described as moving through three levels of relationship maturity: self-focused, role-focused, and individuated-connected.

The **self-focused level** *is the first level of relationship maturity, at which one's perspective on another person or a relationship is concerned only with how it affects oneself.* The individual's own wishes and plans overshadow those of others, and the individual shows little concern for others. Intimate communication skills are in the early, experimental stages. In terms of sexuality, there is little understanding of mutuality or consideration of another's sexual needs.

The **role-focused level** *is the second or intermediate level of relationship maturity, when one begins to perceive others as individuals in their own right. However, at this level, the perspective is stereotypical and emphasizes social acceptability.* Individuals at this level know that acknowledging and respecting another is part of being a good friend or a romantic partner. Yet commitment to an individual, rather than to the romantic partner role, is not articulated. Generalizations about the importance of communication in relationships abound, but underlying this talk is a shallow understanding of commitment.

The **individuated-connected level** *is the highest level of relationship maturity, when one begins to understand oneself, as well as to have consideration for others' motivations and to anticipate their needs. Concern and caring involve emotional support and individualized expressions of interest.* At this level, individuals make a commitment to specific individuals with whom they share a relationship, and they understand the personal time and investment needed to make a relationship work. In White's view, it is not until adulthood that the individuated-connected level is likely to be reached. She believes that most individuals making the transition from adolescence to adulthood are either self-focused or role-focused in their relationship maturity.

Intimacy and Independence

The early adult years are a time when individuals usually develop an intimate relationship with another individual. An important aspect of this relationship is the commitment of the individuals to each other. At the same time, individuals show a strong interest in independence and freedom. Development in early adulthood often involves an intricate balance of intimacy and commitment on the one hand, and independence and freedom on the other (McAdams, 1988).

Recall that intimacy is the aspect of development that follows identity in Erikson's eight stages of development. A related aspect of developing an identity in adolescence and early adulthood is independence. At the same time as individuals are trying to establish an identity, they face the difficulty of having to cope with increasing their independence from their parents, developing an intimate relationship with another individual, and increasing their friendship commitments, while also being able to think for themselves and do things without always relying on what others say or do.

The extent to which the young adult has begun to develop autonomy has important implications for early adulthood maturity. The young adult who has not sufficiently moved away from parental ties may have difficulty in both interpersonal relationships and a career. Consider the mother who overprotects her daughter, continues to support her financially, and does not want to let go of her. In early adulthood, the daughter may have difficulty developing mature intimate relationships and she may have career difficulties. When a promotion comes up that involves more responsibility and possibly more stress, she may turn it down. When

LIFE-SPAN PRACTICAL KNOWLEDGE 15.4

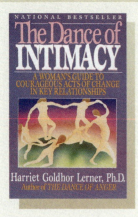

The Dance of Intimacy

(1985) by Harriet Lerner. New York: HarperCollins.

The Dance of Intimacy is written for women and is about women's intimate relationships. The book is subtitled "A Woman's Guide to Courageous Acts of Change in Key Relationships." Drawing on a combination of psychoanalytic and family-systems theories, Lerner weaves together a portrait of a woman's current self and relationships that she believes is derived from long-standing relationships with mothers, fathers, and siblings. Lerner tells women that if they are having problems in intimate relationships with a partner or their families of origin, they need to explore the nature of their family upbringing to produce clues to the current difficulties. Women learn how to distance themselves from their families of origin and how not to overreact to problems. Lerner gives women insights about how to define themselves, how to understand their needs and limits, and how to positively change. The positive change involves moving from being stuck in relationships that are going nowhere or are destructive to intimate connectedness with others and a solid sense of self. Lerner intelligently tells women that they should balance the "I" and the "We" in their lives, becoming neither too self-absorbed nor too other-oriented. To explore unhealthy patterns of close relationships that have been passed down from one generation to the next in their families, women are shown how to create a "genogram," a family diagram that goes back to your grandparents or earlier.

The Dance of Intimacy is an outstanding self-help book for understanding why close relationships are problematic and how to change them in positive ways. It does not give simple, quick-fix solutions. Lerner accurately tells women that change is difficult but possible. Her warm, personal tone helps women to gain the self-confidence necessary to make the changes she recommends. Maggie Scarf (1985), a well-known close relationships writer, said that reading *The Dance of Intimacy* is like having a long, revealing conversation with a wise and compassionate friend.

things do not go well in her relationship with a young man, she may go crying to her mother.

The balance between intimacy and commitment, on the one hand, and independence and freedom, on the other, is delicate. Keep in mind that these important dimensions of adult development are not necessarily opposite ends of a continuum—some individuals are able to experience a healthy independence and freedom along with an intimate relationship. These dimensions may also fluctuate with social and historical change. And keep in mind that intimacy and commitment, and independence and freedom, are not just concerns of early adulthood; they are important themes of development that are worked and reworked throughout the adult years.

Women's Development, Men's Development, and Gender Issues

In chapters 9 and 11 we discussed a number of ideas about gender, many of them about gender development in children. We continue our discussion of important aspects of gender, focusing on women's development and men's development.

Women's Development and Gender Issues

Many feminist scholars believe that historically psychology has portrayed human behavior with a male-dominant theme (DeFour & Paludi, in press; Denmark & Paludi, 1994). They also believe that sexism is still rampant in society and that women continue to be discriminated against in the workplace, in politics, at home, and many other arenas.

> *In the last decade it has become clearer that if women are trying to define and create a full personhood, we are engaged in a huge undertaking. We see that this attempt means building a new way of living which encompasses all realms of life, from global economic, social, and political levels to the most intimate personal relationships.*
>
> —Jean Baker Miller,
> *Toward a New Psychology of Women*, 1986

In chapter 1, we described some of the political, economic, educational, and psychological conditions of women around the world. We indicated that in politics women are too often treated as burdens rather than assets; that women's work is more limiting and narrow than that of men; that in many developing countries, especially in Africa, women do not have adequate opportunities for education; that too many women experience physical and psychological abuse from men; and that women are much more likely to be depressed than men (Culbertson, 1991).

Too many women have low self-esteem from living in a male-dominated society that has discriminated against women and not adequately addressed their economic and emotional

LIFE-SPAN PRACTICAL KNOWLEDGE 15.5

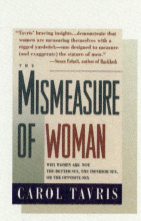

The Mismeasure of Woman

(1992) by Carol Tavris. New York: Simon & Schuster.

The Mismeasure of Woman explores the stereotyping of women and similarities and differences between women and men. Tavris believes that no matter how hard women try, they can't measure up. They are criticized for being too feminine or not feminine enough, but they are always judged and mismeasured by how they fit into a male world.

Tavris believes that more evidence exists for similarities between the sexes than for differences between them. She does not accept female superiority or male superiority. Tavris refutes feminists who say that women are more empathic then men, and she rejects the notion that women are less sexual. She also examines how society "pathologizes" women through psychiatric diagnoses, sexist divorce rulings, and images of women as moody, self-defeating, and unstable. In Tavris's view, if women appear to be different, it is because of the roles they have been assigned. This is an excellent book that cuts through the myths and misunderstandings about women and arrives at some intriguing insights about the nature of women and how women and men relate to each other.

---

needs. Feminists argue that gender stereotyping, male-imposed standards, and devaluation of feminine qualities has made women "second-class" citizens in their countries, their communities, and their homes.

Jean Baker Miller (1976, 1986) has been an important voice in stimulating examination of psychological issues from a female perspective. She believes the study of women's psychological development opens up paths to a better understanding of all psychological development, female and male. She also concludes that what psychologists discover about women, when they examine what women have been doing in life, is that a large part of their activity involves active participation in others' development. In Miller's view, women often interact with others in ways that foster the other person's emotional, intellectual, and social development. She and many others, including Carol Gilligan (1990), argue that society needs to place a higher value on connectedness to others, sensitivity to others' feelings, and close relationships—all of which women are very good at.

Many feminist thinkers believe that it is important for women not only to maintain their competency in relationships but to be self-motivated as well. Miller says that through increased self-determination, coupled with already developed relationship skills, many women will gain greater power in American society. As Harriet Lerner (1989) concluded in her book *The Dance of Intimacy*, it is important for women to bring to their relationships nothing less than a strong, assertive, independent, and authentic self. She believes competent relationships are those in which the separate "I-ness" of both persons can be appreciated and enhanced while the two persons still stay emotionally connected to each other.

Critical Thinking

What gender issues do you believe women will face in the year 2000? Will they be the same issues women face today?

Men's Development and Gender Issues

The male of the species—what is he really like? What does he really want? As a result of the woman's movement and its attack on society's male bias and discrimination against women, men have developed their own movement. The men's movement has not been as political or as activist as the women's movement. Rather, it has been more an emotional, spiritual movement that reasserts the importance of masculinity and urges men to resist women's efforts to turn them into "soft" males. Or it has been a psychological movement that recognizes that men need to be less violent and more nurturant but still retain much of their masculine identity. Many of the men's-movement disciples argue that society's changing gender arena has led many men to question what being a man really means.

Herbert Goldberg became a central figure in the early development of the men's movement in the 1970s and early 1980s, mainly as a result of his writings about men's issues in *The Hazards of Being Male* (1979) and *The New Male* (1980). Goldberg argues that a critical difference between men and women creates a precipitous gulf between them. That difference: Women can sense and articulate their feelings and problems; men, because of their masculine conditioning, can't. The result is an armor of masculinity that is defensive and powerful in maintaining self-destructive patterns. Goldberg says that most men have been effective work machines and performers but most else in their lives suffers. Men die earlier than women on the average, have higher hospitalization rates, and show more behavioral problems. In a word, Goldberg believes, millions of men are killing themselves by striving to be "true" men, a heavy price to pay for masculine privilege and power.

How can men solve their dilemma and live more physically and psychologically healthy lives? Goldberg argues that men need to get in touch with their emotions and their bodies. They can't do this by just piggybacking on the changes that are occurring in women's attitudes, he says. Rather, men need to develop their own realizations of what is critical for their survival and well-being. Goldberg especially encourages men to do the following:

- Recognize the suicidal "success" syndrome and avoid it
- Understand that occasional impotence is nothing serious
- Become aware of their real needs and desires and get in touch with their own bodies
- Elude the binds of masculine role-playing
- Relate to liberated women as their equals rather than serving as their guilty servants or hostile enemies
- Develop friendships with other males

Goldberg's messages to men that they need to become more attuned to their inner selves and emotional makeup, and work on developing more positive close relationships, are important ones.

One author who helped usher in a renewed interest in the men's movement in the 1990s is Robert Bly, a poet, storyteller, translator, and best-selling author who is a disciple of Carl Jung's ideas. In *Iron John* (1990), Bly says we live in a society that hasn't had fathers around since the Industrial Revolution. With no viable rituals for introducing young boys to manhood, today's men are left confused. Bly thinks that too many of today's males are "soft," having bonded with their mothers because their fathers were unavailable. These "soft" males know how to follow instead of lead, how to be vulnerable, and how to go with the flow, says Bly. He believes that what they don't know is what it's like to have a deep masculine identity. Iron John, a hairy mythological creature, has a deep masculine identity. He is spontaneous and sexual, an action taker, a boundary definer, and an earth preserver. He has untamed impulses and thoughtful self-discipline.

Bly not only writes poetry and books. He and his associates conduct 5-week-long gatherings and weekend workshops for men. At these gatherings, the participants try to capture what it is like to be a true man by engaging in such rituals as drum beating and naming ceremonies.

Many critics do not like Bly's strong insistence on the separateness of the sexes. Only masculine men and feminine women populate Bly's world. Feminist critics deplore Bly's approach, saying it is a regression to the old macho model of masculinity. And not everyone applauds Bly's belief that men can learn to become true men by going off into the woods to beat drums, dance around the fire, and bare their souls.

CONTINUITY AND DISCONTINUITY FROM CHILDHOOD TO ADULTHOOD

It is a common finding that the smaller the time intervals over which we measure personality characteristics, the more similar an individual will look from one measurement to the next. Thus, if we measure an individual's self-concept at the age of 20 and then again at the age of 30, we will probably find more stability than if we measured the individual's self-concept at the age of 10 and then again at the age of 30. We no longer believe in the infant determinism of Freud's psychosexual theory, which argued that our personality as adults is virtually cast in stone by the time we are 5 years of age. But the first 20 years of life are not meaningless in predicting an adult's personality. And there is every reason to believe that later experiences in the early adult years are important in determining what the individual is like as an adult. In trying to understand the young adult's personality, it would be misleading to look only at the adult's life in present tense, ignoring the developmental unfolding of personality. So, too, would it be far off target to only search through a 30-year-old's first 5 to 10 years of life in trying to predict why he or she is having difficulty in a close relationship. The truth about adult personality development, then, lies somewhere between the infant determinism of Freud and a contextual approach that ignores the antecedents of the adult years altogether.

At this point we have discussed a number of ideas about the diversity of adult life-styles, intimacy and independence, and continuity and discontinuity. A summary of these ideas is presented in concept table 15.2.

CONCEPT TABLE 15.2

The Diversity of Adult Life-Styles, Intimacy and Independence, and Continuity and Discontinuity

Concept	Processes/Related Ideas	Characteristics/Description
The diversity of adult life-styles	Single adults	Being single has become an increasingly prominent life-style. Myths and stereotypes about singles abound, ranging from "swinging single" to "desperately lonely, suicidal single." There are advantages and disadvantages to being single, autonomy being one of the advantages. Intimacy, loneliness, and finding a positive identity in a marriage-oriented society are concerns of single adults.
	Divorced adults	Divorce has increased dramatically, although its rate of increase has begun to slow. Divorce is complex and emotional. In the first year following divorce, a disequilibrium in the divorced adult's behavior occurs, but by several years after the divorce, more stability has been achieved. The divorced displaced homemaker may encounter excessive stress. Men do not go through a divorce unscathed either.
Intimacy and independence	Intimacy	Erikson argues that intimacy versus isolation, the sixth stage in his eight-stage theory of the life cycle, coincides with early adulthood. Five styles of intimate interaction are intimate style, preintimate style, stereotyped style, pseudointimate style, and isolated style. White proposed a model of relationship maturity in which individuals move through three levels: self-focused, role-focused, and individuated-connected.
	Intimacy and independence	There is a delicate balance between intimacy and commitment, on the one hand, and independence and freedom, on the other. These themes are germane to understanding early adulthood, but they are usually worked and reworked throughout the adult years.
	Women's development and gender issues	Feminist scholars are developing new perspectives that focus on women's experiences and development. Women's strengths have been especially important in relationships and connections with others. A special emphasis is that, while staying emotionally connected to significant others, women can enhance their well-being by developing stronger self-determination.
	Men's development and gender issues	The men's movement has involved several different themes, among them the belief that today's males are too soft. Another branch of the movement argues that males need to be more sensitive and less violent.
Continuity and discontinuity	Their nature	The shorter the time intervals over which we measure personality, the more continuity we find. The first 20 years are important in predicting an adult's personality, but so, too, are continuing experiences in the adult years. The first 5 years are not as powerful as Freud believed in determining an adult's personality.

LIFE-SPAN HEALTH AND WELL-BEING

Reducing Loneliness

oneliness, like depression, can be a dark cloud that enfolds a person's day-to-day life. Feeling lonely should not be confused with being alone. Time spent alone can be quite satisfying and meaningful. But when we find ourselves longing to be with others and feeling unconnected, isolated, and alienated, our loneliness can seriously interfere with our sense of life satisfaction. While most of us may feel lonely from time to time, some people find themselves feeling intensely lonely for long periods of time. For each person, there may be many ways to combat loneliness. But in general, people who find themselves facing loneliness can do some things for themselves.

One way to prevent loneliness in the first place is to become involved in activities with others. For example, many opportunities to meet others and become involved arise through work, school, community announcements, and religious organizations. People also can join organizations and volunteer time for a cause that they believe in. Spending time with others and developing social networks will have the long-term payoff of reducing the chances of finding oneself alone and feeling lonely. One social

gathering can lead to the development of several new social contacts if one takes the initiative to introduce oneself to others and start a conversation. Meeting new people and developing social ties always involves taking some personal risks, but the benefits often outweigh these risks.

Loneliness often occurs as a result of the loss of social contacts. Moving to a new community, changing jobs, and breaking off dating relationships usually decrease the number of social contacts one has. It is therefore important to replace social contacts that have been lost. Of course, lost contacts need not be replaced with the same types of relationships. For example, when a dating relationship is broken off, new nondating friends can fill the social void. Also, social contacts do not necessarily have to be new to meet social needs. Sometimes these can be met by spending more time with old friends.

As with depression, it is important to recognize the warning signs of loneliness early on. Knowing what feelings may come about before one starts to feel lonely can allow a person to take action to head off the loneliness. For example, people who begin to feel somewhat bored and alienated before loneliness

sinks in can learn to recognize these feelings as a warning sign, and take steps to prevent themselves from becoming lonely. This is particularly important because loneliness can become so intense that it can keep a person from acting. Thus, as with depression, heading off loneliness can be much easier than trying to get out of it.

The most effective means of avoiding loneliness, though, is to develop interests and activities that provide the opportunity to develop social contacts. A person's social contacts are referred to as a "social network" because usually contacts are not isolated from each other, but rather are interconnected.

Evaluating your social network shows how your social needs are met. When social contacts change or are lost, knowing your social network can help you make adjustments and avoid loneliness. Take some time and think about the people you see and those you share time with. Construct a social network and think about which relationships are most important to you and which you would like to strengthen (Simons, Kalichman, & Santrock, 1994). ■

CONCLUSIONS

Love and close relationships are a vast territory that has become increasingly complex in recent years. Some of the complexity is due to changes in marriage and the family and the increasing number of individuals who follow different life-styles than did their counterparts of only a generation or two ago.

We began this chapter by exploring the romantic worlds of Edith, Phil, and Sherry. We evaluated what attracts us to each other, the faces of love, and loneliness. Our coverage of marriage and the family focused on the

family life cycle, marital trends, marital expectations and myths, gender, intimacy, family work in marriage, and the parental role. Then we studied the diversity of adult life-styles, especially single adults and divorced adults. We also considered the nature of intimacy, intimacy and independence, and women's and men's gender issues. And we evaluated continuity and discontinuity from childhood to adulthood. At different points in the chapter we read about marriages

around the world, the mother's and the father's roles, and reducing loneliness.

Remember that you can obtain an overall summary of the chapter by again reading the two concept tables on pages 450 and 457. This concludes our discussion of early adulthood. In Section Eight, we continue our journey through adulthood by studying middle adulthood, beginning with chapter 16, "Physical and Cognitive Development in Middle Adulthood."

KEY TERMS

consensual validation Explains why individuals are attracted to people who are similar to them. Our own attitudes and behavior are supported and validated when someone else's attitudes and behavior are similar to our own. (439)

friendship A form of close relationship that involves enjoyment, acceptance, trust, respect, mutual assistance, confiding, understanding, and spontaneity. (440)

romantic love Also called "passionate love" or "Eros," romantic love has strong sexual and infatuation components and often predominates in the early period of a love relationship. (440)

affectionate love In this type of love (also called "companionate love"), an individual desires to have the other person near and has a deep, caring affection for the other person. (441)

triangular theory of love Sternberg's theory that love has three main forms: passion, intimacy, and commitment. (441)

leaving home and becoming a single adult The first stage in the family life cycle and involves launching. (443)

launching The process in which youths move into adulthood and exit their family of origin. (443)

new couple Forming the new couple is the second stage in the family life cycle. Two individuals from separate families of origin unite to form a new family system. (443)

becoming parents and a family with children The third stage in the family life cycle. Adults who enter this stage move up a generation and become caregivers to the younger generation. (445)

family with adolescents The fourth stage of the family life cycle, in which adolescent children push for autonomy and seek to develop their own identities. (445)

family at mid-life The fifth stage in the family life cycle, a time of launching children, linking generations, and adapting to mid-life developmental changes. (445)

family in later life The sixth and final stage in the family life cycle, involving retirement and, in many families, grandparenting. (445)

intimate style According to Jacob Orlofsky's classification of styles in intimate interactions, an individual with the intimate style forms and maintains one or more deep and long-lasting love relationships. (453)

preintimate style According to Orlofsky, an individual with preintimate style shows mixed emotions about commitment, an ambivalence that is reflected in the strategy of offering love without obligations or long-lasting bonds. (453)

stereotyped style According to Orlofsky, an individual with the stereotyped style of intimate relationships has superficial relationships that tend to be dominated by friendship ties with

same-sex rather than opposite-sex individuals. (453)

pseudointimate style According to Orlofsky, an individual with pseudointimate style maintains a long-lasting sexual attachment with little or no depth or closeness. (453)

isolated style According to Orlofsky, an individual with isolated style withdraws from social encounters and has little or no attachment to same- or opposite-sex individuals. (453)

self-focused level In the model of relationship maturity developed by Kathleen White and her colleagues, this is the first level of relationship maturity. At the self-focused level, one's perspective on another or on a relationship is concerned only with how it affects oneself. (453)

role-focused level In White's model, this is the second level of relationship maturity, at which one begins to perceive others as individuals in their own right. One's perspective is still stereotypical and emphasizes social acceptability. (453)

individuated-connected level In White's model, this is the highest level of relationship maturity. One is acquiring an understanding of oneself, as well as consideration for others' motivations and anticipation of their needs. One now feels concern and caring that involve emotional support and individualized expressions of interest. (453)

ANSWERS TO THE MARRIAGE QUIZ (FIGURE 15.4)

1. False
2. True
3. False
4. False
5. True
6. True
7. False
8. False
9. False
10. False
11. False
12. True
13. False
14. False
15. False

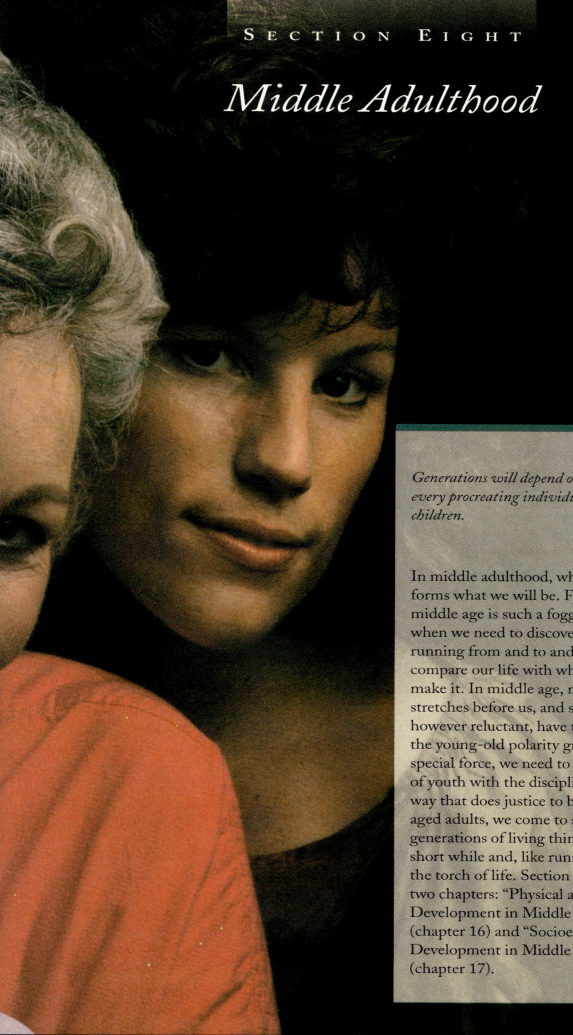

Middle Adulthood

Generations will depend on the ability of every procreating individual to face his children.

—Erik Erikson

In middle adulthood, what we have been forms what we will be. For some of us, middle age is such a foggy place, a time when we need to discover what we are running from and to and why. We compare our life with what we vowed to make it. In middle age, more time stretches before us, and some evaluations, however reluctant, have to be made. As the young-old polarity greets us with a special force, we need to join the daring of youth with the discipline of age in a way that does justice to both. As middle-aged adults, we come to sense that the generations of living things pass in a short while and, like runners, hand on the torch of life. Section Eight consists of two chapters: "Physical and Cognitive Development in Middle Adulthood" (chapter 16) and "Socioemotional Development in Middle Adulthood" (chapter 17).

Salakhov Tair, Ritratto del compositore Kara-Karjev, detail.

16

Physical and Cognitive Development in Middle Adulthood

Chapter Outline

LIFE-SPAN HEALTH AND WELL-BEING

Chapter Boxes

When more time stretches before one, some assessments, however reluctantly and incompletely, begin to be made.

—James Baldwin

*The first forty years of life furnish the text, while
the remaining thirty supply the commentary.*

—Schopenauer

IMAGES OF LIFE-SPAN DEVELOPMENT

Time Perspectives

Our perception of time depends on where we are in the life cycle. We are more concerned about time at some points in life than others. Jim Croce's song "Time in a Bottle" reflects a time perspective that develops in the adult years.

If I could save time in a bottle
the first thing that I'd like to do
is save every day till eternity passes
away
just to spend them with you. . . .
But there never seems to be
enough time to do
the things you want to do once you
find them.

Looked around enough to know
that you're the one
I want to go through time with

Jim Croce, "Time in a Bottle"

When we are young adults, love and intimacy assume prominent roles in our lives. We begin to look back at where we have been. As middle-aged adults, we reflect even more on what we have done with the time we have had. We look toward the future more in terms of how much time remains to accomplish what we wish to do with our lives.

When we think about what happens to us when we become middle-aged, physical changes leap to the forefront of our thoughts—the lessening of physical powers, the arrival of sags, spreads, and lines, the appearance of menopause. Middle age also brings forth thoughts about whether our mind slows down at this point in the life cycle. We wonder, "Will my memory be worse when I become middle-aged?" for example. And we imagine where we will be in our careers in middle age. We think, "Will I be able to reach and maintain satisfaction in my career?" "Will I possibly change careers in mid-life?" "Will I be able to find enough time for leisure and lead a balanced, happy life?"

PREVIEW

The questions just raised reflect some of the main themes of this chapter—physical, cognitive, and career development. Interest in middle age is essentially a late-twentieth-century phenomenon. In 1900, the average life expectancy was 47 years of age; it has only been since a much larger percentage of people began living to older ages that it made any sense to label, describe, and investigate a period in the human life span called "middle adulthood." In this chapter, we will begin by considering whether what constitutes middle age is changing; we will next highlight the physical changes of middle age, then evaluate whether cognitive changes also take place as we make the transition between early adulthood and late adulthood, and finally examine the roles of careers, work, and leisure in middle adulthood.

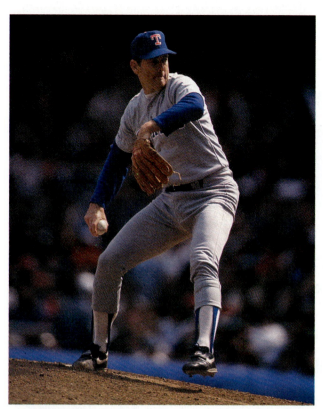

At age 44, Nolan Ryan pitched the seventh no-hit game of his career, and at age 46 he continued to be one of the Texas Rangers' leading pitchers, training vigorously in-season and off-season. In 1993, Ryan retired from professional baseball. The Nolan Ryans of the world are forcing life-span developmentalists to reconsider what constitutes the lower age boundary of middle adulthood.

CHANGING MIDDLE AGE

Each year, for $8, about 2.5 to 3 million Americans who have turned 50 become members of the American Association for Retired Persons (AARP). There is something incongruous about so many 50-year-olds joining a retirement group when hardly any of them are retired. Indeed, many of today's 50-year-olds are in better shape, more alert, and more productive than their 40-year-old counterparts from a generation or two earlier. As more people lead healthier life-styles and medical discoveries help to stave off the aging process, the boundaries of middle age are being pushed upward. It looks like middle age is starting later and lasting longer for increasing numbers of active, healthy, and productive people (Beck, 1992). June Reinisch (1992), director of the Kinsey Institute for Research in Sex, Gender, and Reproduction at Indiana University, recently said, "I'm 49 this year. I wear clothes that my mother would never have thought of wearing when she was this age. When skirts went up, my skirts went up" (p. 42).

Sigmund Freud and Carl Jung studied mid-life transitions around the turn of the twentieth century, but "mid-life" came much earlier back then. In 1900, the average life expectancy was only 47 years of age; only 3 percent of the population lived past 65. Today, the average life expectancy is 75; 12 percent of

the U.S. population is older than 65. As a much greater percentage of the population lives to an older age, the midpoint of life and what constitutes middle age or middle adulthood are getting harder to pin down. In only one century, we have added 30 years to the average life expectancy. Statistically, the middle of life today is about 37 years of age—hardly any 37-year-olds, though, wish to be called "middle-aged"! What we think of as middle age comes later—anywhere from 40 to about 60 to 65 years of age. And as more people live longer, the 60 to 65 years upper boundary will likely be nudged upward. When the American Board of Family Practice asked a random sample of 1,200 Americans when middle age begins, 41 percent said it was when you worry about having enough money for health-care concerns, 42 percent said it was when your last child moves out, and 46 percent said it was when you don't recognize the names of music groups on the radio anymore (Beck, 1992).

Though the age boundaries are not set in stone, we will consider **middle adulthood** *as the developmental period that begins at approximately 35 to 45 years of age and extends into the sixties.* For many people, mid-life is a time of declining physical skills and expanding responsibility; a period in which people become more conscious of the young-old polarity and the shrinking amount of time left in life; a point when individuals seek to transmit something meaningful to the next generation; and a time when people reach and maintain satisfaction in their careers.

But these characteristics don't describe everybody in middle age. As life-span expert Gilbert Brim (1992) commented recently, middle adulthood is full of changes, twists, and turns; the path is not fixed. People move in and out of states of success and failure.

> *I must govern the clock, not be governed by it.*
> —Golda Meir

PHYSICAL DEVELOPMENT

I am 49 years of age at the time of this writing. When I was an adolescent and my father was 49 years old, I thought he was old. I could not conceive of myself ever being that old! But it happened, and now I've got a few gray hairs. I'm wearing reading glasses while I'm typing this sentence, and I can't run as fast as I could, although I still run about 15 miles every week to keep my body from falling apart. At some point in our forties we become middle-aged. What physical changes accompany this change to middle adulthood? What is the health status of middle-aged adults? What kind of sexual changes occur?

Physical Changes

A host of physical changes characterize middle adulthood—some began to appear earlier in the individual's thirties, but at some point in the forties, decline in physical development indicates that middle adulthood has arrived.

FEELING FIFTY (1)

Flop Fat Fake Furious Forgetful Fidgety Fragile Fussy Foolish Frag mented Fossil Free Fall

FEELING FIFTY (2)

Free Frolicsome Focused Fit Fashionable Formidable Forbearing Feminized Fotogenic Fabulous

> *I wear them. They help me. But I don't care for them . . .*
> *My gaze feels aimed. It is as if two manufactured beams*
> *had been lodged in my sockets—hollow stiff and gray. Like*
> *mailing tubes—and when I pivot, vases topple down from*
> *tabletops, and women frown.*
>
> —John Updike

Seeing and hearing are two of the most troublesome and noticeable changes in middle adulthood. Accommodation of the eye—the ability to focus and maintain an image on the retina—experiences its sharpest decline between 40 and 59 years of age. In particular, middle-aged individuals begin to have difficulty viewing close objects (Kline & Schieber, 1985). The eye's blood supply also diminishes, although usually not until the fifties or sixties. The reduced blood supply may decrease the visual field's size and account for an increase in the eye's blind spot. And there is some evidence that the retina becomes less sensitive to low levels of illumination. In one investigation, the effects of illumination level on the work productivity of individuals in early and middle adulthood were studied (Hughes, 1978). The workers were asked to look for 10 target numbers printed on sheets of paper that had a total of 420 numbers printed on them. Each of the workers performed the task under three different levels of illumination. While increased levels of illumination increased performance for both age groups, the performance of middle-aged workers improved the most.

Hearing may also start to decline by the age of 40. Sensitivity to high pitches usually declines first; the ability to hear low-pitched sounds does not seem to decline much in middle adulthood, though. And men usually lose their

LIFE-SPAN PRACTICAL KNOWLEDGE 16.1

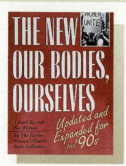

The New Our Bodies, Ourselves (1992) by The Boston Women's Health Book Collective. New York: Simon & Schuster.

This expanded and updated version of *Our Bodies, Ourselves* tackles a wide range of women's health concerns of the 1990s. Among the topics covered are women's changing bodies, sexual myths and realities, menstruation, menopause, and a number of diseases that afflict women. New topics in this edition include female condoms, infection and AIDS, breast reconstruction after a mastectomy, interstitial cystitis (a bladder disease that primarily afflicts women), and chronic fatigue syndrome.

A host of physical changes accompany middle age, among them accommodation of the eye.

sensitivity to high-pitched sounds sooner than women do. However, this sex difference might be due to men's greater exposure to noise in occupations such as mining, automobile work, and so on (Olsho, Harkins, & Lenhardt, 1985).

As individuals go through their adult years, they get shorter—our bodies cannot hold off gravity forever! As muscles weaken, an adult's back weakens. As the disks between the bones of the spine deteriorate, the bones move closer to one another. For example, a man who is 5 feet 10 inches tall at age 30 will probably be 5 feet 9⅞ inches by age 50, and only 5 feet 9¼ inches by age 60.

Health Status

Health status becomes a major concern in middle adulthood. More time is spent worrying about health now than in early adulthood. Because middle adulthood is characterized by a general decline in physical fitness, some deterioration in health is to be expected. The main health nemeses of middle-aged adults are cardiovascular disease, cancer, and weight. Cardiovascular disease is the number one killer in the United States, followed by cancer. Smoking-related cancer often surfaces for the first time in middle adulthood. And the *Harvard Medical School Health Letter* indicates that about 20 million Americans are on a serious diet at any particular moment. Being overweight is a critical health problem in middle adulthood. For individuals who are 30 percent or more overweight, the probability of dying in middle adulthood increases by about 40 percent. Obesity increases the probability that an individual will suffer a number of other ailments, among them hypertension and digestive disorders.

> *Middle age is when your age starts to show around your middle.*
>
> —Bob Hope

Since a youthful appearance is stressed in our culture, many individuals whose hair is graying, whose skin is wrinkling, whose bodies are sagging, and whose teeth are yellowing strive to make themselves look younger. Undergoing cosmetic surgery, dying hair, purchasing wigs, enrolling in weight reduction programs, participating in exercise regimens, and taking heavy doses of vitamins are common in middle age. One investigation found that middle-aged women focus more attention on facial attractiveness than do older or younger women (Nowak, 1977). In this same investigation, middle-aged women were more likely to perceive the signs of aging as having a negative effect on their physical appearance. In our culture, some aspects of aging in middle adulthood are taken as signs of attractiveness in men; similar signs may be perceived as unattractive in women. Facial wrinkles and gray hair symbolize strength and maturity in men but may be perceived as unattractive in women.

How individuals deal with physical change and decline varies greatly from one individual to the next. One individual may be able to function well with severe physical problems or deteriorating health; another with the same problems may be hospitalized and bedridden. Some individuals call a doctor at the slightest hint of something being physically amiss; others ignore serious physical signs that might indicate the presence of a heart condition or cancer.

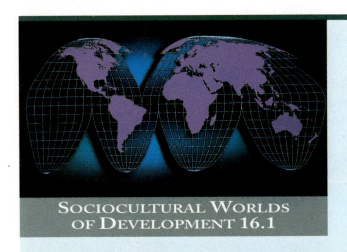

SOCIOCULTURAL WORLDS OF DEVELOPMENT 16.1

Health Promotion in Black Americans, Hispanic Americans, Asian Americans, and Native Americans

There are differences within ethnic groups as well as among them. This is just as true of health among ethnic groups as it is of, say, family structure. The spectrum of living conditions and life-styles within an ethnic group are influenced by social class, immigrant status, social and language skills, occupational opportunities, and such social resources as the availability of meaningful support networks—all of which can play a role in an ethnic minority member's health. Psychologists Felipe Castro and Delia Magaña (1988) developed a course in health promotion in ethnic minority communities, which they teach at UCLA. A summary of some of the issues they discuss in the course follows.

Prejudice and racial segregation are the historical underpinnings for the chronic stress of discrimination and poverty that adversely affects the health of many Black Americans. Support systems, such as an extended family network, may be especially important resources to improve the health of Black Americans and help them cope with stress (Boyd-Franklin, 1989; McAdoo, 1988).

Some of the same stressors mentioned for Black Americans are associated with migration to the United States by Puerto Ricans, Mexicans, and Latin Americans. Language is often a barrier for unacculturated Hispanics in doctor-patient communications. In addition, there is increasing evidence that diabetes occurs at an above-average rate in Hispanics, making this disease a major health problem that parallels the above-average rate of high blood pressure among Blacks (Gardner & others, 1984).

Asian Americans are characterized by their broad diversity in national backgrounds and life-styles. They range from highly acculturated Japanese Americans, who may be better educated than many Anglo-Americans and have excellent access to health care, to the many Indochinese refugees who have few economic resources and may be in poor health.

Cultural barriers to adequate health care include a lack of financial resources and poor language skills. In addition, members of ethnic minority groups are often unfamiliar with how the medical system operates, confused about the need to see numerous people, and uncertain about why they have to wait so long for service (Snowden & Cheung, 1990).

Other barriers may be specific to certain cultures, reflecting differing ideas regarding what causes disease and how it should be treated. For example, there are Chinese herbalists and folk healers in every Chinatown in the United States. Depending on their degree of acculturation to Western society, Chinese Americans may go to either a folk healer or a Western doctor first, but generally they will consult a folk

Life-Style, Personality, and Health

Emotional stability and personality are related to health in middle adulthood. In the California Longitudinal Study, as individuals aged from 34 to 50, those who were the most healthy were also the most calm, the most self-controlled, and the most responsible (Livson & Peskin, 1981). Three clusters of personality characteristics that have been extensively investigated as factors in stress and health are Type A behavior, Type C behavior, and hardiness. And considerable interest has developed in the role of stress and diet in cancer.

Cardiovascular Disease and the Type A Behavior Pattern

The heart and coronary arteries change in middle adulthood. The heart of a 40-year-old pumps only 23 liters of blood per minute; the heart of a 20-year-old pumps 40 liters under comparable conditions. Just as the coronary arteries that supply blood to the heart narrow during middle adulthood, the level of cholesterol in the blood increases with age—at age 20, it is 180 milligrams; at 40, 220 mg; at 60, 230 mg—and begins

to accumulate on the artery walls, which are also thickening. The net result: Arteries are more likely to become clogged, increasing the pressure on the arterial walls, which in turn pushes the heart to work harder to pump blood, thus making a stroke or heart attack more likely. Blood pressure, too, usually rises in the forties and fifties. At menopause, a woman's blood pressure rises sharply and usually remains above that of a man through life's later years.

In one recent 3-year longitudinal study of 500 women 42 to 50 years of age at the onset of the study, those who increased their exercise not only showed the lowest weight gains over the years but also had the lowest decreases in "good" cholesterol (high density lipoprotein—HDL). The types of exercise reported by the women included walking, calisthenics, and aerobic exercise. As women's risk of coronary disease heightens in middle age, there is a growing consensus that even moderate exercise can lower its risk.

Culture also plays an important role in coronary disease. Cross-cultural psychologists believe that studies of migrant ethnic groups help shed light on the role culture plays in health. As

Prejudice and racial segregation provide historical underpinnings for the chronic stress of discrimination and poverty that adversely affects the health of many Black Americans.

Herbalists and folk healers continue to play an important role in the health care of Chinese Americans. For example, there are Chinese herbalists and folk-healers in every Chinatown in the United States.

healer for follow-up care. Chinese medicines are usually used for home care. These include ginseng tea, boiled centipede soup for cancer, and eucalyptus oil for dizziness resulting from hypertension.

Native Americans view Western medicine as a source of crisis intervention, quick fixes for broken legs, or cures for other symptoms. They do not view Western medicine as a source for treating the causes of disease or for preventing disease. For example, they are unlikely to attend a seminar on preventing alcohol abuse. They also are reluctant to become involved in care that requires long-term hospitalization or surgery.

Both Navajo Indians and Mexican Americans rely on family members to make decisions about treatment. Doctors who expect such patients to decide on the spot whether or not to

undergo treatment will likely embarrass the patient or force the patient to give an answer that may lead to canceled appointments. Mexican Americans also believe that some illnesses are due to natural causes whereas others are due to supernatural causes. Depending on their level of acculturation, Mexican Americans may be disappointed and confused by doctors who do not show an awareness of how to treat diseases with supposed supernatural origins.

Health-care professionals can increase their effectiveness with ethnic minority patients by improving their knowledge of patients' attitudes, beliefs, and folk practices regarding health and disease (Anderson, 1991; Martin, 1991). Such information should be integrated into Western treatment rather than ignored at the risk of alienating patients.

ethnic groups migrate, the health practices dictated by their cultures change while their genetic predispositions to certain disorders remains constant (Ilola, 1990). The Ni-Hon-San Study (Nipon-Honolulu-San Francisco), part of the Honolulu Heart Study, is an ongoing study of approximately 12,000 Japanese men in Hiroshima and Nagasaki (Japan), Honolulu, and San Francisco. In the study, the Japanese men living in Japan have had the lowest rate of coronary heart disease, those living in Honolulu have had an intermediate rate, and those living in San Francisco have had the highest rate. Acculturation provides a valuable framework for understanding why the Japanese men's cholesterol level, glucose level, and weight all increased as they migrated and acculturated. As the Japanese men migrated farther away from Japan, their health practices, such as diet, changed. The Japanese men in California, for example, ate 40 percent more fat than the men in Japan.

Conversely, Japanese men in California have much lower rates of cerebrovascular disease (stroke) than Japanese men living in Japan. Businessmen in Japan tend to consume vast quantities of alcohol and to chain-smoke, both of which are high-risk factors for stroke. As a result, stroke was the leading cause

of death in Japan until it was surpassed by cancer in 1981. However, death rates from stroke for Japanese American men are at the same level as those of Anglo-American men. Researchers suspect that this level is related to a change in behavior. That is, Japanese American men consume less alcohol and smoke less than their counterparts in Japan. More about cultural factors in health appears in Sociocultural Worlds of Development 16.1.

Might an individual's personality characteristics contribute to the likelihood of having cardiovascular disease? In the late 1950s a secretary for two California cardiologists, Meyer Friedman and Ray Rosenman, observed that the chairs in their waiting rooms were tattered and worn, but only on the front edge. The cardiologists had noticed the impatience of their cardiac patients, who often arrived exactly on time for an appointment and were in a great hurry to leave. Subsequently they conducted a study of 3,000 healthy men between the ages of 35 and 59 over a period of 8 years (Friedman & Rosenman, 1974). During the 8 years, one group of men had twice as many heart attacks or other forms of heart disease as anyone else. Autopsies of the men who died revealed that this same group had coronary

LIFE-SPAN PRACTICAL KNOWLEDGE 16.2

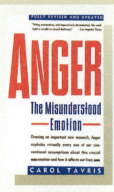

Anger: The Misunderstood Emotion

(1989) by Carol Tavris. New York: Touchstone Books.

Anger: The Misunderstood Emotion covers a wide terrain of anger. Indeed, it is hard to come up with any situations involving anger—from wrecked friendships to wars—that Tavris does not tackle. In addition to extensive coverage of anger between marital partners, she addresses highway anger, violence in sports, and young women's anger. Tavris debunks myths about anger, attacks the catharsis, ventilationist approach to anger, describes the toll of anger on the body, and tells readers how to rethink anger and make more adaptive choices. Anyone wanting to cope more effectively with the anger in their lives will find this book a welcome tonic.

Type Z behavior

Drawing by D. Reilly; © 1987 The New Yorker Magazine, Inc.

arteries that were more obstructed than those of other men. Friedman and Rosenman described the coronary-disease group as characterized by **Type A behavior pattern,** *a cluster of characteristics—excessive competitiveness, hard-drivenness, impatience, and hostility—thought to be related to the incidence of heart disease.*

However, further research on the link between Type A behavior and coronary disease indicates that the association is not as strong as Friedman and Rosenman believed (Edwards & Baglioni, 1991; Siegman & Dembrowski, 1989; Williams, 1989). Researchers have examined the different components of Type A behavior, such as hostility, to determine a more precise link with coronary risk. People who are hostile or consistently turn anger inward, it turns out, are more likely to develop heart disease (Williams, 1989). Such people have been labeled "hot reactors," meaning that they have intense physiological reactions to stress—their hearts race, their breathing quickens, and their muscles tense up—which could lead to heart disease. Redford Williams (1989), a leading researcher in charting the behavioral and psychological dimensions of heart disease, believes each of us has the ability to control our anger and develop more trust in others, which he believes will reduce the risk for heart disease.

> *All men should strive to learn before they die*
> *What they are running from, and to, and why.*
> —James Thurber, *The Shore and the Sea*, 1956

Individuals who display Type A behavior often benefit from stress management programs. By turning to Perspectives on Parenting and Education 16.1, you can read about the nature of these programs and a component that is often present in them—relaxation training.

Type C Behavior

Type C behavior *refers to the cancer-prone personality, which consists of being inhibited, uptight, emotionally inexpressive, and otherwise constrained. This type of individual is more likely to develop cancer than are more expressive people* (Temoshok & Dreher, 1992). Although this is still a very new concept, Type C behavior holds the promise of capturing as much attention as Type A behavior. The concept of Type C behavior fits with the findings of stress and health researchers, who have found that holding in one's problems and being inhibited about talking with others about problems can be an impairment to health.

Hardiness

Hardiness *is a personality style characterized by a sense of commitment (rather than alienation), control (rather than powerlessness), and a perception of problems as challenges (rather than as threats).* In the Chicago Stress Project, male business managers 32 to 65 years of age were studied over a 5-year period (Maddi, 1986). During the 5 years, most of the managers experienced stressful events, such as divorce, job transfers, the death of a close friend, inferior performance evaluations at work, or working for an unpleasant boss. Managers who developed an illness (ranging from the flu to a heart attack) were compared with those who did not. Those in the latter group were more likely to have hardy personalities. Another study investigated whether

LIFE-SPAN PRACTICAL KNOWLEDGE 16.3

Beyond the Relaxation Response
(1984) by Herbert Benson. New York: Times Books.

Beyond the Relaxation Response is Herbert Benson's sequel to *The Relaxation Response.* A decade after he coined the term *relaxation response,* Benson concluded that combining the relaxation response with another strategy is even more powerful in combating stress than the relaxation response alone. The other strategy is faith in a healing power either inside or outside yourself. Benson arrived at this conclusion through his own clinical observations and studies of Tibetan monks in the Himalayas, which are described in detail in *Beyond the Relaxation Response.* This does not mean you have to believe in a certain dogma or a traditional religion—you also can achieve the desired result by having faith in yourself, by moving into that state while exercising, or by simply eliciting the relaxation response itself. Benson tells you how to harness the power of faith in a number of different situations—while jogging or walking, swimming, lying in bed, or praying.

Beyond the Relaxation Response was one of the top 25 books in the recent national survey of clinical and counseling psychologists. It is a very practical book that clearly conveys the healing power of relaxation and mental strategies in improving our well-being.

PERSPECTIVES ON PARENTING AND EDUCATION 16.1

Stress Management

Because many people have difficulty in managing stress themselves, psychologists have developed a variety of stress management programs that can be taught to individuals. Stress management programs are often taught through workshops, which are increasingly offered in the workplace (Taylor, 1991). Aware of the high cost of productivity lost to stress-related disorders, many organizations have become increasingly motivated to help their workers identify and cope with stressful circumstances in their lives. Some stress management programs are broad in scope, teaching a variety of techniques to handle stress; others are more narrow, teaching a specific technique, such as relaxation or assertiveness training. Some stress management programs are also taught to individuals who are experiencing similar kinds of problems—such as migraine headache sufferers or individuals with chronically high blood pressure. Colleges are increasingly developing stress management programs for students. If you are finding the experience of college extremely stressful and are having difficulty coping with taxing circumstances in your life, you might want to consider enrolling in a stress management program at your college or in your community. Let's now examine one of the techniques used in many stress management programs—relaxation training.

How relaxed are you right now? Would you like to feel more tranquil and peaceful? If so, you can probably reach that feeling state by following some simple instructions. First, you need to find a quiet place to sit. Get a comfortable chair and sit quietly and upright in it. Let your chin rest comfortably on your chest, your arms in your lap. Close your eyes. Then pay attention to your breathing. Every time you inhale and every time you exhale, notice it and pay attention to the sensations of air flowing through your body, the feeling of your lungs filling and emptying. After you have done this for several breaths, begin to repeat silently to yourself a single word every time you breathe out. The word you choose does not have to mean anything. You can make the word up, you could use the word *one,* or you could try a word that is associated with the emotion you want to produce, such as *trust, love, patience,* or *happy.* Try several different words to see which one works best for you. At first, you will find that thoughts intrude and you are no longer attending to your breathing. Just return to your breathing and say the word each time you exhale. After you have practiced this exercise for 10 to 15 minutes, twice a day, every day for 2 weeks, you will be ready for a shortened version. If you notice stressful thoughts or circumstances appearing, simply engage in the relaxation response on the spot for several minutes. If you are in public, you don't have to close your eyes, just fix your gaze on some nearby object, attend to your breathing, and say your word silently every time you exhale.

Audiotapes that induce the relaxation response are available in most bookstores. They usually include soothing background music along with instructions for how to induce the relaxation response. These audiotapes can especially help induce a more relaxed state before you go to bed at night.

FIGURE 16.1

Cross-cultural comparisons of diet and cancer. In countries in which individuals have a low daily intake of fat (in Thailand, for example), the rate of breast cancer is low. In countries in which individuals have a high daily intake of fat (in the Netherlands, for example), the rate of breast cancer is high.

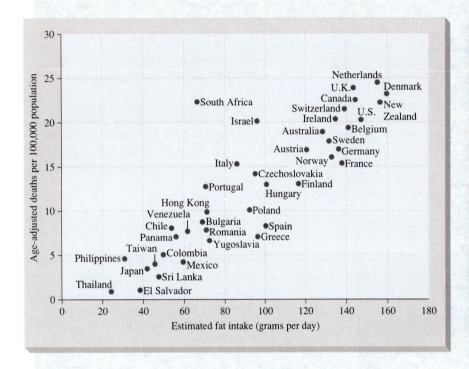

or not hardiness along with exercise and social support buffered stress and reduced illness in executives' lives (Kobasa, Maddi, Kahn, 1982). When all three factors were present in an executive's life, the level of illness dropped dramatically. This suggests the power of multiple buffers against stress, rather than a single buffer, in maintaining health.

Critical Thinking

A sense of commitment, control, and a perception of problems as challenges predicted resistance to illness in middle-aged men. Can you think of other factors that might prevent illness in middle age?

Stress, Diet, and Cancer

If we lead less-stressful lives and improve our diet, are we less likely to develop cancer? Findings that associate stress with cancer are controversial. In one investigation, the Minnesota Multiphasic Personal Inventory (MMPI) personality test was given to 2,018 middle-aged men in 1958 (Persky, Kepthorne-Rawson, & Shekelle, 1987). In the next 20 years, the middle-aged men who were the least depressed were less likely to die of cancer, a finding that was not due to their age, smoking, drinking, or other physical characteristics. And researchers have found that cancer patients who hold their negative emotions

inside and do not psychologically fight the disease have less-effective immune systems and less chance of survival (Jensen, 1987; Levy, 1985).

The relation of emotions to cancer should not be over-stated. There is no evidence that stress causes cancer (Levenson & Bemis, 1991). Rather, stress likely influences how rapidly the cancer spreads by weakening the body's immune system, rendering it less effective in its fight against malignant cells.

Not only is stress related to cancer (although it does not cause it), but so is diet. Researchers have found that mice fed on a high-fat diet are more likely to develop breast cancer than are mice fed on a low-fat diet, and a cross-national study involving women also found a strong positive correlation between fat consumption and death rates from breast cancer (Cohen, 1987) (see figure 16.1).

One of the most telling comparisons to link fat intake and cancer is between the United States and Japan. These countries have similar levels of industrialization and education, and both have high medical standards. Although the overall cancer rates of the two countries are similar, cancers of the breast, colon, and prostrate are common in the United States but rare in Japan. By contrast, cancer of the stomach is common in Japan but rare in the United States. Within two generations, Japanese immigrants to Hawaii and California have breast cancer rates that are significantly higher than those in Japan and that approach those of Americans. Many researchers believe that the high fat intake of Americans and the low fat intake of the Japanese are implicated in the countries' different cancer rates.

The general good health, low cancer rates, and longevity of Seventh Day Adventists, an evangelical Protestant sect, further support the link between cultural factors, especially diet, and cancer. Strict Seventh Day Adventists adhere to biblical precepts that determine diet and other life-style behaviors. Their well-balanced diet includes generous portions of unrefined foods, grains, vegetable protein, fruits, and vegetables. Smoking is prohibited. As a result, there is a very low incidence of lung cancer among Seventh Day Adventists. In addition, Seventh Day Adventists have fewer members with cancer of any type—including breast, pancreas, and colorectal cancer—than do other cultural groups in the United States.

As is the case with any cultural group, some Seventh Day Adventists adhere more strictly to the sect's life-style than do others. Religiously inactive Norwegian Seventh Day Adventists' risk of disease is similar to that of Norwegians who are not Seventh Day Adventists. Similarly, Seventh Day Adventists in the United States who only marginally adhere to the sect's guidelines for physical, mental, and spiritual health have an increased risk of disease (Phillips & others, 1980).

Sexuality

What kind of sexual changes take place during middle adulthood? What are the biological factors involved? What are our sexual attitudes and behavior like as we go through middle adulthood?

Biological Changes

Most of us know something about menopause. But is what we know accurate? Stop for a moment and think about your knowledge of menopause. What is menopause? When does it occur? Can it be treated? Most of us share some assumptions about menopause—we may think that it is a deficiency disease, that it involves numerous complaints, that women who are undergoing menopause deeply regret losing their reproductive capacity, their sexuality, and their femininity, and that they become deeply depressed. Are these assumptions accurate?

Menopause *is the time in middle age, usually in the late forties or early fifties, when a woman's menstrual periods and childbearing capability cease completely.* The average age at which women have their last period is 52. A small percentage of women—10 percent—undergo menopause before 40. There is a dramatic decline in the production of estrogen by the ovaries. Estrogen decline produces some uncomfortable symptoms in some menopausal women—"hot flashes," nausea, fatigue, and rapid heartbeat, for example. Some menopausal women report depression and irritability, but in some instances these feelings are related to other circumstances in the women's life, such as becoming divorced, losing a job, caring for a sick parent, and so on (Dickson, 1990; Strickland, 1987).

The comments of the following two women reveal the extensive variation menopause may bring. One woman commented, "I had hot flashes several times a week for almost 6 months. I didn't get as embarrassed as some of my friends who also had hot flashes, but I found the 'heat wave' sensation uncomfortable." Another woman commented, "I am constantly amazed and delighted to discover new things about my body, something menstruation did not allow me to do. I have new responses, desires, sensations, freed and apart from the distraction of menses [periods]."

Recent research investigations reveal that menopause does not produce psychological problems or physical problems for the majority of women. For example, in a large survey of more than 8,000 randomly selected women, the majority judged menopause to be a positive experience—feeling relief that they no longer had to worry about becoming pregnant or having periods—or a neutral experience—with no particular feelings at all about it (McKinlay & McKinlay, 1984). Only 3 percent said they regretted reaching menopause. Except for some temporary bothersome symptoms, such as hot flashes, sweating, and menstrual irregularity, most women simply said that menopause was not nearly the big deal that a lot of people make it out to be.

Why, then, do so many individuals have the idea that menopause is such a big deal? Why do we have so many erroneous assumptions—that menopausal women will lose their sexuality and femininity, that they will become deeply depressed, and that they will experience extensive physical pain? Much of the research on menopause is based on small, selective samples of women who go to physicians or therapists because they are having problems associated with menopause. These women are unrepresentative of the large population of women in the United States.

The problem of using a small, selective sample was recently reflected in popular author Gail Sheehy's (1991) book *The Silent Passage*. Sheehy writes about her own difficult experiences and reports the frustrations of a few women she chose to interview. Although Sheehy dramatically overstates the percentage of women who have serious problems with menopause, she does not overstate the stigma attached to menopause or the inadequate attention accorded it by the medical community (which is male-dominated).

For the minority of menopausal women whose experiences are physically painful and psychologically difficult, estrogen replacement therapy may be beneficial. The painful symptoms are usually related either to low estrogen levels or to hormonal imbalance. Estrogen replacement therapy has been successful in relieving low-estrogen menopausal symptoms like hot flashes and sweating. Medical experts increasingly recommend that, prior to menopause, women have their level of estrogen monitored. In this way, once menopause occurs and estrogen level declines, the physician knows how much estrogen to replace to maintain a woman's normal level.

While estrogen replacement therapy has a lot going for it, some worries about its use have surfaced. According to Veronica Ravnikar (1992), head of the menopause unit at Massachusetts General Hospital, the biggest worry about estrogen replacement is that it might increase the risk of breast cancer. The results of studies usually show no increased risk of breast cancer, but in a few investigations the risk of the disease has increased from 1 case per 1,000 women to 1.2 cases per 1,000 in women taking estrogen. One negative health consequence of estrogen replacement is undisputed: Given by itself, estrogen can increase the risk of cancer of the uterine lining. To combat this effect, most women also take a synthetic form of a second female hormone, progesterone. This second hormone, though, may lessen estrogen's protection against heart attacks, and in about 25 percent of women it causes PMS-like bloating and irritability.

Our portrayal of menopause has been much more positive than its usual portrayals in the past. While menopause overall is not the negative experience for most women it was once thought to be, the loss of fertility is an important marker for women—it means that they have to make final decisions about having children. Women in their thirties who have never had children sometimes speak about being "up against the biological clock" because they cannot postpone questions about having children much longer (Blechman & Brownell, 1987).

Do men go through anything like the menopause that women experience? That is, is there a male menopause? During middle adulthood, most men do not lose their capacity to father children, although there usually is a modest decline in their sexual potency at this time. Men do experience hormonal changes in their fifties and sixties, but nothing like the dramatic drop in estrogen that women experience. Testosterone production begins to decline about 1 percent a year during middle adulthood, and sperm count usually shows a slow decline, but men do not lose their fertility in middle age. What has been referred to as "male menopause," then, probably has less to do with hormonal change than with the psychological adjustment men must make when they are faced with declining physical energy and family and work pressures. Testosterone therapy has not been found to relieve such symptoms, suggesting that they are not induced by hormonal change.

Sexual Attitudes and Behavior

Although the ability of men and women to function sexually shows little biological decline in middle adulthood, sexual activity usually occurs on a less frequent basis than in early adulthood. Career interests, family matters, energy level, and routine may contribute to this decline. But a large percentage of individuals in middle adulthood continue to engage in sexual activity on a reasonably frequent basis. For example, in one national survey of 502 men and women between 46 and 71 years of age, approximately 68 percent of the 51- to 55-year-old respondents said that they had a moderate or strong interest in sex, and approximately 52 percent said that they had sexual intercourse once a week or more (Pfeiffer, Verwoerdt, & Davis, 1974).

Critical Thinking

What will sex probably be like in the next generation of middle-aged women and men?

In middle age, men's testosterone levels gradually drop, which can reduce their sexual drive. Their erections are less full and less frequent, and require more stimulation to achieve. Researchers once attributed these changes to psychological factors, but increasingly they find that as many as 75 percent of the erectile dysfunctions in middle age stem from physiological problems. According to sexuality expert Laurence Levine (1992), smoking, diabetes, hypertension, and elevated cholesterol levels are at fault in many erectile problems in middle-aged men.

At this point we have discussed a number of ideas about physical development in middle adulthood. A summary of these ideas is presented in concept table 16.1. Next we study the possibility of cognitive change in middle adulthood.

COGNITIVE DEVELOPMENT

We have seen that the decline in some physical characteristics during middle adulthood is not just imagined. Middle-aged adults may not see as well, run as fast, or be as healthy as in their twenties and thirties. But what about cognitive characteristics? In chapter 14, we saw that our cognitive abilities are very strong during early adulthood. Do they decline as we enter and move through middle adulthood?

The aspect of cognition that has been investigated more than any other in this regard is memory. Putting the pieces of this research together, we find that memory decline in middle adulthood is more likely to occur when long-term rather than short-term memory is involved (Craik, 1977). For example, a middle-aged man can remember a phone number he heard 20 seconds ago, but he probably won't remember it as efficiently the next day. Memory is also more likely to decline when organization and imagery are not used (Hultsch, 1971; Smith, 1977). By using memory strategies, such as organizing lists of phone numbers into different categories or imagining that the phone numbers represent different objects around the house, memory in middle adulthood can be improved. Memory also tends to decline when the information to be recalled is recently acquired information or when the information is not used often (Riege & Inman, 1981). For example, a middle-aged adult may easily remember chess moves, baseball rules, or television schedules if she has used this information extensively in the past. And finally, memory tends to decline if recall rather than recognition is required (Mandler, 1980). If the middle-aged man is shown a list of phone numbers and asked to select the numbers

CONCEPT TABLE 16.1

Physical Development in Middle Adulthood

Concept	Processes/Related Ideas	Characteristics/Description
Changing middle age	Its nature	The age boundaries of middle age are not set in stone. As more people live to an older age, what we think of as middle age seems to be occurring later. Middle age is full of twists and turns and changes. With this variation and change in mind, we will consider middle adulthood to be entered at some point between 35 and 45 and exited sometime in the sixties.
Physical changes	Their nature	A host of physical changes occur. At some point in the forties, decline in physical development usually indicates that middle adulthood has arrived. Seeing and hearing decline, and individuals actually become shorter.
	Health status	Health status becomes a major concern in middle adulthood. Some deterioration is to be expected. The main health nemeses of middle adulthood are cardiovascular disease, cancer, and weight. How individuals deal with physical decline varies greatly from one individual to the next.
Life-style, personality, and health	Cardiovascular disease and the Type A behavior pattern	The heart and coronary arteries become less efficient in middle age, and cardiovascular disease is the number one cause of death. Type A behavior pattern involves a cluster of characteristics—being excessively competitive, hard-driven, impatient, and hostile— thought to be related to heart disease. The Type A pattern is controversial, with some researchers arguing that only specific components of the cluster, such as hostility, are associated with heart disease.
	Type C behavior	This refers to the cancer-prone personality, which consists of being inhibited, uptight, lacking in expressiveness, and otherwise constrained. This type of individual is more likely to develop cancer than are more expressive people.
	Hardiness	Hardiness is a personality style characterized by a sense of commitment, control, and a perception of problems as challenges rather than threats. Hardiness is a buffer of stress and is related to reduced illness.
	Stress, diet, and cancer	The link between cancer and stress is controversial. Stress does not cause cancer, but some researchers believe stress is related to how rapidly cancer grows. A high-fat diet is associated with breast cancer.
	Toward healthier lives	Seven of the ten leading causes of death—heart disease, cancer, and stroke, for example—are associated with the absence of health behaviors. The next major improvement in general health may be behavioral, not medical. A number of health goals for the year 2000 have been proposed, and businesses are increasingly interested in improving their employees' health.
Sexuality	Biological changes	Menopause is a marker that signals the cessation of childbearing capability, arriving usually in the late forties and early fifties. The vast majority of women do not have substantial problems with menopause, although the public perception of menopause has often been negative. Estrogen replacement therapy is effective in reducing the physical pain of menopause. Men do not experience an inability to father children, although their testosterone level gradually drops off; clearly, a male menopause, like the dramatic decline in estrogen in women, does not occur.
	Sexual attitudes and behavior	Sexual behavior usually occurs on a less frequent basis in middle adulthood than in early adulthood. Nonetheless, a majority of middle-aged adults show a moderate or strong interest in sex.

LIFE-SPAN PRACTICAL KNOWLEDGE 16.4

Age Wave

(1990) by Ken Dychtwald. New York: Bantam.

This book describes adults between the ages of 35 and 55 as the "Age Wave"—the largest generation in American history. The author discusses new patterns of work and leisure that will expand this cohort's productive years, why national priorities must dramatically shift to take into account the aging of our society, and how to overcome the negative myths of aging and live a longer and healthier life. The aging of America is portrayed as full of challenge and hope.

---

he heard yesterday (recognition), this can be done more efficiently than recalling the numbers without the list. Memory in middle adulthood will also decline if health is poor and attitudes are negative (Poon, 1985; Salthouse, 1989). More about the nature of cognitive changes in adulthood appears in chapter 18, where we discuss general changes in intelligence, problem-solving skills, and further ideas about memory.

CAREERS, WORK, AND LEISURE

Are middle-aged workers as satisfied with their jobs as young adult workers? What is the career ladder in middle adulthood like? How extensive is mid-life career change? What are some different pathways for men and women in the workplace? What is leisure at mid-life like? These are among the most important questions to answer about careers, work, and leisure in middle adulthood—we consider each of them in turn.

> *One of the saddest things is that the only thing a man can do for eight hours a day, day after day, is work. You can't eat eight hours a day nor drink for eight hours a day nor make love for eight hours.*
>
> —William Faulkner, *Writers at Work,* 1958

Job Satisfaction

Work satisfaction increases steadily throughout the work life—from age 20 to at least age 60, for both college-educated and non-college-educated adults (Rhodes, 1983; Tamir, 1982). This same pattern has been found for both women and men. Satisfaction probably increases because as we get older we get paid more, we are in higher positions, and we have more job security. There is also a greater commitment to the job as we get older—we take our jobs more seriously, have lower rates of avoidable absenteeism, and are more involved with our work in middle adulthood than in early adulthood. Younger adults are still experimenting with their work, still searching for the right occupation, so they may be inclined to seek out what is wrong with their current job rather than focusing on what is right about it (Rhodes, 1983).

Critical Thinking

What might be the most important ingredients of job satisfaction in middle adulthood? That is, what is it about jobs in middle age that cause people to enjoy them?

Career Ladders

Many of us think of our adult work life as a series of discrete steps, much like the rungs on a ladder. In a factory, an individual might move from laborer, to foreman, to superintendent, to production manager, and so on up the ladder. In a business, an individual might move from salesperson, to sales manager, to regional sales manager, to national sales manager, to vice president of the company, and then even possibly to president of the company, for example. Not all occupations have such clearly defined steps, but most jobs involve a hierarchy in which low-level workers and high-level workers are clearly distinguished. How can an individual move up the career ladder?

Having a college education helps a great deal; a college degree is associated with earlier career advancement and greater career advancement (Bray & Howard, 1983; Golan, 1986). And individuals who are promoted early go further up the career ladder than those who are promoted late. Most career advancement occurs early in our adult lives. By the ages of 40 to 45, most of us have gone as far as we will up the career ladder. In one investigation of a large corporation, this occurred regardless of whether the positions were nonmanagement, lower management, or foreman (Rosenbaum, 1984).

Mid-Life Career Change

Only about 10 percent of Americans change jobs in mid-life; as we saw earlier, job satisfaction usually increases in mid-life. But for those 10 percent who do change jobs in mid-life, what are some of the psychological reasons behind this dramatic life change? Of course, some of these individuals get fired, but others may change course because of their own motivation. The mid-life career-change experience has been described as a turning point in adulthood by Daniel Levinson (1978). One aspect of the mid-life period involves adjusting idealistic hope to realistic possibilities in light of how much time is left in an

Reprinted with special permission of King Feature Syndicate.

occupation. Middle-aged adults may focus on how much time they have left before retirement and the speed with which they are reaching their occupational goals (Pines & Aronson, 1988). If individuals perceive that they are behind schedule, or if their goals are now perceived as unrealistic, reassessment and readjustment may take place. Levinson (1978) believes this may result in a sadness over unfulfilled dreams. He found that many middle-aged men feel constrained by their bosses, their wives, and their children. Such feelings, he says, may produce rebellion, which can assume several forms—extramarital affairs, divorce, alcoholism, suicide, or career change.

Work Pathways of Men and Women

Most men begin work in early adulthood and work more or less continuously until they retire, unless they return to school or become unemployed. Unstable patterns of work are much more common among low-income workers than among middle-income workers, although a continuous pattern of work is still the norm among low-income workers.

The most common path for the middle-class woman is to work for awhile after finishing high school or even college; to marry and have children; then, when the children are a little older, to go back to part-time work to supplement the husband's income. As the children begin to leave home, the woman goes back to school for some updating of earlier skills or for a retraining program so she can assume a full-time paid job in her forties and fifties, when she is relatively free of responsibilities.

For the professional or career women, the picture is somewhat different, since she has more invested in keeping up her professional skills. Four career patterns among professional women have been identified (Golan, 1986): (1) *regular,* the woman who pursued her professional training immediately after graduation, who began to work and continued to do so without interruption or with minimal interruption throughout the years; (2) *interrupted career,* the woman who began as in the regular pattern but interrupted her career for several years—usually for child rearing—and then went back to work full-time; (3) *second career,* the woman who started her professional training near or after the time the children left home or after a divorce; and (4) *modified second career,* the woman who started her professional training while the children were still at home but old

A number of career patterns may be followed by the professional or career woman during her adulthood years.

enough not to need full-time mothering, then started to work, possibly part-time, until the last child left home or became independent, at which time she shifted to a full-time career.

Why do women go back to work during middle adulthood? What stands out is that reasons are rarely as simple as earning money, although in those families where the husband has become ill or disabled, or for other reasons has not been able to keep up his breadwinner role, income is undoubtedly the main motive. Many middle-aged women enter the labor force when they are confronted with the need to support themselves and their family, but boredom, loneliness, and the desire for new interests are probably involved, too. Today's 50-year-old women are taking courses in computer programming, enrolling in schools of social work, and studying for a real estate salesperson's license in far greater numbers than their mothers or grandmothers did in similar circumstances. The trend toward dual career couples, so prevalent in their children's generation, is also now penetrating middle adulthood.

Sigmund Freud once commented that the two things adults need to do well to adapt to society's demands are to work and to love. To his list we add "to play." In our fast-paced society, it is all too easy to get caught up in the frenzied, hectic pace of our achievement-oriented work world and ignore leisure and play. Imagine your life as a middle-aged adult. What would be the ideal mix of work and leisure? What leisure activities do you want to enjoy as a middle-aged adult?

Researchers who study women at mid-life have found that employment plays an important role in many women's psychological well-being (Baruch & Barnett, 1987). In one investigation, higher earnings were related to life satisfaction, and being overworked was related to unhappiness, in middle-aged women (Crohan & others, 1989).

Leisure

As adults, not only must we learn how to work well, but we also need to learn how to relax and enjoy leisure. Henry Ford was known as a man who emphasized that our salvation rests in our work. Few people were aware of Ford's frequent trips to his mansion in Dearborn, Michigan, where he relaxed and participated extensively in leisure activities. Similarly, former president George Bush seems to have found a better balance between work and leisure than many of us. With the kind of work ethic on which our country is based, it is not surprising to find that many adults view leisure as boring and unnecessary. But even Aristotle recognized leisure's importance in life, stressing

that we should not only work well but use leisure well. He even described leisure as better because it was the end of work. How can we define leisure? **Leisure** *refers to the pleasant times after work when individuals are free to pursue activities and interests of their own choosing—hobbies, sports, or reading, for example.*

Ninety years ago, the average work week was 72 hours. Only in the last three to four decades has it averaged 40 hours. What do most of us do now that we have more free time than cohorts at the beginning of this century? One of the basic themes of research on leisure is the increasing reliance on television over other forms of mass media as a form of entertainment. Sports are also an integral part of the nation's leisure activities, either through direct participation or as a spectator. The diversity of sports allows many individuals to escape the rigors and pressures of everyday life, even if only for a few hours a week.

What is leisure in middle adulthood like? When Mark became 40 years old, he decided that he needed to develop some leisure activities and interests. He bought a personal computer and joined a computer club. Now Mark looks forward to coming

CONCEPT TABLE 16.2

Cognitive Development and Careers, Work, and Leisure

Concept	Processes/Related Ideas	Characteristics/Description
Cognitive development	Its nature	Some decline in memory occurs during middle adulthood, although strategies can be used to reduce the decline. Deficits are greater in long-term than in short-term memory. Processes such as organization and imagery can be used to reduce deficits in memory. Deficits are greater when the information is recently acquired or not used often, and when recall rather than recognition is assessed. Poor health and negative attitudes are related to memory decline.
Careers, work, and leisure	Job satisfaction	Work satisfaction increases steadily throughout life—from age 20 to at least age 60, for both college-educated and non-college-educated adults.
	Career ladders	Many of us think of our adult work life as a series of discrete steps, much like the rungs of a ladder. Having a college education helps us move up the ladder. Most career advancement occurs early in our adult lives, at least by 40 to 45, and individuals who are promoted early go farther.
	Mid-life career change	Only about 10 percent of Americans change jobs in mid-life, some because they are fired, others because of their own motivation. In mid-life, we often evaluate our possibilities in terms of how much time we have left in an occupation.
	Work pathways of men and women	A continuous pattern of work is more common among men than among women, although low-income men have more unstable work patterns than middle-income men. It is not unusual for women to go back to work for reasons other than money.
	Leisure	We not only need to learn to work well, but we also need to learn to enjoy leisure. Mid-life may be an especially important time for leisure because of the physical changes that occur and because of preparation for an active retirement.

home from work and "playing with his toy." At the age of 43, Barbara sent her last child off to college and told her husband that she was going to spend the next several years reading the many books she had bought but had never found time to read. Mark and Barbara chose different leisure activities, but their actions suggest that middle adulthood is a time when leisure activities assume added importance. For example, some developmentalists believe that middle adulthood is a time of questioning how time should be spent and of reassessing priorities (Gould, 1978).

Leisure may be an especially important aspect of middle adulthood because of the changes many individuals experience at this point in the adult life cycle. The changes include physical changes, relationship changes with spouse and children, and career changes. By middle adulthood, more money is available

to many individuals, and there may be more free time and paid vacations. These mid-life changes may produce expanded opportunities for leisure. For many individuals, middle adulthood is the first time in their lives when they have the opportunity to diversify their interests.

Adults at mid-life need to begin preparing both financially and psychologically for retirement. Constructive and fulfilling leisure activities in middle adulthood are an important part of this preparation. If an adult develops leisure activities that can be continued into retirement, the transition from work to retirement may be less stressful.

We have discussed a number of ideas about cognitive development and about careers, work, and leisure. A summary of these ideas is presented in concept table 16.2.

LIFE-SPAN HEALTH AND WELL-BEING

Toward Healthier Lives

We are becoming increasingly aware that our behavior determines whether we will develop a serious illness and when we will die (Minkler, 1989). Seven of the ten leading causes of death in the United States are associated with the *absence* of health behaviors. Diseases such as influenza, polio, and rubella no longer are major causes of death. More deaths now are caused by heart disease (36 percent of all deaths in 1986), cancer (22 percent), and stroke (17 percent).

As we have seen repeatedly in this chapter, personal habits and life-style play key roles in these diseases. These findings lead health psychologists, behavioral medicine specialists, and public health professionals to predict that the next major step in improving the general health of the American population will be primarily behavioral, not medical.

The federal government and the Society for Public Health Education have set health objectives for the year 2000 (Schwartz & Eriksen, 1989). Among them are these:

- The need to develop preventive services targeting diseases and problems such as cancer, heart disease, stroke, unintended pregnancy (especially among adolescents), and AIDS.
- The need for health promotion, including behavior modification and health education. Stronger programs are urged for dealing with smoking, alcohol and drug abuse, nutrition, physical fitness, and mental health.
- The need for cleaner air and water, and the need to improve workplace safety, including reducing exposure to toxic chemicals.
- Meeting the health needs of special populations, such as a better understanding of disease prevention in Black and Hispanic populations (Klonoff, 1991). Ethic minority groups suffer disproportionately from cancer, heart disease, diabetes, and other major diseases.

America's health costs have soared and are moving toward the $1 trillion mark annually. Health experts hope to make a dent in these costs by encouraging people to live healthier lives. Many corporations have begun to recognize that health promotion for their employees is cost-effective. Businesses are increasingly examining their employees' health behavior and the workplace environment as they recognize the role health plays in productive work. Smoke-free work environments, on-site exercise programs, bonuses to quit smoking and lose weight, and company-sponsored athletic events are increasingly found in American businesses. ∎

CONCLUSIONS

In middle age, more time stretches before us, and the young-old polarity greets us with a special force.

We began this chapter by considering the time perspectives of individuals from adolescence through late adulthood, then we explored how middle age is changing. Our coverage of physical development in middle age focused on physical changes, health status, life-style, personality and health, and sexuality. We then studied cognitive development in middle age, as well as careers, work, and leisure. At different points in the chapter you also read about health promotion in different ethnic groups, stress management, and moving toward healthier lives.

Don't forget that you can obtain an overall summary of the chapter by again reading the two concept tables on pages 475 and 479. In the next chapter, we examine some fascinating aspects of middle adulthood that involve socioemotional development.

KEY TERMS

middle adulthood   The developmental period that begins at approximately 35 to 45 years of age and extends into the sixties. (465)

Type A behavior pattern   This cluster of characteristics—being excessively competitive, hard-driven, impatient, and hostile—is thought to be related to the incidence of heart disease. (470)

Type C behavior   Individuals with this personality—inhibited, uptight, emotionally inexpressive, and otherwise constrained—are more likely to develop cancer than are more expressive people. (470)

hardiness   A personality style that is characterized by a sense of commitment rather than alienation, control rather than powerlessness, and a perception of problems as challenges rather than threats. (470)

menopause   A woman's menstrual periods and childbearing capability cease completely during menopause, which usually occurs in the late forties or early fifties. (473)

leisure   The pleasant times after work when individuals are free to pursue activities and interests of their own choosing. (478)

Rufino Tamayo, Man and
Woman, detail.

Socioemotional Development in Middle Adulthood

Perhaps middle-age is, or should be, a period of shedding shells; the shell of ambition, the shell of material accumulations and possessions, the shell of ego.

—Ann Morrow Lindbergh,
Gift from the Sea, 1955

The generations of living things pass in a short time,
and like runners hand on the torch of life.

—Lucretius, 1st Century B.C.

IMAGES OF LIFE-SPAN DEVELOPMENT

Middle-Age Variations

Forty-five-year-old Sarah feels tired, depressed, and angry. She became pregnant when she was 17 and married Ben. They stayed together for 3 years, and then he left her for another woman. Sarah went to work as a salesclerk to help make ends meet. She remarried 8 years later to Alan, who had two children of his own from a previous marriage. Sarah stopped working for several years, but then Alan started going out on her. She found out about it from a friend. Sarah stayed with Alan for another year, but finally he was gone so much that she could not take it anymore and she decided to divorce him. Sarah went back to work again as a salesclerk; she has been in the same position for 16 years now. During those 16 years, she has dated a number of men, but the relationships never seem to work out. Her son never finished high school and

has drug problems. Her father just died last year, and Sarah is trying to help her mother financially, although she can barely pay her own bills. Sarah looks in the mirror and does not like what she sees—she sees her past as a shambles, and the future does not look rosy, either.

Forty-five-year-old Wanda feels energetic, happy, and satisfied. She graduated from college and worked for 3 years as a high school math teacher. She married Andy, who had just finished law school. One year later, they had their first child, Josh. Wanda stayed home with Josh for 2 years, then returned to her job as a math teacher. Even during her pregnancy, Wanda stayed active and exercised regularly, playing tennis almost every day. After her pregnancy, she kept up her exercise habits. Wanda and Andy had another child, Wendy, and now as

they move into their middle-aged years, Josh and Wendy are both off to college, and Wanda and Andy are enjoying spending more time with each other. Last weekend they visited Josh at his college, and the weekend before they visited Wendy at her college. Wanda continued working as a high school math teacher until 6 years ago. She had developed considerable computer skills as part of her job and taken some computer courses at a nearby college, doubling up during the summer months. She resigned her math teaching job and took a job with a computer company, where she has already worked her way into management. Wanda looks in the mirror and likes what she sees—she sees her past as enjoyable, although not without hills and valleys, and she looks to the future with zest and enthusiasm.

PREVIEW

The life paths of Sarah and Wanda have been very different. They represent the individual variation, the divergence, of what middle age is like. For some, middle age is the worst period of life; for others, it is the best. In this chapter, we will explore some of the common themes of middle age—the nature of relationships, whether or not we are likely to experience a mid-life crisis, the personality characteristics that take on greater meaning in mid-life, and the degree to which we change or stay the same as we go through middle adulthood.

CLOSE RELATIONSHIPS

Attachment and love are important to our well-being throughout our lives. What are marital relationships like in middle adulthood? Do our friendships change? What is the nature of sibling relationships in middle adulthood? How do intergenerational relationships contribute to our development? These are among the important questions about relationships in middle adulthood that we address.

Love and Marriage at Mid-Life

Remember from chapter 15 that two major forms of love are romantic love and affectionate love. The fires of romantic love are strong in early adulthood. Affectionate or companionate love increases during middle adulthood. That is, physical attraction, romance, and passion are more important in new relationships, especially in early adulthood, whereas security, loyalty, and mutual emotional interest become more important as relationships mature, especially in middle adulthood. Some developmentalists believe mutuality plays a key role in the maturity of relationships, occurring when partners share knowledge with each other, assume responsibility for each other's satisfaction, and share private information that governs their relationship (Berscheid, 1985; Levinger, 1974). For example, as indicated in figure 17.1, we begin a relationship with someone at a zero point of contact and then gradually move from a surface relationship into more-intense, mutual interaction, sharing ourselves more and more with the other individual as the relationship deepens. At the final stage, a major intersection, we are probably experiencing affectionate or companionate love.

To explore the nature of age and sex differences in satisfying love relationships, in one investigation 102 happily married couples in early adulthood (average age 28), middle adulthood (average age 45), and late adulthood (average age 65) were interviewed (Reedy, Birren, & Schaie, 1981). Passion and sexual intimacy were more important in early adulthood, and tender feelings of affection and loyalty were more important in later-life love relationships. Young adult lovers also rated communication as more characteristic of their love than their older counterparts. Aside from the age differences, however, there were some striking similarities in the nature of satisfying love relationships. At all ages, emotional security was ranked as the most important factor in love, followed by respect, communication, help and play behaviors, sexual intimacy, and loyalty. Clearly, there is more to satisfying relationships than sex. The findings in this research also suggested that women believe emotional security is more important in love than men do.

Even some marriages that were difficult and rocky during early adulthood turn out to be better adjusted during middle adulthood (Rollins, 1989). Although the partners may have lived through a great deal of turmoil, they eventually discover a deep and solid foundation on which to anchor their relationship. In middle adulthood, the partners may have fewer financial worries, less housework and chores, and more time with each other. Partners who engage in mutual activities usually view their marriage as more positive at this time.

FIGURE 17.1

The development of relationships. *One view of how close relationships develop states that we begin a relationship with someone at a zero point of contact (top) and then gradually move from a surface relationship into more intense, mutual interaction, sharing ourselves more and more with the other person as the relationship develops. At the final stage, a major intersection, we are probably experiencing affectionate or companionate love (bottom).*

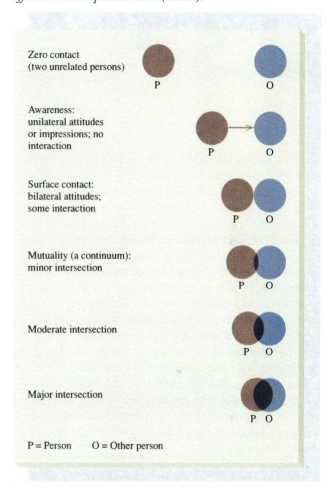

As marital partners grow older, many of their earlier incompatibilities brought about by differences in religion, ethnicity, social class, levels of education, family backgrounds, and personality patterns have either been worked out and adjusted to or have contributed to the breakup of the marriage (Golan, 1986). Divorce in middle adulthood may be more positive in some ways, more negative in others, than divorce in early adulthood. For mature individuals, the perils of divorce may be fewer and less intense than for younger individuals. They have more resources, and they can use this time as an opportunity to simplify their lives by disposing of possessions, such as a large home, which they no longer need. Their children are adults and may be able to cope with their parents' divorce more effectively. The partners may have attained a better understanding of themselves and may be searching for changes that could include the end to a poor marriage.

"Thus ends another evening of dancing on the edge of the volcano."
Drawing by Lorenz; © 1987 The New Yorker Magazine, Inc.

At some point in middle adulthood, couples who have survived intact have often accommodated to changing goals and interests (Birchler, 1992). One family researcher (Campbell, 1980) calls this stage in the family life cycle *stability*, another (Kovacs, 1988) refers to it as *working through*. Stability is accomplished when spouses have progressed through the romance and power-struggle stages to a point of finally accepting the relationship with all of its pluses and minuses. Conflict patterns become more familiar, more predictable, more comfortable, less threatening, and less catastrophic. The mid-life couple's expectations are also more realistic than earlier in their marriage.

In contrast, the emotional and time commitment to marriage that has existed for so many years may not be lightly given up. Many mid-life individuals perceive this as failing in the best years of their lives. The divorcer may see the situation as an escape from an untenable relationship; the divorced partner, however, usually sees it as betrayal, the ending of a relationship that had been built up over many years and that involved a great deal of commitment and trust.

The Empty Nest and Its Refilling

An important event in a family is the launching of a child into adult life, to a career or family independent of the family of origin. Parents face new adjustments as disequilibrium is created by a child's absence (Bassoff, 1988). The **empty nest syndrome** *states that marital satisfaction will decrease because parents derive considerable satisfaction from their children, and therefore, the children's departure will leave parents with empty feelings. While the empty nest syndrome may hold true for some parents who live vicariously through their children, the empty nest usually does not lower marital satisfaction. Rather, just the opposite happens; marital satisfaction increases in the post-childrearing years.* Now with children gone, marital partners have more time to pursue career interests and more time for each other.

In today's uncertain economic climate, the refilling of the empty nest is becoming a common occurrence as adult children return to live at home after an unsuccessful career or a divorce. And some individuals don't leave home at all until their middle to late twenties, because they cannot financially support themselves. The middle generation has always provided support for the younger generation, even after the nest is bare. Through loans and monetary gifts for education, and through emotional support, the middle generation has helped the younger generation. Adult children appreciate the financial and emotional support their parents provide them at a time when they often feel considerable stress about their career, work, and life-style. And parents feel good that they can provide this support.

However, as with most family living arrangements, there are both pluses and minuses when adult children return to live at home. Many parents have developed expectations that their adult children would be capable of supporting themselves. And adult children had expectations that they would be on their own as young adults. In one investigation, 42 percent of middle-aged parents said they had serious conflicts with their resident adult children (Clemens & Axelson, 1985). One of the most common complaints voiced by both adult children and their parents is a loss of privacy. The adult children complain that their parents restrict their independence, cramp their sex lives, reduce their rock music listening, and treat them as children rather than adults. Parents often complain that their quiet home has become noisy, that they stay up late worrying when their adult children will come home, that meals are difficult to plan because of conflicting schedules, that their relationship as a married couple has been invaded, and that they have to shoulder too much responsibility for their adult children. In sum, when adult children return home to live, a disequilibrium in family life is created, which requires considerable adaptation on the part of parents and their adult children. This living arrangement usually works best when there is adequate space, when parents treat their adult children more like adults than children, and when there is an atmosphere of trust and communication. To read further about adult children moving back home, turn to Perspectives on Parenting and Education 17.1.

Sibling Relationships and Friendships

Sibling relationships also persist over the entire life cycle for most adults. Eighty-five percent of today's adults have at least one living sibling. Sibling relationships in adulthood may be extremely close, apathetic, or highly rivalrous. The majority of sibling relationships in adulthood have been found to be close in several investigations (Cicirelli, 1982, 1991; Scott, 1983). Those siblings who are psychologically close to each other in adulthood tended to be that way in childhood; it is rare for sibling closeness to develop for the first time in adulthood (Dunn, 1984).

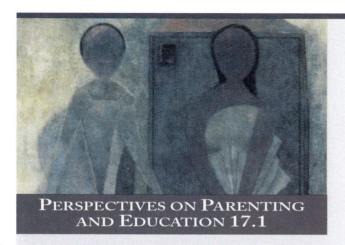

PERSPECTIVES ON PARENTING AND EDUCATION 17.1

When Adult Children Move Back In

More than half of all 20- to 24-year-olds either are living with their parents or are being supported by them (this is an increase from 40 percent in 1960). Eleven percent of all 25- to 34-year-olds either have never left home or have returned home (this is an increase from 9 percent in 1960). When adult children return home, they are no longer teenagers but rather young adults who are accustomed to a great deal of independence and not having to answer to anyone. During the time their adult children have been away from home, parents have gotten used to living on their own and not sharing their home, food, car, and other resources with anyone. The following four recommendations were developed by Laurence Steinberg and Ann Levine (1990) for parents whose adult children move back:

1. *Define your relationship.* A decision needs to be made about whether the family will function as a group or the young adult will come and go like a tenant. Parents and their young adult child who returns home often entertain very different ideas about what coming back home to live means. Such issues as whether adult children will eat with the family or prepare their own meals, do their own laundry, and have access to the family car, need to be explored.

2. *Young adult children need to be allowed to have an independent personal life.* When children are adolescents, parents still have the final say on such issues as curfew and drinking. Boyfriends or girlfriends certainly weren't allowed to spend the night. However, Steinberg and Levine believe it is not appropriate for parents to intervene in their young adult children's personal lives. When they come home, whether they drink, who their friends are, and whom they sleep with should be young adult children's decisions. What parents of young adult children do have the right to expect is common courtesy. If young adult children have an idea that they will not be home until 2 or 3 A.M., they should let their parents know. If they plan to have an overnight guest, they should let their parents know in advance. If parents do not approve of premarital sex, they have the right to ask their adult child not to sleep with a lover in their house. But Steinberg and Levine believe that parents should not forbid their adult children to spend the night at their boyfriend's or girlfriend's apartment, even if they think he or she is not the right person for them.

3. *Discuss how finances will be handled.* If young adult children are working, they should be expected to pay for their own clothes, car expenses, recreation, and such. Steinberg and Levine say that it is also reasonable for young adult children to make a contribution toward household expenses such as food, gas, electricity, and phone bills. If young adult children are saving money to go back to school or to move into an apartment, or if they are working only part-time while going to college or involved in some other educational undertaking, parents may want to cover their adult children's living expenses. If adult children are neither working nor studying and have no immediate plans to do either, parents may decide to offer them an allowance for a limited period of time, clearly specifying when the allowance will end and expecting adult children to do extra work around the house that would normally require outside help to do, such as housecleaning, yard work, and the like. When young adult children are in drifting, temporary life-style circumstances, it is important for parents to provide emotional support for them but also make real-world demands on them. As Steinberg and Levine comment, the real world does demand that adults earn their keep.

4. *A time limit on living at home needs to be established.* Young adult children who are 20 years old or older should not live with their parents indefinitely. Some of young adults' most important life tasks—such as solidifying their identity, becoming independent, and developing mature, intimate relationships—are made more difficult when they live at home for an extended period of time. Unless there are no extenuating circumstances, such as an illness, parents and their adult children should set a time limit for tapering off financial support and specify a deadline for moving out. Steinberg and Levine believe that parents should be prepared to provide their young adult children with one final boost for successfully "launching" them, such as the deposit for an apartment or downpayment on a car, if they can afford such items.

In the investigation by Alice Rossi (1989), mothers and their daughters had much closer relationships during their adult years than mothers and sons, fathers and daughters, and fathers and sons. Married men were more involved with their wives' kin than their own. And maternal grandmothers and maternal aunts were cited twice as often as their counterparts on the paternal side of the family as the most important or loved relative.

Friendships continue to be important in middle adulthood just as they were in early adulthood (Antonucci, 1989; Rook, 1987). It takes time to develop intimate friendships, so friendships that have endured over the adult years are often deeper than those that have just been formed in middle adulthood.

Intergenerational Relationships

In Samuel Butler's novel, *The Way of All Flesh* (1902), Theobold Pontifex had been raised by a harsh father but believed that he would be more lenient toward his own son than his father had been toward him. But he also believed, as had his father, that he must be on guard against being too indulgent. Theobold thrashed his son, Ernest, for mispronouncing a word. With each new generation, personality characteristics, attitudes, and values are replicated or changed. As older family members die, their emotional, intellectual, personal, and genetic legacies are carried on in the next generation. Their children become the oldest generation and their grandchildren the second generation (Datan, Greene, & Reese, 1986).

For the most part, family members maintain considerable contact across generations. As we continue to maintain contact with our parents and our children as we age, both similarity and dissimilarity across generations are found. For example, parent-child similarity is most noticeable in religious and political areas,

least in gender roles, life-style, and work orientation. An example of how relationships are transmitted across generations appeared in the California Longitudinal Study (Elder, Caspi, & Downey, 1986). Children whose parents had a high degree of marital conflict and who were unaffectionate subsequently had tension in their own marriages and were ineffective in disciplining their own children (now the third generation).

Critical Thinking

Are we likely to see more or less contact across generations in future decades? Explain your answer.

Gender differences also characterize intergenerational relationships (Nydegger & Mitteness, 1991; Troll, 1989; Troll & Bengston, 1982). In one investigation, mothers and their daughters had much closer relationships during their adult years than mothers and sons, fathers and daughters, and fathers and sons (Rossi, 1989). Also, in this same investigation, married men were more involved with their wives' kin than their own. And maternal grandmothers and maternal aunts were cited twice as often as their counterparts on the paternal side of the family as the most important or loved relative. These findings underscore the significance of a woman's role as mother in monitoring access to and feelings toward kin (Barnett & others, 1991; Fischer, 1991).

> *In case you're worried about what's going to become of the younger generation, it's going to grow up and start worrying about the younger generation.*
>
> —Roger Allen

Middle-aged adults play an important role in intergenerational relationships (Brody, 1990; Crosby & Ayers, 1991; Richards, Bengston, & Miller, 1989). They have been described as the "sandwich" generation. Their situation has been labeled the "generation squeeze" or "generational overload." The demands they face, as both children of elderly parents and parents of adolescents or young adults, have implications for individual life-course development and for the family systems to which they belong. While middle-aged adults are guiding and financially supporting their adolescents, they may have to support elderly parents who no longer have a secure base in times of emotional difficulties or financial problems. Instead, the older parents may need affection and financial support from their middle-aged children. These simultaneous pressures from adolescents or young adult children and aging parents may contribute to stress in middle adulthood. When adults immigrate to another country, intergenerational stress

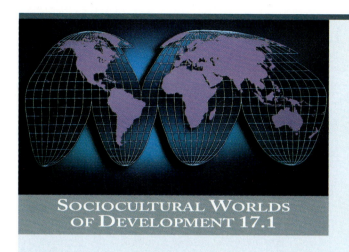

Intergenerational Relationships in Mexican American Families— The Effects of Immigration and Acculturation

In the last several decades, increasing numbers of Mexicans have immigrated to the United States, and their numbers are expected to increase. The pattern of immigration usually involves separation from the extended family. It may also involve separation of immediate family members, with the husband coming first and then later bringing his wife and children. Initially isolated, especially the wife, they experience considerable stress due to relocation and the absence of family and friends. Within several years, a social network is usually established in the ethnic neighborhood.

As soon as some stability in their lives is achieved, Mexican families may sponsor the immigration of extended family members, such as a maternal or paternal sister or mother who provides child care and enables the mother to go to work. In some

cases the older generation remains behind and joins their grown children in old age. The accessibility of Mexico facilitates visits to and from the native village for vacations or at a time of crisis, such as when an adolescent runs away from home.

Three levels of acculturation often exist within a Mexican American family (Falicov & Karrer, 1980). The mother and the grandparents may be at the beginning level, the father at an intermediate level, and the children at an advanced level. The discrepancies between acculturation levels can give rise to conflicting expectations within the family. The immigrant parents' model of child rearing may be out of phase with the dominant culture's model, which may cause reverberations through the family's generations. For example, the mother and grandparents may be especially resistant to the demands for autonomy and dating made by adolescent daughters, and so may the father. And in recent years an increasing number of female youth are leaving their Mexican American homes to further their education, an event that is often stressful for families with strong ties to Mexican values.

As children leave home, parents begin to face their future as a middle-aged couple. This may be difficult for many Mexican American middle-aged couples because their value orientations have prepared them better for parenting than for relating as a married couple. Family therapists who work with Mexican Americans frequently report that a common pattern is psychological distance between the spouses and a type of emotional separation in mid-life, with the marital partners continuing to live together and carrying on their family duties but relating to each other only at a surface level. The younger generation of Mexican Americans may find it difficult to accept their parents' life-style, may question their marital arrangement, and may rebel against their value orientations. Despite the intergenerational stress that may be brought about by immigration and acculturation, the majority of Mexican American families maintain considerable contact across generations and continue to have a strong family orientation.

may also be increased. To read about the role of immigration and acculturation in intergenerational relationships among Mexican Americans, see Sociocultural Worlds of Development 17.1.

At this point we have discussed a number of ideas about close relationships in middle adulthood. A summary of these ideas is presented in concept table 17.1. Now we turn our attention to theories of adult personality development, especially the way they conceptualize the middle adulthood years.

PERSONALITY THEORIES AND DEVELOPMENT IN MIDDLE AGE

How should we conceptualize personality in middle age? Is mid-life a stage that is beset with crisis? How important are life events, like divorce and death, in understanding personality at mid-life? To what extent do social and historical circumstances modify how personality develops in middle adulthood? How much individual variation characterizes middle adulthood?

CONCEPT TABLE 17.1

Close Relationships in Middle Adulthood

Concept	Processes/Related Ideas	Characteristics/Description
Love and marriage at mid-life	Their nature	Affectionate or companionate love increases in middle adulthood, especially in marriages that have endured many years. Divorce in middle adulthood may be more positive or more negative than divorce in early adulthood.
The empty nest and its refilling	The empty nest syndrome	This states that marital satisfaction will decrease when children leave home after adolescence because parents derive considerable pleasure from their children. However, rather than decreasing marital satisfaction, the empty nest usually increases it.
	When adult children return home to live	Increasing numbers of young adult children continue to live with their parents or refill the empty nest by returning home after a failed marriage, economic difficulties, college, or loss of a job. The refilling of the empty nest requires considerable adaptation on the part of parents and their adult children.
Sibling relationships and friendships	Sibling relationships	These continue throughout life. Many sibling relationships in adulthood are close, especially if they were close in childhood, although some are apathetic or highly conflicted.
	Friendships	Friendships continue to be important in middle adulthood. Long-standing friendships are often deeper and more intimate.
Intergenerational relationships	Contact	There is generally continuing contact across generations in families. Greater continuity occurs in political and religious attitudes, lesser continuity occurs in gender roles, life-styles, and work orientation.
	Gender	Mothers and daughters have the closest relationship in adulthood. Women play an important role in the monitoring of access to and feelings toward kin.
	Middle age	The middle-aged generation has been called the "sandwich" generation because financial and caregiving obligations to youth and to aging parents may create stress for middle-aged adults. The middle-aged generation plays an important role in linking generations.

The Adult Stage Theories

Adult stage theories have been plentiful, and they have contributed to the view that mid-life is a crisis in development. Three prominent adult stage theories are Erik Erikson's life-cycle view, Roger Gould's transformations, and Daniel Levinson's seasons of a man's life. George Vaillant's view represents an important expansion of Erikson's theory. We consider each of these perspectives in turn.

Erikson's Stage of Generativity Versus Stagnation

Erikson (1968) believes that middle-aged adults face a significant issue in life—generativity versus stagnation, which is the name Erikson gave to the seventh stage in his life-span theory. Generativity encompasses adults' plans for what they hope to do to leave a legacy of themselves to the next generation. Through generativity, the adult achieves a kind of immortality

FIGURE 17.2

Four paths to developing generativity.

Biological generativity

Adults conceive and give birth to infants

Parental generativity

Adults provide nurturance and guidance to children

Work generativity

Adults develop skills that are passed down to others

Cultural generativity

Adults create, renovate, or conserve some aspect of the culture that survives

by leaving one's legacy to the next generation (McAdams, 1990). By contrast, stagnation (sometimes called "self-absorption") develops when individuals sense that they have done nothing for the next generation.

Middle-aged adults can develop generativity in a number of different ways (Kotre, 1984). Through biological generativity, adults conceive and give birth to an infant. Through parental generativity, adults provide nurturance and guidance to children. Through work generativity, adults develop skills that are passed down to others. The generative individual in this instance is the apprentice who learns the skill. And through cultural generativity, adults create, renovate, or conserve some aspect of culture that ultimately survives. In this instance, the generative object is the culture itself. (Figure 17.2 shows these four different ways middle-aged adults can develop generativity.)

Through generativity, adults promote and guide the next generation through such important aspects of life as parenting,

LIFE-SPAN PRACTICAL KNOWLEDGE 17.1

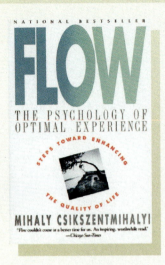

Flow
(1990) by Mihaly Csikszentmihalyi. New York: Harper & Row.

Flow is about the optimal experiencing of life. Author Mihaly Csikszentmihalyi is a professor of psychology at the University of Chicago who for more than two decades has been investigating the concept he calls "flow." Flow is the state of deep enjoyment that people feel when they have mastered something. Flow is a state of concentration in which a person becomes completely absorbed while engaging in an activity. We can develop flow by setting

challenges for ourselves, by stretching ourselves to the limits to achieve something worthwhile, by developing competent coping skills, and by combining life's experiences into a meaningful pattern. Flow is the antidote to the twin evils of boredom and anxiety, says Csikszentmihalyi.

Well-known author and psychologist Carol Tavris (1990) concluded that *Flow* is an important book because it documents that the path to happiness lies not in mindless hedonism but rather in mindful challenge, is found not in having unlimited opportunities but in focused possibilities, and is experienced not in having it done for you, but in doing it yourself.

T ABLE 17.1

Gould's Transformations in Adult Development

Stage	Approximate Age	Development(s)
1	16 to 18	Desire to escape parental control.
2	18 to 22	Leaving the family; peer group orientation.
3	22 to 28	Developing independence; commitment to a career and to children.
4	29 to 34	Questioning self; role confusion; marriage and career vulnerable to dissatisfaction.
5	35 to 43	Period of urgency to attain life's goals; awareness of time limitation; realignment of life's goals.
6	43 to 53	Settling down; acceptance of one's life.
7	53 to 60	More tolerance; acceptance of past; less negativism; general mellowing.

teaching, leading, and doing things that benefit the community (McAdams, 1990). Generative adults commit themselves to the continuation and improvement of society as a whole through their connection to the next generation. Generative adults develop a positive legacy of the self and then offer it as a gift to the next generation.

In one research investigation, Carol Ryff (1984) compared the views of women and men from different age groups. She found that generativity was a major concern of the middle-aged adults in her study. They saw themselves as leaders and decision makers who were interested in helping and guiding younger people.

Gould's Transformations

Psychiatrist Roger Gould (1975, 1978, 1980, 1994) links stage and crisis in his view of developmental transformations. He emphasizes that mid-life is every bit as turbulent as adolescence, with the exception that during middle adulthood striving to handle crisis will probably produce a happier, healthier life. Gould studied 524 men and women, whom he described as going through seven stages of adult life (see table 17.1). He believes that in our twenties we assume new roles; in our thirties we begin to feel stuck with our responsibilities; and in our forties we begin to feel a sense of urgency that our lives are speeding by. Handling the mid-life crisis and realizing that a sense

FIGURE 17.3

Levinson's periods of adult development.

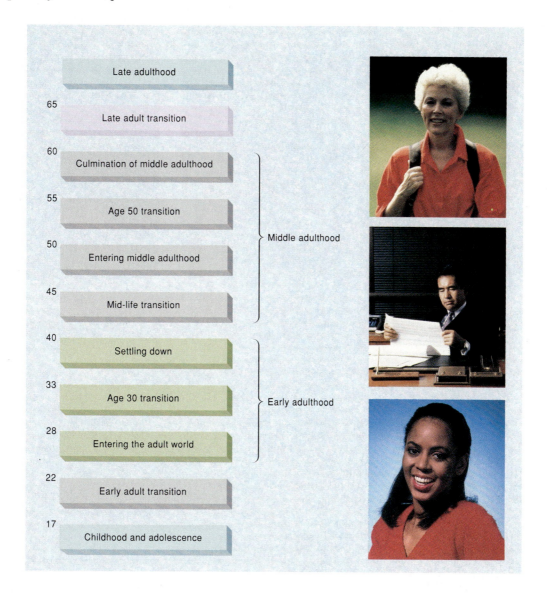

of urgency is a natural reaction to this stage helps to keep us on the path of adult maturity, Gould says. His study has been criticized—it contains middle-class bias, no test of the reliability of clinical judgments was conducted, and no statistical analysis was performed.

> *Whoever, in middle age, attempts to realize the wishes and hopes of his early youth, invariably deceives himself.*
> —Goethe, *Elective Affinities*, 1809

Levinson's Seasons of a Man's Life

In *The Seasons of a Man's Life*, clinical psychologist Daniel Levinson (1978, 1980) and his colleagues at Yale University reported the results of their extensive interviews with 40

middle-aged men. His interviews were conducted with hourly workers, business executives, academic biologists, and novelists. He bolstered his conclusions with information from the biographies of famous men and the development of memorable characters in literature. Although Levinson's major interest focused on mid-life change, he described a number of stages and transitions in the life cycle, ranging from 17 to 65 years of age, which are shown in figure 17.3.

Like Robert Havighurst (1972), Levinson emphasizes that developmental tasks must be mastered at each of these stages. In early adulthood, the two major tasks to be mastered are exploring the possibilities for adult living and developing a stable life structure. Levinson sees the twenties as a *novice phase* of adult development. At the end of one's teens, a transition from dependence to independence should occur. This transition is marked by the formation of a dream—an image of the kind of life the youth wants to have, especially in terms of a career and

Michaelangelo (1475–1574), the great Renaissance sculptor, painter, architect, and poet, hit a terrifying lull at age 40 after a brilliant earlier career. Free of unworthy patrons, he revived his career with his work on the Medici Chapel.

Julia Child, America's master chef, ate her first bite of French food at 37. It was not until her 50s that her books and TV show gained her fame and fortune.

Paul Gauguin (1848–1903), the famous French artist, was a Parisian stockbroker early in his adult years. At age 35, Gauguin left his wife and five children and absorbed himself in the life of an artist; at 43, he left France to live in Tahiti.

marriage. The novice phase is a time of reasonably free experimentation and of testing the dream in the real world.

From about the ages of 28 to 33, the individual goes through a transition period in which he must face the more serious question of determining his goals. During the thirties, the individual usually focuses on family and career development. In the later years of this period, the individual enters a phase of Becoming One's Own Man (or BOOM, as Levinson calls it). By age 40, the individual has reached a stable location in his career, has outgrown his earlier, more tenuous attempts at learning to become an adult, and now must look forward to the kind of life he will lead as a middle-aged adult.

> *Middle age is such a foggy place.*
> —Roger Rosenblatt, 1987

According to Levinson, the change to middle adulthood lasts about 5 years and requires the adult to come to grips with four major conflicts that have existed in his life since adolescence: (1) being young versus being old, (2) being destructive versus being constructive, (3) being masculine versus being feminine, and (4) being attached to others versus being separated from them. Seventy to 80 percent of the men Levinson interviewed found the mid-life transition (ages 40 to 45) tumultuous and psychologically painful, as many aspects of their lives came into

question. According to Levinson, the success of the mid-life transition rests on how effectively the individual reduces the polarities and accepts each of them as an integral part of his being.

> *Midway in life's journey I was made aware*
> *That I had strayed into a dark forest,*
> *And the right path appeared not anywhere.*
> —Dante, *The Inferno*

Because Levinson interviewed middle-aged males, we can consider the data about middle adulthood more valid than the data about early adulthood. When individuals are asked to remember information about earlier parts of their lives, they may distort and forget things. The original Levinson data included no females, although Levinson (1987) reported that his stages, transitions, and the crisis of middle age hold for females as well as males. Like Gould's report, Levinson's work included no statistical analysis. However, the quality and quantity of the Levinson biographies are outstanding in the clinical tradition.

Critical Thinking

Levinson argues that his adult stages are basically the same for women as for men. Can you think of some types of women for whom the stages might not be as accurate?

LIFE-SPAN PRACTICAL KNOWLEDGE 17.2

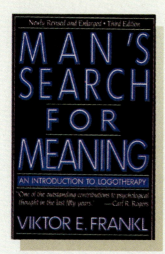

Man's Search for Meaning
(1984) by Victor Frankl. New York: Basic Books.

Man's Search for Meaning is an existentialist approach to the pursuit of self-fulfillment and life's meaning. Author Victor Frankl, M.D., has been a professor of neurology and psychiatry at the University of Vienna Medical School in Austria. After Frankl survived the German concentration camp at Auschwitz, he founded a school of psychotherapy he called "logotherapy," which is based on the view that the desire to find meaning in life is the primary motive in human beings. Frankl stresses each person's uniqueness and the finiteness of life. He thinks that exploring the finiteness of your existence and the certainty of your death adds meaning to the remaining days of your life. If life were not finite, says Frankl, you could spend your time doing just about whatever you pleased, because time would continue forever for you.

Frankl believes that the three most distinct human qualities are spirituality, freedom, and responsibility. In Frankl's system, spirituality does not have a religious underpinning. Rather, it refers to a human being's uniqueness—to spirit, philosophy, and mind. Freedom mainly means having the autonomy to make decisions. And with autonomy to make decisions comes the responsibility for those decisions. Among the questions Frankl thinks you should probe are these: Why do you exist? What do you want from life? What is the meaning of your life? Published originally in 1946, *Man's Search for Meaning* still commands a great deal of respect among many psychologists. The reading is rough going at times, but if you persist and probe Frankl's penetrating analysis, the rewards are well worth the effort.

Vaillant's Expansion of Erikson's Stages

Adult developmentalist George Vaillant (1977; Vaillant & Koury, 1994) believes two additional stages should be added to Erikson's adult stages. **Career consolidation** *is Vaillant's stage that occurs from approximately 23 to 35 years of age. Career consolidation is a period in which an individual's career becomes more stable and coherent.* **Keeping the meaning versus rigidity** *is Vaillant's stage that occurs from approximately 45 to 55 years of age. At this time a more relaxed feeling characterizes adults if they have met their goals, or if they have not, accept the fact. At this time adults become concerned about extracting some meaning from their lives and fight against falling into a rigid orientation.*

> *You come to a place in your life when what you've been is going to form what you will be. If you've wasted what you have in you, it's too late to do much about it. If you've invested yourself in life, you're pretty certain to get a return. If you are inwardly a serious person, in the middle years it will pay off.*
>
> —Lillian Hellman

Conclusions About the Adult Stage Theories

When Vaillant's stages are added to Erikson's stages, there is at least reasonable agreement among Gould, Levinson, and Vaillant about adult stages. All would concur with a general outline of adult development that begins with the change from identity to intimacy, then from career consolidation to generativity, and finally from searching for meaning to some final integration. Thus, although the labels are different, the underlying themes of these adult developmental stage theories are remarkably similar (see figure 17.4).

The adult developmental perspectives of Erikson, Gould, Levinson, and Vaillant emphasize the importance of developmental stages in the life cycle. Though information about stages can be helpful in pinpointing dominant themes that characterize many individuals at particular points in development, there are several important ideas to keep in mind when considering these perspectives as viable models of adult development. First, the research on which they are based has not been very scientific. Second, there has been a tendency to focus on the stages as crises in development, especially the mid-life crisis. Third, there is an alternative perspective that emphasizes the importance of life

FIGURE 17.4

Comparison of the adult developmental stages proposed by Levinson, Gould, and Vaillant.
When Vaillant's stages are added to Erikson's stages, some agreement between the adult stage theories of Levinson, Gould, and Vaillant is apparent. All would concur with a general outline of adult development that begins with a change from identity to intimacy, then from career consolidation to generativity, and finally from searching for meaning to some final integration.

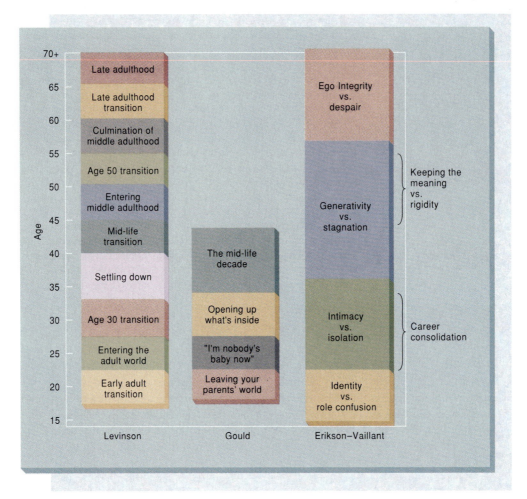

events rather than stages in development. Fourth, there often is considerable individual variation in the way people experience the stages.

Crisis and Cohort

Daniel Levinson (1978, 1987) views mid-life as a crisis, believing that the middle-aged adult is suspended between the past and the future, trying to cope with this gap that threatens life's continuity. George Vaillant (1977) concludes that just as adolescence is a time for detecting parental flaws and discovering the truth about childhood, the forties are a decade of reassessing and recording the truth about the adolescent and adulthood years. However, while Levinson sees mid-life as a crisis, Vaillant believes that only a minority of adults experience a mid-life crisis:

> Just as pop psychologists have reveled in the not-so-common high drama of adolescent turmoil, just so the popular press, sensing good copy, had made all too much of the mid-life crisis. The term mid-life crisis brings to mind some variation of the renegade minister who leaves behind four children and the congregation that loved him in order to drive off in a magenta Porsche with a 25-year-old striptease artiste. . . . As with adolescent turmoil, mid-life crises are much rarer in community samples (pp. 222–223).

"Goodbye, Alice. I've got to get this California thing out of my system."
Drawing by Leo Cullum; © 1984 The New Yorker Magazine, Inc.

Critics say the stage theories of adult development have a male bias by emphasizing career choice and achievement. The stage theories do not adequately address women's concerns about relationships, interdependence, and caring. The stage theories assume a normative sequence of development, but as women's roles have become more varied and complex, determining what is normative is difficult.

Vaillant's study—called the "Grant Study"—involved a follow-up of Harvard University men in their early thirties and in their late forties who initially had been interviewed as undergraduates. In Vaillant's words, "The high drama in Gail Sheehy's best-selling *Passages* was rarely observed in the lives of the Grant Study men" (p. 223).

Some developmentalists believe that changing times and different social expectations influence how different cohorts—remember that these are groups of individuals born in the same year or time period—move through the life cycle. Bernice Neugarten (1964) has been emphasizing the power of age-group or cohort since the 1960s. Our values, attitudes, expectations, and behaviors are influenced by the period in which we live. For example, individuals born during the difficult times of the Great Depression may have a different outlook on life than those born during the optimistic 1950s, says Neugarten.

Neugarten (1986) believes that the social environment of a particular age group can alter its **social clock**—*the timetable according to which individuals are expected to accomplish life's tasks, such as getting married, having children, or establishing themselves in a career.* Social clocks provide guides for our lives; individuals whose lives are not synchronized with these social clocks find life to be more stressful than those who are on schedule, says Neugarten. She argues that today there is much less agreement than in the past on the right age or sequence for the occurrence of major life events. For example, the age at which people get married, have children, become parents, go to school, and retire varies more than in previous decades.

Trying to tease out universal truths and patterns about adult development from one birth cohort is complicated because the findings may not apply to another birth cohort. Most of the individuals studied by Levinson, Gould, and Vaillant, for example, were born before and during the Depression. What was true for these individuals may not be true for today's 40-year-olds, born in the optimistic aftermath of World War II, or the post-

baby-boom generation as they approach the mid-life transition. The mid-life men in Levinson's, Gould's, and Vaillant's studies may have been burned out at a premature age rather than reflect a normal developmental pattern of less stress (Rossi, 1988).

Gender, Culture, and Middle Age

Do women experience middle age differently than men do? How do women in other cultures, especially nonindustrialized cultures, experience middle age? Do most cultures around the world show as much interest in mid-life crises as North Americans do?

Gender

Critics say that the stage theories of adult development have a male bias (Deutsch, 1991; Grambs, 1989; Mercer, Nichols, & Doyle, 1989). For example, the central focus of stage theories is on career choice and work achievement, which historically have dominated men's life choices and life chances more than women's. The stage theories do not adequately address women's concerns about relationships, interdependence, and caring (Gilligan, 1982). The adult stage theories have also placed little importance on childbearing and child rearing. Women's family roles are complex and often have a higher salience in their lives than in men's lives. The role demands that women experience in balancing career and family are usually not experienced as intensely by men.

One of the problems in making stage theory comparisons of males and females is the assumption of a normative sequence of development by the stage theories. That is, the stage theories assume that most people will encounter a given developmental stage at more or less the same time: graduation from high school and college, getting married, starting a family, becoming grandparents, and retiring, for example. However, our contemporary life challenges many of these "normative" experiences. Many women are returning to college to obtain an education and further their career a number of years after starting a family. Many other women are delaying marriage and childbearing until after they have successfully established a career. Yet other women continue in the tradition of women earlier in this century by getting married, having children, and not pursuing a career outside the home. As the roles of women have become more complex and varied, defining a normative sequence of development for them has become difficult, if not impossible.

Many women who are now at mid-life and beyond experienced a role shift in their late twenties, thirties, or beyond (Fodor & Franks, 1990). As they were engaging in traditional roles, the women's movement began and changed the lives of a substantial number of traditionally raised women and their families. Changes are still occurring for many mid-life women. There is an increasing number of late-life divorces. And in an America obsessed with youth and beauty, there is a double standard of aging: Women must stay young, while men are allowed to age. In one study, most mid-life women wanted to be at least 10 years younger (Rossi, 1980).

Is mid-life and beyond to be feared by women as a loss of youth and opportunity, a time of decline, or is it a new prime of life, a time for renewal, for shedding preoccupations with a youthful appearance and body, seeking new challenges, valuing maturity, and enjoying change?

In an investigation by Valory Mitchell and Ravenna Helson (1990), the early fifties were indeed a new prime of life for many women. In a sample of 700 women aged 26 to 80, women in their early fifties most often described their lives as "first-rate." Conditions that distinguished the lives of women in their early fifties from those of women in other age periods included more "empty nests," better health, higher income, and

more concern for parents. Women in their early fifties showed confidence, involvement, security, and breadth of personality.

In sum, the view that mid-life is a negative age period for women is stereotypical, as so many perceptions of age periods are. Mid-life is a diversified, heterogeneous period for women, just as it is for men.

Middle-Aged Women in Nonindustrialized Societies

What is middle age like for women in other cultures? The nature of middle age for women in other cultures depends on the modernity of the culture and the culture's view of gender roles. Anthropologist Judith Brown (1985) believes that middle age has more advantages in many nonindustrialized societies than in industrialized nations like the United States. She argues that as women reach middle age in many nonindustrialized societies, three changes take place that improve their status. First, they are often freed from cumbersome restrictions that were placed on them when they were younger. For example, in middle age they enjoy greater geographical mobility. Child care has ceased or can be delegated, and domestic chores are reduced. Commercial opportunities, visitation of relatives living at a distance, and religious opportunities provide an opportunity to venture forth from the village. A second major change brought on by middle age is a woman's right to exercise authority over specified younger kin. Middle-aged women can extract labor from younger family members. The work of the middle-aged woman tends to be administrative, delegating tasks and making assignments to younger women. The middle-aged woman also makes important decisions for certain members of the younger generation: what a grandchild is to be named, who is ready to be initiated, and who is eligible to marry whom. A third major change brought on by middle age in nonindustrialized societies is the eligibility of the woman for special statuses and the possibility that these provide recognition beyond the household. These statuses include the vocations of midwife, curer, holy woman, and matchmaker.

Cultural Conceptions of Middle Age

We have already seen that mid-life crises are less pervasive in the United States than is commonly believed (Chiriboga, 1989; Haan, 1989). How common are mid-life crises in other cultures? There has been little cross-cultural research on middle adulthood, and adult stage theories, such as Levinson's seasons of a man's life, have not been tested in other cultures. In many cultures, though, especially nonindustrialized cultures, the concept of middle age is not very clear, or in some cases is absent. It is common in nonindustrialized societies to describe individuals as young or old, but not as middle-aged (Foner, 1984; Grambs, 1989). And some cultures have no words for "adolescent," "young adult," or "middle-aged adult."

Gusii dancers perform on habitat day, Nairobi, Kenya. Movement from one status to another in the Gusii culture is due primarily to life events, not age. The Gusii do not have a clearly labeled mid-life transition.

Consider the Gusii culture, located south of the equator in the African country of Kenya. The Gusii divide the life course differently for females and males (LeVine, 1979):

Females	Males
1. Infant	1. Infant
2. Uncircumcised girl	2. Uncircumcised boy
3. Circumcised girl	3. Circumcised boy warrior
4. Married woman	4. Male elder
5. Female elder	

Thus, movement from one status to the next is due primarily to life events, not age, in the Gusii culture. While the Gusii do not have a clearly labeled mid-life transition, some of the Gusii adults do reassess their lives around the age of 40. At this time, these Gusii adults examine their current status and the limited time they have remaining in their lives. Their physical strength is decreasing and they know they cannot farm their land forever, so they seek spiritual powers by becoming ritual practitioners or healers. As in the American culture, however, a mid-life crisis in the Gusii culture is the exception rather than the rule.

At this point we have discussed a number of ideas about adult stage theories, crisis and cohort, and gender and culture. A summary of these ideas is presented in concept table 17.2.

The Life-Events Approach

An alternative to the stage approach to adult development is the life-events approach. In the early version of the life-events approach, life events were viewed as taxing circumstances for individuals, forcing them to change their personality (Holmes & Rahe, 1967). Such events as the death of a spouse, divorce, marriage, and so on were believed to involve varying degrees of stress, and therefore likely to influence the individual's development.

Today's life-events approach is more sophisticated (Brim & Ryff, 1980; Hansell, 1991; Hultsch & Plemons, 1979; Lieberman, 1994). The **contemporary life-events approach** *emphasizes that how life events influence the individual's development depends not only on the life event, but also on mediating factors (physical health, family supports, for example), the individual's adaptation to the life event (appraisal of the threat, coping strategies, for example), the life-stage context, and the sociohistorical context* (see figure 17.5). If individuals are in poor health and have little family support, life events are likely to be more stressful. One individual may perceive a life event as highly stressful, another individual may perceive the same event as a challenge. And a divorce may be more stressful after many years of marriage when adults are in their fifties than when they have only been married several years and are in their twenties (Chiriboga, 1982). Adults may be able to cope more effectively with divorce in the 1990s than in the 1950s because divorce has become more commonplace and accepted in today's society.

Though the life-events approach is a valuable addition to understanding adult development, like other approaches to

CONCEPT TABLE 17.2

Adult Stage Theories, Crisis and Cohort, Gender and Culture

Concept	Processes/Related Ideas	Characteristics/Description
Adult stage theories	Generativity versus stagnation	In middle adulthood, individuals need to assist the next generation in developing and leading useful lives.
	Gould's transformations	Mid-life is as turbulent as adolescence except that during mid-life striving to handle a crisis produces a healthy, happier life. In our forties we begin to feel a sense of urgency as we see our lives speeding by.
	Levinson's seasons of a man's life	Developmental tasks should be mastered at different points in development. Changes in middle adulthood focus on four conflicts; being young vs. being old; being destructive vs. being constructive; being masculine vs. being feminine; being attached to others vs. being separated from them.
	Vaillant's expansion of Erikson's stages	Career consolidation occurs from 23 to 35 years of age; keeping the meaning vs. rigidity occurs from 45 to 55 years of age.
	Conclusions	Adult development begins with a change from identity to intimacy, then from career consolidation to generativity, and finally from searching for meaning to some final integration. Criticisms of the stage theories have been made.
Crisis and cohort	Crisis	A majority of individuals in the United States do not experience a mid-life crisis.
	Cohort	Neugarten believes the social environment of a particular cohort can alter its social clock—the timetable according to which individuals are expected to accomplish life's tasks—such as getting married, having children, or establishing a career.
Gender, culture, and middle age	Gender	Critics say the adult stage theories have a male bias by emphasizing career choice and achievement. The stage theories do not adequately address women's concerns about relationships, interdependence, and caring. The stage theories assume a normative sequence of development, but as women's roles have become more varied and complex, determining what is normative is difficult. Mid-life is a heterogeneous age period for women, just as it is for men. For some women, mid-life truly is the prime of their lives.
	Culture	In many nonindustrialized societies, a woman's status often improves in middle age. In many cultures, the concept of middle age is not clear. Some cultures do not have words for "adolescent," "young adult," or "middle-aged adult." However, most cultures distinguish between the young and the old.

adult development, it has its drawbacks (Dohrenwend & Dohrenwend, 1978). One of the most significant drawbacks is that the life-events approach places too much emphasis on change, not adequately recognizing the stability that, at least to some degree, characterizes adult development. Another drawback is that it may not be life's major events that are the primary sources of stress, but our daily experiences. Enduring a boring but tense job or marriage and living in poverty do not show up on scales of major life events. Yet the everyday pounding we

take from these living conditions can add up to a highly stressful life and eventually illness. Some psychologists believe we can gain greater insight into the source of life's stresses by focusing more on daily hassles and daily uplifts (Kanner & Feldman, 1991; Lazarus & Folkman, 1984).

In one investigation of 210 Florida police officers, the day-to-day friction associated with an inefficient justice system and distorted press accounts of police work were more stressful than responding to a felony in progress or making an arrest

FIGURE 17.5

A contemporary life-events framework for interpreting adult developmental change.

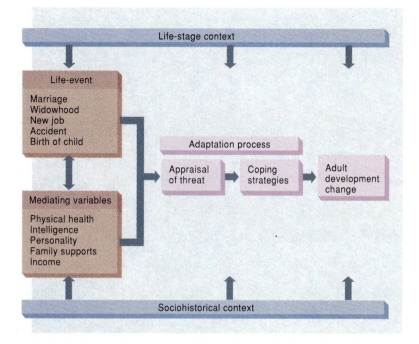

(Spielberger & Grier, 1983). In another investigation, the most frequent daily hassles of college students were wasting time, concerns about meeting high standards, and being lonely (Kanner & others, 1981). Among the most frequent uplifts of the college students were entertainment, getting along well with friends, and completing a task. In this same investigation, the most frequent daily hassles of middle-aged adults were concerns about weight and the health of a family member, while their most frequent daily uplifts involved relating well with a spouse or lover, or a friend (see figure 17.6). And the middle-aged adults were more likely than the college students to report that their daily hassles involved economic concerns (rising prices and taxes, for example). Critics of the daily-hassles approach argue that some of the same problems involved with life-events scales occur when daily hassles are assessed (Dohrenwend & Shrout, 1985). For example, knowing about an adult's daily hassles tells us nothing about physical changes, how the individual copes with hassles, and how the individual perceives hassles.

> *It's not the large things that send a man to the madhouse*
> *. . . no, it's the continuing series of small tragedies that*
> *send a man to the madhouse . . . not the death of his love*
> *but a shoelace that snaps with no time left.*
>
> —Charles Bukowski

Individual Variation

One way to look at personality development is to focus on similarities; another way is to focus on differences (Meyer, 1991; Schooler, 1991). The stage theories of Erikson, Gould, Levinson, and Vaillant all attempt to describe the universals—not the individual variations—in adult development. In an extensive investigation of a random sample of 500 men at midlife, Michael Farrell and Stanley Rosenberg (1981) concluded that extensive individual variation characterized the men. They emphasize the individual as an active agent who interprets, shapes, alters, and gives meaning to his life.

> *If a man does not keep pace with his companions, perhaps it*
> *is because he hears a different drummer. Let him step to the*
> *music he hears, however measured or far away.*
>
> —Henry David Thoreau, 1854

The ability to set aside unproductive worries and preoccupations is believed to be an important factor in functioning under stress. In Vaillant's (1977) Grant Study, pervasive personal preoccupations were maladaptive in both the work and the marriages of college students over a 30-year period after leaving college. Some individuals in the Grant Study had personal preoccupations, while others did not. As Solon put it, while collectively we are geese, each of us, individually, walks with the tread of a fox. In the words of Simon Weil, "Every person cries out to be read differently."

FIGURE 17.6

Ten Most Frequent Daily Hassles and Uplifts of Middle-Aged Adults over a Nine-Month Period.

Daily hassles	% of Times Checked*
1. Concerns about weight	52.4
2. Health of a family member	48.1
3. Rising prices of common goods	43.7
4. Home maintenance	42.8
5. Too many things to do	38.6
6. Misplacing or losing things	38.1
7. Yard work or outside home maintenance	38.1
8. Property, investment, or taxes	37.6
9. Crime	37.1
10. Physical appearance	35.9

Daily uplifts	% of Times Checked*
1. Relating well with your spouse or lover	76.3
2. Relating well with friends	74.4
3. Completing a task	73.3
4. Feeling healthy	72.7
5. Getting enough sleep	69.7
6. Eating out	68.4
7. Meeting your responsibilities	68.1
8. Visiting, phoning, or writing someone	67.7
9. Spending time with family	66.7
10. Home (inside) pleasing to you	65.5

* The "% of times checked" figures represent the mean percentage of people checking the item each month averaged over the nine monthly administrations.

LONGITUDINAL STUDIES OF PERSONALITY DEVELOPMENT IN ADULTHOOD

A number of longitudinal studies have assessed the personality development of adults. These studies are especially helpful in charting the most important dimensions of personality at different points in adult development and in evaluating the degree personality changes or stays the same.

One of the earliest longitudinal studies of adult personality development was conducted by Bernice Neugarten (1964). Known as the "Kansas City Study," it involved the investigation of individuals 40 to 80 years of age over a 10-year period. The adults were given personality tests, they filled out questionnaires, and they were interviewed. Neugarten concluded that both continuity and age changes in personality were present.

Adaptive characteristics showed the most stability—these included styles of coping, attaining life satisfaction, and strength of goal-directed behavior. Some consistent age differences occurred in the individual's inner versus outer orientation and active versus passive mastery. For example, 40-year-olds felt that they had control over their environment, and risk taking did not bother them much. However, 60-year-olds were more likely to perceive the environment as threatening and sometimes dangerous, and they had a more passive view of the self. This personality change in adulthood was described by Neugarten as going from active to passive mastery.

Another major longitudinal study of adult personality development has been conducted by Paul Costa and R. R. McRae at the Veterans Administration Outpatient Clinic in Boston. It involves approximately 2,000 men in their twenties through their eighties. Measures include assessments of personality, attitudes, and values (Costa & McRae, 1980, 1989; Costa & others, 1987).

Costa and McRae believe that personality can be best understood in terms of three dimensions: neuroticism, extraversion, and openness to experience. Neuroticism includes how anxious, stable, depressed, self-conscious, impulsive, and vulnerable the individual is; extraversion includes the individual's attachment, gregariousness, assertiveness, activity, excitement seeking, and positive emotions; and openness to experience includes the individual's openness to fantasy, feelings, ideas, and values. Costa and McRae conclude that considerable stability in these three dimensions of personality—neuroticism, extraversion, and openness to experience—characterizes adult development.

By far the longest longitudinal study is the California Longitudinal Study. Initially, more than 500 children and their parents were studied in the late 1920s and early 1930s. In *Present and Past in Middle Life* (Eichorn & others, 1981), the profile of these individuals' lives was described as they became middle-aged. The results from early adolescence to mid-life did not support either extreme in the debate over whether personality is characterized by stability or change. Some characteristics were more stable than others, however. Dimensions more directly concerned with self (cognitively invested, self-confident, and open or closed self) were more consistent than dimensions more directly concerned with interpersonal relationships (nurturant or hostile and undercontrolled or overcontrolled).

Another longitudinal investigation of adult personality development was conducted by Ravenna Helson and her colleagues (Helson, Mitchell, & Moane, 1984; Helson & Moane, 1987; Helson & Wink, 1987). They initially studied 132 women who were seniors at Mills College in California in the late 1950s; in 1981, when the women were 42 to 45 years old, they were studied again. Helson and her colleagues distinguished three main groups among the Mills women: family-oriented, career-oriented (whether or not they also wanted families), and those who followed neither path (women with children who pursued only low-level work). Despite their different college profiles and their diverging life paths, the women in all three groups experienced some similar psychological changes over their adult years, although the women in the third group changed less than those committed to career or family. Between the ages of 27 and the early forties, there was a shift toward less traditionally feminine attitudes, including greater dominance, greater interest in events outside the family, and more emotional stability. This may have been due to societal changes from the 1950s to the 1980s rather than to age changes.

During their early forties, many of the women shared the concerns that stage theorists such as Levinson and Gould found in men: concern for young and old, introspectiveness, interest in roots, and awareness of limitations and death. However, the researchers in the Mills College study concluded that rather than being in a mid-life crisis, what was being experienced was *mid-life consciousness.* They also indicated that commitment to the tasks of early adulthood—whether to a career or family (or both)—helped women learn to control their impulses, develop interpersonal skills, become independent, and work hard to achieve goals. Women who did not commit themselves to one of these life-style patterns faced fewer challenges and did not develop as fully as the other women (Rosenfeld & Stark, 1987).

What can we conclude from the series of longitudinal studies about constancy and change in personality during the adult years? Richard Alpert was an achievement-oriented, hard-working college professor in the 1960s. In the 1970s, Richard Alpert became Ram Dass, a free-spirited guru in search of an expanded state of consciousness. Most individuals would look at Alpert and Ram Dass and see two very different people. But Harvard psychologist David McClelland, who has known Alpert and Ram Dass well, says that Dass is the same old Richard, still charming, still concerned with inner experience, and still power hungry.

Jerry Rubin views his own transformation from yippie to Wall Street businessman in a way that underscores continuity in personality. Rubin says that discovering his identity was accomplished in a typical Jerry Rubin fashion—trying out anything and everything, jumping around wild-eyed and crazy. Whether yippie or Wall Street businessman, Rubin approached life with enthusiasm and curiosity (Rubin, 1981).

William James (1890/1950) said that our basic personality is set like plaster by the time we are 30 and never softens again. Like Jerry Rubin and David McClelland, James believed that our bodies and attitudes may change through the adult years, but not the basic core of our personality. Paul Costa's (1986) research clearly supports this stability. He believes that whether we are extraverted or introverted, how adjusted we are and how open we are to new experience do not change much during our adult lives. Look at an individual at age 25 who is shy and quiet and then observe the individual again at age 50, says Costa, and you will find the same shy and quiet individual.

Yet many adult developmentalists are enthusiastic about our capacity for change as adults, arguing that too much importance has been attached to personality change in childhood and not enough importance has been placed on change in adulthood. A more moderate view on the stability-change view comes from the California Longitudinal Study (Eichorn & others, 1981; Mussen, Honzik, & Eichorn, 1982). They believe some stability exists over the long course of adult development, but that adults are more capable of change than Costa thinks. For example, shy, introverted individuals at age 25 may not be completely extraverted at age 50, but they may be less introverted than they were when they were 25. Perhaps they married someone who encouraged them to be more outgoing and supported their social ventures; perhaps they changed jobs at age 30 and became a salesperson, placing them in a circumstance that required them to develop their social skills.

(a)

(b)

(c)

How much does personality change and how does it stay the same through adulthood? (a) In the early 1970s, Jerry Rubin was a yippie demonstrator, but (b) in the 1980s Rubin became a Wall Street businessman. Rubin said that his transformation underscored continuity in personality: Whether yippie or Wall Street yuppie, he approached life with curiosity and enthusiasm. (c) At age 55, actor Jack Nicholson (1992) recently said, "I feel exactly the same as I've always felt: a slightly reined-in voracious beast."

CONCEPT TABLE 17.3

The Life–Events Approach, Individual Variation, and Longitudinal Studies

Concept	Processes/Related Ideas	Characteristics/Description
The life-events approach	Early version	Life events produce taxing circumstances that produce stress in individuals' lives.
	Contemporary version	How life events influence the individual's development depends not only on the life event but also on mediating factors, the individual's adaptation to the life event, the life-stage context, and the sociohistorical context.
Individual variation	Its nature	One approach to adult personality development emphasizes similarities, another emphasizes differences. The adult stage approach emphasizes similarities. However, there is substantial individual variation in adult development.
Longitudinal studies of personality development in adulthood	Neugarten's study	The most consistent characteristics were adaptive characteristics—styles of coping, attaining life satisfaction, and strength of goal-directed behavior. Two significant changes in middle age were increases in both passive mastery and interiority.
	Costa and McRae's view	They report extensive stability in adult personality development, especially in neuroticism, extraversion, and openness to experience.
	California longitudinal study	The extremes in the stability-change argument were not supported. Characteristics associated with the self were more stable than those associated with interpersonal relationships.
	Mills College study	In this study of adult women, there was a shift toward less traditionally feminine characteristics from age 27 to the early forties, but this may have been due to societal changes. In their early forties, women experienced many of the concerns stage theorists such as Levinson and Gould found in men. However, rather than a mid-life crisis, this change was described as mid-life consciousness.
	Conclusions	The longitudinal studies portray adults as becoming different but still remaining the same—amidst change there is still some underlying coherence and stability.

October answers to that period in the life of man when he is no longer dependent on his transient moods, when all his experiences ripen into wisdom, but every root, branch, leaf of him glows with maturity. What he has been and done in his spring and summer appears. He bears fruit.

—Ralph Waldo Emerson

Humans are adaptive beings; we are resilient throughout our adult lives. But we do not become entirely new personalities either. In a sense we become different but we are still the same—amidst change is some underlying coherence and stability.

At this point we have discussed a number of ideas about personality theories and development in middle age. A summary of these ideas is presented in concept table 17.3.

LIFE-SPAN HEALTH AND WELL-BEING

Engaging in a Life Review

Frank just turned 45 years old yesterday. As he realizes that he has become "middle aged," he recognizes that his life is, almost certainly, at least half over. As he reflects back on his time, he begins to consider his goals from when he was younger. In doing so he realizes that some of his aspirations have been met with success, others with disappointment. Looking back allows Frank the chance to assess where he has been, where he is now, and where he is headed. Given that he still has, at the most, half of his life to go, he can make some adjustments to reach many of the goals he has not yet achieved.

As you read in this chapter, people frequently engage in a process of reviewing their lives when they enter their middle years and beyond. This process, often referred to as "life review," can be highly beneficial. Although dwelling on the past will rarely result in greater productivity or progress, taking a look at how things are going and how they got there can

help us work toward the future. Of course, it is not necessary for a person to be in the middle years to do something like a life review.

One way you can assess your life situation is to consider each aspect of your life and its history, one segment at a time. For example, think about Frank, discussed above. As he wonders about his life situation, he is likely to take many aspects into account. He may ponder his career, family life, education, relationships, and many other things. However, if his thinking is unorganized, he will probably miss some of the connections among aspects of his life and may not see how he could set a new path. Thus, rather than just thinking about one's life, it is possible to examine its developmental course. One way to do this is to list out several life areas and note how they have gone along throughout life. For example, consider your family. Questions that you could pose to yourself include these: "What was most important about my childhood?" "What major events

have changed my family?" "What aspects of my family life am I most and least satisfied with right now?" "How would I like to see my family life in the future, and what can I do to bring it there?" Regarding your career path, consider questions such as these: "How did I get into the work I am currently in?" "How far along have I progressed with respect to my personal goals?" "What can I do to progress along as I have wished?" "Do I need to adjust my goals for the future?"

A life review also benefits when you identify several areas of your life and then write down your perspectives about the past, present, and future prospects of each. Consider the areas listed in the sample life review chart, as well as others that may hold more personal meaning to you. The end result of this process can be a broader view on life that is put together in a meaningful, whole picture (Simons, Kalichman, & Santrock, 1994).

CONCLUSIONS

For most people, mid-life is not a crisis and turns out to be better than they thought it would be. A minority of people experience a mid-life crisis, but just about everyone in America experiences a mid-life consciousness.

We began this chapter by considering mid-life variations and then read about the following dimensions of close relationships in midlife: love and marriage, the empty nest and its refilling, sibling relationships and friendships, and intergenerational

relationships. We spent considerable time evaluating the adult stage theories—Erikson's, Gould's, Levinson's, and Vaillant's; crisis and cohort; gender, culture, and middle age; the life-events approach; and individual variation. We also studied longitudinal investigations of personality in adulthood. At different points in the chapter we also read about the decisions that need to be made when adult children move back in with their parents, intergenerational

relationships in Mexican American families, and engaging in a life review.

Don't forget that you can obtain an overall summary of the chapter by again reading the three concept tables on pages 490, 500, and 505. This concludes our discussion of middle adulthood. In Section Nine, we continue our journey through the human life-span by moving on to late adulthood, beginning with chapter 18, "Physical Development in Late Adulthood."

Example of Life Review Chart

	Past	Present	Future
Family			
Friends			
Education			
Career			
Travel			
Financial Security			
Religious/Spiritual			

An alternative means of life review would be to take a more chronological approach. For example, a person may construct what could be called a "life-line." Rather than examine specific aspects of your life one at a time, you could evaluate your life one period or phase at a time. Construct a time line, starting as far back as you like—with your birth, say, or even with where your family came from before your birth. Then, looking at your infancy, childhood, adolescence, and adulthood, list out all of the major events of your life and where they brought you. The result would again be a clearer depiction of your life that could have all of the benefits discussed above.

Other strategies you can follow include discussing your life with elder family members, constructing a family tree, and keeping an extensive diary. Regardless of the exact method you use, engaging in a personal life review can give you a clearer picture of yourself and place your life into perspective. ■

KEY TERMS

empty nest syndrome   The hypothesis that marital satisfaction will decrease after children leave home, because parents derive considerable satisfaction from their children. The empty nest syndrome may hold true for some parents who live vicariously through their children, but marital satisfaction usually increases during the post-childbearing years. (486)

career consolidation   One of Vaillant's adult stages of development. It occurs from approximately ages 23 to 35 and is a period during which an individual's career becomes more stable and coherent. (495)

keeping the meaning versus rigidity   Vaillant's stage of adult development that occurs from about 45 to 55 years of age, in which adults are more relaxed if they have met their goals; if they have not met their goals, they accept the fact. At this time adults become concerned about extracting some meaning from their lives, and they resist falling into a rigid orientation. (495)

social clock   The timetable according to which individuals are expected to accomplish life's tasks, such as getting married, having children, or establishing themselves in a career. (497)

contemporary life-events approach   Emphasizes that how a life event influences the individual's development depends not only on the life event, but also on mediating factors, the individual's adaptation to the life event, the life-stage context, and the sociohistorical context. (499)

Late Adulthood

To be seventy years young is sometimes far more cheerful and hopeful than to be forty years old.

—Oliver Wendell Holmes

The rhythm and meaning of human development eventually wend their way to late adulthood, when each of us stands alone at the heart of the earth and suddenly it is evening. We shed the leaves of youth and are stripped by the winds of time down to the truth. We learn that life is lived forward but understood backward. We trace the connection between the end and the beginning of life and try to figure out what this whole show is about before it is out. Ultimately, we come to know that we are what survives of us. Section Nine contains three chapters: "Physical Development in Late Adulthood" (chapter 18), "Cognitive Development in Late Adulthood" (chapter 19), and "Socioemotional Development in Late Adulthood" (chapter 20).

Picasso, The Guitarist, detail.

Physical Development in Late Adulthood

'Tis very certain that the desire for life prolongs it.

—Byron, *Don Juan,* 1819

> *Each of us stands alone at the heart of the earth pierced through by a ray of sunlight: And suddenly it is evening.*
>
> —Salvatore Quasimodo

IMAGES OF LIFE-SPAN DEVELOPMENT

Learning to Age Successfully

Jonathan Swift said, "No wise man ever wished to be younger." Without a doubt, a 70-year-old body does not work as well as it once did. It is also true that an individual's fear of aging is often greater than need be. As more individuals live to a ripe *and* active old age, our image of aging is changing. While on the average a 75-year-old's joints should be stiffening, people can practice not to be average. For example, a 75-year-old man may *choose* to train for and run a marathon; an 80-year-old woman whose capacity for work is undiminished may *choose* to continue making and selling children's toys.

Consider 85-year-old Sadie Halperin, who has been working out for 11 months at a rehabilitation center for the aged in Boston, lifting weights and riding a stationary bike. She says that before she started working out, about everything she did—shopping, cooking, walking—was a major struggle. She says she always felt wobbly and held on to a wall when she walked. Now she walks down

Eighty-five-year-old Sadie Halperin doubled her strength in exercise after just 11 months. Before developing an exercise routine, she felt wobbly and often had to hold on to a wall when she walked. Now she walks down the middle of hallways and says she feels wonderful.

the center of the hallways and reports that she feels wonderful. Initially she could lift only 15 pounds with both legs; now she lifts 30 pounds. At first she could bench-press only 20 pounds; now she bench-presses 50 pounds. Sadie's exercise routine has increased her muscle strength and helps her to battle osteoporosis by slowing the calcium loss from her bones, which can lead to deadly fractures (Ubell, 1992).

PREVIEW

Eighty-five-year-old-Sadie Halperin's physical development and well-being raise some truly fascinating questions about life-span development that we will explore in this chapter, including these: Why do we age, and what—if anything—can we do to slow the process down? How long can we live? What chance do you have of living to be 100? What is the nature of physical changes in late adulthood? Do older adults have sex? What kind of health treatment do the elderly receive? Can better nutrition, as well as exercise, make us healthier in old age and possibly expand the life span?

LIFE-SPAN PRACTICAL KNOWLEDGE 18.1

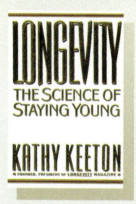

Longevity: The Science of Staying Young
(1992) by Kathy Keeton. New York: Viking Press.

This book provides a guide to recent research and theory about ways to slow the aging process. Author Kathy Keeton provides helpful suggestions for how to live the longest, healthiest, and fullest life possible. Among the topics covered are these: What really happens when the body gets older? How much does life-style influence the aging process? What role does eating play in aging? What role does genetics play in longevity? The research programs of a number of leading scientists who study the aging process are described.

LONGEVITY

Linus Pauling, now in his eighties, believes that vitamin C slows the aging process. Aging researcher Roy Walford fasts 2 days a week because he believes undernutrition (not malnutrition) also slows the aging process. What do we really know about longevity?

Life Expectancy and Life Span

We are no longer a youthful society. Remember from chapter 1 that, as more individuals live to older ages, the proportion of individuals at different ages has become increasingly similar. Indeed, the concept of a period called "late adulthood" is a recent one—until the twentieth century most individuals died before they were 65. In the 1980 census, the number of persons 65 and older had climbed by 28 percent over figures for 1970. In the United States today, there are more than 25 million people in the 65-and-over category.

To me old age is always fifteen years older than I am.
—Bernard Baruch

However, while a much greater percentage of persons live to an older age, the life span has remained virtually unchanged since the beginning of recorded history. **Life span** *is the upper boundary of life, the maximum number of years an individual can live. The maximum life span of human beings is approximately 120 years of age.* **Life expectancy** *is the number of years that will probably be lived by the average person born in a particular year.* Improvements in medicine, nutrition, exercise, and life-style have increased our life expectancy an average of 22 additional years since 1900. However, few of us will live to be 100 (32,000 Americans lived to be 100 in 1980), although the number is increasing.

Supposedly, one American, Charlie Smith (ca. 1842–1979), lived to be 137 years old. Charlie was very, very old, but documentation of his age is sketchy. In 1956, the Social Security Administration began to collect information about American centenarians (those who live to be 100 or older) who were receiving benefits. Charlie Smith was visited in 1961. He gave his birthdate as July 4, 1842, and his place of birth as Liberia. By the end of the nineteenth century, Charlie had settled in Florida. He worked in turpentine camps, and at one point owned a turpentine farm in Homeland, Florida. Smith's records at the Social Security Administration do not provide evidence of his birthdate, but they do mention that he began to earn benefits based on Social Security credits by picking oranges at the age of 113 (Freeman, 1982).

Charlie Smith lived to be very old—exactly how old we will never know. He lived an active life, even after the age of 100. Many other Americans have lived to be 100. In the book *Living to be 100: 1200 Who Did and How They Did It* (Segerberg, 1982), Social Security Administration interviews with 1,127 individuals who lived to be 100 were described. Especially interesting are some of the bizarre reasons several of the centenarians gave as to why they were able to live so long, "because I slept with my head facing the north," "because of eating a lot of fatty pork and salt," and "because I don't believe in germs." More accurate reasons given by these individuals as to why they had lived to be 100 were their organized, purposeful behavior, discipline and hard work, freedom and independence, balanced diet, positive family relations, and the support of friends. In some areas of the world large numbers of individuals reportedly live to be very old. To learn more about these areas, turn to Sociocultural Worlds of Development 18.1.

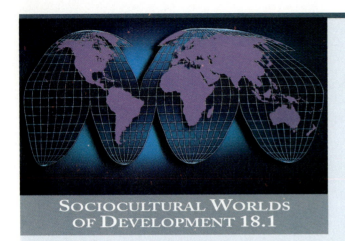

SOCIOCULTURAL WORLDS OF DEVELOPMENT 18.1

Aging in Russia, Ecuador, and Kashmir

Imagine that you are 120 years old. Would you still be able to write your name? Could you think clearly? What would your body look like? Would you be able to walk? To run? Could you still have sex? Would you have an interest in sex? Would your eyes and ears still function? Could you work?

Has anyone ever lived to be 120 years old? Supposedly. In three areas of the world, not just a single person but many people have reportedly lived more than 130 years. These areas are the Republic of Georgia in Russia, the Vilcabamba valley in Ecuador, and the province of Hunza in Kashmir (in Northern India). Three people over 100 years old (centenarians) per 100,000 people is considered normal. But in the Russian region where the Abkhasian people live, approximately 400 centenarians per 100,000 people have been reported. Some of the Abkhasians are said to be 120 to 170 years old (Benet, 1976).

However, there is reason to believe that some of these claims are false (Medvedev, 1974). Indeed, we really do not have sound documentation of anyone living more than 120 years. In the case of the Abkhasians, birth registrations and other documents, such as marriage certificates and military registrations, are not available. In most instances, the ages of the Abkhasians have been based on the individuals' recall of important historical events and interviews with other members of the village (Benet, 1976). In the Russian villages where people have been reported to live a long life, the elderly experience unparalleled esteem and honor. Centenarians are often given special positions in the community, such as the leader of social celebrations. Thus there is a strong motivation to give one's age as older than one really is. One individual who claimed to be 130 years of age was found to have used his father's birth certificate during World War I to escape army duty. Later it was discovered that he only was 78 years old (Hayflick, 1975).

(a) *Selakh Butka, who says he is 113 years old, is shown with his wife, who says she is 101. The Butkas live in the Georgian Republic of Russia, where reports of unusual longevity have surfaced. Why are scientists skeptical about their age?* (b) *Eighty-seven-year-old José Maria Roa is from the Vilcabamba region of Ecuador, which also is renowned for the longevity of its inhabitants.*

What about you? What chance do you have of living to be 100? By taking the test in table 18.1, you can obtain a rough estimate of your chance and discover some of the most important contributors to longevity. According to the questionnaire, heredity and family history, health (weight, diet, smoking, and exercise), education, personality, and life-style are factors in longevity.

Just as actuaries predict longevity for the purpose of estimating insurance risks on the basis of age, sex, and ethnicity, developmentalists have also evaluated the factors that predict longevity. In the most comprehensive investigation of longevity, known as the Duke Longitudinal Study (Palmore, 1982), older adults were assessed over a 25-year period. A total of 270 volunteers were examined for the first time in 1959 with a series of physical, mental, social, and laboratory tasks. At that time, the adults ranged in age from 60 to 94, with a mean age of 70. What were the factors that predicted their longevity 25 years later? Not surprisingly, health was the best predictor. Nonsmoking, intelligence, education, work satisfaction, usefulness, and happiness in 1959 also predicted whether these

TABLE 18.1

Can You Live To Be 100?

The following test gives you a rough guide for predicting your longevity. The basic life expectancy for males is age 71, and for females 78. Write down your basic life expectancy. If you are in your fifties or sixties, you should add ten years to the basic figure because you have already proved yourself to be a durable individual. If you are over age sixty and active, you can even add another two years.

Basic Life Expectancy _____

Decide how each item below applies to you and add or subtract the appropriate number of years from your basic life expectancy.

1. Family history
   Add five years if two or more of your grandparents lived to 80 or beyond.
   Subtract four years if any parent, grandparent, sister, or brother died of heart attack or stroke before 50. _____
   Subtract two years if anyone died from these diseases before 60. _____
   Subtract three years for each case of diabetes, thyroid disorder, breast cancer, cancer of the digestive system, asthma, or chronic bronchitis among parents or grandparents. _____

2. Marital status
   If you are married, add four years.
   If you are over twenty-five and not married, subtract one year for every unwedded decade. _____

3. Economic status
   Add two years if your family income is over $60,000 per year.
   Subtract three years if you have been poor for the greater part of your life. _____

4. Physique
   Subtract one year for every ten pounds you are overweight.
   For each inch your girth measurement exceeds your chest measurement deduct two years. _____
   Add three years if you are over forty and not overweight. _____

5. Exercise
   Add three years if you exercise regularly and moderately (jogging three times a week).
   Add five years if you exercise regularly and vigorously (long-distance running three times a week). _____
   Subtract three years if your job is sedentary. _____
   Add three years if your job is active. _____

6. Alcohol
   Add two years if you are a light drinker (one to three drinks a day).
   Subtract five to ten years if you are a heavy drinker (more than four drinks per day). _____
   Subtract one year if you are a teetotaler. _____

7. Smoking
   Subtract eight years if you smoke two or more packs of cigarettes per day.
   Subtract two years if you smoke one to two packs per day. _____
   Subtract two years if you smoke less than one pack. _____
   Subtract two years if you regularly smoke a pipe or cigars. _____

8. Disposition
   Add two years if you are a reasoned, practical person.
   Subtract two years if you are aggressive, intense, and competitive. _____
   Add one to five years if you are basically happy and content with life. _____
   Subtract one to five years if you are often unhappy, worried, and often feel guilty. _____

9. Education
   Subtract two years if you have less than a high school education.
   Add one year if you attended four years of school beyond high school. _____
   Add three years if you attended five or more years beyond high school. _____

10. Environment
    Add four years if you have lived most of your life in a rural environment.
    Subtract two years if you have lived most of your life in an urban environment. _____

11. Sleep
    Subtract five years if you sleep more than nine hours a day. _____

12. Temperature
    Add two years if your home's thermostat is set at no more than 68°F. _____

13. Health care
    Add three years if you have regular medical checkups and regular dental care. _____
    Subtract two years if you are frequently ill. _____

Your Life Expectancy Total _____

TABLE 18.2

Differences in the Life Expectancies of Females and Males

Sex	Year		
	1950	1985	2020 (projected)
Female	71.0	78.2	82.0
Male	65.5	71.2	74.2

Source: Data from the *Duke Longitudinal Study.*

individuals would still be alive in 1981. Also, finances predicted longevity for men; activity level predicted longevity for women.

Critical Thinking

What factors do you believe will be the most important in increasing longevity 50 years from now, in approximately the year 2040? Will they be any different from those that are the most critical today? Will some factors assume more importance, or less importance?

Beginning at the age of 25, females outnumber males; this gap widens during the remainder of the adult years (see table 18.2). By the time adults are 75 years of age, more than 61 percent of the population is female; for those 85 and over, the figure is almost 70 percent female. Why might this be so? Social factors such as health attitudes, habits, life-styles, and occupation are probably important. For example, men are more likely than women to die from the leading causes of death in the United States, such as cancer of the respiratory system, motor vehicle accidents, suicide, cirrhosis of the liver, emphysema, and coronary heart disease. These causes of death are associated with life-style. For example, the sex difference in deaths due to lung cancer and emphysema is probably associated with men being heavier smokers than women.

However, if life expectancy is influenced extensively by the stress of work, the sex difference in longevity should be narrowing, since so many more women have entered the labor force. Yet in the last 40 years, just the opposite has occurred. Apparently, self-esteem and work satisfaction outweigh the stress of work when the longevity of women is at issue.

The sex difference in longevity is also influenced by biological factors. In virtually all species, females outlive males. Women have more resistance to infections and degenerative diseases. For example, the female's estrogen production helps to protect her from arteriosclerosis (hardening of the arteries). And the X chromosome women carry may be associated with the production of more antibodies to fight off disease.

The Young Old, the Old Old, and the Oldest Old

Late adulthood, which begins in the sixties and extends to approximately 120 years of age, has the longest span of any period of human development—50 to 60 years. The combination of the lengthy span with the dramatic increase in the number of adults living to older ages has led to increased interest in differentiating the late adulthood period. Most of the demarcations involve two subperiods, although exact agreement on the age cutoffs for the subperiods has not been reached. Some developmentalists distinguish between the *young old* or *old age* (65 to 74 years of age) and the *old old* or *late old age* (75 years and older) (Baltes, Smith, & Staudinger, in press; Charness & Bosman, 1992; Neugarten, 1980). Yet others distinguish the *oldest old* (85 years and older) from younger older adults (Johnson, 1994; Pearlin, 1994).

The importance of making such distinctions is especially apparent when we compare the oldest old (85 years and older) with the young old, who are still in their sixties (Suzman, Willis, & Manton, 1992). The oldest old are much more likely to be female, and they have a much higher rate of morbidity and a far greater incidence of disability than do the young old. The oldest old are much more likely to be living in institutions, less likely to be married, and more likely to have low educational attainment. Their needs, capacities, and resources are often different from those of their young old counterparts.

When thinking about the differentiation of late adulthood into subperiods, remember that every period or subperiod of development is heterogeneous. Even the oldest old are a heterogeneous, diversified group (Roberts, Dunkle, & Haug, 1994). Many of the oldest old function effectively, although others have outlived their social and financial supports and depend on society for their daily living. Almost one-fourth of the oldest old are institutionalized (Torrey, 1992), and many report some limitation

One-hundred-year-old Iva Blake is among the oldest old in America. Adapting to her changing circumstances, she still tends to her garden from a wheelchair.

of activity or difficulties in performing personal-care activities (Manton & Soldo, 1992). A significant number are cognitively impaired (Evans & others, 1992).

A substantial portion of the oldest old function effectively. Society's preoccupation with the disability and mortality of the oldest old has concealed the fact that the majority of older adults aged 80 and over continue to live in the community (Kovar & Stone, 1992). More than one-third of older adults 80 and over who live in the community report that their health is excellent or good; 40 percent say they have no activity limitation (Suzman, Harris, & others, 1992). Shakespeare's image of the oldest old, in *As You Like It*—"mere oblivion, sans teeth, sans taste, sans everything"—clearly is not supported by the increasing amount of research evidence that describes a more optimistic picture of a substantial portion of people in their eighties and older (Suzman, Willis, & Manton, 1992).

Biological Theories of Aging

Even if we keep a remarkably healthy profile through our adult lives, we begin to age at some point. What are the biological explanations of aging? **Microbiological theories of aging** *look within the body's cells to explain aging. The label* micro *is used because a cell is a very small unit of analysis.* **Macrobiological theories of aging** *examine life at a more global level of analysis than the cell.* Macro *refers to a larger, more global level of analysis.* Some microbiological and macrobiological theories attribute aging to wear and tear on the body, others to a biological clock within the body.

Microbiological Theories

As cells age, they have more difficulty disposing of their wastes. Eventually this "garbage" takes up as much as 20 percent of a cell's space. Imagine the cell's working molecules as waiters in a nightclub trying to move across a dance floor that becomes increasingly crowded. Service becomes slower and slower, until eventually it might come to a complete standstill. Most scientists view this phenomenon as a result, rather than a cause, of aging, though.

As cells age, their molecules can become linked or attached to each other in ways that stop vital biochemical cycles and create other forms of havoc as they disrupt cell functioning (Bruce, 1991; Ivy & others, 1992; Pacifici & Davies, 1991). "Cross-linkage," like "garbage-accumulation," is now thought to be a consequence rather than a cause of aging.

(a)

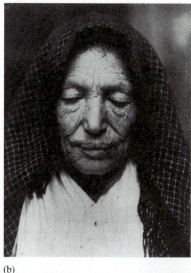
(b)

(c)

(a) *Frenchwoman Jeanne Louise Calment, 118, is said to be the oldest person now alive. Greater ages have been claimed, but scientists say the maximum human life span is about 120.* (b) *Some people age rapidly, like this 40-year-old immigrant from Italy. What is likely to cause such premature aging?* (c) *Heredity is an important component of how long we will live. For example, in table 18.1, you were able to add 5 years to your life expectancy if two or more of your grandparents lived to 80 or beyond. And if you were born a female, you get to start out with a basic life expectancy that is 7 years older than if you were born a male. The three sisters shown above are all in their eighties.*

Might there also be a biological clock within our cells that causes us to age? Leonard Hayflick (1977, 1987) thinks so. He has demonstrated that the body's cells can divide only a limited number of times. Cells from human embryonic tissue can divide only about fifty times, for example. Cells extracted from older individuals still have dividing capability, however, so we rarely live to the end of our life-span potential. Based on the way human cells divide, scientists place the upper limit of the human life span at about 120 years.

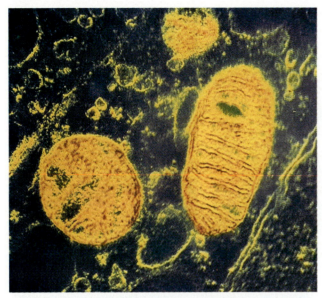

Thousands of mitochondria (magnified here 14,700 times) inhabit every cell in every species. They make adenosine triphosphate (ATP), the chemical that gives us energy. They also age, accumulating damage that can kill cells.

Jere Gottschalk and 11 other men in their sixties and seventies were given human growth hormone three times a week for 6 months in an experiment conducted by Daniel Rudman (1990). In each of the 12 subjects, fat decreased and muscle grew, but when treatment was stopped, all the gains were lost.

Macrobiological Theories

Aging also may be influenced by the immune system, the brain, and homeostasis. Regarding the immune system, in early adulthood, the thymus (a gland in the upper chest whose hormones stimulate the white blood cells needed to fight infection and cancer) has already begun to shrink. As life continues, the immune system loses some of its ability to recognize and attack bacteria and other invaders, as well as cancer cells. The immune cells may also start to attack the body's own healthy cells, possibly producing autoimmune diseases such as rheumatoid arthritis and some kidney ailments (Walford, 1969).

Other scientists argue that the aging timer is located in the brain, more specifically in the hypothalamus and pituitary glands, which are involved in the release of hormones. In this view, beginning at puberty the pituitary gland releases a hormone, or a family of hormones, that causes the body to decline at a programmed rate. This "aging" hormone—which has not yet been isolated or proven to exist—hinders the cell's ability to take in thyroxine, the hormone secreted by the thyroid gland. Thyroxine controls the metabolic rate in the body's key cardiovascular and immune systems, whose failure often is involved in many diseases that kill older individuals.

In an intriguing study conducted to answer the puzzling question of why we age and whether aging can be slowed down, Daniel Rudman and his colleagues (1990) administered human growth hormone (hGH)—a potent secretion of the pituitary gland that helps the body to heal wounds, bolster the immune system, build bones and muscle, and break down fats—to a group of men in their sixties and seventies. A control group of elderly men was not given any human growth hormone. Some members of the control group lost muscle, bone, and organ

mass over the 6-month period of the experiment, while the experimental group that received hGH gained back 10 percent of the muscle mass they had lost through the aging process, had a 9 percent increase in skin thickness, and lost 14 percent of their body fat. Their livers and spleens also regained substantial mass. In effect, says Rudman, the treatment reversed body composition changes that would normally occur in 10 to 20 years of aging.

When the experiment was concluded, every man in the hGH group rapidly lost the youthful characteristics he had gained. Rudman's research documents that more than one aging clock exists. A clock in the genes may ultimately determine the length of our lives, but there is also a clock in the neuroendocrine system that has something to say about aging.

Another part of the neuroendocrine system is also involved in aging. An adrenal hormone, DHEA (short for dehydroepiandrosterone), floods the body while we are young and has a number of beneficial effects on human functioning. When we enter our thirties, production of DHEA begins to ebb. At age 50, most people secrete only about 30 percent of what they produced when they were young, and the loss can be devastating. A DHEA deficiency can increase the risk of breast cancer in women and heart attacks in men. Arthur Schwartz, a researcher on aging, reported that high-dose feedings of DHEA to laboratory animals reduced body fat by one-third, prevented atherosclerosis, alleviated diabetes, reduced the risk of cancer, enhanced the functioning of the immune system, and extended the life span of normal mice by 20 percent. There are side effects: overproduction of sex hormones and liver enlargement. The negative effects of DHEA are reduced to safe levels if appropriate doses of a chemically modified version of the compound are used (Darrach, 1992).

FIGURE 18.1

Biological theories of aging.

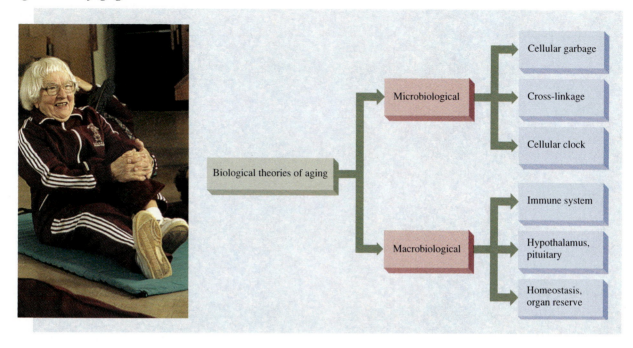

Aging might also be related to the decline in the body's organ reserve. At the level of the organism, life may be defined as internal homeostasis (balance). The body's internal world is balanced and regulated within strict limits. Neural and endocrine systems monitor heart, lungs, liver, kidneys, and other organs to maintain this balance. Biologists estimate that in young adulthood we have an organ reserve that is ten times that required to sustain life. This organ reserve allows a stressed individual to restore homeostasis, or balance, when the body is damaged by something external. But beginning at about 30 years of age, our organ reserve begins a gradual drop that continues through the remainder of our life. Eventually our organ reserve capacity reaches zero, and we die even if a disease is not present. After the age of 30, an individual's mortality rate doubles every 8 years because of this decline in organ reserve (Upton, 1977).

Although no one knows for sure why we age, scientists today believe we have a biological clock that ultimately will be identified. Some scientists argue that the clock resides in the cells of the body, others argue that it lies in the brain or certain glands, and yet others argue that it lies in the homeostatic balance of the body and organ reserve in general. A summary of the theories of aging we have described is shown in figure 18.1.

THE COURSE OF PHYSICAL CHANGES IN LATE ADULTHOOD

Old age does bring greater physical decline than do earlier age periods. We will chronicle these age-related changes in physical decline, but we will emphasize important new developments in aging research that document that bodily powers decline very slowly and that even lost function can sometimes be restored.

The Brain and Nervous System

As we age we lose a number of neurons, the basic cellular units of the nervous system. Some researchers estimate that the loss may be as high as 50 percent over the adult years, although others believe the loss is substantially less and that an accurate assessment of neuron loss has not been made in human brains (Bondareff, 1985). Perhaps a more reasonable estimate is that 5 to 10 percent of our neurons atrophy until we reach the seventies. After that, neuron loss may accelerate.

A significant aspect of the aging process may be that neurons do not replace themselves (Moushegian, 1993). Nonetheless, the brain has remarkable recovery and repair capability, losing only a small portion of its ability to function in the late adulthood years (Labouvie-Vief, 1985). The adaptive nature of the brain was demonstrated in one investigation (Coleman, 1986). From the forties through the seventies, the growth of dendrites increased. Dendrites are the receiving part of the neuron or nerve cell. They are thought to be especially important because they make up approximately 95 percent of the neuron's surface. But in very old people, those in their nineties, dendritic growth was no longer taking place. Dendritic growth may compensate for neuron loss, then, through the seventies, but not when individuals reach their nineties.

Myths have been built up about the aging brain. Among them is the stereotype that all elderly adults lose a majority of their brain cells or experience dramatic deterioration in brain functioning. The welcome news today is that despite some neuron loss, the aging brain can function effectively.

TABLE 18.3

The Perceptual Decline in Old Age and Late Old Age

Perceptual System	Old Age (65–74 years)	Late Old Age (75 years and older)
Vision	Little focusing ability remains, and there is a loss of acuity even with corrective lenses. Less transmission of light occurs through the retina (half as much as in young adults). Greater susceptibility to glare occurs. Color discrimination ability decreases.	There is a significant loss of visual acuity and color discrimination, and a decrease in the size of the perceived visual field. In late old age, people are at significant risk for visual dysfunction from cataracts and glaucoma.
Hearing	There is a significant loss of hearing at high frequencies and some loss at middle frequencies. These losses can be helped by a hearing aid. There is greater susceptibility to masking of what is heard by noise.	There is a significant loss at high and middle frequencies, and a hearing aid is more likely to be needed than in old age.
Taste, smell, and touch	Minor loss.	Significant loss.

Source: Data from N. Charness and E. A. Bosman, "Human Factors and Age" in F. I. M. Craik and T. A. Satthouse (eds.), *The Handbook of Aging, and Cognition,* Lawrence Erlbaum Associates, Inc., 1992, p. 502.

Sensory Development

Sensory physical changes in late adulthood involve vision, hearing, taste, smell, and pain. In late adulthood, the decline in vision that, for most of us, began in early or middle adulthood becomes more pronounced (Kosnick & others, 1989). Night driving becomes especially difficult, to some extent because tolerance for glare diminishes. Dark adaptation is slower, meaning that older individuals take longer to recover their vision when going from well-lighted rooms to semidarkness. The area of the visual field becomes smaller, suggesting that a stimulus's intensity in the peripheral area of the visual field needs to be increased if the stimulus is to be seen. Events taking place away from the center of the visual field may not be detected (Kline & Schieber, 1985).

This visual decline can usually be traced to reduction in the quality or intensity of light reaching the retina. In extreme old age, these changes may be accompanied by degenerative changes in the retina, causing severe difficulty in seeing. Large print books and magnifiers may be needed in such cases. Legal blindness is defined as corrected distance vision of 20/200 in the better eye or a visual field restricted to 20 degrees as large as the diameter. Legal blindness occurs in less than 100 out of every 100,000 individuals under the age of 21; it increases to 1400 out of every 100,000 individuals at the age of 69, still indicating that the vast majority of older adults can see quite well with glasses.

Although hearing impairment may begin in middle adulthood, it usually does not become much of an impediment until late adulthood. Even then, some but not all hearing problems may be corrected by hearing aids. Only 19 percent of individuals from 45 to 54 experience some type of hearing problem, but from 75 to 79 the figure has reached 75 percent (Harris, 1975). It has been estimated that 15 percent of the population over the age of 65 is legally deaf, usually due to the degeneration of the cochlea, the primary neural receptor for hearing in the inner ear (Olsho, Harkins, & Lenhardt, 1985). Wearing two hearing aids that are balanced to correct each ear separately can sometimes help hearing-impaired adults.

Not only do we experience declines in vision and hearing as we age, but we may also become less sensitive to taste and smell. Sensitivity to bitter and sour tastes persists longer than sensitivity to sweet and salty tastes. However, in healthy older adults, there is less decline in sensitivity to taste and smell than in those who are not healthy (Engen, 1977). One loss of sensory sensitivity as we age may be advantageous, though. Older adults are less sensitive to pain and suffer from it less than younger adults. Of course, although decreased sensitivity to pain may help the elderly cope with disease and injury, it can be harmful if it masks injury and illness that need to be treated.

Earlier we indicated that life-span developmentalists are increasingly making distinctions between the young old or old age (ages 65–74) and the old old or late old age (75 years and older). This distinction is important in considering the degree of decline in various perceptual systems. As indicated in table 18.3, the decline in perceptual systems is much greater in late old age than in young old age (Charness & Bosman, 1992).

The Circulatory System

Not long ago it was believed that cardiac output—the amount of blood the heart pumps—declines with age even in healthy adults. However, we now know that when heart disease is absent, the amount of blood pumped is the same regardless of an adult's age. In fact, some experts on aging argue that the healthy heart may even become stronger as we age through the adult years, with capacity increasing, not decreasing (Fozard, 1992).

In the past, a 60-year-old with a blood pressure reading of 160/90 would have been told, "For your age, that is normal." Now medication might be prescribed. Most experts on aging recommend that consistent blood pressures at 160/90 and above should be treated to reduce the risk of heart attack, stroke, or kidney disease (Lakatta, 1992). Blood pressure may rise with age because of illness, obesity, anxiety, stiffening of blood vessels, or lack of exercise. The longer any of these factors persist, the worse the individual's blood pressure gets.

TABLE 18.4

The Six Leading Causes of Death in Americans 65 Years of Age and Older

Rank	Cause of Death	Rate per 100,000 Population in the 65 and Over Age Group
1	Heart disease	2,173
2	Cancer	1,047
3	Cerebrovascular disease (stroke)	464
4	Lung diseases	213
5	Pneumonia and influenza	206
6	Diabetes	96

Source: National Center for Health Statistics, 1987.

The Respiratory System

Lung capacity drops 40 percent between the ages of 20 and 80, even without disease (Fozard, 1992). Lungs lose elasticity, the chest shrinks, and the diaphragm weakens. The good news, though, is that older adults can improve lung functioning with diaphragm-strengthening exercises.

Sexuality

Aging does induce some changes in human sexual performance, more so in the male than in the female. Orgasm becomes less frequent in males, occurring in every second to third act of intercourse rather than every time. More direct stimulation usually is needed to produce an erection. In the absence of two circumstances—actual disease and the belief that old people are or should be asexual—sexuality can be lifelong. Even when actual intercourse is impaired by infirmity, other relationship needs persist, among them closeness, sensuality, and being valued as a man or a woman.

Such a view, of course, is contrary to folklore, to the beliefs of many individuals in society, and even to many physicians and health-care personnel. Fortunately, many elderly individuals went on having sex without talking about it, unabashed by the accepted and destructive social image of the dirty old man and the asexual, undesirable older woman. Bear in mind that many individuals who are now in their eighties were reared when there was a Victorian attitude toward sex. In early surveys of sexual attitudes, older individuals were not asked about their sexuality, possibly because everyone thought they did not have sex or because the investigators believed it would be embarrassing to ask them about sex (Pfeiffer & Davis, 1974).

Various therapies for elderly individuals who report sexual difficulties have been effective. In one investigation, sex education—which consisted largely of simply giving sexual information—led to increased sexual interest, knowledge, and activity in the elderly (White & Catania, 1981).

At this point we have discussed a number of ideas about the nature of longevity and the course of physical decline in late adulthood. A summary of these ideas is presented in concept table 18.1. Now we turn our attention to the nature of health in older adults.

HEALTH

What are the major health problems in old age? What are the main causes of death in older adults?

Health Problems

As we age, the probability we will have some disease or illness increases. For example, the majority of adults who are still alive at the age of 80 are likely to have some impairment.

Chronic disorders *are characterized by a slow onset and a long duration. Chronic disorders rarely develop in early adulthood, increase during middle adulthood, and become common in late adulthood.* As shown in figure 18.2, arthritis is the most common chronic disorder in late adulthood, followed by hypertension. Elderly women have higher incidences of arthritis and hypertension, are more likely to have visual problems, but are less likely to have hearing problems than elderly men are.

> *How many of us older persons have really been prepared for the second half of life, for old age, and eternity?*
> —Carl Jung, *Modern Man in Search of a Soul*, 1933

Although adults over the age of 65 often have a physical impairment, many of them can still carry on their everyday activities or work. Chronic conditions associated with the greatest limitation on work are heart conditions (52 percent), diabetes (34 percent), asthma (27 percent), and arthritis (27 percent) (Harris, 1978). Low income is also strongly related to health problems in late adulthood. Approximately three times as many poor as nonpoor older adults report that their activities are limited by chronic disorders.

Causes of Death in Older Adults

Nearly three-fourths of all older adults die of heart disease, cancer, or cerebrovascular disease (stroke). Chronic lung diseases, pneumonia and influenza, and diabetes round out the six leading causes of death among older adults (see table 18.4). If cancer, the second leading cause of death in older adults, were completely eliminated, the average life expectancy would rise by

CONCEPT TABLE 18.1

Longevity and the Course of Physical Changes in Late Adulthood

Concept	Processes/Related Ideas	Characteristics/Description
Longevity	Life expectancy and life span	Life expectancy is increasing but the life span is not. Among the most important factors in longevity are heredity and family history, health, personality characteristics, and life-style. Beginning at age 25, females outnumber males; this gap widens as individuals age; this sex difference is probably due to social and biological factors.
	The young old, the old old, and the oldest old	Developmentalists are increasingly differentiating the late adult period. Most demarcations involve two subperiods, although agreement on the age cutoffs of these subperiods has not been reached. Distinctions include the young old or old age (65–74 years), the old old or late old age (75 years and older), and the oldest old (85 years and older). The needs, capacities, and resources of the oldest old are often different from those of their young old counterparts. Remember, though, that every period or subperiod of the life span is heterogeneous. Although many of the oldest old have some type of impairment, many others do not. Significant numbers of the oldest old function effectively and are in good health.
	Biological theories of aging	Microbiological theories of aging look within the body's cells for the clues to aging. The most popular microbiological theories are those of cellular garbage, cross-linkage, and the cellular clock. Macrobiological theories look for more global causes of aging than the cellular, microbiological theories. Three popular macrobiological theories involve the immune system, the hypothalamus and pituitary gland, and organ reserve and homeostasis.
The course of physical changes	The brain and nervous system	Although we lose some neurons as we age, the extent to which neuron loss is incapacitating is debated. The brain has remarkable repair capacity. Dendritic growth can take place until adults are very old. Old negative myths about the aging brain are being replaced by more optimistic portrayals.
	Sensory development	The visual system declines in late adulthood, but the vast majority of older adults can have their vision corrected so they can continue to work or function in their world. Hearing decline often begins in middle adulthood, but it usually does not become much of an impediment until late adulthood. Hearing aids can diminish hearing problems for many older adults. Decline in taste and smell may occur, although the decline is barely noticeable in healthy older adults. Sensitivity to pain decreases in late adulthood.
	Circulatory system	When heart disease is absent, the amount of blood pumped is the same regardless of an adult's age. High blood pressure is no longer just accepted in older adults but is treated with medication. Blood pressure can rise in older adults due to a number of factors, many of which can be modified.
	Respiratory system	Lung capacity does drop, but older adults can improve lung functioning with diaphragm-strengthening exercises.
	Sexuality	Aging in late adulthood does include some changes in sexual performance, more so for males than for females. Nonetheless, there are no known age limits to sexual activity.

FIGURE 18.2

The most prevalent chronic conditions in middle and late adulthood.

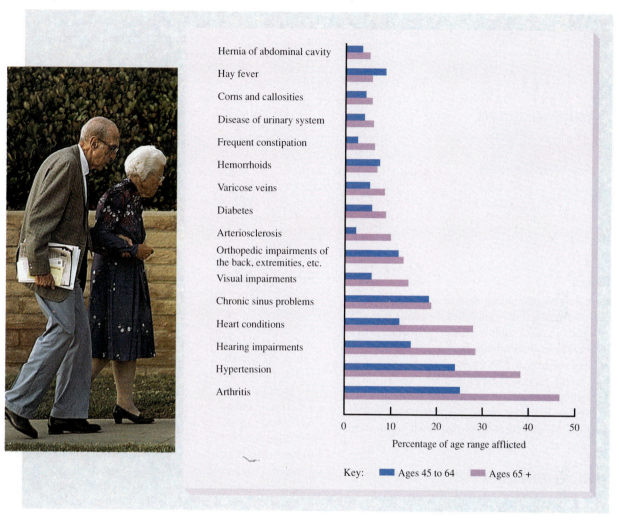

only 1 to 2 years. However, if all cardiovascular and kidney diseases were eradicated, the average life expectancy of older adults would increase by approximately 10 years (Butler, 1975). This increase in longevity is already under way as the number of strokes among older adults has declined considerably in the last several decades. The decline in strokes is due to improved treatment of high blood pressure, a decrease in smoking, better diet, and an increase in exercise.

Arthritis

Arthritis *is an inflammation of the joints accompanied by pain, stiffness, and movement problems. Arthritis is especially common in older adults.* This disorder can affect hips, knees, ankles, fingers, and vertebrae. Individuals with arthritis often experience pain and stiffness, as well as problems in moving about and performing routine daily activities. There is no known cure for arthritis. However, the symptoms of arthritis can be reduced by drugs, such as aspirin, range-of-motion exercises for the afflicted joints, weight reduction, and, in extreme cases, replacement of the crippled joint with a prothesis (Aiken, 1989).

Osteoporosis

Normal aging involves some loss of bone tissue from the skeleton (Kiebzak, 1991). However, in some instances loss of bone tissue can become severe. **Osteoporosis** *is an aging disorder involving an extensive loss of bone tissue. Osteoporosis is the main reason many older adults walk with a marked stoop. Women are especially vulnerable to osteoporosis, the leading cause of broken bones in women.* Almost two-thirds of all women over the age of 60 are affected by osteoporosis. Osteoporosis is more common in White, thin, and small-framed women. This aging disorder is related to deficiencies in calcium, vitamin D, estrogen depletion, and lack of exercise (Dawson-Hughes & others, 1990). To prevent osteoporosis, young and middle-aged women should eat foods rich in calcium, get more exercise, and avoid smoking. Calcium-rich foods include dairy products (low-fat milk and low-fat yogurt, for example) and certain vegetables (such as broccoli, turnip greens, and kale). Estrogen replacement therapy may also be recommended for middle-aged women at especially high risk for developing osteoporosis.

LIFE-SPAN PRACTICAL KNOWLEDGE 18.2

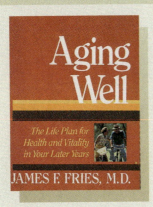

Aging Well

(1989) by James Fries. Reading, MA: Addison-Wesley.

Aging Well explores a number of topics on aging, with a stronger emphasis on the medical and physical dimensions of aging than on the life-style dimensions. Author James Fries is a professor of medicine at Stanford University and a world-renowned expert on aging.

Fries believes we have the capacity to age well—with grace and wisdom, energy and vitality. Aging is not an easy task, he says. It requires a basic understanding of the aging process, a good plan, work, and persistence.

Fries provides a very positive outlook on aging. He believes that even though the aging process may slow us down, our older years can still yield the richest moments of our lives. Fries provides a wealth of information about a number of specific diseases, such as arthritis and osteoporosis, discusses how to deal with doctors, and gives a step-by-step guide to managing a full range of medical problems.

Accidents

Accidents are the seventh leading cause of death among older adults. Injuries resulting from a fall at home or during a traffic accident in which an older adult is a driver or an older pedestrian is hit by a vehicle are common. Each year, approximately 200,000 adults over the age of 65 (most of them women) fracture a hip in a fall. Half of these older adults die within 12 months, frequently from pneumonia. Because healing and recuperation are slower in older adults, an accident that is only a temporary setback for a younger person may result in long-term hospital or home care for an older adult.

The Robust Oldest Old

Our image of the oldest old (eighties and older) is predominantly of being disabled and frail. The implications of the projected rapid growth of the oldest old population have often been unremittingly pessimistic—an expensive burden of chronic disability in which the oldest old often require the everyday help of other persons. However, as we discussed earlier in this chapter, the oldest old are a heterogeneous group, and until recently this diversity has not been adequately recognized. Although almost one-fourth of the oldest old are institutionalized, the majority live in the community and remain independent (Suzman, Harris, & others, 1992).

Because so much attention has been given to chronic disabilities of the oldest old, those who have aged successfully have gone virtually unnoticed and unstudied. An increased interest in successful aging is producing a more optimistic portrayal of the oldest old than was painted in the past (Rowe & Kahn, 1987). Health service researchers are discovering that a relatively large portion of people in old age are low-cost users of medical services; a small percentage account for a large fraction of expenditures, and this usually occurs in the last year of life, a period that is expensive at any age (Scitovsky, 1988). A surprisingly large portion of the oldest old not only do not require personal assistance on a daily basis but also are physically robust, and some who are not initially robust recover their robustness.

In a longitudinal study of a national sample of adults 80 years and older, 33 percent were classified as robust based on the following criteria: no difficulty in walking ¼ mile, stooping, crouching, kneeling, lifting 10 pounds, or walking up 10 steps without resting (Harris & others, 1989; Suzman, Harris, & others, 1992). About three-fourths of the robust older adults had no hospitalizations and had fewer than six doctor visits in the previous 12 months.

In this and other studies of very old adults, a sizable portion of individuals have been discovered to be free of disability, able to cope with their disabilities free of assistance, or able to recover their functioning over time (Harris & others, 1989; Manton, 1989). Cataract surgery and a variety of rehabilitation strategies are being used to improve the functioning of the oldest old. Later in this chapter we will discuss a number of studies that reveal how exercise programs improve strength and mobility in older persons. For example, in one investigation, 8 weeks of leg-strength training markedly improved the walking ability of nursing home residents who averaged 90 years of age (Fiatarone & others, 1990). A number of promising approaches to preventing or intervening in osteoporosis are being developed, including calcium supplementation, estrogen replacement, and other hormone therapies.

In sum, earlier portraits of the oldest old have been stereotypical. A substantial subgroup of the oldest old are robust and active, and there is cause for optimism in the development of new regimens of prevention and intervention (Suzman, Harris, & others, 1992).

HEALTH TREATMENT

What are the health costs of the elderly and how are they handled? What is the quality of nursing homes and other extended care facilities for older adults? What is the nature of the relationship between older adults and health-care providers? We consider each of these questions in turn.

Health Costs

Compared to individuals under the age of 65, the elderly spend more days in bed, visit doctors more often, have longer and more frequent stays in hospitals, and consume more medications (Aiken, 1989). The expenses associated with these health problems would be impossible for most elderly adults and their families to meet without turning to the federal and state government agencies for assistance. Expenditures for health-care costs are heading toward an average of $5,000 per person per year for individuals 65 years and older. Medicare and Medicaid, the federal government's health-care programs for the elderly, account for approximately two-thirds of the elderly's health-care costs. Escalating medical costs are stimulating considerable discussion about better ways to meet the health-care needs of older adults (DeFriese & Womert, 1991). One consideration is for the government to pay for long-term, home-based care, which is much less costly than nursing home residency. Another consideration is some form of national health insurance. Continued reevaluation of the government's role in health care for the elderly is needed because, despite billions of dollars appropriated each year by the federal government for Medicare and Medicaid, medical bills often deplete the savings and income of many older adults.

Nursing Homes

Only about 5 percent of adults 65 years of age and over reside in a nursing home at any point in time in our society. However, as older adults age, their probability of being in a nursing home or other extended care facility increases (Baines, 1991). Twenty-three percent of adults 85 years of age and older live in nursing homes or other extended care facilities.

Three kinds of services or levels of nursing care are provided by various types of nursing homes. In a *skilled* nursing facility, the most extensive nursing care is found. This type of nursing home is carefully reviewed and monitored by federal and state governments. In an *intermediate or ordinary* nursing facility, nursing care is less extensive than in a skilled nursing facility. In a *residential* nursing facility, qualification standards are the least restrictive. Residential nursing care is mainly routine "maintenance" and personal assistance in meeting day-to-day needs. Residential care may include provision for some rehabilitation. The costs for residential care are lower than for the other two types of nursing homes.

The quality of nursing homes and other extended care facilities for elderly adults varies enormously and is a source of continuing national concern (Cherry, 1991; Kanda & Mezey, 1991). Investigations of nursing homes reveal that more than one-third are seriously deficient in one or more areas. Even many of the skilled nursing homes are unaccredited (they fail to pass federally mandated inspections) because they do not meet the minimum standards for physicians, pharmacists, and various rehabilitation specialists (occupational and physical therapists). Further concerns focus on the patient's right to privacy, access to medical information, safety, and life-style freedom within the individual's range of mental and physical capabilities.

Giving nursing home residents options for control and teaching them coping skills are important factors in their health and psychological well-being.

The decision to place an elderly parent or relative in a nursing home or other extended care facility is often preceded by a number of years of attempting to cope with the increasing physical and emotional demands of caretaking (Rybash, Roodin, & Santrock, 1991). The decision to place an elderly person in a nursing home is often a stressful one. Anticipation of a move to a nursing home raises the following concerns among the elderly: How well will I adjust to living in a nursing home? How much independence will I lose and how dependent will I become on the staff? What is the quality and availability of medical care? Will they give me tender loving care? Do they have sufficient space?

Nursing home costs continue to escalate each year. A survey of adults conducted by the American Association of Retired Persons (1990) indicated they believe that protection against the high cost of nursing homes is the most important coverage in a long-term health-care program. The average cost of staying in a nursing home for 1 year ranges from $25,000 to $34,000. Medicare only pays for 100 days a year, and patients must share the cost after 20 days. Most older adults need supplemental nursing home insurance, yet few obtain this coverage. They incorrectly believe that Medicare or other government programs will cover all of their hospital and nursing home expenses, or they find nursing home insurance premiums to be too expensive. In the AARP survey, 88 percent of the adults said they would support a government-sponsored program to cover the costs of nursing home care.

Because of the inadequate quality of many nursing homes and the escalating costs of nursing home care, many gerontologists and geriatric specialists (*geriatrics* is the branch of medicine dealing with the health problems of the aged) believe alternatives to nursing homes need to be considered. These alternatives include home health care, day-care centers, and preventive medicine clinics (Aiken, 1989; Miller, 1991). The alternatives are potentially less expensive than hospitals and nursing homes, and are also less likely to engender feelings of depersonalization and dependency that occur so often among residents of institutions.

Ellen Langer (left) and Judith Rodin conducted a classic study of perceived control in nursing homes. They found that perceived control over their environment literally was a matter of life or death for the elderly nursing home residents.

Giving Options for Control and Teaching Coping Skills

An important factor related to health, and even survival, in a nursing home is the patient's feelings of control and self-determination (Baltes & Wahl, 1991; Schmidt, 1990). In one investigation, a group of elderly nursing home residents were encouraged to make more day-to-day choices and thus feel they had more responsibility for and control over their lives (Rodin & Langer, 1977). They began to decide such matters as what they ate, when their visitors could come, what movies they saw, and who could come to their rooms. A similar group in the same nursing home was told by the administrator how caring the nursing home was and how much the staff wanted to help, but these elderly nursing home residents were given no opportunities to take more control over their lives. Eighteen months later, the residents given responsibility and control were more alert and active, and said they were happier, than the residents who were only encouraged to feel that the staff would try to satisfy their needs. And the "responsible" or "self-control" group had significantly better improvement in their health than did the "dependent" group. Even more important was the finding that after 18 months only half as many nursing home residents in the "responsibility" group had died as in the "dependent" group. Perceived control over one's environment, then, may literally be a matter of life or death.

In another investigation, Richard Schulz (1976) gave nursing home residents different amounts of control over visits they received from local college students. Having control over the visits, or at least advance information about them, made the nursing home residents more active, happier, and healthier, probably because control makes life less stressful by making it more predictable. When the experiment ended, so did the visits by the college students. In a follow-up 2 years later, the researchers found that the nursing home residents who had been given control over scheduling of visits, and then had the visits, and the control, taken away, were doing worse psychologically than the others (Schulz & Hanusa, 1978). Loss of control may even be worse than lack of control in some cases.

How can a psychological factor, such as the feeling of control, have such dramatic effects on health? American psychologist Judith Rodin (1986, 1990; Rodin & Timko, 1991) says that individuals who believe they have a high degree of control are more likely to feel that their actions can make a difference in their lives, so they are more likely to take better care of themselves by eating healthier foods and exercising. In contrast, those who have reduced feelings of control are likely to feel that what they do will not make a difference, and thus do not even bother to try to make a difference. Rodin also believes that the perception of control can have a direct effect on the body. For example, being in control reduces stress and its stress-related hormones. When stress-related hormones remain elevated, there is more wear and tear on the body; high blood pressure, heart disease, arthritis, and certain types of ulcers have all been linked with excessive stress.

Following up on this line of thinking, Rodin (1983) measured stress-related hormones in several groups of nursing home residents and then taught the residents coping skills to help them deal better with day-to-day problems. She taught the residents how to say no when they did not want something, without worrying whether they would offend someone. She gave them assertiveness training, and she also taught them time management skills. After the training, the nursing home residents had greatly reduced levels of cortisol, a hormone closely related to stress that has been implicated in a number of diseases. The cortisol levels of the "assertive training" residents remained lower, even after 18 months. Further, these nursing home residents were healthier and had a reduced need for medication, compared to residents who had not been taught the coping skills. In sum, Rodin's research has shown that simply giving nursing home residents options for control and teaching them coping skills can change their behavior and improve their health (Trotter, 1990).

Critical Thinking

Other than giving options for control and teaching coping skills, can you think of other psychological interventions that could benefit nursing home residents?

In yet another investigation, Charles Alexander and his colleagues (1989) taught transcendental meditation (TM) to a group of octogenarians in eight Boston-area nursing homes. The elderly adults practiced TM for 20 minutes a day for 3 years. One hundred percent of them were still alive after 3 years, while 38 percent of a control group of elderly residents who did not practice TM daily had died during the same period of time. Legends of Himalayan yogis using similar techniques and living for more than 100 years have to be taken with a grain of salt (there is no legitimate documentation of their longevity), but Alexander and Langer's experiment documented that meditation can be added to the list of coping strategies that can help people live longer.

The Older Adult and Health-Care Providers

The attitudes of both the health-care provider and the older adult are important aspects of the older adult's health care (Morse & Johnson, 1991). Unfortunately, health-care providers too often share society's stereotypes and negative attitudes toward the elderly. In a health-care setting, these attitudes can take the form of avoidance, dislike, and begrudged tolerance rather than positive, hopeful treatment. Health-care personnel are more likely to be interested in treating younger persons who more often have acute problems with a higher prognosis for successful recovery than older persons who are more likely to have chronic problems with a lower prognosis for successful recovery (Butler, 1975).

Health-care personnel also report that they have a more difficult time communicating with older persons than younger persons. In one investigation, the communication between a group of middle-aged physicians and their patients of different ages was examined (Greene & others, 1987). The physicians raised fewer psychosocial issues (asking patients questions about their general anxieties and worries, feelings of depression, economic problems, leisure activities, family relationships, and so on) with older patients than younger patients. And when the older patients raised psychosocial concerns, the physicians were less responsive to them than when their younger patients raised such issues. Such findings are important because older adults are more satisfied with their physicians and show better improvement in their health when physicians raise various psychosocial issues or respond positively when older patients want to talk about psychosocial issues.

Not only are physicians less responsive to older patients, but older patients often take a less active role in medical encounters with health-care personnel than do younger patients (Woodward & Wallston, 1987). Older adults should be encouraged to take a more active role in their own health care. To read further about how the elderly can learn to deal with the health-care industry, turn to Perspectives on Parenting and Education 18.1.

EXERCISE, NUTRITION, AND WEIGHT

An important aspect of preventing health problems in older adults and improving their health is to encourage individuals to exercise more and to develop better nutritional habits.

Exercise

Although we may be in the evening of our lives in late adulthood, we are not meant to live out our remaining years passively. Everything we know about older adults suggests they are healthier and happier the more active they are. The possibility that regular exercise can lead to a healthier late adulthood, and possibly extend life, has been raised (O'Brien & Vertinsky, 1991; Schilke, 1991).

In one study, the cardiovascular fitness of 101 older men and women (average age = 67 years) was examined (Blumenthal & others, 1989). The older adults were randomly assigned to an aerobic exercise group, a yoga and flexibility control group, and a waiting list control group. The program lasted 4 months. Prior to and following the 4-month program, the older adults underwent comprehensive physiological examinations. In the aerobic group, the older adults participated in three supervised exercise sessions per week for 16 weeks. Each session consisted of a 10-minute warm-up, 30 minutes of continuous exercise on a stationary bicycle, 15 minutes of brisk walking/jogging, and a 5-minute cool-down. In the yoga and flexibility control group, the older adults participated in 60 minutes of supervised yoga exercises at least twice a week for 16 weeks. Over the 4-month period, the cardiovascular fitness—such as peak oxygen consumption, cholesterol level, and blood pressure—of the aerobic exercise group significantly improved. In contrast, the cardiovascular fitness of the yoga and waiting list groups did not improve.

In another investigation, exercise literally meant a difference in life or death for middle-aged and older adults (Blair, 1990; Blair & Kohl, 1988). More than 17,000 men and women were studied at the Aerobic Institute in Dallas, Texas. Sedentary participants were more than twice as likely to die during the 8-year time span of the study than those who were moderately fit. Examples of exercise programs included running 2 miles in 20 minutes twice a week or walking 3 miles in 45 minutes twice a week. In yet another recent study, changes in level of physical activity and cigarette smoking were associated with risk of death

PERSPECTIVES ON PARENTING AND EDUCATION 18.1

Learning How to Deal With Health-Care Personnel

The elderly should seek out doctors who will fully answer their questions on anything from the implications of physical and mental symptoms to medications and their side effects. The elderly should not be afraid to move on if they don't like a doctor, even though it might be inconvenient. Robert Butler, former head of the National Institute of Aging, says that some doctors put off Medicare and Medicaid patients by offering them appointments weeks or months away. Not much can be done about that, because doctors are not required to take Medicare patients. Doctors who do see the elderly but say their complaints come from being old ("You should just take it easy") should seek another doctor. Being told to take it easy is one of the worst prescriptions a doctor can give to an elderly person, because remaining active is the best medicine for older people, says Butler.

There are good and caring doctors for the elderly. Once elderly people find one, the following rules of thumb can help them cope effectively with their health problems (Podolsky & Silberner, 1993):

Speak Up   If the elderly want more aggressive care, they need to speak up, ask their doctors to give them alternatives for treatment, and ask for explanations of things they don't understand. They can help their doctors by bringing to their office visits all of the drugs they are taking.

Question Assertions Based Solely on Age   Often such statements are based on limited information and subjective expectations. The elderly need to bear in mind that their physiological age—how well their body works—is often more relevant to their treatment than is their chronological age.

Get the Family Involved   Doctors and nurses who care for the elderly say that frustrated families, battling to stave off the death of a loved one who is going to die no matter what, often push medical professionals into giving heroic care that can't help. Both family and doctor need a clear idea of the care patients want, if the patients are unable to speak for themselves. Guessing can be tragic. In a survey of 70 patients, the patients predicted that doctors and loved ones would know what they wanted done if they became senile and then had a heart attack. But the physicians were wrong half the time, and the patients' families were not much better in their predictions.

Decide Now   The Patient Self-Determination Act, which became effective in December 1991, requires hospitals to inform patients on admission that they can refuse life-sustaining treatment. However, only people who are alert and conscious are offered the directives. Filling out a living will while an elderly person is feeling fine may upset the elderly person's family, but it is better than becoming a headline. Once patients are incapacitated, it is too late for them to give instructions about their medical care.

during the middle and late adulthood years (Paffenbarger & others, 1993). Beginning moderately vigorous sports activity from the forties through the eighties was associated with a 23 percent lower risk of death, quitting cigarette smoking with a 41 percent lower death risk.

Gerontologists are increasingly recommending strength training in addition to aerobic activity and stretching for older adults (Butler, 1993; Evans, 1993). The average person's lean body mass declines with age—about 6.6 pounds of lean muscle are lost each decade during the adult years. The rate of loss accelerates after age 45. Also, the average percentage ratio of muscle to fat for a 60- to 70-year-old woman is 44 percent fat. In a 20-year-old woman the ratio is 23 to 24 percent. Weight lifting can preserve and possibly increase muscle mass in older adults. As yet researchers do not know whether muscle loss can be completely stopped through weight lifting, but it is clear that adults in their sixties and seventies who are working out do have considerably more muscle than do their counterparts in their twenties who do no weight lifting.

Exercise is an excellent way to maintain health. Researchers are continuing to document its positive effects in older adults (Kirwan & others, 1993). Exercise helps people to live independent lives with dignity in late adulthood. At 80, 90, and even 100 years of age, exercise can help prevent elderly adults from falling down or even being institutionalized. Being physically fit means being able to do the things you want to do, whether you are young or old. More about researchers' investigations into exercise's positive benefits for health is shown in figure 18.3.

LIFE-SPAN PRACTICAL KNOWLEDGE 18.3

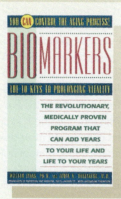

Biomarkers

(1991) by William Evans and Irwin Rosenberg. New York: Simon & Schuster.

Based on recent data from their research on human nutrition and exercise, William Evans and Irwin Rosenberg reveal how 50 minutes a day of aerobic exercise and strength training can slow the aging process. They identify 10 biomarkers—key physiological factors—that are associated with youth and vitality:

- Lean body mass
- Strength
- Basal metabolism rate
- Body fat percentage
- Aerobic capacity
- Blood pressure
- Insulin sensitivity
- Cholesterol/HDL ratio
- Bone density
- Body temperature regulation

The authors provide dietary guidelines, self-tests for evaluating physical fitness, and exercise programs for every fitness level.

All we know about older adults indicates that they are healthier and happier the more active they are. Several decades ago, it was believed that older adults should be more passive and inactive to be well adjusted and satisfied with life. In today's world, we believe that while older adults may be in the evening of life's human cycle, they were not meant to passively live out their remaining years.

FIGURE 18.3

The jogging hog experiment. *Jogging hogs have shown the dramatic effects of exercise on health. In one investigation, a group of hogs were trained to run approximately 100 miles per week (Bloor & White, 1983). Then, the researchers narrowed the arteries that supplied blood to the hogs' hearts. The hearts of the jogging hogs developed extensive alternate pathways for blood supply, and 42 percent of the threatened heart tissue was salvaged compared to only 17 percent in a control group of nonjogging hogs.*

Nutrition and Weight

English philosopher and essayist Francis Bacon (1561–1626) was the first author to recommend scientific evaluation of diet and longevity. He advocated a frugal diet. Does a restricted intake of food increase longevity or could it possibly even extend the human life span?

Scientists have accumulated considerable evidence that food restriction in laboratory animals (in most cases rats) can increase the animals' life span (Adelman, 1988; Dax & others, 1989). Animals fed diets restricted in calories, although adequate in protein, vitamins, and minerals, live as much as 40 percent longer than animals given unlimited access to food. And chronic problems such as kidney disease appear at a later age. Diet restriction also delays biochemical alterations such as the age-related rise in cholesterol observed in both humans and animals. Whether similar very low-calorie diets (in some instances the animals eat 40 percent less than normal) can stretch the human life span is not known. Most nutritional experts do not recommend very low-calorie diets for older adults; rather, they recommend a well-balanced, low-fat diet that includes the nutritional factors needed to maintain good health.

Leaner men do live longer, healthier lives. In one recent study of 19,297 Harvard alumni, those weighing the least were less likely to die over the past three decades (Lee & others, 1993). The men were divided into five categories according to body mass index (a complex formula that takes into account weight and height). As body mass increased, so did risk of death. The most overweight men had a 67% higher risk of dying than the thinnest men. For example, the heaviest men (such as 181 pounds or more for a 5-foot-10-inch man) also had 2½ times the risk of death from cardiovascular disease. Currently, these researchers are studying the relation of body mass index to longevity in women and predict similar results to the study with men.

The Growing Vitamin-and-Aging Controversy

For years, most experts on aging and health argued that a balanced diet was all that was needed for successful aging; vitamin supplements were not recommended. However, an increasing number of research studies are raising questions about the practice of not recommending vitamin supplements for middle-aged and older adults. The new research suggests that some vitamin supplements—mainly a group called "antioxidants," which includes vitamin C, vitamin E, and beta-carotene—may help to slow the aging process and improve the health of older adults (Miller, 1993).

Antioxidants are thought to counteract the cell damage caused by oxygen-free radicals, which are produced both by the body's own metabolism and by environmental factors such as smoking, pollution, and bad chemicals in the diet. When free radicals cause damage (oxidation) in one cell, a chain reaction of damage follows. Antioxidants act much like a fire extinguisher, helping to neutralize free-radical activity. For example, in two recent studies, people who took vitamin E supplements for 2 years significantly reduced their risk of heart disease—by up to 40 percent (Rimm & others, 1993; Stampfer & others, 1993).

There is no evidence that antioxidants can increase the human life span, but an increasing number of aging and health experts believe they can reduce a person's risk of becoming frail and sick in the later adult years. Some experts on aging say that although the vitamin supplement research looks promising, there are still a lot of blanks and uncertainties in what we know (Stern, 1993). That is, we don't know which vitamins should be taken, how large a dose should be taken, what the restraints are, and so on. Critics also argue that the key experimental studies that document the effectiveness of the vitamins in slowing the aging process have not been conducted. The studies in this area so far have been so-called population studies that are correlational rather than experimental in nature. Other factors—such as exercise, better health practices, and good nutritional habits—might be responsible for the positive findings about vitamins and aging rather than vitamins per se. Also, the free radical theory is a theory and not a fact, and is only one of a number of theories about why we age.

With these uncertainties in mind, some aging experts still are recommending that vitamin supplements in the following range are unlikely to be harmful in any way and could benefit the aging process (Blumberg, 1993): 250 to 1000 mg of vitamin C, 100 to 400 IU of vitamin E, and 15 to 30 mg of beta-carotene. In the next several decades we will likely see considerable refinement of our knowledge about vitamin supplements and the aging process.

At this point we have discussed a number of important ideas about health and health treatment, and about excercise, nutrition, and weight, in older adults. A summary of these ideas is presented in concept table 18.2.

LIFE-SPAN HEALTH AND WELL-BEING

Explorations in the Health Care of the Elderly

Too many elderly people get shoddy medical care. Consider the following facts about the elderly and their health care:

- Older adults consume about twice as much medicine as all other age groups combined and fill about 40 percent of the nation's hospital beds.
- Nearly two-thirds of heart-drug trials have excluded older adults over the age of 75—those who are most likely to die from heart disease.
- Half of the elderly population over the age of 75 don't report vision, hearing, walking, or dental problems to medical-care personnel because they think such problems are inevitable.
- In the past 15 years, the cancer rate has dropped 5 percent for people 65 years of age and younger, but it has risen 13 percent for those over the age of 65.
- The elderly do not always experience classic symptoms of medical problems and illnesses. A heart attack may be signaled by fatigue rather than crushing chest pain.
- Women over the age of 65 are twice as likely as younger women to develop breast cancer and are half as likely to be treated appropriately if they do.

Improving the health care of the elderly starts with training. At a time when the nation's elderly population is dramatically increasing, only 8 of the nation's 126 medical schools require separate courses on geriatric medicine. By contrast, pediatrics and obstetrics courses are required at virtually all medical schools. And only now are the elderly just beginning to be included in research trials, which doctors routinely rely on to formulate treatment strategies. Of more than 5,400 patients and 18 types of cancer at the University of Wisconsin Cancer Center, patients over 75 were

Ira Baldwin, age 97, was told he would die, but he chose to fight instead. In 1990, after physicians told him that his rare form of liver cancer was incurable, he searched for a doctor who would help seek a cure. Paul Carbone of the University of Wisconsin Cancer Center took Baldwin's challenge. The drug alpha interferon initially kept the cancer in check, but when the tumor started to grow again, Baldwin was switched to a platinum-based drug. Baldwin says he feels fine after the switch (Podolsky & Silberner, 1993).

one-third as likely as younger patients to be offered radiation and chemotherapy. Such findings may explain why the overall cancer rate during the past 15 years has gone up 13 percent for people over 65 but declined 5 percent for younger people. Ironically, most older people are as likely to benefit from cancer treatments as younger people. Surprisingly, older people may respond *better* to treatment for many tumors of the breast, lung, colon, and prostate, according to William Ershler, director of the University of Wisconsin Institute on Aging. Such tumors appear to be less aggressive in older people, possibly because the levels of body chemicals that stimulate cancer cells to multiply subside with age.

Doctors also undertreat older adults with heart disease, the leading killer of the elderly. The aged are less likely to receive medications that reduce the heart attack death rate, such as clotbusters, aspirin, and rhythm regulators like beta-blockers. In a recent editorial in the *New England Journal of Medicine*, it was concluded that older adults over the age of 75 receive clotbusting drugs one-sixth as often as younger adults do (Topol & Califf, 1992). Why? Doctors may worry about

the risk of bleeding or stroke from the drugs. However, five recent clotbuster trials failed to demonstrate a link between age and either stroke or bleeding. In fact, the trials revealed that the older the clotbuster recipient, the greater the benefit.

Overtreatment of the elderly is often just as much a problem as undertreatment. Older adults are prone to medical overload because they are so extensively exposed to doctors, according to Eugene Robin, professor emeritus of medicine at Stanford University Medical School. In various recent studies of elderly patients, 17 percent of coronary angiographies (X rays of the blood vessels that nourish the heart), one-third of carotid endarterectomies (cholesterol-clearing operations on blood vessels in the neck), 17 percent of upper GI endoscopies (visual inspections of the gastrointestinal tract), and 44 percent of coronary bypasses have been judged to have been superfluous, inappropriate, or questionable.

In summary, we need better and more informed health-care treatment for the elderly. The elderly need to insist on their rights and get careful, competent health-care advice (Podolsky & Silberner, 1993). ■

CONCEPT TABLE 18.2

Health, Health Treatment, and Exercise, Nutrition, and Weight

Concept	Processes/Related Ideas	Characteristics/Description
Health	Health problems	As we age, the probability that we will have some disease or illness increases. Chronic disorders rarely develop in early adulthood, increase in middle adulthood, and become common in late adulthood. The most common chronic problem is arthritis, followed by hypertension.
	Causes of death in older adults	Nearly three-fourths of older adults die of heart disease, cancer, or cerebrovascular disease (stroke).
	Arthritis	Arthritis is an inflammation of the joints accompanied by pain, stiffness, and movement problems. Arthritis is especially common among older adults.
	Osteoporosis	Osteoporosis is an aging disorder involving an extensive loss of bone tissue. Osteoporosis is the main reason many older adults walk with a stoop. Women are especially vulnerable to osteoporosis.
	Accidents	Accidents are the seventh leading cause of death among older adults. Accidents are usually more debilitating to older adults than to younger adults.
	The robust oldest old	Although chronic disorders increase in late adulthood, even a substantial portion of the oldest old are robust. Early portraits of the oldest old were too stereotypical. There is cause for optimism in the development of new regimens of prevention and intervention.
Health treatment	Health costs	Compared to individuals under the age of 65, the elderly spend more days in bed, visit doctors more often, have longer and more frequent stays in the hospital, and consume more medications. Health-care costs for the elderly are escalating. Government programs, such as Medicare and Medicaid, cover approximately two-thirds of the older adult's health-care costs.
	Nursing homes	Although only 5 percent of adults 65 and over reside in nursing homes, 23 percent of adults 85 and over do. Three types of nursing homes are skilled, intermediate or ordinary, and residential. The quality of nursing homes varies enormously. The decision to place an elderly person in a nursing home is often a stressful one. Nursing home costs are escalating, and alternatives to nursing homes are being proposed.

Concept	Processes/Related Ideas	Characteristics/Description
	Giving options for control, and teaching coping skills	Simply giving nursing home residents options for control and teaching coping skills can change their behavior and improve their health.
	The older adult and health-care providers	The attitudes of both the health-care provider and the older adult patient are important aspects of the older adult's health care. Too often health-care personnel share society's negative view of older adults. Discussion of psychosocial issues with the older patient and encouragement of the older adult patient's active role in medical care are recommended strategies.
Exercise, nutrition, and weight	Exercise	Although there may be some need for reduction in exercise in late adulthood, the physical benefits of exercise have been demonstrated. Recently, researchers documented a relation between exercise and longevity, but no evidence exists that exercise can extend the human life span. Weight lifting is increasingly being recommended in addition to aerobic fitness.
	Nutrition and weight	Food restriction in animals can increase the animals' life span, but whether this works with humans is not known. In humans, being overweight is associated with an increased mortality rate. Most nutritional experts recommend a well-balanced, low-fat diet for older adults, but do not recommend an extremely low-calorie diet.
	The growing vitamin-and-aging controversy	For years, vitamin supplements were not recommended for older adults; a healthy, well-balanced diet was all that was needed for successful aging, said the aging experts. However, a growing amount of evidence suggests that vitamin supplements in the form of antioxidants—vitamin C, vitamin E, and beta-carotene—may slow the aging process and improve the health of older adults. Critics, however, caution that the key experimental studies on aging and vitamins have not been conducted and that the free radical theory is but one of a number of theories of aging, none of which have been proven as fact.

CONCLUSIONS

Although we may be in the evening of our lives when we are in late adulthood, there are a number of keys to aging successfully and achieving health and well-being as elderly adults.

We began this chapter by reading about the change that exercise made in the life of 85-year-old Sadie Halperin, then we explored a number of ideas about longevity, including life expectancy and life span, the young old, the old old, and the oldest old, and biological theories of aging. Next, we examined the course of physical changes in late adulthood that involve the brain and nervous system, sensory development, the circulatory system, the respiratory system, and sexuality. Our coverage of health in late adulthood focused on health problems, causes of death in older adults, arthritis, osteoporosis, accidents, and the robust oldest old. Then we studied health treatment of older adults by examining health costs, nursing homes, giving options for control and coping skills, and the older adult and health-care providers. And we evaluated the roles of exercise, nutrition and weight, and the growing vitamin-and-aging controversy in late adulthood. At different points in the chapter we also studied aging in Russia, Ecuador, and Kashmir, learning how to deal with health-care providers, and various dimensions of health care and the elderly.

Don't forget that you can obtain an overall summary of the chapter by again reading the two concept tables on pages 522 and 532. In the next chapter, we consider another important dimension of the journey through late adulthood by exploring the cognitive aspects of late adulthood and aging.

KEY TERMS

life span   The upper boundary of life, the maximum number of years an individual can live. The maximum life span of human beings is about 120 years of age. (513)

life expectancy   The number of years that will probably be lived by the average person born in a particular year. (513)

microbiological theories of aging
Theories that look within the body's cells to explain aging. (517)

macrobiological theories of aging
Theories that examine life at a more global level of analysis than the cell. (517)

chronic disorders   Disorders that are characterized by slow onset and long duration. They rarely develop in early adulthood, they increase during middle adulthood, and they become common in late adulthood. (521)

arthritis   Especially common in older adults, arthritis is an inflammation of the joints that is accompanied by pain, stiffness, and movement problems. (523)

osteoporosis   Disorder of aging that involves an extensive loss of bone tissue and is the main reason many older adults walk with a marked stoop. Women are especially vulnerable to osteoporosis. (523)

Rembrandt, Old Woman
Reading, detail.

Cognitive Development in Late Adulthood

Chapter Outline

LIFE-SPAN HEALTH AND WELL-BEING

*Trends in the Mental Health Care
of Older Adults 551*

Chapter Boxes

*The night hath not yet come: We are not
quite cut off from labor by the failing
light; some work remains for us to do and
dare.*

—Henry Wadsworth Longfellow,
Morituri Salutamous, 1875

It is always in season for the old to learn.

Aeschylus, 524–456 B.C.

IMAGES OF LIFE-SPAN DEVELOPMENT

Facing Retirement

Imagine that you are a healthy 60-year-old faced with the possibility of early retirement from a position with a large corporation. Your career has been successful and you have received steady increases in pay. However, you have not been given a major promotion in the last 10 years. You sense that the company has put you on the shelf and is simply waiting for you to retire so that a younger employee on the way up can fill your position. Further, the company is offering attractive early-retirement options that are beginning to look tempting to you. Indeed, the com-

pany recently paid your way (and that of other employees in their late fifties and early sixties) to a retirement seminar at a golf resort. You attended several sessions led by psychologists that focused on the benefits of early retirement. One psychologist commented, "Early retirement will allow you to travel and pursue your own interests while you are young enough to still have your health." The sessions were thought-provoking. What should you do?

On the one hand, you enjoy your work. You know that you are competent

at your job and do many good things for the company (although you don't think they are always appreciated). You believe that you are every bit as sharp as the younger employees in your department. Your greater experience has been invaluable on countless occasions when critical decisions had to be made. And, aside from a little arthritis, your health is excellent and you have not missed a day of work in 15 years. So, why should you retire?

PREVIEW

Later in this chapter, we will discuss the changing worlds of work and retirement in late adulthood. We also will evaluate the nature of older adults' mental health. But to begin we will examine the debate about whether older adults are less intelligent than younger adults.

COGNITIVE FUNCTIONING IN OLDER ADULTS

At the age of 70, Dr. John Rock introduced the birth control pill. At age 89, Arthur Rubinstein gave one of his best performances at New York's Carnegie Hall. From 85 to 90 years of age, Pablo Picasso completed three sets of drawings. And at age 76, Anna Mary Robertson Moses took up painting: as Grandma Moses, she became internationally famous and staged fifteen one-woman shows throughout Europe. Are these feats rare exceptions?

> *Age only matters when one is aging. Now that I have arrived at a great age, I might just as well be twenty.*
> —Picasso

The Debate About Intellectual Decline in Late Adulthood

The issue of intellectual decline through the adult years is a provocative one. David Wechsler (1972), who developed the Wechsler scales of intelligence, concluded that adulthood is characterized by intellectual decline due to the aging process everyone experiences. But the issue is more complex. For example, John Horn thinks some abilities decline while others do not (Horn & Donaldson, 1980). Horn argues that **crystallized intelligence,** *an individual's accumulated information and verbal skills, increases with age,* while **fluid intelligence,** *one's ability to reason abstractly, steadily declines from middle adulthood* (see figure 19.1).

Paul Baltes and K. Warner Schaie seriously question Horn's claims (Baltes, 1987; Schaie, 1984). They believe that many of the data on intelligence and aging, such as Horn's, are

FIGURE 19.1

Fluid and crystallized intellectual development across the life span.
According to Horn, crystallized intelligence (based on cumulative learning experiences) increases throughout the life span, but fluid intelligence (the ability to perceive and manipulate information) steadily declines from middle adulthood.

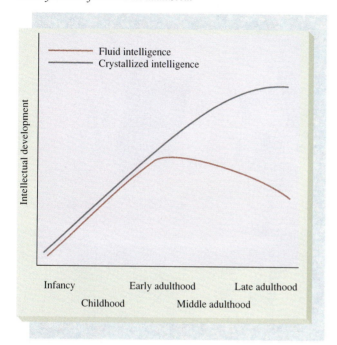

FIGURE 19.2

Intellectual development in adulthood: a comparison of cross-sectional and longitudinal data. *In one investigation involving a test of verbal intelligence, when the cross-sectional strategy was used, test scores decreased in the middle and late adulthood years (Schaie & Strother, 1968). However, when the longitudinal strategy was followed (adults tested over a number of years), intelligence test scores increased until late adulthood, at which point they only slightly decreased.*

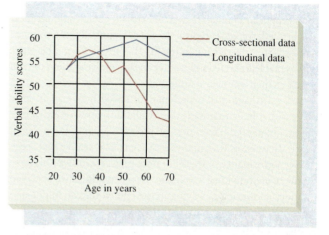

Life-span developmentalist K. Warner Schaie (right) believes there is considerable plasticity in the intelligence of older adults. Schaie and his colleagues have conducted important studies that reveal the role of cohort effects in intelligence.

flawed because they were collected in a cross-sectional manner. Recall from chapter 2 that in a cross-sectional study individuals of different ages are tested at the same time. For example, a cross-sectional study might assess the intelligence of different groups of 40- and 70-year-old individuals in a single evaluation, say in 1986. The average 40-year-old individual and the average 70-year-old individual tested in 1986 were born and reared in different eras, which produced different socioeconomic and educational opportunities. For instance, as the 70-year-old individuals grew up, they had fewer educational opportunities, which probably influenced their scores on intelligence tests; so, if we find differences in intelligence levels of 40- and 70-year-old individuals when we assess them in a cross-sectional manner, the differences may be due to educational opportunities instead of age.

By contrast, a longitudinal study might evaluate the intelligence of the same individuals at age 40 and then again at age 70. Remember from chapter 2 that in a longitudinal study the same individuals are retested after a period of years. The longitudinal data collected by Schaie (1984) and others do not reveal an intellectual decline in adulthood at least up to about 70 years of age (see figure 19.2). In his most recent research, Schaie (1994) has found a decline in mental abilities beginning at an average of 74 years of age. However, the magnitude of the decrement is significantly reduced when age changes and perceptual speed are removed.

In thinking about how to study intelligence in late adulthood, we need to consider what components should be investigated and how they should be measured (Salthouse, 1991, 1992; Perlmutter, 1994). Horn, Baltes, and Schaie, for the most

part, have studied general intelligence and several of its subfactors, such as fluid and crystallized intelligence, through psychometric testing (standardized intelligence tests). Are we likely to find a decline in intelligence if we focus on important intellectual processes such as speed of processing, memory, and problem solving and observe them in different contexts?

Speed of Processing, Memory, and Problem Solving

It is now widely accepted that the speed of processing information declines in late adulthood (Baltes, Smith, & Staudinger, in press; Dobson & others, 1993; Salthouse, 1992, 1993, in press; Salthouse & Coon, 1993; Sternberg & McGrane, 1993). There is also some evidence that older adults are less able to effortfully retrieve information from memory (Sternberg & McGrane, 1993) and to efficiently use mental imagination in memory (Baltes, Smith, & Staudinger, in press).

Although our speed of processing information slows down in late adulthood, there is considerable individual variation in this ability. And when the slowdown occurs, it is not clear that this affects our lives in any substantial way. For example, in one experiment the reaction time and typing skills of typists of all ages were studied (Salthouse, 1984). The older typists usually had slower reactions, but they actually typed just as fast as the younger typists. Possibly the older typists were faster when they were younger and had slowed down, but the results in another condition suggested that something else was involved. When the number of characters that the typists could look ahead at was limited, the older typists slowed substantially; the younger typists were affected much less by this restriction. The older typists had learned to look farther ahead, allowing them to type as fast as their younger counterparts.

A substitution of experience for speed may explain how older individuals maintain their skills in many cognitive domains, among them memory and problem solving (Poon, 1985, 1990). Because of this, many researchers now realize that measuring performance in the laboratory may give only a rough estimate of an individual's ability in the real world. If we observed memory and problem solving in the real world, we might discover less decline in late adulthood. Nancy Denney (1986) pointed out that most tests of memory and problem-solving abilities measure how older adults perform abstract or trivial activities, not unlike those found on school exams.

In her research, Denney assessed cognition among older adults by observing how they handled a landlord who would not fix their stove and what they would do if a Social Security check did not arrive on time. Denney revealed that the ability to solve such practical problems actually increased through the forties and fifties as individuals got practical experience. She also found that individuals in their seventies were no worse at this type of practical problem solving than their counterparts in their twenties, who were quite good at solving practical problems.

We have already seen that understanding the nature of cognitive functioning in late adulthood is not so simple as examining general, overall decline in intelligence on a traditional test of intelligence. We found that some aspects of cognitive functioning (such as speed of processing information) are more likely to decline than others (such as problem solving in natural contexts). Other aspects important for understanding cognitive functioning in older adults include education, health, work, terminal drop, cognitive skills training, and wisdom, each of which we consider in turn.

Education, Work, and Health

Education, work, and health are three important influences on the cognitive functioning of older adults. They are also three of the most important factors involved in understanding why cohort effects need to be taken into account in studying the cognitive functioning of older adults (Baltes, 1987).

Education

Successive generations in America's twentieth century have been better educated. Not only were today's older adults more

Shown here is 77-year-old Etta Kallman, who recently returned to New York University to further her education. She is a straight A student.

likely to go to college when they were young adults than were their parents or grandparents, but more older adults are returning to college today to further their education than in past generations. Educational experiences are positively correlated with scores on intelligence tests and information processing tasks, such as memory (Verhaeghen, Marcoen, & Goossens, 1993).

Older adults may seek more education for a number of reasons (Mullins, 1993; Willis, 1985). They may want to better understand the nature of their aging. They may want to learn more about the social and technological changes that have produced dramatic changes in their lives. They may want to discover relevant knowledge and to learn relevant skills to cope with societal and job demands in later life. They may recognize that they need further education to remain competitive and stay in the work force. Earlier in this century, individuals made career choices in adolescence and young adulthood and never wavered from those choices throughout their adult years. Today, that pattern does not always occur. Technological changes have meant that some of the occupations of 15 years ago no longer exist. And some of today's occupations could not even be identified 15 years ago. Finally, older adults may seek more education to enhance their self-discovery and the leisure activities that will enable them to make a smoother adjustment to retirement.

Work

Successive generations have also had work experiences that include a stronger emphasis on cognitively oriented labor. Our great-grandfathers and grandfathers were more likely to be manual laborers than were our fathers, who are more likely to be involved in cognitively oriented occupations. As the industrial society continues to be replaced by the information society, younger generations will have more experience in jobs that require considerable cognitive investment. The increased emphasis on information processing in jobs likely enhances an individual's intellectual abilities.

Health

Successive generations have also been healthier in late adulthood as better treatments for a variety of illnesses (such as hypertension) have been developed. Many of these illnesses have a negative impact on intellectual performance (Hultsch, Hammer, & Small, 1993). In one investigation, hypertension was related to decreased performance on the WAIS (Wechsler Adult Intelligence Scale) by individuals over the age of 60 (Wilkie & Eisdorfer, 1971). The older the population, the greater the number of persons with health problems will be (Siegler & Costa, 1985). Thus, some of the decline in intellectual performance found for older adults is likely due to health-related factors rather than to age per se.

In chapter 18 we found that exercise is related to longevity. Might exercise also help older adults to think more efficiently while they are living longer? In one investigation, the relation between vigorous physical exercise and cognitive ability in men and women 55 to 91 years of age was examined (Clarkson-Smith & Hartley, 1989). *Vigorous exercisers* were older adults who engaged in at least 1¼ hours of strenuous exercise per week. *Low exercisers* were older adults who spent less than 10 minutes per week exercising. The older adults who exercised vigorously performed better on tests of reasoning, memory, and reaction time than did the older adults who exercised little if at all. These results occurred regardless of the age, educational level, and health status of the older adults. Other researchers have also begun to confirm that exercise is a very important factor in improving the cognitive functioning of older adults (Park, 1992; Stones & Kozman, 1989). Of course, prior to beginning an exercise program, older adults should have a thorough physical examination, and they should begin with a level of exercise that is tailored to their physical status.

Terminal Drop

Related to the idea that health status is an important factor in the cognitive functioning of older adults is the **terminal drop hypothesis,** *which states that death is preceded by a decrease in cognitive functioning over approximately a 5-year period prior to death.* Thus, distance from death in a subsequently deceased population should be correlated with performance on tests of cognitive functioning if they were administered during the critical 5-year period (Riegel & Riegel, 1972). In investigations that compare older and younger adults, many more of the older adults than the younger adults are likely to be within 5 years of their death. The chronic diseases these older adults may have are likely to decrease their motivation, alertness, and energy to perform competently when they are given tests of cognitive functioning. Thus, the negative findings for older adults found

Although the memory of older adults may show some decline, memory activities can be used to improve their memory. The older adults shown here can use the technique of chunking, for example, to improve their memory of such items as telephone numbers, social security numbers, and license plate numbers.

in some investigations that compare older adults with younger adults may be due in part to age from death rather than simply age from birth. One issue in considering terminal drop is in keeping with our emphasis on assessing a number of aspects of cognitive functioning rather than general intelligence alone. In one recent investigation, the terminal drop hypothesis was supported for tests of vocabulary, but not for numerical facility and perceptual speed (White & Cunningham, 1989).

Training Cognitive Skills

If cognitive skills are atrophying in late adulthood, can they be retrained? An increasing number of developmentalists believe they can be (Denney, 1982; Frech & Willis, 1993; Meyer, Young, & Bartlett, 1989; Neely & Bäckman, 1993; Perlmutter, 1990; Schaie, 1994; Willis, 1989, 1990; Willis & Schaie, 1990). For example, in the investigation conducted by life-span developmentalists K. Warner Schaie and Sherry Willis (1986), more than 4,000 adults, most of whom were older adults, were studied. Using individualized training, the researchers improved the spatial orientation and reasoning skills for two-thirds of the adults. Nearly 40 percent of those whose abilities had declined returned to a level they had reached 14 years earlier.

Mnemonics can also be used to improve older adults' cognitive skills. **Mnemonics** *is a term that describes the techniques designed to make memory more efficient.* In the fifth century B.C., the Greek poet Simonides attended a banquet. After he left, the building collapsed, crushing the guests and maiming their bodies beyond recognition. Simonides was able to identify the bodies using a memory technique. He generated vivid images of each individual and pictured where they had sat at the banquet table. The *method of loci,* Simonides' technique, was used in one study to improve the memory of older adults (Kliegl & Baltes, 1987). The method of loci training involved practice with a map of 40 Berlin landmarks. The older adults were also trained to use *chunking*—organizing items into meaningful or manageable units—to improve their memory of Berlin landmarks. Telephone numbers, Social Security numbers, and license plate numbers are common examples of how chunking can help us and elderly adults remember large amounts of information in our everyday lives. Using the method of loci and chunking, the elderly adults could recall more than 32 of the 40 Berlin landmarks. Later they were able to apply what they had learned in their method of loci and chunking training to recall long lists of digits. One 69-year-old woman correctly recalled 120 digits presented in intervals of eights. Such results suggest substantial memory capacity in healthy, mentally fit older adults. In another study, the method of loci was again effective in improving the memory of older adults (Kliegl, Smith, & Baltes, 1990).

In a 7-year-longitudinal study, Sherry Willis and Carolyn Nesselroade (1990) examined the effectiveness of cognitive training on the maintenance of fluid intelligence with advancing age. The older adults were taught strategies for identifying the rule or pattern required in problem solutions. Adults in their seventies and eighties performed at a higher level than they had in their late sixties following the cognitive training, which consisted of the trainer modeling the use of correct strategies in solving tasks, individual practice on training items, feedback about correct solutions of practice problems, and group discussion.

According to Willis (1990), cognitive training research contributes in three ways to understanding the cognitive mechanisms of old age. First, this research underscores the plasticity in older adults' cognitive performance (Lerner, 1990). Second, findings from cognitive training research contribute to an understanding of the cognitive processes associated with developmental change in old age, especially those involved in age-related decline (Campbell & Charness, 1990). Third, cognitive training research has the potential of contributing relevant information to the development of programs and services for older adults that will improve their ability to live independently and productively. To read further about training the elderly, turn to Perspectives on Parenting and Education 19.1.

Wisdom

Wisdom, like good wine, may get better with age. What is this thing we call "wisdom"? **Wisdom** *is expert knowledge about the practical aspects of life that permits excellent judgment about important matters of life* (Baltes, in press; Baltes & Staudinger, in press; Baltes & others, in press; Kliegl, Smith, & Baltes, 1989). This practical knowledge involves exceptional insight into human development and life matters, good judgment, and an understanding of how to cope with difficult life problems. Thus, wisdom, more than standard conceptions of intelligence, focuses on life's pragmatic concerns and human conditions. This practical knowledge system takes many years to acquire, accumulating through intentional, planned experiences and through incidental experiences. Of course, not all older adults solve practical problems in wise ways. In one investigation, only 5 percent of adults' responses to life-planning problems were considered wise, and these wise responses were equally distributed across the early, middle, and late adulthood years (Smith & Baltes, 1990).

> *With the ancient is wisdom; and in the lengths of days understanding.*
> —Job 12:12

Critical Thinking

Do you agree with the components of wisdom we have outlined? What would you add or subtract from the list?

One aspect of wisdom that seems to improve as adults get older is becoming more flexible in transforming and accommodating life goals to new life circumstances and new personal conditions (Brandtstädter & Grieve, in press; Brandtstädter & Renner, 1990). Older adults are also more likely than younger adults to search for contentment than to search for an elusive happiness (Dittman-Kohli, 1992).

What does the possibility that older adults are as wise as, or wiser than, younger adults mean in terms of the basic issue of intellectual decline in adulthood? Remember that intelligence comes in different forms. In many instances, older adults are not as intelligent as younger adults when speed of processing is involved, and this probably harms their performance on many traditional school-related tasks and standardized intelligence tests. But general knowledge and something we call "wisdom" may be an entirely different matter (Baltes & others, in press).

Cognitive Mechanics and Cognitive Pragmatics

Recently, Paul Baltes (1993) further clarified the distinction between those aspects of the aging mind that show decline and those that do not, or even show some improvement. He makes a distinction between "cognitive mechanics" and "cognitive pragmatics." Using computer language as an analogy, **cognitive mechanics** *are the hardware of the mind and reflect the neurophysiological architecture of the brain as developed through*

Older adults may not be as quick with their thoughts as younger adults, but wisdom may be an entirely different matter. This elderly woman shares the wisdom of her experiences with a classroom of children.

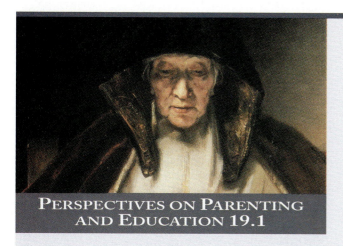

PERSPECTIVES ON PARENTING AND EDUCATION 19.1

Improving Older Adults' Attitudes Toward Computers

The widespread use of computers in our society raises important questions about the willingness and ability of older adults to adapt to this technology. Researchers have found that the elderly can acquire a wide range of computer skills, including word processing (Czaja & others, 1986; Hartley, Hartley, & Johnson, 1984), programming (Yarmon, 1982), and spreadsheet operation (Garfein, Schaie, & Willis, 1988). However, only 1 percent of individuals aged 65 and older actually use a computer (Schwartz, 1988).

Given the limited use of computers by elderly adults, it is important to identify factors associated with computer use. The factor that has been given the most attention is elderly adults' attitudes toward computers. The more experience older adults have with computers, the more positive their attitudes are toward computers (Kerschner & Chelsvig-Hart, 1984; Krauss & Hoyer, 1984).

In one recent investigation, Gina Jay and Sherry Willis (1992) conducted a 2-week computer training program in which older adults aged 57 to 87 learned to use a desktop publishing software program. They found that the older adults' computer attitudes were made more positive by the training experience. After the training the older adults felt more at ease with computers and more confident in their ability to use computers. A posttest 2 weeks after the computer training indicated that the older adults' positive attitudes toward computers as a consequence of the training had been maintained.

Researchers have found that the elderly can acquire a wide range of computer skills, including word processing. The more experience older adults have with computers, the more positive their attitudes toward computers.

FIGURE 19.3

The increase in part-time work among older adults. *McDonald's created McMasters, a 4-week job training program for people over 50. Katherine Galik (shown here) went through the training and was hired to work part-time at McDonald's. The percentage of older adults who work part-time has increased dramatically in the twentieth century.*

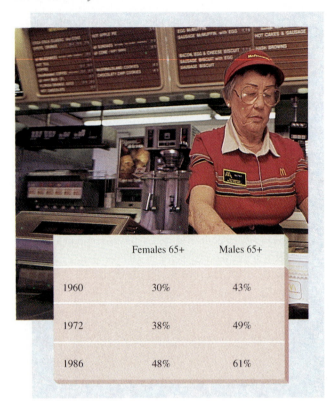

	Females 65+	Males 65+
1960	30%	43%
1972	38%	49%
1986	48%	61%

evolution. *At the operational level, cognitive mechanics involve speed and accuracy of the processes involving sensory input, visual and motor memory, discrimination, comparison, and categorization. Because of the strong influence of biology, heredity, and health on cognitive mechanics, their decline with aging is likely.* Conversely, **cognitive pragmatics** *refer to the culture-based "software" of the mind. At the operational level, cognitive pragmatics include reading and writing skills, language comprehension, educational qualifications, professional skills, and also the type of knowledge about the self and life skills that help us to master or cope with life. Because of the strong influence of culture on cognitive pragmatics, their progress into old age is possible.* Because of the enhancing and compensatory power of cognitive pragmatics, they may increase in old age even in the face of age-related decline in cognitive mechanics. For example, people who can read, a case of cognitive pragmatics, can outperform others who can't read even if they have worse cognitive mechanics.

At this point we have discussed a number of ideas about cognitive functioning in late adulthood. A summary of these issues is presented in concept table 19.1. Now we turn our attention to the nature of work and retirement in older adults.

WORK AND RETIREMENT

What percentage of older adults continue to work? How productive are they? Do older adults go through phases of retirement? Who adjusts best to retirement? What is the changing pattern of retirement in the United States and around the world? These are some of the questions we now examine.

Work

In the 1980s the percentage of men over the age of 65 who continued to work full-time was less than at the beginning of the twentieth century. The decline from 1900 through the 1980s was as much as 70 percent (Douvan, 1983). One important change in older adults' work patterns is the increase in part-time work (Elder & Pavalko, 1993). For example, of the more than 3 million adults over the age of 65 who worked in 1986, more than half were part-time workers. As indicated in figure 19.3, the percentage of older adults who work part-time has steadily increased since 1960.

Some individuals maintain their productivity throughout their lives. These older adults may follow a work agenda that exhausts younger workers, and some older workers demonstrate highly creative skills, at times outperforming their younger counterparts (Landy, 1989). In business and industry, a positive relation between age and productivity favors the older worker. For example, older workers have a 20 percent better attendance record than younger workers. Somewhat surprisingly, they also have fewer disabling injuries, and their frequency of accidents is lower than for young adults. Recent changes in the federal law that allow individuals over the age of 65 to continue working sound wise and humane.

One national survey focused on the characteristics of older workers in the United States (Flanagan, 1981). The individuals ranged in age from 68 to 73. Each of the 500 men and 500 women participated in an extensive 4- to 5-hour interview about their education, family, employment, and quality of life. Only 4 percent of the men were working full-time, while an additional 12 percent were working part-time. The same percentage of women were working full-time, but only 8 percent were working part-time. Most of the men were in jobs that did not require professional training. About 41 percent were in general labor and service-type jobs requiring no special skills. Nearly 14 percent more were in mechanical, technical, or construction trades, while 33 percent were in sales or clerical positions. Only about 12 percent were in jobs

CONCEPT TABLE 19.1

Cognitive Functioning in Older Adults

Concept	Processes/Related Ideas	Characteristics/Description
The debate about intellectual decline in late adulthood	Horn's position	John Horn thinks that some abilities decline but others do not. He argues that fluid intelligence (one's ability to reason abstractly) declines but that crystallized intelligence (an individual's accumulated information and verbal skills) increases.
	Schaie and Baltes's position	They argue that longitudinal data reveal little or no decline in intelligence, while cross-sectional data do because of cohort effects.
Speed of processing, memory, and problem solving	Speed of processing	Speed of processing declines in late adulthood, but strategies can be used to reduce the impact of this decline.
	Memory and problem solving	Memory declines do occur in late adulthood, but recent naturalistic research on memory and problem solving suggests that the decline in these cognitive processes may have been exaggerated.
Education, work, and health	Education	Successive generations of Americans have been better educated. Education is positively correlated with scores on intelligence tests. Older adults may return to education for a number of reasons.
	Work	Successive generations have had work experiences that include a stronger emphasis on cognitively oriented labor. The increased emphasis on information processing in jobs likely enhances an individual's intellectual abilities.
	Health	Successive generations have been healthier. Poor health is related to decreased performance on intelligence tests in late adulthood. Exercise is related to improved cognitive functioning among older adults.
Terminal drop	Its nature	The terminal drop hypothesis states that death is preceded by a decrease in cognitive functioning over approximately a 5-year period prior to death. Probably because of their poor health preceding death, older adults' cognitive functioning declines in this period prior to death.
Training cognitive skills	Its nature	We have increasing evidence that the elderly's cognitive skills can be trained through techniques such as mnemonics.
Wisdom	Its nature	Wisdom, more so than standardly conceived intelligence, focuses on life's pragmatic concerns and human conditions. Many developmentalists believe that wisdom increases in late adulthood.
Cognitive mechanics and cognitive pragmatics	Their nature	Cognitive mechanics are the hardware of the mind and decline with aging, while cognitive pragmatics are the software of the mind and show no decline or can improve with aging. Examples of cognitive mechanics are speed and accuracy of sensory input, and visual and motor memory; examples of cognitive pragmatics are reading and writing skills, professional skills, and life skills that help us to cope more effectively.

At some point in our lives, we face the issue of how to handle retirement in a work-oriented world. Some individuals, such as those shown here, may have looked forward most of their lives to retirement and greatly enjoy its more relaxed freedom. Others may not know what to do with themselves when they retire—their life satisfaction might be improved if they were to continue working.

requiring college training. However, more women (29 percent) were in occupations requiring college training, with teachers accounting for the bulk of these jobs. About 31 percent of the women who worked had unskilled labor jobs, while 39 percent of the women who worked either full- or part-time had sales and clerical jobs. The older adults expressed a great deal of pride and life satisfaction in their ability to continue their work into late adulthood.

Retirement in the United States and Other Countries

A retirement option for older workers is a late-twentieth-century phenomenon in America. Recall from our earlier discussion that a much higher percentage of older Americans worked full-time in the early 1900s than today. The Social Security system, which establishes benefits for older workers when they retire, was implemented in 1935. On the average, today's workers will spend 10 to 15 percent of their lives in retirement.

> *Work is what you do so that some time you won't have to do it anymore.*
>
> —Alfred Polgar

In 1967, the Age Discrimination Act made it a federal policy to prohibit the firing of employees because of their age before they reach the mandatory retirement age. In 1978, Congress extended the mandatory retirement age from 65 to 70 in business, industry, and the federal government. In 1986, Congress voted to ban mandatory retirement for all but a few occupations, such as police officer, firefighter, and airline pilot, where safety is an issue. Federal law now prohibits employers from firing older workers, who have seniority and higher salaries, just to save money. As mandatory retirement

continues to lessen, older workers will face the decision of when to retire rather than be forced into retirement.

Although the United States has extended the retirement age upward, early retirement continues to be followed in large numbers (Stanford & others, 1991). In many European countries—both capitalist and former Communist bloc—officials have experimented with various financial inducements designed to reduce or control unemployment by encouraging the retirement of older workers. West Germany, Sweden, Great Britain, Italy, France, Czechoslovakia, Hungary, and Russia are among the nations that are moving toward earlier retirement. More information about cultural variations in retirement appears in Sociocultural Worlds of Development 19.1.

Phases of Retirement

Gerontologist Robert Atchley (1976) described seven phases of retirement adults can go through—remote, near, honeymoon, disenchantment, reorientation, stability, and termination (see figure 19.4).

Most of us go to work with the vague belief that we will not die on the job but will enjoy the fruits of our labor at some point in the distant future. In the **remote phase,** *most individuals do little in the way of preparing for retirement.* As they age toward possible retirement, they may deny that retirement will ever happen. In the **near phase,** *the worker begins to participate in a preretirement program.* These programs usually help adults decide when and how they should retire by familiarizing them

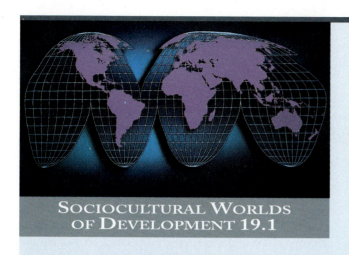

SOCIOCULTURAL WORLDS OF DEVELOPMENT 19.1

Work and Retirement in Japan, The United States, England, and France

Are a larger percentage of older adults in Japan in the labor force than in the United States and other industrialized countries? What are the attitudes of older Japanese adults toward work and retirement compared to their counterparts in other

industrialized countries? To answer these questions, the Japanese Prime Minister's Office (1982) conducted national surveys of adults 60 years of age and older in four industrialized nations—Japan, the United States, England, and France. A much larger percentage of the men over 60 in Japan were in the labor force (57%) than in the United States (33%), England (13%), and France (8%).

When asked, "What do you think is the best age to retire?" a majority of the older men in England and France said 60 years of age. In sharp contrast, only 14 percent of the older men in Japan and 16 percent of the older men in the United States chose such an early age to retire. Another question the older men in the four countries were asked was, "Where should an older person's income come from?" In Japan and the United States, the proportion of older men who favored saving while working was at least twice that advising reliance on social security. In contrast, older adult men in France and England favored reliance on social security.

Sociologists Alex Inkeles and Chikako Usui (1989) believe these cross-cultural data suggest that the marked differences in the rate of employment among those over 60 in Japan and the United States, compared to England and France, are mainly due to attitudes and values about work, and about reliance on oneself (and on relatives, in the case of Japan) rather than on the government and its social security system.

FIGURE 19.4

Seven phases of retirement. Gerontologist Robert Atchley believes individuals experience seven phases of retirement. However, because individuals retire at different ages for different reasons, there is considerable variation in the timing and sequencing of various aspects of retirement.

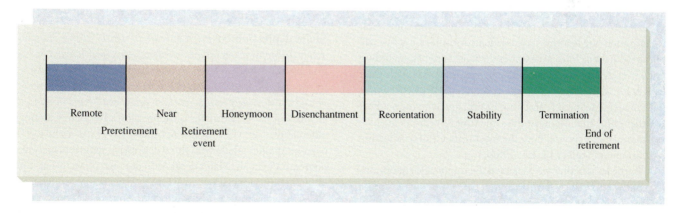

Remote — Preretirement | Near — Retirement event | Honeymoon | Disenchantment | Reorientation | Stability | Termination — End of retirement

with the benefits and pensions they can expect to receive, or involve discussion of more comprehensive issues, such as physical and mental health. As adults have become more aware of the importance of financial planning, a surge of participation in preretirement planning has occurred in the last decade (Anderson & Weber, 1993; Ekerdt & DeViney, 1993).

Five phases occur after retirement. In the **honeymoon phase,** *the earliest phase of retirement, many individuals feel euphoric.* They may be able to do all of the things they never had

time to do before, and they may enjoy leisure activities more. However, adults who are forced to retire, or who retire because they are angry about their job, or because of ill health, are less likely to experience the positive aspects of the honeymoon stage. In the **disenchantment phase,** *older adults recognize that their preretirement fantasies about retirement were unrealistic.* After the honeymoon stage, older adults often fall into a routine. If the routine is satisfying, adjustment to retirement is usually successful. Adults whose life-styles did not entirely revolve around their jobs before retirement are more likely to make the retirement adjustment and develop a satisfying routine than those who did not develop leisure activities during their working years.

> *Even for those who do not move, retirement is a moving experience.*
>
> —Richard Armour

In the **reorientation phase,** *retirees take stock, pull themselves together, and develop more realistic life alternatives.* They explore and evaluate the type of life-style that is likely to bring them life satisfaction. In the **stability phase,** *adults have decided upon a set of criteria for evaluating choices in retirement and how they will perform once they have made these choices.* For some adults, this phase follows the honeymoon phase, but for others the transition is slower and more difficult. In the **termination phase,** *the retirement role is replaced by the sick or dependent role because the older adult can no longer function autonomously and be self-sufficient.*

For some adults, the retirement role may lose its significance and relevance. They may go to work again, often accepting a job that is totally unrelated to what they had done prior to retirement. Full-time leisure may become boring to them, or they may need money to support themselves.

Because individuals retire at different ages and for different reasons, there is no particular timing or sequencing of the seven stages. Nonetheless, the seven phases help us to think about the different ways we can experience retirement and the adjustments that are involved.

Those Who Adjust Best to Retirement

Who adjusts best to retirement? Older adults who adjust best to retirement are healthy, have adequate income, are active, are better educated, have an extended social network including both friends and family, and usually were satisfied with their lives before they retired (Palmore & others, 1985). Older adults with inadequate income and poor health, and who must adjust to other stress that occurs at the same time as retirement, such as the death of a spouse, have the most difficult time adjusting to retirement (Stull & Hatch, 1984).

In the last chapter we discussed the importance of options for control and self-determination in the health, and even the longevity, of nursing home residents. Choice and self-determination are also important factors in successful work and retirement (Herzog, House, & Morgan, 1991; Reis & Gould, 1993). The fewer choices older adults have regarding their retirement, the less satisfied they are with their lives. Options for control and self-determination are important aspects of the mental health of older adults (Fry, Slivinske, & Fitch, 1989).

THE MENTAL HEALTH OF OLDER ADULTS

What is the nature of mental health among older adults? What are the common mental health problems? What are the most effective mental health treatments for older adults?

The Nature of Mental Health in Older Adults

Although a substantial portion of the population can now look forward to a longer life, that life may unfortunately be hampered by a mental disability in old age. This prospect is both troubling to the individual and costly to society. Mental disorders make individuals increasingly dependent on the help and care of others; the cost of mental health disorders in older adults is estimated at more than $40 billion per year in the United States. More important than the loss in dollars, though, is the loss of human potential and the suffering (Gatz, 1989; Siegler, 1989).

Mental health is not only comprised of the absence of mental disorders, difficulties, and frustrations, but also reflects one's ability to deal with life's issues in effective and satisfying ways. Because older adults are more likely to have some type of physical illness, the interweaving of physical and mental problems is more common in later adulthood than in early adulthood (Birren & Sloane, 1985).

How common are mental disorders in older adults? At least 10 percent of individuals over 65 have mental health problems severe enough to warrant professional attention (LaRue, Dessonville, & Jarvik, 1985). Three disorders that are especially prevalent among older adults are depression, anxiety, and Alzheimer's disease.

Depression

Major depression *is a mood disorder in which the individual is deeply unhappy, demoralized, self-derogatory, and bored. The individual with major depression does not feel well, loses stamina easily, has a poor appetite, and is listless and unmotivated. Major depression is so widespread it has been called the "common cold" of mental disorders.* Estimates of depression's frequency among older adults vary (Lewinsohn & others, 1991). As many as 80 percent of older adults who show depressive symptoms receive no treatment at all. Major depression not only may envelop the individual in sadness, but may also evoke suicidal tendencies. Nearly 25 percent of individuals who commit suicide in the United States are older than 65 years of age (Church, Siegel, & Foster, 1988). The four greatest risk factors related to suicide in older adults are living alone, being male, losing a spouse, and experiencing failing health.

Anxiety

Anxiety disorders *are psychological disorders characterized by motor tension (jumpiness, trembling, inability to relax), hyperactivity (dizziness, a racing heart, or perspiration), and apprehensive thoughts and expectations.* Gerontologists have given more attention to problems of depression than to anxiety in older adults, but recent surveys indicate that the elderly may actually have a higher incidence of anxiety disorders than of depression (George & others, 1988). Estimates indicate that approximately 7 percent of older adults have an anxiety disorder (Gatz, 1992).

Alzheimer's Disease

Mary's family thought she was having vision problems when at age 65 she could not remember how to do the crossword puzzles she loved so much. Soon her family detected other symptoms pointing to a more serious condition. Mary no longer recognized her husband and even ran away from him in terror several times. She thought he was a stranger who has going to attack her, although he was an extremely kind and gentle man. Mary's family finally took her to a hospital, where she was diagnosed as having **Alzheimer's disease,** *a progressive, irreversible brain disorder characterized by gradual deterioration of memory, reasoning, language, and eventually physical function.*

Alzheimer's disease was discovered in 1906, and researchers have still not found the causes or cure for it. Approximately 2.5 million individuals over the age of 65 in the United States have this disease. As increasing numbers of individuals live to older ages, it has been predicted that Alzheimer's disease could triple in the next 50 years. Because of the increasing prevalence of Alzheimer's disease, researchers have stepped up their efforts to understand the causes of the disease and to discover more effective ways to treat it (Davidson & Stern, 1991; Growden & others, 1993; Morris & Rubin, 1991).

For roughly one in ten Alzheimer's victims, the disease is clearly inherited. On the average, Alzheimer's will strike 50 percent of the offspring of someone with this hereditary form of the disease. Families with an incidence of Alzheimer's disease are three times as likely to have a case of Down syndrome, a severe form of mental retardation, in their family as well. Scientists have yet to isolate the gene or genetic combination responsible, but they are getting closer—it is on chromosome 21 (Barnes, 1987). The brains of Alzheimer's patients are filled with plaque, formed from pieces of nerve cells and a protein, amyloid. The plaque accumulates at sites of nerve cell connections and chokes off communication between nerve cells (Kosik, 1989). But it is not known whether the plaque causes Alzheimer's or is a secondary effect caused by other factors. Researchers are currently investigating the genes that control amyloid production for possible clues about the cause of Alzheimer's disease.

Written reminders help this Alzheimer's victim lead a relatively normal life. In the early phases of Alzheimer's disease, older adults can often remember how to do something if they are reminded to do it. In the later phases of the disease, they may lose the ability to perform even simple tasks.

Something also goes wrong with the neurotransmitter acetylcholine in Alzheimer's patients; this chemical is especially important in memory and the motor control of muscles (McDonald & Nemeroff, 1991). It may be that the problems in acetylcholine production are due to a defective gene. One strategy for treating Alzheimer's patients involves the use of drugs to block the pathway that leads to acetylcholine breakdown. In one investigation, a drug by the name of THA improved the memory and coping skills of 16 of 17 Alzheimer's patients by increasing acetylcholine production. But most scientists believe that increasing acetylcholine production does not attack the cause of Alzheimer's disease. Eventually, the acetylcholine-producing cells in Alzheimer's patients die, and THA only works as long as there is at least some acetylcholine around.

With more knowledge about the genetic basis of Alzheimer's disease, though, scientists are optimistic that the cause of Alzheimer's disease will be discovered and the expression of the disorder curtailed. Even if the gene defect is discovered, it is clear that more than just a gene defect is involved. Some trigger must set off the disease. What that trigger (or triggers) might be is still not known, although Alzheimer's disease is associated with diet, smoking, stress, head injury, and thyroid problems.

Whether or not special living conditions can improve the motor skills of Alzheimer's patients is being studied, too. Color codes and bright lights may help the daily functioning of the Alzheimer's patient. Dance and exercise may improve motor abilities. The family's role as a support system for Alzheimer's patients is also being evaluated. Psychologists believe the family can help improve the mental outlook of the Alzheimer's patient (Biegel, Sales, & Schulz, 1991; Kinney & Ogrocki, 1991; Zarit, 1993).

LIFE-SPAN PRACTICAL KNOWLEDGE 19.1

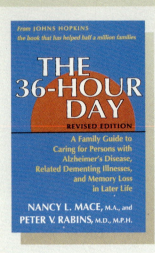

*From JOHNS HOPKINS
the book that has helped half a million families*

THE 36-HOUR DAY
REVISED EDITION

A Family Guide to
Caring for Persons with
Alzheimer's Disease,
Related Dementing Illnesses,
and Memory Loss
in Later Life

NANCY L. MACE, M.A., and
PETER V. RABINS, M.D., M.P.H.

The 36-Hour Day

(1981) by Nancy Mace and Peter Rabins. Baltimore: The Johns Hopkins University Press.

The 36-Hour Day is a family guide to caring for persons with Alzheimer's and related diseases in older adults. The authors say that for those who care for a person with Alzheimer's or related diseases, every day often seems as if it were 36 hours long. *The 36-Hour Day* provides information about home care of older adults who are in the early or middle stages of these diseases. The book helps family members to understand behaviors that seem baffling and unpredictable. It also provides strategies for helping the afflicted relative lead as full and satisfying a life as possible. The family is also helped to recognize the point beyond which home care is no longer enough, and given guidance in choosing a nursing home or other care facility. The authors also describe various support groups that have been formed to help families with a family member who has Alzheimer's.

Fear of Victimization and Crime

Some of the physical decline and limitations that characterize development in late adulthood contribute to a sense of vulnerability and fear among older adults. For some elderly adults, the fear of crime may become a deterrent to travel, attendance at social events, and the pursuit of an active life-style. Almost one-fourth of older adults say they have a basic fear of being the victim of a crime. However, in reality, possibly because of the precautions they take, older adults are less likely than younger adults to be the victim of a crime. However, the crimes committed against the elderly are likely to be serious offenses, such as armed robbery (Cohn & Harlow, 1993). The elderly are also victims of nonviolent crimes such as fraud, vandalism, purse snatching, and harassment. Estimates of the incidence of crimes against the elderly may be low, because older adults may not report crimes, fearing retribution from criminals or believing the criminal justice system cannot help them (Church, Siegel, & Foster, 1988).

Critical Thinking

What can be done to decrease the fear of victimization and crime among the elderly? What role might federal, state, and local governments play?

Margaret Gatz (right) has been a crusader for better mental health treatment of the elderly. She believes that mental health professionals need to be encouraged to include more older adults in their client lists and that we need to better educate the elderly about how they can benefit from therapy.

Meeting the Mental Health Needs of Older Adults

Older adults receive disproportionately fewer mental health services. One estimate is that only 2.7 percent of all clinical services provided by psychologists go to older adults, although individuals aged 65 and over make up more than 11 percent of the population. The proportion of community mental health services rendered to older adults has remained relatively stable—at or about 4 percent in the 1970s and 1980s (Lebowitz, 1987; VandenBos, Stapp, & Kilburg, 1981).

Psychotherapy can be expensive. Although reduced fees and sometimes no fee can be arranged in public hospitals for older adults from low-income backgrounds, many older adults who need psychotherapy do not get it. It has been said that psychotherapists like to work with young, attractive, verbal, intelligent, and successful clients (called YAVISes) rather than those who are quiet, ugly, old, institutionalized, and different (called QUOIDs). While mental health professionals have become increasingly sensitive to such problems, surveys indicate that 70 percent of psychotherapists report never seeing older clients (VandenBos, Stapp, & Kilburg, 1981). Psychotherapists have been accused of failing to see older adults because they perceive that older adults have a poor prognosis for therapy success, they do not feel they have adequate training to treat older adults, who may have special problems requiring special treatment, and they may have stereotypes that label older adults as low-status and unworthy recipients of treatment.

There are many different types of mental health treatment available to older adults. Some common mechanisms of change that improve the mental health of older adults are (Gatz, 1989; Matthews, 1993; Tobin, 1991; Zarit & Pearlin, 1993): (1) fostering a sense of control, self-efficacy, and hope; (2) establishing a relationship with a helper; (3) providing or elucidating a sense of meaning; and (4) promoting educative activities and the development of skills.

How can we better meet the mental health needs of the elderly? First, psychologists must be encouraged to include more older adults in their client lists, and the elderly must be convinced that they can benefit from therapy. Second, we must make mental health care affordable: Medicare currently pays lower percentages for mental health care than for physical health care, for example (Roybal, 1988).

At this point we have discussed a number of ideas about the nature of work and retirement, and about the mental health of older adults. A summary of these ideas is presented in concept table 19.2. In the next chapter we continue our discussion of late adulthood as we describe the socioemotional development of older adults.

LIFE-SPAN HEALTH AND WELL-BEING

Trends in the Mental Health Care of Older Adults

According to mental health and aging expert Margaret Gatz (1992), trends in mental health services for older adults in the 1980s included overreliance on inpatient treatment, increased use of general hospitals as treatment sites, inadequate integration with the nursing home industry, and insufficient mental health referrals from general medical providers.

Gatz especially worries about the lack of coordination or cooperation among components of the health and mental health systems. The upshot is that both everyone and no one is responsible for older adults with mental disorders, a situation that borders on being a nonsystem of mental health care (Swan & McCall, 1987).

Three interrelated points are important when evaluating the intersection of health and mental health systems. First, the mental health system reflects and is affected by trends in the health-care system, especially government determination of payment allowances. Second, older adults are more likely to consult a physician than a mental health professional about their psychological difficulties. And third, there is often a relation between physical and mental problems in older adults (Cohen, 1990).

Physical problems can lead to mental problems, and mental distress can exacerbate physical symptoms. In the National Nursing Home Survey, of all patients with diagnosable mental disorders, more than 80 percent had at least one area of physical functioning in which they required assistance (National Center for Health Statistics, 1989). In the planning of effective services for older adults, the interaction of physical and mental conditions needs to be taken into account.

As the population of older adults increases, so will the number of those who need mental health services. One positive trend is that older adults are getting more access to mental health services in the community than in the past because psychologists are now eligible for reimbursement under Medicare. Gatz (1992) speculated about other possible changes that would benefit the mental health needs of the elderly. Among them are caregiving leaves for workers to care for aging family members with mental disorders, elder day centers in the workplace, and an expansion of tax incentives for family caregiving. ■

CONCEPT TABLE 19.2

Work and Retirement, and the Mental Health of Older Adults

Concept	Processes/Related Ideas	Characteristics/Description
Work and retirement	Work	In the 1980s the percentage of men over the age of 65 who continued to work full-time was less than at the beginning of the twentieth century. One important change in older adults' work patterns is the increase in part-time work. Some individuals continue a life of strong productivity throughout late adulthood.
	Retirement in the United States and other countries	A retirement option for older workers is a late-twentieth-century phenomenon in America. The United States has extended the mandatory retirement age upward, and efforts have been made to reduce age discrimination in work-related circumstances. While the United States has moved toward increasing the age for retirement, many European companies have lowered it.
	Phases of retirement	One theory of retirement emphasizes seven phases: remote, near, honeymoon, disenchantment, reorientation, stability, and termination. Many individuals do not experience the phases in this order, although the phases can help us to think about the different ways we can experience retirement.
	Those who adjust best to retirement	Individuals who are healthy, have adequate income, are active, are better educated, have an extended social network of friends and family, and usually were satisfied with their lives before they retired adjust best to retirement.
The mental health of older adults	Its nature	At least 10 percent of older adults have mental health problems sufficient to require professional help.
	Depression	Depression has been called the "common cold" of mental disorders. However, a majority of older adults with depressive symptoms never receive mental health treatment.
	Anxiety	Recent surveys indicate that anxiety is a more common problem among the elderly than is depression.
	Alzheimer's disease	Approximately 2.5 million older adults have this progressive, irreversible brain disorder characterized by gradual deterioration of memory, reasoning, language, and, eventually, physical function. Special attention is being given to Alzheimer's cellular and genetic basis.
	Fear of victimization and crime	Some of the physical decline and limitations that characterize development in late adulthood contribute to a sense of vulnerability and fear among older adults. Almost one-fourth of older adults say they have a basic fear of being the victim of a crime.
	Meeting the mental health needs of the elderly	A number of barriers to mental health treatment in older adults exist; older adults receive disproportionately less mental health treatment. There are many different ways to treat the mental health problems of the elderly.

CONCLUSIONS

For many years, a stereotype about aging was that all aspects of intelligence go downhill when we get older. Some aspects of our intelligence do decline in late adulthood, but the drop is not as precipitous as was once believed, and in most instances cognitive training can improve the elderly's performance.

We began this chapter by investigating the cognitive functioning of older adults, exploring such topics as the debate about intellectual decline in late adulthood, speed of processing, memory, and problem solving, education, work, and health, terminal drop, training cognitive skills, and wisdom. Then we studied work, retirement in the United States and other countries, phases of retirement, and those who adjust best to retirement. Next, our coverage of the mental health of older adults focused on the nature of their mental health, depression, anxiety, Alzheimer's disease, fear of victimization and crime, and meeting the mental health needs of older adults. At different points in the chapter we discussed how older adults' attitudes toward computers can be improved, work and retirement in Japan, the United States, England, and France, and trends in the mental health care of older adults.

Don't forget that you can obtain an overall summary of the chapter by again reading the two concept tables on pages 545 and 552. In the next chapter we continue our journey through late adulthood by exploring its socioemotional aspects.

KEY TERMS

crystallized intelligence Accumulated information and verbal skills, which increase with age. (538)

fluid intelligence Ability to reason abstractly, which steadily declines from middle adulthood on. (538)

terminal drop hypothesis States that death is preceded by a decrease in cognitive functioning over approximately a 5-year period prior to death. (541)

mnemonics Techniques designed to make memory more efficient. (541)

wisdom According to Baltes, wisdom is expert knowledge about the practical aspects of life. (542)

cognitive mechanics Are the hardware of the mind and reflect the neurophysiological architecture of the brain as developed through evolution. At the operational level, cognitive mechanics involve speed and accuracy of the processes involving sensory input, visual and motor memory, discrimination, comparison, and categorization. (542)

cognitive pragmatics Refer to culture-based "software" of the mind. At the operational level, cognitive pragmatics include reading and writing skills, language comprehension, educational qualifications, professional skills, and also the type of knowledge about the self and life skills that help us to master or cope with life. (544)

remote phase In the first of Robert Atchley's seven phases of retirement, most individuals do little to prepare for retirement. (546)

near phase In the second of Atchley's phases of retirement, the worker begins to participate in a preretirement program. (546)

honeymoon phase The third of Atchley's phases of retirement is the earliest phase of retirement. The retirees may feel euphoric. (547)

disenchantment phase In the fourth of Atchley's phases of retirement, retirees recognize that their preretirement fantasies about retirement were unrealistic. (547)

reorientation phase In the fifth of Atchley's phases of retirement, retirees take stock, pull themselves together, and develop more realistic life alternatives. (548)

stability phase In the sixth of Atchley's phases of retirement, retirees have decided upon a set of criteria for evaluating choices in retirement and how they will perform once they have made these choices. (548)

termination phase In the last of Atchley's phases of retirement, the retirement role is replaced by the role of being sick or dependent because the older adult can no longer function autonomously and be self-sufficient. (548)

major depression An individual suffering from this mood disorder is deeply unhappy, demoralized, self-derogatory, and bored. The person does not feel well, loses stamina easily, has poor appetite, and is listless and unmotivated. Major depression is so widespread that it has been called the "common cold" of mental disorders. (548)

anxiety disorders Psychological disorders that are characterized by motor tension, hyperactivity, and apprehensive thoughts and expectations. (549)

Alzheimer's disease Persons with this progressive, irreversible brain disorder suffer gradual deterioration of memory, reasoning, language, and, eventually, physical function. (549)

Laura Wheeler, Anna Washington Derry, detail.

20

Socioemotional Development in Late Adulthood

LIFE-SPAN HEALTH AND WELL-BEING

Social Support and Health in Late Adulthood 571

I am the family face;
Flesh perishes, I live on,
Projecting trait and trace
Through time to times anon,
And leaping from place to place
Over oblivion.

—Thomas Hardy, 1917

Grow old with me!
The best is yet to be,
The last of life,
For which the first was made.

—Browning

IMAGES OF LIFE-SPAN DEVELOPMENT

Edna, Age 75, and Her Life Review

Edna is a 75-year-old woman who has spent more time reflecting on what her life has been like since she entered late adulthood. Recently, she thought to herself:

> I think about my life a lot—it is in the back of my mind on many occasions. Thoughts of the past come into my mind when I look at my children and their children. When I walk down the street I think back to when I was a young girl . . . to the enjoyable moments with my friends and my parents. I think about my husband, our wedding . . . the times we struggled but made ends meet. He is gone now, but I have so many good memories of him.

On another occasion, Edna passed by a mirror and looked at herself:

> I see all these wrinkles and this little old lady whose body is slumping. I said to myself how old I looked. It made me think of death. It made me think of my past—what I had done wrong, what I had done right.

Several years ago after her husband died, Edna was hospitalized for two months. She thought to herself:

> I feel so unhappy, so depressed. My husband is gone forever. I'm mad. I hate all of this. Why does it have to be this way? I'm mad at myself. When I look myself over, I think, "You could have done things a lot better. Maybe if you had done things differently you wouldn't feel like this."

On yet another occasion, some 6 months after she left the hospital, Edna's reflections revealed some of the adaptive and constructive outcomes a life review can provide:

> I am a lot more optimistic about my life now than I was six months ago. I have six marvelous grandchildren and two great daughters. I decided to get a tape recorder and talk about my positive feelings I had been having lately about my life. I wanted to tell my life story so my grandchildren could listen to it when they grow up. I acted like I was telling the story directly to them. I hope they will listen to it after I am gone.

PREVIEW

In late adulthood, we come to understand that our life is lived forward but understood backward. In this final period of the human life span, we review our lives, looking back through our development files and evaluating what they have been like. Later in the chapter we will explore more fully the pervasive theme of life review in late adulthood. Among the other aspects of late adulthood we will explore our ethnicity, gender, and culture; families and social relationships; and personality development, life satisfaction, and successful aging. But to begin, we will study the social worlds of late adulthood.

THE SOCIAL WORLDS OF OLDER ADULTS

Could social experiences partly explain why we age? Do we stereotype old people in the United States? What social policy issues does an aging society raise? How devastating is poverty to the elderly? What are the living arrangements of older adults?

Social Theories of Aging

For too many years, it was believed that the best way to age was to be disengaged. **Disengagement theory** *argues that as older adults slow down they gradually withdraw from society* (Cumming & Henry, 1961). Disengagement is a mutual activity in which the older adult not only disengages from society, but society disengages from the older adult. According to the theory, the older adult develops an increasing self-preoccupation, lessens emotional ties with others, and shows a decreasing interest in society's affairs. Reduction of social interaction and increased self-preoccupation was thought to increase life satisfaction among older adults.

Disengagement theory predicted that low morale would accompany high activity, that disengagement is inevitable, and that disengagement is sought out by the elderly. Disengagement theory was in error. A series of investigations failed to support these contentions (Maddox, 1968; Neugarten, Havighurst, & Tobin, 1968; Reichard, Levson, & Peterson, 1962). When individuals continue to live active, energetic, and productive lives as older adults, their life satisfaction does not go down; sometimes it even goes up.

According to **activity theory,** *the more active and involved older adults are, the less likely they will age and the more likely they will be satisfied with their lives.* Activity theory suggests that individuals should continue their middle adulthood roles through late adulthood; if these roles are taken away from them (as in forced retirement, for example), it is important for them to find substitute roles that keep them active and involved in society's activities.

A third social theory of aging is **social breakdown-reconstruction theory** (Kuypers & Bengston, 1973). *This theory argues that aging is promoted through negative psychological functioning brought about by negative societal views of older adults and inadequate provision of services for them. Social reconstruction can occur by changing society's view of older adults and by providing adequate support systems for them.* As suggested in figure 20.1, social breakdown begins with negative social views and ends with identifying and labeling oneself as incompetent. Figure 20.2 shows how social reconstruction could reverse social breakdown. Both activity theory and social breakdown-reconstruction theory argue that older adults' capabilities and competence are far greater than society has acknowledged in the past. Encouragement of older adults' active participation in society should increase their life satisfaction and positive feelings about themselves.

Stereotyping Older Adults

Ageism *is prejudice against older adults.* Like sexism, it is one of society's uglier words. Many older adults face painful discrimination and may be too polite and too timid to attack it. Older

FIGURE 20.1

Social breakdown syndrome.

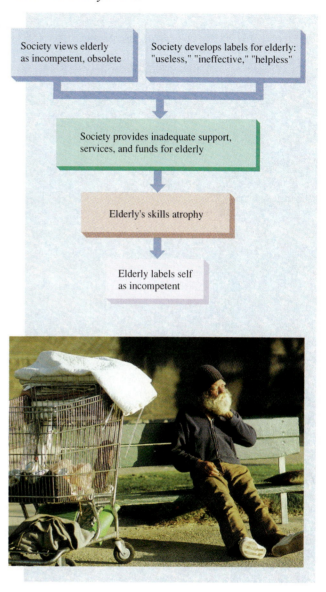

adults may not be hired for new jobs or may be eased out of old ones because they are perceived as too rigid or feebleminded, or because it is cost-effective. They may be shunned socially, possibly because they are perceived as senile or boring. At other times, they may be perceived as children and described with adjectives such as "cute" and "adorable." The elderly may be edged out of their family life by children who see them as sick, ugly, and parasitic. In sum, the elderly may be perceived as incapable of thinking clearly, learning new things, enjoying sex, contributing to the community, and holding responsible jobs—inhumane perceptions to be sure, but often painfully real (Butler, 1987; Chinn, 1991; Cole & others, 1993; Gatz, 1992).

The increased number of adults living to an older age has led to active efforts at improving society's image of the elderly,

FIGURE 20.2

Social reconstruction syndrome.

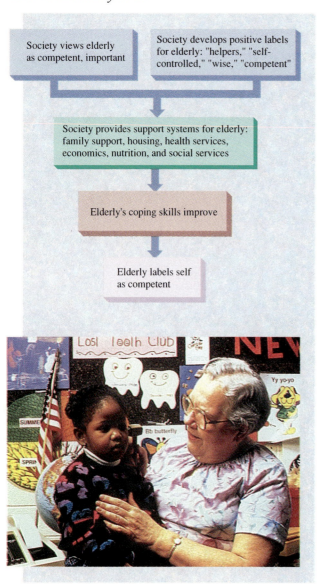

The Gray Panthers are actively involved in pressuring Congress on everything from health insurance to housing costs. Along with the American Association for Retired Persons, they have developed a formidable gray lobbying effort in state and national politics.

obtaining better living conditions for the elderly, and gaining political clout. The American Association of Retired Persons (AARP), with almost 30 million members, is bigger than most countries. The Gray Panthers, with 80,000 members, pressures Congress on everything from health insurance to housing costs. These groups have developed a formidable gray lobbying effort in state and national politics (Kuhn & Sodei, 1993).

Policy Issues in an Aging Society

The aging society and older persons' status in this society raise policy issues about the well-being of older adults, among them the status of the economy and the viability of the Social Security system, the provision of health care, supports for families who care for elderly adults, and generational inequity, each of which we consider in turn (Neugarten, 1988; Neugarten & Neugarten, 1989).

An important issue involving the economy and aging is the concern that our economy cannot bear the burden of so many older persons, who by reason of their age alone are usually consumers rather than producers. However, not all persons 65 and over are nonworkers and not all persons 18 to 64 are workers. And considerably more individuals in the 55 to 64 age group are in the work force—three out of five men—than a decade ago. Thus, it is incorrect to simply describe older adults as consumers and younger adults as producers. Another concern about the economy and aging is the viability of the Social Security system. Scares in the mid- to late-1980s about the Social Security system going bankrupt have now eased, and the Social Security system is no longer in jeopardy.

An aging society also brings with it various problems involving health care (Birren, 1993; Pifer, 1993). Escalating health-care costs are currently causing considerable concern. One factor that contributes to the surge in health costs is the increasing number of older adults. Older adults have more illnesses than younger adults, despite the fact that many older adults report their health as good. Older adults see doctors more often, are hospitalized more often, and have longer hospital stays. Approximately one-third of the total health bill of the United States is for the care of adults 65 and over, who comprise only 12 percent of the population. The health-care needs of the elderly are reflected in Medicare, the program that provides health-care insurance to adults over 65 under the Social Security system. Of interest is the fact that the United States is the only industrialized nation that provides health insurance specifically for older adults rather than to the population at large, and the only industrialized nation currently without a national health-care system. Older adults themselves still pay about one-third of their total health-care costs. Thus, older adults as well as younger adults are adversely affected by rising medical costs.

A special concern is that while many of the health problems of the elderly are chronic rather than acute, the medical system is still based on a "cure" rather than a "care" model. Chronic illness is long-term, often lifelong, and requires long-term, if not life-term, management. Chronic illness often follows a pattern of an acute period that may require hospitalization, followed by a longer period of remission, and then repetitions of this pattern. The patient's home, rather than the hospital, often becomes the center of managing the patient's chronic illness. In a home-based system, a new type of cooperative relationship between doctors, nurses, patients, family members, and other service providers needs to be developed. Health-care personnel need to be trained and be available to provide home services, sharing authority with the patient and perhaps yielding to it over the long term (Corbin & Strauss, 1988; *Quality Health Care,* 1988).

Eldercare *is the physical and emotional caretaking of older members of the family, whether that care is day-to-day physical assistance or responsibility for arranging and overseeing such care.* An important issue involving eldercare is how it can best be provided (Cox, 1993; Franklin, Ames, & King, 1994; Gallagher & Gerstel, 1993; Gonyea, 1994). With so many women in the labor market, who will replace them as caregivers? An added problem is that many caregivers are in their sixties, and many of them are ill themselves. They may find it especially stressful to be responsible for the care of relatives who are in their eighties or nineties.

Some gerontologists advocate that the government should provide financial support to families to help with home services or substitute for the loss of income if a worker reduces outside employment to care for an aging relative (England & others, 1991). Some large corporations are helping workers with parent-caring by providing flexible work schedules and creating more part-time or at-home jobs. Government supports have been slow to develop. One reason for their slow development is that some persons believe such government interventions will weaken the family's responsibility and thus have a negative effect on the well-being of older, as well as younger, adults.

Yet another policy issue involving aging is **generational inequity** (discussed initially in chapter 1), *which states that an aging society is being unfair to its younger members because older adults pile up advantages by receiving an inequitably large allocation of resources* (Bengston, Marti, & Roberts, 1991). Some authors have argued that generational inequity produces intergenerational conflict and divisiveness in the society at large (Longman, 1987). The generational equity issue raises questions about whether the young should be required to pay for the old. One claim is that today's baby boomers, now in their thirties and forties, will receive lower Social Security payments than are presently being paid out, or none at all, when they reach retirement age. However, our earlier comments indicated that this is highly unlikely. The generational equity issue sometimes also takes the form of whether the "advantaged" old population is using up resources that should go to disadvantaged children (Hirshorn, 1991; Sapp, 1991; Welch, 1991). The argument is that older adults are advantaged because they have publicly provided pensions, health care, food stamps, housing subsidies, tax breaks, and other benefits that younger age groups do not have. While the trend of greater services for the elderly has been occurring, the percentage of children living in poverty has been increasing. Distinguished developmentalist Bernice Neugarten (1988) says it is undeniable that the large numbers of poor children are a disgrace to an affluent society like the United States. She stresses that the problem should not be viewed as one of generational equity, but rather as a major shortcoming of our broader economic and social policies. In conclusion, Neugarten envisions that we would do better to think about what a positive spirit of aging would mean to America, and to what extent this positive spirit could improve the range of options for people of all ages. Margaret Gatz (1992), an expert on aging, agrees.

Income

The elderly poor are a special concern (Krause, Jay, & Liang, 1991; McLaughlin & Jensen, 1993). In 1988, 3,482,000 individuals aged 65 and over in the United States were classified as poor by the federal government (U.S. Bureau of the Census, 1990). Poverty level is determined by the minimum income required to sustain families of various sizes. For example, in 1988 the federal poverty level for an elderly person living alone was $5,674 and for an elderly couple it was $7,158. The percentage of elderly poor would be greater if the "hidden poor," those who have been taken in by relatives who are not poor, were included. A special concern is the elderly who are widowed and the elderly who are single, showing poverty rates of 40 percent or higher in various parts of the United States (Hurd & Wise, 1989).

Many older adults are understandably concerned about their income. The average income of retired Americans is only about half of what they earned when they were fully employed. While retired individuals need less income for job-related and social activities, adults 65 and over spend a greater proportion of their income for food, utilities, and health care. They spend a smaller proportion for transportation, clothing, pension and life insurance, and entertainment than do adults under the age of 65. Social Security is the largest contributor to the income of older Americans (38 percent), followed by assets, earnings, and pensions.

The majority of older adults face a life of reduced income. Far too few middle-aged adults adequately plan for this. For instance, middle-aged Americans who will retire in 20 to 25 years will need an income equal to 75 percent of their current annual expenditures (adjusted for inflation) to maintain their current, middle-aged life-style (Taylor, 1988).

Despite the sizable number of elderly adults who still fall below the poverty level, the reduction of poverty among older

Americans is one of the few success stories of the federal government's war on poverty. During the 1970s and 1980s, poverty rates declined for both elderly and nonelderly adults (Aiken, 1989).

Living Arrangements

One stereotype of older adults is that they are often residents in institutions—hospitals, mental hospitals, nursing homes, and so on. However, nearly 95 percent of older adults live in the community. Almost two-thirds of older adults live with family members—spouse, a child, a sibling, for example—while almost one-third live alone (Church, Siegel, & Foster, 1988). The older people become, the greater are their odds for living alone. The majority of older adults living alone are widowed. As with younger adults, living alone as an older adult does not mean being lonely (Kasper, 1988). Elderly adults who can sustain themselves while living alone often have good health and few disabilities, and they may have regular social exchanges with relatives, friends, and neighbors.

For many years researchers who studied the living arrangements of older adults focused on special situations such as nursing homes, public housing, mobile-home parks, welfare hotels, or retirement communities. However, less than 10 percent of older adults live in these types of housing arrangements. Nonetheless, the quality of housing for the elderly is far from perfect (Baker & Prince, 1991; Pastalan, 1991). The vast majority of older adults prefer to live independently—either alone or with a spouse—rather than with a child, with a relative, or in an institution (Beland, 1987).

Only 5 percent of adults 65 years of age and older live in institutions, but the older adults become, the more likely they are to live in an institution. For example, 23 percent of adults 85 years and over live in institutions. The majority of the elderly adults in institutions are widows, many of whom cannot physically navigate their environment, are mentally impaired, or are incontinent (cannot control their excretory functions). Because the population is aging and because wives' life expectations are increasing more rapidly than husbands', we are likely to witness even greater numbers of widows in institutions in the future.

ETHNICITY, GENDER, AND CULTURE

What are the roles of ethnicity and gender in aging? What are the social aspects of aging in different cultures?

Ethnicity and Gender

Of special concern are the ethnic minority elderly, especially Black Americans and Hispanic Americans, who are overrepresented in the elderly poor (Atchley, 1989; Hernandez, 1991). Consider Harry, a 72-year-old Black American who lives in a run-down hotel in Los Angeles. He suffers from arthritis and uses a walker. He has not been able to work for years, and government payments are barely enough to meet his needs. Nearly one-third of elderly Black Americans live on less than $5,300 per year. Among Black American women living alone the figure is 55 percent. Almost one-fourth of elderly Hispanic

Americans are below the poverty line. Only 10 percent of elderly White Americans fall below the poverty line (Bahr, 1989).

Comparative information about Black Americans, Hispanic Americans, and White Americans indicates a possible double jeopardy for elderly ethnic minority individuals, who face problems related to *both* ageism and racism (Brink, 1992; Jackson, Chatters, & Taylor, 1993; Tran, Wright, & Chatters, 1991). Both the wealth and the health of ethnic minority elderly decrease more rapidly than for elderly White Americans (Chatters, 1993; Edmonds, 1993). Ethnic minority elderly are more likely to become ill but less likely to receive treatment. They are also more likely to have a history of less education, unemployment, worse housing conditions, and shorter life expectancies than their elderly White American counterparts. And many ethnic minority workers never enjoy the Social Security and Medicare benefits to which their earnings contribute, because they die before reaching the age of eligibility for benefits (Gibson, 1993; Skinner, 1990; Williams, 1990).

Critical Thinking

Do you have any ideas about how we can intervene to make the lives of low-income and ethnic minority older adults healthier and happier? Describe at least one strategy that could be implemented.

A possible double jeopardy also faces many women—the burden of *both* ageism and sexism (Datan, 1989; Gerlach, 1991; Harrison, 1991; Pifer, 1993; Rayman, Allshouse, & Allen, 1993). The poverty rate for elderly females is almost double that of elderly males. According to Congresswoman Mary Rose Oakar, the number one priority for mid-life and older women should be economic security. She predicts that 25 percent of all women working today can expect to be poor in old age (Porcino, 1983). Yet only recently has scientific and political interest in the aging woman developed. For many years, the aging woman was virtually invisible in aging research and in protests involving rights for the elderly. An important research and political agenda for the 1990s is increased interest in the aging and rights of elderly women.

Not only is it important to be concerned about older women's double jeopardy of ageism and sexism, but special attention also needs to be devoted to the elderly who are female ethnic minority individuals. They face what could be described as triple jeopardy—ageism, sexism, and racism (Edmonds, 1990; Malveaux, 1993). Income is a special problem for these women. For example, more than one-third of older Black American women have incomes below the poverty level (compared to less than one-fourth of older Black American men and approximately 13 percent of older White American women). One-fourth of older Hispanic American women have incomes below the poverty level (compared to 19 percent of Hispanic American men) (United States Bureau of the Census, 1990). More information about being female, ethnic, and old appears in Sociocultural Worlds of Development 20.1.

Despite the stress and discrimination elderly ethnic minority individuals face, many of these older adults have developed coping mechanisms that allow them to survive in the dominant

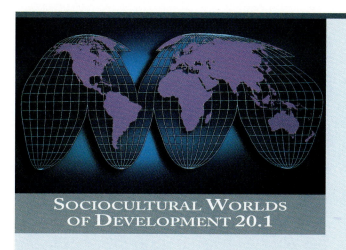

SOCIOCULTURAL WORLDS
OF DEVELOPMENT 20.1

Being Female, Ethnic, and Old

Part of the unfortunate history of ethnic minority groups in the United States has been the negative stereotypes against members of their groups. Many have also been hampered by their immigrant origins in that they are not fluent or literate in English, may not be aware of the values and norms involved in American social interaction, and may have life-styles that differ from those of mainstream America (Brink, 1992; Johnson, 1994; Morycz, 1993; Organista, 1994). Often included in these cultural differences is the role of women in the family and in society. Many, but not all, immigrant ethnic groups traditionally have relegated the woman's role to family maintenance. Many important decisions may be made by a woman's husband or parents, and she is often not expected to seek an independent career or enter the work force except in the case of dire financial need.

Some ethnic minority groups may define an older woman's role as unimportant, especially if she is unable to contribute financially. However, in some ethnic minority groups, an older woman's social status improves. For example, older Black American women can express their own needs and can be given status and power in the community. Despite their positive status in the Black family and the Black culture, Black women over the age of 70 are the poorest population group in the United States. Three of five elderly Black women live alone; most of them are widowed. The low incomes of elderly Black women translate into less than adequate access to health care. Substantially lower incomes for Black American elderly women are related to the kinds of jobs they hold, which either are not covered by Social Security or, in the case of domestic service, are not reported even when reporting is legally required.

A portrayal of older Black women in cities reveals some of their survival strategies. They highly value the family as a system of mutual support and aid, adhere to the American work ethic, and view religion as a source of strength (Perry & Johnson, 1994). The use of religion as a way of coping with stress has a long history in the Black culture, with roots in the slave experience. The Black church came to fulfill needs and functions once met by religion-based tribal and community organizations that Blacks brought from Africa (McAdoo, 1988; Smith, 1993). In one investigation, the elderly Black women valued church organizations more than their male counterparts did, especially valuing the church's group activities and organizations (Taylor, 1982).

In sum, Black elderly women have faced considerable stress in their lives (Edmonds, 1990). In the face of this stress, they have shown remarkable adaptiveness, resilience, responsibility, and coping skills.

A special concern is the stress faced by Black elderly women, many of whom view religion as a source of strength to help them cope with stress.

White American world (Markides & Mindel, 1987). Extension of family networks helps elderly minority-group individuals cope with the bare essentials of living, and gives them a sense of being loved. The Black church, as well as the Catholic church in Hispanic communities, provides avenues for meaningful social participation, feelings of power, and a sense of internal satisfaction. And residential concentrations of ethnic minority groups give their elderly members a sense of belonging. Nonetheless, the income and health of elderly ethnic minority individuals are important concerns in our aging society.

Gender Roles

Do our gender roles change when we become older adults? Some developmentalists believe there is decreasing femininity in women and decreasing masculinity in men when they reach the late adulthood years (Gutmann, 1975). The evidence suggests that older men do become more feminine—nurturant, sensitive, and so on—but it appears that older women do not necessarily become more masculine—assertive, dominant, and so on (Turner, 1982). Keep in mind that cohort effects are especially important to consider in areas like gender roles. As sociohistorical changes take place and are assessed more frequently in life-span investigations, what were once perceived to be age effects may turn out to be cohort effects (Belsky, 1992; Jacobs, 1994; Szinovacz, 1989; Wainrib, 1992).

Culture

For many generations, the elderly in China and Japan experienced higher status than the elderly in the United States (Ikels, 1989; Palmore, 1975; Yu, 1993). In Japan, the elderly are more integrated into their families than are the elderly in most industrialized countries. More than 75 percent live with their children; few single older adults live alone. Respect for the elderly surfaces in many circumstances: The best seats may be reserved for the elderly, cooking caters to the tastes of the elderly, and individuals bow to the elderly.

However, the image of elderly Japanese who are spared the heartbreak associated with aging in the United States by the respect and devotion they receive from children, grandchildren, and society is probably idealized and exaggerated (Tobin, 1987). Americans' images of the elderly in other cultures may be idealized, too—we imagine elderly Eskimos adrift on blocks of ice and 120-year-old Russian yogurt eaters, in addition to the honored elders of Japan. For example, as Japan has become more urbanized and Westernized, fewer elderly live with their children and more elderly adults return to work, usually in a lower-status job, with lower pay, a loss of fringe benefits, and a loss of union membership. The Japanese culture has acted as a powerful brake in slowing the decline in the respect for the elderly—today respect for the elderly is greater in Japan than in the United States, but not as strong as the idealized images we sometimes have (Takada, 1993; Usui, 1989).

What factors are associated with whether the elderly are accorded a position of high status in a culture? Seven factors are most likely to predict high status for the elderly in a culture (Cogwill, 1974; Sangree, 1989; Sokolovsky, 1983):

1. Older persons have valuable knowledge.
2. Older persons control key family/community resources.
3. Older persons are permitted to engage in useful and valued functions as long as possible.
4. There is role continuity throughout the life span.
5. Age-related role changes involve greater responsibility, authority, and advisory capacity.

An older adult fabric weaver in Kyoto, Japan. As Japan has become more urbanized and Westernized, fewer elderly adults live with their children and more elderly adults return to work. Today, respect for the elderly in Japan is greater than in the United States, but not as strong as the idealized images we sometimes have.

6. The extended family is a common family arrangement in the culture, and the older person is integrated into the extended family.
7. The culture is more collectivistic than individualistic.

At this point we have discussed a number of ideas about the social worlds of older adults, and about the roles of ethnicity, gender, and culture in aging. A summary of these ideas is presented in concept table 20.1. Now we turn our attention to the nature of families and social relationships in late adulthood.

FAMILIES AND SOCIAL RELATIONSHIPS

What is the nature of marital relationships in older adults? Do older adults date? What is the nature of their friendships and social networks? What is the grandparent's role? These are some of the important questions to ask about the families and social relationships of older adults.

The Aging Couple, Life-Styles, Dating, and Friendship

The time from retirement until death is sometimes referred to as the "final stage in the marriage process." Retirement alters a couple's life-style, requiring adaptation (Mann, 1991; Vinick & Ekerdt, 1991). The greatest changes occur in the traditional family, in which the husband works and the wife is a homemaker. The husband may not know what to do with his time, and the wife may feel uneasy having him around the house all of the time. In traditional families, both partners may need to

CONCEPT TABLE 20.1

The Social Worlds of Older Adults; and Ethnicity, Gender, and Culture

Concept	Processes/Related Ideas	Characteristics/Description
The social and cultural worlds of older adults	Social theories of aging	Three prominent theories are disengagement theory, activity theory, and social breakdown-reconstruction theory. No support has been found for disengagement theory. Both activity theory and social breakdown-reconstruction theory argue that older adults' capabilities are far greater than was acknowledged in the past.
	Stereotyping of older adults	Ageism is prejudice against older adults. Too many negative stereotypes of older adults still exist.
	Policy issues in an aging society	According to Neugarten, some of the important policy issues in an aging society of the United States are the status of the economy and the viability of the Social Security system, the provision of health care, eldercare, and generational inequity.
	Income	A special concern is the elderly poor. Older adults who are widowed or single have especially high poverty rates, although overall, there are fewer older adults living in poverty today than in earlier decades. Nonetheless, the majority of older adults face a life of reduced income.
	Living arrangements	A stereotype of older adults is that they often live in institutions, but almost 95 percent live in the community. The majority of older adults living alone are widowed. The older adults become, the more likely they are to live in an institution (23 percent of adults 85 and over, for example). Almost two-thirds of older adults live with family members.
Ethnicity, gender, and culture	Ethnicity and gender	The ethnic minority elderly face special burdens, having to cope with the possible double jeopardy of ageism and racism. Many older women also face a possible double jeopardy—ageism and sexism. Only recently have scientific and political interests focused on the aging woman. Older ethnic minority women face a possible triple jeopardy—the burdens of ageism, racism, and sexism. Nonetheless, despite the stress and discrimination elderly ethnic minority persons face, many of these older adults have developed coping mechanisms that allow them to survive in the dominant White American culture.
	Gender roles	There is stronger evidence that men become more "feminine" (nurturant, sensitive) as older adults than there is that women become more "masculine" (assertive, dominant) as older adults.
	Culture	For many generations the elderly in China and Japan have experienced higher status than the elderly in the United States. Today, respect for the elderly in Japan has diminished somewhat, but still remains above that accorded the elderly in the United States. The factors that predict high status for the elderly across cultures include their valuable knowledge, their control of family/community resources, allowing older persons to engage in useful functions, role continuity, age-related role changes that involve greater responsibility, integration in an extended family, and a collectivistic rather than an individualistic cultural orientation.

Friends play an important role in the support system of elderly individuals. In some cases, friendships with unrelated adults may replace the warmth and companionship traditionally provided by family relationships.

move toward more expressive roles. The husband must adjust from being the good provider to being a helper around the house; the wife must change from being only a good home-maker to being even more loving and understanding. Marital happiness as an older adult is also affected by each partner's ability to deal with personal conflicts, including aging, illness, and eventual death (Condi, 1989; Duvall & Miller, 1985; Greenberg, 1994; Starrels, 1994).

So closely interwoven have been our lives, our purposes, and experiences that, separated, we have a feeling of incompleteness—united, such strengths of self-assertion that no ordinary obstacles, differences, or dangers ever appear to us insurmountable.

—Elizabeth Cady Stanton, *Eighty Years and More*

Individuals who are married in late adulthood are usually happier than those who are single (Lee, 1978). Marital satis-faction is greater for women than for men, possibly because women place more emphasis on attaining satisfaction through marriage than men do. However, as more women develop ca-reers, this sex difference may not continue.

The richest love is that which submits to the arbitration of time.

—Lawrence Durrell, *Clea*, 1960

Not all older adults are married. At least 8 percent of all in-dividuals who reach the age of 65 have never been married. Contrary to the popular stereotype, older adults who have never been married seem to have the least difficulty coping with lone-liness in old age. Many of them discovered long ago how to live autonomously and how to become self-reliant (Gubrium, 1975).

Few of us imagine older couples taking an interest in sex rather than only nonsexual companionship—perhaps we see them as being interested in a game of bridge or a conversa-tion on the porch, but not much else. In fact, there are a num-ber of older adults who date. The increased health and longevity of older adults have resulted in a much larger pool of active older adults. And the increased divorce rate has added many more older adults to this pool.

> *I could be handy, mending a fuse when your lights are gone. You can knit a sweater by the fireside, Sunday morning go for a ride. Doing the garden, digging the weeds, who could ask for more? Will you still need me, will you still feed me, when I'm sixty-four?*
>
> —John Lennon and Paul McCartney

Regardless of their age, individuals also seem to place a high value on time spent with friends, at times higher than time spent with relatives. Life events may influence our friendships. In divorce or death, friendship usually provides an important support system; these events may intensify our friendships. Friendships among the elderly may become especially important in the years to come. Because individuals are having fewer children, families are becoming smaller. As individuals age, they will have fewer individuals to depend on for emotional and financial support. The mobility of our society also increases the distance between older and younger adults. Friendships with unrelated adults may help to replace the warmth, companionship, and nurturance traditionally supplied by families. In sum, friends play an important role in the support systems of older adults (Adams, 1989; Crohan & Antonucci, 1989).

Grandparenting

Think for a moment about your images of grandparents. We generally think of grandparents as old people, but there are many middle-aged grandparents too. About three of every four adults over the age of 65 has at least one living grandchild, and most grandparents have some regular contact with their grandchildren (Bahr, 1989). About 80 percent of grandparents say they are happy in their relationships with their grandchildren, and a majority of grandparents say that grandparenting is easier than parenthood and that they enjoy it more than parenthood (Brubaker, 1985). In one investigation, grandfathers were less satisfied with grandparenthood than were grandmothers, and middle-aged grandparents (aged 45–60) were more willing to give advice and to assume responsibility for watching and disciplining grandchildren than were older grandparents (aged 60 and older) (Thomas, 1986). Also, maternal grandparents often interact more with their grandchildren than paternal grandparents (Bahr, 1989).

What is the meaning of the grandparent role? Three prominent meanings are attached to being a grandparent (Neugarten & Weinstein, 1964). For some older adults, being a grandparent is a source of biological reward and continuity. In such cases, feelings of renewal (youth) or extensions of the self and family into the future emerge. For others, being a grandparent is a source of emotional self-fulfillment, generating feelings of companionship and satisfaction that may have been missing in earlier adult-child relationships (Sanders &

At some point in our middle or late adulthood years, the majority of us will become grandparents. What are the different meanings attached to the grandparent role? What do you think you will be like as a grandparent? Would you treat your grandchildren any differently than your grandparents treated you?

Trygstad, 1993; Strom & Strom, 1993). And for yet others, being a grandparent is not as important as it is for some individuals, experienced as a remote role.

The grandparent role may have different functions in different families, in different ethnic groups and cultures, and in different situations. For example, in one investigation of White, Black, and Mexican American grandparents and grandchildren, the Mexican American grandparents saw their grandchildren more frequently, provided more support for the grandchildren and their parents, and had more satisfying relationships with their grandchildren (Bengston, 1985). And in an investigation of three generations of families in Chicago, grandmothers had closer relationships with their children and grandchildren and gave more personal advice than grandfathers did (Hagestad, 1985).

The diversity of grandparenting was also apparent in an early investigation of how grandparents interacted with their grandchildren (Neugarten & Weinstein, 1964). Three styles were dominant—formal, fun-seeking, and distant figure. In the formal style, the grandparent performed what was considered to be a proper and prescribed role. These grandparents showed a strong interest in their grandchildren, but left parenting to the parents and were careful not to give child-rearing advice. In the

At the turn of the century, the three-generation family was common, but now the four-generation family is common as well. Thus, an increasing number of grandparents are also great-grandparents. The four-generation family shown here is the Jordans—author John Santrock's mother-in-law, daughter, granddaughter, and wife.

fun-seeking style, the grandparent was informal and playful. Grandchildren were a source of leisure activity; mutual satisfaction was emphasized. A substantial portion of grandparents were distant figures. In the distant-figure style, the grandparent was benevolent but interaction occurred on an infrequent basis. Grandparents who were over the age of 65 were more likely to display a formal style of interaction; those under 65 were more likely to display a fun-seeking style.

Critical Thinking

How do you think the grandparent's role will change in the future? Consider such factors as the increased mobility of our society, the increased number of people growing up in divorced and stepparent families, the increased longevity of our population, and changing gender roles.

As more individuals live to an old age and as more families live in varied family structures, we can expect the nature of the grandparent's role and social interaction with grandchildren to change (Cherlin & Furstenberg, 1988; Peterson, 1989). Because of the aging of our society, an increasing number of grandparents are also great-grandparents. At the turn of the century, the three-generation family was common, but now the four-generation family is common. As divorce and remarriage have become more common, a special concern of grandparents is visitation privileges with their grandchildren. In the last 10 to 15 years, most states have passed laws giving grandparents the right to petition a court to legally obtain visitation privileges with their

grandchildren. Now, even if a parent objects, grandparents may be permitted to spend time with their grandchildren. Whether such forced visitation rights for grandparents are in the child's best interests is still being debated. More about grandparenting and other aspects of intergenerational relationships appears in Perspectives on Parenting and Education 20.1.

PERSONALITY DEVELOPMENT, LIFE SATISFACTION, AND SUCCESSFUL AGING

Does our personality change when we become old? Do we enter a new stage of personality development? What contributes to our life satisfaction as an older adult? How can we age successfully? Do our gender roles change when we become old? We consider each of these questions in turn.

The Nature of Personality Development

Psychoanalytic theorists Sigmund Freud and Carl Jung saw old age as similar to childhood. For example, Freud believed that in old age we return to the narcissistic interests of early childhood. Jung said that in old age thought is deeply submerged in the unconscious mind; little contact with reality in old age was possible, he thought. More recently, developmentalists have crafted a view of old age that is more constructive and adaptive (Erikson, Erikson, & Kivnick, 1986).

Erikson's Final Stage: Integrity Versus Despair

Erik Erikson (1968) believes that late adulthood is characterized by the last of the eight life cycle stages, *integrity versus despair.* In Erikson's view, the later years of life are a time for looking back at what we have done with our lives. Through many different routes, the older adult may have developed a positive outlook in each of the preceding periods. If so, retrospective glances and reminiscence will reveal a picture of a life well spent, and the older adult will be satisfied (integrity). But if the older adult resolved one or more of the earlier stages in a negative way (being isolated in early adulthood or stagnated in middle adulthood, for example), retrospective glances may reveal doubt, gloom, and despair over the total worth of one's life. Erikson's own words capture the richness of his thought about the crisis of integrity versus despair in older adults:

> A meaningful old age, then . . . serves the need for that integrated heritage which gives indispensable perspective to the life cycle. Strength here takes the form of that detached yet active concern with life bounded by death, which we call *wisdom* in its many connotations from ripened "wits" to accumulated knowledge, mature judgment, and inclusive understanding. Not that each man can evolve wisdom for himself. For most, a living *tradition* provides the essence of it. But the end of the life cycle also evokes "ultimate concerns" for what change may have to transcend the limitations of his identity. . . .

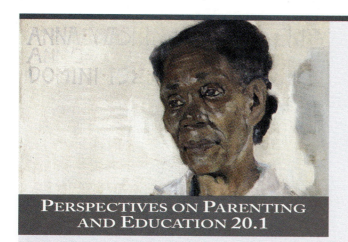

**PERSPECTIVES ON PARENTING
AND EDUCATION 20.1**

Intergenerational Relationships and Diversity in Family Structure and Roles

Sociohistorical changes in the twentieth century have produced varied patterns of intergenerational relationships in families. Among the different intergenerational family structures that have been produced are the age-condensed, age-gapped, truncated, matrilineal, and stepfamily structures (Bengston, Rosenthal, & Burton, 1990).

Age-Condensed. The increase in teenage pregnancy, especially across generations, has created an age-condensed intergenerational pattern in which the distance between generations can be just 15 years. This small distance between generations often blurs generational boundaries. For example, in one study of age-condensed families, the mother-daughter relationship was more intra- than intergenerationally oriented (Burton, 1985). Mothers and daughters perceived themselves as more like sisters than like parent and child. Teenage pregnancy sparked early transitions to grandparenthood that often were not welcomed.

Age-Gapped. While teenage pregnancy produces multiple generations with little age distance between generations and unclear generational boundaries, delayed childbearing has the opposite effect. When women postpone childbearing until their thirties, large age gaps are created across generations. The greater age distance may create strains in the development of bonds across the life course, especially since it may result in parents' experiencing child-rearing difficulties with their adolescents simultaneously with caregiving demands from aging parents (Rossi, 1987). Also, the later the parents have a child, the more likely they are to have fewer total children, which reduces the potential caregiver pool for aging parents.

Truncated (Childless). Childlessness creates the shortest, slimmest lineage across generations (Parke, 1988). Establishing intergenerational ties and the options for receiving care within the family become very limited for older childless adults. The childless elderly often establish bonds with extended family relatives.

Matrilineal. The increase in out-of-wedlock childbearing produces yet another type of intergenerational family structure—matrilineal. Out-of-wedlock childbearing is especially high among Black women. For example, in 1986 one-half of all births to Black American women involved unmarried females (U.S. Bureau of the Census, 1987). In such families, older Black women may be called upon more often by their daughters to serve as the "other parent" for their children. And older women are more likely in these circumstances to share their households with their daughters and grandchildren and help assist in child rearing and alleviating the financial pressures of single parenthood (Wilson, 1986).

Stepfamily. A fifth demographic trend that has produced diversity in intergenerational relationships involves the high rate of divorce. When the children of elderly parents divorce, it has a marked impact on intergenerational relationships. Parents of the adult child who does not receive custody of the child or children are faced with not having the same opportunities to be actively involved in the lives of their grandchildren. And the elderly parents may be forced to restrict their relationship with the former daughter- or son-in-law. If divorce is followed by remarriage, elderly parents are faced with a complex reconstitution of the intergenerational family, and even further complexity when remarriage includes integrating stepchildren into the kinship structure.

In sum, intergenerational patterns of transmission have become more complex as the number of people in diverse family structures has increased.

To whatever abyss ultimate concerns may lead individual men, man as a psychosocial creature will face, toward the end of his life, a new edition of the identity crisis which we may state in the words, "I am what survives of me." (140–141)

Robert Peck's Reworking of Erikson's Final Stage

Robert Peck (1968) reworked Erikson's final stage of development, integrity versus despair, by describing three developmental tasks, or issues, that men and women face when they become old. **Differentiation versus role preoccupation** *is Peck's developmental task in which older adults must redefine their worth in terms of something other than work roles.* Peck believes older adults need to pursue a set of valued activities so that time previously spent in an occupation and with children can be filled. **Body transcendence versus body preoccupation** *is Peck's developmental task in which older adults must cope with declining physical well-being.* As older adults age, they may experience a chronic illness and considerable deterioration in their physical capabilities. For men and women whose identity has revolved around their physical well-being, the decrease in health and deterioration of physical capabilities may present a severe threat to their identity and feelings of life satisfaction. However, while most older adults experience illnesses, many enjoy life through human relationships that allow them to go beyond a preoccupation with their aging body. **Ego transcendence versus ego**

LIFE-SPAN PRACTICAL KNOWLEDGE 20.1

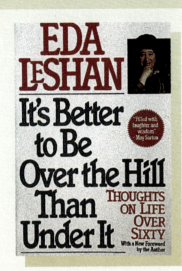

It's Better To Be Over the Hill Than Under the Hill: Thoughts on Life After 60

(1990) by Eda LeShan. New York: Newmarket Press.

This book covers a wide range of topics related to the social, psychological, and life-style dimensions of aging. The book consists of 75 essays written by LeShan that range from "An Open Letter to the Tooth Fairy" to "Nothing Is Simple Anymore" to "Divorce After Sixty." Among the aging issues dealt with are money, love, sex, anger, facing mortality, work, marriage, friendship, retirement, holidays, grandparenting, and children. Woven through the essays is hope for older adults, hope that will allow them to love and to grow and to keep their minds and bodies active and alive. This Erma Bombeck–like version of old age is enjoyable reading. It will be especially helpful to older adults who feel caught in a rut and need their spirits lifted. And it is good reading for the middle-aged and young adult children of aging parents, helping children to become knowledgeable about the changes that are taking place in their aging parents.

preoccupation *is Peck's developmental task in which older adults must recognize that while death is inevitable and probably not too far away, they feel at ease with themselves by realizing that they have contributed to the future through the competent rearing of their children or through their vocation and ideas.*

Life Review

Life review *is a common theme in theories of personality development in late adulthood. Life review involves looking back at one's life experiences, evaluating them, interpreting them, and often reinterpreting them.* Distinguished aging researcher Robert Butler (1975) believes the life review is set in motion by looking forward to death. Sometimes the life review proceeds quietly, at other times it is intense, requiring considerable work to achieve some sense of personality integration. The life review may be observed initially in stray and insignificant thoughts about oneself and one's life history. These thoughts may continue to emerge in brief intermittent spurts or become essentially continuous. One 76-year-old man commented, "My life is in the back of my mind. It can't be any other way. Thoughts of the past play on me. Sometimes I play with them, encouraging and savoring them; at other times I dismiss them."

As the past marches in review (Merriam, 1993; Webster, 1993), the older adult surveys it, observes it, and reflects on it. Reconsideration of previous experiences and their meaning occurs, often with revision or expanded understanding taking place (Haight, 1991). This reorganization of the past may provide a more valid picture for the individual, providing new and significant meaning to one's life. It may also help prepare the individual for death, in the process reducing fear. Remember our description of the 75-year-old woman at the beginning of the chapter, who decided to get a tape recorder and describe her life so her grandchildren would have something to remember her by when she is gone.

As the life review proceeds, the older adult may reveal to a spouse, children, or other close associates unknown characteristics and experiences that previously had been undisclosed. In return, they may reveal previously unknown or undisclosed truths. Hidden themes of great meaning to the individual may emerge, changing the nature of the older adult's sense of self. Successful aging, though, doesn't mean thinking about the past all of the time. In one study, older adults who were obsessed about the past were less well adjusted than older adults who integrated their past and present (Wong & Watt, 1991).

Life Satisfaction

Life satisfaction *is psychological well-being in general or satisfaction with life as a whole. Life satisfaction is a widely used index of psychological well-being in older adults.* Income, health, an active life-style, and a network of friends and family are associated with older adults' life satisfaction in predictable ways. Older adults with adequate income and good health are more likely to be satisfied with their lives than their counterparts who have little income and poor health (Markides & Martin, 1979). An active life-style is associated with psychological well-being in older adults—older adults who go to church, go to meetings, go on trips, play golf, go to dances, and exercise regularly are more satisfied with their lives than older adults who stay at home and wrap themselves in a cocoon. Older adults who have an extended social network of friends and family are also more satisfied with their lives than older adults who are more socially isolated (Chappell & Badger, 1989; Palmore & others, 1985). Some researchers, though, believe a close attachment to one or more individuals is more important than support networks as a whole (Levitt, 1989; Levitt & others, in press).

Interestingly, older adults often have a more optimistic perception of late-life development than do young or middle-aged adults. In one recent study, Joachim Krueger and Jutta

Heckhausen (1993) asked young, middle-aged, and old adults to rate 100 trait descriptions with regard to the decades of adult life. The old adults were more likely to choose optimistic trait descriptions about late-life development than were their younger counterparts.

Successful Aging

The good news about aging is that, barring disease, many of our capabilities decline very slowly, given proper diet, exercise, mental stimulation, and good social relationships and support. Throughout our discussion of late adulthood we have underscored that leading an active rather than a passive life will reap physical and psychological benefits. However, successful aging does require effort and coping skills (Satlin, 1994; Weintraub, Powell, & Whitla, 1994). Engaging in a regular exercise program requires effort for people of any age. So does engaging in effective coping skills. Adopting these strategies for successful aging may be especially difficult in late adulthood because of declining strength and energy. Nonetheless, older adults who do develop a commitment to an active life and to the belief that developing coping skills can produce greater life satisfaction are more likely to age successfully than are older adults who don't make this commitment.

Life-span developmentalist Paul Baltes and his colleagues (Baltes & Baltes, 1990; Baltes, Smith, & Staudinger, in press) believe that successful aging is related to three main factors: selection, optimization, and compensation. Consider the late Arthur Rubinstein, who was interviewed when he was 80 years old. Rubinstein said that three factors were responsible for his ability to maintain his status as an admired concert pianist into old age. First, he mastered the weaknesses of old age by reducing the scope of his repertoire and playing fewer pieces (an example of selection). Second, he spent more time at practice than earlier in his life (an example of optimization). And

third, he used special strategies such as slowing down before fast segments, thus creating the image of faster playing than was objectively true (an example of compensation) (Baltes, Smith, & Staudinger, in press).

The **selective optimization with compensation model** *proposes that successful aging is related to three main factors: selection, optimization, and compensation.* Selection is based on the concept that in old age there is a reduced capacity and loss of functioning, which mandate a reduction of performance in most domains of life. Optimization suggests that it is possible to maintain performance in some areas by practice and the use of new technologies. Compensation becomes relevant when life tasks require a level of capacity beyond the current level of the older adult's performance potential. Older adults especially need to compensate in circumstances with high mental or physical demands, such as when thinking about and memorizing new material very fast, reacting quickly when driving a car, or running fast. Illness in old age makes the need for compensation obvious.

There is an increasing interest in the roles of selective optimization with compensation as a model for successful aging (Heckhausen & Schultz, in press). The process of selective optimization with compensation is likely to be effective whenever loss is an important component of a person's life. Loss is a common dimension of old age, although there are wide variations in the nature of the losses involved. Thus, all aging persons are likely to engage in some form of selection, optimization, and compensation, but the specific form of adaptation will vary depending on each individual's life history, pattern of interests, values, health, skills, and resources.

At this point, we have discussed a number of ideas about families and social relationships, and about personality development, in late adulthood. A summary of these ideas is presented in concept table 20.2.

CONCLUSIONS

In late adulthood, we shed the leaves of youth and adapt to life as older adults. We began this chapter with a description of a 75-year-old woman named Edna and her life review. Then we explored the social worlds of older adults by studying social theories of aging, stereotyping of older adults, policy issues in an aging society, income, and living arrangements. Next, we read about ethnicity, gender, and culture in old age. Our coverage of families and social relationships focused on the

aging couple, life-styles, dating, and friendship, as well as grandparenting. We also studied personality development, life satisfaction, and successful aging. We concluded that successful aging occurs when older adults follow a proper diet, exercise, seek mental stimulation, and have good social relationships and support. Successful aging requires effort and coping skills. There is increasing interest in a model of successful aging that involves selective optimization with compensation. At dif-

ferent points in the chapter we also studied what it is like to be female, ethnic, and old, intergenerational relationships and diversity in family structure and roles, and social support and health in late adulthood.

Remember that you can obtain an overall summary of the chapter by again reading the two concept tables on pages 563 and 570. This concludes our discussion of late adulthood. Next we turn our attention to the book's final section, "Death and Dying."

CONCEPT TABLE 20.2

Families and Social Relationships, and Personality Development

Concept	Processes/Related Ideas	Characteristics/Description
Families and social relationships	The aging couple, life-styles, dating, and friendship	The time from retirement until death is sometimes referred to as the "final stage in the marriage process." Retirement alters a couple's life-style, requiring adaptation. Married adults in old age are usually happier than single adults, although single adults may adjust more easily to loneliness. Dating has become increasingly common among older adults. In some cases it is similar to dating in younger adults, and in other cases it is dissimilar. Regardless of age, friendships are an important dimension of social relationships; they may become more intense in times of loss.
	Grandparenting	About 80 percent of grandparents say they are happy in their relationships with grandchildren. Maternal grandparents interact with grandchildren more than paternal grandparents. The grandparent role has at least three meanings—biological, emotional, and remote; and it has at least three styles of interaction—formal, fun-seeking, and distant. Grandparents' roles may vary across cultures and ethnic groups, and, because of our aging society, an increasing number of grandparents are also great-grandparents. As divorce and remarriage have become more common, a special concern is the visitation rights of grandparents.
Personality development	Its nature	Erikson proposed that late adulthood is characterized by the stage of integrity versus despair, a time when older adults look back and evaluate what they have done with their lives. Peck reworked Erikson's final stage. He proposed three developmental tasks older adults face: differentiation versus role preoccupation, body transcendence versus body preoccupation, and ego transcendence versus ego preoccupation. Life review is a common theme in personality theories of late adulthood.
	Life satisfaction	This refers to psychological well-being in general. Income, health, an active life-style, and a network of family and friends are associated in predictable ways with older adults' life satisfaction.
	Successful aging	Successful aging occurs when older adults follow a proper diet, exercise, seek mental stimulation, and have good social relationships and support. Successful aging requires effort and coping skills. There is increasing interest in a model of successful aging that involves the three factors of selection, optimization, and compensation. It is especially applicable when loss is present.

LIFE-SPAN HEALTH AND WELL-BEING

Social Support and Health in Late Adulthood

How might social support improve the health of older adults? Toni Antonucci (1990) explored this question and arrived at the following conclusions. Possibly social interaction with people who provide social support provides the elderly with a more positive view of themselves. In one study, speaking to a supporting other about a cancer symptom was related to seeking medical attention (Antonucci, Jackson, & Gibson, 1989).

People in crises are also better able to cope with and recover from these events when they have good supportive relationships. This effect has been found in people who experience heart attacks, as well as other health problems such as cancer and diabetes (Atkins, Kaplan, & Toshima, 1989; Litwak & Messeri, 1989).

Social support also affects the mental health of the elderly. Depressed persons have smaller social networks, experience problems in interaction with members of the social network they do have, and often have experienced loss in their lives (Coyne, Wortman, & Lehman, 1988).

Individuals with inadequate social relationships also have reduced immunological functioning. And social support is associated with a reduction in the symptoms of a disease or illness and with the ability to meet one's own health-care needs (Cohen, Teresi, & Holmes, 1985). Social support also decreases the probability of institutionalization (Brubaker, 1987).

A final area of social support and health in the elderly involves the relation between formal and informal caregivers. The aged generally resist the use of formal support, preferring immediate kin for support (Litwak, 1985). With increasing age, however, the elderly choose formal support services, probably because they don't want to burden their children (Marshall, Rosenthal, & Daciuk, 1987). A special concern that has emerged in recent years is the stress on caregivers who care for an elderly person (Brody & others, 1987), a topic we will return to in the final chapter, on death and dying. ■

KEY TERMS

disengagement theory Proposes that as older adults slow down they gradually withdraw from society. (557)

activity theory Proposes that the more active and involved older adults are, the less likely they will age and the more likely they will be satisfied with their lives. (557)

social breakdown-reconstruction theory Argues that aging is promoted through negative psychological functioning brought about by negative societal views of older adults and inadequate provision of services for them. Social reconstruction can occur by changing society's view of older adults and by providing adequate support systems for them. (557)

ageism Ageism is prejudice against older adults. (557)

eldercare Whether by giving day-to-day physical assistance or by being responsible for overseeing such care, eldercare is the physical and emotional caretaking of older members of the family. (559)

generational inequity When older adults in an aging society pile up advantages by receiving an inequitably large allocation of resources, that society is being unfair to its younger members. (559)

differentiation versus role preoccupation One of the three developmental tasks of aging described by Peck. Older adults must redefine their worth in terms of something other than work roles. (567)

body transcendence versus body preoccupation In this developmental task of aging described by Peck, older adults must cope with declining physical well-being. (567)

ego transcendence versus ego preoccupation In this developmental task of aging described by Peck, older adults must come to feel at ease with themselves by recognizing that although death is inevitable and probably not too far away, they have contributed to the future through the competent rearing of their children or through their vocations and ideas. (568)

life review In a life review, one looks back at one's life experiences, evaluating them, interpreting them, and often reinterpreting them. (568)

life satisfaction Is psychological well-being in general or satisfaction with life as a whole; life satisfaction is widely used as an index of psychological well-being in older adults. (568)

selective optimization with compensation model Proposes that successful aging is related to three main factors: selection, optimization, and compensation. (569)

Death and Dying

*Years following years steal something
every day:
At last they steal us from ourselves away.*
—Alexander Pope

Our life ultimately ends—when we
approach life's grave sustained and
soothed with unfaltering trust or rave at
the close of day; when at last years steal
us from ourselves; and when we are
linked to our children's children's children
by an invisible cable that runs from age to
age. This final section contains one
chapter: "Death and Dying"
(chapter 21).

Paul Gauguin, Old Women at Arles, detail.

21

Death and Dying

Sustained and soothed
By an unfaltering trust, approach
thy grave,
Like one who wraps the drapery
of his couch
About him, and lies down to
pleasant dreams.

—William Cullen Bryant,
Thanatopsis, 1811

Man is the only animal that finds his own existence a problem he has to solve and from which he cannot escape. In the same sense man is the only animal who knows he must die.

—Erich Fromm

IMAGES OF LIFE-SPAN DEVELOPMENT

Jack Kevorkian, the "Suicide Doctor"

Dr. Jack Kevorkian has become known as the "suicide doctor" because he has taught so many desperately sick patients how to commit suicide. One Michigan judge dismissed murder charges against Kevorkian but advised him against crusading for his physician-assisted suicide cause. Kevorkian replied that he would never shirk his duty. In the state of Michigan, where Kevorkian lives, legislators temporarily banned physician-assisted suicide until a commission could make a recommendation. Kevorkian said it made no difference to him what the commission might recommend or the legislators might decide—if they passed a law against physician-assisted suicide, he would violate it.

Two out of three Americans say they think doctors should be allowed to help extremely sick patients commit suicide (Gibbs, 1992). But there are some aspects of Kevorkian's mode of operating that bother some experts on biomedical ethics. Kevorkian says he takes precautions in advising potential suicide patients, but he is essentially a maverick who anoints himself as an "outlaw." Even passionate supporters of euthanasia argue that safeguards in physician-assisted suicide should be followed, such as second opinions from disinterested doctors, psychological evaluations, and family consultations. Kevorkian's actions have

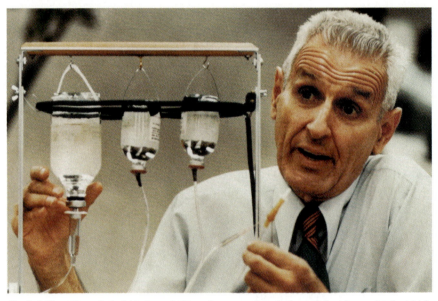

Dr. Jack Kevorkian, the "suicide doctor." Where do you stand on the issue of physician-assisted suicide?

raised concern about his neutrality in counseling potential clients. Critics say that because Kevorkian is a pathologist, he is not in the position to make a judgment about patients who are still alive.

Currently, the law seems clear on one point: "Mercy killing" is illegal. A person may not actively kill another person, regardless of how well established the other person's consent and desire to die may be. "Mercy killing" is considered to be a criminal homicide. However, some biomedical ethicists believe this classification is inconsistent

with individual autonomy and privacy, let alone compassion and common sense (van den Haag, 1992). As increasing numbers of people live to an older age and develop severe disabilities or become desperately sick, the burden of life is likely to become more depressing to increasing numbers of people. As a consequence, the ethical and legal dimensions of physician-assisted suicide will continue to raise considerable controversy in the foreseeable future.

PREVIEW

The issues involved in physician-assisted suicide are difficult ones. We will explore other complex issues in this chapter and evaluate some intriguing questions, such as these: How do we define death? How is death viewed in other cultures? How is death viewed at different points in the life cycle? How do we face our own death? How should we communicate with a dying person? How can we cope with the death of someone else? What are the contexts in which people die?

DEFINING DEATH

Is there one point in the process of dying that is *the* point at which death takes place, or is death a more gradual process? Should we painlessly put to death people who are suffering extensively?

Issues in Determining Death

Twenty-five years ago, determining if someone was dead was simpler than it is today. The end of certain biological functions, such as breathing and blood pressure, and the rigidity of the body (rigor mortis) were considered to be clear signs of death. In the past several decades, defining death has become more complex. Consider the circumstance of Philadelphia Flyers hockey star Pelle Lindbergh, who slammed his Porsche into a cement wall on November 10, 1985. The newspaper headline the next day read "Flyers' Goalie is Declared Brain Dead." In spite of the claim that he was "brain dead," the story reported that Lindbergh was listed in "critical condition" in the intensive care unit of a hospital.

Brain death *is a neurological definition of death, which states that a person is brain dead when all electrical activity of the brain has ceased for a specified period of time. A flat EEG (electroencephalogram) recording for a specified period of time is one criterion of brain death.* The higher portions of the brain often die sooner than the lower portions. Because the brain's lower portions monitor heartbeat and respiration, individuals whose higher brain areas have died may continue breathing and have a heartbeat. The definition of brain death currently followed by most physicians includes the death of both the higher cortical functions and the lower brain stem functions. Currently 36 states and the District of Columbia have adopted a statute endorsing the cessation of brain function as a standard for determining death.

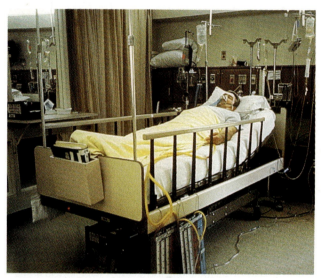

Advances in medical technology have complicated the definition of death. Controversy continues to swirl about what criteria should be used to determine when someone is dead. Most states abide by a statute defining death as death of both higher and lower brain functions, but some medical experts argue that even if lower brain areas are still functioning, the person should be declared dead, because it is the higher brain functions that make us human.

One of the most famous cases of brain death is that of Karen Ann Quinlin, whose higher cortical functioning stopped because she had taken a potent mixture of alcohol and barbiturates. However, because the lower portion of her brain still functioned, she continued to survive on her own. Because of such cases as Karen Ann Quinlin and hockey star Pelle Lindbergh, some medical experts are debating the possibility that the criteria for death should include only higher cortical functioning. If the cortical death definition were adopted, then physicians could claim a person is dead who has no cortical functioning even though the lower brain stem is functioning. Supporters of the cortical death policy argue that the functions we associate with being human, such as intelligence and personality, are located in the higher cortical part of the brain. They believe that when these functions are lost, the "human being" is no longer alive. To date, the cortical definition of death is not a legal definition of death anywhere in America.

Critical Thinking

Considering our discussion of the factors involved in defining death, how would you define death?

Euthanasia

Euthanasia *is the act of painlessly putting to death persons who are suffering from an incurable disease or severe disability. Sometimes euthanasia is called "mercy killing."* Distinctions are made between two types of euthanasia—active and passive. **Active euthanasia** *occurs when death is induced by a deliberate attempt to end a person's life, such as the injection of a lethal dose of a drug.* **Passive euthanasia** *occurs when a person is allowed to die by withholding an available treatment, such as withdrawing a life-sustaining therapeutic device* (turning off a respirator or a heart-lung machine, for example). Some medical ethicists argue that passive euthanasia is not a form of euthanasia at all, but simply letting nature take its course. Today, active euthanasia is illegal in all countries of the world, except in several specific circumstances in the Netherlands (Levinson, 1987).

Technological advances in life-support devices raise the issue of quality of life. Should individuals be kept alive in undignified and hopeless states? The trend is toward acceptance of passive euthanasia in the case of terminally ill patients. The inflammatory argument that once equated this practice with suicide rarely is heard today. However, experts do not yet entirely agree on the precise boundaries or the exact mechanisms by which treatment decisions should be implemented. Can a comatose patient's life-support systems be disconnected when the patient has left no written instructions to that effect? Does the family of a comatose patient have the right to overrule the attending physician's decision to continue life-support systems? These are searching questions with no simple or universally agreed upon answers.

DEATH AND SOCIOHISTORICAL, CULTURAL CONTEXTS

When, where, and how people die have changed historically in the United States, and attitudes toward death vary across cultures.

Changing Historical Circumstances

We have already described one of the historical changes involving death—the increasing complexity of determining when someone is truly dead. Another historical change in death is in the age group it strikes most often. Two hundred years ago, almost one of every two children died before the age of 10, and one parent died before children grew up. Today, death occurs most often among the elderly. Life expectancy has increased from 47 years for a person born in 1900 to 75 years for someone born today. As our population has aged and become more mobile, more older adults die apart from their families. In the United States today, more than 80 percent of all deaths occur in institutions or hospitals. The care of a dying older person has shifted away from the family and minimized our exposure to death and its painful surroundings.

Death in Different Cultures

The ancient Greeks faced death as they faced life—openly and directly. To live a full life and die with glory was the prevailing goal of the Greeks. Individuals are more conscious of death in times of war, famine, and plague. Whereas Americans are conditioned from early in life to live as though they were immortal, in much of the world this fiction cannot be maintained. Death crowds the streets of Calcutta in daily overdisplay, as it does the scrubby villages of Africa's Sahel. Children live with the ultimate toll of malnutrition and disease, mothers lose as many babies as survive into adulthood, and it is rare that a family remains intact for many years. Even in peasant areas where life is better, and health and maturity may be reasonable expectations, the presence of dying people in the house, the large attendance at funerals, and the daily contact with aging adults prepare the young for death and provide them with guidelines on how to die. By contrast, in the United States it is not uncommon to reach adulthood without having seen someone die.

Most societies throughout history have had philosophical or religious beliefs about death, and most societies have a ritual that deals with death (see figure 21.1). For example, elderly Eskimos in Greenland who can no longer contribute to their society may walk off alone, never to be seen again, or they may be given a departure ceremony at which they are honored, then ritually killed. In some tribes, an old man wants his oldest son or favorite daughter to put a string around his neck and hoist him to his death. This may be performed at the height of a party where there is good food, gaiety, and dancing (Freuchen, 1961).

In most societies, death is not viewed as the end of existence—though the biological body has died, the spiritual body is believed to live on. This religious perspective is favored by Americans as well. However, cultures may differ in their perceptions of death and their reactions to it (Bliatoat, 1993; Rosenblatt, 1993; Younoszai, 1993). In the Gond culture of India, death is believed to be caused by magic and demons. The members of the Gond culture react angrily to death. In the Tanala culture of Madagascar, death is believed to be caused by natural forces. The members of the Tanala culture show a much more peaceful reaction to death than their counterparts in the Gond culture. Other cultural variations in attitudes toward death include beliefs about reincarnation, which is an important aspect of the Hindu and Buddhist religions (Truitner & Truitner, 1993).

FIGURE 21.1

Rituals associated with death in different cultures. *(a) Family memorial day at the national cemetery in Seoul, Korea; (b) Chinese burial service in Singapore; and (c) Funeral procession in Haiti.*

Critical Thinking

How many different rituals for death can you think of that take place in the United States? Describe them, and explain their roles in death and life.

Perceptions of death vary and reflect diverse values and philosophies. Death may be seen as a punishment for one's sins, an act of atonement, or a judgment of a just God. For some, death means loneliness; for others, death is a quest for happiness. For still others, death represents redemption, a relief from the trials and tribulations of the earthly world. Some embrace death and welcome it; others abhor and fear it. For those who welcome it, death may be seen as the fitting end to a fulfilled life. From this perspective, how we depart from earth is influenced by how we have lived. In the words of Leonardo da Vinci, death should come to an individual after a full life, just as sleep comes after a hard day's work.

In many ways, we are death avoiders and death deniers in the United States. This denial can take many forms:

- The tendency of the funeral industry to gloss over death and fashion lifelike qualities in the dead
- The adoption of euphemistic language for death—for example, exiting, passing on, never say die, and good for life, which implies forever
- The persistent search for a fountain of youth
- The rejection and isolation of the aged, who may remind us of death
- The adoption of the concept of a pleasant and rewarding afterlife, suggesting that we are immortal
- The medical community's emphasis on the prolongation of biological life rather than an emphasis on diminishing human suffering

Even though we are death avoiders and death deniers, ultimately we face death—others' and our own.

LIFE-SPAN PRACTICAL KNOWLEDGE 21.1

Helping Children Grieve
(1991) by Theresa Huntley.
Minneapolis: Augsburg Press.

Helping Children Grieve addresses helping children cope with either their own death or the death of a loved one. The author presents a developmental approach to helping children cope with death, focusing on the 3 to 6, 6 to 10, 10 to 12, and early and late adolescent periods. Advice is given on how to talk about death with children, and the author discusses common behaviors and feelings children show when faced with death, including denial, panic, anger, guilt, regression, hyperactivity, and withdrawal. Adults are encouraged to get children to ask them questions about death, and to answer those questions as honestly as possible. The dying child's fears are presented, as are ways to care for the dying child's basic needs.

A DEVELOPMENTAL PERSPECTIVE ON DEATH

Do the causes of death vary across the human life cycle? Do we have different expectations about death as we develop through the life span? What are our attitudes toward death at different points in our development?

Causes of Death and Expectations About Death

Although we often think of death as occurring in old age, death can occur at any point in the human life cycle. Death can occur during prenatal development through miscarriages or stillborn births. Death can also occur during the birth process or in the first few days after birth, which usually happens because of a birth defect or because infants have not developed adequately to sustain life outside the uterus. An especially tragic form of death in infants is **sudden infant death syndrome (SIDS),** *which is the sudden death of an apparently healthy infant. SIDS occurs most often between 2 and 4 months of age. The immediate cause of SIDS is that the infant stops breathing, but the underlying cause is not yet known.* An infant's death from SIDS is difficult for parents to cope with because the infant appears to have been very healthy until death suddenly arrived. Thus, the deaths of some persons seem more tragic than those of others. The death of a 90-year-old woman is considered to be natural, since she has lived a long, full life, whereas the death of an infant is considered to be tragic because a life has ended before it has barely begun.

In childhood, death occurs most often because of accidents or illness. Accidental death in childhood can be the consequence of such things as an automobile accident, drowning, poisoning, fire, or a fall from a high place. Major illnesses that cause death in children are heart disease, cancer, and birth defects, and it is not unusual for terminally ill children to distance themselves from their parents as they approach the final phase of their illness (Wass & Stillion, 1988). The distancing may be due to the depression that many dying patients experience, or

it may be a child's way of protecting parents from the overwhelming grief they will experience at the death. Most dying children know they have a terminal illness. Their developmental level, social support, and coping skills influence how well they cope with knowing they will die.

Compared to childhood, death in adolescence is more likely to occur because of suicide, motor vehicle accidents, and homicide. Many motor vehicle accidents that cause death in adolescence are alcohol-related.

Older adults are more likely to die from chronic diseases, such as heart disease and cancer, whereas younger adults are more likely to die from accidents. Older adults' diseases often incapacitate before they kill, which produces a course of dying that slowly leads to death. Of course, many young and middle-aged adults die of diseases, such as heart disease and cancer. Younger adults who are dying often feel cheated more than do older adults who are dying (Kalish, 1987). Younger adults are more likely to feel they have not had the opportunity to do what they want to with their lives. Younger adults perceive they are losing what they might achieve; older adults perceive they are losing what they have (Cavanaugh, 1990).

Attitudes Toward Death at Different Points in the Life Span

The ages of children and adults influence the way they experience and think about death. A mature, adultlike conception of death includes an understanding that death is final and irreversible, that death represents the end of life, and that all living things die (Speece & Brent, 1984). Most researchers have found that, as children grow, they develop a more mature approach to death (Wass & Stillion, 1988).

Childhood

Most researchers believe that infants do not have even a rudimentary concept of death. However, as infants develop an attachment to a caregiver, they can experience loss or separation and an accompanying anxiety. But young children do not perceive time the way adults do. Even brief separations may be experienced as total losses. For most infants, the reappearance of the caregiver provides a continuity of existence and a reduction of anxiety. We know very little about the infant's actual experiences with bereavement, although the loss of a parent, especially if the caregiving is not replaced, can negatively affect the infant's health.

Even children 3 to 5 years of age have little or no idea of what death really means. They may confuse death with sleep or ask in a puzzled way, "Why doesn't it move?" Preschool-aged children rarely get upset by the sight of a dead animal or by being told that a person has died. They believe that the dead can be brought back to life spontaneously by magic or by giving them food or medical treatment (Lonetto, 1980). Young children often believe that only people who want to die, or who are bad or careless, actually die. They also may blame themselves for the death of someone they know well, illogically reasoning that the event may have happened because they disobeyed the person who died.

Sometime in the middle and late childhood years these illogical ways of conceptualizing death give way to more realistic perceptions of death. In one early investigation of children's perception of death, children 3 to 5 years of age denied that death exists, children 6 to 9 years of age believed that death exists but only happens to some people, and children 9 years of age and older recognized death's finality and universality (Nagy, 1948).

Most psychologists believe that honesty is the best strategy in discussing death with children. Treating the concept as unmentionable is thought to be an inappropriate strategy, yet most of us have grown up in a society in which death is rarely discussed. In one investigation, the attitudes of 30,000 young adults toward death were evaluated (Shneidman, 1973). More than 30 percent said they could not recall any discussion of death during their childhood; an equal number said that, although death was discussed, the discussion took place in an uncomfortable atmosphere. Almost one of every two respondents said that the death of a grandparent was their first personal encounter with death.

Adolescence

In adolescence, the prospect of death, like the prospect of aging, is regarded as a notion that is so remote that it does not have much relevance. The subject of death may be avoided, glossed over, kidded about, neutralized, and controlled by a cool, spectatorlike orientation. This perspective is typical of the adolescent's self-conscious thought; however, some adolescents do show a concern for death, both in trying to fathom its meaning and in confronting the prospect of their own demise.

Adolescents develop more abstract conceptions of death than children do. For example, adolescents describe death in terms of darkness, light, transition, or nothingness (Wenestam & Wass, 1987). They also develop religious and philosophical views about the nature of death and whether there is life after death.

Adulthood

There is no evidence that a special orientation toward death develops in early adulthood. An increase in consciousness about death accompanies individuals' awareness that they are aging, which usually intensifies in middle adulthood. In our discussion of middle adulthood, we indicated that mid-life is a time when adults begin to think more about how much time is left in their lives. Researchers have found that middle-aged adults actually fear death more than do young adults or older adults (Kalish & Reynolds, 1976). Older adults, though, think about death more and talk about it more in conversations with others than do middle-aged and young adults. They also have more direct experience with death as their friends and relatives become ill and die. Older adults are forced to examine the meanings of life and death more frequently than are younger adults.

In old age, one's own death may take on an appropriateness it lacked in earlier years. Some of the increased thinking and conversing about death, and an increased sense of integrity developed through a positive life review, may help older adults accept death. Older adults are less likely to have unfinished business than are younger adults. They usually do not have children who need to be guided to maturity, their spouses are more likely to be dead, and they are less likely to have work-related projects that require completion. Lacking such anticipations, death may be less emotionally painful to them. Even among older adults, however, attitudes toward death are sometimes as individualized as the people holding them. One 82-year-old woman declared that she had lived her life and was now ready to see it come to an end. Another 82-year-old woman declared that death would be a regrettable interruption of her participation in activities and relationships.

At this point, we have discussed a number of ideas about defining death; death and sociohistorical, cultural contexts; and a developmental perspective on death. A summary of these ideas is presented in concept table 21.1.

FACING ONE'S OWN DEATH

This chapter opened with a quote from Erich Fromm (1955) about people being the only animals who know they must die. Knowledge of death's inevitability permits us to establish priorities and structure our time accordingly. As we age, these priorities and structurings change in recognition of diminishing future time. Values concerning the most important uses of time also change. For example, when asked how they would spend 6 remaining months of life, younger adults described such activities as traveling and accomplishing things they previously had not done; older adults described more inner-focused activities—contemplation and meditation, for example (Kalish & Reynolds, 1976).

Most dying individuals want an opportunity to make some decisions regarding their own life and death. Some individuals want to complete unfinished business; they want time to resolve

CONCEPT TABLE 21.1

*Defining Death; Death and Sociohistorical, Cultural Contexts;
and Attitudes About Death Across the Life Cycle*

Concept	Processes/Related Ideas	Characteristics/Description
Defining death	Issues in determining death	Twenty-five years ago, determining if someone was dead was simpler than it is today. Brain death is a neurological definition of death, which states that a person is brain dead when all electrical activity of the brain has ceased for a specified period of time. Medical experts debate whether this should mean the higher and lower brain functions or just the higher cortical functions. Currently, most states have a statute endorsing the cessation of brain function (both higher and lower) as a standard for determining death.
	Euthanasia	Euthanasia is the act of painlessly putting to death a person who is suffering from an incurable disease or disability. Distinctions are made between active and passive euthanasia.
Death and sociohistorical, cultural contexts	Changing historical circumstances	When, where, and why people die have changed historically. Today, death occurs most often among the elderly. More than 80 percent of all deaths in the United States now occur in a hospital or an institution. Our exposure to death in the family has been minimized.
	Death in different cultures	Most societies throughout history have had philosophical or religious beliefs about death, and most societies have rituals that deal with death. Most cultures do not view death as the end of existence—spiritual life is thought to continue. The United States has been described as a death-denying and death-avoiding culture.
A developmental perspective on death	Causes of death and expectations about death	Although death is more likely to occur in late adulthood, death can come at any point in development. The deaths of some persons, especially children and younger adults, are often perceived to be more tragic than those of others, such as very old adults, who have had an opportunity to live a long life. In children and younger adults, death is more likely to occur because of accidents but in older adults is more likely to occur because of chronic diseases.
	Attitudes toward death at different points in the life span	Infants do not have a concept of death. Preschool children also have little concept of death, showing no upset at the sight of a dead animal or person. Preschool children sometimes blame themselves for a person's death. In the elementary school years, children develop a more realistic orientation toward death. Most psychologists believe honesty is the best strategy for helping children cope with death. Death may be glossed over in adolescence. Adolescents have more abstract, philosophical views of death than children do. There is no evidence that a special orientation toward death emerges in early adulthood. Middle adulthood is a time when adults show a heightened consciousness about death and death anxiety. Older adults often show less death anxiety than middle-aged adults, but older adults experience and converse about death more. Attitudes about death may vary considerably among adults of any age.

problems and conflicts and to put their affairs in order. Might there be a sequence of stages we go through as we face death?

Kübler-Ross's Stages of Dying

Elisabeth Kübler-Ross (1969) divided the behavior and thinking of dying persons into five stages: denial and isolation, anger, bargaining, depression, and acceptance. **Denial and isolation** *is Kübler-Ross's first stage of dying, in which the person denies that death is really going to take place.* The person may say, "No, it can't be me. It's not possible." This is a common reaction to terminal illness. However, denial is usually only a temporary defense and is eventually replaced with increased acceptance when the person is confronted with such matters as financial considerations, unfinished business, and worry about surviving family members.

Anger *is Kübler-Ross's second stage of dying, in which the dying person recognizes that denial can no longer be maintained. Denial often gives way to anger, resentment, rage, and envy.* The dying person's question is, "Why me?" At this point, the person becomes increasingly difficult to care for as anger may become displaced and projected onto physicians, nurses, family members, and even God. The realization of loss is great, and those who symbolize life, energy, and competent functioning are especially salient targets of the dying person's resentment and jealousy.

Bargaining *is Kübler-Ross's third stage of dying, in which the person develops the hope that death can somehow be postponed or delayed.* Some persons enter into a bargaining or negotiation—often with God—as they try to delay their death. Psychologically, the person is saying. "Yes, me, but. . . ." In exchange for a few more days, weeks, or months of life, the person promises to lead a reformed life dedicated to God or to the service of others.

Depression *is Kübler-Ross's fourth stage of dying, in which the dying person comes to accept the certainty of death. At this point, a period of depression or preparatory grief may appear.* The dying person may become silent, refuse visitors, and spend much of the time crying or grieving. This behavior should be perceived as normal in this circumstance and is actually an effort to disconnect the self from all love objects. Attempts to cheer up the dying person at this stage should be discouraged, says Kübler-Ross, because the dying person has a need to contemplate impending death.

Acceptance *is Kübler-Ross's fifth stage of dying, in which the person develops a sense of peace; an acceptance of one's fate; and, in many cases, a desire to be left alone.* In this stage, feelings and physical pain may be virtually absent. Kübler-Ross describes this fifth stage as the end of the dying struggle, the final resting stage before death. A summary of Kübler-Ross's dying stages is presented in figure 21.2.

FIGURE 21.2

Kübler-Ross's stages of dying. According to Elisabeth Kübler-Ross, we go through five stages of dying: denial and isolation, anger, bargaining, depression, and acceptance. Today's interpretation of Kübler-Ross's stages suggests that adaptation does not require us to go through the stages in the order described by Kübler-Ross.

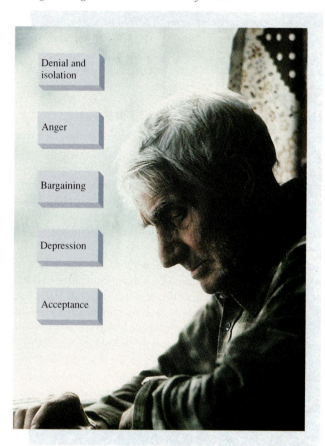

No one has been able to confirm that people go through the stages in the order described by Kübler-Ross. Kübler-Ross herself feels that she has been misread, saying that she never intended the stages to be an invariant sequence of steps toward death. Even though Kübler-Ross (1974) recognizes the importance of individual variation in how we face death, she still believes that the optimal way to face death is in the sequence she has proposed.

> *Do not go gentle into that good night*
> *Old age should burn and rave at close of day;*
> *Rage, rage against the dying of the light.*
>
> —Dylan Thomas

Some individuals, though, struggle until the end, desperately trying to hang on to their lives. Acceptance of death never comes for them. Some psychologists believe that the harder individuals fight to avoid the inevitable death they face and the more they deny it, the more difficulty they will have in dying peacefully and in a dignified way; other psychologists argue that not confronting death until the end may be adaptive for some individuals (Kalish, 1988; Lifton, 1977; Shneidman, 1973). At any one moment, a number of emotions may wax and wane. Hope, disbelief, bewilderment, anger, and acceptance may come and go as individuals try to make sense of what is happening to them.

Perceived Control and Denial

Perceived control and denial may work together as an adaptive strategy for some older adults who face death. When individuals are led to believe they can influence and control events—such as prolonging their lives—they may become more alert and cheerful. Remember from our discussion in chapter 18 that giving nursing home residents options for control improved their attitudes and increased their longevity (Rodin & Langer, 1977).

Denial also may be a fruitful way for some individuals to approach death. It is not unusual for dying individuals to deny death right up until the time they die. Life without hope represents learned helplessness in its most extreme form. Denial can protect us from the torturous feeling that we are going to die. Denial may come in different forms (Weisman, 1972). First, we can deny the facts. For example, a woman who has been told by her physician that a scheduled operation is for cancer may believe that the operation is for a benign tumor. Second, we can deny the implications of a disease or life-threatening situation. For example, a man may accept the fact that he has a disease but may deny that it leads to death. Third, we can deny that we will be extinguished even if we die biologically; we can have faith in our spiritual immortality.

Denial can be adaptive or maladaptive. Denial can be used to avoid the destructive impact of shock by delaying the necessity of dealing with one's death. Denial can insulate the individual from having to cope with intense feelings of anger and hurt; however, if denial keeps us from having a life-saving operation, it clearly is maladaptive. Denial is neither good nor bad; its adaptive qualities need to be evaluated on an individual basis (Kalish, 1981).

The Contexts in Which People Die

For dying individuals, the context in which they die is important. Most deaths in the United States occur in a hospital; a smaller number occur in other institutions such as nursing homes and board-and-care centers. Hospitals offer several important advantages to the dying individual—professional staff members are readily available, and the medical technology present may prolong life, for example, yet a hospital may not be

the best place for many people to die. Most individuals say they would rather die at home (Kalish & Reynolds, 1976). Many feel, however, that they will be a burden at home, that there is limited space there, and that dying at home may alter prior relationships such as being cared for by one's children. Individuals who are facing death also worry about the competency and availability of emergency medical treatment if they remain at home.

In addition to hospital and home, a third context for dying that has received increased attention in recent years is the **hospice,** *a humanized institution committed to making the end of life as free from pain, anxiety, and depression as possible. The hospice's goals contrast with those of a hospital, which are to cure illness and prolong life.* The hospice movement began toward the end of the 1960s in London, when a new kind of medical institution, St. Christopher's Hospice, opened. Little effort is made to prolong life at St. Christopher's—there are no heart-lung machines and there is no intensive care unit, for example. A primary goal is to bring pain under control and to help dying patients face death in a psychologically healthy way. The hospice also makes every effort to include the dying individual's family; it is believed that this strategy benefits not only the dying individual but family members as well, probably diminishing their guilt after the death.

The hospice movement has grown rapidly in the United States. In 1987, there were close to 200 hospices (Kitch, 1987). The hospice advocates continue to underscore that it is possible to control pain for almost any dying individual and that it is possible to create an environment for the patient that is superior to that found in most hospitals.

COPING WITH THE DEATH OF SOMEONE ELSE

Loss can come in many forms in our lives—divorce, a pet's death, loss of a job—but no loss is greater than that which comes through the death of someone we love and care for—a parent, sibling, spouse, relative, or friend. In the ratings of life's stresses that require the most adjustment, death of a spouse is given the highest number. How should we communicate with a dying individual? How do we cope with the death of someone we love?

> *One must have looked into the greyness of the night that every man passes through and not flinch in order to hold the hands of those who are making the great transition. All of the defenses and denials we ascribe to others may in reality be projections of our own extinction. When one has achieved some composure about his own death, he may finally be able to listen creatively with responses and silences that help others have an appropriate death.*
>
> —James Peterson, 1980

LIFE-SPAN PRACTICAL KNOWLEDGE 21.2

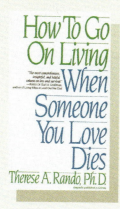

How To Go On Living When Someone You Love Dies

(1991) by Therese Rando.
New York: Bantam.

This book suggests ways to effectively grieve when someone you love dies. Rando believes there is no right or wrong way to grieve, because people are so different. She describes a variety of ways to grieve and encourages you to select the coping strategy that is best for you. Rando tells you what grief is and how it affects you, informs you about grieving different forms of death, explains the inevitable family reorganization following a family member's death, advises you on how to resolve your own grief, and gives suggestions for how to obtain additional help.

This is an excellent book for learning how to cope with the death of someone close to you. Unlike many other writers in this area, Rando does not give pat, overgeneralized recommendations.

Communicating with a Dying Person

Most psychologists believe that it is best for dying individuals to know that they are dying and that significant others know they are dying so they can interact and communicate with each other on the basis of this mutual knowledge. What are some of the advantages of this open awareness context for the dying individual? Four such advantages are these: Dying individuals can close their lives in accord with their own ideas about proper dying; dying individuals may be able to complete some plans and projects, can make arrangements for survivors, and can participate in decisions about a funeral and burial; dying individuals have the opportunity to reminisce, to converse with others who have been important individuals in their life, and to end life conscious of what life has been like; and dying individuals have more understanding of what is happening within their bodies and what the medical staff is doing to them (Kalish, 1981).

In addition to an open communication system, what are some other suggestions for conversing with a dying individual? Some experts believe that conversation should not focus on mental pathology or preparation for death but should focus on strengths of the individual and preparation for the remainder of life. Since external accomplishments are not possible, communication should be directed more at internal growth. Keep in mind also that caring does not have to come from a mental health professional only; a concerned nurse, an attentive physician, a sensitive spouse, or an intimate friend can provide an important support system for a dying individual.

Critical Thinking

Consider your close relationships with the people in your life. How would you communicate with them if they were dying? Would their developmental status affect how you talked to them? If so, how?

Stages and Dimensions of Grief

Grief *is the emotional numbness, disbelief, separation anxiety, despair, sadness, and loneliness that accompany the loss of someone we love.* One view indicates that we go through three stages of grief after we lose someone we love: shock, despair, and recovery (Averill, 1968). Another perspective indicates that we go through four stages: numbness, pining, depression, and recovery (Parkes, 1972).

In the first view of grief, at stage 1 the survivor feels shock, disbelief, and numbness, often weeping or becoming easily agitated. This stage occurs just after death and usually lasts for 1 to 3 days. It is like the denial and anger stages Kübler-Ross proposed for the dying individual. At stage 2, there is painful longing for the dead, memories and visual images of the deceased, sadness, insomnia, irritability, and restlessness. Beginning not long after the death, this stage often peaks in the second to fourth weeks following the death and may subside after several months, although it can persist for 1 to 2 years. Elements of bargaining for the return of the deceased person may appear, again corresponding to one of Kübler-Ross's stages. Stage 3 usually appears within a year after the death. Analogous to Kübler-Ross's acceptance stage, this grief resolution stage is marked by a resumption of ordinary activities, a greater probability of recalling pleasant memories about the deceased, and the establishment of new relationships with others.

It is sweet to mingle tears with tears; griefs, where they wound in solitude, wound more deeply.

—Senaca

However, just as we found that Kübler-Ross's stages of dying are not invariant and that individuals do not have to go through them in the order she suggested to adapt effectively, the same can be said for grief's stages (Campbell, Swank, & Vincent, 1991;

Klass, 1988). Rather than talking about grief's stages, perhaps it is more accurate to talk about grief's dimensions. One description emphasized that grief is not a simple, decrescendoing emotional state but, rather, a complex, evolving process with multiple dimensions (Jacobs & others, 1987). In this view, pining for the lost person is one important dimension. Pining or yearning reflects an intermittent, recurrent wish or need to recover the lost person. Another important dimension of grief is separation anxiety, which not only includes pining and preoccupation with thoughts of the deceased person but also focuses on places and things associated with the deceased, as well as crying or sighing as a type of suppressed cry. Another dimension of grief is the typical immediate reaction to a loss discussed earlier—emotional blunting, numbness, disbelief, and outbursts of panic or extreme tearfulness. Yet another dimension of grief involves despair and sadness, which include a sense of hopelessness and defeat, depressive symptoms, apathy, loss of meaning for activities that used to involve the person who is gone, and growing desolation. This dimension does not represent a clear-cut stage but, rather, occurs repeatedly in one context or another shortly after a loss. Nonetheless, as time passes, pining and protest over the loss tend to diminish, although episodes of depression and apathy may remain or increase. The sense of separation anxiety and loss may continue to the end of one's life, but most of us emerge from grief's tears, turning our attention once again to productive tasks and regaining a more positive view of life (Morycz, 1992; Powers & Wampold, 1994).

Everyone can master grief but he who has it.
—Shakespeare

Making Sense of the World

One beneficial aspect of grieving is that it stimulates many individuals to try to make sense of their world. A common occurrence is to go over again and again all of the events that led up to the death. In the days and weeks after the death, the closest family members share experiences with each other, sometimes reminiscing over family experiences (Kalish, 1981).

Each individual may offer a piece of death's puzzle. "When I saw him last Saturday, he looked as though he were rallying," says one family member. "Do you think it might have had something to do with his sister's illness?" remarks another. "I doubt it, but I heard from an aide that he fell going to the bathroom that morning," comments yet another. "That explains the bruise on his elbow," says the first individual. "No wonder he told me that he was angry because he could not seem to do anything right," chimes in a fourth family member. So it goes in the attempt to understand why someone who was rallying on Saturday was dead on Wednesday.

When a death is caused by an accident or a disaster, the effort to make sense of it is pursued more vigorously. As added pieces of news come trickling in, they are integrated into the puzzle. The bereaved want to put the death into a perspective that they can understand—divine intervention, a curse from a neighboring tribe, a logical sequence of cause and effect, or whatever it may be.

In some instances, when famous individuals die, solving the puzzle of the death may become a national obsession and can drag on for years. Such was the case in the assassination of President John F. Kennedy. Some individuals are still trying to make sense of the event. That the death was the act of one unstable man working alone strikes many individuals as improbable. "How can such an absurd set of circumstances destroy such a powerful man?" ask some individuals.

Eventually, each of us finds an adequate "story" of the dying and death—of John F. Kennedy, of our father, or of our friend. Versions of the death may differ—whether their doctors did all they could to save the patient, whether Aunt Bertha showed up frequently at the hospital or not, whether the operation succeeded or not, whether the individual was ready to die or not. Each individual develops a satisfactory version, and, with slight modifications, it becomes the official version for the teller.

Widowhood

Usually the most difficult loss is the death of a spouse. There are more than 12 million widowed people in the United States; widows outnumber widowers about fivefold. The death of a spouse is usually unpreventable, may involve the shattering of a long-term bond, may require the pursuit of new roles and statuses, may lead to financial hardship, and may leave the survivor without a major support system. Thus, it is not surprising that a spouse's death is associated with depression, increases in physician consultations, hospitalization, increases in health-compromising behaviors such as smoking and drinking, and mortality rates above the expected norm (Zisook, Schuchter, & Lyons, 1987).

Widowhood may be experienced differently depending on sociohistorical circumstances. Modernization of societies has resulted in many widows living independently, free from the control of the patriarchal family and able to maintain themselves economically through paid employment or the Social Security system, in the United States. Although there are isolated widows—unable to reengage in social relations and social roles after a past tie is broken through death—many widows have support systems and eventually reimmerse themselves in their families, their neighborhood, friendship networks, or occupations and organizations. Social support for caregivers of dying individuals helps them adjust to the death (Bass, Bowman, & Noelker, 1991; Morgan & Silverman, 1993; Worden, 1991).

Keep in mind that widowhood may be experienced in many different ways (Lopata, 1987; O'Bryant, 1991). Some widows are passive, accepting changes produced by the death of a husband. Others acquire personal abilities and may even bloom in widowhood. Some stay in pockets of high tradition, surrounded by, but almost oblivious to, changes around them. Others eagerly seek new resources and social roles. Sometimes

LIFE-SPAN PRACTICAL KNOWLEDGE 21.3

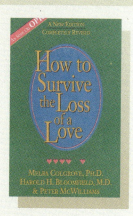

How To Survive the Loss of a Love

(1991) by Melba Colgrove, Harold Bloomfield, and Peter McWilliams. Los Angeles: Prelude Press.

This book provides messages about how to cope with the loss of a loved one. The authors address loss through death as well as other types of loss, such as divorce, rape, loss of long-term goals, and loss through aging. The presentation is unusual—poetry, common sense, and psychologically based advice are interwoven throughout the brief discussions of more than 100 topics. The overriding themes are understanding loss, surviving, healing, and growing. Specific topics include these: It's OK to feel; tomorrow will come; seek the comfort of others; touching and hugging; do the mourning now; when you might want counseling or therapy; nutrition; pray; meditate; contemplate; keep a journal; your happiness is up to you.

How To Survive the Loss of a Love covers a vast territory of circumstances and feelings in a brief format. This is a good self-help book to keep at your fingertips and use as a guide when loss comes into your life.

---

the initiative to cope with widowhood comes from within; at other times it comes from support systems.

Forms of Mourning and the Funeral

Suttee *is the now-outlawed Hindu practice of burning to death a dead man's widow to increase his family's prestige and firmly establish an image of her in his memory.* In some cultures, a ceremonial meal is held. In others, a black armband is worn for 1 year following a death (see figure 21.3). From these examples, it is obvious that cultures vary in how they practice mourning.

The funeral is an important aspect of mourning in many cultures. One consideration involves what to do with the body. In the United States, most bodies are placed in caskets under the earth or in mausoleums. About 9 percent are cremated. Most individuals who are cremated have their ashes spread in the crematorium's garden; others wish their ashes to be taken to specific locations. A viewing of the body occurs after about 75 percent of the deaths in the United States.

The funeral industry has been the source of controversy in recent years (Fulton, 1988). Funeral directors and their supporters argue that the funeral provides a form of closure to the relationship with the deceased, especially when there is an open casket. Their dissenters, however, stress that funeral directors are just trying to make money; they further argue that the art of embalming is grotesque.

One way to avoid the exploitation that may occur because bereavement may make us vulnerable to more expensive funeral arrangements is to purchase them in advance. However, most of us do not follow this procedure. In one survey, only 24 percent of individuals 60 and over had made any funeral arrangements (Kalish & Reynolds, 1976).

Some cultures have elaborate mourning systems. To learn about two cultures with extensive mourning systems, turn to Sociocultural Worlds of Development 21.1.

FIGURE 21.3

Cultural comparisons of the rituals surrounding death. A New Orleans street funeral, a ritual that includes a march through the streets with music and dancing.

DEATH EDUCATION

Thanatologists, *persons who study death and dying,* believe that death education provides a positive preparation for both dying and living. Many of them stress that confronting one's own mortality and that of others is important for developing the mature perspective necessary for making decisions about crucial life and death events (Durlak & Riesenberg, 1991; Wass, Berardo, & Neimeyer, 1988). Some thanatologists also argue that, although our society has developed greater permissiveness toward the open discussion of formerly taboo topics, we may

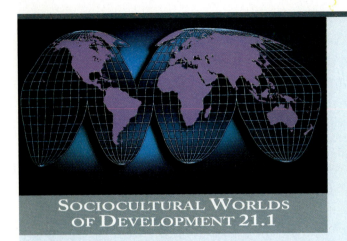

SOCIOCULTURAL WORLDS OF DEVELOPMENT 21.1

The Family and the Community in Mourning —The Amish and Traditional Judaism

The family and the community have important roles in mourning in some cultures. Two of those cultures are the Amish and traditional Judaism (Worthington, 1989).

The Amish are a conservative group with approximately 80,000 members in the United States, Ontario, and several small settlements in South and Central America. The Amish live in a family-oriented society in which family and community support are essential for survival. Today, they live at the same unhurried pace as that of their ancestors, using horses instead of cars and facing death with the same steadfast faith as their forebears. At the time of death, close neighbors assume the responsibility of notifying others of the death. The Amish community handles virtually all aspects of the funeral. Family members dress the body in white garments—the wearing of white clothes signifies the high ceremonial emphasis on death as the final rite of passage to a new and better life (Bryer, 1979). The funeral service is held in a barn in warmer months and in a house during colder months. Calm acceptance of death, influenced by a deep religious faith, is an integral part of the Amish culture. Following the funeral, a high level of support is given to the bereaved family for at least a year. Visits to the family, special scrapbooks and handmade items for the family, new work projects started for the widow, and quilting days that combine fellowship and productivity are among the supports given to the bereaved family.

The family and community also have specific and important roles in mourning in traditional Judaism. The program of mourning is divided into graduated time periods, each with its appropriate practices (Gerson, 1977). The observance of these practices is required of the spouse and the immediate blood relatives of the deceased. The first period is *aninut*, the period between death and burial. The next two periods make up *avelut*, or mourning proper. The first of these is *shivah*, a period of 7 days, which commences with the burial. This is followed by *sheloshim*, the 30-day period following the burial, including shivah. At the end of sheloshim, the mourning process is considered over for all but one's parents. In this case, mourning continues for 11 months, although observances are minimal. The 7-day period of the shivah is especially important in mourning in traditional Judaism. The Jewish community provides considerable support during the mourning process (Kidorf, 1966). The mourners, sitting together as a group through an extended period, have an opportunity to project their feelings to the group as a whole. Visits from others during shivah may help the mourner deal with feelings of guilt. After shivah, the mourner is encouraged to resume normal social interaction. In fact, it is customary for the mourners to walk together a short distance as a symbol of their return to society. In its entirety, the elaborate mourning system of traditional Judaism is designed to promote personal growth and to reintegrate the individual into the community.

An Amish funeral procession in Pennsylvania. The funeral service is held in the barn in the warmer months and in the house during the colder months. Following the funeral, a high level of support is given to the bereaved family for at least a year.

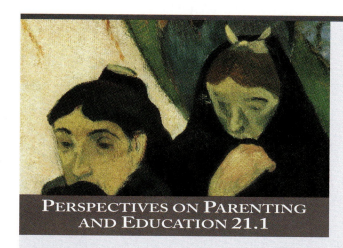

PERSPECTIVES ON PARENTING AND EDUCATION 21.1

Exploring Death Education

One study found diminished mourning by adult children and a decrease in ceremonial grief expressions throughout our American culture (Fulton, 1988). Children are often kept from attending funerals, so they may not even learn the *forms* of our rituals for death. Television also gives minimal attention to such rituals. In an investigation of more than 1,500 commercial television programs aired at prime time and on weekday afternoons,

there were approximately 300 incidents of one death or multiple deaths, 80 percent of them caused by violence. However, grief reactions were shown in fewer than 30 of the deaths, and only 9 funerals were shown (Wass, 1985).

Despite the efforts of thanatologists to educate children more extensively about death, death education has not received widespread acceptance in elementary schools (Wass, Berardo, & Neimeyer, 1988). How death-related crises are handled in schools is related more to teachers' qualities, including their rapport with children, their comfort with the topic, and their degree of empathy, than to any special preparation or curriculum.

High school students are more likely to be exposed to some death education, although sometimes it is only a brief presentation as part of a health class. In one survey, 14 percent of the health educators in high schools in the state of New York taught a unit on death, and another 64 percent discussed death as part of another unit (Cappiello & Troyer, 1979). Many colleges and universities now have one or more courses in death or dying. These courses are taught in a variety of disciplines such as psychology, sociology, religion, anthropology, the humanities, and philosophy. Death educators hope that such courses provide students with important information about the nature of death and dying, help them clarify their values, and improve their coping skills (Knott, 1979).

have merely developed a more sophisticated level of denial (Morgan, 1988). The avoidance of discussing death and dying that characterized the American culture two decades ago still appears in too many instances today. To read further about death education, turn to Perspectives on Parenting and Education 21.1.

> *The art of living well and the art of dying well are one.*
> —Epicurus, 3rd Century B.C.

Critical Thinking

Imagine that you have been hired as a consultant to an elementary school system as an expert on death education. Design a curriculum of death education for elementary school children.

At this point, we have discussed a number of ideas about facing one's own death, coping with the death of someone else, and death education. A summary of these ideas is presented in concept table 21.2.

CONCLUSIONS

People have diverse ways of adapting to death and dying. The meaning of death, and coping with death and dying, are best understood when they are considered in culturally embedded settings. We began this chapter by exploring the complex issues involved in physician-assisted suicide, especially the circumstances involving Jack Kevorkian, the "suicide doctor." Then we turned our attention to variations in how death can be defined and euthanasia. We also studied death in changing historical circumstances and in different cultures. Our coverage of facing one's own death focused on Kübler-Ross's stages of

dying, perceived control and denial, and the contexts in which people die. We also explored the following aspects of coping with the death of someone else: communicating with the dying person, stages and dimensions of grief, making sense of the world, widowhood, and forms of mourning and the funeral. And we examined the nature of death education. At different points in the chapter you also read about the family and the community in mourning (the Amish and traditional Judaism), explorations in death education, and how the diversity in healthy grieving reflects culturally embedded practices.

Don't forget that you can obtain an overall summary of the chapter by again reading the two concept tables on pages 582 and 590. This concludes the last of *Life-Span Development's* 21 chapters. However, there is one final, brief part of the book yet to come: an epilogue on the journey of life. This is a combination of words and photographs that I hope will stimulate you to look back and review what you have read and thought about in this book and in the course on life-span development you are taking.

CONCEPT TABLE 21.2

Facing One's Own Death, Coping With the Death of Someone Else, and Death Education

Concept	Processes/Related Ideas	Characteristics/Description
Facing one's own death	Kübler-Ross's stages of dying	She proposed five stages: denial and isolation, anger, bargaining, depression, and acceptance. Not all individuals go through the same sequence. Some individuals may struggle to the end.
	Perceived control and denial	Perceived control and denial may work together as an adaptive orientation for the dying individual. Denial can be adaptive or maladaptive, depending on the circumstance.
	The contexts in which people die	Most deaths in the United States occur in hospitals; this has advantages and disadvantages. Most individuals say they would rather die at home, but they worry that they will be a burden and they worry about the lack of medical care. The hospice is a humanized environment with a commitment to making the end of life as free from pain and depression as possible; the hospice movement has grown rapidly.
Coping with the death of someone else	Communicating with a dying person	Most psychologists recommend an open communication system; this system should not dwell on pathology or preparation for death but should emphasize the dying person's strengths.
	Stages and dimensions of grief	Grief is the emotional numbness, disbelief, separation, anxiety, despair, sadness, and loneliness that accompany the loss of someone we love. One view suggests we go through three stages of grief: shock, despair, and recovery. Another indicates that we go through four stages: numbness, pining, depression, and recovery. We do not necessarily go through the stages in order; many developmentalists believe we should understand grief's dimensions rather than grief's stages. In some cases, grieving may last for years.
	Making sense of the world	The grieving process may stimulate individuals to strive to make sense out of their world; each individual may contribute a piece to death's puzzle.
	Widowhood	Usually the most difficult loss is the death of a spouse. A spouse's death is associated with depression, health-compromising behavior, and increased mortality rates. Widowhood is experienced differently depending on sociohistorical circumstances.
	Forms of mourning and the funeral	They vary from culture to culture. The most important aspect of mourning in most cultures is the funeral. In recent years, the funeral industry has been the focus of controversy.
Death education	Its nature	Thanatologists, persons who study death and dying, believe death education provides a positive preparation for both dying and living. In many ways, we still are a death-avoiding society.

LIFE-SPAN HEALTH AND WELL-BEING

Diversity in Healthy Grieving

Contemporary orientations on grieving emphasize the importance of breaking bonds with the deceased and the return of survivors to autonomous lifestyles (Golan, 1975; Lopata, 1988; Parkes, 1972/1986; Raphael & Nunn, 1988). People who persist in holding on to the deceased are believed to be in need of therapy. Recent conceptual and research analyses, however, have cast doubt on whether this uniform recommendation is always the best therapeutic advice (Stroebe & others, 1992).

Analyses of non-Western cultures suggest that beliefs about continuing bonds with the deceased vary extensively. In contrast with Western beliefs, maintenance of ties with the deceased is accepted and sustained in the religious rituals of Japan. In the Hopi of Arizona, the deceased are forgotten as quickly as possible and life is carried on as usual. Their funeral ritual concludes with a breakoff between mortals and spirits. The diversity of grieving is nowhere more clear than in two Muslim societies—one in Egypt, the other in Bali. In Egypt, the bereaved are encouraged to dwell at length on their grief, surrounded by others who relate similarly tragic accounts and express their own sorrow. By contrast, in Bali, the bereaved are encouraged to laugh and be joyful rather than be sad.

In a recent longitudinal study of bereavement in the Netherlands, many people tended to maintain contact with the deceased, despite the contemporary emphasis on breaking such bonds (Stroebe & Stroebe, 1991, in press). Many of the widowed persons were not planning a major break with their pasts, but rather were integrating the loss experience into their life-styles and trying to carry on much as before the death of a loved one. Well over half "consulted" the deceased when having to make a decision. One widow said that she gained considerable comfort from knowing that this is exactly what her deceased husband would have wanted her to do. Similar findings have recently been reported regarding American widows (Shuchter & Zisook, in press). A similar picture emerges in another recent study of parents of sons who died in two Israeli wars, 13 and 4 years earlier (Rubin, in press). Even many years after the death of their son, the Israeli parents showed a strong involvement with and valuation of the son. They especially idealized the lost son in ways that were not present in the descriptions by a control group of parents of sons who had recently left home.

In summary, detailed inquiry into grieving around the world suggests that diverse groups of people grieve in a variety of ways (Stroebe, in press). The diverse grieving patterns are culturally embedded practices. Thus, there is no one right, ideal way to grieve. There are many different ways to feel about a deceased person and no set series of stages that the bereaved must pass through to become well adjusted. The stoic widower may need to cry out over his loss at times, and the weeping widow may need to put her husband's wishes aside as she becomes the financial manager of her estate. What is needed is an understanding that healthy coping with the death of a loved one involves growth, flexibility, and appropriateness within a cultural context. This orientation is just beginning to appear in the fields of bereavement research and clinical practice (Stroebe, Stroebe, & Hanson, in press). ■

KEY TERMS

brain death   By this neurological definition of death, a person is brain dead when all electrical activity of the brain has ceased for a specified period of time. A flat EEG recording is one criterion of brain death. (577)

euthanasia   Sometimes called "mercy killing," euthanasia is the act of painlessly putting to death persons who are suffering from incurable diseases or severe disabilities. (578)

active euthanasia   Death is induced by a deliberate attempt to end a person's life, as by injecting a lethal dose of a drug. (578)

passive euthanasia   Available treatments, such as life-sustaining therapeutic devices, are withheld, allowing a person to die. (578)

sudden infant death syndrome (SIDS)   The sudden death of an apparently healthy infant, occurring most often in infants between 2 and 4 months of age. The immediate cause of SIDS is that the infant stops breathing, but the underlying cause is not yet known. (580)

denial and isolation   In Kübler-Ross's first stage of dying, the dying person denies that she or he is really going to die. (583)

anger   In Kübler-Ross's second stage of dying, the dying person's denial gives way to anger, resentment, rage, and envy. (583)

bargaining   In Kübler-Ross's third stage of dying, the dying person develops the hope that death can somehow be postponed. (583)

depression   In Kübler-Ross's fourth stage of dying, the dying person comes to accept the certainty of her or his death. A period of depression or preparatory grief may appear. (583)

acceptance   In Kübler-Ross's fifth stage of dying, the dying person develops a sense of peace, an acceptance of his or her fate, and, in many cases, a desire to be left alone. (583)

hospice   A hospice is a humanized institution committed to making the end of life as free from pain, anxiety, and depression as possible. The hospice's goals contrast with those of a hospital, which are to cure disease and prolong life. (584)

grief   The emotional numbness, disbelief, separation anxiety, despair, sadness, and loneliness that accompany the loss of someone we love. (585)

suttee   Now outlawed, suttee was the Hindu practice of burning to death a dead man's widow to increase his family's prestige and firmly establish an image of her in his memory. (587)

thanatologists   Persons who study death and dying. (587)

The Journey of Life

We have come to the end of this book. I leave you with the following montage of thoughts and images that convey the power, complexity, and beauty of human development.

Life-Span Development has been about life's rhythm and meaning, about turning mystery into understanding, and about weaving together a portrait of who we were, are, and will be. From the first cries of a newborn baby to the final prayers of an elderly adult, we arrive, laugh, grow, play, seek, work, question, hope, mate, quarrel, sing, achieve, and care.

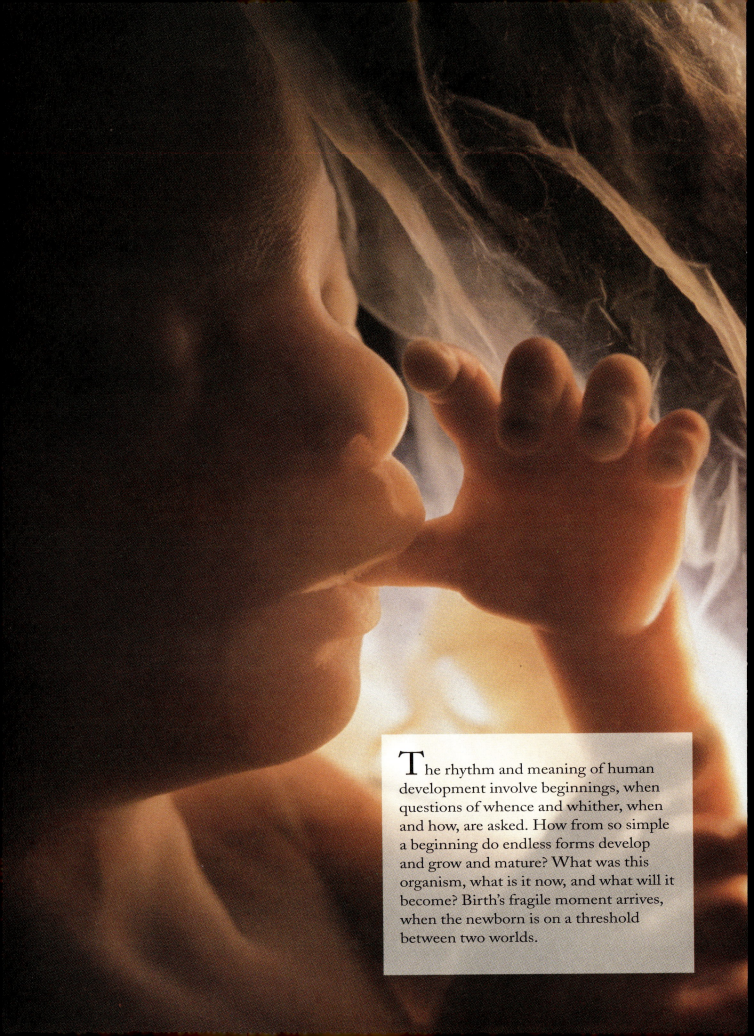

The rhythm and meaning of human development involve beginnings, when questions of whence and whither, when and how, are asked. How from so simple a beginning do endless forms develop and grow and mature? What was this organism, what is it now, and what will it become? Birth's fragile moment arrives, when the newborn is on a threshold between two worlds.

As newborns, we were not empty-headed organisms. We cried, kicked, coughed, sucked, saw, heard, and tasted. We slept a lot, and occasionally we smiled, although the meaning of our first smiles was not entirely clear. We crawled and then we walked, a journey of a thousand miles beginning with a single step. With each forward step we left some ghost of ourselves behind. Sometimes we conformed, sometimes others conformed to us. Our development was a continuous creation of more-complex forms, and our helpless kind demanded the meeting eyes of love. We split the universe into two halves: "me" and "not me." And we juggled the need to curb our own will with becoming what we could will freely.

In early childhood, our greatest untold poem was being only 4 years old. We skipped, played, and ran all the day long, never in our lives so busy, busy becoming something we had not quite grasped yet. Who knew our thoughts, which we worked up into small mythologies all our own. While our thoughts and feelings took wings, the blossoms of our heart no wind could touch. Our small world widened as we discovered new refuges and new people. When we said "I," we meant something totally unique, not to be confused with any other.

In middle and late childhood, we were on a different plane, belonging to a generation and a feeling properly our own. It is the wisdom of human development that at no other time are we more ready to learn than at the end of early childhood's period of expansive imagination. Our thirst was to know and to understand. Our parents continued to cradle our lives, but our growth was also being shaped by successive choirs of friends. We did not think much about the future or the past, but enjoyed the present.

In no order of things was adolescence the simple time of life for us. We clothed ourselves with rainbows and went "brave as the zodiac," flashing from one end of the world to the other. We tried on one face after another, searching for a face of our own. We wanted our parents to understand us and hoped they would give us the privilege of understanding them. We wanted to fly but found that first we had to learn to stand and walk and climb and dance. In our most pimply and awkward moments we became acquainted with sex. We played furiously at adult games but were confined to a society of our own peers. Our generation was the fragile cable by which the best and the worst of our parents' generation was transmitted to the present. In the end, there were but two lasting bequests our parents could leave us—one being roots, the other wings.

Early adulthood is a time for work and a time for love, sometimes leaving little time for anything else. For some of us, finding our place in adult society and committing to a more stable life take longer than we imagine. We still ask ourselves who we are and wonder if it isn't enough just to be. Our dreams continue and our thoughts are bold, but at some point we become more pragmatic. Sex and love are powerful passions in our lives—at times angels of light, at others fiends of torment. And we possibly will never know the love of our parents until we become parents ourselves.

In middle adulthood, what we have been forms what we will be. For some of us, middle age is such a foggy place, a time when we need to discover what we are running from and to and why. We compare our life with what we vowed to make it. In middle age, more time stretches before us and some evaluations have to be made, however reluctantly. As the young/old polarity greets us with a special force, we need to join the daring of youth with the discipline of age in a way that does justice to both. As middle-aged adults, we come to sense that the generations of living things pass in a short while and, like runners, hand on the torch of life.

The rhythm and meaning of human development eventually wend their way to late adulthood, when each of us stands alone at the heart of the earth, and "suddenly it is evening." We shed the leaves of youth and are stripped by the winds of time down to the truth. We learn that life is lived forward but understood backward. We trace the connection between the end and the beginning of life and try to figure out what this whole show is about before it is over. Ultimately, we come to know that we are what survives of us.

Our life ultimately ends—when we approach life's grave sustained and soothed with unfaltering trust or rave at the close of day; when, at last, years steal us from ourselves; and when we are linked to our children's children's children by an invisible cable that runs from age to age.

I hope that this book has been not only a window to the life span of *Homo sapiens* but also a window to your own personal journey in life.

John W. Santrock

GLOSSARY

A

ABC method A learning-to-read technique that emphasizes memorizing the names and letters of the alphabet. (299)

acceptance In Kübler-Ross's fifth stage of dying, the dying person develops a sense of peace, an acceptance of his or her fate, and, in many cases, a desire to be left alone. (583)

accommodation Occurs when individuals adjust to new information. (39)

acculturation Cultural change that results from continuous, firsthand contact between two distinctive cultural groups. Acculturative stress is the negative consequence of acculturation. (278)

achievement motivation (or **need for achievement**) The desire to accomplish something, to reach a standard of excellence, and to expend effort to excel. (301)

achieving stage Schaie's early adulthood stage that involves the application of intelligence to situations that have profound consequences for achieving long-term goals, such as those involving careers and knowledge. (423)

active euthanasia Death is induced by a deliberate attempt to end a person's life, as by injecting a lethal dose of a drug. (578)

active (niche-picking) genotype environment interactions When children seek out environments they find compatible and stimulating. "Niche-picking" means finding a niche or setting that is especially suited to the child's abilities. (89)

activity level The tempo and vigor of movement. (187)

activity theory Proposes that the more active and involved older adults are, the less likely they will age and the more likely they will be satisfied with their lives. (557)

addiction Physical dependence on a drug. (414)

adolescence The developmental period of transition from childhood to early adulthood, entered at approximately 10 to 12 years of age and ending at 18 or 22 years of age. (21)

adolescent egocentrism David Elkind believes that adolescent egocentrism has two parts: an imaginary audience and a personal fable. (353)

adoption study Investigators seek to discover whether the behavior and psychological characteristics of adopted children are more like their adoptive parents, who provided a home environment, or their biological parents, who contributed their heredity. (86)

aerobic exercise Sustained exercise, such as jogging, swimming, or cycling, that stimulates heart and lung activity. (412)

affectionate love In this type of love (also called "companionate love"), an individual desires to have the other person near and has a deep, caring affection for the other person. (441)

afterbirth The third stage of birth, at which time the placenta, umbilical cord, and other membranes are detached and expelled. (110)

ageism Ageism is prejudice against older adults. (557)

AIDS (acquired immune deficiency syndrome) A sexually transmitted disease that is caused by a virus, human immunodeficiency virus (HIV), that destroys the body's immune system. It is also transmitted by sharing needles and other contact with an infected person's blood. (418)

altruism An unselfish interest in helping someone. (337)

Alzheimer's disease Persons with this progressive, irreversible brain disorder suffer gradual deterioration of memory, reasoning, language, and, eventually, physical function. (549)

amniocentesis A prenatal medical procedure in which a sample of amniotic fluid is withdrawn by syringe and tested to discover if the fetus is suffering from any chromosomal or metabolic disorders. (80)

amnion A bag or envelope that contains a clear fluid in which the developing embryo floats and is another important life-support system. (98)

anal stage The second Freudian stage of development, occurring between 1½ and 3 years of age, in which the child's greatest pleasure involves the anus or the eliminative functions associated with it. (35)

androgen The main class of male sex hormones. (257)

androgyny The presence of desirable masculine and feminine characteristics in the same individual. (330)

anger cry A variation of the basic cry. However, in the anger cry more excess air is forced through the vocal cords. The anger cry gets its name from mothers who infer exasperation or rage from it. (190)

anger In Kübler-Ross's second stage of dying, the dying person's denial gives way to anger, resentment, rage, and envy. (583)

animism Another facet of preoperational thought is the belief that inanimate objects have "lifelike" qualities and are capable of action. (212)

anorexia nervosa Eating disorder that involves the relentless pursuit of thinness through starvation. (368)

anoxia The insufficient supply of oxygen to the infant. (110)

anxiety disorders Psychological disorders that are characterized by motor tension, hyperactivity, and apprehensive thoughts and expectations. (549)

Apgar scale A method widely used to assess the health of newborns at one and five minutes after birth. The Apgar scale evaluates infants' heart rate, respiratory effort, muscle tone, body color, and reflex irritability. (116)

aptitude-treatment interaction (ATI) Stresses the importance of children's aptitudes or characteristics and the treatments or experiences they are given in classrooms. (318)

arthritis Especially common in older adults, arthritis is an inflammation of the joints that is accompanied by pain, stiffness, and movement problems. (523)

assimilation   Occurs when individuals incorporate new information into their existing knowledge, and the absorption of ethnic minority groups into the dominant group, which often involves the loss of some or virtually all of the behavior and values of the ethnic minority group. (39, 391)

associative play   Occurs when play involves social interaction with little or no organization. (251)

attachment   A close emotional bond between the infant and the caregiver. (180)

attention-deficit hyperactivity disorder   Commonly called "hyperactivity." This disorder is characterized by a short attention span, distractibility, and high levels of physical activity. (281)

authoritarian parenting   A restrictive, punitive style that exhorts the child to follow the parent's directions and to respect work and effort. The authoritarian parent places firm limits and controls on the child with little verbal exchange allowed. Authoritarian parenting is associated with children's social incompetence. (237)

authoritative parenting   Encourages children to be independent but still places limits and controls on their actions. Extensive verbal give-and-take is allowed, and parents are warm and nurturant toward the child. Authoritative parenting is associated with children's social competence. (237)

autonomous morality   The second stage of moral development in Piaget's theory, displayed by older children (about 10 years of age and older). The child becomes aware that rules and laws are created by people and that, in judging an action, one should consider the actor's intentions as well as the consequences. (263)

autonomy versus shame and doubt   Erikson's second stage of development, occurring in late infancy and toddlerhood (1-3 years). (37)

B

bargaining   In Kübler-Ross's third stage of dying, the dying person develops the hope that death can somehow be postponed. (583)

basal metabolism rate (BMR)   The minimum amount of energy a person uses in a resting state. (208, 411)

basic cry   A rhythmic pattern that usually consists of a cry, followed by a briefer silence, then a shorter inspiratory whistle that is somewhat higher in pitch than the main cry, then another brief rest before the next cry. (189)

Bayley Scales of Infant Development   Scales developed by Nancy Bayley that are widely used in the assessment of infant development. The current version has three components: a mental scale, a motor scale, and an infant behavior profile. (163)

becoming parents and a family with children   The third stage in the family life cycle. Adults who enter this stage move up a generation and become caregivers to the younger generation. (445)

behavior genetics   The branch of genetics that is concerned with the degree and nature of behavior's hereditary basis. (86)

behaviorism   Emphasizes the scientific study of observable behavioral responses and their environmental determinants. (44)

bilingual education   Refers to programs for students with limited proficiency in English that instruct students in their own language part of the time while they learn English. (300)

biological processes   Involve changes in the individual's physical nature. (20)

blastocyst   The inner layer of cells that develops during the germinal period. These cells later develop into the embryo. (96)

body transcendence versus body preoccupation   In this developmental task of aging described by Peck, older adults must cope with declining physical well-being. (567)

bonding   The occurrence of close contact, especially physical, between parents and newborn in the period shortly after birth. (120)

boundary ambiguity   The uncertainty in stepfamilies of who is in or out of the family and who is performing or responsible for certain tasks in the family system. (312)

brain death   By this neurological definition of death, a person is brain dead when all electrical activity of the brain has ceased for a specified period of time. A flat EEG recording is one criterion of brain death. (577)

Brazelton Neonatal Behavioral Assessment Scale   Given several days after birth to assess the newborn's neurological development, reflexes, and reactions to people. (116)

breech position   The baby's position in the uterus that causes the buttocks to be the first part to emerge from the vagina. (110)

bulimia   Eating disorder that involves a binge-and-purge sequence on a regular basis. (368)

burnout   A feeling of hopelessness and helplessness brought on by relentless, work-related stress. (408)

C

canalization   Describes the narrow path or developmental course that certain characteristics take. Apparently, preservative forces help to protect or buffer a person from environmental extremes. (86)

care perspective   A moral perspective that views people in terms of their connectedness with others and emphasizes interpersonal communication, relationships with others, and concern for others. Gilligan's theory is a care perspective. (336)

career consolidation   One of Vaillant's adult stages of development. It occurs from approximately ages 23 to 35 and is a period during which an individual's career becomes more stable and coherent. (495)

career self-concept theory   In Donald Super's view, an individual's self-concept plays a central role in career choice. Super believes that a number of developmental changes in vocational self-concept take place during the adolescent and young adulthood years. (425)

case study   An in-depth look at one individual; it is used mainly by clinical psychologists when the unique aspects of an individual's life cannot be duplicated, for either practical or ethical reasons. (52)

centration   The focusing or centering of attention on one characteristic to the exclusion of all others. (213)

cephalocaudal pattern   The sequence in which the greatest growth always occurs at the top—the head—with physical growth in size, weight, and feature differentiation gradually working its way down from top to bottom (to neck, shoulders, middle trunk, and so on). (134)

cesarean section   The surgical removal of the baby from the uterus. (110)

child-centered kindergarten   Education that involves the whole child and that includes concern for the child's physical, cognitive, and social development. Instruction is organized around the child's needs, interests, and learning styles. The process of learning, rather than what is learned, is emphasized. (222)

chorionic villus test   A prenatal medical procedure in which a small sample of the placenta is removed at some point between the 8th and 11th week of pregnancy. (81)

chromosomes   Threadlike structures that come in 23 pairs, one member of each pair coming from each parent. Chromosomes contain the remarkable genetic substance deoxyribonucleic acid or DNA. (77)

chronic disorders Disorders that are characterized by slow onset and long duration. They rarely develop in early adulthood, they increase during middle adulthood, and they become common in late adulthood. (521)

chronosystem The patterning of environmental events and transitions over the life course and sociohistorical circumstances. (49)

cliques Smaller groups that involve greater intimacy among members and have more cohesion than crowds. (384)

cognitive appraisal Lazarus's term that describes children's interpretations of events in their lives as harmful, threatening, or challenging and their determination of whether they have the resources to effectively cope with the events. (277)

cognitive developmental theory of gender Children's gender typing occurs after they have developed a concept of gender. Once they consistently conceive of themselves as male or female, children often organize their world on the basis of gender. (261)

cognitive mechanics Are the hardware of the mind and reflect the neurophysiological architecture of the brain as developed through evolution. At the operational level, cognitive mechanics involve speed and accuracy of the processes involving sensory input, visual and motor memory, discrimination, comparison, and categorization. (542)

cognitive monitoring The process of taking stock of what you are currently doing, what you will do next, and how effectively the mental activity is unfolding. (289)

cognitive pragmatics Refer to culture-based "software" of the mind. At the operational level, cognitive pragmatics include reading and writing skills, language comprehension, educational qualifications, professional skills, and also the type of knowledge about the self and life skills that help us to master or cope with life. (544)

cognitive processes Involve changes in the individual's thought, intelligence, and language. (20)

cohort effects Effects that are due to a subject's time of birth or generation but not to actual age. (58)

commitment James Marcia defines commitment as the part of identity development in which adolescents show a personal investment in what they are going to do. (394)

community rights versus individual rights The fifth stage in Kohlberg's theory of moral development. At this stage, the person understands that values and laws are relative and that standards may vary from one person to another. (335)

concrete operational stage (Lasts from approximately 7 to 11 years of age) the third Piagetian stage; children can perform operations, and logical reasoning replaces intuitive thought as long as reasoning can be applied to specific or concrete examples. (42)

connectedness According to Cooper and her colleagues, connectedness consists of two dimensions: mutuality (sensitivity to and respect for others' views) and permeability (openness to others' views). (395)

consensual validation Explains why individuals are attracted to people who are similar to them. Our own attitudes and behavior are supported and validated when someone else's attitudes and behavior are similar to our own. (439)

conservation A belief in the permanence of certain attributes of objects or situations in spite of superficial changes. (213)

constructive play Combines sensorimotor/practice repetitive activity with symbolic representation of ideas. Constructive play occurs when children engage in self-regulated creation or construction of a product or a problem solution. (252)

constructivist view A view advocated by Piaget that states that the main perceptual abilities—visual, auditory, and tactile, for example—are completely uncoordinated at birth and that young infants do not have intermodal perception. (147)

contemporary life-events approach Emphasizes that how a life event influences the individual's development depends not only on the life event, but also on mediating factors, the individual's adaptation to the life event, the life-stage context, and the sociohistorical context. (499)

context Is the setting in which development occurs, a setting that is influenced by historical, economic, social, and cultural factors. (15)

continuity of development This view states that development involves gradual, cumulative change from conception to death. (24)

control processes Are cognitive processes that do not occur automatically but require work and effort. They are under the learner's conscious control and they can be used to improve memory. They are also appropriately called "strategies." (287)

conventional reasoning The second or intermediate level in Kohlberg's theory of moral development. At this level, the individual's internalization is intermediate. The person abides by certain standards (internal), but they are the standards of others (external), such as parents or the laws of society. (334)

convergent thinking Is characteristic of the kind of thinking on standardized intelligence tests, that produces one correct answer. (299)

cooperative play Involves social interaction in a group with a sense of group identity and organized activity. (251)

coordination of secondary circular reactions Piaget's fourth sensorimotor substage that develops between 8 and 12 months of age. In this substage, several significant changes take place involving the coordination of schemes and intentionality. (156)

correlational strategy The goal is to describe the strength of the relation between two or more events or characteristics. This is a useful strategy because the more strongly events are correlated (related, or associated), the more effectively we can predict one from the other. (54)

creativity The ability to think about something in novel and unusual ways and to come up with unique solutions to problems. (299)

crisis James Marcia defines crisis as a period of identity development during which the adolescent is choosing among meaningful alternatives. (393)

critical period A fixed time period very early in development during which certain behaviors optimally emerge. (47)

critical thinking Involves grasping the deeper meaning of problems, keeping an open mind about different approaches and perspectives, and thinking reflectively rather than accepting statements and carrying out procedures without significant understanding and evaluation. (289)

cross-cultural studies The comparison of a culture with one or more other cultures, which provides information about the degree to which development is similar (universal) across cultures or the degree to which it is culture-specific. (15, 388)

cross-sectional approach A research strategy in which individuals of different ages are compared at one time. (56)

crowd The largest and least personal of adolescent groups. (384)

crystallized intelligence Accumulated information and verbal skills, which increase with age. (538)

cultural-familial retardation A mental deficit in which no evidence of organic brain damage can be found; individuals' IQs range from 50 to 70. Psychologists suspect that such mental deficits result from the normal variation that distributes people along the range of intelligence scores above 50, combined with growing up in a below-average intellectual environment. (297)

culture-fair tests   Tests that are designed to reduce cultural bias. (296)

culture   The behavior patterns, beliefs, and all other products of a particular group of people that are passed on from generation to generation. (15)

D

date or acquaintance rape   Coercive sexual activity directed at someone with whom the individual is at least casually acquainted. (421)

dating scripts   The cognitive models that adolescents and adults use to guide and evaluate dating interactions. (385)

deep structure   The syntactic relation of words in a sentence. (166)

defense mechanisms   The psychoanalytic term for unconscious methods, the ego distorts reality, thereby protecting it from anxiety. (35)

deferred imitation   Imitation that occurs after a time delay of hours or days. (162)

denial and isolation   In Kübler-Ross's first stage of dying, the dying person denies that she or he is really going to die. (583)

dependent variable   The factor that is measured in an experiment; it may change because of the manipulation of the independent variable. (56)

depression   In Kübler-Ross's fourth stage of dying, the dying person comes to accept the certainty of her or his death. A period of depression or preparatory grief may appear. (583)

deprivation dwarfism   A type of growth retardation caused by emotional deprivation; children are deprived of affection, which causes stress and alters the release of hormones by the pituitary gland. (206)

development   The pattern of movement or change that begins at conception and continues through the life cycle. (20)

developmentally appropriate practice   Schooling based on the knowledge of the typical development of children within an age span (age appropriateness) as well as the uniqueness of the child (individual appropriateness). Developmentally appropriate practice contrasts with developmentally inappropriate practice, which ignores the concrete,

hands-on approach to learning. Direct teaching largely through abstract, paper-and-pencil activities presented to large groups of young children is believed to be developmentally inappropriate. (222)

developmental quotient (DQ)   An overall developmental score that combines subscores in motor, language, adaptive, and personal-social domains in the Gesell assessment of infants. (163)

developmental theory of career choice   In Eli Ginzberg's view, individuals go through three career choice stages: fantasy, tentative, and realistic. (425)

dialectical model   States that each individual is continually changing because of various forces that push and pull development forward. In the dialectical model, each person is viewed as acting on and reacting to social and historical conditions. (24)

differentiation versus role preoccupation   One of the three developmental tasks of aging described by Peck. Older adults must redefine their worth in terms of something other than work roles. (567)

difficult child   A child who tends to react negatively and cry frequently, engages in irregular daily routines, and is slow to accept new experiences. (186)

direct-perception view   A view that states that infants are born with intermodal perception abilities that enable them to display intermodal perception early in infancy. (147)

discontinuity of development   This view states that development involves distinct stages in the life span. (24)

disenchantment phase   In the fourth of Atchley's phases of retirement, retirees recognize that their preretirement fantasies about retirement were unrealistic. (547)

disengagement theory   Proposes that as older adults slow down they gradually withdraw from society. (557)

dishabituation   An infant's renewed interest in a stimulus. (160)

divergent thinking   Produces many answers to the same question and is more characteristic of creativity. (299)

DNA   A complex molecule that contains genetic information. (77)

dominant-recessive genes principle   If one gene of the pair is dominant and one is recessive (goes back or recedes), the dominant gene exerts its effect, overriding the potential influence of the other, recessive gene. A recessive gene exerts its influence only if the two genes of a pair are both recessive. (84)

Down syndrome   The most common genetically transmitted form of mental retardation is caused by the presence of an extra (47th) chromosome. (80)

E

early adulthood   The developmental period beginning in the late teens or early twenties and lasting through the thirties. (21)

early childhood   The developmental period extending from the end of infancy to about 5 or 6 years; this period is sometimes called the "preschool years." (20)

easy child   A child who is generally in a positive mood, quickly establishes regular routines in infancy, and adapts easily to new experiences. (186)

echoing   Repeating what the child says to you, especially if it is an incomplete phrase or sentence. (168)

echolalia   A speech disorder associated with autism in which children echo what they hear. (195)

eclectic theoretical orientation   Does not follow any one theoretical approach, but rather selects and uses whatever is considered the best in all theories. (49)

ecological theory   Bronfenbrenner's sociocultural view of development consists of five environmental systems ranging from the fine-grained inputs of direct interactions with social agents to the broad-based inputs of culture. (47)

ectoderm   The outermost layer, which will become the nervous system, sensory receptors (ear, nose, and eyes, for example), and skin parts (hair and nails, for example.) (97)

ego transcendence versus ego preoccupation   In this developmental task of aging described by Peck, older adults must come to feel at ease with themselves by recognizing that although death is inevitable and probably not too far away, they have contributed to the future through the competent rearing of their children or through their vocations and ideas. (568)

ego   The Freudian structure of personality that deals with the demands of reality. (34)

egocentrism   A salient feature of preoperational thought. It is the inability to distinguish between one's own perspective and someone else's perspective. (212)

eldercare   Whether by giving day-to-day physical assistance or by being responsible for overseeing such care, eldercare is the physical and emotional caretaking of older members of the family. (559)

embryonic period   The period of prenatal development that occurs from two to eight weeks after conception. During the embryonic period, the rate of cell differentiation intensifies, support systems for the cells form, and organs appear. (97)

emic approach   The goal is to describe behavior in one culture or ethnic group in terms that are meaningful and important to the people in that culture or ethnic group, without regard to other cultures or ethnic groups. (53)

emotion   Feeling or affect that involves a mixture of physiological arousal (a rapid heartbeat, for example) and overt behavior (a smile or grimace, for example). (187)

emotionality   The tendency to be distressed. (186)

empathy   Reacting to another's feelings with an emotional response that is similar to the other's feelings. (264)

empty nest syndrome   The hypothesis that marital satisfaction will decrease after children leave home, because parents derive considerable satisfaction from their children. The empty nest syndrome may hold true for some parents who live vicariously through their children, but marital satisfaction usually increases during the post-childbearing years. (486)

endoderm   The inner layer of cells, which will develop into the digestive and respiratory systems. (97)

erogenous zones   The parts of the body that have especially strong pleasure-giving qualities at each stage of development. (35)

estradiol   Hormone is associated with breast, uterine, and skeletal development in girls. (349)

estrogen   The main class of female sex hormones. (257)

ethnic gloss   Using an ethnic label, such as Black, Hispanic, Asian, or Native American, in a superficial way that makes an ethnic group seem more homogeneous than it actually is. (54)

ethnic identity   A sense of membership based on the shared language, religion, customs, values, history, and race of an ethnic group. (15)

ethnicity   Is based on cultural heritage, nationality characteristics, race, religion, and language. (15)

ethnocentrism   The tendency to favor one's own group over other groups. (325)

ethology   Stresses that behavior is strongly influenced by biology, is tied to evolution, and is characterized by critical or sensitive periods. (46)

etic approach   The goal is to describe behavior so that generalizations can be made across cultures. (53)

euthanasia   Sometimes called "mercy killing," euthanasia is the act of painlessly putting to death persons who are suffering from incurable diseases or severe disabilities. (578)

evocative genotype-environment interactions   When a child's genotype elicits certain types of physical and social environments. (89)

executive stage   Schaie's middle adult stage in which people are responsible for societal systems and organizations. The individual develops an understanding of how societal organizations work and the complex relationships that are involved. (424)

exosystem   When experiences in another social setting—in which the individual does not have an active role—influence what the individual experiences in an immediate context. (49)

expanding   Restating what the child has said in a linguistically sophisticated form. (168)

experimental strategy   Allows investigators to precisely determine behavior's causes. The psychologist accomplishes this task by performing an experiment, a carefully regulated setting in which one or more of the factors believed to influence the behavior being studied is manipulated and all others are held constant. (55)

extrinsic motivation   Motivation influenced by external rewards and punishments. (302)

F

family at mid-life   The fifth stage in the family life cycle, a time of launching children, linking generations, and adapting to mid-life developmental changes. (445)

family in later life   The sixth and final stage in the family life cycle, involving retirement and, in many families, grandparenting. (445)

family structure model   States that any differences in children from different family structures are due to the family structure variations, such as the father's being absent in one set of the families. (244)

family with adolescents   The fourth stage of the family life cycle, in which adolescent children push for autonomy and seek to develop their own identities. (445)

fetal alcohol syndrome (FAS)   A cluster of abnormalities that appear in the offspring of mothers who drink alcohol heavily during pregnancy. (105)

fetal period   The prenatal period of development that begins two months after conception and lasts for seven months, on the average. (98)

fine motor skills   Skills that involve more finely tuned movements, such as finger dexterity. (135)

first habits and primary circular reactions   Piaget's second sensorimotor substage that develops between one and four months of age. In this substage, the infant learns to coordinate sensation and types of schemes or structures—that is, habits and primary circular reactions. (156)

fluid intelligence   Ability to reason abstractly, which steadily declines from middle adulthood on. (538)

formal operational stage   (Appears between the ages of 11 and 15) the fourth and final Piagetian stage; individuals move beyond the world of actual, concrete experiences and think in abstract and more logical terms. (42)

fraternal twins   (Called "dizygotic" twins) develop from separate eggs, making them genetically less similar than identical twins. (86)

friendship   A form of close relationship that involves enjoyment, acceptance, trust, respect, mutual assistance, confiding, understanding, and spontaneity. (440)

G

games   Activities engaged in for pleasure that include rules and often competition with one or more individuals. (253)

gametes   Human reproduction cells created in the testes of males and the ovaries of females. (78)

gender identity   The sense of being male or female, which most children acquire by the time they are 3 years old. (257)

gender role   A set of expectations that prescribe how females and males should think, act, and feel. (257)

gender schema theory   States that an individual's attention and behavior are guided by an internal motivation to conform to gender-based sociocultural standards and stereotypes. (261)

gender schema   Organizes the world in terms of female and male. (261)

gender-role stereotypes   These are broad categories that reflect our impressions and beliefs about females and males. (326)

gender-role transcendence   The belief that, when an individual's competence is at issue, it should not be conceptualized on the basis of masculinity, femininity, or androgyny, but rather on a person basis. (331)

gender   The social dimension of being male or female. (15, 257)

generational inequity   A social policy concern which is the condition in which an aging society is being unfair to its younger members because older adults pile up advantages by receiving inequitably large allocations of resources, such as Social Security and Medicare. (17, 559)

generativity versus stagnation Erikson's seventh developmental stage, which individuals experience during middle adulthood. (39)

genes The units of hereditary information are short segments of the DNA "staircase." Genes act as a blueprint for cells to reproduce themselves and manufacture the proteins that maintain life. (77)

genital stage The fifth and final Freudian stage of development, occurring from puberty on. The genital stage is a time of sexual reawakening; the source of sexual pleasure now becomes someone outside of the family. (36)

genotype The person's genetic heritage, the actual genetic material. (84)

germinal period The period of prenatal development that takes place in the first two weeks after conception. It includes the creation of the zygote, continued cell division, and the attachment of the zygote to the uterine wall. (96)

gifted Have above-average intelligence (an IQ of 120 or higher) and/or superior talent for something. (298)

grammar The formal description of syntactical rules. (166)

grasping reflex A reflex that occurs when something touches the infants' palms. The infant responds by grasping tightly. (133)

grief The emotional numbness, disbelief, separation anxiety, despair, sadness, and loneliness that accompany the loss of someone we love. (585)

gross motor skills Skills that involve large muscle activities such as moving one's arms and walking. (135)

H

habituation Repeated presentation of the same stimulus that causes reduced attention to the stimulus. (160)

hardiness A personality style that is characterized by a sense of commitment rather than alienation, control rather than powerlessness, and a perception of problems as challenges rather than threats. (470)

helpless orientation Describes children who seem trapped by the experience of difficulty. They attribute their difficulty to a lack of ability. (303)

heteronomous morality The first stage of moral development in Piaget's theory, occurring from approximately 4 to 7 years of age. Justice and rules are conceived of as unchangeable properties of the world, removed from the control of people. (263)

holophrase hypothesis The concept that a single word is used to imply a

complete sentence; this is characteristic of an infant's first words. (171)

honeymoon phase The third of Atchley's phases of retirement is the earliest phase of retirement. The retirees may feel euphoric. (547)

hospice A hospice is a humanized institution committed to making the end of life as free from pain, anxiety, and depression as possible. The hospice's goals contrast with those of a hospital, which are to cure disease and prolong life. (584)

hypotheses Assumptions that can be tested to determine their accuracy. (33)

hypothetical-deductive reasoning According to Piaget's formal operational concept, adolescents have the cognitive ability to develop hypotheses, or best guesses, about ways to solve problems, such as an algebraic equation. They then systematically deduce, or conclude, which is the best path for solving the problem. (352)

I

id The Freudian structure of personality that consists of instincts, which are an individual's reservoir of psychic energy. (34)

identical twins (Called "monozygotic" twins) develop from a single fertilized egg that splits into two genetically identical replicas, each of which becomes a person. (86)

identification theory Stems from Freud's view that the preschool child develops a sexual attraction to the opposite-sex parent, then by approximately 5 or 6 years of age renounces this attraction because of anxious feelings, and subsequently identifies with the same-sex parent, unconsciously adopting the same-sex parent's characteristics. (258)

identity achievement Marcia's term for adolescents who have undergone a crisis and made a commitment. (394)

identity diffusion James Marcia uses this term to describe adolescents who have not yet experienced a crisis (explored meaningful alternatives) or made any commitments. (394)

identity foreclosure Marcia uses this term to describe adolescents who have made a commitment but have not experienced a crisis. (394)

identity moratorium Marcia uses this term to describe adolescents who are in the midst of a crisis, but their commitments are either absent or vaguely defined. (394)

identity versus identity confusion Erikson's fifth developmental stage,

which individuals experience during the adolescent years. At this time individuals are faced with finding out who they are, what they are all about, and where they are going in life. (37)

idiographic needs Needs that refer to what is important for the individual, not the group. (61)

imaginary audience According to Elkind, adolescents believe that others are as preoccupied with them as they are with themselves. (353)

immanent justice The concept that if a rule is broken, punishment will be meted out immediately. (263)

implantation The attachment of the zygote to the uterine wall, which takes place about ten days after conception. (97)

imprinting The ethological concept of rapid, innate learning within a limited critical period of time that involves attachment to the first moving object seen. (46)

in vitro fertilization Conception outside the body. (78)

independent variable The manipulated, influential, experimental factor in the experiment. (55)

index offenses Criminal acts, whether committed by juveniles or by adults. They include robbery, aggravated assault, rape, and homicide. (362)

individualism and purpose The second stage in Kohlberg's theory of moral development. At this stage, moral thinking is based on rewards and self-interest. (334)

individuality According to Cooper and her colleagues, individuality consists of two dimensions: self-assertion (the ability to have and communicate a point of view) and separateness (the use of communication patterns to express how one is different from others). (395)

individuated-connected level In White's model, this is the highest level of relationship maturity. One is acquiring an understanding of oneself, as well as consideration for others' motivations and anticipation of their needs. One now feels concern and caring that involve emotional support and individualized expressions of interest. (453)

industry versus inferiority Erikson's fourth developmental stage, occurring approximately in the elementary school years. (38)

infancy The developmental period extending from birth to 18 or 24 months. (20)

infantile autism A severe developmental disorder that includes deficiencies in social relationships, abnormalities in communication, and restricted, repetitive, and stereotyped patterns of behavior; onset is in infancy. (195)

infinite generativity An individual's ability to generate an infinite number of meaningful sentences using a finite set of words and rules, which makes language a highly creative enterprise. (164)

information-processing approach Concerned with how individuals process information about their world—how information enters our minds, how it is stored and transformed, and how it is retrieved to perform such complex activities as problem solving and reasoning. (42)

initiative versus guilt Erikson's third stage of development, occurring during the preschool years. (37)

innate goodness View presented by Swiss-born French philosopher Jean Jacques Rousseau, who stressed that children are inherently good. (8)

integrity versus despair Erikson's eighth and final developmental stage, which individuals experience during late adulthood. (39)

intelligence quotient (IQ) Was devised by William Stern. IQ is the child's mental age divided by chronological age multiplied by 100. (290)

intelligence Verbal ability, problem-solving skills, and the ability to learn from and adapt to the experiences of everyday life. (290)

intermodal perception The ability to relate and integrate information about two or more sensory modalities, such as vision and hearing. (147)

internalization The developmental change from behavior that is externally controlled to behavior that is internally controlled. (334)

internalization of schemes Piaget's sixth and final sensorimotor substage that develops between 18 and 24 months of age. In this substage, the infant's mental functioning shifts from a purely sensorimotor plane to a symbolic plane, and the infant develops the ability to use primitive symbols. (156)

interpersonal norms The third stage in Kohlberg's theory of moral development. At this stage, the person values trust, caring, and loyalty to others as the basis of moral judgments. (334)

intimacy in friendships Self-disclosure and the sharing of private thoughts. (315)

intimacy versus isolation Erikson's sixth developmental stage, which individuals experience during the early adulthood years. At this time, individuals face the developmental task of forming intimate relationships with others. (39)

intimate style According to Jacob Orlofsky's classification of styles in intimate interactions, and individual with the intimate style forms and maintains one or more deep and longlasting love relationships. (453)

intrinsic motivation The internal desire to be competent and to do something for its own sake. (302)

intuitive thought substage The second substage of preoperational thought occurring between approximately 4 and 7 years of age. In this substage, children begin to use primitive reasoning and want to know the answers to all sorts of questions. Piaget called this time period *intuitive* because young children seem so sure about their knowledge and understanding, yet are so unaware of how they know what they know. (213)

involution The process by which the uterus returns to its prepregnant size five to six weeks after birth. (119)

isolated style According to Orlofsky, an individual with isolated style withdraws from social encounters and has little or no attachment to same- or opposite-sex individuals. (453)

J

justice perspective A moral perspective that focuses on the rights of the individual; individuals stand alone and independently make moral decisions. Kohlberg's theory is a justice perspective. (336)

juvenile delinquency Refers to a broad range of behaviors, from socially unacceptable behavior (such as acting out in school) to status offenses (such as running away) to criminal offenses (such as burglary). (362)

K

keeping the meaning versus rigidity Vaillant's stage of adult development that occurs from about 45 to 55 years of age, in which adults are more relaxed if they have met their goals; if they have not met their goals, they accept the fact. At this time adults become concerned about extracting some meaning from their lives, and they resist falling into a rigid orientation. (495)

Klinefelter syndrome A genetic disorder in which males have an extra X chromosome, making them XXY instead of XY. (80)

L

labeling Identifying the names of objects. (168)

laboratory A controlled setting from which many of the complex factors of the "real world" are removed. (52)

Lamaze method A widely used childbirth strategy developed by Fernand Lamaze, a pioneering French obstetrician, that is a form of natural childbirth. (112)

language acquisition device (LAD) A biological prewiring that enables the child to detect certain language categories, such as phonology, syntax, and semantics. (166)

language A system of symbols used to communicate with others. In humans, language is characterized in infinite generativity and rule systems. (164)

late adulthood The developmental period beginning in the sixties or seventies and lasting until death. (21)

latency stage The fourth Freudian stage of development, which occurs between approximately 6 years of age and puberty; the child represses all interest in sexuality and develops social and intellectual skills. (36)

launching The process in which youths move into adulthood and exit their family of origin. (443)

learning disabilities (1) Are of normal intelligence or above, (2) have difficulties in several academic areas but usually do not show deficits in others, and (3) are not suffering from some other conditions or disorders that could explain their learning problems. (281)

leaving home and becoming a single adult The first stage in the family life cycle and involves launching. (443)

Leboyer method A childbirth strategy developed by Frederick Leboyer that intends to make the birth process less stressful for infants. Leboyer's procedure is referred to as "birth without violence." (111)

leisure The pleasant times after work when individuals are free to pursue activities and interests of their own choosing. (478)

life expectancy The number of years that will probably be lived by the average person born in a particular year. (513)

life review In a life review, one looks back at one's life experiences, evaluating them, interpreting them, and often reinterpreting them. (568)

life satisfaction Is psychological well-being in general or satisfaction with life as a whole; life satisfaction is widely used as an index of psychological well-being in older adults. (568)

life span   The upper boundary of life, the maximum number of years an individual can live. The maximum life span of human beings is about 120 years of age. (513)

life-span perspective   Involves seven basic contentions: development is lifelong, multidimensional, multidirectional, plastic, historically embedded, multidisciplinary, and contextual. (11)

long-term memory   A relatively permanent and unlimited type of memory. (287)

longitudinal approach   A research strategy in which the same individuals are studied over a period of time, usually several years or more. (57)

low-birthweight infants   Infants born after a regular gestation period (the length of time between conception and birth) of 38 to 42 weeks, but who weigh less than 5 1/2 pounds. (114)

M

macrobiological theories of aging   Theories that examine life at a more global level of analysis than the cell. (517)

macrosystem   The culture in which individuals live. (49)

mainstreaming   Occurs when handicapped children attend regular school classes with nonhandicapped children. In this way handicapped children enter the "mainstream" of education in the school and are not separated from nonhandicapped students. (280)

major depression   An individual suffering from this mood disorder is deeply unhappy, demoralized, self-derogatory, and bored. The person does not feel well, loses stamina easily, has poor appetite, and is listless and unmotivated. Major depression is so widespread that it has been called the "common cold" of mental disorders. (548)

marasmus   A wasting away of body tissues in the infant's first year, caused by severe deficiency of protein and calories. (139)

mastery orientation   Describes children who are task oriented. Instead of focusing on their ability, they become concerned about their learning strategies. (303)

maternal blood test   (Alpha-fetoprotein test—AFP) a prenatal diagnostic technique that is used to assess blood alphaprotein level, which is associated with neural tube defects. (83)

maturation   The orderly sequence of changes dictated by each person's genetic blueprint. (23)

Maximally Discriminative Facial Movement Coding System ("MAX"

for short)   Izard's system of coding facial expressions related to emotion. Using MAX, coders watch slow-motion and stop-action videotapes of infants' facial reactions to stimuli. (189)

mean length of utterance (MLU)   An index of language development based on the number of words per sentence a child produces in a sample of about 50 to 100 sentences; is a good index of language maturity. (171)

meiosis   The process of cell division in which each pair of chromosomes in the cell separates, with one member of each pair going into each gamete, or daughter cell. (78)

memory   A central feature of cognitive development, pertaining to all situations in which an individual retains information over time. (161)

menarche   A girl's first menstruation. (349)

menopause   A woman's menstrual periods and childbearing capability cease completely during menopause, which usually occurs in the late forties or early fifties. (473)

mental age (MA)   An individual's level of mental development relative to others. (290)

mental retardation   A condition of limited mental ability in which the individual has a low IQ, usually below 70 on a traditional intelligence test, and has difficulty adapting to everyday life. (297)

mesoderm   The middle layer, which will become the circulatory system, bones, muscle, excretory system, and reproductive system. (97)

mesosystem   Relations between microsystems or connections between contexts, such as the relation of family experiences to school experiences, school experiences to church experiences, or family experiences to peer experiences. (49)

metacognitive knowledge   Knowledge about cognition, the knowledge children have accumulated through experience, and stored in long-term memory about the human mind and its workings. (288)

microbiological theories of aging   Theories that look within the body's cells to explain aging. (517)

microsystem   The setting in which the individual lives; includes the person's family, peers, school, and neighborhood. It is in the microsystem that the most direct interactions with social agents take place—with parents, peers, and teachers, for example. (47)

middle adulthood   The developmental period that begins at approximately 35 to 45 years of age and extends into the sixties. (21, 465)

middle and late childhood   The developmental period extending from about 6 to 11 years of age, approximately corresponding to the elementary school years; this period is sometimes called the "elementary school years." (21)

mnemonics   Techniques designed to make memory more efficient. (541)

moral development   Concerns rules and conventions about what people should do in their interactions with other people. (263)

Moro reflex   A neonatal startle response that occurs in response to sudden, intense noise or movement. When startled, the newborn arches its back, throws its head back, and flings out its arms and legs. Then the newborn rapidly closes its arms and legs to the center of its body. (133)

morphology   The rules for combining morphemes; a morpheme is the smallest string of sounds that gives meaning to what we say and hear. (164)

motherese   The way mothers and other adults often talk to babies in a higher-than-normal frequency, greater-than-normal pitch, and simple words and sentences. (168)

multiple-factor model of divorce   Takes into account the complexity of the divorce context and examines a number of influences on the child's development, including not only family structure, but also the strengths and weaknesses of the child prior to the divorce, the nature of the events surrounding the divorce itself, the type of custody involved, visitation patterns, socioeconomic status, and postdivorce family functioning. (244)

myelination   A process in which nerve cells are covered and insulated with a layer of fat cells. This process has the effect of increasing the speed of information traveling through the nervous system. (206)

N

natural selection   The evolutionary process that favors individuals of a species that are best adapted to survive and reproduce. (75)

naturalistic observation   A method in which the scientist observes behavior in real world settings and makes no effort to manipulate or control the situation. (52)

near phase   In the second of Atchley's phases of retirement, the worker begins to participate in a preretirement program. (546)

negative affectivity (NA)   Emotions that are negatively toned, such as anxiety, anger, guilt, and sadness. (187)

neglected children These children receive little attention from their peers but they are not necessarily disliked by their peers. (314)

neo-Piagetians Are developmentalists who have elaborated on Piaget's theory, believing children's cognitive development is more specific in many respects than he thought. (286)

new couple Forming the new couple is the second stage in the family life cycle. Two individuals from separate families of origin unite to form a new family system. (443)

nomothetic research Research conducted at the level of the group. (61)

nonnormative life events Are unusual occurrences that have a major impact on an individual's life. The occurrence, pattern, and sequence of these events are not applicable to many individuals. (12)

nonnutritive sucking Sucking behavior unrelated to the infants' feeding. (134)

nonshared environmental influences The child's own unique experiences, both within the family and outside the family, that are not shared with another sibling. (89)

normal distribution Is symmetrical with a majority of cases falling in the middle of the possible range of scores and a few scores appearing toward the extremes of the range. (292)

normative age-graded influences Are biological and environmental influences that are similar for individuals in a particular age group. (12)

normative history-graded influences Are biological and environmental influences that are associated with history. These influences are common to people of a particular generation. (12)

O

object permanence The Piagetian term for one of an infant's most important accomplishments: understanding that objects and events continue to exist even when they cannot directly be seen, heard, or touched. (156)

Oedipus complex The Freudian concept in which the young child develops an intense desire to replace the parent of the same sex and enjoy the affections of the opposite-sexed parent. (36)

onlooker play Occurs when the child watches other children play. (251)

operations Internalized sets of actions that allow the child to do mentally what was done physically before. (210)

oral rehydration therapy (ORT) A treatment involving a range of techniques designed to prevent dehydration during episodes of diarrhea by giving the child fluids by mouth. (208)

oral stage The first Freudian stage of development, occurring during the first 18 months of life, in which the infant's pleasure centers around the mouth. (35)

organic retardation Mental retardation caused by a genetic disorder or by brain damage; organic refers to the tissues or organs of the body, so there is some physical damage in organic retardation. (297)

organogenesis The process of organ formation that takes place during the first two months of prenatal development. (98)

original sin Philosophical view that children are born into the world as basically bad, evil beings. (8)

osteoporosis Disorder of aging that involves an extensive loss of bone tissue and is the main reason many older adults walk with a marked stoop. Women are especially vulnerable to osteoporosis. (523)

oxytocin A hormone that stimulates and regulates the rhythmicity of uterine contractions, has been widely used as a drug to speed delivery. Controversy surrounds the use of this drug. (110)

P

pain cry Stimulated by high intensity stimuli and differs from other types of cries in that there is a sudden appearance of loud crying without preliminary moaning, and a long initial cry followed by an extended period of breath holding. (190)

parallel play Occurs when the child plays separately from others, but with toys like those the others are using or in a manner that mimics their play. (251)

passive euthanasia Available treatments, such as life-sustaining therapeutic devices, are withheld, allowing a person to die. (578)

passive genotype-environment interactions When parents who are genetically related to the child provide a rearing environment for the child. (87)

peers Children of about the same age or maturity level. (246)

perception The interpretation of what is sensed. (142)

permissive-indulgent parenting A style of parenting in which parents are highly involved with their children but place few demands or controls on them. Permissive-indulgent parenting is associated with children's social incompetence, especially lack of self-control. (238)

permissive-indifferent parenting A style of parenting in which the parent is very involved in the child's life; it is associated with children's social incompetence, especially a lack of self-control. (238)

personal fable According to Elkind, the adolescent's egocentrism involves a sense of uniqueness so that others cannot truly understand how she or he feels. (353)

personality type theory In John Holland's view, it is important to match an individual's personality with a particular career. (425)

perspective taking The ability to assume another person's perspective and understand his or her thoughts and feelings. (321)

phallic stage The third Freudian stage of development, which occurs between the ages of 3 and 6; its name comes from the Latin word phallus, which means "penis." (35)

phenotype The way an individual's genotype is expressed in observed and measurable characteristics. (84)

phenylketonuria A genetic disorder in which the individual cannot properly metabolize protein. Phenylketonuria is now easily detected, but if left untreated, mental retardation and hyperactivity result. (80)

phonics method A learning-to-read technique that emphasizes the sounds that letters make when in words (such sounds can differ from the names of these letters, as when the sound of the letter C is not found in cat). (299)

phonology The study of a language's sound system. (164)

placenta A life-support system that consists of a disk-shaped group of tissues in which small blood vessels from the mother and the offspring intertwine but do not join. (97)

play therapy Allows the child to work off frustrations and is a medium through which the therapist can analyze the child's conflicts and ways of coping with them. Children may feel less threatened and be more likely to express their true feelings in the context of play. (251)

play A pleasurable activity that is engaged in for its own sake. (250)

pluralism The coexistence of distinct ethnic and cultural groups in the same society. Individuals with a pluralist stance usually advocate that cultural differences should be maintained and appreciated. (391)

polygenic inheritance A genetic principle describing the interaction of many genes to produce a particular characteristic. (84)

positive affectivity (PA) The range of positive emotions, from high energy, enthusiasm, and excitement, to calm, quiet, and withdrawn. Joy, happiness, and laughter involve positive affectivity. (187)

postconventional reasoning   The highest level in Kohlberg's theory of moral development. At this level, morality is completely internalized and not based on others' standards. (335)

postpartal period   The period after childbirth or delivery that is also called the "postpartum period." It is a time when the woman adjusts, both physically and psychologically, to the process of childbearing. It lasts for about six weeks or until the body has completed its adjustment and has returned to a near prepregnant state. (118)

practice play   Involves the repetition of behavior when new skills are being learned or when physical or mental mastery and coordination of skills are required for games or sports. Sensorimotor play, which often involves practice play, is primarily confined to infancy, while practice play can be engaged in throughout life. (252)

pragmatics   The ability to engage in appropriate conversation. (166)

precipitate delivery   A form of delivery that takes place too rapidly. A precipitate delivery is one in which the baby takes less than ten minutes to be squeezed through the birth canal. (110)

preconventional reasoning   The lowest level in Kohlberg's theory of moral development. At this level, the child shows no internalization of moral values—moral reasoning is controlled by external rewards and punishments. (334)

preintimate style   According to Orlofsky, an individual with preintimate style shows mixed emotions about commitment, an ambivalence that is reflected in the strategy of offering love without obligations or longlasting bonds. (453)

prejudice   An unjustified negative attitude toward an individual because of that person's membership in a group. (325)

prenatal period   The time from conception to birth. (20)

preoperational stage   (Lasts from approximately 2 to 7 years of age) the second Piagetian stage; children begin to represent the world with words, images, and drawings. (42)

prepared, or natural, childbirth   Includes being informed about what will happen during the procedure, knowing about comfort measures for childbirth, anticipating that little or no medication will be used, and if

complications arise, expecting to participate in a decision. (111)

pretense/symbolic play   Occurs when the child transforms the physical environment into a symbol. (252)

preterm infant   An infant who is born prior to 38 weeks (also called a "premature" infant). (114)

primary appraisal   Children interpret whether an event involves harm or loss that has already occurred, a threat to some future danger, or a challenge to be overcome. (277)

primary circular reaction   A scheme based upon the infants attempt to reproduce an interesting or pleasurable event that initially occurred by chance. (156)

Project Follow Through   Implemented in 1967 as an adjunct to Project Head Start. In Project Follow Through, different types of educational programs were devised to determine which programs were most effective. In the Follow Through programs, the enriched programs were carried through the first few years of elementary school. (227)

Project Head Start   A compensatory education program designed to provide children from low-income homes the opportunity to acquire skills and experiences important for success in school. (227)

proximodistal pattern   The sequence in which growth starts at the center of the body and moves toward the extremities. (135)

pseudointimate style   According to Orlofsky, an individual with pseudointimate style maintains a longlasting sexual attachment with little or no depth or closeness. (453)

psychoactive drug   Any drug that acts on the nervous system to alter states of consciousness, modify perceptions, and change moods. (414)

psychological dependence   The need to take a drug to cope with problems and stress. (414)

puberty   A period of rapid skeletal and sexual maturation that occurs mainly in early adolescence. (349)

Public Law 94-142   The federal government's mandate to all states to provide a free, appropriate education for all children. This law, also called the "Education for All Handicapped Children Act," was passed by Congress in 1975. A key provision of the bill was the development of an individualized education program for each identified handicapped child. (280)

punishment and obedience orientation   The first stage in Kohlberg's theory of moral development. At this stage, moral thinking is based on punishment. (334)

Q

questionnaire   Similar to a highly structured interview except that respondents read the questions and mark their answers on paper rather than respond verbally to the interviewer. (52)

R

random assignment   When researchers assign subjects by chance to experimental and control conditions, thus reducing the likelihood that the results of the experiment will be due to some preexisting differences in the two groups. (55)

rape   Forcible sexual intercourse with a person who does not give consent. (421)

reaction range   Used to describe the range of phenotypes for each genotype, suggesting the importance of an environment's restrictiveness or enrichment. (85)

recasting   Phrasing the same or similar meaning of a sentence in a different way; perhaps turning it into a question. (168)

receptive vocabulary   The words an individual understands. (171)

reciprocal socialization   The view that socialization is bidirectional; children socialize parents just as parents socialize children. (179)

reciprocal teaching   An instructional procedure used by Brown and Palincsar to develop cognitive monitoring; it requires that students take turns in leading a study group in the use of strategies for comprehending and remembering text content. (289)

reflexive smile   A smile that does not occur in response to external stimuli. It appears during the first month after birth, usually during irregular patterns of sleep, not when an infant is in an alert state. (190)

reintegrative stage   Schaie's late adulthood, or final, stage, in which older adults choose to focus their energy on the tasks and activities that have meaning for them. (424)

rejected children   These children are more likely to be disruptive and aggressive than neglected children and are often disliked by their peers. (314)

remote phase   In the first of Robert Atchley's seven phases of retirement, most individuals do little to prepare for retirement. (546)

reorientation phase   In the fifth of Atchley's phases of retirement, retirees take stock, pull themselves together, and develop more realistic life alternatives. (548)

repression The most powerful and pervasive defense mechanism, (according to Freud) it works to push unacceptable id impulses out of awareness and back into the unconscious mind. (35)

reproduction When a female gamete (ovum) is fertilized by a male gamete (sperm), the reproduction process begins. (78)

responsibility stage Schaie's adult stage when a family is established and attention is given to the needs of a spouse and offspring. (424)

rite of passage A ceremony or a ritual that marks an individual's transition from one status to another. Most rites of passage focus on the transition to adult status. (388)

role-focused level In White's model, this is the second level of relationship maturity, at which one begins to perceive others as individuals in their own right. One's perspective is still stereotypical and emphasizes social acceptability. (453)

romantic love Also called "passionate love" or "Eros," romantic love has strong sexual and infatuation components and often predominates in the early period of a love relationship. (440)

rooting reflex A reflex that occurs when the infant's cheek is stroked or the side of the mouth is touched. In response, the infant turns its head toward the side that was touched, in an apparent effort to find something to suck. (133)

S

scaffolding An important caregiver's role in early parent-child interaction. Through their attention and choice of behaviors, caregivers provide a framework around which they and their infants interact. One function scaffolding serves is to introduce infants to social rules, especially turntaking. (179)

schema A cognitive structure, a network of associations that organizes and guides an individual's perceptions. (261)

scheme (or schema) Stage that refers to the basic unit (or units) for an organized pattern of sensorimotor functioning. (155)

scientific method An approach, that can be used to discover accurate information about behavior and development, it includes the following steps: identify and analyze the problem, collect data, draw conclusions, and revise theories. (33)

script A schema for an event. (288)

secondary appraisal Children evaluate their resources and determine how effectively they can cope with the event. (277)

secondary circular reaction Piaget's third sensorimotor substage that develops between four and eight months of age. In this substage, the infant becomes more object-orientated or focused on the world, moving beyond preoccupation with the self in sensorimotor interactions. (156)

secure attachment Infants use the caregiver, usually the mother, as a secure base from which to explore the environment. Ainsworth believes that secure attachment in the first year of life provides an important foundation for psychological development later in life. (181)

selective optimization with compensation model Proposes that successful aging is related to three main factors: selection, optimization, and compensation. (569)

self-concept Domain-specific evaluations of the self. (323)

self-esteem The global evaluative dimension of the self. Self-esteem is also referred to as "self-worth" or "self-image." (323)

self-focused level In the model of relationship maturity developed by Kathleen White and her colleagues, this is the first level of relationship maturity. At the self-focused level, one's perspective on another or on a relationship is concerned only with how it affects oneself. (453)

Self-Perception Profile for Children This self-concept measure has five specific domains—scholastic competence, athletic competence, social acceptance, physical appearance, and behavioral conduct—plus general self-worth. (324)

self-understanding The child's cognitive representation of self, the substance and content of the child's self-conceptions. (257)

semantics The meaning of words and sentences. (166)

sensation Sensation occurs when information contacts sensory receptors—the eyes, ears, tongue, nostrils, and skin. (142)

sensorimotor play Behavior engaged in by infants to derive pleasure from exercising their existing sensorimotor schemas. (252)

sensorimotor stage (Lasts from birth to about 2 years of age) the first Piagetian stage; infants construct an understanding of the world by coordinating sensory experiences (such as seeing and hearing) with physical, motoric actions—hence the term sensorimotor. (39)

sequential approach Combined cross-sectional, longitudinal design. (57)

set point The weight one maintains when one makes no effort to gain or lose weight. (410)

shared environmental influences Children's common experiences, such as their parents' personalities and intellectual orientation, the family's social class, and the neighborhood in which they live. (89)

short-term memory Individuals retain information for up to 15 to 30 seconds, assuming there is no rehearsal. (217)

sickle-cell anemia Occurs most often in Blacks that is a genetic disorder affecting the red blood cells. (80)

simple reflexes Piaget's first sensorimotor substage that corresponds to the first month after birth. In this substage, the basic means of coordinating sensation and action is through reflexive behaviors, such as rooting and sucking, which the infant has at birth. (156)

slow-to-warm-up child A child who has a low activity level, is somewhat negative, shows low adaptability, and displays a low intensity of mood. (186)

sociability The tendency to prefer the company of others to being alone. (187)

social breakdown-reconstruction theory Argues that aging is promoted through negative psychological functioning brought about by negative societal views of older adults and inadequate provision of services for them. Social reconstruction can occur by changing society's view of older adults and by providing adequate support systems for them. (557)

social clock The timetable according to which individuals are expected to accomplish life's tasks, such as getting married, having children, or establishing themselves in a career. (497)

social identity theory Social psychologist Henry Tajfel's (1978) theory that, when individuals are assigned to a group, they invariably think of that group as an in-group for them. This occurs because individuals want to have a positive image. (324)

social learning theory of gender Emphasizes that children's gender development occurs through observation and imitation of gender behavior, and through the rewards and punishments children experience for gender appropriate and inappropriate behavior. (258)

social learning theory The view of psychologists who emphasize behavior, environment, and cognition as the key factors in development. (44)

social play   Play that involves social interactions with peers. (252)

social policy   A national government's course of action designed to influence the welfare of its citizens. (17)

social smile   A smile that occurs in response to an external stimulus, which, early in development, typically is in response to a face. (190)

social system morality   The fourth stage in Kohlberg's theory of moral development. At this stage, moral judgments are based on understanding the social order, law, justice, and duty. (334)

sociobiology   Emphasizes the power of genes in determining behavior and explains complex social interactions that natural selection cannot. It states that all behavior is motivated by the desire to contribute one's genetic heritage to the greatest number of descendants. (75)

socioemotional processes   Involve changes in the individual's relationships with other people, changes in emotions, and changes in personality. (20)

solitary play   Occurs when the child plays alone and independently of others. (251)

stability phase   In the sixth of Atchley's phases of retirement, retirees have decided upon a set of criteria for evaluating choices in retirement and how they will perform once they have made these choices. (548)

stability-change issue   Addresses whether development is best described by stability or by change. The stability-change issue involves the degree to which we become older renditions of our early experience or whether we develop into someone different from who we were at an earlier point in development. (24)

standardized tests   Require people to answer a series of written or oral questions. They have two distinct features; first, psychologists usually total an individual's score to yield a single score, or a set of scores, that reflects something about the individual; second, psychologists compare the individual's score to the scores of a large group of similar people to determine how the individual responded relative to others. (53)

status offenses   Juvenile offenses such as running away, truancy, underage drinking, sexual promiscuity, and uncontrollability. They are less serious than index offenses. (362)

stereotyped style   According to Orlofsky, an individual with the stereotyped style of intimate relationships has superficial relationships that tend to be dominated by friendship ties with same-sex rather than opposite-sex individuals. (453)

storm-and-stress view   G. Stanley Hall's concept that adolescence is a turbulent time charged with conflict and mood swings. (8)

stress   The response of individuals to the circumstances and events (called "stressors") that threaten them and tax their coping abilities. (277)

sucking reflex   A reflex that occurs when newborns automatically suck an object placed in their mouth. The sucking reflex enables newborns to get nourishment before they have associated a nipple with food. (133)

sudden infant death syndrome (SIDS)   The sudden death of an apparently healthy infant, occurring most often in infants between 2 and 4 months of age. The immediate cause of SIDS is that the infant stops breathing, but the underlying cause is not yet known. (138, 580)

superego   The Freudian structure of personality that is the moral branch of personality. (34)

surface structure   The actual order of words in a sentence. (166)

suttee   Now outlawed, suttee was the Hindu practice of burning to death a dead man's widow to increase his family's prestige and firmly establish an image of her in his memory. (587)

symbolic function substage   The first substage of preoperational thought, occurring roughly between the ages of 2 and 4. In this substage, the young child gains the ability to mentally represent an object that is not present. (211)

syntax   The way words are combined to form acceptable phrases and sentences. (164)

T

tabula rasa   View proposed by English philosopher John Locke. He argued that children are not innately bad, but instead they are like a "blank tablet," a "tabula rasa" as he called it. (8)

telegraphic speech   The use of short and precise words to communicate; it is characteristic of young children's two-word utterances. (171)

temperament   An individual's behavioral style and characteristic way of responding. (186)

teratogen   (The word comes from the Greek word *tera* meaning "monster.") Any agent that causes a birth defect. The field of study that investigates the causes of birth defects is called "teratology." (102)

terminal drop hypothesis   States that death is preceded by a decrease in cognitive functioning over approximately a 5-year period prior to death. (541)

termination phase   In the last of Atchley's phases of retirement, the retirement role is replaced by the role of being sick or dependent because the older adult can no longer function autonomously and be self-sufficient. (548)

tertiary circular reactions, novelty, and curiosity   Piaget's fifth sensorimotor substage that develops between 12 and 18 months of age. In this substage, infants become intrigued by the variety of properties that objects possess and by the multiplicity of things they can make happen to objects. (156)

testosterone   Hormone is associated with the development of genitals, an increase in height, and a change of voice in boys. (349)

thanatologists   Persons who study death and dying. (587)

theory   A coherent set of ideas that helps to explain data and to make prediction. (33)

top-dog phenomenon   Includes the circumstance of moving from the top position (in elementary school, being the oldest, biggest, and most powerful students in the school) to the lowest position (in middle or junior high school, being the youngest, smallest, and least powerful students in the school). (358)

toxoplasmosis   A mild infection that causes coldlike symptoms or no apparent illness in adults. However, toxoplasmosis can be a teratogen for the unborn baby, causing possible eye defects, brain defects, and premature birth. (108)

triangular theory of love   Sternberg's theory that love has three main forms: passion, intimacy, and commitment. (441)

triarchic theory   Sternberg's theory that intelligence consists of componential intelligence, experiential intelligence, and contextual intelligence. (293)

trophoblast   The outer layer of cells that develops during the germinal period. It later provides nutrition and support for the embryo. (97)

trust versus mistrust   Erikson's first psychosocial stage, which is experienced in the first year of life. A sense of trust requires a feeling of physical comfort and a minimal amount of fear and apprehension about the future. (37)

Turner syndrome   A genetic disorder in which females are missing an X chromosome, making them XO instead of XX. (80)

twin study When the behavior of identical twins is compared with the behavior of fraternal twins. (86)

type A babies Babies who exhibit insecurity by avoiding the mother (for example, ignoring her, avoiding her gaze, and failing to seek proximity). (181)

Type A behavior pattern This cluster of characteristics—being excessively competitive, hard-driven, impatient, and hostile—is thought to be related to the incidence of heart disease. (470)

type B babies Babies who use the mother as a secure base from which to explore the environment. (181)

type C babies Babies who exhibit insecurity by resisting the mother (for example, clinging to her but at the same time fighting against the closeness, perhaps by kicking and pushing away). (181)

Type C behavior Individuals with this personality—inhibited, uptight, emotionally inexpressive, and otherwise constrained—are more likely to develop cancer than are more expressive people. (470)

U

ultrasound sonography A prenatal medical procedure in which high-frequency sound waves are directed into the pregnant woman's abdomen. (81)

umbilical cord A life-support system, containing two arteries and one vein, that connects the baby to the placenta. (97)

universal ethical principles The sixth and highest stage in Kohlberg's theory of moral development. At this stage, persons have developed a moral standard based on universal human rights. (335)

unoccupied play Occurs when the child is not engaging in play as it is commonly understood and may stand in one spot, look around the room, or perform random movements that do not seem to have a goal. (251)

W

whole-word method A learning-to-read technique that emphasizes learning direct associations between whole words and their meanings. (299)

wisdom According to Baltes, wisdom is expert knowledge about the practical aspects of life. (542)

withdrawal The undesirable, intense pain and craving experienced by an addict when the addictive drug is withheld. (414)

X

XYY syndrome A genetic disorder in which the male has an extra Y chromosome. (80)

Y

youth Kenneth Kenniston's term for the transitional period between adolescence and adulthood, which is a time of extended economic and personal temporariness. (407)

Z

zone of proximal development (ZPD) Vygotsky's term for tasks too difficult for children to master alone, but that can be mastered with the guidance and assistance of adults or more skilled children. (220)

zygote A single cell formed through fertilization. (78)

REFERENCES

A

Aber, J. L. (1993, March). *Poverty and child development: The policy implications of understanding causal mechanisms.* Paper presented at the biennial meeting of the Society for Research in Child Development, New Orleans.

Aboud, F., & Skerry, S. (1983). Self and ethnic concepts in relation to ethnic constancy. *Canadian Journal of Behavioral Science, 15,* 3–34.

Abramovitch, R., Corter, C., Pepler, D. J., & Stanhope, L. (1986). Sibling and peer interaction: A final follow-up and comparison. *Child Development, 47,* 217–229.

Abrams, R. (1990). *Will it hurt the baby?* Reading, MA: Addison-Wesley.

Achenbach, T. M., Phares, V., Howell, V. A., & Nurcombe, B. (1990). Seven-year outcome of the Vermont Intervention Program for Low-Birthweight Infants. *Child Development, 61,* 1672–1681.

Ackerman, B. P. (1988). Thematic influences on children's judgments about story accuracy. *Child Development, 59,* 918–938.

Acredolo, L. P., & Hake, J. L. (1982). Infant perception. In B. B. Wolman (Ed.), *Handbook of developmental psychology.* Englewood Cliffs, NJ: Prentice-Hall.

Adams, R. G. (1989). Conceptual and methodological issues in studying friendships of older adults. In R. G. Adams & R. Blieszner (Eds.), *Other adult friendships.* Newbury Park, CA: Sage.

Adamson, L. B. (1992). Variations in the early use of language. In J. Valsiner & L. T. Winegar (Eds.), *Children's development within social context* (Vol. 1). Hillsdale, NJ: Erlbaum.

Adelman, R. C. (1988). The importance of basic biological science to gerontology. *Journal of Gerontology: Biological Sciences, 43,* B1–2.

Adler, T. (1991, January). Seeing double? Controversial twins study is widely reported, debated. *APA Monitor, 22,* 1, 8.

Ahl, V. A. (1993, March). *Classification of infants prenatally exposed to cocaine.* Paper presented at the biennial meeting of the Society for Research in Child Development, New Orleans.

Ahrons, C. R., & Rodgers, R. H. (1987). *Divorced families.* New York: W. W. Norton.

Aiken, L. R. (1989). *Later life* (3rd ed.). Hillsdale, NJ: Erlbaum.

Ainsworth, M. D. S. (1979). Infant-mother attachment. *American Psychologist, 34,* 932–937.

Alan Guttmacher Institute. (1990). *Adolescent sexuality.* New York: Author.

Alan Guttmacher Institute. (1993). *National survey of the American male's sexual habits.* Unpublished data. New York: Author.

Albrecht, H. T., & Silbereisen, R. K. (1992, March). *Antecedents of adolescent peer rejection.* Paper presented at the meeting of the Society for Research on Adolescence, Washington, DC.

Alcoholics Anonymous. (3rd ed.). (1976). New York: Alcoholics Anonymous World Services.

Alexander, C. N., Langer, E. J., Newman, R. I., Chandler, H. M., & Davies, J. L. (1989). Transcendental meditation, mindfulness, and longevity: An experimental study with the elderly. *Journal of Personality and Social Psychology, 57,* 950–964.

Alexander, K. L., & Entwisle, D. R. (1988). Achievement in the first two years of school: Patterns and processes. *Monographs of the Society for Research in Child Development, 53* (2, Serial No. 218).

Allen, J., & Allen, R. F. (1986). From short-term compliance to long-term freedom: Culture-based health promotion by health professionals. *American Journal of Health Promotion, 12,* 46–47.

Allen, J. P., Bell, K. L., & Boykin, K. A. (1994, February). *Autonomy and relatedness in adolescent–mother interactions and social functioning with peers.* Paper presented at the meeting of the Society for Research on Adolescence, San Diego, CA.

Allen, J. P., Hauser, S. T., Bell, K. L., & O'Connor, T. G. (1994). Longitudinal assessment of autonomy and relatedness in adolescent-family interactions as predictors of adolescent ego development and self-esteem. *Child Development, 65,* 179–194.

Allen, L., & Majidi-Ahi, S. (1989). Black American children. In J. T. Gibbs & L. N. Huang (Eds.), *Children of color.* San Francisco: Jossey-Bass.

Allen, L., & Santrock, J. W. (1993). *Psychology: The contexts of behavior.* Dubuque, IA: Brown & Benchmark.

Alymer, R. C. (1989). The launching of the single young adult. In B. Carter & M. McGoldrick (Eds.), *The changing family life cycle* (2nd ed.). Boston: Allyn & Bacon.

America in transition. (1989). Washington, DC: National Governors' Association Task Force on Children.

American Association for Protecting Children. (1986). *Highlights of official child neglect and abuse reporting: 1984.* Denver: American Humane Association.

American Association of Retired Persons. (1990, January). *Survey of the most important coverages in long-term health care.* Washington, DC: AARP.

American College Health Association. (1989, May). *Survey of AIDS on American college and university campuses.* Washington, DC: Author.

Ames, C., & Ames, R. (Eds.). (1989). *Research on motivation in education: Vol. 3. Goals and cognitions.* San Diego: Academic Press.

Amsterdam, B. K. (1968). *Mirror behavior in children under two years of age.* Unpublished doctoral dissertation, University of North Carolina, Chapel Hill.

Anastasi, A. (1988). *Psychological testing* (6th ed.). New York: Macmillan.

Anderson, C. E., & Weber, J. A. (1993). Preretirement planning and perceptions of satisfaction among retirees. *Educational Gerontology, 19,* 397–406.

Anderson, D. R., Lorch, E. P., Field, D. E., Collins, P. A., & Nathan J. G. (1985, April). *Television viewing at home: Age trends in visual attention and time with TV.* Paper presented at the biennial meeting of the Society for Research in Child Development, Toronto.

Anderson, E. A., & Leslie, L. A. (1991). Coping with employment and family stress: Employment arrangement and gender differences. *Sex Roles, 24,* 223–237.

Anderson, E. R. (1992, March). *Consistency of parenting in stepfather families.* Paper presented at the meeting of the Society for Research on Adolescence, Washington, DC.

Anderson, L. W. (1989, April). *The impact of sex and age on the resolutions of preschool children's conversational disagreements.* Paper presented at the biennial meeting of the Society for Research in Child Development, Kansas City.

Anderson, N. (1991, August). *Sociodemographic aspects of hypertension in African Americans: A research agenda for health psychology.* Paper presented at the meeting of the American Psychological Association, San Francisco.

Andersson, B. (1992). Effects of day care on cognitive and socioemotional competence of thirteen-year-old Swedish schoolchildren. *Child Development, 63,* 20–36.

Andres, R. (1989). Does the "best" body weight change with age? In A. J. Stunkard & A. Baum (Eds.), *Perspectives on behavioral medicine.* Hillsdale, NJ: Erlbaum.

Andrews, J., & Conte, R. (1993, March). *Enhancing the social cognition of learning disabled children through a cognitive strategies* *approach.* Paper presented at the biennial meeting of the Society for Research in Child Development, New Orleans.

Angoff, W. (1989, August). *Perspectives on bias in mental testing.* Paper presented at the meeting of the American Psychological Association, New Orleans.

Antonucci, T. C., Jackson, T. C., & Gibson, R. (1989). Social relations, productive activities, and coping with stress in late life. In M. A. P. Stephens, J. H. Crowther, S. E. Hobfoll, & D. L. Tennenbaum (Eds.), *Stress and coping in later life families.* Washington, DC: Hemisphere.

Antonucci, T. C. (1989). Understanding adult social relationships. In K. Kreppner & R. M. Lerner (Eds.), *Family systems and life-span development.* Hillsdale, NJ: Erlbaum.

Antonucci, T. C. (1990). Social supports and relationships. In R. H. Binstock & L. K. George (Eds.), *Handbook of aging and the social sciences.* San Diego: Academic Press.

Archer, S. L., & Waterman, A. S. (1994). Adolescent identity development: Contextual perspectives. In C. Fisher & R. Lerner (Eds.), *Applied developmental psychology.* New York: McGraw-Hill.

Archer, S. L. (1989). The status of identity: Reflections on the need for intervention. *Journal of Adolescence, 12,* 345–359.

Archer, S. L. (1992). A feminist's approach to identity research. In G. R. Adams, T. P. Gullotta, & R. Montemayor (Eds.), *Adolescent identity formation.* Newbury Park, CA: Sage.

Arehart, D. M., & Smith, P. H. (1990). Identity in adolescence: Influences on dysfunction and psychosocial task issues. *Journal of Youth and Adolescence, 19,* 63–72.

Aries, P. (1962). *Centuries of childhood* (R. Baldrick, Trans.). New York: Knopf.

Arman-Nolley, S. (1989, April). *Vygotsky's perspective on development of creativity and imagination.* Paper presented at the biennial meeting of the Society for Research on Child Development, Kansas City.

Armsden, G. C., & Greenberg, M. T. (1987). The inventory of parent and peer attachment: Individual differences and their relationship to psychological well-being in adolescence. *Journal of Youth and Adolescence, 16,* 427–454.

Arnett, J. (1990). Contraceptive use, sensation seeking, and adolescent egocentrism. *Journal of Youth and Adolescence, 19,* 171–180.

Aronson, E. (1986, August). *Teaching students things they think they already know about: The case of prejudice and desegregation.* Paper presented at the meeting of the American Psychological Association, Washington, DC.

Asarnow, J. R., & Callan, J. W. (1985). Boys with peer adjustment problems: Social cognitive processes. *Journal of Consulting and Clinical Psychology, 53,* 80–87.

Asher, J., & Garcia, R. (1969). The optimal age to learn a foreign language. *Modern Language Journal, 53,* 334–341.

Astin, A. W., Green, K. C., & Korn, W. S. (1987). *The American freshman: Twenty year trends.* Los Angeles: UCLA Higher Education Research Institute.

Astin, A. W., Green, K. C., & Korn, W. S. (1989). *The American freshman, 1988.* Unpublished manuscript. Higher Education Institute, University of California, Los Angeles.

Atchley, R. C. (1976). *The sociology of retirement.* Cambridge, MA: Schenkman.

Atchley, R. C. (1989). Demographic factors and adult psychological development. In K. W. Schaie & C. Schooler (Eds.), *Social structure and aging.* Hillsdale, NJ: Erlbaum.

Atkins, C. J., Kaplan, R. M., & Toshima, M. T. (1989). Close relationships in the epidemiology of cardiovascular disease. In W. H. Jones & D. Perlman (Eds.), *Advances in personal relationships.* Greenwich, CT: JAI Press.

Atkinson, D. R., Morten, G., & Sue, D. W. (1989). *Counseling American minorities: A cross-cultural perspective.* (3rd ed.). Dubuque, IA: Brown & Benchmark.

Atkinson, D. R., Morten, G., & Sue, D. W. (1993). *Counseling American minorities* (4th ed.). Dubuque, IA: Brown & Benchmark.

Atkinson, J. W., & Raynor, I. O. (1974). *Motivation and achievement.* New York: Wiley.

Averill, J. R. (1968). Grief: Its nature and significance. *Psychological Bulletin, 6,* 721–748.

B

Baca Zinn, M. (1980). Employment and education of Mexican-American women: The interplay of modernity and ethnicity in eight families. *Harvard Educational Review, 50,* 47–62.

Bachman, J., O'Malley, P., & Johnston, L. (1978). *Youth in transition: Vol. 6. Adolescence to adulthood—change and stability of the lives of young men.* Ann Arbor: University of Michigan, Institute of Social Research.

Baer, J. (1993). *Creativity and divergent thinking.* Hillsdale, NJ: Erlbaum.

Bahr, S. J. (1989). Prologue: A developmental overview of the aging family. In S. J. Bahr & E. T. Peterson (Eds.), *Aging and the family.* Lexington, MA: Lexington Books.

Bahrick, L. E. (1988). Intermodal learning in infancy: Learning on the basis of two kinds of invariant relations in audible and visual events. *Child Development, 59,* 197–209.

Bahrick, L. E. (1992). Infants' perceptual differentiation of amodal and modality-specific audio-visual relations. *Journal of Experimental Child Psychology, 53,* 180–199.

Bailey, C. (1991). *The new fit or fat* (rev. ed.). Boston: Houghton Mifflin.

Baillargeon, R. (1987). Object permanence in 3.5- 4.5-month-old infants. *Developmental Psychology, 23,* 655–664.

Baillargeon, R. (1991, April). *Infants' reasoning about collision events.* Paper presented at the Society for Research in Child Development, Seattle.

Baines, E. M. (1991). *Perspectives on gerontological nursing.* Newbury Park, CA: Sage.

Bakeman, R., & Brown, J. V. (1980). Early interaction: Consequences for social and mental development at three years. *Child Development, 51,* 437–447.

Baker, L., & Brown, A. L. (1984). Metacognitive skills and reading. In P. D. Pearson (Ed.), *Handbook of reading research, Part 2.* New York: Longman.

Baker, P. M., & Prince, M. J. (1991). Supportive housing preferences among the elderly. *Journal of Housing for the Elderly, 7,* 5–24.

Ballenger, M. (1983). Reading in the kindergarten: Comment. *Childhood Education, 59,* 187.

Baltes, M. M., & Wahl, H. W. (1991). The behavior system of dependency in long-term care institutions. In M. G. Ory, R. P. Abeles, & P. D. Lipman (Eds.), *Aging, health, and behavior.* Newbury Park, CA: Sage.

Baltes, P. B., & Baltes, M. M. (1990). Psychological perspectives on successful aging: The model of selective optimization with compensation. In P. B. Baltes & M. M. Baltes (Eds.), *Successful aging: Perspectives from the behavioral sciences.* New York: Cambridge University Press.

Baltes, P. B., & Smith, J. (1990). The psychology of wisdom and its ontogenesis. In R. J. Sternberg (Ed.), *Wisdom: Its nature, origins, and development.* New York: Cambridge.

Baltes, P. B., & Smith, J. (in press). Toward a psychology of wisdom and its ontogenesis. In R. J. Sternberg (Ed.), *Wisdom: Its nature, origins, and development.* New York: Cambridge University Press.

Baltes, P. B., & Staudinger, U. M. (1993). The search for a psychology of wisdom. *Current Directions in Psychological Science, 2,* 75–80.

Baltes, P. B., Featherman, D. L., & Lerner, R. M. (1990). *Life-span development and behavior* (Vol. 10). Hillsdale, NJ: Erlbaum.

Baltes, P. B., Smith, J., & Staudinger, U. M (in press). Wisdom and successful aging. *Nebraska Symposium of Motivation, 39.*

Baltes, P. B., Smith, J., Staudinger, U. M., & Sowarka, D. (in press). Wisdom: One facet of successful aging? In M. Perlmutter (Ed.), *Late-life potential.* Washington, DC: Gerontological Association of America.

Baltes, P. B. (1987). Theoretical propositions of life-span developmental psychology: On the dynamics between growth and decline. *Developmental Psychology, 23,* 611–626.

Baltes, P. B. (1989). The dynamics between growth and decline. *Contemporary Psychology, 34,* 983–984.

Baltes, P. B. (in press). The aging mind: Potential and limits. *Gerontologist.*

Bancroft, J., & Reinisch, J. M. (1990). *Adolescence and puberty.* New York: Oxford University Press.

Bandura, A. (1965). Influence of models' reinforcement contingencies on the acquisition of imitative responses. *Journal of Personality and Social Psychology, 1,* 589–595.

Bandura, A. (1977). *Social learning theory.* Englewood Cliffs, NJ: Prentice-Hall.

Bandura, A. (1986). *Social foundations of thought and action: A social cognitive theory.* Englewood Cliffs, NJ: Prentice-Hall.

Bandura, A. (1989). Social cognitive theory. In R. Vasta (Ed.), *Six theories of child development.* Greenwich, CT: JAI Press.

Bandura, A. (1991). Self-efficacy: Impact of self-beliefs on adolescent life paths. In R. M.

Lerner, A. C. Petersen, & J. Brooks-Gunn (Eds.), *Encyclopedia of adolescence* (Vol. 2). New York: Garland.

Bandura, A. (1994). Social cognitive theory of mass communication. In J. Bryant & D. Zillman (Eds.), *Media effects.* Hillsdale, NJ: Erlbaum.

Banks, E. C. (1993, March). *Moral education curriculum in a multicultural context: The Malaysian primary curriculum.* Paper presented at the biennial meeting of the Society for Research in Child Development, New Orleans.

Banks, M. S., & Salapatek, P. (1983). Infant visual perception. In P. H. Mussen (Ed.), *Handbook of child psychology* (4th ed., Vol. 2). New York: Wiley.

Barbach, L. (1975). *For yourself.* New York: Doubleday.

Barbach, L. (1982). *For each other.* New York: Doubleday.

Barber, B. L., & Eccles, J. S. (1992). Long-term influence of divorce and single parenting on adolescent family- and work-related values, behaviors, and aspirations. *Psychological Bulletin, 111,* 108–126.

Barber, B. L., Clark, J. J. Clossick, M. L., & Wamboldt, P. (1992, March). *The effects of parent-adolescent communication on adjustment: Variations across divorced and intact families.* Paper presented at the meeting of the Society for Research on Adolescence, Washington, DC.

Bardwick, J. (1971). *The psychology of women: A study of biocultural conflicts.* New York: Harper & Row.

Barenboim, C. (1981). The development of person perception in childhood and adolescence: From behavioral comparisons to psychological constructs to psychological comparisons. *Child Development, 52,* 129–144.

Barenboim, C. (1985, April). *Person perception and interpersonal behavior.* Paper presented at the biennial meeting of the Society for Research in Child Development, Toronto.

Barkeley, R. (1989). Attention deficit disorders: History, definition, diagnosis. In M. Lewis, & S. Miller (Eds.), *Handbook of developmental psychopathology.* New York: Plenum.

Barker, R., & Wright, H. F. (1951). *One boy's day.* New York: Harper.

Barnes, D. M. (1987). Defect in Alzheimer's is on Chromosome 21. *Science, 235,* 846–847.

Barness, L. A., & Gilbert-Barness, E. (1992). Cause of death: SIDS or something else? *Contemporary Pediatrics, 9,* 13–31.

Barnet, B., Joffe, A., Duggan, A., & Repke, J. (1992, March). *Depressive symptoms, stress, and social support in pregnant and postpartum adolescents.* Paper presented at the meeting of the Society for Adolescent Medicine, Washington, DC.

Barnett, R. C., Kibria, N., Baruch, G. K., & Pleck, J. H. (1991). Adult daughter-parent relationships and their associations with daughters' subjective well-being and psychological distress. *Journal of Marriage and the Family, 53,* 29–42.

Barr, R. G., Desilets, J., & Rotman, A. (1991, April). *Parsing the normal crying curve: Is it really the evening fussing curve?* Paper presented at the biennial meeting of the Society for Research in Child Development, Seattle.

Barrett, D. E., Radke-Yarrow, M., & Klein, R. E. (1982). Chronic malnutrition and child behavior: Effects of calorie supplementation on social and emotional functioning at school age. *Developmental Psychology, 18,* 541–556.

Barron, F. (1989, April). The birth of a notion: Exercises to tap your creative potential. *Omni,* pp. 112–119.

Barron, J., & Tabor, M. B. W. (1991, August 4). Clues in the life of an accused mass killer. *The New York Times,* p. N1.

Bartsch, K., & Wellman, H. (1993, March). *Before belief: Children's early psychological theory.* Paper presented at the biennial meeting of the Society for Research in Child Development, New Orleans.

Baruch, G. K., & Barnett, R. C. (1987). Role quality and psychological well-being. In F. J. Crosby (Ed.), *Spouse, parent, worker: On gender and multiple roles.* New Haven, CT: Yale University Press.

Baskett, L. M., & Johnson, S. M. (1982). The young child's interaction with parents versus siblings. *Child Development, 53,* 643–650.

Bass, D. M., Bowman, K., & Noelker, L. S. (1991). The influence of caregiving and bereavement support on adjusting to an older relative's death. *Gerontologist, 31,* 32–41.

Bassoff, E. (1988) *Mothers and daughters: Loving and letting go.* New York: New American Library.

Bassuk, E. L., Carman, R. W., & Weinreb, L. F. (Eds.). (1990). *Community care for homeless families: A program design manual.* Washington, DC: Better Homes Foundation, Interagency Council on the Homeless.

Bassuk, E. L. (1991, December). Homeless families. *Scientific American,* pp. 66–74.

Bateson, G. (1956). The message, "This is play." In B. Schaffner (Ed.), *Group processes.* New York: Josiah Macy Foundation.

Batshaw, M. L., & Perret, Y. M. (1986). *Children and handicaps.* Baltimore: Paul H. Brookes.

Batson, C. D. (1989). Personal values, moral principles, and the three path model of prosocial motivation. In N. Eisenberg & J. Reykowski (Eds.), *Social and moral values.* Hillsdale, NJ: Erlbaum.

Baumrind, D. (1971). Current patterns of parental authority. *Developmental Psychology Monographs, 4* (1, Pt. 2).

Baumrind, D. (1989, April). *Sex-differentiated socialization effects in childhood and adolescence.* Paper presented at the biennial meeting of the Society for Research in Child Development, Kansas City.

Baumrind, D. (1993). The average expectable environment is not good enough: A response to Scarr. *Child Development, 64,* 1299–1317.

Baumrind, D. (in press). The average expectable environment is not good enough: A response to Scarr. *Child Development.*

Bayley, N. (1969). *Manual for the Bayley Scales of infant development.* New York: Psychological Corporation.

Bayley, N. (1970). Development of mental abilities. In P. H. Mussen (Ed.), *Manual of child psychology* (3rd ed., Vol. 1). New York: Wiley.

Beal, C. R. (1994). *Boys and girls: The development of gender roles.* New York: McGraw-Hill.

Bean, C. R. (1990). *Methods of childbirth* (rev. ed.). New York: Quill.

Beck, M. (1992, December 7). Middle Age. *Newsweek,* pp. 50–56.

Becker, J. A. (1991). Processes in the acquisition of pragmatic competence. In G. Conti-Ramsden & C. E. Snow (Eds.), *Children's language* (Vol. 7). Hillsdale, NJ: Erlbaum.

Bedmar, R. L., Wells, M. G., & Peterson, S. R. (1989). *Self-esteem.* Washington, DC: American Psychological Association.

Behnke, M., & Eyler, F. D. (1991, April). *Issues in perinatal cocaine abuse research: The interface between medicine and child development.* Paper presented at the biennial meeting of the Society for Research in Child Development, Seattle.

Beilin, H. (1992). Piaget's enduring contribution to developmental psychology. *Developmental Psychology, 28,* 191–204.

Beland, F. (1987). Living arrangement preferences among elderly people. *Gerontologist, 27,* 797–803.

Bell, A. P., & Weinberg, M. S. (1978). *Homosexualities.* New York: Simon & Schuster.

Bell, A. P., Weinberg, M. S., & Mammersmith, S. K. (1981). *Sexual preference: Its development in men and women.* New York: Simon & Schuster.

Bell, S. M., & Ainsworth, M. D. S. (1972). Infant crying and maternal responsiveness. *Child Development, 43,* 1171–1190.

Bell-Scott, P., & Taylor, R. L. (1989). Introduction: The multiple ecologies of black adolescent development. *Journal of Adolescent Research, 4,* 117–118.

Belle, D., & Paul, E. (1989, April). *Structural and functional changes accompanying the transition to college.* Paper presented at the biennial meeting of the Society for Research in Child Development, Kansas City.

Belle, D. (1990). Poverty and women's mental health. *American Psychologist, 45,* 385–389.

Bellinger, D., Leviton, A., Waternaux, C., Needleman, H., & Rabinowitz, M. (1987). Longitudinal analysis of prenatal and postnatal lead exposure and early cognitive development. *New England Journal of Medicine, 316,* 1037–1043.

Belloc, N. B., & Breslow, L. (1972). Relationships of physical health status and health practices. *Preventive Medicine, 1,* 409–421.

Belmont, J. M. (1989). Cognitive strategies and strategic learning: The socio-instructional approach. *American Psychologist, 44,* 142–148.

Belsky, J., Rovine, M., & Fish, M. (1989). The developing family system. In M. R. Gunnar & E. Thelen (Eds.), *Systems and development: The Minnesota Symposia on Child Psychology Series* (Vol. 22). Hillsdale, NJ: Erlbaum.

Belsky, J. (1981). Early human experience: A family perspective. *Developmental Psychology, 17,* 3–23.

Belsky, J. (1989). Infant-parent attachment and day care: In defense of the strange situation. In J. S. Lande, S. Scarr, & N. Gunzenhauser (Eds.), *Caring for children:*

Challenge to America. Hillsdale, NJ: Erlbaum.

Belsky, J. (1992). The research findings on gender issues in aging men and women. In B. R. Rubin (Ed.), *Gender issues across the life cycle.* New York: Springer.

Belson, W. (1978). *Television violence and the adolescent boy.* London: Saxon House.

Bem, S. L. (1977). On the utility of alternative procedures for assessing psychological androgyny. *Journal of Consulting and Clinical Psychology, 45,* 196–205.

Bem, S. L. (1979). Theory and measurement of androgyny: A reply to the Pedhazur-Tetenbaum and Locksley-Colten critiques. *Journal of Personality and Social Psychology, 37,* 1047–1054.

Bem, S. L. (1981). Gender schema theory: A cognitive account of sex typing. *Psychological Review, 88,* 354–364.

Benet, S. (1976). *How to live to be 100.* New York: Dial Press.

Bengston, V., Rosenthal, C., & Burton, L. (1990). Families and aging: Diversity and heterogeneity. In R. H. Binstock & L. K. George (Eds.), *Handbook of aging and the social sciences.* San Diego: Academic Press.

Bengston, V. L. Marti, G., & Roberts, R. E. L. (1991). Age group relationships: Generational equity and inequity. In K. Pillemer & K. McCartney (Eds.), *Parent-child relations throughout life.* Hillsdale, NJ: Erlbaum.

Bengston, V. L. (1985). Diversity and symbolism in grandparental roles. In V. L. Bengston & J. Robertson (Eds.), *Grandparenthood.* Newbury Park, CA: Sage.

Bennet, S. K. (1994). The American Indian: A psychological overview. In W. J. Lonner & R. Malpass (Eds.), *Psychology and culture.* Needham Heights, MA: Allyn & Bacon.

Bennett, W. I., & Gurin, J. (1982). *The dieter's dilemma: Eating less and weighing more.* New York: Basic Books.

Benson, H. (1984). *Beyond the relaxation response.* New York: Times Books.

Berardo, F. M. (1990). Trends and directions in family research in the 1980s. *Journal of Marriage and the Family, 52,* 809–817.

Berensen, G. (1989, February). *The Bogalusa heart study.* Paper presented at the science forum, American Heart Association, Monterey, CA.

Berg, W. K., & Berg, K. M. (1987). Psychophysiological development in infancy: State, startle, and attention. In J. D. Osofsky (Ed.), *Handbook of infant development* (2nd ed.). New York: Wiley.

Bergin, D. (1988). Stages of play development. In D. Bergin (Ed.), *Play as a medium for learning and development.* Portsmouth, NH: Heinemann.

Berk, S. F. (1985). *The gender factory: The apportionment of work in American households.* New York: Plenum.

Berko, J. (1958). The child's learning of English morphology. *Word, 14,* 150–177.

Berlin, L. (1993, March). *Attachment and emotions in preschool children.* Paper presented at the biennial meeting of the Society for Research in Child Development, New Orleans.

Berlyne, D. E. (1960). *Conflict, arousal, and curiosity.* New York: McGraw-Hill.

Berman, B. D. (1992, June). *Attention deficit disorder: Early indicators and treatment strategies.* Paper presented at the conference on issues in early child development, San Diego.

Bernard, H. S. (1981). Identity formation in late adolescence: A review of some empirical findings. *Adolescence, 16,* 349–358.

Bernard, J. (1972). *The future of marriage.* New York: Bantam.

Berndt, T. J., & Perry, T. B. (1990). Distinctive features and effects of early adolescent friendships. In R. Montemayor (Ed.), *Advances in adolescent research.* Greenwich, CT: JAI Press.

Berndt, T. J. (1979). Developmental changes in conformity to peers and parents. *Developmental Psychology, 15,* 608–616.

Berndt, T. J. (1982). The features and effects of friendships in early adolescence. *Child Development, 53,* 1447–1460.

Bernhardt, B. A., & Pyeritz, R. E. (1992). The organizations and delivery of clinical genetic services. *Pediatric Clinics of North America, 39,* 1–12.

Berry, J. W. (1990). Psychology of acculturation: Understanding individuals moving between cultures. In R. W. Brislin (Ed.), *Applied cross-cultural psychology.* Newbury Park, CA: Sage.

Berry, J. W., Poortinga, Y. H., Segall, M. H., & Dasen, P. R. (in press). *Cross-cultural psychology: Theory, method, and applications.* Cambridge, England: Cambridge University Press.

Berry, J. W. (1969). On cross-cultural comparability. *International Journal of Psychology, 4,* 119–128.

Berry, J. W. (1980). Introduction to methodology. In H. C. Triandis & J. W. Berry (Eds.), *Handbook of cross-cultural psychology: Methodology* (Vol. 2). Boston: Allyn & Bacon.

Berscheid, E., & Fei, J. (1977). Sexual jealousy and romantic love. In G. Clinton & G. Smith (Eds.), *Sexual jealousy.* Englewood Cliffs, NJ: Prentice-Hall.

Berscheid, E., Snyder, M., & Omoto, A. M. (1989). Issues in studying close relationships: Conceptualizing and measuring closeness. In C. Hendrick (Ed.), *Close relationships.* Newbury Park, CA: Sage.

Berscheid, E. (1985). Interpersonal attraction. In G. Lindzey & E. Aronson (Eds.), *Handbook of social psychology* (3rd ed., Vol. 2). New York: Random House.

Berscheid, E. (1988). Some comments on love's anatomy: Or, whatever happened to an old-fashioned lust? In R. J. Sternberg & M. L. Barnes (Eds.), *Anatomy of love.* New Haven, CT: Yale University Press.

Bertenthal, B. (1993, March). *Emerging themes in perceptual development.* Paper presented at the biennial meeting of the Society for Research in Child Development, New Orleans.

Berzon, B. (1988). *Permanent partners.* New York: Dutton.

Beth-Marom, R., Austin, L., Fischoff, B., Palmgren, C., & Quadrel, M. J. (in press). Perceived consequences of risky behaviors: Adolescents and adults. *Developmental Psychology.*

Bianchi, S. M., & Spani, D. (1986). *American women in transition.* New York: Russell Sage Foundation.

Bidell, T. (1993, March). *The contructive web: Understanding cultural diversity in developmental pathways.* Paper presented at the biennial meeting of the Society for Research in Child Development, New Orleans.

Biegel, D. E., Sales, E., & Schulz, R. (1991). *Family caregiving in chronic illness.* Newbury Park, CA: Sage.

Bierman, K. L., Smoot, D. L., & Aumiller, K. (1993). Characteristics of aggressive-rejected, aggressive (nonrejected), and rejected (nonaggressive) boys. *Child Development, 64,* 139–151.

Bigler, R. S., & Liben, L. S. (in press). Cognitive mechanisms in children's gender stereotyping: Theoretical and educational implications of a cognitive-based intervention. *Child Development.*

Bigler, R. S., Liben, L. S., & Yekel, C. A. (1992, August). *Developmental patterns of gender-related beliefs: Beyond unitary constructs and measures.* Paper presented at the meeting of the American Psychological Association, Washington, DC.

Biller, H. B. (1993). *Fathers and families: Paternal factors in child development.* Westport, CT: Auburn House.

Birchler, G. R. (1992). Marriage. In V. B. Van Hasselt & M. Hersen (Eds.), *Handbook of social development: A life-span perspective.* New York: Plenum.

Birren, J. E., & Sloane, R. B. (Eds.). (1985). *Handbook of mental health and aging.* Englewood Cliffs, NJ: Erlbaum.

Birren, J. E. (1993). Fifteen commandments for responsible old age. In R. N. Butler & K. Kiikuni (Eds.), *Who is responsible for my old age?* New York: Springer.

Bishop, S. M., & Ingersoll, G. M. (1989). Effects of marital conflict and family structure on the self-concepts of pre- and early adolescents. *Journal of Youth and Adolescence, 18,* 25–38.

Black, A. E., & Pedro-Carroll, J. L. (1993, March). *The long-term effects of interpersonal conflict and parental divorce among late adolescents.* Paper presented at the biennial meeting of the Society for Research in Child Development, New Orleans.

Blair, S. N., & Kohl, H. W. (1988). Physical activity: Which is more important for health? *Medicine and Science and Sports and Exercise, 20,* (2, Suppl.), 5–7.

Blair, S. N. (1990, January). Personal communication. Aerobics Institute, Dallas, TX.

Blash, R., & Unger, D. G. (1992, March). *Cultural factors and the self-esteem and aspirations of African-American adolescent males.* Paper presented at the meeting of the Society for Research on Adolescence, Washington, DC.

Blatt, R. J. R. (1988). *Prenatal tests.* New York: Vintage Books.

Blechman, E. A., & Brownell, K. D. (Eds.). (1987). *Handbook of behavioral medicine for women.* Elmsford, NY: Pergamon.

Bliatout, B. T. (1993). Hmong death customs: Traditional and acculturated. In D. P. Irish & K. F. Lundquist (Eds.), *Ethnic variations in dying, death, and grief:*

Diversity in universality. Washington, DC: Taylor & Francis.

Bloch, M. (1992, August/September). Tobacco control advocacy: Winning the war on tobacco. *Zero to Three, 13,* 29–34.

Block, J. H., Block, J., & Gjerde, P. F. (1986). The personality of children prior to divorce: A prospective study. *Child Development, 57,* 827–840.

Block, J. (1992, March). *Parental and personality antecedents of early menarche.* Paper presented at the meeting of the Society for Research in Adolescence, Washington, DC.

Bloom, L. (1992, August). *Racism in developmental research.* Paper presented at the meeting of the American Psychological Association, Washington, DC.

Blos, P. (1989). The inner world of the adolescent. In A. H. Esman (Ed.), *International annals of adolescent psychiatry.* Chicago: University of Chicago Press.

Blumberg, J. (1993, June 2). Commentary in "Lowly vitamin supplements pack a big health punch." *USA Today,* p. 3D.

Blumenfeld, P. C., Pintrich, P. R. Wessles, K., & Meece, J. (1981, April). *Age and sex differences in the impact of classroom experiences on self-perceptions.* Paper presented at the biennial meeting of the Society for Research in Child Development, Boston.

Blumenthal, J. A., Emery, C. F., Madden, D. J., George, L. K., Coleman, R. E., Riddle, M. W., McKee, D. C., Reasoner, J., & Williams, R. S. (1989). Cardiovascular and behavioral effects of aerobic exercise training in healthy older men and women. *Journal of Gerontology: Medical Sciences, 44,* M147–157.

Blumstein, P., & Schwartz, P. (1983). *American couples: Money, work, sex.* New York: Morrow.

Blundell, J. E. (1984). Systems and interactions: An approach to the pharmacology of feeding. In A. J. Stunkard & E. Stellar (Eds.), *Eating and its disorders.* New York: Raven Press.

Bly, R. (1990). *Iron John.* New York: Vintage Books.

Blyth, D. A. Bulcroft, R., & Simmons, R. G. (1981, August). *The impact of puberty on adolescents: A longitudinal study.* Paper presented at the meeting of the American Psychological Association, Los Angeles.

Bohannon, J. N., III, & Stanowicz, L. (1988). The issue of negative evidence: Adult responses to children's language errors. *Developmental Psychology, 24,* 684–689.

Boller, K., & Rovee-Collier, C. (1992). Contextual coding and recoding of infants' memories. *Journal of Experimental Child Psychology, 53,* 1–23.

Bolles, R. N. (1994). *What color is your parachute? A practical manual for job-hunters and career-changers.* Berkeley, CA: Ten Speed Press.

Bondareff, W. (1985). The neural basis of aging. In J. E. Birren & K. W. Schaie (Eds.), *Handbook of the psychology of aging.* (2nd ed.). New York: Van Nostrand Reinhold.

Bonvillian, J. D., Orlansky, M. D., & Novack, L. L. (1983). Developmental milestones: Sign language and motor development. *Child Development, 54,* 1435–1445.

Bornstein, M. H., & Krasnegor, N. A. (1989). *Stability and continuity in mental development.* Hillsdale NJ: Erlbaum.

Bornstein, M. H., & Sigman, M. D. (1986). Continuity in mental development in infancy. *Child Development, 57,* 251–274.

Bornstein, M. H. (1989). Stability in early mental development. In M. H. Bornstein, & N. A. Krasnegor (Eds.), *Stability and continuity in mental development.* Hillsdale, NJ: Erlbaum.

Borovsky, D., Hill, W., & Rovee-Collier, C. (1987, April). *Developmental changes in infant long-term memory.* Paper presented at the biennial meeting of the Society for Research in Child Development, Baltimore.

Borstelmann, L. J. (1983). Children before psychology: Ideas about children from antiquity to the late 1800s. In P. H. Mussen (Ed.), *Handbook of child psychology* (4th ed., Vol. 1). New York: Wiley.

Boston Women's Health Book Collective. (1984). *The new our bodies, ourselves.* New York: Simon & Schuster.

Boston Women's Health Book Collective. (1987). *Ourselves growing older.* New York: Simon & Schuster.

Boston Women's Health Book Collective. (1992). *The new our bodies, ourselves.* New York: Simon & Schuster.

Botvin, G. (1986). Substance abuse prevention efforts: Recent developments and future directions. *Journal of School Health, 56,* 369–374.

Botvin, G. (1987, April 28). *Infancy to adolescence: Opportunities for success.* Paper presented to the Select Committee on Children, Youth, and Families, Washington, DC.

Bouchard, T. J., Heston, L., Eckert, E., Keyes, M., & Resnick, S. (1981). The Minnesota study of twins reared apart: Project description and sample results in the developmental domain. *Twin Research, 3,* 227–233.

Bouchard, T. J., Lykken, D. T., McGue, M., Segal, N. L., & Tellegen, A. (1990). Source of human psychological differences: The Minnesota Study of Twins Reared Apart. *Science, 250,* 223–228.

Bowen, M. (1978). *Family therapy in clinical practice.* New York: Aronson.

Bower, B. (1985). The left hand of math and verbal talent. *Science News, 127,* p. 263.

Bower, T. G. R. (1977). *A primer of infant development.* New York: W. H. Freeman.

Bower, T. G. R. (1989). *The rational infant.* San Francisco: W. H. Freeman.

Bower, T. G. R. (1991, May). Personal communication, Program in Psychology. University of Texas at Dallas, Richardson.

Bower, T. G. R. (1993, January). Personal communication. Program in Psychology and Human Development, University of Texas at Dallas, Richardson, TX.

Bowlby J. (1969). *Attachment and loss* (Vol. 1). London: Hogarth.

Bowlby, J. (1989). *Secure and insecure attachment.* New York: Basic Books.

Bowman, P. J., & Howard, C. (1985). Race-related socialization, motivation, and academic achievement: A study of Black youths in three-generation families. *Journal of the American Academy of Child Psychiatry, 24,* 134–141.

Boyce, T. (1991, May). Commentary. In D. Gelman, "The miracle of resiliency." *Newsweek Special Issue,* pp. 44–47.

Boyd-Franklin, N. (1989). *Black families in therapy: A multisystems approach.* New York: Guilford Press.

Boyer, C. B. & Hein, K. (1991). AIDS and HIV infection in adolescents: The role of education and antibody testing. In R. M. Lerner, A. C. Petersen, & J. Brooks-Gunn (Eds.), *Encyclopedia of adolescence* (Vol. 1). New York: Garland.

Brackbill, Y. (1979). Obstetric medication and infant behavior. In J. D. Osofsky (Ed.), *Handbook of infant development.* New York: Wiley.

Bracken, M. B., Eskenazi, B., Sachse, K., McSharry, J., Hellenbrand, K., & Leo-Summers, L. (1990). Association of cocaine use with sperm concentration, motility, and morphology. *Fertility and Sterility, 53,* 315–322.

Brady, M. P., Swank, P. R., Taylor, R. D., & Freiberg, H. J. (1988). Teacher-student interactions in middle school mainstreamed classes: Differences with special and regular students. *Journal of Educational Research, 81,* 332–340.

Brandtstädter, J., & Greve, B. (in press). The aging self: Stabilizing and protective processes. *Developmental Review.*

Brandtstädter, J., & Renner, G. (1990). Tenacious goal pursuit and flexible goal adjustment: Explication and age-related analysis of assimilative and accommodative strategies of coping. *Psychology and Aging, 5,* 58–67.

Braungart, J. M., Plomin, R., DeFries, J. C., & Fulker, D. W. (1992). Genetic influence on the tester-rated infant temperament as assessed by Bayley's Infant Behavior Record: Nonadaptive and adoptive siblings and twins. *Developmental Psychology, 28,* 40–47.

Bray, D. W., & Howard, A. (1983). The AT&T longitudinal studies of managers. In K. W. Schaie (Ed.), *Longitudinal studies of adult psychological development.* New York: Guilford Press.

Brazelton, T. B., Nugent, J. K., & Lester, B. M. (1987). Neonatal Behavioral Assessment Scale. In J. D. Osofsky (Ed.), *Handbook of infant development* (2nd ed.). New York: Wiley.

Brazelton, T. B. (1956). Sucking in infancy. *Pediatrics, 17,* 400–404.

Brazelton, T. B. (1973). *Neonatal behavioral assessment scale.* London: Heinemann Medical Books.

Brazelton, T. B. (1983). *Infants and mothers: Differences in development.* New York: Delta.

Brazelton, T. B. (1984). *To listen to a child.* Reading, MA: Addison-Wesley.

Brazelton, T. B. (1990a). Cover commentary. In R. Abrams, *Will it hurt the baby?* Reading, MA: Addison-Wesley.

Brazelton, T. B. (1990b). Saving the bathwater. *Child Development, 61,* 1661–1671.

Brazelton, T. B. (1992). *Touchpoints.* Reading, MA: Addison-Wesley.

Bredekamp, S., & Rosegrant, T. (Eds.). (1992). *Reaching potentials: Appropriate curriculum and assessment for young children.* Washington, DC: National Association for the Education of Young Children.

Bredekamp, S., & Shepard, L. (1989). How to best protect children from inappropriate school expectations, practices, and policies. *Young Children, 44,* 14–24.

Bredekamp, S. (1987). *Developmentally appropriate practice in early childhood programs serving children from birth through age 8.* Washington, DC: National Association for the Education of Young Children.

Brent, D. A. (1989). Suicide and suicidal behavior in children and adolescents. *Pediatrics in Review, 10,* 269–275.

Bretherton, I., Fritz, J., Zahn-Waxler, C., & Ridgeway, D. (1986). Learning to talk about emotions. *Child Development, 57,* 529–548.

Bridges, S. (1973). *IQ–150.* London: Priory Press.

Brim, G. (1992, December 7). Commentary, *Newsweek,* p. 52.

Brim, O. G., & Ryff, C. D. (1980). On the properties of life events. In P. B. Baltes & O. G. Brim (Eds.), *Life-span development and behavior.* New York: Academic Press.

Brink, T. L. (Ed.). (1994). *Hispanic aged mental health.* New York: Haworth Press.

Brislin, R. (1993). *Culture's influence on behavior.* Fort Worth, TX: Harcourt Brace Jovanovich.

Brislin, R. (1993). *Understanding culture's influence on human behavior.* San Diego: Harcourt Brace Jovanovich.

Broberg, A. G., Hwang, C. P., & Chase, S. V. (1993, March). *Effects of day care on school performance and adjustment.* Paper presented at the biennial meeting of the Society for Research in Child Development, New Orleans.

Brody, E. M., Kleban, M. H., Johnsen, P. T., Hoffman, C., & Schoonover, C. B. (1987). Work status and parent care: A comparison of four groups of women. *Gerontologist, 27,* 201–208.

Brody, E. M. (1990). *Women in the middle: Their parent-care years.* New York: Springer.

Brodzinsky, D., Schechter, M., & Henig, R. (1992). *Being adopted.* New York: Doubleday.

Brodzinsky, D. M., Schechter, D. E., Braff, A. M., & Singer, L. M. (1984). Psychological and academic adjustment in adopted children. *Journal of Consulting and Clinical Psychology, 52,* 582–590.

Brone, R. J., & Fisher, C. B. (1988). Determinants of adolescent obesity: A comparison with anorexia nervosa. *Adolescence, 23,* 155–169.

Bronfenbrenner, U. (1974). *Is early intervention effective?* (DHEW Publication No. OHD 74-25). Washington, DC: U.S. Government Printing Office.

Bronfenbrenner, U. (1979). Contexts of child rearing: Problems and prospects. *American Psychologist, 34,* 844–850.

Bronfenbrenner, U. (1986). Ecology of the family as a context for human development: Research perspectives. *Developmental Psychology, 22,* 723–742.

Bronfenbrenner, U. (1989, April). *The developing ecology of human development.* Paper presented at the biennial meeting of the Society for Research in Child Development, Kansas City.

Bronfenbrenner, U. (1993). Ecological systems theory. In R. K. Wozniak & K. Fischer

(Eds.), *Development in context.* Hillsdale, NJ: Erlbaum.

Bronstein, P., & Paludi, M. (1988). The introductory course from a broader human perspective. In P. A. Bronstein & K. Quina (Eds.), *Teaching a psychology of people.* Washington, DC: American Psychological Association.

Bronstein, P. (1988). Marital and parenting roles in transition. In P. Bronstein & C. P. Cowen (Eds.), *Contemporary fatherhood.* New York: Wiley.

Brook, D. W., & Brook, J. S. (in press). Family processes associated with alcohol and drug use and abuse. In E. Kaufman & P. Kaufman (Eds.), *Family therapy of drug and alcohol abuse: Ten years later.* New York: Gardner.

Brook, J. S., Brook, D. W., Gordon, A. S., Whiteman, M., & Cohen P. (1990). The psychological etiology of adolescent drug use: A family interactional approach. *Genetic, Social, and General Psychology Monographs, 116,* 110–267.

Brooks-Gunn, J., & Paikoff, R. L. (1993). "Sex is a gamble, kissing is a game": Adolescent sexuality and health promotion. In S. G. Millstein, A. C. Petersen, & E. O. Nightingale (Eds.), *Promoting the health of adolescents.* New York: Oxford University Press.

Brooks-Gunn, J., Klebanov, P. K., Liaw, F., & Spiker, D. (in press). Enhancing the development of low birth weight, premature infants: Changes in cognition and behavior over the first three years. *Child Development.*

Brooks-Gunn, J., McCarton, C., & Tonascia, J. (1992, May). *Enhancing the development of LBW, premature infants: Defining risk and targeting subgroups in the Infant Health and Development Program.* Paper presented at the International Conference on Infant Studies, Miami Beach.

Brooks-Gunn, J., McCormick, M. C., Benasich, A. A., Shapiro, S., & Black, G. (1992). Secondary effects: Maternal education, maternal employment, and fertility. In R. T. Gross, (Ed.), *Infant health and development program.* Stanford, CA: Stanford University Press.

Brooks-Gunn, J. (1988). Antecedents and consequences of variations in girls' maturational timing. In M. D. Levine & E. R. McAnarney (Eds.), *Early adolescent transitions.* Lexington, MA: Lexington Books.

Brooks-Gunn, J. (1992, March). *Revisiting theories of "storm and stress": The role of biology.* Paper presented at the meeting of the Society for Research in Adolescence, Washington, DC.

Brooks-Gunn, J. (1993, March). *Adolescence.* Paper presented at the biennial meeting of the Society for Research in Child Development, New Orleans.

Broughton, J. M. (1978). Development of concepts of self, mind, reality, and knowledge. In W. Damon (Ed.), *Social cognition.* San Francisco: Jossey-Bass.

Broverman, I., Broverman, D., Clarkson, F., Rosenkrantz, P., & Vogel, S. 1970. Sex-role stereotypes and clinical judgments of mental health. *Journal of Consulting and Clinical Psychology, 34,* 1–7.

Broverman, I., Vogel, S., Broverman, D., Clarkson, F., & Rosenkranz, P. (1972). Sex-role stereotypes: A current appraisal. *Journal of Social Issues, 28,* 59–78.

Brown, A. L., & Palincsar, A. M. (1989). Guided, cooperative learning and individual knowledge acquisition. In L. B. Resnick (Ed.), *Knowing and learning: Essays in honor of Robert Glaser.* Hillsdale, NJ: Erlbaum.

Brown, A. L., Campione, J. C., Reeve, R. A., Ferrara, R. A., Palincsar, A. S. (in press). Interactive learning, individual understanding: The case of reading and mathematics. In L. T. Landsmann (Ed.), *Culture, schooling, and psychological development.* Hillsdale, NJ: Erlbaum.

Brown, B. B., & Lohr, M. J. (1987). Peer-group affiliation and adolescent self-esteem: An integration of ego-identity and symbolic-interaction theories. *Journal of Personality and Social Psychology, 52,* 47–55.

Brown, B. B., & Mounts, N. (1989, April). *Peer group structures in single vs. multiethnic high schools.* Paper presented at the biennial meeting of the Society for Research in Child Development, Kansas City.

Brown, B. B. (1994, February). *Family-peer linkages in adolescence: New directions for research.* Paper presented at the meeting of the Society for Research on Adolescence, San Diego, CA.

Brown, D. R., & Gary, L. E. (1985). Social support network differentials among married and nonmarried Black females. *Psychology of Women Quarterly, 9,* 229–241.

Brown, F. (1973). *The reform of secondary education: Report of the national commission on the reform of secondary education.* New York: McGraw-Hill.

Brown, J. D. (1991). Staying fit and staying well: Physical fitness as a moderator of life stress. *Journal of Personality and Social Psychology, 60,* 555–561.

Brown, J. K. (1985). Introduction. In J. K. Brown & V. Kerns (Eds.), *In her prime: A new view of middle-aged women.* South Hadley, MA: Bergin & Garvey.

Brown, J. L., & Pizer, H. F. (1987). *Living hungry in America.* New York: Macmillan.

Brown, J. L. (1964). States in newborn infants. *Merrill-Palmer Quarterly, 10,* 313–327.

Brown, L., & Brown, M. (1986). *Dinosaurs divorce.* Boston: Little, Brown.

Brown, L. (1989). New voice, new visions: Toward a lesbian/gay paradigm for psychology. *Psychology of Women Quarterly, 13,* 445–458.

Brown, L. (1992). [Interview]. In M. A. Paludi, *The psychology of women.* Dubuque, IA: Brown & Benchmark.

Brown, R. (1973). *A first language: The early stages.* Cambridge, MA: Harvard University Press.

Brown, R. (1986). *Social psychology* (2nd ed.). New York: Free Press.

Browne, A., & Williams, K. R. (1993). Gender, intimacy, and lethal violence: Trends from 1976 through 1987. *Gender and Society, 7,* 78–98.

Browne, C. R., Brown, J. V., Blumenthal, J., Anderson, L., & Johnson, P. (1993, March). *African-American fathering: The perception of mothers and sons.* Paper presented at the biennial meeting of the

Society for Research in Child Development, New Orleans.

Brownell, K. D. (1990, August). *Dieting, weight, and body image: Where culture and physiology collide.* Paper presented at the meeting of the American Psychological Association, Boston.

Brownell, K. D. (1991). Dieting and the search for the perfect body: Where physiology and culture collide. *Behavior Therapy, 22,* 1–12.

Brubaker, T. H. (1985). *Later life families.* Newbury Park, CA: Sage.

Brubaker, T. (1987). *Aging, health and family, and long-term care.* Newbury Park, CA: Sage.

Bruce, S. A. (1991). Ultrastructure of dermal fibroblasts during development and aging: Relationship to in vitro senescence of dermal fibroblasts. *Experimental Gerontology, 26,* 3–16.

Bruner, J. S. (1989, April). *The state of developmental psychology.* Paper presented at the biennial meeting of the Society for Research in Child Development, Kansas City.

Bryant, D. M., & Ramey, C. T. (1987). An analysis of the effectiveness of early intervention programs for high-risk children. In M. Guralnick & C. Bennett (Eds.), *The effectiveness of early intervention for at-risk and handicapped children* (pp. 33–78). San Diego, CA: Academic Press.

Bryer, K. B. (1979). The Amish way of death: A study of family support systems. *American Psychologist, 34,* 255–261.

Buchanan, C. M., & Maccoby, E. E. (1990, March). *Characteristics of adolescents and their families in three custodial arrangements.* Paper presented at the meeting of the Society for Research in Adolescence, Atlanta.

Buchannan, C. M., Maccoby, E. E., & Dornbusch, S. M. (1992). Adolescents and their families after divorce: Three residential arrangements compared. *Journal of Research on Adolescence, 2,* 261–292.

Buck, G. M., Cookfair, D. L., Michalek, A. M., Nasca, P. C., Standfast, S. J., Sever, L. E., & Kramer, A. A. (1989). Intrauterine growth retardation and risk of sudden infant death syndrome (SIDS). *American Journal of Epidemiology, 129,* 874–884.

Buhrmester, D., (1989). *Changes in friendship, interpersonal competence, and social adaptation during early adolescence.* Unpublished manuscript, Department of Psychology, University of California, Los Angeles.

Buhrmester, D. (1993, March). *Adolescent friendship and the socialization of gender differences in social interaction styles.* Paper presented at the biennial meeting of the Society for Research in Child Development, New Orleans.

Burley, K. A. (1991). Family-work spillover in dual-career couples: A comparison of two time perspectives. *Psychological Reports, 68,* 471–480.

Bursik, K. (1991). Adaptation to divorce and ego development in adult women. *Journal of Personality and Social Psychology, 60,* 300–306.

Burton, L. M. (1985). *Early and on-time grandmotherhood in multigenerational Black families.* Unpublished doctoral dissertation,

University of Southern California, Los Angeles.

Burts, D. C., Charlesworth, R., & Fleege, P. O. (1991, April). *Achievement in kindergarten children in developmentally appropriate and developmentally inappropriate classrooms.* Paper presented at the biennial meeting of the Society for Research in Child Development, Seattle.

Burts, D. C., Hart, C. H., Charlesworth, R., Fleege, P. O., Mosley, J., & Thomasson, R. (in press). Observed activities and stress behaviors of children in developmentally appropriate and inappropriate kindergarten classrooms. *Early Childhood Research Quarterly.*

Burts, D. C., Hart, C. H., Charlesworth, R., Hernandez, S., Kirk, L., & Mosley, J. (1989, March). *A comparison of the frequencies of stress behaviors observed in kindergarten children in classrooms with developmentally appropriate vs. developmentally inappropriate instructional practices.* Paper presented at the annual meeting of the American Educational Research Association, San Francisco.

Buss, A. H., & Plomin, R. (1984). *A temperament theory of personality development.* New York: Wiley-Interscience.

Buss, A. H., & Plomin, R. (1987). Commentary. In H. H. Goldsmith, A. H. Buss, R. Plomin, M. K. Rothbart, A. Thomas, A. Chess, R. R. Hinde, & R. B. McCall (Eds.), Roundtable: What is temperament? Four approaches. *Child Development, 58,* 505–529.

Buss, D. M., & others. (1990). International preferences in selecting mates: A study of 37 cultures. *Journal of Cross-Cultural Psychology, 21,* 5–47.

Buss, R. R., Yussen, S. R., Mathews, S. R., Miller, G. E., & Rembold, K. L. (1983). Development of children's use of a story schema to retrieve information. *Developmental Psychology, 19,* 22–28.

Bussey, K., & Maughan, B. (1982). Gender differences in moral reasoning. *Journal of Personality and Social Psychology, 42,* 701–706.

Butler, R. N. (1975). *Why survive? Being old in America.* New York: Harper & Row.

Butler, R. N. (1987). Ageism. In G. L. Maddox (Ed.), *The encyclopedia of aging.* New York: Springer.

Butler, R. N. (1993). Did you say 'sarcopenia'? *Geriatrics, 48,* 11–12.

Butler, S. (1902). The way of all flesh. Vol. 17 in *The works of Samuel Butler* (Shrewsbury, Ed.). New York: AMS Press.

Butterworth, G. (1993). Context and cognition in models of cognitive growth. In P. Light & G. Butterworth (Eds.), *Context and cognition.* Hillsdale, NJ: Erlbaum.

Byer, C. O., & Shainberg, L. W. (1991). *Dimensions of human sexuality* (3rd ed.). Dubuque, IA: Brown & Benchmark.

Byrnes, J. P. (1988). Formal operations: A systematic reformulation. *Developmental Review, 8,* 66–87.

Byrnes, J. P. (1993). Analyzing perspectives on rationality and critical thinking: A commentary on the Merrill-Palmer Quarterly invitational issue. *Merrill-Palmer Quarterly, 39,* 159–171.

C

Cairns, R. B. (1991). Multiple metaphors for a singular idea. *Developmental Psychology, 27,* 23–26.

Caldwell, B. (1964). The effects of infant care. In M. Hoffman & L. Hoffman (Eds.), *Review of child development research* (Vol. 1). New York: Russell Sage.

Caldwell, B. (1991, October). *Impact on the child.* Paper presented at the symposium on day care for children, Arlington, VA.

Caldwell, M. B., & Rogers, M. F. (1991). Epidemiology of pediatric HIV infection. *Pediatrics Clinics of North America, 38,* 1–16.

Calkins, S. D., & Fox, N. A. (1992). The relations among infant temperament, security of attachment, and behavioral inhibition at twenty-four months. *Child Development, 63,* 1456–1472.

Camara, K. A., & Resnick, G. (1988). Interparental conflict and cooperation: Factors moderating children's post-divorce adjustment. In E. M. Hetherington & J. D. Arasteh (Eds.), *Impact of divorce, single parenting, and stepparenting on children.* Hillsdale, NJ: Erlbaum.

Camarena, P. M. (1991). Conformity in adolescence. In R. M. Lerner, A. C. Petersen, & J. Brooks-Gunn (Eds.), *Encyclopedia of adolescence* (Vol. 1). New York: Garland.

Cameron, D. (1988, February). Soviet schools. *NEA Today,* p. 15.

Cameron, J., Cowan, L., Holmes, B., Hurst, P., & McLean, M. (Eds.). (1983). *International handbook of educational systems.* New York: Wiley.

Campbell, J., Swank, P., & Vincent, K. (1991). The role of hardiness in the resolution of grief. *Omega, 23,* 53–65.

Campbell, J. I. D., & Charness, N. (1990). Age-related declines in working-memory skills: Evidence from a complex calculation task. *Developmental Psychology, 26,* 879–888.

Campbell, S. B., Meyers, T., Ross, S., & Flanagan, C. (1993, March). *Chronicity of maternal depression and mother-infant interaction.* Paper presented at the biennial meeting of the Society for Research in Child Development, New Orleans.

Campbell, S. (1980). *The couple's journey: Intimacy as a path to wholeness.* San Luis Obispo, CA: Impact.

Campos, J. J., Langer, A., & Krowitz, A. (1970). Cardiac responses on the visual cliff in prelocomotor human infants. *Science, 170,* 196–197.

Cancian, F. M., & Gordon, S. L. (1988). Changing emotion norms in marriage: Love and anger in U.S. women's magazines since 1900. *Gender and Society, 2,* 308–342.

Canfield, R. L., & Haith, M. M. (1991). Young infants' visual expectations for symmetric and asymmetric stimulus sequences. *Developmental Psychology, 27,* 198–208.

Cantor, M. H. (1991). Family and community: Changing roles in an aging society. *Gerontologist, 31,* 337–346.

Caplan, P. J., & Caplan, J. B. (1994). *Thinking critically about research on sex and gender.* New York: HarperCollins.

Cappiello, L. A., & Troyer, R. E. (1979). A study of the role of health educators in teaching about death and dying. *Journal of School Health, 49*, 397–399.

Carbo, M. (1987). Reading styles research: "What works" isn't always phonics. *Phi Delta Kappan*, pp. 431–435.

Cardon, L. R., Fulker, D. W., DeFries, J. C., & Plomin, R. (1992). Continuity and change in cognitive ability from 1 to 7 years of age. *Developmental Psychology, 28*, 64–73.

Carey, J. C. (1992). Health supervision and anticipatory guidance for children with genetic disorders. *Pediatric Clinics of North America, 39*, 35–54.

Carey, S. (1977). The child as word learner. In M. Halle, J. Bresman, & G. A. Miller (Eds.), *Linguistic theory and psychological reality*. Cambridge: Massachusetts Institute of Technology Press.

Carlson, C., Cooper, C., & Hsu, J. (1990, March). *Predicting school achievement in early adolescence: The role of family process.* Paper presented at the meeting of the Society for Research in Adolescence, Atlanta.

Carnegie Corporation. (1989). *Turning points: Preparing youth for the 21st century.* New York: Author.

Carson, D., & Bittner, M. (1993, March). *Creative thinking and temperament as predictors of school-aged children's coping abilities and response to stress.* Paper presented at the biennial meeting of the Society for Research in Child Development, New Orleans.

Carter, B., & McGoldrick, M. (1989). Overview: The changing family life cycle—a framework for family therapy. In B. Carter & M. McGoldrick (Eds.), *The changing family life cycle* (2nd ed.). Boston: Allyn & Bacon.

Carter, D. B., & Levy, G. D. (1988). Cognitive aspects of children's early sex-role development: The influence of gender schemas on preschoolers' memories and preference for sex-typed toys and activities. *Child Development, 59*, 782–793.

Carter, D. B., & Taylor, R. D. (in press). The development of children's awareness and understanding of flexibility in sex-role stereotypes: Implications for preferences, attitude, and behavior. *Sex Roles*.

Case, R., Kurland, D. M., & Goldberg, J. (1982). Operational efficiency and the growth of short-term memory span. *Journal of Experimental Child Psychology, 33*, 386–404.

Case, R. (1985). *Intellectual development: Birth to adulthood.* New York: Academic Press.

Case, R. (1987). Neo-Piagetian theory: Retrospect and prospect. *International Journal of Psychology, 22*, 773–791.

Case, R. (1993, March). *Central conceptual structures and their manifestation in specific task performance.* Paper presented at the biennial meeting of the Society for Research in Child Development, New Orleans.

Case, R. (Ed.). (1992). *The mind's staircase: Exploring the conceptual underpinnings of children's thought and knowledge.* Hillsdale, NJ: Erlbaum.

Castro, F. G., & Magaña, D. (1988). A course in health promotion in ethnic minority populations. In P. A. Bronstein & K. Quina (Eds.), *Teaching a psychology of*

people. Washington, DC: American Psychological Association.

Caughy, M. O., DiPietro, J. A., & Strobino, D. M. (in press). Day-care participation as a protective factor in the cognitive development of low-income children. *Child Development*.

Cavanaugh, J. C. (1990). *Adult development and aging.* Belmont, CA: Wadsworth.

Cavett, D. (1974). *Cavett.* San Diego: Harcourt Brace Jovanovich.

Ceballo, R., & Olson, S. L. (1993, March). *The role of alternative caregivers in the lives of children poor, single-parent families.* Paper presented at the biennial meeting of the Society for Research in Child Development, New Orleans.

Chalfant, J. C. (1989). Learning disabilities. Policy issues and promising approaches. *American Psychologist, 44*, 392–398.

Chan, W.-S. (1963). *A source book in Chinese philosophy.* Princeton, NJ: Princeton University Press.

Chappell, N. L., & Badger, M. (1989). Social isolation and well-being. *Journal of Gerontology, 14*, S169–S176.

Charlesworth, R., Hart, C. H., Burts, D. C., & Hernandez, S. (in press). Kindergarten teachers' beliefs and practices. *Early Child Development and Care*.

Charlesworth, R. (1987). *Understanding child development* (2nd ed.). Albany, NY: Delmar.

Charlesworth, R. (1989). "Behind" before they start? *Young Children, 44*, 5–13.

Charlesworth, W. R. (1992). Commentary: Can biology explain human development? *Human Development, 35*, 9–11.

Charness, N., & Bosman, E. A. (1992). Human factors and aging. In F. I. M. Craik & T. A. Salthouse (Eds.), *The handbook of aging and cognition.* Hillsdale, NJ: Erlbaum.

Chase-Lansdale, P. L., & Hetherington, E. M. (in press). The impact of divorce on life-span development: Short- and long-term effects. In P. B. Baltes, D. L. Featherman, & R. M. Lerner (Eds.), *Life-span development and behavior.* Hillsdale, NJ: Erlbaum.

Chase-Lansdale, P. L., Brooks-Gunn, J., & Zamsky, E. S. (in press). Young African-American multigenerational families in poverty: Quality of mothering and grandmothering. *Child Development*.

Chasnoff, I. J., Griffith, D. R., Freier, C., & Murray, J. (1992). Cocaine/polydrug use in pregnancy: Two-year follow-up. *Pediatrics, 89*, 284–289.

Chasnoff, I. J., Griffith, D. R., MacGregor, S., Dirkes, K., & Burns, K. A. (1989). Temporal patterns of cocaine use in pregnancy. *Journal of the American Medical Association, 261*, 1741–1744.

Chasnoff, I. J. (1991, April). *Cocaine versus tobacco: Impact on infant and child outcome.* Paper presented at the biennial meeting of the Society for Research in Child Development, Seattle.

Chatters, L. M. (1993). Health disability and its consequences for subjective stress. In J. S. Jackson, L. M. Chatters, & R. J. Taylor (Eds.), *Aging in Black America.* Newbury Park, CA: Sage.

Cherlin, A. J., & Furstenberg, F. F. (1988). *The new American grandparent.* New York: Basic Books.

Cherry, R. L. (1991). Agents of nursing home quality of care: Ombudsmen and staff ratios revisited. *Gerontologist, 31*, 302–308.

Chesney-Lind, M. (1989). Girls' crime and woman's place: Toward a feminist model of female delinquency. *Crime and Delinquency, 35*, 5–30.

Chess, S., & Thomas, A. (1977). Temperamental individuality from childhood to adolescence. *Journal of Child Psychiatry, 16*, 218–226.

Chi, M. T. (1978). Knowledge structures and memory development. In R. S. Siegler (Ed.), *Children's thinking: What develops?* Hillsdale, NJ: Erlbaum.

Children's Defense Fund. (1990). *Children, 1990.* Washington, DC: Author.

Children's Defense Fund. (1992). *Children, 1992.* Washington, DC: Author.

Children's Defense Fund. (1993). *Children, 1993.* Washington, DC: Author.

Chinn, P. L. (1991). Aging and ageism. *Advances in Nursing Science, 13*, vii.

Chiriboga, D. A. (1982). Adaptation to marital separation in later and earlier life. *Journal of Gerontology, 37*, 109–114.

Chiriboga, D. A. (1989). Mental health at the midpoint: Crisis, challenge, or relief? In S. Hunter & M. Sundel (Eds.), *Midlife myths.* Newbury Park, CA: Sage.

Chodorow, N. J. (1978). *The reproduction of mothering.* Berkeley: University of California Press.

Chodorow, N. J. (1989). *Feminism and psychoanalytic theory.* New Haven, CT: Yale University Press.

Chomsky, N. (1957). *Syntactic structures.* The Hague: Mouton.

Christiansen, A., & Pasch, L. (1993). The sequence of marital conflict. *Clinical Psychology Review, 13*, 3–14.

Church, D. K., Siegel, M. A., & Foster, C. D. (1988) *Growing old in America.* Wylie, TX: Information Aids.

Cicirelli, V. G. (1982). Sibling influence throughout the life span. In M. E. Lamb & B. Sutton-Smith (Eds.), *Sibling relationships.* Hillsdale, NJ: Erlbaum.

Cicirelli, V. G. (1991). Sibling relationships in adulthood. *Marriage and Family Review, 16*, 291–310.

Cicirelli, V. G. (1994). Sibling relationships in cross-cultural perspective. *Journal of Marriage and the Family, 56*, 7–20.

Cicirelli, V. (1977). Family structure and interaction: Sibling effects on socialization. In M. McMillan & M. Sergio (Eds.), *Child psychiatry: Treatment and research.* New York: Brunner/Mazel.

Clark, E. V. (1983). Meanings and concepts. In P. H. Mussen (Ed.), *Handbook of child psychology* (4th ed., Vol. 4). New York: Wiley.

Clark, K. B., & Clark, M. P. (1939). The development of self and the emergence of racial identification in Negro preschool children. *Journal of Social Psychology, 10*, 591–599.

Clarke-Stewart, A. (1993). *Daycare* (rev. ed.). Cambridge, MA: Harvard University Press.

Clarke-Stewart, K. A., & Fein, G. G. (1983). Early childhood programs. In P. H.

Mussen (Ed.), *Handbook of child psychology* (4th ed., Vol. 2). New York: Wiley.

Clarke-Stewart, K. (1989) Infant day care: Maligned or malignant? *American Psychologist, 44,* 266–273.

Clarkson-Smith, L., & Hartley, A. A. (1989). Relationships between physical exercise and cognitive abilities in older adults. *Psychology and Aging, 4,* 183–189.

Clemens, A. W., & Axelson, L. J. (1985). The not-so-empty nest: The return of the fledgling adult. *Family Relations, 34,* 259–264.

Cochran, S. D., & Mays, V. M. (1990). Sex, lies, and HIV. *New England Journal of Medicine, 322* (11), 774–775.

Cogwill, D. O. (1974). Aging and modernization: A revision of theory. In J. Gubrium (Ed.), *Late life.* Springfield, IL: Charles C Thomas.

Cohen, C. I., Teresi, J., & Holmes, D. (1985). Social networks, stress, adaptation, and health. *Research on Aging, 7,* 409–431.

Cohen, C. P., & Naimark, H. (1991). United Nations convention on the rights of the child: Individual rights concepts and their significance for social scientists. *American Psychologist, 46,* 60–65.

Cohen, G. D. (1990). Psychopathology and mental health in the mature and elderly adult. In J. E. Birren & K. W. Schaie (Eds.), *Handbook of the psychology of aging* (3rd ed.). San Diego: Academic Press.

Cohen, L. A. (1987, November). Diet and cancer. *Scientific American,* pp. 128–137.

Cohen, P., Brook, J. S., & Kandel, D. B. (1991). Drug use, predictors and correlates of. In R. M. Lerner, A. C. Petersen, & J. Brooks-Gunn (Eds.), *Encyclopedia of adolescence* (Vol. 1). New York: Garland.

Cohen, S. E. (1994, February). *High school dropouts.* Paper presented at the meeting of the Society for Research on Adolescence, San Diego, CA.

Cohn, E., & Harlow, K. (1993, October). *Elders as victims: Randomized studies in two states.* Paper presented at the meeting of the Gerontological Association of America, New Orleans.

Cohn, J. F., & Tronick, E. Z. (1988). Mother-infant face-to-face interaction: Influence is bidirectional and unrelated to periodic cycles in either partner's behavior. *Developmental Psychology, 24,* 396–397.

Coie, J. D., & Koeppl, G. K. (1990). Adapting intervention to the problems of aggressive and disruptive rejected children. In S. R. Asher & J. D. Coie (Eds.), *Peer rejection in childhood.* New York: Cambridge University Press.

Colby, A., Kohlberg, L., Gibbs, J., & Lieberman, M. (1983). A longitudinal study of moral judgment. *Monographs of the Society for Research in Child Development* (Serial No. 201).

Cole, D. A. (1991). Suicide, adolescent. In R. M. Lerner, A. C. Petersen, & J. Brooks-Gunn (Eds.), *Encyclopedia of adolescence* (Vol. 2). New York: Garland.

Cole, M. (1993, March). *A cultural-historical goal for developmental research: Create sustainable model systems of diversity.* Paper presented at the biennial meeting of the Society for Research in Child Development, New Orleans.

Cole, T. R., Achenbaum, W. A., Jakobi, P. L., & Kastenbaum, R. (Eds.). *Voices and visions of aging: Toward a critical gerontology.* New York: Springer.

Coleman, J. S., & others. (1974). *Youth: Transition to adulthood.* Report of the Panel on Youth of the President's Science Advisory Committee. Chicago: University of Chicago Press.

Coleman, J. S. (1961). *The adolescent society.* New York: Free Press.

Coleman, L. L., & Coleman, A. D. (1991). *Pregnancy: The psychological experience* (rev. ed.). New York: Noonday Press.

Coleman, M., & Ganong, L. H. (1990). Remarriage and stepfamily research in the 1980s: Increased interest in an old form. *Journal of Marriage and the Family, 52,* 925–939.

Coleman, P. D. (1986, August). *Regulation of dendritic extent: Human aging brain and Alzheimer's disease.* Paper presented at the meeting of the American Psychological Association, Washington, DC.

Coles, C. D., Platzman, K. A., & Smith, I. E. (1991, April). *Substance abuse and neonates: Alcohol and cocaine effects.* Paper presented at the biennial meeting of the Society for Research in Child Development, Seattle.

Coles, R. (1970). *Erik H. Erikson: The growth of his work.* Boston: Little, Brown.

Coles, R. (1986). *The political life of children.* Boston: Little, Brown.

Colgrove, M., Bloomfield, H., & McWilliams, P. (1991). *How to survive the loss of a love.* Los Angeles: Prelude Press.

Collins, A., Brown, J. S., & Newman, S. E. (1989). Cognitive apprenticeship: Teaching the craft of reading, writing, and mathematics. In L. B. Resnick (Ed.), *Knowing and learning: Essays in honor of Robert Glaser.* Hillsdale, NJ: Erlbaum.

Collins, W. A., & Luebker, C. (1993, March). *Parental behavior during adolescence: Individual and relational significance.* Paper presented at the biennial meeting of the Society for Research in Child Development, New Orleans.

Collins, W. A. (1990). Parent-child relationships in the transition to adolescence: Continuity and change in interaction, affect, and cognition. In R. Montemayor, G. R. Adams, & T. P. Gullotta (Eds.), *From childhood to adolescence: A transitional period?* Newbury Park, CA: Sage.

Colombo, J., Moss, M., & Horowitz, F. D. (1989). Neonatal state profiles: Reliability and short-term prediction of neurobehavioral status. *Child Development, 60,* 1102–1110.

Colt, G. H. (1991, April). The birth of a family. *Life Magazine,* pp. 28–38.

Columbo, J., & Fagen, J. W. (Eds.). (1991). *Individual differences in infancy.* Hillsdale, NJ: Erlbaum.

Comas-Diaz, L. (1993). Hispanic/Latino communities: Psychological implications. In D. R. Atkinson, G. Morten, & D. W. Sue (Eds.), *Counseling American minorities.* Dubuque, IA: Brown & Benchmark.

Comer, J. P., & Poussaint, A. B. (1992). *Raising black children.* New York: Plume.

Comer, J. P. (1988). Educating poor minority children. *Scientific American, 259,* 42–48.

Committee for Economic Development. (1987). *Children in need: Investment strategies for the educationally disadvantaged.* Washington, DC: Author.

Compas, B. (1989, April). *Vulnerability and stress in childhood and adolescence.* Paper presented at the biennial meeting of the Society for Research in Child Development, Kansas City.

Comstock, G. (1991). *Television and the American child.* San Diego, CA: Academic Press.

Conant, J. B. (1959). *The American high school today.* New York: McGraw-Hill.

Condi, S. J. (1989). Older married couples. In S. J. Bahr & E. T. Peterson (Eds.), *The aging family.* Lexington, MA: Lexington Books.

Condry, J. C. *The psychology of television.* Hillsdale, NJ: Erlbaum.

Conger, J. J. (1988). Hostages to the future: Youth, values, and the public interest. *American Psychologist, 43,* 291–300.

Conger, R. D., Conger, K. J., & Simons, R. L. (1992, March). *Family economic stress, parenting behavior, and adolescent drinking.* Paper presented at the meeting of the Society for Research on Adolescence, Washington, DC.

Connolly, J. A., & Johnson, A. M. (1993, March). *The psychosocial context of adolescent romantic relationships.* Paper presented at the biennial meeting of the Society for Research in Child Development, New Orleans.

Conti-Ramsden, G., & Snow, C. E. (1991). Children's language: How it develops and how it is used. In G. Conti-Ramsden & C. E. Snow (Eds.), *Children's language* (Vol. 7). Hillsdale, NJ: Erlbaum.

Coombs, R. H. (1991). Marital status and personal well-being: A literature review. *Family Relations, 40,* 97–102.

Coons, S., & Guilleminault, C. (1984). Development of consolidated sleep and wakeful periods in relation to the day/night cycle of infancy. *Developmental Medicine and Child Neurology, 26,* 169–176.

Cooper, C. R., & Grotevant, H. D. (1989, April). *Individuality and connectedness in the family and adolescents' self and relational competence.* Paper presented at the biennial meeting of the Society for Research in Child Development, Kansas City.

Cooper, C. R., Grotevant, H. D., Moore, M. S., & Condon, S. M. (1982, August). *Family support and conflict: Both foster adolescent identity and role taking.* Paper presented at the meeting of the American Psychological Association, Washington, DC.

Cooper, K. (1970). *The new aerobics.* New York: Bantam.

Coopersmith, S. (1967). *The antecedents of self-esteem.* San Francisco: W. H. Freeman.

Corbin, J., & Strauss, A. (1988). *Unending work and care: Managing chronic illness at home.* San Francisco: Jossey-Bass.

Cornell, D. G., & Grossberg, I. N. (1986). Siblings of children in gifted programs. *Journal for the Education of the Gifted, 9* (4), 253–264.

Corrigan, R. (1981). The effects of task and practice on search for invisibly displaced objects. *Developmental Review, 11,* 1–17.

Costa, P. T., & McRae, R. R. (1980). Still stable after all these years: Personality as a key to some issues in aging. In P. B. Baltes & O. G. Brim (Eds.), *Life-span development and behavior.* New York: Academic Press.

Costa, P. T., & McRae, R. R. (1989). Personality continuity and the changes of adult life. In M. Storandt & G. R. VandenBos (Eds.), *The adult years: Continuity and change.* Washington, DC: American Psychological Association.

Costa, P. T., Zonderman, A. B., McCrae, R. R., Cornon-Huntely, J., Locke, B. Z., & Barbano, H. E. (1987). Longitudinal analyses of psychological well-being in a national sample: Stability and mean levels. *Journal of Gerontology, 42,* 50–55.

Costa, P. T. (1986, August). *The scope of individuality.* Paper presented at the meeting of the American Psychological Association, Washington, DC.

Cowley, G. (1988, May 23). The wisdom of animals. *Newsweek,* pp. 52–58.

Cox, B. D. (1993, March). *Internalization through the reinterpretation of spontaneous invention: The examples of mathematics and metamemory.* Paper presented at the biennial meeting of the Society for Research in Child Development, New Orleans.

Cox, C. (1993). *The frail elderly: Problems, needs, and community responses.* Westport, CT: Auburn House.

Cox, F. D. (1994). *The AIDS booklet* (3rd ed.). Dubuque, IA: Brown & Benchmark.

Coyne, J. C., Wortman, C. B., & Lehman, D. R. (1988). The other side of support: Emotional overinvolvement and miscarried helping. In B. Gottlieb (Ed.), *Marshaling social support: Formats, processes, and effects.* Newbury Park, CA: Sage.

Craik, F. I. M. (1977). Age differences in human memory. In J. E. Birren & K. W. Schaie (Eds.), *Handbook of the psychology of aging.* New York: Van Nostrand Reinhold.

Creasy, G. L., Mitts, N., Catanzaro, L. E., & Lustig, K. (1993, March). *Associations among daily hassles, coping, and behavior problems among kindergartners.* Paper presented at the biennial meeting of the Society for Research in Child Development, New Orleans.

Crick, N. R., & Dodge, K. A. (1994). A review and reformulation of social information-processing mechanisms in children's social adjustment. *Psychological Bulletin, 115,* 74–101.

Crisafi, M. A., & Driscoll, J. M. (1991, April). *Developmental outcome in very low birthweight infants at three years of age.* Paper presented at the biennial meeting of the Society for Research in Child Development, Seattle.

Crittenden, P. (1988a). Family and dyadic patterns of functioning in maltreating families. In K. Browne, C. Davies, & P. Stratton (Eds.), *Early prediction and prevention of child abuse.* New York: Wiley.

Crittenden, P. (1988b). Relationships at risk. In J. Belsky & T. Nezworksi (Eds.), *The clinical implications for attachment.* Hillsdale, NJ: Erlbaum.

Crockenberg, S., & Lourie, A. (1993, March). *Conflict strategies: Parents with children and children with peers.* Paper presented at the biennial meeting of the Society for Research in Child Development, New Orleans.

Crockett, L. J., & Chopak, J. S. (1993). Pregnancy prevention in early adolescence. In R. M. Lerner (Ed.), *Early adolescence: Perspectives on research, policy, and intervention.* Hillsdale, NJ: Erlbaum.

Crohan, S. E., & Antonucci, T. C. (1989). Friends as a source of social support in old age. In R. G. Adams & R. Blieszner (Eds.), *Older adult friendships.* Newbury Park, CA: Sage.

Crohan, S. E., Antonucci, T. C., Adelmann, P. K., & Coleman, L. M. (1989). Job characteristics and well-being at mid-life: Ethnic and gender comparisons. *Psychology of Women Quarterly, 13,* 223–235.

Cronbach, L. J., & Snow, R. E. (1977). *Aptitudes and instructional methods.* New York: Irvington Books.

Crosby, F., & Ayers, L. (1991). In the middle. *Contemporary Psychology, 36,* 565–566.

Crosby, F. J., & Jaskar, K. L. (1993). Women and men at home and at work: Realities and illusions. In S. Oskamp & M. Costanzo (Eds.), *Gender issues in contemporary society.* Newbury Park, CA: Sage.

Culbertson, F. M. (1991, August). *Mental health of women: An international journey.* Paper presented at the meeting of the American Psychological Association, San Francisco.

Cumming, E., & Henry, W. (1961). *Growing old.* New York: Basic Books.

Cummings, E. M. (1987). Coping with background anger in early childhood. *Child Development, 58,* 976–984.

Curtiss, S. (1977). *Genie.* New York: Academic Press.

Cutrona, C. E. (1982). Transition to college: Loneliness and the process of social adjustment. In L. A. Peplau & D. Perlman (Eds.), *Loneliness: A sourcebook of current theory, research and therapy.* New York: Wiley.

Czaja, S. J., Hammond, K., Blascovich, J. J., & Swede, H. (1986). Learning to use a work-processing system as a function of training strategy. *Behaviour and Information Technology, 5,* 203–216.

Czikszentmihalyi, M. (1990). *Flow.* New York: Harper & Row.

D

Damon, W., & Hart, D. (1988). *Self-understanding in childhood and adolescence.* New York: Cambridge University Press.

Damon, W., & Hart, D. (1992). Self-understanding and its role in social and moral development. On M. H. Bornstein & M. E. Lamb (Eds.), *Developmental psychology: An advanced textbook* (3rd ed.). Hillsdale, NJ: Erlbaum.

Damon, W. (1988). *The moral child.* New York: Free Press.

Danner, F. (1989). Cognitive development in adolescence. In J. Worrell & F. Danner (Eds.), *The adolescent as decision maker.* New York: Academic Press.

Darling, C. A., Kallon, D. J., & Van Duesen, J. E. (1984). Sex in transition, 1900–1984. *Journal of Youth and Adolescence, 13,* 385–399.

Darlington, R. B. (1991). The long-term effects of model preschool programs. In L. Okagaki & R. J. Sternberg (Eds.), *Directors of development: Influences on the development of children's thinking.* Hillsdale, NJ: Erlbaum.

Darrach, B. (1992, October). The war on aging. *Life,* pp. 33–43.

Darwin, C. (1859). *On the origin of species.* London: John Murray.

Dash, L. (1986, January 26). Children's children: The crisis up close. *The Washington Post,* pp. A1, A12.

Datan, N., Greene, A. L., & Reese, H. W. (1986). *Life-span developmental psychology.* Hillsdale, NJ: Erlbaum.

Datan, N. (1989). Aging women: The silent majority. *Women's Studies Quarterly,* 12–19.

Davidson, M., & Stern, R. G. (1991). The treatment of cognitive impairment in Alzheimer's disease: Beyond the cholinergic approach. *Psychiatric Clinics of North America, 14,* 461–482.

Davis, J. M., & Mercier, C. E. (1992). The effects of drugs and other substances on the fetus. In R. A. Hoekelman, S. B. Friedman, N. M. Nelson, & H. M. Seidel (Eds.), *Primary Pediatric care* (2nd ed.). St. Louis: Mosby Yearbook.

Davis, K. E. (1985, February). Near and dear: Friendship and love compared. *Psychology Today,* pp. 22–29.

Dawson, G. (Ed.). (1989). *Autism: Nature, diagnosis, and treatment.* New York: Guilford Press.

Dawson-Hughes, B., Dallal, G. E., Krall, E. A., Sadowski, L., Sahyoun, N., & Tannebaum, S. (1990). A controlled trial of the effect of calcium supplementation on bone density in postmenopausal women. *New England Journal of Medicine, 323* 878–883.

Dax, E. M., Ingram, D. K., Partilla, J. S., & Gregerman, R. I. (1989). Food restriction prevents an age-associated increase in rat liver beta-adrenergic receptors. *Journal of Gerontology: Biological Sciences, 44,* B72–76.

Day, N. (1991, April). *Effects of alcohol and marijuana on growth and development.* Paper presented at the biennial meeting of the Society for Research in Child Development, Seattle.

de Jong-Gierveld, J. (1987). Developing and testing a model of loneliness. *Journal of Personality and Social Psychology, 53,* 119–128.

de Villiers, J. G., & de Villiers, P. A. (1978). *Language acquisition.* Cambridge, MA: Harvard University Press.

de Villiers, P. A., & de Villiers, J. G. (1992). Language development. In M. H. Bornstein & M. E. Lamb (Eds.), *Developmental psychology* (3rd ed.). Hillsdale, NJ: Erlbaum.

Dean, A. L. (1993, March). *Putting the pieces of the adolescent pregnancy puzzle together.* Paper presented at the biennial meeting of the Society for Research in Child Development, New Orleans.

DeAngelis, T. (1990, June). House child-care bill ignores quality issue. *APA Monitor,* p. 21.

DeCasper, A. J., & Spence, M. J. (1986). Prenatal maternal speech influences newborn's perception of speech sounds. *Infant Behavior and Development, 9,* 133–150.

DeCorte, W. (1993). Estimating sex-related bias in job evaluation. *Journal of Occupational and Organizational Psychology, 66,* 83–96.

DeFour, D. C., & Paludi, M. A. (in press). Integrating scholarship on ethnicity into the psychology of women course. *Teaching of Psychology.*

DeFriese, G. H., & Womert, A. (1991). Informal and formal health care systems serving older people. In M. G. Ory, R. P. Abeles, & P. D. Lipman (Eds.), *Aging, health, and behavior.* Newbury Park, CA: Sage.

DeHart, G., & Smith, B. (1991, April). *The role of age and gender composition in sibling pretend play.* Paper presented at the biennial meeting of the Society for Research in Child Development, Seattle.

DelCielo, D., Castaneda, M., Hui, J., & Frye, D. (1993, March). *Is theory of mind related to categorization?* Paper presented at the biennial meeting of the Society for Research in Child Development, New Orleans.

DeLoache, J. S., Cassidy, D. J., & Carpenter, C. J. (1987). The Three Bears are all boys: Mothers' gender labeling of neutral picture book characters. *Sex Roles, 17,* 163–178.

DeLoache, J. (1993, March). *What do young children understand about symbolic representations?* Paper presented at the biennial meeting of the Society for Research in Child Development, New Orleans.

Demetriou, A., & Efklides, A. (in press). Experiential structuralism: A frame for unifying cognitive developmental theories. *Monographs of the Society for Research in Child Development.*

Dempster, F. N. (1981). Memory span: Sources of individual and developmental differences. *Psychological Bulletin, 80,* 63–100.

Denmark, F. L., & Paludi, M. A. (Eds.). (1993). *Psychology of women: A handbook of issues and theories.* Westport, CT: Greenwood Press.

Denmark, F. L., & Paludi, M. A. (Eds.). (in press). *Handbook on the psychology of women.* Westport, CT: Greenwood Press.

Denmark, F. L., Russo, N. F., Frieze, I. H., & Sechzur, J. (1988). Guidelines for avoiding sexism in psychological research: A report of the ad hoc committee on nonsexist research. *American Psychologist, 43,* 582–585.

Denmark, F. L. (1993, August). *Women in psychology: Past, present, and future.* Paper presented at the meeting of the American Psychological Association, Toronto, Canada.

Denney, N. (1982). Aging and cognitive changes. In B. B. Wolman (Ed.), *Handbook of developmental psychology.* Englewood Cliffs, NJ: Prentice-Hall.

Denney, N. (1986, August). *Practical problem solving.* Paper presented at the meeting of the American Psychological Association, Washington, DC.

Dennis, W. (1966). Creative productivity between the ages of 20 and 80 years. *Journal of Gerontology, 21,* 1–18.

Deutsch, F. M. (1991). Women's lives: The story not told by theories of development. *Contemporary Psychology, 36,* 237–238.

Deutsch, M. (Ed.). (1967). *The disadvantaged child: Selected papers of Martin Deutsch and his associates.* New York: Basic Books.

DeVault, M. L. (1987). Doing housework: Feeding and family life. In N. Gerstel & H. E. Gross (Eds.), *Families and work.* Philadelphia: Temple University Press.

Dewey, J. (1933). *How we think: A restatement of the relation of reflective thinking to the educative process.* Lexington, MA: D. C. Heath.

Diaz, R. M. (1983). Thought and two languages: The impact of bilingualism on cognitive development. *Review of Research in Education, 10,* 23–54.

Dickerscheid, J. D., Schwarz, P. M., Noir, S., & El-Taliawy, T. (1988). Gender concept development of preschool-aged children in the United States and Egypt. *Sex Roles, 18,* 669–677.

Dickinson, G. E. (1975). Dating behavior of black and white adolescents before and after desegregation. *Journal of Marriage and the Family, 37,* 602–608.

Dickson, G. L. (1990). A feminist post-structuralist analysis of the knowledge of menopause. *Advances in Nursing Science, 12,* 15–31.

Dietz, W. (1986, March). *Comments at the workshop on childhood obesity.* Washington, DC: National Institute of Health.

Dishion, T. J. (1992, March). *Parental factors in early adolescent substance use: Correlational and experimental evidence.* Paper presented at the meeting of the Society for Research on Adolescence, Washington, DC.

Dittman-Kohli, F. (1992). *The personal system of sense of life: A comparison between early and late adulthood.* Unpublished manuscript, Free University, Berlin, Germany.

Dixon, S. D. (1991, April). *Infants exposed perinatally to cocaine or methamphetamine demonstrate behavioral and neurophysiologic changes.* Paper presented at the biennial meeting of the Society for Research in Child Development, Seattle.

Dobson, S. H., Binder, K. S., Kirasic, K. C., & Allen, G. L. (1993, October). *The role of working memory, information-processing speed, health, and activity level on verbal learning.* Paper presented at the meeting of the Gerontological Association of America, New Orleans.

Dodge, K. A., Petit, G. S., McClaskey, C. L., & Brown, M. M. (1986). Social competence in children. *Monographs of the Society for Research in Child Development, 55,* 1646–1650.

Dodge, K. A. (1983). Behavioral antecedents of peer social status. *Child Development, 54,* 1386–1399.

Dohrenwend, B. S., & Dohrenwend, B. P. (1978). Some issues in research on stressful life events. *Journal of Nervous and Mental Disease, 166,* 7–15.

Dohrenwend, B. S., & Shrout, P. E. (1985). "Hassles" in the conceptualization and measurement of life stress variables. *American Psychologist, 40,* 780–785.

Dolcini, M. M., Coh, L. D., Adler, N. E., Millstein, S. G., Irwin, C. E., Kegeles, S. M., & Stone, G. C. (1989). Adolescent egocentrism and feelings of

invulnerability: Are they related? *Journal of Early Adolescence, 9,* 409–418.

Dolgin, K. G., & Behrend D. A. (1984). Children's knowledge about animates and inanimates. *Child Development, 55,* 1646–1650.

Doll, G. (1988, Spring). Day care. *Vanderbilt Magazine,* p. 29.

Domino, G. (1992). Acculturation of Hispanics. In S. B. Knouse, P. Rosenfeld, & A. Culbertson (Eds.), *Hispanics in the workplace.* Newbury Park, CA: Sage.

Donat, P. L. N., & D'Emilio, J. D. (1992). A feminist redefinition of rape and sexual assault: Historical foundations and change. *Journal of Social Issues, 48,* 9–22.

Dornbusch, S. M., Carlsmith, J. M., Bushwall, S. J., Ritter, P. I, Leidman, P. H., Hastorf, A. H., & Gross, R. T. (1985). Single parents, extended households, and the control of adolescents. *Child Development, 56,* 326–341.

Dornbusch, S. M., Ritter, P. L., Leiderman, P. H., Roberts, D. F., & Fraleigh, M. J. (1987). The relation of parenting style to adolescent school performance. *Child Development, 58,* 1244–1257.

Douvan, D. (1983). Listening to a different drummer. *Contemporary Psychology, 28,* 261–262.

Douvan, E., & Adelson, J. (1966). *The adolescent experience.* New York: Wiley.

Dowd, J. J., & Bengston, V. L. (1978). Aging in minority populations: An examination of the double jeopardy hypothesis. *Journal of Gerontology, 30,* 584–593.

Dowdy, B. B., & Howard, C. W. (1993, March). *The effects of dating and parent-adolescent consultant preferences during adolescence.* Paper presented at the biennial meeting of the Society for Research in Child Development, New Orleans.

Downey, A. M, Frank, G. C., Webber, L. S., Harsha, D. W., Virgilio, S. J., Franklin, F. A., & Berenson, G. S. (1987). Implementation of "Heart Smart": A cardiovascular school health promotion program. *Journal of School Health, 57,* 98–104.

Downey, G., & Coyne, J. C. (1990). Children of depressed parents: An integrative review. *Psychological Bulletin, 108,* 50–76.

Doyne, E. J., Ossip-Klein, D. J., Bowman, E. D., Osborne, K. M., McDougall-Wilson, I. B., & Neimeyer, R. A. (1987). Running versus weight lifting in the treatment of depression. *Journal of Consulting and Clinical Psychology, 55,* 748–754.

Draper, T. W., Larsen, J. M., Haupt, J. H., Robinson, C. C., & Hart, C. (1993, March). *Family emotional climate as a mediating variable between parent education and child social competence in an advantaged subculture.* Paper presented at the biennial meeting of the Society for Research in Child Development, New Orleans.

Dreikurs, R. (1964). *Children: The challenge.* New York: Hawthorn Books.

Drew, P. J., & Luftig, R. L. (1993, March). *Factors related to loneliness in students with and without learning disabilities at four developmental levels.* Paper presented at the biennial meeting of the Society for Research in Child Development, New Orleans.

Dreyer, P. H., Jennings, T., Johnson, L., & Evans, D. (1994, February). *Culture and personality in urban schools: Identity status, self-concept, and locus of control among high school students in monolingual and bilingual homes.* Paper presented at the meeting of the Society for Research on Adolescence, San Diego, CA.

Dryfoos, J. G. (1990). *Adolescents at risk: Prevalence and prevention.* New York: Oxford University Press.

Dryfoos, J. G. (1992, March). *Integrating services for adolescents: The community schools.* Paper presented at the meeting of the Society for Research on Adolescence, Washington, DC.

Dryfoos, J. G. (1993). Schools as places for health, mental health, and special services. In R. Takanishi (Ed.), *Adolescence in the 1990s.* New York: Teachers College Press.

Duck, S., & Pond, K. (1989). Friends, Romans, countrymen, lend me your retrospections: Rhetoric and reality in personal relationships. In C. Hendrick (Ed.), *Close relationships.* Newbury Park, CA: Sage.

Duck, S. W. (1975). Personality similarity and friendship choices by adolescents. *European Journal of Social Psychology, 5,* 351–365.

Duck, S. W. (1988). Child and adolescent friendships. In P. Marsh (Ed.), *Eye to eye: How people interact.* Topsfield, MA: Salem House.

Duck, S. (1993). *Individuals in relationships.* Newbury Park, CA: Sage.

Duke, D. L., & Canady, R. L. (1991). *School policy.* New York: McGraw-Hill.

Duncan, G. J. (1993, March). *Economic deprivation and child development.* Paper presented at the biennial meeting of the Society for Research in Child Development, New Orleans.

Duncan, R. M. (1991, April). *An examination of Vygotsky's theory of children's private speech.* Paper presented at the biennial meeting of the Society for Research in Child Development, Seattle.

Dunn, J., & Kendrick, C. (1982). *Siblings.* Cambridge, MA: Harvard University Press.

Dunn, J. (1984). Sibling studies and the developmental impact of critical incidents. In P. B. Baltes & O. G. Brim (Eds.), *Life-span development and behavior* (Vol. 6). Orlando, FL: Academic Press.

Dunphy, D. C. (1963). The social structure of urban adolescent peer groups. *Society, 26,* 230–246.

Durkin, K. (1985). Television and sex-role acquisition: 1. Content. *British Journal of Social Psychology, 24,* 101–113.

Durlak, J. A., & Riesenberg, L. A. (1991). The impact of death education. *Death Studies, 15,* 39–58.

Duvall, E. M., & Miller, B. C. (1985). *Marriage and family development* (6th ed.). New York: Harper & Row.

Duxbury, L. E., & Higgins, C. A. (1991). Gender differences in work-family conflict. *Journal of Applied Psychology, 76,* 60–74.

Dychtwald, K. (1990). *Age wave.* New York: Bantam.

Dyk, P. K. (1993). Anatomy, physiology, and gender issues in adolescence. In T. P. Gullotta, G. R. Adams, & R. Montemayor (Eds.), *Adolescent sexuality.* Newbury Park, CA: Sage.

E

Eagly, A. H., & Crowley, M. (1986). Gender and helping behavior: A meta-analytic review of the social psychological literature. *Psychological Bulletin, 100,* 283–308.

Eccles, J., MacIver, D., & Lange, L. (1986). *Classroom practices and motivation to study math.* Paper presented at the annual meeting of the American Educational Research Association, San Francisco.

Eccles, J. S., & Buchanan, C. M. (1992, March). *Hormones and behavior at early adolescence: A theoretical overview.* Paper presented at the biennial meeting of the Society for Research in Adolescence, Washington, DC.

Eccles, J. S., & Midgley, C. (1990). Changes in academic motivation and self-perception during early adolescence. In R. Montemayor, G. R. Adams, & T. P. Gullotta (Eds.), *From childhood to adolescence: A transitional period?* Newbury Park, CA: Sage.

Eccles, J. S., Harold-Goldsmith, R., & Miller, C. R. (1989, April). *Parents' stereotyping beliefs about gender differences in adolescence.* Paper presented at the biennial meeting of the Society for Research in Child Development, Kansas City.

Eccles, J. S. (1987). Gender roles and achievement patterns: An expectancy value perspective. In J. M. Reinisch, L. A. Rosenblum, & S. A. Sanders (Eds.), *Masculinity/Femininity.* New York: Oxford University Press.

Edelman, M. W. (1987). *Families in peril.* Cambridge, MA: Harvard University Press.

Edelman, M. W. (1992). *The state of America's children, 1992.* Washington, DC: Children's Defense Fund.

Edelman, M. W. (1994). *The state of America's children, 1994.* Washington, DC: Children's Defense Fund.

Edmonds, M. M. (1993). Physical health. In J. S. Jackson, L. M. Chatters, & R. J. Taylor (Eds.), *Aging in Black America.* Newbury Park, CA: Sage.

Edmonds, M. Mc. (1990). The health of the black aged female. In Z. Harel, E. A. McKinney, & M. Williams (Eds.), *Black aged.* Newbury Park, CA: Sage.

Educational Testing Service. (1992, February). *Cross-national comparisons of 9–13 year-olds' science and math achievement.* Princeton, NJ: Author.

Edwards, J. R., & Baglioni, A. J. (1991). Relation between Type A behavior pattern and mental and physical symptoms: A comparison of global and component measures. *Journal of Applied Psychology, 76,* 276–290.

Egeland, B. (1989, January). *Secure attachment in infancy and competence in the third grade.* Paper presented at the meeting of the American Association for the Advancement of Science, San Francisco.

Ehrhardt, A. A. (1987). A transactional perspective on the development of gender differences. In J. M. Reinisch, L. A. Rosenblum, & S. A. Sanders (Eds.), *Masculinity/femininity: Basic perspectives.* New York: Oxford University Press.

Eichorn, D. H., Clausen, J. A., Haan, N., Honzik, M. P., & Mussen, P. H. (Eds.). (1981). *Present and past in middle life.* New York: Academic Press.

Eiferman, R. R. (1971). Social play in childhood. In R. E. Herron & B. Sutton-Smith (Eds.), *Child's play.* New York: Wiley.

Eiger, M. S. (1992). The feeding of infants and children. In R. B. Hoekelman, S. B. Friedman, N. M. Nelson, & H. M. Seidel (Eds.), *Primary pediatric care* (2nd ed.). St. Louis: Mosby Yearbook.

Einstein, E., & Albert, L. (1986). *Strengthening your stepfamily.* Circle Pines, MN: American Guidance Service.

Eisenberg, A., Murkoff, H. E., & Hathaway, S. E. (1989). *What to expect in the first year.* New York: Workman.

Eisenberg, A. R., Wolfe, P., & Mick, M. (1993, March). *Who makes a good sibling? Personality and the quality of sibling relationships.* Paper presented at the biennial meeting of the Society for Research in Child Development, New Orleans.

Eisenberg, N. (1992, Fall). Social development: Current trends and future possibilities. *SRCD Newsletter,* pp. 1, 10–11.

Eisenberg, N. (Ed.). (1982). *The development of prosocial behavior.* New York: Wiley.

Ekerdt, D. J., & DeViney, S. (1993). Evidence for a preretirement process among older male workers. *Journal of Gerontology, 48,* S35–S43.

Elder, G. H., & Pavalko, E. K. (1993). Work careers in men's later years: Transitions, trajectories, and historical change. *Journal of Gerontology, 48,* S180–S191.

Elder, G. H., Caspi, A., & Burton, L. M. (1988). Adolescent transition in developmental perspective: Sociological and historical insights. In M. R. Gunnar & W. A. Collins (Eds.), *Development during the transition to adolescence.* Hillsdale, NJ: Erlbaum.

Elder, G. H., Caspi, A., & Downey, G. (1986). Problem behavior and family relationships: A multigenerational analysis. In A. Sorensen, F. Weinert, & L. Sherrod (Eds.), *Human development and the life course.* Hillsdale, NJ: Erlbaum.

Elkind, D. (1970, April 5). Erik Erikson's eight ages of man. *New York Times Magazine.*

Elkind, D. (1976). *Child development and education: A Piagetian perspective.* New York: Oxford University Press.

Elkind, D. (1978). Understanding the young adolescent. *Adolescence, 13,* 127–134.

Elkind, D. (1981). *The hurried child.* Reading, MA: Addison-Wesley.

Elkind, D. (1985). [Reply to D. Lapsley and M. Murphy's *Developmental Review* paper.] *Developmental Review, 5,* 218–226.

Elkind, D. (1987). *Miseducation: Preschoolers at risk.* New York: Knopf.

Elkind, D. (1988, January). Educating the very young: A call for clear thinking. *NEA Today,* pp. 22–27.

Elkind, D. (1988). *The hurried child* (rev. ed.). Reading, MA: Addison-Wesley.

Elkind, D. (1991). *All grown up and no place to go: Teenagers in crisis.* Reading, MA: Addison-Wesley.

Ellis, A., & Velton, E. (1992). *When AA doesn't work for you: Rational steps to quitting alcohol.* Fort Lee, NJ: Barricade Books.

Ellis, A. (1991). Cover notes. In S. Peele & A. Brodsky, *The truth about addiction and recovery.* New York: Simon & Schuster.

Ellis, L., & Ames, M. A. (1987). Neurohormonal functioning and sexual orientation: A theory of homosexuality-heterosexuality. *Psychological Bulletin, 101,* 233–258.

Emde, R. N., Gaensbauer, T. G., & Harmon, R. J. (1976). Emotional expression in infancy: A biobehavioral study. *Psychological Issues: Monograph Series, 10* (No. 37).

Emde, R. N., Plomin, R., Robinson, J., Corley, R., DeFries, J., Fulker, D. W., Reznick, J. S., Campos, J., Kagan, J., & Zahn-Waxler, C. (1992). Temperament, emotion, and cognition at fourteen months: The McArthur longitudinal twin study. *Child Development, 63,* 1437–1455.

Emery, R. E. (1989). Family violence. *American Psychologist, 44,* 321–328.

Emmerich, W., Goldman, K. S., Kirsch, B., & Sharabany, R. (1977). Evidence for a transitional phase in the development of gender constancy. *Child Development, 48,* 930–936.

Engen, T. (1977). Taste and smell. In J. E. Birren & K. W. Schaie (Eds.), *Handbook of the psychology of aging.* New York: Van Nostrand.

England, S. E., Linsk, N. L., Simon-Rusinowitz, L., & Keigher, S. M. (1991). Paying kin for care: Agency barriers to formalizing informal care. *Journal of Aging and Social Policy, 2,* 63–86.

Engle, P. L. (1991, April). *The effects of nutritional supplementation on cognitive functioning of preschoolers in Guatemala.* Paper presented at the biennial meeting of the Society for Research in Child Development, Seattle.

Enkin, M. W. (1989). Cesarean section: Why do the rates differ? *Birth, 16,* 207–208.

Ennis, R. H. (1991). Critical thinking: Literature review and needed research. In L. Idol & B. F. Jones (Eds.), *Educational values and cognitive instruction.* Hillsdale, NJ: Erlbaum.

Enright, R. D., Lapsley, D. K., Dricas, A. S., & Fehr, L. A. (1980). Parental influence on the development of adolescent autonomy and identity. *Journal of Youth and Adolescence, 9,* 529–546.

Entwisle, D., & Alexander, K. (1992, March). *School organization and adolescent development.* Meet-the-scientist luncheon at the Society for Research on Adolescence, Washington, DC.

Entwisle, D. R. (1990). Schools and the adolescent. In S. S. Feldman & G. R. Elliott (Eds.), *At the threshold: The developing adolescent.* Cambridge, MA: Harvard University Press.

Epstein, C. F. (1987). Multiple demands and multiple roles: The conditions of successful management. In F. J. Crosby (Ed.), *Spouse, Parent, Worker: On gender and multiple roles.* New Haven, CT: Yale University Press.

Epstein, N., & Eidelson, R. J. (1981). Unrealistic beliefs of clinical couples: Their relationship to expectations, goals, and satisfaction. *American Journal of Family Therapy, 9,* 13–21.

Erickson, P. I., & Rapkin, A. J. (1991). Unwanted sexual experiences among middle and high school youth. *Journal of Adolescent Health, 12,* 319–325.

Erikson, E. H., Erikson, J. M., & Kivnick, H. Q. (1986). *Vital involvement in old age.* New York: W. W. Norton.

Erikson, E. H. (1950). *Childhood and society.* New York: W. W. Norton.

Erikson, E. H. (1968). *Identity: Youth and crisis.* New York: W. W. Norton.

Espin, O. M. (1993). Psychological impact of migration on Latinos. In D. R. Atkinson, G. Morten, & D. W. Sue (Eds.), *Counseling American minorities.* Dubuque, IA: Brown & Benchmark.

Esty, E. T., & Fisch, S. M. (1991, April). *SQUARE ONE TV: Using television to enhance children's problem solving.* Paper presented at the Society for Research in Child Development meeting, Seattle.

Evans, B. J., & Whitfield, J. R. (Eds.). (1988). *Black males in the United States: An annotated bibliography from 1967 to 1987.* Washington, DC: American Psychological Association.

Evans, D. A., & others. (1992). The impact of Alzheimer's disease in the United States population. In R. M. Suzman, D. P. Willis, & K. G. Manton (Eds.), *The oldest old.* New York: Oxford University Press.

Evans, W., & Rosenberg, I. (1991). *Biomarkers: The 10 keys to prolonging vitality.* New York: Simon & Schuster.

Eyler, F. D., Behnke, M. L., & Stewart, N. J. (1990). *Issues in identification and follow-up of cocaine-exposed neonates.* Unpublished manuscript, University of Florida, Gainesville.

F

Fagot, B. I., Leinbach, M. D., & O'Boyle, C. (1992). Gender labeling, gender stereotyping, and parenting behaviors. *Developmental Psychology, 28,* 225–230.

Falbo, T., & Polit, D. F. (1986). A quantitative review of the only-child literature. Research evidence and theory development. *Psychological Bulletin, 100,* 176–189.

Falbo, T., & Poston, D. L. (1993). The academic, personality, and physical outcomes of only children in China. *Child Development, 64,* 18–35.

Falbo, T. L., & Romo, H. D. (1994, February). *Hispanic parents and public education: The gap between cultures.* Paper presented at the meeting of the Society for Research on Adolescence, San Diego, CA.

Falicov, C. J., & Karrer, B. M. (1980). Cultural variations in the family life cycle: The Mexican-American family. In E. A. Carter & M. McGoldrick (Eds.), *The family life cycle: A framework for family therapy.* New York: Gardner Press.

Fallon, A. (1990). Culture in the mirror: Sociocultural determinants of body image. In T. F. Cash & T. Pruzinsky (Eds.), *Body images: Development, deviance, and change.* New York: Guilford Press.

Fantz, R. L. (1963). Pattern vision in newborn infants. *Science, 140,* 296–297.

Farrell, M. P., & Rosenberg, S. D. (1981). *Men at mid-life.* Boston: Auburn House.

Fasick, F. A. (1988). Patterns of formal education in high school as rites of passage. *Adolescence, 23,* 457–468.

Fasick, F. A. (1994). On the "invention" of adolescence. *Journal of Early Adolescence, 14,* 4–5.

Fein, G. G. (1986). Pretend play. In D. Görlitz & J. F. Wohlwill (Eds.), *Curiosity, imagination, and play.* Hillsdale, NJ: Erlbaum.

Feldman, S. S., & Elliott, G. R. (1990). Progress and promise of research on normal adolescent development. In S. S. Feldman & G. Elliott (Eds.), *At the threshold: The developing adolescent.* Cambridge, MA: Harvard University Press.

Feldman, S. S., & Elliott, G. R. (Eds.). (1990). *At the threshold: The developing adolescent.* Cambridge, MA: Harvard University Press.

Feldman, S. S., & Rosenthal, D. A. (1990a). *The influence of family variables and adolescents' values on age expectations of behavioral autonomy: A cross cultural study of Hong Kong, Australian, and American youth.* Unpublished manuscript, Stanford Center for the Study of Families.

Feldman, S. S., & Rosenthal, D. A. (1990b). The acculturation of autonomy expectations in Chinese high schoolers residing in two Western nations. *International Journal of Psychology, 25,* 259–281.

Ferber, R. (1985). *Solve your child's sleep problems.* New York: Simon & Schuster.

Ferguson, D. M., Harwood, L. J., & Shannon, F. T. (1987). Breastfeeding and subsequent social adjustment in 6- to 8-year-old children. *Journal of Child Psychology and Psychiatry, 28,* 378–386.

Fernandez, J. (1993). *Tales out of school.* Boston: Little, Brown.

Fiatarone, M. A., Marks, E. C., Meredith, C. N., Lipsitz, L. A., & Evans, W. J. (1990). High intensity strength training in nonagenarians: Effects on skeletal muscle. *Journal of the American Medical Association, 263,* 3029–3034.

Field, T., Scafidi, F., & Schanberg, S. (1987). Massage of preterm newborns to improve growth and development. *Pediatric Nursing, 13,* 385–387.

Field, T. M. (1979). Visual and cardiac responses to animate and inanimate faces by young term and preterm infants. *Child Development, 50,* 188–194.

Field, T. M. (1987, January). Interview. *Psychology Today,* p. 31.

Field, T. M. (1990). Alleviating stress in newborn infants in the intensive care unit. In B. M. Lester & E. Z. Tronick (Eds.), *Stimulation and the preterm infant: The limits of plasticity.* Philadelphia: Saunders.

Field, T. M. (1991). Reducing stress in child and psychiatric patients by massage and relaxation therapy. In T. M. Field, P. M. McCabe, & N. Schneiderman (Eds.), *Stress and coping infancy and childhood* (Vol. 4). Hillsdale, NJ: Erlbaum.

Field, T. M. (1992a, May). *Massaging high-risk infants.* Paper presented at the International Conference on Infant Studies, Miami Beach.

Field, T. (1992b, September). Stroking babies helps growth, reduces stress. *The Brown University Child and Adolescent Behavior Letter,* pp. 1, 6.

Field, T. (in press), Quality infant daycare and grade school behavior and performance. *Child Development.*

Fillmore, L. W. (1989). Teachability and second language acquisition. In M. L. Rice & R. L. Schiefelbusch (Eds.), *The teachability of language.* Baltimore: Paul H. Brookes.

Fincham, F. D. (1993). Introduction to special issue on marital violence. *Clinical Psychology Review, 13,* 1–2.

Firush, R., & Cobb, P. A. (1989, April). *Developing scripts.* Paper presented at the Society for Research in Child Development meeting, Kansas City.

Fischer, K. W., & Farrar, M. J. (1987). Generalizations about generalization: How a theory of skill development explains both generality and specificity. *International Journal of Psychology, 22,* 643–677.

Fischer, L. R. (1991). Between mothers and daughters. *Marriage and Family Review, 16,* 237–248.

Fish, M. (1989, April). *Temperament and attachment of separation intolerance at three years.* Paper presented at the Society for Research in Child Development meeting, Kansas City.

Fisher, C. B., & Brone, R. J. (1991). Eating disorders in adolescence. In R. M. Lerner, A. C. Petersen, & J. Brooks-Gunn (Eds.), *Encyclopedia of adolescence* (Vol. 1). New York: Garland.

Fisher, D. (1990, March). *Effects of attachment on adolescents' friendships.* Paper presented at the meeting of the Society for Research in Adolescence, Atlanta.

Fisher, J. D., & Fisher, W. A. (1992). Changing AIDS-risk behavior. *Psychological Bulletin, 111,* 455–474.

Flanagan, J. (1981, August). *Some characteristics of 70-year-old workers.* Paper presented at the meeting of the American Psychological Association, Los Angeles.

Flannagan, D. A., & Tate, C. S. (1989, April). *The effects of children's script knowledge on their communication and recall of scenes.* Paper presented at the Society for Research in Child Development meeting, Kansas City.

Flavell, J. H., Beach, D. R., & Chinsky, J. M. (1966). Spontaneous verbal rehearsal in a memory task as a function of age. *Child Development, 37,* 283–299.

Flavell, J. H., Miller, P. H., & Miller, S. A. (1993). *Cognitive development* (3rd ed.). Cognitive development. Englewood Cliffs, NJ: Prentice-Hall.

Flavell, J. H. (1979). Metacognition and cognitive monitoring: A new area of psychological inquiry. *American Psychologist, 34,* 906–911.

Flavell, J. H. (1985). *Cognitive development* (2nd ed.). Englewood Cliffs, NJ: Prentice-Hall.

Flavell, J. H. (1992). Cognitive development: Past, present, and future. *Developmental Psychology, 28,* 998–1005.

Fodor, I. G., & Franks, V. (1990). Women in midlife and beyond: The new prime of life? *Psychology of Women Quarterly, 14,* 445–449.

Fogel, A., Toda, S., & Kawai, M. (1988). Mother-infant face-to-face interaction in Japan and the United States: A laboratory

comparison using 3-month-old infants. *Developmental Psychology, 24,* 398–406.

Folkman, S., & Lazarus, R. (1991). Coping and emotion. In N. Stein, B. L. Leventhal, & T. Trabasso (Eds.), *Psychological and biological approaches to emotion.* Hillsdale, NJ: Erlbaum.

Foner, N. (1984). *Ages in conflict.* New York: Columbia University Press.

Forrester, M. A. (1992). *The development of young children's social-cognitive skills.* Hillsdale, NJ: Erlbaum.

Forsyth, B. W. C., Leventhal, J. M., & McCarthy, P. L. (1985). Mothers' perceptions of feeding and crying behaviors. *American Journal of Diseases of Children, 139,* 269–272.

Foster-Clark, F. S., & Blyth, D. A. (1991). Peer relations and influences. In R. M. Lerner, A. C. Petersen, & J. Brooks-Gunn (Eds.), *Encyclopedia of adolescence* (Vol. 2). New York: Garland.

Fox, L. H., Brody, L., & Tobin, D. (1979). *Women and mathematics.* Baltimore: The Johns Hopkins University, Intellectually Gifted Study Group.

Fox, N. A., Sutton, B., Aaron, N., & Luebering, A. (1989, April). *Infant temperament and attachment: A new look at an old issue.* Paper presented at the Society for Research in Child Development meeting, Kansas City.

Fozard, J. L., & Popkin, S. J. (1978). Optimizing adult development. *American Psychologist, 33,* 975–989.

Fozard, J. (1992, December 6). Commentary in "We can age successfully." *Parade Magazine.* pp. 14–15.

Fraiberg, S. (1959). *The magic years.* New York: Charles Scribner's Sons.

Francis, J., Fraser, G., & Marcia, J. E. (1989). *Cognitive and experimental factors in moratorium-achievement (MAMA) cycles.* Unpublished manuscript, Department of Psychology, Simon Fraser University, Burnaby, British Columbia.

Frankel, A., & Prentice-Dunn, S. (1990). Loneliness and the processing of self-relevant information. *Journal of Social and Clinical Psychology, 9,* 303–315.

Frankl, V. (1984). *Man's search for meaning.* New York: Basic Books.

Franklin, S. T., Ames, B. D., & King, S. (1994). Acquiring the family eldercare role: Influence on female employment adaptation. *Research on Aging, 16,* 27–42.

Fraser, K. (1994, February). *Ethnic differences in adolescents' possible selves: The role of ethnic identity in shaping self-concept.* Paper presented at the meeting of the Society for Research on Adolescence, San Diego, CA.

Frech, C. D., & Willis, S. L. (1993, October). *Training on health problem solving tasks.* Paper presented at the meeting of the Gerontological Association of America, New Orleans.

Freedman, J. L. (1984). Effects of television violence on aggressiveness. *Psychological Bulletin, 96,* 227–246.

Freeman, H. S. (1993, March). *Parental control of adolescents through family transitions.* Paper presented at the biennial meeting of the Society for Research in Child Development, New Orleans.

Freeman, J. (1982). The old, old, very old Charlie Smith. *Gerontologist, 22,* 532.

Freuchen, P. (1961). *Book of the Eskimos.* Cleveland: World Press.

Freud, A., & Dann, S. (1951). Instinctual anxiety during puberty. In A. Freud (Ed.), *The ego and its mechanisms of defense.* New York: International Universities Press.

Freud, S. (1917). *A general introduction to psychoanalysis.* New York: Washington Square Press.

Fried, P., & O'Connell, C. (1991, April). *Marijuana and tobacco as prenatal correlates of child behavior: Follow-up to school age.* Paper presented at the biennial meeting of the Society for Research in Child Development, Seattle.

Fried, P. A., & Watkinson, B. (1990). 36- and 48-month neurobehavioral follow-up of children prenatally exposed to marijuana, cigarettes, and alcohol. *Developmental and Behavioral Pediatrics, 11,* 49–58.

Fried, P. A., Watkinson, B., & Dillon R. F. (1987). Neonatal neurological status in a low-risk population after prenatal exposure to cigarettes, marijuana, and alcohol. *Journal of Developmental and Behavioral Pediatrics, 8,* 318–326.

Friedman, H., & Caron, B. (1991, April). *Trends in outcome of very low birthweight (VLBW) children.* Paper presented at the biennial meeting of the Society for Research in Child Development, Seattle.

Friedman, M., & Rosenman, R. (1974). *Type A behavior and your heart.* New York: Knopf.

Friedrich, L. K., & Stein, A. H. (1973). Aggressive and prosocial TV programs and the natural behavior of preschool children. *Monographs of the Society for Research in Child Development, 38* (4, Serial No. 151).

Fries, J. (1989). *Aging well.* Reading, MA: Addison-Wesley.

Fromm, E. (1955). *The same society.* New York: Fawcett.

Fry, P. S., Slivinske, L. R., & Fitch, V. L. (1989). Power, control, and well-being of the elderly: A critical reconstruction. In P. S. Fry (Ed.), *Psychological perspectives of helplessness and control in the elderly.* Amsterdam: North Holland.

Fulton, R. (1988). The funeral in contemporary society. In H. Wass, F. M. Berardo, & R. A. Neimeyer (Eds.), *Dying: Facing the facts* (2nd ed.). Washington, DC: Hemisphere.

Furman, L. N., & Walden, T. A. (1989, April). *The effect of script knowledge on children's communicative interactions.* Paper presented at the Society for Research in Child Development meeting, Kansas City.

Furman, L. N., & Walden, T. A. (1990). Effect of script knowledge on preschool children's communicative interactions. *Developmental Psychology, 26,* 227–233.

Furstenberg, F. F., Brooks-Gunn, J., & Chase-Lansdale, L. (1989). Teenage pregnancy and childbearing. *American Psychologist, 44,* 313–320.

Furstenberg, F. F. (1988). Child care after divorce and remarriage. In E. M. Hetherington & J. Arasteh (Eds.), *Impact of divorce, single parenting, and stepparenting on children.* Hillsdale, NJ: Erlbaum.

Furstenberg, F. F. (1991). Pregnancy and childbearing: Effects on teen mothers. In R. M. Lerner, A. C. Petersen, & J. Brooks-Gunn (Eds.), *Encyclopedia of adolescence* (Vol. 2). New York: Garland.

Furth, H. G., & Wachs, H. (1975). *Thinking goes to school*. New York: Oxford University Press.

G

Gage, N. L. (1965). Desirable behaviors of teachers. *Urban Education, 1*, 85–96.

Galambos, N. L., & Maggs, J. L. (1989, April). *The after-school ecology of young adolescents and self-reported behavior*. Paper presented at the biennial meeting of the Society for Research in Child Development, Kansas City.

Galinsky, E., & David, J. (1988). *The preschool years: Family strategies that work—from experts and parents*. New York: Times Books.

Gallagher, J. J., Trohanis, P. L., & Clifford, R. M. (1989). *Policy implementation and PL 99-457*. Baltimore: Paul H. Brookes.

Gallagher, S. K., & Gerstel, N. (1993). Kinkeeping and friend keeping among older women: The effect of marriage. *The Gerontologist, 33*, 675–681.

Gallup, A. M., & Clark, D. L. (1987). The 19th annual Gallup poll of the public's attitude toward the public schools. *Phi Delta Kappan, 69*, 17–30.

Gallup Report. (1987). *Legalized gay relations* (Gallup Report No. 254, p. 25).

Galotti, K. M., Kozberg, S. F., & Appleman, D. (in press). Younger and older adolescents' thinking about commitments. *Journal of Experimental Child Psychology*.

Galotti, K. M., Kozberg, S. F., & Farmer, M. C. (1990, March). *Gender and developmental differences in adolescents' conceptions of moral reasoning*. Paper presented at the meeting of the Society for Research in Adolescence, Atlanta.

Galotti, K. M. (1989). Approaches to studying formal and everyday reasoning. *Psychological Bulletin, 105*, 331–351.

Ganzel, A. K., & Jacobs, J. E. (1992, March). *Everyday decision-making by families: A comparison of outcomes and processes*. Paper presented at the meeting of the Society for Research on Adolescence, Washington, DC.

Garbarino, J. (1976). The ecological correlates of child abuse: The impact of socioeconomic stress on mothers. *Child Development, 47*, 178–185.

Garden, A. (1989). Burnout: The effect of psychological type on research findings. *Journal of Occupational Psychology, 62*, 223–234.

Gardner, B. T., & Gardner, R. A. (1971). Two-way communication with an infant chimpanzee. In A. Schrier & F. Stollnitz (Eds.), *Behavior of nonhuman primates* (Vol. 4). New York: Academic Press.

Gardner, H. (1983). *Frames of mind*. New York: Basic Books.

Gardner, H. (1993, March). *A developmental approach to understanding developmental constraints and disciplinary opportunities*. Paper presented at the biennial meeting of the Society for Research in Child Development, New Orleans.

Gardner, H. (1989). Beyond a modular view of mind. In W. Damon (Ed.), *Child development today and tomorrow*. San Francisco: Jossey-Bass.

Gardner, L. I., Stern, M. P., Haffner, S. M., Gaskill, S. P., Hazuda, H. P., Relethford, J. H., & Eifter, C. W. (1984). Prevalence of diabetes in Mexican Americans: Relationships to percent of gene pool derived from Native American sources. *Diabetes, 33*, 86–92.

Gardner, R. (1983). *The boys and girls book about divorce*. Northvale, NJ: Jason Aronson.

Garfein, A. J., Schaie, K. W., & Willis, S. L. (1988). Microcomputer proficiency in later-middle-aged adults: Teaching old dogs new tricks. *Social Behaviour, 3*, 131–148.

Gargiulo, J., Attie, I., Brooks-Gunn, J., & Warren, M. P. (1987). Girls' dating behavior as a function of social context and maturation. *Developmental Psychology, 23*, 730–737.

Garrison, W. T., & McQuiston, S. (1989). *Chronic illness during childhood and adolescence*. Newbury Park, CA: Sage.

Garton, A. F. (1992). *Social interaction and the development of language and cognition*. Hillsdale, NJ: Erlbaum.

Garvey, C. (1977) *Play*. Cambridge, MA: Harvard University Press.

Garwood, S. G., Phillips, D., Hartman, A., & Zigler, E. F. (1989). As the pendulum swings: Federal agency programs for children. *American Psychologist, 44*, 434–440.

Gatz, M., Popkin, S. J., Pino, C. D., & VandenBos, G. R. (1985). Psychological interventions with older adults. In J. E. Birren & K. W. Schaie (Eds.), *Handbook of the psychology of aging* (2nd ed.). New York: Van Nostrand Reinhold.

Gatz, M. (1989). Clinical psychology and aging. In M. Storandt & G. R. VandenBos (Eds.), *The adult years: Continuity and change*. Washington, DC: American Psychological Association.

Gatz, M. (1992). The mental health system and older adults. *American Psychologist, 47*, 741–751.

Gelfand, D. E. (1982). *Aging: The ethnic factor*. Boston: Little, Brown.

Gelfand, D. M., Teti, D. M., & Fox, C. E. R. (1992). Sources of parenting stress for depressed and nondepressed mothers of infants. *Journal of Clinical Child Psychology, 21*, 262–272.

Gelles, R. J., & Conte, J. R. (1990). Domestic violence and sexual abuse of children: A review of research in the eighties. *Journal of Marriage and the Family, 52*, 1045–1058.

Gelman, R., & Baillargeon, R. (1983). A review of some Piagetian concepts. In P. H. Mussen (Ed.), *Handbook of child psychology* (4th ed., Vol. 3). New York: Wiley.

Gelman, R. (1969). Conservation acquisition: A problem of learning to attend to relevant attributes. *Journal of Experimental Child Psychology, 7*, 67–87.

Gelman, R. (1972). Logical capacity of very young children: Number invariance rules. *Child Development, 43*, 75–90.

Gelman, R. (1991). Epigenetic foundations of knowledge structures: Initial and transcendent constructions. In S. Carey and R. Gelman (Eds.), *The epigenesis of mind: Essays on biology and cognition*. Hillsdale, NJ: Erlbaum.

George, L. K., Blazer, D. F., Winfield-Laird, I., Leaf, P. J., & Fischbach, R. L. (1988). Psychiatric disorders and mental health service use in later life: Evidence from the Epidemiologic Catchment Area program. In J. Brody and G. Maddox (Eds.), *Epidemiology and aging*. New York: Springer.

George, R. (1987). *Youth policies and programs in selected countries*. Washington, DC: William T. Grant Foundation.

Gerber, A. (1992). *Language-related learning disabilities*. Baltimore: Paul H. Brookes.

Gerlach, J. (1991). Introduction: Women, education, and aging. *Educational Gerontology, 17*, iii.

Gerson, G. S. (1977). The psychology of grief and mourning in Judaism. *Journal of Religion and Health, 16*, 260–274.

Gerson, K. (1986). *Hard choices: How women decide about work, career, and motherhood*. Berkeley: University of California Press.

Gesell, A. (1934). *An atlas of infant behavior*. New Haven, CT: Yale University Press.

Gewirtz, J. (1977). Maternal responding and the conditioning of infant crying: Directions of influence within the attachment-acquisition process. In B. C. Etzel, J. M. LeBlanc, & D. M. Baer (Eds.), *New developments in behavioral research*. Hillsdale, NJ: Erlbaum.

Gibbs, J. T., & Huang, L. N. (1989). A conceptual framework for assessing and treating minority youth. In J. T. Gibbs & L. N. Huang (Eds.), *Children of color*. San Francisco: Jossey-Bass.

Gibbs, N. (1992, December 28). Mercy's friend or foe? *Time*, pp. 36–37.

Gibson, E. J., & Spelke, E. S. (1983). The development of perception. In P. H. Mussen (Ed.), *Handbook of child psychology* (4th ed., Vol. 3). New York: Wiley.

Gibson, E. J., & Walk, R. D. (1960). The "visual cliff." *Scientific American, 202*, 64–71.

Gibson, E. J. (1969). *The principles of perceptual learning and development*. New York: Appleton-Century-Crofts.

Gibson, E. J. (1989). Exploratory behavior in the development of perceiving, acting, and the acquiring of knowledge. *Annual Review of Psychology, 39*. Palo Alto, CA: Annual Reviews.

Gilligan, C., & Attanucci, J. (1988). Two moral orientations. In C. Gilligan, J. V. Ward, J. M. Taylor, and B. Bardige (Eds.), *Mapping the moral domain*. Cambridge, MA: Harvard University Press.

Gilligan, C., Brown, L. M., & Rogers, A. G. (1990). Psyche embedded: A place for body, relationships, and culture in personality theory. In A. I. Rabin, R. A. Zucker, R. A. Emmons, & S. Frank (Eds.), *Studying persons and lives*. New York: Springer.

Gilligan, C. (1982). *In a different voice*. Cambridge, MA: Harvard University Press.

Gilligan, C. (1990). Teaching Shakespeare's sister. In C. Gilligan, N. Lyons, & T. Hammer (Eds.), *Making connections: The relational worlds of adolescent girls at Emma Willard School*. Cambridge, MA: Harvard University Press.

Gilligan, C. (1991, April). *How should "we" talk about development?* Paper presented at the biennial meeting of the Society for Research in Child Development, Seattle.

Gilligan, C. (1992, May). *Joining the resistance: Girls' development in adolescence.* Paper presented at the symposium on development and vulnerability in close relationships, Montreal.

Ginott, H. (1969). *Between parent and teenager.* New York: Avon.

Ginsburg, H., & Opper, S. (1988). *Piaget's theory of intellectual development.* Englewood Cliffs, NJ: Prentice-Hall.

Ginzberg, E., Ginzberg, S. W., Axelrad, S., & Herman, J. L. (1951). *Occupational choice.* New York: Columbia University.

Ginzberg, E. (1972). Toward a theory of occupational choice: A restatement. *Vocational Guidance Quarterly, 20,* 169–176.

Gladden, W. G. (1991). *Planning and building a stepfamily.* Huntington, NY: William Gladden Foundation.

Glaser, R. (1989). The reemergence of learning theory within instructional research. *American Psychologist, 45,* 29–39.

Glasser, W. (1990). The quality school. *Phi Delta Kappan,* pp. 424–435.

Glick, J. (1991, April). *The uses and abuses of Vygotsky.* Paper presented at the Society for Research in Child Development meeting, Seattle.

Gnepp, J. (1989). Children's use of personal information to understand other people's feelings. In C. Saarni & P. L. Harris (Eds.), *Children's understanding of emotion.* Cambridge, England: Cambridge University Press.

Golan, N. (1975). Wife to widow to woman. *Social Work, 20,* 369–374.

Golan, N. (1986). *The perilous bridge.* New York: Free Press.

Gold, M., & Petronio, R. J. (1980). Delinquent behavior in adolescence. In J. Adelson (Ed.), *Handbook of adolescent psychology.* New York: Wiley.

Goldberg, H. (1979). *The hazards of being male.* New York: Signet.

Goldberg, H. (1980). *The new male.* New York: Signet.

Goldsmith, H. H., & Gottesman, I. I. (1981). Origins of variation in behavioral style: A longitudinal study of temperament in young twins. *Child Development, 52,* 91–103.

Goldsmith, H. H., Rothbart, M. K., Crowley, J. M., Harmon-Losova, S. G., & Bowden, L. M. (1991, April). *Behavioral assessment of early temperament in the laboratory.* Paper presented at the biennial meeting of the Society for Research in Child Development, Seattle.

Goldsmith, H. H. (1988, August). *Does early temperament predict late development?* Paper presented at the meeting of the American Psychological Association, Atlanta.

Goldsmith, H. H. (1994, Winter). The behavior-genetic approach to development and experience: Contexts and constraints. *SRCD Newsletter, 1, 6,* 10–11.

Goleman, D. (1991, August 7). Child's love of cruelty may hint of the future killer. *The New York Times,* p. A10.

Golombok, S., & Fivush, R. (1994). *Gender development.* New York: Cambridge University Press.

Gonyea, J. G. (1994). Introduction to the special issue on work and eldercare. *Research on Aging, 16,* 3–6.

Goodchilds, J. D., & Zellman, G. L. (1984). Sexual signaling and sexual aggression in adolescent relationships. In N. M. Malamuth & E. D. Donnerstein (Eds.), *Pornography and sexual aggression* New York: Academic Press.

Goodman, G., Andrews, T., Jones, S., Weinstein, J., & Weissman, A. (1993, March). *Maternal depression and behavioral sensitivity, and children's attachment representations and behavioral outcomes.* Paper presented at the biennial meeting of the Society for Research in Child Development, New Orleans.

Goodman, R. A., Mercy, J. A., Loya, F., Rosenberg, M. L., Smith, J. C., Allen, N. H., Vargas, L., & Kolts, R. (1986). Alcohol use and interpersonal violence: Alcohol detected in homicide victims. *American Journal of Public Health, 76,* 144–149.

Goodman, S. (1979). *You and your child: From birth to adolescence.* Skokie IL: Rand McNally.

Gopnik, A., & Wellman, H. (1993, March). *The child's theory of mind.* Paper presented at the biennial meeting of the Society for Research in Child Development, New Orleans.

Gorman, K., & Pollitt, E. (1991, April). *The effects of early supplementary feeding on cognitive outcomes in adolescence in rural Guatemala.* Paper presented at the biennial meeting of the Society for Research in Child Development, Seattle.

Goswami, U., & Bryant, P. (1990). *Phonological skills and learning to read.* Hillsdale, NJ: Erlbaum.

Gottfredson, G. D., & Holland, J. L. (1989). *Dictionary of Holland occupational titles* (2nd ed.). Odessa, FL: Psychological Assessment Resources.

Gottfredson, L. (1980). Construct validity of Holland's occupational typology in terms of prestige, census, Department of Labor, and other classification systems. *Journal of Applied Psychology, 65,* 697–714.

Gottfried, A. E., & Gottfried, A. W. (1989, April). *Home environment and children's academic intrinsic motivation: A longitudinal study.* Paper presented at the biennial meeting of the Society for Child Development, Kansas City.

Gottfried, A. E., Fleming, J. S., & Gottfried, A. W. (in press). Role of parental motivational practices in children's academic intrinsic motivation and achievement. *Educational Psychology.*

Gottfried, A. E., Gottfried, A. W., & Bathurst, K. (1988). Maternal employment, family environment, and children's development: Infancy through the school years. In A. E. Gottfried & A. W. Gottfried (Eds.), *Maternal employment and children's development: Longitudinal research.* New York: Plenum.

Gottfried, A. W., & Lussier, C. M. (1993, March). *Continuity, stability, and change in temperament: A 10-year longitudinal investigation from infancy through adolescence.* Paper presented at the biennial meeting of the Society for Child Development, New Orleans.

Gottlieb, D. (1966). Teaching and students: The views of Negro and white teachers. *Sociology of Education, 37,* 345–353.

Gottlieb, G. (1991a). Epigenetic systems view of human development. *Developmental Psychology, 27,* 33–34.

Gottman, J. M., & Parker, J. G. (Eds.). (1987). *Conversations of friends.* New York: Cambridge University Press.

Gould, R. L. (1975). Adult life stages: Growth toward self-tolerance. *Psychology Today, 8,* 74–78.

Gould, R. L. (1978). *Transformations: Growth and change in adult life.* New York: Simon & Schuster.

Gould, R. L. (1980). Transformations during early and middle adult years. In N. J. Smelser & E. H. Erikson (Eds.), *Themes of work and love in adulthood.* Cambridge, MA: Harvard University Press.

Gould, R. L. (1994). Transformational tasks in adulthood. In G. H. Pollock & S. I. Greenspan (Eds.), *The course of life.* Madison, CT: International Universities Press.

Gould, S. J. (1981). *The mismeasure of man.* New York: W. W. Norton.

Graham, S. (1986, August). *Can attribution theory tell us something about motivation in blacks?* Paper presented at the meeting of the American Psychological Association, Washington, DC.

Graham, S. (1987, August). *Developing relations between attributions affect and intended social behavior.* Paper presented at the meeting of the American Psychological Association, New York.

Graham, S. (1990). Motivation if Afro-Americans. In G. L. Berry & J. K. Asamen (Eds.), *Black students: Psychosocial issues and academic achievement.* Newbury Park, CA: Sage.

Grambs, J. D. (1989). *Women over forty* (rev. ed.). New York: Springer.

Granott, N. (1993, March). *Co-construction of knowledge: Interaction model, types of interaction, and a suggested method of analysis.* Paper presented at the biennial meeting of the Society for Research in Child Development, New Orleans.

Grant, J. P. (1993). *The state of the world's children.* New York: UNICEF and Oxford University Press.

Grant, J. P. (1994). *The state of the world's children.* New York: UNICEF and Oxford University Press.

Grant, J. (1986). *The state of the world's children.* New York: UNICEF and Oxford University Press.

Green, J. (1991). Analyzing individual differences in development. In J. Columbo & J. W. Fagen (Eds.), *Individual differences in infancy.* Hillsdale, NJ: Erlbaum.

Greenberg, B. S., & Brand, J. E. (1994). Minorities and the mass media. In J. Bryant & D. Zillman (Eds.), *Media effects.* Hillsdale, NJ: Erlbaum.

Greenberg, J. S., Bruess, C. E., Mullen, K. D., & Sands, D. W. (1989). *Sexuality* (2nd ed.). Dubuque, IA: Brown & Benchmark.

Greenberg, S. (1994). Mutuality in families. *Journal of Geriatric Psychiatry, 27,* 79–96.

Greene, B. (1988, May). The children's hour. *Esquire,* pp. 47–49.

Greene, M. G., Hoffman, S., Charon, R., & Adelman, R. (1987). Psychosocial concerns in the medical encounter: A comparison of the interaction of doctors with their old and young patients. *Gerontologist, 27,* 164–168.

Grotevant, H. D., Cooper, C. R. (1985). Patterns of interaction in family relationships and the development of identity exploration in adolescence. *Child Development, 56,* 415–428.

Growden, J. H., Corkin, S., Ritter-Walker, E., & Wurtman, R. J. (Eds.). (1993). *Aging and Alzheimer's disease.* New York: New York Academy of Sciences.

Gruskin, E. (1994, February). *A review of research on self-identified gay, lesbian, and bisexual youth from 1970–1993.* Paper presented at the meeting of the Society for Research on Adolescence, San Diego, CA.

Gruys, A. (1993, March). *Security of attachment and its relation to quantitative and qualitative aspects of friendship.* Paper presented at the biennial meeting of the Society for Research in Child Development, New Orleans.

Gubrium, J. F. (1975). *Living and dying at Murray Manor.* New York: St. Martin's Press.

Guilford, J. P. (1967). *The structure of intellect.* New York: McGraw-Hill.

Guisinger, S., Cowan, P., & Schuldberg, D. (1989). Changing parent and spouse relations in the first years of remarriage of divorced fathers. *Journal of Marriage and the Family, 51,* 445–456.

Gunnar, M. R., Malone, S., & Fisch, R. O. (1987). The psychobiology of stress and coping in the human neonate: Studies of the adrenocortical activity in response to stress in the first week of life. In T. Field, P. McCabe, & N. Scheiderman (Eds.), *Stress and coping.* Hillsdale, NJ: Erlbaum.

Gunnoe, M. L. (1994, February). *Noncustodial parents: Main effects or interactions?* Paper presented at the meeting of the Society for Research on Adolescence, San Diego, CA.

Gunter, B. (1994). The question of media violence. In J. Bryant & D. Zillman (Eds.), *Media effects.* Hillsdale, NJ: Erlbaum.

Gustafson, G. E., Green, J. A., & Kalinowski, L. L. (1993, March). *The development of communicative skills: Infants' cries and vocalizations in social context.* Paper presented at the biennial meeting of the Society for Research in Child Development, New Orleans.

Gustafson, S. B., & Magnusson, D. (1991). *Female life careers: A pattern approach.* Hillsdale, NJ: Erlbaum.

Gutek, B. A. (1993). Responses to sexual harassment. In S. Oskamp & M. Costanzo (Eds.), *Gender issues in contemporary society.* Newbury Park, CA: Sage.

Gutherie, G. M., Masanagkay, Z., & Gutherie, H. A. (1976). Behavior, malnutrition, and mental development. *Journal of Cross-Cultural Psychology, 7,* 169–180.

Gutmann, D. L. (1975). Parenthood: A key to the comparative study of the life cycle. In N. Datan & L. Ginsberg (Eds.), *Life-span developmental psychology: Normative life crises.* New York: Academic Press.

Guttman, J. (1993). *Divorce in psychosocial perspective.* Hillsdale, NJ: Erlbaum.

H

Haan, N. (1989). Personality at midlife. In S. Hunter & M. Sundel (Eds.), *Midlife myths.* Newbury Park, CA: Sage.

Haffner, D. (1993, August). *Sex education: Trends and issues.* Paper presented at the meeting of the American Psychological Association, Toronto, Canada.

Hagestad, G. O. (1985). Continuity and connectedness. In V. L. Bengston (Ed.), *Grandparenthood.* Beverly Hills, CA: Sage.

Hahn, A. (1987, December). Reaching out to America's dropouts: What to do? *Phi Delta Kappan,* pp. 256–263.

Haight, B. K. (1991). Reminiscing: The state of the art as a basis for practice. *International Journal of Aging and Human Development, 33,* 1–32.

Haith, M. H. (1991, April). *Setting a path for the '90s: Some goals and challenges in infant sensory and perceptual development.* Paper presented at the Society for Research in Child Development meeting, Seattle.

Haith, M. M. (1992, May). *The nature of expectations in early infancy.* Paper presented at the International Conference on Infant Studies, Miami Beach.

Hakuta, K., & Garcia, E. E. (1989). Bilingualism and education. *American Psychologist, 44,* 374–379.

Halford, G. S. (in press). *Children's understanding: The development of mental models.* Hillsdale, NJ: Erlbaum.

Hall, C. C. I., Evans, B. J., & Selice, S. (Eds.). (1989). *Black females in the United States.* Washington, DC: American Psychological Association.

Hall, W. S. (1989). Reading comprehension. *American Psychologist, 44,* 157–161.

Hallahan, D. P., Kauffman, J. M., Lloyd, J. W., & McKinney, J. D. (1988). Questions about the regular education initiative. *Journal of Learning Disabilities, 21,* 3–5.

Hamburg, D. A. (1993). The opportunities of early adolescence. In R. Takanishi (Ed.), *Adolescence in the 1990s.* New York: Teachers College Press.

Hammen, C. (1993, March). *Risk and resilience in children and their depressed mothers.* Paper presented at the biennial meeting of the Society for Research in Child Development, New Orleans.

Hans, S. (1989, April). *Infant behavioral effects of prenatal exposure to methadone.* Paper presented at the biennial meeting of the Society for Research in Child Development, Kansas City.

Hansell, S. (1991). The meaning of stress. *Contemporary Psychology, 36,* 112–114.

Hanson, R. A., & Mullis, R. L. (1985). Age and gender differences in empathy and moral reasoning among adolescents. *Child Study Journal, 15,* 181–188.

Hardyck, C., & Petrinovich, L. F. (1977). Left-handedness. *Psychological Bulletin, 84,* 385–404.

Hare-Muston, R., & Marecek, J. (1988). The meaning of difference: Gender theory, postmodernism, and psychology. *American Psychologist, 43,* 455–464.

Harlow, H. F., & Zimmerman, R. R. (1959). Affectional responses in the infant monkey. *Science, 130,* 421–432.

Harris, C. S. (1978). *Fact book on aging: A profile of America's older population.* Washington, DC: National Council on Aging.

Harris, L. (1975). *The myth and reality of aging in America.* Washington, DC: National Council on Aging.

Harris, L. (1987, September 3). The latchkey child phenomena. *Dallas Morning News,* pp. 1A, 10A.

Harris, P. L. (1989). *Children and emotion.* London: Basil Blackwell.

Harris, T., Kovar, M. G., Suzman, R., Kleinman, J. C. & Feldman, J. J. (1989). Longitudinal study of physical ability in the oldest old. *American Journal of Public Health, 79,* 698–702.

Harrison, C. A. (1991). Older women in our society: America's silent, invisible majority. *Educational Gerontology, 17,* 111–122.

Hart, C. H., Charlesworth, R., Butts, D. C., & DeWolf, M. (1993, March). *The relationship of attendance in developmentally appropriate or inappropriate kindergarten classrooms to first-grade behavior.* Paper presented at the biennial meeting of the Society for Research in Child Development, New Orleans.

Harter, S., Alexander, P. C., & Neimeyer, R. A. (1988). Long-term effects of incestuous child abuse in college women. Social adjustment, social cognition, and family characteristics. *Journal of Consulting and Clinical Psychology, 56,* 5–8.

Harter, S. (1985). *Self-perception Profile for Children.* Denver: University of Denver, Department of Psychology.

Harter, S. (1988). Developmental processes in the construction of self. In T. D. Yawkey & J. E. Johnson (Eds.), *Integrative processes and socialization. Early to middle childhood.* Hillsdale, NJ: Erlbaum.

Harter, S. (1989). *Self-perception profile for adolescents.* Denver, University of Denver.

Harter, S. (1990a). Processes underlying adolescent self-concept formation. In R. Montemayor, G. R. Adams, & T. P. Gullotta (Eds.), *From childhood to adolescence: A transitional period?* Newbury Park, CA: Sage.

Harter, S. (1990b). Self and identity development. In S. S. Feldman & G. R. Elliott (Eds.), *At the threshold: The developing adolescent.* Cambridge, MA: Harvard University Press.

Hartley, A. A., Hartley, J. A., & Johnson, S. A. (1984). The older adult as computer user. In P. K. Robinson, J. Livingston, & J. E. Birren (Eds.), *Aging and technological advances* (pp. 347–348). New York: Plenum.

Hartshorne, H., & May, M. S. (1928–1930). *Moral studies in the nature of character: Studies in the nature of character.* New York: Macmillan.

Hartup, W. W. (1976). Peer interaction and the development of the individual child. In E. Schopler & R. J. Reichler (Eds.), *Psychopathology and child development.* New York: Plenum.

Hartup, W. W. (1983). Peer relations. In P. H. Mussen (Ed.), *Handbook of child psychology* (4th ed., Vol. 4). New York: Wiley.

Hartup, W. W. (1989). Social relationships and their developmental significance. *American Psychologist, 44,* 120–126.

Haskins, R. (1989). Beyond metaphor: The efficacy of early childhood education. *American Psychologist, 44,* 274–282.

Hauser, S. T., & Bowlds, M. K. (1990). Stress, coping, and adaptation. In S. S. Feldman & G. R. Elliott (Eds.), *At the threshold: The developing adolescent.* Cambridge, MA: Harvard University Press.

Hauser, S. T., Powers, S. I., Noam, G. G., Jacobson, A. M., Weisse, B., & Follansbee, D. J. (1984). Familial contexts of adolescent ego development. *Child Development, 55,* 195–213.

Havighurst, R. J. (1972). *Developmental tasks and education* (3rd ed.). New York: McKay.

Havighurst, R. J. (1973). History of developmental psychology: Socialization and personality development through the life span. In P. B. Baltes & K. W. Schaie (Eds.), *Life-span developmental psychology.* New York: Academic Press.

Havighurst, R. J. (1976). A cross-cultural view. In J. F. Adams (Ed.), *Understanding adolescence.* Boston: Allyn & Bacon.

Hawkins, J., Pea, R. D., Glick, J., & Scribner, S. (1984). "Merds that laugh don't like mushrooms": Evidence for deductive reasoning by preschoolers. *Developmental Psychology, 20,* 584–594.

Hawkins, J. A., & Berndt, T. J. (1985, April). *Adjustment following the transition to junior high school.* Paper presented at the Society for Research in Child Development meeting, Toronto.

Hawley, T. L. (1993, March). *Maternal cocaine addiction: Correlates and consequences.* Paper presented at the biennial meeting of the Society for Research in Child Development, New Orleans.

Hayden-Thomson, L., Rubin, K. M., & Hymel, S. (1987). Sex preferences in sociometric choices. *Developmental Psychology, 23,* 558–562.

Hayflick, L. (1975, September). Why grow old? *Stanford Magazine,* pp. 36–43.

Hayflick, L. (1977). The cellular basis for biological aging. In C. E. Finch & L. Hayflick (Eds.), *Handbook of the biology of aging.* New York: Van Nostrand.

Hayflick, L. (1987). The cell biology and theoretical basis of aging. In L. Carstensen & B. A. Edelstein (Eds.), *Handbook of clinical gerontology.* New York: Pergamon.

Haynie, D., & McLellan, J. (1992, March). *Continuity in parent and peer relationships.* Paper presented at the meeting of the Society for Research on Adolescence, Washington, DC.

Hazan, C., & Shaver, P. (1987). Romantic love conceptualized as an attachment process. *Journal of Personality and Social Psychology, 51,* 511–524.

Heath, S. B., & McLaughlin, M. W. (Eds.). (1993). *Identity and inner-city youth.* New York: Teachers College Press.

Heath, S. B. (1983). *Ways with words: Language, life, and work in communities and classrooms.* Cambridge, MA: Cambridge University Press.

Heath, S. B. (1989). Oral and literate traditions among Black Americans living in poverty. *American Psychologist, 44,* 367–373.

Heath, S. B. (in press). The children of Trackton's children: Spoken and written language in social change. In J. Stigler, G.

Herdt, & R. A. Shweder (Eds.), *Cultural psychology: The Chicago symposia.* New York: Cambridge University Press.

Hechinger, F. (1992). *Fateful choices.* New York: Hill & Wang.

Hechinger, F. (1992). *Fateful choices: Healthy youth for the 21st century.* New York: Carnegie Corporation.

Heckhausen, J., & Schultz, R. (in press). Optimization by selection and compensation: Balancing primary and secondary control in life-span development. *International Journal of Behavioral Development.*

Heinicke, C. M., Beckwith, L., & Thompson, A. (1988). Early intervention in the family system: A framework and review. *Infant Mental Health Journal, 9,* 2.

Heise, D. R. (1991). Careers, career trajectories and the self. In J. Rodin, C. Schooler, & K. W. Schaie (Eds.), *Self-directedness and efficacy.* Hillsdale, NJ: Erlbaum.

Helson, R., & Moane, G. (1987). Personality change in women from college to midlife. *Journal of Personality and Social Psychology, 53,* 176–186.

Helson, R., & Wink, P. (1987). Two conceptions of maturity examined in the findings of a longitudinal study. *Journal of Personality and Social Psychology, 53,* 531–541.

Helson, R., Mitchell, V., & Moane, G. (1984). Personality change in women from college to midlife. *Journal of Personality and Social Psychology, 53,* 176–186.

Henderson, V. L., & Dweck, C. S. (1989, April). *Predicting individual differences in school anxiety in early adolescence.* Paper presented at the meeting of the Society for Research in Child Development, Kansas City.

Henderson, V. L., & Dweck, C. S. (1990). Motivation and achievement. In S. S. Feldman & G. R. Elliott (Eds.), *At the threshold: The developing adolescent.* Cambridge, MA: Harvard University Press.

Hendrix, H. (1988). *Getting the love you want.* New York: Henry Holt.

Hendry, J. (1986). *Becoming Japanese: The world of the preschool child.* Honolulu: University of Hawaii Press.

Hepworth, J. (1994). Qualitative analysis and eating disorders: Discourse analytic research on anorexia nervosa. *International Journal of Eating Disorders, 15,* 179–186.

Hernandez, G. G. (1991). Not so benign neglect: Researchers ignore ethnicity in defining family caregiver burden and recommending services. *Gerontologist, 31,* 271.

Hertzig, M., & Shapiro, T. (in press). Autism and pervasive developmental disorders. In M. E. Lewis & S. Miller (Eds.), *Handbook of developmental psychopathology.* New York: Plenum.

Herzog, A. R., House, J. S., & Morgan, J. N. (1991). Relation of work and retirement to health and well-being in older age. *Psychology and Aging, 6,* 202–211.

Hess, R. D., Holloway, S. D., Dickson, W. P., & Price, G. G. (1984). Maternal variables as predictors of children's school readiness and later achievement in vocabulary and mathematics in the sixth grade. *Child Development, 55,* 1902–1912.

Hetherington, E. M, Hagan, M. S., & Anderson, E. R. (1989). Family transitions: A child's perspective. *American Psychologist, 44,* 303–312.

Hetherington, E. M., & Clingempee, W. G. (1992). Coping with marital transitions: A family systems perspective. *Society for Research in Child Development Monographs* (Serial No. 227).

Hetherington, E. M., Anderson, E. R., & Hagan, M. S. (1991). Divorce: Effects of adolescents. In R. M. Lerner, A. C. Petersen, & J. Brooks-Gunn (Eds.), *Encyclopedia of adolescence* (Vol. 1). New York: Garland.

Hetherington, E. M., Cox, M., & Cox, R. (1978). The aftermath of divorce. In J. H. Stevens & M. Mathews (Eds.), *Mother-child/father-child relations.* Washington, DC: National Association for the Education of Young Children.

Hetherington, E. M., Cox, M., & Cox, R. (1979). Play and social interaction in children following divorce. *Journal of Social Issues, 35,* 26–49.

Hetherington, E. M., Cox, M., & Cox, R. (1982). Effects of divorce on children and parents. In M. E. Lamb (Ed.), *Nontraditional families.* Hillsdale, NJ: Erlbaum.

Hetherington, E. M. (1989). Coping with family transitions: Winners, losers, and survivors. *Child Development, 60,* 1–14.

Hetherington, E. M. (1993, March). *An overview of the Virginia longitudinal study of divorce and remarriage with a focus on early adolescence.* Paper presented at the biennial meeting of the Society for Research in Child Development, New Orleans.

Hetherington, E. M. (1994, February). *The role of parents, siblings, peers, and schools in the development of behavior problems in nondivorced, divorced, and remarried families.* Paper presented at the meeting of the Society for Research on Adolescence, San Diego, CA.

Hetherington, E. M. (in press). An overview of the Virginia longitudinal study of divorce and remarriage with a focus on early adolescence. *Journal of Family Psychology.*

Hiester, M., Carlson, E., & Sroufe, L. A. (1993, March) *The evolution of friendships in preschool, middle childhood, and adolescence: Origins in attachment history.* Paper presented at the biennial meeting of the Society for Research in Child Development, New Orleans.

Hightower, E. (1990). Adolescent interpersonal and familial precursors of positive mental health at midlife. *Journal of Youth and Adolescence, 19,* 257–275.

Hill, C. R., & Stafford, F. P. (1980). Parental care of children: Time diary estimate of quantity, predictability, and variety. *Journal of Human Resources, 15,* 219–239.

Hill, J. P., Holmbeck, G. N., Marlow, L., Green, T. M., & Lynch, M. E. (1985). Pubertal status and parent-child relations in families of seventh-grade boys. *Journal of Early Adolescence, 5,* 31–44.

Hill, J. P. (1980). The early adolescent and the family. In M. Johnson (Ed.), *The 79th yearbook of the National Society for the Study of Education.* Chicago: University of Chicago Press.

Hill, J. P. (1983, April). *Early adolescence: A research agenda.* Paper presented at the biennial meeting of the Society for Research in Child Development, Detroit.

Hinde, R. A., & Gorebel, J. (1989). The problem of aggression. In J. Gorebel & R. A. Hinde (Eds.), *Aggression and war: Their biological bases.* New York: Cambridge University Press.

Hinde, R. A. (1984). Why do the sexes behave differently in close relationships? *Journal of Social and Personal Relationships, 1,* 471–501.

Hinde, R. A. (1992a). Commentary: Can biology explain human development? *Human Development, 35,* 34–39.

Hinde, R. A. (1992b). Developmental psychology in the context of other behavioral sciences. *Developmental Psychology, 28,* 1018–1029.

Hines, M. (1982). Prenatal gonadal hormones and sex differences in human behavior. *Psychological Bulletin, 92,* 56–80.

Hiraga, Y., Cauce, A. M., Mason, C., & Ordonez, N. (1993, March). *Ethnic identity and the social adjustment of biracial youth.* Paper presented at the biennial meeting of the Society for Research in Child Development, New Orleans.

Hirsch, B. J., & Rapkin, B. D. (1987). The transition to junior high school: A longitudinal study of self-esteem, psychological symptomatology, school life, and social support. *Child Development, 58,* 1235–1243.

Hirsch, B. J. (1989, April). *School transitions and psychological well-being in adolescence: Comparative longitudinal analyses.* Paper presented at the biennial meeting of the Society for Research in Child Development, Kansas City.

Hirschhorn K. (1992). Genetic counseling in chromosomal disorders. In R. E. Behrman (Ed.), *Nelson textbook of pediatrics* (14th ed.). Philadelphia: Saunders.

Hirsh-Pasek, K., Hyson, M., Rescorla, L., & Cone, J. (1989, April). *Hurrying children: How does it affect their academic, social, creative, and emotional development?* Paper presented at the biennial meeting of the Society for Research in Child Development, Kansas City.

Hirshorn, B. (1991). Sharing or competition: Multiple views of the intergenerational flow of society's resources. *Marriage and Family Review, 16,* 175–192.

Hobbs, N. (Ed.). (1975). *Issues in the classification of children.* (Vol. 1). San Francisco, Jossey-Bass.

Hobfoll, S. E. (1989). Conservation of resources: A new attempt at conceptualizing stress. *American Psychologist, 44,* 513–524.

Hodapp, R. M., Burack, J. A., & Zigler, E. (Eds.). (in press). *Issues in the developmental approach to mental retardation.* New York: Cambridge University Press.

Hodgman, C. H. (1992). Child and adolescent depression and suicide. In D. E. Greydanus & M. L. Wolraich (Eds.), *Behavioral pediatrics.* New York: Springer-Verlag.

Hofferth, S. L. (1990). Trends in adolescent sexual activity, contraception, and pregnancy in the United States. In J. Bancroft & J. M. Reinisch (Eds.), *Adolescence and puberty.* New York: Oxford University Press.

Hoffman, L. W. (1989). Effects of maternal employment in two-parent families. *American Psychologist, 44,* 283–293.

Hoffnung, M. (1984). Motherhood: Contemporary conflict for women. In J. Freeman (Eds.), *Women: A feminist perspective* (3rd ed.). Palo Alto, CA: Mayfield.

Holland, J. L. (1973). *Making vocational choices: A theory of careers.* Englewood Cliffs, NJ: Prentice-Hall.

Holland, J. L. (1987). Current status of Holland's theory of careers: Another perspective. *Career Development Quarterly, 36,* 24–30.

Holmes, L. B. (1992). General clinical principles in genetic disorders. In R. E. Behrman (Ed.), *Nelson textbook of pediatrics* (14th ed.). Philadelphia: Saunders.

Holmes, T. H., & Rahe, R. H. (1967). The social readjustment rating scale. *Journal of Psychosomatic Research, 11,* 213–218.

Holt, S. A., & Fogel, A. (1993, March). *Emotions as components of dynamic systems.* Paper presented at the biennial meeting of the Society for Research in Child Development, New Orleans.

Holtzman, W. H. (Ed.). (1992). *School of the future.* Washington, DC: American Psychological Association.

Holtzmann, W. H. (1982). Cross-cultural comparisons of personality development in Mexico and the United States. In D. A. Wagner & H. W. Stevenson (Eds.), *Cultural perspectives on child development.* New York: W. H. Freeman.

Holzman, M. (1983). *The language of children: Development in home and school.* Englewood Cliffs, NJ: Prentice-Hall.

Hommerding, K. D., & Kriger, M. (1993, March). *Stability and change in infant-mother attachment: A study of low-income families.* Paper presented at the biennial meeting of the Society for Research in Child Development, New Orleans.

Hood, J. C. (1993). *Men, work, and family.* Newbury Park, CA: Sage.

Hood, K. E. (1991). Menstrual cycle. In R. M. Lerner, A. C. Petersen, & J. Brooks-Gunn (Eds.), *Encyclopedia of adolescence* (Vol. 1). New York: Garland.

Horn, J. L., & Donaldson, G. (1980). Cognitive development II: Adulthood development of human abilities. In O. G. Brim & J. Kagan (Eds.), *Constancy and change in human development.* Cambridge, MA: Harvard University Press.

Horne, M. D. (1988). Handicapped, disabled, or exceptional: Terminological issues. *Psychology in the Schools, 25,* 419–421.

Horney, K. (1967). *Feminine psychology.* New York: W. W. Norton.

Horowitz, F. D., & O'Brien, M. (1989). In the interest of the nation: A reflective essay on the state of knowledge and the challenges before us. *American Psychologist, 44,* 441–445.

Horowitz, F. (1991). Developmental models of early individual differences. In J. Columbo & J. W. Fagen (Eds.), *Individual differences in infancy.* Hillsdale, NJ: Erlbaum.

Hort, B. E., & Leinbach, M. D. (1993, March). *Children's use of metaphorical cues in gender-typing of objects.* Paper presented at the biennial meeting of the society for Research in Child Development, New Orleans.

Houston, A. C., McLoyd, V. C., & Coll, C. G. (in press). Children and poverty: Issues in contemporary research. *Child Development.*

Howard, J. (1982). Counseling: A developmental approach. In E. E. Bleck & D. A. Nagel (Eds.), *Physically handicapped children.* New York: Grune & Stratton.

Howe, C. J. (1992). *Language learning.* Hillsdale, NJ: Erlbaum.

Howes, C., Unger, O., & Seidner, L. B. (1989). Social pretend play in toddlers: Parallels with social play and solitary pretend. *Child Development, 60,* 77–84.

Howes, C. (1988, April). *Can the age of entry and the quality of infant child care predict behaviors in kindergarten?* Paper presented at the International Conference on Infant Studies, Washington, DC.

Hoyert, D. L. (1991). Financial and household exchanges between generations. *Research on Aging, 13,* 205–226.

Huang, L. N., & Gibbs, J. T. (1989). Future directions: Implications for research, training, and practice. In J. T. Gibbs & L. N. Huang (Eds.), *Children of color.* San Francisco: Jossey-Bass.

Huang, L. N., & Ying, Y. (1989). Japanese children and adolescents. In J. T. Gibbs & L. N. Huang (Eds.), *Children of color.* San Francisco: Jossey-Bass.

Hudson, L. M., Forman, E. R., & Brion-Meisels, S. (1982). Role-taking as a predictor of prosocial behavior in cross-age tutors. *Child Development, 53,* 222–234.

Huebner, A. M., Garrod, A. C., & Snarey, J. (1990, March). *Moral development in Tibetan Buddhist monks: A cross-cultural study of adolescents and young adults in Nepal.* Paper presented at the meeting of the Society for Research in Adolescence, Atlanta.

Huesmann, L. R., Eron, L. D., Klein, R., Brice, P., & Fischer, P. (1983). Mitigating the imitation of aggressive behaviors by changing children's attitudes about media violence. *Journal of Personality and Social Psychology, 44,* 899–910.

Huesmann, L. R. (1986). Psychological processes promoting the relation between exposure to media violence and aggressive behavior by the viewer. *Journal of Social Issues, 42,* 125–139.

Hughes, S. O., Power, T. G., & Francis, D. J. (1992, March). *Attachment, autonomy, and adolescent drinking: Differentiating abstainers, experimenters, and heavy users.* Paper presented at the meeting of the Society for Research on Adolescence, Washington, DC.

Hultsch, D. F., & Plemons, J. K. (1979). Life events and life-span development. In P. B. Baltes & O. G. Brim (Eds.), *Life-span development and behavior.* New York: Academic Press.

Hultsch, D. F., Hammer, M., & Small, B. J. (1993). Age differences in cognitive performance in later life: Relationships to self-reported health and activity life style. *Journal of Gerontology, 48,* P1–P11.

Hultsch, D. F. (1971). Adult age differences in free classification and free recall. *Developmental Psychology, 4,* 338–342.

Hunt, M. (1974). *Sexual behavior in the 1970s.* Chicago: Playboy.

Huntley, T. (1991). *Helping children grieve.* Minneapolis: Augsburg Press.

Hurd, M. D., & Wise, D. A. (1989). The wealth and poverty of widows: Assets before and after the husband's death. In D. A. Wise (Ed.), *The economics of aging.* Chicago: University of Chicago Press.

Huston, A. C., Seigle, J., & Bremer, M. (1983, April). *Family environment and television use by preschool children.* Paper presented at the Society for Research in Child Development meeting, Detroit.

Huston, A. C. (1983). Sex-typing. In P. H. Mussen (Ed.), *Handbook of child psychology* (4th ed., Vol. 4). New York: Wiley.

Huston-Stein, A., & Higgens-Trenk, A. (1978). Development of females from childhood through adulthood: Career and feminine role orientations. In P. Baltes (Ed.), *Life-span development and behavior* (Vol. 1). New York: Academic Press.

Hutchings, D. E., & Fifer, W. P. (1986). Neurobehavioral effects in human and animal offspring following prenatal exposure to methadone. In E. P. Riley & C. V. Vorhees (Eds.), *Handbook of behavioral teratology.* New York: Plenum.

Hyatt, C. (1990). *Shifting gears: How to master career change and find the work that's right for you.* New York: Simon & Schuster.

Hyde, J. S. (1981). How large are cognitive gender differences? A meta-analysis using w^2 and d. *American Psychologist, 36,* 892–901.

Hyde, J. S. (1985). *Half the human experience* (3rd ed.). Lexington, MA: D.C. Heath.

Hyde, J. S. (1990). Meta-analysis and the psychology of gender differences. *Signs: Journal of Women in Culture and Society, 16,* 55–69.

Hyde, J. S. (in press). Meta-analysis and the psychology of women. In F. L. Denmark & M. A. Paludi (Eds.), *Handbook on the psychology of women.* Westport, CT: Greenwood Press.

Hynd, G. W., & Obrzut, J. E. (1986). Exceptionality: Historical antecedents and present positions. In R. T. Brown & C. R. Reynolds (Eds.), *Psychological perspectives on childhood exceptionality: A handbook.* New York: Wiley.

I

Ikels, C. (1989). Becoming a human being in theory and practice: Chinese views of human development. In D. I. Kertzer & K. W. Schaie (Eds.), *Age structuring in comparative perspective.* Hillsdale, NJ: Erlbaum.

Ilola, L. M. (1990). Culture and health. In R. W. Brislin (Ed.), *Applied cross-cultural psychology.* Newbury Park, CA: Sage.

Infant Health and Development Program Staff. (1990). Enhancing the outcomes of low birthweight, premature infants: A multisite randomized trial. *Journal of the American Medical Association, 263*(22), 3035–3042.

Ingelhart, R., & Rabier, J. (1986). Aspirations adapt to situations–but why are the Belgians so much happier than the French? A cross-cultural analysis of the subjective quality of life. In F. M. Andrews (Ed.), *Research on the quality of life.* Ann Arbor: University of Michigan, Institute of Social Research.

Inkeles, A., & Usui, C. (1989). Retirement patterns in cross-national perspective. In D. I. Kertzer & K. W. Schaie (Eds.), *Age structuring in comparative perspective.* Hillsdale, NJ: Erlbaum.

Irvine, M. J., Johnston, D. W., Jenner, D. A., & Marie, G. V. (1986). Relaxation and stress management in the treatment of essential hypertension. *Journal of Psychosomatic Research, 30,* 437–450.

Ishii-Kuntz, M. (1994). Paternal involvement and perception toward fathers' roles. *Journal of Family Issues, 15,* 30–48.

Ivy, G. O., MacLeod, C. M., Petit, T. L., & Markus, E. J. (1992). A physiological framework for perceptual and cognitive changes in aging. In F. I. M. Craik & T. A. Salthouse (Eds.), *The handbook of aging and cognition.* Hillsdale, NJ: Erlbaum.

Izard, C. E. (1982). *Measuring emotions in infants and young children.* New York: Cambridge University Press.

J

Jackson, I. I., Breitmeyer, B. G., & Fletcher, J. M. (1993). *Effects of color transparencies on reading in learning disability subgroups.* Paper presented at the biennial meeting of the Society for Research in Child Development, New Orleans.

Jackson, J. F. (1993). Human behavioral genetics, Scarr's theory, and her views on interventions: A critical review and commentary on their implications for African American children. *Child Development, 64,* 1318–1332.

Jackson, J. S., Chatters, L. M., & Taylor, R. J. (Eds.). (1993). *Aging in Black America.* Newbury Park, CA: Sage.

Jackson, J. S. (Ed.). (1992). *Life in Black America.* Newbury Park, CA: Sage.

Jacobs, F. H., & Davies, M. W. (1991, Winter). Rhetoric or reality? Child and family policy in the United States. *Social Policy Report, Society for Research in Child Development,* pp. 1–25.

Jacobs, F. H., Little, P., & Almeida, C. (1993). *Supporting family life: A survey of homeless shelters.* Unpublished manuscript, Department of Child Study, Tufts University, Medford, MA.

Jacobs, J. E., & Potenza, M. (1990, March). *The use of decision making strategies in late adolescence.* Paper presented at the meeting of the Society for Research in Adolescence, Atlanta.

Jacobs, R. H. (1994). His and her aging: Differences, difficulties, dilemmas, delights. *Journal of Geriatric Psychiatry, 27,* 113–128.

Jacobs, S. C., Dosten, T. R., Kasl, S. V., Ostfield, A. M. Berkman, L., & Charpentier, M. P. H. (1987). Attachment theory and multiple dimensions of grief. *Omega, 18,* 41–52.

Jacobson, J. L., Jacobson, S. W., Fein, G. G., Schwartz, P. M., & Dowler, J. K. (1984). Prenatal exposure to an environmental toxin: A test of the multiple-effects model. *Developmental Psychology, 20,* 523–532.

Jacobson, J. L., Jacobson, S. W., Padgett, R. J., Brumitt, G. A., & Billings, R. L. (1992). Effects of prenatal PCB exposure on cognitive processing efficiency and sustained attention. *Developmental Psychology, 28,* 297–306.

Jaffe, D. T., & Scott, C. D. (1991). Career development for empowerment in a changing work world. In J. M. Jummerow (Ed.), *New directions in career planning and the work place.* Palo Alto, CA: Consulting Psychologists Press.

Jagacinski, C. M., & Nicholls, J. G. (1990). Reducing effort to protect perceived ability: "They'd do it but I wouldn't." *Journal of Educational Psychology, 82,* 15–21.

James, W. (1890/1950). *The principles of psychology.* New York: Dover.

Janos, P. M., & Robinson, N. N. (1985). Psychosocial development in intellectually gifted children. In F. D. Horowitz & M. O'Brien (Eds.), *The gifted and the talented.* Washington, DC: American Psychological Association.

Janzen, L., & Nanson, J. (1993, March). *Neuropsychological evaluation of preschoolers with fetal alcohol syndrome.* Paper presented at the biennial meeting of the Society for Research in Child Development, New Orleans.

Japanese Prime Minister's Office. (1982). *International comparative survey of life and perception of the old.* Tokyo: Office of the Aged, Prime Minister's Office.

Jarvik, L. F., Winograd, C. H. (1988). *Treatments for the Alzheimer's patient.* New York: Springer.

Javernik, E. (1988, January). Johnny's not jumping: Can we help obese children? *Young Children,* pp. 18–23.

Jay, G. M., & Willis, S. L. (1992). Influence of direct computer experience on older adults' attitudes toward computers. *Journal of Gerontology, 47,* P250–P257.

Jeans, P. C., Smith, M. B., & Stearns, G. (1955). Incidence of prematurity in relation to maternal nutrition. *Journal of the American Dietary Association, 31,* 576–581.

Jemmot, J. B., & Jones, J. M. (1993). Social psychology and AIDS among ethnic minorities. In J. B. Pryor & G. D. Reeder (Eds.), *The social psychology of HIV infection.* Hillsdale, NJ: Erlbaum.

Jensen, L. C., & Kingston, M. (1986). *Parenting.* Fort Worth, TX: Holt, Rinehart, & Winston.

Jensen, M. R. (1987). Psychobiological factors predicting the course of breast cancer. *Journal of Personality, 55,* 317–342.

Jensen, R. A. (1969). How much can we boost IQ and scholastic achievement? *Harvard Educational Review, 39,* 1–123.

Johnson, C. L. (1994). Introduction: Social and cultural diversity of the oldest-old. *International Journal of Aging and Human Development, 38,* 1–12.

Johnson, C. (1990, May). The new woman's ethics report. *New Woman,* p. 6.

Johnson, D. D. L., Swank, P., Howie, V. M., Baldwin, C., & Owen, M. (1993, March).

Tobacco smoke in the home and child intelligence. Paper presented at the biennial meeting of the Society for Research in Child Development, New Orleans.

Johnson, D. L., & McGowan, R. J. (1984). Comparison of three intelligence tests as predictors of academic achievement and classroom behaviors of Mexican-American children. *Journal of Psychosexual Assessment, 2,* 345–352.

Johnston, L., O'Malley, P., & Bachman, G. (1994, January 31). *Drug use rises among American teenagers.* Institute of Social Research, University of Michigan, Ann Arbor, MI.

Johnston, L., O'Malley, P., & Bachman, J. G. (1993, March). *Drug use rises among the nation's eighth-grade students.* Ann Arbor: University of Michigan, Institute of Social Research.

Johnston, L. D., O'Malley, P. M., & Bachman, J. G. (1987). *National trends in drug use and related factors among American high school students and young adults, 1975–1986.* Ann Arbor: University of Michigan, Institute of Social Research.

Johnston, L. D., O'Malley, P. M., & Bachman, J. G. (1991, January 23). *News release on national drug use by young Americans.* Ann Arbor: University of Michigan, Institute for Social Research.

Johnston, L. D., O'Malley, P. M., & Bachman, J. G. (1992, January 25). *Most forms of drug use decline among American high school and college students.* News release, Institute of Social Research, University of Michigan, Ann Arbor.

Jones, B. F., Idol, L., & Brandt, R. S. (1991). Dimensions of thinking. In B. F. Jones & L. Idol (Eds.), *Dimensions of thinking and cognitive instruction.* Hillsdale, NJ: Erlbaum.

Jones, J. M. (1990, August). *Psychological approaches to race: What have they been and what should they be?* Paper presented at the meeting of the American Psychological Association, Boston.

Jones, J. M. (1993, August). *Racism and civil rights: Right problem, wrong solution.* Paper presented at the meeting of the American Psychological Association, Toronto.

Jones, J. M. (1994). The African American: A duality dilemma? In W. J. Lonner & R. Malpass (Eds.), *Psychology and culture.* Needham Heights, MA: Allyn & Bacon.

Jones, M. C. (1965). Psychological correlates of somatic development. *Child Development, 36,* 899–911.

Jones, W. H., Hobbs, S. A., & Hockenbury, D. (1982). Loneliness and social skills deficits. *Journal of Personality and Social Psychology, 42,* 682–689.

Jorgenson, S. R. (1993). Adolescent pregnancy and planning. In T. P. Gullotta, G. R. Adams, & R. Montemayor (Eds.), *Adolescent sexuality.* Newbury Park, CA: Sage.

K

Kagan, J., & Snidman, N. (1991). Temperamental factors in human development. *American Psychologist, 46,* 856–862.

Kagan, J., Kearsley, R. B., & Zelazo, P. R. (1978). *Infancy.* Cambridge, MA: Harvard University Press.

Kagan, J. (1984). *The nature of the child.* New York: Basic Books.

Kagan, J. (1987). Perspectives on infancy. In J. D. Osofsky (Ed.), *Handbook on infant development* (2nd ed.). New York: Wiley.

Kagan, J. (1989). *Unstable ideas: Temperament, cognition, and self.* Cambridge, MA: Harvard University Press.

Kagan, J. (1992). Yesterday's premises, tomorrow's promises. *Developmental Psychology, 28,* 990–997.

Kagan, S. L. (1988, January). Current reforms in early childhood education: Are we addressing the issues? *Young Children, 43,* 27–38.

Kalichman, S. (1994). Sexuality. In J. A. Simons, S. Kalichman, & J. W. Santrock, *Human Adjustment.* Dubuque, IA: Brown & Benchmark.

Kalish, R. A., & Reynolds, D. K. (1976). *An overview of death and ethnicity.* Farmingdale, NY: Baywood.

Kalish, R. A. (1981). *Death, grief, and caring relationships.* Monterey, CA: Brooks/Cole.

Kalish, R. A. (1987). Death. In G. L. Maddox (Ed.), *Encyclopedia of aging.* New York: Springer.

Kalish, R. A. (1988). The study of death: A psychosocial perspective. In H. Wass, F. M. Berardo, & R. A. Niemeyer (Eds.), *Dying: Facing the facts* (2nd ed.). Washington, DC: Hemisphere.

Kalter, N. (1990). *Growing up with divorce.* New York: Free Press.

Kamerman, S. B., & Kahn, A. J. (Eds.). (1978). *Family policy: Government and families in fourteen countries.* New York: Columbia University Press.

Kamo, Y. (1988). Determinants of the household division of labor: Resources, power, and ideology. *Journal of Family Issues, 9,* 177–200.

Kanda, K., & Mezey, M. (1991). Registered nursing staffing in Pennsylvania nursing homes: Comparison before and after implementation of Medicare's prospective payment system. *Gerontologist, 31,* 318–324.

Kandel, D. B. (1974). The role of parents and peers in marijuana use. *Journal of Social Issues, 30,* 107–135.

Kanner, A. D., & Feldman, S. S. (1991). Control over uplifts and hassles and its relationship to adaptational outcomes. *Journal of Behavioral Medicine, 14,* 187–196.

Kanner, A. D., Coyne, J. C., Schaefer, C., & Lazarus, R. S. (1981). Comparison of two modes of stress measurement: Daily hassles and uplifts versus major life events. *Journal of Behavioral Medicine, 4,* 1–39.

Kantrowitz, B., & Wingert, P. (1989, April 17). How kids learn. *Newsweek,* pp. 4–10.

Karlin, R., & Karlin, A. R. (1987). *Teaching elementary reading.* San Diego: Harcourt Brace Jovanovich.

Kart, C. S. (1990). *Diversity among aged black males.* In Z. Harel, E. A., McKinney, & M. Williams (Eds.), *Black aged.* Newbury Park, CA: Sage.

Kaslow, N. J., Deering, C. G., & Racusin, G. R. (1994). Depressed children and their families. *Clinical Psychology Review, 14,* 39–59.

Kasper, J. D. (1988). *Aging alone: Profiles and projections.* Report of the Commonwealth Fund Commission: Elderly People Living Alone. Baltimore: Commonwealth Fund Commission.

Katz, L., & Chard, S. (1989). *Engaging the minds of young children: The project approach.* Norwood, NJ: Ablex.

Katz, P. A. (1987, August). *Children and social issues.* Paper presented at the meeting of the American Psychological Association, New York.

Kavanaugh, K. H., & Kennedy, P. H. (1992). *Promoting cultural diversity.* Newbury Park, CA: Sage.

Kavin, E. J., & Parcell, S. R. (1977). Sexual aggression: A second look at the offended female. *Archives of Sexual Behavior, 6,* 67–76.

Kearns, D. T. (1988, April). An education recovery plan for America. *Phi Delta Kappan,* pp. 565–570.

Keating, D. P., Menna, R., & Matthews, S. J. (1992, March). *Adolescent cognitive development in everyday life: Dealing with stress.* Paper presented at the meeting of the Society for Research on Adolescence, Washington, DC.

Keating, D. P. (1990). Adolescent thinking. In S. S. Feldman & G. R. Elliott (Eds.), *At the threshold: The developing adolescent.* Cambridge, MA: Harvard University Press.

Keating, D. P. (in press). Structuralism, deconstruction, reconstruction: The limits of reasoning. In W. F. Overton (Ed.), *Reasoning, necessity, and logic: Developmental perspectives.* Hillsdale, NJ: Erlbaum.

Keating, D. (1980). Thinking processes in adolescence. In J. Adelson (Ed.), *Handbook of adolescent psychology.* New York: Wiley.

Keefe, S. E., & Padilla, A. M. (1987). *Chicago ethnicity.* Albuquerque: University of New Mexico Press.

Keeton, K. (1992). *Longevity: The science of staying young.* New York: Viking Press.

Keirouz, K. S. (1990). Concerns of parents of gifted children: A research review. *Gifted Child Quarterly, 34,* 56–62.

Keith, T. Z., Cool, V. A., Novak, C. G., White, L. J., & Pottebaum, S. M. (1988). Confirmatory factor analysis of the Stanford-Binet Fourth Edition: Testing the theory-test match. *Journal of School Psychology, 26,* 253–274.

Keller, A., Ford, L., & Meacham, J. (1978). Dimensions of self-concept in preschool children. *Developmental Psychology, 14,* 483–489.

Kelly, J. A., & de Armas, A. (1989). Social relationships in adolescence: Skill development and training. In J. Worell & F. Danner (Eds.), *The adolescent as decision-maker.* San Diego: Academic Press.

Kennedy, J. H. (1990). Determinants of peer social status: Contributions of physical appearance, reputation, and behavior. *Journal of Youth and Adolescence, 19,* 233–244.

Kenniston, K. (1970). Youth: A "new" stage of life. *American Scholar, 39,* 631–654.

Kephart, W. M. (1967). Some correlates of romantic love. *Journal of Marriage and the Family, 29,* 470–474.

Kerr, B. A. (1983). Raising the career aspirations of gifted girls. *Vocational Guidance Quarterly, 32,* 37–43.

Kerschner, P. A., & Chelsvig Hart, K. (1984). The aged user and technology. In R. E. Dunkel, M. R. Haug, & M. Rosenberg (Eds.), *Communications technology and the elderly: Issues and forecasts.* New York: Springer.

Kessen, W., Haith, M. M., & Salapatek, P. (1970). Human infancy. In P. H. Mussen (Ed.), *Manual of child psychology* (3rd ed., Vol. 1). New York: Wiley.

Kidorf, I. W. (1966). The shiva: A form of group psychotherapy. *Journal of Religion and Health, 5,* 43–46.

Kiebzak, G. M. (1991). Age-related bone changes. *Experimental Gerontology, 26,* 171–188.

Kiecolt-Glaser, J. K., & Glaser, R. (1988). Behavioral influences on immune function. In T. Field, P. McCabe, & N. Schneiderman(Eds.), *Stress and coping across development.* Hillsdale, NJ: Erlbaum.

King, N. (1982). School uses of materials traditionally associated with children's play. *Theory and Research in Social Education, 10,* 17–27.

Kinney, J. M., & Ogrocki, P. K. (1991). Stressors and well-being among caregivers to older adults with Dementia: The in-home versus nursing home experience. *Gerontologist, 31,* 217–223.

Kinsey, A. C., Pomeroy, W. B., & Martin, E. E. (1948). *Sexual behavior in the human male.* Philadelphia: Saunders.

Kirwan, J. P., Kohrt, W. M., Wojta, D. M., Bourey, R. E., & Holloszy, J. O. (1993). Endurance exercise training reduces glucose-stimulated insulin levels in 60- to 70-year-old men and women. *Journal of Gerontology, 48,* M84–M90.

Kitch, D. L. (1987). Hospice. In R. J. Corsini (Ed.), *Concise encyclopedia of psychology.* New York: Wiley.

Kite, M. E., Deaux, K., & Miele, M. (1991). Stereotypes of young and old: Does age outweigh gender? *Psychology and Aging, 6,* 19–27.

Klahr, D. (1989). Information-processing approaches. In R. Vasta (Ed.), *Six theories of child development: Revised formulations and current issues.* Greenwich, CT: JAI Press.

Klass, D. (1988). *Parental grief.* New York: Springer.

Klaus, M., & Kennell, H. H. (1976). *Maternal-infant bonding.* St. Louis: Mosby.

Kliegl, R., Smith, J., & Baltes, P. B. (1989). Testing-the-limits and the study of age differences in cognitive plasticity of a mnemonic skill. *Developmental Psychology, 25,* 247–256.

Kliegl, R., Smith, J., & Baltes, P. B. (1990). On the locus and process of magnification of age differences during mnemonic training. *Developmental Psychology, 26,* 894–904.

Kline, D. W., & Schieber, F. (1985). Vision and aging. In J. E. Birren & K. W. Schaie (Eds.), *Handbook of the psychology of aging* (2nd ed.). New York: Van Nostrand Reinhold.

Klonoff, E. A. (1991, August). *Ethnicity and women's health: The neglected women.* Paper

presented at the meeting of the American Psychological Association, San Francisco.

Knight, R. A., Rosenberg, R., & Schneider, B. (1985). Classification of sexual offenders: Perspectives, methods, and validation. In A. W. Burgess (Ed.), *Rape and sexual assault.* New York: Garland.

Knott, J. E. (1979). Death education for all. In H. Wass (Ed.), *Dying: Facing the facts.* Washington, DC: Hemisphere.

Knouse, S. B. (1992). Hispanics and work: An overview. On S. B. Knouse, R. Rosenfeld, & A. Culbertson (Eds.), *Hispanics in the workplace.* Newbury Park: CA: Sage.

Kobak, R., & Cole, C. (in press). Attachment and meta-monitoring: Implications for adolescent autonomy and psychopathology. In D. Cicchetti (Ed.), *Rochester Symposium on Development and Psychopathology: Vol. 5: Disorders of the Self.* Rochester, NY: University of Rochester Press.

Kobak, R., Cole, C., Fleming, W., Ferenz-Gilles, R., & Bamble, W. (1993). Attachment and emotional regulation during mother-teen problem-solving: A control theory analysis. *Child Development, 64,* 231–245.

Kobak, R., Ferenz-Gillies, R., Everhart, E., & Seabrook, L. (1992, March). *Maternal attachment strategies and autonomy among adolescent offspring.* Paper presented at the meeting of the Society for Research on Adolescence, Washington, DC.

Kobak, R. (1992, March). *Autonomy as self-regulation: An attachment perspective.* Paper presented at the meeting of the Society for Research on Adolescence, Washington, DC.

Kobasa, N., Maddi, S., & Kahn, S. (1982). Hardiness and health: A prospective study. *Journal of Personality and Social Psychology, 42,* 168–177.

Kohlberg, L. (1958). *The development on modes of moral thinking and choice in the years 10 to 16.* Unpublished doctoral dissertation. University of Chicago.

Kohlberg, L. (1966). A cognitive-developmental analysis of children's sex-role concepts and attitudes. In E. E. Maccoby (Ed.), *The development of sex differences.* Palo Alto, CA: Stanford University Press.

Kohlberg, L. (1969). Stage and sequence: The cognitive-developmental approach to socialization. In D. A. Goslin (Ed.), *Handbook of socialization theory and research.* Chicago: Rand McNally.

Kohlberg, L. (1976). Moral stages and moralization: The cognitive-developmental approach. In T. Lickona (Ed.), *Moral development and behavior.* New York: Holt, Rinehart & Winston.

Kohlberg, L. (1986). A current statement on some theoretical issues. In S. Modgil & C. Modgil (Eds.), *Lawrence Kohlberg.* Philadelphia: Falmer.

Kohn, M. L. (1977). *Class and conformity: A study in values.* (2nd ed.). Chicago: University of Chicago Press.

Kopp, C. B., & Kaler, S. R. (1989). Risk in infancy: Origins and implications. *American Psychologist, 44,* 224–230.

Kopp, C. B. (1983). Risk factors in development. In P. H. Mussen (Ed.), *Handbook of child psychology* (4th ed., Vol. 2). New York: Wiley.

Kopp, C. B. (1987). Developmental risk: Historical reflections. In J. D. Osofsky (Ed.), *Handbook of infant development* 2nd ed.). New York: Wiley.

Kopp, C. B. (1992, October). *Trends and directions in studies of developmental risk.* Paper presented at the 27th Minnesota Symposium on Child Psychology, University of Minnesota, Minneapolis.

Korner, A. F. (1971). Individual differences at birth: Implications for early experience and later development. *American Journal of Orthopsychiatry, 41,* 608–619.

Kosik, K. S. (1989). The molecular and cellular pathology of Alzheimer neurofibrillary lesions. *Journal of Gerontology: Biological Sciences, 44,* B55–58.

Kosnik, W., Winslow, L., Kline, D., Rasinski, K., & Sekuler, R. (1989). Visual changes in daily life through adulthood. *Journal of Gerontology: Psychological Sciences, 43,* P63–P70.

Koss, M. P. (1990). The women's mental health research agenda: Violence against women. *American Psychologist, 45,* 374–380.

Kotre, J. (1984). *Outliving the self: Generativity and the interpretation of lives.* Baltimore: The Johns Hopkins University Press.

Kovacs, L. (1988). Couple therapy: An integrated developmental and family system model. *Family Therapy, 15,* 133–155.

Kovar, M. G., & Stone, R. I. (1992). The social environment of the very old. In R. M. Suzman, D. P. Willis, & K. G. Manton (Eds.), *The oldest old.* New York: Oxford University Press.

Krackow, E. (1991, April). *Preschool children's memory for repeated changes in the lunch routine.* Paper presented at the biennial meeting of the Society for Research in Child Development, Seattle.

Krause, N., Jay, G., & Liang, J. (1991). Financial strain and psychological well-being among the American and Japanese elderly. *Psychology and Aging, 6,* 17–181.

Krauss, I. K, & Hoyer, W. J. (1984). Technology and the older person: Age, sex and experience as moderators of attitudes toward computers. In P. K. Robinson, J. Livingston, & J. E. Birren (Eds.), *Aging and technological advances.* New York: Plenum.

Kreutzer, J. C., & Fritz, J. J. (in press). Infusing a diversity perspective into human development courses. *Child Development.*

Krijnen, P., van den Hoek, J. A. R., & Coutinho, R. A. (1994). Do bisexual men play a significant role in the heterosexual spread of HIV? *Sexually Transmitted Diseases, 21,* 24–25.

Krueger, J., & Heckhausen, J. (1993). Personality development across the adult life span: Subjective conceptions vs. cross-sectional contrasts. *Journal of Gerontology, 48,* P100–P108.

Kübler-Ross, E. (1969). *On death and dying.* New York: Macmillan.

Kübler-Ross, E. (1974). *Questions and answers on death and dying.* New York: Macmillan.

Kuhn, D. (1991). Education for thinking: What can psychology contribute? In M. Schwebel, C. A., Maher, & N. S. Fagley (Eds.), *Promoting cognitive growth over the life span.* Hillsdale, NJ: Erlbaum.

Kuhn, D. (1993, March). *Missing links in the education equation.* Paper presented at the biennial meeting of the Society for Research in Child Development, New Orleans.

Kuhn, M., & Sodei, T. (1993). Gray panthers, red kimonos: Perspectives on aging. In R. N. Butler & K. Kiikuni (Eds.), *Who is responsible for my old age?* New York: Springer.

Kupersmidt, J. B., & Coie, J. D. (1990). Preadolescent peer status, aggression, and school adjustment as predictors of externalizing problems in adolescence. *Child Development, 61,* 1350–1363.

Kupersmidt, J. B., Burchinal, M. R., Leff, S. S., & Patterson, C. J. (1992, March). *A longitudinal study of perceived support and conflict with parents from middle childhood through early adolescence.* Paper presented at the meeting of the Society for Research on Adolescence, Washington, DC.

Kurdek, L. A., & Krile, D. (1982). A developmental analysis of the relation between peer acceptance and both interpersonal understanding and perceived social self-competence. *Child Development, 53,* 1485–1491.

Kurtines, W. M., & Gewirtz, J. (Eds.). (1991). *Oral behavior and development: Advances in theory, research, and application.* Hillsdale, NJ: Erlbaum.

Kuypers, J. A., & Bengston, V. L. (1973). Social breakdown and competence. A model of normal aging. *Human Development, 16,* 181–201.

L

Labouvie-Vief, G. (1982). Dynamic development and mature autonomy: A theoretical prologue. *Human Development, 25,* 161–191.

Labouvie-Vief, G. (1985). Intelligence and cognition. In J. E. Birren & K. W. Schaie (Eds.), *Handbook on the psychology of aging* (2nd ed.). New York: Van Nostrand Reinhold.

Labouvie-Vief, G. (1986, August). *Modes of knowing and life-span cognition.* Paper presented at the meeting of the American Psychological Association, Washington, DC.

Ladd, G., & Hart, C. H. (1992). Creating informal play opportunities: Are parents' and preschoolers' initiations related to children's competence with peers? *Developmental Psychology, 28,* 1179–1187.

LaFromboise, T. D., & Low, D. G. (1989). American Indian children and adolescents. In J. T. Gibbs & L. N. Huang (Eds.), *Children of color.* San Francisco: Jossey-Bass.

LaFromboise, T. (1993). American Indian mental health policy. In D. R. Atkinson, G. Morten, & D. W. Sue (Eds.), *Counseling American minorities.* Dubuque, IA: Brown & Benchmark.

LaGrand, L. E. (1991). United we cope: Support groups for the dying and bereaved. *Death Studies, 15,* 207–230.

Lakatta, E. S. (1992, December 6). Commentary in "We can age successfully." *Parade Magazine,* p. 15.

Lally, J. R., Mangione, P., & Honig, S. (1987). *The Syracuse University family development research program.* Unpublished manuscript, Syracuse University, Syracuse, NY.

Lamb, M. E., & Sternberg, K. J. (1992). Sociocultural perspectives on nonparental child care. In M. E. Lamb, K. J. Sternberg, C. Hwang, & A. G. Broberg (Eds.), *Child care in context.* Hillsdale, NJ: Erlbaum.

Lamb, M. E., Frodi, A. M., Hwang, C. P., Frodi, M., & Steinberg, J. (1982). Mother- and father-infant interaction involving play and holding in traditional and nontraditional Swedish families. *Developmental Psychology, 18,* 215–221.

Lamb, M. E., Sternberg, K. J., & Prodromidis, M. (1992). Nonmaternal care and the security of infant-mother attachment: A reanalysis of data. *Infant Behavior and Development, 15,* 71–83.

Lamb, M. E., Sternberg, K. J., Hwang, C., & Broberg, A. G. (Eds.). (1992). *Child care in context.* Hillsdale, NJ: Erlbaum.

Lamb, M. E. (1977). The development of mother-infant and father-infant attachments in the second year of life. *Developmental Psychology, 13,* 637–648.

Lamb, M. E. (Ed.). (1986). *The father's role: Applied perspectives.* New York: Wiley.

Lamb, M. (1994). Infant care practices and the application of knowledge. In C. Fisher & R. Lerner (Eds.), *Applied developmental psychology.* New York: McGraw-Hill.

Landesman-Dwyer, S., & Sackett, G. P. (1983, April). *Prenatal nicotine exposure and sleep-wake patterns in infancy.* Paper presented at the biennial meeting of the Society for Research in Child Development, Detroit.

Landy, F. J. (1989). *Psychology of work behavior* (4th ed.). Chicago: Dorsey Press.

Lane, H. (1976). *The wild boy of Aveyron.* Cambridge, MA: Harvard University Press.

Langer, J. (1969). *Theories of development.* New York: Holt, Rinehart & Winston.

Langlois, S. (1992). Genetic diagnosis based on molecular analysis. *Pediatric Clinics of North America, 39,* 91–110.

Lapsley, D. G. (1989). Continuity and discontinuity in adolescent social cognitive development. In R. Montemayor, G. Adams, & T. Gullotta (Eds.), *Advances in adolescence research* (Vol. 2). Orlando, FL: Academic Press.

Lapsley, D. K., & Murphy, M. N. (1985). Another look at the theoretical assumptions of adolescent egocentrism. *Developmental Review, 5,* 201–217.

Lapsley, D. K., & Rice, K. G. (1988). The "new look" at the imaginary audience and personal fable: Toward an integrative model of adolescent ego development. In D. K. Lapsley & F. C. Power (Eds.), *Self, ego, and identity: Integrative approaches.* New York: Springer-Verlag.

Lapsley, D. K., Enright, R. D., & Serlin, R. C. (1985). Toward a theoretical perspective on the legislation of adolescence. *Journal of Early Adolescence, 5,* 441–466.

Lapsley, D. K., Milstead, M., Quintana, S. M., Flannery, D., & Buss, R. R. (1986). Adolescent egocentrism and formal operations: Tests of a theoretical

assumption. *Developmental Psychology, 22,* 800–807.

Lapsley, D. K. (1991). Egocentrism theory and the "new look" at the imaginary audience and personal fable in adolescence. In R. M. Lerner, A. C. Petersen, & J. Brooks-Gunn (Eds.), *Encyclopedia of adolescence.* New York: Garland.

Larson, J. H. (1988). The Marriage Quiz: College students' beliefs in selected myths about marriage. *Family Relations, 37,* 3–11.

LaRue, A., Dessonville, C., & Jarvik, L. F. (1985). Aging and mental disorders. In J. E. Birren & K. W. Schaie (Eds.), *Handbook of the psychology of aging* (2nd ed.). New York: Van Nostrand Reinhold.

LaVoie, J. (1976). Ego identity formation in middle adolescence. *Journal of Youth and Adolescence, 5,* 371–385.

Lawton, M. P. (1989). Behavior-relevant ecological factors. In K. W. Schaie & C. Schooler (Eds.), *Social structure and aging.* Hillsdale, NJ: Erlbaum.

Lay, K., Waters, E., & Park, K. A. (1989). Maternal responsiveness and child compliance: The role of mood as a mediator. *Child Development, 60,* 1405–1411.

Lazar, I., & Darlington, R. (1982). Lasting effects of early education: A report from the consortium for longitudinal studies. *Monographs of the Society for Research in Child Development, 47* (2–3, Serial No. 195).

Lazar, I., Darlington, R., & Collaborators. (1982). Lasting effects of early education: A report from the consortium for longitudinal studies. *Monographs of the Society for Research in Child Development, 47.*

Lazarus, R. S., & Folkman, S. (1984). *Stress, appraisal, and coping.* New York: Springer.

Lazarus, R. S. (1966). *Psychological stress and the coping process.* New York: McGraw-Hill.

Lazarus, R. S. (1990, August). *Progress on a cognitive-motivational-relational theory of emotion.* Paper presented at the meeting of the American Psychological Association, Boston.

Lazarus, R. S. (1993a). From psychological stress to the emotions: A history of a changing outlook. *Annual Review of Psychology, 44,* 1–21.

Lazarus, R. S. (1993b). Coping theory and research: Past, present, and future. *Psychosomatic Medicine, 55,* 234–247.

Leach, P. (1990). *Your baby & child: From birth to age five.* New York: Knopf.

Leafgren, A. (1989). Health and wellness programs. In M. L. Upcraft & J. N. Gardner (Eds.), *The freshman year experience.* San Francisco: Jossey-Bass.

Leamer, I. (1986). *As time goes by.* New York: Harper & Row.

Lebowitz, B. D. (1987). Mental health services. In G. L. Maddox (Ed.), *The encyclopedia of aging.* New York: Springer.

Leboyer, F. (1975). *Birth without violence.* New York: Knopf.

Lee, D. J., & Hall, C. C. I. (1994). Being Asian in North America. In W. J. Lonner & R. Malpass (Eds.), *Psychology and culture.* Needham Heights, MA: Allyn & Bacon.

Lee, G. R. (1978). Marriage and morale in late life. *Journal of Marriage and the Family, 40,* 131–139.

Lee, I. M., Manson, J. E., Hennekens, C. H., & Paffenbarger, R. S. (1993). Bodyweight and mortality: A 27-year-follow-up. *Journal of the American Medical Association, 270*, 2823–2828.

Lee, L. C. (1992, August). *In search of universals: Whatever happened to race?* Paper presented at the meeting of the American Psychological Association, Washington, DC.

Lee, V. E., Brooks,-Gunn, J., & Schnur, E. (1988). Does Head Start work? A 1-year follow-up comparison of disadvantaged children attending Head Start, no preschool, and other preschool programs. *Developmental Psychology, 24*, 210–222.

LeGall, S. (1990). Academic achievement orientation and help-seeking behavior in early adolescent girls. *Journal of Early Adolescence, 10*, 176–190.

Lehman, H. C. (1960). The age decrement in outstanding scientific creativity. *American Psychologist, 15*, 128–134.

Leibert, R. M., & Sprafkin, J. N. (1988). *The early window: Effects of television on children and youth* (3rd ed.). Elmsford, NY: Pergamon.

Leifer, A. D. (1973). *Television and the development of social behavior.* Paper presented at the meeting of the International Society for the Study of Behavioral Development, Ann Arbor.

Leigh, B. C., Temple, M. T., & Trocki, K. F. (1993). The sexual behavior of U.S. adults: Results from a national survey. *American Journal of Public Health, 83*, 1400–1408.

Lempers, J. D., Flavel, E. R., & Flavel, J. H. (1977). The development in very young children of tacit knowledge concerning visual perception. *Genetic Psychology Monographs, 95*, 3–53.

Lennenberg, E. H., Rebelsky, R. G., & Nichols, I. A. (1965). The vocalization of infants born to deaf and hearing parents. *Human Development, 8*, 23–37.

Leonoff, D. J. (1993, March). *Parental and peer factors in adolescent academic underachievement.* Paper presented at the biennial meeting of the Society for Research in Child Development, New Orleans.

Lepper, M., Greene, D., & Nisbett, R. R. (1973). Undermining children's intrinsic interest with extrinsic rewards. *Journal of Personality and Social Psychology, 28*, 129–137.

Lerner, H. G. (1989). *The dance of intimacy.* New York: HarperCollins.

Lerner, J. V., & Abrams, A. (1994). Developmental correlates of maternal employment: Influences on children. In C. Fisher & R. Lerner (Eds.), *Applied developmental psychology.* New York: McGraw-Hill.

Lerner, J. W. (1988). *Learning disabilities.* Boston: Houghton Mifflin.

Lerner, J. W. (1989). Educational interventions in learning disabilities. *Journal of the American Academy of Child and Adolescent Psychiatry, 28*, 326–331.

Lerner, R. M., Entwisle, D. R., & Hauser, S. T. (1994). The crisis among contemporary American adolescents: A call for the integration of research, policies, and programs. *Journal of Research on Adolescence, 4*, 1–4.

Lerner, R. M., Petersen, A. C., & Brooks-Gunn, J. (Eds.). (1991). *Encyclopedia of adolescence.* New York: Garland.

Lerner, R. M. (1990). Plasticity, person-context relations, and cognitive training in the aged years: A developmental contextual perspective. *Developmental Psychology, 26*, 911–915.

Lerner, R. M. (1991). Changing organism-context relations as the basic process of development: A developmental-contextual perspective. *Developmental Psychology, 27*, 27–32.

LeShan, E. (1990). *It's better to be over the hill than under the hill: Thoughts on life after 60.* New York: Newmarket Press.

Lester, B. M., & Tronick, E. Z., (1990). Introduction. In B. M. Lester & E. Z. Tronick (Eds.), *Stimulation and the preterm infant: The limits of plasticity.* Philadelphia: Saunders.

Lester, B. M., Boukydis, C. F., McGarth, M., Censullo, M., Zahr, L., & Brazelton, T. B. (1990). Behavioral and psychophysiologic assessment of the newborn. In B. M. Lester & E. Z. Tronick (Eds.), *Stimulation and the preterm infant: The limits of plasticity.* Philadelphia: Saunders.

Lester, B. M. (1991, April). *Neurobehavioral syndromes in cocaine-exposed newborn infants.* Paper presented at the biennial meeting of the Society for Research in Child Development, Seattle.

Levenson, J. L., & Bemis, C. (1991). The role of psychological factors in cancer onset and progression. *Psychosomatics, 32*, 124–132.

Leventhal, A. (1994, February). *Peer conformity during adolescence: An integration of developmental, situational, and individual characteristics.* Paper presented at the meeting of the Society for Research on Adolescence, San Diego, CA.

Levin, J. (1980). *The mnemonic '80s: Keywords in the classroom.* Theoretical paper No. 86. Madison: Wisconsin Research and Development Center for Individualized Schooling.

Levine, L. (1992, December 7). Commentary, *Newsweek*, p. 54.

LeVine, S. (1979). *Mothers and wives: Gusii women of East Africa.* Chicago: University of Chicago Press.

Levinger, G. (1974). A three-level approach to attraction: Toward an understanding of pair relatedness. In T. Huston (Ed.), *Foundations of interpersonal attraction.* New York: Academic Press.

Levinson, D. J. (1978). *The seasons of a man's life.* New York: Knopf.

Levinson, D. J. (1980). Toward a conception of the adult life course. In N. J. Smelser & E. H. Erikson (Eds.), *Themes of work and love in adulthood.* Cambridge, MA: Harvard University Press.

Levinson, D. J. (1987, August). *The seasons of a woman's life.* Paper presented at the meeting of the American Psychological Association, New York.

Levinson, R. J. (1987). Euthanasia. In G. L. Maddox (Ed.), *The encyclopedia of aging.* New York: Springer.

Levitt, M. J., Clark, M. C., Rotton, J., & Finley, G. E. (in press). Social support, perceived control, and well-being: A study of an environmentally distressed population. *International Journal of Aging and Human Development.*

Levitt, M. J. (1989). Attachment and close relationships: A life-span perspective. In J. L. Gewirtz & W. F. Kurtines (Eds.), *Intersections with attachment.* Hillsdale, NJ: Erlbaum.

Levy, A. B., Dixon, K. N., & Stern, S. L. (1989). How are depression and bulimia related? *American Journal of Psychiatry, 146*, 162–169.

Levy, G. D., & Carter, D. B. (1989). Gender schema, gender constancy, and gender-role knowledge: The roles of cognitive factors in preschoolers' gender-role steriotype attributions. *Developmental Psychology, 25*, 444–449.

Levy, G. D. (1991, April). *Effects of gender constancy, figure's sex and size on preschoolers' gender constancy: Sometimes big girls do cry.* Paper presented at the Society for Research in Child Development meeting, Seattle.

Levy, S. M. (1985). *Behavior and cancer.* San Francisco: Jossey-Bass.

Lewinsohn, P. M., Rohde, P., Seeley, J. R., & Fischer, S. A. (1991). Age and depression: Unique and shared effects. *Psychology and Aging, 6*, 246–260.

Lewis, C. G. (1981). How adolescents approach decisions: Changes over grades seven to twelve and policy implications. *Child Development, 52*, 538–554.

Lewis, M., & Brooks-Gunn, J. (1979). *Social cognition and the acquisition of the self.* New York: Plenum.

Lewis, M., & Feinman, S. (Eds.). (1991). *Social influences and socialization in infancy.* New York: Plenum.

Lewis, M., Sullivan, M. W., Sanger, C., & Weiss, M. (1989). Self development and self-conscious emotions. *Child Development, 60*, 146–156.

Lewkowicz, D. J. (1988). Sensory dominance in infants: 1. Six-month-old infants' response to auditory-visual compounds. *Developmental Psychology, 24*, 155–171.

Liaw, F., Meisels, S. J., & Brooks-Gunn, J. (1994). *Intervention with low birth weight, premature children: An examination of the experience of intervention.* Unpublished manuscript.

Liaw, F., Meisels, S. J., & Brooks-Gunn, J. (1994). *Intervention with low-birth weight, premature children: An examination of the experience of intervention.* New York: Columbia University, Department of Psychology.

Liben, L. S., & Signorella, M. L. (1993). Gender-schematic processing in children: The role of initial presentation of stimuli. *Developmental Psychology, 29*, 141–149.

Liben, L. S., & Signorella, M. L. (Eds.). (1987). *Children's gender schemata: New directions in child development.* San Francisco: Jossey-Bass.

Lieberman, M. A. (1994). A reexamination of adult life crises. In G. H. Pollock & S. I. Greenspan (Eds.), *The course of life.* Madison, CT: International Universities Press.

Lifton, R. J. (1977). The sense of immortality: On death and the continuity of life. In H. Feifel (Ed.), *New meanings of death.* New York: McGraw-Hill.

Light, P., & Butterworth, G. (1993). (Eds.). *Context and cognition.* Hillsdale, NJ: Erlbaum.

Lightfoot, C. (1993, March). *Playing with desire.* Paper presented at the biennial meeting of the Society for Research in Child Development, New Orleans.

Lindner, M. S. (1992, March). *When dad and mom and adolescent makes four: Adolescents' perceptions of relationships with three parents.* Paper presented at the meeting of the Society for Research on Adolescence, Washington, DC.

Linn, M. C., & Peterson, A. C. (1986). A meta-analysis of gender differences in spatial ability: Implications for mathematics and science achievement. In J. S. Hyde & M. C. Linn (Eds.), *The psychology of gender: Advances through meta-analysis.* Baltimore: The Johns Hopkins University Press.

Linney, J. A., & Seidman, E. (1989). The future of schooling. *American Psychologist, 44,* 336–340.

Lipsitt, L. P., Reilly, B. M., Butcher, M. J., & Greenwood, M. M. (1976). The stability and interrelationships of newborn sucking and heart rate. *Developmental Psychology, 9,* 305–310.

Lipsitz, J. (1983, October). *Making it the hard way: Adolescents in the 1980s.* Testimony presented at the Crisis Intervention Task Force, House Select Committee on Children, Youth, and Families, Washington, DC.

Lipsitz, J. (1984). *Successful schools for young adolescents.* New Brunswick, NJ: Transaction.

Lipson, E. (1991). *The New York Times guide to the best books for children.* New York: Random House.

Little, B. B., Snell, L. M., Klein, V. R., & Gilstrap, L. C. (1989). Cocaine abuse during pregnancy: Maternal and fetal implications. *Obstetrics and Gynecology, 73,* 157–160.

Little, G. A. (1992). The fetus at risk. In R. A. Hoekelman, S. B. Friedman, N. M. Nelson, & H. M. Seidel (Eds.), *Primary pediatric care* (2nd ed.). St. Louis: Mosby Yearbook.

Little, P. (in press). Homeless families in four cities: A multiple-site case study in policy formation. In F. H. Jacobs & M. Davies (Eds.), *Casebook in child and family policy.*

Litwak, E., & Messeri, P. (1989). Organization theory, social supports, and mortality rates: A theoretical convergence. *American Sociological Review, 54,* 49–67.

Litwak, E. (1985). *Helping the elderly: The complementary role of informal networks and formal system.* New York: Guilford Press.

Lively, W., & Bromley, D. (1973). *Person perception in childhood and adolescence.* New York: Wiley.

Livson, N., & Peskin, H. (1981). Psychological health at age 40. Prediction from adolescent personality. In D. M. Eichorn, J. Clausen, N. Haan, M. Honzik, & P. Mussen (Eds.), *Present and past in middle life.* New York: Academic Press.

Lloyd, S. A. (1991). The darkside of courtship: Violence and sexual exploitation. *Family Relations, 40,* 14–20.

Lobstein, D. D., Ismail, A. H., & Rasmussen, C. L. (1989). Beta-endorphin and components of emotionality discriminate between physically active and sedentary men. *Biological Psychiatry, 26,* 3–14.

Lock, R. D. (1988). *Job search and taking care of your career direction.* Pacific Grove, CA: Brooks/Cole.

Loehlin, J. C. (1992). *Genes and environment in personality development.* Newbury Park, CA: Sage.

Logue, A. W. (1986). *Eating and drinking.* New York: W. H. Freeman.

London, M., & Greller, M. M. (1991). Demographic trends and vocational behavior: A twenty year retrospective and agenda for the 1990s. *Journal of Vocational Behavior, 38,* 125–164.

Lonetto, R. (1980). *Children's conception of death.* New York: Springer.

Long, B. C. (1989). Sex-role orientation, coping strategies, and self-efficacy of women in traditional and nontraditional occupations. *Psychology of Women Quarterly, 13,* 307–324.

Long, T., & Long, L. (1983). *Latchkey children.* New York: Penguin.

Longman, P. (1987). *Born to pay: The new politics of aging in America.* Boston: Houghton Mifflin.

Lonner, W. J., & Malpass, R. (Eds.). (1994). *Psychology and culture.* Needham Heights, MA: Allyn & Bacon.

Lopata, H. Z. (Ed.). (1987). Widowhood. In G. L. Maddox (Ed.), *The encyclopedia of aging.* New York: Springer.

Lopata, H. (1988). Support systems of American urban widowhood. *Journal of Social Issues, 44,* 113–128.

Lorenz, K. Z. (1965). *Evolution and the modification of behavior.* Chicago: University of Chicago Press.

Louv, R. (1990). *Childhood's future.* Boston: Houghton Mifflin.

Lowman, R. L. (1991). *The clinical practice of career assessment.* Washington, DC: American Psychological Association.

Luria, A., & Herzog, E. (1985, April). *Gender segregation across and within settings.* Paper presented at the biennial meeting of the Society for Research in Child Development, Toronto.

Lyle, J., & Hoffman, H. R. (1972). Children's use of television and other media. In E. A. Rubenstein, G. A. Comstock, & J. P. Murray (Eds.), *Television and social behavior* (Vol. 4). Washington, DC: U.S. Government Printing Office.

Lynch, M. A., & Roberts, J. (1982). *The consequences of child abuse.* New York: Academic Press.

Lyons, J. M., & Barber, B. L. (1992, March). *Family environment effects on adolescent adjustment: Differences between intact and remarried families.* Paper presented at the meeting of the Society for Research on Adolescence, Washington, DC.

Lyons, N. P. (1983). Two perspectives: On self, relationships, and morality. *Harvard Educational Review, 53,* 125–145.

Lyons, N. P. (1990). Listening to voices we have not heard. In C. Gilligan, N. P. Lyons, & T. J. Hanmer (Eds.), *Making connections.* Cambridge, MA: Harvard University Press.

Lyytinen, P., Rasku-Puttonen, H., Poikkeus, A., Laakso, M., & Ahonen, T. (1994).

Mother-child teaching strategies and learning disabilities. *Journal of Learning Disabilities, 27,* 186–192.

M

Maccoby, E. E., & Jacklin, C. N. (1974). *The psychology of sex differences.* Palo Alto, CA: Stanford University Press.

Maccoby, E. E., & Martin, J. A. (1983). Socialization in the context of the family: Parent-child interaction. In P. H. Mussen (Ed.), *Handbook of Child Psychology* (4th ed., Vol. 4). New York: Wiley.

Maccoby, E. E. (1980). *Social development.* San Diego: Harcourt Brace Jovanovich.

Maccoby, E. E. (1984). Middle childhood in the context of the family. In *Development during middle childhood.* Washington, DC: National Academy Press.

Maccoby, E. E. (1987a, November). Interview with Elizabeth Hall: All in the family. *Psychology Today,* pp. 54–60.

Maccoby, E. E. (1987b). The varied meanings of "masculine" and "feminine." In J. M. Reinisch, L. A. Rosenblum, & S. A. Sanders (Eds.), *Masculinity/femininity: Basic perspectives.* New York: Oxford University Press.

Maccoby, E. E. (1989, August). *Gender and relationships: A developmental account.* Paper presented at the meeting of the American Psychological Association, New Orleans.

Maccoby, E. E. (1992a). The role of parents in the socialization of children: An historical overview. *Developmental Psychology, 28,* 1006–1018.

Maccoby, E. E. (1992b). Trends in the study of socialization: Is there a Lewinian heritage? *Journal of Social Issues, 48,* 171–185.

Maccoby, E. E. (1993, March). *Trends and issues in the study of gender role development.* Paper presented at the biennial meeting of the Society for Research in Child Development, New Orleans.

MacDonald, B. (1989). Outside the sisterhood: Ageism in women's studies. *Women's Studies Quarterly,* 6–11.

MacDonald, K. (1991). Rites of passage. In R. M. Lerner, A. C. Petersen, & J. Brooks-Gunn (Eds.), *Encyclopedia of adolescence* (Vol. 2). New York: Garland.

Mace, N., & Rabins, P. (1981). *The 36-hour day.* Baltimore: The Johns Hopkins University Press.

MacFarlane, J. A. (1975). Olfaction in the development of social preferences in the human neonate. In *Parent-infant interaction,* Ciba Foundation Symposium, 33. Amsterdam: Elsevier.

MacIver, D., Urban, T., Beck, J., Midgley, C., Reuman, D., Tasko, A., Fenzel, L. M., Arhar, J., & Kramer, L. (1992, March). *Changing schools and classrooms in the middle grades: Research on new partnerships, processes, practices, and programs.* Paper presented at the meeting of the Society for Research on Adolescence, Washington, DC.

MacPhee, D., Fritz, J. J., & Miller-Heyl, J. (1993, March). *Ethnic variations in social support networks and child rearing.* Paper presented at the biennial meeting of the Society for Research in Child Development, New Orleans.

Maddi, S. (1986, August). *The great stress-illness controversy.* Paper presented at the meeting of the American Psychological Association, Washington, DC.

Maddox, G. L. (1968). Disengagement theory: A critical evaluation. *Gerontologist, 4,* 80–83.

Magnusson, D., Stattin, H., & Allen, V. L. (1985). Biological maturation and social development: A longitudinal study of some adjustment processes from mid-adolescence to adulthood. *Journal of Youth and Adolescence, 14,* 267–283.

Mahler, M. (1979). *Separation-individuation* (Vol. 2). London: Jason Aronson.

Malina, R. M. (1991). Growth spurt, adolescent (II). In R. M. Lerner, A. C. Petersen, & J. Brooks-Gunn (Eds.), *Encyclopedia of adolescence* (Vol. 1). New York: Garland.

Malinowski, B. (1927). *Sex and repression in savage society.* New York: Humanities Press.

Maltsberger, J. T. (1988). *Suicide risk.* New York: Human Sciences Press.

Malveaux, J. (1993). Race, poverty, and women's aging. In J. Allen & A. Pifer (Eds.), *Women on the front line: Meeting the challenge of an aging America.* Washington, DC: Urban Institute Press.

Mandler, G. (1980). Recognizing the judgment of previous occurrence. *Psychology Review, 87,* 252–271.

Mandler, J. M. (1990). A new perspective on cognitive development. *American Scientist, 78,* 236–243.

Mandler, J. M. (1992, Spring). The precocious infant revisited. *SRCD Newsletter,* pp. 1, 10, 11.

Mandler, J. M. (in press, a). How to build a baby II: Conceptual primitives. *Psychological Review.*

Mandler, J. M. (in press, b). The foundations of conceptual thought in infancy. *Cognitive Development.*

Mann, J. (1991). Discussion—Retirement: What happens to husband-wife relationships? *Journal of Geriatric Psychiatry, 24,* 41–46.

Mann, L., Harmoni, R., & Power, C. N. (in press). Adolescent decision making: The development of competence. *Journal of Adolescence.*

Manton, K. G., & Soldo, G. J. (1992). Disability and mortality among the oldest old: Implications for current and future health and long-term care service needs. In R. M. Suzman, D. P. Willis, & K. G. Manton (Eds.), *The oldest old.* New York: Oxford University Press.

Manton, K. G. (1989). Epidemiological, demographic, and social correlates of disability among the elderly. *Milbank Quarterly, 67,* 13–58.

Maratsos, M. P. (1983). Some current issues in the study of the acquisition of grammar. In P. H. Mussen (Ed.), *Handbook of child psychology* (4th ed., Vol. 3). New York: Wiley.

Maratsos, M. P. (1991). How the acquisition of nouns may be different from that of verbs. In N. A. Krasnegor, D. M. Rumbaugh, M. Studdert-Kennedy, & R. L. Schiefelbusch (Eds.), *Biological and behavioral determinants of language development.* Hillsdale, NJ: Erlbaum.

Marcia, J. E. (1966). Identity six years after: A follow-up study. *Journal of Youth and Adolescence, 5,* 145–160.

Marcia, J. E. (1980). Ego identity development. In J. Adelson (Ed.), *Handbook of adolescent psychology.* New York: Wiley.

Marcia, J. E. (1987). The identity status approach to the study of ego identity development. In T. Honess & K. Yardley (Eds.), *Self and identity: Perspectives across the lifespan.* London: Routledge & Kegan Paul.

Marcia, J. E. (1991). Identity and self-development. In R. M. Lerner, A. C. Petersen, & J. Brooks-Gunn (Eds.), *Encyclopedia of adolescence* (Vol. 1). New York: Garland.

Margolin, G., & Burman, B. (1993). Wife abuse versus marital violence. *Clinical Psychology Review, 13,* 49–74.

Margolin, L. (1994). Child sexual abuse by uncles. *Child Abuse & Neglect, 18,* 215–224.

Marieskind, H. L. (1989). Cesarean section in the United States: Has it changed since 1979? *Birth, 16,* 196–202.

Marin, G. (1994). The expereience of being a Hispanic in the United States. In W. J. Lonner & R. Malpass (Ed.), *Psychology and culture.* Needham Heights, MA: Allyn & Bacon.

Markides, K., & Martin, H. (1979). A causal mode of life satisfaction among the elderly. *Journal of Gerontology, 34,* 86–93.

Markides, K. S., & Mindel, C. H. (1987). *Aging and ethnicity.* Newbury Park, CA: Sage.

Marquis, K. S., & Detweiler, R. A. (1985). Does adopted mean different? An attributional analysis. *Journal of Personality and Social Psychology, 48,* 1054–1066.

Marshall, N. L., & Barnett, R. C. (1993). Work-family strains and gains among two-earner couples. *Journal of Community Psychology, 21,* 64–72.

Marshall, V. W., Rosenthal, C. J., & Daciuk, J. (1987). Older parents' expectations for support. *Social Justice Research, 1,* 405–424.

Martin, B. (1991, August). *Challenges of using the theory of reasoned action in Hispanic health research.* Paper presented at the meeting of the American Psychological Association, San Francisco.

Martin, C. L., & Halverson, C. F. (1987). The role of cognition in sex role acquisition. In D. B. Carter (Ed.), *Current conceptions of sex roles and sex typing: Theory and research.* New York: Praeger.

Martin, C. L., & Rose, H. A. (1991, April). *Children's gender-based distinctive theories.* Paper presented at the Society for Research in Child Development, Seattle.

Martin, C. L. (1989, April). *Beyond knowledge-based conceptions of gender schematic processing.* Paper presented at the biennial meeting of the Society for Research in Child Development, Kansas City.

Martin, C. L. (1993, March). *The influence of children's theories about groups on gender-based inferences.* Paper presented at the biennial meeting of the Society for Research in Child Development, New Orleans.

Martin, H. P. (1992). Child abuse and neglect. In R. A. Hoekelman, S. B. Friedman, N. M. Nelson, & H. M. Seidel (Eds.), *Primary pediatric care* (2nd ed.). St. Louis: Mosby Yearbook.

Martin, J. (1976). *The education of adolescents.* Washington, DC: U.S. Office of Education.

Matas, L., Arend, R. A., & Sroufe, L. A. (1978). Continuity in adaptation: Quality of attachment and later competence. *Child Development, 49,* 547–556.

Matheny, A. P., Dolan, R. S., & Wilson, R. S. (1976). Relation between twins' similarity: Testing an assumption. *Behavior Genetics, 6,* 343–351.

Matthews, A. M. (1993). Issues in the examination of the caregiving relationship. In S. H. Zarit, L. I. Pearlin, & K. W. Schaie (Eds.), *Caregiving systems.* Hillsdale, NJ: Erlbaum.

Mays, V. M. (1991, August). *The role of sexual orientation and ethnic identification in HIV health risk.* Paper presented at the meeting of the American Psychological Association, San Francisco.

Mays, V. (1993, August). *Ethnic identification in the therapeutic process.* Paper presented at the meeting of the American Psychological Association, Toronto, Canada.

McAdams, D. P. (1988). *Power, intimacy, and the life story.* New York: Guilford Press.

McAdams, D. P. (1990). Unity and purpose in human lives: The emergence of identity as a life story. In A. I. Rabin, R. A. Zucker, R. A. Emmons, & S. Frank (Eds.), *Studying persons and lives.* New York: Springer.

McAdoo, H. P., & McAdoo, J. L. (Eds.). (1985). *Black children: Social, educational, and parental environments.* Beverly Hills, CA: Sage.

McAdoo, H. P. (Ed.). (1988). *Black families.* Newbury Park, CA: Sage.

McAdoo, H. P. (Ed.). (1993). *Black families* (2nd ed.). Newbury Park, CA: Sage.

McBride, B. A. (1991, April). *Variations in father involvement with preschool-aged children.* Paper presented at the biennial meeting of the Society for Research in Child Development, Seattle.

McCall, R. B., & Carriger, M. S. (1993). A meta-analysis of infant habituation and recognition memory performance as predictors of later IQ. *Child Development, 64,* 57–79.

McCandless, B. R., & Trotter, R. J. (1977). *Children* (3rd ed.). New York: Holt, Rinehart & Winston.

McCartney, K., Rocheleau, A., Rosenthal, S., & Keefe, N. (1993, March). *Social development in the context of center based on care and family factors.* Paper presented at the biennial meeting of the Society for Research in Child Development, New Orleans.

McClelland, D. C. (1955). Some social consequences of achievement motivation. In M. R. Jones (Ed.), *The Nebraska Symposium on Motivation.* Lincoln: University of Nebraska Press.

McCormick, N. B., & Jessor, C. J. (1983). The courtship game. In E. R. Allgeier & N. B. McCormick (Eds.), *Changing boundaries: Gender roles and behavior.* Palo Alto, CA: Mayfield.

McDaniel, M. A., & Pressley, M. (1987). *Imagery and related mnemonic processes.* New York: Springer-Verlag.

McDonald, W. M., & Nemeroff, C. B. (1991). Neurotransmitters and neuropeptides in Alzheimer's disease. *Psychiatric Clinics of North America, 14,* 421–442.

McGhee, P. E. (1984). Play, incongruity, and humor. In T. Yawkey & A. D. Pellegrini (Eds.), *Child's play: Developmental and applied.* Hillsdale, NJ: Erlbaum.

McGoldrick, M. (1989). The joining of families together through marriage. In B. Carter & M. McGoldrick (Eds.), *The changing family cycle* (2nd ed.). Boston: Allyn & Bacon.

McGrath, J. E., Kelly, J. R. & Rhodes, J. E. (1993). A feminist perspective on research methodology. In S. Oskamp & M. Costanzo (Eds.), *Gender issues in contemporary society.* Newbury Park, CA: Sage.

McGue, M., Pickens, R. W., & Svikis, D. S. (1992). Sex and age effects on the inheritance of alcohol problems: A twin study. *Journal of Abnormal Psychology, 101,* 3–17.

McHugh, M., Koeske, R., & Frieze, I. H. (1986). Issues to consider in conducting nonsexist psychological research: A guide for researchers. *American Psychologist, 41,* 879–890.

McKey, R. H., Condelli, L., Ganson, H., Barrett, B. J., McConkey, C., & Plantz, M. C. (1985). *The impact of Head Start on children, family, and communities: Head Start Synthesis Project* (DHHS Publication No. ODHS 85-31193). Washington, DC: U.S. Government Printing Office.

McKinlay, S. M., & McKinlay, J. B. (1984). *Health status and health care utilization by menopausal women.* Unpublished manuscript, Cambridge Research Center, American Institutes for Research, Cambridge, MA.

McKnight, C. C., Crosswhite, F. J., Dossey, J. A., Kifer, E., Swafford, J. O., Travers, K. J., & Cooney, T. J. (1987). *The underachieving curriculum: Assessing U.S. school mathematics from an international perspective.* Champaign, IL: Stipes.

McLaughlin, D. K., & Jensen, L. (1993). Poverty among older Americans: The plight of nonmetropolitan elders. *Journal of Gerontology, 48,* S44–S54.

McLellan, J. A., Haynie, D., & Strouse, D. (1993, March). *Membership in high school crowd clusters and relationships with family and friends.* Paper presented at the biennial meeting of the Society for Research in Child Development, New Orleans.

McLoyd, V. (1993, March). *Direct and indirect effects of economic hardship on socioemotional functioning in African-American adolescents.* Paper presented at the biennial meeting of the Society for Research in Child Development, New Orleans.

McLoyd, V. (in press). The declining fortunes of Black children: Psychological distress, parenting, and socioemotional development in the context of economic hardship. *Child Development.*

McMaster, L. E., & Wintre, M. G. (1994, February). *The link between parental reciprocity, parental approval, and adolescent substance abuse.* Paper presented at the meeting of the Society for Research on Adolescence, San Diego, CA.

McWhirter, B. T. (1990). Loneliness: A review of current literature, with implications for counseling and research. *Journal of Counseling and Development, 68,* 417–422.

McWhirter, D. P., Reinisch, J. M., & Sanders, S. A. (1989). *Homosexuality/heterosexuality.* New York: Oxford University Press.

Medrich, E. A., Rossen, J., Rubin, V., & Buckley, S. (1982). *The serious business of growing up.* Berkeley: University of California Press.

Medvedev, Z. A. (1974). The nucleic acids in the development of aging. In B. L. Strehler (Ed.), *Advances in gerontological research* (Vol. 1). New York: Academic Press.

Mehegany, D. V. (1992). The relation of temperament and behavior disorders in a preschool clinical sample. *Child Psychiatry and Human Development, 22,* 129–136.

Meltzoff, A., & Kuhl, P. (1989). Infants' perceptions of faces and speech sounds: Challenges to developmental theory. In P. R. Zelazo & R. Barr (Eds.), *Challenges to developmental paradigms.* Hillsdale, NJ: Erlbaum.

Meltzoff, A. N., & Moore, M. K. (1992, May). *Placing imitation within a broader developmental framework: The role of person, movement, social communication, and identity.* Paper presented at the International Conference on Infant Studies, Miami Beach.

Meltzoff, A. N. (1988). Infant imitation and memory: Nine-month-old infants in immediate and deferred tests. *Child Development, 59,* 217–225.

Meltzoff, A. N. (1990, June). *Infant imitation.* Invited address at the University of Texas at Dallas, School of Human Development and Communication Sciences, Richardson, TX.

Meltzoff, A. N. (1992, May). *Cognition in the service of learning.* Paper presented at the International Conference on Infant Studies, Miami Beach.

Mercer, R., Nichols, E. G., & Doyle, G. C. (1989). *Transitions in a woman's life: Major life events in developmental context.* New York: Springer.

Meredith, H. V. (1978). Research between 1960 and 1970 on the standing height of young children in different parts of the world. In H. W. Reece & L. P. Lipsitt (Eds.), *Advances in child development and behavior* (Vol. 12). New York: Academic Press.

Merriam, S. B. (1993). The uses of reminiscence in older adulthood. *Educational Gerontology, 19,* 441–450.

Meyer, B. J. F., Young, C. J., & Bartlett, B. J. (1989). *Memory improved: Reading and memory enhancement across the life span through strategic text structures.* Hillsdale, NJ: Erlbaum.

Meyer, J. W. (1991). Individualisms: Social experience and cultural formulation. In J. Rodin, C. Schooler, & K. W. Schaie (Eds.), *Self-directedness and efficacy.* Hillsdale, NJ: Erlbaum.

Michel, G. L. (1981). Right-handedness: A consequence of infant supine head-orientation preference? *Science, 212,* 685–687.

Miller, C. A. (1987). A review of maternity care programs in Western Europe. *Family Planning Perspectives, 19,* 207–211.

Miller, G. (1981). *Language and speech.* New York: W. H. Freeman.

Miller, J. A. (1991). *Community-based long-term care.* Newbury Park, CA: Sage.

Miller, J. B. (1976). *Toward a new psychology of women.* Boston: Beacon Press.

Miller, J. B. (1986). *Toward a new psychology of women* (2nd ed.). Boston: Beacon Press.

Miller, J. G., & Bersoff, D. M. (in press). Culture and moral judgment: How are conflicts between justice and interpersonal responsibilities resolved? *Journal of Personality and Social Psychology.*

Miller, J. G. (1991). A cultural perspective on the morality of beneficence and interpersonal responsibility. In S. Ting-Toomey & F. Korzenny (Eds.), *International and intercultural communication annual, 15.* Newbury Park, CA: Sage.

Miller L. (1993, June 2). Lowly vitamin supplements pack a big punch. *USA Today,* p. 3D.

Miller, M. E. (1992). Genetic disease. In R. A. Hoekelman (Ed.), *Primary pediatric care* (2nd ed.). St. Louis: Mosby Yearbook.

Miller, P. A., Kliewer, W., & Burkeman, D. (1993, March). *Effects of maternal socialization on children's learning to cope with divorce.* Paper presented at the biennial meeting of the Society for Research in Child Development, New Orleans.

Miller-Jones, D. (1989). Culture and testing. *American Psychologist, 44,* 360–366.

Milligan, S. E. (1990). Understanding diversity of the urban black aged: Historical perspectives. In Z. Harel, E. A., McKinney, & M. Williams (Eds.), *Black aged.* Newbury Park, CA: Sage.

Minkler, M. (1989). Health education, health promotion and the open society: A historical perspective. *Health Education Quarterly, 16,* 17–30.

Minnett, A. M., Vandell, D. L, & Santrock, J. W. (1983). The effects of sibling status on sibling interaction: Influence of birth order, age spacing, sex of the child, and sex of the sibling. *Child Development, 54,* 1064–1072.

Minuchin, P. P., & Shapiro, E. K. (1983). The school as a context for social development. In P. H. Mussen (Ed.), *Handbook of child psychology* (4th ed., Vol. 4). New York: Wiley.

Mischel, W., & Patterson, C. J. (1976). Substantive and structural elements of effective plans for self-control. *Journal of Personality and Social Psychology, 34,* 942–950.

Mischel, W. (1970). Sex-typing and socialization. In P. H. Mussen (Ed.), *Manual of child psychology* (Vol. 2, 3rd ed.). New York: Wiley.

Mischel, W. (1973). Toward a cognitive social learning reconceptualization of personality. *Psychological Review, 80,* 252–283.

Mischel, W. (1984). Convergences and challenges in the search for consistency. *American Psychologist, 39,* 351–364.

Mitchell, V., & Helson, R. (1990). Women's prime of life: Is it the 50s? *Psychology of Women Quarterly, 14,* 451–470.

Mize, J., Pettit, G. S., Laird, R. D., & Lindsey, E. (1993, March). *Mothers' coaching of social skills and children's peer competence: Independent contributions of content and style.* Paper presented at the biennial meeting of the Society for Research in Child Development, New Orleans.

Moely, B. E., Olson, F. A., Halwes, T. G., & Flavell, J. H. (1969). Production deficiency in young children's clustered recall. *Developmental Psychology, 1,* 26–34.

Moll, I. (1991, April). *The material and the social in Vygotsky's theory of cognitive development.* Paper presented at the Society for Research in Child Development meeting, Seattle.

Monagle, K. (1990, October). Women around the world. *New Woman,* pp. 195–197.

Money, J. (1987). Sin, sickness, or status? Homosexual gender identity and psychoneuroendocrinology. *American Psychologist, 42,* 384–389.

Montemayor, R., Adams, G. R., & Gullotta, T. P. (Eds.). (1990). *From childhood to adolescence: A transitional period?* Newbury Park, CA: Sage.

Montemayor, R. (1982). The relationship between parent-adolescent conflict and the amount of time adolescents spend with parents, peers, and alone. *Child Development, 53,* 1512–1519.

Morgan, D. L., & Silverman, R. (1993, October). *Sources of satisfaction with social support among recent widows.* Paper presented at the meeting of the Gerontological Association of America, New Orleans.

Morgan, J. D. (1988). Living our dying: Social and cultural considerations. In H. Wass, F. N. Berardo, & R. A. Neimeyer (Eds.), *Dying: Facing the facts* (2nd ed.). Washington, DC: Hemisphere.

Morris, J. C., & Rubin, E. H. (1991). Clinical diagnosis and course of Alzheimer's disease. *Psychiatric Clinics of North America, 14,* 223–236.

Morrison, A. M., & Von Glinow, M. A. (1990). Women and minorities in management. *American Psychologist, 45,* 200–208.

Morrison, A. M. (1993, August). *Best practices for developing diversity.* Paper presented at the meeting of the American Psychological Association, Toronto, Canada.

Morrongiello, B. A., Fenwick, K. D., & Chance, G. (1990). Sound localization acuity in very young infants: An observer-based testing procedure. *Developmental Psychology, 26,* 75–84.

Morse, J. M., & Johnston, J. L. (Eds.). (1991). *The illness experience.* Newbury Park, CA: Sage.

Mortimer, E. A. (1992). Child health in the developing world. In R. E. Behrman, R. M. Kliegman, W. E. Nelson, & V. C. Vaughan (Eds.), *Nelson textbook of pediatrics* (14th ed.). Philadelphia: Saunders.

Morycz, R. K. (1992). Bereavement to widowhood in later life. In V. B. Van Hasselt & M. Hersen (Eds.), *Handbook of social development.* New York: Plenum.

Morycz, R. (1993). Caregiving families and cross-cultural perspectives. In S. H. Zarit, L. I. Pearlin, & K. W. Schaie (Eds.), *Caregiving systems.* Hillsdale, NJ: Erlbaum.

Moses, J., Steptoe, A., Mathews, A., & Edwards, S. (1989). The effects of exercise training of mental well-being in the normal population: A controlled trial. *Journal of Psychosomatic Research, 33,* 47–61.

Mott, F. L., & Marsiglio, W. (1985, September/October). Early childbearing and completion of high school. *Family Planning Perspectives,* p. 234.

Mounts, N. S. (1992, March). *An ecological analysis of peer influence on adolescent academic achievement and delinquency.* Paper presented at the meeting of the Society for Research on Adolescence, Washington, DC.

Moushegian, G. (1993, January). Personal communication, Program in Psychology and Human Development, University of Texas at Dallas, Richardson, TX.

Moyer, J., Egertson, H., & Isenberg, J. (1987). The child-centered kindergarten. *Childhood Education, 63,* 235–242.

Mullins, L. C. (1993). Reflections on gerontological education into the twenty-first century. *Gerontology and Geriatrics Education, 14,* 11–17.

Munroe, R. H., Himmin, H. S., & Munroe, R. L. (1984). Gender understanding and sex role preference in four cultures. *Developmental Psychology, 20,* 673–682.

Munsch, J., Wampler, R. S., & Dawson, M. (1992, March). *Coping with school-related stress in multi-ethnic sample of early adolescents.* Paper presented at the meeting of the Society for Research on Adolescence, Washington, DC.

Murphy, S. O. (1993, March). *The family context and the transition to siblinghood: Strategies parents use to influence sibling-infant relationships.* Paper presented at the biennial meeting of the Society for Research in Child Development, New Orleans.

Murray, H. A. (1938). *Explorations in personality.* New York: Oxford University Press.

Mussen, P. H., Honzik, M., & Eichorn, D. (1982). Early adult antecedents of life satisfaction at age 70. *Journal of Gerontology, 37,* 316–322.

Myers, D. G. (1992). *The pursuit of happiness.* New York: William Morrow.

Myers, N. A., Clifton, R. K., & Clarkson, M. G. (1987). When they were very young: Almost-threes remember two years ago. *Infant Behavior and Development, 10,* 123–132.

N

Nagy, M. (1948). The child's theories concerning death. *Journal of Genetic Psychology, 73,* 3–27.

National Advisory Council on Economic Opportunity. (1980). *Critical choices for the 80s.* Washington, DC: U.S. Government Printing Office.

National Association for the Education of Young Children. (1986a). *How to choose a good early childhood program.* Washington, DC: NAEYC.

National Association for the Education of Young Children. (1986b). Position statement on developmentally appropriate practice in programs for 4- and 5-year olds. *Young Children, 41,* 20–29.

National Association for the Education of Young Children. (1988). NAEYC position statement on developmentally appropriate practices in the primary grades, serving 5- through 8-year-olds. *Young Children, 43,* 64–83.

National Association for the Education of Young Children. (1990). NAEYC position statement on school readiness. *Young Children, 46,* 21–28.

National Center for Health Statistics. (1989, June). *Statistics on marriage and divorce.* Washington, DC: U.S. Government Printing Office.

National Center for Health Statistics (1989). *National nursing home survey* (DHHS Publication No. PHS 89-1758, Series 13, No. 97). Washington, DC: U.S. Government Printing Office.

Needle, R. H., Su, S. S., & Doherty, W. J. (1990). Divorce, remarriage, and adolescent substance use: A prospective longitudinal study. *Journal of Marriage and the Family, 52,* 157–169.

Neely, A. S., & Bäckman, L. (1993). Long-term maintenance of gains from memory training in older adults: Two 3½-year follow-ups. *Journal of Gerontology, 48,* P233–P237.

Nelson, N. M. (1992). Perinatal medicine. In R. B. Hoekelman, S. B. Friedman, N. M. Nelson, & H. M. Seidel (Eds.), *Primary pediatric care* (2nd ed.). St Louis: Mosby Yearbook.

Neugarten, B. L., & Neugarten, D. A. (1989). Policy issues in an aging society. In M. Storandt & G. R. VandenBos (Eds.), *The adult years: Continuity and change.* Washington, DC: American Psychological Association.

Neugarten, B. L., & Weinstein, K. K. (1964). The changing American grandparent. *Journal of Marriage and the Family, 26,* 199–204.

Neugarten, B. L. Havighurst, R. J., & Tobin, S. S. (1968). Personality and patterns of aging. In B. L. Neugarten (Ed.), *Middle age and aging.* Chicago: University of Chicago Press.

Neugarten, B. L. (1964). *Personality in middle and late life.* New York: Atherton Press.

Neugarten, B. L. (1986). The aging society. In A. Pifer & L. Bronte (Eds.), *Our aging society: Paradox and promise.* New York: W. W. Norton.

Neugarten, B. L. (1988, August). *Policy issues for an aging society.* Paper presented at the meeting of the American Psychological Association, Atlanta.

Neugebauer, B. (Ed.). (1992). *Alike and different.* Washington, DC: National Association for the Education of Young Children.

Newcomb, M. D., & Bentler, P. M. (1988). Substance use and abuse among children and teenagers. *American Psychologist, 44,* 242–248.

Newcomb, M. D., & Bentler, P. M. (1989). Substance use and abuse among children and teenagers. *American Psychologist, 44,* 242–248.

Nicholls, J. G. (1984). Conceptions of ability and achievement motivation. In R. E.

Ames & C. Ames (Eds.), *Motivation in education*. New York: Academic Press.

Nickman, S. L. (1992). Adoption and foster care. In R. A. Hoekelman (Ed.), *Primary pediatric care* (2nd ed.). St. Louis: Mosby Yearbook.

Nitz, V., & Lerner, J. V. (1991). Temperament during adolescence. In R. M. Lerner, A. C. Petersen, & J. Brooks-Gunn (Eds.), *Encyclopedia of adolescence* (Vol. 2), New York: Garland.

Nolen-Hoeksema, S. (1990). *Sex differences in depression.* Stanford, CA: Stanford University Press.

Nottelmann, E. D., Susman, E. J., Blue, J. H., Inoff-Germain, G., Dorn, L. D., Loriaux, D. L., Cutler, G. B., & Chrousos, G. P. (1987). Gonadal and adrenal hormone correlates of adjustment in early adolescence. In R. M. Lerner & T. T. Foch (Eds.), *Biological-psychological interactions in early adolescence.* Hillsdale, NJ: Erlbaum.

Novak, W. (1983). *The great man shortage.* New York: Rawson.

Novy, D. M., Gaa, J. P., Frankiewicz, R. G., Liberman, D., & Amerikaner, M. (1992). The association between patterns of family functioning and ego development of the juvenile offender. *Adolescence, 27,* 25–36.

Nowak, C. A. (1977). Does youthfulness equal attractiveness? In L. E. Troll, J. Israel, & K. Israel (Eds.), *Looking ahead: A woman's guide to the problems and joys of growing older.* Englewood Cliffs, NJ: Prentice-Hall.

Nydegger, C. N., & Mitteness, L. S. (1991). Fathers and their adult sons and daughters. *Marriage and Family Review, 16,* 249–266.

O

O'Brien, M. (1993, March). *Are working mothers different? Attitudes toward parenthood in employed and nonemployed mothers of infants and toddlers.* Paper presented at the biennial meeting of the Society for Research in Child Development, New Orleans.

O'Brien, S. J., & Vertinsky, P. A. (1991). Unfit survivors: Exercise as a resource for aging women. *Gerontologist, 31,* 347–357.

O'Bryant, S. L. (1991). Older widows and independent life-styles. *International Journal of Aging and Human Development, 32,* 31–52.

O'Conner, B. P., & Nikolic, J. (1990). Identity development and formal operations as sources of adolescent egocentrism. *Journal of Youth and Adolescence, 19,* 149–158.

O'Conner, T. G. (1992, March). *Validating a closeness to stepfather scale.* Paper presented at the meeting of the Society for Research on Adolescence, Washington, DC.

O'Connor, E., Crowell, J. A., & Sprafkin, J. (1993, March). *Mother-child interaction in ADHD boys and its relation to secondary symptoms.* Paper presented at the biennial meeting of the Society for Research in Child Development, New Orleans.

O'Donnel, B. (1989, April). *Altering children's gender stereotypes about adult occupations with nonsexist books.* Paper presented at the biennial meeting of the Society for Research in Child Development, Kansas City.

O'Hara, M. (1986). Social support, life events, and depression during pregnancy and the puererium. *Archives of General Psychiatry, 43,* 569–573.

Offer, D., & Church, R. B. (1991). Turmoil, adolescent. In R. M. Lerner, A. C. Petersen, & J. Brooks-Gunn (Eds.), *Encyclopedia of adolescence* (Vol. 2). New York: Garland.

Offer, D., Ostrov, E., Howard, K. I., & Atkinson, R. (1988). *The teenage world: Adolescents' self image in ten countries.* New York: Plenum.

Ogbu, J. U. (1974). *The next generation: An ethnography of education in an urban neighborhood.* New York: Academic Press.

Ogbu, J. U. (1986). The consequences of the American caste system. In U. Neisser (Ed.), *The school achievement of minority children: New perspectives.* Hillsdale, NJ: Erlbaum.

Ogbu, J. U. (1989, April). *Academic socialization of Black children: An inoculation against future failure?* Paper presented at the biennial meeting of the Society for Research in Child Development, Kansas City.

Ogden, J., & Wardle, J. (1991). Cognitive and emotional responses to food. *International Journal of Eating Disorders, 10,* 297–311.

Okun, B. F., & Rappaport, L. J. (1980). *Working with families: An introduction to family therapy.* North Scituate, MA: Duxbury Press.

Olds, S. B., London, M. L., & Ladewig, P. A. (1988). *Maternal newborn nursing: A family-centered approach.* Menlo Park, CA: Addison-Wesley.

Olds, S. W. (1986). *Working parents' survival guide.* New York: Bantam.

Olsho, L. W., Harkins, S. W., & Lenhardt, M. L. (1985). Aging and the auditory system. In J. E. Birren & K. W. Schaie (Eds.), *Handbook of the psychology of aging* (2nd ed.). New York: Van Nostrand Reinhold.

Olson, D. R. (1993, March). *What are beliefs and why can a 4-year-old but not a 3-year-old understand them?* Paper presented at the biennial meeting of the Society for Research in Child Development, New Orleans.

Olweus, D. (1980). Bullying among schoolboys. In R. Barnen (Ed.), *Children and violence.* Stockholm: Adaemic Litteratur.

Onishi, M., & Gjerde, P. F. (1994, February). *Attachment styles: A multi-method examination of concurrent and prospective personality characteristics.* Paper presented at the meeting of the Society for Research on Adolescence, San Diego, CA.

Organista, K. C. (1994). Overdue overview of elderly Latino mental health. *Contemporary Psychology, 39,* 61–62.

Orlofsky, J., Marcia, J., & Lesser, I. (1973). Ego identity status and the intimacy vs. isolation crisis of young adulthood. *Journal of Personality and Social Psychology, 27,* 211–219.

Orlofsky, J. (1976). Intimacy status: Relationship to interpersonal perception. *Journal of Youth and Adolescence, 5,* 73–88.

Ornstein, R., & Sobel, D. (1989). *Healthy pleasures.* Reading, MA: Addison-Wesley.

Osmond, M. W., Wambach, K. G., Harrison, D. F., Byers, J., Levine, P., **Imershein, A., & Quadagno, D. M.** (1993). The multiple jeopardy of race, class, and gender for AIDS risk among women. *Gender and Society, 7,* 99–120.

Ossip-Klein, D. J., Doyne, E. J., Bowman, E. D., Osborn, K. M., McDougall-Wilson, I. B., & Neimeyer, R. A. (1989). Effects of running or weight lifting on self-concept in clinically depressed women. *Journal of Consulting and Clinical Psychology, 57,* 158–161.

Osterkamp, L. (1991). *How to deal with your parents.* New York: Berkley Books.

Ottinger, D. R., & Simmons, J. E. (1964). Behavior of human neonates and prenatal maternal anxiety. *Psychological Reports, 14,* 391–394.

Overton, W. F., & Byrnes, J. P. (1991). Cognitive development. In R. M. Lerner, A. C. Petersen, and J. Brooks-Gunn (Eds.), *Encyclopedia of adolescence* (Vol. 1). New York: Garland.

Overton, W. F., & Montangero, J. (1991). Piaget, Jean. In R. M. Lerner, A. C. Petersen, & J. Brooks-Gunn (Eds.), *Encyclopedia of adolescence* (Vol. 2). New York: Garland.

P

Pacifici, R. E., & Davies, K. J. A. (1991). Protein, lipid and DNA repair systems in oxidative stress: The free-radical theory of aging revisited. *Gerontology, 37,* 166–182.

Padilla, A. M., & Lindholm, K. J. (1992, August). *What do we know about culturally diverse children?* Paper presented at the meeting of the American Psychological Association, Washington, DC.

Paffenbarger, R. S., Hyde, R. T., Wing, A. L, & Hsieh, C. (1986). Physical activity, all-cause mortality, and longevity of college alumni. *New England Journal of Medicine, 314,* 605–612.

Paffenbarger, R. S., Hyde, R. T., Wing, A. L., Lee, I., Jung, D. L., & Kampter, J. B. (1993). The association of changes in physical-activity level and other life-style characteristics with morality among men. *New England Journal of Medicine, 328,* 538–545.

Paikoff, R. L., Buchanan, C. M., & Brooks-Gunn, J. (1991). Hormone-behavior links at puberty, methodological links in the study of. In R. M. Lerner, A. C. Petersen, & J. Brooks-Gunn (Eds.), *Encyclopedia of adolescence* (Vol. 1). New York: Garland.

Palmore, E. B., Burchett, B. M., Fillenbaum, C. G., George, L. K., & Wallman, L. M. (1985). *Retirement: Causes and consequences.* New York: Springer.

Palmore, E. B. (1975). *The honorable elders: A cross-cultural analysis of aging in Japan.* Durham, NC: Duke University Press.

Palmore, E. B. (1982). Predictors of the longevity difference: A 25-year follow-up. *Gerontologist, 22,* 513–518.

Paludi, M. A. (1992). *The psychology of women.* Dubuque, IA: Brown & Benchmark.

Papini, D. R., Micka, J., & Barnett, J. (1989). Perceptions of intrapsychic and extrapsychic functioning as bases of adolescent ego identity statuses. *Journal of Adolescent Research, 4,* 460–480.

Papini, D. R., Roggman, L. A., & Anderson, J. (1990). *Early adolescent perceptions of attachment to mother and father: A test of the emotional distancing hypothesis.* Paper presented at the meeting of the Society for Research in Adolescence, Atlanta.

Parcel, G. S., Simons-Morton, G. G., O'Hara, N. M., Baranowski, T., Kolbe, L. J., & Bee, D. E. (1987). School promotion of healthful diet and exercise behavior: An integration of organizational change and social learning theory interventions. *Journal of School Health, 57,* 150–156.

Parham, T. A., & McDavis, R. J. (1993). Black men, an endangered species: Who's really pulling the trigger. In D. R. Atkinson, G. Morten, & D. W. Sue (Eds.), *Counseling American minorities.* Dubuque, IA: Brown & Benchmark.

Paris, S. C., & Lindauer, B. K. (1982). The development of cognitive skills during childhood. In B. B. Wolman (Ed.), *Handbook of developmental psychology.* Englewood Cliffs, NJ: Prentice-Hall.

Park, D. C. (1992). Applied cognitive aging research. In F. I. M. Craik & T. A. Salthouse (Eds.), *The handbook of aging and cognition.* Hillsdale, NJ: Erlbaum.

Park, K. J., & Honig, A. S. (1991, August). *Infant child care patterns and later ratings of preschool behaviors.* Paper presented at the meeting of the American Psychological Association, San Francisco.

Parke, R. D., & Sawin, D. B. (1980). The family in early infancy. In F. Pedersen (Ed.), *The father-infant relationship: Observational studies in family context.* New York: Praeger.

Parke, R. D., & Stearns, P. N. (1993). Fathers and child rearing. In G. H. Elder, J. Modell, & R. D. Parke (Eds.), *Children in time and place.* New York: Cambridge University Press.

Parke, R. D. (1988). Families in lifespan perspective: A multilevel developmental approach. In E. M. Hetherington, R. M Lerner, & M. Perlmutter (Eds.), *Child development in life span perspective.* Hillsdale, NJ: Erlbaum.

Parker, J. G., & Asher, S. R. (1987). Peer relations and later personal adjustment: Are low accepted children at risk? *Psychological Bulletin, 102,* 357–389.

Parker, S. J., & Barrett, D. E. (1992). Maternal type A behavior during pregnancy, neonatal crying, and infant temperament: Do type A women have type A babies? *Pediatrics, 89,* 474–479.

Parkes, C. M. (1972). *Bereavement: Studies of grief in adult life.* New York: International University Press.

Parkes, C. M. (1986). *Bereavement: Studies of grief in adult life.* London: Penguin. (Original work published 1972).

Parlee, M. B. (1979, April). The friendship bond: PT's survey report on friendship in America. *Psychology Today,* pp. 43–54, 113.

Parmalee, A., Wenner, W., & Schulz, H. (1964). Infant sleep patterns from birth to 16 weeks of age. *Journal of Pediatrics, 65,* 572–576.

Parten, M. (1932). Social play among preschool children. *Journal of Abnormal and Social Psychology, 27,* 243–269.

Pascual-Leone, J. (1987). Organismic processes for neo-Piagetian theories: A dialectical causal account of cognitive development. *International Journal of Psychology, 22,* 531–570.

Pasley, K., & Ihinger-Tallman, M. (Eds.). (1987). *Remarriage and stepparenting.* New York: Guilford Press.

Pastalan, P. M. (1991). Introduction: Optimizing housing for the elderly. *Journal of Housing for the Elderly, 7,* 1–4.

Patterson, G. R., & Stouthamer-Loeber, M. (1984). The correlation of family management practices and delinquency. *Child Development, 55,* 1299–1307.

Patterson, G. R., Capaldi, D., & Bank, L. (1991). An early starter model for predicting delinquency. In D. Pepler & K. Rubin (Eds.), *The development and treatment of aggression in childhood.* Hillsdale: NJ: Erlbaum.

Paul, E. L., & White, K. M. (1990). The development of intimate relationships in late adolescence. *Adolescence, 25,* 375–400.

Pearl, R., Bryan, T., & Herzog, A. (1990). Resisting or acquiescing to peer pressure to engage in misconduct: Adolescents' expectations of probable consequences. *Journal of Youth and Adolescence, 19,* 43–55.

Pearlin, L. I. (1994). The study of the oldest-old: Some promises and puzzles. *International Journal of Aging and Human Development, 38,* 91–98.

Peck, M. S. (1978). *The road less traveled.* New York: Simon & Schuster.

Peck, R. C. (1968). Psychological developments in the second half of life. In B. L. Neugarten (Ed.), *Middle age and aging.* Chicago: University of Chicago Press.

Pederson, D. R., Moran, G., Sitko, C., Campbell, K., Ghesquire, K., & Acton, H. (1989, April). *Maternal sensitivity and the security of infant-mother attachment.* Paper presented at the biennial meeting of the Society for Research in Child Development, Kansas City.

Peele, S., & Brodsky, A. (1991). *The truth about addiction and recovery.* New York: Simon & Schuster.

Pennebaker, J. (1992). Commentary. In J. W. Santrock, *Psychology: The science of mind and behavior* (4th ed.). Dubuque, IA; Brown & Benchmark.

Penner, S. G. (1987). Parental responses to grammatical and ungrammatical child utterances. *Child Development, 58,* 376–384.

Pentz, M. A. (1994). Primary prevention of adolescent drug abuse. In C. Fisher & R. Lerner (Eds.), *Applied developmental psychology.* New York: McGraw-Hill.

Peplau, L. A., & Gordon, S. L. (1985). Women and men in love: Gender differences in close heterosexual relationships. In V. E. O'Leary, R. K. Unger, & B. S. Wallston (Eds.), *Women, gender, and social psychology.* Hillsdale, NJ: Erlbaum.

Peplau, L. A., & Perlman, D. (Eds.). (1982). *Loneliness: A sourcebook of current theory, research and therapy.* New York: Wiley.

Perkins, D. N., Jay, E., & Tishman, S. (1993). Beyond abilities: A dispositional theory of thinking. *Merrill-Palmer Quarterly, 39,* 1–21.

Perkinson, H. J. (1991). The imperfect panacea: America faith in education, 1865–1990 (3rd ed.). New York: McGraw-Hill.

Perlmutter, M. (1990, April). *Practical intelligence across adulthood.* Paper presented at the 12th West Virginia conference on life-span developmental psychology, Morgantown.

Perlmutter, M. (1994). Cognitive skills within the context of adult development and old age. In C. Fisher & R. Lerner (Eds.), *Applied developmental psychology.* New York: McGraw-Hill.

Perris, E. E., Myers, N. A., & Clifton, R. K. (1990). Long-term memory for a single experience. *Child Development, 61,* 1796–1807.

Perry, C. M., & Johnson, C. L. (1994). Families and support networks among African American oldest-old. *International Journal of Aging and Human Development, 38,* 41–50.

Perry, W. G. (1970). *Forms of intellectual and ethical development in the college years.* New York: Holt, Rinehart & Winston.

Persky, V. W., Kepthorne-Rawson, J., & Shekelle, R. B. (1987). Personality and risk of cancer: 20-year follow-up of the Western Electric study. *Psychosomatic Medicine 49,* 435–449.

Peskin, H. (1967). Pubertal onset and ego functioning. *Journal of Abnormal Psychology, 72,* 1–15.

Petersen, A. C. (1979, January). Can puberty come any faster? *Psychology Today,* pp. 45–56.

Petersen, A. C. (1993). Creating adolescents: The role of context and process in developmental trajectories. *Journal of Research on Adolescence, 3,* 1–18.

Peterson, E. T. (1989). Grandparenting. In S. J. Bahr & E. T. Peterson (Eds.), *Aging and the family.* Lexington, MA: Lexington Books.

Peterson, P. L. (1977). Interactive effects of student anxiety, achievement orientation, and teacher behavior on student achievement and attitude. *Journal of Educational Psychology, 69,* 779–792.

Pettit, G. S., Dodge, K. A., & Brown, M. M. (1988). Early family experience, social problem solving patterns, and children's social competence. *Child Development, 59,* 107–120.

Pfeiffer, E., & Davis, G. (1974). Determinants of sexual behavior in middle and old age. In E. Palmore (Ed.), *Normal aging II.* Durham NC: Duke University Press.

Pfeiffer, E., Verwoerdt, A., & Davis, G. C. (1974). Sexual behavior in middle life. In E. Palmore (Ed.), *Normal aging II: Reports from the Duke longitudinal studies, 1970–1973.* Durham, NC: Duke University Press.

Phillips, D. A. (in press). Child care for children in poverty: Opportunity or inequity? *Child Development.*

Phillips, D. (1989). Future directions and needs for child care in the United States. In J. Lande, S. Scarr, & N. Gunzenhauser (Eds.), *Caring for children: Challenge to America.* Hillsdale, NJ: Erlbaum.

Phillips, R. L., & others. (1980). Influence of selection versus lifestyle on risk of fatal cancer and cardiovascular disease among

Seventh-Day Adventists. *American Journal of Epidemiology, 112,* 296–314.

Phinney, J. S., & Alipura, L. L. (1990). Ethnic identity in college students from four ethnic groups. *Journal of Adolescence, 13,* 171–183.

Phinney, J. S., & Cobb, N. J. (1993, March). *Adolescents' reasoning about discrimination: Ethnic and attitudinal predictors.* Paper presented at the biennial meeting of the Society for Research in Child Development, New Orleans.

Phinney, J. S., & Rosenthal, D. A. (1992). Ethnic identity in adolescence: Process, context, and outcome. In G. R. Adams, T. P. Gullotta, & R. Montemayor (Eds.), *Adolescent identity formation.* Newbury Park, CA: Sage.

Phinney, J. S., Chavira, V., & Williamson, L. (1992). Acculturation attitudes and self-esteem among high school and college students. *Youth and Society, 25,* 299–312.

Phinney, J. S., Dupont, S., Landin, J., & Onwughalu, M. (1994, February). *Social identity orientation, bicultural conflict, and coping strategies among minority adolescents.* Paper presented at the meeting of the Society for Research on Adolescence, San Diego, CA.

Phinney, J. S. (1989). Stages of ethnic identity development in minority group adolescents. *Journal of Early Adolescence, 9,* 34–49.

Piaget, J., & Inhelder, B. (1969). *The child's conception of space* (F. J. Langdon & J. L. Lunzer, Trans.). New York: W. W. Norton.

Piaget, J. (1932). *The moral judgment of the child.* New York: Harcourt Brace Jovanovich.

Piaget, J. (1936). *The origins of intelligence in children.* New York: W. W. Norton.

Piaget, J. (1952). *The origins of intelligence in children.* New York: International Universities Press.

Piaget, J. (1952a). Jean Piaget. In C. A. Murchison (Ed.), *A history of psychology in autobiography* (Vol. 4). Worcester, MA: Clark University Press.

Piaget, J. (1954). *The construction of reality in the child.* New York: Basic Books.

Piaget, J. (1962). *Play, dreams, and imitation in childhood.* New York: W. W. Norton.

Piaget, J. (1967). *The child's conception of the world.* Totowa, NJ: Littlefield, Adams.

Piers, E. V., & Harris, D. V. (1964). Age and other correlates of self-concept in children. *Journal of Educational Psychology, 55,* 91–95.

Pifer, A. (1993). Meeting the challenge: Implications for policy and practice. In J. Allen & A. Pifer (Eds.), *Women on the front line: Meeting the challenge of an aging America.* Washington, DC: Urban Institute Press.

Pifer, A. (1993). The public sector: "We the people" and our government's role. In R. N. Butler & K. Kiikuni (Eds.), *Who is responsible for my old age?* New York: Springer.

Pines, A., & Aronson, E. (1988). *Career burnout: Causes and cures.* New York: Free Press.

Piotrowski, C. S., Collins, R. C., Knitzer, J., & Robinson, R. (1994). Strengthening mental health services in Head Start: A challenge for the 1990s. *American Psychologist, 49,* 133–139.

Pipes, P. (1988). Nutrition in childhood. In S. R. Williams & B. S. Worthington-Roberts (Eds.), *Nutrition throughout the life cycle.* St. Louis: Times Mirror/Mosby.

Plante, T. G., & Rodin, J. (1990). Physical fitness and enhanced psychological health. *Current Psychology Research and Reviews, 9,* 3–24.

Pleck, J. (1981). *Three conceptual issues in research on male roles.* Working paper no.98, Wellesley College Center for Research on Women, Wellesley, MA.

Plomin, R., & Daniels, D. (1987). Why are children in the same family so different from one another? *Behavioral and Brain Sciences, 10,* 1–60.

Plomin, R., & Thompson, L. (1987). Life-span developmental behavior genetics. In P. B. Baltes, D. L. Featherman, & R. M. Lerner (Eds.), *Life-span development and behavior* (Vol. 7). Hillsdale, NJ: Erlbaum.

Plomin, R., DeFries, J. C., & McClearn, G. E. (1990). *Behavioral genetics: A primer.* New York: W. H. Freeman.

Plomin, R., Emde, R. N., Braungart, J. M., Campos, J., Corley, R., Fulkder, D. W., Kagan, J., Reznick, J. S., Robinson, J., Zahn-Waxler, C., & DeFries, J. C. (1993). Genetic change and continuity from fourteen to twenty months: The MacArthur Longitudinal Twin Study. *Child Development, 64,* 1354–1376.

Plomin, R., Reiss, D., Hetherington, E. M., & Howe, G. W. (1994). Nature and nurture: Contributions to measures of the family environment. *Developmental Psychology, 30,* 32–43.

Plomin, R. (1989). Environment and genes: Determinants of behavior. *American Psychologist, 44,* 105–111.

Plomin, R. (1991, April). *The nature of nurture: Genetic influence on "environmental" measures.* Paper presented at the biennial meeting of the Society for Research in Child Development, Seattle.

Plomin, R. (1993, March). *Human behavioral genetics and development: An overview and update.* Paper presented at the biennial meeting of the Society for Research in Child Development, New Orleans.

Podolsky, D., & Silberner, J. (1993, January 18). How medicine mistreats the elderly. *U.S. News and World Report,* pp. 72–79.

Poest, C. A., Williams, J. R., Witt, D. D., & Atwood, M. E. (1990). Challenge me to move: Large muscle development in young children. *Young Children, 45,* 4–10.

Polivy, J., & Herman, C. P. (1991). Good and bad dieters: Self-perception and reaction to a dietary challenge. *International Journal of Eating Disorders, 10,* 91–99.

Polivy, J., & Thomsen, L. (1987). Eating, dieting, and body image. In E. A. Blechman & K. D. Brownell (Eds.), *Handbook of behavioral medicine for women.* Elmsford, NY: Pergamon.

Pollitt, E. P., Gorman, K. S., Engle, P. L., Martorell, R., & Rivera, J. (1993). Early supplementary feeding and cognition. *Monographs of the Society for Research in Child Development, 58,* (7, Serial No. 235).

Pollock, G. H., & Greenspan, S. I. (Eds.). (1994). *The course of life.* Madison, CT: International Universities Press.

Pomerleau, A. (1989). Commentary. *Human Development, 32,* 167–191.

Poon, L. W. (1985). Differences in human memory with aging: Nature causes, and clinical implications. In J. E. Birren & K. W. Schaie (Eds.), *Handbook of the psychology of aging* (2nd ed.). New York: Van Nostrand Reinhold.

Poon, L. W. (1990, April). *What is everyday cognition? Some validity and generalization considerations.* Paper presented at the 12th West Virginia conference on life-span developmental psychology, Morgantown.

Porcino, J. (1983). *Growing older, getting better: A handbook for women in the second half of life.* Reading, MA: Addison-Wesley.

Porter, F. L., Porges, S. W., & Marshall, R. E. (1988). Newborn pain cries and vagal tone: Parallel changes in response to circumcision. *Child Development, 59,* 495–515.

Posner, J. K., & Vandell, D. L. (in press). Low-income children's after-school care: Are there beneficial effects of after-school programs? *Child Development.*

Potter, J. F., Schafer, D. F., & Bohi, R. L. (1988). In-hospital mortality as a function of body mass index: An age-dependent variable. *Journal of Gerontology: Medical Sciences, 43,* 559–632.

Potthof, S. J. (1992, March). *Modeling family planning expertise to predict oral contraceptive discontinuance in teenagers.* Paper presented at the meeting of the Society for Research on Adolescence, Washington, DC.

Potvin, L., Champagne, F., & Laberge-Nadeau, C. (1988). Mandatory driver training and road safety: The Quebec experience. *American Journal of Public Health, 78,* 1206–1212.

Powell, G. J., & Fuller, M. (1972). The variables for positive self-concept among young southern Black adolescents. *Journal of the National Medical Association, 43,* 72–79.

Powers, L. E., & Wampold, B. E. (1994). Cognitive-behavioral factors in adjustment to adult bereavement. *Death Studies, 18,* 1–24.

Premack, D. (1986). *Gavagai! The future history of the ape language controversy.* Cambridge, MA: MIT Press.

Prescott, C. A., Hewitt, J. K., Heath, A. C., Truett, K. R., Neale, M. C., & Eaves, L. J. (1994). Environmental and genetic influence on alcohol use in a volunteer sample of older twins. *Journal of Studies on Alcohol, 55,* 18–33.

Price, R., Cowen, E., Lorion, R., & Ramos-McKay, J. (Eds.). (1988). *14 ounces of prevention.* Washington, DC: American Psychological Association.

Pryor, J. B., Reeder, G. D., Vinacco, R., & Kott, T. L. (1989). The instrumental and symbolic functions of attitudes toward persons with AIDS. *Journal of Applied Social Psychology, 19,* 377–404.

Puka, B. (1991). Toward the redevelopment of Kohlberg's theory: Preserving essential structure, removing controversial content. In W. M. Kurtines & J. Gewirtz (Eds.), *Moral behavior and development: Advances in theory, research, and application.* Hillsdale, NJ: Erlbaum.

Q

Quadrel, M. J., Fischoff, B., & Davis, W. (1993). Adolescent (in)vulnerability. *American Psychologist, 48,* 102–106.

Quality health care: Critical issues before the nation. (1988, March). Washington, DC: Health Care Quality Alliance.

Quay, L. C., Minore, D. A., & Fraizer, L. M. (1993, March). *Sex typing in stories and comprehension, recall, and sex-typed beliefs in young children.* Paper presented at the biennial meeting of the Society for Research in Child Development, New Orleans.

Quiggle, N. L., Garber, J., Panak, W. F., & Dodge, K. A. (1992). Social information processing in aggressive and depressed children. *Child Development, 63,* 1305–1320.

Quina, K. (1986). *Teaching research methods: A multidimensional feminist curricular transformation plan.* Wellesley College Center for Research on Women. Working Paper No. 164.

R

Rabin, D. S., & Chrousos, G. P. (1991). Androgens, gonadal. In R. M. Lerner, A. C. Petersen, & J. Brooks-Gunn. (Eds.), *Encyclopedia of adolescence* (Vol. 1). New York: Garland.

Rabinowitz, V. C., & Sechzur, J. (1994). Feminist methodologies. In F. L. Denmark & M. A. Paludi (Eds.), *Handbook on the psychology of women.* Westport, CT: Greenwood Press.

Rachels, J. (1986). *The end of life.* New York: Oxford University Press.

Radke-Yarrow, M., Nottlemann, E., Martinez, P., Fox, M. B., & Belmont, B. (1992). Young children of affectively ill parents: A longitudinal study of psychosocial development. *Journal of the American Academy of Child and Adolescent Psychiatry, 31,* 68–77.

Rafferty, Y., & Shinn, M. (1991). The impact of homelessness on children. *American Psychologist, 46,* 1170–1179.

Rahman, T., & Bisanz, G. L. (1986). Reading ability and use of a story schema in recalling and reconstructing information. *Journal of Educational Psychology, 5,* 323–333.

Ramey, C. T., Bryant, D. M., Campbell, F. A., Sparling, J. J., & Wasik, B. H. (1988). Early intervention for high-risk children: The Carolina Early Intervention Program. In R. H. Price, E. L. Cowen, R. P. Lorion, & J. Ramos-McKay (Eds.), *14 ounces of prevention.* Washington, DC: American Psychological Association.

Ramirez, O., & Arce, C. Y. (1981). The contemporary Chicano family: An empirically based review. In A. Baron (Ed.), *Explorations in Chicano psychology.* New York: Praeger.

Ramirez, O. (1989). Mexican American children and adolescents. In J. T. Gibbs & L. N. Huang (Eds.), *Children of color.* San Francisco: Jossey-Bass.

Ramirez, O. (1989). Mexican American children and adolescents. In J. T. Gibbs & L. N. Huang (Eds.), *Children of color.* San Francisco: Jossey-Bass.

Ramsay, D. S. (1980). Onset of unimanual handedness in infants. *Infant Behavior and Development, 3,* 377–385.

Rando, T. (1991). *How to go on living when someone you love dies.* New York: Bantam.

Raphael, B., & Nunn, K. (1988). Counseling the bereaved. *Journal of Social Issues, 44,* 191–206.

Ratcliff, K. S., & Bogdan, J. (1988). Unemployed women: When 'social support' is not supportive. *Social Problems, 35,* 54–63.

Ravnikar, V. (1992, May 25). Commentary, *Newsweek,* p. 82.

Rayman, J. R., & Garis, J. W. (1989). Counseling. In M. L. Upcraft & J. N. Gardner (Eds.), *The freshman year experience.* San Francisco: Jossey-Bass.

Rayman, P., Allshouse, K., & Allen, J. (1993). Resiliency amidst inequity: Older women workers in an aging society. In J. Allen & A. Pifer (Eds.), *Women on the front line: Meeting the challenge of an aging America.* Washington, DC: Urban Institute Press.

Reedy, M. N., Birren, J. E., & Schaie, K. W. (1981). Age and sex differences in satisfying relationships across the adult life span. *Human Development, 24,* 52–66.

Reichard, S., Levson, F., & Peterson, P. (1962). *Aging and personality: A study of 87 older men.* New York: Wiley.

Reilly, R. (1988, August 15). Here no one is spared. *Sports Illustrated,* pp. 70–77.

Reinherz, H. Z., Giaconia, R. M., Silverman, A. B., & Friedman, A. C. (1994, February). *Early psychosocial risks for adolescent suicide ideation and attempts.* Paper presented at the meeting of the Society for Research on Adolescence, San Diego, CA.

Reinisch, J. M. (1990). *The Kinsey Institute new report on sex: What you must know to be sexually literate.* New York: St. Martin's Press.

Reinisch, J. (1992, December 7). Commentary, *Newsweek,* p. 54.

Reis, M., & Gold, D. P. (1993). Retirement and life satisfaction: A review and two models. *Journal of Applied Gerontology, 12,* 261–282.

Remafedi, G. (1991). Homosexuality, adolescent. In R. M. Lerner, A. C. Petersen, & J. Brooks-Gunn (Eds.), *Encyclopedia of adolescence* (Vol. 1). New York: Garland.

Revitch, E., & Schlesinger, L. B. (1978). Murder: Evaluation, classification, and prediction. In I. L. Kutash, S. B. Kutash, & L. B. Schlesinger (Eds.), *Violence.* San Francisco: Jossey-Bass.

Rhodes, S. R. (1983). Age-related differences in work attitudes and behavior: A review and conceptual analysis. *Psychological Bulletin, 93,* 329–367.

Rice, M. B. (1991). Preschoolers' QUIL: Quick incidental learning of words. In G. Conti-Ramsden & C. E. Snow (Eds.), *Children's language* (Vol. 7). Hillsdale, NJ: Erlbaum.

Rice, M. L. (1989). Children's language acquisition. *American Psychologist, 44,* 149–156.

Rice, M. (1993, November). Review of *Child Development,* 6th ed. Dubuque, IA: Brown & Benchmark.

Rich, C. L., Young, D., & Fowler, R. C. (1986). San Diego suicide study. *Archives of General Psychiatry, 43,* 577–582.

Richards, L. N., Bengston, V. L., & Miller, R. B. (1989). The "generation in the middle": Perceptions of changes in adults' intergenerational relationships. In K. Kreppner & R. M. Lerner (Eds.), *Family systems and life-span development.* Hillsdale, NJ: Erlbaum.

Richards, M., Suleiman, L., Sims, B., & Sedeno, A. (1994, February). *Experiences of ethnically diverse young adolescents growing up in poverty.* Paper presented at the meeting of the Society for Research on Adolescence, San Diego, CA.

Richards, M. H., & Duckett, E. (1994). The relationship of maternal employment to early adolescent daily experience with and without parents. *Child Development, 65,* 225–236.

Rick, K., & Foward, J. (1992). Acculturation and perceived intergenerational differences among Hmong youth. *Journal of Cross-Cultural Psychology, 23,* 85–94.

Rieben, L., & Perfetti, C. A. (1991). *Learning to read: Basic research and its implications.* Hillsdale, NJ: Erlbaum.

Riege, W. H., & Inman, V. (1981). Age differences in nonverbal memory tasks. *Journal of Gerontology, 36,* 51–58.

Riegel, K. F., & Riegel, R. M. (1972). Development, drop, and death. *Developmental Psychology, 6,* 306–319.

Riegel, K. F. (1975). Toward a dialectical theory of development. *Human Development, 18,* 50–64.

Riegel, K. F. (1977). The dialectics of time. In N. Datan & H. W. Reese (Eds.), *Life-span developmental psychology: Dialectical perspective on experimental research.* New York: Academic Press.

Riley, M. W. (1989). Foreword: Why this book? In K. W. Schaie, & C. Schooler (Eds.), *Social structure and aging: Psychological processes.* Hillsdale, NJ: Erlbaum.

Rimm, E. B., Stampfer, M. J., Ascherio, A., Giovannucci, E., Colditz, G. A., & Willett, W. C. (1993). Vitamin E consumption and the risk of coronary heart disease in men. *New England Journal of Medicine, 328,* 1450–1456.

Rivers, P. C. (1994). *Alcohol and human behavior.* Englewood Cliffs, NJ: Prentice-Hall.

Roberts, B. L., Dunkle, R., & Haug, M. (1994). Physical, psychological, and social resources as moderators of stress to mental health of the very old. *Journal of Gerontology, 49,* S35–S43.

Roberts, D. F. (1993). Adolescents and the mass media: From "Leave It to Beaver" to "Beverly Hills 90210." In R. Takanishi (Ed.), *Adolescence in the 1990s.* New York: Teachers College Press.

Roberts, W. L. (1993, March). *Programs for the collection and analysis of observational data.* Paper presented at the biennial meeting of the Society for Research in Child Development, New Orleans.

Robinson, D. P., & Greene, J. W. (1988). The adolescent alcohol and drug problem: A practical approach. *Pediatric Nursing, 14,* 305–310.

Robinson, I., Ziss, K., Ganza, B., Katz, S., & Robinson, E. (1991). Twenty years of the sexual revolution, 1965–1985: An update. *Journal of Marriage and the Family, 53,* 216–220.

Robinson, J. L., Kagan, J., Reznick, J. S., & Corley, R. (1992). The heritability of inhibited and uninhibited behavior: A twin study. *Developmental Psychology, 28,* 1030–1037.

Rode, S. S., Chang, P., Fisch, R. O., & Sroufe, L. A. (1981). Attachment patterns of infants separated at birth. *Developmental Psychology, 17,* 188–191.

Rodin, J., & Langer, E. J. (1977). Long-term effects of a control relevant intervention with the institutionalized aged. *Journal of Personality and Social Psychology, 35,* 397–402.

Rodin, J., & Timko, C. (1991). Sense of control, aging, and health. In M. G. Ory, R. P. Abeles, & P. D. Lipman (Eds.), *Aging, health, and behavior.* Newbury Park, CA: Sage.

Rodin, J. (1983). Behavioral medicine: Beneficial effects of self-control training in aging. *International Review of Applied Psychology, 32,* 153–181.

Rodin, J. (1986). Health, control, and aging. In M. M. Baltes & P. B. Baltes (Eds.), *The psychology of control and aging.* Hillsdale, NJ: Erlbaum.

Rodin, J. (1990, January). Conversation with Robert Trotter. *Longevity,* pp. 60–67.

Rodman, H., Pratto, D. J., & Nelson, R. S. (1988). Toward a definition of self-care children: A commentary on Steinberg (1986). *Developmental Psychology, 24,* 292–294.

Rodriguez-Haynes, M., & Crittenden, P. M. (1988). *Ethnic differences among abusing, neglecting, and non-maltreating families.* Paper presented at the Southeastern Conference on Human Development, Charleston, SC.

Roedel, T., & Bendixen, L. D. (1992, March). *A case study approach to description of behaviorally distinct subgroups of peer rejected adolescents.* Paper presented at the meeting of the Society for Research on Adolescence, Washington, DC.

Roff, M., Sells, S. B., & Golden, M. W. (1972). *Social adjustment and personality development in children.* Minneapolis: University of Minnesota Press.

Rogers, A. (1987). *Questions of gender differences: Ego development and moral voice in adolescence.* Unpublished manuscript, Department of Education, Harvard University.

Rogers, C. S., & Sawyers, J. K. (1988) *Play in the lives of children.* Washington, DC: National Association for the Education of Young Children.

Rogoff, B., & Morelli, G. (1989). Perspectives on children's development from cultural psychology. *American Psychologist, 44,* 343–348.

Rogoff, B. (1993, March). *Whither cognitive development in the 1990s?* Paper presented at the biennial meeting of the Society for Research in Child Development, New Orleans.

Rohner, R. P., & Rohner, E. C. (1981). Parental acceptance-rejection and parental

control: Cross-cultural codes. *Ethnology, 20,* 245–260.

Rokach, A. (1990). Surviving and coping with loneliness. *Journal of Psychology, 124,* 39–54.

Rollins, B. C. (1989). Marital quality at mid-life. In S. Hunter & M. Sundel (Eds.), *Midlife myths.* Newbury Park, CA: Sage.

Rook, K. (1987). Reciprocity of social exchange and social satisfaction among older women. *Journal of Personality and Social Psychology, 52,* 145–154.

Root, M. P. P. (1993). Guidelines for facilitating therapy with Asian-American clients. In D. R. Atkinson, G. Morten, & D. W. Sue (Eds.), *Counseling American minorities.* Dubuque, IA: Brown & Benchmark.

Root, M. P. (Ed.). (1992). *Racially mixed people in America.* Newbury Park, CA: Sage.

Rose, H. A., & Martin, C. L. (1993, March). *Children's gender-based inferences about others' activities, emotions, and occupations.* Paper presented at the biennial meeting of the Society for Research in Child Development, New Orleans.

Rose, S., & Frieze, I. R. (1993). Young singles' contemporary dating scripts. *Sex Roles, 28,* 499–509.

Rose, S. A., & Ruff, H. A. (1987). Cross-modal abilities in human infants. In J. D. Osofsky (Ed.), *Handbook of infant development* (2nd ed.). New York: Wiley.

Rose, S. A., Feldman, J. F., McCarton, C. M., & Wolfson, J. (1988). Information processing in seven-month-old infants as a function of risk status. *Child Development, 59,* 489–603.

Rose, S. A. (1989). Measuring infant intelligence: New perspectives. In M. H. Bornstein & N. A. Krasnegor (Eds.), *Stability and continuity in mental development.* Hillsdale, NJ: Erlbaum.

Rose, S. A. (1992, May). *Infancy: The roots of cognition.* Paper presented at the International Conference of Infant Studies, Miami Beach.

Rosenbaum, J. E. (1984). *Career mobility in a corporate hierarchy.* New York: Academic Press.

Rosenblatt, P. C. (1993). Cross-cultural variation in the experience, expression, and understanding of grief. In D. P. Irish & K. F. Lundquist (Eds.), *Ethnic variations in dying, death, and grief: Diversity in universality.* Washington, DC: Taylor & Francis.

Rosenblith, J. F., & Sims-Knight, J. E. (1985). *In the beginning: Development in the first two years.* Monterey, CA: Brooks/Cole.

Rosenblith, J. F., & Sims-Knight, J. E. (1992). *In the beginning* (2nd ed.). Newbury Park, CA: Sage.

Rosenblith, J. F. (1992). *In the beginning* (2nd ed.). Newbury Park, CA: Sage.

Rosenfeld, A., & Stark, E. (1987, May). The prime of our lives. *Psychology Today.* pp. 62–72.

Rosenthal, R., & Jacobsen, L. (1968). *Pygmalian in the classroom.* New York: Holt, Rinehart & Winston.

Rossi, A. S. (1988). A life-course approach to gender, aging, and intergenerational relations. In K. W. Schaie & C. Schooler (Eds.), *Social structure and aging.* Hillsdale, NJ: Erlbaum.

Rossi, A. (1980). Aging and parenthood in the middle years. In P. Baltes & O. Brim (Eds.), *Life-span development and behavior* (Vol. 3). New York: Academic Press.

Rosso, P. (1992). Maternal nutritional status and fetal growth. In R. Hoekleman, S. B. Friedman, N. M. Nelson, & H. M. Seidel (Eds.), *Primary pediatric care* (2nd ed.). St. Louis: Mosby Yearbook.

Rothbart, M. K, Hanley, D., & Albert, M. (1986). Gender differences in moral reasoning. *Sex Roles, 15,* 645–653.

Rothbart, M. K., & Ahadi, S. A. (1993, March). *Temperament and socialization.* Paper presented at the biennial meeting of the Society for Research in Child Development, New Orleans.

Rothbart, M. K. (1988). Temperament and the development of inhibited approach. *Child Development, 59,* 1241–1250.

Rothbart, M. L. K. (1971). Birth order and mother-child interaction. *Dissertation Abstracts, 27,* 45–57.

Rothstein, W. G. (1980). The significance of occupations in work careers: An empirical and theoretical review. *Journal of Vocational Behavior, 17,* 343–378.

Rotter, J. B. (1989, August). *Internal versus external locus of control of reinforcement: A case history of a variable.* Paper presented at the meeting of the American Psychological Association, New Orleans.

Rovee-Collier, C. K. (1992, April). *Relating cognition and learning to information acquisition.* Paper presented at the International Conference on Infant Studies, Miami Beach.

Rovee-Collier, C. (1987). Learning and memory in children. In J. D. Osofsky (Ed.), *Handbook of infant development* (2nd ed.). New York: Wiley.

Rowe, D. C. (in press). As the twig is bent? The myth of child-rearing influences on personality development. *Journal of Counseling and Development.*

Rowe, J., & Kahn, R. (1987). Human aging: Usual and successful. *Science, 237,* 143–149.

Rowlett, J. D., Patel, D., & Greydanus, D. E. (1992). Homosexuality. In D. E. Greydanus & M. L. Wolraich (Eds.), *Behavioral pediatrics.* New York: Springer-Verlag.

Roybal, E. R. (1988). Mental health and aging: The need for an expanded federal response. *American Psychologist, 43,* 189–194.

Rubin, K. H., Maioni, T. L., & Hornung, M. (1976). Free play behaviors in middle and lower social class preschoolers: Parten and Piaget revisited. *Child Development, 47,* 414–419.

Rubin, K. N., Fein, G. G., & Vandenberg, B. (1983). Play. In P. H. Mussen (Ed.), *Handbook of child psychology* (4th ed., Vol. 4). New York: Wiley.

Rubin, L. B. (1984). *Intimate strangers: Men and women working together.* New York: Harper & Row.

Rubin, S. (in press). The death of a child is forever: The life course impact of child loss. In M. Stroebe, W. Stroebe, & R. O. Hanson (Eds.), *Handbook of bereavement.* New York: Cambridge University Press.

Rubin, Z., & Mitchell, C. (1976). Couples research as couples counseling. *American Psychologist, 31,* 17–25.

Rubin, Z., & Sloman, J. (1984). How parents influence their children's friendships. In M. Lewis (Ed.), *Beyond the dyad.* New York: Plenum.

Rubin, Z. (1970). Measurement of romantic love. *Journal of Personality and Social Psychology, 16,* 265–273.

Rubin, Z. (1981, May). Does personality really change after 20? *Psychology Today.*

Ruble, D. N., Boggiano, A. K., Feldman, N. S., & Loebl, J. H. (1989). Developmental analysis of the role of social comparison in self-evaluation. *Developmental Psychology, 16,* 105–115.

Rudman, D., & others. (1990). Effects of human growth hormone in men over 60 years of age. *New England Journal of Medicine, 323,* 1–6.

Ruebenstein, J., Heeren, T., Housman, D., Rubin, C., & Stechler, G. (1989). Suicidal behavior in "normal" adolescents: Risk and protective factors. *American Journal of Orthopsychiatry, 59,* 59–71.

Rumbaugh, D. M., & Savage-Rumbaugh, E. S. (1990, June). *Chimpanzees: Language, speech, counting, and video tasks.* Paper presented at the meeting of the American Psychological Society, Dallas.

Rumbaugh, D. M., Hopkins, W. D., Washburn, D. A., & Savage-Rumbaugh, E. S. (1991). Comparative perspectives of brain, cognition, and language. In N. A. Krasnegor, D. M. Rumbaugh, M. Studdert-Kennedy, & R. L. Schiefelbusch (Eds.), *Biological and behavioral determinants of language development.* Hillsdale, NJ: Erlbaum.

Rumberger, R. W. (1983). Dropping out of high school: The influence of race, sex, and family background. *American Educational Research Journal, 20,* 199–220.

Rumberger, R. W. (1987). High school dropouts: A review of the issues and evidence. *Review of Educational Research, 57,* 101–121.

Russo, N. F. (1990). Overview: Forging research priorities for women's mental health. *American Psychologist, 45,* 368–374.

Rutter, M., & Schopler, E. (1987). Autism and pervasive developmental disorders: Concepts and diagnostic issues. *Journal of Autism and Developmental Disorders, 17,* 159–186.

Rutter, M. (1983, April). *Influences from family and school.* Paper presented at the meeting of the Society for Research in Child Development, Detroit.

Ryan, R. A. (1980). Strengths of the American Indian family: State of the art. In F. Hoffman (Ed.), *The American Indian family: Strengths and stresses.* Isleta, NM: American Indian Social Research and Development Association.

Ryan, R. M., & Lynch, J. H. (1989). Emotional autonomy versus detachment: Revisiting the vicissitudes of adolescence and young adulthood. *Child Development, 60,* 340–356.

Rybash, J. W., Roodin, P. A., & Santrock, J. W. (1991). *Adult development and aging* (2nd ed.). Dubuque, IA: Brown & Benchmark.

Ryff, C. D. (1984). Personality development from the inside: The subjective experience of change in adulthood and aging. In P. B. Baltes & O. G. Brim (Eds.), *Life-span*

development and behavior. New York: Academic Press.

S

Saarni, C. (1988). Children's understanding of the interpersonal consequences of dissemblance of nonverbal emotional-expressive behavior. *Journal of Nonverbal Behavior, 12,* 275–294.

Sadik, N. (1991, March–April). Success in development depends on women. In *Popline.* New York: World Population News Service.

Sadker, M., & Sadker, D. (1986, March). Sexism in the classroom: From grade school to graduate school. *Phi Delta Kappan.* pp. 512–515.

Sadker, M., Sadker, D., & Klein, S. S. (1986). Abolishing misperceptions about sex equity in education. *Theory Into Practice, 25,* 219–226.

Sagan, C. (1977). *Dragons of Eden.* New York: Random House.

Salk, L. (1992). *Familyhood.* New York: Simon & Schuster.

Salthouse, T. A., & Coon, V. E. (1993). Influence of task-specific processing speed on age differences in memory. *Journal of Gerontology, 48,* P245–P255.

Salthouse, T. A. (1984). Effects of age and skill in typing. *Journal of Experimental Psychology: General, 113,* 345–371.

Salthouse, T. A. (1989). Age-related changes in basic cognitive processes. In M. Storandt & G. R. VandenBos (Eds.), *The adult years: Continuity and change.* Washington, DC: American Psychological Association.

Salthouse, T. A. (1991). *Theoretical perspectives on cognitive aging.* Hillsdale, NJ: Erlbaum.

Salthouse, T. A. (1992). Reasoning and spatial abilities. In F. I. M. Craik & T. A. Salthouse (Eds.), *The handbook of aging and cognition.* Hillsdale, NJ: Erlbaum.

Salthouse, T. A. (1993). Speed and knowledge as determinants of adult age differences in verbal tasks. *Journal of Gerontology, 48,* P29–P36.

Salthouse, T. A. (in press). The nature of the influence of speed on adult age differences in cognition. *Developmental Psychology.*

Sameroff, A. J., Dickstein, S., Hayden, L. C., & Schiller, M. (1993, March). *Effects of family process and parental depression on children.* Paper presented at the biennial meeting of the Society for Child Development, New Orleans.

Sampson, R. J., & Laub, J. H. (in press). Urban poverty and the family context of delinquency. *Child Development.*

Sanders, G. F., & Trygstad, D. W. (1993). Strengths in the grandparent-grandchild relationship. *Activities, Adaptation and Aging, 17,* 43–50.

Sangree, W. H. (1989). Age and power: Life-course trajectories and age structuring of power relations in East and West Africa. In D. I. Kertzer & K. W. Schaie (Eds.), *Age structuring in comparative perspective.* Hillsdale, NJ: Erlbaum.

Sankar, A. (1991). Ritual and dying: A cultural analysis of social support for caregivers. *Gerontologist, 31,* 43–50.

Santrock, J. W., & Sitterle, K. A. (1987). Parent-child relationships in stepmother

families. In K. Pasley & M. Ihinger-Tallman (Eds.), *Remarriage and stepparenting.* New York: Guilford Press.

Santrock, J. W., & Warshak, R. A. (1979). Father custody and social development in boys and girls. *Journal of Social Issues, 35,* 112–125.

Santrock, J. W., & Warshak, R. A. (1986). Development, relationships, and legal/clinical considerations in father custody families. In M. E. Lamb (Ed.), *The father's role: Applied perspectives.* New York: Wiley.

Santrock, J. W., Minnett, A., & Campbell, B. D. (1993). *The authoritative guide to self-help books.* New York: Guilford Press.

Santrock, J. W., Sitterle, K. A., & Warshak, R. A. (1988). Parent-child relationships in stepfather families. In P. Bronstein & C. P. Cowan (Eds.), *Fatherhood today.* New York: Wiley.

Santrock, J. W. (1993). *Adolescence* (5th ed.). Dubuque, IA: Brown & Benchmark.

Santrock, J. W. (1993). *Children* (3rd ed.). Dubuque, IA: Brown & Benchmark.

Sapp, S. (1991). Ethical issues in intergenerational equity. *Journal of Religious Gerontology, 7,* 1–16.

Sarrel, P., & Masters, W. (1982). Sexual molestation of men and women. *Archives of Human Sexuality, 11,* 117–131.

Satlin, A. (1994). The psychology of successful aging. *Journal of Geriatric Psychiatry, 27,* 3–8.

Sattler, J. (1988). *Assessment of children* (3rd ed.). San Diego: Jerome Sattler.

Sauber, M., & Corrigan, E. M. (1970). *The six year experience of unwed mothers as parents.* New York: Community Council of Greater New York.

Savage-Rumbaugh, E. S., Murphy, J., Sevick, R. A., Brakke, K. E., Williams, S. L., & Rumbaugh, D. (1993). Language comprehension in ape and child. *Monographs of the Society for Research in Child Development, 58,* (3–4, Serial No. 233).

Savage-Rumbaugh, E. S. (1991). Language learning in the Bonobo: How and why they learn. In N. A. Krasnegor, D. M. Rumbaugh, M. Studdert-Kennedy, & R. L. Schiefelbusch (Eds.), *Biological and behavioral determinants of language development.* Hillsdale, NJ: Erlbaum.

Savin-Williams, R., & Rodriguez, R. G. (1993). A developmental clinical perspective on lesbian, gay male, and bisexual youths. In T. P. Gullotta, G. R. Adams, & R. Montemayor (Eds.), *Adolescent sexuality.* Newbury Park, CA: Sage.

Saxe, G. B., & Guberman, S. R. (1993, March). Peers' emergent arithmetical goals in a problem-solving game. Paper presented at the biennial meeting of the Society for Research in Child Development, New Orleans.

Saxe, G. B., Guberman, S. R., & Gearhart, M. (1987). Social processes in early number development. *Monographs of the Society for Research in Child Development, 52* (2, Serial No. 216).

Scafidi, F., & Wheeden, A. (1993, March). *Perinatal complications and Brazelton performance of cocaine-exposed preterm infants.* Paper presented at the biennial meeting of the Society for Research in Child Development, New Orleans.

Scales, P. C. (1992). *A portrait of young adolescents in the 1990s: Implications for promoting healthy growth and development.* Carrboro, NC: Center for Early Adolescence.

Scardamalia, M., Bereiter, C., & Steinbach, R. (1984). Teachability of reflective processes in written composition. *Cognitive Science, 8,* 173–190.

Scarf, M. (1985). Cover notes. In H. Lerner. *The dance of intimacy.* New York: HarperCollins.

Scarr, S., & McCartney, K. (1983). How people make their own environments: A theory of genotype-environment effects. *Child Development, 54,* 424–435.

Scarr, S., & Ricciuti, A. (in press). What effects do parents have on their children? In L. Okagaki & R. J. Sternberg (Eds.), *Directors of development: Influences on the development of children's thinking.*

Scarr, S., & Weinberg, R. A. (1980). Calling all camps! The war is over. *American Sociological Review, 45,* 859–865.

Scarr, S., & Weinberg, R. A. (1983). The Minnesota adoption studies: Genetic differences and malleability. *Child Development, 54,* 253–259.

Scarr, S., Lande, J., & McCartney, K. (1989). Child care and the family: Complements and interactions. In J. Lande, S. Scarr, & N. Gunzenhauser (Eds.), *Caring for children: Challenge to America.* Hillsdale, NJ: Erlbaum.

Scarr, S. (1984, May). Interview. *Psychology Today,* pp. 59–63.

Scarr, S. (1984). *Mother care/other care.* New York: Basic Books.

Scarr, S. (1992). Developmental theories for the 1990s: Development and individual differences. *Child Development, 63,* 1–19.

Scarr, S. (1993). Biological and cultural diversity: The legacy of Darwin for development. *Child Development, 64,* 1333–1353.

Schaff, E. A. (1992). Abortion. In R. A. Hoekleman, S. B. Friedman, N. M. Nelson, & H. M. Seidel (Eds.), *Primary pediatric care* (2nd ed.). St. Louis: Mosby Yearbook.

Schaie, K. W., & Strother, C. R. (1968). A cross-sequential study of age changes in cognitive behavior. *Psychological Bulletin, 70,* 671–680.

Schaie, K. W., Willis, S. L., & O'Hanlon, A. M. (in press). Perceived intellectual performance change over seven years. *Journal of Gerontology: Psychological Sciences.*

Schaie, K. W. (1973). Methodological problems in descriptive developmental research on adulthood and aging. In J. R. Nesselroade & H. W. Reese (Eds.), *Life-span developmental psychology: Methodological issues.* New York: Academic Press.

Schaie, K. W. (1977). Toward a stage theory of adult cognitive development. *Aging and Human Development, 8,* 129–138.

Schaie, K. W. (1984). The Seattle Longitudinal Study: A 21-year exploration of psychometric intelligence in adulthood. In K. W. Schaie (Ed.), *Longitudinal studies of adult psychological development.* New York: Guilford Press.

Schaie, K. W. (1989). Introduction. In K. W. Schaie & C. Schooler (Eds.), *Social structure and aging: Psychological processes.* Hillsdale, NJ: Erlbaum.

Schaie, K. W. (1993). *The course of adult intellectual development.* Unpublished manuscript, Pennsylvania State University, University Park, PA.

Schaie, K. W. (1993). The Seattle longitudinal studies of adult intelligence. *Current Directions in Psychological Science, 2,* 171–175.

Schaie, K. W. (1994). *The course of adult intellectual development.* Unpublished manuscript, Department of Psychology, Pennsylvania State University, University Park.

Schaie, K. W. (1994). Developmental designs revisited. In S. H. Cohen & H. W. Reese (Eds.), *Life-span developmental psychology: Methodological contributions.* Hillsdale, NJ: Erlbaum.

Schank, R., & Abelson, R. (1977). *Scripts, plans, goals, and understanding.* Hillsdale, NJ: Erlbaum.

Schegloff, E. A. (1989). Reflections on language, development, and the interactional character of talk-interaction. In M. H. Bornstein & J. S. Bruner (Eds.), *Interaction in human development.* Hillsdale, NJ: Erlbaum.

Scheidel, D. G., & Marcia, J. E. (1985). Ego identity, intimacy, sex-role orientation, and gender. *Developmental Psychology, 21,* 149–160.

Schilke, J. M. (1991). Slowing the aging process with physical activity. *Gerontological Nursing, 17,* 4–8.

Schirmer, G. J. (Ed.). (1974). *Performance objectives for preschool children.* Sioux Falls, SD: Adapt Press.

Schlenker, E. D. (1988). Nutrition for aging and the aged. In S. R. Williams & B. S. Worthington-Roberts (Eds.), *Nutrition throughout the life cycle.* St. Louis: Times Mirror/Mosby.

Schmich, M. T. (1987, July 29). Living alone. *Dallas Morning News,* Section C, pp. 1, 4.

Schmidt, M. G. (1990). *Negotiating a good old age.* San Francisco: Jossey-Bass.

Schnorr, T. M., & others. (1991). Videodisplay terminals and the risk of spontaneous abortion. *New England Journal of Medicine, 324,* 727–733.

Schoendorf, K. C., & Kiely, J. L. (1992). Relationship of sudden infant death syndrome to maternal smoking during and after pregnancy. *Pediatrics, 90,* 905–908.

Schoenfeld, A. H. (1985). *Mathematical problem solving.* Orlando, FL: Academic Press.

Schooler, C. (1991). Individualism and the historical and social structural determinants of people's concern over self-directedness and efficacy. In J. Rodin, C. Schooler, & K. W. Schaie (Eds.), *Self-directedness and efficacy.* Hillsdale, NJ: Erlbaum.

Schorr, L. B. (1989, April). *Within our reach: Breaking the cycle of disadvantage.* Paper presented at the biennial meeting of the Society for Research in Child Development, Kansas City.

Schorr, L. (1988). *Within our reach: Breaking the cycle of disadvantage.* New York: Anchor.

Schrag, S. G., & Dixon, R. L. (1985). Occupational exposure associated with male reproductive dysfunction. *Annual Review of Pharmacology and Toxicology, 25,* 467–592.

Schuckit, M. A. (1994). A clinical model of genetic influences in alcohol dependence. *Journal of Studies on Alcohol, 55,* 5–17.

Schultz, R., & Curnow, C. (1988). Peak performance and age among super athletes: Track and field, swimming, baseball, tennis, and golf. *Journal of Gerontology, 43,* P113–P120.

Schultz, R., & Hanusa, B. H. (1978). Long-term effects of control and predictability-enhancing interventions: Findings and ethical issues. *Journal of Personality and Social Psychology, 11,* 1194–1201.

Schulz, R. (1976). Effects of control and predictability on the physical and psychological well-being of the institutionalized aged. *Journal of Personality and Social Psychology, 33,* 563–573.

Schunk, D. H. (1983). Developing children's self-efficacy and skills: The roles of social comparative information and goal-setting. *Contemporary Educational Psychology, 8,* 76–86.

Schunk, D. H. (1990). Introduction to the special section on motivation and efficacy. *Journal of Educational Psychology, 82,* 3–6.

Schwartz, D., & Mayaux, M. J. (1982). Female fecundity as a function of age: Results of artificial insemination in nulliparous women with azoospermic husbands. *New England Journal of Medicine, 306,* 304–406.

Schwartz, J. (1988). The computer market. *American Demographics, 10* (9), 38–41.

Schwartz, R., & Eriksen, M. (1989). Statement of the Society for Public Health Education on the national health promotion disease prevention objectives for the year 2000. *Health Education Quarterly, 16,* 3–7.

Scitovsky, A. A. (1988). Medical care in the last twelve months of life: Relation between age, functional status, and medical care expenditures. *Milbank Quarterly, 66,* 640–660.

Scott, J. P. (1983). Siblings and other kin. In T. Brubaker (Ed.), *Family relationships in later life.* Beverly Hills, CA: Sage.

Scott-Jones, D., & White, A. B. (1990). Correlates of sexual activity in early adolescence. *Journal of Early Adolescence, 10,* 221–238.

Scribner, S. (1977). Modes of thinking and ways of speaking: Culture and logic reconsidered. In F. N. Johnson-Laird & P. C. Wason (Eds.), *Thinking: Readings in cognitive science.* New York: Cambridge University Press.

Seager, J., & Olson, A. (Eds.). (1986). *Women of the world: An international atlas.* New York: Simon & Schuster.

Sears, R. R., & Feldman, S. S. (Eds.). (1973). *The seven ages of man.* Los Altos, CA: Kaufmann.

Segerberg, O. (1982). *Living to be 100: 1200 who did and how they did it.* New York: Charles Scribner's Sons.

Seidman, E., Allen, L., Aber, J. L., Mithcell, C., & Feinman, J. (in press). The impact of school transitions in early adolescence on the self-system perceived social context of poor urban youth. *Child Development.*

Selman, R. L. (1976). Social-cognitive understanding. In T. Lickona (Ed.), *Moral development and behavior.* New York: Holt, Rinehart & Winston.

Selman, R. L. (1980). *The growth of interpersonal understanding.* New York: Academic Press.

Semaj, L. T. (1985). Afrikanity, cognition, and extended self-identity. In M. B. Spencer, G. K. Brookins, & W. R. Allen (Eds.), *Beginnings: The social and affective development of Black children.* Hillsdale. NJ: Erlbaum.

Serbin, L. A., & Sprafkin, C. (1986). The salience of gender in the process of sex-typing in three- to seven-year-old children. *Child Development, 57,* 1188–1209.

Serdula, M., Williamson, D. F., Kendrick, J. S., Anda, R. F., & Byers, T. (1991). Trends in alcohol consumption by pregnant women: 1985 through 1988. *Journal of the American Medical Association, 265,* 876–879.

Sexton, M., & Hebel, J. R. (1984). A clinical trial of change in maternal smoking and its effects on birth weight. *Journal of the American Medical Association, 251,* 911–915.

Shakeshaft, C. (1986, March). A gender at risk. *Phi Delta Kappan,* pp. 499–503.

Shantz, C. O. (1988). Conflicts between children. *Child Development, 59,* 283–305.

Shantz, C. U. (1983). Social cognition. In P. H. Mussen (Ed.), *Handbook of child psychology* (4th ed., Vol. 3). New York: Wiley.

Shaver, P. (1986, August). *Being lonely, falling in love: Perspectives from attachment theory.* Paper presented at the meeting of the American Psychological Association, Washington, DC.

Shaver, P. (1993, March). *Where do adult romantic attachment patterns come from?* Paper presented at the biennial meeting of the Society for Research in Child Development, New Orleans.

Shaw, S. M. (1988). Gender differences in the definition and perception of household labor. *Family Relations, 37,* 333–337.

Sheehy, G. (1991). *The silent passage.* New York: Random House.

Sherwood, A., Light, K. C., & Blumenthal, J. A. (1989). Effects of aerobic exercise training on hemodynamic responses during psychosocial stress in normotensive and borderline hypertensive Type A men: A preliminary report. *Psychosomatic Medicine, 51,* 123–136.

Shields, S. A. (1991a, August). *Doing emotion/doing gender.* Paper presented at the meeting of the American Psychological Association, San Francisco.

Shields, S. A. (1991b). Gender in the psychology of emotion: A selective research review. In K. T. Strongman (Ed.), *International review of studies on emotion* (Vol. 1). New York: Wiley.

Shinn, M., & Gillespie, C. (1994). The roles of housing and poverty in the origins of homelessness. *American Behavioral Scientists, 37,* 505–521.

Shneidman, E. S. (1971). Suicide among the gifted. *Suicide and Life-threatening Behavior, 1,* 23–45.

Shneidman, E. S. (1973). *Deaths of man.* New York: Quadrangle/New York Times.

Shonkoss, J. P. (in press). Health surveillance and the development of children. In S. L. Friedman & H. C. Haywood (Eds.), *Developmental follow-up: Concepts, genres,*

domains, and methods. New York: Academic Press.

Shuchter, S., & Zisook, S. (in press). The course of normal grief. In M. Stroebe, W. Stroebe, & R. O. Hanson (Eds.), *Handbook of bereavement.* New York: Cambridge University Press.

Shugar, G. W., & Kmita, G. (1991). The pragmatics of collaboration: Participant structure and the structure of participation. In G. Conti-Ramsden & C. E. Snow (Eds.), *Children's language* (Vol. 7). Hillsdale, NJ: Erlbaum.

Siegel, L. S. (1989, April). *Perceptual-motor, cognitive, and language skills as predictors of cognitive abilities at school age.* Paper presented at the biennial meeting of the Society for Research in Children, Kansas City.

Siegler, I. C., & Costa, P. T. (1985). Health behavior relationships. In J. E. Birren & K. W. Schaie (Eds.), *Handbook of the psychology of aging* (2nd ed.). New York: Van Nostrand Reinhold.

Siegler, I. C. (1989). Developmental health psychology. In M. Storandt & G. R. VandenBos (Eds.), *The adult years: Continuity and change.* Washington, DC: American Psychological Association.

Siegler, R. S. (1991). *Children's thinking* (2nd ed.). Englewood Cliffs, NJ: Prentice-Hall.

Siegman, A. W., & Dembrowski, T. (Eds.). (1989). *In search of coronary-prone behavior: Beyond Type A.* Hillsdale, NJ: Erlbaum.

Sigman, M., Asarnow, R., Cohen, S., & Parmalee, A. H. (1989, April). *Infant attention as a measure of information processing.* Paper presented at the biennial meeting of the Society for Research in Child Development, Kansas City.

Silverberg, S. B., & Steinberg, L. (1990). Psychological well-being of parents with early adolescent children. *Developmental Psychology, 26,* 658–666.

Simkin, P., Whalley, J., & Keppler, A. (1984). *Pregnancy, childbirth, and the newborn.* New York: Simon & Schuster.

Simmons, R. G., & Blyth, D. A. (1987). *Moving into adolescence.* Hawthorne, NY: Aldine.

Simons, J., Finlay, B., & Yang, A. (1993). *The adolescent and young adult fact book.* Washington, DC: Children's Defense Fund.

Simons, J., Kalichman, S., & Santrock, J. W. (1994). *The psychology of human adjustment.* Dubuque, IA: Brown & Benchmark.

Simons, J. M., Finlay, B., & Yang, A. (1991). *The adolescent and young adult fact book.* Washington, DC: Children's Defense Fund.

Simonton, D. K. (1989). Age and creative productivity: Nonlinear estimation of an information-processing model. *International Journal of Aging and Human Development, 29,* 23–27.

Simopoulos, A. P., & VanItallie, T. B. (1984). Body weight, health, and longevity. *Annual of Internal Medicine, 100,* 285.

Simpson, J. A., Campbell, B., & Berscheid, E. (1986). The association between love and marriage: Kephart (1967) twice revisited. *Personality and Social Psychology Bulletin, 12,* 363–372.

Singer, J. L., & Singer, D. G. (1988). Imaginative play and human development:

Schemas, scripts, and possibilities. In D. Bergin (Ed.), *Play as a medium for learning and development.* Portsmouth, NH: Heinemann.

Singer, M. (1991). *Psychology of language: An introduction to sentence and discourse processes.* Hillsdale, NJ: Erlbaum.

Skinner, B. F. (1957). *Verbal behavior.* New York: Appleton-Century-Crofts.

Skinner, E. A., Wellborn, J. G., & Connell, J. P. (1990). What it takes to do well in school and whether I've got it: A process model of perceived control and children's engagement and achievement in school. *Journal of Educational Psychology, 82,* 22–32.

Skinner, J. H. (1990). Targeting benefits for the black elderly: The Older Americans Act. In Z. Harel, E. A. McKinney, & M. Williams (Eds.), *Black aged.* Newbury Park, CA: Sage.

Skoe, E. E., & Marcia, J. E. (1988). *Ego identity and care-based moral reasoning in college women.* Unpublished manuscript, Acadia University.

Slater, A., Cooper, R., Rose, D., & Morrison, V. (1989). Prediction of cognitive performance from infancy to early childhood. *Human Development, 32,* 137–147.

Slaughter-Defoe, D. T., Nakagawa, K., Takanishi, R., & Johnson, D. J. (1990). Toward cultural/ecological perspectives on schooling and achievement in African- and Asian-American children. *Child Development, 61,* 363–383.

Slavin, R. E. (1987). Developmental and motivational perspectives on cooperative learning: A reconciliation. *Child Development, 58,* 1161–1167.

Slavin, R. E. (1988). *Educational psychology* (2nd ed.). Englewood Cliffs, NJ: Prentice-Hall.

Slavin, R. E. (1989). Cooperative learning and student achievement. In R. E. Slavin (Ed.), *School and classroom organization.* Hillsdale, NJ: Erlbaum.

Slobin, D. (1972, July) Children and language: They learn the same way all around the world. *Psychology Today,* pp. 71–76.

Smith, A. D. (1977). Adult age differences in cued recall. *Developmental Psychology, 13,* 326–331.

Smith, B. A., Fillion, T. J., & Blass, E. M. (1990). Orally mediated sources of calming in 1- to 3-day-old human infants. *Developmental Psychology, 26,* 731–737.

Smith, H. L., & Morgan, S. P. (1994). Children's closeness to father as reported by mothers, sons, and daughters. *Journal of Family Issues, 15,* 3–29.

Smith, J., & Baltes, P. B. (1991). A life-span perspective on thinking and problem solving. In M. Schwebel, C. A. Maher, & N. S. Fagley (Eds.), *Promoting cognitive growth over the life span.* Hillsdale, NJ: Erlbaum.

Smith, J., & Baltes, P. B. (in press). A study of wisdom-related knowledge: Age-cohort differences in responses to life-planning problems. *Developmental Psychology.*

Smith, J. M. (1993). Function and supportive roles of church and religion. In J. S. Jackson, L. M. Chatters & R. J. Taylor (Eds.). *Aging in Black America.* Newbury Park, CA: Sage.

Smith, L., Ulvund, S. E., & Lindemann, R. (1994). Very low birth weight infants at double risk. *Journal of Developmental and Behavioral Pediatrics, 15,* 7–13.

Smither, R. D. (1988). *The psychology of work and human performance.* New York: Harper & Row.

Smolucha, F. (1989, April). *Vygotsky's theory of creative imagination and its relevance for research on play.* Paper presented at the biennial meeting of the Society for Research on Child Development, Kansas City.

Snarey, J. (1987, June). A question of morality. *Psychology Today,* pp. 6–8.

Snow, C. E. (1989, April). *Imitation as one path to language acquisition.* Paper presented at the biennial meeting of the Society for Research in Child Development, Kansas City.

Snow, D. A., & Bradford, M. G. (1994). Broadening perspectives on homelessness. *American Behavioral Scientists, 37,* 451–452.

Snowden, L. R., & Cheung, F. K. (1990). Use of inpatient mental health services by members of ethnic minority groups. *American Psychologist, 45,* 347–355.

Sokolovsky, J. (1983). *Growing old in different societies: Cross-cultural perspectives.* Belmont, CA: Wadsworth.

Sommer, B. B. (1978). *Puberty and adolescence.* New York: Oxford University Press.

Sorenson, S. B., & White, J. W. (1992). Adult sexual assault: Overview of research. *Journal of Social Issues, 48,* 1–8.

Spade, J. Z., & Reese, C. A. (1991). We've come a long way, maybe: College students' plan for work and family. *Sex Roles, 24,* 309–322.

Spear-Swerling, L., & Sternberg, R. J. (1994). The road not taken: An integrative theoretical model of reading disability. *Journal of Learning Disabilities, 27,* 91–103.

Speece, M., & Brent, S. (1984). Children's understanding of death: A review of three components of a death concept. *Child Development, 55,* 1671–1686.

Spelke, E. S. (1988). The origins of physical knowledge. In L. Weiskrantz (Ed.), *Thought without language.* New York: Oxford University Press.

Spelke, E. S. (1991). Physical knowledge in infancy: Reflections on Piaget's theory. In S. Carey & R. Gelman (Eds.), *The epigenesis of mind: Essays on biology and cognition.* Hillsdale, NJ: Erlbaum.

Spence, J. T., & Helmreich, R. (1978). *Masculinity and femininity: Their psychological dimensions.* Austin: University of Texas Press.

Spence, J. T. (1984). Masculinity, femininity, and gender-related traits: A conceptual analysis and critique of current research. In B. A. Maher & W. B. Maher (Eds.), *Progress in experimental personality research* (Vol. 13, pp. 1–97). Orlando, FL: Academic Press.

Spence, J. T. (1985). Gender identity and its implications for the concepts of masculinity and femininity. In T. B. Sonderegger (Ed.), *Psychology and gender: Nebraska Symposium on Motivation* (pp. 59–96). Lincoln: University of Nebraska Press.

Spencer, M. B., & Dornbusch, S. M. (1990). Challenges in studying minority youth. In S. S. Feldman & G. R. Elliott (Eds.), *At the threshold: The developing adolescent.*

Cambridge, MA: Harvard University Press.

Spencer, M. B., & Markstrom-Adams, C. (1990). Identity processes among racial and ethnic minority children in America. *Child Development, 61,* 290–310.

Spencer, M. B. (1987). Black children's ethnic identity formation: Risk and resilience of castelike minorities. In J. S. Phinney & M. J. Rotheram (Eds.), *Children's ethnic socialization: Pluralism and development.* Newbury Park, CA: Sage.

Spielberger, C. D., & Grier, K. (1983). Unpublished manuscript, University of South Florida, Tampa.

Sprecher, S., & McKinney, K. (1993). *Sexuality.* Newbury Park, CA: Sage.

Sprei, J. E., & Courtois, C. A. (1988). The treatment of women's sexual dysfunctions arising from sexual assault. In R. A. Brown & J. R. Field (Eds.), *Treatment of sexual problems in individual and couples therapy.* Great Neck, NY: PMA.

Sroufe, L. A., & Waters, E. (1976). The ontogenesis of smiling and laughter: A perspective on the organization of development in infancy. *Psychological Review, 83,* 173–198.

Sroufe, L. A. (1985). Attachment classification from the perspective of infant-caregiver relationships and infant temperament. *Child Development, 49,* 547–556.

Sroufe, L. A. (1990). Considering normal and abnormal together: The essence of developmental psychopathology. *Development and Psychopathology, 2,* 335–347.

Sroufe, L. A. (in press). Pathways to adaptation and maladaptation: Psychopathology as developmental deviation. In D. Cicchetti (Ed.), *Developmental psychopathology: Past, present, and future.* Hillsdale, NJ: Erlbaum.

Stallings, J. (1975). Implementation and child effects of teaching practices in Follow Through classrooms. *Monographs of the Society for Research in Child Development, 40* (Serial No. 163).

Stampfer, M. J., Hennekens, C. H., Manson, J. E., Colditz, G. A., Rosner, B., & Willett, W. C. (1993). Vitamin E consumption and the risk of coronary disease in women. *New England Journal of Medicine, 328,* 1444–1449.

Stanford, E. P., Happersett, C. J., Morton, D. J., Molgaard, C. A., & Peddecord, K. M. (1991). Early retirement and functional impairment from a multi-ethnic perspective. *Research on Aging, 13,* 5–38.

Stanford, E. P. (1990). Diverse Black aged. In Z. Harel, E. A. McKinney, & M. Williams (Eds.), *Black aged.* Newbury Park, CA: Sage.

Stanhope, L., & Corter, C. (1993, March). *The mother's role in the transition to siblinghood.* Paper presented at the biennial meeting of the Society for Research in Child Development, New Orleans.

Starrels, M. (1994, January 18). Retirement and marital quality. Invited presentation, School of Social Sciences, University of Texas at Dallas, Richardson, TX.

Stattin, H., & Magnusson, D. (1990). Pubertal maturation in female development. *Paths through life* (Vol. 2). Hillsdale, NJ: Erlbaum.

Steil, J. M., & Weltman, K. (1991). Marital inequality: The importance of resources, personal attributes, and social norms on career valuing and the allocation of domestic responsibilities. *Sex Roles, 24,* 161–180.

Stein, N. L., & Glenn, C. G. (1979). An analysis of story comprehension in elementary school children. In R. O. Freedle (Ed.), *Discourse processing: Multidisciplinary perspectives* (pp. 53–120). Norwood, NJ: Ablex.

Steinberg, L. D., & Levine, A. (1990). *You and your adolescent.* New York: Harper.

Steinberg, L. D. (1981). Transformations in family relations at puberty. *Developmental Psychology, 17,* 833–840.

Steinberg, L. D. (1986). Latchkey children and susceptibility to peer pressure: An ecological analysis. *Developmental Psychology, 22,* 433–439.

Steinberg, L. D. (1988). Reciprocal relation between parent-child distance and pubertal maturation. *Developmental Psychology, 24,* 122–128.

Steinberg, L. (1993). *Adolescence* (3rd ed.). New York: McGraw-Hill.

Steiner, J. E. (1979). Human facial expressions in response to taste and smell stimulation. In H. Reese & L. Lipsitt (Eds.), *Advances in child development and behavior* (Vol. 13). New York: Academic Press.

Stern, D. N., Beebe, B., Jaffe, J., & Bennett, S. L. (1977). The infant's stimulus world during social interaction: A study of caregiver behaviors with particular reference to repetition and timing. In H. R. Schaffer (Ed.), *Studies in mother-infant interaction.* London: Academic Press.

Stern, J. S. (1984). Is obesity a disease of inactivity? In A. J. Stunkard & E. Stellar (Eds.), *Eating and its disorders.* New York: Raven Press.

Stern, J. S. (1993, June 2). Commentary in "Lowly vitamin supplements pack a big health punch." *USA Today,* p. 3D.

Sternberg, R. J., & McGrane, P. A. (1993). *Intellectual development across the life span.* Unpublished manuscript, Yale University, New Haven, CT.

Sternberg, R. J., & Okagaki, L. (1989). Continuity and discontinuity in intellectual development are not a matter of 'either-or.' *Human Development, 32,* 158–166.

Sternberg, R. J. (1986). *Intelligence applied.* San Diego: Harcourt Brace Jovanovich.

Sternberg, R. J. (1987a). A day at developmental downs: Sportscast for race #2—neo-Piagetian theories of cognitive development. *International Journal of Psychology, 22,* 507–529.

Sternberg, R. J. (1987b). Teaching intelligence: The application of cognitive psychology of intellectual skills. In J. B. Baron & R. J. Sternberg (Eds.), *Teaching thinking skills: Theory and practice.* New York: W. H. Freeman.

Sternberg, R. J. (1988). *The triangle of love.* New York: Basic Books.

Sternberg, R. J. (1989). Introduction. In R. J. Sternberg (Ed.), *Advances in the psychology of human intelligence* (Vol. 5). Hillsdale, NJ: Erlbaum.

Sternberg, R. J. (1993, August). *Recent advances in the psychology of love.* Paper presented at the meeting of the American Psychological Association, Toronto, Canada.

Sternglanz, S. H., Serbin, L. A. (1974). Sex-role stereotyping in children's television programming. *Developmental Psychology, 10*, 710–715.

Steur, F. B., Applefield, J. M., & Smith, R. (1971). Televised aggression and interpersonal aggression of preschool children. *Journal of Experimental Child Psychology, 11*, 442–447.

Stevens, J. H. (1984). Black grandmothers' and black adolescents mothers' knowledge about parenting. *Developmental Psychology, 20*, 1017–1025.

Stevens-Simon, C., & McAnarney, E. R. (1992). Adolescent pregnancy: Continuing challenges. In D. E. Greydanus & M. L. Wolraich (Eds.), *Behavioral pediatrics.* New York: Springer-Verlag.

Stevenson, H. W., Chen, C., & Lee, S. Y. (1993). Mathematics achievement of Chinese, Japanese, & American Children: Ten years later. *Science, 259.* 53–58.

Stevenson, H. W., Lee, S., Chen, C., Stigler, J. W., Hsu, C., & Kitamura, S. (1990). Contexts of achievement. *Monograph of the Society for Research in Child Development, 55* (Serial No. 221).

Stevenson, H. W. (1992, December). Learning from Asian schools. *Scientific American,* pp. 6, 70–76.

Steward, E. P. (1994). *Beginning writers in the zone of proximal development.* Hillsdale, NJ: Erlbaum.

Stewart, N. (1990, January 27). *The effects of cocaine use by pregnant mothers on the development of their offspring.* Invited presentation, School of Human Development, University of Texas at Dallas, Richardson, TX.

Stine, E. L., & Bohannon, J. N., III. (1984). Imitations, interactions, and language acquisition. *Journal of Child Language, 10*, 589–603.

Stipek D. J., & Hoffman, J. M. (1980). Children's achievement-related expectancies as a function of academic performance histories and sex. *Journal of Educational Psychology, 72*, 861–865.

Stipek, D. (1992). The child at school. In M. H. Bornstein & M. E. Lamb (Eds.), *Developmental psychology: An advanced textbook* (3rd ed.). Hillsdale, NJ: Erlbaum.

Stock, W. A., Okum, M. A., Haring, M. J., & Witter, R. A. (1983). Age and subjective well-being: A meta-analysis. In R. J. Light (Ed.), *Evaluation studies: Review annual* (Vol. 8). Newbury Park, CA: Sage.

Stocker, C., & Dunn, J. (1991). Sibling relationships in adolescence. In R. M. Lerner, A. C. Petersen, & J. Brooks-Gunn (Eds.), *Encyclopedia of adolescence* (Vol. 2). New York: Garland.

Stones, M. J., & Kozman, A. (1989). Age, exercise, and coding performance. *Psychology and Aging. 4*, 190–194.

Strawn, J. (1992, Fall). *The states and the poor: Child poverty rises as the safety net shrinks.* (Social Policy Report, Society for Research in Child Development, pp. 1–19). Chicago: University of Chicago Press.

Streissguth, A. P., Carmichael-Olson, H., Sampston, P. D., & Barr, H. M. (1991, April). *Alcohol vs. tobacco as prenatal correlates of child behavior.* Paper presented at the biennial meeting of the Society for Research in Child Development, Seattle.

Streissguth, A. P., Martin, D. C., Barr, H. M., Sandman, B. M., Kirshner, G. L., & Darby, B. L. (1984). Intrauterine alcohol and nicotine exposure: Attention and reaction time in 4-year-old children. *Developmental Psychology, 20*, 533–541.

Strickland, B. R. (1987). Menopause. In E. A. Blechaman & K. D. Brownell (Eds.), *Handbook of behavioral medicine for women.* Elmsford, NY: Pergamon.

Strickland, B. (1988). Sex-related differences in health and illness. *Psychology of Women Quarterly, 12*, 381–399.

Striegel-Moore, R., Pike, K., Rodin, J., Schreiber, G., & Wilfley, D. (1993, March). *Predictors and correlates of drive for thinness.* Paper presented at the biennial meeting of the Society for Research in Child Development, New Orleans.

Stroebe, M., & Stroebe, W. (1991). Does "grief work" work? *Journal of Consulting and Clinical Psychology, 59*, 57–65.

Stroebe, M., Gergen, M. H., Gergen, K. J., & Stroebe, W. (1992). Broken hearts or broken bonds: Love and death in historical perspective. *American Psychologist, 47* 1205–1212.

Stroebe, M., Stroebe, W., & Hanson, R. O. (Eds.). (in press). *Handbook of bereavement.* New York: Cambridge University Press.

Stroebe, M. (in press). Coping with bereavement: A review of the grief work hypothesis. *Omega.*

Stroebe, W., Stroebe, M. (in press). Determinants of adjustment to bereavement in young widows and widowers. In M. Stroebe, W. Stroebe, & R. O. Hanson (Eds.), *Handbook of bereavement.* New York: Cambridge University Press.

Strom, R. D., & Strom, S. K. (1993). Grandparents raising grandchildren: Goals and support groups. *Educational Gerontology, 19*, 705–716.

Stull, D. E., & Hatch, L. R. (1984). Unravelling the effects of multiple life changes. *Research on Aging, 6*, 560–571.

Stunkard, A. J. (1987). The regulation of body weight and the treatment of obesity. In H. Weiner & A. Baum (Eds.), *Eating regulation and discontrol.* Hillsdale, NJ: Erlbaum.

Sue, D., & Sue, D. W. (1993). Ethnic identity: Cultural factors in the psychological development of Asians in America. In D. R. Atkinson, G. Morten, & D. W. Sue (Eds.), *Counseling American minorities.* Dubuque, IA: Brown & Benchmark.

Sue, D. W. (1989). Ethnic identity: The impact of two cultures on the psychological development of Asians in America. In D. R. Atkinson, G. Morten, & D. W. Sue (Eds.), *Counseling American minorities* (3rd ed.). Dubuque, IA: Brown & Benchmark.

Sue, S., & Okazaki, S. (1990). Asian-American educational achievements. *American Psychologist, 45*, 913–920.

Sue, S. (1990, August). *Ethnicity and culture in psychological research and practice.* Paper presented at the meeting of the American Psychological Association, Boston.

Suitor, J. J. (1991). Marital quality and satisfaction with the division of household labor across the family life cycle. *Journal of Marriage and the Family, 53*, 221–230.

Sullivan, H. S. (1953). *The interpersonal theory of psychiatry.* New York: W. W. Norton.

Sullivan, K., & Sullivan, A. (1980). Adolescent-parent separation. *Developmental Psychology, 16*, 93–99.

Suomi, S. J., Harlow, H. F., & Domek, C. J. (1970). Effect of repetitive infant-infant separations of young monkeys. *Journal of Abnormal Psychology, 76*, 161–172.

Super, C. M., Herrera, M. G., & Mora, J. O. (1990). Long-term effects of food supplementation and psychosocial intervention on the physical growth of Colombian infants at risk of malnutrition. *Child Development, 61*, 29–49.

Super, C. M., Herrera, M. G., & Mora, J. O. (1991, April). *Cognitive outcomes of early nutritional intervention in the Bogota study.* Paper presented at the biennial meeting of the Society for Research in Child Development, Seattle.

Super, C. M. (1980). Cross-cultural research on infancy. In H. C. Triandis & A. Heron (Eds.), *Handbook of cross-cultural psychology, developmental psychology* (Vol. 4). Boston: Allyn & Bacon.

Super, D. E., Kowalski, R., & Gotkin, E. (1967). *Floundering and trial after high school.* Unpublished manuscript, Columbia University.

Super, D. E. (1967). *The psychology of careers.* New York: Harper & Row.

Super, D. E. (1976). *Career education and the meanings of work.* Washington, DC: U.S. Office of Education.

Susman, E. J., & Dorn, L. (1991). Hormones and behavior in adolescence. In R. M. Lerner, A. C. Petersen, & J. Brooks-Gunn (Eds.), *Encyclopedia of adolescence* (Vol. 1). New York: Garland.

Susman, E. J., & Dorn, L. (1991). Hormones and behavior in adolescence. In R. M. Lerner, A. C. Petersen, & J. Brooks-Gunn (Eds.), *Encyclopedia of adolescence* (Vol. 1). New York: Garland.

Suzman, R. M., Harris, T., Hadley, E. C., Kovar, M. G., & Weindruch, R. (1992). The robust oldest old: Optimistic perspectives for increasing healthy life expectancy. In R. M. Suzman, D. P. Willis, & K. G. Manton (Eds.), *The oldest old.* New York: Oxford University Press.

Swan, J. H., & McCall, M. E. (1987). Mental health system components and the aged. In E. E. Lurie, J. H. Swan, & Associates (Eds.), *Serving the mentally ill elderly.* Lexington, MA: Lexington Books.

Swick, K. J., & Manning, M. L. (1983). Father involvement in home and school settings. *Childhood Education, 60*, 128–134.

Szinovacz, M. E. (1984). Changing family roles and interactions. In B. B. Hess & M. B. Sussman (Eds.), *Women and the family: Two decades of change.* New York: Hayworth Press.

Szinovacz, M. E. (1989). Retirement, couples, and household work. In S. J. Bahr & E. T. Peterson (Eds.), *Aging and the family.* Lexington, MA: Lexington Books.

T

Tager-Flusberg, H. (in press). A psycholinguistic perspective on language development in autistic children. In G. Dawson (Ed.), *Autism: New directions on diagnosis, nature, and treatment.* New York: Guilford Press.

Tajfel, H. (1978). The achievement of group differentiation. In H. Tajfel (Ed.), *Differentiation between social groups: Studies in the social psychology of intergroup relations.* London: Academic Press.

Takada, K. (1993). Aging workers in Japan: From reverence to redundancy. *Aging International, 20,* 17–20.

Takanishi, R., & DeLeon, P. H. (1994). A Head Start for the 21st century. *American Psychologist, 49,* 127–132.

Takanishi, R. (1993). Changing views of adolescence in contemporary society. In R. Takanishi (Ed.), *Adolescence in the 1990s.* New York: Teachers College Press.

Tamir, L. M. (1982). *Men in their forties.* New York: Springer.

Tannen, D. (1990). *You just don't understand.* New York: Ballantine.

Tanner, J. M. (1978). *Fetus into man: Physical growth from conception into maturity.* Cambridge, MA: Harvard University Press.

Tanner, J. M. (1991). Growth spurt, adolescent (I). In R. M. Lerner, A. C. Petersen, & J. Brooks-Gunn (Eds.), *Encyclopedia of adolescence* (Vol. 1). New York: Garland.

Tavris, C., & Wade, C. (1984). *The longest war: Sex differences in perspective* (2nd ed.). San Diego: Harcourt Brace Jovanovich.

Tavris, C. (1989). *Anger: The misunderstood emotion* (2nd ed.). New York: Touchstone.

Tavris, C. (1990). Cover commentary. In M. Csikszentmihalyi, *Flow.* New York: Harper & Row.

Tavris, C. (1992). *The mismeasure of women.* New York: Simon & Schuster.

Taylor, S. E. (1991). *Health psychology* (2nd ed.). New York: McGraw-Hill.

Taylor, S. P. (1982). Mental health and successful coping among Black women. In R. C. Manuel (Ed.), *Minority aging.* Westport, CT: Greenwood Press.

Taylor, W. (1988). Real problems, real answers. *Boston Magazine, 80,* 176–228.

Temoshok, L., & Dreher, H. (1992). *The Type C syndrome.* New York: Random House.

Terman, L. (1925). *Genetic studies of genius: Vol. 1. Mental and physical traits of a thousand gifted children.* Stanford, CA: Stanford University Press.

Teti, D. M., Sakin, J., Kucera, E., Caballeros, M., & Corns, K. M. (1993, March). *Transitions to siblinghood and security of firstborn attachment: Psychosocial and psychiatric correlates of changes over time.* Paper presented at the biennial meeting of the Society for Research in Child Development, New Orleans.

Tharp, R. G. (1989). Psychocultural variables and constants: Effects on teaching and learning in schools. *American Psychologist, 44,* 349–359.

The health of America's children. (1992). Washington, DC: Children's Defense Fund.

Thoman, E. B. (1992, May). *Individualizing intervention for premature infants.* Paper presented at the International Conference on Infant Studies, Miami Beach.

Thomas, A., & Chess, A. (1991). Temperament in adolescence and its functional significance. In R. M. Lerner, A. C. Petersen, & J. Brooks-Gunn (Eds.), *Encyclopedia of adolescence* (Vol. 2). New York: Garland.

Thomas, A., & Chess, S. (1987). Commentary. In H. H. Goldsmith, A. H. Buss, R. Plomin, M. K. Rothbart, A. Thomas, A. Chess, R. R. Hinde, & R. B. McCall (Eds.), Roundtable: What is temperament? Four approaches. *Child Development, 58,* 505–529.

Thomas, C. W., Coffman, J. K., & Kipp, K. L. (1993, March). *Are only children different from children with siblings? A longitudinal study of behavioral and social functioning.* Paper presented at the biennial meeting of the Society for Research in Child Development, New Orleans.

Thomas, G. (Ed.). (1988). *World education encyclopedia.* New York: Facts on File Publications.

Thomas, J. L. (1986). Age and sex differences in perceptions of grandparenting. *Journal of Gerontology, 41,* 417–423.

Thompson, L., & Walker, A. J. (1989). Gender in families: Women and men in marriage, work, and parenthood. *Journal of Marriage and the Family, 51,* 845–871.

Thompson, R. A. (1991). Construction and reconstruction of early attachments: Taking perspective on attachment theory and research. In D. P. Keating & H. G. Rosen (Eds.), *Constructivist perspectives on atypical development.* Hillsdale, NJ: Erlbaum.

Thompson, R. J., & Oehler, J. M. (1991, April). *Very low birthweight (VLBW) infants: Maternal stress, coping, and psychological adjustment.* Paper presented at the biennial meeting of the Society for Research in Child Development, Seattle.

Thorndike, R. L., Hagan, E. P., & Sattler, J. M. (1985). *Stanford-Binet* (4th ed.). Chicago: Riverside.

Tildesley, E. A., & Duncan, T. E. (1994, February). *Family and peer influences on the developmental trajectories of substance use in adolescence.* Paper presented at the meeting of the Society for Research on Adolescence, San Diego, CA.

Tishler, C. L. (1992). Adolescent suicide: Assessment of risk, prevention, and treatment. *Adolescent Medicine, 3,* 51–60.

Tobin, J. J., Wu, D. Y. H., & Davidson, D. H. (1989). *Preschool in three cultures.* New Haven, CT: Yale University Press.

Tobin, J. J. (1987). The American idealization of old age in Japan. *Gerontologist, 27,* 53–58.

Tobin, S. S. (1991). *Personhood in advanced old age.* New York: Springer.

Tomlinson-Keasey, C., Warren, L. W., & Elliott, J. E. (1986). Suicide among gifted women: A prospective study. *Journal of Abnormal Psychology, 95,* 123–130.

Topol, E. J., & Califf, R. M. (1992). Thrombolytic therapy for elderly patients. *New England Journal of Medicine, 327,* 45–47.

Torrey, B. B. (1992). Sharing increasing costs on declining income: The visible dilemma of the invisible aged. In R. M. Suzman, D. P. Willis, & K. G. Manton (Eds.), *The oldest old.* New York: Oxford University Press.

Toth, A. (1991). *The fertility solution.* New York: Atlantic Monthly Press.

Tran, T. V., Wright, R., & Chatters, L. (1991). Health, stress, psychological resources, and subjective well-being among older Blacks. *Psychology and Aging, 6,* 100–108.

Trankina, F. (1983). Clinical issues and techniques in working with Hispanic children and their families. In G. J. Powell, J. Yamamoto, A. Romero, & A. Morales (Eds.), *The psychosocial development of minority group children.* New York: Brunner/Mazel.

Treboux, D. A., & Busch-Rossnagel, N. A. (1991). Sexual behavior, sexual attitudes, and contraceptive use, age differences in adolescents. In R. M. Lerner, A. C. Petersen, & J. Brooks-Gunn (Eds.), *Encyclopedia of adolescence* (Vol. 2). New York: Garland.

Trehub, S. E., Schneider, B. A., Thorpe, L. A., & Judge, P. (1991). Observational measures of auditory sensitivity in early infancy. *Developmental Psychology, 27,* 40–49.

Triandis, H. C. (1990). Theoretical concepts that are applicable to the analysis of ethnocentrism. In R. W. Brislin (Ed.), *Applied cross-cultural psychology.* Newbury Park, CA: Sage.

Triandis, H. C. (1994). *Culture and social behavior.* New York: McGraw-Hill.

Trimble, J. E. (1989). *The enculturation of contemporary psychology.* Paper presented at the meeting of the American Psychological Association, New Orleans.

Troll, L. E., & Bengston, V. L. (1982). Intergenerational relations through the life span. In B. B. Wolman (Ed.), *Developmental psychology.* Englewood Cliffs, NJ: Prentice-Hall.

Troll, L. E. (1989). Myths of mid-life intergenerational relationships. In S. Hunter & M. Sundel (Eds.), *Mid-life myths.* Newbury Park, CA: Sage.

Tronick, E. Z. (1989). Emotions and emotional communication in infants. *American Psychologist, 44,* 112–119.

Trotter, R. J. (1987, December). Project day-care. *Psychology Today,* pp. 32–38.

Trotter, R. J. (1990, January). Regaining control. *Longevity,* pp. 60–67.

Truitner, K., & Truitner, N. (1993). Death and dying in Buddhism. In D. P. Irish & K. F. Lundquist (Eds.), *Ethnic variations in dying, death, and grief: Diversity in universality.* Washington, DC: Taylor & Francis.

Tucker, L. A. (1987). Television, teenagers, and health. *Journal of Youth and Adolescence, 16,* 415–425.

Tudge, J., & Winterhoff, P. (1993, March). *The cognitive consequences of collaboration: Why ask how?* Paper presented at the biennial meeting of the Society for Research in Child Development, New Orleans.

Turk, D. C., Rudy, T. E., & Salovey, P. (1984). Health protection: Attitudes and behaviors of LPN's teachers, and college students. *Health Psychology, 3,* 189–210.

Turner, B. F. (1982). Sex-related differences in aging. In B. B. Wolman (Ed.), *Handbook* *of developmental psychology.* Englewood Cliffs, NJ: Prentice-Hall.

Tyack, D. (1976). Ways of seeing: An essay on the history of compulsory schooling. *Harvard Educational Review, 46,* 355–389.

U

U.S. Bureau of the Census. (1987). *Fertility of American Women: June, 1986.* (Current Population Reports, Series P-20, No. 421). Washington, DC: U.S. Government Printing Office.

U.S. Bureau of the Census. (1990). *Statistical abstracts of the United States, 1990.* Washington, DC: U.S. Department of Commerce.

Ubell, C. (1992, December 6). We can age successfully. *Parade,* pp. 14–15.

Ulbrich, P. M. (1988). The determinants of depression in two-income marriages. *Journal of Marriage and the Family, 50,* 121–131.

United States Commission on Civil Rights. (1975). *A better chance to learn: Bilingual bicultural education.* Washington, DC: U.S. Government Printing Office.

Upcraft, M. L., & Gardner, J. N. (Eds.). (1989). *The freshman year experience.* San Francisco: Jossey-Bass.

Upton, A. C. (1977). Pathology. In L. E. Finch & L. Hayflick (Eds.), *Handbook of the biology of aging.* New York: Van Nostrand.

Usui, C. (1989). Can Japanese society promote individualism? In D. I. Kertzer & K. W. Schaie (Eds.), *Age structuring in comparative perspective.* Hillsdale, NJ: Erlbaum.

V

Vaillant, G. E., & Koury, S. H. (1994). Late midlife development. In G. H. Pollock & S. I. Greenspan (Eds.), *The course of life.* Madison, CT: International Universities Press.

Vaillant, G. E. (1977). *Adaptation to life.* Boston: Little, Brown.

van den Haag, E. (1992, October 13). At the final exit, in need of help. *Wall Street Journal,* A20.

Van Deusen-Henkel, J., & Argondizza, M. (1987). Early elementary education: Curriculum planning for the primary grades. In *A framework for curriculum design.* Augusta, ME: Maine Department of Educational and Cultural Services, Division of Curriculum.

Vandell, D. L., & Corasaniti, M. A. (1988). Variations in early child care: Do they predict subsequent social, emotional, and cognitive differences? *Child Development, 59,* 176–186.

Vandell, D. L., & Wilson, K. S. (1988). Infants' interactions with mother, sibling, and peer: Contrasts and relations between interaction systems. *Child Development, 48,* 176–186.

VandenBos, G. R., Stapp, J., & Kilburg, R. R. (1981). Health service providers in psychology: Results of the 1978 APA Human Resources Survey. *American Psychologist, 36,* 1395–1418.

VanItallie, T. B. (1984). The enduring storage capacity for fat: Implications for treatment

of obesity. In A. J. Stunkard & F. Stellar (Eds.), *Eating and its disorders.* New York: Raven Press.

Vannoy-Hiller, D., & Philliber, W. W. (1989). *Equal partners: Successful women in marriage.* Newbury Park, CA: Sage.

Vaughn, S. (1993, March). *A prospective investigation of the social competence of youngsters with learning disabilities.* Paper presented at the biennial meeting of the Society for Research in Child Development, New Orleans.

Verhaeghen, P., Marcoen, A., & Goossens, L. (1993). Facts and fiction about memory aging: A quantitative integration of research findings. *Journal of Gerontology, 48,* P157–P171.

Vinick, B. H., & Ekerdt, D. J. (1991). Retirement: What happens to husband-wife relationships? *Journal of Geriatric Psychiatry, 24,* 23–40.

Vining, E. P. G. (1992). Down syndrome. In R. A. Hoekelman (Ed.), *Primary pediatric care* (2nd ed.). St. Louis: Mosby Yearbook.

Visher, E. B., & Visher, J. (1992). Why stepfamilies need your help. *Contemporary Pediatrics, 9,* 146–165.

Voight, J., & Hans, S. (1993, March). *The mothers of adolescent mothers: Support and conflict in grandmother's social networks.* Paper presented at the biennial meeting of the Society for Research in Child Development, New Orleans.

von Tetzchner, S., & Siegel, L. S. (1989). *The social and cognitive aspects of normal and atypical language development.* New York: Springer-Verlag.

Vondracek, F. W. (1991). Vocational development and choice in adolescence. In R. M. Lerner, A. C. Petersen, & J. Brooks-Gunn (Eds.), *Encyclopedia of adolescence* (Vol. 2). New York: Garland.

Vorhees, C. V., & Mollnow, E. (1987). Behavioral teratogenesis: Long-term influences in behavior from early exposure to environmental agents. In J. D. Osofsky (Ed.), *Handbook of infant development.* New York: Wiley.

Vygotsky, L. S. (1962). *Thought and language.* Cambridge: Massachusetts Institute of Technology Press.

W

Waddington, C. H. (1957). *The strategy of the genes.* London: Allen & Son.

Wagner, B. M., Cole, R. E., & Schwartzman, P. (1993, March). *Prediction of suicide attempts among junior and senior high school youth.* Paper presented at the biennial meeting of the Society for Research in Child Development, New Orleans.

Wainrib, B. R. (Ed.). (1992). *Gender issues across the life cycle.* New York: Springer.

Walford, R. L. (1969). *The immunologic theory of aging.* Baltimore: Williams & Wilkins.

Walker, L. J. (1984). Sex differences in the development of moral reasoning. A critical review. *Child Development, 51,* 131–139.

Walker, L. J. (1991a). Sex differences in moral development. In W. M. Kurtines & J. Gewirtz (Eds.), *Moral behavior and development* (Vol. 2). Hillsdale, NJ: Erlbaum.

Walker, L. J. (1991b, April). *The validity of an ethic of care.* Paper presented at the Society for Research in Child Development meeting, Seattle.

Wall, J. A. (1993, March). *Susceptibility to antisocial peer pressure in Mexican-American adolescents and its relation to acculturation.* Paper presented at the biennial meeting of the Society for Research in Child Development, New Orleans.

Wallerstein, J. S., & Kelly, J. B. (1980). *Surviving the breakup: How children cope with divorce.* New York: Basic Books.

Wallerstein, J. S., Corbin, S. B., & Lewis, J. M. (1988). Children of divorce: A 10-year study. In E. M. Hetherington & J. D. Arasteh (Eds.), *Impact of divorce, single parenting, and stepparenting on children.* Hillsdale, NJ: Erlbaum.

Wallerstein, J. S. (1989). *Second chances.* New York: Ticknor & Fields.

Wallis, C. (1985, December 9). Children having children. *Time,* pp. 78–88.

Warner, R. L. (1986). Alternative strategies for measuring household division of labor: A comparison. *Journal of Family Issues, 7,* 179–185.

Warshak, R. A. (1993, January 15). Personal communication, Department of Psychology, University of Texas at Dallas, Richardson, TX.

Wass, H., & Stillion, J. M. (1988). Death in the lives of children and adolescents. In H. Wass, F. M. Berardo, & R. A. Neimeyer (Eds.), *Dying: Facing the facts* (2nd ed.). Washington, DC: Hemisphere.

Wass, H., Berardo, F. N., & Neimeyer, R. A. (1988). Dying: Integrating the facts. In H. Wass, F. N. Berardo, & R. A. Neimeyer (Eds.), *Dying: Facing the facts* (2nd ed.). Washington, DC; Hemisphere.

Wass, H. (1985). Depiction of death, grief, and funerals on national television. *Research Record, 2,* 81–82.

Wasz-Hockert, O., Lind, J., Vuorenkoski, V., Partanen, T., & Valanne, E. (1968). *The infant cry.* London: Spastics International Medical Publications.

Waterman, A. S. (1985). Identity in the context of adolescent psychology. In A. S. Waterman (Ed.), *Identity in adolescence: Processes and contents.* San Francisco: Jossey-Bass.

Waterman, A. S. (1992). Identity as an aspect of optimal psychological functioning. In G. R. Adams, T. P. Gullotta, & R. Montemayor (Eds), *Adolescent Identity formation.* Newbury Park, CA: Sage.

Waterman, A S. (1989). Curricula interventions for identity change: Substantive and ethical considerations. *Journal of Adolescence, 12,* 389–400.

Waters, E., Posada, G., Crowell, J. A., & Lay, K. L. (1994). The development of attachment. *Psychiatry: Interpersonal and Biological Processes, 57,* 32–42.

Waters, E. B., & Goodman, J. G. (1990). *Empowering older adults: Practical strategies for counselors.* San Francisco: Jossey-Bass.

Watson, J. B. (1928). *Psychological care of infant and child.* New York: W. W. Norton.

Watson, W. H. (1990). Family care, economics, and health. In Z. Harel, E. A. McKinney, & M. Williams (Eds.), *Black aged.* Newbury Park, CA: Sage.

Webster, J. D. (1993, October). *Adult age differences in reminiscence functions.* Paper presented at the meeting of the Gerontological Association of America, New Orleans.

Wechsler, D. (1949). *Wechsler Intelligence Scale for Children.* New York: Psychological Corporation.

Wechsler, D. (1955). *Wechsler Adult Intelligence Scale manual.* New York: Psychological Corporation.

Wechsler, D. (1967). *Wechsler Preschool and Primary Scale of Intelligence.* New York: Psychological Corporation.

Wechsler, D. (1972) "Hold" and "Don't Hold" test. In S. M. Chown (Ed.), *Human aging.* New York: Penguin.

Wechsler, D. (1974). *Wechsler Intelligence Scale for Children—Revised.* New York: Psychological Corporation.

Wechsler, D. (1981). *Wechsler Adult Intelligence Scale—Revised.* New York: Psychological Corporation.

Wechsler, D. (1989). *Wechsler Preschool and Primary Scale of Intelligence—Revised.* San Antonio, TX: Psychological Corporation.

Wechsler, D. (1991). *Wechsler Intelligence Scale for Children—Third Edition.* San Antonio, TX: Psychological Corporation.

Wegman, W. E. (1986). Annual summary of vital statistics—1985. *Pediatrics, 78,* 983–984.

Weikert, D. P. (1982). Preschool education for disadvantaged children. In J. R. Travers & R. J. Light (Eds.), *Learning from experience: Evaluating early childhood demonstration programs.* Washington, DC: National Academy Press.

Weikert, D. P. (1993). *Long-term positive effects in the Perry Preschool Program.* Unpublished data. The High Scope Foundation, Ypsilanti, MI.

Weinstein, N. D. (1984). Reducing unrealistic optimism about illness susceptibility. *Health Psychology, 3,* 431–457.

Weintraub, S., Powell, D. H., & Whitla, D. K. (1994). Successful cognitive aging. *Journal of Geriatric Psychiatry, 27,* 15–34.

Weisman, A. T. (1972). On dying and denying: A psychiatric study of terminality. In M. Lowenthal, M. Turnher, & D. Chiriboga (Eds.), *Four stages of life.* San Francisco: Jossey-Bass.

Weiss, B., Dodge, K. A., Bates, J. E., & Pettit, G. S. (1992). Some consequences of early harsh discipline: Child aggression and a maladaptive social information processing style. *Child Development, 63,* 1321–1335.

Weissberg, R. P., Caplan, M. Z., & Sivo, P. J. (1989). A new conceptual framework for establishing school-based social competence promotion programs. In L. A. Bond, B. E. Compas, & C. Swift (Eds.), *Prevention in the schools.* Menlo Park, CA: Sage.

Welch, H. G. (1991). Comparing apples and oranges: Does cost-effectiveness analysis deal fairly with the old and young? *Gerontologist, 31,* 332–336.

Wellman, H. H. (1988). First steps in theorizing about the mind. In J. W. Astington, P. L. Harris, & D. R. Olson (Eds.), *Developing theories of mind.* Cambridge, England: Cambridge University Press.

Wellman, H. M., & Estes, D. (1986). Early understanding of mental entities: A reexamination of childhood realism. *Child Development, 57,* 910–923.

Wellman, H. M., & Gelman, S. A. (1992). Cognitive development: Foundational theories of core domains. *Annual Review of Psychology, 43,* 337–375.

Wellman, H. M., & Woolley, J. D. (1990). From simple desires to ordinary beliefs: The early development of everyday psychology. *Cognition, 35,* 245–275.

Wellman, H. M. (1990). *The child's theory of mind.* Cambridge, MA: M.I.T. Press.

Wender, P. H., Kety, S. S., Rosenthal, D., Schulsinger, F., Ortmann, J., & Lunde, I. (1986). Psychiatric disorders in the biological and adoptive families of adopted individuals with affective disorder. *Archives of General Psychiatry, 43,* 923–929.

Wenestam, C. G., & Wass, H. (1987). Swedish and U.S. Children's thinking about death: A qualitative study and cross-cultural comparison. *Death Studies, 11,* 99–121.

Wenzlaff, R. M., & Prohaska, M. L. (1989). When misery loves company: Depression, attributions, and responses to others' moods. *Journal of Experimental Social Psychology, 25,* 220–223.

Werner, E. E., & Smith, R. S. (1982). *Vulnerable but invincible: A longitudinal study of resilient children and youth.* New York: McGraw-Hill.

Werner, E. E. (1979). *Cross-cultural child development: A view from planet earth.* Monterey, CA: Brooks/Cole.

Wertheimer, M. (1945). *Productive thinking.* New York: Harper.

Wertsch, J. V., & Tulviste, P. (1992). L. S. Vygotsky and contemporary developmental psychology. *Developmental Psychology, 28,* 548–557.

Whalen, C. K., & Henker, B. (1994). Commentary: When the unexpected happens: Harnessing serendipity or following the text. *Journal of Pediatric Psychology, 19,* 23–26.

Whaley, L. F., & Wong, D. L. (1988). *Essentials of pediatric nursing* (3rd ed.). St. Louis: Mosby.

White, B. L., & Held, R. (1966). Plasticity of sensorimotor development in human infants. In J. Rosenblith & W. Allinsmith (Eds.), *The causes of behavior.* Boston: Allyn & Bacon.

White, B. L. (1988). *Educating the infant and toddler.* Lexington, MA: Lexington Books.

White, B. L. (1990). *The first three years of life.* New York: Prentice-Hall.

White, C. B., & Catania, J. (1981). Psychoeducational intervention for sexuality with the aged, family members of the aged, and people who work with the aged. *International Journal of Aging and Human Development.*

White, K. M., Speisman, J. C., Costos, D., & Smith, A. (1987). Relationship maturity: A conceptual and empirical approach. In J. Meacham (Ed.), *Interpersonal relations: Family, peers, friends.* Basel, Switzerland; Karger.

White, K. M., Speisman, J. C., Jackson, D., Bartis, S., & Costos, D. (1986). Intimacy maturity and its correlates in young married couples. *Journal of Personality and Social Psychology, 50,* (1), 152–162.

White, M. (1993). *The material child.* New York: The Free Press.

White, N., & Cunningham, W. R. (1989). Is terminal drop pervasive or specific? *Journal of Gerontology: Psychological Sciences, 43,* P141–144.

Whitehurst, G. J., & Valdez-Menchaca, M. C. (1988). What is the role of reinforcement in early language acquisition? *Child Development, 59,* 430–440.

Whiting, B. B., & Edwards, C. P. (1988). *Children of different worlds.* Cambridge, MA: Harvard University Press.

Whiting, B. B. (1989, April). *Culture and interpersonal behavior.* Paper presented at the biennial meeting of the Society for Research in Child Development, Kansas City.

Whitman, F. L., Diamond, M., & Martin, J. (1993). Homosexual orientation in twins: A report of 61 pairs and three triplet sets. *Archives of Sexual Behavior, 22,* 187–198.

Widmayer, S., & Field, T. (1980). Effects of Brazelton demonstrations on early patterns of preterm infants and their teenage mothers. *Infant Behavior and Development, 3,* 79–89.

Wiesenfeld, A. R., Malatesta, C. Z., & DeLoache, L. L. (1981). Differential parental response to familiar and unfamiliar infant distress signals. *Infant Behavior and Development, 4,* 281–295.

Wilkie, F., & Eisdorfer, C. (1971). Intelligence and blood pressure in the aged. *Science, 172,* 959–962.

Wilkinson, S., & Kitzinger, C. (1993). *Heterosexuality.* Newbury Park, CA: Sage.

Willer, B., & Bredekamp, S. (1990). Redefining readiness: An essential requisite for educational reform. *Young Children, 45,* 22–26.

William T. Grant Foundation Commission on Work, Family, and Citizenship. (1988, February). *The forgotten half: Non-college-bound youth in America.* Washington, DC: William T. Grant Foundation.

Williams, J. E., & Best, D. L. (1982). *Measuring sex stereotypes: A thirty-nation study.* Newbury Park, CA: Sage.

Williams, J. E., & Best, D. L. (1989). *Sex and psyche: Self-concept viewed cross-culturally.* Newbury Park, CA: Sage.

Williams, J. (1979). Reading instruction today. *American Psychologist, 34,* 917–922.

Williams, M. F., & Condry, J. C. (1989, April). Living color: Minority portrayals and cross-racial interactions on television. Paper presented at the Society for Research in Child Development meeting, Kansas City.

Williams, M. H. (1990). *Lifetime fitness and wellness* (2nd ed.). Dubuque, IA: Brown & Benchmark.

Williams, M. (1990). African American elderly experiences with Title II: Program assumptions and economic well-being. In Z. Harel, E. A. McKinney, & M. Williams, (Eds.), *Black aged.* Newbury Park, CA: Sage.

Williams, R. B. (1989). Biological mechanisms mediating the relationship between behavior and coronary prone behavior. In A. W. Siegman & T. Dembrowski (Eds.),

In search of coronary-prone behavior: Beyond Type A. Hillsdale, NJ: Erlbaum.

Willis, S. L., & Nesselroade, C. S. (1990). Long-term effects of fluid ability training in old age. *Developmental Psychology, 26,* 905–910.

Willis, S. L., & Schaie, K. W. (1986). Training the elderly on the ability factors of spatial orientation and inductive reasoning. *Psychology and Aging, 1,* 239–247.

Willis, S. L., & Schaie, K. W. (1990, April). *Methodological and taxonomic considerations in research on everyday cognition.* Paper presented at the 12th West Virginia conference on life-span developmental psychology, Morgantown.

Willis, S. L., & Schaie, K. W. (1994). Assessing everyday competence in the elderly. In C. Fisher & R. Lerner (Eds.), *Applied developmental psychology.* Hillsdale, NJ: Erlbaum.

Willis, S. L. (1985). Towards an educational psychology of the adult learner. In J. E. Birren & K. W. Schaie (Eds.), *Handbook of the psychology of aging* (2nd ed.). New York: Van Nostrand Reinhold.

Willis, S. L. (1989). Cohort differences in cognitive aging: A sample case. On K. W. Schaie & C. Schooler (Eds.), *Social structure and aging: Psychological processes.* Hillsdale, NJ: Erlbaum.

Willis, S. L. (1990). Introduction to the special section on cognitive training in later adulthood. *Developmental Psychology, 26,* 875–879.

Wilson, E. O. (1975). *Sociobiology: The new synthesis.* Cambridge, MA: Harvard University Press.

Wilson, L. C. (1990). *Infants and toddlers: Curriculum and teaching.* Albany, NY: Delmar.

Wilson, M. N. (1986). The Black extended family: An analytical consideration. *Developmental Psychology, 22,* 246–256.

Wilson, W. J., & Neckerman, K. M. (1986). Poverty and family structure: The widening gap between evidence and public policy issues. In S. Danziger & D. Weinberg (Eds.), *Fighting poverty.* Cambridge, MA: Harvard University Press.

Windle, W. F. (1940). *Physiology of the human fetus.* Philadelphia: Saunders.

Winner, E., & Gardner, H. (1988). Creating a world with words. In F. Kessel (Ed.), *The development of language and language researchers.* Hillsdale, NJ: Erlbaum.

Winner, E. (1986, August). Where pelicans kiss seals. *Psychology Today,* pp. 24–35.

Witkin, H. A., Mednick, S. A., Schulsinger, R., Bakkestrom, E., Christiansen, K. O., Goodenbough, D. R., Hirschhorn, K., Lunsteen, C., Owen, D. R., Philip, J., Ruben, D. B., & Stocking, M. (1976). Criminality in XYY and XXY men. *Science, 193* 547–555.

Wolff, P. H. (1969). The natural history of crying and other vocalizations in early infancy. In B. M. Foss (Ed.), *Determinants of infant development* (Vol. 4). London: Methuen.

Wolters, P. M., Brouwers, P., Moss, H. A., & Pizzo, P. A. (1994). Adaptive behavior of children with symptomatic HIV infection before and after Zidovudine therapy. *Journal of Pediatric Psychology, 19,* 47–62.

Wong, P. T. P., & Watt, L. M. (1991). What types of reminiscence are associated with successful aging? *Psychology and Aging, 6,* 272–279.

Wood, F. H. (1988). Learners at risk. *Teaching Exceptional Children, 20,* 4–9.

Woodward, N. J., & Wallston, B. S. (1987). Age and health-care beliefs: Self-efficacy as a mediator of low desire for control. *Psychology and Aging, 2,* 3–8.

Woolsey, S. F. (1992). Sudden infant death syndrome. In R. B. Hoekelman, S. B. Friedman, N. M. Nelson, & H. M. Seidel (Eds.), *Primary pediatric care* (2nd ed.). St. Louis: Mosby Yearbook.

Wootton, J., & Miller, S. I. (1994). Cocaine: A review. *Pediatrics in Review, 15,* 89–92.

Worden, J. W. (1991). *Grief and counseling and grief therapy* (2nd ed.). New York: Springer.

Worobey, J., & Belsky, J. (1982). Employing the Brazelton Scale to influence mothering: An experimental comparison of three strategies. *Developmental Psychology, 18,* 736–743.

Worschel, S., & Cooper, J. (1979). *Understanding social psychology.* Homewood, IL: Dorsey Press.

Worthington, E. L. (1989). Religious faith across the life span: Implications for counseling and research. *Counseling Psychologist, 17,* 555–612.

Worthington-Roberts, B. S. (1988). Lactation and human milk. In S. R. Williams & B. S. Worthington-Roberts (Eds.), *Nutrition throughout the life cycle.* St. Louis: Times Mirror/Mosby.

Wright, M. R. (1989). Body image satisfaction in adolescent girls and boys. *Journal of Youth and Adolescence, 18,* 71–84.

Wroblewski, R., & Huston, A. C. (1987). Televised occupational stereotypes and their effects on early adolescents: Are they changing? *Journal of Early Adolescence, 7,* 283–297.

Wylie, R. (1979). *The self concept. Vol. 2.: Theory and research on selected topics.* Lincoln: University of Nebraska Press.

X

Xiaohe, X., & Whyte, M. K. (1990). Love matches and arranged marriages. *Journal of Marriage and the Family, 52,* 709–722.

Y

Yardley, K. (1987). What do you mean "Who am I?": Exploring the implications of a self-concept measurement with subjects. In K. Yardley & T. Honess (Eds.), *Self and identity: Psychosocial perspectives.* New York: Wiley.

Yarmon, M. (1982). The new computers need you. *50 Plus, 22,* 60–61.

Young, K. T. (1990). American conceptions of infant development from 1955 to 1984: What the experts are telling parents. *Child Development, 61,* 17–28.

Youngblade, L., & Belsky, J. (1992). Parent-child antecedents of 5-year-olds' close friendships: A longitudinal analysis. *Developmental Psychology, 28,* 700–713.

Younoszai, B. (1993). Mexican American perspectives related to death. In D. P. Irish

& K. F. Lundquist (Eds.), *Ethnic variations in dying, death, and grief: Diversity in universality.* Washington, DC: Taylor & Francis.

Ysseldyke, J. E., Algozzine, B., & Thurlow, M. L. (1992). *Critical issues in special education* (2nd ed.). Boston: Houghton Mifflin.

Yu, L. C. (1993). Intergenerational transfer of resources within policy and cultural contexts. In S. H. Zarit, L. I. Pearlin, & K. W. Schaie (Eds.), *Caregiving systems.* Hillsdale, NJ: Erlbaum.

Yussen, S. R., & Levy, V. (1975). Developmental changes in predicting one's own span of short-term memory. *Journal of Experimental Child Psychology, 19,* 502–508.

Yussen, S. R., Mathews, S. R., Huang, S., & Evans, R. (1988). The robustness and temporal course of the story schema's influence on recall. *Journal of Experimental Psychology: Learning, Memory, and Cognition, 14,* 173–179.

Z

Zahn-Waxler, C. (1990, May 28). Commentary. *Newsweek,* p. 61.

Zarit, S. H., & Pearlin, L. I. (1993). Family caregiving: Integrating informal and formal systems for care. In S. H. Zarit, L. I. Pearlin, & K. W. Schaie (Eds.), *Caregiving systems.* Hillsdale, NJ: Erlbaum.

Zarit, S. H., & Reid, J. D. (1994). Family caregiving and the older family. In D. Fisher & R. Lerner (Eds.), *Applied developmental psychology.* Hillsdale, NJ: Erlbaum.

Zarit, S. (1993). Interview on caring for an Alzheimer's patient. *Aging, 363–364,* 18–21.

Zedeck, S., & Mosier, K. L. (1990). Work in the family and employing organization. *American Psychologist, 45,* 240–251.

Zeiss, A. M., Lewinsohn, P. M. (1986, Fall). Adapting behavioral treatment of depression to meet the needs of the elderly. *Clinical Psychologist.* 98–100.

Zelazo, P. D., & Frye, D. (1993, March). *Cognitive complexity and changes in children's theory of mind.* Paper presented at the biennial meeting of the Society for Research in Child Development, New Orleans.

Zelnik, M., & Kantner, J. F. (1977). Sexual and contraceptive experiences of young unmarried women in the United States, 1976 and 1971. *Family Planning Perspectives, 9,* 55–71.

Zeskind, P. S., Klein, L., & Marshall, T. R. (1992). Adults' perceptions of experimental modifications of durations and expiratory sounds in infant crying. *Developmental Psychology, 28,* 1153–1162.

Zigler, E., & Styfoc, S. J. (1994). Head Start: Criticisms in a constructive context. *American Psychologist, 49,* 127–132.

Zigler, E. E., & Muenchow, S. (1992). *The story of Head Start.* New York: Basic Books.

Zigler, E. (1987, April). *Child care for parents who work outside the home: Problems and solutions.* Paper presented at the biennial meeting of the Society for Research in Child Development, Baltimore.

Zilbergeld, B. (1992). *The new male sexuality.* New York: Bantam.

Zisook S., Schuchter, S. R., & Lyons, L. E. (1987). Predictors of psychological reactions during the early stages of widowhood. *Psychiatric Clinics of North America, 10,* 355–368.

Zuckerman, M. (1979). *Sensation seeking: Beyond the optimal level of arousal.* Hillsdale, NJ: Erlbaum.

CREDITS

PHOTOGRAPHS

Section Openers

Section 1: © Jay Maisel; **Section 2:** © Petit Format/Nestle/Photo Researchers; **Section 3:** © Courtesy of Northern Telecom; **Section 4:** © David Burnett/Contact Press; **Section 5:** © Francois Dardelet/Image Bank

Chapter 1

Opener: © Giraudon/Art Resource; **p. 6:** © Wide World Photo; **1.1a:** © Erich Lessing/Art Resource; **1.1b:** © Scala/Art Resource; **1.4a:** Art Wolfe/The Image Bank; **1.4b:** R. Kawakami/The Image Bank; **1.4c:** Eric Meola/The Image Bank; **p. 11:** Courtesy of Paul Baltes; **1.5b:** © Ted Horowitz/The Stock Market; **1.6b:** © Courtesy of Nancy Agostini; **p. 16:** © James Pozarik/Gamma Liason; **p. 17 left:** © Courtesy of Miriam Wright Edelman, The Children's Defense Foundation. Photo by Rick Reinhard; **p. 17 right:** © Dennis Brack/Black Star; **p. 18:** © Renato Rotola/Gamma Liason; **1.8b:** © Elyse Lewin/Image Bank; **1.8c:** © Rhoda Sidney/Leo de Wys; **1.8d:** © Dan Esgro/Image Bank; **1.8e:** © James Shaffer; **1.8f:** © Michael Salas/Image Bank; **1.8g:** © Joe Sohm/Image Works; **1.8h:** Courtesy of John Santrock; **1.8i:** © Landrum Shettles; **p. 21:** Courtesy of Bernice Neugarten

Chapter 2

Opener: Romare Beardon Estate, ACA Galleries New York; **p. 34:** Bettmann Newsphotos; **p. 37 left:** Courtesy of Karen Horney; **p. 37 right:** Courtesy of Nancy Chodorow, Photo by Jean Margolis; **38b:** © Sarah Putnam/Picture Cube; **2.2 top:** © William Hopkins; **2.2 top middle:** © Suzanne Szasz/Photo Researchers; **2.2 bottom middle:** © Suzanne Szasz/Photo Researchers; **2.2e:** © Mel Digiacomo/Image Bank; **2.2 top:** © Sam Zarember/The Image Bank; **2.2 top middle:** © Brett Froomer/The Image Bank; **2.2 bottom middle:** © Alan Carey/The Image Works; **2.2 bottom:** © Art Kane/The Image Bank; **2.3a:** © Paul Conklin; **p. 42:** © Yves de Braine/Black Star; **p. 44:** Courtesy of Albert Bandura; **p. 45:** © Brian ViKander/West Light; **2.5:** Photo by Nina Leen/Time/Life Magazine © Time Inc.; **2.6:** © David Austen/Stock Boston; **p. 47:** Courtesy of Urie Bronfenbrenner; **2.7:** © Patricia A. McConville/The Image Bank; **2.8:** © Gary Chapman/The Image Bank; **2.10a:** © Photo Researchers, Inc.; **2.10b:** AP/Wide World Photos; **2.10c:** AP/Wide World Photos; **2.10d:**

The Bettmann Archive; **2.10e:** © Suki Hill Photographer; **2.10f:** © Lawrence Migdale/Photo Researchers, Inc.; **p. 58:** Courtesy of Dr. Florence L. Denmark/Photo by Robert Wesner

Chapter 3

Opener: © Private Collection National Gallery London/Superstock; **p. 74:** © Enrico Ferorelli; **p. 76:** © Explorer/Vincent Hazat/Photo Researchers; **3.1 top:** © R. Heinzen/Superstock; **3.1 bottom:** © Elyse Lewin/The Image Bank; **3.2 left:** © Sundstrom/Gamma Liason; **3.3:** © Alexandria Tsiaras/Photo Researchers; **3.4:** © Will and Deni McIntyre/Photo Researchers; **3.5:** © J. Pavlousky/Sygma; **3.7 top:** © Tim Davis/ Photo Researchers; **3.7 bottom:** © Sandy Roessler/The Stock Market; **p. 86:** © Myrleen Ferguson/Photo Edit; **p. 88:** © Elizabeth Crews/Image Works; **p. 89:** Courtesy of Sandra Scarr

Chapter 4

Opener: © Musee d'Orsay/Art Resource; **p. 99 all:** © Lennart Nilsson; **4.3 large:** © Petit Format Nestle Science Source/Photo Researchers; **4.3 top:** © Lennart Nilsson; **4.3 middle:** © Nestle/ Photo Researchers; **4.3 bottom:** © Nestle/Photo Researchers; **4.5a:** © Will Deni McIntyre/Photo Researchers; **p. 107:** © Chas Cancellare/Picture Group; **p. 110:** © G. Hofstetter/Photo Network; **p. 115:** © Charles Gupton/Stock Boston; **4.6:** © Comstock; **p. 124:** Courtesy of Dr. Tiffany Fields

Chapter 5

Opener: Courtesy of Michael McCormick Gallery; **5.1 left:** © Elizabeth Crews/The Image Works; **5.1 middle:** © James G. White Photography; **5.1 right:** © Petit Format/Photo Researchers; **5.2:** © Nancy Brown/The Image Bank; **5.3:** © Bruce McAllister/Image Works; **p. 139:** © C. Vergara/Photo Researchers; **5.5b:** © David Linton; **5.6 right:** © Enrico Ferorelli; **p. 144:** © George Goodwin/Monkmeyer; **p. 145 left:** © Joe McNally/Sygma; **5.7a:** © Michael Siluk; **5.7b:** © Dr. Melanie Spence, University of Texas; **5.8:** © Jean Guichard/ Sygma; **p. 149:** © Bob Daemmrich/Image Works

Chapter 6

Opener: © National Gallery of Art; **p. 154:** © Jacques Chenet/Woodfin Camp; **6.1 top:** © C&W Shields; **6.1 middle:** © C&W Shields; **6.1 bottom:** © Gabor Demjen/Stock Boston; **6.1 top:** © Sally & Richard Greenhill; **6.1f:**

© Joel Gordon; **6.1g:** © Eric Wheater/The Image Bank; **6.2 both:** © D. Goodman/Monkmeyer Press; **6.3 bottom:** © Denise Marcotte/The Picture Cube; **6.4:** Courtesy of Rovee-Collier; **p. 161 bottom:** © Joe McNally/Sygma; **6.5:** © Enrico Ferorelli; **6.6:** © Enrico Ferorelli; **p. 169:** © Katrina Thomas/Photo Researchers; **p. 170:** © John Carter/ Photo Researchers; **p. 171:** © Anthony Bannister/Earth Scenes; **p. 174:** © Les Stone/Sygma

Chapter 7

Opener: © Mills College Art Gallery; **p. 178a:** © Leonard Lee Rue/Photo Researchers; **p. 178b:** © Mitch Reardon/Photo Researchers; **p. 178c:** © Anthony Boccaccio/Image Bank; **7.1 left:** © Comstock; **7.2:** © Martin Rogers/Stock Boston; **p. 181:** © Chris Hackett/The Image Bank; **p. 183:** © Cesar Lucas/Image Bank; **p. 191:** © Tom/Image Bank; **p. 193:** Courtesy of Dr. Dante Cicchetti

Chapter 8

Opener: © McNay Art Museum, San Antonio; **8.1:** © Walter Imber; **p. 209:** © William Campbell/Time Magazine; **8.6:** © Paul Fusco/Magnum Photos; **8.8:** © Owen Franken/Stock Boston; **p. 219:** Courtesy of Roger Brown; **8.10 top:** © Elizabeth Crews/Image Works; **p. 221 bottom:** © James Wertsch/Clark University; **8.11 top:** © Elizabeth Crews/The Image Works; **8.11 middle:** © Jeffry W. Myers/The Stock Market; **8.11 bottom:** © Paul Conklin; **8.11 top:** © Elizabeth Crews/The Image Works; **8.11 middle:** © G. Hofstetter/Photo Network; **8.11 bottom:** © Leo de Wys; **p. 226:** © Robert Wallis/SIPA Press, Newsweek, April 17, 1989, p. 8; **p. 227:** © R. Knowles/Black Star

Chapter 9

Opener: Courtesy of John Santrock; **9.1:** © Eri Heller/The Picture Group; **p. 240 top:** © Bob Daemmrich/The Image Works; **p. 241:** © Karen Kasmauski/Woodfin Camp; **p. 243:** © Richardson Photography; **9.3 bottom:** © Erik Anderson/Stock Boston; **p. 249 top:** © Bill Foley/BlackStar; **9.4a:** © Superstock; **9.4b:** © Comstock; **9.4c:** © Stephen Marks/The Image Bank; **9.4d:** © Elizabeth Crews/Image Works; **9.4e:** © Patrick Watson/Image Works; **9.4 large:** © Schuster/Photo Researchers; **9.5:** © Larry Voight/Photo Researchers; **p. 260 left:** © Suzanne Szasz/Photo Researchers; **p. 260 right:** Courtesy of Eleanor Maccoby; **9.6:** © Ken Gaghan/Jeroboam

Chapter 10

Opener: © Superstock; **p. 274:** © Joe McNally/Sports Illustrated; **p. 275:** © Bob Daemmrich/The Image Works; **p. 277:** © Pat Lacroix/The Image Bank; **p. 279:** © Photo Edit; **p. 280 top:** © Will McIntyre/Photo Researchers; **p. 280 bottom:** © Richard Hutchings/Photo Researchers; **10.2:** © Richard Hutchings/Photo Researchers; **p. 286:** © Yves DeBraine/Black Star; **p. 287:** © M&E Bernheim/Woodfin Camp; **p. 288:** Courtesy of John Flavell; **10.5a:** Mark Antman/The Image Works; **10.5b:** © Dr. Rose Gantner/Comstock; **10.5c:** © Meike Mass/The Image Bank; **10.8a:** © David Austen/Stock Boston; **10.8b:** © Ben Simmons/Stock Market; **10.9:** © Jill Cannefax/EKM Nepenthe; **p. 301:** © Lawrence Migdale/Photo Researchers; **p. 304:** © Eiji Miyazawa/Black Star; **p. 306:** Courtesy of Madeline Cartwright

Chapter 11

Opener: © Worcester Art Museum; **11.1:** © Sumo/The Image Bank; **p. 320 top:** © Bob Daemmrich/Image Works; **p. 320 bottom:** © John S. Abbott; **p. 324:** Courtesy of Susan Harter; **11.2:** © Eddie Adams/Time Picture; **p. 329:** © Jeff Smith/Image Bank; **p. 332 top:** © B. P. Wolff/Photo Researchers; **p. 332 bottom:** © Catherine Gehm; **p. 336:** © Margaret Finefrock/Unicorn Stock Photos; **p. 337:** © Keith Carter Photography; **p. 339:** © Bob Daemmrich/Image Works

Chapter 12

Opener: © Superstock; **12.1:** © Alan Carey/The Image Works; **12.4:** © Paul Conklin; **p. 353:** © Gio Barto/Image Bank; **p. 357:** © H. Yamaguchi/Gamma Liaison; **12.5:** © Alan Carey/Image Works; **p. 367:** © William Hopkins; **p. 368:** © George Zimbel/Monkmeyer Press; **p. 374:** © Bob Daemmrich/Stock Boston

Chapter 13

Opener: © Vincent van Gogh Foundation/ Van Gogh Museum, Amsterdam; **13.1:** © Richard Hutchings/Photo Researchers; **p. 383 left:** © Nills Jorgensen/Rex Features; **p. 383 right:** © Tony Freeman/Photo Edit; **13.2 top:** © Mary Kate Denny/PhotoEdit; **13.2 top middle:** © Jean Claude Lejeune; **13.2 middle:** © Peter Vandermark/Stock Boston; **13.2 bottom middle:** © David De Lossy/The Image Bank; **13.2 bottom:** © Myrleen Ferguson/PhotoEdit; **p. 388:** © Daniel Laine; **p. 391:** Courtesy of Stanley Sue; **p. 392 left:** © Joan Marcus; **p. 392 right:** © Bob Daemmrich/Image Works; **13.3:** © Jeff Persons/Stock Boston; **p. 395:** Courtesy of Margaret Beale Spencer; **p. 397:** © Bob Daemmrich/The Image Works; **p. 400:** © 1988 by Warner Bros. Inc., Photo by Tony Friedkin

Chapter 14

Opener: Miami University Art Museum, Oxford, Ohio; **p. 408:** © Alvis Upitis/The Image Bank; **p. 412 insert:** © Jamie Villasseca/The Image Bank; **p. 412 right:** © David Frazier Photo Library; **p. 413 top:** © Douglas J. Fisher/Image Bank; **p. 413 bottom:** © W. Woodworth/ Superstock; **p. 416 bottom:** © Barry O'Rourke/The Stock Market; **p. 417:** © Randy

Taylor/Sygma; **14.3:** © Alan Reininger/Contact Press; **14.5a:** © Marc Romanelli/The Image Bank; **p. 430:** © Shooting Star

Chapter 15

Opener: Art Resource; **15.2:** © Robert Farber/The Image Bank; **15.3b:** © Tony Freeman/Photo Edit; **15.3c:** © Alan Oddie/Photo Edit; **15.3d:** © Anthony A. Boccaccio/The Image Bank; **15.3e:** © Kenneth Redding/Image Bank; **15.3f:** © Woodfin Camp; **15.3g:** After: Carter, B., McGoldrick, M. Overview: Carter & M. McGoldrick (Eds.) *The Changing Family Life Cycle 2/e*, 1989 Allyn & Bacon: Boston p. 15; **p. 446a:** © Explorer/J. P. Nacivet/Photo Researchers; **p. 446b:** © Jean Buldain/Berg & Associates; **p. 446c:** © Dean Press Images/The Image Works; **p. 452:** © David Schaefer Photography

Chapter 16

Opener: © Scala/Art Resource; **p. 465:** © Focus on Sports; **p. 467 bottom:** © M. Milford/Image Bank; **p. 469 left:** Roy Morsch/The Stock Market; **p. 469 right:** Comstock; **16.1:** © John Elk, III; **p. 477:** © Benn Mitchell/The Image Bank; **p. 478 top:** © Chuck Kuhn/The Image Bank; **p. 478 bottom:** © Colin M. Olyneux/The Image Bank

Chapter 17

Opener: © Tate Gallery/Art Resource; **p. 491:** © William Hubbell/Woodfin Camp and Assoc.; **17.2:** © Henley & Savage/The Stock Market; **17.3 top:** © Walter Bibikow/The Image Bank; **17.3 middle:** © Kaz Mori/The Image Bank; **17.3 bottom:** © Kaz Mori/Image Bank; **p. 494 left:** © UPI/Bettmann; **p. 494 middle:** © UPI/Bettmann; **p. 494 right:** © UPI/Bettmann; **p. 497:** © Nancy Anne Dawe; **p. 499:** © Betty Press/Picture Group; **17.6:** © Don Klumpp/Image Bank; **p. 504a:** © Owen Franken/Stock Boston; **p. 504b:** © Bettman Archives; **p. 504c:** © UPI/Bettmann

Chapter 18

Opener: © Superstock; **p. 512:** © John Goodman; **p. 514a:** © John Launois/Black Star. **p. 514b:** © John Launois/Black Star; **p. 516:** © Jim Richardson/West Light; **p. 517a:** © Pascal Parrot/Sygma; **p. 517b:** Courtesy Kelmscott Gallery, Chicago; **p. 517c:** © Thomas Braise/The Stock Market; **p. 518 left:** © CNRI/ Science Photo Library/Photo Researchers; **p. 518 right:** © Kevin Horan Photography; **18.1:** © James Schnepf/Woodfin Camp; **18.2:** © George Gardner/Image Works; **p. 525:** © Sal Dimarco/Black Star; **p. 526:** Courtesy of Ellen Langer; **p. 529 large:** © Bob Daemmrich/Stock Boston; **p. 529 insert:** © Bruce Kliewe/Jeroboam; **18.3:** Courtesy of University of California; **p. 531:** © Linda Creighton/U.S. News and World Report

Chapter 19

Opener: © Superstock; **p. 539:** Courtesy of K. Warner Shaie; **p. 540:** © Yvonne Hemsy/ Gamma Liaison; **p. 541:** © J. Isaac/Helena Frost Associates; **p. 543:** © Sobel/Klonsky/Image Bank; **p. 542:** © Elizabeth Crews; **19.3:** © Kevin

Horan/Picture Group; **p. 546:** © Carter, B., McGoldrick; **p. 549:** © Ira Wyman/Sygma; **p. 550 bottom:** Courtesy of Margaret Gatz

Chapter 20

Opener: © Superstock; **p. 558 right:** © Mario Ruiz/Time Magazine; **20.1:** © Jay Lurie Photography; **20.2 left:** © D. Gorton/Time Magazine; **p. 561:** © Wayne Floyd/Unicorn Stock Photos; **p. 562:** © Comstock; **p. 564:** © Ivor Sharp/Image Bank; **p. 565:** © David Brownell/Image Bank; **p. 566:** Courtesy of Dr. John Santrock

Chapter 21

Opener: © The Art Institute of Chicago; **p. 576:** © Detroit News/Gamma-Liasion; **p. 577:** © Herb Snitzer/Stock Boston; **21.1b:** © Patrick Ward/Stock Boston; **21.1a:** © David Burnett/Stock Boston; **21.1c:** Stock Boston; **21.2:** © Eastcott/Momatwick/Image Works; **21.3:** © Jackson Hill/Southern Lights; **p. 588:** © Hermine Dreyfuss/Monkmeyer Press

Epilogue

Opener top left: © Lennart Nilsson; **top middle** © Niki Mareschal/Image Bank; **top right:** © Barbara Feigles/Stock Boston; **middle left:** © Sumo/The Image Bank-Texas; **middle middle:** © A. Upitis/Image Bank; **middle right:** © John Kelly/Image Bank-Texas; **bottom left:** © Micke Mass/Image Bank; **bottom middle:** © Dick Durrance II/Woodfin Camp; **bottom right:** © Dennis Stock/Magnum Photos

LINE ART, EXCERPTS, POEMS

Chapter 1

excerpt, p. 6: From the Prologue by Carl Sandburg to *The Family of Man*, edited by Edward Steichen. Copyright © 1955, renewed 1983, The Museum of Modern Art, New York. Reprinted by permission.
figure 1.2: Source: Data from Monroe Lerner, "When, Why, and Where People Die" in E. S. Shneidman (ed.), *Death: Current Perspectives*, 2d ed., pp. 89–91, 1980.
figure 1.3: Source: U.S. Census Data: Social Security Administration, *The Statistical History of the United States, 1976.*
figure 1.4: Source: Data from Kirkwood, "Comparative and Evolutionary Aspects of Longevity" in C. E. Finch and E. L. Schneider (eds.), *Handbook of the Biology of Aging*, p. 34, Van Nostrand Reinhold Company, 1985.
p. 13: From Lee Salk, *Familyhood.* COVER COPYRIGHT © 1992 by Simon & Schuster Inc. Reprinted by permission of Simon & Schuster Inc.

Chapter 2

figure 2.1: From L. S. Wrightsman and C. K. Sigelman, *Psychology: A Scientific Study of Human Behavior*, 5th ed. Copyright © 1979 Wadsworth Publishing Company. Reprinted by permission of Brooks/Cole Publishing Company.
poem, p. 35: From *The Poetry of Robert Frost* edited by Edward Connery Lathem. Copyright 1936 by Robert Frost. Copyright © 1964 by

Lesley Frost Ballantine. Copyright © 1969 by Henry Holt and Company, Inc. Reprinted by permission of Henry Holt and Company, Inc.
p. 38: From Erik H. Erikson, *Identity: Youth & Crisis.* Copyright © 1968 W. W. Norton & Company, Inc., New York, NY. Reprinted by permission.
figure 2.6 (text): Claire B. Kopp and Joanne B. Krakow, *The Child.* (p. 648). © 1982 by Addison-Wesley Publishing Company, Inc. Reprinted by permission of the publisher.
excerpt, p. 64: From J. Allen and R. Allen, "From Short-Term Compliance to Long-Term Freedom: Culture-Based Health Promotion by Health Professionals" in *American Journal of Health Promotion,* 12:46–47. Copyright © 1986 American Journal of Health Promotion, Rochester Hills, MI.

Chapter 3

poem, p. 78: From *Verses From 1929 On* by Ogden Nash. Copyright 1940 by Ogden Nash. By permission of Little, Brown and Company; Reprinted by permission of Curtis Brown, Ltd. Copyright © 1945 by Ogden Nash, *Many Long Years Ago;* Reprinted by permission of Andre Deutsch Ltd., *Ave Ogden: Nash in Latin.*
p. 79: From *Being Adopted* (JACKET COVER) by Dr. David Brodzinsky, M. Schechter & R. Henig. Copyright © 1992 by David Brodzinsky, Marshall Schechter, Robin M. Henig. Used by permission of Doubleday, a division of Bantam Doubleday Dell Publishing Group, Inc.
p. 82: From Robin J. R. Blatt, *Prenatal Tests.* Copyright © Vintage Books, New York, NY.
figure 3.8: From I. Gottesman, "Genetic Aspects of Intellectual Behavior" in *Handbook of Mental Deficiency,* Norman R. Ellis (ed.). Copyright © McGraw-Hill, Inc., New York, NY. Reprinted by permission of Norman R. Ellis.

Chapter 4

figure 4.1: From Charles Carroll and Dean Miller, *Health: The Science of Human Adaptation,* 5th ed. Copyright © 1991 Wm. C. Brown Communications, Inc., Dubuque, Iowa. All Rights Reserved. Reprinted by permission.
p. 102: *What To Expect When You're Expecting* by Arlene Eisenberg, Heidi E. Murkoff, and Sandee E. Hathaway © 1984, 1988, 1991. Cover reprinted by permission of Workman Publishing Company, Inc. All rights reserved.
figure 4.3: Copyright © 1991 by the Childbirth Education Association of Seattle. Reprinted from *Pregnancy, Childbirth and the Newborn* with the permission of its publisher, Meadowbrook Press.
figure 4.4: From Keith L. Moore, *The Developing Human: Clinically Oriented,* 4th ed. Copyright © 1988 W. B. Saunders, Philadelphia, PA. Reprinted by permission.
figure 4.5: From Queenan and Queenan, *A New Life: Pregnancy, Birth and Your Child's First Year.* Copyright © 1986 Marshall Cavendish Ltd, London, England. Reprinted by permission.
p. 108: *Will It Hurt the Baby?* © 1990 by Richard S. Abrams, M.D. Reprinted by permission of Addison-Wesley Publishing Company, Inc.
figure 4.6: From Virginia A. Apgar, "A Proposal for a New Method of Evaluation of a Newborn Infant" in *Anesthesia and Analgesia,* 32:260–267, 1975. Reprinted by permission of Williams & Wilkins, Baltimore, MD.

Chapter 5

p. 133: *What To Expect The First Year* by Arlene Eisenberg, Heidi E. Murkoff, and Sandee E. Hathaway © 1989. Cover reprinted by permission of Workman Publishing Company, Inc. All rights reserved.
figure 5.2: Source: National Center for Health Statistics, NCHS Growth Charts, *Monthly Vital Statistics Report.*
figure 5.3: From W. K. Frankenburg and J. B. Dodds, "The Denver Development Screening Test" in *Journal of Pediatrics,* 71:181–192. Copyright © 1967 Mosby-Year Book, Inc., St. Louis, MO. Reprinted by permission.
figure 5.4: Reprinted by permission of the publishers from *Postnatal Development of the Human Cerebral Cortex* by Jesse LeRoy Conel, Cambridge, Mass.: Harvard University Press. Copyright © President and Fellows of Harvard College and Jesse LeRoy Conel.
p. 138: From Richard Ferber, *Solve Your Child's Sleep Problems.* COVER COPYRIGHT © 1985 by Simon & Schuster Inc. Reprinted by permission of Simon & Schuster Inc.

Chapter 6

excerpt, p. 154: Source: Walt Whitman, *Leaves of Grass,* 1945. Random House Modern Library, New York, NY.
p. 163: From Burton White, *The First Three Years of Life.* COVER COPYRIGHT © 1993 by Simon & Schuster Inc. Reprinted by permission of Simon & Schuster Inc.
figure 6.7: From J. U. Dumtschin, "Recognize Language Development and Delay in Early Childhood" in *Young Children,* March 1988:16–24. Copyright © 1988 by the National Association for the Education of Young Children. Reprinted by permission.
figure 6.8: From R. Brown, C. Cazden, and U. Bella-Klima, "The Child's Grammar from 1–3" in *Minnesota Symposium on Child Psychology,* Vol. 2, J. P. Hill, (ed.), University of Minnesota Press, Minneapolis. Copyright © 1969 by the University of Minnesota. Reprinted by permission.

Chapter 7

figure 7.1: From Jay Belsky, "Early Human Experiences: A Family Perspective" in *Developmental Psychology,* 17:3-23. Copyright 1981 by the American Psychological Association. Reprinted by permission.
p. 185: Kathleen Alison Clarke-Stewart, *Daycare.* Copyright © 1993 Harvard University Press, Cambridge, MA. Reprinted by permission.
p. 192: 1992 © Hornick/Rivlin. Reprinted by permission.

Chapter 8

figure 8.1: Source: National Center for Health Statistics, NCHS Growth Charts, *Monthly Vital Statistics Report,* 25(3).
figure 8.2: Reprinted from *Human Biology and Ecology* by Albert Damon with the permission of W. W. Norton & Company, Inc. Copyright © 1977 by W. W. Norton & Company, Inc.
figure 8.3a: D. Wolf/J. Nove.
figure 8.3b: Reprinted by permission of Ellen Winner.

p. 223: From S. Bredekamp and T. Rosengrant (eds.), *Reaching Potentials: Appropriate Curriculum and Assessment for Young Children,* Vol. I. Copyright © 1992 National Association for the Education of Young Children, Washington, DC. Reprinted by permission.
figure 8.11: Excerpted with permission from "NAEYC Position Statement on Developmentally Appropriate Practice in Programs for 4- and 5-Year-Olds," 1986, *Young Children,* 41(6), pp. 23-76. Copyright © 1986 by the National Association for the Education of Young Children. All rights reserved.
p. 228: From Bonnie Neugebauer (ed.), *Alike and Different.* Copyright © 1992 National Association for the Education of Young Children, Washington, DC. Reprinted by permission.

Chapter 9

p. 238: From *Children: The Challenge* by Rudolf Dreikurs, M.D. with Vicki Soltz, R.N. Copyright © 1964 by Rudolf Dreikurs, M.D. Used by permission of Dutton Signet, a division of Penguin Books USA Inc.
p. 240: From *Raising Black Children* by James P. Comer and Alvin F. Poussaint. Copyright © 1975, 1992 by James P. Comer and Alvin F. Poussaint. Used by permission of Dutton Signet, a division of Penguin Books USA Inc.
figure 9.2: Source: Data from Government Printing Office, Washington, DC.
p. 244: From Richard Gardner, *The Boys and Girls Book about Divorce.* Copyright © 1983 Jason Aronson, Inc., Northvale, NJ 07647
p. 245: Reprinted with the permission of The Free Press, a Division of Macmillan, Inc. from *Growing Up With Divorce* by Neil Kalter. Copyright © 1990 Macmillan, Inc.
p. 250: From *The Preschool Years* by Ellen and David Galinsky. Copyright © 1988 by Ellen Galinsky. Reprinted by permission of Times Books, a division of Random House, Inc.

Chapter 10

p. 278: © Hornick/Rivlin, Boston.
figure 10.3: From Joel Levin, et al., "The Keyword Method in the Classroom" in *Elementary School Journal,* 80:4. Copyright © 1980 University of Chicago Press, Chicago, IL. Reprinted by permission.
figure 10.4: From Steven R. Yussen, et al., "The Robustness and Temporal Cause of the Story Schemics Influence on Recall" in *Journal of Experimental Psychology: Learning, Memory, and Cognition,* 14:173–179. Copyright 1988 by the American Psychological Association. Reprinted by permission.
p. 300: From Eden Lipson, *The New York Times Parents' Guide to the Best Books for Children.* Copyright © 1991 Random House, Inc. Reprinted by permission of Random House, Inc.
p. 302: *The Hurried Child,* © 1988 by David Elkind. Reprinted by permission of Addison-Wesley Publishing Company, Inc.

Chapter 11

p. 312: Reproduced with permission of publisher American Guidance Service, Inc., 4201 Woodland Road, Circle Pines, MN 55014–1796.
excerpt, p. 313: From Carle F. O'Neil and Waln K. Brown, "Planning and Building a Stepfamily,"

William Gladden Foundation, 1991. Reprinted by permission.

p. 317: From Joseph Fernandez and John Underwood, *Tales Out of School,* Copyright © Little, Brown and Company, Boston, MA. Reprinted by permission.

figure 11.3: From Janet S. Hyde, et al., "Gender Differences in Mathematics Performance" in *Psychological Bulletin,* 107:139–155. Copyright 1990 by the American Psychological Association. Reprinted by permission.

Chapter 12

figure 12.1: From J. M. Tanner, R. H. Whitehouse, and M. Takaishi, "Standards from Birth to Maturity for Height, Weight, Height Velocity, and Weight Velocity: British Children 1965" in *Archives of Diseases in Childhood,* 41. Copyright © British Medical Association, London, England. Reprinted by permission.

figure 12.5: Source: Data from Johnston, Bachman, and O'Malley, Institute for Social Research, University of Michigan, 1993.

p. 361: Jacket design from *Fateful Choices* by Fred Hechinger. Jacket design © 1992 by Meadows and Wiser. Cover photograph © 1992 by Harold Feinstein from *Children of War.* Reprinted by permission of Hill and Wang, a division of Farrar, Straus & Giroux, Inc.

p. 369: From Laurence Steinberg and Ann Levine, *You & Your Adolescent.* Copyright © Harper Perennial, New York, NY.

p. 370: *All Grown Up and No Place to Go,* © 1984 by David Elkind. Reprinted by permission of Addison-Wesley Publishing Company, Inc.

Chapter 13

p. 381: From Haim Ginott, *Between Parent and Teenager.* Copyright © 1969 Avon Books.

figure 13.2: Source: Data from Dexter C. Dunphy, "The Social Structure of Urban Adolescent Peer Groups" in *Sociometry,* Vol. 26, American Sociological Association, 1963.

p. 389: From Simons, Finlay, and Yang, *The Adolescent and Young Adult Fact Book.* Copyright © 1991 The Childrens' Defense Fund, Washington, DC. Reprinted by permission.

Chapter 14

lyric, p. 403: Copyright © 1962 by WARNER BROS. MUSIC. COPYRIGHT RENEWED 1990 by SPECIAL RIDER MUSIC. All rights reserved. International copyright secured. Reprinted by permission.

excerpt, p. 406: From S. Christ and G. Meyer, "10 Reasons Not to Get a Job" in *The Harvard Lampoon Big Book of College Life.* Copyright © The Harvard Lampoon, Cambridge, MA.

p. 407: From M. Scott Peck, *The Road Less Travelled.* COVER COPYRIGHT © 1978 by Simon & Schuster Inc. Reprinted by permission of Simon & Schuster Inc.

figure 14.2: From L. L. Langley, *Physiology of Man.* Copyright © 1971 Van Nostrand Reinhold Company, New York, NY. Reprinted by permission.

p. 412: From Covert Bailey, *The New Fit or Fat,* revised. Copyright © 1991 Houghton Mifflin Company, Boston, MA. Reprinted by permission.

p. 414: From *The New Aerobics* (Jacket Cover) by Kenneth Cooper. Copyright © 1970 by Kenneth Cooper. Used by permission of Bantam Doubleday Dell Publishing Group, Inc.

p. 415: From Stanton Peele and Archie Brodsky, *The Truth About Addiction and Recovery.* COVER COPYRIGHT © by Simon & Schuster Inc. Reprinted by permission of Simon & Schuster Inc.

p. 416: From *For Yourself: The Fulfillment of Female Sexuality* by Lonnie Garfield Barbach. Copyright © 1975 by Lonnie Garfield Barbach. Used by permission of Dutton Signet, a division of Penguin Books USA Inc.

p. 418: From *Permanent Partners* by Betty Berzon, Ph.D. Copyright © 1988 by Betty Berzon, Ph.D. Used by permission of Viking Penguin, a division of Penguin Books USA Inc.

p. 420: From *The New Male Sexuality* (JACKET COVER) by Bernie Zilberg. Copyright © 1992 by Bernie Zilberg. Used by permission of Bantam Books, a division of Bantam Doubleday Dell Publishing Group, Inc.

poem, p. 423: "Once More, The Round," copyright © 1962 by Beatrice Roethke, Administratrix of the Estate of Theodore Roethke. Used by permission of Doubleday, a division of Bantam Doubleday Dell Publishing Group, Inc.

figure 14.4: Reproduced by special permission of the Publisher, Psychological Assessment Resources, Inc., from *Making Vocational Choices,* copyright 1973, 1985 by Psychological Assessment Resources, Inc. All rights reserved.

p. 427: Reprinted with permission from *What Color is Your Parachute?* 1993, by Richard Bolles, published by Ten Speed Press, PO Box 7123, Berkeley, CA 94707. Copyright 1993.

Chapter 15

figure 15.1: From Zick Rubin, "Measurement of Romantic Love" in *Journal of Personality and Social Psychology,* 16:267. Copyright © 1970 American Psychological Association. Reprinted by permission of Zick Rubin.

p. 441: From Harville Hendrix, *Getting the Love You Want.* Copyright © HarperCollins Publishers, New York, NY. Reprinted by permission.

figure 15.2: Source: Data from R. J. Sternberg, *The Triangle of Love,* Basic Books, New York, 1988.

figure 15.4: From J. Larson, "The Marriage Quiz: College Students' Beliefs in Selected Myths about Marriage" in *Family Relations,* 37:4. Copyrighted 1988 by the National Council on Family Relations, 3989 Central Ave. NE, Suite 550, Minneapolis, MN 55421. Reprinted by permission.

p. 447: From Deborah Tannen, *You Just Don't Understand.* Copyright © 1990 Ballantine Books, a Division of Random House, Inc. Reprinted by permission.

p. 448: From Lynn Osterkamp, *How to Deal with Your Parents.* Copyright © 1991 The Putnam Berkley Group, New York, NY. Reprinted by permission.

p. 454: From Harriet Lerner, *The Dance of Intimacy.* Copyright © 1989 HarperCollins Publishers, Inc., New York, NY. Reprinted by permission.

p. 455: From Carol Tavris, *The Mismeasure of Women.* COVER COPYRIGHT © 1992 by Simon & Schuster Inc. Reprinted by permission of Simon & Schuster Inc.

Chapter 16

lyric, p. 464: © 1972, 1985 Denjac Music Co.

p. 467: COVER COPYRIGHT © 1992 by Simon & Schuster, Inc. Reprinted by permission of Simon & Schuster, Inc.

p. 470: From Carol Tavris, *Anger: The Misunderstood Emotion.* COVER COPYRIGHT © 1989 by Simon & Schuster Inc. Reprinted by permission of Simon & Schuster Inc.

p. 471: From Herbert Benson, *Beyond the Relaxation Response.* Copyright © 1984 Times Books, New York, NY.

p. 476: From *Age Wave* (Jacket Cover) by Ken Dychtwald and Joe Flower. Copyright © 1989 by Ken Dychtwald, Joe Flower. Used by permission of Bantam Books, a division of Bantam Doubleday Dell Publishing Group, Inc.

Chapter 17

figure 17.1: From George Levinger and Diedrick Snoek, *Attraction in Relationship: A New Look at Interpersonal Attraction.* Copyright © 1972 George Levinger and Diedrick Snoek. Reprinted by permission.

figure 17.3: Reprinted by permission of the publishers from *Themes of Work and Love in Adulthood* edited by Neil J. Smelser and Erik H. Erickson, Cambridge, Mass.: Harvard University Press, Copyright © 1980 by the President and Fellows of Harvard College.

p. 492: From Mihaly Csikszentmihalyi, *Flow.* Copyright © 1990 Harper & Row, Publishers, Inc. Reprinted by permission.

p. 495: From Viktor E. Frankl, *Man's Search for Meaning.* COVER COPYRIGHT © 1984 by Simon & Schuster Inc. Reprinted by permission of Simon & Schuster Inc.

excerpt, p. 499: From S. LeVine, *Mothers and Wives: Gusii Women of East Africa.* Copyright © 1979 University of Chicago Press, Chicago, IL. Reprinted by permission.

figure 17.5: From D. F. Hultsch and J. K. Plemons, "Life Events and Life Span Development" in *Life Span Development and Behavior,* Vol. 2, P. B. Baltes and O. G. Brun (eds.). Copyright © 1979 Academic Press, Orlando, FL. Reprinted by permission.

figure 17.6: From A. D. Kanner, et al., "Comparison of Two Modes of Stress Management: Daily Hassles and Uplifts Versus Major Life Events" in *Journal of Behavioral Medicine,* 4. Copyright © 1981 Plenum Publishing Corporation, New York, NY. Reprinted by permission.

Chapter 18

p. 513: From *Longevity* by Kathy Keeton. Copyright © 1992 by Kathy Keeton. Used by permission of Viking Penguin, a division of Penguin Books USA Inc.

figure 18.2: Source: Data from Advocate for the U.S. Senate Special Committee on Aging, "Aging in America," p. 50, U.S. Government Printing Office, Washington, DC, 1983.

p. 524: Copyright © Superstock, Jacksonville, FL. Reprinted by permission.

p. 529: From Irwin H. Rosenberg, William J. Evans, and Jacqueline Thompson, *Biomarkers.* COVER COPYRIGHT © 1992 by Simon & Schuster Inc. Reprinted by permission of Simon & Schuster Inc.

Chapter 19

figure 19.2: From K. W. Schaie and C. R. Strother, "A Cross-Sequential Study of Age Changes in Cognitive Behavior" in *Psychological Bulletin,* 70:671–680. Copyright 1968 by the American Psychological Association. Reprinted by permission.

figure 19.3: Source: U.S. Bureau of Labor Statistics, 1986.

figure 19.4: From Robert C. Atchley, *The Social Forces in Later Life.* Copyright © 1977 Wadsworth Publishing Company. Reprinted by permission.

p. 550: From Peter Rabins, *The 36-Hour Day.* Copyright © 1981 The Johns Hopkins University Press, Baltimore, MD. Reprinted by permission.

Chapter 20

lyric, p. 565: From John Lennon and Paul McCartney, "When I'm Sixty-Four." Copyright © MCA Music Publishing, New York, NY. Reprinted by permission.

p. 568: From *IT'S BETTER TO BE OVER THE HILL THAN UNDER IT: Thoughts on Life Over Sixty,* by Eda LeShan. Copyright © 1990 Eda LeShan. Jacket photograph © Scott Hagendorf; Jacket design © Andrew Newman. Reprinted by permission of Newmarket Press, 18 E. 48th St., New York, NY 10017.

Chapter 21

p. 580: Reprinted by permission from *Helping Children Grieve* by Theresa Huntley, copyright © 1991 Augsburg Fortress.

poem, p. 583: Dylan Thomas:*Poems of Dylan Thomas.* Copyright 1952 by Dylan Thomas. Reprinted by permission of New Directions Publishing Corp.; Reprinted by permission of David Higham Associates Limited, London, England.

p. 585: From *How to Go on Living When Someone You Love Dies* by Therese A. Rando, Ph.D. Cover by Richard Rossiter. Copyright © 1988 by Lexington Books, Cover type and Design © 1991 Richard Rossiter. Used by permission of Bantam Books, a division of Bantam Doubleday Dell Publishing Group.

p. 587: From *How to Survive the Loss of a Love* by Melba Colgrove, Ph.D., Harold H. Bloomfield, M.D., and Peter McWilliams, published by Prelude Press, 8159 Santa Monica Boulevard, Los Angeles, CA 90046, 1–800–LIFE–101.

Name Index

SUBJECT INDEX